PAGE 38

ON THE ROAD

YOUR COMPLETE DESTINATION GUIDE
In-depth reviews, detailed listings
and insider tips

Malawi p112

Zambia p549

Mozambique p167

Victoria Falls p533

Zimbabwe p602

Namibia p244

Botswana p40

Swaziland p515

Lesotho p94

South Africa p322

PAGE 695

SURVIVAL GUIDE

VITAL PRACTICAL INFORMATION TO
HELP YOU HAVE A SMOOTH TRIP

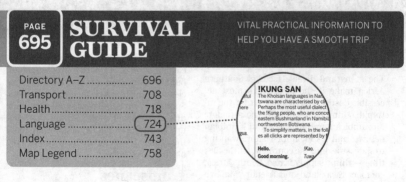

!KUNG SAN
The Khoisan languages in Nam...
tswana are characterised by cl...
Perhaps the most useful dialect...
the !Kung people, who are conce...
eastern Bushmanland in Namibi...
northwestern Botswana.
To simplify matters, in the foll...
es all clicks are represented by !

Hello.   !Kao.
Good morning.   Tuwa...

THIS EDITION WRITTEN AND RESEARCHED BY

Alan Murphy,

Kate Armstrong, Lucy Corne, Mary Fitzpatrick,

Michael Grosberg, Anthony Ham, Trent Holden,

Kate Morgan, Richard Waters

welcome to Southern Africa

Accessible Africa

The many and diverse faces of Southern Africa make it the continent's most accessible destination. It's perfect for the intrepid – think Zambian wilderness, remote Mozambican archipelagoes and Namibian deserts; and it's ideal for visitors wanting to slide a toe onto the continent for the first time – think sophisticated South Africa, compact Swaziland and friendly Malawi. From Okavango Delta luxury lodges to Cape Town budget digs, this is truly Africa.

Wildlife Watching

Southern Africa has some of Africa's great safari destinations: Kruger, Etosha, South Luangwa and Hwange National Parks, and the Okavango Delta. The sheer number of elephants, lions, leopards, hyenas, rhinos, buffaloes, antelope and myriad other species will quickly overwhelm your camera. Spot them on self-drives, guided wildlife drives or charter flights...and if that's not up close and personal enough, what about the chance to track the highly endangered black rhino...on foot?

Landscapes

There's famous Table Mountain, the mighty Fish River Canyon, and the desertscapes of the Kalahari, but the lonely rural tracks that expose visitors to a wandering wilderness are just as memorable. In Namibia, huge slabs of flat-topped granite rise from

An astonishingly diverse region fused by its prolific wildlife, breathtaking landscapes and remnants of ancient culture, Southern Africa will etch itself onto your heart.

(left) Okavango Delta, Botswana
(below) Himba children, Opuwo, Namibia

mists of wind-blown sand dust. And Zambian flood plains are dotted with acacia trees and flanked by escarpments of dense woodland. Want to see all the landscapes the region has to offer? Put aside a lifetime.

Cultural Experiences

For insight into extraordinary rock art left by ancestors of the San, an ancient people with direct links to the Stone Age, visit Tsodilo Hills in Botswana and the extensive rock art galleries in Namibia, South Africa and Zimbabwe. Step back through the centuries in the cultural melting pot of Mozambique Island; stay in a mud hut in Zimbabwe and watch Shona sculptors at work; prop up the bar at a *shebeen* in Soweto; or mingle with Basotho people in highland villages in Lesotho.

Adventure Activities

Namibia is Southern Africa's headquarters for adrenaline-pumping fun, but there's adventure to be had all over the region. Sail by dhow past remote islands off Mozambique's jagged coastline, abseil Livingstonia in Malawi, tackle the ferocious rapids down the Zambezi River or bungee from a bridge at Victoria Falls. In South Africa, the Garden Route with its old-growth forests offers shark-cage diving, surfing, skydiving, canoeing and kloofing (canyoning). And that's just scratching the surface.

› Southern Africa

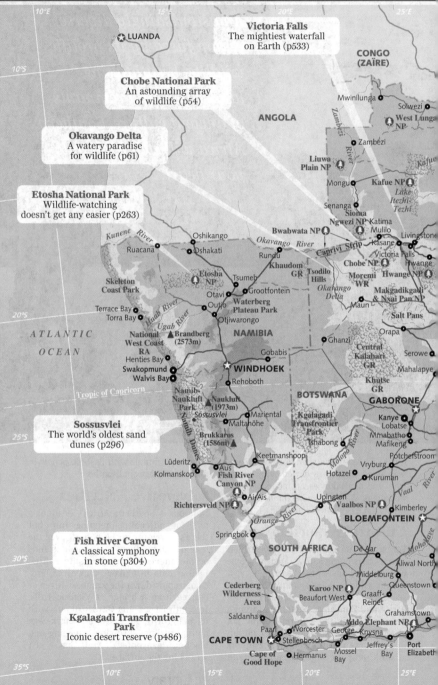

Victoria Falls
The mightiest waterfall on Earth (p533)

Chobe National Park
An astounding array of wildlife (p54)

Okavango Delta
A watery paradise for wildlife (p61)

Etosha National Park
Wildlife-watching doesn't get any easier (p263)

Sossusvlei
The world's oldest sand dunes (p296)

Fish River Canyon
A classical symphony in stone (p304)

Kgalagadi Transfrontier Park
Iconic desert reserve (p486)

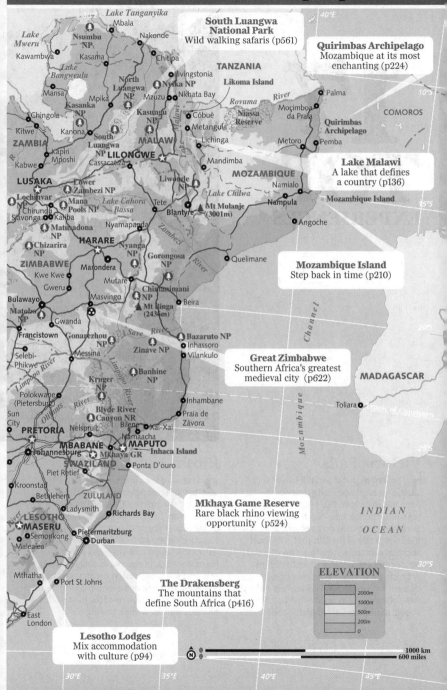

South Luangwa National Park
Wild walking safaris (p561)

Quirimbas Archipelago
Mozambique at its most enchanting (p224)

Lake Malawi
A lake that defines a country (p136)

Mozambique Island
Step back in time (p210)

Great Zimbabwe
Southern Africa's greatest medieval city (p622)

Mkhaya Game Reserve
Rare black rhino viewing opportunity (p524)

The Drakensberg
The mountains that define South Africa (p416)

Lesotho Lodges
Mix accommodation with culture (p94)

ELEVATION

	2000m
	1000m
	500m
	200m
	0

0   1000 km
0   600 miles

17 TOP EXPERIENCES

Victoria Falls

1 The largest, most beautiful and simply the greatest waterfall in the world. As iconic to Africa as 'Dr Livingstone, I presume', thunderous Victoria Falls (p533) will blow your mind and soak your shirt. It's the sheer scale of the falls that is its most impressive feature. A million litres of water per second are funnelled over the 108m drop, creating a plume of spray that can be seen for kilometres. This really is a sight that, when you're in Southern Africa, you should move heaven and earth to see.

Etosha National Park

2 There are few places in Southern Africa that can compete with the wildlife prospects of extraordinary Etosha National Park (p263), Namibia. A network of waterholes dispersed among the bush and grasslands surrounding the pan – a blindingly white, flat, saline desert that stretches into the horizon – attracts enormous congregations of animals. A single waterhole can render thousands of sightings over the course of a day. Etosha is simply one of the best places on the planet for wildlife viewing

Fish River Canyon

3 The enormous gash in the surface of the planet in the south of Namibia is an almost implausible landscape. Seen most clearly in the morning, Fish River Canyon (p304) is desolate, immense and seemingly carved into the earth by a master builder. The exposed rock and lack of plantlife is quite startling, and any attempt to take pictures is soon replaced with thoughtful reflection and a quiet sense of awe. The canyon's rounded edges and sharp corners create a symphony in stone of gigantic and imposing proportions.

Sossusvlei

4 The towering red dunes of Sossusvlei (p296) consist of incredibly fine sand that feels soft when it falls through your fingers and changes hue with the light. It's astounding, especially given that the sands originated in the Kalahari millions of years ago. The valley is dotted by hulking dunes, and interspersed with unearthly, dry *vleis* (low, open landscapes). Clambering up the face of these constantly moving giants is a uniquely Namibian experience. Survey the seemingly endless swath of nothingness that surrounds you, and feel as though time itself has slowed.

ARIADNE VAN ZANDBERGEN/GETTY IMAGES©

JANE SWEENEY/ROBERT HARDING/GETTY IMAGES©

DAVE HAMMAN/GETTY IMAGES©

Okavango Delta

5 The Okavango (p61) in Botswana is an astonishing, beautiful and wild place. Home to wildlife spectacles of rare power and drama, the delta changes with the seasons as flood waters ebb and flow, creating islands, river channels and pathways for animals that move this way and that at the waters' behest. No visit to the delta is complete without drifting in a traditional *mokoro* (dugout canoe). Exclusive and remote lodges are an Okavango speciality, and self-drivers can find outstanding campsites in the heart of the Okavango's Moremi Game Reserve.

Chobe National Park

6 Botswana's Chobe National Park (p54) ranks among the elite of African safari destinations. For a start, there are more elephants here than anywhere else on earth, numbering in the tens of thousands. And they're big – really big. Then you have the iconic landscapes of Savuti with its elephant-eating lions. There's Linyanti, one of the best places on the continent to see the highly endangered African wild dog. And finally the Chobe Riverfront, where most of Africa's charismatic megafauna come to drink.

Lessons in History

7 The impact of apartheid on present-day South Africa is impossible to measure as it informs so much of daily life. Yet trying to understand this history should be a priority for every visitor. Exceptional museums, informative and moving in equal parts, dot the country, with the best of the best – the Apartheid Museum (p442), Constitution Hill (p439), Liliesleaf Farm (p437) and the Hector Pieterson Museum (p452) – located in Gauteng. Elsewhere, visit Robben Island (p329) and District Six (p323) in Cape Town, the South End Museum (p379) in Port Elizabeth and KwaMuhle Museum (p397) in Durban.
Apartheid Museum

Quirimbas Archipelago

8 Idyllic islands strewn amid azure seas, dense mangrove channels opening onto pristine patches of soft, white sand, dhows silhouetted against the horizon and magical Ibo Island, with its silversmiths, fort and crumbling mansions – the remote Quirimbas Archipelago (p224) in Mozambique is a time and place set apart, accessed with difficulty, and invariably left behind with regret. Whether you dive and snorkel amid the wealth of corals and fish, wander Ibo's sandy lanes, relax in a luxury lodge or explore on a dhow, the archipelago never fails to enchant.

Mozambique Island

9 There are no crowds and few vehicles, but Mozambique Island (p210) is hardly silent. Echoes of its past mix with the squawking of chickens, the sounds of children playing and the calls of the muezzin to remind you that the island is still very much alive. Wander along cobbled streets, past graceful praças (town squares) rimmed by once-grand churches and stately colonial-era buildings. This Unesco World Heritage site, with its time-warp atmosphere and backdrop of turquoise seas, is a Mozambique highlight, and not to be missed

South Luangwa National Park

10 Stroll single file through Zambia's South Luangwa National Park (p561) with a rifle-carrying scout in the lead, no 4WD engine sounds, no obstructed sight lines and no barrier between you and the wildlife, both predator and prey. The focus here is on the little things, including the medicinal uses of native flora and a CSI-like investigation of animal dung. Simply sitting under a tree and looking out over a plain filled with munching grazers is an opportunity for a quasi-meditative immersion in South Luangwa.

Kgalagadi Transfrontier Park

11 Kgalagadi (p486) covers almost 40,000 sq km of raw Kalahari in the Northern Cape and Botswana, roamed by some 2000 predators. But such statistics, albeit impressive, barely scrape the surface of this immense land of sizzling sunsets, velvety night skies and rolling red dunes. You might spot black-maned lions napping under thorn trees or purring along the road; the park is one of the world's best places to spot big cats, home to about 800 lions, cheetahs and leopards.

The Drakensberg

12 Majestic, stunning and mysterious, the mountains and surrounds of the World Heritage–listed uKhahlamba-Drakensberg Park (p416) in South Africa are among the country's most awe-inspiring landscapes. The region is best known as a hikers' utopia, with walks ranging from day-trails taking in waterfalls to challenging ten-day treks tackling some of the loftier peaks. Less-energetic travellers are equally well-catered for with picturesque picnic spots, scenic drives, and easy hour-long walks to visit some of the region's many millennia-old San rock art sites.

11

ANJA TUZEL/GETTY IMAGES©

12

SHAEN ADEY/GETTY IMAGES©

Lesotho Lodge Living

13 There are few places where lodge accommodation and village experiences are integrated. A trip to Semonkong (p103), Malealea (p103), Roma (p100) and Ramabanta (p100) in Lesotho not only provides you with opportunities to stay in historic buildings – generally, former trading posts – but also offers chances to mingle with locals, head off on guided pony treks and enjoy village life at a *shebeen*. Also on tap are hiking and abseiling, San rock art, dinosaur prints, and wonderful plants and birdlife. Malealea

Majete Wildlife Reserve

14 Deep in the heartland of southern Malawi lies one of the country's most exciting reserves, thanks to its massively reinvigorated wildlife population, fenced perimeter, finessed infrastructure and a determined antipoaching program. It's official: Malawi finally has the Big Five again, since lions were introduced into Majete (p153) in 2012, joining the ranks of leopards, buffaloes, elephants and rhino. Stay at the blissfully comfortable Mkulumadzi Lodge for up-close animal encounters, and track their newly ensconced lion pride on a game drive.

PHOTOSHOT HOLDINGS LTD/ALAMY©

TODD LAWSON/GETTY IMAGES©

DENNIS K. JOHNSON/GETTY IMAGES©

Mkhaya Game Reserve

15 Top of the conservation pops, Swaziland's stunning Mkhaya private reserve (p524) was established in 1979 to save the pure Nguni breed of cattle from extinction. It's known, however, for its preservation of both the black and white rhino population. The reserve is staffed entirely by Swazis from neighbouring communities who run an extremely effective antipoaching unit. That's not all: roan and sable antelopes, *tsessebis* and elephants roam the reserve. A bird hide, too, gives you an opportunity to get up close and personal with rare species.

Lake Malawi

16 The emerald jewel in Malawi's crown is undoubtedly its interior sea, Lake Malawi (p136). Fringed by golden beaches, the 'calendar lake' – so-called because it measures 365 miles long and 52 miles wide – offers travellers an underwater palace to swim among brilliantly coloured cichlid fish and desert islands to escape to. The resorts of Chintheche Strip, Nkhata Bay and Cape Maclear also offer a spectrum of great accommodation and activities such as kayaking and windsurfing to ensure you can make the best of it.

Great Zimbabwe

17 Clamber around boulders, step past teetering rocks, slip through narrow stone crevices and take in the stunning views as you explore the architectural feat that is Great Zimbabwe (p622). These 11th century mysterious ruins lend the nation its name and provide evidence that ancient Africa reached a level of civilisation not suspected by earlier scholars. Come for sunset and watch in awe as the sun sinks behind the majestic walls of the greatest medieval city in sub-Saharan Africa.

need to know

Currency

» US dollar ($) the most recognised international currency; euros (€) and UK pounds (£) often also accepted. South African rand (R) widely recognised.

Language

» English is an official language in every Southern African country except Mozambique (where it's Portuguese). Afrikaans is widely spoken.

When to Go

Tropical climate, wet and dry seasons
Warm to hot summers, mild winters
Desert, dry climate

Lusaka
GO Apr–Aug

Harare
GO Apr–Oct

Livingstone
GO Jul–Oct

Windhoek
GO May–Oct

Cape Town
GO Nov–Apr

High Season

(Apr–Aug)

» Most places bask in temperate sunshine, with comfortable (but often very chilly) nights.

» Cape Town (a more Mediterranean climate) is characterised by rain and blustery winds.

Shoulder

(Feb & Mar, Sep & Oct)

» Usually quite comfortable in the central part of the region.

» Great time to visit with good wildlife viewing but fewer tourist numbers.

Low Season

(Nov–Jan)

» In the north, plan for inclement weather.

» Heat can be oppressive and travel more difficult due to washed-out roads.

» Birdwatching and thunderstorms at their best.

Your Daily Budget

» Cape Town and the Garden Route are more expensive. Prices vary considerably between countries.

Budget less than R450

» Dorm beds: from R150

» Four-hour minibus taxi ride: R200

» Free entry to many museums

Midrange from R450

» Guesthouse, B&B or hotel double: from R400

» Wildlife drive: R250

» Single room supplements common

Top End more than R1500

» Guesthouse, B&B or hotel double: from R1000

» Jo'burg–Cape Town flight: from R80

» Luxury lodges offer all-inclusive packages

Money

» ATMs widely available in larger towns and cities. Credit cards widely accepted in most shops, restaurants and hotels (especially in South Africa, Swaziland, Botswana and Namibia).

Visas

» Generally not required (or free on arrival) for stays of between 30 and 90 days – depending on the country. Exceptions are Mozambique, Zambia and Zimbabwe.

Mobile Phones

» Local SIM cards are available across the region and can be used in unlocked Australian and European phones. Top-up vouchers are widely available.

Driving

» Drive on the left; steering wheel is on the right side of the car. Conditions vary widely but include well-developed road networks.

Websites

» **Lonely Planet** (www.lonelyplanet. com) Destination information, hotel bookings, traveller forum and more.

» **Regional Tourism Organisation of Southern Africa** (www. retosa.co.za) Promotes tourism in the region.

» **Southafrica.info** (www.southafrica.info) South African news with articles relating to the wider region and good links.

» **Zambezi Traveller** (www.zambezitraveller. com) Travel info for destinations along the Zambezi River.

Best Sources for Regional News

» **African Encounter** (www.africaencounter.com) Run by a travel agent specialising in itineraries of Southern Africa. Good for info on getting around Zimbabwe.

» **All Africa** (http://allafrica.com) Posts around a thousand articles a day, collated from more than 125 different news organisations.

» **iafrica.com** (www.iafrica.com) Includes travel, news and lifestyle content.

» **Integrated Regional Information Network** (www.irinnews.org) Regional humanitarian news.

» **Open Africa** (www.openafrica.org) Excellent site detailing off-the-beaten track tourism supporting job creation and conservation.

» **Political Africa** (www.politicalafrica.com) Latest stories on Africa from various news services around the world, plus links to sport, economics and the UN in Africa.

Arriving in Southern Africa

» **OR Tambo International Airport, Johannesburg**
Main gateway to region; regular connections to Southern African capitals
Gautrain – Jo'burg/ Pretoria R115/125; 25/35 minutes, every 12 to 30 minutes
Taxi or shuttle to Jo'burg R400

» **Cape Town International Airport**
Growing in popularity; better intro to Africa than Jo'burg
MyCiTi bus – R55; 20 to 60 minutes, departing every 20 minutes
Taxi/shuttle into town R220/180

Driving in Remote Areas

Careful preparations for any remote trips in Southern Africa are required. You will need a robust 4WD vehicle and enough supplies to see you through the journey – this includes food and water for the entire trip. You should also travel in a convoy of at least two vehicles. Carry several spare tyres for each vehicle, a tyre iron, a good puncture-repair kit and a range of vehicle spares, as well as twice as much petrol as the distances would suggest. For navigation, use a compass or preferably a global positioning system (GPS). Relevant topographic sheets are also extremely helpful. Be careful where you camp; always ask permission on private land, and think twice about pitching a tent in shady and inviting riverbeds as large animals often use them as thoroughfares, and they can also be subject to flash floods.

if you like...

Adventure Activities

Adventure sports thrive in Southern Africa and enthusiasts find ways to raise their heart rate in most countries. Try sandboarding an ancient desert, throwing yourself out of a plane, surfing the Atlantic or shooting down foaming white-water rapids.

Middle Zambezi (Zimbabwe) Multiday canoe safaris down an incredible wilderness route: the Chirundu to Mana Pools offers the best scenery and diversity of wildlife (p616).

Northern Mozambique Sail by dhow past remote islands or venture into trackless bush in the interior (p207).

Semonkong (Lesotho) Take a plunge on the longest commercially operated single-drop abseil (204m) down the Maletsunyane Falls (p103).

Swakopmund Namibia's, and indeed Southern Africa's, capital of adventure sports, this is adrenaline-junkie heaven (p281).

Usutu River (Swaziland) White-water rafting including Grade IV rapids, which aren't for the faint-hearted (p520).

Victoria Falls (Zimbabwe) Tackle the Grade V rapids down the Zambezi River or bungee from Victoria Falls bridge (p534).

Beaches

Coastal beaches and miles of inland lakeshore mean there are no excuses not to wet your toes. Turquoise waters, coral reefs and sandy beaches are ideal for swimming, snorkelling, diving or just good ole sunbathing.

Cape Town and the Cape Peninsula (South Africa) Sunbathe with the beautiful people in Camps Bay, with penguins in Simon's Town (p342) or swap the towel for a surfboard in Muizenberg.

Lake Niassa (Mozambique) Revel in the remoteness, snorkelling in crystal-clear waters and kayaking past quiet coves (p216).

Mumbo Island (Malawi) This gem of an island fringed by sugary sand and turquoise water adazzle with cichlids is a traveller's fantasy (p132).

Ponta d'Ouro (Mozambique) The country's southernmost tip features a long, dune-fringed beach with reliable surf and the chance to spot dolphins (p181).

Tofo (Mozambique) A lovely arc of white sand with azure waters, fine surfing and diving with manta rays and whale sharks (p188).

Cultural Interactions

Experiencing the rich tapestry of Southern African culture will enhance any visit to the region. There are myriad ways of accessing the region's peoples, their traditions and way of life.

Bairro Mafalala (Mozambique) Learn about the rich history and culture of Maputo's Mafalala neighbourhood during a walking tour (p171).

Mozambique Island (Mozambique) Step back through the centuries in this historical treasure trove and cultural melting pot (p210).

Soweto (South Africa) Stay the night in a backpackers or B&B and learn local history from the residents over a *shebeen* beer (p451).

Tengenenge (Zimbabwe) An open-air gallery, home to more than 120 Shona sculptors, where you can see the artists at work and stay in a traditional mud hut (p614).

The Kalahari (Botswana) Numerous lodges and camps employ San guides and trackers to take you out onto their ancestral lands and introduce you to their culture (p72).

» Local children, Tengenenge (p614), Zimbabwe

Hiking

A great way to experience the magic of the region is to hear the crunch of the earth beneath your boots. Here are some of Southern Africa's great hikes.

Chimanimani Mountains (Mozambique) Get to know local culture while hiking through lush, seldom-visited forest areas (p200).

Drakensberg (South Africa) From day-hikes to week-long treks, the dramatic Drakensberg creates happy hikers (p416).

Fish River Canyon (Namibia) The best way to get a feel for this massive gash in the earth is to embark on a five-day hike along the valley floor (p304).

Kgalagadi Transfrontier Park (Bostwana) In a remote Botswanan corner of the park there are some challenging multiday hikes along wilderness tracks.

Lesotho A country 'made' for hiking (p94).

Mt Mulanje & the Zomba Plateau (Malawi) The country's best spots for hiking (p151) (p143).

Wild Coast (South Africa) Strap a pack to your back and take a hike past rugged cliffs, remote beaches and Xhosa villages (p391).

Landscapes

One of the best things about exploring the region is discovering its array of landscapes: from swirling desert sands and slabs of ancient granite mountain, to jagged coastlines, rock-strewn moonscapes and lush savannah.

Drakensberg (South Africa) Awesome peaks and formations, such as the Ampitheatre, are fronted by rolling hills (p416).

Mutinondo Wilderness (Zambia) Mutinondo offers soul-stirring landscapes dotted with huge purple-hued *inselbergs* (isolated ranges) and laced with meandering rivers (p580).

Northwestern Namibia Encountering the enigmatic Skeleton Coast and the Kaokoveld with its lonely desert roads is like driving through a picture book (p275).

Nyika National Park (Malawi) The rolling grasslands of Nyika, with their heather and wildflowers, are otherworldy (p125).

Savuti (Botswana) The heart and soul of Chobe National Park, with dramatic rocky outcrops and savannah-like swamps (p59).

Wild Coast (South Africa) The green hills dotted with pastel *rondavels*, rugged cliffs and empty Indian Ocean beaches are unforgettable (p391).

Mountains

Some of Africa's finest peaks scrape the cloud line in Southern Africa. Who hasn't heard of Table Mountain? But the region is peppered with plenty of other massive mounds ideal for climbing, ogling and snapping.

Mt Mulanje (Malawi) Surrounded by majestically rolling green tea plantations, it's the country's best climb. It has decent walking routes and cabins to overnight in (p151).

Mt Gorongosa (Mozambique) Steeped in local lore and wonderful for birdwatchers; also an off-the-beaten-track hiking destination (p200).

Sani Pass (Lesotho) Shouldn't be missed for its exhilarating hair-raising bends, stupendous views and on-top-of-the-world pub (p101).

Table Mountain (South Africa) Whether you take the easy way up in a revolving cable car, or put in the leg work on one of many hiking trails to the top, attaining the summit of Table Mountain is a Capetonian rite of passage (p340).

VINCENT TALBOT/GETTY IMAGES©

» Cederberg Wilderness Area (p373), South Africa

Off-Road Driving

This is adventure country for 4WD enthusiasts. In many remote places age-old tracks are the only way to navigate through the African wilderness.

Kaokoveld (Namibia) A true wilderness, the beguiling Kaokoveld is crisscrossed by sandy tracks laid down decades ago (p277).

Khaudum National Park (Namibia) With virtually no signage, and navigation dependent on GPS coordinates and topographical maps, Khaudum is a wildlife and off-road adventure (p269).

Makgadikgadi Pans (Botswana) If the notion of exploring 12,000 sq km of disorientating saltpans is your idea of an adventure, then calibrate your GPS and head straight here (p53).

North Luangwa National Park (Zambia) Simply making it to this remote park in your own vehicle is an achievement. You'll have to navigate rough tracks while dodging the diverse wildlife (p566).

Richtersveld (South Africa) This wild frontier is a moonlike swatch of land accessible only by 4WD (p489).

Rock Art

The rock art of Southern Africa is an extraordinary chronology of an ancient people and a link to our ancient ancestors. Dotted around the region in hills and caves, these are sacred works of art.

Cederberg (South Africa) The fiery orange peaks of the barren Cederberg are dotted with craggy rock formations and dozens of easily accessible rock art sites (p373).

Game Pass Shelter (South Africa) Guides lead informative walks to this Drakensberg cave, often referred to as the 'Rosetta Stone' of San rock art (p423).

Matobo National Park (Zimbabwe) Some of Zimbabwe's oldest San paintings are hidden in caves here (p628).

Quthing (Lesotho) Authentic in-your-face San rock art is a feature here (p104).

Tsodilo Hills (Botswana) These dramatic rock formations in northeastern Botswana, known as the 'Louvre of the Desert', shelter around 4000 paintings and carvings (p69).

Twyfelfontein (Namibia) One of Africa's most extensive galleries of rock art (p276).

Wildlife Safaris

Some of the best wildlife viewing on the continent is at your fingertips. Unique opportunities abound while on safari.

Chobe Riverfront (Botswana) Africa's largest elephants draw near to the water's edge with predators prowling nearby (p58).

Etosha National Park (Namibia) Incredible wildlife viewing with animals crowding around easily seen waterholes (p263).

Kgalagadi Transfrontier Park (South Africa) Deep in the Kalahari is one of the world's best places to spot big cats, from cheetahs to black-maned lions (p486).

Kruger National Park South Africa's famous park has 5000 rhinos alone, and landscapes ranging from woodland to mopane-veld (p458).

Mana Pools (Zimbabwe) For the wild at heart – you're almost guaranteed to see lions; unguided walks allowed (p615).

Okavango Delta (Botswana) One of the world's largest inland river deltas; the life-sustaining waters ebb and flow, supporting vast quantities of wildlife (p61).

South Luangwa National Park (Zambia) Abundant wildlife, wonderful scenery and walking safaris (p561).

month by month

Top Events

1 **Minstrel Carnival**, January

2 **Maitisong Festival**, March

3 **National Arts Festival**, July

4 **Umhlanga Dance**, August

5 **Oktoberfest**, October

January

With Christmas over the party in the Cape is only just beginning; it's smack-bang in the middle of summer and high season.

Street Party!

The Mother City's most colourful street party, the Cape Town Minstrel Carnival (Kaapse Klopse) runs for a month from 2 January. With sequin-and-satin-clad minstrel troupes, ribald song and dance parades and general revelry, it's the Cape's Mardi Gras.

February

Rains in the northern part of the region can make travel difficult. Wildlife is hard to spot in the tall grass but it's a great time for bird watching. Some parks close down.

Gwaza Muthini

This early February celebration in Marracuene, Mozambique, commemorates the colonial resistors who lost their lives in the 1895 Battle of Marracuene. It also marks the start of the *ukanhi* season, a traditional brew made from the fruit of the canhoeiro tree.

Marrabenta Festival

To hear *marrabenta* – Mozambique's national music – at its best, don't miss the annual Marrabenta Festival (www.ccfmoz.com). It's held mostly in Maputo, but also in Beira, Inhambane and several other locations. The timing is set to coincide with Marracuene's Gwaza Muthini commemorations.

N'cwala

A Ngoni festival held near Chipata in eastern Zambia on 24 February. Food, dance and music are all enjoyed to celebrate the end of the rainy season and pray for a successful harvest.

March

The rains are petering out and the sizzling temperatures are coming to an end. Keep in mind South African school holidays begin in late March when accommodation can be hard to find.

Enjando Street Festival

The Namibian capital's biggest street party, also known as Mbapira, occurs in March every year. It's also a good excuse for people to dress in extravagant ethnic clothes that bring the streets to life.

Maitisong Festival

Botswana's largest performing arts festival (www.maitisong.org) is held annually over several days from mid-March to early April in Gaborone. The festival features an outdoor program of film, music, theatre and dance, with top performing artists from around Africa.

Ditshwanelo Human Rights Film Festival

Screenings on human rights topics are held at the AV Centre, Maru a Pula School in Gaborone, Botswana, during the festival (www.ditshwanelo.org.bw), and guest speakers are invited to talk about their experiences.

Kuomboka Ceremony

Celebrated by the Lozi people of western Zambia to mark the ceremonial journey of the *litunga* (the Lozi king) from his dry-season palace to his wet-season palace on higher ground at Limulunga. It usually takes place in late March or early April.

April

The end of the low season – parks have new growth, the rains are finishing and the temperatures are becoming more pleasant but tourist numbers are still down. South African school holidays continue until mid April.

Windhoek Karnival

Established in 1953 by a small group of German immigrants, Windhoek's April Karnival (WIKA; www.windhoek-karneval.com) is now one of the highlights of Namibia's cultural calendar, culminating in the Royal Ball.

Maun Festival

A two-day celebration with plenty of music, parades, poetry, theatre, craftwork, dance and food; visual arts also feature. Held in Maun, the festival raises funds for local schools while commemorating northwestern Botswana's rich cultural roots.

AfrikaBurn

This subcultural blowout features art installations and themed camps as a corner of the Karoo in South Africa is temporarily turned into a surreal paradise. If you're in the area in April make a beeline here.

Harare HIFA

A not-to-be-missed event in Zimbabwe, Harare International Festival of Art features local and international performers in opera, jazz, classical music, funk, theatre and dance.

May

Beginning of winter and the dry season, and a great time to visit. Snow may fall on the highlands of South Africa and Lesotho where it is much wetter.

Wild Cinema Festival

Just a few years old but proving popular is this film festival held in May. It showcases the work of local and South African talent at cinemas throughout Windhoek, Namibia.

Maputo International Music Festival

This festival (www.maputomusic.com) – held as much to celebrate the charms of Maputo as to celebrate music itself – consists of a series of concerts by classical and contemporary musicians at various venues around the city.

July

High season is beginning to crank up – expect warm clear days and ideal conditions; and combined with South African school holidays until mid-July, it's busy so book accommodation in advance.

Lake Malawi Yachting Marathon

This international event – a gruelling 8-day and 560km race – is the longest fresh-water contest in Africa. Starting at Club Macacola it ends at the Chintheche Inn. A great time to be on one of the lake's islands.

Mulanje Porter's Race

Formerly just for porters, the race is now open to anyone with the lungs and legs to make it 25km up the staggeringly steep Mt Mulanje in Malawi. A great spectacle, participation is not for the faint of heart.

National Arts Festival

Feel South Africa's creative pulse at the country's premier arts festival from late June to early July in studenty Grahamstown. Performers from every conceivable discipline descend on the refined city, hijacking space from squares to sports fields.

August

Wildlife watching is at its best as water sources become limited in the parks, so it's a popular time for visitors on safari. Temperatures on the rise across the region.

Maherero Day

One of Namibia's largest festivals falls on the weekend nearest 26 August. Dressed in traditional garb, the Red Flag Herero people gather in Okahandja for a memorial service to commemorate their chiefs killed in the Khoikhoi and German wars.

Timbilas Festival

Watch Chopi musicians play intricate rhythms on large marimbas, often in orchestras consisting of 20 or more instruments, plus singers and dancers. While the Mozambican festival (www.amizava.org) is not always well organised, the musical tradition is fascinating. It's held in Quissico.

Umhlanga Dance

A showcase of potential wives for the king; young Swazi women of marriageable age journey from all over the kingdom, carrying reeds, to help repair the queen mother's home (around August or September; dates vary).

September

Temperatures are rising but it's still a popular time for travel to the region and tourist numbers are high. South African school holidays in late September can jam accommodation.

 /Ae//Gams Arts Festival

Windhoek's main arts festival is held in September, and includes troupes of dancers, musicians, poets and performers all competing for various prizes. The best of Namibian food is also on show.

Dockanema

This Mozambican festival (www.dockanema.org) showcases documentary films from Southern Africa and from other Lusophone countries, and is a real highlight for both history and cinematography buffs. Maputo is the place to be, with many free screenings and discussion forums.

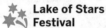 Lake of Stars Festival

'Glastonbury on the beach'; this brilliant three-day Malawian festival bubbles with stellar UK and African bands, and a host of celebrated global DJs. Money raised goes toward the Children in the Wilderness charity.

Morija Arts & Cultural Festival

This annual five-day event held in September/October in Lesotho showcases the diversity of Sotho culture through dance, music and theatre.

October

The end of high season, but Windhoek is a magnet for beer drinkers and it is a popular time especially for German tourists. First rains arrive in the northernmost regions.

Oktoberfest

Windhoek in Namibia stages its own Oktoberfest – an orgy of food, drink and merrymaking in an event that showcases the best in German beer, usually drunk at tables set up inside large marquees. There's plenty of traditional German dress on display, too.

itineraries

Whether you've got six days or 60, these itineraries provide a starting point for the trip of a lifetime. Want more inspiration? Head online to lonelyplanet. com/thorntree to chat with other travellers.

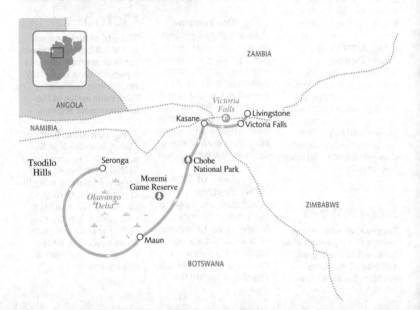

One Week
Natural Wonder & Sensational Safaris

> Start your trip at one of the great natural wonders of the world, **Victoria Falls**. For the best perspectives, visit from both **Livingstone** (Zambia) and the town of **Victoria Falls** (Zimbabwe). There's a plethora of activities on offer, including serene canoe trips on top of the falls and, for those after an adrenalin rush, rafting below the falls down the churning Zambezi. From the Zambian side, cross the nearby border at Kazungula and head for **Kasane** in Botswana, the gateway town to the stunning, wildlife-rich **Chobe National Park**. Here you can organise wildlife drives and river cruises along the Chobe River front, where nearly every Southern African mammal species is represented. From Chobe it's an easy hop, skip and jump southwest to **Maun** and the vast **Okavango Delta**, where one of the world's most impressive ecosystems breathes life into the Kalahari sands and attracts astonishing amounts of wildlife and incalculable numbers of birds. From Maun, take a minibus clockwise around the delta towards Namibia, perhaps stopping in Sepupa to take a boat to **Seronga** and do a *mokoro* (dug-out canoe) trip in the Okavango Panhandle.

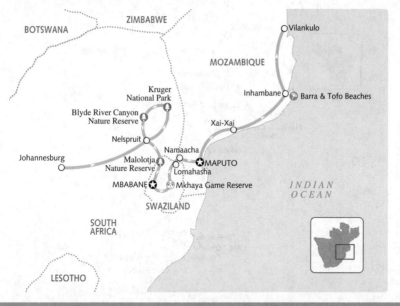

Three Weeks
Nature & Fun in the Sun

> This 2000km-plus route serves up delightful variety, and you can get a good sampling of wildlife and local culture and still have time to laze on the beach. Short on time? Whiz through the Swaziland leg and stick to motorways where possible. Using **Johannesburg** as a gateway, head east via **Nelspruit** to world-renowned **Kruger National Park** (Great Limpopo Transfrontier Park). The teeming wildlife will undoubtedly mesmerise you for several days. One option here is to cross into Mozambique via official border posts within the park, taking a look around in the Mozambiquan side of this gigantic transfrontier park. The wildlife is sparse but it's a serious bush adventure. Then you could nip across to the coast and do the rest of this itinerary in reverse, making a nice loop back through Swaziland and into South Africa again. Otherwise, if you've time, duck out of Orpen Gate for a look at remote and off-the-tourist-radar **Blyde River Canyon**. This awe-inspiring natural sight has good access points such as the Three Rondavels and Gods Window, and if you're really captivated, consider a 2½-day walk along the valley floor. Continue south into Swaziland, where you can spend a few days hiking through the grasslands and forests of **Malolotja Nature Reserve** before heading on via **Mbabane** to the tiny, but brilliant **Mkhaya Game Reserve**, noted for its black rhinos. After sampling the fine hospitality and food of this tiny mountain kingdom, it's time to get your feet wet. Head for the border town of **Lomahasha** in Swaziland and cross into the former Portuguese colony of Mozambique (formalities are straighforward) via the Mozambican border town of **Namaacha**. Motor down approximately 50km to culturally intriguing **Maputo** and then head north on the EN1 and, if you're getting desperate for a dip, stop to enjoy the quiet beaches at **Xai-Xai**. Continue up the EN1 to **Inhambane**, one of the country's oldest and most charming towns. Beaches close by include legendary **Tofo**, with azure waters, and the more sedate **Barra**. If you've more steam, trundle a bit further north to **Vilankulo**, the gateway to the tropical paradise of the Bazaruto Archipelago.

Three Weeks
A Southern African Slice

> For road-trip lovers. Even if you can't squeeze in all of this 3000km-plus journey, you'll come away with an immense appreciation of this remarkable region. Looking to make cuts? Shave some kilometres off the Western Cape loop. A car (4WD useful but not necessary) is definitely your best bet for this mega road trip. After a few days in **Cape Town**, ogling Table Mountain from various vantage points around town, tear yourself away from this wonderful city and head to the fertile valleys of the Winelands, with a night or two in **Stellenbosch** or **Franschhoek**.

From here, continue east to the artists enclave of **Montagu**, and then via the scenic Route 62 through the Little Karoo to **Oudtshoorn**, South Africa's ostrich capital. Some possible detours along the way include a trip to **Hermanus** for whale-watching if the season is right, or to **Cape Agulhas** for the thrill of standing at Africa's southernmost point.

From Oudtshoorn take the N12 north and then loop back towards Cape Town via the N1, link up with the N7 and head for **Namakwa** to see the fabulous wildflower displays, which are especially good in August and September.

Keep tracking up the N7, cross into Namibia at **Vioolsdrif** and head to **Hobas** to see the **Fish River Canyon National Park** – a mighty gash hacked out of the Earth's surface – one of the continent's great natural wonders. The best way to appreciate this work of a master builder is a five-day trek along the valley floor.

Further north along the B1, **Keetmanshoop** has some colonial architecture; but don't linger, head west along the B4 to surreal **Lüderitz**, a coastal colonial relic sandwiched between the desert and the Atlantic seaboard. Heading back to the B1, turn north at the C13 and make a beeline for the baroque **Duwisib Castle**, which is well worth exploring. You can stay 300m from the castle on a rustic farm or camp. From there head to **Mariental** back on the B1, and it's another couple of hours to **Windhoek**, the small but colourful and cosmopolitan capital city with its bracing highland climate.

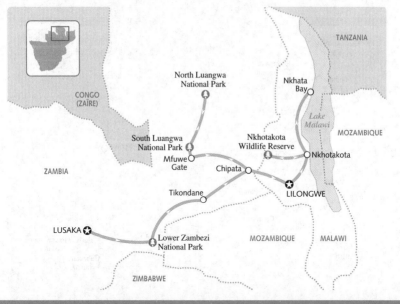

Three Weeks
Dusty Roads & Shimmering Waters

A 2000km route through the Southern African outback. Travelling in Zambia offers a taste of the real Africa, though the dusty roads will become a distant memory once you're lazing by the crystal-clear waters of Lake Malawi. Start with a few days in Zambia's cosmopolitan capital, **Lusaka**, with its genuine African feel and the country's best nightlife. Then head out on the highway to the stunning **Lower Zambezi National Park**, with its beautiful flood plain that's dotted with acacias and other large trees. There's no public transport to the park, so you'll need your own car to get there, or go on an organised tour.

Hook up with the Great East Rd and head to chaotic **Chipata**. Before you get here, you'll come across **Tikondane**, a small grassroots NGO working with local communities that has decent budget accommodation and meals. At Chipata you can organise a trip to **South Luangwa National Park**, one of the most majestic parks on the continent. Make sure you do a walking safari when you're here – it's one of the best places in Southern Africa to do it. From Chipata you can drive to **Mfuwe Gate**, or take one of the minibuses that make the trip to Mfuwe village. The really adventurous could try to reach the wild and spectacular **North Luangwa National Park**, but it's important that you seek local advice before doing this; you need to be well prepared.

Then it's on to Malawi and the town of **Lilongwe**, which is worth a day or two to check out the old town and the local Nature Sanctuary. From Lilongwe strike out north along the M1 to **Nkhata Bay** on Lake Malawi, which is perfect for swimming, kayaking or just lazing about after some hard weeks on the road. A possible detour on the way to/from Nkhata is historic **Nkhotakota** from where you can organise a trip to the revitalised **Nkhotakota Wildlife Reserve**. The reserve offers a good chance of seeing elephants and roan and sable antelope and there's excellent lodge accommodation available in the park.

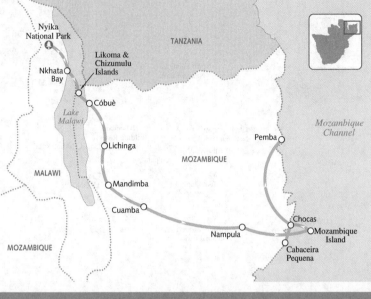

Three Weeks
Lakeshore to Seashore

> This 1500km Mozambican bush adventure could be tacked onto the Dusty Roads and Shimmering Waters itinerary, but it also stands well alone. Mozambique Island makes a wonderful contrast to the bush, and you can finish on the beach in the tropical island paradise of Quirimbas Archipelago.

Drag yourself out of the crystal waters at **Nkhata Bay** and, if you have time before heading across the lake, make a beeline to the enigmatic **Nyika National Park**. Here, you can briefly forget you're in Africa on a multiday hike among rolling grasslands and a surprisingly cool climate. When you're ready, hop on the *Ilala* ferry for the blissful **Likoma Island**, where swimming, snorkelling and local cultures are the star attractions. Splash out for a night at Kaya Mawa if you've the pennies – it's one of Africa's finest paradise retreats. Take the ferry over to the Mediterranean-esque **Chizumulu Island**, with its idyllic beaches, and return by dhow (if the waters are calm enough). From Likoma hop back on the ferry to Metangula and from there take a *chapa* up towards **Cóbuè**, on the other side of the lakeshore in Mozambique. (Or take a dhow direct from Likoma to Cóbuè). Stay the night just south of Cóbuè at Nkwichi Lodge, a magnificent bush retreat that is part of an important development and conservation project; it's well worth a splurge. If your budget isn't up to Nkwichi, try one of several backpacker-friendly places in Cóbuè itself.

After exploring the lake area, head south to cool **Lichinga**. Surrounded by scenic, rugged terrain, it is the capital of remote Niassa province. Carry on through to **Mandimba** and on to bustling **Cuamba**, where you can pick up a train all the way through to **Nampula**. Then jump on a bus to magnificent **Mozambique Island**, with its intriguing architecture and time-warp atmosphere. If you need a beach break after exploring the island, hire a dhow to take you over to **Chocas** and the lovely nearby beach at **Cabaceira Pequena**. The trip finishes up a bit further north at **Pemba**, which is the gateway to the superb Quirimbas Archipelago.

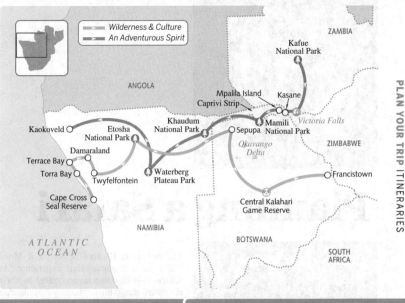

- Wilderness & Culture
- An Adventurous Spirit

One Month
Wilderness & Culture

Starting on Namibia's Skeleton Coast, a treacherous coastline with rusting shipwrecks and desert wilderness, check out the **Cape Cross Seal Reserve**. Track north along the coast to **Torra Bay**, where you can camp, or head for **Terrace Bay** for more luxurious accommodation. Then travel east into the wonders of **Damaraland**, with its wild, open spaces, and make a beeline for **Twyfelfontein**, one of the most extensive galleries of rock art in Africa. Then journey further east into **Etosha National Park**, teeming with animals and one of the continent's great wildlife-viewing areas. Exit Etosha via von Linqequist Gate. Track along the B8 into Botswana at the Mahango–Mohembo border crossing. Drive down the west side of the **Okavango Delta**, perhaps stopping in **Sepupa** to do a boat trip in the Okavango Panhandle. The last leg of this ambitious trip is the iconic **Central Kalahari Game Reserve** to the southeast, lying at the heart of Botswana. Enter at the Matswere Gate at the northeastern end of the reserve: wildlife includes lions and brown hyenas. You can finish your trip by exiting the same gate and travelling east to **Francistown**.

One Month
An Adventurous Spirit

Starting in the magnificent **Kafue National Park** in Zambia – classic wildlife country and one of the largest parks in the world – head south to the iconic **Victoria Falls**, a thunderous sight that will blow your mind and soak your T-shirt. From here head into **Kasane** in Botswana to duck your head into the Chobe Riverfront. Wildlife is prolific and includes huge elephant herds. Charter a plane or boat to **Mpalila Island**, a luxuriously remote retreat stranded in the middle of the Zambezi. From here, head into Namibia's **Caprivi Strip** and visit the mini-Okavango of the **Mamili National Park**, where the rains bring a delta-like feel to the forested islands. Then drive to the untamed wilderness that is **Khaudum National Park**, a serious adventure destination. From Khaudum the road will take you south through Grootfontein, from where it's worth making a short detour to the **Waterberg Plateau Park**. North of Grootfontein the road takes you into Namibia's cultural heartland, the Owambo region, from where you can access the remote and mysterious **Kaokoveld**, homeland to the Himba people and possibly one of the last true wildernesses left in Southern Africa.

Planning a Safari

Best Safari to Spot the Big Five

Kruger National Park (p459), South Africa
Etosha National Park (p263), Namibia
Chobe National Park (p54), Botswana

Best Short Safari

Kruger National Park (p459), South Africa
Chobe National Park (p54), Botswana
Mkhaya Game Reserve (p525), Swaziland

Best Adventure Safari

Any park or wildlife reserve in Zambia (p590)
Kgalagadi Transfrontier Park (p75), Botswana
Mana Pools (p615), Zimbabwe

Most Remote Safari

Khaudum National Park (p269), Namibia
North Luangwa National Park (p566), Zambia
Gorongosa National Park (p199), Mozambique

The unique landscapes of Southern Africa make for a magical safari experience. As safaris have become more crafted to their clientele, the typical image of khaki-clad tourists bush-whacking through the scrub becomes more obsolete. These days a safari can incorporate anything from ballooning over the undulating dunes of the Namib, to scooting along the lush channels of the Okavango in a traditional *mokoro* (dugout canoe). Horse riding, trekking, birding, fishing, night-drives and camel safaris are all on the agenda.

Wildlife watching tops the region's list of attractions and forms the basis of most safaris – and little wonder. Etosha National Park in Namibia, Botswana's Okavango Delta and Chobe National Park, South Africa's Kruger National Park and Zambia's South Luangwa (to name just a few) are packed with animals – at times the density and diversity of wildlife in Southern Africa is astonishing.

It's good to keep in mind that although there are safaris catering to most budgets, in countries such as Botswana, most safari experiences are skewed towards the top end of the market.

This chapter provides an overview of the factors to consider when planning a safari. There is a lot more to choose from at the higher end of the price spectrum, where ambience, safari style and the operator's overall focus are important considerations. However, good, reliable budget operators can also be found across the region.

Wildlife Watching

Wildlife and birdwatching are two of the main activities that lure travellers to Southern Africa. The obvious place to spot the region's furred, feathered and scaled delights is in one of the numerous national parks.

In most places in Southern Africa, large animals are confined to national parks (or similar conservation areas), and the only way to see them is by vehicle – this is both by law and by default, as there's rarely any public transport. If you don't have a vehicle (motorcycles and bicycles don't count), your only option is to join an organised safari.

The range of wildlife-viewing safaris available in Southern Africa is enormous. They can last from a day to a month, and participants may camp outside and cook over an open fire or stay in luxury lodges and be served gourmet meals. You could charter a safari customised to your group's interests or join an already established group or prescheduled safari. You could spend a frantic day ticking species off a list or spend hours by a single waterhole watching the comings and goings.

And of course, there's also a range of prices available. The best value will be participation safaris, in which clients muck in to pack and unpack the vehicle, put up their own tents and help with cooking and washing up. These are typically good value, and are almost always highly rewarding, especially when you get off the beaten track. At the other end of the spectrum, you can pay up to US$500 per person per day and enjoy all the comforts of home, with camp staff to take care of all the chores.

Lots of overseas agencies organise programs using local operators, but these are typically quite expensive. Packages are generally more economical when organised on site (the exception is for safaris involving upmarket lodges, which are often block-booked by overseas agents who can get deals that are lower than rack rates). Locally, the best places to organise safaris are Cape Town, Windhoek in Namibia, Harare, and the tourist towns of Livingstone and Victoria Falls.

When to Go

Getting around is easier in the dry season (May to October), and in many parks this is when animals are easier to find around waterholes and rivers. Foliage is also less dense, making wildlife spotting simpler. However, as the dry season corresponds in part with the high-travel season, lodges and camps in some areas get crowded and accommodation prices are at a premium.

Apart from these general considerations, the ideal time to make a safari very much depends on which parks and reserves you want to visit and your particular interests. For example, the wet season is the best time for birdwatching in many areas, although some places may be inaccessible during the rains. Wildlife concentrations also vary markedly, depending on the season. See the country chapters for more information.

Choosing an Operator

A good operator is the single most important variable for your safari, and it's worth spending time thoroughly researching those you're considering. At the budget level in particular, you may find operators who cut corners, so be careful to go with a reputable outfit. There are many high quality companies that have excellent track records. Operators recommended throughout this guidebook enjoyed a good reputation at the time of research, as do many others that couldn't be listed due to space considerations. However, we can't emphasise enough the need to check on the current situation with all of the listed companies and any others you may hear about.

Do some legwork (the internet is a good start) before coming to Southern Africa. Get personal recommendations – this can be done on Lonely Planet's Thorn Tree forum (lonelyplanet.com/thorntree) – and, once in the region, talk with as many travellers as you can who have recently returned from a safari or trek with the company you're considering.

Be sceptical of price quotes that sound too good to be true, and don't rush into any deals, no matter how good they sound.

Also, take the time to go through the itinerary in detail, confirming what is expected and planned for each stage of the trip. Be sure that the number of wildlife drives per day and all other specifics appear in the written contract, as well as the starting and ending dates and approximate times.

Safari Style

While price can be a major determining factor in safari planning, there are other considerations that are just as important:

A BEGINNER'S GUIDE TO TRACKING WILDLIFE

Visitors to Africa are always amazed at the apparent ease with which professional guides locate and spot wildlife. While most of us can't hope to replicate their skills in a brief visit, a few pointers can hone your approach.

Time of day This is possibly the most important factor for determining animal movements and behaviours. Dawn and dusk tend to be the most productive periods for mammals and many birds. They're the coolest parts of the day, and also produce the richest light for photographs. Although the middle of the day is usually too hot for much action, this is when some antelopes feel less vulnerable at a waterhole, and when raptors and reptiles are most obvious.

Weather Prevailing conditions can greatly affect your wildlife-viewing experience. For example, high winds may drive herbivores and birds into cover, so concentrate your search in sheltered areas. Summer thunderstorms are often followed by a flurry of activity as insect colonies and frogs emerge, followed by their predators. Overcast or cool days may prolong activity such as hunting by normally crepuscular predators, and extremely cold winter nights force nocturnal species to stay active at dawn.

Water Most animals drink daily when water is available, so water sources are worthwhile places to invest time, particularly in the dry season. Predators and very large herbivores tend to drink early in the day or at dusk, while antelopes tend to drink from the early morning to midday. On the coast, receding tides are usually followed by the appearance of wading birds and detritus feeders such as crabs.

Food sources Knowing what the different species eat will help you to decide where to spend most of your time. A flowering aloe might not hold much interest at first glance, but knowing that it is irresistible to many species of sunbirds might change your mind. Fruiting trees attract monkeys, while herds of herbivores with their young are a predator's dessert cart.

Habitat Knowing which habitats are preferred by each species is a good beginning, but just as important is knowing where to look in those habitats. Animals aren't merely randomly dispersed within their favoured habitats. Instead, they seek out specific sites to shelter – hollows, trees, caves and high points on plains. Many predators use open grasslands but also gravitate towards available cover, such as large trees, thickets or even grass tussocks. Ecotones – where one habitat merges into another – can be particularly productive because species from both habitats will be present.

Tracks & signs Even when you don't see animals, they leave many signs of their presence. Spoor (tracks), scat (droppings), pellets, nests, scrapes and scent marks provide information about wildlife, and may even help to locate it. Check dirt and sand roads when driving – it won't take long for you to recognise interesting spoor. Elephant footprints are unmistakable, and large predator tracks are fairly obvious. Also, many wild cats and dogs use roads to hunt, so look for where the tracks leave the road – often they mark the point where they began a stalk or sought out a nearby bush for shade.

Equipment Probably the most important piece of equipment you can have is a good pair of binoculars. These help you not only spot wildlife but also correctly identify it (this is essential for birding). Binoculars are also useful for viewing species and behaviours where close approaches are impossible. Field guides, which are pocket-sized books that depict mammals, birds, flowers etc of a specific area with photos or colour illustrations, are also invaluable. These guides also provide important identification pointers and a distribution map for each species.

» (above) Sossusvlei sand dune (p296),
  Namibia
» (left) South Luangwa National Park
  (p561), Zambia

BUSH DRIVING & CAMPING IN SOUTHERN AFRICA

Below are road-tested tips to help you plan a safe and successful 4WD expedition.

» Invest in a good Global Positioning System (GPS). You should always be able to identify your location on a map, though, even if you're navigating with a GPS. We found the Tracks4Africa (www.tracks4africa.co.za) program to be the best.

» Stock up on emergency provisions, even on main highways. Fill up whenever you pass a station. For long expeditions, carry the requisite amount of fuel in metal jerry cans or reserve tanks (off-road driving burns nearly twice as much fuel as highway driving). Carry 5L of water per person per day, as well as plenty of high-calorie, nonperishable emergency food items.

» You should have a tow rope, a shovel, an extra fan belt, vehicle fluids, spark plugs, bailing wire, jump leads, fuses, hoses, a good jack and a wooden plank (to use as a base in sand and salt), several spare tyres and a pump. A good Swiss Army knife or Leatherman and a roll of gaffer tape can save your vehicle's life in a pinch.

» Essential camping equipment includes a waterproof tent, a three-season sleeping bag (or a warmer bag in the winter), a ground mat, fire-starting supplies, firewood, a basic first-aid kit and a torch (flashlight) with extra batteries.

» Natural water sources are vital to local people, stock and wildlife, so please don't use clear streams, springs or waterholes for washing yourself or your gear. Similarly, avoid camping near springs or waterholes lest you frighten the animals and inadvertently prevent them from drinking. You should always ask permission before entering or camping near a settlement. Please be considerate and respect the local environment and culture.

» In the interests of the delicate landscape and flora, keep to obvious vehicle tracks; in this dry climate, damage caused by off-road driving may be visible for hundreds of years to come.

» Sand tracks are least likely to bog vehicles in the cool mornings and evenings, when air spaces between sand grains are smaller. Move as quickly as possible and keep the revs up, but avoid sudden acceleration. Shift down gears before deep sandy patches or the vehicle may stall and bog.

» When negotiating a straight course through rutted sand, allow the vehicle to wander along the path of least resistance. Anticipate corners and turn the wheel slightly earlier

Ambience Will you be staying in or near the park? (If you stay well outside the park, you'll miss the good early morning and evening wildlife-viewing hours.) Are the surroundings atmospheric? Will you be in a large lodge or an intimate private camp?

Equipment Mediocre equipment and vehicles can significantly detract from your experience. In remote areas, lack of quality equipment or vehicles and appropriate backup arrangements can be a safety risk.

Access & activities If you don't relish the idea of spending hours on bumpy roads, consider parks and lodges where you can fly in. To get out of the vehicle and into the bush, target areas offering walking and boat safaris.

Guides A good driver/guide can make or break your safari.

Community commitment Look for operators that do more than give lip-service to ecotourism principles, and that have a genuine, long-standing commitment to the communities where they work. In addition to being more culturally responsible, they'll also be able to give you a more authentic and enjoyable experience.

Setting the agenda Some drivers feel that they have to whisk you from one good 'sighting' to the next. If you prefer to stay in one strategic place for a while to experience the environment and see what comes by, discuss this with your driver. Going off in wild pursuit of the Big Five (elephant, lion, rhino, leopard and buffalo) means you'll miss the more subtle aspects of your surroundings.

Less is more If you'll be teaming up with others to make a group, find out how many people will be in your vehicle, and try to meet your travelling companions before setting off.

Special interests If birdwatching or other special interests are important, arrange a private safari with a specialised operator.

than you would on a solid surface – this allows the vehicle to skid round smoothly – then accelerate gently out of the turn.

» Driving in places such as the Kalahari, often through high grass, the seeds can quickly foul radiators and cause overheating; this is a problem especially near the end of the dry season. If the temperature gauge begins to climb, remove as much plant material as you can from the grille.

» Keep your tyre pressure slightly lower than on sealed roads (around half on sandy tracks), but don't forget to reinflate upon returning to the tarmac.

» When driving in a pan, even if it seems dry, it can still be wet underneath – vehicles can break through the crust and become irretrievably bogged. Foul-smelling salt can mean the pan is wet and potentially dangerous. If in doubt, follow the tracks of other drivers (unless, of course, you see bits of vehicle poking above the surface).

» Avoid travelling at night, when dust and distance may create confusing mirages.

» Follow ruts made by other vehicles.

» If the road is corrugated, gradually accelerate until you find the correct speed – it'll be obvious when the rattling stops.

» If you have a tyre blowout, do not hit the brakes or you'll lose control and the car will roll. Instead, steer straight ahead as best you can, and let the car slow itself down before you bring it to a complete stop.

» In rainy weather, gravel roads can turn to quagmires and desert washes may fill with water. If you're uncertain, get out and check the depth, and only cross when it's safe for the type of vehicle you're driving.

» Always be on the lookout for animals.

» Avoid swerving sharply or braking suddenly on a gravel road or you risk losing control of the vehicle. If the rear wheels begin to skid, steer gently in the direction of the skid until you regain control. If the front wheels skid, take a firm hand on the wheel and steer in the opposite direction of the skid.

» In dusty conditions, switch on your headlights so you can be seen more easily.

Fly-In Safaris

If the world is your oyster, then the sheer sexiness of taking off in a little six-seater aircraft to nip across to the next remote safari camp or designer lodge is a must. It also means you'll be able to maximise your time and cover a selection of parks and reserves to give yourself an idea of the fantastic variety of landscapes on offer.

The biggest temptation will be to cram too much into your itinerary, leaving you rushing from place to place. Be advised, it's always better to give yourself at least three days in each camp or lodge in order to really avail yourself of the various activities on offer.

While a fly-in safari is never cheap, they are all-inclusive and what you pay should cover the cost of your flight transfers as well as meals, drinks and activities in each camp. Obviously, this all takes some planning and the earlier you can book a fly-in safari the

better – many operators advise on at least six to eight months' notice if you want to pick and choose where you stay.

Fly-in safaris are particularly popular and sometimes a necessity in the Delta region of Botswana. Given the country's profile as a top-end safari destination, many tour operators specialise in fly-in safaris or include a fly-in element in their itineraries.

Overland Safaris

Given the costs and complex logistics of arranging a big safari, many budget travellers opt for a ride on an overland expedition, run by specialists like Africa in Focus (www.africa-in-focus.com) and Dragoman (www.dragoman.com). Most of these expeditions are multicountry affairs starting in either Cape Town (South Africa) or Nairobi (Kenya) and covering a combination of countries, such as Namibia, Botswana, Zimbabwe, Zambia, Malawi and Tanzania.

The subject of overlanding often raises passionate debate among travellers. For some the massive trucks and concentrated numbers of travellers herded together are everything that's wrong with travel. They take exception to the practice of rumbling into tiny villages to 'gawk' at the locals and then roaring off to party hard in hostels and bush camps throughout the host countries. Often the dynamics of travelling in such large groups (15 to 20 people at least) creates a surprising insularity resulting in a rather reduced experience of the countries you're travelling through.

For others, the overland truck presents an excellent way to get around on a budget and see a variety of parks and reserves whilst meeting up with people from different walks of life. Whatever your view, bear in mind that you're unlikely to get the best out of any particular African country by racing through on such inflexible itineraries.

Self-Drive Safaris

It's possible to arrange an entire safari from scratch if you hire your own vehicle. This has several advantages over an organised safari, primarily total independence and being able to choose your travelling companions. However, as far as costs go, it's generally true to say that organising your own safari will cost nearly as much as going on a cheap organised safari. Also bear in mind that it's wise to make all your campsite bookings (and pay for them) in advance, which means that you'll need to stick to your itinerary.

Apart from the cost, vehicle breakdowns, accidents, security, weather conditions and local knowledge are also major issues. It's not just about hiring a 4WD, but having the confidence to travel through some pretty rough terrain and handle anything it throws at you. If you don't have 4WD off-roading experience, Africa is not the place to start! However, if all this doesn't put you off then it can be a great adventure.

Your greatest priority will be finding a properly equipped 4WD, including all the necessary tools you might need in case of a breakdown.

You can find pretty much all the camping essentials you need in major supermarket chains, which have outlets in most cities and some larger towns throughout the region.

Walking & Hiking Safaris

At many national parks, you can arrange walks of two to three hours in the early morning or late afternoon, with the focus on watching animals rather than covering distance. Following the walk, you'll return to the main camp or lodge.

It's also possible in Namibia to arrange safaris on foot to track black rhino in the wild. This presents a unique opportunity to see one of Africa's most endangered animals in the wild. This type of safari usually takes place on a private concession.

Desert Hiking

While desert areas of Southern Africa – especially parts of Namibia, Botswana and South Africa – offer a host of hiking opportunities, the conditions are quite different from those to which most visitors are accustomed. Take note of the following:

» In national parks, summer hiking is officially forbidden, and most hiking trails are closed from November or December to April or May.

» In the desert heat, hikers should carry 4L of water per person per day.

» Wear light-coloured and lightweight clothing, use a good sunscreen (at least UV Protection Factor 30) and never set off without a hat that shelters your neck and face from the direct sun.

» Rise before the sun and hike until the heat becomes oppressive. You may then want to rest through the heat of midday and begin again after about 3pm. (Note, however, that summer thunderstorms often brew up at around this time and may continue into the night.)

» During warmer months, it may also be worthwhile timing your hike with the full moon, which will allow you to hike at night.

» Never camp in canyons or dry riverbeds, and always keep to higher ground whenever there's a risk of flash-flooding.

countries at a glance

Before delving into some of the best landscapes, wildlife-watching and cultural experiences on the continent, remember that together these countries make up a huge area, and even crossing overland between them requires careful planning.

Wildlife regions abound, with South Africa, Botswana and Zambia offering the greatest diversity and numbers. Incredible landscapes just seem to pop up, but Namibia's north, the Kalahari, and South Africa's Drakensberg – to name but a few – are the stuff of legend. Many of the countries offer access to some of the best galleries of San rock art in Africa, while cities such as Cape Town, Windhoek and Maputo provide opportunities to delve deeper into the cultural fabric of the region.

Botswana

Landscape ✓✓✓
Wildlife ✓✓✓
Lodges ✓✓✓

Delta & Desert
Two of the continent's iconic landscapes, the shifting waters of the Okavango Delta and the vast emptiness of the Kalahari Desert, provide more than merely a backdrop to some of Africa's best wildlife spectacles.

Wildlife Watching
One of the greatest wildlife-watching shows on earth, from black-maned Kalahari lions to the largest elephant population on the planet.

Lodges & Campsites
Botswana is renowned for having some of the most exclusive lodges in Africa with unimpeachable levels of luxury. For self-drivers, campsites are widespread and often outstanding.

p40

Lesotho

Adventure ✓✓✓
Culture ✓✓✓
Wilderness ✓✓✓

Pony Adventures
Malealea, Ramabanta and Semonkong wow adventurers. Sturdy Basotho ponies take travellers to another level, as does Southern Africa's highest waterfall.

Cultural Interaction
Traditional Basotho life remains strong, and the art of the San people is present throughout the country; lowland craft villages produce weavings, and dancing and music abounds at Morija Arts and Cultural Festival.

Remote & Rugged
Sehlabathebe National Park is beautifully remote, Ts'ehlanyane National Park is lush and rugged, while the central highlands afford intense on-road driving.

p94

Malawi

The Lake ✓✓✓
Walking ✓✓
Safaris ✓✓✓

Diving & Kayaking
Lake Malawi, carved out by the Rift Valley, is a bottle-green paradise swarming with fish and desert islands. It's perfect for diving, with crystal-clear depths and the most diverse freshwater fish on the planet.

Trekking Malawi
The otherworldly landscapes of the soaring Mulanje massif and Zomba Plateau are perfect places to trek, with decent cabins to stay in, well-marked trails and reliable guides.

Reinvigorated Wildlife
Malawi is firmly back on the map with restocked parks throughout the country, reintroduced lions, world class safari lodges and excellent tour operators.

p112

Mozambique

Beaches ✓✓✓
Culture ✓✓
Adventure ✓✓✓

Beaches & Islands
From the pounding surf and windswept dunes of Ponta d'Ouro to the turquoise waters and white sand of the Quirimbas Archipelago, Mozambique offers some of the continent's best beaches.

Culture
Mozambique's cultures have returned with full force after years of suppression. Sample this vibrancy in Maputo, with dance, theatre and other cultural offerings.

Bush Adventure
Northern Mozambique is one of the continent's last adventure frontiers, with unspoiled beaches and islands, and trackless bush. Sail on a dhow to uninhabited islands, relax on pristine beaches or track wildlife in the interior.

p167

Namibia

Adventure ✓✓✓
Landscape ✓✓✓
Desert ✓✓✓

Heart-Stoppers
Namibia is southern Africa's hub for adrenaline-pumping fun. Shoot down a dune on a sandboard, fling yourself out of an aircraft or go camel-riding into a desert sunset.

Canyons & Lonely Roads
Namibia is simply stunning – granite monoliths rise from the desert plains through mists of windblown sand. The enormous gash hacked out of the planet at Fish River Canyon should not be missed.

Shifting Sands
Namib-Naukluft Park is one of the world's largest national parks. This is desert country and the swirling sand dunes here are mesmerising – silent, constantly shifting and gently hued in colour – and a highlight of Namibia.

p244

South Africa

Cuisine ✓✓✓
Wildlife ✓✓✓
History ✓✓✓

Culinary Diversity
Experience Indian-style curries in Durban, hearty meaty fare inland, seafood along the coast and Cape Malay cuisine in and around Cape Town.

Creatures Great & Small
The self-drive safari is South Africa's wildlife-watching trump card. As well as its diverse wildlife, including the Big Five, it has enough birds to keep twitchers smiling for months.

Lest We Forget
To understand South Africa, you must understand its recent past. Even small-town museums have an apartheid exhibit, while larger cities have dedicated vast spaces to documenting the country's darkest era.

p322

Swaziland

Handicrafts ✓✓✓
Activities ✓✓
Culture ✓✓

Handicrafts & Textiles

Outlets such as Manzini Market abound, its handicrafts and textiles supplied by rural sellers, while the Ezulwini and Malkerns Valleys have a well-earned reputation for their craft centres and markets.

Adventure Activities

Choose between Malolotja Nature Reserve's hiking and canopy tours; walks, mountain biking and horse riding in Mlilwane Wildlife Sancturay; Great Usutu River rafting; caving in Gobholo; and tracking black rhino in Mkhaya.

Famous Festival

Swaziland's ceremonies are famous, among them is the Umhlanga Dance, essentially a debutante ball for Swazi maidens.

p515

Zambia

Wildlife ✓✓✓
Adventure ✓✓✓
Waterfalls ✓✓✓

Wildlife Utopia

A wealth of animals and a network of bush camps make Zambia an alluring wildlife-watching destinations. South Luangwa National Park is the highlight, but there are many more, including Kafue, known for its leopards.

Wild Africa Calls

Outside Lusaka, almost everywhere in Zambia is bush. Once you're out in the wild, the logistical hassles fade away as the raw beauty of the landscape takes over.

Vic Falls

The world's largest waterfall assaults the senses: get drenched by the spray, fill your ears with its roar and feast your eyes on its magnificence. Raft the rapids, cruise the Zambezi or simply stand awestruck on the sidelines.

p549

Zimbabwe

Wildlife ✓✓✓
Adventure ✓✓✓
Archaeology ✓

Wild Safaris

It doesn't get much wilder than the parks of Zimbabwe. Hwange is home to one of the largest elephant populations in Africa, while Mana Pools offers unguided walking in a park with predators.

White-Water Adventures

Zimbabwe is the perfect base for some serious adrenaline rushes. Bungee off Victoria Falls Bridge or tame the rapids on the Zambezi River.

Rock Art & Ruins

Landscapes of natural granite boulders in the Matobo National Park are the canvas for ancient rock paintings by the San people, while Great Zimbabwe is the site of the greatest medieval city in sub-Saharan Africa.

p602

> Reviews are organised by author preference, except Eating and Sleeping reviews, which are organised first by budget, and then by author preference.

> Look out for these icons:

TOP CHOICE Our author's top recommendation

A green or sustainable option

FREE No payment required

On the Road

Botswana

Best for Wildlife

» Moremi Game Reserve (p70)

» Chobe National Park (p54)

» Makgadikgadi Pans National Park (p53)

» Central Kalahari Game Reserve (p72)

Best of the Outdoors

» Mokoro trip, Okavango Delta (p68)

» Kgalagadi Transfrontier Park (p75)

Why Go

Blessed with some of the greatest wildlife spectacles on earth, Botswana is one of the foremost safari destinations in Africa. There are more elephants in Botswana than in any other country, the big cats roam free and there's everything from endangered African wild dogs to aquatic antelopes, from rhinos (which are making a comeback) to abundant bird life at every turn.

This is also the land of the Okavango Delta and the Kalahari Desert, at once iconic African landscapes and vast stretches of wilderness. Combine these landscapes and the wildlife that inhabits them and it's difficult to escape the conclusion that this is wild Africa at its best.

Botswana may rank among Africa's most exclusive destinations – accommodation prices at most lodges are once-in-a-lifetime propositions – but self-drive expeditions are also possible. And whichever way you visit, Botswana is a truly extraordinary place.

When to Go

Gaborone

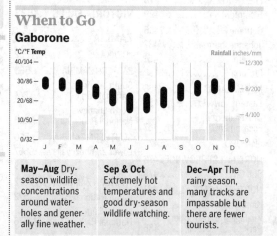

May–Aug Dry-season wildlife concentrations around waterholes and generally fine weather.

Sep & Oct Extremely hot temperatures and good dry-season wildlife watching.

Dec–Apr The rainy season, many tracks are impassable but there are fewer tourists.

GABORONE

POP 231,626

Botswana's small capital may be the country's largest city, but it's a pretty low-key place. There aren't that many reasons to come here – it's a world of government ministries, shopping malls and a seemingly endless urban sprawl with outer neighbourhoods known as 'Phases' and 'Extensions' – most travellers either fly to Maun or cross overland elsewhere. But if you do find yourself here, 'Gabs' has a handful of decent restaurants and good hotels.

◎ Sights

Gaborone Game Reserve   WILDLIFE RESERVE
(☑318 4492; adult/child/vehicle P10/5/10; ◎6.30am-6.30pm) This small reserve was established in 1988 to give locals an opportunity to view Botswana's wildlife in a natural and accessible location. It boasts elands, wildebeest, gemsboks, kudus, ostriches and warthogs, as well as plenty of bird life. All roads are accessible by 2WD. It is 1km east of Broadhurst Mall and can be accessed from Limpopo Dr.

FREE **National Museum &**
Art Gallery   MUSEUM
(Map p46; ☑397 4616; 331 Independence Ave; ◎9am-6pm Tue-Fri, to 5pm Sat & Sun) This small, neglected museum has exhibits of stuffed animals, as well as on precolonial and colonial history. In the Art Gallery section, there's a permanent collection of traditional and modern African and European art.

☞ Tours

Garcin Safaris   GUIDED TOUR
(☑393 8190; www.garcinsafaris.com; 1-/2-day tours €126/402) Local resident and Gaborone expert Marilyn Garcin does great tours of the city, including a *No. 1 Ladies Detective Agency*–focused jaunt.

Africa Insight   GUIDED TOUR
(☑7265 4323; www.africainsight.com; half-/full-day tours P495/860) *No. 1 Ladies Detective Agency* tours endorsed by the author himself with more wide-ranging excursions also possible.

✹ Festivals & Events

Maitisong Festival   PERFORMING ARTS
(www.maitisong.org) Established in 1987, the Maitisong Festival is the largest performing-arts festival in Botswana and is held annually for seven days during the last week of March or the first week of April.

🛏 Sleeping

Mokolodi Backpackers   BACKPACKERS $
(☑7716 8685; admin@backpackers.co.bw; campsites/dm/s P95/165/220, chalets P370-525; @☒) This excellent place around 10km south of the city centre is the only place with a real backpacker vibe around Gaborone. It has attractive chalets and good campsites and dorms. It's handy for the Mokolodi Game Reserve, which is 1km away.

TOP
CHOICE **Metcourt Inn**   HOTEL $$
(☑363 7907; www.peermont.com; r from P720; ✱☏) Located within the Grand Palm Hotel complex and part of the reliable Peermont suite of hotels, this affordable business hotel has classy rooms with a hint of Afro-chic in the decor. If you've been out in the bush, it's heaven on a midrange budget.

Motheo Apartments   APARTMENT $$
(Map p44; ☑318 1587; www.motheoapartments. co.bw; Moremi Rd; apt P420-820; ✱☏☒) This well-run place has good self-catering apartments with internet, DSTV and other mod cons.

Brackendene Lodge   HOTEL $$
(Map p46; ☑391 2886; www.brackendenelodge. com; Tati Rd; r from P250, s/d with bathroom & breakfast P420/458, with kitchen P433/475; ✱☏) Brackendene is one of the better-value hotels in town. Rooms are simple but large and kitted out with TVs and air-con; there's reasonably reliable wi-fi. It's quiet, but you're within walking distance of the Mall.

Walmont Ambassador
at the Grand Palm   HOTEL $$$
(☑363 7777; www.walmont.com; Molepolole Rd; r from P1755; ✱☏☒) Located 4km west of the city centre, this resolutely modern and polished hotel is situated in a Las Vegas–inspired minicity complete with restaurants, bars, a casino, a cinema and a spa. You'll pay to stay, but it's worth it for the pampering.

✗ Eating

Cafe Dijo   CAFE $
(☑315 0575; Old Lobatse Rd, Kgale View Shopping Mall; mains P62; ◎7am-4pm Mon-Fri, 9am-1pm Sat; ☏) Next door to Kalahari Quilts (p45) in the

Botswana Highlights

1 Enjoying the ultimate safari at the **Moremi Game Reserve** (p70), which has some of the best wildlife watching on earth

2 Gliding gently through the vast unspoiled wilderness of the **Okavango Delta** (p61) in a wooden *mokoro* (dugout canoe)

3 Getting up close and personal with Africa's largest elephant herds at the **Chobe National Park** (p54)

4 Looking for black-maned lions at the **Central Kalahari Game Reserve** (p72) in the heart of the Kalahari Desert

5 Watching the wildlife gather by the banks of the Boteti River in the **Makgadikgadi Pans National Park** (p53)

6 Exploring the Kalahari's best dune scenery in the **Kgalagadi Transfrontier Park** (p75) in Botswana's deep south

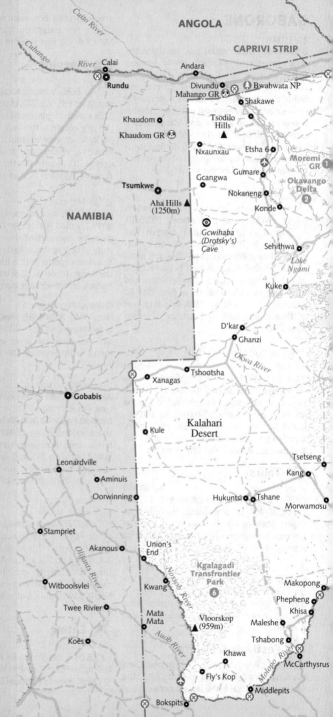

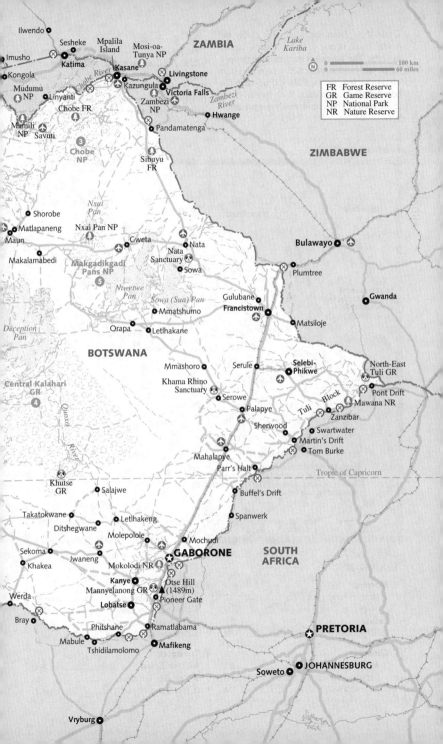

Kgale View Shopping Mall, this classy but casual place is one of our favourite haunts in Gabs. The lunch specials include pepper-steak pie, tandoori-chicken wraps and light Thai-inflected dishes, followed up with Gaborone's best carrot cake. With free wi-fi and great coffee, you could easily spend hours here.

TOP CHOICE Courtyard
Restaurant   AFRICAN, INTERNATIONAL **$$**
(☑392 2487; www.botswanacraft.bw; Western Bypass, off Airport Rd; mains P55-85; ⊗8am-4pm) In the garden area out the back of Botswanacraft (p45), this tranquil spot serves up imaginative African cooking (including impala stew and guinea fowl pot) with other local

Gaborone

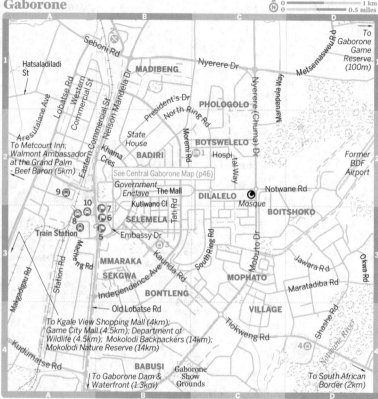

See Central Gaborone Map (p46)

Gaborone

staples making the occasional appearance. They also do a mean lamb curry, salads and sandwiches.

Bull & Bush Pub
INTERNATIONAL $$

(Map p44; ☑397 5070; www.bullandbush.net; mains P85-110; ☺noon-10.30pm Mon-Fri, to 11.30pm Sat & Sun) This long-standing Gaborone institution off Nelson Mandela Dr is deservedly popular with expats, tourists and locals alike. Renowned for its thick steaks and cold beers, they have some themed nights – Wednesday is BBQ night, Thursday is pizzas – while on any given night, the outdoor beer garden is buzzing with activity. It's also the main place for expat nightlife in Gabs.

Beef Baron
BUFFET $$

(☑363 7777; Grand Palm Resort; mains P65-190; ☺6.30-10.30pm Mon-Sat) With a name like this, there's no mystery about the menu, with Gaborone's finest cuts of Botswana beef served in upmarket surrounds. It's inside the Grand Palm complex. Part of the same complex, Mokolwane's Restaurant (buffet P199) has an excellent buffet.

🔒 Shopping

Botswanacraft Marketing
HANDICRAFTS

(☑392 2487; www.botswanacraft.bw; Western Bypass, off Airport Rd; ☺8am-6pm Mon-Fri, to 5pm Sat, 9am-1pm Sun) Botswana's largest craft emporium sells traditional souvenirs from all over the country, including pottery from Gabane and Thamaga, San jewellery, and baskets from across the country at fixed prices. There's also the good on-site Courtyard Restaurant (p44).

Kalahari Quilts
ARTS & CRAFTS

(☑7261 8711; www.kalahariquilts.com; Unit 7A, Kgale Hill Shopping Mall; ☺9am-5pm Mon-Fri, to 2pm Sat) These stunning quilts are made by Batswana women overseen by Jenny Healy and are a genuine and unique craft to take home. Each quilt is unique, although all do a good job at capturing the primary-colour palette that defines Botswana's sensory assault.

Exclusive Books
BOOKS

(Map p44; ☑370 0130; Riverwalk Mall; ☺9am-5pm Mon-Fri, to 2pm Sat) Easily Gaborone's best bookshop, this large shop in the Riverwalk Mall (Map p44; Tlokweng Rd) has literature, nonfiction and travel books, with excellent sections focused on Africa.

ℹ️ Information

Emergency

Ambulance (☑997)
Fire (☑998)
Police (☑999)

Internet Access

Wireless (usually but not always free) is now almost standard in most Gaborone hotels. Most internet cafes rarely survive long.

Moby Trek (1st fl, Unit 24, Embassy Chambers, The Mall; per hr P10; ☺8am-7.30pm Mon-Fri, 9am-7.30pm Sat, 10am-7.30pm Sun)

Medical Services

Gaborone Hospital Dental Clinic (☑395 3777; Segoditshane Way)
Gaborone Private Hospital (☑300 1999; Segoditshane Way) The best facility in town; opposite Broadhurst Mall.

Money

American Express (Map p44; 1st fl, Riverside Mall; ☺9am-5pm Mon-Fri, to 1.30pm Sat)
Barclays Bank (Map p46; The Mall; ☺8.30am-3.30pm Mon-Fri, 8.15-10.45am Sat)
Standard Chartered Bank (Map p46; The Mall; ☺8.30am-3.30pm Mon-Fri, 8.15-11am Sat)

Tourist Information

Tourist Office (Map p46; ☑395 9455; www.botswanatourism.co.bw; Botswana Rd; ☺7.30am-6pm Mon-Fri, 8am-1pm Sat) Moderately useful collection of brochures; next to the Cresta President Hotel.

Department of Wildlife & National Parks (DWNP; ☑381 0774; www.mewt.gov.bw/DWNP) One of two accommodation booking offices – the other is in Maun (p67) – for all national parks and reserves run by the DWNP.

ℹ️ Getting There & Away

Air

From Sir Seretse Khama International Airport, 14km northeast of the centre, **Air Botswana** (Map p46; ☑368 0900; www.airbotswana.co.bw; Matstitam Rd; ☺9.30am-5pm Mon-Fri, 8.30-11.30am Sat) operates international services to Harare, Johannesburg and Lusaka, as well as domestic services to Francistown (from P680), Kasane (from P1050) and Maun (from P882).

Bus

Domestic buses leave from the **main bus terminal** (Map p44). To reach Maun or Kasane, you'll need to change in Francistown. Destinations include Francistown (P60, six hours) and Ghanzi

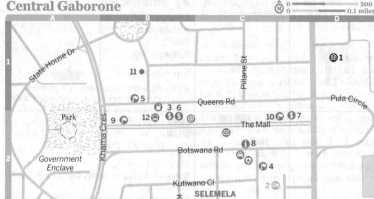

Central Gaborone

⊙ Sights
1 National Museum & Art Gallery D1

🛏 Sleeping
2 Brackendene Lodge C2

ⓘ Information
3 Barclays Bank B2
4 French Embassy C2

5 South African Embassy B1
6 Standard Chartered ATM B2
7 Standard Chartered Bank D2
8 Tourist Office C2
9 UK Embassy B2
10 Zambian Embassy C2

ⓘ Transport
11 Air Botswana B1
12 Intercape Mainliner Bus Office B2

(P130, 11 hours). For details of international bus services to Johannesburg, see p89.

ⓘ Getting Around

To/From the Airport

Taxis rarely turn up at the airport; if you do find one, you'll pay around P70 to Gaborone's centre. Otherwise, try the courtesy minibuses operated by the top-end hotels for their guests. If there's space, nonguests may talk the driver into a lift.

Combi

Packed white combis circulate according to set routes and cost P5. They pick up and drop off only at designated lay-bys marked 'bus/taxi stop'. The new Riverwalk Mall and the Kgale Centre are on the Tlokweng and Kgale routes respectively.

Taxi

Taxis, which can also be easily identified by their blue number plates, are surprisingly difficult to come by in Gabs. Arrange one through your hotel. Fares (negotiable) are generally P40 to P75 per trip around the city.

Final Bravo Cabs (☎312 1785)
Speedy Cabs (☎390 0070)

AROUND GABORONE

Mokolodi Nature Reserve

This 3000-hectare private reserve (☎316 1955; www.mokolodi.com; per vehicle per day P60, day/night game drives per person P140/200, giraffe/rhino tracking P490/590; ⊘7.30am-6pm, often closed Dec-Mar) was established in 1991 and is home to giraffes, elephants, zebras, baboons, warthogs, rhinos, hippos, kudu, impala, waterbucks and klipspringers. The reserve also protects a few retired cheetahs, leopards, honey badgers, jackals and hyenas, as well as over 300 bird species. Mokolodi also operates a research facility, a breeding centre for rare and endangered species, a community-education centre, a sanctuary for orphaned, injured or confiscated birds and animals, and is the base for Cheetah Conservation Botswana (www.cheetahbotswana.com). Among the activities on offer is rhino- and giraffe-tracking – check the website for details.

Visitors are permitted to drive their own vehicles around the reserve (you'll need a 4WD in the rainy season), though guided tours by 4WD or on foot are available. If you're self-driving, pick up a map from the reception office.

The entrance to the reserve is 12km south of Gaborone.

⌊▭ Sleeping

Mokolodi Nature
Reserve Campsite   CAMPGROUND $$
(campsite per adult/child P120/60, chalets P680-1240) Spending the night in the reserve is a refreshing and highly recommended alternative to staying in Gaborone. The campsites are secluded and well groomed, and feature *braai* (barbecue) pits, thatched bush showers (with steaming-hot water) and toilets. There are also three- to eight-person chalets in the middle of the reserve; prices increase significantly on weekends. Advance bookings are necessary.

EASTERN BOTSWANA

Khama Rhino Sanctuary

The 4300-hectare Khama Rhino Sanctuary (⌨463 0713; www.khamarhinosanctuary.org.bw; adult/child P52/26, vehicle under/over 5 tonnes P65/190; ⊘7am-7pm) protects 40 white and four black rhinos; the sanctuary was not originally set up for black rhinos but when one wandered across the border from Zimbabwe it was the start of a beautiful friendship. The sanctuary is also home to impalas, wildebeest, ostriches, brown hyenas, leopards and over 230 bird species.

The best time for spotting rhinos is late afternoon or early morning, with Malemás Pan, Serwe Pan and the waterhole at the bird hide the most wildlife-rich areas of the sanctuary; these locations are clearly marked on the sanctuary map (P10) available at the park entrance.

Two-hour wildlife drives (day/night drive P460/635) can take up to four people. Nature walks and rhino-tracking excursions can also be arranged.

⌊▭ Sleeping

Rhino Sanctuary Trust   CAMPGROUND, CHALETS $
(campsite per adult/child P68/34, dm P317, chalets P470-710; ✱) Shady campsites with *braai* (barbecue) pits are adjacent to clean toilets and steaming-hot showers, while there are also some six-person dorms. For a little more comfort, there are rustic four-person chalets and six-person A-frames; both have basic kitchen facilities and private bathrooms. There's also a restaurant, bar and swimming pool.

❶ Getting There & Away

The sanctuary is 26km northwest of Serowe along the road to Orapa (turn left at the poorly signed T-junction about 5km northwest of Serowe). Khama is accessible by any bus or combi heading towards Orapa.

Francistown

POP 98,963

Francistown is Botswana's second-largest city and an important regional centre – there's a fair chance you'll overnight here if you're on your way north coming from South Africa. There's a small museum, a handful of decent restaurants and plenty of supermarkets.

⌊▭ Sleeping

Grand Lodge   HOTEL $
(⌨241 2300; Haskins St; s/d P275/350; ✱) This is an excellent choice if you want to stay in the city centre. Standard rooms wouldn't win a style award but they're elevated above the norm by the presence of air-con, cable TV, a fridge and a hotplate.

⎡TOP⎤
⎣CHOICE⎦ Woodlands
Stop Over   CAMPGROUND, CHALET $$
(⌨244 0131; www.woodlandscampingbots.com; campsite per person P83, s/d chalets P330/475, r from P685; ✱) A wonderfully tranquil place

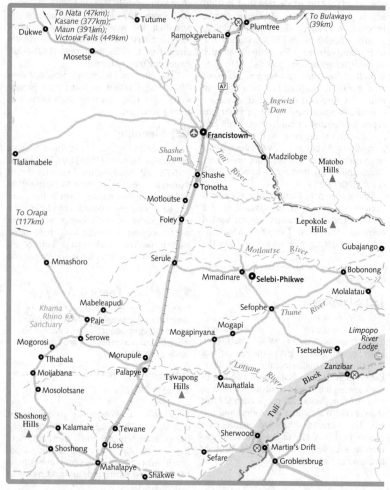

Map locations shown:
To Nata (47km); Kasane (377km); Maun (391km); Victoria Falls (449km)
Dukwe
Tutume
Ramokgwebana
Plumtree
To Bulawayo (39km)
Mosetse
A7
Ingwizi Dam
Francistown
Shashe Dam
Tati River
Madzilobge
Matobo Hills
Tlalamabele
Shashe
Tonotha
Motloutse
To Orapa (117km)
Foley
Lepokole Hills
Motloutse River
Gubajango
Mmashoro
Serule
Bobonong
Mmadinare
Selebi-Phikwe
Molalatau
Mabeleapudi
Sefophe
Thune River
Khama Rhino Sanctuary
Paje
Mogapinyana
Mogapi
Limpopo River Lodge
Mogorosi
Serowe
Tsetsebjwe
Tlhabala
Morupule
Lotsane River
Zanzibar
Block
Moijabana
Palapye
Tswapong Hills
Maunatlala
Tuli
Mosolotsane
Shoshong Hills
Kalamare
Tewane
Sherwood
Shoshong
Lose
Martin's Drift
Sefare
Groblersbrug
Mahalapye
Shakwe

10km north of town off the road to Maun, Woodlands is the pick of the places to stay around Francistown if you have your own wheels. The chalets are nicely appointed, the campsites a wonderful respite from dusty Botswana trails, and Anne and Mike are welcoming hosts.

Digger Inn   HOTEL $$
(244 0107; www.diggerinn.co.bw; St Patrick St, Village Mall; d/f P705/860;) At the northern end of the city centre, Diggers Inn is at once quiet, central and part of the most happening expat enclave (Village Mall) in the city. The rooms here are large if a little careworn and the decor evokes Francistown's mining heyday.

Cresta Marang Gardens   HOTEL $$$
(241 3991; www.crestahotels.com; Old Gaborone Rd; s/d from US$144/169;) One of the better hotels in the Cresta chain in Botswana, this excellent hotel has expansive grounds, standard rooms and some lovely thatched cottages on stilts.

✖ Eating

Thorn Tree TOP CHOICE   CAFE $
(St Patrick St, Village Mall; mains P35-60; ◷6am-3pm Mon-Sat;) An oasis of sophistication

at the northern end of Francistown, Thorn Tree (no relation to Lonely Planet's famous online bulletin board) does burgers, salads, jacket potatoes, fresh fish and great coffee.

Barbara's Bistro INTERNATIONAL **$**
(Francistown Sports Club; mains from P55; ☻noon-2pm & 7-10pm Mon-Sat) Located in the eastern outskirts of town, this quaint, leafy spot is a good choice for a casual atmosphere and good international-style food.

Savanna INTERNATIONAL **$$**
(St Patrick St, 1st fl, Village Mall; mains P55-110; ☻10am-10pm Mon-Sat; 🛜) Probably the pick

of Francistown's sit-down restaurants, this place serves up the town's best steaks, but watch out also for their daily specials. The bar is also one of few expat haunts in town.

ℹ️ Information
Kokela Internet Café (St Patrick St, Village Mall; per hr P12; ☻8am-5pm Mon-Sat)
Tourist Office (☎244 0113; St Patrick St, Village Mall; ☻7.30am-6pm Mon-Fri, 9am-2pm Sat)

ℹ️ Getting There & Away
AIR You can fly between Francistown and Gaborone with **Air Botswana** (☎241 2393; Francis Ave) for around P680.
BUS & COMBI From the **main bus terminal**, located between the train line and **Blue Jacket Plaza**, buses and combis connect Francistown with Gaborone (P60, six hours), Kasane (P106, seven hours), Maun (P90, five hours) and Nata (P41, two hours). For international services to Zimbabwe, see p90.

ℹ️ Getting Around
Francistown's airport is 5.5km west of the city centre. A taxi into town shouldn't cost more than P50.

Tuli Block

This 10km- to 20km-wide swath of free-hold farmland extends over 300km along the northern bank of the Limpopo River and is made up of a series of private properties, many of which have a conservation bent. Wildlife is a big attraction here, but so too is the landscape of muddy oranges and browns, and *kopjes* (small rocky hills) overlooked by deep blue sky. Elephants, hippos, kudu, wildebeest and impalas as well as small numbers of lions, cheetahs, leopards and hyenas circle each other among the *kopjes* scattered with artefacts from the Stone Age onwards. More than 350 species of bird have also been recorded here.

🛏️ Sleeping
Wild at Tuli TENTED CAMP **$$**
(☎7211 3688; www.wildattuli.com; Kwa-Tuli Game Reserve; per person self-catering/full board P595/960) This fabulous camp on an island in a branch of the Limpopo River is run by respected conservationists Judi Gounaris and Dr Helena Fitchat and they bring a winning combination of warmth and

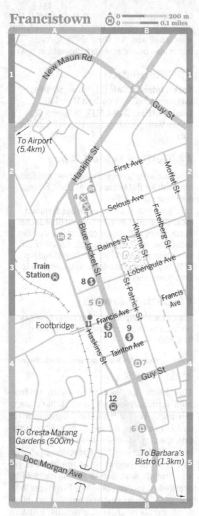

Francistown

conservation knowledge to the experience. Meals are home-cooked and eaten around the communal table, the tents are comfortable and game drives on the 5000-hectare property are included in the price.

Tuli Safari Lodge LODGE $$$
(✆264 5303; www.tulilodge.com; ste with full board P820-2410; ✳☀) In the Northern Tuli Game Reserve, this fine lodge is set in a riverine oasis and surrounded by red rock country that teems with wildlife. The game reserve is just beyond the Pont Drift border post.

Mashatu Game Reserve TENTED CAMP $$$
(✆in South Africa 011-442 2267; www.mashatu. com; chalet s/d US$660/880, luxury tent US$480/640; ✳☀) One of the largest private wildlife reserves in Southern Africa, Mashatu is renowned for its big cats and frighteningly large elephant population. Accommodation is in enormous luxury suites decorated with impeccable taste in the main camp. The wildlife reserve is close to the Pont Drift border post.

ⓘ Information

Entrance to the Tuli Game Reserve is free and night drives (not permitted in government-controlled parks and reserves) are allowed. The best time to visit is May to September, when animals congregate around permanent water sources.

Please note that the Tuli Block is private land, so visitors are not allowed to venture off the main roads or camp outside the official campsites and lodges.

ⓘ Getting There & Away

There are daily flights between Johannesburg and the Limpopo Valley Airport at Polokwane, which is convenient for the Mashatu Game Reserve and Tuli Safari Lodge; flights can sometimes be booked as part of a package with either reserve. Otherwise you'll need your own vehicle to reach the Tuli Block.

From inside Botswana, the lodges can be accessed from the west via the paved road from Bobonong.

MAKGADIKGADI & NXAI PANS

Within striking distance of the water-drowned terrain of the Okavango Delta, Chobe River and Linyanti Marshes lies Makgadikgadi, the largest network of salt pans in the world. It's as much an emptiness as a place, an area larger than Switzerland, mesmerising in scope and in beauty.

Two protected areas – Makgadikgadi Pans National Park and Nxai Pan National Park, separated only by the asphalted A3 – protect large tracts of salt pans, palm forests, grasslands and savannah. The horizonless pans of Nxai Pan have a reputation for cheetah sightings, while the return of waters to the Boteti River in the west can lead to a wildlife bonanza of wildebeest, zebra and antelope species pursued by lions. But there are also some fabulous areas outside park boundaries, with iconic stands of baobab trees and beguiling landscapes.

Nata

Dusty Nata serves as the eastern gateway to the Makgadikgadi Pans, as well as an obligatory fuel stop if you're heading to either Kasane or Maun.

◉ Sights

Nata Bird Sanctuary WILDLIFE RESERVE
(☏7154 4342; admission P55; ⊙7am-7pm) This 230-sq-km community-run wildlife sanctuary 15km southeast of Nata draws over 165 species of bird, with water birds (especially flamingos and pelicans in the rainy season) a speciality. In the dry season (May to October), it's possible to drive around the sanctuary in a 2WD with high clearance, though it's best to enquire about the condition of the tracks in the sanctuary before entering. During the rainy season, however, a 4WD is essential.

☐ Sleeping

Nata Bird Sanctuary Campsite CAMPGROUND $
(☏7154 4342; campsite per person/vehicle P35/15; ⊜) Nata Bird Sanctuary offers several serene and isolated campsites with clean pit toilets, *braai* pits and cold showers. From the campsites, it's possible to access the pan on foot (7km) – bring a compass.

Nata Lodge LODGE $$
(☏620 0070; www.natalodge.com; campsite per adult/child P70/45, d luxury tents/chalets P635/800; ✲⊛) The Nata Lodge has luxury wood-and-thatch chalets, stylish safari tents and a good campsite all set amid a verdant oasis of monkey thorn, marula and mokolane palms. Game drives into the pans start at P165 per person; they also organise cultural tours of Nata village (P115), while dinner costs P140.

Northgate Lodge LODGE $$
(☏621 1156; www.northgate.co.bw; s/d/f P555/636/945; ✲⊛) In the heart of town next to

BOTSWANA NATA

WORTH A TRIP

KUBU ISLAND

Along the southwestern edge of Sowa Pan is a ghostly, baobab-laden rock, entirely surrounded by a sea of salt. Once a real island on a real lake (in Setswana, *kubu* means 'hippopotamus') and inhabited by people as recently as 500 years ago, Kubu is now protected as a national monument, administered by the local Gaing-O-Community Trust.

The community-run **Kubu Island Campsite** (☏7549 4669; www.kubuisland.com; Lekhubu, GPS: S 20°53.460', E 25°49.318'; campsite per adult/child P100/50) is one of Botswana's loveliest with baobabs as a backdrop to most campsites, many of which have sweeping views of the pan. There are bucket showers and pit toilets.

Access to Kubu Island (S 20°53.740', E 25°49.426') involves negotiating a maze of grassy islets and salty bays. Increased traffic has now made the route considerably more obvious, but drivers still need a 4WD and a compass or GPS.

Makgadikgadi & Nxai Pans National Parks

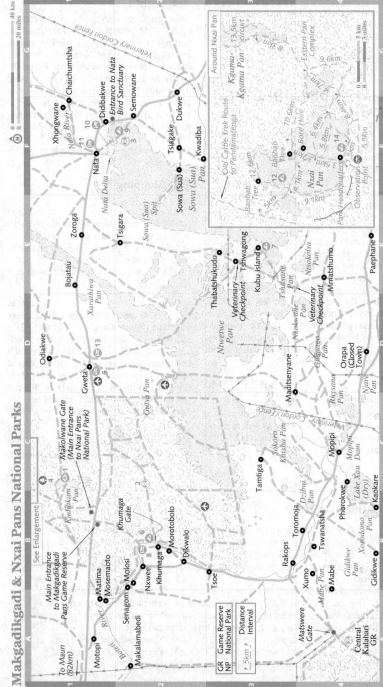

Around Nxai Pan

Eastern Pan Complex

Kgama-Kgama Pan circuit 13.5km

9.6km

Old Cattle Trek Route to Pandamatenga

Baobab Tree 12.6km

Baobab Tree 10.6km

Bore Hole

Nxai Pan

Park Headquarters

Observation Point

GR Game Reserve
NP National Park

5km Distance Interval

To Maun (82km)

Motopi

Makalamabedi

Senagom Molosi

Matima Mosemaoto

Nxwee Khumaga

Morotobolo

Dikwalo

Tsoe

Main Entrance to Makgadikgadi Pans Game Reserve

Makolwane Gate (Main Entrance to Nxai Pans National Park)

Kudiakam Pan

Khumaga Gate

See Enlargement

Matswere Gate

Central Kalahari GR

Xumo

Mabe

Gidikwe

Tswanatsha

Rakops

Toromoja

Tamtiga

Phorokwe

Kaokare

Mopipi

Orapa (Closed Town)

Maditsenyane

Kubu Island

Veterinary Checkpoint

Tshwagong

Thabatshukudu

Gweta

Odiakwe

Bojatau

Zoroga

Tsigara

Xhongwane

Chaichumtsha

Didibakwe

Entrance to Nata Bird Sanctuary

Semowane

Dukwe

Tsiagake

Kwadiba

Nata

Sowa (Sua)

Sowa (Sua) Pan

Sowa (Sua) Spit

Nata Delta

Nata River

Veterinary Cordon Fence

Xarathiwa Pan

Ntwetwe Pan

Nwetwe Pan

Ntwetswe Pan

Gidikwe Pan

Xobdomo Pan

Mabe Pan

Dzibui Pan

Sokoro Ktusha Pan

Nnamatshumo

Nsokotsa Pan

Tshitsane Pan

Nhokwane Pan

Gkgagga Pan

Rhysana Pan

Njare Pan

Paephane

Lake Xau (Dry)

Mopipi Dam

Veterinary Cordon Fence

Boteti River

40 km
20 miles

the petrol stations, Northgate Lodge is more about breaking up the journey than finding a remote base for a few days. The rooms are pleasant enough and excellent value. Depending on your perspective, the location is either too busy or convenient, standing as it does at the crossroads of roads that lead to all corners of the country. We lean towards the former unless you're travelling by public transport, but make up your own mind.

❶ Getting There & Away

Regular combis (minibuses) travelling en route to Kasane (P88, five hours), Francistown (P41, two hours) and Maun (P76, five hours) pass by the **Northgate Lodge**.

Gweta

Gweta is an obligatory fuel stop if you're heading to either Kasane or Maun, although be warned – its petrol station was closed for repairs when we passed through. The village itself is a dusty and laidback crossroad on the edge of the pans framed by bushveld and big skies.

⊨ Sleeping

Gweta Lodge   LODGE **$$**
(☎621 2220; www.gwetalodge.com; d safari tents P350, s/d/f P390/525/795; ✱🛜🏊) In the centre of town, Gweta Lodge is a friendly place with a vaguely colonial air and a poolside bar. The rooms are large and comfortable and there are plans for an overhaul of their campsites. They organise a range of activities, and lunch (P22 to P80) and dinner (P140) are served by the pool.

Planet Baobab   LODGE, CAMPGROUND **$$**
(☎in South Africa 011-447 1605; www.unchar tedafrica.com; campsite per adult/child P45/68, d tents P450, s/d/q huts from P1010/1120/1760; 🛜🏊) About 4km east of Gweta, funky and

friendly Planet Baobab is an inventive lodge with a great open-air bar-restaurant (meals P49 to P90). Outside, *rondavels* and chalets are scattered over the gravel and campers can pitch a tent beneath the shade of a baobab tree. There's an excellent range of activities.

❶ Getting There & Away

Hourly combis travelling to Francistown (P44, three hours) and Maun (P47, four hours) pass along the main road.

Makgadikgadi Pans National Park

This 3900-sq-km park extends from the Boteti River in the west to the Ntwetwe Pan in the east. The return of water to the Boteti River in recent years has drawn plenty of wildlife, particularly in the dry season from May to October (including one of southern Africa's most spectacular wildebeest and zebra migrations) when the river is the only source of permanent water in the reserve.

⊨ Sleeping

Khumaga Campsite   CAMPGROUND **$**
(www.sklcamps.com;GPS:S20°27.311,'E24°30.968';
campsite per adult/child US$50/25) The Khumaga campsite sits high above the bank of the Boteti and is an attractive site with good shade, *braai* pits and an excellent ablutions block with flush toilets and hot showers.

Leroo-La-Tau   LODGE **$$$**
(☎686 1559; www.desertdelta.com; per person Jan-Apr US$476, s/d May-Dec US$1113/1712; 🏊) Luxury East African–style canvas tents with private verandahs overlooking the Boteti riverbed make for some of the best views in the Kalahari – sunset when the animals

---

Makgadikgadi & Nxai Pans National Parks

⊙ Sights		
1 Baines' Baobabs		C1
2 Makgadikgadi Pans Game Reserve		C2
3 Nata Bird Sanctuary		F2
4 Nxai Pan National Park		C1

⊨ Sleeping		
Baines' Baobab		(see 1)
5 Gweta Lodge		D1
6 Khumaga Campsite		B2
7 Kubu Island Campsite		E3
8 Leroo-La-Tau		B2
9 Nata Bird Sanctuary Campsite		F2
10 Nata Lodge		F1
11 Northgate Lodge		F1
12 Nxai Pan Camp		F3
13 Planet Baobab		D1
14 South Camp		F4

come down to drink is the time to nurse a sundowner on the verandah.

ℹ️ Getting There & Away

The main entrance to the wildlife reserve is 141km west of Nata and 164km east of Maun. A 4WD is needed to drive around the park, and the road from the main gate to the Khumaga campsite is deep sand. There's another entrance close to Khumaga campsite, but you'll need to cross the river on a pontoon ferry (per vehicle P120).

Nxai Pan National Park

The grassy expanse of this 2578-sq-km park is interesting during the rains, when large animal herds migrate from the south and predators arrive to take advantage of the bounty, but it's also impressive when the land is dry and dust clouds migrate over the scrub and salt pans. The region is specked with umbrella acacias, and cheetah and elephant sightings are common.

◎ Sights

Baines' Baobabs   OUTDOORS
(GPS: S 20°06.726', E 24°46.136') In the south of the Nxai Pan National Park are the famous Baines' Baobabs, which were immortalised in paintings by the artist and adventurer Thomas Baines in 1862. Today, a comparison with Baines' paintings reveals that in almost 150 years, only one branch has broken off.

🛏️ Sleeping

South Camp   CAMPGROUND $
(www.xomaesites.com; GPS: S 19°56.159', E 24°46.598'; campsite per adult/child P226/113) Around 37km from the park gate along a sandy track, South Camp has 10 sites clustered quite close together behind some trees at the edge of one of the pans. There's a good ablutions block with flush toilets and hot showers, as well as *braai* pits.

Baines' Baobab   CAMPGROUND $
(www.xomaesites.com; GPS: S 20°08.362', E 24°46.213'; campsite per adult/child P350/175) Just three sites sit close to the famed baobabs, a wonderfully evocative site once the day trippers go home. There are bucket showers and pit toilets.

Nxai Pan Camp   TENTED CAMP $$$
(☑686 1449; www.kwando.co.bw; s/d per person from US$620/880; 🐾) Eight rooms done up in a chic modern-African style curve in a crescent around an open plain; inside, smooth

linens and indoor and outdoor showers do a good job of pushing the whole rustic-luxury vibe. The large, polished deck or pool are fine vantage points.

ℹ️ Getting There & Away

The entrance to the park is at Makolwane Gate, which is about 140km east of Maun and 60km west of Gweta. A 4WD is required to get around the national park.

Two tracks lead from the main track to Baines' Baobab; when we visited, the longer, northernmost of the two was much easier to traverse, but ask at the park gate.

CHOBE NATIONAL PARK & KASANE

Chobe National Park is one of *the* great wildlife destinations of Africa. Famed for its enormous population of massive elephants, Chobe, which encompasses nearly 11,000 sq km, is itself the size of a small country and an important epicentre of Botswana's safari industry.

The park has three major sections for wildlife-watching:

Chobe Riverfront Supports the largest wildlife concentration in the park; within easy striking distance of the gateway town of Kasane.

Linyanti Marshes Predator-rich and a wonderfully remote feel.

Savuti Reached from Maun or Kasane, Savuti has prolific wildlife, and the miraculous return of waters to the Savuti Channel has restored the region to its former glory.

Kasane & Around

Kasane lies at the meeting point of four countries – Botswana, Zambia, Namibia and Zimbabwe – and the confluence of two major rivers – the Chobe and the Zambezi.

Chobe National Park

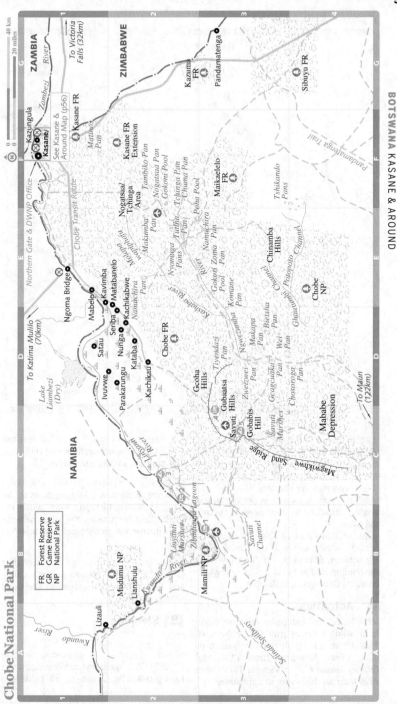

Chobe National Park

FR	Forest Reserve
GR	Game Reserve
NP	National Park

ZAMBIA

ZIMBABWE

NAMIBIA

0   20 miles
0   40 km

To Victoria
Falls (32km)

Zambezi River

Kazungula
Kasane
See Kasane &
Around Map (p56)

Kasane FR

Matwea
Pan

Kazuma
FR

Pandamatenga

Sibuyu FR

Pandamatenga Trail

Chobe Transit Route

Northern Gate & DWNP Office

Kasane FR
Extension

Nogatsaa/
Tchinga
Area

Nogatsaa Pan
Gokomi Pool
Tambiko Pan
Tchinga Pan
Chuma Pan
Peha Pool

Maikaelelo
FR

Tshikando
Pans

Ngoma Bridge

Mabele
Kavimba
Matabanelo
Kachikabwe
Namachira

Mukumba
Pan
Tutlha
Pan
Nyomuga
Pans

Gokori Zoma Pan

Chinamba
Hills

Chobe
NP

Satau
Seritbe
Nunga
Kataba
Kachikau

Parakarungu
Ivuvwe

Mohupiu

Mohupiu

Kasikubu River

Nogi Zoma
Pool Pan
Komane
Pan
Ngwezumba River

Gokori
Pan

Ghanwi Potopoto Channel

To Katima Mulilo
(70km)

Lake
Liambezi
(Dry)

Chobe FR

Gcoha
Hills

Tiyendazi
Pan

Gubaatsa
Hills

Gobabis
Hill

Savuti

Zweizwei
Pan
Gcagcakaa
Pan

Makapa
Pan
Bietsha
Pan
Wei Pan

Chosoroga
Pan

Mababe
Depression

To Maun
(122km)

Magwikhwe Sand Ridge

Kwando River

Linyanti River

Linyanti
Marshes

Zibadianja Lagoon

Savuti
Marshes

Savuti Channel

Selinda Spillway

Kwando River

Mudumu NP

Lianshulu

Mamili NP

Lizauli

Savuti Channel

Kasane & Around

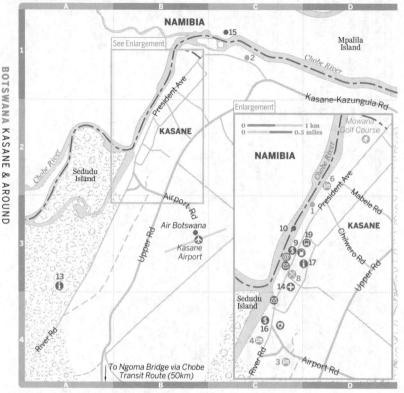

It's also the northern gateway to Chobe National Park and the jumping-off point for excursions to Victoria Falls. Although it's nowhere near as large or developed as Maun, there's certainly no shortage of lodges and safari companies, as well as petrol stations and supermarkets for those heading out into the wilds.

About 12km east of Kasane is tiny Kazungula, which serves as the border crossing between Botswana and Zimbabwe, and the landing for the Kazungula ferry, which connects Botswana and Zambia.

🏃 Activities

Most lodges and campsites organise three-hour wildlife drives into Chobe National Park (from P195), three-hour boat trips along Chobe Riverfront (from P190) and full-day excursions to Victoria Falls (from P1250) across the border in Zimbabwe.

Kalahari Holiday Tours WILDLIFE TOUR
(☑625 0880; www.kalaharichobe.com) Half-, full- and multiday safaris into Chobe.

Pangolin Photography Safaris GUIDED TOUR
(www.pangolinphoto.com; 3hr game drives or boat trips US$120) Photography tours along the Chobe Riverfront using the latest cameras with instruction thrown in; park fees cost extra.

Gecko GUIDED TOUR
(☑625 2562; www.oldhousekasane.com) Canoe and fishing trips add variety to the usual wildlife drives.

🛏 Sleeping

TOP
CHOICE **Senyati Safari Camp** CAMPGROUND, CHALETS $$
(☑7188 1306; www.senyatisafaricamp.com; off Kazungula-Nata Rd; campsite per adult/child from

Kasane & Around

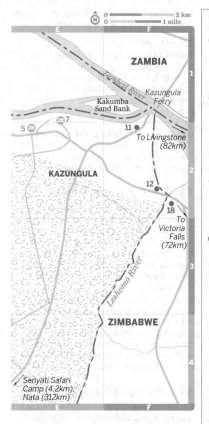

P63/115, s/d/f chalets P400/520/690; ❄❄) Off the main highway south of Kazungula (the turn-off is well-signposted 6.8km south of Kazungula, from where it's a further 1.6km off road), this wonderful spot has comfy chalets and some of northern Botswana's best campsites, each with their own ablutions block. The bar and some of the chalets overlook a waterhole where elephants congregate in large numbers nightly, and wild dogs have also been known to pass by for a drink.

Old House
GUESTHOUSE $$

(☑625 2562; www.oldhousekasane.com; President Ave; r P550-900; ❄❄❄) Close to the centre and with a nice intimate feel, the Old House has lovely rooms adjacent to a quiet garden by the riverbank. The bar-restaurant is one of Kasane's best and the rooms are stylish and comfortable without being overdone.

Toro Safari Lodge
LODGE, CAMPGROUND $$

(☑625 2694; www.torolodge.co.bw; off Kasane-Kazungula Rd; campsite per person P81, chalets from P671, apt P1003; ❄@❄) Down a side road off the main Kasane-Kazungula Rd, this excellent place has campsites beneath maturing trees, comfortable chalets (some with river views) and attractive grounds that run along the riverbank.

Chobe Safari Lodge
LODGE $$$

(☑625 0336; www.chobesafarilodge.com; President Ave; campsite per adult/child P75/60, r P975-1175; ❄❄) One of the more affordable upmarket lodges in Kasane (or Botswana for that matter), Chobe Safari Lodge has understated but comfortable rooms, which are priced according to size and location, though all feature attractive mosquito-netted beds and modern furnishings.

Kubu Lodge   LODGE $$$
(✆625 0312; www.kubulodge.net; Kasane-Kazungula Rd; s/d US$255/310; ✼✖) Located 9km east of Kasane, this riverside option lacks the stuffiness and formality found in most other top-end lodges but is their match for quality. Rustic wooden chalets are lovingly adorned with thick rugs and wicker furniture, and scattered around an impeccably manicured lawn dotted with fig trees.

✖ Eating

Coffee & Curry   INDIAN $
(✆625 2237; Shop 1AB, Hunters' Africa Mall, off President Ave; mains P45-70; ⊙9am-10pm Mon-Sat, 11am-9pm Sun) They do just about everything (except African!) at this simple Indian-run place with an especially good selection of curries and other Indian dishes, as well as a few pizzas and Southeast Asian–inspired dishes.

TOP CHOICE **Old House**   INTERNATIONAL $$
(✆625 2562; www.oldhousekasane.com; President Ave; breakfast P45-60, light meals P30-60, mains P45-85) This open-air bar-restaurant close to the riverbank is every bit as good as the guesthouse it inhabits. The menu contains all the usual suspects such as burgers, toasted sandwiches, salads, steaks and pizzas, with fish and chips not forgotten either. There's also a kids' menu.

❶ Information

Emergency
Chobe Private Clinic (✆625 1555; President Ave)
Kasane Hospital (✆625 0333; President Ave)

Internet Access
Chobe Post Office (Hunters' Africa Mall, off President Ave; per hr P40; ⊙9am-5pm Mon-Fri, to noon Sat)
Cape to Cairo Bureau de Change & Internet (Hunters' Africa Mall, off President Ave; per hr P40; ⊙8.30am-5pm Mon-Fri, to 4.30pm Sat)

Money
Barclays Bank (Hunters' Africa Mall, off President Ave; ⊙8.30am-3.30pm Mon-Fri, 8.15-10.45am Sat) Be sure to stock up on US dollars (post-1996) if you're heading to Zimbabwe.
Open Door Bureau de Change (President Ave; ⊙8.30am-5pm Mon-Fri, to 4.30pm Sat) Next

to Choppies supermarket; charges 2% commission on cash, 3% on travellers cheques.

Tourist Information
Tourist Office (✆625 0555; Hunters' Africa Mall, off President Ave; ⊙7.30am-6pm Mon-Fri, 9am-2pm Sat) Plenty of brochures for lodges and safari companies and generally helpful, although you're better off visiting the park gate for information on Chobe National Park.
Department of Wildlife & National Parks (DWNP; ✆625 0235; Sedudu Gate) This is the place to pay for your park permit and get information on visiting Chobe National Park.

❶ Getting There & Away

AIR **Air Botswana** (✆625 0161; www.airbotswana.co.bw) connects Kasane to Maun (from P369) and Gaborone (from P1050).

BUS & COMBI Combis heading to Francistown (P106, seven hours), Maun (P96, six hours) and Nata (P88, five hours) run when full from the **Shell petrol station** and **bus terminal** on Mabele Rd.

CAR & MOTORCYCLE The direct route between Kasane and Maun is only accessible by 4WD, and may be almost impassable after heavy rains. Also remember that there is nowhere along the Kasane–Maun road to buy fuel, food or drinks, or to get vehicle repairs. All other traffic between Kasane and Maun travels via Nata.

❶ Getting Around

Combis travel regularly between Kasane and Kazungula, and continue to the immigration posts for Zambia and Zimbabwe if requested. The standard fare for anywhere around Kasane and Kazungula is about P35.

Chobe Riverfront

The Chobe Riverfront rarely disappoints with arguably Botswana's densest concentration of wildlife. Although animals are present along the riverfront year-round, the density of wildlife can be overwhelming during the dry season, especially during September and October. Whether you cruise along the river in a motorboat, or drive along the banks in a 4WD, you're almost guaranteed an up-close encounter with some of the largest elephant herds on the continent.

If you don't have your own wheels, any of the hotels and lodges in Kasane can help you organise a wildlife drive or boat cruise along the riverfront.

CHOBE RIVERFRONT (DE)CONGESTION

Chobe is one of few national parks in Botswana where you may enter as a day tripper without a confirmed lodge or campsite reservation (although you will be expected to leave the park prior to closing if you do not have one). But overcrowding along Chobe Riverfront's safari trails has prompted park officials to institute a controversial system aimed at reducing the number of vehicles during peak times. Under the strategy, tour operators are allowed to visit the park from dawn until 9am and from 2.30pm to sunset. Self-drivers and day trippers are left with the wholly unappealing hours of 9am to 2.30pm.

However, when we visited (self-driving) during a particularly busy period, we were allowed in at 3pm and allowed to stay until sunset. Confused? Our advice is to turn up at the Chobe Riverfront (Sedudu) gate of the park almost immediately after you arrive in Kasane to enable you to plan your visit. And it's always worth trying to discuss the situation with the rangers at the gate if at first they refuse you entry.

🛏 Sleeping

Ihaha Campsite   CAMPGROUND $
(kwalatesafari@gmail.com; GPS: S 17°50.487', E 24°52.754'; campsite per adult/child P260/130) Ihaha campsite is the only camping ground for self-drivers along the Chobe Riverfront – staying here gives you the run of the park without having to negotiate the decongestion strategy. The trees need more time to mature but the location is excellent – it's by the water's edge about 27km from the Northern Gate. There's an ablutions block and *braai* areas.

Chobe Game Lodge   LODGE $$$
(☑625 1761, 625 0340; www.chobegamelodge.com; River Rd; per person Jan-Apr US$476, s/d May-Dec US$1113/1712; ❀) This highly praised safari lodge, 9km west of the Northern Gate, has individually decorated rooms that are elegant yet soothing, and some have views of the Chobe River and Namibian flood plains. Service is attentive and professional, and there's a good chance you'll spot herds of elephants along the riverfront as you walk around the hotel grounds.

Chobe Chilwero Lodge   LODGE $$$
(☑in South Africa 011-438 4650; www.sanctuarylodges.com; Airport Rd; per person Jan-Apr US$620, May-Dec US$1055; ❀❀❀) *Chilwero* means 'place of high view' in Setswana, and indeed this exclusive lodge boasts panoramic views across the Chobe River. Accommodation is in one of 15 elegant bungalows featuring romantic indoor and outdoor showers, private terraced gardens and colonial fixtures adorned with plush linens. There's a well-reviewed gourmet restaurant.

❶ Getting There & Away

From central Kasane, the park's Northern Gate is about 6km to the southwest. All tracks along the riverfront require a 4WD vehicle. If you exit via Ngoma, you can return to Kasane via the Chobe transit route.

Savuti

Savuti, in the southwestern corner of Chobe National Park, is one of Africa's great safari destinations. Flat, wildlife-packed expanses are awash with distinctly African colours and vistas. Although home to its share of elite lodges, there is also an excellent campsite for self-drivers.

◉ Sights

The southernmost of the rocky monoliths that rise up from the Savuti sand is aptly known as **Leopard Rock** and sightings of the most elusive of Africa's big cats are reasonably common here. The **Savuti Marshes** in southern Savuti is where once-dry tracks now disappear into standing water. The marshes lie between the Savuti Channel and the main Savuti–Maun track. Another of the rocky monoliths, **Gobabis Hill** is home to several sets of signposted 4000-year-old rock paintings of San origin.

🛏 Sleeping

Savuti Campsite   CAMPGROUND $
(www.sklcamps.com; GPS: S 18°34.014', E 24°03.905'; campsite per adult/child US$50/20) One of the best campsites in northern Botswana, five of the seven sites overlook the river – sites one to four could do with a little more shade but are otherwise lovely, while

THE SAVUTI CHANNEL

One of northern Botswana's strangest natural phenomena, the Savuti Channel, which miraculously began flowing again in 2008, links the Savuti Marshes with the Linyanti Marshes and – via the Selinda Spillway – the Okavango Delta. At times it will stop flowing for years at a stretch (eg from 1888 to 1957, 1966 to 1967 and 1982 until 2008). When flowing, the channel changes the entire ecosystem, creating an oasis that provides water for thirsty wildlife. According to the only feasible explanation thus far put forward, the phenomenon may be attributed to tectonics – the flow of the Savuti Channel must be governed by an imperceptible flexing of the surface crust. The minimum change required to open or close the channel would be at least 9m, and there's evidence that this has happened at least five times in the past 100 years.

Paradise camp is our pick. The ablutions block has sit-down flush toilets, *braai* pits and (usually hot) showers. Be careful of wandering baboons and elephants.

Camp Savuti　　　　　　TENTED CAMP **$$$**
(www.sklcamps.com; s/d May-Dec full board US$500/700) Given a licence to run the public campsites, cheeky SKL has also taken on the big boys with some beautifully appointed canvas tents overlooking the Savuti Channel. Prices are a touch below the longer-established camps but the quality is pretty much on a par.

Savute Safari Lodge　　　　LODGE **$$$**
(☏686 1559; www.desertdelta.com; per person Jan-Apr US$476, s/d May-Dec US$1113/1712) Next to the former site of the legendary Lloyd's Camp, this upmarket retreat consists of 12 contemporary thatched chalets in neutral tones. The main safari lodge is home to a sitting lounge, an elegant dining room, a small library, a cocktail bar and a breathtaking viewing deck.

Savute Elephant Camp　　　LODGE **$$$**
(☏686 0302; www.savuteelephantcamp.com; s/d May-Dec full board US$1856/2650; ❇☲) The premier camp in Savuti is made up of 12 lavishly appointed East African–style linen tents on raised wooden platforms and complete with replica antique furniture. The main tent houses a dining room, lounge and bar, and is next to a swimming pool that overlooks a pumped waterhole.

❶ Getting There & Away
Under optimum conditions, it's a four-hour slog from Kasane's Sedudu Gate to Savuti, though be advised that this route is often unnavigable from January to March. Access is also possible from Maun or the Moremi Game Reserve via Mababe Gate. All of these routes require a 4WD vehicle.

Chartered flights use the airstrip several kilometres north of the lodges in Savuti. Check with your lodge regarding booking a flight.

Linyanti Marshes
In the northwest corner of Chobe National Park, the Linyanti River spreads into a 900-sq-km flooded plain that attracts stunning concentrations of wildlife during the dry season. Wildlife trails run along the marsh shoreline and sightings of the area's stable populations of elephants, lions, wild dogs, cheetahs and leopards are fairly common, although you'll need to be patient, especially for big cats. Given that most of the luxury lodges are outside the national park, night drives are a highlight.

🛏 Sleeping

Linyanti Campsite　　　　CAMPGROUND **$**
(www.sklcamps.com; GPS: S 18°16.228', E 23°56.163'; campsite per adult/child US$50/25) Most of the sites at this camping ground run by the excellent SKL sit on a shady and gentle rise just up from the water's edge, with good views of the marshes costing nothing extra. There are all the usual *braai* pits, hot showers, sit-down flush toilets and, in the dry season, lots of elephants and baboons.

Camp Linyanti　　　　TENTED CAMP **$$$**
(www.sklcamps.com; GPS: S 18°16.228', E 23°56.163'; s/d May-Dec full board US$500/700) SKL has set up a luxury tented camp within earshot of the cheaper public sites. The camps are luxurious without being overdone; with prices significantly less than their near neighbours they're well worth considering.

Duma Tau　　　　　　TENTED CAMP **$$$**
(☏in South Africa 011-807 1800; www.wilderness -safaris.com; s/d Jan-Apr US$1123/1736, May-Dec

US$1588/2666; ❄❄) This 10-room camp was rebuilt completely in 2012 with a commitment to sustainability; all of the camp's power comes from solar energy and waste disposal is state of the art. The raised tents overlook the hippo-filled Zibadianja Lagoon from a mangosteen grove. The lagoon can be explored by boat when the water levels are high, or you can kick back in a luxury tent under thatch.

King's Pool Camp   TENTED CAMP **$$$**
(✐in South Africa 011-807 1800; www.wilderness -safaris.com; s/d Jan-Apr US$1495/2388, May-Dec US$2287/3972; ❄❄) Occupying a magical setting on a Linyanti River oxbow overlooking a lagoon, this nine-room camp is one of the most luxurious properties in Linyanti with private plunge pools in the rooms and an overall stunning attention to detail and service. Accommodation at King's Pool is in private thatched chalets featuring indoor and outdoor showers. This place almost prides itself on being noisy – you will almost certainly be woken up by the nearby hippos, elephants, baboons and lions.

ℹ️ Getting There & Away

From the south, the track from Savuti is a hard slog of deep sand. The track running east towards Kachikau (where it meets the paved road to Kasane) is only slightly better. Most guests choose to fly into their camp on a chartered flight from Maun or Kasane.

OKAVANGO DELTA

Welcome to one of Africa's most iconic landscapes. The waters of the Okavango sustain vast quantities of wildlife and the Okavango's fly-in luxury lodges make a strong claim to be Africa's most exclusive safari destinations. Fork out a fortune for nights spent deep in the inner delta and you're unlikely to regret it. And yet, it is possible to gain a delta foothold for those on a smaller budget through a combination of mobile safaris from Maun and self-driving to the campsites of the Moremi Game Reserve.

Maun

As the main gateway to the Okavango Delta, Maun (pronounced 'mau-UUnn') is Botswana's primary tourism hub. The town itself has little going for it – it's strung out over kilometres with not much of a discernible centre –

but accommodation is excellent and some hotels and camps have lovely riverside vantage points. Many of these are in Matlapaneng, around 2.5km northwest of Maun centre.

🚩 Tours

Maun is brimful of travel agencies and safari companies. Most delta lodges are affiliated with specific agencies, so it pays to shop around and talk to a few different tour operators. And for extended trips into the delta or stays at a luxury lodge, contact one or more recommended agencies or operators *before* you arrive if possible – don't come to Maun and expect to jump on a plane to a safari lodge or embark on an overland safari the next day.

An excellent place to start is at Travel Wild (✆686 0822; www.travelwildbotswana.com; Mathiba I St), opposite the airport, which serves as a central booking and information office for lodges, safaris and other adventures. It can't provide you with direct bookings, but it has great contacts with all local safari providers.

Safaris

African Animal Adventures   WILDLIFE TOUR
(✆7230 1054; www.africananimaladventures.com) Horse safaris into the delta and the salt pans of Makgadikgadi. Can also be contacted through the Old Bridge Backpackers (p63) and Gweta Lodge (p53).

African Secrets   WILDLIFE TOUR
(Map p67; ✆686 0300; www.africansecrets.net; Mathiba I St, Matlapaneng) This excellent operation is run out of the Island Safari Lodge.

Audi Camp Safaris   WILDLIFE TOUR
(Map p67; ✆686 0599; www.okavangocamp.com; Shorobe Rd, Matlapaneng) Well-run safaris into the delta and further afield.

Crocodile Camp Safaris   WILDLIFE TOUR
(Map p67; ✆686 0222; www.crocodilecamp.com; Shorobe Rd, Matlapaneng) Budget operator at the Crocodile Camp.

Nxuma Adventure Safaris   WILDLIFE TOUR
(✆7646 2829; nxumu@hotmail.com) *Mokoro* and other boat trips in the Okavango, as well as guided walks; ask for Oscar.

Okavango River Lodge   WILDLIFE TOUR
(Map p67; ✆686 3707; www.okavango-river-lodge. com; Shorobe Rd, Matlapaneng) Reliable safaris run out of the Okavango River Lodge.

Okavango Delta

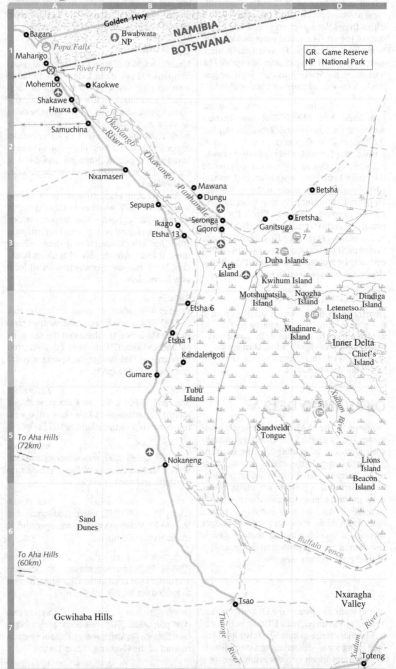

GR Game Reserve
NP National Park

Old Bridge Backpackers WILDLIFE TOUR

(Map p67; ☑686 2406; www.maun-backpackers. com; Shorobe Rd, Matlapaneng) Experienced budget operation run from the Old Bridge Backpackers.

Scenic Flights

Flying over the delta in a light plane or helicopter is the experience of a lifetime. To join a scenic flight you can either contact one of the following charter companies or simply ask at the front desk of your accommodation.

Per-hour prices for scenic flights in a three-/five-/seven-seater plane start at P2000/2650/3400, but shop around for the best quote. In most cases, a departure tax of P50 must be added per person to the quoted prices. The offices for all air-charter companies in Maun are either in or next to the airport. Bring your passport when making a booking.

Delta Air SCENIC FLIGHTS

(Map p64; ☑686 0044; synergy@info.bw; Mathiba I St) Near the Bushman Craft Shop inside the airport gate.

Helicopter Horizons SCENIC FLIGHTS

(Map p64; ☑680 1186; www.helicopterhorizons. com; per person from US$110) A range of helicopter options, all with the passenger doors removed to aid photography.

Mack Air SCENIC FLIGHTS

(Map p64; ☑686 0675; www.mackair.co.bw; Mathiba I St) Across the road from the airport.

🛏 Sleeping

TOP CHOICE **Old Bridge Backpackers** CAMPGROUND $

(Map p67; ☑686 2406; www.maun-backpackers. com; Hippo Pools, Old Matlapaneng Bridge; campsite per person P60, dm P155, s/d tents without bathroom P225/348, d tents with bathroom P505;

Maun

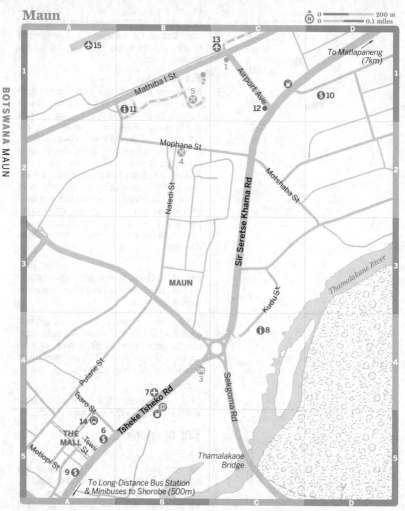

@⧆) One of the great boltholes on southern African overland trails, 'The Bridge', as it's known, has a great bar-at-the-end-of-the-world kind of vibe. Accommodation ranges from dorms by the riverbank, well-appointed campsites and some more private tents to retreat to at day's end. A good range of *mokoro* trips and the like is on offer. In short, this is a place that understands travellers and doesn't make them pay over the odds for it.

Okavango River Lodge CAMPGROUND, CHALETS **$**
(Map p67; ☑686 3707; www.okavango-river-lodge. com; Matlapaneng; campsite per person P70, s/d/f chalets P250/330/400, s/d tents P150/280) This down-to-earth spot off Shorobe Rd has a lovely setting on the riverbank. The owners are friendly and pride themselves on giving travellers useful (and independent) information on trips through the delta.

Island Safari Lodge CAMPGROUND, CHALETS **$$**
(Map p67; ☑686 0300; www.africansecrets. net; Matlapaneng; campsite per person P60, s/d P375/580, s/d chalets P560/870; ⧆⧆) One of the original lodges in Maun, Island Safari Lodge is also still one of its best with a range of accommodation that nicely spans differ-

Maun

ent budgets. The campsites have ablutions blocks and give access to the lodge's pool, restaurant and bar. The budget rooms are run-down but well-priced, while the chalets are excellent value. They also run a professional, well-established series of safaris, the riverside location is ideal on lazy Okavango afternoons and the restaurant is excellent.

Crocodile Camp   CAMPGROUND, CHALETS $
(Map p67; ☎7560 6864; www.crocodilecamp.com; Matlapaneng; campsite per person P60, chalets per person incl breakfast P400; ☒) 'Croc Camp' occupies a superb spot right on the river and is a quieter place than some other riverside places. Off Shorobe Rd, the campsite is excellent and secure while there are also thatched riverside chalets with en suite bathrooms.

Audi Camp   CAMPGROUND $$
(Map p67; ☎686 0599; www.okavangocamp.com; Matlapaneng; campsite per person from P60, s/d tents without bathroom from P140/170, with bathroom P540/640; @☒) Off Shorobe Rd, Audi Camp is a fantastic campsite that's become increasingly popular with families, although independent overlanders will feel welcome as well. Management is friendly and helpful, and there's a wide range of safari activities. The restaurant does a mean steak as well.

Discovery Bed & Breakfast   B&B $$
(off Map p67; ☎7244 8298; www.discoverybedand breakfast.com; Matlapaneng; s/d from P275/425; ☒) Dutch-run Discovery does a cool job of creating an African-village vibe in the midst of Maun – they strive for and achieve 'affordable accommodation with a traditional touch'. The thatched, *rondavel*-style (traditional circular houses with thatched roofs) housing looks pretty bush from the outside and feels as posh as a nice hotel on the inside.

Cresta Riley's Hotel   HOTEL $$$
(Map p64; ☎686 0204; www.crestahotels.com; Tsheke Tsheko Rd; s/d P1039/1444; ❋☎☒) Riley's is the only hotel or lodge in central Maun and it has been here since before tourists began arriving. It offers comfortable rooms in a convenient setting in leafy grounds – just don't expect a lodge/wilderness experience.

Royal Tree Lodge   LODGE $$$
(☎680 0757; www.royaltreelodge.com; per person low season full board US$262, s/d high season from US$395/610; ❋@☒) This private farm-reserve, about 13km west of the airport, is a lovely luxury option that maintains a good crew of regular visitors. These returnees are probably impressed by the resident wandering giraffe, kudu and ostrich, the large, beautifully decked out private cabins and the utter sense of calm and quiet here far away from Maun's bustle.

Eating & Drinking

Many of the lodges and camps have accomplished kitchens, particularly the Island Safari Lodge and Audi Camp. Otherwise, Maun has versions of every *peri-peri*–obsessed fast-food chain in Southern Africa. There are good supermarkets all over town.

The majority of lodges have their own bar, most of which are fairly sedate; if you're after a more overland and expat scene, try the Old Bridge Backpackers or Okavango River Lodge. Of the restaurants, the Sports

Bar has the best and liveliest bar. For a more African vibe, there are, of course, numerous *shebeen* (illegal drinking establishments) serving home-brewed sorghum beer to a local crowd; the staff at your hotel or lodge can point you in the right direction for this sort of off-licence fun.

Motsana Arts Cafe
CAFE $

(Map p67; www.motsana.com; Shorobe Rd, Matlapaneng; meals P45-60; ☺8am-8pm; ☜) Housed in an innovative new arts complex northeast of town on the road to Shorobe, this cool, casual and sophisticated cafe serves up burgers, salads, paninis, cajun chicken with avocado and all-day breakfasts, with free wi-fi thrown in.

French Connection
FRENCH $

(Map p64; Mophane St; meals from P45; ☺8.30am-5pm Mon-Sat) Close to the airport but on a quieter back street, this fine little place serves up salads, baguettes and other light meals in a shady garden setting. The roast beef sandwich is perfectly executed.

Hilary's
INTERNATIONAL $$

(Map p64; meals from P50; ☺8am-4pm Mon-Fri, 8.30am-noon Sat; ☜) Just off Mathiba I St, this homey place offers a choice of wonderfully earthy meals, including homemade bread, baked potatoes, soups and sandwiches. It's ideal for vegetarians and anyone sick of greasy sausages and soggy chips. We're just sorry they don't open in the evenings.

Bon Arrivee
INTERNATIONAL $$

(Map p64; Mathiba I St; meals P60-120; ☺8am-10pm) They lay on the pilot puns and flight-deck jokes very thick at this airport-themed place, which sits, of course, right across from the airport. The food is good – lots of pasta, steak and seafood – but don't come here an hour before your flight expecting a quick turnaround.

Sports Bar & Restaurant
INTERNATIONAL $$

(Map p67; Shorobe Rd, Matlapaneng; meals P50-80; ☺5-10pm) Bucking the trend by only opening for dinner, Sports Bar does the usual pasta and pizza suspects with occasional curries and some excellent Botswana-bred steaks. When the kitchen closes the place morphs into an expat-filled bar with music you can dance to on Friday and Saturday. You'll need a taxi (P40 from the city centre) or your own wheels to get here.

ⓘ Information

Emergency

Delta Medical Centre (☏686 1411; www.delta medicalcentre.org; Tsheke Tsheko Rd) Along the main road; this is the best medical facility in Maun. It offers a 24-hour emergency service.

Maun General Hospital (☏686 0661; Shorobe Rd) About 1km southwest of the town centre.

MedRescue (☏390 1601, 680 0598, 992; www.mri.co.bw) For evacuations in the bush.

Internet Access

Many hotels now offer internet access, either in the form of wireless or a publicly accessible computer.

Open Door Bureau de Change (Tsheke Tsheko Rd; per hr P30; ☺7.30am-6pm Mon-Fri, 8am-4pm Sat, 9am-4pm Sun)

Money

Barclays Bank (Tsheke Tsheko Rd; ☺8.30am-3.30pm Mon-Fri, 8.15-10.45am Sat)

Standard Chartered Bank (Tsheke Tsheko Rd; ☺8.30am-3.30pm Mon-Fri, 8.15-11am Sat)

Sunny Bureau de Change (Sir Seretse Khama Rd, Ngami Centre; ☺8am-6pm) Less favourable exchange rates than at the banks, but a convenient option if lines at the banks are long.

ZONES OF THE OKAVANGO

Eastern Delta This part of the delta is far more accessible (and therefore cheaper to reach) from Maun than the Inner Delta and Moremi.

Inner Delta The area west and north of Moremi is classic delta scenery. Accommodation is mostly in top-end luxury lodges, almost all of which are only accessible by expensive chartered flights.

Moremi Game Reserve This region is one of the most popular destinations within the delta. Moremi Game Reserve is the only officially protected area within the delta, so wildlife is plentiful. Moremi has a few campsites as well as several truly decadent lodges with prices to match.

Okavango Panhandle This swampy extension of the Inner Delta stretches northwest towards Namibia. As a general rule, this is better known for birdwatching and fishing than wildlife safaris.

Matlapaneng

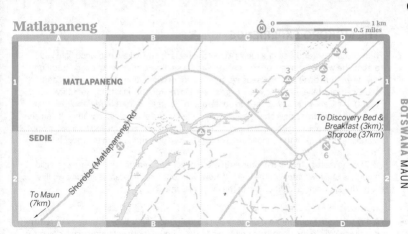

Tourist Information

Department of Wildlife & National Parks
(DWNP; ☎686 1265; Kudu St; ☺7.30am-
4.30pm Mon-Fri, 7.30am-12.45pm & 1.45-
4.30pm Sat, 7.30am-12.45pm Sun) Pay national
park entry fees and book those park campsites
not in private hands; it's in a separate compound behind the main department building
and is well signposted.

Tourist Office (☎686 1056; Off Mathiba I
St; ☺7.30am-6pm Mon-Fri, 9am-2pm Sat)
Provides information on the town's many tour
companies and lodges.

ⓘ Getting There & Away

Air

Air Botswana (☎686 0391; www.airbotswana.
co.bw) offers flights to Gaborone (from P882)
and Kasane (from P369). In addition to domestic
flights, there are international flights between
Maun and Johannesburg (South Africa), Victoria
Falls (Zimbabwe) and Livingstone (Zambia).

Bus & Combi

The **bus station** (Tsheke Tsheko Rd) for long-
distance buses and combis (minibuses) is southwest of the centre. For Gaborone, you'll need to
change in Ghanzi or Francistown.

TO	FARE (P)	DURATION (HOURS)
D'kar	43	four
Francistown	89.90	five
Ghanzi	63	five
Gweta	47	four
Kasane	96	six
Nata	76	five
Shakawe	108	seven

Matlapaneng

Activities, Courses & Tours

African Secrets	(see 3)
Audi Camp Safaris	(see 1)
Crocodile Camp Safaris	(see 2)
Okavango River Lodge	(see 3)
Old Bridge Backpackers	(see 5)

Sleeping

1	Audi Camp	C1
2	Crocodile Camp	D1
3	Island Safari Lodge	C1
4	Okavango River Lodge	D1
5	Old Bridge Backpackers	C2

Eating

6	Motsana Arts Cafe	D2
7	Sports Bar & Restaurant	B2

Car & Motorcycle

The direct route between Kasane and Maun
is only accessible by 4WD and may be almost
impassable after heavy rains. Also, remember
that there is nowhere along the Kasane–Maun
road to buy fuel, food or drinks, or to get vehicle
repairs. All other traffic between Kasane and
Maun travels via Nata.

ⓘ Getting Around

To/From the Airport

Maun **airport** is close to the town centre. If you
have prebooked accommodation at an upmarket
hotel or lodge in Maun or the Okavango Delta,
make sure it provides a (free) courtesy minibus
from the **terminal**. Otherwise, walk about 300m
down Airport Rd to Sir Seretse Khama Rd and
catch a combi.

THE MOKORO EXPERIENCE

One of the best (and also cheapest) ways to experience the Okavango Delta is to glide across the waters in a *mokoro* (plural *mekoro*), a shallow-draft dugout canoe traditionally hewn from an ebony or a sausage-tree log; for conservation reasons (ebony and sausage trees take over 100 years to grow while a *mokoro* only lasts for about five years), the Batswana have begun to construct more *mekoro* from fibreglass.

A *mokoro* is amazingly stable and ideally suited to the shallow delta waters. It can accommodate two passengers and some limited luggage, and is propelled by a poler who stands at the back of the canoe with a *ngashi*, a long pole made from the mogonono tree.

The main attraction of a *mokoro* trip is the peace and serenity you'll feel as you glide along the shallow waters of the delta. If, however, your main interest is viewing wildlife, consider spending a night or two in the Moremi Game Reserve.

Booking a Mokoro Trip

A day trip from Maun into the Eastern Delta usually includes a two- to three-hour return drive in a 4WD to the departure point, two to three hours (perhaps longer each day on a two- or three-day trip) in a *mokoro* (dugout canoe), and two to three hours of hiking. At the start of a *mokoro* trip, ask the poler what they have in mind, and agree to the length of time spent per day in the *mokoro*, out hiking and relaxing at the campsite – bear in mind that travelling by *mokoro* is tiring for the poler.

All polers operating *mokoro* trips out of Maun are represented by the Okavango Kopano Mokoro Community Trust (☎686 4806; off Mathiba 1 St; ☺8am-5pm Mon-Fri, to noon Sat), which sets daily rates for the polers (P180 per poler per day, plus a P55 daily membership fee for the trust) by which all safari operators must abide.

A few things to remember when you're planning your trip:

» 'Self-catering' means you must bring your own food as well as cooking, sleeping and camping equipment – you shave a little off the cost although most travellers prefer catered trips.

» It's easier to get a lower price if you're booking as part of a group or if you plan a multiday tour.

» Ask the booking agency if you're expected to provide food for the poler (usually you're not).

» Bring good walking shoes and long trousers for hiking, a hat and plenty of sunscreen and water.

» Water from the delta (despite its unpleasant colour) can be drunk if boiled or purified.

» Most campsites are natural, so take out all litter and burn toilet paper.

» Bring warm clothes for the evenings between about May and September.

» Wildlife can be dangerous, so make sure to never swim anywhere without checking with the poler first.

Combis & Taxis

Combis marked 'Maun Route 1' or 'Sedie Route 1' travel every few minutes during daylight hours between the station in town and a stop near Crocodile Camp in Matlapaneng. The standard fare for all local trips is P5.

Taxis also ply the main road and are the only form of public transport in the evening. They also hang around a stand along Pulane St in the town centre. A typical fare from central Maun to Matlapaneng costs about P15/40 in a shared/private taxi. To pre-order a taxi, ask your hotel or campsite for a recommendation.

Inner Delta

Welcome to the heart of the Okavango, a world inaccessible by road and inhabited by some of the richest wildlife concentrations on earth. Although budget trips are possible in some areas, the quintessential delta experience is staying in one of the fly-in luxury lodges – if you're going to make a splash with your money in Botswana, make it here.

Roughly defined, the Inner Delta occupies the areas west of Chief's Island and between Chief's Island and the base of the Okavango Panhandle. *Mokoro* trips through the Inner Delta operate roughly between June and December, depending on water levels. To see the most wildlife you'll have to pay park fees to land on Chief's Island or other parts of Moremi Game Reserve.

🛏 Sleeping

Gunn's Camp   TENTED CAMP $$$
(Map p62; ☎686 0023; www.gunns-camp.com; per person low season US$371, s/d high season US$672/1102) Gunn's is a beautiful option for those wanting the amenities of a high-end safari – expertly cooked meals, attentive service and wonderful views over its island location in the delta – with a more rugged sense of place. The elegant tented rooms are as comfy as you'll find anywhere, but there is more of a feeling of being engaged with the wilderness. Compared with prices elsewhere, Gunn's represents fabulous value.

Kanana Camp   TENTED CAMP $$$
(Map p62; ☎686 0375; www.kerdowneybotswana. com; per person low season US$495, s/d high season US$1050/1640) This classy retreat occupies a watery site in a maze of grass- and palm-covered islands. It's an excellent base for wildlife-viewing by *mokoro* around Chiefs Island or fishing in surrounding waterways.

Accommodation is in eight well-furnished linen tents that are shaded by towering riverine forest.

Mapula Lodge   TENTED CAMP $$$
(Map p62; ☎686 3369; www.mapula-lodge.com; per person low season US$415, s/d high season US$936/1440) Located on the fringe of the Moremi Game Reserve, this lodge has a style all its own. African hardwoods dominate the decor with zinc bathtubs adding to a more rustic, *Out of Africa* feel without ever compromising on comfort.

Moremi Crossing   TENTED CAMP $$$
(Map p62; ☎686 0023; www.moremicrossing.com; per person low season US$321, s/d high season US$567/892; 🐜) Part of the well-regarded portfolio of Under One Botswana Sky, this well-priced collection of lovely chalets flanks a simply gorgeous (and enormous) thatched dining and bar area that overlooks a long flood plain where you can often see wandering giraffes and elephants. The camp is to be commended for pioneering a plumbing system that minimises environmental impact (it's also quite a feat of engineering – ask to see how it all works).

Duba Plains   TENTED CAMP $$$
(Map p62; ☎686 0086; www.wilderness-safaris. com; s/d low season US$963/1416, high season US$1473/2436; 🐜) North of the Moremi Game Reserve, Duba Plains is one of the most remote camps in the delta. Both the intimate layout of the grounds and the virtual isolation of this part of the delta contribute to a unique wilderness experience.

WORTH A TRIP

TSODILO HILLS

The Unesco World Heritage–listed Tsodilo Hills rise abruptly from the northwestern Kalahari, west of the Okavango Panhandle. Rare outposts of vertical variety in this extremely flat country, these lonely chunks of quartzite schist are dramatic and beautiful, distinguished by streaks of vivid natural hues. The hills are also a site of huge spiritual significance for the region's original inhabitants, the San. The major drawcards are more than 4000 prehistoric rock paintings spread over 200 sites throughout the hills. The hills can be explored along any of five walking trails. Although there are some signposts, most trails require a guide (expect to pay around P50 to P60 for a two- to three-hour hike, or P100 per day), which can be arranged at the Main (Rhino) Camp.

The Tsodilo Hills are signposted off the Sehitwa–Shakawe road (which connects Maun with Namibia) along a good gravel track. The turn-off is just south of Nxamasere village. It's around 35km from the main road to the entrance to the site. Once there, camping is free but facilities are minimal and you'll need to be self-sufficient in food and water.

Oddball's TENTED CAMP **$$$**
(Map p62; ☎686 1154; www.oddballscamp.com; tents low/high season US$240/340) For years Oddball's was a well-regarded budget lodge and although it's still way below lodge prices elsewhere in the delta, we reckon they're asking too much considering you're still staying in budget dome tents. It occupies less-than-exciting woodland beside an airstrip but is within walking distance of some classic delta scenery.

ⓘ Getting There & Away

The only way into and out of the Inner Delta for most visitors is by air. This is an expensive extra, but the pain is alleviated if you look at it as two scenic flights. Chartered flights to the lodges typically cost about US$150 to US$200 return. A *mokoro* or 4WD vehicle will meet your plane and take you to the lodge.

Moremi Game Reserve

Moremi Game Reserve covers 5000 sq km, or one-third of the Okavango Delta, and is home to some of the densest concentrations of wildlife in Africa. Best of all, it's one of the most accessible corners of the Okavango with well-maintained trails and accommodation that ranges from luxury lodges to public campsites for self-drivers. Habitats in the reserve range from mopane woodland and thorn scrub to dry savannah, riparian woodland, grassland, flood plain, marsh, permanent waterways, lagoons and islands.

With the recent reintroduction of the rhino, Moremi is now home to the Big Five (lion, leopard, buffalo, elephant and rhino), and the largest population of red lechwe in the whole of Africa. The reserve also protects one of the largest remaining populations of endangered African wild dogs. Bird life in Moremi is incredibly varied and rich.

◉ Sights

The largest island in the Okavango Delta, **Chiefs Island** (70km long and 15km wide) was once the sole hunting preserve of the local chief. Raised above the water level by tectonic activity in ancient times, it's here that so much of the delta's wildlife retreats as water levels rise. The combination of reed-fringed waters, grasslands and light woodlands makes for game viewing that can feel like a BBC wildlife documentary brought to life.

Literally the third log bridge after entering the reserve at **South Gate**, rustic and rather ramshackle **Third Bridge** spans a reed-filled, tannin-coloured pool on the Sekiri River. The neighbouring campsite is one of our favourites in the Okavango. The grassy savannah of 100-sq-km **Mboma Island**, a long extension of the Moremi Tongue, contrasts sharply with the surrounding landscapes and it provides some excellent dry season wildlife watching. The 32km sandy Mboma Loop starts about 2km west of Third Bridge and is a pleasant side trip. Boat trips from the Mboma Boat Station on the island's northwestern tip are highly recommended.

With one of Africa's largest heronries, **Xakanaxa Lediba** (Xakanaxa Lagoon) is renowned as a birdwatchers' paradise. There are myriad trails around the Xakanaxa backwaters – the Shell Map of the Moremi Game Reserve is the most detailed resource. One of the loveliest corners of Moremi, the nearby area known as **Paradise Pools** is as lovely as the name suggests with forests of dead trees, waterholes and reed-filled swamps.

The drive between **North Gate** (including Khwai) and Xakanaxa Lediba follows one of Botswana's more scenic tracks, although the exact route changes with the years depending on flood levels. Worthwhile stops en route include **Dombo Hippo Pool** (about 14km southwest of North Gate), where hippos crowd along the shore.

🏃 Activities

Moremi is the launching point for some wonderful boat excursions into the delta. Although *mokoro* trips may be possible, most of what's on offer is in open-sided motor-propelled boats. More jetties spring up with

---

ⓘ WHEN TO VISIT MOREMI

The best time to see wildlife in Moremi is the late dry season (July to October), when animals are forced to congregate around the permanent water sources accessible to wildlife (and humans). September and October are optimum times for spotting wildlife and bird life, but these are also the hottest two months. January and February are normally very wet and tracks are frequently impassable during these months.

Moremi Tongue

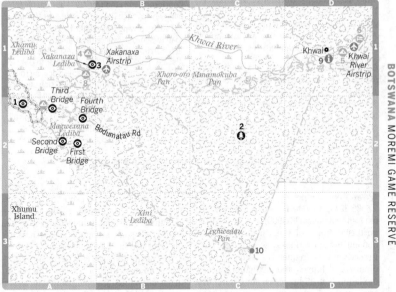

each passing year, but at the time of writing there were two in the Xakanaxa area with a further site at the Mboma Boat Station on Mboma Island. Prices start at P520/544/627 per hour for an 8-/12-/16-seater craft.

🛏 Sleeping

Third Bridge Campsite   CAMPGROUND $
(www.xomaesites.com; Third Bridge; GPS: S 19°14.340', E 23°21.276'; per adult/child P226/113) The favourite campsite for many self-drivers in the region, Third Bridge has sites that are away from the main track and set on the edge of a lagoon (watch out for hippos and crocs). It's a beautiful place to pitch for the night.

Xakanaxa Campsite   CAMPGROUND $
(Xakanaxa Lediba; kwalatesafari@gmail.com; GPS: S 19°10.991', E 23°24.937'; campsite per adult/child P260/130) Another favourite Moremi camping ground, Xakanaxa occupies a narrow strip of land surrounded by marshes and lagoons. It's no coincidence that many up-market lodges are located nearby – the wild-life in the area can be prolific. Boat journeys onto the lagoon are also possible.

Khwai Campsite   CAMPGROUND $
(www.sklcamps.com; GPS: S 19°10.359', E 23°45.122'; campsite per adult/child US$50/25)

Moremi Tongue

The campsites at this expansive camping ground are shady and well developed with some lovely sites close to the riverbank; others are a little further inland. There was a nonfatal leopard attack on a lone camper at this camping ground; always drive to the ablutions block from your campsite after dark.

Camp Moremi   TENTED CAMP $$$
(☏686 1559; www.desertdelta.com; per person low season US$476, s/d high season US$1113/1712; ☒)

This long-standing wilderness retreat sits amid giant ebony trees next to Xakanaxa Lediba and is surrounded by wildlife-rich grasslands. Accommodation is in East African–style linen tents that are attractively furnished with wooden fixtures.

Camp Okavango
TENTED CAMP $$$

(☎686 1559; www.desertdelta.com; per person low season US$476, s/d high season US$1113/1712; ☎) Set amid sausage and jackalberry trees on Nxaragha Island just outside Moremi, this charming lodge is elegant and the staff are famous for their meticulous attention to detail. If you want Okavango served up with silver tea service, candelabras and fine china, this is the place for you.

Khwai River Lodge
LODGE $$$

(☎686 1244; www.khwairiverlodge.com; per person high season from US$900) Perched on the northern shores of the Khwai River, this opulent lodge overlooks the Moremi Game Reserve and is frequently visited by large numbers of hippos and elephants. Accommodation is in 15 luxury en suite tents that are larger and more extravagant than most upmarket hotel rooms.

Mombo Camp
TENTED CAMP $$$

(☎686 0086; www.wilderness-safaris.com; s/d low season US$2230/3430, high season US$3026/4862; ☎) Ask anyone in Botswana for the country's most exclusive camp and they're likely to nominate Mombo, situated (with its sister camp, Little Mombo) are on the northwest corner of Chiefs Island. The surrounding delta scenery is some of the finest in the Okavango and the wildlife watching is almost unrivalled. The rooms are enormous and the entire package – from the service to the comfort levels and attention to detail – never misses a beat.

ⓘ Information

Entry fees to the reserve should be paid for in advance at the Department of Wildlife & National Parks (p67) office in Maun, although these can be paid at the gate if you have no other choice. Self-drivers will, however, only be allowed entry to the reserve if you have a confirmed reservation at one of the four public campsites.

If you're coming from Maun, the reserve entrance is located at South (Maqwee) Gate, about 99km north of Maun via Shorobe. From Kasane and the east, a track links Chobe National Park with the other gate at North (Khwai) Gate.

ⓘ Getting There & Away

Chartered flights (and/or 4WD) are usually the only way to reach the luxury lodges of Moremi.

If you're driving from Maun, take the paved road to Shorobe, where the road turns into awfully corrugated gravel. Once inside the park, it's about 52km (two hours) from South Gate to Third Bridge along a reasonable track, en route passing through beautiful, wildlife-rich country. It's about 25km (one hour) from Third Bridge to Xakanaxa Lediba, and another 45km (1.5 hours) from there to North Gate. Some tracks can still be impassable well into the dry season.

THE KALAHARI

The parched alter ego of the Okavango Delta, the Kalahari is a primeval landscape. The Tswana call this the Kgalagadi (Land of Thirst). And this is indeed dry, parched country. By some accounts the Kalahari has the largest volume of sand of any desert on earth. Such statistics can be misleading – this is no desert of rolling sand dunes. But this is undoubtedly a land painted by a sand palette: blood and mud reds and bleached bone yellow; dust that bites you back as you taste it in the morning. But come the nights this hard end of the colour wheel shifts into its cooler, sometimes white-cold shades: indigo nights that fade to deepest black, and blue stars ice-speckling the impossibly long horizon.

Central Kalahari Game Reserve

The dry heart of the dry south of a dry continent, the Central Kalahari Game Reserve (CKGR) is epic in scale and, at all times, awe inspiring. If remoteness, desert silence and the sound of lions roaring in the night are your thing, this could become one of your favourite places in Africa. Covering 52,000 sq km (about the size of Denmark), this is one of Africa's largest protected areas. The CKGR is perhaps best known for Deception Valley, the site of Mark and Delia Owens' 1974 to 1981 brown hyena and lion study, which is described in their book *Cry of the Kalahari*. Three similar fossil valleys – the Okwa, the Quoxo (Meratswe) and the Passarge – also bring topographical relief to the virtually featureless expanses, although the rivers ceased flowing more than 16,000 years ago.

🛏 Sleeping

There are dozens of campsites dotted around the reserve. While most lack facilities, they usually have a *braai* pit, bucket showers and a pit toilet. You'll need to be fully self-sufficient for water, food and petrol. The more expensive lodges within the CKGR are usually accessed via charter flight.

Central Kalahari & Khutse Game Reserves

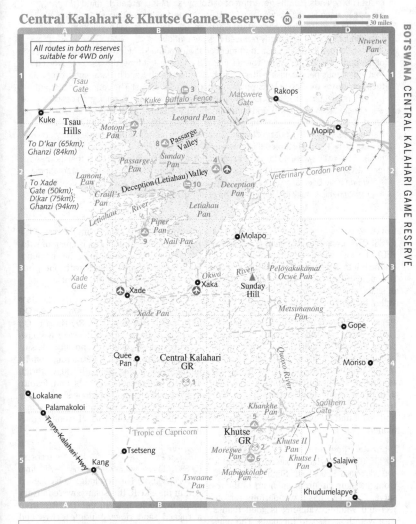

Central Kalahari & Khutse Game Reserves

◉ Sights

1 Central Kalahari Game Reserve............ B4
2 Khutse Game Reserve C5

🛏 Sleeping

3 Deception Valley Lodge B1
4 Kori Campsite...................................... C2
5 Molose Pan Campsite.......................... C5
6 Moreswe Pan Campsite C5
7 Motopi Campsite.................................. B2
8 Passarge Valley Campsites B2
9 Piper Pan Campsite............................. B3
10 Tau Pan Camp B2

THE SAN & THE KALAHARI

The CKGR was originally established in 1961 as a private reservation for the San in order to protect them from the encroachments of the modern world and to protect their ancestral homelands. But the government of Botswana later changed its mind (primarily, critics say, because diamonds were found within the park's boundaries) and although the southern and western parts of the CKGR are still home to small populations of San, forced relocations have greatly reduced this population.

After South Africa's highest court found in favour of the Richtersveld people (relatives of the San) of Northern Cape Province in 2003 – for the first time, the court recognised that indigenous people have both communal land ownership and mineral rights over their territory – the San of Botswana launched a similar appeal. The court case brought by the First People of the Kalahari (FPK) against the government's relocation policies was concluded in May 2006, and approximately 1000 San attached their names to the effort. During the proceedings many San tried to return home to the Central Kalahari Game Reserve (CKGR), but most were forced off the grounds of the reserve. In December 2006 the high court ruled that the eviction of the San was 'unlawful and unconstitutional'. One justice went so far as to say that not allowing the San to hunt in their homeland 'was tantamount to condemning the residents of the CKGR to death by starvation'. A few San have been allowed back into the reserve although the government continues to drag its heels in fully implementing the court ruling.

Kori Campsite CAMPGROUND $
(✆381 0774; dwnp@gov.bw; campsite per person P30) The four campsites known as Kori sit on the hill that rises gently from the western shoreline of Deception Valley. There's plenty of shade and some have partial views of the valley, making it a wonderful base.

Passarge Valley Campsite CAMPGROUND $
(✆395 3360; www.bigfoottours.co.bw; campsite per adult/child P200/100) These three campsites have no facilities, but their location on the valley floor (some kilometres apart) is amongst the best in the Kalahari. Site No 2, under a shady stand of trees in the centre of the valley floor, is simply wonderful and you'll find the world is yours and yours alone.

Piper Pan Campsite CAMPGROUND $
(✆395 3360; www.bigfoottours.co.bw; campsite per adult/child P200/100) Slightly removed from the main circuit in the heart of the reserve, Piper Pan has a wonderfully remote feel and wildlife watching is good thanks to a waterhole next to the pans. The pans are 26km southwest off the main Leatihau track. Check the Bigfoot Tours website for GPS coordinates.

Motopi Campsite CAMPGROUND $
(✆395 3360; www.bigfoottours.co.bw; campsite per adult/child P200/100) In the northwestern corner of the reserve, these three campsites are wonderfully isolated from the rest of the reserve. Nearby Motopi Pan is great for wildlife, and lions are common in the surrounding area – we spent hours with one pride here without seeing another vehicle.

Deception Valley Lodge LODGE $$$
(www.deceptionvalley.co.za; s/d Jun-Oct US$546/840, Nov-May US$458/704; ✹) On the edge of the reserve, this exclusive bush retreat was designed to blend into the surrounding nature without detracting from its ambience. Soothing rooms blend Victorian and African design elements and feature a private lounge and outdoor shower. The lodge is about 120km south of Maun, and the route is accessible to 2WD vehicles during the dry season.

Tau Pan Camp LODGE $$$
(✆686 1449; www.kwando.co.bw; s/d from US$620/880; ✹) The first lodge to be opened within the CKGR, this solar-powered luxury lodge overlooks magnificent Tau Pan from a rugged sand ridge. Wildlife drives and San-led bushwalks are the order of the day, and neither disappoint, especially when the rains hit and this becomes one of Southern Africa's best wildlife-viewing locations. The lodge maintains a strong eco sensibility, and comes highly recommended by former guests.

ℹ Information

Camping is only allowed at designated campsites, which must be booked in advance. You will not be permitted into the park without a campsite reservation. The nearest reliable petrol supplies are located in Ghanzi, Maun and Rakops.

Collecting firewood is banned in the CKGR, so bring your own.

ℹ Getting There & Away

Many Maun tour operators offer mobile safaris to the reserve. A 4WD is essential to get around the reserve, and a compass (or GPS equipment) and petrol reserves are also recommended.

Khutse Game Reserve

This 2500-sq-km reserve, which is an extension of the southern boundary of the Central Kalahari Game Reserve, is a popular weekend excursion for residents of Gaborone, but it's still deliciously remote and crowds are rare. It has all the attractions of the Kalahari, including good wildlife watching (although population densities are low), well-maintained trails and around 60 mineralised clay pans that once belonged to Africa's largest inland lake. Leopard and lion sightings in particular are possible.

The pans at the western end of the reserve provide good wildlife watching thanks to the waterholes, one at each pan; the Moreswe waterhole was being repaired when we visited but there were still lions in the vicinity. Molose is busier, whereas Moreswe feels more remote. Pick up the free photocopied map of the reserve from the park entrance.

🛏 Sleeping

Khutse boasts several superbly located campsites, which are all administered by Big Foot Tours (☑395 3360; www.bigfoottours. co.bw; camping per adult/child P200/100).

Moreswe Pan Campsite   CAMPGROUND $
(☑395 3360; www.bigfoottours.co.bw; campsite per adult/child P200/100) Our pick of the campsites in Khutse, these four sites far from civilisation are fine places to rest, and some have terrific, sweeping views over the pan, with the waterhole nearby. Each site has a *braai* pit, bucket showers and a pit toliet. We stayed in Site No 2 on our most recent visit and thought it one of the loveliest campsites in the country.

Molose Pan Campsite   CAMPGROUND $
(☑395 3360; www.bigfoottours.co.bw; campsite per adult/child P200/100) Busier than the campsites at Moreswe (the four sites here are 24km closer to the entrance gate), these sites are nonetheless excellent with a nearby waterhole maintained by the park authorities and open plains country offering good wildlife visibility.

ℹ Getting There & Away

The entrance gate and park office are 210km from Gaborone. The road is paved until Letlhakeng (109km from the park entrance), whereafter it's around 100km on a patchy gravel road to the turn-off to Kaudwane, then a sandy track for the last few kilometres to the park entrance. A 4WD vehicle is necessary for exploring the reserve.

Kgalagadi Transfrontier Park

In 2000 the former Mabuasehube-Gemsbok National Park was combined with South Africa's former Kalahari Gemsbok National Park to create the new Kgalagadi Transfrontier Park. The result is a 28,400-sq-km binational park that is one of the largest and most pristine arid wilderness areas on the continent. The park is also the only place in Botswana where you'll see the shifting sand dunes that many mistakenly believe to be typical of the Kalahari. This is true desert; in the summer it can reach 45°C, and at night it can drop to -10°C.

◉ Sights

The Mabuasehube section of the park covers 1800 sq km and focuses on the low red dunes around three major and several minor salt-pan complexes. The largest, Mabuasehube Pan, is used as a salt lick by migrating herds in late winter and early spring. Although you can now reach the Two Rivers section from either Kaa or Mabuasehube, access is still easiest from South Africa. The pools of rainwater that collect in the dry riverbeds of the Auob and Nossob Rivers provide the best opportunities for wildlife viewing in the park. The Kalahari Gemsbok National Park section is characterised by a semidesert landscape of Kalahari dunes, camelthorn-dotted grasslands and the dry beds of the Auob and Nossob Rivers. One advantage of visiting this side of the park is that many roads are accessible by 2WD.

🛏 Sleeping

All campsites in the Botswana sections of the park must be booked in advance through the Department of Wildlife & National Parks (DWNP; ☎381 0774; dwnp@gov.bw; camping per person P30).

Bookings for huts and chalets on the South African side are recommended from June to September and during all weekends and public and school holidays. Contact the National Parks Board (☑in South Africa 012-428 9111; www.sanparks.org).

Mabuasehube Section

There are rudimentary campsites at Lesholoago Pan, Khiding Pan, Mabuasehube Pan, Mpaathutlwa Pan, Monamodi Pan and Bosobogolo Pan. Facilities are limited to pit latrines, but most have waterholes for viewing wildlife.

On the road between Mabuasehube and the Two Rivers section of the park you'll find Motopi 1 and Motopi 2 campsites. The former is 71km west of Mabuasehube (95km from Two Rivers), while Motopi 2 is 60km from Mabuasehube and 106km from Two Rivers.

Two Rivers Section

In the western area of the Botswana section of the park, campsites are found along the Nossob Valley at Two Rivers. Although within Botswana territory, these campsites must be accessed from the South African side of the border.

Two Rivers   CAMPGROUND $
(DWNP; ☑381 0774; dwnp@gov.bw; campsite per person P30) This site has cold showers and sit-down flush toilets and may be accessible from north of Bokspits in Botswana without having to go into South Africa first; check when making your booking.

Polentswa   CAMPGROUND $
(DWNP; ☑381 0774; dwnp@gov.bw; campsite per person P30) This simple campsite has shade and latrines but no running water.

Kalahari Gemsbok National Park

Huts and chalets are all equipped with bedding and cooking equipment. Each place has a shop that sells basic supplies, such as food, drinks (including alcohol) and usually petrol. For information on all of the following camps, visit www.sanparks.org.za/parks/kgalagadi/tourism/accommodation.php.

Twee Rivieren   CAMPGROUND, CHALETS $$
(campsites R155-180, chalets R715-1040; ❄❄) The most accessible and popular rest camp on either side of the river, Twee Rivieren features a swimming pool and, unusually for this area, an outdoor bar-restaurant. Rustic chalets have modern amenities including air-con, hot showers and a full kitchen. This is the only one of the Kgalagadi camps to have 24-hour electricity and a relatively strong mobile (cellphone) signal.

Bitterpan Wilderness Camp   CABINS $$$
(2-bed reed cabins R945) Getting out here requires coming through Nossob on a one-way 4WD-only route, but damn if these stilted cabins hovering over a shimmering waterhole and within sight of red sand dunes aren't worth it for their sheer romance. The sense of isolation makes this the perfect Kalahari retreat.

!Xaus Lodge   LODGE $$$
(☑in South Africa 021-701 7860; www.xauslodge.co.za; s/d R4030/6200; ❄❄) If you're after a more luxurious experience, book a night in Kgalagadi's only upmarket lodge accommodation. Owned and operated by the local San community, the lodge is a dry, dreamy fantasy in ochre, decorated with wall hangings made by a local women's sewing collective and overlooking an evocative circular pan. The on-site pool feels a little much in these dry lands, but the San staff, cultural activities and excellent wildlife drives round out a wonderful package.

ℹ Getting There & Away

The Two Rivers Section is accessible from the south via Two Rivers and from the north via Kaa. Access to the Kalahari Gemsbok National Park is via Twee Rivieren – both are about 53km north of the Bokspits border crossing. Access to the Mabuasehube Section is possible from the south (via Tshabong), north (via Tshane) and east (via Werda).

UNDERSTAND BOTSWANA

Botswana Today

By any standards, Botswana's recent history is a lesson for other African countries. Instead of suffering from Africa's oft-seen resource curse, Botswana's government has used the ongoing windfall from diamond mines to build a stable and, for the most part, egalitarian country, one whose economic growth rates have, for decades, been among the world's highest. This is a place where things work, where education, health and environmental protection are government priorities, and even when faced with one of the most serious challenges faced by Africa in the 20th century – HIV/AIDS – the government broke new ground by making antiretroviral treatment available to all.

For all such promising news, Botswana is far from perfect. In late 2010, Survival International called for a boycott of Botswanan diamonds, accusing the government of trying to force the San from their ancestral lands. In the economic sphere, the country's dependence on diamonds is also a major concern when looking towards Botswana's future; diamond production is expected to peak and then decline over the next 20 years. The dependence on diamonds makes the economy vulnerable to a fluctuating world economy – when world demand contracted in 2009, so too did Botswana's economy (by almost 5%) for the first time in living memory, a cautionary tale for the government. Unemployment stands officially at around 7.5%, but unofficially it could be closer to 40%.

History

Rise of the Tswana

The San (p79) may have been Botswana's first known inhabitants, but it's the Tswana who have come to dominate modern Botswana.

One of the most significant developments in Botswana's human history was the evolution of the three main branches of the Tswana tribe during the 14th century. It's a typical tale of family discord, where three brothers – Kwena, Ngwaketse and Ngwato – broke away from their father, Chief Malope, to establish their own followings in Molepolole, Kanye and Serowe respectively. The Ngwato clan split further in the late 18th century following a quarrel between Chief Khama I and his brother Tawana, who subsequently left Serowe and established his chiefdom in the area around Maun. The four major present-day Batswana groups – the Batawana, Bakwena, Bangwaketse and Bangwato – trace their ancestry to these splits and Botswana's demographic make-up owes much to the dispersal of the various groups.

Botswana Takes Shape

In the 19th century the Zulu warlord Shaka, the new chief of the Zulu confederation, launched a series of ruthless campaigns aimed at forcibly amalgamating or destroying all tribes and settlements in his way. By 1830, the Bakwena and Bangwato areas had been overrun and survivors had started the difaqane (literally 'the scattering' or exodus). In his wake came his equally ruthless Ndebele general, Mzilikazi, who continued to send raiding parties into the villages of Botswana and forced villagers to flee as far as Ghanzi and Tshane in the heart of the Kalahari.

The Tswana states of Ngwaketse, Kwena and Ngwato were only reconstituted in the 1840s after the ravages of the difaqane had passed. Realising from their experience that their divided nation was vulnerable to attack, they began to regroup under the aegis of King Segkoma I. These new states were then organised under their own chiefs, who then paid tribute (based on labour and cattle) to the king. Botswana may have begun to unite, but the states were also highly competitive, vying with each other for the increasing trade in ivory and ostrich feathers being carried down new roads to the Cape Colony in the south. Those roads also brought Christian missionaries into Botswana for the first time and enabled the Boer trekkers to begin their migrations further north. The Boers were farmers from the Eastern Cape in southern Africa, the descendants of Dutch-speaking settlers, and their northward migration was prompted by increasing conflict with British colonial settlers.

The Boers & the British

When in the 19th century around 20,000 Boers set out on the Great Trek across the Vaal River into Batswana and Zulu territory, the Batswana chiefs petitioned the British government for protection from the Boers. As the threat of a German–Boer alliance across the Kalahari grew, cutting the British off from their dreams of expanding their interests into mineral-rich Rhodesia (Zimbabwe), the British government started to look seriously at the Batswana petitions for protection. And in 1885 they proclaimed a protectorate over their Setswana allies,

DIAMONDS: A COUNTRY'S BEST FRIEND

In the early 1960s, Botswana ranked as one of the world's poorest countries, with GDP per capita of less than US$200. Less than 2% of the population had completed primary school and fewer than 100 students were enrolled in university. In the entire country there was only one 12km-long paved road. Then, in 1967, everything changed with the discovery of diamonds at Orapa. Two other major mines followed at Letlhakane in 1977 and Jwaneng in 1982, making Botswana the world's leading producer of gem-quality stones – Botswana still extracts around one-quarter of the world's diamond supply.

Where other African countries have squandered the proceeds of bountiful natural resources or descended into conflict, Botswana has bucked the trend. The government has spread this wealth throughout Botswana's small population fairly equitably, and diamond dollars have been ploughed into infrastructure, education (adult literacy stands at 84.4%) and health. In 1994, Botswana became the first country in the world to graduate from the UN's Least Developed Country Status, a league table of development based around key economic, social and quality-of-life indicators. From 1966 to 2005, Botswana's economy grew faster than any other in the world.

In 2011, Botswana ranked 32nd on Transparency International's Corruption Perception Index, the highest ranking of any country in Africa. In the same year, Botswana's GDP per capita was a respectable US$16,200, compared with US$500 in Zimbabwe, US$1600 in Zambia, US$7500 in Namibia and US$11,100 in South Africa.

known as the British Crown Colony of Bechuanaland.

British expansion in southern Africa came in the form of a private venture under the auspices of the British South Africa Company (BSAC), owned by millionaire businessman Cecil John Rhodes. Rhodes exploited a colonial system of land concessions that offered cheap land to private companies in order to colonise new land for the Crown and he fraudulently obtained large tracts of land from local chiefs by passing off contracts as treaties. For their part, the British turned a blind eye as they eventually hoped to transfer the entire Bechuanaland protectorate to the BSAC and relieve themselves of the expense of colonial administration.

Realising the implications of Rhodes' aspirations, three Batswana chiefs, Bathoen, Khama III and Sebele, accompanied by a sympathetic missionary, WC Willoughby, sailed to England to appeal directly to the British parliament for continued government control of Bechuanaland. With Colonial Minister Joseph Chamberlain unresponsive, the delegation turned to the London Missionary Society (LMS) who, through a campaign, took the matter to the British public. Fearing that the BSAC would allow alcohol in Bechuanaland, the LMS and other Christian groups backed the devoutly Christian Khama and his entourage. Public pressure mounted to such a level that the government was forced to concede to the chiefs. Chamberlain agreed to continue British administration of Bechuanaland, ceding only a small strip of the southeast (now known as the Tuli Block) to the BSAC for the construction of a railway line to Rhodesia.

By selling cattle, draught oxen and grain to the Europeans streaming north in search of farming land and minerals, Bechuanaland had enjoyed an initial degree of economic independence. However, the construction of the railway through Bechuanaland to Rhodesia, and a serious outbreak of foot-and-mouth disease in the 1890s, destroyed the transit trade. This new economic vulnerability, combined with a series of droughts and the need to raise cash to pay British taxes, sent many Batswana to South Africa to look for work on farms and in mines. This accelerated the breakdown of traditional land-use patterns and eroded the chiefs' powers.

Independent Botswana

The extent of Botswana's subordination to the interests of South Africa during this period became clear in 1950 when the British government banned Seretse Khama from the chieftainship of the Ngwato and exiled him for six years. This, as secret documents have since revealed, was in order to appease the South African government, which objected to Seretse's marriage to a British woman at a time when racial segregation was enforced in South Africa.

Such meddling only increased growing political agitation and throughout the 1950s and '60s Batswana political parties started to surface and promote the idea of independence. In 1962, Seretse Khama and Kanye farmer Ketumile 'Quett' Masire formed the moderate Bechuanaland Democratic Party (BDP). The BDP formulated a schedule for independence, drawing on support from local chiefs such as Bathoen II of the Bangwaketse, and traditional Batswana. The BDP also called for the transfer of the capital into Botswana (from Mafikeng in South Africa to Gaborone) and a new nonracial constitution.

The British accepted the BDP's peaceful plan for a transfer of power, and Khama was elected president when general elections were held in 1965. On 30 September 1966, the country – now called the Republic of Botswana – was granted full independence. With a steady hand, Seretse Khama steered Botswana through its first 14 years of independence. He guaranteed continued freehold over land held by white ranchers and adopted a strictly neutral stance (at least until near the end of his presidency) towards South Africa and Rhodesia. The reason, of course, was Botswana's economic dependence on the giant to the south, from where they imported the majority of their foodstuffs and where many Batswana worked in the diamond mines. Nevertheless, Khama refused to exchange ambassadors with South Africa and officially disapproved of apartheid in international circles.

Sir Seretse Khama died in 1980 but his Botswana Democratic Party (BDP), formerly the Bechuanaland Democratic Party, continues to command a substantial majority in the Botswana parliament. Sir Ketumile 'Quett' Masire, who succeeded Khama as president from 1980 to 1998, followed the path laid down by his predecessor and continued to cautiously pursue pro-Western policies. Festus Mogae largely continued this trend from 1998 to 2008. Mogae handed over the presidency to Vice President Ian Khama (son of Sir Seretse Khama) on 1 April 2008, a move that generated some grumbles as Khama was never elected as president. Since assuming power Khama has cracked down on drinking, demanding earlier curfews in bars. On 16 October 2009, Ian Khama was sworn in after his BDP party dominated the election as predicted. The party won 45 out of 57 seats in parliament.

People of Botswana

All citizens of Botswana – regardless of colour, ancestry or tribal affiliation – are known as Batswana (plural) or Motswana (singular). Almost everyone, including members of non-Tswana tribes, communicates via the lingua franca of Tswana, a native language, rather than the official language of English. Alongside language, education has played an important role in building a unified country, and the government proudly claims that its commitment of over 30% of its budget to education is the highest per capita in the world.

Tswana

Botswana means 'land of the Tswana' and about 80% of the country's population claims Tswana heritage. In Batswana society, traditional culture acts as a sort of societal glue. Villages grew up around reliable water sources and developed into complex settlements with *kgosi* (chiefs) ultimately responsible for the affairs of the community. Respect for one's elders, firmly held religious beliefs, traditional gender roles and the tradition of the *kgotla* – a specially designated meeting place in each village where social and judicial affairs are discussed and dealt with – created a well-defined social structure with some rigid customs at its core. At a family level, in Batswana village life each family was entitled to land, and traditional homesteads were social affairs consisting of communal eating places and separate huts for sleeping, sometimes for several family members. Historically, the Batswana are farmers and cattle herders. Cattle, and to a lesser extent goats and sheep, are still in many ways the measure of a family's status.

The San

The San were living in the Kalahari and Tsodilo Hills as far back as 30,000 years ago. Of the 100,000 remaining San, which may include many mixed San, around 60% live in Botswana (the !Kung, G//ana, G/wi and !xo being the largest groups) where they make up just 3% of Botswana's population, with the remainder scattered throughout Namibia, South Africa, Angola, Zimbabwe and Zambia.

Traditionally San were nomadic hunter-gatherers who travelled in small family bands (usually between around 25 and 35 people) within well-defined territories. They had no chiefs or hierarchy of leadership and decisions were reached by group consensus. With no animals, crops or possessions, the San were highly mobile. Everything that they needed for their daily existence they carried with them.

Initially the San's social flexibility enabled them to evade conquest and control. But as other powerful tribes with big herds of livestock and farming ambitions moved into the area, inevitable disputes arose over the land. The San's wide-ranging, nomadic lifestyle (some territories extended over 1000 sq km) was utterly at odds with the settled world of the farmers and soon became a source of bitter conflict. This situation was rapidly accelerated by European colonists, who arrived in the area during the mid-17th century. The early Boers pursued an extermination campaign that lasted for 200 years and killed as many as 200,000 indigenous people.

Like so many indigenous peoples the world over, the San are largely impoverished. Many work on farms and cattle posts or live in squalid, handout-dependent and alcohol-plagued settlements centred on boreholes in western Botswana and northeastern Namibia as debate rages around them as to their 'place' in modern African society. Tourism provides some measure of economic opportunity for the San, who are often employed in Ghanzi- and Kalahari-based lodges as wildlife guides and trackers.

And a word on terminology: in Botswana you'll often hear the term 'Basarwa' being used to describe the San, but this is considered by the San to be pejorative as it literally means 'people of the sticks'.

Arts & Crafts

Handicrafts

Botswana is most famous for the basketry produced in the northwestern regions of the Okavango Delta by Wayeyi and Mbukushu women. Like most material arts in Africa they have a practical purpose, but their intricate construction and evocative designs are anything but. In the watery environs of the delta the baskets serve as watertight containers for grains and seeds. The weaving is so tight on some that they were also used as beer kegs. All the baskets are made from the leaf fibre of the real fan palm (mokolane) and colours are derived from soaking the fibres in natural plant dyes.

Traditional San crafts include ostrich-eggshell jewellery, leather aprons, and bags and strands of seeds and nuts (some of which may be not be imported into certain countries).

Literature

Botswana's most famous modern literary figure is South African–born Bessie Head (1937–86), who fled apartheid in South Africa and settled in Sir Seretse Khama's village of Serowe. Her writings, many of which are set in Serowe, reflect the harshness and beauty of African village life and the physical attributes of Botswana itself. Her most widely read work is *Serowe: Village of the Rain Wind*.

Since the 1980s Setswana novel writing has had something of a revival with the publication in English of novels like Andrew Sesinyi's *Love on the Rocks* (1983) and Gaele Sobott-Mogwe's haunting collection of short stories, *Colour Me Blue* (1995), which blends fantasy and reality with the everyday grit of African life. Other novels that lend insight into contemporary Batswana life are *Jamestown Blues* (1997) and *Place of Reeds* (2005) by Caitlin Davies, who was married to a Motswana and lived in Botswana for 12 years.

Unity Dow, Botswana's first female high court judge, has also authored four books to date, all of them dealing with contemporary social issues in the country; we recommend *Far and Beyon'* (2002).

Environment

The Land

Landlocked Botswana is the geographic heart of sub-Saharan Africa, extending over 1100km from north to south and 960km from east to west, an area of 582,000 sq km that's equivalent in size to France.

THE KALAHARI

Around 100 million years ago the supercontinent Gondwanaland dramatically broke up. As the land mass ripped apart, the edges of the African continent rose up, forming the mountain ranges of southern and central Africa. Over millennia, water and wind weathered these highlands, carrying the fine dust inland to the Kalahari Basin. At 2.5 million sq km it's the earth's largest unbroken tract of sand. Depending on who you believe, between 68% and 85% of the country, including the entire central and southwestern regions, is occupied by the Kalahari. The shifting sand dunes that compose a traditional desert are found only in the far southwest, in the Kgalagadi Transfrontier Park. In the northeast are the great salty deserts of the Makgadikgadi Pans; in ancient times part of a vast superlake, they're now the largest (about 12,000 sq km) complex of saltpans in the world and considered to be part of the Kalahari.

In Botswana, large tracts of the Kalahari are protected, with at least five protected areas. From north to south:

» Nxai Pan National Park (p54)
» Makgadikgadi Pans National Park (p53)
» Central Kalahari Game Reserve (p72)
» Khutse Game Reserve (p75)
» Kgalagadi Transfrontier Park (p75)

OKAVANGO DELTA

The Okavango Delta is one of Africa's most extraordinary landscapes. Covering between 13,000 and 18,000 sq km, it snakes into the country from Angola to form a watery paradise of convoluted channels and islands that appear and disappear depending on the water levels. The delta is home to more than 2000 plant species, 450 bird species and 65 fish species, not to mention an estimated 200,000 large mammals.

The delta owes its existence to a tectonic trough in the Kalahari basin, a topographical depression that ensures that the waters of the Okavango River evaporate or are drunk by plants without ever reaching the sea; the delta is extremely flat with no more than 2m of variation in the land's altitude, which means that the waters simply come to a halt. The delta's waters surge and subside at the behest of the rains in far-off Angola, and every year around 11 cubic kilometres of water flood into the delta. The flooding is seasonal, beginning in the Angolan highlands in January and February, with the waters travelling approximately 1200km in a month. Having reached the delta, the waters disperse across the delta from March to June, before peaking in July and August – during these months, the water surface area of the delta can be three times that of the nonflooding periods.

Wildlife

Botswana is home to anywhere between 160 and 500 different mammal species, 593 species of bird, 150 different reptiles, over 8000 species of insect and spider and more than 3100 types of plants and trees. Because the Okavango Delta and the Chobe River provide an incongruous water supply in the otherwise dry savanna, nearly all southern African mammal species, including such rarities as pukus, red lechwes, sitatungas and wild dogs, are present in Moremi Game Reserve, parts of Chobe National Park and the Linyanti Marshes. In the Makgadikgadi & Nxai Pan National Park, herds of wildebeest, zebras and other hoofed mammals migrate between their winter range on the Makgadikgadi plains and the summer lushness of the Nxai Pan region.

National Parks

Around one-third of Botswana's land mass is officially protected in some form, representing one of the highest proportions of protected areas on in the world. All public national parks and reserves in Botswana are run by the Department of Wildlife & National Parks (p45). In addition to the main office in Gaborone, there are other park offices in Maun (p67) and Kasane (p58).

There are a few things worth remembering about visiting Botswana's national parks and reserves:

» Park fees were slated for a significant rise at the time of writing – don't be surprised if they're significantly above those listed here by the time you arrive.
» Although there are exceptions (such as the Chobe Riverfront section of Chobe National Park) and it may be possible on rare occasions to get park rangers to bend the rules, no one is allowed into a national park or reserve without an accommodation booking for that park. For more information, see p83.
» The gates for each DWNP park are open 6am to 6.30pm from 1 April to 30 September and 5.30am to 7pm from

NATIONAL PARK FEES PER DAY

Infants and children up to the age of seven are entitled to free entry into the national parks.

	FOREIGNER PRICE
adult	P120
child (8-17)	P60
camping	P50
vehicles <3500kg	P50

MAJOR NATIONAL PARKS

PARK	FEATURES	ACTIVITIES	BEST TIME
Central Kalahari Game Reserve	52,800 sq km; one of the largest protected areas in the world; semi-arid grassland	wildlife viewing; walking; visiting San villages	Jun-Oct
Chobe National Park	11,700 sq km; mosaic of grassland & woodland; high elephant population	wildlife viewing; bird-watching; fishing	year-round
Kgalagadi Transfrontier Park	38,000 sq km; straddles the South African border; semi-arid grassland	wildlife viewing; bird-watching	Dec-May
Khutse Game Reserve	2590 sq km; adjoins Central Kalahari Game Reserve; same features	wildlife viewing; walking; visiting San villages	Jun-Oct
Makgadikgadi & Nxai Pans NPs	7300 sq km; largest saltpans in the world; migratory zebra & wildebeest; flamingos	wildlife viewing; trekking with San; quad biking	Mar-Jul
Moremi Game Reserve	3800 sq km; grassland, flood plains & swamps; high wild-life density	wildlife viewing; walking; scenic flights; boating	Aug-Dec
Northern Tuli Game Reserve	collection of private reserves; unique rock formations	wildlife viewing; horse riding; walking; night drives	May-Sep
Khama Rhino Sanctuary	4300 hectares; last refuge of Botswana's rhinos	wildlife viewing; bird-watching	May-Sep

1 October to 31 March. It is vital that all visitors be out of the park or settled into their campsite outside of these hours. Driving after dark is strictly forbidden (although it is permitted in private concessions).

CAMPING & BOOKING

The DWNP ran all of the campsites within national parks and reserves until a recent shift in policy saw most of these tendered out to private companies. For information on which companies run which sites and how to make bookings, see p84.

The DWNP still runs a small number of campsites (especially in the Central Kalahari Game Reserve and Kgalagadi Transfrontier Park) and reservations for any DWNP campsite can be made up to 12 months in advance at the DWNP offices in Maun or Gaborone; Chobe National Park bookings are also possible at the Kasane DWNP office. It's at these offices that you also pay the park entry fees (upon presenting proof of a confirmed campsite reservation).

We recommend that, wherever possible, you make the bookings in person or arrange for someone to do so on your behalf. In theory the DWNP also allows you to make bookings over the phone or via email, but in practice getting anyone to answer the phone or reply to emails is far more challenging than it should be. If you do manage to make a phone or email booking, insist on receiving (either by fax, email or letter) a receipt with a reference number on it that you must keep and quote if you need to change your reservation.

When making the reservation, you need to tell the DWNP the name of the preferred campsite(s) within the park, in order of preference.

Environmental Issues

As a relatively large country with a very low population density, Botswana is one of Africa's most unpolluted and pristine regions. Even so, Botswana faces most of the ecological problems experienced elsewhere in Africa, such as land degradation and desertification, deforestation (around 21% of the country is covered by forests), water scarcity and urban sprawl.

In November 2012, Botswana's government announced a ban on all commercial hunting from January 2014.

FENCES
If you've been stopped at a veterinary checkpoint, or visited the eastern Okavango Delta, you'll be familiar with the country's 3000km of 1.5m-high 'buffalo fence', officially called the Veterinary Cordon Fence. It's not a single fence but a series of high-tensile steel-wire barriers. The fences were first erected in 1954 to segregate wild buffalo herds from domestic free-range cattle in order to thwart the spread of foot-and-mouth disease. Botswana's beef-farming industry is one of the most important in the country, both economically and in terms of the status conferred by cattle upon their owners in Batswana society. The fences, however, often block important wildlife migration corridors. Balancing these two significant yet sometimes conflicting imperatives is one of the most complicated challenges facing Botswana's government.

THE DELTA
Despite its status as a biodiversity hotspot and the largest Ramsar Wetland Site on the planet, the Okavango Delta has no international protection (apart from the Moremi Game Reserve), although many prominent conservationists consider it to be critically endangered and argue that it should be awarded Unesco World Heritage status. A survey team from the DWNP and BirdLife Botswana has concluded that the delta is shrinking. The Kubango River – originating in the highlands of Angola – carries less water and floods the delta for a shorter period of the year. Other key threats include overgrazing, which is already resulting in accelerated land and soil degradation, and the proposed extraction of water from the Okavango River to supply the growing needs of Namibia.

SURVIVAL GUIDE

Directory A–Z

Accommodation
The story of Botswana's accommodation is the story of extremes. At one end, there are fabulously sited campsites for self-drivers

---

> ### ℹ BED LEVY & GOVERNMENT TAX
>
> Please note that all hotels, lodges, campsites and other forms of accommodation are required by the government to charge a P10 bed levy per person per night. This levy is rarely if ever included in quoted accommodation rates.
>
> In addition to the levy, a 12% government tax is levied on hotels and lodges (but not all campsites); this, unlike the levy, is usually included in prices.

(the closest the country comes to budget accommodation). At the other extreme, there are top-end lodges where prices can be eye-wateringly high. In between, you will find some midrange options in the major towns and places like the Okavango Panhandle, but elsewhere there's very little for the midrange (and nothing for the noncamping budget) traveller.

SEASONS
While most budget and midrange options tend to have a standard room price, many top-end places change their prices according to season. High season is usually from June to November (and may also apply to Christmas, New Year and Easter, depending on the lodge), low season corresponds to the rains (December to March or April) and the shoulder is a short April and May window. The only exception is the Kalahari, where June to November is generally (but not always) considered to be low season.

CAMPING
Just about everywhere of interest, including all major national parks, has a campsite. Once the domain of the Department

---

> ### SLEEPING PRICE RANGES
>
> The following price ranges refer to a high-season double room with private bathroom and, unless stated otherwise, include breakfast. Upmarket places tend to price in US dollars as opposed to pula.
>
> **$** Less than US$50
> **$$** From US$50 to US$100
> **$$$** More than US$100

of Wildlife & National Parks (DWNP), most of the campsites are now privately run. Many sites have ablutions blocks with sit-down flush toilets and hot showers, as well as *braai* pits, while others, particularly in remote regions, have basic pit latrines and cold bucket showers.

All campsites must be booked in advance and they fill up fast in busy periods, such as during South African school holidays. And

SELF-DRIVE CAMPSITES: AN OVERVIEW

PARK/RESERVE/ SECTOR	CAMPSITE	OPERATOR	PRICE PER ADULT/ CHILD
Makgadikgadi Pans National Park	Khumaga	**SKL** (www.sklcamps.com)	P240/120 (US$50/25)
Nxai Pan National Park	South Camp	**Xomae** (www.xomaesites. com)	P226/113
	Baines' Baobab	**Xomae** (www.xomaesites. com)	P350/175
Chobe Riverfront	Ihaha	**Kwalate** (for bookings email kwalatesafari@ gmail.com)	P260/130 (US$40/20)
Savuti	Savuti Camp	**SKL** (www.sklcamps.com)	P240/120 (US$50/25)
Linyanti	Linyanti Camp	**SKL** (www.sklcamps.com)	P240/120 (US$50/25)
Moremi Game Reserve	Xakanaxa	**Kwalate** (for bookings email kwalatesafari@ gmail.com)	P260/130 (US$40/20)
	Khwai	**SKL** (www.sklcamps.com)	P240/120 (US$50/25)
	Third Bridge	**Xomae** (www.xomaesites. com)	P226/113
	South Camp	**Kwalate** (for bookings email kwalatesafari@ gmail.com)	P260/130 (US$40/20)
Kubu Island	Kubu Island	**Gaing-O-Community Trust** (www.kubuisland. com)	P100/50
Central Kalahari Game Reserve	Kori, Deception Valley, Leopard Pan, Phokoje Pan, Xade, Bape and Xaka	**DWNP** (for bookings email dwnp@gov.bw or 📞318 0774 Gaborone office)	P200/100
	Passarge Valley, Piper Pan, Motopi, Lekhubu, Leatihau and Sunday Pan	**Big Foot Tours** (www. bigfoottours.co.bw)	P200/100
Khutse Game Reserve	All sites	**Big Foot Tours** (www. bigfoottours.co.bw)	P200/100
Kgalagadi Transfrontier Park	All sites	**DWNP** (for bookings email dwnp@gov.bw or 📞318 0774 Gaborone office)	P30/15

it is very important to remember that you will not be allowed into any park run by the DWNP without a reservation for a campsite.

SAFARI CAMPS & LODGES

Botswana's claim to being Africa's most exclusive destination is built around its luxury lodges (sometimes called 'camps'). You'll find them anywhere that there are decent concentrations of wildlife, most notably in Chobe National Park, the Tuli Block, Moremi Game Reserve, all over the Okavango Delta and, to a lesser extent, the parks and reserves of the Kalahari. It's impossible to generalise about them, other than to say that most pride themselves on their isolation, exclusivity, luxury and impeccable service. Most feature permanent or semi-permanent luxury tents, a communal dining area overlooking a waterhole or other important geographical feature and a swimming pool.

For many visitors, they're once-in-a-lifetime places with accommodation rates to match – some start at around US$1000/1500 per person per night in the low/high season, but many cost considerably more than that. Usually included in these rates are all meals, some drinks and most wildlife drives and other activities. Most places are only accessible by 4WD transfer or air; the latter will cost an extra US$100 to US$200.

🏃 Activities

Apart from wildlife viewing and 4WD safaris, some safaris include a hiking component, while other possibilities include elephant or horseback safaris in the Okavango, quadbiking on the Makgadikgadi Pans, fishing in the Okavango Panhandle, or scenic flights from Maun.

Travelling around the channels of the Okavango Delta in a *mokoro* is a wonderful experience that is not to be missed. The *mokoro* is poled along the waterways by a skilled poler, much like an African gondola. Although you won't be spotting much wildlife from such a low viewpoint, it's a great way to appreciate the delta's bird life and gain an appreciation, hopefully from a distance, of the formidable bulk of hippos.

Business Hours

Reviews in this guidebook won't list business hours unless they differ significantly from the following standards. The whole country practically closes down on Sunday.

Banks 8.30am to 3.30pm Monday to Friday, 8.15am to 10.45am Saturday

National Parks 6am to 6.30pm April to September, 5.30am to 7pm October to March

Post Offices 9am to 5pm Monday to Friday, 9am to noon Saturday or 7.30am to noon and 2pm to 4.30pm Monday to Friday, 7.30am to 12.30pm Saturday

Restaurants 11am to 11pm Monday to Saturday; some are also open the same hours on Sunday

Children

Botswana can be a challenging destination for families travelling with children. That's primarily because the distances here can be epic and long days in the vehicle along bumpy trails will test the patience of most kids. It's also worth remembering that many upmarket lodges and safari companies won't accept children under a certain age (sometimes seven, more often 12), and those that do will probably require you to book separate wildlife drives. National park entry is free for children under eight and half-price for those aged from eight to 17 years old.

Customs Regulations

Most items from elsewhere in the Southern African Customs Union (SACU) – Namibia, South Africa, Lesotho and Swaziland – may be imported duty free. You may be asked to declare new laptops and cameras, but this is rarely enforced.

Visitors may bring into Botswana the following amounts of duty-free items: up to 400 cigarettes, 50 cigars or 250g of tobacco; 2L of wine or 1L of beer or spirits; and 50mL of perfume or 250mL of eau de cologne.

The most rigorous searches at customs posts are for fresh meat products – don't buy succulent steaks in South Africa for your camping barbecue and expect them to be allowed in.

Embassies & High Commissions

French Embassy (Map p46; ☑397 3863; www.ambafrance-bw.org; 761 Robinson Rd, Gaborone; ⊘8am-4pm Mon-Fri)

German Embassy (☑395 3143; www.gaborone.diplo.de; Segoditshane Way, 3rd fl, Professional

House, Broadhurst Mall, Gaborone; ⊗9am-noon Mon-Fri)

Namibian Embassy (Map p44; ☑390 2181; nhc.gabs@info.bw; Plot 186, Morara Close, Gaborone; ⊗7.30am-1pm & 2-4.30pm Mon-Fri)

South African Embassy (Map p46; ☑390 4800; sahcgabs@botsnet.bw; 29 Queens Rd, Gaborone; ⊗8am-12.45pm & 1.30-4.30pm Mon-Fri)

UK Embassy (Map p46; ☑395 2841; www.ukinbotswana.fco.gov.uk/en/; Queens Rd, Gaborone; ⊗8am-12.30pm & 1.30-4.30pm Mon-Thu, to 1pm Fri)

US Embassy (Map p44; ☑395 3982; http://botswana.usembassy.gov; Embassy Dr, Government Enclave, Gaborone; ⊗7.30am-5pm Mon-Thu, to 1.30pm Fri)

Zambian Embassy (Map p46; ☑395 1951; Plot No 1118 Queens Rd, the Mall, Gaborone; ⊗8.30am-12.30pm & 2-4.30pm Mon-Fri)

Zimbabwean Embassy (Map p44; ☑391 4495; www.zimgaborone.gov.zw; Plot 8850, Orapa Cl, Government Enclave, Gaborone; ⊗8am-1pm & 2-4.30pm Mon-Fri)

Food

The following price ranges are used for Eating reviews in this chapter.

$	Less than US$10 per meal
$$	US$10-20 per meal
$$$	More than US$20 per main dish

Internet Access

Cyber cafes Common in large and medium-sized towns; connection speeds fluctuate wildly and prices range from P12 per hour in Gaborone to P40 elsewhere.

Post Offices Some post offices, including in Kasane, have a few internet-enabled PCs.

Wireless Reasonably common in mid-range and top-end hotels in towns, but very rarely available in safari lodges.

Maps

The best paper map of Botswana is the *Botswana* (1:1,000,000) map published by Tracks4Africa (www.tracks4africa.co.za). Updated every couple of years using detailed traveller feedback, the map is printed on tear-free, waterproof paper and includes distances and estimated travel times. Used in conjunction with their unrivalled GPS maps, it's far and away the best mapping

product on the market. Even so, be aware that, particularly in the Okavango Delta, last year's trails may this year be underwater depending on water levels, so these maps should never be a substitute for expert local knowledge.

If for some reason you are unable to get hold of the Tracks4Africa map the only other maps that we recommend are those published by Shell Oil Botswana and Veronica Roodt. Their *Shell Tourist Map of Botswana* (1:1,750,000) is available at major bookshops in Botswana and South Africa.

Probably of more interest are Shell's zoomed-in maps (with varying scales) of the various reserves and other popular areas. These include numerous GPS coordinates for important landmarks and the tracks are superimposed onto satellite images of the area in question. Some are a little out of date, but they're still excellent. Titles include: *Okavango Delta, Chobe National Park, Moremi Game Reserve* and *Kgalagadi Transfrontier Park.*

Money

The unit of currency is the Botswanan pula (P). Pula means 'blessings' or 'rain', the latter of which is as precious as money in this largely desert country. Notes come in denominations of P10, P20, P50 and P100, and coins (thebe, or 'shield') are in denominations of 5t, 10t, 25t, 50t, P1, P2 and P5.

Prices can be quoted in US dollars and pula. At top-end hotels, lodges and camps, things are often priced in US dollars; you can also pay in US dollars. Otherwise, you'll be making most transactions in Botswana pula.

Most banks and foreign exchange offices won't touch Zambian kwacha and (sometimes) Namibian dollars; in border areas you can sometimes pay for things with the latter.

ATMS

Credit cards can be used in ATMs displaying the appropriate sign or to obtain cash advances over the counter in many banks – Visa and MasterCard are among the most widely recognised. Transaction fees can be prohibitive and usually apply per transaction rather than the amount you're withdrawing – take out as much as you can each time.

You'll find ATMs at all the main bank branches throughout Botswana, including in Gaborone, Maun, Francistown and Kas-

> ### ℹ CHANGING MONEY AT THE BORDER
>
> A word of warning: if you're changing money at or near border posts and not doing so through the banks, be aware that local businesses (sometimes bureaux de change, sometimes just shops with a sideline in currencies so that arriving travellers can pay their customs duties) usually have abysmal rates. Change the minimum that you're likely to need and change the rest at a bank or bureaux de change in the nearest large town.

ane, and this is undoubtedly the simplest (and safest) way to handle your money while travelling.

CASH

Most common foreign currencies can be exchanged, but not every branch of every bank will do so. Therefore, it's best to stick to US dollars, euros, UK pounds and South African rand, which are all easy to change.

There are five commercial banks in the country with branches in all the main towns and major villages. Although you will get less favourable rates at a bureau de change, they are a convenient option if the lines at the banks are particularly long.

There is no black market in Botswana. Anyone offering to exchange money on the street is doing so illegally and is probably setting you up for a scam, the exception being the guys who change pula for South African rand in front of South Africa–bound minibuses – locals use their services, so they can be trusted.

CREDIT CARDS

Most major credit cards (especially Visa and MasterCard) are accepted at the tourist hotels and restaurants in the larger cities and towns.

TIPPING

While tipping isn't obligatory, the government's official policy of promoting upmarket tourism has raised expectations in many hotels and restaurants. A service charge may be added as a matter of course, in which case there's no need to leave a tip. If there is no service charge and the service has been good, leave around 10%.

It is also a good idea to tip the men who watch your car in public car parks and the attendants at service stations who wash your windscreens. A tip of around P5 to P10 is appropriate.

Guides and drivers of safari vehicles will also expect a tip, especially if you've spent a number of days under their care.

TRAVELLERS CHEQUES

Travellers cheques can be cashed at most banks and exchange offices. American Express (Amex), Thomas Cook and Visa are the most widely accepted brands. Banks charge anywhere between 2% and 3% commission to change the cheques; Barclays usually offers the most efficient service and charges 2.5% commission for most brands. You must take your passport with you when cashing cheques.

Post

Botswana Post (www.botspost.co.bw) is generally reliable, although it can be slow, so allow at least two weeks for delivery to or from any overseas address.

Public Holidays

New Year's Day 1 January

Day after New Year's Day 2 January

Easter March/April – Good Friday, Holy Saturday and Easter Monday

Labour Day 1 May

Ascension Day April/May

Sir Seretse Khama Day 1 July

President's Day July

Botswana/Independence Day 30 September

Day after Independence Day 1 October

Christmas 25 December

Boxing Day 26 December

Safe Travel

Crime is rarely a problem in Botswana, and what crime there is rarely extends beyond occasional pickpocketing and theft from parked cars.

Although vehicle traffic is light on most roads outside of the major towns and cities, the main concern for most travellers is road safety. Botswana has one of the highest accident rates in the world, and drunk and reckless driving are common, especially at month's end (wage day). Cattle, goats, sheep, donkeys and even elephants are deadly hazards on the road, especially at dusk and after dark when visibility is poor. Never drive at night unless you absolutely have to.

Telephone

Botswana Telecom (www.btc.bw) is the operator of Botswana's fixed-line telephone service. Local and domestic calls at peak times start at P35 per minute and rise according to the distance.

Botswana's two main mobile (cell) phone networks are Mascom Wireless (www.mascom.bw) and Orange Botswana (www.orange.co.bw), of which Mascom is by far the largest provider. Both providers have dealers where you can buy phones, SIM cards and top up your credit in most large and medium-sized towns. The coverage map for these two providers is improving with each passing year, but there's simply no mobile coverage across large swaths of the country (including much of the Kalahari and Okavango Delta). The main highway system is generally covered. Most Botswana mobile numbers begin with ☎071 or ☎072.

There are no internal area codes in Botswana.

Country code ☎267

International access code ☎00

Tourist Information

The Department of Tourism, rebranded in the public sphere as Botswana Tourism (www.botswanatourism.co.bw), has an excellent website and a growing portfolio of tourist offices around the country; we list some of these throughout this chapter. These tourist offices don't always have their finger on the pulse, but they can be an extremely useful source of brochures from local hotels, tour operators and other tourist services.

For information on national parks, you're better off contacting the Department of Wildlife & National Parks (DWNP; ☎381 0774; www.mewt.gov.bw/DWNP).

Another useful resource is the Regional Tourism Organisation of Southern Africa (☎in South Africa 011-315 2420; www.retosa.co.za), which promotes tourism throughout Southern Africa, including Botswana.

Visas

Most visitors can obtain tourist visas at the international airports and borders (and the nearest police stations in lieu of an immigration official at remote border crossings). Visas on arrival are valid for 30 days – and possibly up to 90 days if requested at the time of entry – and are available for free to passport holders from most Commonwealth countries (but not Ghana, India, Nigeria, Pakistan and Sri Lanka); all EU countries; the USA; and countries in the Southern African Customs Union (SACU), ie South Africa, Namibia, Lesotho and Swaziland. If you hold a passport from any other country, apply for a 30-day tourist visa at an overseas Botswanan embassy or consulate.

Getting There & Away

Entering the Country

Entering Botswana is usually straightforward provided you are carrying a valid passport. Visas are available on arrival for most nationalities and are issued in no time. If you're crossing into the country overland and in your own (or rented) vehicle, expect to endure (sometimes quite cursory) searches for fresh meat and fruit and dairy products, most of which will be confiscated if found. For vehicles rented in South Africa, Namibia or another regional country, you will need to show a letter from the owner that you have permission to drive the car into Botswana, in addition to all other registration documents.

At all border posts you must pay P120 (a combination of road levy and third-party insurance) if you're driving your own vehicle. Hassles from officialdom are rare.

The Tracks4Africa *Botswana* map (p86) has opening hours for all border posts.

PASSPORT

All visitors entering Botswana must hold a passport that is valid for at least six months. Also, allow a few empty pages for stamp-happy immigration officials, especially if you plan on crossing over to Zimbabwe and/or Zambia to Victoria Falls.

Air

AIRPORTS

Sir Seretse Khama International Airport (GBE; ☎391 4401) Botswana's main airport is located 11km north of Gaborone. Although this is well served with flights from Johannesburg and Harare, it's seldom used by tourists as an entry point into the country.

Maun Airport (MUB; ☑686 1559) Air Botswana uses this busy provincial airports, as do numerous charter airlines.

Kasane Airport (BBK; ☑625 0133) Quieter airport with mostly domestic flights and a few charters.

AIRLINES FLYING TO/FROM BOTSWANA

The national carrier is **Air Botswana** (BP; ☑390 5500; www.airbotswana.co.bw), which flies routes within southern Africa. Air Botswana has offices in Gaborone, Francistown, Maun, Kasane and Victoria Falls (Zimbabwe). It's generally cheaper to book Air Botswana tickets online than it is through one of their offices.

The only scheduled international flights into Botswana come from Jo'burg and Cape Town (South Africa), Victoria Falls and Harare (Zimbabwe), Lusaka (Zambia) and Windhoek (Namibia).

South African Airways (☑in Gaborone 397 2397; www.flysaa.com)

Air Namibia (☑in Maun 686 0391; www.airnamibia.com)

Land

NAMIBIA

Border Crossings

There are five border crossings between Botswana and Namibia:

Gcangwa–Tsumkwe Little-used crossing along a 4WD-only track close to Botswana's Tsodilo Hills

Kasane/Mpalila Island Only for guests with prebooked accommodation at upmarket lodges on the island

Mamuno Remote crossing on the road between Ghanzi and Windhoek

Mohembo Connects Shakawe, Maun and the Okavango Panhandle with northeastern Namibia

Ngoma Bridge East of Kasane and connects to Namibia's Caprivi Strip

Bus

One option is to catch the daily combi (minibus) from Ghanzi to Mamuno (three hours) and then to cross the borders on foot, bearing in mind that this crossing is about a kilometre long. You will then have to hitch a ride from the Namibian side at least to Gobabis, where you can catch a train or other transport to Windhoek. It's time-consuming and unreliable at best.

Car & Motorcycle

Drivers crossing the border at Mohembo must secure an entry permit for Mahango Game Reserve at Popa Falls. This is free if you're transiting or N$80 per person per day plus N$40 per vehicle per day if you want to drive around the reserve (which is possible in a 2WD).

From Divundu turn west towards Rundu and then southwest for Windhoek, or east towards Katima Mulilo (Namibia), Kasane (Botswana) and Victoria Falls (Zimbabwe), or take the ferry to Zambia.

SOUTH AFRICA

Gaborone is only 280km as the crow flies from Jo'burg, or 379km along a good road link.

Border Crossings

There are 14 border crossings between South Africa and Botswana. Five of these provide access of sorts from the South African side of the Kgalagadi Transfrontier Park, five are handy for Gaborone and the remaining four are good for Eastern Botswana and the Tuli Block.

The major crossings are:

Bokspits The best South African access to the Kgalagadi Transfontier Park

Martin's Drift, Zanzibar, Platjan & Pont Drift Eastern Botswana and the Tuli Block from the Northern Transvaal

Pioneer Gate Connects Gaborone (via Lobatse and Zeerust) with Jo'burg

Ramatlabama Connects Gaborone with Mafikeng

Tlokweng Connects Gaborone and Jo'burg via the Madikwe Game Reserve in South Africa

Bus & Combi

Intercape Mainliner (☑397 4294, in South Africa 021-380 4400; www.intercape.co.za) runs a service from Jo'burg to Gaborone (from R240, 6.5 hours, one daily); while you need to get off the bus to sort out any necessary visa formalities, you'll rarely be held up for too long at the border. From Gaborone, the Intercape Mainliner runs from the petrol

i RENTING A 4WD IN SOUTH AFRICA

Renting in South Africa is cheaper and more reliable than doing so in Botswana, even accounting for the extra distance you'll need to drive just to get into Botswana. While you could rent from one of the mainstream car rental agencies, there are some specialist 4WD operators that can set you up perfectly for almost any self-drive expedition into Botswana. You may be able to arrange to pick up the vehicle within Botswana itself, but this will, of course, cost extra.

On our most recent research trip we used a 4WD Land Rover Defender camper from Explorer Safaris (in South Africa 082-855 1574; www.explorersafaris.co.za). All of their vehicles are two years old or less and are fitted with a fold-out camper, rooftop tent, gas cookers, a fridge and all necessary camping equipment. We have no hesitation in recommending either their vehicles or standards of professionalism. Rates start at R995 up to R1575 per day, depending on the vehicle and the duration of the rental period, plus petrol and insurance. Booked in conjunction with Drive Botswana (in Palapye 492 3416; www.drivebotswana.com), it's an excellent overall package. It is important to note that we received no discounts from Explorer Safaris.

Other South African companies that rent 4WDs with camping equipment include Around About Cars (in South Africa 0860 422 4022; www.aroundaboutcars.com), Britz (in South Africa 011-396 1860; www.britz.co.za) and Buffalo Campers (in South Africa 011-021 0385; www.buffalo.co.za).

station beside the Mall and tickets should be booked a week or so in advance; this can be done online.

You can also travel between South Africa and Botswana by combi. From the far (back) end of the bus station in Gaborone, combis leave when full to a number of South African destinations including Jo'burg (P210/R220, six to seven hours). Be warned that you'll be dropped in Jo'burg's Park Station, which is not a safe place to linger.

Car & Motorcycle

Most border crossings are clearly marked, but it is vital to note that some crossings over the Limpopo and Molopo Rivers (the latter is in Botswana's south) are drifts (river fords) that cannot be crossed by 2WD in wet weather. In times of very high water, these crossings may be closed to all traffic.

ZIMBABWE

Border Crossings

There are three land border crossings between Botswana and Zimbabwe.

Kazungula The main crossing point from Kasane to Victoria Falls

Pandamatenga A little-used backroads crossing off the road between Kasane and Nata

Ramokgweban/Plumtree Connects Francistown with Bulawayo and Harare

Bus

Incredibly, there is no public transport between Kasane, the gateway to one of Botswana's major attractions (ie Chobe National Park), and Victoria Falls. Other than hitching, the only cross-border option is the 'tourist shuttle' minibuses that take about one hour and can be arranged through most hotels, camps and tour operators in Kasane. There is little or no coordination between combi companies in either town, so combis often return from Victoria Falls to Kasane empty. Most combis won't leave unless they have at least two passengers. Some hotels and lodges in Kasane also offer private transfers to Livingstone/Victoria Falls (from P1250, two hours). They usually pick up booked passengers at their hotels around 10am.

Elsewhere, buses leave early to mid-afternoon from the bus station in Francistown bound for Bulawayo (P60, two hours) and Harare (P160, five hours). For anywhere else in western Zimbabwe, get a connection in Bulawayo.

River

Botswana and Zambia share one of the world's shortest international borders: about 750m across the Zambezi River. The only way across the river is by ferry from Kazungula, which normally operates from 6am to 6pm daily.

If you're driving, ferry costs depend on which ferry you catch. The Botswana-registered ferry costs P80 for Botswana-registered vehicles to make the crossing, P200 for foreign vehicles. The Zambian-run ferry charges ZK134,000 per vehicle. Note, however, that the Zambian currency was due to be revalued in January 2013 with three zeros to be knocked off.

At the time of writing there was no cross-border public transport. A combi from Kasane to the border post at Kasungula should cost no more than P35. Once there, you'll need to complete the formalities and take the ferry on foot. There is no regular public transport from the Zambian side of the river, although there is one combi that goes to Dambwa, 3km west of Livingstone. If you don't have a vehicle, ask for a lift to Livingstone, Lusaka or points beyond at the ferry terminal or on the ferry itself.

Getting Around

Air

Air Botswana (BP; ✆390 5500; www.airbotswana.co.bw) operates a limited number of domestic routes. It's usually much cheaper to purchase the tickets online than in person at one of their offices. Sample one-way fares at the time of writing:

Gaborone–Francistown (from P680)

Gaborone–Kasane (from P1050)

Gaborone–Maun (from P882)

Kasane–Maun (from P369)

One-way fares are usually more expensive than return fares, so plan your itinerary accordingly; children aged under two sitting on the lap of an adult cost 10% of the fare and children aged between two and 12 cost 50% of the fare. Passengers are allowed 20kg of luggage.

CHARTER FLIGHTS

Charter flights are often the best – and sometimes the only – way to reach remote lodges, but they are an expensive extra cost; fares are not usually included in the quoted rates for most lodges. On average, a one-way fare between Maun and a remote lodge in the Okavango Delta will set you back around US$150 to US$250. These services are now highly regulated and flights must be booked as part of a safari package with a mandatory reservation at one of the lodges.

It is very important to note that passengers on charter flights are only allowed 10kg to 12kg (and rarely 20kg) of luggage each; check the exact amount when booking.

Bus & Combi

Buses and combis regularly travel to all major towns and villages throughout Botswana but are less frequent in sparsely populated areas such as western Botswana and the Kalahari. Public transport to smaller villages is often nonexistent, unless the village is along a major route. The extent and frequency of buses and combis also depends on the quantity and quality of roads – for example, there is no public transport along the direct route between Maun and Kasane (ie through Chobe National Park) – and services elsewhere can be suspended if roads are flooded.

Buses are usually comfortable and normally leave at a set time regardless of whether they're full or not – ask around the bus station for bus departure times. Combis leave when full, usually from the same station as the buses. Tickets for all public buses and combis cannot be bought in advance; they can only be purchased on board.

Car & Motorcycle

The best way to travel around Botswana is to hire a vehicle. Remember, however, that distances are long and we generally recommend that you rent a vehicle outside the country (preferably South Africa) where the range of choice is greater and prices generally lower.

DRIVING LICENCE

Your home driving licence is valid for six months in Botswana, but if it isn't written in English you must provide a certified translation. In any case, it is advisable to obtain an International Driving Permit (IDP). Your national automobile association can issue this and it is valid for 12 months.

FUEL & SPARE PARTS

Fuel (petrol) is relatively expensive in Botswana – at the time of writing it was P9.15 for petrol, P9.40 for diesel – but prices vary according to the remoteness of the petrol station. Petrol stations are open 24 hours in Gaborone, Francistown, Maun, Mahalapye and Palapye; elsewhere, they open from about 7am to 7pm daily.

HIRE

If you're looking to rent a car for exploring Botswana, consider renting a vehicle in South Africa (see the boxed text, p90).

Otherwise, we recommend the following companies who offer specialist rental of fully equipped 4WDs with all camping equipment:

Drive Botswana (☎in Palapye 492 3416; www.drivebotswana.com) Arranges 4WDs through Explorer Safaris (☎in South Africa 082-855 1574; www.explorersafaris.co.za) in South Africa, but also organises a complete package itinerary including maps, trip notes and bookings for campsites, all at no extra cost. We made our booking through them (we received no discounts or other preferential treatment) and found them to be outstanding and unfailingly professional. They should declare the owner Andy Raggett a national treasure.

Self Drive Adventures (☎in Maun 686 3755; www.selfdriveadventures.com) A recommended self-drive operator that can make most of the arrangements.

Mainstream international car-rental agencies have offices in Botswana. That said, most only have a handful of 4WDs and you should always read the fine print of any rental contracts – some agencies are known for including a clause that forbids off-road driving!

INSURANCE

Insurance is strongly recommended. No matter who you hire your car from, make sure you understand what is included in the price (such as unlimited kilometres, tax and so on) and what your liabilities are. Most local insurance policies do not include cover for damage to windshields and tyres. Third-party motor insurance is a minimum requirement in Botswana. However, it is also advisable to take Damage (Collision) Waiver, which costs around P150 extra per day for a 2WD and about P300 per day for a 4WD. Loss (Theft) Waiver is an extra worth having.

ROAD CONDITIONS

With the upgrading of the road between Kasane and Nata, good paved roads link most major population centres. The most notable exception is the direct route between Kasane and Maun – a horribly corrugated gravel track. The road from Maun to Shakawe past the Okavango Panhandle is generally reasonable but beware of potholes.

ROAD RULES

To drive a car in Botswana, you must be at least 18 years old. Like most other Southern African countries, traffic keeps to the left side of the road. The national speed limit is 60km/h up to 120km/h on paved roads; when passing through towns and villages, assume a speed limit of 60km/h. Mobile police units routinely set up speed cameras along major roads, particularly between Gaborone and Francistown – fines operate on a sliding scale, but can go as high as P500 if you're 30km/h over the limit, and you'll be expected to pay on the spot. On gravel roads, limits are set at 60km/h to 80km/h, while it's 40km/h in all national parks and reserves.

Other road conditions to be aware of:
» Seat belt usage (where installed) is compulsory in the front (but not back) seats.
» If you have an accident causing injury, it must be reported to the authorities within 48 hours. If vehicles have sustained only minor damage and there are no injuries – and all parties agree – you can exchange names and addresses and sort it out later through your insurance companies.
» In theory, owners are responsible for keeping their livestock off the road, but in practice animals wander wherever they want.
» The chance of hitting a wild or domestic animal is far, far greater after dark, so driving at night is definitely not recommended.
» At the so-called 'buffalo fences' (officially called Veterinary Cordon Fences), your vehicle may be searched (they're looking for fresh meat or dairy products) and you may have to walk through a soda solution and drive your car through soda-treated water.

Local Transport

COMBI (MINIBUS)

Combis, recognisable by their blue number plates, circulate according to set routes around major towns: Gaborone, Kasane, Ghanzi, Molepolole, Mahalapye, Palapye, Francistown, Selebi-Phikwe, Lobatse and Kanye. They are very frequent, inexpensive and generally reliable. However, they aren't terribly safe (most drive too fast), especially on long journeys, and they only serve the major towns. They can also be crowded.

TAXI

Licensed taxis are also recognisable by their blue number plates. They rarely bother hanging around the airports at Gaborone, Francistown, Kasane and Maun, so the only reliable transport from the airport is usually a courtesy bus operated by a top-end hotel or lodge.

It is not normal for taxis to cruise the streets for fares – even in Gaborone. If you need one, telephone a taxi company to arrange a pick-up or go to a taxi stand (usually near the bus or train stations).

Lesotho

Best Things to Do

» Malealea (p103)
» Semonkong (p103)
» Ramabanta (p100)
» Thaba-Bosiu (p100)
» Quthing (p104)

Best Places to Stay

» Malealea Lodge (p103)
» Maliba Mountain Lodge (p102)
» Semonkong Lodge (p103)

Why Go?

Lesotho (le-soo-too) is a vastly underrated travel destination. It's beautiful, culturally rich, safe, cheap and easily accessible from Durban and Johannesburg.

The contrast with South Africa could not be more striking, in both post-apartheid attitude and topographical extremes. Even a few days spent in Lesotho's mountain air will give you a fresh perspective on the continent.

This is essentially an alpine country where villagers on horseback in multicoloured balaclavas and blankets greet you round precipitous bends. The hiking and trekking – often on a famed Basotho pony – is world-class and the infrastructure of the four national parks continues to improve.

The 1000m-high 'lowlands' are the scene of low-key Lesotho life, with good craft shopping around Teyateyaneng and the cruisy capital, Maseru. But be sure to ascend inland into the ethereal rock-strewn, bowling-green valleys and stone-faced mountains, where blue streams traverse an ancient dinosaur playground. This is genuine adventure travel.

When to Go

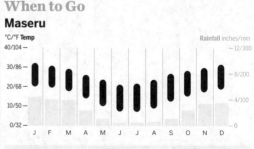

Maseru

Sep Celebrate Lesotho culture at the renowned Morija Arts & Cultural Festival

Dec & Jan Feel the full force of Maletsunyane, the region's highest waterfall

Year-round Experience year-round contrasting temperatures in the highlands and lowlands

MASERU

POP 430,000 / ELEV 1600M

Maseru is one of the world's more low-key capital cities. It sprawls across Lesotho's lower-lying western edge, rimmed by the Berea and Qeme Plateaus. While the city has few sights, Maseru is where you can get your bearings, sort out logistics and stock up on supplies before heading into the highlands and beyond.

🛏 Sleeping

Maseru Backpackers & Conference Centre   BACKPACKERS $

(☑2232 5166; www.maserubackpackers.com; Airport Rd; dm M150, 2- to 4-person r M400) The best budget choice, which is run by a British NGO, has sparse, clean backpackers' dorms, twins and doubles. The main reason to stay here is for outdoor activities, including canoeing trips on the Caledon River (M200). It's 3km from the city centre and popular with large groups.

Foothills Guesthouse   GUESTHOUSE $

(☑5870 6566; melvin@xsi net.co.za; 121 Maluti Rd; s/d incl breakfast M380/550) This converted, sandstone house offers something different to the fairly bland capital-city standard. The small, kitschy rooms have garden aspects and guests mingle on the verandah each morning over breakfast. You'll need a taxi to get here.

Lesotho Sun   HOTEL $$$

(☑2224 3000; www.suninternational.com; r M1505; ❄@🏊) The moderately radiant Sun is a punter's paradise perched on a hill. A thorough spruce-up has lifted the premier hotel in Lesotho up a notch. It boasts the ubiqui-tous casino and two restaurants, and offers a typical modern motel experience. Sundowners by the pool are a Maseru must for nonguests.

🍴 Eating

Ouh La La   CAFE $

(☑2832 3330; Cnr Kingsway & Pioneer Rd; breakfast, lunch & dinner M25-50) Locals and expats mix easily in this streetside garden cafe on the doorstep of Alliance Francais.

Mediterranée's Restaurant Pizzeriaé   PIZZERIA $

(☑2231 2960; LNDC Centre; mains M45-75; ⊙lunch & dinner) The Med cooks up yummy wood-fired pizzas and grilled meats and smoking jazz soundtracks.

Regal   INDIAN $$

(☑2231 3930; Level 1, Basotho Hat; mains M45-85; ⊙lunch & dinner; ☑) Regal serves surprisingly delicious British-style Indian food (think 'butter chicken' and 'spicy kormas') at the smartest restaurant in town.

🔒 Shopping

The **Basotho Hat** (☑2232 2523; Kingsway; ⊙8am-5pm Mon-Fri, 8am-4.30pm Sat) have a supply of woven Basotho hats and other souvenirs. For tapestries try **Maseru Tapestries & Mats** (☑2231 1773; Raboshabane Rd) or **Seithati Weavers** (☑2231 3975), about 7km from town.

❶ Information

Dangers & Annoyances

Maseru is reasonably safe but watch for bag-snatching and pickpocketing. Walking around at night is *not* recommended; the city and streets are deserted.

WORTH A TRIP

TEYATEYANENG

If heading west – or for a day drive from Maseru – Teyateyaneng (Place of Quick Sands) is the craft centre of Lesotho. Some of the best crafts come from: **Helang Basali Crafts** (⊙8am-5pm) at St Agnes Mission, about 2km before Teyateyaneng; Setsoto Design, near Blue Mountain Inn; Hatooa Mose Mosali; and Elelloang Basali Weavers about 4km to the north of TY. At most places you can watch the weavers at work.

Minibus taxis run between Teyateyaneng and Maseru (M14, 45 minutes, 35km). Chartering a taxi from Maseru costs around M150 one way.

En route are the **Ha Kome cave houses** (⊙8am-4.30pm Mon-Fri, 8.30am-noon Sat), 21km from TY and several kilometres from Mateka village. These extraordinary inhabited mud dwellings are nestled under a rock overhang, hidden within the pink and orange cliffs. There's a small information centre; 4WD required.

Lesotho Highlights

1 Experiencing a unique lodge-village experience at **Semonkong** (p103), **Malealea** (p103), **Roma** (p100) or **Ramabanta** (p100)

2 Absorbing the awesome vistas from **Sani Pass** (p101) and hiking the challenging wilderness hikes of the **northern highlands** (p102)

3 Revelling in the nature and hikes (and luxury lodge) of the underrated **Ts'ehlanyane National Park** (p102)

4 Hiking from Semonkong in the beautiful Thaba Putsoa mountains to the **Ketane Falls** (p103)

5 Stomping for dinosaur prints in **Quthing** (p104)

6 Climbing **Thaba-Bosiu** (p100), a place of pilgrimage outside Maseru

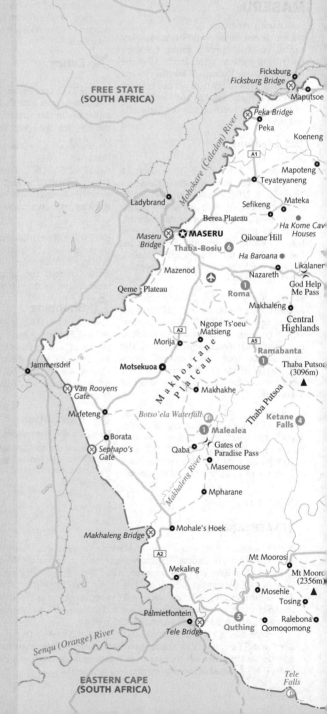

Maseru

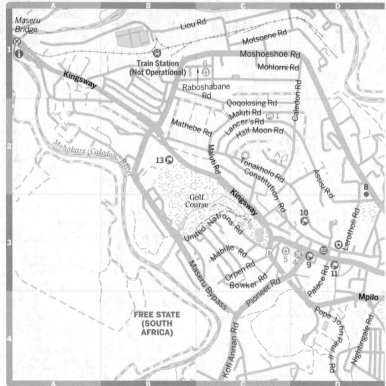

Maseru

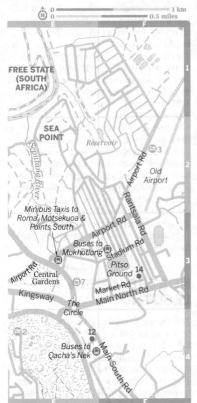

International Business Centre (Kingsway, Ground fl, Lesotho Bank Tower; ⊘8.30am-3.30pm Mon-Fri, 8.30am-noon Sat)

Post

Post Office (cnr Kingsway & Palace Rd)

Tourist Information

Tourist Information Office (☑2231 2427; Maseru Bridge Border Post; ⊘8am-5pm Mon-Fri, 8.30am-1pm Sat) Has lists of tour guides, information on transport and, if in stock, Maseru city maps. This border crossing is where many travellers arrive.

Travel Agencies

City Centre Maseru Travel (☑2231 4536; Kingsway, Maseru Book Centre) Next to Nedbank, does regional and international flight bookings and tickets for Intercape buses.

Shoprite Money Market (LNDC Centre) The easiest place to buy Greyhound, Intercape, Cityliner, Translux and SA Roadlink bus tickets.

ⓘ Getting There & Away

Bus & Minibus Taxi

There are three main transport stands to the northeast of the main roundabout: behind Sefika Mall (the 'new' taxi rank) for **minibus taxis** to Roma (M12) and points south including Motsekuoa (M13, for Malealea); just off Main North Rd near Pitso Ground for **minibus taxis** to points north; and a block away, for large Lesotho Freight Service buses to points south and north. These also depart for **Mokhotlong** (M80) from Stadium Rd behind Pitso Ground, while those to **Qacha's Nek** (M100) depart from next to St James Primary and High Schools on Main Rd South.

ⓘ Getting Around

Taxi

Taxi companies include **Planet** (☑2231 7777), **Luxury** (☑2232 6211) and **Executive Car Hire & Travel** (☑2231 4460). These can also be chartered for long-distance transport elsewhere in the country.

AROUND MASERU

Morija

Morija, 40km from Maseru, is the site of the first European mission in Lesotho. **Morija Museum & Archives** (☑2236 0308; www.morijafestival.wordpress.com; admission M10; ⊘8am-5pm Mon-Sat, noon-5pm Sun), Lesotho's unofficial

Emergency

Ambulance (☑2231 2501)

Fire (☑115)

Police (☑2231 9900)

Internet Access

999 Internet (Kingsway; per hr M10; ⊘8am-8pm Mon-Fri, 8am-6pm Sat, 9am-5pm Sun) Opposite post office.

Medical Services

For anything serious, you'll need to go to South Africa. In an emergency, also try contacting your embassy.

Maseru Private Hospital (☑2231 3260) In Ha Thetsane, about 7km south of Maseru.

Money

The top-end hotels will exchange foreign currency (at poor rates). Otherwise try **Nedbank** (Kingsway) and **Standard Bank** (Kingsway) on Kingsway.

MORIJA ARTS FESTIVAL

The annual Morija Arts & Cultural Festival is organised by the museum. This popular, annual event is held around late September/early October and showcases the diversity of Sotho culture through dance, music and theatre. For more information, check out www.morijafest.wordpress.com.

national one, is a small, considered place with ethnographical exhibits, archives and artefacts.

Morija Guest House (☑6306 5093; www.morijaguesthouses.com; r per person without bathroom M210-245) is a comfortable and attractive stone-and-thatch house with great views, a kitchen, and selection of sleeping options. **Lindy's B&B** (☑5885 5309; www.lindysbnb.co.ls; modern house per person M180, historic home per person M220) is another appealing option.

Minibus taxis run throughout the day between Maseru and Morija (M13, 45 minutes, 40km).

Roma

Roma, 35km from Maseru, is Lesotho's centre of learning, with the country's only university. Several attractive sandstone buildings are dotted around the town, and the entry to town by the southern gorge is spectacular. **Roma Trading Post Guest House** (☑082 773 2180, 2234 0202; www.trading post.co.za; campsites per person M75, dm M125, r per person M175, s with half board M375; ☒) is a charming fifth-generation trading post operated since 1903 by the Thorn family. The attached guesthouse includes garden rooms, *rondavels* (round, traditional-style huts), and the original sandstone homestead, set in a lush garden. Pony trekking, hiking, 4WD trails and even *minwane* (dinosaur footprints) nearby.

About 40km further along and owned by the same crew is **Ramabanta Guest House** (☑2234 0267; tradingpost@leo.co.ls; campsites per person M100, rondavel with half board per person M440, dm per person M150; rondavel w/half board per person M455). The views here are to diefor. Staying here provides the chance to link up Roma, Ramabanta and other places in the area on overnight hikes and pony treks.

Minibus taxis run throughout the day to/from Maseru (M18, 30 minutes).

NORTHEASTERN LESOTHO

The awesome northeastern area is defined by the rugged escarpment of the Drakensberg. It's best known for Sani Pass, but it also boasts the highest mountain in Southern Africa, the 3482m Thabana-Ntlenyana. This stunning mountain region features highland villages, *rondavels*, shepherds and sandstone rock shelters. It's *the* place for serious hikers.

Regular minibus taxis run between Maseru and the towns. Maputsoe is a major transport junction, and for northbound transport from Maseru, you'll usually need to change

THABA-BOSIU

Moshoeshoe the Great's mountain stronghold, first occupied in July 1824, is about 16km east of Maseru. Thaba-Bosiu (Mountain at Night) played a pivotal role in the consolidation of the Basotho nation. The name may be a legacy of the site being first occupied at night, but many legends exist.

At the mountain's base is a **visitors information centre** (☑2835 7207; admission M10; ☺8am-5pm Mon-Fri, 9am-1pm Sat) where you can organise an official guide to accompany you on the short walk to the top of the mountain.

Good views from here include those of the **Qiloane Hill** (inspiration for the Basotho hat), along with the remains of fortifications, Moshoeshoe's grave and parts of the original settlement.

Minibuses to Thaba-Bosiu (M10, 30 minutes) depart from Maseru at the Sefika Mall transport stand. If you're driving, take the Mafeteng Rd for about 13km and turn left at the Roma turn-off; ask for directions.

vehicles there. Minibus taxis to Maseru (M17, one hour), Butha-Buthe (M13, 45 minutes) and Leribe (M7, 30 minutes) run throughout the day from the Total petrol station.

Oxbow

Situated over the dramatic 2820m Moteng Pass, Oxbow consists of several lodges and huts nestled amid some wonderful mountain scenery. (Beware the treacherous hairpin bends in winter.) Skiing is available through Afri-Ski (☑086 123 747 54; www.afriski.co.za; 1-/3-day pass M350/750), 11km past Oxbow.

New Oxbow Lodge (☑in South Africa 051-933 2247; www.oxbow.co.za; s/d incl breakfast M462/759) is an incongruous Austrian-style chalet on the banks of the Malibamat'so River, with accommodation and a cosy restaurant-bar.

A bus between Maseru and Mokhotlong goes via Oxbow (M70, 4½ hours). Several minibus taxis run daily between Butha-Buthe and Oxbow (M35, 1½ hours).

Mokhotlong

Mokhotlong (Place of the Bald Ibis) is situated 270km from Maseru and is the first major town north of Sani Pass. It has an appealing Wild West feel to it, with locals – sporting Basotho blankets – on their horses, and basic shops.

Molumong Guesthouse & Backpackers (☑in South Africa 033-394 3072; www.molumonglodge.com; campsites per person M80, s/d M150/300) is a rustic lodge and former colonial trading post, about 15km southwest of Mokhotlong. It's a basic (electricity-free) self-catering stay. Pony trekking is a feature.

St James Lodge (☑071-672 6801, in South Africa 033-326 1601; www.stjameslodgeco.za; r per person M100-200), a working mission, is a humble yet somehow stylish place to say (note: it's self-catering). Pony trekking and scenic walks are available. It's 12km south of Mokhotlong on the road to Thaba-Tseka.

The Senqu Hotel (☑2292 0330; s M260-320, d M320-380) is 2.5km from the buses on the western end of town. Nearby Grow (☑2292 0205; dm R90), a Lesotho-registered development office, has basic dorms and a simple kitchen.

Public transport runs to/from Butha-Buthe (M55, six hours), Maseru (M90, eight hours), Linakaneng (for Molumong Lodge; M35) and Sani Top (M75).

Sani Top

Sani Top sits atop the steep Sani Pass, the only dependable (albeit steeply winding) road into Lesotho through the uKhahlamba-Drakensberg mountain range in KwaZulu-Natal. It offers stupendous views on clear days and unlimited hiking possibilities.

From the Sani Top Chalet at the top of the pass there are several day walks, including a long and arduous trek to Thabana-Ntlenyana (3482m), the highest peak in Southern Africa. A guide is handy.

Hodgson's Peaks (3257m) is a much easier hike 6km south, from where you can see into Sehlabathebe National Park and KwaZulu-Natal.

Other hikes in this area are outlined in the excellent *A Backpackers' Guide to Lesotho* by Russell Suchet, available through the Morija Museum (p99) or Sani Lodge (☑in South Africa 033-702 0330; www.sanilodge.co.za) at Sani Pass.

🛏 Sleeping & Eating

Sani Top Chalet   CHALET $$
(☑in South Africa 033-702 1158; www.sanitopchalet.co.za; campsites per person M80, dm M150, rondavel s/d M650/1000) At 2874m, Sani Top Chalet stakes a peculiar claim to the highest drinking hole in Southern Africa. Booze trivia aside, cosy *rondavels* and excellent meals reward those who make the steep ascent. Backpackers doss down the road in modern rooms that hold between two and six people. In winter the snow is sometimes deep enough for skiing; pony trekking can be arranged with advance notice.

❶ Getting There & Away

A minibus taxi runs daily from Mokhotlong via Sani Top down to Underberg (South Africa) and back (five hours). From Butha-Buthe (north) taxis cost M53.

If you're driving, you'll need a 4WD to go on the pass. The border crossings are open 6am to 6pm daily. Note: allow enough time at either end and check the border times – they do change.

SOUTHERN LESOTHO

Southern Lesotho – from Semonkong to Morija and southeast to Quthing – is less developed than the northwest between Maseru and Butha-Buthe, with massive mountain

HIGHLAND PARKS & RESERVES

Lesotho Northern Parks (☑2246 0723) handles all accommodation bookings for the following parks (except Maliba Mountain Lodge):

Bokong Nature Reserve

The bearded vulture, the ice rat and the Vaal rhebok are just some of the denizens of this reserve (adult/child M10/5, campsites M40, basic 4-person huts M250; ⊗8am-5pm), at the top of the 3090m Mafika-Lisiu Pass, near the Bokong River. There are a number of day walks, a visitors centre and an overnight camping ground. Guides (per person M30) and pony trekking (per day M180) can be arranged.

Ts'ehlanyane National Park

Deep in the rugged Maluti Mountains this 5600-hectare national park (admission per person/vehicle M40/10, campsite from M50) protects a beautiful, high-altitude patch of rugged wilderness, including one of Lesotho's only stands of indigenous forest. This underrated and underused place is about as far away from it all as you can get and is perfect for hiking.

In addition to day walks, there's a challenging 39km hiking trail from Ts'ehlanyane southwest to Bokong Nature Reserve through some of Lesotho's most dramatic terrain (guides to here can be arranged). Pony trekking (per half-/full day M150/180) can be arranged through Lesotho Northern Parks with advance notice or through Maliba Mountain Lodge.

Maliba Mountain Lodge (☑in South Africa 031-266 1344; www.maliba-lodge.com; d per person incl full board from M2990) is Lesotho's finest accommodation in Lesotho.

---

ranges, awesome valleys, and villages that have an enticing off-the-beaten-track feel.

Qacha's Nek

This pleasant town was founded in 1888 as a mission station near the pass (1980m) of the same name. It has an attractive church, colonial-era sandstone buildings and California redwood trees.

Hotel Nthatuoa (☑2295 0260; s M320-460, d M400-550, all incl breakfast) has simple rooms.

Minibus taxis go from Qacha's Nek and Maseru via Quthing (M110, six hours). A daily bus runs between Maseru and Qacha's Nek (M110, nine hours), and another between Qacha's Nek and Sehlabathebe National Park, departing Qacha's Nek around noon (M35, five hours).

Sehlabathebe National Park

Lesotho's first national park, proclaimed in 1970, is isolated, rugged and beautiful. Getting there is a worthwhile adventure, especially for wilderness, seclusion and fishing. Hiking (and horse riding from Sani Top or

the Drakensberg) is the main way to explore the waterfalls and surrounds.

You'll need to bring all your food, and be well prepared for the elements (summer sees frequent thick mists; winter nights are cold and snow is also possible).

🛏 Sleeping & Eating

Buses reach Sehlabathebe in the evening, which means you'll need to stay overnight in or near Mavuka village. Mabotle Hotel consists of neat *rondavels* with no water (staff will bring you a bucket). Within the park is the self-catering Sehlabathebe Park Lodge (☑2232 6075, 223 11767; campsites per person M30, r per person M80), a large time-warped house set on flat grasslands, 12km into the park (4WD required); reserve ahead.

Camping is permitted throughout the park, though there are no facilities besides plenty of water.

ℹ Getting There & Away

A daily bus connects Qacha's Nek and Sehlabathebe, departing from Qacha's Nek at around noon and Sehlabathebe at 5.30am (M40, five hours). The bus terminates in Mavuka village, near the park gate. From here, it's about 12km further on foot to the lodge. If you're driving, the main route into the park is via Quthing and

Qacha's Nek. The road from Qacha's Nek is unpaved but in reasonable condition, and negotiable at most times of the year in 2WD. You can arrange to leave your vehicle at the police station in Paolosi village while you're in the park.

Keen walkers can hike the 10km up the escarpment from Bushman's Nek in KwaZulu-Natal. From Bushman's Nek to the Nkonkoana Gate border crossing takes about six hours. Horses can also be arranged through **Khotso Trails** (⌨ in South Africa 033-701 1502; www.khotso trails.co.za) in Underberg.

Semonkong

Semonkong (Place of Smoke) is a one-horse town in the serene and lofty Thaba Putsoa range. Maletsunyane Falls (Lebahane Falls; 204m) are a 1½-hour walk away and are at their most awesome in summer, especially from the bottom of the gorge. Ketane Falls (122m) are an exciting day's ride (30km) from Semonkong.

Semonkong Lodge (⌨ 6202 1021, 266 2700 6037; www.placeofsmoke.co.ls; campsites per person M60, dm/s/d M100/395/660, rondavels s/d M465/720), near the Maletsunyane River, is a model of community tourism. The three- to eight-hour trawl up the mountain (depending on what form of transport you take) is worth the effort. There's a kitchen for those who want to self-cater, but the bar-restaurant serves possibly the best (Westernised) food in Lesotho. Staff arrange a smorgasbord of activities, from day and overnight hikes to a pub crawl on the back of a donkey. Plus the world's longest commercially operated single-drop abseil (204m) down the Maletsunyane Falls.

Buses between Maseru and Semonkong (M110) leave from either town in the morning, arriving in late afternoon.

Malealea

Just outside Malealea is the Gates of Paradise Pass. A plaque announces 'Wayfarer – pause and look upon a Gateway of Paradise'. This says it all – about the region, village and the lodge. The breathtaking mountains feature caves with San rock art.

Today, the heart of the village is Malealea Lodge, which offers a variety of cultural and outdoor activities.

This is one of the best places in Lesotho to arrange pony trekking and experience the awesome scenery. It also offers a good chance to meet Basotho villagers.

For walkers, Malealea Lodge has route maps for short walks (two hours) to overnight and longer hikes and can arrange pack ponies for your gear. The walks incorporate waterfalls, gorges, plateaus and surrounding villages and San rock art sites.

Village visits provide a stimulating insight into the local people and their customs. You can visit the tiny museum, housed in a traditional Basotho hut, a *sangoma* (witchdoctor) and a reclaimed donga.

🛏 Sleeping

TOP CHOICE **Malealea Lodge** LODGE **$**
(⌨ in South Africa 082 552 4215; www.malealea. co.ls; campsites M75, backpackers hut M135-155, r M220-275) Malealea Lodge is the rightful poster child for the 'Kingdom in the Sky'. The lodge began life in 1905 as a trading post. These days it offers delightful accommodation, with everything from campsites and two-person 'forest', or backpacker, huts in a pretty wooded setting away from the lodge, to simple, cosy rooms and *rondavels* with ensuites.

Hungry hikers love the bar, hearty meals (breakfast/lunch/dinner M60/70/95) and self-catering facilities. A village shop stocks basic goods.

There's intermittent mobile-phone connection at the lodge. September to November are the busy months; reserve ahead through South Africa.

ⓘ Getting There & Away

Regular minibus taxis connect Maseru and Malealea (M36, 2½ hours, 83km). Otherwise, catch a minibus taxi from Maseru or Mafeteng to the junction town of Motsekuoa (M13, two hours), from where there are frequent connections to Malealea (M22, 30 minutes).

If you're driving, head south from Maseru on Mafeteng Rd (Main Rd South) for 52km to Motsekuoa. Here, look for the Malealea Lodge sign and the collection of minibus taxis. Turn left (east) onto a tarmac road. Ten kilometres further on take the right fork and continue another 15km. At the Malealea sign it's another 7km along an unsealed road to the lodge.

Mafeteng

Mafeteng (Place of Lefeta's People) is named after an early magistrate Emile Rolland, who was known to the local Basotho as

Lefeta (One Who Passes By). It's is an important transport interchange and a border junction (it's 22km to Wepener in Free State) and a possible stocking-up point.

If you are stuck here for the night, the polygon-shaped Mafeteng Hotel (☎2270 0236; s/d/tr from M220/280/360; ☒) is one of Lesotho's better hotels, albeit a blast from the past. There's a restaurant, plus thatched rooms in a garden.

Frequent minibus taxis connect Mafeteng with Maseru (M25, 1½ hours) and Mohale's Hoek (M16, 30 minutes). For Quthing, change at Mohale's Hoek.

Mohale's Hoek

More agreeable than Mafeteng, this comfortable town is 125km from Maseru. The younger brother of Moshoeshoe the Great, Mohale gave this land to the British for administrative purposes in 1884.

The best bet of a motley lot is Hotel Mount Maluti (☎2278 5224; mmh@leo.co.ls; s/d incl breakfast M257/380), with motel-style rooms plus a restaurant.

Quthing

Quthing, the southernmost major town in Lesotho, is also known as Moyeni (Place of the Wind). It was established in 1877, abandoned during the Gun War of 1880 and then rebuilt at the present site.

About 1.5km off the highway, 5km west of Quthing, is the intriguing Masitise Cave House Museum (☎5879 4167; admission by donation), built into a San rock shelter in 1866 by Reverend Ellenberger. Ask for the key from the local pastor in the house next to the church. Accommodation is available on a B&B basis and in the unrenovated *rondavels*. There are San rock art paintings nearby.

Quthing's other claim to fame is a proliferation of dinosaur footprints. The most easily accessible are just off the main road to Mt Moorosi; watch for the small, pink building to your left. These footprints are believed to be 180 million years old.

Between Quthing and Masitise, and visible from the main road, is Villa Maria Mission, with a striking, twin-spired sandstone church.

At Qomoqomong, 10km from Quthing, there's a collection of San rock art paintings; ask at the General Dealers store about

a guide for the 20-minute walk to the paintings.

The road from Quthing to Qacha's Nek, along the winding Senqu (Orange) River Gorge, is one of Lesotho's most stunning drives.

En route is the village of Mt Moorosi, named after a Basotho chieftain who in 1879 stuck it out for eight months against the British on his fortified mountain until he was killed; the pretty Mphaki village, a possible base for hiking; and Christ the King Mission, with wide views over the Senqu River valley. It's a good two- to three-day hike from the mission, north to Semonkong.

🛏 Sleeping & Eating

Fuleng Guest House GUESTHOUSE $
(☎2275 0260; r per person M280-350) Perched on a hill, this is the place for rooms and *rondavels*-with-a-view plus a friendly local experience. It's signposted from the main road just before the bend to Upper Quthing.

Moorosi Chalets CHALET $
(☑in South Africa 082 552 4215; www.moorosi chalets.com; campsites M60; rondavel per person M175-225; hut without bathroom per person M150; self-catering house per person M150) Go fishing or ride ponies with local villagers courtesy of this partnership between Malealea and the Quthing Wildlife Development Trust. The fees go directly to the villages for equipment and supplies. Basic *rondavel* accommodation is also offered in the main camp area. The chalets are 6km from Mt Moorosi village; take the turn-off to Ha Moqalo 2km out of the village in the direction of Qacha's Nek.

❶ Getting There & Away

Minibus taxis run daily between Quthing and Maseru (M65, 3½ hours) and Qacha's Nek (M75, three hours). The Quthing–Qacha's Nek road is sealed the entire way despite what many maps indicate.

UNDERSTAND LESOTHO

Lesotho Today

Lesotho ranks among the region's poorer countries, and has few natural resources. During the last century, Lesotho's main export was labour – approximately 60% of males worked mainly in mining in South Africa. In the late 1990s the restructuring of the South African gold-mining industry, mechanisation and the closure of mines resulted in massive job losses. Meanwhile, the Lesotho economy – under transformation due to a rapid growth of the textile industry – collapsed.

It is hoped that economic initiatives, such as the Economic Partnership Agreement (EPA), signed with the EU in 2007 to create free trade zones, will help revive the local business sector.

In June 2012 Thomas Thabane, a former foreign minister and leader of the All Basotho Convention (ABC), the biggest opposition party, was appointed prime minister. He heads a coalition government along with two opposition parties, the Lesotho Congress for Democracy (LCD) and the Basotho National Party (BNP).

History

Lesotho was settled by Sotho peoples as late as the 16th century. The Khoisan, and possibly some Nguni people, lived among them, intermarrying and mingling their languages.

The early society was made up of small chiefdoms. Cattle and cultivation were the economy's mainstays. Their products were traded for iron from the northeast of South Africa.

By the early 19th century white traders were on the scene, exchanging beads for cattle. They were soon followed by the Voortrekkers and pressure on Sotho grazing lands grew. Even without white encroachment, Sotho society had to accept that it had expanded as far as it could and would have to adapt to living in a finite territory. On top of this came the disaster of the *difaqane* (forced migration).

The rapid consolidation and expansion of the Zulu state under the leadership of Shaka, and later Dingaan, resulted in a chain reaction of turmoil throughout the whole of Southern Africa. That the loosely organised Southern Sotho society survived this period was largely due to the abilities of Moshoeshoe (pronounced mo-shesh-way) the Great.

Moshoeshoe the Great

Moshoeshoe began as a leader of a small village and in around 1820 he led his villagers to Butha-Buthe (Place of Lying Down). From this mountain stronghold his people

survived the first battles of the *difaqane* and in 1824 Moshoeshoe began his policy of assisting refugees who helped in his defence. Later in the same year he moved his people to Thaba-Bosiu (Mountain at Night), a more easily defendable mountain top.

From Thaba-Bosiu, Moshoeshoe played a patient game of placating the stronger local rulers and granting protection, land and cattle to refugees. These people were to form Basotholand. At the time of Moshoeshoe's death in 1870, the population was more than 150,000.

The welcome Moshoeshoe gave to missionaries, and his ability to take their advice without being dominated by them, was another factor in Basotholand's emergence and survival. The first missionaries arrived in 1833 from the Paris Evangelical Missionary Society. In return for a degree of Christianisation of Sotho customs, the missionaries were disposed to defend the rights of 'their' Basotho against the new threat – British and Boer expansion.

The Boers had crossed the Orange River in the 1830s, and by 1843 Moshoeshoe was sufficiently concerned by their numbers to ally himself with the British Cape government. The British Resident, installed in Basotholand as a condition of the treaties, decided Moshoeshoe was too powerful and engineered an unsuccessful attack on his kingdom.

In 1854 the British withdrew from the area, having fixed the boundaries of Basotholand. The Boers pressed their claims on the land, and increasing tension led to the Free State-Basotho Wars of 1858 and 1865. After success in the first war, Moshoeshoe was forced in the second to sign away much of his western lowlands.

Moshoeshoe again called on British assistance in 1868, this time on the imperial government in London. A high commission adjudicated the dispute and the result was the loss of more Basotho land. It was obvious that no treaty between Boers and Basotho would hold for long. Continual war between the Free State and Basotholand was not good for British interests, so the British annexed Basotholand and handed it to the Cape Colony to run in 1871.

After Moshoeshoe the Great

The year after Moshoeshoe the Great's death, squabbles over succession divided the country. The Cape government exploited this and reduced the powers of chiefs, limiting them to their individual areas.

The Gun War of 1880 began as a protest against the Cape government's refusal to allow the Basotho to own firearms, but it quickly became a battle between the rebel chiefs on one side and the government and collaborating chiefs on the other. The war ended in a stalemate with the Cape government being discredited.

A shaky peace followed; in 1884 the British government again took control of Basotholand. Its decision to back strong local leaders helped to stabilise the country. One unexpected benefit of direct British rule was that when the Union of South Africa was created, Basotholand was classified as a British Protectorate and was not included in the Union.

Home Rule & Independence

In 1910 the advisory Basotholand National Council was formed from members nominated by the chiefs. After decades of allegations of corruption and favouritism, reforms in the 1940s introduced some democratic processes into council appointments.

In the mid-1950s the council requested internal self-government from the British. In 1960 a new constitution was in place and elections were held for a Legislative Council.

Meanwhile, political parties had formed, including the Basotholand Congress Party (BCP), similar to South Africa's African National Congress (ANC), and the Basotholand National Party (BNP), a conservative party headed by Chief Leabua Jonathan.

The BCP won the 1960 elections, then demanded, and won, a new constitution that paved the way to full independence from Britain in 1966. However, after the 1965 elections the BCP lost power to the BNP, and Chief Jonathan became the first prime minister of the new Kingdom of Lesotho. During the election campaign the BNP promised cooperation with the South African apartheid regime and in turn received massive support from it.

As most of the civil service was still loyal to the BCP, Jonathan did not have an easy time. Stripping King Moshoeshoe II of the few powers that the new constitution had left him did not endear Jonathan's government to the people, and the BCP won the 1970 election.

Jonathan responded to the election results by suspending the constitution, arresting and expelling the king, and banning opposition parties. The king was eventually allowed to return from exile in Holland, and Jonathan attempted to form a government of national reconciliation. This ploy was partly successful, but some BCP members, including the leader Ntsu Mokhehle, resisted and attempted to stage a coup in 1974. The coup failed miserably and resulted in the death of many BCP supporters and the jailing or exile of the BCP leadership.

Jonathan changed tack in his attitude to South Africa, calling for the return of land in the Orange Free State that had been stolen from the original Basotholand, and criticising apartheid, allegedly offering refuge to ANC guerrillas, and flirting with Cuba. Relations soured; South Africa closed Lesotho's borders, strangling the country.

The Lesotho military took action. Jonathan was deposed in 1986 and the king was restored as head of state. This was a popular move, but eventually agitation for democratic reform rose again. In 1990 King Moshoeshoe II was deposed by the army in favour of his son, Prince Mohato Bereng Seeisa (Letsie III). Elections in 1993 resulted in the return of the BCP.

The BCP was split between those who wanted Prime Minister Ntsu Mokhehle to remain as leader and those who didn't. Mokhehle formed the breakaway Lesotho Congress for Democracy (LCD) party and continued to govern.

In 1995 Letsie III abdicated in favour of his father and, five years after being deposed, Moshoeshoe II was reinstated. He restored calm to Lesotho after a year of unrest. Tragically, less than a year later he was killed when his 4WD plunged over a cliff in the Maluti Mountains. Letsie III was again made the king.

Elections & Invasion

Elections were held in 1998 amid accusations of widespread cheating by the LCD, which won with a landslide. Tensions arose and meanwhile, Mokhehle handed over to his successor Pakalitha Mosisili.

In September 1998, following months of protests, the government called on the Southern African Development Community (SADC) treaty partners, Botswana, South Africa and Zimbabwe, to help restore order. Troops invaded the kingdom and fighting ensued in Maseru.

In May 2002 Mosisili's LCD party won again and he began a second five-year term.

FAMINE IN LESOTHO

Lesotho, particularly rural Lesotho, is extremely vulnerable to food shortages; the mountain kingdom's annual cereal production is declining because of unpredictable weather, long-term soil erosion and the impact of HIV/AIDS. On top of this, the country faces trade constraints and declining employment opportunities, leaving many vulnerable to food insecurity. Subsistence farming used to be the main food source for most people, but today many rent out their land for others to cultivate, thereby losing their ability to grow their own food. Per capita agricultural production in real terms has been falling for decades, and today tens of thousands of the most vulnerable people are relying on external food aid. Many people in the country's lowlands do not have access to water for domestic use, and travel long distances each day to fetch it – an irony given that the Lesotho Highlands Water Project supplies South Africa with millions of cubic metres of water each year.

The 2007 elections were highly controversial, with the newly formed All Basotho Convention (ABC) party accusing the LCD party of manipulating the allocation of seats. National strikes ensued and several ministers were allegedly attacked by gunmen. There was an assassination attempt on ABC's leader, Thomas Thabane, and many people were detained and tortured.

The Culture

Pride is at the core of the Basotho people, which is not surprising given the incredible history of their nation. The Basotho are remarkably free of the effects of apartheid and warmly welcome travellers to their kingdom. The traditional class system has altered – herding, once a revered position, is done by the poorest boys (many families are said to sell their sons to wealthy families to be herders), although the population continues to rely on and respect its community chiefs. The Basotho blanket, worn proudly by many in the rural areas, reflects one's status in the community, according to the quality, material and design of the blanket itself.

Daily Life

Traditional culture, which is still strong, consists largely of the customs, rites and superstitions with which the Basotho explain and enrich their lives. Music also plays an important part in their lives.

Traditional medicine mixes rites and customs with *sangoma*s, who develop their own charms and rituals.

Poverty and death is ever-present in Lesotho. Life for most people is harsh, with the majority trying to eke out a living through subsistence agriculture, especially livestock; unemployment currently stands at about 45%. The spectre of HIV/AIDS is high – the infection rate (adult prevalence) is estimated at 24%.

Most Lesotho in rural communities live in *rondavels*, round huts with mud walls (often decorated) and thatched roofs.

Population

The citizens of Lesotho are known as the Basotho people. Most are Southern Sotho and most speak South Sotho. The melding of the Basotho nation was largely the result of Moshoeshoe the Great's 19th-century military and diplomatic triumphs; many diverse subgroups and peoples have somehow merged into a homogeneous society.

Religion

Around 80% of the population is believed to be Christian (mainly Roman Catholic, Anglican and Episcopalian). The remaining 20% live by traditional Basotho beliefs. There are many churches throughout the country, many of which were (or continue to be) built by missionaries.

Arts & Crafts

Music and dance are important components of ceremony and everyday life. There are various musical instruments, from the lekolulo (a flutelike instrument played by herd boys), to the thomo (a stringed instrument) and the *setolo-tolo* (a stringed instrument played with the mouth).

Tapestry and rug weaving is practised in many regions of Lesotho and good-quality items can be found around Teyateyaneng and the fringes of Maseru. Other handicrafts specific to the area include Basotho hat baskets, and grass and clay products.

Environment

Land & Wildlife

All of Lesotho exceeds 1000m in altitude, with peaks in the central ranges and near the Drakensberg reaching to more than 3000m. The tallest mountain in Southern Africa (the highest point south of Mt Kilimanjaro) is the 3482m Thabana-Ntlenyana.

Due mainly to its altitude, Lesotho is home to fewer animals than many Southern African countries. The bird life is rich, with just under 300 species recorded. The Drakensberg is an excellent place for birdwatching, and bearded vultures and black eagles are both found here. Lesotho is one of the few places you may spot the extremely rare bald ibis.

The high plains and mountains are home to Cape alpine flowers. The national flower, spiral aloe, is a strange plant unique to Lesotho. Its leaves form rows of striking, spiral patterns and you'll see it in left- and right-handed varieties on the slopes of the Maluti Mountains.

National Parks

Sehlabathebe, under the jurisdiction of the Ministry of Tourism, Environment & Culture (☑2232 6075, 2231 1767; Kingsway, New Postal Office Bldg, 6th fl, Maseru), is Lesotho's most famous national park.

The country's other main conservation areas – Ts'ehlanyane National Park, Bokong Nature Reserve and the Liphofung Cave Cultural Historical Site – are under the jurisdiction of Lesotho Northern Parks (p102), which handles all accommodation bookings. All have simple accommodation (except Bokong, which has camping only), established trails and helpful staff, and are relatively easy to access, making them well worth visiting.

Environmental Issues

This high, corrugated and often freezing kingdom is a tough environment at the best of times. Serious erosion exists in Lesotho due to the pressures of modern farming techniques and overgrazing.

There are also environmental concerns about the controversial Lesotho Highlands Water Project, which provides water and electricity to South Africa.

SURVIVAL GUIDE

Directory A–Z

Accommodation

Maseru has a reasonable range of accommodation ranging from Farmer Training Centres to lodges, to former trading posts.

If camping, always ask permission of the local landowners and chief, and expect to pay a small fee.

The order of accommodation listings follows author's preference within each budget category ($, $$, $$$).

🏃 Activities

Activities abound in Lesotho. You can hit the heights at Semonkong Lodge for the longest commercially operated single-drop abseil (204m) down the Maletsunyane Falls or catch the local horse races here, too. Elsewhere, birdwatchers will appreciate the 280 bird species. Trout fishing is very popular in Lesotho; the season runs from September to the end of May. There is a nominal licence fee, a bag limit of 12 fish and a minimum size limit of 25cm; only rod and line and artificial nonspinning flies may be used. For more information contact the Livestock Division of the Ministry of Agriculture (☑2232 3986; Private Bag A82, Maseru).

Lesotho offers great remote-area trekking in a landscape reminiscent of the Tibetan plateau. The eastern highlands and the Drakensberg crown attract serious hikers, with the walk between Qacha's Nek and Butha-Buthe offering the best challenge. You'll need serious gear, a compass and your own supplies. Caution: walking can be dangerous due to harsh conditions.

SLEEPING PRICE RANGES

The following price ranges refer to a double room with bathroom in high season.

$ less than M400
$$ M400 to M1000
$$$ more than M1000

Pony trekking is an excellent and popular way of seeing the Lesotho highlands, and is offered by Malealea Lodge, Ramabanta Guest House and Semonkong Lodge.

Books

A Backpacker's Guide to Lesotho by Russell Suchet features walks around Lesotho and is a must for hikers. Poignant personal accounts by Basotho include *Singing Away the Hunger* by Mpho Matsepo Nthunya et al, and *Shepherd Boy of the Maloti* by Thabo Makoa. For history, read *A Short History of Lesotho* by Stephen Gill.

Business Hours

Most businesses are open from 8am to 5pm weekdays (8.30am to 1pm Wednesday) and 8am to 1pm Saturday. The civil service works between 8am and 4.30pm weekdays with a break for lunch from 12.45pm to 2pm.

Customs Regulations

Visitors from the Southern African Customs Union – Botswana, Swaziland and South Africa – cannot bring in alcohol.

Embassies & Consulates

A number of countries have representation in Maseru.

Chinese Embassy (☎2231 6521; http://ls.china-embassy.org/eng; United Nations Rd)

French Consulate (☎2232 5722; www.alliance.org.za/consular-services.html; Alliance Française, cnr Kingsway & Pioneer Rd)

German Consulate (☎2233 2983, 2233 2292; www.southafrica.diplo.de; Alliance Française, cnr Kingsway & Pioneer Rd)

Irish Embassy (☎2231 4068; www.embassyofireland.org.ls; Tonakholo Rd)

Dutch Embassy (☎2231 2114; www.dutchembassy.co.za; c/o Lancer's Inn)

South African Embassy (☎2231 5758; www.dfa.gov.za; cnr Kingsway & Old School Rd)

USA Embassy (☎2231 2666; maseru.usembassy.gov; 254 Kingsway Rd)

✿ Festivals & Events

The Morija Arts & Cultural Festival (www.morijafest.com) is an annual five-day event held in September/October that showcases the diversity of Sotho culture through dance, music and theatre.

Food

The following price ranges are used for Eating reviews in this chapter.

$	Less than M70 per main
$$	M70-110 per main
$$$	More than M110 per main

Holidays

Lesotho's public holidays:

New Year's Day 1 January

Moshoeshoe Day 11 March

Good Friday March/April

Easter Monday March/April

Hero's Day 25 May

Workers' Day 1 May

Ascension Day May

King's Birthday 17 July

Independence Day 4 October

Christmas Day 25 December

Boxing Day 26 December

Language

The official languages are South Sotho and English.

Money

The unit of currency is the loti (plural maloti; M), which is divided into 100 liesente. The loti is fixed at a value equal to the South African rand, which is accepted everywhere (however, maloti are not accepted outside Lesotho).

ATMS & CASH

If changing foreign currency, do it in South Africa before you come – rates are better. There are a few ATMs in Maseru.

The only banks where you can reliably change foreign currency, including travellers cheques, are in Maseru.

CREDIT CARDS

Most hotels, restaurants and travel agencies will accept credit cards. As a last resort, you can change money for low rates at larger hotels.

TIPPING

Wages are low in Lesotho. In rural parts of Lesotho it's normal to round up the bill, and in tourist areas it's usual to tip around 10%.

PRACTICALITIES

» Several newspapers such as *Southern Star* are available in Maseru and other towns. Day-old South African newspapers are also available in Maseru.

» Lesotho's electricity is generated at 220V. Appliances have three round prongs as used in South Africa.

» Lesotho uses the metric system.

Post

Post offices are open from 8am to 4.30pm weekdays and 8am to noon Saturday.

Safe Travel

You may receive unmenacing requests for money, especially if hiking somewhere without a guide. In the highlands, you'll receive incessant requests for 'sweets! sweets!' from school children and herd boys; it causes begging so please refrain. Children throwing stones at cars sometimes occurs in the highlands.

Several lives (mainly those of herd boys) are lost each year from lightning strikes. Keep off high ground during electrical storms and avoid camping in the open.

Never go out into the mountains, even in summer or for an afternoon, without a sleeping bag, tent and sufficient food for a couple of days in case you get fogged in.

There's a slight risk of being robbed in Lesotho; muggings are common in Maseru.

Telephone

Lesotho's telephone system works reasonably well, but only where there is access – it is limited in the highlands. International phone calls are expensive; if possible, wait until you are in South Africa. Note: no telephone networks function in the highlands. Mobile-phone signals are extremely rare and can be picked up on a few mountain passes only. They should not be relied upon.

Tourist Information

The only tourist information office (☎2231 2427; Maseru Bridge Border Post; ☻8am-5pm Mon-Fri, 8.30am-1pm Sat) is near Maseru and is managed by the Lesotho Tourism Development Corporation. It provides brochures, lists of tour guides, information on public transport and basic maps.

Visas

Citizens of most Western European countries, the USA and most Commonwealth countries are granted an entry permit (free) at the border or airport. The standard stay permitted is between 14 and 28 days and is renewable by leaving and re-entering the country or by application to the Director of Immigration & Passport Services (☎2232 1110, 2232 3771; PO Box 363, Maseru 100).

No vaccination certificates are required unless you have recently been in a yellow-fever area.

Getting There & Away

Entering the Country

Most travellers enter Lesotho overland from South Africa, although it's also possible to fly in from Johannesburg. A passport is required.

Air

Lesotho's Moshoeshoe I International Airport is 21km from Maseru.

South African Airways (SAA; ☎in South Africa 011-978 5313; www.flysaa.com) flies daily between Moshoeshoe I International Airport and Johannesburg for around R2000, one way.

Border Crossings

All Lesotho's borders are with South Africa. Most people enter via Maseru Bridge (open 24 hours). Other main border crossings include Ficksburg Bridge (open 24 hours), Makhaleng Bridge (open 8am to 4pm), and Sani Pass (6am to 6pm, but check, as times alter), but these often have long queues.

Most of the other entry points in the south and the east of the country involve very difficult, rough roads.

Bus

Intercape (www.intercape.co.za) offers bus services to a changing timetable between Bloemfontein and Maseru (from M550, 1¾ hours). After your passport is stamped you need to catch a car taxi (called a four-by-one) from the Lesotho border to the Maseru taxi rank.

DEPARTURE TAX

A M50 departure tax is payable on leaving the airport.

Via minibus taxi, daily minibuses run between Bloemfontein and Maseru (two hours). Another option is to head from Bloemfontein to Botshabelo (one hour) from where you can catch a connection to Maseru (1½ hours), though direct services may be available. Other useful connections include a daily minibus taxi between Mokhotlong (Lesotho) and Underberg (South Africa) via Sani Pass; and several minibus taxis daily between Qacha's Nek (Lesotho) and Matatiele (South Africa).

There are at least three buses weekly between Johannesburg and Maseru (six to seven hours), as well as daily minibus taxis between both Johannesburg and Ladybrand (16km from the Maseru Bridge border crossing) and Maseru. All these services will bring you into Maseru coming from South Africa; if you are leaving Maseru, you'll need to go to the South Africa side of Maseru Bridge.

Car

You can't enter Lesotho via Sani Pass unless your vehicle is 4WD.

It is far more economical to use a car hired in South Africa; you will need a written agreement from the hirer for which you pay a small fee. There is an entry road tax of around M5.

A licence is required; insurance is strongly recommended.

Getting Around

Bus & Minibus Taxi

A good network of slow, no-frills buses and faster minibus taxis access many towns. Minibuses leave when full; no reserva-tions are necessary. You'll be quoted long-distance fares on the buses but it's best to just buy a ticket to the next major town, as most of the passengers will get off there and you might be stuck waiting for the bus to fill up again, while other buses leave before yours.

Car & Motorcycle

FUEL & SPARE PARTS

Fuel – including unleaded fuel and diesel – is available in the major towns, but diesel and unleaded is not always available in the highlands; fill up whenever possible and carry a jerry can with extra fuel. Carry tools and spare tyres; tyre repairers are as common as mountains in 'them-thar parts'.

ROAD CONDITIONS & HAZARDS

Driving in Lesotho is getting easier with new sealed roads in the country's north, but a 4WD is obligatory for the country's rough unsealed roads. Motorcycles are fine on the sealed roads. Beware of treacherously slippery roads in winter.

Unsealed roads can be rough. Before attempting a difficult drive, try to get local info on current conditions: ask at a police station as no warning signs are displayed. Major hazards are steep hairpin bends, flooding rivers (after summer storms), ice and snow in winter, people and animals. Police roadblocks do random checks, usually for stolen cars.

ROAD RULES

In Lesotho, vehicles are driven on the left-hand side. The national speed limit is 80km/h and the speed limit in villages is 50km/h. Seat belts must be worn at all times. It's obligatory to carry your licence, a vehicle registration booklet and safety triangle.

LESOTHO GETTING AROUND

Malawi

Includes »

Best Places to Eat

» Latitude 13° (p116)
» Buchanan's Grill (p117)
» Casa Mia (p147)
» Kaya Mawa (p132)

Best Places to Stay

» Kaya Mawa (p132)
» Mumbo Camp (p138)
» Mkulumadzi Lodge (p154)
» Latitude 13° (p116)

Why Go?

Malawi has been previously overlooked as a mere snack at the table of epic safari destinations. That is until Majete Wildlife Reserve, debilitated by underfunding and poaching, was thoroughly restocked and a lion reintroduction program began in 2012. The country now has its Big Five again and travel editors are salivating with excitement. Add to this some new world-class boutique hotels and luxury safari lodges, and you can see why Malawi may just be Africa's next big destination.

Unforgettable landscapes also await. Slicing through the landscape in a trough formed by the Great Rift Valley is Lake Malawi – Africa's third largest – a glittering vision swarming with colourful cichlid fish, and ideal for diving, snorkelling, kayaking or chilling on its desert islands.

Suspended in the clouds in the deep south are the dramatic peaks of Mt Mulanje and Zomba Plateau; both a trekker's dream with mist-cowled forests. Head further north and you'll witness the otherworldly beauty of Nyika Plateau, its grasslands reminiscent of the Scottish Highlands.

When to Go

Lilongwe

May–mid-Nov The dry season is the best time to visit.

May–Jul National parks like Nyika are a blaze of wild flowers.

Oct–Nov Wildlife viewing is at its peak though temperatures can be hot.

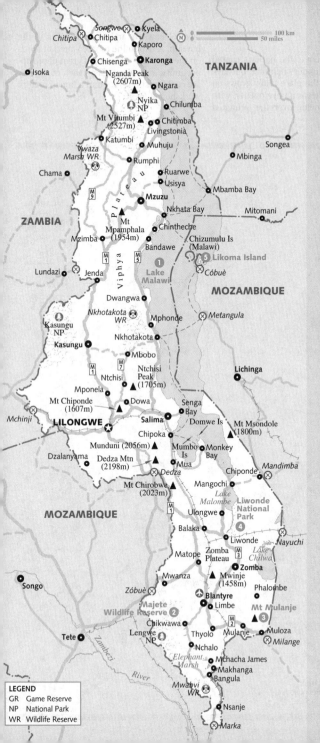

Malawi Highlights

❶ Soaking up the sun in the private coves of **Lake Malawi** (p159), gliding over glassy waters by kayak, or heading beneath the surface and discovering a world of brilliantly coloured fish

❷ Visiting the first of Malawi's reintroduced lions and staying at gorgeous Mkulumadzi Lodge in **Majete Wildlife Reserve** (p153)

❸ Scrambling up twisted peaks, sleeping in mountain huts and soaking up the astounding views of **Mt Mulanje** (p151)

❹ Spotting hippos, crocs and kingfishers on the Shire River, or getting up close to elephants on foot in **Liwonde National Park** (p141)

❺ Escaping to dreamy beaches and exploring traditional villages, panoramic walks and the magnificent cathedral on **Likoma Island** (p131)

LEGEND
GR   Game Reserve
NP   National Park
WR   Wildlife Reserve

LILONGWE

Sprawling and chaotic, the nation's capital is initially a little underwhelming, but give it a few days and the place really grows on you. The city market is an eye opener, with African music dancing over the animated faces of hawkers and fruit gleaming in the hot sun. A trip to the tobacco auction floors on the outskirts of town is a great photo opportunity, and within easy reach of the city are cool forest reserves and a famed pottery workshop at Dedza.

Lilongwe

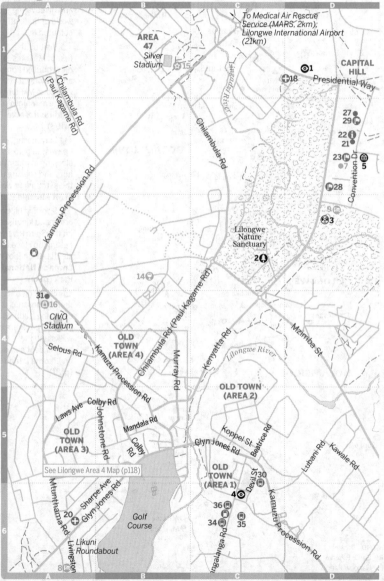

See Lilongwe Area 4 Map (p118)

Lilongwe has two centres: City Centre (Capital City), home to ministries, embassies, smart hotels, airline offices and travel agents; and Old Town, with its guesthouses, backpackers hostels and campsites, bus station, main market, banks, tour companies and malls. The two centres are 3km apart

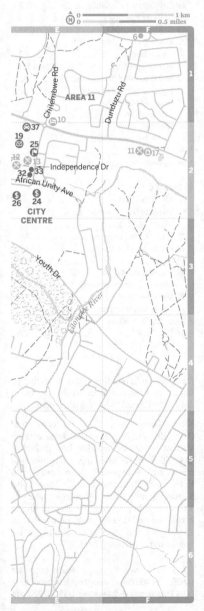

and minibuses frequently run between them.

⊙ Sights & Activities

Market   MARKET
(Map p114; Malangalanga Rd) The main market near the bus station in Old Town is worth a visit, and you'll find everything from bicycle parts, live chickens, vegetables, dustbins, underwear...the list goes on. Watch out for pickpockets.

Tobacco Auction Floors   NOTABLE BUILDING
(☑01-710377) To get an in-depth look at Malawi's most important cash crop, go to the public gallery at the Auction Holdings warehouse about 7km north of the city centre, east of the main road towards Kasungu and Mzuzu. The auction season is April or May to September.

Lilongwe Nature Sanctuary   PARK
(Map p114) In between City Centre and Old Town and alongside the Lingadzi River is the 180-hectare Lilongwe Nature Sanctuary, a great spot for walks and picnics.

Lilongwe Wildlife Centre   WILDLIFE RESERVE
(Map p114; ☑01-757120; www.lilongwewildlife.org; Kenyatta Rd; admission MK1500; ⊗8am-4pm Mon-Fri, to noon Sat) Lilongwe Wildlife Centre is an animal rescue and educational facility. The centre's ultimate aim is to rehabilitate animals in the wild and it has a strict no-unessential-contact, no-breeding and no-trade policy. Tours operate on the hour from 9am to 2pm then at 3.30pm and 4.30pm. Inspiring.

Kamuzu Mausoleum   SHRINE
(Map p114; Presidential Way) Dr Hastings Kamuzu Banda's marble-and-granite mausoleum is in Heroes Acre. Construction finished in 2006 at a whopping cost of US$600,000.

⌔ Sleeping

Old Town is the most convenient area of the city to stay due to its eating, drinking and transport facilities.

Mabuya Camp   HOSTEL, CAMPGROUND **$**
(Map p114; ☑01-754978; www.mabuyacamp.com; Livingstone Rd; campsite per person US$4, dm US$6, d/tw US$18, chalet d $45; ⓟ@🛜🏊) Lilongwe's liveliest backpacker spot has dorms and a double in the main house, as well as chalets and camping pitches in the garden. Rooms share clean showers set in thatched *rondavels* (round, traditional-style huts).

Lilongwe

There's also a bar with sport on TV; its menu features wraps, salads, breakfasts and sandwiches. A 15-minute walk from the Old Town centre.

St Peter's Guesthouse   GUESTHOUSE **$**
(Map p118; ☎08-317769, 01-752812; Glyn Jones Rd; d MK1000, r without bathroom MK2000; ☐) St Peter's has four pleasant rooms next to a red-brick chapel and a four-bed dorm with shared bathroom. It's very peaceful with a tranquil, leafy garden.

Mufasa Lodge   GUESTHOUSE **$**
(Map p118; ☎09 99071665; www.mufasamalawi. com; Kamuzu Procession Rd, Area 4; dm from US$8, s/d US$21/33; ☐@☎) Friendly Mufasa has small singles, dorms and spacious double rooms, plus twins with bathrooms. There's a little kitchen, storage lockers, laundry serv-

ice, tourist info point as well as an exchange library and bags of space in the garden to chill. Continental breakfast is included.

Kiboko Town Hotel   GUESTHOUSE **$$**
(Map p118; ☎01-751226; www.kiboko-safaris.com; Mandala Rd; s/d incl breakfast from US$59/69; @☎) This fresh mid-ranger has pleasant rooms with four-posters, ochre walls, fresh linen, mozzie nets and cable TV. There's also a great adjoining cafe in their courtyard – as well as a kids playground – serving up big breakfasts and decent coffee. Come evening the bar is a real traveller/expat magnet. Kiboko Safaris are based here.

TOP CHOICE **Latitude 13°**   BOUTIQUE HOTEL **$$$**
(☎09 96403159; www.thelatitudehotels.com; 60/43 Mphonongo Rd; s/d suites US$170/220, gar-

ITINERARIES

Three Days

Spend a day getting acclimatised in Lilongwe before going down to Liwonde National Park for two days of elephant and hippo spotting.

One Week

Head down from Blantyre to the woodland and streams of the Zomba Plateau, then make for Mulanje for three or four days' hiking across the mountain's twisted peaks.

Two Weeks

Head south from Lilongwe to Majete Wildlife Reserve, Malawi's new home for lions. After this make north for mysterious Nyika Plateau and the colonial hilltop town of Livingstonia. Then head for Nkhata Bay for some beachside frolics, before catching the *Ilala* ferry over to Likoma or Chizumulu Island. Charter a flight or wait for the *Ilala* to take you back to the mainland.

One Month

With more time on your hands you can take in all of the highlights above and add a few more: perhaps the southern beach resorts of Cape Maclear, Mumbo Island or Senga Bay; or head to the newly revived Nkhotakota Wildlife Reserve.

den suites US$220/270; P⊖❄@📶) The city's only boutique hotel has sumptuous rooms with buffed cement floors, four-posters, black walls and plunge baths.

Resident chef Richard Greenhall trained under Jamie Oliver and alchemises in the kitchen. The ever-changing menu (MK10,000) never gets tired, but try the lamb cutlets in red wine and pureed mash. And we haven't even started on the wine list. Always full, this low-lit and beguilingly romantic place is easily the most stylish option in the city.

Sunbird Capital Hotel HOTEL **$$$**
(Map p114; ☎01-773388; www.sunbirdmalawi.com; Chilembwe Rd; s/d US$175/205; P⊖❄@📶≋) Set in lush gardens, rooms here are tastefully conservative with bureaus, bouncy beds and large bathrooms. The main restaurant dishes up Italian and Indian cuisine. There's also a gym, pool, hairdresser, shops and travel agents here.

Kumbali Country Lodge LODGE **$$$**
(☎09 99963402; www.kumbalilodge.com; Capital Hill Dairy Farm, Plot 9 & 11, Area 44; s/d from US$180/220; P❄@📶≋) In a rural setting, these swanky thatched chalets have beautiful views all the way to nearby Nkhoma Mountain. There are also plenty of nature trails and bird-spotting opportunities here.

Sunbird Lilongwe Hotel HOTEL **$$$**
(Map p118; ☎01-756333; Kamuzu Procession Rd; s/d from US$109/134; P❄@📶≋) With a whiff of colonial chic, the Sunbird's international-standard rooms are well furnished with fridges, and bathrooms are spotless. There's a classy restaurant, as well as a gym and pool to cool off in.

Crossroads Hotel HOTEL **$$$**
(Map p114; ☎01-750333; www.crossroadshotel.net; Mchinji Roundabout, Crossroads Complex; r MK26,000, deluxe r MK33,000; P⊖❄@📶≋) Crossroads has all the facilities from internet cafes, bars, swimming pool and 100-rooms based around a pleasant courtyard. Rooms have cable TV and are very comfy indeed. Crossroads Car Hire (p165) is based here.

Sanctuary Lodge LODGE **$$$**
(Map p114; ☎01-775200; www.thesanctuarylodge.net; Youth Dr; campsite per adult/child US$9/6, s/d incl breakfast from US$135/160; P❄@📶≋) These chalets – just outside Lilongwe Nature Sanctuary – are well appointed with boutique flair; tiled floors, step in showers, wicker chairs and African chic decor. Add to this the peaceful setting in quiet leafy gardens and you have a winner.

There's also a campsite with hot showers, while the lodge's restaurant is equally charming.

Eating

Buchanan's Grill STEAKHOUSE **$**
(Map p114; Presidential Way, Four Seasons Centre; mains MK1500-2300; ⏰lunch & dinner Mon-Sat)

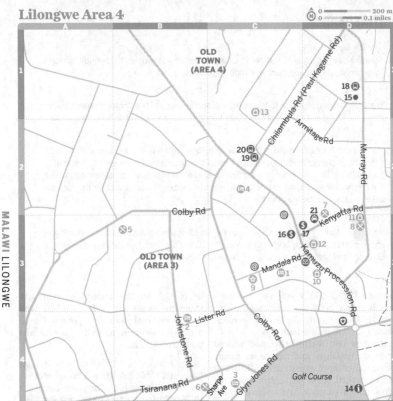

Lilongwe Area 4

OLD TOWN (AREA 4)

Chilambula Rd (Paul Kagame Rd)

Armitage Rd

Murray Rd

Colby Rd

Kenyatta Rd

Mandala Rd

Kamuzu Procession Rd

OLD TOWN (AREA 3)

Lister Rd

Johnstone Rd

Colby Rd

Tsiranana Rd

Sharpe Ave

Glyn Jones Rd

Golf Course

Eat in the old-world style restaurant (with a sports bar attached), or outside beside an ornamental pool. It's a carnivore-friendly menu with rump, sirloin and fillet steaks.

TOP CHOICE Don Brioni's Bistro   BISTRO $

(Map p118; Mandala Rd; mains from MK2500; ☺lunch & dinner; 🕾) Burgers, steaks, spaghetti, T-bone, spare ribs. Don Brioni's, an expat magnet, has check-cloth tables bathed in low-lit ambience. Take a pew in the atmospheric dining room or outside on the candlelit terrace.

Korea Garden Restaurant   KOREAN $

(Map p118; 3056 Tsiranana Rd; mains MK3000; ☺breakfast, lunch & dinner; 🅿🕾) This poolside affair has Korean-style grub like chicken in sesame seeds and soy sauce, or fried fish, pepper steaks and *chambo* (a breamlike fish).

Ama Khofi   CAFE $

(Map p114; Presidential Way, Four Seasons Centre; mains MK2300; ☺7.30am-5pm Mon-Sat, 9am-5pm Sun; 🅿🕾🖉) Delightful Parisian-style cafe with wrought iron chairs and pretty gardens. It has a menu of carrot cake, ice cream and salads, and main courses like beef burgers.

Mamma Mia   ITALIAN $

(Map p118; Old Town Mall; mains from MK1400; ☺lunch & dinner; 🅿🕾🖉) Mamma's has a wide-ranging menu featuring antipasti, salads, panini and homemade pasta. The pizza dough is delicious.

Sanctuary Restaurant   INTERNATIONAL $

(Map p114; www.thesanctuarylodge.net; meals from MK2000; ☺10am-10.30pm Mon-Sat, 9am-4pm Sun; 🅿🕾🖉) Shaded by mature fig trees singing with cicadas, Sanctuary boasts a veggie menu as well as breakfasts, meatballs, fish

Lilongwe Area 4

MALAWI LILONGWE

and steaks. At night the restaurant is romantically candlelit.

Monsoon THAI $
(Pacific Parade Shopping Mall; mains from MK1750; ⊙10.30am-2pm & 6-11pm; ☎🖬) This new Thai restaurant in the Pacific Parade Shopping Mall is a pleasant spot for faves like *tom yum* soup, Thai green curry and satay. Head north on the Chilembwe Rd to Area 10.

Bohemian Cafe CAFE $
(Map p118; Land & Lake Safaris, 84 Laws Ave, Area 3; snacks from MK450; ⊙8am-4.30pm Mon-Fri, 9am-2pm Sat; P☎🖬) This tempting garden cafe has very tasty, choc-infused coffees, as well as homemade cakes, bagels, healthy sandwiches and salads.

Self-Catering

There are decent supermarkets all over the city, the newest and best being **Spar** (Map p118; Lilongwe City Mall, Kenyatta Rd) in Old Town.

Drinking & Entertainment

Chameleon Bar BAR, LIVE MUSIC
(Map p114; Presidential Way, Four Seasons Centre; ⊙11am-midnight Mon-Sat, to 10pm Sun; ☎) This effervescent cocktail bar sits opposite Buchanan's Grill in a leafy compound, and puts on live music, DJ nights, poetry readings and theme parties.

Harry's Bar BAR
(Map p114; ⊙6pm-late) This lively wood shack dishes up a bubbling atmosphere and live jazz in the garden. A Lilongwe institution.

Chez Ntemba NIGHTCLUB
(Map p114; Area 47; ⊙6pm-late) Live acts – with a distinctly African flavour – and disco magnetises locals and *wazungu* (white foreigners) in a fleshpot of sweaty bodies. Great fun.

Umunthu Theatre THEATRE
(Map p118; ☎01-757979; www.umunthu.com) Off Mandala Rd, Umunthu is the highlight of Lilongwe's cultural scene. It puts on regular live music, films, club nights and variety shows, showcasing the best of Malawian talent.

Shopping
Malls

Four Seasons Centre MALL
(Map p114; Presidential Way; ☎) An oasis of fine dining and upscale shopping, featuring clothing and design boutiques, a couple of bars, restaurants and a tempting cafe, Four Seasons is a restful one-stop shop.

Lilongwe City Mall
MALL

(Map p118; Kenyatta Rd) The newest and best mall in the city for fast food joints, supermarkets and dead-central location in Old Town.

Crossroads Complex
MALL

(Map p114; Mchinji Roundabout) This houses banks, a swanky hotel, minigolf, Crossroads Car Hire (p165), a variety of upmarket shops, supermarkets and services, and a branch of the South African Steers.

Old Town Mall
MALL

(Map p118; off Chilambula Rd) Off Chilambula Rd, this small mall has a couple of bookshops and craft stores as well as the Mamma Mia restaurant. Chic and quiet.

Arts & Crafts

Ishq
HANDICRAFTS

(Map p114; Four Seasons Centre; ⊙9am-5.30pm Mon-Sat, 10.30am-4pm Sun) Selling a range of recycled mahogany and glass tables, stylish natural-coloured linen chemises, bespoke jewellery, hand-woven throws, bags and pasminas, Ishq is pure style. Cheap it isn't.

African Habitat
HANDICRAFTS

(Map p118; Old Town Mall; ⊙8.30am-5pm Mon-Fri, to 1pm Sat) Excellent for sculpture, woodcarvings, sarongs, cards and jewellery, as well as T-shirts and bags.

La Galleria
HANDICRAFTS

(Map p118; lacaverna@malawi.net; Old Town Mall; ⊙9am-4.30pm Mon-Fri, to 1pm Sat) Pleasant boutique selling vivid African paintings, masks, bags and jewellery by local artists.

Markets

The city's main market is by the bus station. There's also a craft market (Map p118; Kamuzu Procession Rd) outside the Old Town post office, where vendors sell everything from woodcarvings to basketware and jewellery.

ℹ Information

Bookshops

Central Africana (Map p118; www.centralafricana.com; Old Town Mall; ⊙8.30am-5pm Mon-Fri, to 1pm Sat) Has a small selection of English language novels, pictorial travel books and some very nice prints of Malawi as keepsakes.

Grey Matter (Map p118; Lilongwe City Mall) Great range of thrillers, biographies, kids books and travel titles.

Emergency
Ambulance (☑998)
Fire (☑01-757999)
Police (☑01-753333)
Rapid Response Unit (☑01-794254)

Internet Access

Internet is readily available in Lilongwe with Skyband wi-fi hotspots across the city.

Comptech (per 10min MK75) Fast internet connection, printing and photocopying as well as Skype web telephone service, with branches at Mandala Rd and Kamuzu Procession Rd.

Medical Services

Adventist Health Centre (Map p114; ☑01-775680; Presidential Way) Good for consultations, plus eye and dental problems.

Dr Peter Kalungwe (Map p114; ☑09 99969548, 01-750404) Available for private consultations.

Likuni Mission Hospital (☑01-766574, 01-766602; Glyn Jones Rd) Public wards, private rooms and some expat European doctors on staff; 7km southwest of Old Town.

Lilongwe Private Clinic (☑01-774972, 01-927035; Plot 10131, Mphonongo Rd, Area 10) Ask for Dr Chirwa.

Michiru Pharmacy (Map p118; ☑01-754294; Nico Shopping Centre; ⊙8am-5pm Mon-Fri, to 1pm Sat & Sun) Sells antibiotics and malaria pills as well as the usual offerings.

Money

Money Bureau (Map p114; ☑01-750789; Mchinji Roundabout, Crossroads Complex, Crossroads) Has good rates, doesn't charge commission and does cash advances on credit cards.

National Bank of Malawi (Map p118; Kamuzu Procession Rd, Old Town) You can change money here and get a cash advance on your Visa card. There's also a 24-hour ATM that accepts Visa. There's also another branch in City Centre (Map p114; African Unity Ave, City Centre).

Standard Bank (Map p118; Kamuzu Procession Rd, Old Town) Offers the same facilities as National Bank of Malawi but the ATM also accepts MasterCard and Maestro. There's another branch in City Centre (Map p114; African Unity Ave, City Centre).

Post

Post office (⊙7.30am-noon, 1-5pm Mon-Fri) Branches at City Centre (Map p114), next to the City Centre Shopping Centre, and Old Town (Kamuzu Procession Rd).

Safe Travel

You definitely don't want to be around Lilongwe Nature Sanctuary after dark thanks to late night appearances of hyenas. Also there have been isolated cases of muggings around the Sanctuary Lodge – so ask for a security guard to escort you to your cabana.

During the day it's fine to walk everywhere around Old Town and City Centre. At night Malangalanga Rd can be dangerous, and walking to Area 3 is not recommended. The bridge between Area 2 and Area 3 is still a favourite haunt for muggers. Always watch out for your things when at the city's main bus station, and if you arrive on a bus after dark take a taxi to your accommodation. As a general rule it isn't safe to walk around anywhere in the city after dark.

Tourist Information

Department of Surveys Map Sales Office (Map p118) Survey maps of Malawi and some of its cities are available from the Department of Surveys Map Sales Office, about 500m south of the roundabout where Glyn Jones Rd meets Kamuzu Procession Rd.

Immigration Office (Map p118; ☑01-754297; Murray Rd)

Ministry of Tourism, Wildlife & Culture (Map p114; ☑01-755499; Tourism House; ⊙7.30am-5pm Mon-Fri, 8-10am Sat) Information and advice is minimal at this tourist office; you're better off at a travel agency.

Travel Agencies

Barefoot Safaris & Adventure Tours (☑01-707346, in South Africa 0027-78-630 9734; www.barefoot-safaris.com) Organises horse riding, hiking, climbing, walking and 4WD safaris throughout Malawi and beyond. Based at the Barefoot Safari Lodge 10km out of the city.

Kiboko Safaris (Map p118; ☑01-751226; www.kiboko-safaris.com; Mandala Rd) Specialises in budget camping safaris throughout Malawi and Zambia; a four-day southern Malawi trip is US$450.

Land & Lake Safaris (Map p118; ☑01-757120; www.landlake.net; 84 Laws Rd, Area 3) This trusted company has tours for all budgets in both Malawi and Zambia; a four-day trip to South Luangwa National Park is US$590.

Robin Pope Safaris (☑01-795483; www.robinpopesafaris.net; Plot 10/144, Tsoka Road, Area 10) Robin Pope and African Parks have put Majete Wildlife Reserve back on the map with its dazzling new lodge, Mkulumadzi. It also operates tours in Zambia.

Ulendo Travel Group (Map p114; ☑01-794555; www.ulendo.net; 441 Chilanga Drive, Area 10) Trustworthy Ulendo organises accommodation, pre-books flights (it also has its own airline, Ulendo Airlink (p162), ferrying travellers to safari parks and Likoma Island), car hire and a variety of expertly tailored tours and safaris in Malawi and Zambia.

Wilderness Safaris (Map p114; ☑01-771153, 01-771393; www.wilderness-safaris.com; Bisnowaty Complex, Kenyatta Rd) Specialising in safari trips to their high-lux lodges in Liwonde and Nyika National Parks, Wilderness is the country's top safari operator. It also provides top-end safaris and lodge bookings throughout Southern Africa.

❶ Getting There & Away

Air
Airline offices in Lilongwe:

Air Malawi (☑01-700811; www.flyairmalawi.com; Kamazu International Airport)

Kenya Airways (Map p114; www.kenya-airways.com; Independence Dr)

KLM (Map p114; ☑01-774227; www.klm.com; Independence Dr)

South African Airways (Map p114; ☑01-770307, 01-772242; www.flysaa.com; Sunbird Capital Hotel, Chilembwe Rd)

Bus
AXA City Trouper and commuter buses leave from the **main bus station** (Map p114) where you'll find their **ticket office** (Map p114), though you can also buy tickets at Postdotnet inside the City Centre Peoples Supermarket at **Nico Shopping Centre** (Map p118; Kamuzu Procession Rd) and at Crossroads Complex.

AXA executive coaches (Map p118) depart from outside the City Centre Peoples Supermarket before stopping at the immigration office on Murray Rd and making their way to Blantyre. An executive ticket between the two cities costs MK6000.

Destinations from the main bus station include Mzuzu (MK3500, five hours, two or three daily), Blantyre (MK2000, four hours, three daily), Kasungu (MK1500, two hours, two daily), Nkhotakota (MK3500, three hours, two daily), Nkhata Bay (MK900, five hours, one daily), Salima (MK390, one hour, two daily) and Dedza (MK1300, one hour).

A number of other bus companies, including Coachline and Zimatha, also leave from the main bus station at similar rates and times. **Super Sink** (Map p114) buses depart for Mzuzu (MK2000, six hours) and Songwe (MK5000) on the Tanzanian border from the **Engen petrol station** next to the main bus station between 7am and 8am.

Long-distance minibuses (Map p114) depart from behind the bus station to nearby destinations such as Zomba (MK2500, four to five hours), Dedza (MK1000, 45 minutes to one hour), the Zambian border (MK1500, two hours), Nchitsi (MK1200, 2½ hours), Mangochi (MK2500, 4½ hours), Limbe (MK1900, three to four hours), Mangochi (MK1200, four hours) and Nkhotakota (MK1800, three hours).

Intercape Mainliner (p163) has modern buses and leaves from the Total petrol station in Old Town on Tuesday, Wednesday, Saturday and Sunday at 6am, arriving in Johannesburg at 6am the following day (one way MK29,500). Chiwale Bus Co (p163) leaves for Johannesburg at 6am on Saturday from the same location (one way MK21,000).

Buses to Dar Es Salaam and Lusaka (Map p114; Devil St) leave from Devil St. The **Zambia−Botswana Coach** (☑09 99405340) leaves Wednesday and Saturday at 6am arriving in Lusaka at 5pm (MK9500). Kob's Coach leaves the same days, same price, at 6am. The Tarqwa coach departs from Devil St at 7pm on Saturday, Sunday and Tuesday for the 27-hour journey to Dar Es Salaam, continuing on to Nairobi.

❶ Getting Around

To/From the Airport

Lilongwe International Airport is 21km north of the city. A taxi from the airport into town costs MK8000. Maddeningly, there is currently no airport bus.

Bus

The most useful local minibus service for visitors is between Old Town and City Centre. From Old Town, local minibuses (marked Area 12) leave from either the bus rank near the market or next to **Shoprite** (Map p118; Kenyatta Rd). They then head north up Kenyatta Rd, via Youth and Convention Drs or via Independence Dr, to reach City Centre. From City Centre back to Old Town, the bus stop for the return journey is at the northern end of Independence Dr.

Taxi

The best places to find taxis are the main hotels. There's a **rank** (Map p114) on Presidential Way, just north of City Centre Shopping Centre. Taxis also congregate outside Shoprite in Old Town. The fare between Old Town and City Centre is about MK2500. Short journeys within City Centre or Old Town cost around MK1500. Particularly reliable is **Charlie Kandoje** (☑08 88853373, 09 99935281; half day around the city of Lilongwe MK6500).

NORTHERN MALAWI

Out of the way and sometimes forgotten, northern Malawi is where ravishing highlands meet hippo-filled swamps, vast mountains loom over empty beaches, and colonial relics litter pristine islands and hilltop villages. This part of Lake Malawi is lined with gleaming coves and beaches straight out of a Caribbean dream. Budget travellers will do particularly well here with beachfront accommodation and backpacker-friendly activities.

Karonga

Dusty little Karonga is the first place you'll come across if making the journey down from Tanzania and suffices for an overnight stay of checking emails, stocking up on cash and having a close encounter with a 100-million-year-old dinosaur. Karonga has the proud title of Malawi's 'fossil district', with well-preserved remains of dinosaurs and ancient man. Its most famous discovery is the Malawisaurus (Malawi lizard) – a fossilised dino skeleton found 45km south of the town. See it at the Culture and Museum Centre Karonga (CMCK; ☑01-362579; www.palaeo.net/cmck; ⊗8am-5pm Mon-Sat, 2-5pm Sun).

If you do decide to stay, opt for Sumuka Inn (☑0999-444816; standard/deluxe/executive r MK8500/10,500/12,500, ste from MK15,000) or Safari Lodge Annex (☑01-362340; standard/executive/chalet MK4500/4800/6500); apart from the Mbande Cafe (⊗8am-5pm Mon-Sat, 2-5pm Sun), eating options are slim. There's a Standard Bank and National Bank of Malawi, internet at the museum and the locals are friendly.

Super Sink Buses leave at 8pm for Lilongwe. Alternatively head to Mzuzu (MK1600, four hours) from where AXA City Trouper buses also leave for Lilongwe and Blantyre. Minibuses go to numerous destinations, including Songwe (MK1200, 45 minutes) and Mzuzu (MK1600, four hours). Taxis to Nakonde on the Tanzanian border go from the main bus station and cost MK1200.

If you've got a 4WD, you can cross into northern Zambia via Chitipa in northern Malawi. It's four hours from Karonga to Chitipa on a rough dirt road (there's no public transport but you might be able to get a lift on a truck). After going through customs it's another 80km or four hours' drive to the Zambian border post at Nakonde.

Livingstonia

Built by missionaries, mountain-top Livingstonia feels sanctified and otherworldly; its main street graced with colonial-style buildings and smartly attired folk who look as if

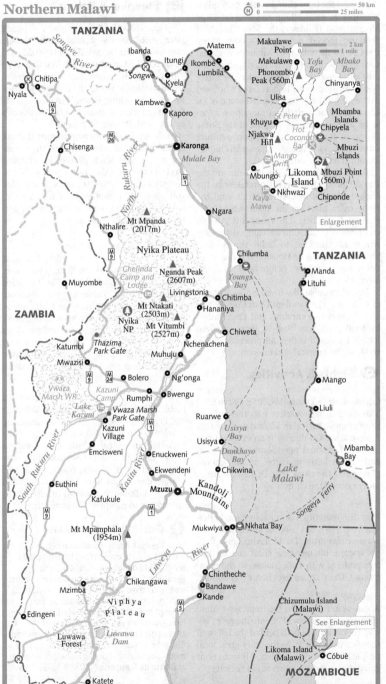

Northern Malawi

0 — 50 km
0 — 25 miles

TANZANIA

Songwe River

Chitipa
Nyala
M9

Ibanda
Itungi
Songwe
Kyela
Ikombe
Lumbila
Matema

Kambwe
Kaporo
M26
Chisenga

Karonga
Mulale Bay

Rukuru River
M1

Ngara

Nthalire
Mt Mpanda (2017m)
Nyika Plateau

Muyombe
Chelinda Camp and Lodge
Nganda Peak (2607m)

ZAMBIA

Livingstonia
Youngs Bay

Chilumba

TANZANIA

Manda
Lituhi

Mt Ntakati (2503m)
Nyika NP
Mt Vitumbi (2527m)
Nchenachena
Muhuju
Ng'onga

Chitimba
Hananiya

Chiweta

Katumbi
Thazima Park Gate
Mwazisi
M9
Bolero
Kazuni Camp
Rumphi
Bwengu

M24

Vwaza Marsh WR
Lake Kazuni
Vwaza Marsh Park Gate
Kazuni Village

Emcisweni
Enuckweni
Ekwendeni

Kasitu River

Ruarwe
Usisya
Usisya Bay
Dankhayo Bay

Chikwina

Mango

Liuli

Mbamba Bay

South Rukuru River
Euthini
M9
Kafukule
M1
Mzuzu
Kandoli Mountains

Lake Malawi

Songeya Ferry

Mt Mpamphala (1954m)
M1
Mukwiya
Nkhata Bay

Luweza River

Chikangawa
Mzimba
Viphya Plateau
Luwawa Dam
M5
Chintheche
Bandawe
Kande

Chizumulu Island (Malawi)
See Enlargement

Edingeni
Luwawa Forest

Likoma Island (Malawi)
Cóbuè

Katete

MÓZAMBIQUE

Enlargement

Makulawe Point
0 — 2 km
0 — 1 mile

Makulawe
Phonombo Peak (560m)
Yofu Bay
Mbako Bay

Chinyanya

Ulisa

St Peter
Khuyu
Njakwa Hill
Hot Coconut Bar
Mango Drift

Mbamba Islands
Chipyela

Mbuzi Islands

Mbungo
Likoma Island
Mbuzi Point (560m)

Kaya Mawa
Nkhwazi
Chiponde

they're en route to church. After two failed attempts at establishing missions at Cape Maclear and Bandawe, the Free Church of Scotland moved its mission 900m above the lake to the village of Khondowe. Called Livingstonia after Dr David Livingstone, the mission was built in 1884 under the direction of missionary Dr Robert Laws who lived in the Stone House (the original home of Dr Laws and now a national monument, museum and guesthouse). Staying at the Stone House, or at one of the nearby permaculture farms, makes for a magical, peaceful chapter in your northern journey.

Down the road from the museum are the David Gordon Memorial Hospital, once the biggest hospital in Central Africa, and the stone cairn marking the place where missionary Dr Robert Laws and his African companion Uriah Chirwa camped in 1894 when they decided to build the mission here. Also nearby is House No 1, the original home of Dr Laws before he moved into Stone House.

You might also like to take a look at the clock tower. The excellent Craft Coffee Shop sells inexpensive carvings and crafts made by local people, as well as their excellent locally produced coffee; all proceeds go directly to the hospital and mission.

◉ Sights & Activities

Stone House Museum   MUSEUM
(admission MK250, photos MK100; ⊙7.30am-5pm) This fascinating museum tells the story of the European arrival in Malawi and the first missionaries. On display is an excellent collection of original magic-lantern slides, an early anaesthesia machine, an old gramophone and the cloak that Dr Laws wore as moderator of the church.

Church   CHURCH
Near the museum, the mission church, dating from 1894, has a beautiful stained-glass window featuring David Livingstone with his sextant, his medicine chest and his two companions, with Lake Malawi in the background. There are services here every Sunday.

Manchewe Falls   WATERFALL
About 4km from town the impressive Manchewe Falls thunders 125m into the valley below. Follow a small path behind the falls and there's a cave where, as the story goes, local people hid from slave-traders. Allow an hour going down and 1½ hours to get back up.

🛏 Sleeping & Eating

Mushroom Farm   LODGE $
(☑09 99652485; www.themushroomfarmmalawi. com; campsite per person US$5, tent hire US$6, s/d US$16.50/23.50, cob chalet s/d US$33/41; P@🛜) This permaculture campsite perched on the mountainside is worth the arduous journey for the astonishing views. Three chalets offer simple accommodation – best is the cob cottage with its own bathroom.

Wake up in the morning to mist drifting up the mountain, Miles Davis on the speakers, and owner Mick dishing up amazing food. If you've got the energy you can abseil and rock-climb (US$40). Mick can also pick you up (US$50 each way for four people) from Chitimba (at the base of the mountain) to save you the horrible drive.

TOP CHOICE **Lukwe Permaculture Camp**   CAMPING, ECOLODGE
(☑09 99434985, 09 99792311; www.lukwe. com; campsites US$5, tent hire US$6, s/d cabins US$12/20; 🛜) Ten kilometres from Chitimba, above the zigzag hairpins, or an hour's downhill walk east from Livingstonia (about 5km), Lukwe has extraordinary unbroken views from its funky timber verandah. The cafe serves delectable grub while their four superclean chalets are set in leafy terraced gardens, and enjoy mozzie nets and balconies.

Stone House   GUESTHOUSE $
(☑01-368223; campsite per person MK900, r MK1500-2000; ⊜@🛜) This atmospheric granite house was built on the crest of the mountain in the early 20th century and its rooms are still redolent with history; cosy rugs, shadowy hardwood floors and a twee lounge that might have been transplanted from an Edinburgh tearoom (it also serves scones just to complete the conceit!).

ⓘ Getting There & Away

From the main north–south road between Karonga and Mzuzu, the road to Livingstonia turns off at Chitimba, forcing its way up the escarpment in a series of lethal hairpins, with a mainly unpaved surface – at times single track – with the drop abysmally close to you. Don't attempt this in anything but a 4WD and never in rain. And only if you possess nerves of steel. Ask Mick at the Mushroom Farm to collect you from Chitimba, or walk the 15km (2½ hours) up the mountain, leaving your bag in the lock-up room at **Chitimba Campsite** (☑0888-387116; www.

chitimba.com; Chitimba; campsite per person MK1200, dm MK2400, chalets with bathroom MK5400; P @ 🛜 🐾). Take care on this road though as isolated incidents of muggings have occurred.

The other way to reach Livingstonia is to take the dirt road from Rumphi. It's also possible to get a truck here from outside the Peoples Supermarket in Rumphi (leaves 2pm Tuesday and Thursday, five hours).

A third option is to walk to Livingstonia from the Nyika Plateau, which can by done through Chelinda Camp (p126).

Nyika National Park

Burnt amber by the afternoon sun, Nyika's highland grass flickers with the stripes of zebras and is punctuated by glittering boulders. Towering 2500m above sea level, 3200-sq-km Nyika National Park is enigmatic; one moment its rolling grasslands resem-

ble the Yorkshire Dales, then an antelope leaps across the car bonnet and you know you're in Africa.

There are plenty of zebras, bushbucks, roan antelopes and elephants here and you may also spot elands, warthogs, klipspringers, jackals, duikers, hyenas and leopards. If you're a twitcher, more than 400 species of birds have been recorded here. After the wet season the landscape bursts into life in a blaze of wildflowers – around 200 species of orchids grow on the plateau.

You can take a game drive, explore on a mountain bike, or ramble through the hills on foot. It can get surprisingly cold on the Nyika Plateau though, especially at night from June to August when frost is not uncommon. Log fires are provided in the chalets and rooms, but bring a warm sleeping bag if you're camping. In 2013 lions are due for reintroduction (and possibly cheetahs).

MALAWI NYIKA NATIONAL PARK

Nyika National Park

TREKKING ON THE NYIKA PLATEAU

Routes to viewpoints on the western and northern escarpments are especially popular and Wilderness Safaris (see below) can avail you with obligatory guides and porters for a number of memorable treks. The hugely rewarding and spectacular three-day route from Chelinda Camp to Livingstonia heads east through grassland, then steeply down through wooded escarpment to Livingstonia.

🏃 Activities

Wildlife Watching

Day game drives start from Wilderness Safaris' Chelinda Camp or Lodge at 8am every morning. The most exciting drives are by night, with a 40% chance of your guide scoping out leopards. Nurse a Carlsberg 'green' as you take in the panorama of stars above the open-top Landcrusier and watch the animals appear – unforgettable!

Wildlife viewing is good year-round, although in July and August the cold weather means the animals move to lower areas. Birdwatching is particularly good between October and April when migratory birds are on the move.

Wilderness Safaris ADVENTURE TOUR
(☎01-771393; www.wilderness-safaris.com) Wilderness Safaris has run Nyika's concession since 2009, and provides some enticingly cosy lodge accommodation in the park. As well as treks, fishing and game drives it also offers mountain biking, and hopefully soon will resurrect horse riding on the plateau.

🛏 Sleeping

All self-caterers should stock up in either Mzuzu or Rumphi. There's a small shop at Chelinda for national park staff but provisions are often basic and supplies sporadic.

Camping Ground CAMPING $
(campsites per person US$15) About 2km from the main Chelinda Camp, this camping ground is set in a secluded site with vistas of rolling hills. It has permanent security, clean toilets, hot showers, endless firewood, and shelters for cooking and eating.

TOP CHOICE Chelinda Lodge LODGE $$$
(☎01-771393; www.wilderness-safaris.com; Nyika National Park; chalets US$450; 🅿🍴@📶) A kilometre from Chelinda Camp and sitting on a hillside in a clearing of pine trees, upscale Chelinda Lodge is a traveller's dream. The main building crackles with a fiery hearth casting its glow on exquisite chandeliers and lush wildlife photography.

After a day's hiking or biking settle back for a candlelit dinner, or train your binoculars on the opposite valley for passing zebra. No less enchanting are their Swiss-style timber chalets with roaring fires, wood floors, clawed baths and hot water bottles in beds! Chelinda's elevated views are best enjoyed at dawn when the surrounding grasslands are cloaked in blue mist. Bliss.

Chelinda Camp CHALETS $$$
(☎01-771393; www.wilderness-safaris.com; Nyika National Park; chalets US$160; 🅿📶) Nestled into the lee of a valley beside a small lake, Chelinda Camp (run by Wilderness Safaris) is insanely picturesque. Its chalets have an unfussy '70s aspect to them and are ideal for families, with decent self-catering facilities, cosy sitting rooms and stone fireplaces.

Keep your eyes peeled for leopards drinking at the lake come dawn. Reception and a welcoming restaurant are but a few yards away.

ℹ Getting There & Away

The main Thazima Gate is 54km from Rumphi; once inside the park it's another 60km or so (about two hours' drive) to Chelinda Camp.

You can cycle the 60km from the Thazima Gate to Chelinda (but start early!). The nearest public bus is via the service from Mzuzu to Rumphi. From there find a truck or *matola* (pick-up truck) going to Chitipa to drop you off at the turn-off to Chelinda Camp (MK1500), from where you'll still have 20km to walk. From the camp itself you can catch a lift out of the park on a timber truck bound for Rumphi (MK1500).

Entry into Nyika is US$10 per person and an additional US$3 per vehicle. Petrol is available at Chelinda but in limited supply, so fill up before you enter the park.

Charter flights from Lilongwe to Nyika are now operating through Ulendo Airlink (p162), the aviation wing of Ulendo Travel Group (p121), and cost US$500 each way, per person.

Vwaza Marsh Wildlife Reserve

Despite being assailed by poachers, Vwaza boasts a healthy population of around 2000 buffaloes and 300 elephants. It's also one of the best places in Malawi to see waders. The park ranges in appearance from large flat areas of mopane woodland to open swamp and wetlands, and its main focus is Lake Kazuni.

Just sitting around Vwaza's main camp will bring plenty of animal sightings as it looks over the lake, and on most days you'll see crocodiles lying out in the sun, hippos popping their heads out of the water and a steady parade of animals coming down to the lake to drink.

The best time of year to visit is in the dry season (the rainy season's high grass restricts visibility). The park entry fee is US$10 per person and US$3 per vehicle.

🛏 Sleeping

Lake Kazuni Safari Camp　　　BUSH CAMP **$$**
(☏08 84462518; huts US$40; **P**) The camp's basic thatch and brick cabanas with bathrooms are well positioned on the lakeshore for viewing wildlife. Although the management are seriously depleted in their offerings, the National Parks skeleton staff can cook you dinner in the camp's kitchen (if you stock up on grub in nearby Rumphi).

There are no vehicles to take you on a game drive but guide **Godwin** (☏09 94418625; US$10 per 1½ hour trip, walking safari $10 per trip) can accompany you in your own vehicle (as long as it's a 4WD). Before heading here, check to see whether the lodge is still open.

❶ Getting There & Away

If you're travelling by public transport, first get to Rumphi (reached from Mzuzu by minibus for MK1000). From Rumphi there are plenty of *matola* travelling to and from the Kazuni area and you should be able to get a lift to the main gate for around MK1000. Otherwise buses and minibuses to Mzimba might drop you at Kazuni village, which is about 1km from the park gate.

By car, head west from Rumphi. Turn left after 10km (Vwaza Marsh Wildlife Reserve is signposted) and continue for about 20km. Where the road swings left over a bridge, go straight on to reach the park gate and camp after 1km.

Mzuzu

Dusty, busy Mzuzu is northern Malawi's largest town and serves as the transport hub for the region. Travellers heading to Blantyre, Lilongwe, Nkhata Bay, Nyika or Viphya, or to and from Tanzania are likely to spend a night or two here. Mzuzu has banks, shops, a post office, supermarkets, pharmacies, petrol stations and other facilities, which are especially useful if you've come into Malawi from the north.

Internet access is available at **Postdotnet** (Boardman Rd; per 30 min MK300; ⊙8am-5pm Mon-Fri, to 12.30pm Sat).

◎ Sights & Activities

Museum　　　MUSEUM
(M'Mbelwa Rd; admission MK200; ⊙7.30am-noon & 1-5pm, tours at 9am, 11am, 1.30pm & 2pm) The museum has displays on the people and the land of northern Malawi including the Tumbuka, the Tonga and the Ngoni. If you're planning to go to Livingstonia, there's an interesting exhibition telling the story of the missionaries' journey.

🛏 Sleeping

TOP CHOICE Mzoozoozoo　　　HOSTEL **$**
(☏08 88864493; campsite MK500, dm MK1400, r MK3800; **P@🛜**) This funky backpackers haven delights with its lovely garden, quiet location (a few minutes' walk out of town) and colourful basic rooms. The friendly vibe, art-spattered walls and warm management, plus the terrific comfort food (steaks, chicken) may change your travel plans by a night or two.

Sunbird Mzuzu Hotel　　　HOTEL **$$$**
(☏01-332622; www.sunbirdmalawi.com; s/d from US$160/180; **P✳@🛜**) Easily the plushest digs in the city, this large hotel is set in imposing grounds and has huge rooms with DSTV, and views of the town's golf course. The service is friendly and efficient and the place feels of an international standard. There's also a cosy cafe with wi-fi for laptops.

Mzuzu Lodge　　　LODGE **$$$**
(☏01-310224/226; Orton Chewa Ave; s/d standard US$50/65, executive US$65/95; **P✳@🛜**) If you stay in these motel-style digs, go for an executive room – away from the noise of

Mzuzu

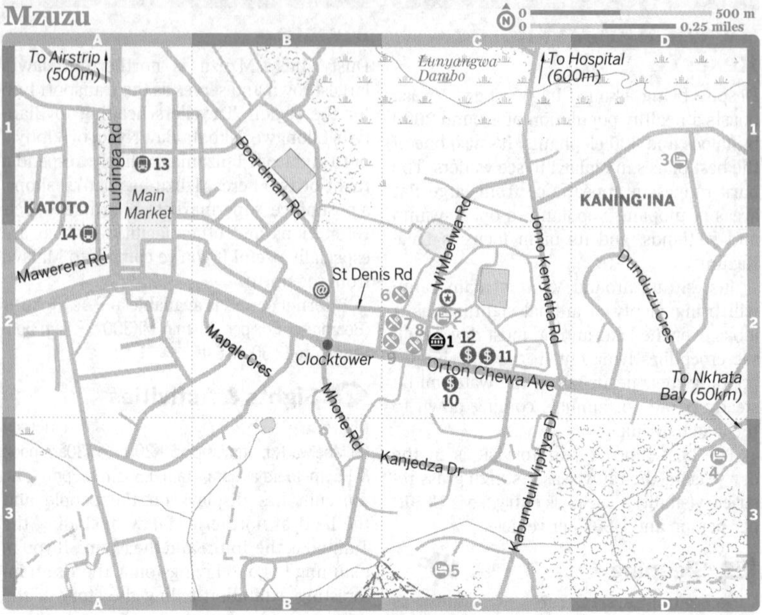

Mzuzu

Sights

1 Museum C2

Sleeping

2 Mimosa Court Hotel C2
3 Mzoozoozoo D1
4 Mzuzu Lodge D3
5 Sunbird Mzuzu Hotel C3

Eating

6 A1 Restaurant C2
7 Greenvee Restaurant C2
8 Metro Cash & Carry C2
9 Peoples Supermarket C2
Sombrero Restaurant .... (see 2)

Information

10 First Merchant Bank C2
11 National Bank of Malawi C2
12 Standard Bank C2

Transport

13 Bus Station A1
14 Local Minibuses A2

the bar and with all the hotel amenities you could want like armoires and TVs. Standard rooms, however, are dingy and overpriced.

Mimosa Court Hotel HOTEL $$$
(01-312609, 01-312833; off Orton Chewa Ave; s/d MK12,700/14,500; P) Mimosa is friendly and has a decent restaurant and bar. Rooms are scrupulously clean, with mozzie net, DSTV and fan. It's in a convenient location right in the centre of town.

Eating

Self-caterers can stock up at the **Peoples Supermarket** (Orton Chewa Ave) or **Metro Cash & Carry** (M'Mbelwa Rd).

TOP CHOICE **A1 Restaurant** INDIAN $
(St Denis Rd; mains around MK1000; 11.45am-2pm & 6-10pm;) Superfresh indigo-walled A1 has DSTV on the wall, abstract art and a menu featuring classic North Indian cuisine. The chicken korma is tasty.

Greenvee Restaurant INDIAN, MALAWIAN $
(08 88899666; St Denis Rd; mains from MK800; 6am-10pm) With its red check-cloth tables, airy interior and verandah, Greenvee is a nice spot to tuck into *nshima* (maize porridge), Indian curries, steak, and chicken and chips.

Sombrero Restaurant MALAWIAN $
(01-312833; off Orton Chewa Ave, Mimosa Court Hotel; mains MK800; breakfast, lunch & dinner;

P📶) The small sunny terrace and congenial atmosphere make Sombrero a fun place to eat steaks, fish and curries.

❶ Getting There & Away

AXA City Trouper buses go to Lilongwe at 7am and 5pm (MK3500, five hours) and local buses leave at 7.30am and 6pm (MK2200, six to seven hours). AXA buses also go to Karonga, leaving at 6.30am and 10am (MK1500, four hours) and local buses leave to Karonga at 6.30am (MK700, five hours) via Rumphi (MK1000) and Chitimba (MK540).

Minibuses go to Nkhata Bay (MK850, one to two hours), Karonga (MK2000, three to four hours), Chitimba (MK1700, two hours), Rumphi (MK1000, one hour) and Mbeya on the Tanzanian border (MK2500, four hours).

National Bus Company has daily departures to Lilongwe (MK2250), Blantyre (MK3000) and Salima (MK3000).

The **Taqwa bus** (📞09 99334538), originating in Lilongwe, travels between Mzuzu and Nairobi daily (MK24,000), calling at Songwe for the Tanzanian border (MK5000), Mbeya (MK7000) and Dar Es Salaam (MK13,000). You should report to the station at 11.30pm for a midnight departure. The bus crosses the border at first light, goes through Mbeya in the morning, gets to Dar Es Salaam at around 10pm and leaves for Nairobi the next morning.

KM Bus Services (📞0888-639363) leaves from the forecourt of Mbacheda Guesthouse at 7pm on Fridays, going to Harare (MK1700) and Johannesburg (MK23,000).

Nkhata Bay

With its fishing boats, vivid market and perfectly positioned guesthouses perched on cliffs overlooking the glittering lake, Nkhata Bay feels distinctly Caribbean. There's also loads of activities to enjoy before you hammock flop; be it snorkelling, diving, kayaking, fish-eagle feeding or forest walks.

Strung along the coast from the town centre most lodges are nestled into small bays. All are reached via a road that climbs up and down a hill between bays.

🏃 Activities

Swimming
On the southern side of Nkhata Bay, Chikale Beach is a popular spot for swimming and lazing on the sand, especially at weekends. Snorkelling equipment is free for guests at most of the lodges.

Kayaking
Monkey Business (📞0999-437247; blondie leap@hotmail.com; Butterfly Space) and Chimango Tours (📞09 99268595; Mayoka Village), can organise paddling excursions personally tailored to your needs – anything from half a day to a few days down the coast. Typical itineraries include idyllic spots along the northern lakeshore such as Usisya and Ruarwe. A full day usually costs US$40.

Diving
Aqua Africa Diving   DIVING
(📞09 99921418, 01-852284; www.aquaafrica.co.uk) The bay's only dive operator, this dependable Western-run outfit offers casual dives for certified divers (US$50) and full PADI four-day beginner courses (US$375). Colourful chiclid fish, the kind you've probably seen in a dentist's aquarium, swim throughout the lake but more spectacular are the schools of dolphinfish who are drawn to your torch on night dives. Aqua Africa also rents snorkelling gear (US$15 per half day).

🧭 Tours

Nkhata Bay Safari
(📞09 99265064; daviemzungu@yahoo.co.uk; 5-day safari per person US$500; ⏰office 7am-5pm) Nkhata runs a five-day trip to Vwaza Marsh Wildlife Reserve, Nyika National Park and Livingstonia, as well as tailored trips further afield. It can also arrange bus bookings for Tanzania, cabins for the *Ilala* ferry, flights and lodges. Sunset cruises cost US$20.

🛏 Sleeping

TOP CHOICE ⭐ **Butterfly Space**   GUESTHOUSE $
(📞09 99265065; www.butterfly-space.com; campsite per person MK750, dm MK1500, chalet with/without bathroom MK4000/2500; P@📶) Ispiring, socially committed Butterfly Space is a backpackers' oasis. There's a spacious beachfront bar to chill in; a private beach, internet cafe, media centre, self-catering block and a restaurant serving authentic Tonga cuisine. Rooms in A-frame cabanas are basic but very clean.

There's a youth centre onsite and volunteers can help with computer, painting or English lessons. There's also a handicrafts shop.

Aqua Africa   LODGE $$
(📞09 99921418, 01-352284; www.aqua-africa. co.uk; r from US$35-80; ❄@📶) Cosy rooms

Nkhata Bay

Ⓝ 0 ————— 200 m
0 ————— 0.1 miles

Njaya Lodge   LODGE $
(☎09 99409878, 01-352342; www.njayalodge.
com; camping MK800, reed/stone chalets
MK2000/2000, family chalets MK4500-7000;
℗❋@⊛) Set in terraced gardens bursting
with frangipani trees and palms, and manicured lawns tumbling down to the lake,
Njaya has tasteful family-sized chalets up on
the hill, cosy reed huts, and striking stone
cottages right by the lake.

It also has a restaurant that serves great
seafood.

Big Blue Star   GUESTHOUSE $
(☎01-352316; campsite per person MK1000,
dm/s/d without bathroom MK1500/1700/3750;
℗@⊛) Occupying a hillside spot with great
lake views, Big Blue Star has a lively bar,
book exchange, free storage, a boho chill-out
lounge, overlander parking spaces and free
wi-fi.

Accommodation comes in small colourful
dorms (with mozzie nets) or reed huts, plus
a few shaded spots for tents. The staff are
friendly too.

with private balconies, huge beds and step-
in mozzie nets; this is lovely accommodation
often used by resident divers. The Dive Deck
Cafe complete with wicker loungers and
viewing deck, has an excellent menu ranging from full breakfasts to salads, tortilla
wraps and muffins. Staff are equally friendly
and helpful.

Mayoka Village   LODGE $$
(☎09 99268595, 01-994025; www.mayokavil
lage.com; dm US$8, s/d chalet without bath-
room US$15/28, US$20/40; ℗@⊛) Cleverly
shaped around the rocky topography of a
cliff, boutique-style Mayoka cascades down
in a series of beautiful bamboo and stone
chalets, some with wraparound verandahs.
Interiors are nicely finished with taste-
ful furniture and fans. There's also a great
waterfront bar. Lovely.

✖ Eating & Drinking

TOP CHOICE **Kaya Papaya**   THAI, MALWIAN $
(mains from MK900; ◷7am-late, food served to
9pm; ⊛✍) With its purple and orange col-
our scheme and shadowy interior, there's

more than a touch of Afro-chic here, which is matched by a Thai-accented menu of zesty salads, pizza and Malawian fare like butterfish with *nshima*.

Mayoka Village INTERNATIONAL $
(mains from MK950; ⊙7am-3pm & 6-8.30pm; P🔊⏃) This guacamole-green bar is infused with African sounds and the lapping waves of the lake a few feet away. Enjoy organic salads, breakfasts, baguettes and stir-fries. The staff may even be dancing!

Take Away Palace INDIAN $
(MK1000; ⏃) Run by a local Indian family, sit in the diner-style interior or outside, feasting on a menu spanning Northern Indian cuisine to Western dishes. It also does take-aways.

❶ Information

There's nowhere to change money but there are two ATMs at the top of the hill (50m before you reach Big Blue Star guesthouse). While they accept Visa, they don't accept MasterCard. Alternatively, some of the lodges accept credit cards, US currency and travellers cheques for payment. Internet access is available at Aqua Africa and **L-Net Internet Cafe** (MK250 per 30min; ⊙7am-5pm Mon-Fri, 8am-12.30pm Sat & Sun).

Dangers & Annoyances

Be careful of walking between town and your lodge at night; the hilly road to Chikale Beach is unlit and muggings are not infrequent (walk in numbers or take a guard from your lodge with you).

❶ Getting There & Away

All buses and minibuses go from the bus stand on the main road. AXA buses run to Mzuzu (MK800, two hours) and minibuses run to Nkhotakota (MK1000, five hours), Chintheche (MK600, one hour) and Mzuzu (MK700, one to two hours). To reach Lilongwe the quickest option is to go to Mzuzu and change buses.

Many come or go on the *Ilala* ferry which arrives at 1am on Sunday then heads for Ruarwe and Usiya at 7am.

Likoma Island

Seventeen-square-kilometre Likoma is a dream of turquoise waters and desert island calm that peels away crow's feet with every minute passed here. The island is peppered with sublime crescent bays and outstanding views out to Mozambique. About 6000 people make their home here, and the island's relative isolation from the rest of Malawi has allowed the locals to maintain their reserved culture, shaped partly by the religious legacy of missionaries, but also by the lack of any transient population. It's absolutely worth the effort to get here.

⊙ Sights

Down on the lakeshore is a beach where local boats come and go, and the people wash and sell fish. The *Ilala* stops at another beach about 1km to the south.

Cathedral of St Peter CHURCH
In Chipyela, this Anglican cathedral built by missionaries between 1903 and 1905 should not be missed; its stained-glass windows, crumbling masonry and sheer scale are a testament to the zeal of its creators' religious conviction. You can climb the tower for spectacular views and you're welcome to join in the vibrant Sunday morning service.

Marketplace MARKET
Near the cathedral, the marketplace contains a few shops and stalls.

ACTIVITIES

Swimming is best enjoyed on the long stretches of beach here. Thanks to the local tropical fish the **snorkelling** is excellent. Kaya Mawa arranges three-day open water PADI **scuba-diving** courses (US$315), while the island's compact size is perfect for **walking** or **mountain biking** – you can bring bikes across on the ferry or hire them from Mango Drift for US$10 per day.

🛏 Sleeping & Eating

Mango Drift HOSTEL $$
(☎09 99746122; www.mangodrift.com; campsite per person US$6, dm US$8, chalets without

> ### ❶ IMMIGRATION OFFICE: GETTING TO MOZAMBIQUE
>
> The only Mozambique border crossing on the east where you can get a visa on arrival is Cóbuè, a short ride over the water from Likoma Island. Local boats will take you there for US$3 and you pay US$30 for a visa. By the cathedral in the market there's an immigration office to fill in your exit pass. Right beside the office are the boatmen.

bathroom US$30, double chalets US$70; @ 🛜) Mango has gorgeous stone chalets boasting boutique genes – hibiscus petals scattered on snow-white linen, painted wicker sofas, and sundowner verandahs. Tempted?

The shared toilets and shower block are immaculate. Double chalets are a few yards up the hill. Chill out in the bar, grab a book from the exchange, scuba dive or just flop on the golden beach shaded by mango trees.

TOP CHOICE **Kaya Mawa** BOUTIQUE HOTEL $$$
(📞09 99318359; www.kayamawa.com; per person chalets with full board US$375-435; 🌐@🛜) Kaya Mawa, sitting on a beach lapped by turquoise water, has remarkable cliffside chalets cleverly moulded around the landscape. They're so beautiful you'll never want to leave – think plunge baths, the gentle lap of waves and tinkle of a waiter quietly appearing with a bottle of chilled champagne at your verandah.

Dinner is set by candlelight on the beach, staff are almost elfin in their diplomacy and discretion, while the food is sublime. It's only when you leave Kaya Mawa you truly appreciate how special it is.

Hunger Clinic MALAWIAN $
(mains MK750; ⏱6am-6pm; 🍴) Right by the water near the Immigration Office, this simple cafe serves up *nshima* with vegetables, and great fish and chips.

ⓘ Getting There & Away

Ulendo Airlink (p162) provides charter flights to Likoma. A one-way flight from Lilongwe to Likoma ranges from US$210 to US$320 per person depending on passenger numbers.

The *Ilala* ferry stops at Likoma Island twice a week, usually for three to four hours. Heading south, the ferry then sails to Metangula on the Mozambique mainland. Local dhows also sail to Cóbuè for MK500 and for a little extra can pick you up or drop you off from Mango Drift on Likoma.

Chizumulu Island

Stretches of azure water and white rocky outcrops give Chizumulu island a Mediterranean flavour, while the backdrop of dry scrub is positively antipodean.

Chill out at **Wakwenda Retreat** (📞09 99348415; campsite per person US$3.50, dm US$6, r from US$14), smack bang on a postcardperfect beach. The sizeable bar, constructed around a massive, hollow baobab tree, is perfect for sundowners, while the shaded lounge area is often the focus of lazy activities such as barbecues. The restaurant (meals from MK500) serves food communal style, so it's easy to get to know the other guests.

The *Ilala* ferry stops right outside. There are daily dhow ferries between Likoma and Chizumulu costing around MK500 per person. The trip can take anything from one to three hours depending on the weather; it's an extremely choppy ride when the wind is blowing, and potentially dangerous if a storm comes up.

CENTRAL MALAWI

Central Malawi is famed for its dazzling white beaches, like the backpacker magnet, Cape Maclear, and for its desert islands like Mumbo and Domwe – perfect places to flop in a hammock, or kayak and snorkel among brilliantly coloured chiclid fish. Just a short drive up from the lake is the Viphya Plateau, a haunting wilderness of mountains, grasslands and mist-shrouded pines. And nearby Nkhotakota Wildlife Reserve now has fine lodges, improved access and increased wildlife stocks.

Viphya Plateau

The Viphya Plateau forms the spine of central and northern Malawi, snaking a cool path past flat scrubland and sunny beaches. Tightly knit forests give way to gentle valleys and rivers, and huge granite domes rise softly from the earth like sleeping beasts. Indigenous woodland bristles with birds and wildflowers, and antelope and monkeys are often spotted darting through the trees.

Activity junkies should head for Luwawa Forest Lodge, where activities organised on the plateau include rock climbing and mountain biking.

🛏 Sleeping

TOP CHOICE **Luwawa Forest Lodge** LODGE $$
(📞01-342333, 01-991106; www.luwawaforestlodge.com; campsite per person US$7, tw/tr without bathroom per person US$40, chalets with half board/full board per person US$68/75, cottages per night US$160; 🅿@🛜) Homely Luwawa sits in a clearing of pine trees and boasts gorgeous

Central Malawi

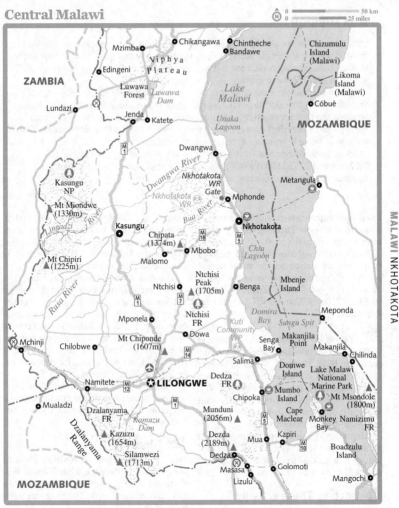

views of the forests and nearby lake. There are four chalets – with bunk beds, en suites, self-catering facilities and swallow-you-up four-posters – which are perfect for families (sleep up to six), as well as three new cottages and a well-shaded camping area.

Activities include mountain biking with a guide (US$10 per person), abseiling and rock climbing (US$40 per person, half day) with an experienced instructor, and three-day treks to Lake Malawi. With its cosy lounge and the warm service of its staff and owner, George, Luwawa is a rare treat.

There's no public transport to this lodge, so you'll have to ask the bus driver to drop you at the Luwawa turn-off and either walk from the main road or call the lodge for a pick-up (US$10 per group). The lodge lies 10km east of the main M1 road between Kasungu and Mzuzu and is well signposted.

Nkhotakota

Unassuming Nkhotakota played a sinister part in Malawi's history during the 1800s as the town was home to a huge slave market.

MUA MISSION

Sitting on a hill aglow with flame trees, Mua is a rare treat; its red-brick terracotta-tiled mission seemingly transplanted from Tuscany, its church strangely beautiful. Mua Mission houses a school, hospital and the fascinating **Kungoni Centre of Culture and Art** (📞01-262706; www.kungoni.org; ⏲7.30am-4pm Mon-Sat).

The main attraction is the **Chamare Museum** (admission MK900; ⏲7.30am-4pm Mon-Sat), which concentrates on the region's three main cultural groups (Chewa, Ngoni and Yao) and their approach to traditional beliefs. A guide is included in the entrance fee (tour takes one hour). Also check out the **Kungoni Art Gallery** (admission MK1500) and the **Carving Workshop**, both close by the museum.

For accommodation head to the magical eyrie of **Namalikhate Hostel** (📞01-262706; s/d MK9750/13,000; 🅿@🛜), which sits picturesquely over a gorge and has sumptuously appointed cabanas and friendly staff.

From here captives were shipped annually across the lake to Tanzania, before being forced to march to the coast.

Buses and minibuses stop and pick up from the fuel station on the main north–south road. You can get online at the **Nkhotakota Internet Café** (📞01-292284; per min MK300; ⏲7.30am-4.30pm Mon-Fri, 8am-6pm Sat, 2-6pm Sun).

Stima Inn HOTEL $$
(📞09 99260005; www.sanibeachresort.com; dm per person US$8, standard r US$40-55, superior r US$75; 🅿@🛜) Within staggering distance of the *Ilala* ferry, this cream building with art deco aspirations is quirky; adorned with nautical motifs it sits in isolation looking out over sand-flats to the nearby lake.

Atmospheric, houseproud rooms come in all shapes and sizes. The central courtyard lounge is a good place to feast on intrepid dishes like crocodile tail in honey.

❶ Getting There & Away

You can get to Nkhotakota by the *Ilala* ferry. AXA buses go to and from Lilongwe (MK2000, three hours). The bus will drop you off roughly outside Nkhotakota's Shell petrol station, which is on the highway. Minibuses also leave from here and go to Salima (MK1100, two hours) and Nkhata Bay (MK1500, four to five hours).

Nkhotakota Wildlife Reserve

Nkhotakota Wildlife Reserve – 1800 sq km of dense *miombo* (moist woodland) forests, bush and a couple of navigable roads – is back on the map thanks to Bua River Lodge and Tongole Wilderness Lodge. Indeed thanks to increased funding, successful wildlife conservation programs and increased road networks, the reserve is coming back into its own.

The Bua River is choking on crocs, and come evening there's a very good chance you will see elephants crossing the river at either lodge. There are also roan and sable antelope here, buffaloes, baboons, waterbucks and leopards. Several large rivers cross the reserve, so the birdlife is varied, with more than 200 species. The Bua River is also excellent for salmon fishing.

Tongole Wilderness Lodge has just opened its own airstrip for private charters. For more information contact Ulendo Airlink (p162).

🛌 Sleeping

Bua River Lodge sits conveniently close to the entrance of the park, while Tongole Wilderness Lodge is a further hour's drive into the heart of the reserve. The roads are navigable with a normal car.

Tongole Wilderness Lodge LODGE $$$
(📞09 91337681, 08 81433168; www.tongole.com; adult/child per night US$345/172; 🅿@🛜) The lodge sits above the Bua River and a well-worn elephant crossing. Its thatched, church-high lodge is stunning, as are its chalets. Crafted from local materials, they include plunge baths, rain showers and wrought iron doors that fully immerse you in the widescreen views.

Activities (all included) on offer are fishing, trekking and kayaking past crocs. Style meets adrenalin.

Bua River Lodge LODGE $$$

(☎08 8803981, 09 95476887; island/riverside tents US$115/95, basic rooms half-board US$17, hillside rooms US$75; P@�) On the Bua River, this cosy lodge boasts safari tents kitted out with alfresco rain showers, African chic decor and thick quilts. The multilevel central lodge is a thatched, open-sided affair. Its excellent restaurant serves up tenderised steaks by candlelight (a three-course dinner is included in the price). It's probable you'll see crocs, lots of them, on the sandbars next to the river. Heavenly.

❶ Getting There & Away

The turn-off to Bua is 10km north of Nkhotakota town, followed by a rough dirt track. You will need your own wheels to get here. AXA buses headed from Mzuzu can drop you off at the park gate (ask to be dropped at the Lozi Trading centre) then call John at Bua River Lodge for a lift (MK2000 per person). To walk to to Bua River Lodge it's about 10km.

Senga Bay

Sitting at the eastern end of a broad peninsula that juts into the lake, by night Senga Bay thrums with music; by day fishing nets dry on the beach, boats are propped up photogenically on the shore and backstreets are vivid with chirruping kids. There are a couple of pretty beaches, nice hotels and great budget digs.

◉ Sights & Activities

Windsurf, snorkel, take a boat ride or learn to dive. You can also take a trip out to nearby Lizard Island to see its population of giant monitor lizards and its cormorant colony. Many lodges and local guides can arrange this for about US$60.

Alternatively, head for the hippo pools about half an hour's walk up the lakeshore beyond Steps Campsite (also reached by descending the north side of the Senga Hills). Again, a local guide is recommended.

If you're looking for souvenirs, there's a strip of craft stalls a few kilometres out of Senga Bay on the Salima road.

About 10km south of Senga Bay is Stewart Grant's Tropical Fish Farm (☎01-263165; fax 01-263165), which breeds and exports cichlids. You can take a half-hour tour of the farm.

⌂ Sleeping

Steps Campsite CAMPGROUND $

(campsite per person MK1500; P@�) Perfectly situated by the giant boulders that bookend its golden stretch of beach, this campsite has loads of shaded pitches, hot showers, individual power points and round-the-clock security; there's also a beach bar that leaps from a Martini ad, a volleyball court, and a spotless ablutions block.

TOP CHOICE Cool Runnings GUESTHOUSE, CAMPGROUND $$

(☎09 99915173, 01-263398; coolrunnings@malawi.net; campsite per person US$5, tent hire US$7, dm US$10, fixed trailer per person US$12, r US$35; P@�) Run by warm host Sam, this is excellent value beachside accommodation. Camp or sleep in their fixed trailer in the main building, or in a comfortable dorm.

There's also an inviting bar and tin-roofed cafe featuring fresh fish and chicken. Boat charters can be arranged as well as car hire. Cool Runnings is involved in community development programs; it's set up a volunteer police force, built a school and a library, and runs a football team!

TOP CHOICE Safari Beach Lodge LODGE $$$

(☎09 99365494, 01-263143; www.safaribeachlodge.net; s/d US$110/140, children under 12 US$60; P❋@�) Safari's magical hillside gardens cascade in a riot of bougainvillea down to the beach. There are four rooms in the lodge, five stone chalets and two family-sized chalets (hut 7 is the best).

The rooms themselves are delightful; with colourful-patterned bedspreads, choice art, fridges, air-con and driftwood bureaus and DSTV. You'll also find free kayaks and snorkels. The lodge is 1km off the main road; turn off just before the gates to the Sunbird Livingstonia Beach Hotel.

Sunbird Livingstonia Beach Hotel HOTEL $$$

(☎01-263444, 01-263222; www.sunbirdmalawi.com; standard s/d from US$100/130, deluxe US$145/175; P❋@�) With its columned entrance and manicured lawns, this spearmint-white 1920s pile reeks of old world charm. Take dinner on the alfresco terrace, plunge in the spotless pool, lounge on the sugar-fine-sand beach or head for a massage. Rooms vary in size but are traditional with international standard furnishings.

Eating & Drinking

Red Zebra Cafe MALAWIAN $
(mains MK1000; ⏲7am-10.30pm; P ✓) In a garden off the main road, this zesty Caribbean-infused restaurant covers the bases with grilled chops, steak, fruit salads, ice cream and cupcakes. Eat within its colourful interior or alfresco.

Information

Dangers & Annoyances

Take great care when swimming near the large rocks at the end of the beach at Steps Campsite; there's a surprisingly strong undertow. Some of the beaches here are flat and reedy – perfect conditions for schistosomiasis (bilharzia; p721), so get advice from your hotel or lodge to see if it's safe. Finally, never swim in the lake at dusk (from then on and through the night) as this is when crocs and hippos are at large;

Getting There & Away

First get to Salima. From there, local *matolas* run to Senga Bay (MK250), dropping you in the main street. If you want a lift all the way to Steps Campsite, negotiate an extra fee with the driver. If you're travelling to/from Cape Maclear, consider chartering a boat; it's not too expensive (around US$250-300) if you get a group together. Ask at Cool Runnings.

Monkey Bay

Sultry-paced Monkey Bay is enchanting; languid locals, a gas station, a few shops and a couple of magic beachside traveller joints where you can snorkel or flop in the sun. Conveniently the *Ilala* ferry stops at Monkey Bay's quaint harbour. There's a Peoples Supermarket nearby and one ATM that sometimes works.

Sleeping

Mufasa Rustic Camp CAMPGROUND, CABANAS $
(☎09 93080057; campsite per person MK850, dm MK2250, s/d MK5250/6750; P) Mufasa has its own beach and is only 400m from the main harbour. Rooms are basic bamboo affairs, but the bar is much more appealing; with lounging cushions, wicker swing chairs and a relaxed vibe.

The owners can arrange snorkel and boat trips for around MK3500. There's also a rowing boat you can use (MK2500). Be careful though of swimming over to the reedy inlet next to the camp's main beach – a traveller was recently mauled by a croc there.

Venice Beach Backpackers HOSTEL $
(☎08 4416541; campsite per person MK800, dm MK2000, r MK4000; P @ ☎) This thatched building has a selection of beach-facing dorms and doubles as well as a top-floor viewing deck with plenty of hammocks. Kayak (MK5000), dive, spear fish or find your rhythm with drumming classes and a reggae-fuelled bar. About 1.5km from the main road.

Getting There & Away

From Lilongwe, AXA buses go to Monkey Bay, usually via Mua and the southern lakeshore (MK1800, four hours). From Lilongwe you're probably better off going by minibus to Salima (MK1500, one hour), from where you might find a minibus or *matola* going direct to Monkey Bay.

It's much easier to reach Monkey Bay from Blantyre on the ordinary bus that travels via Liwonde and Mangochi (MK2500, five to six hours). A quicker option is to go by minibus (MK2500, four to five hours), but you'll need to leave early in the morning and you might have to change at Mangochi. Many travellers also use the *Ilala* ferry to travel up and down the country to or from Monkey Bay.

From Monkey Bay, a *matola* ride to Cape Maclear should cost MK600. Although not far away, it can take forever to get there and you could have to wait hours for a *matola* departure. To Mangochi, a minibus costs around MK600 and the AXA bus MK550.

Cape Maclear

A long stretch of powder-fine sand bookended by mountains and lapped by dazzling water, Cape Maclear is studded by nearby islands and puttering, crayon-coloured boats. On shore women wash clothes while fishermen spread out nets to dry. And there's bags of things to do, be it kayaking, sailing, snorkelling, walking or diving.

There are plenty of sleeping options here to keep all sorts happy – from reed huts and tents on the beach to upmarket lodges serving fine French cuisine.

Sights

Much of the area around Cape Maclear, including several offshore islands, is part of **Lake Malawi National Park** (per person/car US$5/1), designated a Unesco World Heritage Site back in 1986. The **park headquarters** (⏲7.30am-noon & 1-5pm Mon-Sat, 10am-noon & 1-4pm Sun) are just inside the gate, where

Cape Maclear

◎ Sights
1 Missionary Graves A5

✦ Activities, Courses & Tours
2 Billy Riordan Memorial Trust A5
3 Danforth Yachting A5
4 Frogman Scuba...................................A5
5 Kayak Africa A5
6 Panda Garden.....................................A5

▭ Sleeping
  Danforth Yachting ....(see 3)
7 Domwe Island Adventure Camp......... A1
8 Fat Monkeys B4
9 Gecko Lounge B5
10 Mgoza Lodge......................................B5

◈ Eating
11 Boma/Hiccups Pub.............................B5
  Mgoza Restaurant ....(see 10)
12 Thomas's Grocery Restaurant
   and Bar..A5

ⓘ Information
13 Billy Riordan Clinic............................A5

to a set price list and circulate at different resorts along the beach on a weekly basis.

Water Sports

Guides can organise half- and full-day **snorkelling** trips to Thumbi Island West (US$45 per person including food, snorkel hire, park fees and fish-eagle feeding). If you prefer to go snorkelling on your own, many places rent gear for about US$10; Otter Point, less than 1km beyond the Golden Sands holiday resort, is a small rocky peninsula vivid with fish. Several of the lodges rent out kayaks.

Frogman Scuba   DIVING
(☏09 99952488, 01-599156; casual dives $US40, PADI 4-day open water course US$375)

Kayak Africa   KAYAK
(☏09 99942661; www.kayakafrica.co.za) This eco tour operator organises kayaking to their beautiful camps on Domwe and Mumbo Islands, or between the two.

Danforth Yachting   SAILING, DIVING
(☏09 99960770, 09 99960077; www.danforth yachting.com; sunset cruise per person US$50) Yet another option is sailing on a yacht with Danforth Yachting. A sunset cruise around Cape Maclear aboard the *Mufasa* requires a minimum of six people; a full-day

you'll also find a visitor centre that doubles as a small museum and aquarium.

Just before the entrance gate to the park a path leads towards a group of **missionary graves**, marking the last resting place of the missionaries who attempted to establish the first Livingstonia Mission here in 1875.

🏃 Activities

The **Cape Maclear Tour Guide Association** is a membership organisation for local guides, ensuring business is fairly distributed among them. All registered guides work

island-hopping cruise costs US$900 per boat, including lunch. Danforth also organises diving trips.

Hiking

There's a range of hikes and walks in the hills, but it's better to hire a guide. The national park's guide rate is US$15 per person for a full-day trip. There are also hippo trips (US$45 per person, minimum three people).

The main path starts by the missionary graves and leads up through woodland to a col below Nkhunguni Peak, the highest on the Nankumba Peninsula, with great views over Cape Maclear, the lake and surrounding islands. It's six hours' return to the summit; plenty of water and a good sun hat are essential.

Volunteering

Billy Riordan Memorial Trust
VOLUNTEERING
(www.billysmalawiproject.org) The inspiring Billy Riordan Memorial Trust always needs medical volunteers (doctors, nurses, lab technicians, dentists) for their invaluable work in the area. It prefers skilled volunteers who can commit for a minimum of four months.

Panda Garden
VOLUNTEERING
(☑09 99140905; www.heedmalawi.net; Main St, Chembe village) Help out with art classes (artists very welcome), gardening and bilharzia research on the lake, identifying host-carrying snail areas (scuba divers welcome).

🛏 Sleeping

Mgoza Lodge
LODGE $$
(☑09 95632105; www.mgozalodge.com; dm MK1500, chalets US$55; P@🛜) More low-key than nearby Gecko, Mgoza has charming brick-and-thatch cottages spaced around a leafy garden. Rooms are cool and split-level with wood-panel baths, huge beds, and billowing step-in mozzie nets. There's also an inviting restaurant with an upstairs viewing deck, perfect for sundowners.

Fat Monkeys
GUESTHOUSE $$
(☑09 99948501; campsite per person US$3, vehicle US$6, dm US$10, s/d US$55/75; P@🛜) Cape Mac's most popular mid-scale place to eat, Monkeys has tasty salads, pizza and excellent *chambo*. The dorms and rooms are clean and cool with fans, while pitches are shaded. Come evening the bar is lively.

TOP CHOICE Mumbo Camp
BUSH CAMP $$$
(☑09 99942661, in South Africa 0027-21-783 1955; www.kayakafrica.co.za; adult/child with full board US$290/145, family tent with full board US$725) On Mumbo Island, this terrific eco boutique campsite has seven walk-in tents on wooden platforms, tucked beneath trees and above rocks, with spacious decks and astounding views. The cost also includes snorkel gear and park fees. Indulge in that castaway feeling on hammocks and loungers, or kayak, snorkel or take a scuba course with Frogman Scuba. A maximum of 14 people can stay here. You can reach the island by kayak leaving from Kayak Africa (camp staff will bring along your stuff separately), or by boat. Impossibly romantic.

TOP CHOICE Danforth Yachting
LODGE $$$
(☑09 99960770, 09 99960077; www.danforthyachting.com; per person with full board US$190; P✳❄🛜) Danforth has stylish, mint-fresh rooms set in lush gardens. There's also a topnotch restaurant. Mainly an active crowd stay here to take advantage of the various yachting options on offer. The rooms themselves are sumptuous, with nautical-blue linen contrasting with white walls.

Gecko Lounge
LODGE $$$
(☑09 99787322, 01-599188; www.geckolounge.net; r s/d US$80/90, chalet d/tr US$110/120; P@🛜) Gecko sports chalets with kitchenettes and self-catering facilities. There are bunk beds too for large families; fridges, fans, cool tile floors and mozzie nets, as well as plenty of hammocks and swing chairs outside. The restaurant serves tasty pizza and burgers, as well as being the perfect sundowner spot. You can also rent kayaks and snorkel gear.

Domwe Island Adventure Camp
BUSH CAMP $$$
(☑in South Africa 0027-21-783 1955; www.kayakafrica.co.za; camp tents US$25, safari tents s/d US$75/120) Based on nearby Domwe Island, this is the smaller and more rustic of Kayak Africa's two lodges. It runs on solar power and is romantically lit by paraffin lamps. It's self-catering, with furnished safari tents, fridges, shared ecoshowers and toilets. It also has a bar and a beautiful staggered dining area, open to the elements and set among boulders. It costs US$30 each way to be dropped off/picked up at the

island. Kayaks cost US$30 to hire, snorkel gear US$15.

✗ Eating & Drinking

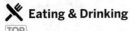 Mgoza Restaurant INTERNATIONAL $
(mains MK1300; ▣🛜🖋) Mgoza has shaded open-sided shelters in a garden facing the lake, or you can eat in the friendly bar.

The restaurant serves up excellent full English breakfasts, healthy fruit smoothies and perhaps the best homemade hamburgers in Malawi.

Thomas's Grocery Restaurant and Bar MALAWIAN $
(dishes from MK1000) This simple joint sells toiletries, and dishes up chicken curry, chipatis, *chambo*, catfish and chips.

Boma/Hiccups Pub INTERNATIONAL, BAR $$
(dishes MK1500; ⊘noon-late; ✳🛜🖋) This is a great place for dinner and a cool Carlsberg 'green'; feast on salads, Hungarian goulash, veggie lasagne, steak and chips or *chambo*. A projector screens live sport. Stylish.

ℹ Information

The **Billy Riordan Clinic** (consultations child/adult US$40/80; ⊘minor complaints 8am-noon & 2-4pm Mon-Fri, emergency also 10am-noon & 3-4pm Sat & Sun) offers bilharzia medicine on weekdays from 8am to noon and 2pm to 4pm; on weekends it's 10am to noon and 2pm to 3pm.

Skyband has come to Cape Maclear so most of the lodges have wi-fi and many will lend you a laptop to check your emails. You can also buy Airtel phone vouchers at the more upscale lodges.

Dangers & Annoyances
Travellers sometimes receive hassle from beach boys selling jewellery – a firm 'No' should suffice.

ℹ Getting There & Away

By public transport, first get to Monkey Bay, from where a *matola* should cost MK400. If you're driving from Mangochi, the dirt road to Cape Maclear (signposted) turns west off the main road, about 5km before Monkey Bay.

From Cape Maclear, if you're heading for Senga Bay, ask around about chartering a boat. It will cost around US$300, but it's not bad when split between four to six people and much better than the long, hard bus ride. *Matolas* leave for Monkey Bay from around 6am, on a fill-up-and-go basis, and take about an hour. From there you can get onward transport.

SOUTHERN MALAWI

Southern Malawi is home to the country's commercial capital and an incredibly diverse landscape. To its eastern border with Mozambique, and flanked by tea plantations, is mist-shrouded Mt Mulanje. A short way north is the Zomba Plateau, a stunning highland area, while safari lovers can head to two of the country's best parks: Liwonde, where you can get up close to elephants, hippos, rhinos and crocodiles; and Majete, newly invigorated with reintroduced lions. Blantyre, the country's most dynamic city, is a pit stop for restaurants and bars.

Liwonde

Straddling the Shire River, the small town of Liwonde is one of the gateways to Liwonde National Park. The river divides the town in two; to the east you'll find the main bus stations, the market, supermarkets and the train station. West of the river are several tourist lodges.

🛏 Sleeping

Shire Camp GUESTHOUSE $
(☑09 99210532, 08 88909236; campsite per person MK500, chalet incl breakfast MK3500; ▣) Shire Camp has a colourful restaurant/bar and meticulously clean cabanas with tiled floors, fan and hot-water bathrooms. The campsite has a basic ablutions block. River Safaris (US$25 per person) deep into Liwonde National Park are run from here. The camp is on the river's north bank; take the dirt road on the right just before the National Bank.

Hippo View Lodge LODGE $$$
(☑01-542116/8, 01- 542255; www.hippoviewlodge.com; s/d MK14,500/23,000; ▣✳@🛜) Hippo has a volleyball court, decent restaurant, pretty gardens, DSTV and respectable river-view rooms. To reach it turn right down the dirt road just before the National Bank and look out for the two hippos flanking the road just before the entrance.

ℹ Getting There & Away

Lakeshore AXA buses pass by Liwonde on their way up to Mangochi but most drop off passengers at the turn-off and not in the town itself, so you're better off using a minibus. Minibuses run regularly from Zomba (MK250, 45 minutes), Limbe (MK500, three hours) and Mangochi (MK450, two hours). You can also get a minibus

Southern Malawi

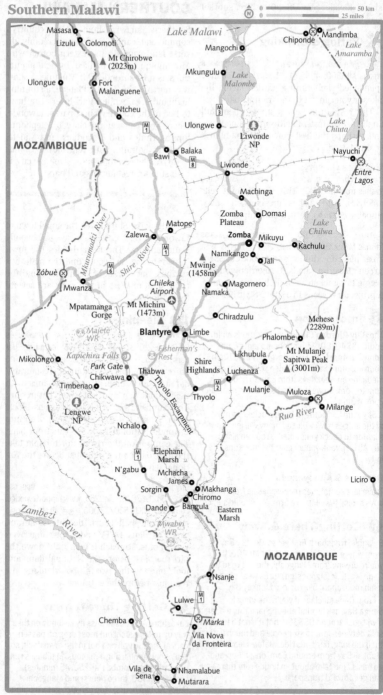

to the Mozambique border at Nayuchi (MK850, 2½ to three hours).

Liwonde National Park

Liwonde National Park has some 545 elephants, 1900 hippos, 500 water buffalo and 1800 crocs. It's a comparatively small reserve set in dry savannah and forest over 584 sq km, and you can walk, drive and putter along the Shire River to make the best of it. Excitingly, 2013 is the year lions are being reintroduced.

The Shire River dominates the park. Unsurprising then, that it's prime hippo- and croc-spotting territory (midday sun is the best time to see crocs sunning themselves, and late afternoon to see the hippos rising from the river). Waterbucks are also common, while sable and roan antelopes, zebras and elands populate the flood plains in the east. Night drives often reveal bushbabies, side-striped jackals and even spotted hyenas. The main event here though is the elephants, and you'll get very close indeed.

☂ Activities

Mvuu Camp   TOUR
(www.wilderness-safaris.com; dawn walks/night drives per person US$20/30, boat safari US$30 per person) Night drives take you past flashing crocs' eyes, ninja-quiet elephants and grunting hippos, finishing by a romantic sundowner by the Shire. Dawn walks are magical as you wander the savannah with a guide learning about trees and wildlife tracks (occasionally hiding behind a tree as a bull elphant appears!). Finally, you can take a boat safari, which will take you past braces of hippos and elephants close to the riverbank.

Bushman's Baobabs   TOUR
(www.bushmansbaobabs.com; tours $25 per person) Bushman's Baobabs offer a range of tours from game drives, village walks, boat trips and kayaking excursions.

Hippo View Lodge   TOUR
(☎01-542255; www.hippoviewlodge.com; 1hr boat tour per person US$90) Hippo View in Liwonde runs wildlife-viewing boat trips along the Shire River into Liwonde National Park.

☘ Njobvu Cultural Village   CULTURAL TOUR
(☎08 88623530, through Mvuu Camp reception 01-542135; www.njobvuvillage.com; r per person US$16, all inclusive US$50) Near the park's Makanga Gate, Njobvu offers visitors a rare opportunity to stay in a traditional Malawian village, sleeping in mud-brick huts. Take part in the villagers' daily lives, visiting traditional doctors, the village school and eating traditional food like *nshima*. All proceeds go directly to the community.

⛏ Sleeping

☘ Bushman's Baobabs   LODGE $$
(☎09 95453324, 08 88838159; www.bushmans baobabs.com; per person campsite/dm/tent US$7.50/15/45, per person tented chalet US$60; P@☏☂) Bushman's lies in the south of the park, and has comfortable rooms in the main house as well as a number of walk-in safari tents with bathrooms. There's also a pool and a large viewing deck. The nearby campsite has plenty of pitches, a dorm and a bar and restaurant.

TOP CHOICE Mvuu Camp   LODGE $$$
(☎01-771153, 01-771393; www.wilderness-safaris. com; campsite per person US$15, all-inclusive chalets per person US$260; @☏) Magical Mvuu sits in the realm of myriad hippos and crocs. The inviting camp has a scattering of chalets with cosy interiors; step-in mozzie nets, comfy beds, immaculate linen and stone-walled bathrooms. There's also a small campsite with spotless ablutions blocks and self-catering facilities.

Eat at the open-plan, thatched restaurant; dinner is communal and the food is hearty. Look out for the nightly firepit.

MALAWI LIWONDE NATIONAL PARK

LIWONDE RHINO SANCTUARY

The rhino sanctuary (www.wilderness-safaris.com; admission US$3) is a fenced-off area within the park developed for breeding rare black rhinos. Ten black rhinos currently live in the enclosure. Organised in conjunction with Wilderness Safaris at Mvuu Camp and Lodge, you can go on three-hour early morning treks with scouts (US$45) searching for the rhinos in the 48-sq-km reserve.

Mvuu Wilderness Lodge
LODGE **$$$**

(☎01-771153, 01-771393; all inclusive chalets per person US$445; ▣) This upscale lodge is full of romantic atmosphere. Sumptuous safari tents have huge beds with billowing mosquito nets and semi-alfresco roofs and bathrooms.

Private balconies overlook a waterhole where crocs sun themselves, and there's a small swimming pool, a restaurant serving excellent food and a raised lounge area overlooking the lagoon. Rates include all wildlife excursions.

❶ Getting There & Away

The main park gate is 6km east of Liwonde town. There's no public transport beyond here, though you might find a *matola* to take you as far as Bushman's Baobabs for around MK600. From the gate to Mvuu Camp is 28km along the park track (closed in the wet season); a 4WD vehicle is recommended for this route.

Another way in for vehicles is via the dirt road (open all year) from Ulongwe, a village between Liwonde town and Mangochi. This leads for 14km through local villages to the western boundary. A few kilometres inside the park is a car park and boat jetty, where a watchman hails a boat from Mvuu Camp to come and collect you. This service is free if you're staying at the camp.

Alternatively, if you make a booking in advance for Mvuu Camp through **Wilderness Safaris** (Map p114; ☎01-771393; www.wilderness-safaris.com; Kenyatta Rd, Bisnowaty Service Centre, Lilongwe), the camp can arrange a boat transfer from Liwonde town for US$80.

For those without wheels, the best option is to get any bus or minibus between Liwonde town and Mangochi and get off at Ulongwe (make sure you say this clearly, otherwise the driver will think you want to go to Lilongwe). In Ulongwe local boys wait by the bus stop and will sometimes take you by bicycle to the park (takes about an hour).

Zomba

With its chilly elevation, decrepit red-brick church, faded cricket club and old colonial buildings, Zomba feels like a ghostly lost chapter of British Empire. And the higher you head up to the Zomba Plateau, the more stunning and pristine the scenery becomes. The capital of Malawi from 1891 until the mid-1970s, Zomba town is home to wide, tree-lined streets, and has an easy charm. East of the main road is the commercial centre where you'll find a lively market, banks, bureaux de change, internet cafes and a couple of decent eateries.

🛌 Sleeping

TOP CHOICE Annie's Lodge
LODGE **$$**

(☎01-527002; Livingstone Rd; s/d from MK8250/9400; ▣▣@�) Set in the foothills, Annie's has appealing black-and-white brick chalets with green roofs, swallowed in palm trees and flowers.

Rooms are carpeted, clean and welcoming with DSTV, air-con and en suites. More expensive rooms are in a new wing and sit at the top of the plot with great views. There's a bar and restaurant too.

Hotel Masongola
HOTEL **$$**

(☎01-524688; hotelmasongola@clcom.net; Livingstone Rd; s/d from MK10,600/15,300; ▣�) Built in 1886, this tin-roofed, turreted old dame has bags of charm. Choose between a superior room with an aerial view or one of the brick-red chalets set in gardens of roses and geraniums. Rooms are cosy and clean.

🍴 Eating & Drinking

TOP CHOICE Tasty Bites
INTERNATIONAL **$**

(Kamuzu Hwy; dishes from MK1000; ⊙9.30am-8pm Mon-Sat, 10.30am-8pm Sun; ▣▣☞) This expat hangout is a sanctuary for pizzas, burgers, curries, *chambo* and chips, and various delicious desserts.

Dominos
INTERNATIONAL **$**

(Macleod Rd; mains MK1000; ⊙10am-midnight; ▣☞) In a leafy part of town, Domino's is fun for lunch, dinner or sundowners, thanks to its lushly gardened outside patio and excellent wood-fired pizzas, *chambo*, steak and fries.

❶ Getting There & Away

Zomba is on a main route between Lilongwe and Blantyre. The bus station is in the town centre, off Namiwawa Rd. AXA buses run to/from Zomba and Lilongwe (MK2000, five to six hours), Blantyre (MK750, 1½ to two hours), Liwonde (MK650, one hour) and Nkhata Bay (MK3950) via Mangochi (MK1000) and Mzuzu (MK4000).

Minibuses go every hour or so to Limbe (MK1000, one hour) and also head to Lilongwe (MK2000, four to five hours) Liwonde (MK700, 45 minutes) and Mangochi (MK800).

Zomba

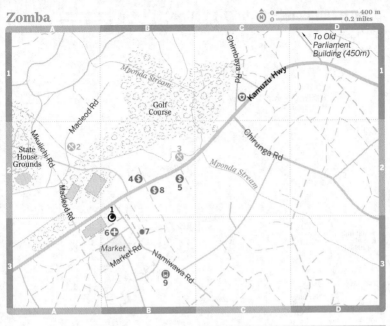

Zomba Plateau

Carpeted in pine and rising nearly 1800m (7000 feet), Zomba Plateau is beguilingly pretty. As you ascend the snaking road past wildflowers, locals heaving huge burdens of timber, and roadside strawberry vendors, the atmosphere is very much like alpine France; then a monkey jumps out, a pocket of blue mist envelops your car, and you realise you're in Africa. This highland paradise, crisscrossed by streams, lakes and tumbling waterfalls, is home to leopards, bushbucks and birds like mountain wagtail and Bertram's weaver.

The plateau can be covered on foot, by car (4WD on the backroads), and myriad winding trails that ring and cross the mountain. Horse riding with **Zomba Plateau Stables** (☎08 88714443, 08 88714445; maggieparsons@ iwayafrica.com; per person per hour US$35) is also an option.

🛏 Sleeping

Ku Chawe
Trout Farm　CAMPGROUND, BUNGALOWS $
(campsite per person MK600, chalets per person MK2000, 4-bed self-contained chalets MK7000; P) This idyllic campsite in the lee of a valley has barbecue facilities, and while the toilets

Zomba

◉ Sights
1 Mosque...B2

🍴 Eating
2 Dominos...A2
3 Tasty Bites..B2

ℹ Information
4 First Merchant Bank...........................B2
5 National Bank......................................B2
6 One Stop Community Drugstore........B3
7 Peoples..B3
8 Standard Bank....................................B2

ℹ Transport
9 Bus Station..B3

are onsite, showers are inconveniently located behind the cottages on the other side of the complex. Alternatively, experience the Camp Crystal–meets–Norman Bates chalet on the hill, with its creaky verandah (complete with rocking chair!), bunk beds and kitchenette.

TOP
CHOICE **Ku Chawe Inn**　HOTEL $$$
(☎01-773388, 01-514237; s/d US$125/160, hilltop rooms s/d US$185/210; ❀✱@?) Set in elevated botanical gardens dripping with

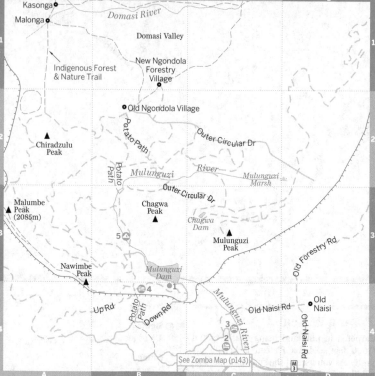

Zomba Plateau (Southern Section)

honeysuckle, Ku Chawe boasts amazing views of the distant plain. Inside, its red-brick exterior rooms are equally appealing, with outside verandahs, international decor and cosy stone fireplaces.

There are two restaurants dishing up sirloin steaks, pork chops and king-sized prawns. There's also bags to do, like mountain biking and trekking the plateau.

ⓘ Getting There & Away

A sealed road leads steeply up the escarpment from Zomba town to the top of the plateau (about 4km). After passing the Wico Sawmill,

a two-way sealed road, known as the Down Rd, veers east and continues for another 2km before turning into a dirt track. Up Rd is now open only to walkers.

Take a taxi (negotiable from around MK6000 to MK8000) all the way.

Blantyre & Limbe

Founded by Scottish missionaries in 1876, and named after the town in South Lanarkshire, Scotland, where explorer David Livingstone was born, with an estimated 728,000 citizens, Blantyre is Malawi's second-

HIKING ON THE ZOMBA PLATEAU

The southern half of the plateau is ideal for hiking. The network of tracks can be confusing though, so for more help with orientation there's a 3D map of the plateau in the Model Hut. There are also guides based here who charge around US$20 per day.

The Potato Path is the most popular hike at Zomba. It's a direct route from town all the way up to the plateau. To find the path, head up the main road from town leading up to the plateau and look for the signpost – it's at a sharp bend in the road some 2km from Zomba town. The path climbs steeply through woodland to reach the plateau near Ku Chawe Inn.

From near Ku Chawe Inn, the Potato Path then goes straight across the southern half of the plateau, sometimes using the park tracks, sometimes using narrow shortcuts, and leads eventually to Old Ngondola village, from where it descends quite steeply into the Domasi Valley.

Allow two to three hours for the ascent, and about 1½ hours coming down.

largest city. It's more appealing and cohesive than Lilongwe thanks to its compact size and hilly topography, and though there's not much to do, it makes for a useful springboard when exploring areas such as Mulanje and the Lower Shire Valley. Attached to the city's eastern side (as of 1956) is Limbe. Unlike Blantyre, which has seen a finessing of its restaurants and hotels, Limbe has fallen into disrepair.

Blantyre has the most diverse choice of restaurants in the country. Add to that tour operators, banks, internet cafes and other practicalities, and it makes for a pleasant stopover. The main focus of shops, cafes and banks is on Victoria Ave and adjoining Glyn Jones Rd.

◉ Sights & Activities

CCAP Church   CHURCH
(Map p148) Blantyre's most magnificent building is the red-brick CCAP Church, officially called St Michael & All Angels Church. Built in the late 19th century, it's an impressive feat of elaborate brickwork moulded into arches, buttresses, columns and towers, topped with a grand basilica dome.

National Museum   MUSEUM
(Map p146; Kasungu Cres; admission MK200; ⊙7.30am-5pm) Malawi's National Museum is a modest affair, but has a fascinating display on Gule Wamkulu – an important traditional dance of the Chewa people. The museum is midway between Blantyre and Limbe, 500m from the Chichiri Shopping Mall. Take a minibus headed for Limbe and ask to be let off at the museum.

Mandala House   HISTORIC BUILDING
(Map p148; ☎01-871932; Mackie Rd; ⊙8.30am-4.30pm Mon-Fri, to 1pm Sat) This is the oldest building standing in Malawi and was built back in 1882 as a home for the managers of the Mandala Trading Company. It's a quietly grand colonial house, encased in wraparound verandahs and set in lovely gardens. Inside the house is the eclectic shop, La Galleria, and the **Society of Malawi Library & Archive** (Map p148; Mandala House, Mackie Rd; ⊙9am-noon Mon-Fri & 6-7.30pm Thu), which contains journals, books and photographs dating as far back as the 19th century.

Blantyre Sports Club   HEALTH & FITNESS
(Map p148; ☎01-835095, 01-821172; cnr Victoria Ave & Independence Dr; daily membership MK2000) If you're feeling active for a game of squash, swim, a round of golf or a spot of tennis, head here, where there's also a great restaurant.

🛏 Sleeping

Kabula Lodge   LODGE $
(☎01-821216; www.kabulalodge.co.mw; off Michiru Rd, Kabula Hill; dm/s/d without bathroom, incl breakfast US$10/15/30, r incl breakfast US$40; @ 🛜) On the crest of a hill, Kabula enjoys scenic mountain views on both sides. The rooms have wrought iron beds, DSTV and fans. Dinner can be requested, alternatively there's a TV lounge and a self-catering kitchen.

Doogles   GUESTHOUSE, CAMPGROUND $$
(Map p148; ☎09 99186512, 01-621128; www.doogles lodge.com; Mulomba Pl; campsite MK1250, dm MK2000, chalets with/without bathroom US$35/25; P @ 🛜 ⓢ) Magnetising backpackers with its centerpiece pool, bar and lush

Greater Blantyre & Limbe

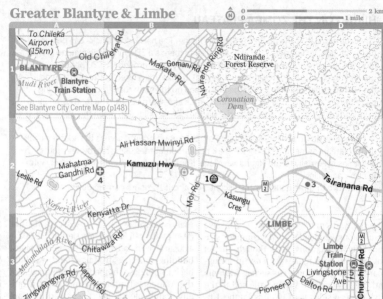

gardens, Doogles is a good place to stay and is right near the bus station. It has super fresh rooms, clean dorms and chalets. It also has bikes for hire, internet and wi-fi. Finally, you can pitch your tent here.

House Five　　　　　　　GUESTHOUSE **$$$**
(☎08 88901762; www.housefivemw.com; Kabula Hill Rd; s/d incl breakfast US$100/120; P🛜🏊) This hillside accommodation sits in a lush garden and brims with charm, from its outdoor bistro serving up pizza and pasta, to its friendly staff. Rooms excel with parquet floors and old world furniture. Romantic.

Protea Hotel Ryalls　　　　HOTEL **$$$**
(Map p148; ☎01-820955; ryalls@proteamalawi.com; 2 Hanover Ave; s/d US$215/245; P🐕❄@🛜🏊) With its wood-panelled lobby, elegant restaurant, pool, gym and bar, this remains the businessman's premier choice. Rooms deserve the four-star rating with stylish fittings, huge beds and sumptuous decor. There's also a Wilderness Safaris (p150) office here.

Sunbird Mount Soche Hotel　　HOTEL **$$$**
(Map p148; ☎01-820071; www.sunbirdmalawi.com; Glyn Jones Rd; s/d US$185/210; P🐕❄@🛜🏊) Lovely international-style rooms – somewhat on the small side – in the centre of town; think thick carpets, DSTV, biscuit-coloured walls, darkwood furniture, desk and air-con. There's an internet cafe here too, as well as Pablo's Lounge, a new sports bar. Quality.

Hostellerie de France　　GUESTHOUSE **$$$**
(☎01-669626; www.hostellerie-de-france.com; cnr Chilomoni Ring Rd & Kazuni Cl; standard d/tr/f from US$60/70/100; P@🛜🏊) You'll find everything here from standard rooms, to executive doubles, apartments and family suites,

and there are discounts for long stayers. The swimming pool (and attached Jacuzzi) looks out across the valley to Mt Ndirande and there's a restaurant with a sophisticated menu. Car rental is possible.

Malawi Sun Hotel HOTEL $$$
(Map p148; ☑01-824808; www.malawisunhotel. com; Robins Rd; s/d from US$126/160; P☼☀@ ☀☼) Plenty to tempt here with a swimming pool, flavoursome Deepend Grill, and rooms with DSTV, comfy beds and air-con. Choose from the main building or chalets. Also on-site, the Aamari restaurant serves everything from pasta and curries to beef stew and *nshima* (mains MK1000).

Pedro's Lodge LODGE $$$
(☑01-833430; www.pedroslodge.com; 9 Smythe Rd, Sunnyside; s/d US$75/105; P☀@☀☼) There are eight rooms in this large house set in leafy gardens. Rooms have homely interiors and tasteful fresh linen, DSTV and restful views. Best of all it's peaceful.

✗ Eating

TOP CHOICE **21 Grill on Hanover** STEAKHOUSE $
(Map p148; ☑01-820955; 2 Hanover Ave, Protea Hotel Ryalls; mains around MK3000; ☉noon-2pm & 6.30-10pm; P☀☀♪) Fit for a senator, this fine restaurant opened in '69 is showing no signs of fatigue. Sit at the granite-topped bar, or get sucked into a comfy Chesterfield before you tuck into a flame-grilled steak or the signature '21 spare ribs dipped in bourbon sauce'.

Mandala Cafe CAFE $
(Map p148; Mackie Rd, Mandala House; mains MK1200; ☉8.30am-4.30pm Mon-Fri, 8.30am-12.30pm Sat; P☼♪) Sit on a breezy stone terrace in the grounds of Mandala House, or inside at this chilled cafe within the old house itself. There are swings and a see-saw to keep the kids happy, and speedy wi-fi. Regulars love the Italian cuisine and freshly brewed coffee.

Hong Kong Restaurant CHINESE $
(Map p148; ☑01-820859; Robins Rd; mains MK1000; ☉noon-2pm & 6-10pm Tue-Sun; P☀☼) Hong Kong is an atmospheric pagoda-style building with a red wooden ceiling festooned in lanterns, and walls dancing with dragon murals. Food includes the usual dishes rendered with flair.

Bombay Palace INDIAN $
(Map p148; ☑08 88200200; Hanover Ave; mains MK2300; ☉noon-1.45pm Tue-Sun, 6.30-10pm daily;

☀☼) This classy Indian restaurant, with mushroom-grey walls and vivid artwork, spans chicken tikka massala to tandori, prawns and sizzling mutton dishes to plenty of veggie choices.

Food Court FAST FOOD $
(Map p148; Robins Rd, Malawi Sun Hotel; dishes around MK700; ☉10am-10pm) This breezy alfresco courtyard is surrounded by a fried chicken joint (Blue Savannah), an ice cream parlour (Scoops) and cafe (Shakes), where can get your favourite chocolate bar whizzed into a milkshake. It's a nice spot for kids and an alcohol-free zone.

Casa Mia INTERNATIONAL $$$
(☑01-915559; casamia@africa-online.net; Kabula Hill Rd; mains: MK2500-5000; P☀☼♪) Within Casa Mia's wine-stacked interior are antique Cinzano prints, white-cloth tables and an exclusive menu of dishes like grilled *chambo*, smoked salmon and risotto. Eat inside or outside.

☻ Drinking & Entertainment

Garden Terrace Bar BAR
(Map p148; Glyn Jones Rd, Sunbird Mount Soche Hotel) Catering to a more sophisticated market, its tranquil surrounds are appealing. At the same hotel, the Sportsman's Bar is favoured by local businessmen and other movers and shakers.

Cine City Cinema CINEMA
(Map p146; ☑01-912873; Kamuzu Hwy, Chichiri Shopping Mall; ☉closed Tue) Big-name films are shown at 5.30pm and 8.30pm daily with an extra 2.30pm session at the weekend. It's in the basement of the mall, underneath Game supermarket.

Warehouse Cultural Centre THEATRE
(Map p148; www.thewarehouse-malawi.net) This former depot consists of a theatre, cafe and bar, and is a staunch supporter of Malawian music, art, dance, theatre and literature. Expect poetry readings, comedy shows, screenings, writing workshops and live-music events.

🛍 Shopping

There are a number of low pressure craft stalls on Chilembwe Rd. Two kilometres out of town is the Chichiri Shopping Mall (Map p146; Kamuzu Hwy), which has bookshops, pharmacies, boutiques and large Shoprite and Game supermarkets.

MALAWI BLANTYRE & LIMBE

Blantyre City Centre

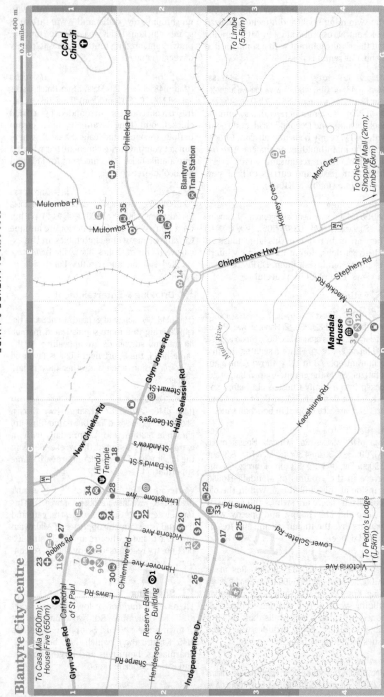

0.2 miles
400 m

To Casa Mia (600m);
House Five (650m)

CCAP
Church

Chileka Rd

To Limbe
(5.5km)

19

16

Mulomba Pl

5
35

Blantyre
Train Station

32

Moir Cres

Kidney Cres

31

To Chichiri
Shopping Mall (2km);
Limbe (6km)

Mulomba Pl

M 2

Chipembere Hwy

14

Stephen Rd

Mulombwe Rd

Glyn Jones Rd

Mudi River

Machie Rd

Mandala
House

3 15 12

New Chileka Rd

Stewart St

Haile Selassie Rd

St George's

St Andrew's

St David's St

Kaoshiung Rd

M 1

Hindu
Temple
18

34

28

Livingstone Ave

29

8

24

22

33

Browns Rd

To Pedro's Lodge
(1.5km)

23

Robins Rd

6
27

11

7

4
9

10

20

21

17

25

Victoria Ave

13

Lower Sclater Rd

Victoria Ave

Cathedral
of St Paul

Chilembwe Rd

30

Hanover Ave

26

1

Reserve Bank
Building

Laws Rd

Sharpe Rd

Henderson St

Independence Dr

Blantyre City Centre

MALAWI BLANTYRE & LIMBE

La Galleria ARTS & CRAFTS
(Map p148; Mackie Rd, Mandala House; ☺9am-5.30pm Mon-Sun) This eclectic gallery features vividly coloured, contemporary artwork by local artists, as well as sculptures, bedspreads, curtains and huge carved wooden thrones.

African Habitat HANDICRAFT
(Map p148; ☑01-873642; Kidney Cres, Uta Waleza Shopping Centre; ☺7.30am-4.30pm Mon-Fri, 8am-noon Sat) For high-end craft hunters, this is a good bet – it's a cavernous boutique crammed full of furniture, jewellery, sculpture, art, textiles and books.

Central Africana Bookshop BOOKSHOP
(Map p148; centralafricana@africa-online.net; Uta Waleza Centre, Kidney Cres) This old established bookshop is an excellent spot for picking up pictorials of the lake as souvenirs of your

stay. There are also charming old prints and maps.

ℹ Information

DANGERS & ANNOYANCES

It's not safe to walk around the city alone at night; always use a taxi after dark. Also watch your valuables when using the busy bus and minibus stations at Blantyre and Limbe. Bag snatching occasionally happens in daylight.

EMERGENCY

Emergency numbers are as follows:
Ambulance (☑998)
Fire (☑01-871999)
Police (☑01-823333)
Rapid Response Unit (☑997)

INTERNET ACCESS

There are plenty of internet cafes and wi-fi hotspots in Blantyre.

Tusa Internet Café (off Livingstone Ave; per min MK6) High-speed internet access.

MEDICAL SERVICES

One Stop Pharmacy (Map p148; Chilembwe Rd; ⏱8am-6pm Mon-Fri, 9am-2pm Sat) This well-stocked pharmacy sells bilharzia and malaria prophylactics.

Mwaiwathu Private Hospital (Map p148; ☎01-834989, 01-822999; Chileka Rd; ⏱24hr) Useful for private medical consultations. A consultation is US$10; all drugs and treatment are extra. East of the city.

Seventh Day Adventist Clinic (Map p148; ☎01-820399; Robins Rd) For medical or dental problems, this clinic charges US$10 for a doctor's consultation and US$10 for a malaria test.

Queen Elizabeth Central Hospital (Map p146; ☎01-874333; ⏱24hr) The malaria test centre at this government-run hospital, off Chipembere Hwy, charges US$10 for a malaria test. Ask for directions as the test centre is hard to find.

MONEY

There are a couple of branches of the National Bank of Malawi and one branch of the Standard Bank on Victoria Ave. They all change cash and travellers cheques and have 24-hour ATMs.

POST

Post Office (Glyn Jones Rd; ⏱7.30am-4.30pm Mon-Fri, 8am-10am Sat) Has poste restante and EMS express mail.

TOURIST INFORMATION

Immigration Office (Map p148; Victoria Ave, Government Complex) If you need to extend your visa, Blantyre has an immigration office.

Tourist Office (Map p148; ☎08 88304362; 2nd fl, Victoria Ave, Government Complex; ⏱7.30am-5pm Mon-Fri) This small office in the Department of Tourism stocks a few leaflets, sells maps of Malawi (MK500) and can offer limited advice.

TRAVEL AGENCIES

Jambo Africa (Map p148; ☎01-835356; www.jambo-africa.com; SS Rent A Car building, Glyn Jones Rd) This is a great one-stop shop for travel tickets, car hire and accommodation.

Responsible Safari Company (Map p148; ☎01-602407; www.responsiblesafaricompany.com) This eco conscious safari tour operator has three-day trips to Lake Malawi, three-day hiking adventures on Mt Mulanje and many more. Beyond this there are specialised tours of southern and northern Malawi.

Wilderness Safaris (Map p148; ☎01-820955; www.wilderness-safaris.com; 2 Hanover Ave, Protea Hotel Ryalls) The country's leading light in adventure travel can organise excursions for Liwonde National Park staying at magical Mvuu Camp (p141).

ⓘ Getting There & Away

AIR

Blantyre's Chileka Airport is about 15km north of the city centre.

Airline offices in Blantyre include the following:

Air Malawi (Map p148; ☎01-820811; Robins Rd; ⏱7.30am-4.30pm Mon-Fri, 8am-noon Sat)

British Airways (Map p148; ☎01-820811; www.britishairways.com; Livingstone Towers, Glyn Jones Rd)

KLM & Kenya Airways (Map p148; ☎01-824524; 2 Hanover Ave, Protea Hotel Ryalls)

South African Airways (Map p148; ☎01-820627; Livingstone Towers, Glyn Jones Rd)

BUS & MINIBUS

Blantyre's main bus station for long-distance buses is **Wenela Bus Station** (Map p148; Mulomba Pl), east of the centre. National Bus Company and AXA City Trouper buses run from here to Lilongwe (MK1800, four hours), Mzuzu (MK4000, nine to 10 hours), Monkey Bay (MK1800, five to six hours) via Zomba (MK750, 1½ to two hours) and Mangochi (MK1500, four to five hours), Mulanje (MK1000, 1½ hours) and Karonga (MK5500, 14 hours, change at Mzuzu).

AXA Executive coaches depart from the Automotive Centre, where you'll also find their ticket office, and call at the Chichiri Shopping Mall and the car park outside Blantyre Lodge (near the main bus station) before departing the city. They leave twice daily to Lilongwe (MK1800, four hours).

Long-distance minibuses go from **Limbe Bus Station** (Map p146); most leave on a fill-up-and-go basis. It's often quicker to get a local minibus to Limbe Bus Station and then a long-distance bus or 'half-bus' from there rather than wait for AXA or other bus services in Blantyre. Routes include Zomba (MK1000, one hour), Mulanje (MK1500, 1¼ hours), Mangochi (MK2000) and the border at Muloza (MK2200, 1½ hours).

Long distance **minibuses for Nchalo & Nsanje** (Map p148) to the Lower Shire leave from the **City Bus Station** (Map p148) near Victoria Ave in Blantyre, between 8am and 5pm; Nchalo (MK1000, two hours) and Nsanje (MK2000, four hours).

The car park next to Blantyre Lodge is the pick-up and drop-off point for long-distance bus companies headed for Jo'burg. **Intercape** (Map p148; ☎09 99403398) goes to Jo'burg at 8.30am on Tuesday, Thursday, Saturday and Sunday (MK27,000, 25 hours). **KJ Transways** (Map p148; ☎01-877738, 01-914017) leaves for Lilongwe every morning at 7.30am (MK2000).

❶ Getting Around

TO/FROM THE AIRPORT

A taxi from the airport to the city costs around MK8000. Frequent local buses between the City Bus Station and Chileka Township pass the airport gate. The fare is MK800.

BUS

Blantyre is a compact city, so it's unlikely you'll need to use public transport to get around, apart from the minibuses that shuttle along Chipembere Hwy between Wenela Bus Station and Limbe bus station.

TAXI

You can find private-hire taxis at the Sunbird Mount Soche Hotel or at the bus stations. A taxi across the city centre costs around MK800; between the centre and the main bus station costs from MK1000; and from Blantyre to Limbe costs around MK2000.

Mulanje

This lively small town sits in the shadow of Mt Mulanje at the centre of Malawi's tea industry – the surrounding hills are covered in vibrant green tea plantations. If coming from the direction of Blantyre, you'll first hit the Chitakale Trading Centre. Here you'll find the Mulanje Infocentre, a Peoples supermarket and two petrol stations. Continue on for 2km to reach Mulanje's centre, where you'll find the main bus station, hotels and banks.

Close to Likhubula on the main road, Mulanje Motel (☎01-466245; r with/without bathroom MK3000/2500; ℗) is a decent budget option, while Mulanje View (☎01-466348; s/d without bathroom MK1050/3000; ℗) is an old red-brick guesthouse with shared bathrooms, basic rooms and views of the towering massif. It's on the main road into town.

For more comfort, Kara O' Mula (☎01-466515; www.karaomula.com; s/d US$50/65; ℗@🛇🛇), hidden up a dirt road at the foot of the mountain, with its leafy grounds and wide terrace restaurant, is a perfect place to relax after a hard day's hiking.

❶ Getting There & Away

AXA buses go to/from Blantyre (MK850, 1½ hours), as do minibuses (MK700, 1¼ hours). If you're heading for the border with Mozambique, minibuses and *matolas* run to Muloza (MK400, 30 minutes).

Mt Mulanje

A huge hulk of twisted granite rising from the surrounding plains, Mt Mulanje towers over 3000m high. All over the mountain are dense green valleys, and rivers drop from sheer cliffs to form dazzling waterfalls. The locals call it the 'Island in the Sky', and on misty days it's easy to see why – the mountain is shrouded in a cotton-wool haze, and its highest peaks burst through the cloud to touch the heavens.

Mulanje measures about 30km from west to east and 25km from north to south, with an area of at least 600 sq km. The highest peak is Sapitwa (3001m), the highest point in Malawi and in all Southern Africa north of the Drakensberg. There are other peaks on the massif above 2500m, and you can reach most of the summits without technical climbing.

🛏 Sleeping

Below the Mountain

Thuchila Tourist Lodge   LODGE **$**
(☎08 81103353; thuchilatlodge@africa-online. net; r from MK6500, r with TV from MK7500; ℗@) Twenty kilometres past Likhubula on the

MALAWI MULANJE

HIKING ON MULANJE

There are about six main routes up and down Mulanje. The three main ascent routes go from Likhubula: the Chambe Plateau Path (also called the Skyline Path), the Chapaluka Path and the Lichenya Path. Other routes, more often used for the descent, are Thuchila Hut to Lukulezi Mission, Sombani Hut to Fort Lister Gap, and Minunu Hut to the Lujeri Tea Estate.

Once you're on the massif, a network of paths links the huts and peaks, and many different permutations are possible. Be warned that some of the routes are impassable or otherwise dangerous. The route from Madzeka Hut to Lujeri is very steep, for example, as are the Boma Path and the path from Lichenya to Nessa on the southwestern side of Mulanje. It takes anything from two to six hours to hike between one hut and the next.

Mt Mulanje

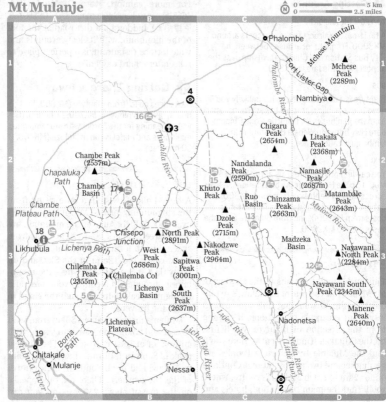

road to Phalombe, you reach a rocky turn-off to Thuchila. It has a decent restaurant and chalets. Convenient for walkers, the lodge is at the base of the path to Thuchila Hut.

Likhubula Forest Lodge　　　　LODGE $$
(☑01-467737, 09 99220560; campsite per person US$6, s/d without bathroom incl breakfast US$25/31, s/d incl breakfast US$31/37, whole lodge US$240; P@) This faded but lovely old colonial house has a homely kitchen, five clean rooms (two with bathroom) and a communal lounge with rocking chairs and a nightly fire crackling.

On the Mountain

Forestry Huts　　　　CHALET $
(campsite per adult/child MK400/200, huts per adult/child MK700/350) On Mulanje are eight forestry huts: Chambe, Chisepo, Lichenya, Thuchila, Chinzama, Minunu, Madzeka and Sombani. Each is equipped with benches, tables and open fires with plenty of wood.

Some have sleeping platforms (no mattresses); in others you just sleep on the floor. You provide your own food, cooking gear, candles, sleeping bag and stove (although you can cook on the fire). A caretaker chops wood, lights fires and brings water, for which a small tip should be paid.

Payments must be made at Likhubula Forestry Office – show your receipt to the hut caretaker.

CCAP Cottage　　　　CHALET $
(dm MK700) On the Lichenya Plateau, this cottage is similar to the forestry huts but there are utensils in the kitchen, plus mattresses and blankets. You can make reservations at the CCAP Mission in Likhubula.

France's Cottage　　　　CHALET $
(☑01-821269; www.mcm.org.mw; Mountain Club of Malawi; dm MK700) This two-bedroom cottage sleeps six and comes with a living room complete with cooking fireplace. It's

Mt Mulanje

in the Chambe basin near the Chambe hut. Ask at the Likhubula Forestry Office or contact the Mountain Club of Malawi for further information.

ℹ Information

Hiking on Mt Mulanje is controlled by the **Likhubula Forestry Office** (PO Box 50, Mulanje; ⊘7.30am-noon & 1-5pm), at the small village of Likhubula, about 15km north of Mulanje town. Entry fees are MK100 per person; vehicle entry costs MK200 and the forestry office car park is MK100 a day. The friendly and helpful staff can arrange guides and porters from an official list. You must register here and make reservations for the mountain huts (you can also call or write in advance). Camping is permitted near huts only and only when huts are full.

Also good for information is the **Mulanje Infocentre** (☑01-466506, 01-466466; infomulanje@malawi.net; Phalombe Rd, Chitakale Trading Centre). Set up to give travellers information on hiking, it carries a selection of books and maps, rents out sleeping bags (per day MK800), and tents (two-/eight-man per day MK1500/2500), and can also arrange mountain guides and porters. Tours to the nearby Dziwe la Nkhalamba waterfall (MK2500) and to the **Lujeri** (☑01-460243, 01-460266) and Mulli Brothers tea estates (per person US$25) are also arranged.

Stock up on supplies at Chitakale (which has shops, stalls and a small supermarket) or in Blantyre.

Dangers & Annoyances

Mulanje has notoriously unpredictable weather, and after rain streams can become impassable, and the mountain's granite surface slippery and dangerous when wet. Even during the dry season, it's not uncommon to get rain, cold winds and thick mists, which make it easy to get lost. Between May and August, periods of low cloud and drizzle (called *chiperone*) can last several days, and temperatures drop below freezing. *Always* carry a map, a compass and warm and waterproof clothing should the weather change.

ℹ Getting There & Away

There are bus services that run between Blantyre and Mulanje town. The dirt road to Likhubula turns off the main sealed Blantyre–Mulanje road at Chitakale, about 2km west of the centre of Mulanje town – follow the signpost to Phalombe. If you're coming from Blantyre on the bus, ask to be dropped at Chitakale. From here, irregular *matolas* run to Likhubula (MK300). If you're in a group, you can hire the whole *matola* to Likhubula for around MK2000. Alternatively, you can walk (10km, two to three hours); it's a pleasant hike with good views of the southwestern face of Mulanje on your right.

Lower Shire

This is a baking stretch of flat plains, swampland, sugar cane and maize fields, where the Shire River makes its final journey before plunging into the great Zambezi.

MAJETE WILDLIFE RESERVE

A rugged wilderness of hilly *miombo* woodland and savannah, Majete Wildlife Reserve (www.majete.org; adult/child MK2000/1000, vehicle MK200, maps MK100) hugs the west bank of the Shire River. Since it was taken over by African Parks (www.africanparks-conservation.com) in 2003, things have really been looking up for the once heavily poached park. A perimeter fence has been erected around the constantly patrolled reserve, while accommodation and roads have been massively upgraded. With Majete's lion reintroduction program, and the establishment of the sumptuous Mkulumadzi Lodge, this terrific reserve now makes for an exciting destination.

There are over 3000 animals in Majete (most translocated from other parks), including hyenas, sable, nyalas, bushbuck, impalas, serval, civets, zebras, antelopes, black rhinos, buffaloes, elephants, hippos and leopards.

◉ Sights & Activities

Mkulumadzi Lodge has a 7000-hectare slice of the 70,000-hectare park, and is bursting with animals. There are 250km of tracks in the park, and you'll need a 4WD to get around – especially during the wet season. The two main routes here are the Mkulumadzi Rd, which runs parallel to the Shire River and Namitsempha Rd, heading west from the entrance. Along Mkulumadzi Rd, just past the park entrance, are the grand Kapichira Falls; further on is Mvuu Spot, a small hide from where you can watch hippos.

If you'd rather your activities were organised there is plenty on offer, including bush walks (per person US$20), game drives (per person US$25), and night game drives (US$35). You can also opt to have a scout join you in your own car (US$15). Hiking Majete Hill is also possible (US$40), as are boat rides past hippos on the Shire River (US$20).

At the entrance to the park is a small open-air heritage centre and gift shop featuring a display of art and craftwork made in and around Majete by local people. There's also a little museum with displays on the region's heritage as well as information on local conservation projects.

🛏 Sleeping

Community Campsite CAMPGROUND $
(campsite s/d US$10/15, tent hire US$25; P) Enabling visitors on a budget to stay in the park, there are shady places to pitch up, or you can sleep on a stilted deck under the stars. There's also clean ablutions blocks and hot showers, as well as cooking facilities. You do need to bring your own food though.

Staying here helps the local community and the park itself. To get here turn left just before the heritage centre.

Mkulumadzi Lodge (TOP CHOICE) LODGE $$$
(☏01-794491; www.mkulumadzi.com; mid/high season per person all inclusive US$337/378; P❄@☏☎) This romantic lodge is reached by a suspension bridge, and has a high thatched ceiling strung with contemporary lights, driftwood art installations, and a kidney-shaped pool outside. Chalets look out onto the Shire River with step-in rain showers, widescreen views and sunken baths.

The camp offers morning walks to a hide close to the river (it's well situated for spotting black rhinos taking a dawn drink); or night drives to see hippos rising from the bank. All game drives are included, as are meals. If you're coming by bus, free transfers are available from Chikwawa village.

Thawale Camp BUSH CAMP $$$
(☏01-835356; www.african-parks.org; luxury tent per person with full board from US$170; P@) Set up around a floodlit waterhole, this bush camp is about 3km from Majete's main entrance. There are six double and twin tented chalets on raised wooden platforms, and each has its own verandah overlooking the waterhole.

There's a central lodge for meals, and a stone terrace with outdoor fire pit. The camp isn't fenced so expect regular visits from elephants, buffaloes and other creatures. All of the camp's revenue is ploughed straight back into conserving Majete.

❶ Getting There & Away

Majete lies west of the Shire River, some 70km south of Blantyre. Follow the road to Chikwawa from where signs will direct you to the reserve. By public transport, the nearest you can get is Chikwawa.

UNDERSTAND MALAWI

Malawi Today

The last couple of years in Malawi have been colourful to say the least, with the reign of its controversial president, Bingu wa Mutharika, coming to an end amid an economic fiasco. In April 2012, when Mutharika's heart gave out, fresh blood was pumped into the political system in the form of its new premier: women's rights activist and former vice president, Dr Joyce Banda.

As Banda came to power the country was in the grip of a fuel crisis, and nepotism and corruption in the ruling elite were rife. More worryingly, confidential files revealed by the *Sunday Times* in November 2012 proved that her predecessor had tried to have her killed to block her becoming prime minister (as vice president she would have automatically succeeded him in the event of his demise). A truck had been arranged to crash into her car; fortunately for Banda, she switched vehicles at the last moment.

Banda has some serious challenges on her hands: Malawi remains one of the world's poorest countries (with a per capita GNP of less than US$250), nearly half the population is chronically malnourished and life expectancy is only 53 years (owing in large part to the HIV/AIDS infection rate in Malawi, which is estimated to run at almost 12%). Increased immunisation and improved access to running water have helped reduce the infant mortality rate, though according to Unicef it still sits at about one in eight children under the age of five dying of preventable causes such as pneumonia, malaria, malnutrition and HIV-related illnesses.

Malawi is urbanising rapidly, and the rate of population growth in the cities is far higher than that in rural areas. The burgeoning population is straining natural resources, and schools and hospitals are overflowing. According to the CIA World Factbook, Malawi's population is around 16.3 million and is growing at an unsustainable 2.8% a year. Because the country is so small, this creates one of the highest population densities in Africa.

History

The precolonial history of Malawi is linked to the history of Southern Africa as a whole.

Early Migrations

Since the first millennium the Bantu people migrated from Central Africa into the area now occupied by Malawi. Migration to the area stepped up with the arrival of the Tumbuka and Phoka groups, who settled around the highlands of Nyika and Viphya during the 17th century, and the Maravi people (from whom the modern-day Chewa people are descended), who established a large and powerful kingdom in the south.

The early 19th century brought with it two more significant migrations. The Yao invaded southern Malawi from western Mozambique, displacing the Maravi, while groups of Zulu migrated northward to settle in central and northern Malawi (where they became known as the Ngoni).

The Rise of Slavery

Slavery, and a slave trade, had existed in Africa for many centuries, but in the early 19th century demand from outside Africa increased considerably. Swahili-Arabs, who dominated the trade on the east coast of Africa, pushed into the interior, using powerful local tribes such as the Yao to raid and capture their unfortunate neighbours. Several trading centres were established in Malawi, including Karonga and Nkhotakota, towns that still bear a strong Swahili-Arab influence today.

Livingstone & the First Missionaries

The first Europeans to arrive in Malawi were Portuguese explorers who reached the interior from Mozambique in the early 1600s. Its most famous explorer though, was David Livingstone from Scotland, whose exploration heralded the arrival of Europeans in a way that was to change Malawi forever.

In 1858 when Livingstone found his route up the Zambezi blocked, he followed a major Zambezi tributary called the Shire into southern Malawi, reached Lake Malawi in September 1859, and provided fodder for thousands of tourist brochures to come by reportedly dubbing it the 'lake of stars'.

He died in Zambia in 1873. In 1875 a group from the Free Church of Scotland built a new mission at Cape Maclear, which they named Livingstonia, and in 1876 the Established Church of Scotland built a mission in the Shire Highlands, which they called Blantyre. Cape Maclear proved to be malarial, so the mission moved to Bandawe, then finally in 1894 to the high ground of the eastern escarpment. This site was successful; the Livingstonia mission flourished and is still there today.

The Colonial Period

By the 1880s competition among European powers in the area was fierce. In 1889 Britain allowed Cecil Rhodes' British South Africa Company to administer the Shire Highlands, and in 1891 the British Central Africa (BCA) Protectorate was extended to include land along the western side of the lake. In 1907 the BCA Protectorate became the colony of Nyasaland.

Colonial rule brought with it an end to slave-traders and intertribal conflicts, but also brought a whole new set of problems. As the European settlers' demand for land grew, the hapless local inhabitants found themselves labelled as 'squatters' or tenants of a new landlord, and were forced to seek work on the white-settler plantations or to become migrant workers in Northern and Southern Rhodesia (present-day Zambia and Zimbabwe) and South Africa. By the

MOVERS & SHAKERS: JOHN CHILEMBWE

Heroic revolutionary John Chilembwe led Malawi's first fight against colonial rule. Born in 1871, he attended the Church of Scotland mission and later worked for Baptist missionary Joseph Booth, with whom he travelled to Virginia in 1897. A spell at an African American theological college lit his revolutionary spark, and when he returned to Nyasaland as an ordained Baptist minister in 1900 he set about establishing independent African schools and preaching self-reliance to his fellow Africans.

When famine struck in 1913, causing immigrants to pour in from Mozambique, Chilembwe was disgusted by the way plantation owners exploited not only his parishioners but also the refugees in the fight to secure land. When, shortly afterwards, the British conscripted local men to fight against the Germans in Tanzania during WWI, Chilembwe complained of exploitation.

On 23 January 1915, he and 200 followers attacked local plantations. Three white plantation staff were killed, as were several African workers. When the uprising failed to gain local support, a distraught Chilembwe tried to flee to Mozambique; however, he was captured and killed by soldiers.

Today, John Chilembwe is immortalised on Malawi's banknotes and John Chilembwe Day is commemorated annually on 15 January.

turn of the 19th century some 6000 Africans were leaving the country every year; escalating to 150,000 by the 1950s.

Transition & Independence

After WWI the British began allowing the African population a part in administering the country, although it wasn't until the 1950s that Africans were actually allowed to enter the government.

In 1953, in an attempt to boost its sluggish development, Nyasaland was linked with Northern and Southern Rhodesia in the Federation of Rhodesia and Nyasaland. But the federation was opposed by the pro-independence Nyasaland African Congress (NAC) party, led by Dr Hastings Kamuzu Banda. The colonial authorities declared a state of emergency and Banda was jailed.

By mid-1960 Britain was losing interest in its colonies. Banda was released, and returned to head the now renamed Malawi Congress Party (MCP), which won elections held in 1962. The federation was dissolved, and Nyasaland became the independent country of Malawi in 1964. Two years later, Malawi became a republic and Banda was made president.

Banda: Hero to Villain

Banda swiftly forced members of the opposition into exile, banning political parties, declaring himself 'president for life', and outlawing the foreign press. Women in trousers, long hair for men and other such signs of Western debauchery were also banned.

Alongside this move towards dictatorship, Banda remained politically conservative, giving political support to apartheid South Africa, which, in turn, rewarded Malawi with aid and trade.

With the end of the East–West 'cold war' in the 1990s, South Africa and the West no longer needed to support Banda, and within the country opposition was swelling. In 1992 the Catholic bishops of Malawi condemned the regime and called for change, and demonstrations, both peaceful and violent, added their weight to the bishops' move. As a final blow, donor countries restricted aid until Banda agreed to relinquish total control.

In June 1993 a referendum was held for the people to choose between a multiparty political system and Banda's autocratic rule. Over 80% of eligible voters took part; those voting for a new system won easily, and Banda accepted the result.

The 1990s: Fresh Hope

At Malawi's first full multiparty election in May 1994, the victor was the United Democratic Front (UDF), led by Bakili Muluzi. He quickly closed political prisons, encouraged freedom of speech and print, and initiated free primary school education; as well as several economic reforms with the help of the World Bank and the IMF.

In November 1997 Dr Banda finally died. His age was unknown, but he was certainly over 90.

In 2002 after failing to pass a bill that would have given him life presidency, Muluzi chose Bingu wa Mutharika as his successor, and in 2004 he duly won the election. Mutharika quit the UDF and set up his own party, the Democratic Progressive Party (DPP). The massive famine in 2005 saw Malawi bear the brunt of crop failure and drought in the region and, in 2006, under the Highly Indebted Poor Country Initiative, Malawi qualified for debt relief.

Mutharika: Malawi's New Dictator

In 2010 Mutharika expelled his deputy Joyce Banda from the party, but had no choice but to retain her as vice-president as she was elected in 2009 as his running mate. Then in 2011 a diplomatic spat erupted between Mutharika and Great Britain, after a leaked document accused him of being autocratic. Mutharika hit back expelling the British High Commisioner, and immediately Malawi's biggest donor froze millions of dollars of aid.

By the end of 2011 Malawi was crippled by soaring fuel prices of up to 150% – and terrible shortages that ground the country's already ailing industry to a halt. Foreign exchange was also banned as Mutharika took the inflammatory measure of inflating Malawi's currency on the international markets.

On 5 April 2012 Mutharika suffered a heart attack. In the following days the Army placed a cordon around Joyce Banda's house to assist her constitutional succession to power (lest Mutharika's supporters enact a coup). She was sworn in as Malawi's first female president on 7 April.

A New Beginning

In 2012 Banda took some very brave steps to get her house in order; first up she devalued the *kwacha* by 40%, next she attempted to sell the US$8.4 million presidential jet, whilst also proving herself a shrewd international diplomat; foreign funding to Malawi swiftly resumed, with the IMF agreeing to a donation of US$157 million.

The Culture

The National Psyche

Fact: Malawians are among the friendliest people in Africa, avoid conflict and often use humour to diffuse tension. And while they're also laid-back and patient, conversely Malawians are quite conservative; women tend to dress modestly and respectable ladies are not seen in bars unaccompanied.

Daily Life

Malawi remains one of the world's poorest countries, with a per capita gross national product (GNP) of less than US$250. Nearly half the population is chronically malnourished and life expectancy is only 53 years, due in large part to the HIV/AIDS infection rate in Malawi, which runs at almost 12%.

Over 80% of the population live in rural areas and are engaged in subsistence farming or fishing, or working on commercial farms and plantations. Malawi is urbanising rapidly.

Population

Malawi's total population is around 16.3 million and is growing at an unsustainable 2.8% a year. Because the country is small, this creates one of the highest population densities in Africa. Around half the population is under 15 years of age.

Multiculturalism

Malawi's main ethnic groups are Chewa, dominant in the centre and south; Yao in the south; and Tumbuka in the north. Other groups include the Ngoni (also spelt Angoni), inhabiting parts of the central and northern provinces; the Chipoka (or Phoka) in the central area; the Lambya; the Ngonde (also called the Nyakyusa) in the northern region; and the Tonga, mostly along the lakeshore.

There are small populations of Asian and European people living mainly in the cities and involved in commerce, farming (mainly tea plantations) or tourism.

Sport

The most popular sport in Malawi is football (soccer), which is played throughout the country at all levels, from young boys on makeshift pitches to the national team. Malawi's national team is nicknamed the Flames.

Religion

Around 75% of Malawians are Christians. Some are Catholic, while many Malawians follow indigenous Christian faiths that have been established locally.

Malawi has a significant Muslim population of around 20%. Alongside the established churches, many Malawians also follow traditional animist religions.

The Arts

Music & Dance

Traditional music and dance in Malawi, as elsewhere in Africa, are closely linked and often form an important social function, beyond entertainment. In Malawi there are some countrywide traditions, and also some regional specialities where local ethnic groups have their own tunes and dances.

Modern home-grown contemporary music is growing in Malawi due largely to influential and popular musicians such as Lucius Banda, who performs soft 'Malawian-style' reggae, and the late Evison Matafale. Look out too for the Black Missionaries and Billy Kaunda. And last but not least is the new World Music star, The Very Best.

Environment

The Land

Pint-sized, landlocked Malawi is no larger than the US state of Pennsylvania. It's wedged between Zambia, Tanzania and Mozambique, measuring roughly 900km long and between 80km and 150km wide, with an area of 118,484 sq km.

Lying in a trough formed by the Rift Valley, Lake Malawi makes up over 75% of Malawi's eastern boundary. Beyond the lake, escarpments rise to high rolling plateaus covering much of the country.

Wildlife

In 2012 Malawi began reintroducing lions at Majete Wildlife Reserve, finally giving the country its 'Big Five' stamp. Many head for Liwonde National Park, noted for its herds of elephants and myriad hippos. Along with Majete, it's the only park in the country where you might see rhinos.

Elephants are also regularly seen in Nkhotakota Wildlife Reserve, Majete and Nyika National Park – with Nyika also having the country's heaviest population of leopards. Nearby Vwaza Marsh is known for its hippos as well as elephants, buffaloes and waterbucks, but is currently in poor shape due to poor management.

Lake Malawi has more fish species than any other inland body of water in the world, with a total of over 600, of which more than 350 are endemic. The largest family of fish in the lake is the Cichlidae (cichlids).

For birdwatchers, Malawi is rewarding; over 600 species have been recorded and birds rarely spotted elsewhere in Southern Africa are easily seen here including the African skimmer, Böhm's bee-eater and the wattled crane.

National Parks

Malawi has five national parks. These are (from north to south) Nyika, Kasungu, Lake Malawi (around Cape Maclear), Liwonde and Lengwe. There are also four wildlife reserves – Vwaza Marsh, Nkhotakota, Mwabvi and Majete – making 16.4% of Malawi's land protected.

Food & Drink

The staple diet for most Malawians is *nshima*, a thick, doughy maize porridge that's bland but very filling. It's eaten with the hands and always accompanied by beans or vegetables and a hot relish, and sometimes meat or fish.

Fish is particularly good in Malawi, and *chambo,* the popular breamlike variety, and *kampango*, a lake fish similar to catfish, are both popular.

Most travellers enjoy the beer produced by Carlsberg at its Blantyre brewery. The most popular brew is Carlsberg 'green' (lager).

SURVIVAL GUIDE

Directory A–Z

Accommodation

BUDGET

In national parks and along the lakeshore, many places offer camping as well as self-catering chalets or cabins. Camping costs around US$5 to US$10 and usually involves hot showers and power points. You'll also find funky backpacker hostels all over the

---

SLEEPING PRICE RANGES

The following price ranges refer to a double room with bathroom in high season.

$ US$10-20
$$ US$30-80
**$$$** US$ 100-250

country, in the major cities as well as at popular lakeshore destinations such as Cape Maclear and Nkhata Bay. Prices range from US$5 to US$10 for a dorm up to about US$10 to US$20 per person for a double or triple with shared facilities, and around US$30 for an en suite room. Ordinary guesthouses are less inspiring.

MIDRANGE

Midrange hotels and lodges start from about US$30 up to US$80 for a double, including taxes, usually with private bathroom and breakfast, sometimes with air-con. Additionally, some backpackers lodges have stylish en suite options for around US$30 to US$50 for a double.

TOP END

Standard top-end hotels in the cities and at beach resorts range from US$100 to US$250 for a double room, with all the mod cons, plus hotel facilities such as swimming pools, tennis courts and boutiques. The price normally includes taxes and breakfast. Then there are the exclusive beach hotels and safari lodges, which charge anything from US$100 to US$450 per person, per night, though this usually includes all meals and some activities.

🏃 Activities

» Lake Malawi is reckoned as among the best freshwater diving areas in the world. Places where you can hire scuba gear and take a PADI Open Water course include Nkhata Bay (Aqua Africa (☑09 99921418, 01-852284; www.aquaafrica.co.uk)), Cape Maclear (Frogman Scuba (☑09 99952488, 01-599156; casual dives $US40, PADI 4-day open water course US$375)), Likoma Island and Senga Bay. If you don't want to dive, snorkelling gear can be hired from dive centres and most lakeside hotels.

» Many of the more upmarket places along the lake have facilities for water-skiing or windsurfing. Kayaking is available at Cape Maclear and Nkhata Bay and at many of the lodges that dot the lakeshore.

» You can go fishing in Lake Malawi, and salmon fishing on the Bua River (Nkhotakota Wildlife Reserve) with Tongole Wilderness Lodge (☑09 91337681, 08 81433168; www.tongole.com; adult/child per night US$345/172; P@🛜). There are trout streams in Nyika, Zomba and Mulanje

Plateaus. Anglers can contact the Angling Society of Malawi (www.anglingmalawi.com) for further details.

» For horse riding there's a stables on the Zomba Plateau (Zomba Plateau Stables (☑08 88714443, 08 88714445; maggieparsons@iwayafrica.com; per person per hour US$35)), and Kande Beach (Kande Horse (☑08 88 500416; www.kandehorse.com; Chinteche strip)) near Chintheche.

» Several of the lakeshore lodges hire out mountain bikes, usually for about US$10 a day. Areas that are great for mountain biking include Nyika National Park (Chelinda Camp (☑01-771393; www.wilderness-safaris.com; Nyika National Park; chalets US$160; P🛜)) and the Viphya Plateau (Luwawa Forest Lodge (☑01-342333, 01-991106; www.luwawaforestlodge.com; campsite per person US$7, tw/tr without bathroom per person US$40, chalets with half board/full board per person US$68/75, cottages per night US$160; P@🛜)). Both hire bikes.

» The main areas for trekking are Nyika, Mulanje and Zomba. Mulanje is Malawi's main rock-climbing area. Rock climbing can also be arranged in Livingstonia and in the Viphya Plateau. The Mountain Club of Malawi (☑01-821269; www.mcm.org.mw) provides a wealth of information about hiking on Mt Mulanje.

Books

FIELD GUIDES, GUIDEBOOKS AND TRAVEL

» *Birds of Malawi: A Supplement to Newman's Birds of Southern Africa*, by KB Newman, 'bridges the bird gap' between species covered in Southern and East Africa guides.

» *Guide to the Fishes of Lake Malawi National Park*, by L Digby, sometimes called the 'WWF guide' as this organisation was the publisher. This guide is small, portable and perfect for amateurs, although not easy to find as it was published in 1986.

» Lonely Planet's *Zambia & Malawi* guide gives more in-depth coverage of Malawi. *Trekking in East Africa* includes a good section on Malawi and is recommended for trekkers and hikers.

» *Venture to the Interior*, by Laurens van der Post, describes the author's 'exploration' of Mt Mulanje and the Nyika Plateau in the 1940s, although in reality this was hardly trailblazing stuff.

THE BOY WHO HARNESSED THE WIND

When the drought of 2001 brought famine, William Kamkwamba's parents could no longer afford the annual fees and the 14-year-old was forced from school. Self-educating at his old primary school, one book in particular spoke to him; it was about electricity generation through windmills.

A light-bulb moment flashed. Exhausted from his work in the fields every day, William picked around for scrap and painstakingly began his creation; a four-bladed windmill. Soon neighbours were coming to see *him* to charge their phones on his windmill.

When news of William's invention spread, people from across the globe offered to help him. He was shortly re-enrolled in college and travelling to America to visit wind-farms, and has since been mentoring kids on how to create their own independent electricity sources. *The Boy Who Harnessed The Wind* (William Kamkwamba and Bryan Mealer) is his amazing story.

Business Hours

Offices and shops in the main towns are usually open from 8am to 5pm weekdays, with an hour for lunch between noon and 1pm. Many shops are also open Saturday morning. In smaller towns, shops and stalls are open most days, but keep informal hours. Bank hours are usually from 8am to 3.30pm weekdays. Post and telephone offices are generally open from 7.30am to 5pm weekdays, sometimes with a break for lunch. In Blantyre and Lilongwe, they also open Saturday morning.

Children

There are few formal facilities for children in Malawi, but it is generally a safe and friendly place for children to visit. Most of the big international hotels in Blantyre and Lilongwe can provide babysitting services, family rooms and cots for babies, as can several of the tourist lodges up and down the coast. Similarly, many of the big city restaurants will be able to provide high chairs. Disposable nappies and formula are widely available in supermarkets in Lilongwe, Blantyre and Mzuzu but can be difficult to find elsewhere.

Customs Regulations

Like any country, Malawi doesn't allow travellers to import weapons, explosives or narcotics. Plants and seeds, livestock and live insects or snails are also prohibited. It is illegal to take products made from endangered animals or plants out of the country. A yellow-fever certificate is required from people arriving from an infected area.

Embassies & Consulates

The following countries have diplomatic representation in Malawi:

Mozambique Embassy (Map p114; ☎01-774100; Convention Dr, City Centre) **Consulate** (Map p146; ☎01-843189; Rayner Ave, 1st fl, Celtel Bldg)

UK High Commission (Map p114; ☎01-772400; off Kenyatta Rd, City Centre) **Consulate** (Map p148; Hanover Ave, Blantyre)

Germany (☎01-772555; Convention Dr, City Centre, Lilongwe)

South Africa (☎01-773722; sahe@malawi.net; Kang'ombe Bldg, City Centre, Lilongwe)

USA (Map p114; ☎01-773166; Convention Dr, City Centre, Lilongwe)

Zambia (☎01-772590; Convention Dr, City Centre, Lilongwe)

✨ Festivals & Events

Lake of Stars Music Festival (www.lakeofstarsfestival.co.uk) takes place each October at various locations around the lake and attracts live-music acts from around Africa and the UK. It last for three days and proceeds go to charity.

Food

The following price ranges are used for Eating reviews in this chapter.

$	Less than US$10 per meal (MK315-3150)
$$	US$10-20 per meal (MK3150-6300)
$$$	More than US$20 per main dish (MK6300-12,600)

Holidays

Public holidays in Malawi:

New Year's Day 1 January

John Chilembwe Day 15 January

Martyrs' Day 3 March

Easter March/April – Good Friday, Holy Saturday and Easter Monday

Labour Day 1 May

Freedom Day 14 June

Republic Day 6 July

Mother's Day October – second Monday

National Tree Planting Day December – second Monday

Christmas Day 25 December

Boxing Day 26 December

Internet Access

You'll find several internet cafes in Lilongwe, Blantyre, and Mzuzu and most towns. Most hotels and restaurants in Lilongwe, Blantyre and Mzuzu have broadband wifi, as do myriad hotels around the country. To get online, buy prepaid Skyband vouchers – MK600 for one hour, MK2400 for five hours.

Money

Malawi's unit of currency is the Malawi kwacha (MK). This is divided into 100 tambala (t).

Bank notes include MK200, MK100, MK50, MK20, MK10 and MK5. Coins are MK1, 50t, 20t, 10t, 5t and 1t, although the small tambala coins are virtually worthless.

At big hotels and other places that actually quote in US dollars you can pay in hard currency or kwacha at the prevailing exchange rate. At the current time there is limited foreign exchange in the country.

ATMS

Standard and National Banks are the best bet for foreigners wishing to withdraw cash, and accept Visa, MasterCard, Cirrus and Maestro cards at their ATMs. ATMs are found in most cities and towns including Lilongwe, Blantyre, Mzuzu, Karonga, Liwonde, Salima, Mangochi, Kasungu and Zomba, as well as a couple in Nkhata Bay and Monkey Bay.

CREDIT CARDS

You can use Visa cards at some but not all of the large hotels and top-end restaurants (be warned that this may add a 5% to 10% surcharge to your bill). It seems even harder to use a MasterCard.

You can change travellers cheques at most major banks and bureaux de change, although you will need to show them the original purchase receipt. You can sometimes use travellers cheques to pay at large hotels and lodges.

TIPPING & TRAVELLERS CHEQUES

In Malawi tipping is not generally expected, as many restaurants and services will add a service charge to your bill.

You can change travellers cheques at most major banks and foreign exchange bureaus, although you will need to show them the original purchase receipt.

Post

Some letters get from Lilongwe to London in three days, others take three weeks. Post offices in Blantyre and Lilongwe have poste restante services.

To African destinations, letters less than 10g and postcards cost MK80. To Europe, India, Pakistan and the Middle East it's MK150 and to the Americas, Japan or Australasia postage is MK200. It's quicker (and probably more reliable) to use the EMS Speedpost service at post offices. Letters up to 500g cost MK750 to Europe and MK1000 to Australia and the USA.

Airmail parcels now cost about MK2000 plus MK500 per kilo to send items outside Africa. Surface mail is cheaper.

Safe Travel

CRIME

In recent years incidences of robberies or muggings have increased. However, these are still rare compared with other countries, and violence is not the norm.

MALAWI DIRECTORY A–Z

PRACTICALITIES

» Malawi's main newspapers are the *Daily Times*, the *Malawi News* and the *Nation*. Watch out too for the *Eye*, a quarterly directory of the best things to see and do.

» TV Malawi was launched in 1999 and consists mostly of imported programs, news, regional music videos and religious programs. International satellite channels are available in most midrange and top-end hotels.

WILDLIFE

Potential dangers at Lake Malawi include encountering a hippo or crocodile, but for travellers the chances of being attacked are extremely remote, so long as you don't go in the water after dusk which is when they are most active. Crocodiles tend to be very wary of humans and are generally only found in quiet vegetated areas around river mouths (although they may sometimes be washed into the lake by floodwater). Therefore, you should be careful if you're walking along the lakeshore or have to wade through a river. Popular tourist beaches are safe, but, to be sure, you should seek local advice before diving in.

Telephone

Telephone calls within Malawi are inexpensive, around MK50 per minute depending on the distance, and the network between main cities is reliable, although the lines to outlying areas are often not working. Calls to mobiles within Malawi cost around MK70 per minute.

MOBILE PHONES

Mobile phone coverage is extensive in Malawi. Mobile phone prefixes are ✆08 88 or ✆09 99 and the major network is Airtel. Sim cards are readily available from street vendors for around MK1500 and include a small amount of airtime. You can buy top-up cards from supermarkets, internet cafes and petrol stations.

PHONE CODES

The international code for Malawi if you're dialling from abroad is ✆265. Malawi does not have area codes, but all landline numbers begin with 01, so whatever number you dial within the country will have eight digits. Numbers starting with 7 are on the Lilongwe exchange; those starting with 8 are in Blantyre; 5 is around Zomba; 4 is the south; 3 is the north; and 2 is the Salima area.

Tourist Information

There are tourist information offices in Blantyre and Lilongwe but you're much better off asking advice from your hostel or hotel, or from a travel agency. Outside Malawi, tourism promotion is handled by UK-based Malawi Tourism (✆0115-982 1903; www.malawitourism.com).

Visas

Visas are not required by citizens of Commonwealth countries, the USA and most European nations. On entering the country you'll be granted a 30-day entry stamp, which can easily be extended at immigration offices in Blantyre (Map p148; Victoria Ave, Government Complex) or Lilongwe (Map p118; ✆01-754297; Murray Rd); however the next month requires a fee of MK5000.

Getting There & Away

The main way to get to Malawi is by land or air. Overland, travellers might enter the country from Zambia, Mozambique or Tanzania. Boats also bring travellers over Lake Malawi from Mozambique. There are no direct flights to Malawi from Europe or the United States. The easiest way to reach the country by air is via Kenya, Ethiopia or South Africa. Flights, tours and rail tickets can be booked online at www.lonelyplanet.com/travel_services.

Air

AIRPORTS & AIRLINES IN MALAWI

Kamuzu International Airport (LLW; ✆01-700766), 19km north of Lilongwe city centre, handles the majority of international flights. Flights from South Africa, Kenya, Zambia and Tanzania also land in Blantyre at Chileka International Airport (BLZ; ✆01-694244).

The country's national carrier is Air Malawi. Ulendo Airlink (✆01-794555; www.ulendo.net; 441 Chilanga Drive, Area 10, Lilongwe) operates domestic flights.

AIRLINES FLYING TO/FROM MALAWI

Air Malawi (☎01-773680, 01-820811; www.air malawi.com) has a decent regional network, with flights heading to Dar es Salaam, Johannesburg, Nairobi, Lusaka and Harare from Blantyre and Lilongwe.

South African Airways (☎01-772242, 01-620617; www.flysaa.com) Flies twice weekly between Blantyre and Jo'burg, and five times weekly between Lilongwe and Jo'burg (with connections to Durban, Cape Town etc).

Kenya Airways (☎01-774524, 01-774624, 01-774227; www.kenya-airways.com) Flies four times per week to/from Nairobi and six times per week to/from Lusaka.

Ethiopian Airways (☎01-771308, 01-771002; www.flyethiopian.com) Flies four times a week from Addis Ababa.

DEPARTURE TAX

The US$35 departure tax is now included in the price of your ticket.

Border Crossings

MOZAMBIQUE

Bus

» South Take a minibus to the Mozambican border crossing at Zóbuè (zob-way; MK3000) and then a minibus to Tete (US$6), from where buses go to Beira and Maputo. You could also get a Blantyre–Harare bus to drop you at Tete and then get a bus to Beira or Maputo.

» Central For central Mozambique, there are several buses per day from Blantyre to Nsanje (MK4500), or all the way to the Malawian border at Marka (ma-ra-ka; MK5500). It's a few kilometres between the border crossings – you can walk or take a bicycle taxi. From here pick-ups go to Mutarara and Vila de Sena.

» North There are three border crossings from Malawi into northern Mozambique: Muloza, from where you can reach Mocuba in Mozambique, and Nayuchi and Chiponde, both of which lead to Cuamba in Mozambique.

Regular buses run from Blantyre, via Mulanje, to Muloza (MK1500). From here, you walk 1km to the Mozambican border crossing at Melosa, from where it's another few kilometres into Milange. From Milange there's usually a *chapa* (pick-up or converted minibus) every other day in the dry season to Mocuba, where you can find transport on to Quelimane or Nampula.

Further north, minibuses and *matolas* run a few times per day between Mangochi and the border crossing at Chiponde (MK3500). It's then 7km to the Mozambican border crossing at Mandimba and the best way to get there is by bicycle taxi (MK650). Mandimba has a couple of *pensãos*, and there's at least three vehicles daily, usually a truck, between here and Cuamba (US$6).

The third option is to go by minibus or passenger train from Liwonde to the border at Nayuchi (MK2000). You can then take a *chapa* from the Mozambican side of the border to Cuamba.

Boat

The Lake Malawi ferry *Ilala* stops at Metangula on the Mozambican mainland. If you're planning a visit you must get a visa in advance and make sure to get your passport stamped at Malawian immigration on Likoma Island or in Nkhata Bay.

Train

If you're heading to northern Mozambique, a freight train sometimes departs from Limbe on Wednesdays at 7am, travelling via Balaka and Liwonde to the border at Nayuchi. That said it's unreliable and you're better off taking the bus.

SOUTH AFRICA

Intercape Mainliner (Map p118; ☎09 99403398) operates a service between Lilongwe and Johannesburg on Tuesday, Wednesday, Saturday and Sunday (US$78), leaving at 6am; as does **Chiwale Bus Co** (Map p118; ☎09 99034014), which leaves from the same location at 6am on Saturday only (US$68). From Blantyre, try **Ingwe Coach** (☎01-822313). Buses from Lilongwe leave from outside the petrol station on Paul Kagame Rd in Old Town. In Blantyre, most Johannesburg-bound buses depart from the car park outside Blantyre Lodge.

TANZANIA

To get from Lilongwe to Dar es Salaam, there are five **Taqwa** (☎09 99334538) buses per week (US$50, Tuesday, Wednesday, Saturday and Sunday) that depart from Devil St in Lilongwe. These buses also pick up and drop off in Mzuzu (US$30) leaving at midnight and arriving in Dar Es Salaam around 2pm the next day. Mbeya (Tanzania) is handy for going between northern Malawi and southern Tanzania.

If you're going in stages, buses and minibuses run between Mzuzu and Karonga

(MK2000, three to four hours), from where you can get a taxi to the Songwe border crossing (MK1200). It's 200m across the bridge to the Tanzanian border crossing.

Once on the Tanzanian side of the border, minibuses travel to Kyela (7km) and on to Mbeya, where you will need to overnight before continuing on the next morning to Dar es Salaam. You can change money with the bicycle-taxi boys.

ZAMBIA

There are four direct buses per week (two on Tuesday and two on Friday) between Lilongwe and Lusaka (MK6000), also departing from Devil St – the journey takes at least 12 hours. Regular minibuses run between Lilongwe and Mchinji (MK400). From here, it's 12km to the border. Local shared taxis shuttle between Mchinji and the border post for around MK200 per person, or MK1000 for the whole car.

From the Zambian side of the border crossing, shared taxis run to Chipata (US$2), which is about 30km west of the border, from where you can reach Lusaka or South Luangwa National Park.

If you've got a 4WD you can cross into Northern Zambia via Chitipa in northern Malawi. It's four hours from Karonga to Chitipa on a rough dirt road, and then the Malawian border post is 5km out of town. After going through customs it is another 80km or four hours' drive to the Zambian border post at Nakonde.

Getting Around

Air

For domestic flights, departure tax is US$5.

AIRLINES IN MALAWI

Air Malawi (☎01-788415, 01-753181, 01-772123; www.airmalawi.com) Air Malawi's domestic schedule only operates regular flights between Lilongwe and Blantyre (MK43,000 one way).

Ulendo Airlink (☎01-794555; www.ulendo.net; 441 Chilanga Dr, Area 10, Lilongwe)

Boat

The Ilala ferry (☎01-587311; ilala@malawi.net) chugs up and down Lake Malawi once a week in each direction. Travelling between Monkey Bay in the south and Chilumba in the north, it makes 12 stops at lakeside villages and towns in between.

The whole trip, from one end of the line to the other, takes about three days. The official schedules are detailed in the table below (only selected ports are shown).

NORTHBOUND

PORT	ARRIVAL	DEPARTURE
Monkey Bay	–	10am (Fri)
Chipoka	1pm (Fri)	4pm (Fri)
Nkhotakota	12am (Sat)	2am (Sat)
Metangula	6am (Sat)	8am (Sat)
Likoma Island	1.30pm	6pm (Sat)
Nkhata Bay	1am (Sun)	5am (Sun)
Ruarwe	10.15am	11.15am (Sun)
Chilumba	5pm (Sun)	

SOUTHBOUND

PORT	ARRIVAL	DEPARTURE
Chilumba	–	1am (Mon)
Ruarwe	6.45am (Mon)	8am (Mon)
Nkhata Bay	12.45pm (Mon)	8pm (Mon)
Likoma Island	3.15am (Tue)	6.15am (Tue)
Metangula	noon (Tue)	2.00pm (Tue)
Nkhotakota	5.30pm (Tue)	7.30pm (Tue)
Chipoka	3.30am (Wed)	7.30am (Wed)
Monkey Bay	10.30am (Wed)	–

The *Ilala* has three classes:

» **Cabin Class** So-so cabins in reasonable condition.

» **First Class** The deck has a sociable bar, seats, a shaded area and mattresses for hire (MK500).

» **Economy** Dark and crowded, and engine fumes permeate from below.

Cabin Class and First Class passengers can dine in the ferry's restaurant, where a meal costs about MK800. Food is also served from a galley on the Economy deck.

Reservations are usually required for Cabin Class. For other classes, tickets are sold only when the boat is sighted.

SAMPLE ROUTES & FARES

All of the following sample fares are from Nkhata Bay.

DESTINATION	CABIN CLASS (MK)	FIRST CLASS (MK)	ECONOMY (MK)
Nkhotakota	MK14,900	MK6820	MK1190
Ruarwe	MK12,500	MK3000	MK1140
Monkey Bay	MK28,240	MK16,110	MK2710

Bus & Minibus

BUS

Malawi's main bus company is AXA Coach Services (☏01-876000; agma@agmaholdings. net). AXA operates three different classes. Coaches are the best and the most expensive. It's a luxury nonstop service with air-con, toilet, comfortable reclining seats, snacks and fresh coffee. Services operate between Blantyre and Lilongwe twice a day from special departure points in each city (not the main bus stations).

AXA Luxury Coach and City Trouper services are the next in line. These buses have air-con and reclining seats as well as TVs, but don't have toilets. They ply the route between Blantyre and Karonga, stopping at all the main towns with limited stops elsewhere.

Lastly, there are the country commuter buses, handy for backpackers as they cover the lakeshore route. If you're headed for Mzuzu another alternative is the comfortable Super Sink Bus between Lilongwe and Mzuzu.

There are also local minibus services which operate on a fill-up-and-go basis.

In rural areas, the frequency of buses and minibuses drops dramatically, and said 'bus' is often a truck or pick-up, with people just piled in the back. In Malawi this is called a *matola*.

RESERVATIONS

You can buy a ticket in advance for AXA Executive, Luxury Coach and City Trouper services, all of which have set departure times. They have offices at the main bus stations and departure points or you can also buy tickets at branches of Postdotnet, post-internet-business centres found in Malawi's major towns. A week's notice is sometimes needed for the Executive Coach, particularly for Friday and Sunday services.

Car & Motorcycle

The majority of main routes are sealed roads, though the roads along less major routes are potholed, making driving slow and dangerous. Secondary roads are usually graded dirt and also vary in condition. Rural routes after heavy rain are often impassable, sometimes for weeks. Several of the lodges along the lakeshore have poor access roads that need a 4WD. The same goes for the country's national parks and wildlife reserves.

BRING YOUR OWN VEHICLE

If you're bringing a car into Malawi from any other country without a carnet, a temporary import permit costs US$3 (payable in *kwacha*) and compulsory third-party insurance is US$25 for one month. There's also a US$20 road tax fee – you must produce the documentation for this if you are driving the car out. When you leave Malawi, a permit handling fee of US$5 is payable. Receipts are issued.

DRIVING LICENCE

You need a full driver's licence (an international driving licence is not necessary), which normally requires a minimum age of 23 and two years' driving experience.

FUEL & SPARE PARTS

Fuel costs around US$1.54 per litre of diesel. Supplies are subject to shortages so always keep your tank no lower than half full (how's that for optimism!). Spare parts are available in Lilongwe, Blantyre and Mzuzu.

HIRE

Most car-hire companies are based in Blantyre and Lilongwe and can arrange pick-up-drop-off deals. International names include Avis (☏in Blantyre 01-892368, in Lilongwe 01-756105/03), and there are several independent outfits like Crossroads Car Hire (Map p114; ☏01-750333; Mchinji Roundabout, Crossroads Complex, Lilongwe; 2WD/4WD with fully comprehensive insurance per day US$100/149; ⏰9am-5pm Mon-Fri) and Sputnik Rent-a-Car (☏01-761563; www.sputnik-car-hire.mw; Lilongwe). Check the tyres – bald tread will not get you up the mountain to Livingstonia.

Self-drive rates for a small car with unlimited mileage start at around US$50 per day. For a 4WD you're looking at around US$150 per day. To this add 17.5% government tax, plus another US$3 to US$7 a day for insurance. There will usually be a fee of about 5% for using a credit card. Also, most companies will quote you in dollars but if you pay by card they'll have to exchange this into *kwacha* first – usually at a hugely unfavourable rate.

If you'd rather not drive yourself, most companies will arrange a driver for you at a cost of around US$45 a day.

MALAWI GETTING AROUND

INSURANCE

Third-party insurance is a requirement for all drivers, but this can be arranged through car-rental companies or purchased at border posts.

ROAD RULES

Malawians drive on the left, and seat belts are compulsory. Speed limits are 80km/h (main roads) and 60km/h (built-up areas).

☞ Tours

Major tour operators in Malawi, with a variety of budgets to suit most pockets, include Ulendo Travel Group (Map p114; ☎01-794555; www.ulendo.net; 441 Chilanga Drive, Area 10), Wilderness Safaris (Map p114; ☎01-771393; www.wilderness-safaris.com; Kenyatta Rd, Bisnowaty Service Centre, Lilongwe) and Robin Pope Safaris (☎01-795483; www.robinpopesafaris.net; Plot 10/144, Tsoka Rd, Area 10).

Mozambique

Why Go?

Mozambique beckons with its coastline and swaying palms, its traditions, its cultures, its vibe and – most of all – its adventure. This enigmatic southeast African country is well off most travellers' maps, but it has much to offer those who venture here: long, dune-fringed beaches; turquoise waters abounding in shoals of colourful fish; well-preserved corals; remote archipelagos in the north; pounding surf in the south; graceful dhows with billowing sails; colonial-style architecture; pulsating nightlife; vast tracks of bush populated with elephants, lions and birds galore; and an endlessly fascinating cultural mix. Discovering these attractions is not always easy, but it is unfailingly rewarding. Bring along some patience, a tolerance for long bus rides and a sense of adventure and jump in for the journey of a lifetime.

Best of Nature

» Gorongosa National Park (p199)

» Chimanimani Mountains (p202)

» Quirimbas Archipelago (p224)

» Lake Niassa (p216)

Best of Culture

» Mozambique Island (p210)

» Ibo Island (p224)

» Maputo (p170)

» Inhambane (p186)

When to Go

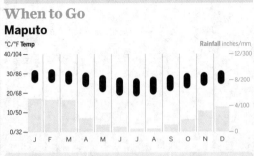

Maputo

Dec–Apr Heavy rains bring flooding in some areas, especially during February and March.

May–Oct Cooler and dry. In August, advance bookings are essential for the southern coastal resorts.

Nov Mostly dry and increasingly warm, but without the holiday crowds of December and January.

Mozambique Highlights

1 Discovering enchanting **Mozambique Island** (p210), with its time-warp atmosphere, cobbled streets and colonial-era buildings

2 Getting to know **Maputo** (p170). Mozambique's waterside capital with flame-tree-lined avenues, lively sidewalk cafes and museums

3 Exploring the **Quirimbas Archipelago** (p224), including magical Ibo Island, with its silversmiths, fort and crumbling mansions

4 Relaxing along the ruggedly beautiful shoreline of **Lake Niassa** (p216)

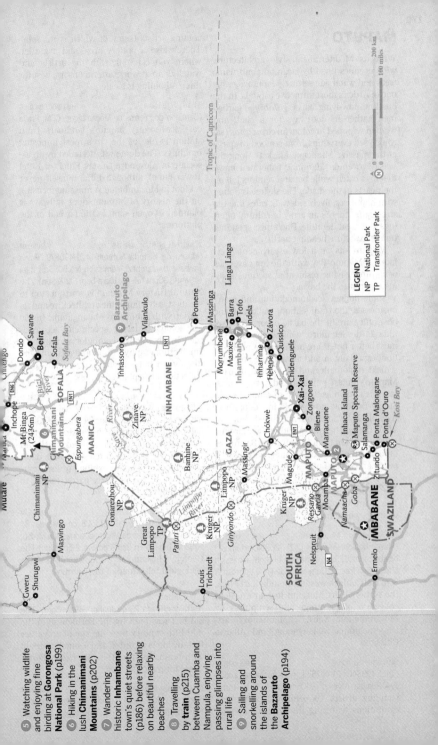

5 Watching wildlife and enjoying fine birding at **Gorongosa National Park** (p199)

6 Hiking in the lush **Chimanimani Mountains** (p202)

7 Wandering historic **Inhambane** town's quiet streets (p186) before relaxing on beautiful nearby beaches

8 Travelling by **train** (p215) between Cuamba and Nampula, enjoying passing glimpses into rural life

9 Sailing and snorkelling around the islands of the **Bazaruto Archipelago** (p194)

LEGEND
NP National Park
TP Transfrontier Park

Tropic of Capricorn

200 km
100 miles

MAPUTO

With its Mediterranean-style architecture, wide avenues lined by jacaranda and flame trees and waterside setting, Maputo is easily one of Africa's most attractive capitals. In the bustling, low-lying baixa, *galabiyya*-garbed men gather in doorways for a chat, and women wrapped in colourful *capulanas* (sarongs) sell everything from seafood to spices at the massive Municipal Market. Along the seaside Avenida Marginal, fishermen hawk the day's catch while banana vendors loll on their carts in the shade. The skyline is dotted with high-rises, lively sidewalk cafes line the streets and there's an array of cultural offerings and great nightlife. Don't miss spending time here before heading north.

Maputo sits on a low escarpment overlooking Maputo Bay, with the long avenues of its upper-lying residential sections spilling down into the baixa.

Some budget accommodation and many businesses, the train station, banks and the post office are in the baixa, on or near Avenida 25 de Setembro, while embassies and most better hotels are in the city's upper section, especially in and around the Sommerschield diplomatic and residential quarter. Maputo's tallest building and a good landmark is known as 'trinta e trés andares' (33 Storey Building, now Mcel), in the baixa at Avenida 25 de Setembro and Rua da Imprensa. At the northernmost end of the Marginal and about 7km from the centre is Bairro Triunfo and the Costa do Sol area, with a small beach and several places to stay and eat.

◉ Sights

The heart of old Maputo is in the baixa, which is where most of the sights are.

National Art Museum   MUSEUM
(Museu Nacional de Arte; ☑21-320264; artemus@ tvcabo.co.mz; 1233 Avenida Ho Chi Minh; admission Mtc20, Sun free; ☺11am-6pm Tue-Fri, 2-6pm Sat & Sun) Half a block west of Avenida Karl Marx, the National Art Museum has an excellent collection of paintings and sculptures by Mozambique's finest contemporary artists, including Malangatana and Alberto Chissano.

Núcleo de Arte   ARTS CENTRE
(☑21-499840, 21-492523; www.nucleodarte.com; 194 Rua da Argélia; ☺10am-8pm) This longstanding artists' cooperative has frequent exhibitions featuring the work of up-and-

coming artists (some of which is for sale). There's also a pottery area, and a garden where you can talk with the artists and watch them at work (afternoons are best for this). Adjoining is a cafe.

Train Station   HISTORIC BUILDING
(Caminho dos Ferros de Moçambique, CFM; Praça dos Trabalhadores) Maputo's landmark train station is one of the city's most imposing buildings. The dome was designed by an associate of Alexandre Gustav Eiffel (of Eiffel Tower fame), although Eiffel himself never set foot in Mozambique. A museum focusing on the history of Mozambique's railways is planned to open soon at the far end of the platforms.

Natural History Museum   MUSEUM
(Museu de História Natural; ☑21-490879; Praça Travessa de Zambezi; admission Mtc50, Sun free; ☺9am-3.30pm Tue-Fri, 10am-5pm Sat & Sun) The Natural History Museum is worth a stop to see its stately Manueline architecture and its garden with a mural by Malangatana. Inside are some taxidermy specimens accompanied by interactive computer terminals, a small ethnography exhibit and a fascinating display of what is probably the region's only collection of elephant foetuses.

National Money Museum   MUSEUM
(Museu Nacional da Moeda; Praça 25 de Junho; admission Mtc20; ☺11am-5pm Tue-Fri, 9am-3.30pm Sat, 2-5pm Sun) Housed in a restored yellow building on the corner of Rua Consiglieri Pedroso, the National Money Museum dates from 1860. Inside are exhibits of local currency, ranging from early barter tokens to modern-day bills.

Geology Museum   MUSEUM
(Museu da Geologia; ☑21-313508; cnr Avenidas 24 de Julho & Mártires de Machava; admission Mtc50; ☺9am-5pm Tue-Fri, 9am-2pm Sat, 2-5pm Sun) The Geology Museum has mineral exhibits and a geological relief map of the country.

FREE Fort   FORTRESS
(Fortaleza; Praça 25 de Junho; ☺9am-5pm) The old fort was built by the Portuguese in the mid-19th century near the site of an earlier fort. Inside is a garden and a small museum with remnants from the era of early Portuguese forays to the area.

Municipal Market   MARKET
(Mercado Municipal; Avenida 25 de Setembro; ☺from about 8am) The Municipal Market,

with its long rows of vendors, tables piled high with produce, fresh fish and colourful spices, and stalls overflowing with everything from brooms to plastic buckets, is Maputo's main market, and well worth a stroll. Get there early in the morning when everything is still fresh, and before the crowds.

Praça da Independência PLAZA
This wide plaza is rimmed on one side by the white, spired Cathedral of Nossa Senhora da Conceição and on the other by the hulking, neoclassical City Hall (Conselho Municipal). Just off the square is the Iron House (Casa de Ferro), which was designed by Eiffel in the late 19th century as the governor's residence, though its metal-plated exterior proved unsuitable for tropical conditions.

Activities

For lap swimming, try the 25m pool at Clube Marítimo de Desportos (Avenida Marginal; per day Mtc200; ⏰5am-8pm). Swimming at the beach along Avenida Marginal is inadvisable due to considerations of cleanliness, currents and occasional rumours of sharks.

Tours

Mozambique City Tours GUIDED TOUR
(☎21-333531; www.mozambiquecitytours.com; per adult/child/family Mtc855/685/995) Mozambique City Tours, with a kiosk at the train station entrance, has a hop-on-hop-off 'train' that runs in a two-hour loop to all the city's main sites, with 10 scheduled stops and four circuits daily.

Bairro Mafalala
Walking Tour CULTURAL TOUR
(☎82-418 0314; www.iverca.org; ⏰3hr tour per person Mtc1000-1500) Walking tours through Mafalala bairro focusing on the area's rich historical and cultural roots.

Jane Flood Walking Tours CULTURAL TOUR
(jane.flood@gmail.com) Specialist walking tours focusing on Maputo's architecture and art.

Festivals & Events

There's almost always an art or music festival happening in Maputo. For upcoming events check with Centro-Cultural Franco-Moçambicano, Kulungwana Espaço Artístico (www.kulungwana.org.mz) and the 'Living in Maputo' pages on Club of Mozambique (www.clubofmozambique.com).

Sleeping

If you want to be in the thick of things, choose somewhere in or near the baixa or in the central area just above the baixa. For sea breezes and more tranquillity, head to the upper part of town in and around Sommerschield and the Polana neighbourhood, or to Avenida Marginal and Costa do Sol.

BAIXA
Base Backpackers BACKPACKERS $
(☎82-452 6860, 21-302723; thebasebp@tvcabo.co.mz; 545 Avenida Patrice Lumumba; dm/d Mtc350/900; @) Small but popular and often full, with a convenient, quiet location on the edge of the baixa. It has a kitchen, a backyard bar, a terrace and a *braai* (barbecue) area with views to the port in the distance. Via public transport from Junta, take a 'Museu' *chapa* (converted passenger truck or minivan) to the final Museu stop, from where it is a short walk.

Residencial Palmeiras BOUTIQUE HOTEL $$
(☎82-306 9200, 21-300199; www.palmeiras-guesthouse.com; 948 Avenida Patrice Lumumba; s/d Mtc2500/3100; ❀🛜) This popular place has bright decor, comfortable, good-value rooms (all but one with private bathroom, and all with TV) and a tiny garden. It is near the British High Commission, and about 10 minutes on foot from the Luciano, Maning Nice and TCO bus company offices.

MAPUTO FOR CHILDREN

There's a large lawn, a playground, arcade games and several eateries at Jardim dos Namorados (Avenida Friedrich Engels). Just next door are the municipal gardens, overlooking the bay. There's also a small playground attached to Mundo's restaurant and another, larger outdoor playground at Jardim dos Professores (Avenida Patrice Lumumba) near Hotel Cardoso.

The swimming pool (☎21-498765; www.girassolhoteis.co.mz; 99 Rua Dom Sebastião; adult/child Mtc400/200) at Girassol Indy Congress Hotel has an attached play area and large surrounding gardens.

Central Maputo

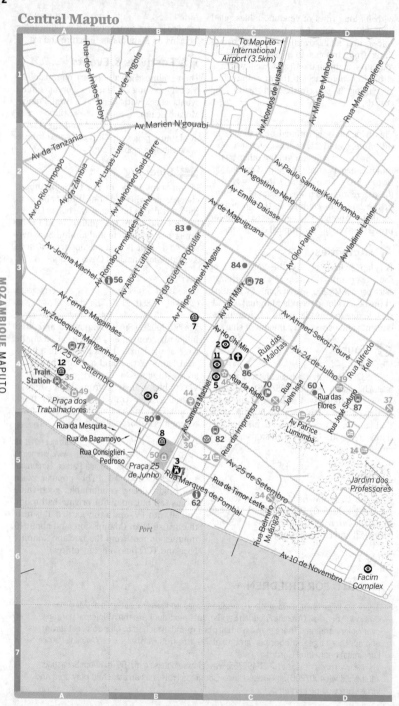

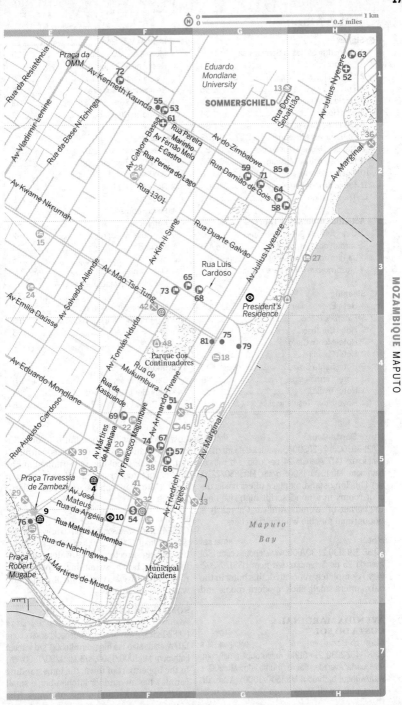

Central Maputo

Hotel Santa Cruz   HOTEL **$$**
(☎21-303006, 21-303004; www.teledata.mz/hotel
santacruz; 1417 Avenida 24 de Julho; s/d without
bathroom Mtc1000/1600, d/ste Mtc1850/2220;
✳) This long-standing place offers basic, de-
cent rooms in a nondescript high-rise near
the corner of Avenida Amilcar Cabral. It is
not optimal for solo women travellers.

Hotel Tivoli   HOTEL **$$$**
(☎82-319 3130, 21-307600; www.tdhotels.com; 1321
Avenida 25 de Setembro; s/d from US$170/202;
✳🖥) Completely renovated, this hotel in the
baixa offers small, slick, modern rooms and
a gym.

AVENIDA MARGINAL & COSTA DO SOL

Maputo Backpackers   BACKPACKERS **$**
(☎82-467 2230, 21-451213; maputobp@gmail.com;
95 Quarta Avenida, Bairro Triunfo; dm Mtc600, r
with/without bathroom Mtc1500/1000) A small,
quiet place well away from the centre near

Costa do Sol, with a handful of rooms (including eight- and 10-bed dorms) with fans
but no nets. Cooking is permitted if the
house isn't too crowded. *Chapas* to/from
town (Mtc7.50) stop nearby. Taxis charge
Mtc300.

Southern Sun   HOTEL **$$$**
(☎21-495050; www.southernsun.com; Avenida Mar-
ginal; s/d from US$270/300; ✳@🖥✈) An attrac-
tive setting directly on the water (although
there's no beach swimming), comfortable
rooms, attentive service, a small gym and a
waterside restaurant.

SOMMERSCHIELD & POLANA

Fatima's Place   BACKPACKERS **$**
(☎82-1851577; www.mozambiquebackpackers.com;
1317 Avenida Mao Tse Tung; dm Mtc500, s/d without
bathroom Mtc1000/1500, s/d Mtc1250/1800; 🖥)
In the upper part of town, the long-standing
Fatima's has an outdoor kitchen-bar, a small
courtyard garden and a mix of rooms. The

same management operates Fatima's Nest in Tofo, and there's a daily shuttle between the two.

Hotel Monte Carlo HOTEL $$
(☎82-312 8160, 21-304048; www.montecarlo.co.mz; 620 Avenida Patrice Lumumba; r Mtc2800-4000; ✳@🖥❄) A convenient central location, efficient staff, tidy rooms (some of the higher-priced ones are quite spacious) and a restaurant make this business travellers hotel overall good value.

Hoyo-Hoyo Residencial HOTEL $$
(☎82-300 9950, 21-490701; www.hoyohoyo.odline.com; 837 Avenida Francisco Magumbwe; s/d Mtc2000/2400; ✳🖥) This solid, no-frills hotel lacks pizzazz, but its 36 small rooms are comfortable, serviceable and fairly priced and the ambience is familial. The location, just back from Avenida Julius Nyerere, is convenient, and there's a good restaurant.

Sundown Guesthouse HOTEL $$
(☎21-497543; www.hotelmaputo.com; 107 Rua 1301; s/d from US$108/128; ✳@🖥) This popular place offers good-value, well-appointed rooms in a small apartment block on a quiet street in the Sommerschield residential area. Meals are available on order and full breakfast is included in the price.

Hotel Polana HOTEL $$$
(☎21-491001; www.serenahotels.com; 1380 Avenida Julius Nyerere; s/d from US$295/330; ✳@🖥❄) In a prime location on the cliff top with uninterrupted views over the sea, the Polana is Maputo's classiest hotel. It has rooms in the elegant main building or in the 'Polana Mar' section closer to the water. There's a large pool set amid lush gardens, a business centre, and a restaurant.

Hotel Cardoso HOTEL $$$
(☎21-491071; www.hotelcardoso.co.mz; 707 Avenida Mártires de Mueda; s/d from US$240/260;

✻@🛜🏊) Opposite the Natural History Museum, and on the cliff top overlooking the bay, this 130-room hotel is a Maputo classic, with good service, well-appointed rooms, a business centre and a bar with views over the water and port area.

Residencial Duqueza de Connaught
BOUTIQUE HOTEL $$$

(✏21-492190; duqueza@tdm.co.mz; 290 Avenida Julius Nyerere; s/d Mtc3500/4500; ✻@) This lovely, quiet, eight-room boutique hotel is in a restored home with polished wood, linen bedding and spotless rooms. Meals can be arranged with advance order.

Mozaika
BOUTIQUE HOTEL $$$

(✏21-303965, 21-303939; www.mozaika.co.mz; 769 Avenida Agostinho Neto; s/d from Mtc3125/4610, apt Mtc7900; ✻@🛜🏊) This boutique hotel – in a convenient central location one block west of Central Hospital – is justifiably popular, with eight small rooms, each decorated with its own theme and set around a small garden courtyard with a tiny pool. There's also a self-catering apartment and a bar, although no restaurant.

Hotel Terminus
HOTEL $$$

(✏21-491333; www.terminus.co.mz; cnr Avenidas Francisco Magumbe & Ahmed Sekou Touré; s/d from Mtc3250/4300; ✻@🛜🏊) This three-star establishment in the upper part of town has small but well-appointed rooms with TV, plus good service and facilities, a business centre, a small garden, a tiny pool and a restaurant. It is popular with business travellers and often fully booked.

Mangas Villa Hotel
HOTEL $$$

(Villa das Mangas; ✏21-497078; www.hipchic hotels.com; 401 Avenida 24 de Julho; s/d from Mtc3630/3990; ✻❄🏊) The pluses at this tidy, whitewashed establishment are its aesthetics and its convenient central location. Rooms – most clustered around the pool in a tiny garden area – are small, with TV and mosquitoes. There's an adjoining restaurant-bar.

✖ Eating

BAIXA

Café Continental
CAFE $

(cnr Avenidas 25 de Setembro & Samora Machel; light meals Mtc150-200; ⊙6am-10pm) This classic place in the baixa is a Maputo landmark, with a good selection of well-prepared pastries, plus light meals, a large seating area and lots of ambience.

Pastelaria Bico d'Ouro
CAFE $

(cnr Avenida Patrice Lumumba & Rua John Issa; meals from Mtc130) A working-person's cafe, with sandwiches, soups and inexpensive but filling set menus.

Kampfumo
PUB $$

(✏82-986 0137; meals Mtc350-400; ⊙12.30-3pm & 6-10.30pm Mon-Fri) At the train station, this former jazz cafe has a set daily menu for lunch, and a selection of well-prepared grilled meat and seafood in the evenings.

AVENIDA MARGINAL & COSTA DO SOL

Dock's
SEAFOOD $$

(✏82-325 5120, 21-493204; Avenida Marginal; meals Mtc350-500; ⊙9am-2am) At Clube Naval, with a daily seafood special, seafood grills and burgers; breezy, waterside seating; and a late-night bar. The Mtc20 Clube Naval compound entry is deducted from your meal bill.

Restaurante Costa do Sol
SEAFOOD $$

(✏21-450115, 21-450038; Avenida Marginal; meals Mtc350-500; ⊙noon-11pm; ℙ) A Maputo classic, this beachside place draws the crowds on weekend afternoons. There's seating on the large sea-facing porch or indoors, and an array of seafood dishes and grills, with prawns the speciality. It's about 5km from the centre at the northern end of Avenida Marginal.

Fish Market
SEAFOOD $$

(Mercado da Peixe; off Avenida Marginal) En route to Costa do Sol (the turnoff is opposite Clube Marítimo), you buy your fish fresh here, then choose a restaurant stall in the enclosed adjoining area to cook it. Cooking prices average about Mtc120 per kilo. The best time to visit is late afternoon.

Feira Popular
INTERNATIONAL $$

(cnr Avenida 25 de Setembro & Rua Belmiro Muanga; admission Mtc20; ⊙lunch & dinner; ℙ) Mix and mingle with the crowds as you wander amid dozens of small bars and restaurants set inside a large, walled compound. O Escorpião (✏21-302180; meals Mtc250-450; ⊙lunch & dinner Tue-Sun), with hearty Portuguese fare, is one of the most popular. Taxis wait outside until the early hours.

Marisqueira Sagres
SEAFOOD $$$

(✏21-495201; 4272 Avenida Marginal; seafood meals from Mtc400; ⊙lunch & dinner Wed-Mon) This waterside place is popular for dinners, and Sunday lunch, with a large menu of well-prepared seafood platters, plus meat grills and continental fare, and a small pool (per adult/child Mtc180/100).

SOMMERSCHIELD & POLANA

Pizza House
CAFE $

(☎21-485257; 601/607 Avenida Mao Tse Tung; pizzas & light meals Mtc170-270; ☺6.30am-10.30pm; ✽) Popular with locals and expats, this place has outdoor seating, plus reasonably priced pastries, sandwiches, burgers, grilled chicken and other meals. Upstairs is an internet cafe.

Surf
CAFE $

(Jardim dos Namorados, Avenida Friedrich Engels; snacks & light meals from Mtc150; ⊞) Surf is a large, amenable place with indoor and garden seating, views from the escarpment over the bay, a children's play area and fast service. It's very popular on weekends, and with families.

Mimmo's
PIZZERIA $

(☎21-309491; cnr Avenidas 24 de Julho & Salvador Allende; meals Mtc200-350) This bustling street-side pizzeria also has pastas, and seafood and meat grills. It's worth checking your bill and change carefully.

Pastelaria & Restaurante Cristál
CAFE, EUROPEAN $$

(☎84-302 3560, 82-281 5180; restaurantecristal@hotmail.com; 554 Avenida 24 de Julho; meals from Mtc300; ☺6.30am-11pm) This long-standing place has delicious pastries and breads, light meals, indoor and street-side seating and a popular, reasonably priced restaurant serving well-prepared local and continental dishes.

Café Acacia
CAFE $$

(Jardim dos Professores, Avenida Patrice Lumumba; light meals from Mtc250; ☺7am-9pm; ⊞) A tranquil garden setting with a children's play area and bay views, plus tasty pastries and coffees.

Piri-Piri Chicken
FAST FOOD $$

(Avenida 24 de Julho; meals from Mtc200; ☺11am-midnight) A Maputo classic, with grilled chicken – with or without *piri-piri* (spicy chilli sauce) – plus spicy shrimp curry, cold beers and a good local vibe. It also does takeaway.

Mundo's
BURGERS, PUB $$

(☎21-494080; www.mundosmaputo.com; cnr Avenidas Julius Nyerere & Eduardo Mondlane; meals Mtc350-500; ☺8am-midnight; ☎⊞) Burritos, burgers, pizzas and other hearty fare – all served up in large portions on wooden tables

set around a street-side verandah. There's also all-day breakfast and a small play area for children.

Self-Catering

Deli-cious Deli
DELI $

(Ground fl, Polana Shopping Centre, cnr Avenidas Julius Nyerere & 24 de Julho) Fresh breads, cheeses and sliced meats.

Deli 698
DELI $

(698 Avenida Julius Nyerere) Gourmet items and fresh bread.

Shoprite
SUPERMARKET $

(Avenida Acordos de Lusaka; ☺9am-8pm Mon-Sat, to 1pm Sun) Just outside the city centre and en route to the airport, with ATMs in the same shopping complex.

Supermares
SUPERMARKET $

(Avenida Marginal, Costa do Sol; ☺9am-7pm Mon-Sat, to 1pm Sun) A large mall with ATMs and many shops, including a Shoprite.

☕ Drinking

Thursday through Saturday are the main nights for Maputo's nightlife scene, with things only getting going after 11pm. Cover charges range from Mtc50 to Mtc250.

Café Camissa
CAFE

(194 Rua da Argélia; admission Mtc100; ☺10am-8pm, later for live music) At Núcleo d'Arte with live music on Friday and Sunday evenings.

Café-Bar Gil Vicente
BAR

(43 Avenida Samora Machel) A popular place with a constantly changing array of performers.

La Dolce Vita Café-Bar
CAFE

(822 Julius Nyerere; ☺10am-late Tue-Sun) This sleek tapas and late-night place near Xenon cinema has live music on Thursday evening. By day, try the juices and smoothies.

Coconuts Live
LOUNGE, DISCOTHEQUE

(Complexo Mini-Golfe, Avenida Marginal; disco Mtc250, lounge free; ☺disco Fri & Sat, lounge Wed-Sun) A weekend disco catering to a younger, less formal crowd, plus a popular chill-out lounge.

☆ Entertainment

Centro Cultural Franco-Moçambicano
CULTURAL CENTRE

(☎21-314590; www.ccfmoz.com; Praça da Independência) Art exhibitions, music and dance performances, films and theatre.

Shopping

Artedif
ARTS & CRAFTS

(☎21-495510; Avenida Marginal; ☺9am-3.30pm)
This cooperative for disabled people is about
400m south of Southern Sun hotel. Crafts
sold here are slightly more expensive than
those at the street markets, but tend to be of
higher quality. Prices are fixed.

Saturday Morning Craft Market
ARTS & CRAFTS

(Praça 25 de Junho; ☺about 8am-1pm Sat) Woodcarvings, batiks and many other items.

Feira de Artesanato, Flôres e Gastronomia de Maputo
ARTS & CRAFTS

(Avenida Mártires da Machava, Parque dos Continu-
adores; ☺9am-5pm) Batiks, woodcarvings and
more.

Himbe
ARTS & CRAFTS

(Train Station, Praça dos Trabalhadores) A small
selection of lovely handicrafts made by local
women.

ℹ Information

Emergency
Official emergency numbers rarely work. It's better to seek help from your hotel or embassy.

Internet Access
Cafetíssimo (Polana Shopping Centre, 3rd
Fl, cnr Avenidas Julius Nyerere & 24 de Julho;
☺8.30am-9pm Mon-Sat; 🛜) Free wi-fi for cafe
customers (note there is no internet cafe).

Pizza House Internet Café (Avenida Mao Tse
Tung; per hr Mtc60; ☺8am-10pm; 🛜) Upstairs
at Pizza House.

Medical Services
AMI Specialist Hospital (Maputo Trauma
Centre; ☎82-302 0999, 82-000 2999, 82-000
1999; 2986 Avenida Julius Nyerere; ☺24hr)
Western standards and facilities; meticais, dol-
lars or Visa card accepted.

Farmácia Dia e Noite (☎84-505 8238, 82-832
3250; 764 Avenida Julius Nyerere; ☺24hr) Opposite the South African High Commission.

Instituto do Coração (☎82-305 3097, 82-
327 4800, 21-416347; 1111 Avenida Kenneth
Kaunda; ☺24hr) Western standards and facilities for all ailments (not just cardiac issues);
meticais, dollars or Visa card accepted.

Money
There are 24-hour ATMs all over town, including
at the airport and at both Shoprites. Only Millennium BIM ATMs accept MasterCard; the rest
accept Visa only. BIC machines dispense up to

Mtc5000 per transaction, Millennium BIM ATMs
up to Mtc3000 per transaction.

Cotacambios City (Gr Fl, Polana Shopping
Centre, cnr Avenida Julius Nyerere & Mao Tse
Tung; ☺9am-9pm Mon-Sat, 10am-8pm Sun);
Airport (Main terminal; ☺open for international
arrivals and departures) All change cash only.
Cotacambios' airport branch also does reverse
exchanges.

Post
Main Post Office (CTT; Avenida 25 de Setembro; ☺8am-6pm Mon-Sat, 9am-noon Sun)

Safe Travel
Although most tourists visit Maputo without
mishap, be vigilant when out and about both
during the day and at night, and take sensible
precautions. In particular, avoid carrying a bag,
wearing expensive jewellery or otherwise giving
a potential thief reason to think that you might
have something of value. Don't put yourself in
isolating situations, and at night, always take a
taxi. Areas to avoid during the day: the isolated
stretches of the Marginal between Praça Robert
Mugabe and the Southern Sun hotel, and the
access roads leading down to the Marginal from
Avenida Friedrich Engels. Also avoid the area
below the escarpment just south of Avenida
Patrice Lumumba.

DOCUMENTS

Carry a notarised copy of your passport
(photo and Mozambique visa pages)
when out and about, rather than the
original. It's rarely checked, but when it
is, it's usually by underpaid policemen
looking to top up their meagre salaries
with bribes. Keep the notarised copy
handy (and away from your other valuables). The more you can do to minimise
the impression that you're a newly arrived tourist, the lower your chances of
getting stopped for a document check.
If you do get stopped, always insist
on going to the nearest police station
(esquadrão), and try to avoid handing
over your actual passport, especially on
the street. The notarised copy should be
used instead.

Documents can be notarised at various points around the city (including
some embassies), and at **4° Cartário
Notarial** (Avenida Armando Tivane;
☺7.30am to 3pm Mon-Fri), between Ruas
Kassuende and Mukumbura.

Restricted areas that are off-limits to pedestrians (no photos) include the eastern footpath on Avenida Julius Nyerere in front of the president's residence and the Ponta Vermelha zone in the city's southeastern corner.

Travel Agencies

Dana Agency (☏21-484300; travel@dana.co.mz; Ground fl, 1170 Avenida Kenneth Kaunda) Domestic and international flight bookings.

Dana Tours (☏21-495514; info@danatours.net; 1st Fl, 1170 Avenida Kenneth Kaunda) Specialises in travel to the coast, and can also sort you out for destinations throughout Mozambique plus in Swaziland and South Africa. Midrange and up.

Mozaic Travel (☏21-451376; www.mozaictravel.com; 240 Rua de Massala, Bairro Triunfo) Excursions, including to Limpopo National Park and Bazaruto Archipelago.

Visas

Immigration Department (Departmento Nacional de Migração; Avenida Ho Chi Minh; ◷7.30am-2pm to receive requests) Allow five to seven days for processing visa extensions.

❶ Getting There & Away

Air

Kenya Airways (p238) and **LAM** (☏21-468800; www.lam.co.mz) have regular flights to Maputo. **South African Airways** (☏84-389 9287, 21-488970/3; www.flysaa.com; Avenida do Zimbabwe, Sommerschield) are located near the South African High Commissioner's residence. **TAP Air Portugal** (☏21-303928, 21-303927; www.flytap.com; 114 Rua da Sé) can be found at the Hotel Pestana Rovuma.

Bus

Maputo's main long-distance bus depot for upcountry arrivals and departures is **Junta** (Avenida de Moçambique), about 7km (Mtc300 in a taxi) from the city centre. Most departures are very early, between 2.30am and 5.30am. Some buses coming into Maputo continue into the city to Ponto Final (p180), from where it's about Mtc150 in a taxi to central hotels. Time your travels to avoid arriving at night.

TCO (☏82-891 3020, 82-956 0600; Avenida Zedequias Manganhela) and **Maning Nice** (☏82-706 2820; Avenida Zedequias Manganhela; ◷8am-5pm) have their ticket offices and arrival/departure point in the baixa, which is much more convenient and without the chaos of Junta. TCO is the most comfortable option to Xai-Xai (Mtc280, four hours), Maxixe (Mtc475, 6½ hours), Massinga (Mtc550, eight hours), Pambara Junction (for Vilankulo; Mtc700, nine hours) and Beira (Mtc1780, 16 hours), with an air-con bus with bathroom two to three times weekly departing at 5am. Departure days vary; confirm when booking and expect last-minute changes.

Private, reasonably priced minivan transport for individuals or groups to Inhambane (about Mtc700) and Massinga can be arranged through Residencial Palmeiras. Fatima's Place has a daily shuttle between Maputo and Tofo (Mtc700).

To Nampula (Mtc2500), Maning Nice goes twice weekly, departing Maputo at 3.30am and arriving around 10am the next morning in Nampula with an overnight stop in Nicoadala. From Nampula, Maning Nice has a connection on to Pemba, departing Nampula around noon and arriving in Pemba around 7pm.

Other transport terminals include **Benfica** (Avenida de Moçambique) for *chapas* to Marracuene and **Fábrica de Cerveja Laurentina** ('Feroviario'; cnr Avenidas 25 de Setembro & Albert Luthuli) for *chapas* to Swaziland, South Africa, Namaacha, Boane and Goba.

Departure and ticketing points for express buses to Johannesburg include Cheetah Express (p239) and the following:

Greyhound (☏21-355700, 21-302771; www.greyhound.co.za; 1242 Avenida Karl Marx) At Cotur Travel & Tours, on the corner with Avenida Eduardo Mondlane.

Luciano Luxury Coach (☏82-769 9830, 84-860 2100, 21-752711; 273 Avenida Zedequias Manganhela; ◷8am-5pm for ticketing) Behind the main post office.

Translux (☏21-303829, 21-303825; www.translux.co.za; 1249 Avenida 24 de Julho) At Simara Travel & Tours.

Train

Slow trains (3rd-class only) connect Maputo with several destinations. Rehabilitation plans are underway; get an update on routes, fares and journey times at the information window, to the left in the main train station entrance, or – with luck – at www.cfmnet.co.mz.

Chicualacuala (on the Zimbabwe border) Departing at 1pm on Wednesday from Maputo and at 1pm on Thursday from Chicualacuala (1st/3rd class Mtc500/182, 20 hours).

Ressano-Garcia (South African border) Departing Maputo at 7.45am, and Ressano Garcia at 12.10pm (Mtc15, four hours).

❶ Getting Around

To/From the Airport

Maputo International Airport is 6km northwest of the city centre (Mtc400 to Mtc500 in a taxi).

Bus & Chapa

Buses have name boards with their destination. City rides cost about Mtc5.

Chapas go everywhere, with the average price for town trips from Mtc5. Most are marked with route start and end points, but also listen for the destination called out by the conductor. To get to Junta, look for a *chapa* going to 'Jardim'; coming from Junta into town, look for a *chapa* heading to 'Museu'. *Chapas* to Costa do Sol leave from the corner of Avenidas Mao Tse Tung and Julius Nyerere, and from Praça dos Trabalhadores.

Other useful *chapa* stops include the following:

Museu (Natural History Museum) *Chapas* to the airport and Junta (Mtc5 from Museu to Junta). *Chapas* marked 'Museu-Benfica' go along Avenida Eduardo Mondlane.

Ponto Final (cnr Avenidas Eduardo Mondlane & Guerra Popular) Terminus for some upcountry buses, and for *chapas* running along Avenida Eduardo Mondlane. Also *chapas* to Costa do Sol.

Ronil (cnr Avenidas Eduardo Mondlane & Karl Marx) *Chapas* to Junta, Benfica and Matola.

Car

Park in guarded lots when possible, or tip the young boys on the street to watch your vehicle. Rental agencies include the following:

Avis (☑21-465498, 82-328 4560, 21-465497; maputo.airport@avis.co.za) Offices also in Beira, Nampula and Tete.

Europcar (☑21-497338, 82-300 2410; www.europcar.co.mz; 1418 Avenida Julius Nyerere) Next to Hotel Polana and at the airport. Offices also in Beira, Nampula and Tete.

Expresso Rent-A-Car (☑21-493619; timisay@tropical.co.mz) At Hotel Cardoso; 2WD vehicles only; unlimited kilometre packages available.

Premium Rent-a-Car (☑82-527 6355, 82-762 9600, 21-466034; www.carpremium.co.mz; Airport) Offices also in Nampula, Beira, Tete and Pemba.

Sixt (☑82-300 5180, 21-465250; www.sixt.com; Airport) Offices also in Nampula, Beira, Tete and Pemba.

Taxi & Tuk-Tuk

Taxi ranks include the **Hotel Polana taxi rank** (☑21-493255) and those in front of most other top-end hotels.

Taxis also park at the Municipal Market and on Avenida Julius Nyerere in front of Mundo's restaurant. Town trips start at Mtc100.

From central Maputo to Costa do Sol costs Mtc300. From Junta to anywhere in the city centre costs Mtc350 to Mtc400.

Tuk-tuks are less expensive than taxis (town trips from Mtc50). Look for them opposite Hotel Cardoso, and on Avenida Julius Nyerere, just up from the South African High Commission.

AROUND MAPUTO

Inhaca Island

Just 7000 years ago – almost like yesterday in geological terms – Inhaca (Ilha de Inhaca) was part of the Mozambican mainland. Today, this wayward chunk of Mozambican coastline lies about 40km offshore from Maputo, and is an enjoyable weekend getaway. It's also an important marine research centre, known in particular for its offshore coral reefs. The reefs are among the most southerly in the world, and since 1976 parts of the island and surrounding waters have been designated a marine reserve (per person US$10). Over 300 species of bird have also been recorded on the island. On Inhaca's southwestern edge (a 50-minute walk from the ferry dock) is a marine biology research station and a small museum (☑21-760009; admission Mtc75; ⊗8.30-11.30am & 2-3.30pm Mon-Fri, from 9.30am Sat, Sun & holidays) with specimens of local fauna.

About 3km northwest of Inhaca is tiny, uninhabited Portuguese Island (Ilha dos Portuguêses), a beautiful white patch of sand surrounded by clear waters.

🛏 Sleeping & Eating

Pestana Inhaca Lodge　　　　　HOTEL $$$
(☑21-760003; www.pestana.com; s/d/f with half board from US$174/259/259; ❄@🐾) Set in expansive, shaded gardens just north of the ferry pier on the island's western side, this four-star establishment is Inhaca's main hotel. Rooms are bright and cheery, with mosquito nets, fan and air-con. Note that there's a two-night minimum stay during peak periods.

Restaurante Lucas　　　　　SEAFOOD $$
(☑21-760007; meals Mtc250-450; ⊗from 7am) This long-standing local-style restaurant is the main place to eat. Order in advance if you're in a rush or if you fancy a particular dish. It's next to Pestana Inhaca Lodge.

ℹ Getting There & Away

The **Vodacom ferry** (☑84-220 1610; www.inhaca.co.mz; ⊗10.30am-5pm Mon, Wed, Thu & Fri) departs from Maputo's Porto da Pesca (off Rua Marques de Pombal) at 8am on Saturday and Sunday (Mtc1700 return, two hours). Departures from Inhaca are at 3pm.

There is also a boat departing from the Catembe ferry pier at 7am on Tuesday, Thursday, Saturday and Sunday (Mtc550 one way, 1½ to two hours). Departures from Inhaca are at 2pm.

Mozambique Yachting (☑84-900 9899; www.maputoyachting.com) does sailing charters to Inhaca. For speedboat charters, contact **Mozambique Charters** (☑84-323 6420; www.mozambiquecharters.com)

Marracuene & Macaneta Beach

Macaneta is the closest open-ocean beach to Maputo, with stiff sea breezes and long stretches of dune-fringed coast. It's on a narrow peninsula divided from the mainland by the Nkomati River, and is reached via Marracuene, 35km north of Maputo along the N1.

Jay's Beach Lodge (☑84-863 0714; www.jaysbeachlodge.co.za; per vehicle for day visitors Mtc200, campsite per person Mtc275, 2-/4-person chalet Mtc1400/2800), just behind the dunes on a long, beautiful beach, has a restaurant and *braai* facilities available for day visitors, and camping and chalets for overnight. Pick-ups from Marracuene can be arranged for those without 4WD. The day visitor fee is waived if you eat at the restaurant.

❶ Getting There & Away

Take any northbound *chapa* from Benfica (Mtc60, one hour) to Marracuene, from where it's a 10-minute walk through town to the **Nkomati River ferry** (return per person/vehicle Mtc4/180, 5min; ⊙6am to 6pm). On the other side, follow the rutted road for about 5km to a junction of sorts, from where you'll find most of the Macaneta places about 5km to 8km further, and signposted. There's no public transport; hitching is slow except at weekends. For drivers, a 4WD is essential, except to get to Macaneta Lodge.

North of Marracuene

About 20km north of Marracuene and signposted just off the N1 are several useful places for breaking up your travel if you're doing a self-drive visit from South Africa, including **Blue Anchor Inn** (☑82-325 3050, 21-900559; www.blueanchorinn.com; adult/child Mtc1106/553), which has pleasant rooms and cottages in large grounds, and a restaurant. Breakfast costs extra.

SOUTHERN MOZAMBIQUE

Long, dune-fringed stretches of white sand, heaping plates of prawns, diving and snorkelling, an established tourism infrastructure, and straightforward road and air access from South Africa make Mozambique's southern coast an ideal destination if you're seeking a beach holiday.

Ponta d'Ouro & Ponta Malongane

The sleepy colonial-era town of Ponta d'Ouro has boomed in popularity in recent years and is the first Mozambique stop on many southern Africa overland itineraries. Its best asset is its excellent beach – long, wide and surf-pounded. Offshore waters host abundant sea life, including dolphins and whale sharks and – from July to October – whales. Thanks to Ponta d'Ouro's proximity to South Africa, it fills up completely on holiday weekends.

About 5km north is the quieter and even more beautiful Ponta Malongane, with a seemingly endless stretch of windswept coastline fringed by high, vegetated dunes and patches of coastal forest.

🏃 Activities

Diving

The Tandje Beach Resort compound is the base for **Scuba Adventures** (☑21-900430; www.africasafaris.co.za) and the **Whaler** (☑84-604 4369; www.thewhaler.co.za) dive operators. Both offer simple tented and/or reed or wooden hut accommodation sharing ablutions with the camping ground, catered or self-catering options, diving courses and equipment rental.

Other local dive bases include **Devocean Diving** (www.devoceandiving.com), in the town centre next to the police station, **Ponta Malongane** (www.malongane.co.za) and **Simply Scuba** (www.simplyscuba.co.za) at Motel do Mar.

Dolphin Tours

Dolphins frequent the waters offshore from Ponta d'Ouro, and catching a glimpse of these beautiful creatures can be a wonderful experience. Prices are about Mtc1100 per person for a two-hour excursion, generally also involving snorkelling near Ponta Malongane and sailing down towards the lighthouse. Dolphins can be spotted year-round (although there are no guarantees, and no refunds if you don't spot any). Whale sharks are most easily seen between July and November. Between June and August it's chilly in the boats, so bring a windbreaker. If conditions are stormy or too windy, the boats don't go out. From October/November to February the sea tends to be calmest.

Dolphin Encountours BOAT TOUR
(☑84-330 3859; www.dolphin-encountours.co.za) Based at Dolphin House in the town centre.

Somente Aqua Dolphin Centre BOAT TOUR
(☑84-242 9864; www.somenteaqua.com) Just before Tandje Beach Resort. Also has self-catering accommodation.

🛏 Sleeping

PONTA D'OURO

Café PENSION $
(☑84-827 5275, 21-650048; pontacafe@yahoo.com; r per person Mtc875; 🐾) Café has small rooms in reed chalets closely spaced around a tiny garden behind the restaurant. All have nets, fans and shared bathrooms with hot water. It's perched on a hilltop in the town centre about 200m in from the beach; look for the bright orange building. If you're after some quiet, midweek is best; on weekends the bar has music until dawn.

Tandje Beach Resort CAMPGROUND $
(☑'Campismo' 21-900430; campsite per person/vehicle Mtc520/15, 2-/4-person bungalow from Mtc1880/4600) In addition to the facilities of the dive camps located on its grounds, both of which have budget accommodation, Tandje has a shaded, seaside camping area with shared ablutions and basic bungalows, including a few beach-facing. All the bungalows have a small gas stove, but only the six-person bungalow has hot water and fridge. It's at the southern end of town. Contact them through Scuba Adventures.

Motel do Mar Beach Resort HOTEL $$
(☑21-650000; www.pontadoouro.co.za; 4-person chalets with/without sea view US$105/85; 🐾) In a fine seaside location (though not all rooms manage to have full sea views), this motel is a throwback to colonial days. It has a restaurant that does seafood grills, a 1960s ambience and blocks of faded but nevertheless quite pleasant two-storey self-catering chalets.

Kaya Kweru BUNGALOW $$
(☑82-527 6378, 21-758403; www.kaya-kweru.com; dm with bathroom US$18, 2-/4-person cottage from US$102/163; 🐾@🐾) About 200m north of the town centre past the Catholic church, this efficient place has rows of closely spaced stone-and-thatch cottages with bathrooms, all set in a rather featureless compound redeemed by its location just in from the beach and its good facilities. The dorm rooms have air-con and private bathroom.

PONTA MALONGANE

Ponta Malongane CAMPGROUND $
(☑in South Africa 013-741 1975; www.malongane.co.za; campsite per adult/child US$21/13, dive-camp tents US$30-60, 4-person self-catering chalets from US$161) This long-running, laid-back place is based at the sprawling and shaded Parque de Malongane. It has various accommodation options, including camping, four-person *rondavels* and chalets and small, rustic twin-bedded log huts. There's also a restaurant, and a large self-catering area. Breakfast costs extra.

Tartaruga Marítima
Luxury Camp TENTED CAMP $$
(☑84-373 0067; www.tartaruga.co.za; s/d US$104/160; 🐾) About 2km further north, Tartaruga is a lovely, tranquil self-catering retreat (no restaurant), with spacious, comfortable safari-style tents tucked away in the coastal forest behind the dunes and just a few minutes' walk from a wonderful stretch of beach.

🍴 Eating

Bula-Bula CONTINENTAL $$
(meals Mtc200-450; ☺lunch & dinner Thu-Tue) The popular Bula-Bula has a large selection of well-prepared continental and Mozambican cuisine, including pastas, salads and seafood grills.

Café CAFE $$
(☑21-650048; pontacafe@yahoo.com; meals from Mtc250; ☺lunch & dinner Wed-Mon; 🐾) The orange Café, perched on the hilltop in the town centre with views to the sea, has tasty pancakes, prawns and other fare, plus a bar with a daily happy hour and live music most weekends.

ℹ Information

There's a BIC ATM just below Café (Visa card only). South African rands are accepted everywhere; meticais and US dollars can also be used.

MAPUTO SPECIAL RESERVE

En route to Ponta d'Ouro and just two hours from the capital is the 90-sq-km **Maputo Special Reserve** (adult/child/vehicle Mtc200/100/200), known until recently as the Maputo Elephant Reserve. The elephants, who suffered from the effects of the war and poaching, are estimated to number only about 180 today, most quite skittish and seldom seen, but planned restocking should improve chances of sightings. There are also small populations of antelopes, hippos and smaller animals. The main attractions are the pristine wilderness feel (it offers a true bush adventure close to the capital) and the birding. Over 300 different types of birds have been identified, including fish eagles and many wetland species. The coastline here is also an important nesting area for loggerhead and leatherback turtles; peak breeding season is November to January.

The heart of the reserve is Ponta Milibangalala, about 35km from the main gate along the sea, where there is a basic beachside **camping ground** (campsite adult/child Mtc200/100). You'll need to be completely self-sufficient, including food and water (water suitable for washing is sometimes available at the main entrance).

Maputo travel agencies operate day and overnight trips to the reserve. Otherwise, you'll need your own transport (4WD). The main entrance ('*campeamento principal*') is 65km from Catembe along the Ponta d'Ouro road. From here, it's 3km to the park gate, and then 35km further along a rough road to the coast and the camping ground. There's a second entrance further along the Ponta d'Ouro road, marked with a barely legible signpost, from where it's 22km into the reserve.

ⓘ Getting There & Away

Ponta d'Ouro is 120km south of Maputo. The road is potholed but in decent shape for the first 60km, but it's slow going through soft, deep sand thereafter. Allow about three hours in a private vehicle (4WD only).

Direct *chapas* depart Maputo's Catembe ferry pier by about 6am or earlier on Tuesday and Friday (Mtc175, five hours). Departures from Ponta d'Ouro are on Wednesday and Saturday from in front of the market. Otherwise, take the ferry to Catembe, where there are several direct *chapas* daily. From Ponta d'Ouro back to Catembe, there is a *chapa* most weekdays departing at 4am. Arrange with the driver the evening before to pick you up at your hotel.

Kaya Kweru has a twice-weekly shuttle from Maputo (Mtc4000 per person return).

Kosi Bay border post is 11km south of Ponta d'Ouro along a sandy track (4WD), and most *chapas* from Catembe pass here first, before stopping at Ponta d'Ouro (Mtc50 from the border to Ponta d'Ouro). Coming from South Africa, there's a guarded lot just over the border where you can leave your vehicle in the shade for R30 per day. All the hotels do pick-ups from the border from about US$10 to US$15 per person, minimum two. Allow about five hours for the drive to/from Durban (South Africa).

There's no public transport to Ponta Malongane, though *chapas* between Maputo and Ponta d'Ouro stop at the signposted turn-off, about 5km before Ponta Malongane. To get between Ponta d'Ouro and Ponta Malongane, you can walk along the beach at low tide (7km) or go via the road.

Namaacha

Cool Namaacha lies on the border with Swaziland, about 70km west of Maputo, its streets lined with lavender jacaranda and bright-orange flame trees.

Located on the main road in the town centre, **Hotel Libombos** (☎21-960102; d/ste Mtc3000/3500; ❊) has comfortable rooms, some with views over the hills, plus a restaurant and a casino.

Chapas run throughout the day to/from Maputo (Mtc70, 1½ hours), departing Namaacha from the border, and stopping in front of the market on the main road.

Bilene

This small resort town sits on the large Uembje Lagoon, which is separated from the open sea by a narrow, sandy spit. If you're based in Maputo with a car at your disposal, it makes an enjoyable getaway, but if you're touring and want some sand, head further north to the beaches around Inhambane or south to Ponta d'Ouro.

Sleeping & Eating

Complexo Palmeiras CAMPGROUND $
(✆82-304 3720, 282-59019; http://complexopal
meiras.blogspot.com; campsite US$6, plus per
person US$5, 4-person chalets US$97) At the
northern edge of town on the beach, with
camping, no-frills chalets with fridge, *braai*
facilities and a restaurant. Bring your own
towels, linens, pans and cutlery. It's about
500m past the market and transport stand:
follow the main road into town to the final
T-junction, then go left for 1km.

Praia do Sol RESORT $$
(✆82-319 3040; www.pdsol.co.za; s/d US$67/133,
chalets per person US$67; ✖) About 4km south
of town along the beach, this place has a col-
lection of spacious two- and four-person A-
frame chalets overlooking the lagoon, plus
some double rooms, larger self-catering cha-
lets, and a restaurant-bar. Turn right onto
the beachfront road and continue for about
3km, staying right at the fork. Prices for the
rooms and non-self-catering chalets include
breakfast.

Café O Bilas CAFE $
(pizzas from Mtc120) This long-standing place
next to the petrol station is good for pizzas
and snacks.

ⓘ Getting There & Away

Bilene is 140km north of Maputo and 35km off
the main road. A direct bus departs Maputo's
Praça dos Combatentes ('Xikelene') at about
7am (Mtc130, five hours). Otherwise, go to Junta
and have any northbound transport drop you
at the Macia junction, from where pick-ups run
throughout the day to/from Bilene (Mtc25, 30
minutes).

Leaving Bilene, direct departures are daily at
6am (and sometimes again at 1pm) from the
town centre near the market.

If you're driving, the road to Bilene is tarmac
throughout. With a 4WD (or by chartering a
boat – possible at most hotels), it's possible to
reach the other side of the lagoon and beach on
the open sea. Boats can also be arranged with
local fishermen from about Mtc250 return.

Limpopo National Park

Together with South Africa's Kruger National
Park and Zimbabwe's Gonarezhou National
Park, Limpopo National Park (Parque Nacion-
al do Limpopo; ✆21-713000; www.limpopopn.gov.
mz; adult/child/vehicle Mtc200/100/200, payable in
meticais or South African rand) forms part of the
Great Limpopo Transfrontier Park. Gona-
rezhou connections are still in the future, but
Kruger and Limpopo are now linked via two
fully functioning border posts.

Wildlife on the Mozambique side can't
compare with that in South Africa's Kruger,
and sightings are still very hit and miss:
it's quite possible to spend time in the park
without seeing large animals. Yet, Limpopo's
bush ambience is alluring, and the park area
also offers the chance for cultural and ad-
venture tourism.

Most visitors use Limpopo as a transit
corridor between Kruger and the coast.
There's also the five-day Shingwedzi 4WD
Trail, starting at Kruger's Punda Maria camp
and continuing south through Limpopo
park to the Lebombo/Ressano Garcia border
post (book through www.dolimpopo.com or
www.sanparks.org).

Sleeping & Eating

Campismo Aguia Pesqueira CAMPGROUND $
(campsite per person Mtc210, 2-person cha-
let Mtc1500) This good park-run camping
ground is along the edge of the escarpment
overlooking Massingir Dam, about 50km
from Giriyondo border post. All campsites
have views over the dam, plus *braai* facili-
ties. There's a communal kitchen and ablu-
tions, plus several rustic self-catering chalets,
also with views.

Covane Fishing & Safari Lodge LODGE $$
(✆in South Africa 011-023 9901; www.covanelodge.
com; campsite per person US$12, tw in traditional
house US$60) This place – jointly run by
Barra Resorts and the local community – is
about 13km outside Limpopo's Massingir
gate on a rise overlooking the dam. It was
in the process of being upgraded as this
book was researched, and price changes are
likely. Currently on offer are camping and
accommodation in local-style bungalows or
twin-bedded chalets plus the chance to rent
houseboats. Boat excursions, fishing trips,
village walks and visits to the park can be
arranged. Breakfast costs US$5 extra and
local-style lunch and dinner are available.
Advance bookings are recommended.

**Machampane
Wilderness Camp** TENTED CAMP $$$
(www.dolimpopo.com; s/d tent with full board
US$363/558) The upmarket Machampane has
five spacious, well-appointed safari tents in a
tranquil setting directly overlooking a section
of the Machampane River where you're likely

to see (or at least hear) hippos plus a variety of smaller wildlife and many birds. Additional offerings include a multinight hiking trail and a four-day canoe expedition along the Elefantes River. Machampane Camp is about 20km from Giriyondo border post, and pickups can be arranged from Massingir village or from Kruger park's Letaba camp (where you can leave your car).

❶ Getting There & Away

The main park entrance on the Mozambique side is **Massingir Gate** (⏱6am-6pm), about 5km from Massingir town (which has an ATM). It's reached via a signposted turn-off from the N1 at Macia junction that continues through Chókwé town (where there's also an ATM) on to Massingir. While daily *chapas* go between Maputo's Junta and Massingir (Mtc180), there is currently no possibility for onward transport within the park, so Limpopo remains at the moment primarily a self-drive destination.

To enter Limpopo from South Africa's Kruger park, you'll also need to pay Kruger park entry fees, and Kruger's gate quota system applies (see www.sanparks.org for information).

The closest tanking up stations on the Mozambique side are in Xai-Xai, Chókwé and Massingir. Travelling via Mapai, there is no fuel until Mapinhane.

Xai-Xai

Xai-Xai (pronounced 'shy-shy') is a long town, stretching for several kilometres along the N1. It's of little interest to travellers, but the nearby Xai-Xai Beach (Praia do Xai-Xai), about 10km from the town centre, has invigorating sea breezes, and is an agreeable overnight stop if you're driving to/from points further north.

🛏 Sleeping

Kaya Ka Hina PENSION $
(☏282-22391; N1; s/d without bathroom Mtc750/850, tw/d from Mtc1200/1500; ❄) The no-frills but centrally located Kaya Ka Hina is convenient if you're trying to catch an early bus or if you don't want to drive down to the beach. Downstairs is a restaurant. It's about 100m north of the praça transport stand.

Complexo Halley HOTEL $$
(☏282-35003; complexohalley1@yahoo.com.br; Xai-Xai Beach; d Mtc2250-2750; ❄) This long-standing and amenable beachfront hotel is the first place you reach coming down the beach access road from town. It has stiff sea

breezes, a seaside esplanade, a good restaurant and pleasant, homey rooms (ask for one that's sea-facing). On Friday evening there's a disco at the hotel; on Saturday it's across the road at the beachside esplanade.

🍴 Eating

Pastelaria Chave CAFE $
(EN1; meals from Mtc150) Inexpensive local dishes and snacks.

Pastelaria Mukokwene CAFE $
(snacks & light meals from Mtc50) Pastries, breads and light meals. It's one block east of the main street.

KFC FAST FOOD $
(just off EN1) For those missing American-style fried chicken.

❶ Information

There are ATMs at **Millennium BIM** (N1, near Kaya Ka Hina); at **Standard Bank** (one block behind Kaya Ka Hina); and at **Barclays** (N1, opposite the church). For internet access try **Telecomunicações de Moçambique** (per min Mtc1; ⏱7.30am-7pm), diagonally opposite Standard Bank and just behind the central market.

❶ Getting There & Away

The main praça transport stand is near the old Pôr do Sol complex on the main road at the southern end of town. Buses to Maputo depart daily at about 6am (Mtc280, four hours). It's marginally faster to take one of the north–south through buses, although getting a seat can be a challenge. Wait by the Pôr do Sol complex on the main road at the southern end of town or, better, take a *chapa* to the *pontinha* (bridge control post), where all traffic needs to stop.

To Xai-Xai Beach (Mtc5), *chapas* depart from the praça transport stand, or catch them anywhere along the main road. They run at least to the roundabout, about 700m uphill from the beach, and sometimes further.

Around Xai-Xai

The lagoon-studded coast north and south of Xai-Xai has a string of attractive beaches – all quiet, except during South African school holidays. The area is particularly suited to travellers with their own vehicle, as many of the lodges are located well off the N1.

The beach is particularly lovely at Chidenguele, about 70km north of Xai-Xai and just 5km off the N1 down an easy access road.

Paraíso de Chidenguele (☑84-390 9999; www.chidbeachresort.com; r per person US$36, 2-/4-/6-person chalets US$85/121/204; ☒) is a lovely place with accommodation in simple, twin-bed rooms, or in spacious, well-equipped self-catering cottages – some with stunning views over the sea, others nestled in the coastal forest. There's a restaurant-bar and a large swimming pool.

Quissico

About 130km northeast of Xai-Xai on the N1 is Quissico, capital of Zavala district. It is noteworthy for being one of the main meal and bathroom stops on long-haul bus routes along the N1. Quissico's other claim to fame is that it is the centre of the famed Chopi *timbila* (marimba) orchestras, and the site of an annual *timbila* festival (last weekend in August).

Lagoa Eco Village (☑84-577 2946; info@lagoaecovillage.com; campsite per person Mtc300, dm/d Mtc400/1750, 5-/8-person self-catering chalet Mtc4300/5940), on the edge of the lagoon about 7km from Quissico town down a rough track, has a lagoon-side setting, swimming and kite-surfing (with your own equipment) on the lagoon and various types of rustic, thatched accommodation and camping. Bring your own food and drink, or book meals with them in advance. Via public transport, take a *chapa* from the main Quissico junction heading to Macomane. Get off at the T-junction, from where it is about 1km further on foot to the right. Driving, the turn-off is signposted opposite the hospital.

Inhambane

With its serene waterside setting, tree-lined avenues, faded colonial-style architecture and mixture of Arabic, Indian and African influences, Inhambane is one of Mozambique's most charming towns and well worth a visit. It has a history that reaches back at least 10 centuries, making it one of the oldest settlements along the coast. It is also the gateway to a fine collection of beaches, including Tofo and Barra.

◉ Sights & Activities

In addition to the general ambience and the bayside setting, Inhambane's attractions include the 18th-century cathedral of Nossa Senhora de Conceição, near the water, the old mosque (1840) on the waterfront, the new mosque, several blocks further east, and the tiny museum (Avenida da Vigilância; admission free, donations welcome; ⊙9am-5pm Tue-Fri, 2-5pm Sat & Sun), near the new mosque.

🛏 Sleeping

Pensão Pachiça   BACKPACKERS $
(☑84-389 5217, 84-412 5297, 293-20565; www.barralighthouse.com; Rua 3 de Fevereiro; dm/s/d Mtc400/900/1500) This backpackers on the waterfront has clean rooms and dorm beds (the family room has its own bathroom), a restaurant-bar and a rooftop terrace overlooking the bay. From the ferry, take a left coming off the jetty and continue about 300m.

Hotel Africa Tropical   PENSION $
(Sensasol; ☑82-777 4871; s/d/tr Mtc500/1200/1700; ☒) The Tropical has a row of tidy rooms facing a small garden. Some have a double bed, others have a double bed plus a single bed. All have fan, net and hot water, and most also have TV and minifridge. Breakfast costs extra, and there's a small restaurant. It's just off Avenida da Independência.

**Escola Superior de
Hotelaria e Turismo**   HOSTEL $
(☑293-20755, 293-20781; www.eshti.uem.mz; Avenida de Moçambique; tw/q Mtc1125/2250) By the train station at the eastern edge of town, this place has functional attached twins (no nets), with each two-room (four-bed) unit sharing a bathroom. Unless they are full, you can often negotiate to only be charged per occupied bed, rather than for the entire room. From the ferry jetty, continue straight through town to the end of the main road.

Hotel Inhambane   HOTEL $$
(☑84-389 3837, 293-21225; www.hotelinhambane.co.mz; Avenida da Independência; d/tr/ste Mtc2200/3200/5900; ☒) Simple, clean, mostly spacious rooms with minifridge, TV and hot water. It's in the town centre.

Casa do Capitão   HOTEL $$$
(☑293-21409, 293-21408; www.hotelcasadocapitao.com; s/d from Mtc4800/6750; ☒🕾) This beautiful new hotel is in a fantastic location with Inhambane Bay on two sides. Views are wonderful, and rooms are beautifully appointed. It's a nice treat if you're in Inhambane on a honeymoon or if you just want pampering. There's also a good

restaurant. Significant low season and weekend discounts are available.

🍴 Eating

TakeAway Sazaria CAFE $
(Avenida da Independência; meals from Mtc80; ☺8am-5pm Mon-Fri) At Fatima's Paradise, with tasty, inexpensive soups, *pregos* (thin steak sandwiches) and sandwiches to eat there or take away.

Café d'Hotel AFRICAN $
(Avenida da Independência; meals Mtc150-200) Inexpensive, tasty daily menus and local dishes.

Padaria de Inhambane BAKERY $
(Avenida da Revolução) For hot, fresh rolls. It's next to the market, and close enough to dash over to from the bus stand.

Famous Fried Chicken FAST FOOD $
(Avenida da Independência; fried chicken from Mtc140) American-style fried chicken and clean bathrooms.

Verdinho's CONTINENTAL $$
(📱82-389 9038; Avenida Acordos de Lusaka; salads from Mtc185, meals from Mtc280; ☺8am-10pm Mon-Sat; 🛜) A large menu, including meze, gourmet salads and burgers, pizzas and

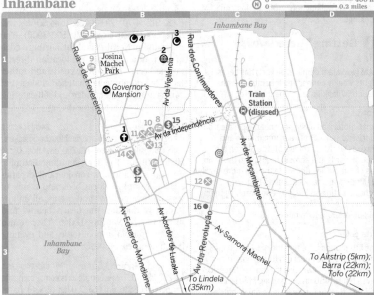

Inhambane

MOZAMBIQUE INHAMBANE

Inhambane

⊙ Sights

1 Cathedral of Nossa Senhora de Conceição	B2
2 Museum	B1
3 New Mosque	B1
4 Old Mosque	B1

🛏 Sleeping

5 Casa do Capitão	A1
6 Escola Superior de Hotelaria e Turismo	C1
7 Hotel Africa Tropical	B2
8 Hotel Inhambane	B2
9 Pensão Pachiça	A1

🍴 Eating

10 Café d'Hotel	B2
11 Famous Fried Chicken	B2
12 Padaria de Inhambane	C2
13 TakeAway Sazaria	B2
14 Verdinho's	B2

ℹ Information

15 Barclays Bank	B2
16 Litanga Travel & Services	C3
17 Millennium BIM	B2

continental dishes and seating indoors or at shaded tables outside on the patio where you can watch the passing scene.

❶ Information

Immigration (for visa extensions) is in Maxixe.

Barclays Bank (Avenida da Independência) ATM.

Centro Provincial de Recursos Digitais de Inhambane (Avenida da Revolução; per min Mtc1; ☺8am-8pm Mon-Fri, 9am-4pm Sat) Internet access.

Millennium BIM (Avenida Acordos de Lusaka) ATM.

Litanga Travel & Services (✆293-21024; litangaservicos@gmail.com; Avenida da Revolução) Near the entrance to the central market, for walking tours, dhow trips and LAM bookings.

❶ Getting There & Away

Air

LAM (www.lam.com.mz; airport) has several flights weekly connecting Inhambane with Maputo, Vilankulo and Johannesburg.

Boat

Small motorised passenger boats operate from sunrise to sunset between Inhambane and Maxixe (Mtc10, 25 minutes). The pier on the Maxixe side is just across the N1 from the main bus stand. Sailing dhows do the trip more slowly for Mtc5, and one of Inhambane's great morning sights is sitting on the jetty and watching them load up. It's also possible to charter a motorboat (about Mtc200, 10 minutes).

Bus & Car

The bus station is behind the market. Chapas to Tofo (Mtc15, one hour) run throughout the day. There is a daily direct bus to Maputo (Mtc500, seven hours, 450km), departing at 5.30am. Fatima's Nest in Tofo also has a daily shuttle to Maputo (Mtc700) that stops by Inhambane. For other southbound buses, and for all northbound transport, you'll need to head to Maxixe.

Coming from Maputo, a direct bus departs Junta between 5am and 6am, or take any northbound bus to Maxixe.

There's at least one daily *chapa* to Maxixe (Mtc40 to Mtc50) via the shortcut road; the turnoff from the N1 is at Agostinho Neto area, 20km south of Maxixe.

Tofo

Tofo has long been legendary on the Southern Africa holidaymakers' scene, with its azure waters, long arc of beach, easy access and party-time atmosphere.

🏃 Activities

Tofo is Mozambique's unofficial diving capital. Operators include the following (all also organise whale shark snorkelling safaris):

Diversity Scuba　　　　　　　DIVING
(✆293-29002; www.diversityscuba.com; town centre) A long-standing operator.

Liquid Adventures　　　　　　DIVING
(✆84-060 9218; www.divingtofo.com) Behind Tofo OnLine in the town centre.

Peri-Peri Divers　　　　　　　DIVING
(www.peri-peridivers.com) At Albatroz Lodge.

🛏 Sleeping

Nordin's Lodge　　　　　BUNGALOW $
(✆82-312 4770, 293-29009; binos50@hotmail. com; 2-/4-person chalets Mtc1500/3000) The unassuming Nordin's is at the northern edge of town in a good, shaded location directly on the beach. It has four rustic and rather faded but decent-value thatched chalets that come with hot water, fridge and self-catering facilities. There are no meals.

Fatima's Nest　　　　　BACKPACKERS $
(✆82-185 1575; www.mozambiquebackpackers. com; campsite per person Mtc250, dm Mtc400, s/d Mtc1000/1600) The long-standing Fatima's, ever popular and now considerably expanded, has camping, dorm beds and a mix of very basic bungalows and rooms, all on low dunes overlooking the beach behind and just north of Nordin's Lodge. There's also a kitchen, a bar, a pool table, and evening beach bonfires.

Bamboozi Beach Lodge　　　BACKPACKERS $
(✆293-29040; www.barraresorts.com; campsite per person US$16, dm US$17, d hut US$36) Bamboozi has dorm beds and basic reed huts – some with floor mattresses and others with beds, and all with just a bottom sheet and net – set down low behind the dunes and sharing rather scruffy ablutions. There are also five stilted reed A-frame 'chalets' with bathrooms and a better sea-view chalet up on the dune. It's 3km north of town along a sandy road. The views from the dune-top bar-restaurant are magnificent, but prices are high for what is on offer. Wednesday and Friday are party nights.

Casa do Mar　　　　　　　　B&B $$
(✆in South Africa 82-455 7481; www.casa-do-mar. co.za; s/d from Mtc1600/2700; ❋▨) This is a beautiful B&B-style place, with bright, spot-

less and impeccably decorated rooms in a large private home, some with sea views, and a chef who prepares delicious gourmet meals. Breakfast costs extra (Mtc250 per person).

Casa Azul   GUESTHOUSE $$
(☏82-821 5921; www.casa-azul-tofo.com; s US$72-108, d US$80-150) Casa Azul, a lovely converted colonial-era house on the beach at the southeastern end of Tofo, is bright and cheery, with white and blue trim outside, and pleasant rooms named for different colours. There are semi-open-air bathrooms, each one different, and a 'treehouse' room with its own verandah, plus a small garden in front and meals.

Aquático Ocean Annex   PENSION $$
(☏82-857 2850; www.aquaticolodge.com; tr Mtc1700; ❄) This place has four attached, spacious self-catering rooms in a good location directly on the beach. Each has one double and one twin bed, fan, nets, a refrigerator and a mini-cooker. There are no meals, but there's a restaurant next door.

Albatroz Lodge   LODGE $$$
(☏293-29005; www.albatrozlodge.com; 4-/6-/8-person chalets Mtc3800/4600/5850) Large, rustic, thatched self-catering cottages in a quiet setting on the bluff overlooking the beach. There's a restaurant and an onsite dive operator. Some cottages are well ventilated, while others have an exterior window and a semi-interior one covered with thatching that can block ventilation.

✖ Eating & Drinking

Tofo Tofo   AFRICAN $
(meals from Mtc150) Inexpensive snacks and local food, and a small grocery store.

Blend   CAFE $
(at Liquid Adventure; snacks from Mtc70) This sandwich and smoothie shop also has good breakfasts, burgers and more.

Casa de Comer   FUSION $$
(☏293-29004; meals from Mtc300-450; ◷9am-10pm Wed-Mon; ☏) Tasty Mozambique-French fusion cuisine, including vegetarian dishes, and some local artwork on display in the small adjoining garden. Found in the town centre.

Dino's Beach Bar   CAFE $$
(www.dinosbeachbar.com; meals from Mtc200; ◷10am-late Thu-Tue) One of Tofo's main hangouts, Dino's is on the beach just past

Fatima's Nest, with good vibes, good music and tasty food (pizzas, seafood, toasted sandwiches, desserts and more).

ℹ Information

The closest ATMs and banks are in Inhambane. There is also an ATM in Barra. **Tofo On-Line** (per min Mtc3) town (◷9am-6pm Wed-Mon; 📶) and beach (◷10am-6pm Thu-Tue) has internet access. The town branch also has pre-paid wireless access.

ℹ Getting There & Away

Chapas run throughout the day along the 22km sealed road between Tofo and Inhambane, departing Tofo from about 5am (Mtc15, Mtc10 for a large bus, one hour). To Maputo's Junta, there's usually one direct bus daily, departing Tofo by about 4.30am (Mtc500, 7½ hours). Fatima's Nest also has a daily shuttle to Maputo (Mtc700). Otherwise, you'll need to go via Inhambane or Maxixe. If you do this and want to catch an early north/southbound bus, it's possible in theory to sleep in Tofo, but for a more sure connection, stay in Inhambane the night before.

If you leave early from Maputo, it's possible to get to Inhambane in time to continue straight on to Tofo that day, with time to spare.

Tofinho

Just around the point (to the south) and easily accessed from Tofo (by walking or catching a lift) is Tofinho, Mozambique's unofficial surfing capital.

Turtle Cove Surf & Yoga Lounge (☏82-719 4848; www.turtlecovetofo.com; campsite per person US$8.50, dm US$12-18, d chalet US$48-60; ❄) is the spot to go if you're interested in surfing or chilling, with Moorish-style stone houses with bathrooms, a few very basic grass huts, camping, a yoga centre and a restaurant. Breakfast is extra. There's a 20% discount for longer stays.

Barra

Barra sits at the tip of the Barra Peninsula, where the waters of Inhambane Bay mix with those of the Indian Ocean. Many self-drivers prefer Barra's quieter scene and its range of midrange accommodation options, but Tofo is a better bet if you're backpacking or relying on public transport. There's an ATM at Barra Lodge. For diving and instruction, contact **Barra Dive** (www.barradiveresorts.com; Barra Lodge).

🛏 Sleeping & Eating

Barra Lighthouse CAMPGROUND $
(Farol de Barra; ☎84-389 5217, 84-573 4525; www.
barralighthouse.com; campsite per person US$12)
Under the same management as Pensão
Pachiça in Inhambane, this place has rustic camping next to the lighthouse at Barra
point, with hot and cold ablutions and plug
points. Boats can be launched; quad bikes
aren't permitted. Take the signposted sandy
right off the Barra road (4WD only), when
coming from Bar Babalaza.

Barra Lodge LODGE $$$
(☎293-20561; www.barraresorts.com; 6-person
self-catering cottages US$173; s/d beach chalet
US$216/400; ❄🛜🌊) One of Barra's largest,
longest-running and most outfitted places,
with a range of accommodation – from
small twin-bedded reed *casitas* with bathroom, to larger, well-equipped self-catering
cottages – plus a beachside bar-restaurant
and a full range of activities.

Flamingo Bay Water Lodge LODGE $$$
(☎293-56007, 293-56005; www.barraresorts.com;
s/d with half board US$177/327; ❄@🌊) Well-appointed wood-and-thatch stilt houses lined
up in a row directly over the bay. There's also
a good restaurant known for its 'double meat
pizzas'. No children under 12 permitted. It's
under the same management as the nearby
Barra Lodge, and transfers to/from the Barra
Lodge beach are provided.

❶ Getting There & Away

Air
Barra Lodge and Flamingo Bay offer fly-in packages from Johannesburg.

Bus
Daily *chapas* go between Inhambane and Conguiana village along the Barra road. From here,
you'll need to sort out a pick-up or walk (about
4km to Barra Lodge).

Car & Motorcycle
The turn-off for Barra is about 15km from Inhambane en route to Tofo; go left at the Bar Babalaza
junction. You can easily make it in a 2WD most
of the way, but you'll need a 4WD to reach Barra
lighthouse. Hitching is easy in high season from
Bar Babalaza.

Maxixe

Maxixe (pronounced ma-sheesh) is about
450km northeast of Maputo on the N1, and
convenient as a stopping point for traffic up

and down the coast. It's also the place to get
off the bus and onto the boat if you're heading to Inhambane, across the bay.

🛏 Sleeping

Maxixe Camping CAMPGROUND $
(☎293-30351; N1; campsite per person Mtc130)
Maxixe Camping, just south of the jetty,
has an enclosed and scruffy but serviceable
camping ground overlooking the bay with
reasonable ablutions. You can leave your vehicle here while visiting Inhambane (Mtc75
per vehicle per day).

Stop Residencial MOTEL $$
(☎82-125 2010, 293-30025; stopmaxixe96@hotmail.com; d/tw/ste Mtc1500/1500/1800; ❄) Tidy,
functional rooms with hot-water bathrooms.
For bookings, directions and check-in, go to
Restaurante Stop next to the ferry.

🍽 Eating

Restaurante Stop CONTINENTAL $$
(☎293-30025; N1; meals from Mtc225; ⊙6am-10pm) Stop, on the north side of the jetty,
has prompt service, clean toilets, tasty meals
and a swimming pool (per person Mtc100).

❶ Information

Inhambane Province's **Department of Immigration** (Migração; ⊙7.30am-3.30pm), for visa
extensions, is in Maxixe, one block back from the
main road. Turn at Barclay's Bank, then take the
first left; Immigration is just up on the left. No
visa extensions are done in Inhambane town.

There are ATMs at Millennium BIM, just in from
the main road near Pousada de Maxixe, and at
Barclays Bank, about 600m further north and
just off the N1.

❶ Getting There & Away

Buses to Maputo (Mtc475, 6½ hours, 450km)
depart from the bus stand by the Tribunal
(court) from 6am. There are no buses to Beira
originating in Maxixe; you'll need to try to get
space on one of those coming from Maputo
that stop at Maxixe's main bus stand (Mtc1000
from Maxixe to Beira). Thirty-seater buses to
Vilankulo originating in Maputo depart Maxixe
from about 10am from the main bus stand.
Otherwise, *chapas* to Vilankulo (Mtc180, 3½
hours) depart throughout the day from Praça
25 de Setembro (Praça de Vilankulo), a couple
of blocks north of the bus stand in front of the
Conselho Municipal.

If you're driving to Inhambane, take the short-cut road signposted to the east about 20km
south of Maxixe in the Agostinho Neto area.

Massinga & Morrungulo

The bustling district capital of Massinga is a convenient stocking-up point, with numerous shops, a petrol station and a garage. There are several ATMs, including Millennium BIM (one block west of the N1) and BCI (N1), at the southern end of town.

About 8km north of Massinga is the signposted turn-off for Morrungulo Beach (Praia de Morrungulo), a stunning stretch of coastline. Ponta Morrungulo (☏293-70101; www.pontamorrungulo.co.za; campsite adult/child Mtc400/200, 4-person garden/seafront chalet Mtc4500/5000) has a mix of rustic, thatched beachfront and garden self-catering chalets and camping, all on a large, manicured bougainvillea- and palm-studded lawn running directly onto the beach with magnificent views of Morrungulo Bay from the top of the escarpment. There's also a restaurant (closed Monday). The setting is outstanding, although the antiquated colonial-era ambiance may be a turn-off for some.

About 1.5km north of here is the unassuming Sylvia Shoal (☏in South Africa 083-270 7582; www.mozambique1.com; campsite per person US$13, barracas US$22, 2-/4-person chalet US$82/107), with shaded campsites, a handful of self-catering chalets set behind low dunes and a restaurant (open during low season with advance bookings only).

❶ Getting There & Away

Most north–south buses stop at Massinga. The first departure to Maputo (Mtc550, eight hours) is by about 6am. Going north, buses from Maputo begin to arrive in Massinga by about 11am, en route to Vilankulo.

Morrungulo is 13km from the main road down a good dirt track that is negotiable with a 2WD. Sporadic *chapas* (Mtc30) run from the Massinga transport stand (on the N1) to Morrungulo village, close to Ponta Morrungulo, and within about 3km walk of Sylvia Shoal.

Pomene

Pomene, the site of a colonial-era beach resort, is known for its fishing and birding, and its striking estuarine setting. The area is part of the Pomene Reserve (per adult/child above 12/vehicle Mtc200/50/200). The beach here is beautiful, especially up near the point by the lighthouse and the now derelict Pomene Hotel.

Pomene Lodge   LODGE $$
(☏82-369 8580, in South Africa 011-023 9901; www.barraresorts.com; campsite per person US$18, s/d water chalet US$145/245; ⚡) Pomene Lodge, in a fine setting on a spit of land between the estuary and the sea, has no-frills self-catering reed bungalows just back from the beach, plus a row of newer, spacious and very lovely 'water chalets' directly over the estuary. There's also camping (hot and cold water), and a restaurant-bar.

Pomene View   LODGE $$
(☏84-465 4572; www.pomeneview.co.za; 5-/6-person chalets US$152/182; ⚡) Pomene View, on a rise amid the mangroves and coastal vegetation on the mainland side of the estuary, is small and tranquil, with its own special appeal and wide views. Accommodation is in self-catering brick-and-thatch chalets, and there's a bar and restaurant. Take the signposted turn-off north of Massinga, and then follow the Pomene View signs.

❶ Getting There & Away

Pomene is on the coast about halfway between Inhambane and Vilankulo off the N1. The turn-off is about 11km north of Massinga (which is the best place to stock up) and signposted immediately after the Morrungulo turn-off. From the turn-off, which is also the end of the tarmac, it's about 58km (1½ to two hours) further along an unpaved road to Pomene Lodge, and about 54km to Pomene View (branch left at the small signpost). In the dry season it's possible to reach Pomene View with a 2WD with clearance. For Pomene Lodge you'll need a 4WD. There's an airstrip for charter flights from Inhambane and Vilankulo.

Via public transport, there are one or two *chapas* weekly from Massinga to Pomene village (Mtc120), which is a few kilometres before Pomene Lodge. Most locals prefer to take a *chapa* from Massinga to Mashungo village (Mtc100, daily) on the north shore, and then a boat across the estuary to Pomene Lodge and village. However, the *chapa* departs Massinga about 3pm, reaching Mashungo about 8pm or 9pm. There is nowhere in Mashungo village to sleep, although you could try your luck asking locally for permission to camp.

Vilankulo

Vilankulo is the finishing (or starting) point of Mozambique's southern tourism circuit, and an institution on the Southern Africa backpackers' and overlanders' scenes. It's also the gateway for visiting the nearby

Vilankulo

To Aguia Negra (1km);
Big Blue (1km); Vila Ia Mar (1.2km);
Vilanculos Beach Lodge (2km)

INDIAN
OCEAN

Harbour
Dona
Ana
Hotel

BAIRRO
MUKOKE

New Market
(Mercado Novo)

Av. Eduardo Mondlane

To Airport (3.5km);
Chibuene (7km);
N1 (20km)

Município

Old
Market

To Complexo
Muha (350m);
Baobab Beach
Backpackers (500m);
Odyssea Dive (500m)

Bazaruto Archipelago. During South African holidays, Vilankulo is overrun with pick-ups and 4WDs, but otherwise it's a quiet, slow-paced town with some lovely nearby beaches.

Activities

Diving
Diving is very good, although the main sites are well offshore (about a 45-minute boat ride), around the Bazaruto Archipelago.

Big Blue DIVING
(www.bigbluevilankulo.com) Located next to Aguia Negra.

Odyssea Dive DIVING
(www.odysseadive.com) Based next to Baobab Beach Backpackers.

Dhow Safaris
For day or overnight dhow safaris around the Bazaruto Archipelago, there are several outfits, including the recommended **Sailaway** (☑82-387 6350, 293-82385; www.sailaway. co.za), on the road paralleling the beach road, about 400m south of the Dona Ana Hotel. Prices average from US$70 to US$80 for a daytime snorkelling excursion to Magaruque, including park fees, snorkelling equipment, protective footwear (important, as the rock ledge can be sharp) and lunch; and, from US$120 per person per day for overnight safaris. There is officially no camping on the islands in the park; most operators camp along the mainland coast.

There are also many independent dhow operators in Vilankulo. If you go with a freelancer, remember that while some are reliable, others may quote tempting prices, and then ask you to 'renegotiate' things once you're well away from shore. Check with the tourist information office or with your hotel for recommendations and don't pay until you're safely back on land. For nonmotorised dhows, allow plenty of extra time to account for wind and water conditions; it can take two to three hours (sometimes longer) under sail from Vilankulo to Magaruque, and much longer to the other islands.

Kite Surfing

Kite Surfing Vilankulo   WINDSURFING
(www.kitesurfingvilankulo.com) At Casa Rex.

Kite Surfing Centre   WINDSURFING
(www.kitesurfingcentre.com) On the beach north of town.

🛏 Sleeping

Complexo Turístico Josef e Tina BUNGALOW $
(✆82-789 7879; www.joseftina.com; campsite per person Mtc200, chalet r Mtc800) Just back from the sea is this tidy, peaceful, locally run place with camping in the enclosed garden, reed chalets sharing bathrooms, and simple rooms in a small self-catering house. All rooms have nets, there's a small kitchen area and meals can be arranged.

Baobab Beach Backpackers   BACKPACKERS $
(✆82-731 5420; www.baobabbeach.net; campsite per person Mtc200, dm Mtc270, d bungalow with bathroom Mtc1400) With its waterside setting, chilled vibe and straightforward bungalows, Baobab Beach is a favourite with the party set. Walking here from town is fine by day; at night, always take a taxi.

**Zombie Cucumber
Backpackers**   BACKPACKERS $
(✆82-804 9410, 84-686 9870; www.zombiecucum ber.com; dm Mtc350, chalet d Mtc1500; ❋) Chilled vibe, hammocks, a bar, circular dorm, small chalets and meals on order. Very relaxing. It's just back from the beach road.

Muha Backpackers   BACKPACKERS $
(✆84-577 8394; s/d with fan Mtc400/800; ❋) This locally run place has eight simple but tidy rooms (a mix of twins and doubles) with fans and nets, a small restaurant and a rooftop terrace. It's around the corner from Baobab Beach Backpackers. Next door is an internet cafe.

Smugglers   LODGE $$
(✆84-071 0792, 293-82253; www.smugglers.co.za; d with/without bathroom Mtc2900/1800, 6-person cottage Mtc4500; ❋@) Just southwest of the Dona Ana Hotel on the inland side of the road, this place has seen better days, although it remains an amenable choice. Rooms are set around large, lush gardens with two small pools (not operational at the time of our vis-

it). Most of the rooms are twin-bedded with shared hot-water bathrooms, fans and nets. There are also larger rooms with bathrooms, a two-room family cottage and a scruffy restaurant. Breakfast costs extra.

Luxus   MOTEL $$
(✆82-851 1301, 84-030 3151; r/apt Mtc2500/3500; ❋) This place has soulless albeit spacious rooms (no nets), most with the main window opening on to a hallway. There's also a two-room apartment with cooking facilities (although no pans). It's located in a small shopping mall at the end of the main street and just opposite Taurus Supermarket.

Vilanculos Beach Lodge   LODGE $$$
(✆293-82388; www.vilanculos.co.za; s/d US$207/ 354; ❋@🛜❄) This place, about 3km north of the Dona Ana hotel along the water, has large, manicured grounds sloping down to the beach, a garden swing, a large infinity pool and spacious, well-appointed rooms.

Aguia Negra   LODGE $$$
(✆293-82387; www.amazingmozambique.com; d US$206, 4-person chalet per person from US$73; ❋) Aguia Negra has breezy, rustic, thatched A-frame chalets, each with an open loft area and all set around a large, grassy compound overlooking the sea. There are also double rooms with air-con, TV and minifridge, a restaurant and a dive operator next door. It's about 2km north of the Dona Ana Hotel.

Casa Rex   BOUTIQUE HOTEL $$$
(✆293-82048; www.casa-rex.com; s from US$140, d US$220-360, f US$360; ❋🛜❄) This lovely, midsized boutique hotel, 500m north of the Dona Ana Hotel, is the place to go if you're after an upmarket getaway. Meals are homemade and excellent, and the hotel is known for its personalised style.

Palmeiras Lodge   LODGE $$$
(✆84-380 2842, 293-82050; www.palmeiras-lodge. net; s/d from Mtc2700/4320) Just in from the beachfront road, this place is light, bright, airy and clean, with well-appointed whitewashed stone-and-thatch cottages set in lush, green grounds, and a restaurant.

🍴 Eating

Café Zambeziana   CAFE $
(light meals from Mtc120) Immediately to your right when exiting the old market, this local place has tasty but inexpensive grilled chicken and BBQ sandwiches.

Café Moçambicano CAFE $
(Avenida Eduardo Mondlane; pastries from Mtc15)
Pastries, bread, yoghurt, juice and a bakery
next door. It's opposite Barclays Bank.

Taurus Supermarket SUPERMARKET $
(Avenida Eduardo Mondlane; ⊘closed Sun) Well
stocked for self-catering. It's near the end of
the tarmac road, diagonally opposite Millennium BIM.

Kilimanjaro Café CAFE $$
(breakfast Mtc140-280, sandwiches & light meals
Mtc200-300; ⊘7.30am-6pm Mon-Sat; ⊛) Salads,
sandwiches, pizza, pasta, and a changing
daily menu plus smoothies and gourmet cof-
fees. It's in the Lexus shopping mall opposite
Taurus supermarket.

Complexo Âncora SEAFOOD, PIZZERIA $$
(✐293-82444; pizzas & meals Mtc200-350; ⊘7am-
10pm Wed-Mon) This waterside place near the
port has pizzas, plus continental dishes. Portions are large, and there's an eating area
overlooking the water. Everything is halal
(no alcohol) and there's a takeaway service.

❶ Information

Internet
Barbylon Internet Café (per hr Mtc100;
⊘9am-noon & 2-7pm) Internet access; next to
Muha Backpackers. Also rents mountain bikes
and snorkelling gear.
iCloud Internet Café (Avenida Eduardo Mondlane; per min Mtc3; ⊘9am-noon & 2pm-7pm
Mon-Fri, 9am-noon Sat) Internet access; at
Lexus Shopping Centre.

Money
Barclays Bank (Avenida Eduardo Mondlane)
ATM; near the town entrance, diagonally op-
posite Café Moçambicano.
BCI (Avenida Eduardo Mondlane) ATM; near the
town entrance, just down from Barclays.
Millennium BIM (Avenida Eduardo Mondlane,
Bairro Mukoke) ATM (Visa & MasterCard).

Tourist Information
Tourist Information Office (www.vilankulo.
com; Rua da OMM; ⊘8am-3.30pm Mon-Fri,
9am-1pm Sat) A helpful stop, with town maps,
general info and sometimes internet access.
It's in the town centre.

❶ Getting There & Away

Air
Offices for all airlines are at the airport, which
also has an ATM. The airport turn-off is along the
road running to Pambara junction, 1.5km from

the main roundabout at the entrance to town.
From the turn-off, it is 2km further.
LAM (www.lam.com.mz) Five times weekly to/
from Maputo (from about US$200 one way).
Federal Air (www.fedair.com) Daily between
Johannesburg and Vilankulo, sometimes via
Nelspruit.

Bus
Vilankulo is 20km east of the N1 down a tarmac
access road, with the turn-off at Pambara junction. *Chapas* run between the two throughout
the day (Mtc15). Except for large buses to
Maputo, all transport departs from the **transport stand** at the new market ('Mercado Novo')
on Avenida Eduardo Mondlane.
　To Maputo (Mtc750, nine to 10 hours), there
are usually two buses daily, departing by
4.30am, and sometimes as early as 2am; book
your ticket with the drivers the afternoon before
and verify the time. Departures are from in front
of the small red shop one block up from the old
market, opposite the tribunal and to the west of
the main road. Coming from Maputo, departures
from Junta are between 2.30am and 3.30am.
More comfortable TCO buses running between
Maputo and Beira stop only at Pambara junction,
and need to be booked in advance.
　To Beira (Mtc550, 10 hours), buses depart
Vilankulo at 4.30am at least every second day;
book the afternoon before.
　There's no direct bus to Chimoio. You'll need
to take a Beira bus as far as Inchope junction
(Mtc550 from Vilankulo), and then get a minibus
from there.
　To Maxixe (for Inhambane and Tofo), several
minibuses depart each morning (Mtc180, three
to four hours). Allow six to seven hours for the
entire journey from Vilankulo to Tofo.
　To Inhassoro (Mtc75, 1½ hours), minibuses
depart from just east of the market.

❶ Getting Around
Vilankulo is very spread out. For a taxi, try contacting **Sr Eusébio** (✐82-681 3383), or arrange
through your hotel. Occasional *chapas* run along
the main road, but not out to the beach places
on the northeastern edge of town, and not to the
airport.
　At night, always take a taxi in the area near
Baobab Beach Backpackers, to/from the
Maputo bus terminus and near the old market
and anywhere near the beachfront.

Bazaruto Archipelago
The Bazaruto Archipelago has clear, turquoise waters filled with colourful fish,
and offers diving, snorkelling and birding.

It makes a fine upmarket holiday if you're looking for the quintessential Indian Ocean getaway.

The archipelago consists of five main islands: Bazaruto, Benguera (also spelled Benguerra, and formerly known as Santo António), Magaruque (Santa Isabel), Santa Carolina (Paradise Island or Ilha do Paraíso) and tiny Bangué.

Since 1971 much of the archipelago has been protected as Bazaruto National Park (Parque Nacional de Bazaruto; adult/child Mtc200/100).

🏃 Activities

Dives, equipment rental and certification courses can be organised at any of the lodges, or in Vilankulo.

Sailing trips around the archipelago can be arranged with island hotels, and with the Vilankulo-based dhow safari operators. Magaruque – the closest island to Vilankulo and the main destination for day sailing/snorkelling safaris from the mainland – has a rock shelf with lots of fish, although only isolated coral patches, on its western side. Surf shoes or other protective footwear are essential, as there are many sharp edges; most operators provide these.

🛏 Sleeping & Eating

There is no budget accommodation on the islands. The best options if you have limited purse strings are arranging an island dhow cruise from Vilankulo, or visiting in the off-season, when some of the lodges offer special deals.

BAZARUTO ISLAND

Pestana Bazaruto Lodge LODGE $$$
(☑84-308 3120, 21-305000; www.pestana.com; s/d with full board from US$359/446; 🕸@🛜🌊) This unpretentious four-star getaway is at the northwestern end of the island overlooking a small, tranquil bay. Accommodation is in two dozen A-frame chalets amid lush gardens beneath the sand dunes. There is also a honeymoon suite and some family-style chalets. There's a two-night minimum stay.

Indigo Bay Island Resort & Spa RESORT $$$
(☑21-301618; www.indigobayresort.com; r per person with full board from US$545; 🕸@🛜🌊) Indigo Bay is the largest and most outfitted lodge in the archipelago. It offers a mix of villas and beachfront chalets, and a range of activities. While it lacks the laid-back island touch of some of the other places, for some

visitors this will be compensated for by the high level of comfort and amenities.

BENGUERA ISLAND

Benguerra Lodge LODGE $$$
(☑in South Africa 011-452 0641; www.benguerra.co.za; r per person with full board from US$575; @🌊) Generally considered to be one of the most intimate of the island lodges, with well-spaced and spacious luxury chalets and villa near the beach. It's at the centre of the island's western coastline, and offers the usual activities.

Azura at Gabriel's RESORT $$$
(☑in South Africa 0767-050599; www.azura-retreats.com; r per person with full board US$575-875; 🕸@🛜🌊) A lovely setting, full facilities and accommodation in villas of varying degrees of luxury.

ℹ️ Information

Entry fees are normally collected by the island hotels, and in advance by most Vilankulo-based dhow safari operators. Park headquarters are located at Sitone, on the western side of Bazaruto Island. While fees for diving, walking and other activities within the archipelago have been approved in principle, they are not currently being enforced.

ℹ️ Getting There & Away

Air

Federal Air (www.fedair.com) flies between Johannesburg, Nelspruit and Vilankulo, from where you can arrange island helicopter or boat transfers with the lodges. **CFA Charters** (☑293-82055; www.cfa.co.za; Vilankulo Airport) has flights connecting Bazaruto Island with Vilankulos (about US$200 one way).

Boat

All the top-end lodges arrange speedboat transfers for their guests. Most day visitors reach the islands by dhow from Vilankulo, where there are a number of sailing safari operators.

Inhassoro

Sleepy Inhassoro – the last of the 'main' coastal towns before the N1 turns inland – is a popular destination for South African anglers. BCI and Millennium BIM have ATMs.

Complexo Turístico Seta (☑293-91001, 82-302 0990, 293-91000; www.inhassorosetahotel.co.cc; campsite per person Mtc300, tw chalet Mtc2500, 6-person self-catering chalet Mtc6000; 🕸), a long-standing place at the end of the main road leading into town from the N1, has large, quiet grounds, a restaurant-bar overlooking the sea, campsites (towards the back of the property), and accommodation in small sea-facing chalets (several sizes available).

❶ Getting There & Away

Inhassoro is 15km east of the main road. *Chapas* run daily to/from Vilankulo (Mtc70, 45 minutes). To Beira, go to Vulanjane (the junction with the N1, Mtc10 in a *chapa*) and wait for passing northbound buses from there; ask staff at your hotel to help with the timing so you're not sitting there all day. Driving northwards, there's a bridge across the Save River.

CENTRAL MOZAMBIQUE

Central Mozambique – Sofala, Manica, Tete and Zambézia provinces – doesn't draw the tourist crowds, although it's a convenient transit zone and has several attractions. These include lovely Gorongosa National Park, hill landscapes and hiking, Cahora Bassa lake and dam, and prime birding.

Beira

Beira, Mozambique's second-largest city and busiest port, is as known for its steamed crabs and prawns as for its tawdry nightlife.

About 40km south of the city is the site of the ancient gold-trading port of Sofala. In its 15th-century heyday, it was one of East Africa's most influential centres, with links to Madagascar, India and beyond, although nothing remains of this today.

The heart of the city is the area around the squares of Praça do Município and Praça do Metical. North of the two squares is the old commercial area of the baixa, while about 1km east is Maquinino, the main bus and transport hub. From Praça do Município, tree-lined streets lead south and east through the shady and charming Ponta Gêa residential area to Avenida das FPLM. This then runs for several kilometres along the ocean to Makuti and the old red-and-white Makuti lighthouse, dating to 1904.

◉ Sights & Activities

Beira's spired cathedral (Avenida Eduardo Mondlane), southeast of the centre, was built in the early 20th century with stones taken from the ruins of San Caetano fort in Sofala.

Makuti Beach (Praia de Makuti; Avenida das FPLM) is one of the better places in town to relax, though it can't compare with the coastline further south or north.

⌂ Sleeping

Rio Savane   CAMPGROUND $
(☏82-596 2560, 23-323555; campsite per person Mtc300) This rustic place, 40km north of town in a serene setting on the Savane River, is separated from the sea by a narrow peninsula. It has camping, *barracas* (thatched shelters) with mattresses and bedding, a couple of self-catering chalets, and meals. Follow the Dondo road past the airport to the right-hand turn-off for Savane. Continue 35km to the estuary, where there's secure parking and a small boat (until 5pm) to take you to the camp.

Hotel Miramar   HOTEL $
(☏23-322283; http://miramar.no.sapo.pt; Rua Vilas Boas Truão; s/d Mtc800/1600; ❄) The Miramar offers reasonably priced, no-frills rooms – some with private bathroom and most with TV – near the water (no beach), but inconvenient for the rest of town.

Beira

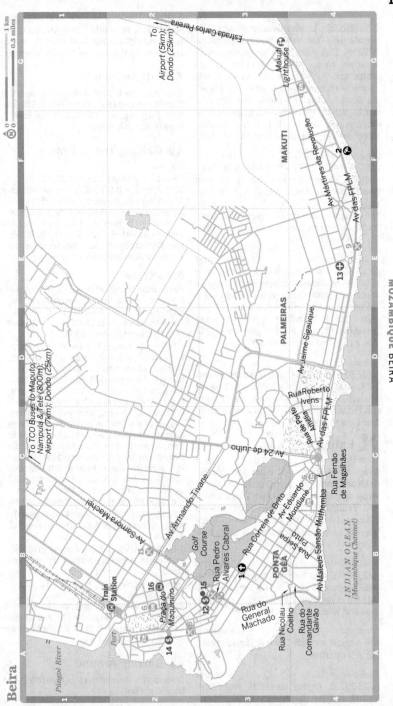

Beira

Púngoè River

Train Station

INDIAN OCEAN
(Mozambique Channel)

1 km
0.5 miles

To TCO Buses to Maputo;
Nampula & Tete (800m);
Airport (7km); Dondo (25km)

Av Samora Machel

Av Armando Tivane

Golf Course

Praça do Maquinino

Rua Pedro Alvares Cabral

Rua Correia de Brito

Rua do General Machado

Rua Nicolau Coelho

Rua do Comandante Gaivão

Rua Mateus Sansão Muthemba

Av Eduardo Mondlane

Rua Serpa Pinto

PONTA GÊA

Rua Fernão de Magalhães

Av 24 de Julho

Rua do Porto

Rua Amélia

Rua Roberto Ivens

Av das FPLM

PALMEIRAS

Av Jaime Sigaúque

MAKUTI

Av das FPLM

Av Mártires da Revolução

Makuti Lighthouse

To Airport (5km);
Dondo (25km)

Estrada Carlos Pereira

14

16

6

8

12

15

1

13

9

2

MOZAMBIQUE BEIRA

Jardim das Velas
HOTEL **$$**

(☎23-312209; jardimdasvelas@gmail.com; 282 Avenida das FPLM, Makuti Beach; d/f Mtc3325/3850; ❄) This quiet place has spotless, well-equipped rooms with views to the sea upstairs, and a couple of four-person family rooms with bunk beds downstairs. There's no breakfast and no meals, but there's a small garden with *braai* facilities, and filtered water. The beach is just across the street. It's very popular and often full.

Residencial BeiraSol
GUESTHOUSE **$$**

(☎82-492 4848, 23-236420; 168 Rua da Madeira; r Mtc1700-2500; ❄) Opposite Hotel Tivoli, with small, modern rooms, although most have only interior windows; ask for a room to the front for more views. Despite this drawback, it is a clean, secure option in the baixa. There is no breakfast.

Pousada Tropical
GUESTHOUSE **$$$**

(☎23-327202; Rua Fernão de Magalhás; r Mtc3500-4000; ❄) Spacious, well-appointed rooms in a restored private villa with polished wood floors and lots of windows. It's just off Avenida Eduardo Mondlane, on the side street immediately next to the governor's residence *(palácio do governador)*.

VIP Inn Beira
HOTEL **$$$**

(☎82-305 4753, 23-340100; www.viphotels.com; 172 Rua Luís Inácio; s/d from Mtc4100/4400; ❄🖥) Modern, comfortable rooms in the heart of the baixa, one and a half blocks north of Praça do Metical.

✕ Eating

Café Riviera
CAFE **$**

(Praça do Município; light meals from Mtc150; ⏰7.30am-9pm) This classic, pink, Old World street-side cafe is a good spot to sit with a cup of coffee and *bolo de mandioca* (almond cake) and watch the passing scene. There are soft, plump sofas inside and tables outdoors overlooking the plaza.

Restaurante Kanimambo
CHINESE **$**

(☎23-323132; Rua Pero de Alenquer; meals from Mtc200; ⏰lunch & dinner Sun-Fri) Down a small side street opposite LAM, with tasty Chinese food and a friendly proprietor.

Shoprite
SUPERMARKET **$**

(cnr Avenidas Armando Tivane & Samora Machel) For self-catering.

Clube Náutico
SEAFOOD **$$**

(☎23-311720; Avenida das FPLM; meals from Mtc200, plus per person entry Mtc20; ⏰lunch & dinner) This colonial-era swimming and social club is another popular waterside hangout, with average food and slow service redeemed by the relaxing beachside setting.

ℹ Information

There are many ATMs, including at the airport; at **Shoprite** (Avenida Samora Machel); at **BCI** (Rua Major Serpa) opposite LAM; and at **Standard Bank** (Praça do Metical).

ℹ Getting There & Away

Air

There are flights on **LAM** (☎23-324142, 23-303112, 23-306000, 23-324141; www.lam.co.mz; 85 Rua Major Serpa) twice weekly to/from Johannesburg, daily to/from Maputo, and several times weekly to/from Tete, Nampula, Pemba and Lichinga. **SAAirlink** (☎23-301570, 23-301569; www.flyairlink.com; Airport) flies several times weekly between Beira and Johannesburg.

Bus & Chapa

Beira's **main transport stand** is in the Praça do Maquinino area, in the area bounded by Avenida Daniel Napatima and Avenida Samora Machel. There's no real order to things; ask locals where to go for buses to your destination.

TCO (☎82-304 8163; tcobeira@tdm.co.mz; 28 Rua dos Irmãos Roby) departs several times weekly at 4am to Maputo (Mtc1780, 15 to 16 hours) and Nampula (Mtc1900, 16 to 17 hours) and three times weekly to Tete (Mtc890, seven hours). All departures are from the TCO office in Bairro dos Pioneiros, 1km north of the centre, and just off Avenida Samora Machel. For intermediate stops between Beira and Maputo (including Pambara junction, for Vilankulo, and Maxixe, for Inhambane), you'll still be charged the full Maputo fare. For Quelimane (Mtc650, 10 hours) direct buses leave daily by 5.30am. Alternatively, TCO en route to Nampula stops at Nicoadala, from where you can get a *chapa* the remaining 40km.

To Vilankulo (Mtc550, seven to eight hours), there's a direct bus daily departing by about 4.30am.

To Chimoio (Mtc200, three hours), minibuses go throughout the day from the main transport stand.

Another option for any northbound or southbound transport is to go to Inchope, a scruffy junction 130km west of Beira (Mtc130, three hours), where the EN6 joins the N1, and try your luck with passing buses there, although they are often full and waits are long.

ℹ Getting Around

The airport is 7km northwest of town (Mtc200 to Mtc250 in a taxi).

Chapas to Makuti (Mtc5) depart from the main transport stand.

For vehicle rentals, head to **Sixt** (📞23-302 651, 23-302 650, 82-300 5190; www.sixt.com) or **Europcar** (📞23-303 090), both at the airport.

The main taxi stand is at the western edge of Praça do Maquinino. Taxis don't cruise for business, and companies come and go, so ask your hotel for the updated numbers.

Around Beira

GORONGOSA NATIONAL PARK

About 170km northwest of Beira is **Gorongosa National Park** (Parque Nacional de Gorongosa; 📞82-308 2252; www.gorongosa.net; adult/child/vehicle per day US$20/10/45; ⊙6am-6pm Apr-Dec), which was gazetted in 1960 and soon made headlines as one of Southern Africa's premier wildlife parks. It was renowned for its large prides of lions, as well as for its elephants, hippos, buffaloes and rhinos. During the 1980s and early 1990s, hungry soldiers and poachers brought an end to this abundance. Because Renamo headquarters was nearby, the surrounding area was heavily mined and the park's infrastructure was destroyed. Rehabilitation work began in 1995, and in 1998 Gorongosa reopened to visitors. In recent years the park has received a major boost thanks to assistance from the US-based Carr Foundation, which has joined with the government of Mozambique to fund Gorongosa's long-term restoration and ecotourism development.

Animal numbers still pale in comparison with those of earlier times, and can't compare with those in other Southern African safari destinations. However, wildlife is making a definite comeback and the park is highly recommended on any Mozambique itinerary. It's likely that you will see impalas, waterbucks, sable antelopes, warthogs, hippos, crocodiles and perhaps even elephants and lions. Another major attraction is the birdlife, with over 300 species, including many endemics and near-endemics, and an abundance of water birds in the wetland areas to the east around the Urema River.

🛏 Sleeping & Eating

🏕 Gorongosa Adventures Campsite   CAMPGROUND $
(📞82-957 1436; http://gorongosa-adventures.blogspot.com) About 9km outside the park's main gate, and 500m off the park access road is this unsignposted, unnamed campsite, with lovely camping, twin-bedded permanent tents under bamboo roofs, clean, hot showers, well-equipped cooking facilities and a small shop selling basic supplies. Staff can also help you organise walks and excursions in the area, including birding trips to Mt Gorongosa, as well as transport to the park gate (where you can then hire a park vehicle for a safari). Accommodation prices were still being sorted out as this book was researched, so you'll need to contact the campsite, but everything is very reasonable, and considerably less expensive than the park accommodation. Meals can be arranged with advance notice for about Mtc300 per person.

Girassol Gorongosa Lodge   LODGE $$
(📞82-308 2252; www.gorongosa.net; campsite per person Mtc320, s/d tent Mtc1480/2100, s/d room from Mtc2600/3500; ❊❊) At Chitengo park headquarters, with comfortable, recently renovated *rondavels* scattered around an expansive, grassy compound, a handful of rooms and a camping ground with ablutions blocks and hot water. There's also a restaurant and a swimming pool.

Explore Gorongosa   TENTED CAMP $$$
(www.exploregorongosa.com; s/d with full board US$728/970; ⊙Apr-Nov) Explore Gorongosa runs walking safaris and canoe trips from its base in a semipermanent tented camp in one of the most scenic sections of the park. For multinight bush walks, it operates a series of fly camps. Everything is custom-tailored; rates include accommodation, meals, beverages and safari activities. Children below 10 years of age by advance arrangement only.

❶ Information

Park headquarters (📞82-302 0604, 23-535010; contact@gorongosa.net) are in Chitengo, about 15km east of the entry gate, from where rough tracks branch out to other park areas. Vehicle rental, guides for wildlife drives, and excursions to a nearby village can be arranged at park headquarters.

❶ Getting There & Away

AIR

CFA Charters (📞21-466 881, 293-82055; www.cfa.co.za) flies on request between Vilankulo and Gorongosa National Park.

ROAD

The park turn-off is at Inchope, about 130km west of Beira, from where it's 43km north along good tarmac to Nota village and then 17km east along an all-weather gravel road to the park gate.

You can easily reach the park entrance with a 2WD, but for exploring, you'll need a 4WD. *Chapas* heading north from Inchope to Gorongosa town (Vila Gorongosa), about 25km beyond the park turn-off, will drop you at the turn-off, from where you can arrange a pick-up with staff (advance booking essential). Pick-ups are also possible from Beira, Chimoio and Inchope; see the park website for prices.

MT GORONGOSA

Outside the park boundaries to the northwest is Mt Gorongosa (1862m), Mozambique's fourth-highest mountain. Steeped in local lore, it's known for its rich plant and birdlife (it's the only place in Southern Africa for spotting the green-headed oriole) and its abundance of lovely waterfalls.

A base camp for hikers and birdwatchers has been set up near the beautiful Morumbodzi Falls, which are on the mountain's western side at about 950m. From the camp, there are paths to the falls (about one hour's easy walk away), birding walks and overnight climbs to the summit (about six hours one way). Hikes to the falls can be organised through park headquarters (p199) for about US$70 including transport. Gorongosa Adventures Campsite (p199) outside the park gate can also help with hikes to the falls, as well as to the summit, as can the small community-based group, Mangwana (www.ecomangwana.com). Note that the climb is quite steep on the mountain's upper reaches.

To get to the Morumbodzi base camp area, follow the N6 from Beira to the turn-off at Inchope. Continue north along the tarmac road, passing the turn-off for Gorongosa park and continuing another 25km or so further to Gorongosa town. About 10km beyond Gorongosa town, turn off the main highway to the right, and continue 10km along an unpaved track to the base camp. Transport from the park can be organised through park staff.

Chimoio

Low-key Chimoio is the jumping-off point for exploring the Chimanimani Mountains to the southwest, on the Zimbabwe border.

🛏 Sleeping

Pink Papaya   BACKPACKERS $
(☎82-555 7310; http://pinkpapaya.atspace.com; cnr Ruas Pigivide & 3 de Fevereiro; dm Mtc400, s/d/q Mtc800/1000/2000; P) Pink Papaya is the best budget option, with helpful management, a convenient central location, clean dorm beds and doubles, a well-equipped kitchen and *braai* area and breakfast available on request. Note that there is no camping. It's about 10 minutes on foot from the bus stand: with the bus stand to your right and train station to your left, walk straight and take the fourth right into Rua 3 de Fevereiro. Go one block to Rua Pigivide. On request, staff will accompany you to the bus stop for early morning departures.

Residencial Dabhad   PENSION $$
(☎82-385 5480, 251-23264; http://dabhad.com; cnr Ruas do Bárue & dos Agricultores; r Mtc1500; P❄) This friendly, no-frills place has a mix of twin- and double-bedded rooms with aircon, TV and hot water. Continental breakfast is included; there are no other meals.

Hotel-Residencial Castelo Branco   HOTEL $$$
(☎82-522 5960, 251-23934; Rua Sussundenga; s/d Mtc3800/4200; P❄🛜) Catering to business travellers, this place has modern, comfortable twin- and double-bedded rooms – all with minifridge and satellite TV – around a small garden, and a breakfast buffet. There's also a restaurant, and apartments available for long-term rentals. It's signposted just off Praça dos Heróis and is often full.

Hotel Inter   HOTEL $$$
(☎84-242 0000, 251-24200; www.interhotels.co.mz; Avenida 25 de Setembro, near Rua Cidade de Lichinga; r/ste from Mtc4000/5200; ❄🛜≋) This multistorey place in the town centre compensates for its lack of ambience with comfortable, modern rooms and good facilities. There's also a restaurant.

🍴 Eating

For self-catering, try Shoprite (N6), 2km east of the town centre.

Café Atlântida   AFRICAN $
(cnr Ruas do Bárue & Dr Araújo de la Cerda; meals from Mtc130) Inexpensive local meals in a rather cavernous interior.

La Plaza   CONTINENTAL $
(☎82-601 4980, 251-23716; Praça da OMM; meals from Mtc150; ⏱lunch & dinner Mon-Sat) The recently renovated La Plaza has good, reasonably priced pizzas, plus Portuguese cuisine and seafood.

Shawarma Castle   FELAFEL $
(☎84-282 0285; Manica Shopping Centre, Rua dos Operários, N6; ⏱lunch & dinner) Good, reason-

ably priced Lebanese food. When heading out of town towards Shoprite, cross the railroad tracks. Manica Shopping Centre is at the next intersection to your right, by the petrol station.

Café-Bar Xeirinho EUROPEAN $$
(☑82-384 7950; Avenida 25 de Setembro; meals about Mtc250; ☺lunch & dinner Wed-Mon) This Portuguese-run place has an amenable ambience, a pool table and tasty food – ranging from coffees and milkshakes to continental dishes. It's just before Rua Cidade de Lichinga.

❶ Information

Internet
Internet Café (KEEP; cnr Ruas do Bárue & Dr Araújo de la Cerda; per min Mtc1) Above Café Atlântida.
Teledata (cnr Avenida 25 de Setembro & Rua Mossurize; per min Mtc1; ☺8.30am-6pm Mon-Fri, 9am-noon Sat; ☎) Slow, but also has wi-fi.

Money
Barclays Bank (Rua Dr Araújo de la Cerda) ATM.
Chimoio Forex (N6) At Manica Shopping Centre, just beyond the railway tracks and next to the petrol station; changes cash.
Standard Bank (cnr Avenida 25 de Setembro & Rua Patrice Lumumba) ATM.

Tourist Information
Mozambique Ecotours (www.mozecotours. com), reachable through the **Eco-Micaia office** (☑251-23759; www.micaia.org; just off Rua Josina Machel, behind the Chimoio International School), is the best source of information on hiking in the Chimanimani Mountains. To get here, follow Avenida Liberdade north past the church. After crossing Rua Sussundenga, continue for three more blocks to Rua Josina Machel, where you take a left. Continue along Rua Josina Machel until the paved road turns right, and Eco-Micaia is immediately on your right.

❶ Getting There & Around

Air
There are three flights weekly on **LAM** (☑82-392 6000, 251-24715; tandamoia@tandamoia.co.mz; Shoprite Complex, N6) to Maputo. The airfield is 10km from town, and signposted about 5km west of Chimoio along the Manica road.

Bus & Chapa
All transport leaves from the main bus station, near the train station.

Buses depart daily at 4am to Tete (Mtc400, seven hours) and between 2.30am and 4am to Maputo (Mtc1200, 14 hours).

For Vilankulo, there's no direct bus; take the Maputo bus and get dropped at Pambara junction. While the price should be prorated, it's difficult from Chimoio to get the drivers to come down from the full Mtc1200.

To Beira (Mtc200, three hours) and Manica (Mtc25, one hour), *chapas* run throughout the day.

To Quelimane (Mtc550, eight hours) and Nampula (Mtc1200, 15 hours), there are departures three times weekly on Maning Nice.

Taxi
Chimoio has a few taxis; look for them in front of the park on Avenida 25 de Setembro or by the market.

Manica

Tiny Manica, 70km west of Chimoio, is situated in what was once the heart of the kingdom of Manica and an important gold-trading area.

Millennium BIM (N6) and **Barclays** (N6) both have ATMs.

About 5km from town and signposted *(pinturas rupestres)* are the **Chinamapere rock paintings**.

About 20km north of Manica and straddling the Zimbabwe border is the scenic **Penha Longa** area, with good walking.

🛏 Sleeping & Eating

Pensão Flamingo PENSION $
(☑251-62385; EN6; r Mtc1100) On the main road a few blocks west of the Millennium BIM bank, this spiffy place has simple rooms with bathroom and fan, plus a garden and a restaurant.

Quinta da Fronteira BUNGALOW $
(Penha Longa Inn; ☑84-839 5311; penhalongainn@gmail.com; campsite per person Mtc250, s/d Mtc600/1350) An old mansion with a once-lovely botanical garden, camping and a few basic rooms in darkish thatch and brick cottages. Bring all your own food and drink.

Manica Lodge LODGE $$
(☑82-872 6668, 251-62452; d in small/large rondavel Mtc1117/1755) At the western end of town, and about 400m off the main road (watch for the signposted turn-off just after the immigration office), this amenable establishment has stone *rondavels* scattered

MOZAMBIQUE MANICA

CHIMANIMANI MOUNTAINS

Silhouetted against the horizon on the Zimbabwe border southwest of Chimoio are the beautiful Chimanimani Mountains, with Mt Binga (2436m), Mozambique's highest peak, rising up on their eastern edge. Much of the range is encompassed by the **Chimanimani National Reserve** (Reserva Nacional de Chimanimani; www.actf.gov.mz; adult/child/vehicle Mtc200/50/200), which is part of the larger Chimanimani Transfrontier Conservation Area (ACTF), together with Chimanimani National Park in Zimbabwe.

It's possible to hike throughout the mountains, with plenty of suitable camping sites on the high plateaus close to mountain streams, and Mt Binga can be climbed in two days, with one night spent on the mountain. The best contact for getting started is the highly recommended Mozambique Ecotours (p201).

Once up in the mountains you have to be entirely self-sufficient. Also, be prepared for sudden changes in weather, especially for mist, rain and cold, and keep in mind that the routes are physically demanding, with hikes beginning at about 700m in altitude and the highest peaks well above 2000m.

Ndzou Camp (www.mozecotours.com; campsite per tent Mtc400, 3-person tent Mtc1300, d rondavel Mtc2150, 6-person self-catering house Mtc3200), a joint venture between Eco-Micaia and the local community, is a wonderful place in the middle of Moribane Forest Reserve with camping, *rondavels* and a small family lodge. Also on offer at Ndzou are guided forest walks, eco-learning activities and the chance to track the local population of forest elephants.

The **main reserve entrance** ('*portão*'), where you pay your entry fees, and where you can arrange a guide (Mtc450 per day), is at the Mussapa Pequeno River, about 70km southwest of Chimoio off the road to Rotanda. To reach here via public transport, take a *chapa* from Chimoio to Sussundenga. Once in Sussundenga, you'll need to wait for another vehicle going towards Rotanda. After passing Muoha, watch for the signposted Chimanimani turn-off. Ask the bus driver to drop you at the 'container', from where you'll have to walk 4km along a track through lovely miombo woodland to the entrance.

For Ndzou Camp, there's usually at least one direct *chapa* daily from Chimoio to Dombe, leaving Chimoio by 8am or earlier, which can drop you. It's often just as fast to take a *chapa* to Sussundenga, from where you can catch onward transport to Dombe and the camps. It's approximately 60km from Chimoio to Sussundenga, and about 40km from Sussundenga to Ndzou.

around tranquil, manicured gardens and a restaurant.

❶ Getting There & Away

All transport departs from the market, diagonally opposite Millennium BIM. *Chapas* run frequently to/from Chimoio (Mtc65, one hour) and to the Zimbabwe border (Mtc25, 30 minutes), and several times daily between Manica and Penha Longa (Mtc25, one hour). From the *chapa* terminus in Penha Longa, it's a 20-minute walk to Mutombomwe and from there, about 3km further to Quinta da Fronteira.

Tete

Dry, dusty Tete doesn't have much in the way of tourist attractions and its reputation as one of the hottest places in Mozambique often discourages visitors. Yet the arid, brown landscape, dotted with baobab trees and cut by the wide swath of the Zambezi River, gives it a unique charm and an atmosphere quite unlike that of Mozambique's other provincial capitals.

🛏 Sleeping

Prédios Univendas   GUESTHOUSE **$$**
(☏252-23199, 252-22670, 252-23198; Avenida Julius Nyerere; s/d without bathroom Mtc1300/1550, s/d from Mtc1550/1750; ✴) Straightforward, clean rooms in the town centre. The entrance to the rooms (most with fan, aircon and TV) is just around the corner from the Univendas shop on Avenida da Independência.

Hotel Sundowner   HOTEL **$**
(☏82-306 1589; N103; r Mtc1000; ✴) Just back from the river and just up from Motel Tete,

with OK rooms (inspect a few, as they're not the cleanest) and meals.

Park Inn Tete
HOTEL $$$

(☎84-337 2009, 252-27900; www.parkinn. com/hotel-tete; Zambia Rd; s/d weekdays from Mtc8400/9000, weekends from Mtc6000/7000; ❂@🛜❄) This new place is a welcome addition to Tete's hotel scene, with modern, wheelchair-friendly rooms and a quiet location outside the city centre on the other side of the bridge. It's 3km from the town centre, just off the N103, along the road to Moatize and the airport.

Hotel Zambeze
HOTEL $$$

(☎252-24000, 252-23101; Avenida Eduardo Mondlane; s/d Mtc4500/5500; ❄) This large, multistorey place in the centre of town has straightforward, rather overpriced rooms with TV and minifridge, but it's often the only place with availability. There's also a restaurant and snack bar. It's next to Standard Bank.

🍴 Eating & Drinking

Le Petit Café
CAFE $

(cnr Avenidas Julius Nyerere & Liberdade; snacks & light meals from Mtc150; ⏱7.30am-8pm Mon-Sat; ❄) In Centro Comercial Fatima, with light meals, pastries, snacks and juices.

Paraíso Misterioso
CONTINENTAL $

(Avenida Liberdade; meals from Mtc170; ⏱lunch & dinner) On the riverbank just below the bridge, with a small garden, river views and good meals. It also has rooms.

ℹ Information

Barclays (Avenida Eduardo Mondlane) ATM; diagonally opposite Hotel Zambeze.

Immigration Office (Rua Macombre) A few blocks up from Hotel Zambeze.

Millennium BIM (Avenida Julius Nyerere) ATM; around the corner from Hotel Zambeze.

Standard Bank (cnr Avenidas Julius Nyerere & Eduardo Mondlane) ATM; next to Hotel Zambeze.

ℹ Getting There & Away

Air

LAM (☎252-22056; Avenida 24 de Julho) flies several times weekly to/from Maputo, Beira, Lichinga, Nampula, Quelimane and Chimoio. The airport is 6km from town on the Moatize road (from Mtc100 in a taxi); take any *chapa* heading to Moatize.

Bus & Chapa

To/from Beira, the best option is **TCO** (☎252-22191; cnr Avenidas Julius Nyerere & Liberdade), departing Tete Tuesday, Thursday and Saturday at 5am (Mtc890, seven to eight hours) from the TCO ticketing office opposite the gas station by Clube de Chingale. Departures from Beira are Monday, Wednesday and Friday at 6am. Travellers to Chimoio will be charged the full Beira fare.

To/from Chimoio (Mtc400, six to seven hours), transport leaves from opposite Prédio Emose on Avenida da Independência, just down from Smart Naira hotel and near Univendas. The first departures in each direction are between 4.30am and 5am, which means that if you're travelling from Chimoio to Blantyre (Malawi) via Tete, you'll be able to make the journey in one long day without overnighting in Tete, after walking across the bridge to catch transport to Zóbuè.

To Songo (for Cahora Bassa Dam), several pick-ups daily depart from the old *correios* (post office) building in the lower part of town near the cathedral (Mtc150).

For Moatize (Mtc10), *chapas* depart throughout the day from the Moatize bus stand on Rua do Qua.

For Malawi, *chapas* run to Zóbuè (Mtc150, 1½ to two hours, 115km northeast of Tete) from the far (Moatize) side of the bridge (to your left, just after crossing the bridge). After crossing the border and passing through 'no man's land', you'll need to switch to Malawi transport on the other side.

For Harare (Zimbabwe), take a *chapa* to Changara (Mtc100, 1½ hours) from Mercado 1 de Maio, and get transport from there.

For Zambia, take a Moatize *chapa* over the bridge past the SOS compound to the petrol station, where you'll find *chapas* to Matema, and from there, infrequent transport to Cassacatiza on the border.

ℹ Getting Around

Sixt Car Rental (☎82-302 1344, 252-20261; www.sixt.com) and **Europcar** (☎252-20171; www.europcar.com) are at the airport.

Taxis are at the airport, and near the intersection of Avenidas Julius Nyerere and Avenida Liberdade.

Cahora Bassa Dam & Songo

About 150km northwest of Tete at the head of a magnificent gorge in the mountains is Cahora Bassa, the fifth-largest dam in the world. It harnesses the waters of the

Zambezi River, creating the massive Cahora Bassa Lake, a prime angling destination.

To arrange visits to the dam, contact **Hidro-eléctrica de Cahora Bassa** (HCB; ☎252-82221, 252-82224, 252-8257) in Tete or in Songo town and ask for Relações Públicas.

Anglers, or anyone wanting an escape to nature, will love **Ugezi Tiger Lodge** (☎84-599 8410; www.ugezitigerlodge.co.za; campsite per person Mtc350, s/d Mtc1500/2280; ❀❀), a rustic fishing camp perched on a hill overlooking Lake Cahora Bassa. There's a choice of camping, basic, somewhat faded chalets on the densely vegetated hillside, or two eight- to 12-person self-catering houses. It's 14km from Songo town and 6km beyond the dam.

❶ Getting There & Away

Chapas run several times daily between Tete and Songo (Mtc150, three to four hours), departing Tete from the old *correios* building. Once in Songo, it's another 7km down to the dam, which you'll have to either walk or hitch.

Caia

This village is the main north–south crossing point over the Zambezi River. About 32km south of Caia along the main road in Catapu is the good **M'phingwe Camp** (☎82-301 6436; www.dalmann.com; s/tw without bathroom Mtc600/850, s/d from Mtc850/1150), which has spotless double cabins, meals and birding.

Quelimane

Quelimane is the capital of Zambézia province and heartland of the Chuabo people. It stands on the site of an old Muslim trading settlement built on the banks of the Bons Sinais (Qua Qua) River in the days when it was linked to the Zambezi River. At one time it was the main entry port to the interior. Few traces of Quelimane's long history remain, but the town's compact size and energetic atmosphere make it an agreeable enough stop for a night or two.

About 30km northeast of town through the coconut plantations is the wide **Zalala beach**, a worthwhile excursion.

🛏 Sleeping

Hotel 1 de Julho   HOTEL **$**
(☎24-213067; cnr Avenidas Samora Machel & Filipe Samuel Magala; tw without bathroom Mtc1000, with bathroom & air-con Mtc1500; ❀) Near the old cathedral, this faded budget choice has reasonable rooms with fan, sink and bucket showers, a central location near the river and offers inexpensive meals. Breakfast costs extra.

Hotel Flamingo   HOTEL **$$**
(☎82-552 7810, 24-215602; www.hotelflamingo-quelimane.com; cnr Avenidas Kwame Nkrumah & 1 de Julho; s Mtc2000-3200, d Mtc2500-3800; ❀❀❀) This popular midrange hotel opposite Praça dos Heróis has bland but good-value rooms, efficient staff, a small pool, a tiny gym and a restaurant. It's often fully booked.

Residencial Millénio   HOTEL **$$**
(☎82-305 6331, 21-213314; Rua Zedequias Manghanela; s/d/tw from Mtc2200/2850/3000; ❀❀) The Millénio, on a small side street next to the unmissable Café Águila, is a business travellers' hotel with modern, comfortable rooms in tiny grounds, and a restaurant.

🍴 Eating

Estilo China   CHINESE **$**
(Bar Refeba, cnr Avenida Marginal & Rua Kwame Nkrumah; meals Mtc190-350) In an ideal location just back from the river, Estilo China has Chinese food plus seafood and meat grills and terrace seating with amenable views.

❶ Getting There & Away
Air

LAM (☎84-307 0737, 24-212801; Avenida 1 de Julho) flies several times weekly to/from Maputo, Beira, Nampula and Tete. The airport is about 3km northwest of town at the end of Avenida 25 de Junho (Mtc150 to Mtc200 in a taxi).

Bus & Chapa

The transport stand (known locally as 'Romoza') is at the northern end of Avenida Eduardo Mondlane. *Chapas* run frequently to/from Nicoadala at the junction with the main road (Mtc30, 45 minutes).

To Nampula, a Grupo Mecula bus departs daily at 4.30am (Mtc480, 10 hours). Several vehicles also run daily to Mocuba (Mtc200, two to three hours), from where you can get onward transport to Nampula via Alto Molócuè, or to the Malawi border at Milange (Melosa). Another option is to take a *chapa* to Nicoadala, and from there, catch the Beira–Nampula **TCO** (☎82-304 8163, 23-354822; tcobeira@tdm.co.mz) bus; advance bookings are essential.

To Gurúè (Mtc300, six to seven hours), there's a bus daily at 4.30am; buy your ticket the day before. Even with a ticket, it's best to show up early at the bus stand to be sure of a seat.

Quelimane

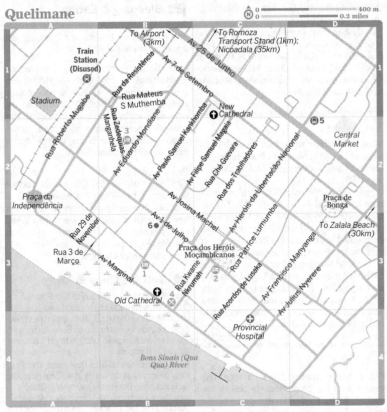

To Beira (Mtc650, 10 hours), there's a daily bus leaving by 5am. Alternatively, TCO passes Nicoadala from about 1pm, but advance booking is necessary.

To Chimoio (Mtc550, eight hours), Maning Nice departs daily at 3am from its office on Avenida Eduardo Mondlane, about 1km past the Romoza transport stand and on the opposite side of the road.

Chapas to Zalala (Mtc25, one hour) depart Quelimane from next to the central market, at the corner of Avenida Heróis da Libertação Nacional and Avenida 25 de Junho.

Quelimane

Sleeping
1 Hotel 1 de Julho	B3
2 Hotel Flamingo	C3
3 Residencial Millénio	B2

Eating
4 Estilo China	B3

Transport
5 Chapas to Zalala Beach	D2
6 LAM	B3

Mocuba

The large, lively town of Mocuba is the junction for travel between Quelimane and Nampula or Malawi.

Pensão Cruzeiro (☏24-810184; Avenida Eduardo Mondlane; tw/d Mtc1000/1200; 🅿) on the main street has decent rooms and meals.

Padaria e Pastelaria Zambeze (Avenida Eduardo Mondlane; snacks from Mtc50), about 400m further north along the main road and near Millennium BIM, has samosas, burgers, yoghurt and other light meals.

Transport to Quelimane (Mtc120, two to three hours) leaves from the market throughout the day. For Nampula (Mtc350), the best bet is to try to get a seat on the Mecula bus from Quelimane, which passes Mocuba from about 7am. There are several vehicles daily in the morning between Mocuba and Milange (Mtc200, four hours) departing from Mocuba's market. Mocuba to Gurúè costs Mtc200.

Milange

Milange is a busy town with more than its share of hustlers about 3km from the border (Melosa) with southeastern Malawi. Millennium BIM has an ATM.

Pensão Reis (r Mtc1100), with hot running water, and **Pensão Lili** (r Mtc750) are both centrally located and have been recommended as safe, although it's better to push on if possible and stay in either Mocuba or over the border in Mulanje (Malawi).

The road between Milange and Mocuba is fairly well travelled, and finding a lift usually isn't a problem. To Gurúè, there is sporadic public transport along a road to Molumbo, and from there to Lioma, from where you can get a *chapa* to Gurúè.

Gurúè

Gurúè sits picturesquely amid lush vegetation and tea plantations in one of the coolest, highest and rainiest parts of the country. The surrounding area offers fine walking and, if you don't mind foregoing the comforts, it would be easy to spend a week or more here hiking in the hills. Rising up from the hills about 15km northeast of Gurúè are the mist-shrouded slopes of **Mt Namúli** (2419m). The climb (allow two days and one night) is detailed in Lonely Planet's *Mozambique* guidebook.

Millennium BIM (Avenida Eduardo Mondlane), in the lower part of town, and **BIC** (Avenida Samora Machel), in the upper part of town, both have ATMs.

◎ Sights & Activities

A good place to start is with a walk through the jacarandas on the northern edge of town. To get here, find the small church in the centre of Gurúè and head north along the road running in front of it. Continue for five to 10 minutes, following the edge of the hill and staying on the uphill side at the forks.

🛏 Sleeping & Eating

For meals, other than what you can arrange at the hotels, try Restaurante Zamzam, just up from Pensão Gurúè.

Catholic Mission   GUESTHOUSE $
(Centro Polivalente Leão Dehon; 📞24-910096; cpld-gurue@gmail.com; dm Mtc300, tw without bathroom Mtc600, d from Mtc1000) Located on the edge of town in Bairro Artes e Ofício, this tranquil place has clean, good-value rooms, meals with advance notice and hot-water bathrooms. The gates close at 9pm.

Pensão Gurúè   PENSION $
(📞82-576 0040, 24-910050; Avenida Eduardo Mondlane; s/tw without bathroom Mtc800, d Mtc1200) On the main street in the lower part of town, this guesthouse offers clean, cheery rooms and a restaurant next door. It's also possible to arrange to pitch a tent in the small gardens behind.

❶ Getting There & Away

From Nampula, take any bus to Alto Molócuè (Mtc200), where you can then get a waiting *chapa* on to Gurúè (Mtc200). Going in the other direction, you'll need to depart Gurúè by 5am at the latest for Nampevo junction to get a connection on to Nampula.

For connections to/from Quelimane, there's a daily direct *chapa* departing at 4.30am (Mtc300, six hours); buy tickets the day before. Otherwise there are several vehicles daily to Mocuba (Mtc200, 3½ to four hours), from where you can continue to Quelimane.

It's also possible to take the train from either Nampula or Cuamba to Mutuali, where you'll find a waiting open-backed pick-up truck on to Gurúè (Mtc150, four to five hours). This works best coming from Cuamba; coming from Nampula, most of the journey to Gurúè will be at night. There's also usually one vehicle daily between Cuamba and Gurúè (Mtc200 to Mtc250, five hours). To Milange, it's fastest to go via Mocuba.

Transport in Gurúè departs from near the market at the lower end of town.

Alto Molócuè

This agreeable town is a refuelling point between Mocuba and Nampula. **Pensão Famba Uone** (d Mtc700), just up from the market, has extremely basic doubles and meals with advance notice. Several vehicles daily go to/from Nampula (Mtc200, 3½ hours) and Mocuba (four hours). There's also at least one vehicle daily to Gurúè via Nauela (50km from

Alto Molócue to Nauela, 56km from Nauela to Gurúè) along a wonderfully scenic route.

NORTHERN MOZAMBIQUE

Lake Niassa to the west, wild Niassa Reserve in the centre and palm-fringed beaches and magical archipelagos along the coast combine to make the north one of Mozambique's most alluring and adventurous destinations.

Nampula

Nampula is a crowded city with a hard edge – although these negatives are redeemed somewhat by the lush surrounding countryside dotted with soaring *inselbergs* (isolated ranges and hills), and by its proximity to Mozambique Island.

⊙ Sights & Activities

National Ethnography Museum MUSEUM
(Museu Nacional de Etnografia; Avenida Eduardo Mondlane; admission Mtc100; ⊙9am-5pm Tue-Fri, 2-5pm Sat & Sun) The National Ethnography Museum is worth a visit, with a collection documenting various aspects of local life and culture, and explanations in English and Portuguese.

Complexo Bamboo Swimming Pool SWIMMING
(Ribáuè Rd; adult/child Mtc200/100) A good spot to cool off.

🛏 Sleeping

Ruby Nampula BACKPACKERS $
(☎82-717 9923; claudilhas@hotmail.com; Rua Daniel Napatima; dm/d Mtc700/1600; ☎) This backpackers in a reconverted private house is highly recommended, especially for travellers using Nampula as a jumping-off point for Mozambique Island. It has spotless, good-value rooms and dormitories, plus hot water, a self-catering kitchen and a small bar selling snacks and cakes. Staff are helpful with onward travel information. It's a block from the National Ethnography Museum, next to the well-signposted offices of World Vision.

Residencial da Universidade Pedagógica HOSTEL $
(☎82-833 7434; 840 Avenida 25 de Setembro; s/d/tw Mtc1400/2000/2400) This university hous-

ing is in a quiet area next to Hotel Milénio, with simple, secure, good-value rooms and breakfast. It's also convenient to the Mecula bus depot.

Complexo Bamboo CHALET $$
(☎26-216595, 26-217838; bamboo@teledata.mz; Ribáuè Rd; s/d/tw Mtc1950/2450/2450; P❉❉) Pleasant, well-maintained rooms (the twins are nicer than the doubles) in expansive grounds with a children's playground and a restaurant make this a good choice for families. It's about 5km out of town; follow Avenida do Trabalho west from the train station, then right onto the Ribáuè Rd; Bamboo is 1.5km down on the left.

Residencial Expresso HOTEL $$
(☎26-218809, 26-218808; 574 Avenida da Independência; tw Mtc2200-2500; P❉) A dozen large, spotless, modern twin-bedded rooms with fridge and TV. Breakfast is included and meals can be arranged.

Hotel Milénio HOTEL $$
(☎26-218989, 26-218877; hotelmilenio@tdm.co.mz; 842 Avenida 25 de Setembro; tw/d/ste Mtc3200/3200/4500; ❉@☎) Large, modern rooms convenient to the Mecula bus garage, and a pricey restaurant downstairs. Wi-fi is in the lobby only.

🍴 Eating

Self-caterers can try the **Supermarket** (Avenida 25 de Setembro; ⊙9am-8pm Mon-Sat, to 3pm Sun) at the lower end of Avenida 25 de Setembro near the junction with Rua dos Continuadores or **Supermercado Ideal** (326 Avenida Eduardo Mondlane), in the Hotel Girassol building.

Café Atlântico CAFE $
(Centro Comercial de Nampula, Avenida Eduardo Mondlane; snacks & meals from Mtc150; ⊙6am-9pm; ❉) Burgers, pizzas and other light meals.

Restaurante Dona Amélia AFRICAN $$
(Casa Fabião, Avenida da Independência; daily menu Mtc300-400; ⊙lunch&dinner; ❉) This small place is hidden away almost in the Galp Fabião petrol station, and next to the TCO booking office. Just ask the gas station attendants to point you to the right doorway. Inside, Dona Amélia prepares soup and one or two different lunch and dinner specials each day. The food is good and reasonably priced, and the ambience authentic, with

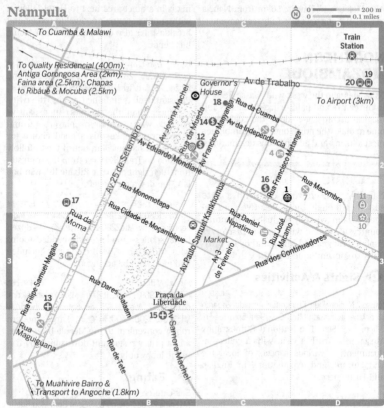

Nampula

To Cuamba & Malawi

Train Station

To Quality Residencial (400m);
Antiga Gorongosa Area (2km);
Faina area (2.5km); Chapas
to Ribáuè & Mocuba (2.5km)

Governor's House

Av de Trabalho

To Airport (3km)

Nampula

⊚ Sights
1 National Ethnography Museum............C2

🛏 Sleeping
2 Hotel Milénio......................................A3
3 Residencial da Universidade
   Pedagógica......................................A3
4 Residencial Expresso..........................C2
5 Ruby Nampula....................................C3

⊗ Eating
6 Café Atlântico....................................B2
7 Copacabana.......................................D2
8 Restaurante Dona Amélia....................C2
9 Supermarket......................................A4
   Supermercado Ideal.......................(see 6)

✪ Entertainment
10 Stadium 25 de Septembro..................D3

🛍 Shopping
11 Sunday Morning Craft
   Market..D2

ℹ Information
12 Centro Comercial de
   Nampula...C2
13 Farmácia 25 de
   Setembro..A3
14 Millennium BIM................................C2
15 Provincial Hospital...........................B4
16 Standard Bank.................................C2

ℹ Transport
17 Grupo Mecula..................................A2
18 LAM...C1
19 Maning Nice....................................D1
20 Nagi Trans......................................D1
   TCO..(see 8)

a TV in the background and locals coming and going.

Copacabana CONTINENTAL **$$**
(Rua Macombre; meals Mtc200-350; ☺7am-9pm Mon-Fri, until 11pm Sat & Sun) This popular place behind the museum has outdoor seating under a large thatched roof, tasty pizzas and seafood and meat grills.

🛍 Shopping

Sunday Morning Craft Market ARTS & CRAFTS
(Stadium; ☺dawn-dusk) In the large stadium downhill from Copacabana restaurant. Go early, before things get hot and crowded.

ℹ Information

Internet Access

There's wi-fi access in the lobby of Hotel Milénio.

Teledata (Centro Comercial de Nampula, Avenida Eduardo Mondlane; per hr Mtc1; ☺8am-noon & 2-8pm Mon-Fri, 9am-5pm Sat) Internet access.

Medical Services

Consultório Médico Boa Saude (☎84-460 5170, 84-601 5600; Rua dos Viveiros, Bairro Muahivire) One of the better bets if you're ill. Just off Avenida das FPLM.

Farmácia 25 de Setembro (Avenida 25 de Setembro; ☺8am-6pm Mon-Sat, 9am-1pm Sun) Just down from Hotel Milénio.

Provincial Hospital (Praça da Liberdade) Malaria testing.

Money

Centro Comercial de Nampula (Avenida Eduardo Mondlane) ATM inside; same location as Hotel Girassol.

Millennium BIM (cnr Avenidas da Independência & Francisco Manyanga) ATM.

Standard Bank (Avenida Eduardo Mondlane) ATM; just up from the museum.

ℹ Getting There & Away

Air

There are flights on **LAM** (☎26-212801, 26-213322; Avenida Francisco Manyanga; ☺7.30am-12.30pm & 2.30-5.30pm Mon-Fri) to Maputo (daily), Beira, Lichinga, Quelimane, Tete and Pemba (all several times weekly).

The airport is about 4km northeast of town (Mtc150 in a taxi).

Bus & Chapa

The main bus companies currently serving Nampula:

To Pemba (Mtc350, seven to eight hours): Grupo Mecula (daily); Maning Nice (three times

weekly, with one bus at 4.30am and one at noon, which awaits the Maning Nice bus arriving from Maputo); Nagi Trans (daily at noon).

To Quelimane (Mtc480, 11 hours): Grupo Mecula (daily); Maning Nice (daily); Nagi Trans (daily).

To Moçimboa da Praia (Mtc500, 13 hours), Mueda (Mtc500) and Montepuez (Mtc300, nine hours): Maning Nice (daily).

To Mozambique Island (Mtc140, three to four hours): *chapas* depart between 5am and 11am from the Padaria Nampula transport stand along Avenida do Trabalho east of the train station. Look for one that's going direct; many go only to Monapo, where you'll need to stand on the roadside and wait for another vehicle. The best connections are on one of the *tanzaniano chapas*, which depart Nampula between about 7am and 10am, depending on how early they arrive from Mozambique Island, and which continue more or less nonstop to the island. The Padaria Nampula transport stand is also the place to find *chapas* to Mossuril, Namapa, and other points north and east.

To Beira (Mtc1900, 16 hours): TCO and Maning Nice (both twice weekly).

To Mocuba (Mtc350): *chapas* leave from the 'Faina' area, about 2.5km west of the train station along Avenida do Trabalho near the Ribáuè road junction, but it's faster to take the Mecula bus to Quelimane and have them drop you.

To Cuamba: it's possible in theory to get transport from the Faina area, although most people go via Gurúè or by train.

To Chimoio (Mtc1200): Maning Nice (three times weekly).

To Maputo (Mtc2500, 30 hours): TCO, Maning Nice and Nagi Trans (all twice weekly).

To Vilankulo: there are no direct buses. The best connection is Nampula to Chimoio on Maning Nice, and then continuing from Chimoio to Vilankulo.

Grupo Mecula (☎26-213772; grupomecula@teledata.mz; Rua da Moma) Departures and ticketing from the Grupo Mecula garage, just off Avenida 25 de Setembro and one block south of Rua Cidade de Moçambique in the area known as 'Roman'. All departures at 5am. Ticketing office opens at 3pm.

Maning Nice (☎82-706 2820; Avenida do Trabalho) Departures and ticketing from Padaria Nampula transport stand, in the same place as *tanzaniano chapas* to Mozambique Island. All departures between 3am and 5am.

TCO (☎84-601 6861, 82-509 2180) Ticketing office adjoins Galp petrol station ('Casa Fabião') on Avenida da Independência, just east of Avenida Paulo Samuel Kankhomba. Departures are from 'Antiga Gorongosa', about 2km from the train station along Avenida do Trabalho, between the Sasol and Galp petrol stations

MOZAMBIQUE NAMPULA

on your left as you're heading to Quelimane. Schedules vary on a weekly basis.

Nagi Trans (☑86-318 4004, 84-265 7082, 84-955 1669; Avenida do Trabalho) Ticketing and departures from Nagi Investimentos, next to the Millennium BIM branch in the Antiga Gorongosa area.

Train

A six-times-weekly passenger train connects Nampula and Cuamba, see p215.

ⓘ Getting Around

The main **taxi rank** (Avenida Paulo Samuel Kankhomba) is near the market. For car hire, **Sixt** (☑82-300 5170, 26-216312; www.sixt. com), **Europcar** (☑84-322 3473; www.europ car.com), **Safari Rent-a-Car** (☑84-333 3555, 26-12255; safari@tdm.co.mz) and **Premium Rent-a-Car** (☑26-217864; www.carpremium. co.mz) are all at the airport.

Mozambique Island (Ilha de Moçambique)

Mozambique Island (Ilha de Moçambique), about 3km off the mainland, is a Unesco World Heritage Site and one of Mozambique's most fascinating destinations. In the staid Stone Town, quiet, cobbled streets lead onto graceful praças rimmed by once-grand churches and stately colonial buildings. In the adjoining Makuti Town, narrow alleyways echo with the sounds of playing children and squawking chickens, while fishermen sit on the sand repairing their nets.

History

As early as the 15th century Mozambique Island was an important boat-building centre, and its history as a trading settlement – with ties to Madagascar, Persia, Arabia and elsewhere – dates back well before that. Vasco da Gama landed here in 1498, and in 1507 a Portuguese settlement was established on

MUSIRO

On Mozambique Island and along the northern coast, you'll often see women with their faces painted white. The paste is known as *musiro*, and is used as a facial mask to beautify the skin, and sometimes as a medicinal treatment (though the medicinal paste usually has a yellowish tinge).

the island. Unlike Sofala to the south, where the Portuguese established a settlement at about the same time, Mozambique Island prospered as both a trading station and a naval base. In the late 16th century the fort of São Sebastião was constructed. The island soon became the capital of Portuguese East Africa – a status that it held until the end of the 19th century when Lourenço Marques (now Maputo) moved into the spotlight.

Over the years various small waves of immigration from East Africa, Goa, Macau and elsewhere have all contributed to the ethnic mix on the island. Today this heterogeneity continues to be one of Mozambique Island's most marked characteristics, although Muslim influence, together with local Makua culture, now dominates.

ⓞ Sights

Palace & Chapel of São Paulo MUSEUM
(Palácio de São Paulo; ☑26-610081; adult/child Mtc100/50; ⊗8am-4.30pm) This imposing edifice – the former governor's residence and now a museum – dates from 1610 and is the island's historical showpiece. The interior, which is currently under renovation and closed to the public, gives a remarkable glimpse into what upper-class life must have been like during the island's 18th-century heyday. In addition to knick-knacks from Portugal, Arabia, India and China, there are many pieces of original furniture, including an important collection of heavily ornamented Indo-Portuguese pieces. In the chapel (currently open), don't miss the altar and the pulpit, the latter of which was made in the 17th century by Chinese artists in Goa. On the ground floor is the small but fascinating Maritime Museum (Museu da Marinha), with gold coins, ship compasses, Chinese porcelain and other items recovered from local shipwrecks. Behind the palace are the Church of the Misericórdia (still in active use) and the Museum of Sacred Art (Museu de Arte Sacra), containing religious ornaments, paintings and carvings. The ticket price includes entry to all three museums and an English-speaking guide.

Other Sights

Dominating the island's northern end, the Fort of São Sebastião (per adult/child Mtc100/50; ⊗8am-4.30pm) is the oldest complete fort still standing in sub-Saharan Africa. Immediately beyond, on the island's tip, is the Chapel of Nossa Senhora de Balu-

Mozambique Island

Mozambique Island

◎ Sights

BIM	(see 24)
1 Camões Statue	A2
2 Chapel of Nossa Senhora de Baluarte	B1
3 Church of Santo António	B6
4 Church of the Misericórdia	A1
5 Colonial Administration Offices	A5
6 Fort of São Sebastião	B1
7 Hindu Temple	A4
Maritime Museum	(see 9)
8 Mosque	A5
Museum of Sacred Art	(see 4)
9 Palace & Chapel of São Paulo	A1

🛏 Sleeping

10 Amakuthini	A5
11 Casa Branca	A2
12 Casa de Dona Chamo	A4
13 Casa de Yasmin	B2
14 Mooxeleliya	A1
15 O Escondidinho	A4
16 Patio dos Quintalinhos	A5
17 Residencial Amy	A4
18 Ruby Backpacker	A2
19 Villa Sands	A4

🍽 Eating

20 Bar Flôr de Rosa	A5
21 Café-Bar Áncora d'Ouro	A1
22 O Paladar	A4
23 Relíquias	A1

ℹ Information

24 BIM	A4
25 Immigration Office	A1

arte, built in 1522 and considered to be the oldest European building in the southern hemisphere.

At the island's southern end is the **Church of Santo António**, while in the Stone Town are many interesting buildings, including the restored **bank** (Avenida Amilcar Cabral) and the ornate **colonial administration offices**. Nearby is a **Hindu temple**

🏃 Activities

Excursions to nearby **Goa Island** can be arranged through most hotels (from about Mtc1000 for four passengers). For beautiful, clean sand, head across Mossuril Bay to Chocas and Cabaceira Pequena.

MOZAMBIQUE MOZAMBIQUE ISLAND (ILHA DE MOÇAMBIQUE)

🛏 Sleeping

Casa Branca
GUESTHOUSE $

(☑82-454 3290, 26-610076; http://ilhamocam
bique.com.sapo.pt; Rua dos Combatentes; r without bathroom Mtc1100, with minifridge & bathroom
Mtc1600) On the island's eastern side near
the Camões statue, Casa Branca has three
simple but spotless rooms with views of the
turquoise sea just a few metres away and
a shared kitchen. One room has its own
bathroom, and the other two share. Rates
include breakfast.

Mooxeleliya
GUESTHOUSE $

(☑82-454 3290, 26-610076; http://ilhamocam
bique.com.sapo.pt; d with/without air-con Mtc1500/
1000, f Mtc2000) Mooxeleliya (the Makua
name translates roughly as, 'Did you rest
well?') has five simple but spacious high-
ceilinged rooms upstairs and two darker,
three- to four-person family-style rooms
downstairs. All rooms have their own bathroom, breakfast is included and there's a
small cooking area with refrigerator and a
communal TV/sitting area. It's just down
from the Church of the Misericórdia.

Patio dos Quintalinhos
GUESTHOUSE $

(Casa de Gabriele; ☑82-419 7610, 26-610090;
www.patiodosquintalinhos.com; Rua do Celeiro; s/d
without bathroom US$26/30, d/q from US$42/64,
ste US$64; P@🛜🏊) Opposite the green
mosque, with a handful of comfortable,
creatively designed rooms around a small
courtyard, including one with a loft, and
a suite with its own skylight and private
rooftop balcony with views to the water. All
have bathroom, except for two small rooms
to the back. There's also a rooftop terrace,
a pool and secure parking; breakfast is included. Staff can help with bicycle rental
and excursions.

Ruby Backpacker
BACKPACKER $

(☑84-398 5862; ruby@themozambiqueisland.com;
Travessa da Sé; dm Mtc500, d Mtc1100; @🛜) This
place – in a renovated 400-year-old house –
has dorm beds upstairs and downstairs, twin
and double rooms, a self-catering kitchen,
hot showers, a bar, a rooftop terrace, bicycle
rental, laundry service, a traveller's bulletin
board and information about onward travel.
From the 'arcade' street, take the first left after passing the Missanga craft shop (to your
right), and then take the next left.

Casa de Yasmin
GUESTHOUSE $

(☑82-676 8850, 26-610073; Rua dos Combatentes; r Mtc750-1500, ste Mtc2000; ✴) Near the
cinema at the island's northern end, with a
handful of clean rooms – some with bathroom and some with air-con – in an annex
next to the family house. The larger double
suite has air-con and a glimpse of the sea.
There's no food.

Casuarina Camping
CAMPGROUND $

(☑84-616 8764; casuarina.camping@gmail.com;
campsite per person Mtc200, d with/without bathroom from Mtc1000/800; 🛜) Casuarina – on
the mainland opposite Mozambique Island,
and just a two minute walk from the bridge
(to your right, coming from the island) – has
a well-maintained camping ground on a
small, clean beach, plus simple bungalow-
style rooms, ablutions blocks with bucket-
style showers and a restaurant with pizza
oven, local dishes, seafood and ice cream.

Amakuthini
GUESTHOUSE $

(Casa de Luís; ☑82-540 7622, 82-436 7570; dm
Mtc350, s/d without bathroom Mtc600/800) Very
basic and rough around the edges, but welcoming, and the only accommodation in
the midst of crowded Makuti Town. It has
an eight-bed dorm and several small, dark
rooms with fan in a tiny garden behind the
family house. There are also basic cooking
facilities, laundry service and a refrigerator.
Take the first left after passing the green
mosque (to your right), make your way
down the narrow, rocky path to the first corner and turn right.

Residencial Amy
GUESTHOUSE $

(Avenida dos Heróis; d Mtc500-700, tr Mtc800)
Near the park, with several basic, dark
rooms (most lacking exterior windows) in
the main house and a common area with TV.
There's no food.

Casa de Dona Chamo
GUESTHOUSE $

(☑84-747 1200, 82-130 3346; Avenida dos Heróis;
d without bathroom Mtc600-700, d/tr with air-con
Mtc1200/1500) This place near the park has
basic, darkish rooms, a common area and a
friendly proprietress. There's no food.

O Escondidinho
HOTEL $$

(☑26-610078; www.escondidinho.net; Avenida dos
Heróis; s Mtc1400-2700, d Mtc1600-2900, extra
bed Mtc650; ✴) This atmospheric place has
spacious, high-ceilinged rooms, all with
nets, ceiling fans and mosquito netting in
the windows, plus a garden courtyard, and
a good restaurant. A few rooms have private
bathroom. It's near the public gardens.

Villa Sands   BOUTIQUE HOTEL $$
(☎82-744 7178; www.villasands.com; d Mtc3200-
3700, ste Mtc4500; ❄🛜🏊) This sleek, boutique
hotel overlooks the water on the northwest-
ern side of the island. Most ground-floor
rooms have only a skylight, although they are
light and airy, with ceiling fans. The upstairs
suite has wide views. The upstairs rooms
have their own pool, and there's a restaurant
(meals from Mtc400) and a rooftop terrace.

Eating

Ask around for the '*barraca* restaurants'
near the hospital, especially Barraca Sara.

O Paladar   AFRICAN $
(meals Mtc250; ☺lunch & dinner Thu-Tue) At the
eastern corner of the old market, O Paladar
is the place to go for local cuisine. Stop by
in the morning and place your order with
Dona Maria for lunchtime or evening meals.

Relíquias   FUSION $$
(☎82-5252318; Avenida da República; meals
Mtc260-600; ☺10am-10pm Tue-Sun) This popular spot has well-prepared seafood and meat
dishes, plus delicious prawn curry, *matapa*
(cooked cassava leaves with peanut sauce)
and coconut rice. It's near the museum, and
has seating indoors or outside overlooking
the water.

Café-Bar Áncora d'Ouro   CAFE $$
(☎26-610006; meals about Mtc350; ☺8am-11pm
Thu-Tue) Muffins, pizzas, sandwiches, soups,
homemade ice cream, waffles and other
goodies, plus more substantial fare, prompt
service and airy seating. It's opposite the
Church of the Misericórdia.

Bar Flôr de Rosa   ITALIAN $$
(☎82-745 7380; meals Mtc300-350; ☺5pm-
midnight Mon-Sat) This small, chic Italian-run
place has coffees and espressos, a selection of
pastas, soups and sandwiches, and a rooftop
terrace for sundowners, plus live music on
Friday and Saturday in season. It's near the
hospital.

ℹ Information

Visa extensions are handled only in Nampula.

BIM (Avenida Amilcar Cabral) Has an ATM (Visa
and MasterCard), and changes cash (US dollars, euro and rand).

Mcel (per min Mtc1; ☺9.30am-6pm Mon-Fri)
Internet access; just down from the police
station.

Telecomunicações de Moçambique (per min
Mtc1; ☺8am-8pm Mon-Fri, to 1pm Sat) Internet

access; near the Palace and Chapel of São
Paulo.

ℹ Getting There & Away

Bus & Chapa

Mozambique Island is joined by a 3.5km bridge
(built in 1967) to the mainland. Most *chapas* stop
about 1km before the bridge in Lumbo, where
you'll need to get into a smaller pick-up to cross
over Mossuril Bay, due to vehicle weight restrictions on the bridge.

Leaving Mozambique Island, all transport
departs from the bridge. The only direct cars to
Nampula (Mtc140, three hours) are the *tanza-
niano* minibuses, with one or two departing daily
between 3am and 5am. The best thing to do is to
ask at your hotel for help to get a message to the
driver to collect you at your hotel pre-dawn. For
all later departures, you will need to change vehicles at Monapo and sometimes also at Namialo.

For travel direct to Pemba, take the 4am *tanza-
niano* to the main junction in Namialo (Mtc100,
one hour). Large buses from Nampula start
passing the Namialo junction from about 6am
and usually have space (about Mtc300, six hours
from Namialo to Pemba). If you miss these, there
are always smaller vehicles going north, and by
2pm or earlier you should be in Pemba. For travel
south to Quelimane, you'll need to overnight in
Nampula.

If you're driving, wide vehicles won't pass over
the bridge, and maximum weight is 1.5 tonnes.
There's a Mtc10 toll per vehicle payable on arrival on the island.

Chartering a vehicle from Nampula to Mozambique Island costs from about Mtc3000 one way.

Around Mozambique Island

North of Mozambique Island and across
Mossuril Bay is the old Portuguese holiday town of Chocas. The town itself is of
minimal interest, but just south along a
sandy track roughly paralleling the beach is
Cabaceira Pequena, with a long, beautiful
white-sand beach and views across the bay
to Mozambique Island. Just inland are the
ruins of an old Swahili-style mosque and the
ruins of a cistern used as a watering spot
by Portuguese sailors. Carrusca Mar & Sol
(☎26-213302, 82-516 0173; 4-/7-person bungalows
Mtc1750/3500) has a handful of rustic but
spacious, nicely outfitted bungalows with
hammocks and terraces, all set on a rise
between the mangroves and one of the best
stretches of beach. There's also a restaurant.

It's about 2km south of Chocas town, en route to Cabaceira Pequena.

About 2km further up the beach is Coral Lodge 15.41 (☏82-902 3612; www.coral lodge1541.com; s/d US$595/900; ❄@☂), an upmarket spot with 10 luxury villas and snorkelling in the lagoon just in front.

Further along (northwest) from Cabaceira Pequena is Cabaceira Grande, with a small treasure-trove of ruins, including a well-preserved church (Nossa Senhora dos Remédios) dating from the late 16th century and the ruins of the mid-19th-century governor-general's palace.

❶ Getting There & Away

BOAT

There's at least one dhow daily connecting Mozambique Island with Cabaceira Grande and Mossuril village (1½ hours on foot from Cabaceira Grande), departing the island between about noon and 1pm from the beach down from BIM bank next to Villa Sands, and departing Mossuril about 6am (Mtc25). If you want to return the same day, you'll need to charter a boat (about Mtc1500 for a motorised dhow). Hotels on Mozambique Island can also organise Chocas/Cabaceira excursions. For all travel to/from the Cabaceiras, be prepared for lots of wading and walking.

BUS

There's one daily direct *chapa* between Nampula and Chocas, departing Nampula between 10am and noon, and departing Chocas about 4am (Mtc150, five hours). Otherwise, take any transport between Nampula or Monapo and Mozambique Island to the signposted Mossuril turn-off, 25km southeast of Monapo (Mtc100 from Nampula to the Mossuril turn-off). Sporadic *chapas* go from here to Mossuril (20km), and on to Chocas (12km further, Mtc50), with no vehicles after about 3pm. From Chocas, it's a 30-minute walk at low tide to Cabaceira Pequena, and from one hour to 1½ hours to Cabaceira Grande.

NACALA

Nacala is northern Mozambique's busiest port, and a gateway to diving and beaches, including at Fernão Veloso, 12km north.

🛏 Sleeping & Eating

Libélula   LODGE $$
(☏82-306 6473, 82-304 2909; www.divelibelula.com; Fernão Veloso; campsite per person US$10, dm US$15, d US$60-70; ☂) Most travellers head to Libélula, about 10km outside town in Fernão Veloso in a fine setting on an escarpment overlooking the beach and the aqua waters of Nacala Bay. On offer are rustic reed-and-thatch chalets, dorm beds, camping, a waterside restaurant, snorkelling and diving. Pick-ups can be arranged from Nacala town or Nampula.

Hotel Maiaia   HOTEL $$
(☏82-601 5440, 26-526842; Rua Principal; s/d Mtc3040/3400; ❄) This centrally located three-star establishment caters to business travellers, with simple rooms with TV (some also have a tiny balcony) and a restaurant. It's on the main street diagonally opposite the central market.

🌿 Nuarro Lodge   LODGE $$$
(☏82-305 3028; www.nuarro.com; per person with full board and activities US$295) This laudable eco venture is a lovely place with 12 rustic but comfortable and spacious chalets. All are constructed out of traditional materials and use solar power, all are beautifully decorated, and each is set on its own along a low vegetated dune overlooking the sea. Activities include sea kayaking, diving, snorkelling and village visits. It's about 90km north of Nacala in Memba on the Baixa do Pindo peninsula; transfers can be arranged from Nacala, Nampula and Pemba.

❶ Getting There & Around

Grupo Mecula buses to Pemba (Mtc350, seven hours) depart Nacala daily at 5am from the Mecula garage. Head down Rua Principal to the large roundabout, then follow the street going left and uphill next to Mozstar. Mecula is about 400m up on the left, behind an unmarked wall.

There are *chapas* each morning to Nampula (Mtc160), Namialo (Mtc80) and Monapo (Mtc75, one hour), departing from the big tree next to Telecomunicações de Moçambique. Once in Monapo (ask your hotel for help in timing the connection), there's onward transport to Mozambique Island and Namialo (the junction town for Pemba).

To get to Fernão Veloso and Libélula: after entering Nacala, the road splits – follow the left fork, and continue for 2km to the unmarked airport and military base turn-off to the right. Go right here. After about 9km watch for the signposted Libélula left-hand turn-off opposite the base, from where it's another 1.5km.

Cuamba

This lively rail and road junction, with its dusty streets, flowering trees and large university student population, is the economic centre of Niassa province and a convenient stop-off if you're travelling to/from Malawi.

🛏 Sleeping & Eating

Quinta Timbwa
CHALETS $

(☎82-300 0752, 82-692 0250; quintatimbwa@yahoo.com.br; tw without bathroom Mtc750, rondavel with/without air-con Mtc2000/1500; ❄) This place is set on a large estate about 2.5km from town, and signposted. It has pleasant rooms (some in attached rows, some in small *rondavels*) surrounded by expansive grounds and a small lake, plus a restaurant.

Hotel Vision 2000
HOTEL $

(☎271-62632; cnr Avenidas Eduardo Mondlane & 25 de Junho; r Mtc1400; ❄) Vision 2000, at the main intersection, is rather down at the heel these days, although the shower-bidet combo in a few of the rooms might be an attraction for some. There's also a restaurant.

Pensão São Miguel
PENSION $

(☎271-62701; r without bathroom Mtc500, r with fan/air-con Mtc800/1000; ❄) A long-standing, local-style guesthouse with small, clean rooms crowded behind the restaurant-bar area.

❶ Information

Millennium BIM (Avenida Eduardo Mondlane) ATM; near the post office.

Telecomunicações de Moçambique (Avenida Eduardo Mondlane; per min Mtc1; ⏱8am-noon & 2-6pm Mon-Sat) Internet access; a few doors up from Millennium BIM.

❶ Getting There & Away

Bus, Car & Chapa

Most transport leaves from Maçaniqueira market, at the southern edge of town and just south of the railway tracks. *Chapas* also come to meet arriving trains. The best times to find transport are between 5am and 6am, and again in the afternoon at the station, when the train from Nampula arrives.

To Gurúè, the best routing is via train to Mutuali, from where you can find waiting pick-ups on to Gurúè. This generally works best going from Cuamba to Gurúè; going in the other direction entails long waits and travel at night. There's also a direct pick-up most days to Gurúè (Mtc200 to Mtc250), departing Cuamba by about 6am. Once in Gurúè, you can connect to Mocuba (Mtc200 Gurúè to Mocuba) and Nampula (Mtc350 Mocuba to Nampula) the same day. At the time of research, there were only sporadic direct vehicles from Cuamba to Nampula. You'll need to take the train, or go via Gurúè (Mtc400 Gurúè to Nampula direct).

To Lichinga (Mtc500, seven hours), there are several trucks daily via Mandimba, with the first departure at about 4am.

To Malawi, there is at least one pick-up daily from Cuamba to Entre Lagos (Mtc170, 1½ hours). Once at Entre Lagos, you'll need to walk across the border, where there's a weekly train on the Malawi side to Liwonde.

Train

A train connects Cuamba with Nampula (Mtc350/140 for 2nd/3rd class, 10 to 12 hours), departing in each direction daily except Monday at 5am. Second class only runs in each direction on alternate days (currently from Cuamba on Wednesday, Friday and Sunday and from Nampula on Tuesday, Thursday and Saturday). It's well worth planning your travels to coincide with a day when 2nd class is running, as 3rd class is crowded and uncomfortable. Second-class tickets can be purchased between 2pm and 5pm on the day before travel (but not earlier). Third-class tickets are available up until the time of departure.

It's a great ride, with the train stopping at many villages along the way and offering a fine taste of rural Mozambican life.

Vendors sell food at every stop, but it's worth supplementing this by bringing some snacks along, and you should bring enough bottled water for the trip as well.

To transport your vehicle on the train (about US$100), you'll need to load it the night before and arrange a guard. During the journey you can ride with the car.

Mandimba

Mandimba is a small, bustling border town and transport junction. Bar-Restaurante Ngame (Senhor Liton's; d Mtc500), near the transport stop, has basic rooms looking out on a small courtyard, and meals with advance notice.

Vehicles go daily to Lichinga (Mtc250) and Cuamba (Mtc250). Expect to pay Mtc30/50/100 for a bicycle/motorbike/taxi lift to cover the approximately 4km from Mandimba to the border, and Mtc50 for a moto-taxi across the 1500m of no-man's land to the Malawi border post (although frequently the moto-taxi drivers will stop in the middle and demand that the price be 'renegotiated').

Lichinga

Niassa's capital is pretty, low-key Lichinga (formerly Vila Cabral), which sits at about 1300m altitude, with an invigorating, cool climate and quiet, jacaranda-lined streets. It's worth a day or two in its own right and is also the best jumping-off point for exploring the lake. The surrounding area – home mainly to Yao people, as well as smaller numbers of Nyanja and Makua people – is dotted with pine groves and ringed by distant hills.

🛏 Sleeping

Ponto Final   HOTEL $
(☎82-304 3632, 271-20912; Rua Filipe Samuel Magaia; s without bathroom Mtc800, d Mtc1200) At the northeastern edge of town, this longstanding place has clean, low-ceilinged rooms and a restaurant-bar. Turn down the road at the small green-and-white Telecomunicações de Moçambique satellite office.

Residencial 2+1   HOTEL $$
(☎82-381 1070; angelina.rosario.guita@gmail.com; Avenida Samora Machel; s/d Mtc1500/1800) Clean, efficient and central – within easy walking distance of the bus stand. Attached is a reasonably priced restaurant.

Hotel Girassol Lichinga   HOTEL $$$
(☎271-21280; www.girassolhoteis.co.mz; Rua Filipe Samuel Magaia; s/d Mtc3750/4200; ❇@⚛) Lichinga's most upmarket option, with satellite TV, huge rooms, a restaurant and a tennis court. Book in advance for a discount; walk-in rates are higher.

🍴 Eating

O Chambo   AFRICAN $
(☎84-319 8800, 271-21354; meals from Mtc150) A cosy place in the Feira Exposição Niassa (FEN) compound next to the market, with soups and local meals. The owner also rents out rooms.

Padaria Mária   CAFE $
(Avenida Samora Machel; snacks & light meals from Mtc100) Opposite Residencial 2+1, with a good selection of pastries, plus light meals and yoghurt.

ℹ Information

Barclays (Main Roundabout) ATM.

BCI (Rua Filipe Samuel Magaia) ATM; in the Hotel Girassol complex, next to the hotel entrance.

Lúrio Empreendimentos (☎84-308 4080, 82-492 3780, 271-21705; lempreendimentos@teledata.mz; Main Roundabout; ⊙8am-noon & 2-5.30pm Mon-Fri, 9am-noon Sat) Next to Barclays, for car rentals, LAM bookings, dropoffs and pick-ups in Cóbuè (for Nkwichi Lodge)

and transport to/from and within the Niassa Reserve.

Millennium BIM (cnr Avenida Samora Machel & Rua Filipe Samuel Magaia) ATM.

Standard Bank (Rua Filipe Samuel Magaia) ATM.

Sycamore Services (Avenida Samora Machel; per min Mtc1; ⊙10am-6pm Mon-Fri, to noon Sat) Internet access.

ℹ Getting There & Away

Air

LAM (☎271-20847, 271-20434; Rua da LAM), just off the airport road, operates several flights weekly to/from Maputo, going via Tete (weekly) or Nampula (three times weekly) and sometimes Beira. Flights out of Lichinga tend to be heavily booked, so reconfirm your reservation and show up early at the airport.

Bus & Truck

All transport departs from beside the market, with vehicles to most destinations leaving by around 6am.

To Cuamba (Mtc500, seven hours), trucks go daily via Mandimba (Mtc250), with the first vehicle departing between 3am and 4am.

To Metangula (Mtc150, 2½ hours), several vehicles go daily.

To Segundo Congresso/Matchedje and the Rovuma River (Mtc500, six hours), at least one pick-up truck goes daily, leaving anywhere between 7am and noon from the dusty street just before the transport stand; look for the blue *barracas* near Safi Comercial and enquire there. Once over the bridge, you can get transport to Songea for about US$7. In both directions, you'll need to have your visa in advance if using this crossing.

To Marrupa (Mtc500, three hours), there's a daily vehicle. However, there is no public transport from Marrupa onwards, either to Niassa Reserve or to Montepuez.

Lake Niassa (Lake Malawi)

The Mozambican side of Lake Niassa (Lago Niassa) is much less developed than the Malawian side, and sees a small but steady stream of adventure travellers.

When venturing onto the lake, keep in mind that squalls can arise suddenly, often with strong winds.

METANGULA

Metangula is the largest Mozambican lakeshore town, with little to offer visitors. About

NKWICHI LODGE

The highly recommended Nkwichi Lodge (www.mandawilderness.org; s/d with full board in chalet US$395/640, in private house US$450/700) – located on the shore of Lake Niassa about 15km south of Cóbuè – is one of the most appealing and genuinely community-integrated lodges we've seen in the region. It is well worth the splurge, and also benefits the local community and environment. The lodge is linked with the Manda Wilderness Community Conservation Area, a privately initiated conservation area that also promotes community development and responsible tourism.

Accommodation is in six spacious handcrafted bungalows, with private outdoor baths and showers built into the bush, and several looking out onto their own white-sand coves. The lake at Nkwichi is crystal clear and there's a dhow for sails and sunset cruises. Boat transfers from Cóbuè and Likoma Island can be arranged.

8km north is the tiny village of Chuwanga, which is on an attractive beach, and is a popular weekend getaway from Lichinga.

🛏 Sleeping & Eating

Chuwanga Beach Hotel BUNGALOW $
(Complexo Cetuka, Catawala's; Chuwanga Beach; ☺campsite per person Mtc150, d Mtc500) About 8km from Metangula on Chuwanga beach, with camping and basic reed bungalows on the sand, with shared, scruffy ablutions (bucket baths). Meals and drinks are available and there's a grill.

🖉 Mbuna Bay CHALET $$$
(☑82-536 7781; www.mbunabay.ch; s/d with full board in bush bungalow US$140/220, in beach chalet US$180/280) About 15km south of Metangula, the eco-friendly Mbuna Bay has four wooden beachfront cottages, four brick cottages set back in the bush, and one wattle-and-daub cottage. All have creatively designed bathrooms, and all are comfortable in a rustic way. Snorkelling, dhow sails, kayaking and yoga can all be arranged, as can transfers from Lichinga.

ℹ Getting There & Away

Daily *chapas* connect Metangula and Lichinga (Mtc150, 2½ to three hours), most departing Lichinga early. There's also one *chapa* daily between Metangula and Cóbuè (Mtc170, four hours). Departures in Metangula are from the fork in the road just up from the market at Bar Triângulo.

There are occasional *chapas* between Metangula and Chuwanga.

The *Ilala* ferry is currently out of service; when running, it connects Metangula and Malawi. At the time of research, a new ferry was supposed to start 'soon' serving ports on the Mozambican side of the lake, including Metangula and Cóbuè.

Check with local lodges if it has begun service. Departures in Metangula are from the small dhow port just down from Bar Triângulo and below the Catholic church.

CÓBUÈ

Tiny Cóbuè is the gateway into Mozambique if you're travelling from Malawi via Likoma Island, about 10km offshore.

🛏 Sleeping & Eating

Khango Beach BUNGALOW $
(☑99-962 0916, in Malawi 88-856 7885, in Mozambique 00-265-856 7885; r without bathroom per person Mtc250; Ⓟ) This rustic place, run by the affable, English-speaking Julius, has simple reed bungalows directly on the sand. All have nets and clean shared ablutions. Meals can be arranged with advance notice.

ℹ Getting There & Away

AIR

There's an airstrip in Cóbuè for charter flights. More common is to charter a flight from Lilongwe (Malawi) to Likoma Island (about US$300 per person one way, book through Nkwichi Lodge) and then arrange a boat transfer from there with the lodge.

BOAT

The *Ilala* ferry was out of service at the time of research. Meanwhile, fishing boats ply daily in the mornings between Cóbuè and Likoma Island (about US$7 one way). Mozambique visas are issued in Cóbuè. If you're travelling to/from Malawi, you'll need to go to Immigration (on the hill near the large antenna) to get your passport stamped.

Ferry service is supposed to restart imminently at ports on the Mozambican side of the lake, including Cóbuè, so check with the lodges for an update.

BUS & CAR

A daily *chapa* runs between Metangula and Cóbuè, departing Metangula about 7am and Cóbuè about 8am (Mtc150, four to five hours).

The road between Cóbuè and Metangula (75km) is unpaved but in good condition, and there's secure parking at Khango Beach and Rest House Mira Lago in Cóbuè. Walking between Cóbuè and Metangula takes about two days, going along the river via the villages of Ngoo and Chia.

Niassa Reserve

About 160km northeast of Lichinga on the Tanzanian border is the Niassa Reserve (Reserva do Niassa; www.niassareserve.org; adult/child/vehicle per day Mtc200/50/200), a vast tract of wilderness with the largest wildlife populations in Mozambique, although the animals are often difficult (or impossible) to spot. Wildlife includes elephants (estimated to number about 16,000), sable antelopes (14,000), lions (800), buffaloes and zebras. There are also duikers, elands, leopards, wildebeest, hippos and a population of the endangered African wild dog, as well as over 400 different types of birds. However, ongoing poaching and hunting in reserve areas has contributed to great skittishness on the part of wildlife; go to Niassa primarily for adventure, rather than for wildlife watching.

An estimated 35,000 people live within the reserve's boundaries, which also encompass a 20,000 sq km buffer zone. You'll undoubtedly come into contact with locals setting their fish traps, walking, or paddling in dugout canoes (for which a few words of Swahili or Yao will stand you in better stead than Portuguese).

🛏 Sleeping & Eating

At the time of writing there was no official public camping ground, although there is a rudimentary area near Mbatamila headquarters where you can pitch a tent, and another camping area at Kiboko, on the Lugenda River by the park gate. Bring all food, drinking water and supplies with you.

Lugenda Bush Camp   TENTED CAMP $$$
(☎21-301618; www.lugenda.com; per person with full board from US$500; ☺Jun-Nov) This lovely place on the Lugenda River near the eastern edge of the park caters primarily to fly-in guests, and offers a unique safari experience that's likely to appeal to well-heeled safari connoisseurs seeking an 'unpackaged' adventure experience with all the amenities. There's a set of maintained roads around the camp to facilitate wildlife tracking.

ℹ Information

Reserve headquarters are about 40km southwest of Mecula at Mbatamila.

Wildlife in Niassa Reserve is spread relatively thinly over a vast area, with dense foliage and only a skeleton network of bush tracks. As a result, most tourism to date has been exclusively for the well-heeled, with the most feasible way to visit by charter plane from Pemba. With the gradual upgrading of road connections linking Cabo Delgado and Niassa provinces, this is beginning to change, although the reserve's main market is likely to remain top end for the foreseeable future.

For self-drivers it is possible in theory to do drive-in visits. However, given the lack of a developed network of tracks, this is only recommended for the adventure and the wilderness, rather than for the safari or Big Five aspects. Note that Niassa's tsetse flies are aggressive and numerous. Any activity in a vehicle will need to be done with windows up.

At the time of research, fees were not being collected at the reserve entrance, but rather are payable in advance – in person or via cheque – through the Maputo office of the **Sociedade para a Gestão e Desinvolvimento da Reserva do Niassa** (SGN; ☎21-329807; sgdrn.map@tvcabo.co.mz; 1031 Avenida Mao Tse Tung) – the entity charged with managing the reserve. The receipt should then be presented when you reach the reserve. That said, the entire reserve infrastructure is still in very early stages, and we haven't heard of anyone being turned away at the gate for lack of a receipt.

ℹ Getting There & Around

Air

The reserve sits roughly midway between Lake Niassa to the west and the Indian Ocean to the east, both about an hour's flight away via small plane. **CFA Charters** (☎82-575 2125; www.cfa.co.za) flies three times weekly between Lugenda Camp and Pemba (US$538/889 one way/return). Book directly, or through Kaskazini in Pemba.

Car

By road, it's possible to reach Mbatamila in the dry season via Montepuez, Balama and Marrupa. The Balama–Marrupa section is in poor condition, although currently being rehabilitated. Allow a full day from Pemba, with bush camping the only accommodation en route. Approaching the reserve from Lichinga, there is good tarmac as far as Marrupa, where there is petrol.

At Marrupa, there is camping and basic accommodation with bucket baths at **Quinta Manlia** (campsite per person Mtc100, r Mtc600), about 3km out along the Pemba route. From Marrupa, the remaining 100km stretch up to the Lugenda River and on into the reserve is dirt but in reasonable shape. The unpaved road from Cuamba to Marrupa is another doable option, especially during the dry season. Petrol is generally also available on the roadside in Mecula, although this should not be relied upon, and on the whole, driving itineraries in the reserve will be limited by how much extra fuel you can carry.

Once across the Lugenda, you'll need to sign in at the reserve, before continuing on towards Mecula and Mbatamila park headquarters – about 45km from the gate, and set in the shadow of the 1441m-high Mt Mecula – where you can arrange a guide.

Montepuez

Montepuez, a busy district capital, is the start of the wild 'road' west across Niassa province towards Lichinga. It would also be the overland gateway to the Niassa Reserve, were it not for a challenging 100-or-so kilometre stretch of road to the west from Balama to Marrupa that is currently just a bush track, although in the process of being rehabilitated. Allow one full day for this section.

🛏 Sleeping & Eating

For meals, there's a **refrigerator** (⊙from 7am Mon-Sat) next to the bakery (which is on a side street one block before the bus stand) with juice, yoghurt and (sometimes) apples. Also try the small **cafe** (light meals from Mtc100) behind the park with the aeroplane.

Vivenda Angelina　　　　　GUESTHOUSE $
(Avenida Julius Nyerere; r Mtc600) Vivenda Angelina is considerably nicer than Residencial do Geptex, with clean, quiet rooms in a private house sharing a bathroom, and (often) running water. There's no food and no signpost. Coming from the main road, turn right at the Plexus signboard at the western end of town, go two short blocks, and then turn left onto Avenida Julius Nyerere. It's the second house on the left.

Residencial do Geptex　　　　PENSION $
(☎272-51114; Avenida Julius Nyerere; d with/without bathroom Mtc500/400) Residencial do Geptex has very basic rooms with double beds, bucket baths, fans and no nets. It's at the western end of town, two blocks north of the main road.

❶ Getting There & Away

The transport stand is about two blocks south of Avenida Eduardo Mondlane; turn down the street with Millennium BIM. Several *chapas* daily go between Pemba and Montepuez (Mtc170, three hours). Heading west, there's regular transport to Balama (Mtc160), but from there to Marrupa (for Niassa Reserve) there is no option other than hitching a lift with a tractor or a truck. If you're driving, the Balama–Marrupa stretch is only feasible in the dry season.

Pemba

Pemba sprawls across a peninsula jutting into the enormous and magnificent Pemba Bay, one of the world's largest natural harbours. It's the capital of Cabo Delgado province, the main town in Mozambique's far north, and gateway to the Quirimbas Archipelago and an endless string of white-sand beaches. Although lacking the charm to be a destination in itself, the town makes for a relaxing and enjoyable stop, with almost perpetual sunshine and blue skies, a long beach nearby and a lazy, languid ambience. About 5km east of the town centre is Wimbi (also spelled Wimbe) Beach, the main hub of tourist activity.

Beginning about 10km south of town is a string of tranquil, attractive beaches, including **Murrébuè**, ideal for kite surfing.

🏃 Activities

There's a small **swimming pool** (per adult/child Mtc200/100; ⊙10am-6pm) at Clube Naval.

Diving

There's rewarding diving around Pemba. Pemba Beach Hotel has resident dive instructors available for its guests.

CI Divers　　　　　　　　　DIVING
(☎272-20102; www.cidivers.co.za; Complexo Náutilus, Avenida Marginal, Wimbi Beach) The main operator, offering PADI open-water certification, equipment rental and boat charters.

Dhow Safaris & Sailing

For day trips around Pemba Bay or multi-night dhow safaris to the Quirimbas Archipelago, contact **Pemba Sailing Safaris** (☎82-408 6694; www.pembasailingsafaris.com).

🛏 Sleeping

TOWN CENTRE

For most travellers, it's only worth considering staying in town if you can't find anything

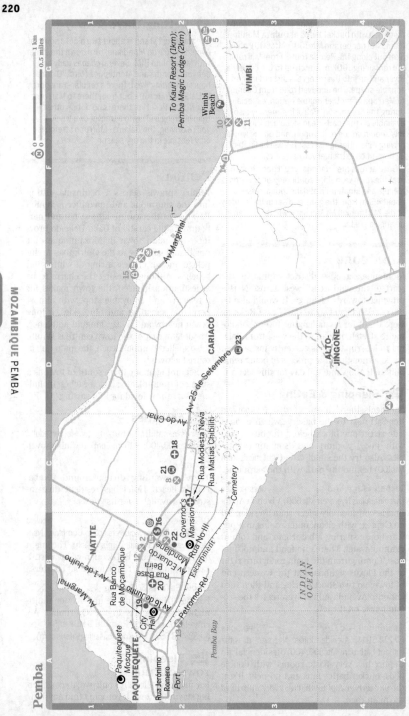

Pemba

MOZAMBIQUE PEMBA

Pemba

Activities, Courses & Tours
CI Divers..................................(see 14)
1 Swimming Pool..................................E2

Sleeping
2 Hotel Cabo Delgado..................................B2
3 Pemba Beach Hotel..................................E1
4 Pemba Dive & Bushcamp..................................D4
5 Pieter's Place..................................G2
6 Residencial Reggio Emilia..................................G2

Eating
7 Clube Naval..................................E2
8 Osman's..................................C2
9 Pastelaria Flor d'Avenida..................................B2
10 Pemba Dolphin..................................F3
Procongel..................................(see 13)
11 Restaurante Rema..................................F3
12 Restaurante-Bar Samar..................................B2
13 Wilson's Wharf..................................A2

Shopping
14 Artes Maconde Complexo
Náutilus Branch..................................F2
15 Artes Maconde Pemba Beach
Hotel Branch..................................E1

Information
16 Barclay's..................................B2
17 Clínica de Cabo Delgado..................................C2
18 Farmácia São Carlos Lwanga..................................C2
19 Immigration Office..................................B2
Kaskazini..................................(see 3)
Millennium BIM..................................(see 16)
20 Provincial Hospital..................................B2
Standard Bank..................................(see 16)

Transport
21 Grupo Mecula..................................C2
22 LAM..................................B2
23 Main Transport Stand..................................D3
Safi Rentals..................................(see 14)

MOZAMBIQUE PEMBA

at Wimbi Beach or if you have an early morning bus.

Hotel Cabo Delgado HOTEL $
(☑272-21552; cnr Avenidas 25 de Setembro & Eduardo Mondlane; s/d Mtc700/1000) This ageing hotel on the main street is well past its prime, although the central location (diagonally opposite Mcel) is convenient. The faded rooms come with bathroom (though not always with water) and fan (though not always with electricity). There's no food.

OUTSIDE THE TOWN CENTRE

Pemba Dive &
Bushcamp CAMPGROUND, BUNGALOW $
(Nacole Jardim; ☑82-661 1530; www.pembadive camp.com; campsite per person US$10, dm US$20, d/q chalet US$100/160) Ideal for families and overlanders, with Pemba's best camping, plus dorm beds, rustic chalets, a beachside bar and *braai* area, and botanical walking tours on request. It's about 10 minutes from town (Mtc400 in a taxi), behind the airport in an excellent setting on the bay, and about 3km off the main road down an unpaved track.

WIMBI BEACH

Pemba Magic Lodge CAMPGROUND $
('Russell's Place'; ☑82-527 7048, 82-686 2730; pembamagic@gmail.com; campsite per person

US$10, dm/d US$20/65; ☎) About 3.5km beyond Complexo Náutilus along the beach road extension, this place has campsites with ablutions (although no cooking facilities) just next to the very busy restaurant, plus a handful of simple chalets with fan and bathroom. There's also a bar-restaurant with a large menu, including pizzas (full breakfast costs Mtc300). The beach is just a few minutes' walk away (high-tide swimming only). Security here is on-again/off-again. Take good care of your valuables.

Residencial Reggio Emilia GUESTHOUSE $$
(☑82-888 0800, 272-21297; www.wix.com/akeelz/ Residencial-Reggio-Emilia; 8696 Avenida Marginal; r Mtc3000, 4-person self-catering chalet Mtc7000; ℗❀☎) This tranquil spot next door to Pieter's Place has clean, spacious rooms – all with hot water, air-con, satellite TV, minifridge and quality mattresses – and a few self-catering chalets in quiet grounds. All are nicely decorated with locally sourced materials such as Palma mats, and all have mosquito screens on the windows. Breakfast costs extra, and the restaurant should be open by the time you read this.

Kauri Resort HOTEL $$
(☑82-151 4222, 272-20936; www.kauriresort.com; r Mtc3000-4000; ❀☎☒) A newish place along the extension of Wimbi beach, with small,

clean, modern rooms and a restaurant (closed Monday).

Pieter's Place
GUESTHOUSE $$

(☑82-682 2700, 272-20102; cidivers@teledata.mz; Avenida Marginal; s/d from US$45/60) Along the extension of the Wimbi beach road with a few small, airy rooms in the shaded grounds of a private residence. Breakfast costs extra. There's also an open-air restaurant (closed Monday), and a huge baobab tree in the courtyard, with a treehouse sitting area built into its upper branches.

Pemba Beach Hotel
HOTEL $$$

(☑272-21770; www.pembabeachresort.com; 5470 Avenida Marginal; s/d from Mtc7076/8613, 4-6 bed self-catering apartment Mtc13,833; P❄️@🛜🏊) This five-star establishment has expansive grounds overlooking the water, well-equipped rooms, a restaurant (closed at the time of research) and a yacht for charters around the Quirimbas Archipelago. Package deals from Johannesburg are available that also include sister lodges in the Quirimbas and Bazaruto archipelagos.

✖️ Eating

TOWN CENTRE & BAIXA

For self-catering try Osman's (Avenida 25 de Setembro; ☺8.30am-6pm Mon-Fri, 9am-4pm Sat), about 1.5km east of the main junction, or the pricey but well-stocked Procongel (Petromoc road; ☺9am-1pm & 2-5pm Mon-Fri, 9am-1pm Sat) attached to Wilson's Wharf restaurant in the Baixa, with produce, imported cheeses and gourmet items.

Pastelaria Flor d'Avenida
CAFE $

(☑272-20514; Avenida Eduardo Mondlane; meals Mtc180-220; ☺7am-9pm Mon-Sat) This long-standing, informal eatery offers outdoor tables on a small, street-side plaza, and a selection of standards and pastries.

Restaurante-Bar Samar
SEAFOOD $

(☑272-20415; Avenida 25 de Setembro; meals Mtc180-220; ☺9am-10pm Sun-Fri) Tucked away in the car park of the Igreja Reino de Deus, this place features hearty Portuguese cuisine served on a shaded porch.

Wilson's Wharf
SEAFOOD, BURGERS $$

(☑84-303 8197, 84-742 2909; Petromoc road; breakfast Mtc200-250, meals Mtc250-750; ☺8am-late Mon-Sat; ❄️🛜) Burgers, seafood and meat grills and hearty breakfasts and views over the port. Rooms are planned.

WIMBI BEACH

Restaurante Rema
AFRICAN $

(Avenida Marginal; meals from Mtc170) A good spot for local meals and local vibes. It's just opposite Pemba Dolphin.

Clube Naval
SEAFOOD, CONTINENTAL $$

(☑82-304 4887, 272-21770; Avenida Marginal; meals from Mtc250; ☺10am-11pm) This waterside restaurant-bar has a beachside setting and a large menu featuring salads, seafood, chicken, ribs, pizzas and desserts. There's a volleyball area on the sand, a swimming pool and a small children's playground.

Pemba Dolphin
SEAFOOD $$

(☑272-20937; Avenida Marginal; pizza Mtc150-250, seafood grills Mtc250-550; ☺from 7am) Directly on the beach, with music and a beach-bar ambience, plus seafood grills and pizzas.

🛍️ Shopping

Artes Maconde Pemba
Beach Hotel Branch
ARTS & CRAFTS

Good crafts at Pemba Beach Hotel.

Artes Maconde Complexo
Náutilus Branch
ARTS & CRAFTS

Good craft located next to CI Divers at Complexo Náutilus.

ℹ️ Information

Immigration
Immigration Office (Avenida 16 de Junho; ☺7.30-11am & 2-4pm Mon-Fri) Just off Rua Base de Moçambique.

Internet Access
Sycamore Services (☑272-21999; 1282 Avenida 25 de Setembro; per hr Mtc100; ☺7.30am-8pm Mon-Sat, 8am-noon Sun) Internet connection; it's just after Mcel.

Medical Services
Clínica de Cabo Delgado (☑272-21462; Rua Modesta Neva 10) For basic medical treatment, although quality is erratic.

Farmácia São Carlos Lwanga (☺7am-6.30pm Mon-Fri, 8am-5pm Sat) One block back from Avenida 25 de Setembro, on the same street as the Mecula bus office.

Provincial Hospital (cnr Ruas Base Beira & 1 de Maio) Malaria tests and basic medical treatment.

Money
Millennium BIM (Avenida Eduardo Mondlane) ATM; there's also a Millennium BIM ATM in front of Complexo Náutilus at Wimbi Beach.

Standard Bank (Avenida Eduardo Mondlane) ATM.

Barclay's (Avenida Eduardo Mondlane) ATM.

Tourist Information
Kaskazini (☑82-309 6990, 272-20371; www.kaskazini.com; Pemba Beach Hotel, Avenida Marginal, Wimbi Beach; ⏰8am-3pm Mon-Fri, 8.30am-noon Sat) Efficient, knowledgeable and a good first stop. It gives free information on Pemba and elsewhere in northern Mozambique, helps with accommodation and flight bookings, and can organise everything from dhow safaris to sunset cruises.

❶ Getting There & Away
Air
LAM (☑272-21251; Avenida Eduardo Mondlane; ⏰7am-4.30pm Mon-Fri, 9.30-11.30am Sat) flies daily to/from Maputo (via Nampula and/or Beira), and twice weekly to/from Dar es Salaam (Tanzania).

SAAirlink (☑272-21700; www.flyairlink.com; Airport) flies twice weekly between Johannesburg and Pemba.

CFA (☑82-575 2125; www.cfa.co.za) flies five times weekly to the Quirimbas Archipelago and three times weekly to Niassa Reserve. Book directly, or through Kaskazini.

Expect to pay from Mtc350 to Mtc500 for a taxi from the airport to town.

Bus & Chapa
Grupo Mecula (☑272-20821; grupomecula@teledata.mz; Rua Josina Machel) has daily buses to Nampula (Mtc350, seven hours), Moçimboa da Praia (Mtc270, seven hours) and Mueda (Mtc280, nine hours), with the same bus going first to Moçimboa da Praia and then on to Mueda. There's also a daily bus to Nacala (Mtc350, seven hours); otherwise take the Nampula bus to Namialo junction and wait there for onward transport. All of Mecula's Pemba departures are at 4.45am from the Grupo Mecula office, just off the main road and about 1.5km from the centre on a small side street behind Osman's supermarket.

For Mozambique Island, the best bet is to continue to Nampula, and then get onward transport from there the next day. You can also try your luck getting out at Namialo junction and looking for onward transport from there, but the timing often doesn't work out, and Namialo is unappealing as an overnight spot.

For other destinations, head to the **main transport stand** (Rodoviario) about 2km from the centre (Mtc100 in a taxi) along the extension of Avenida 25 de Setembro, where there are vehicles in all directions, including to Macomia (Mtc170, two hours) and Montepuez (Mtc170,

three hours). Maning Nice and Nagi Trans buses also depart from here to Nampula daily.

❶ Getting Around
Bus & Taxi
There are taxi ranks on Avenida Eduardo Mondlane just down from Mcel and at the same junction along Avenida 25 de Setembro, or call ☑84-600 0008. Town to Wimbi Beach costs Mtc150 to Mtc200. There's also a public bus that runs between 6am and 7pm from town to Wimbi Beach and beyond (Mtc10), and the occasional *chapa* from the Mcel corner to Complexo Náutilus roundabout (Mtc7.50).

Rental Car
Safi Rentals (☑82-380 8630; www.pembarentacar.com)comes highly recommended, offering reliable car rentals at very reasonable prices. Rates include unlimited kilometres, and open the door to many attractions in the north that would be otherwise inaccessible for budget and midrange travellers. It is based at Complexo Náutilus. It's also possible to arrange car rentals through Kaskazini.

Murrébuè
About 12km south of Pemba is Murrébuè, a lovely, long and undeveloped stretch of white sand fringed by turquoise waters that is famed for its optimal kite surfing conditions.

🛏 Sleeping & Eating
Upeponi GUESTHOUSE $
(☑82-669 8540, 82-397 2659; r with/without aircon Mtc1500/750) This relaxed, locally run place is a popular weekend destination for day visitors, offering a pleasant stretch of beach and a restaurant (weekends only) for lunch and dinner.

Ulala BUNGALOWS $$
(☑82-710 9117, 82-741 5104; www.ulala-lodge.com; s/d in bungalow Mtc2400/2800, in stilt bungalow Mtc3600/4000) This new place has a lovely beachside setting, a large dining/relaxing area, and accommodation in two spacious, breezy stilt houses just back from the beach, or two other nonstilted family bungalows somewhat further back. All have hot water and nets, and the whole setting is lovely. Airport transfers are free for stays of two or more nights.

Il Pirata BUNGALOWS $$
(☑82-380 5790; www.murrebue.com; d with full board US$135-180) Il Pirata, at the northern

end of the beach and about 3km north of Ulala, is the hub of activity. It also has three lovely bungalows and delicious Italian meals. Airport transfers can be arranged.

❶ Getting There & Away

To reach Murrébuè, head out of town along the main road for about 5km; turn left at the signposted Mecufi district road and wind your way along the sandy road downhill. At the T-junction at the bottom, after the police station, Ulala and Upeponi are signposted to the right. Il Pirata is to the left.

Quirimbas Archipelago

The Quirimbas Archipelago consists of about two dozen islands and islets strewn along the 400km stretch of coastline between Pemba and the Rovuma River. Some are waterless and uninhabited, while others have histories as long as the archipelago itself.

Ibo, the best known of the islands, was already an important Muslim trading post when the Portuguese arrived in the 15th century, and by the late 18th century it had become a major slave-trading port and the second-most important town in Mozambique after Mozambique Island. Today, it's a fascinating place with wide streets lined with dilapidated villas and crumbling, moss-covered buildings. At its northern end is the star-shaped fort of São João dating from the late 18th century, known now for its silversmiths. While there are no good beaches near town, there are several secluded spots around the island where you can swim.

Other islands include Quirimba, with extensive coconut plantations, and Matemo and Medjumbe, both with luxury resorts. Quilaluia is now a protected marine sanctuary. Vamizi, Rongui and Macaloé Islands are part of a privately funded, community-based conservation project.

While there are many beautiful patches of white, soft sand, the archipelago is also known for its vegetation, and many of the islands are fringed in part by mangroves. Dense mangrove forests also link some of the islands to each other, and with the coast. Only skilled dhow captains are able to navigate among the intricate channels that were cut during Portuguese times. The archipelago is also known for its diving, and for its birding.

Many of the southern islands, including Ibo and Matemo, are part of Quirimbas National Park (Parque Nacional das Quirimbas; adult/child Mtc200/100), which also includes large inland areas on the fringing coastline. The one-time entry fee is collected by hotels within the park area. There are also various other park fees, including Mtc100 per person per day for camping, but their enforcement status is still in flux.

🛏 Sleeping & Eating

IBO ISLAND

It's possible to arrange homestays ([☎]82-551 1919; r Mtc250-400) with local families; contact Ibraimo Assane directly at this booking number. You'll get a taste for how locals live, and get to sample local meals. Be prepared for extremely basic conditions.

Tikidiri   HOSTEL $

([☎]82-590 3944; Airfield Rd; campsite per person Mtc100, s/d Mtc150/300) This community-run place, 2km from the dhow port along the path leading to the airfield, has basic but clean stone-and-thatch bungalows with nets and bucket baths and clean drop toilet. There's no electricity and no breakfast, but good local meals can be arranged (from Mtc100), as can guides for exploring the island and elsewhere in the archipelago.

Casa de Lucy   GUESTHOUSE $

([☎]82-815 2892; d Mtc800) Just up from the dhow port and before Ibo Island Lodge, with just two nice rooms (one overlooking the water) and some more under construction. Meals can be arranged.

Panela Africana Guesthouse & Restaurant   GUESTHOUSE $

(African Pot; [☎]82-535 3113; sstephanec@hotmail.com; d US$30-40, meals Mtc250-350, set menu Mtc500; ⊘restaurant noon-3pm & 6pm-late) About 75m past and diagonally opposite Santo António fort in Bairro Rituto, with three rooms attached to the family house and a gourmet restaurant, featuring Mozambican-French fusion cuisine. During the dry season, Stephane, the owner, can also arrange dhow safaris to the other islands on his sleeper dhow, *Maisha*.

Pensão Café do Ibo   PENSION $

(Ibo Coffee Guesthouse; [☎]82-551 7501, 82-658 7111; Airfield Rd; r Mtc1200-1500) About 500m up from Miti Miwiri on the water side of the road, with small, clean rooms opposite a small coffee plantation.

Karibuni HOSTEL $
(Campsite do Janine; ☑82-703 2200; campsite per person Mtc120, r Mtc400-800) This place is next to Ibo Island Lodge and just up from the dhow port. It has some very basic rooms and space in a small garden to pitch your tent. Meals can be prepared, but you'll need to bring your own food..

Miti Miwiri GUESTHOUSE $$
(☑82-543 8564, 26-960530; www.mitimiwiri. com; d/tr/f US$65/75/80, 3-course dinner about Mtc500; ⊛) A lovely, atmospheric place in a restored house with a handful of spacious, good-value rooms with bathroom and fan, including one family room with two double beds. There's a large, walled garden with three swings, a bar and sheesha lounge, and a restaurant with excellent meals, including vegetarian selections. Staff can also help with tourist information and excursions, flight bookings to/from Pemba and international telephone calls. It's in the heart of the town, and about 10 minutes on foot from the dhow port – ask any of the children who come to meet the boat to show you the way. Continental/full breakfast costs Mtc150/250 extra.

Cinco Portas GUESTHOUSE $$
(www.cincoportas.net; s US$50-80, d US$65-100, 4-person house US$180-250; ⊛) This comfortable place is in a restored mansion with a lovely garden. It's just up the road from Miti Miwiri, and has a variety of rooms, some with sea-facing verandahs, and a restaurant (breakfast costs extra).

Ibo Island Lodge LODGE $$$
(www.iboisland.co.za; s/d with full board US$460/720; ⊛) This nine-room luxury boutique hotel – the most upmarket accommodation on Ibo – is housed in two restored mansions in a prime setting overlooking the water near the dhow port. Relax on the sea-facing verandahs, enjoy a sundowner overlooking the water, or luxuriate in the comforts of the rooms.

OTHER ISLANDS
It's possible to arrange camping on Matemo at Sr Dade's campsite near Matemo Island Resort; arrange visits through Miti Miwiri on Ibo.

MONEY MATTERS

There are no ATMs or banks on Ibo, and most places on the island do not accept credit cards. Bring sufficient cash, or arrange to pay in advance.

Quilálea LUXURY HOTEL $$$
(www.azura-retreats.com/quilalea; r per person with full board US$665-795) A luxurious private resort with nine sea-facing villas and prime diving and snorkelling immediately offshore.

Medjumbe Island Resort LUXURY HOTEL $$$
(www.medjumbe.com; per person with full board from US$530; ✳✳) Thirteen thatched wooden chalets set directly on the sand, plus diving and fishing.

Matemo Island Resort LUXURY HOTEL $$$
(www.matemoresort.com; per person with full board from US$440; ✳✳) Two dozen beachfront chalets, all with indoor and outdoor showers and Moorish overtones in the common areas.

❶ Getting There & Away
Air

CFA Charters (☑82-575 2125; www.cfa.co.za) flies five times weekly between Ibo and Pemba (US$310 return, 25 minutes), with stops on request at Matemo, Medjumbe and several other islands. Book directly or through Kaskazini in Pemba.

Boat

To reach the island on your own steam, you'll need to go first to Quissanga, on the coast north of Pemba. A direct *chapa* departs Pemba from the fish market behind the mosque in Paquitequete *bairro* (Mtc200, five to six hours) at about 4.30am daily. Once in Quissanga, most vehicles continue on to Tandanhangue village (Mtc200 from Pemba), 5km further, which is the departure point for dhows to Ibo (Mtc50). In a private car, the trip to Quissanga and Tandanhangue takes about 3½ hours. For drivers (4WD), there's secure parking at Gringo's (James') Place next to the Tandanhangue dhow port for Mtc100 per day.

Dhows leave Tandanhangue only at high tide (with a window of about two hours on either side of the high-tide point), and nonmotorised boats take from one to six hours to Ibo (about 45 minutes with motor). There's no accommodation in Tandanhangue. Chartering a motorised boat for yourself to Ibo will cost about Mtc1500 one way. Kaskazini offers road transfers between Pemba and Tandanhangue followed by a motorboat

MAPIKO DANCING

If you hear drumming in the late afternoons while travelling around Cabo Delgado, it likely means *mapiko* – the famed masked dancing of the Makonde.

The dancer – always a man – wears a special wooden mask or *lipiko* (plural: *mapiko*), decorated with wildly exaggerated features, hair (often real) and facial etchings. Before *mapiko* begins, the dancer's body is completely covered with large pieces of cloth wrapped around the legs, arms and body so that nothing can be seen other than the fingers and toes. All evidence that there is a person inside is supposed to be hidden. *Mapiko* supposedly grew out of male attempts to limit the power of women in matrilineal Makonde society. The idea is that the dancer represents the spirit of a dead person who has come to do harm to the women and children, from which only the men of the village can protect them. While boys learn the secret of the dance during their initiation rites, women are never supposed to discover it, remaining in fear of the *mapiko*.

Once the dancer is ready, distinctive rhythms are beaten on special *mapiko* drums. The dance is usually performed on weekend afternoons, and it must be finished by sunset.

transfer to Ibo for US$270 one way for up to four people.

Dhows to Quirimba Island depart from Quissanga. Alternatively, you can inquire with Pensão Quirimba about space on its boat.

For overnight sailing charters from Pemba direct to the islands, contact Kaskazini.

Mueda

Mueda – the main town on the Makonde Plateau and the centre of Mozambique's Makonde people – is rather lacking in charm. However, this is compensated for by a wonderfully cool climate, a rustic, highland feel and an attractive setting, with views down from the escarpment along the southern and western edges of town. It's the first (or last) major town on the Mozambique side if crossing to/from Tanzania on the Unity Bridge. In 1960 it was the site of the infamous massacre of Mueda. There's a statue commemorating Mueda's role in Mozambican independence and a mass grave for the 'martyrs of Mueda' at the western end of town. The closest ATM is in Moçimboa da Praia.

On the main road, **Pensão Mtima** (☏86-314 5303; Rua 1 de Maio; r with/without bathroom Mtc800/500) has basic, clean rooms with bucket baths and meals on order.

❶ Getting There & Away

Grupo Mecula has a daily bus between Pemba and Mueda via Moçimboa da Praia (Mtc280, nine

hours), departing at 5am. Several vehicles go each morning between Mueda and Moçimboa da Praia (Mtc150, two hours). There's also one vehicle daily to the Negomano border (Mtc500), departing between about 8am and 9am. All transport leaves from the main road opposite the market. After about 10am, it's difficult to find vehicles to any destination.

If you're driving, there are two roads connecting Mueda with the main north–south road. Most traffic uses the good road via Diaca (50km). The alternate route via Muidumbe (about 30km south of Diaca) is scenic, winding through hills and forests, but rougher. Near Muidumbe is **Nangololo**, a mission station and an important base during the independence struggle, with an old airstrip large enough to take jets.

Moçimboa da Praia

This bustling outpost – home to the Mwani ('People of the Sea') – is the last major town before the Rovuma River and the Tanzanian border if travelling via public transport and the Kilambo border crossing.

The town itself is long, stretched over several kilometres between the main road and the sea. In the upper-lying section is a small market, several *pensões* (inexpensive hotels), a petrol station and the transport stand. About 2km east near the water are a few more places to stay, police and immigration, a lively fish market and the colourful dhow port.

Together with nearby Palma, Moçimboa da Praia has become a hub for the current influx of oil money in northern Mozambique, so expect changes here.

🛏 Sleeping & Eating

Pensão Leeta, at the town entrance opposite the transport stand, is currently rented out in its entirety, but you may still be able to pitch a tent in its grounds.

Pensão-Residencial Magid   PENSION $
(☑272-81099; Avenida Samora Machel; r Mtc500) A short walk downhill from the transport stand and convenient to the Grupo Mecula bus 'garage', with basic rooms sharing facilities.

Hotel Chez Natalie   CHALET $$
(☑82-439 6080, 272-81092; natalie.bockel@gmail. com; campsite per person Mtc300, d without bathroom Mtc800, 4-person chalets with/without internet & hot water Mtc2200/2000; ⊛) The best bet in town if you have your own transport, with large grounds overlooking the estuary, camping, a handful of spacious family-style four-person chalets with running water and mosquito nets, and a grill. Breakfast and other meals are available with advance arrangement only. It's 2.5km from the town centre; watch for the barely signposted left-hand turn-off from Avenida Samora Machel onto Avenida Eduardo Mondlane just after passing Clubé de Moçimboa. Continue along Avenida Eduardo Mondlane past the small Praça do Paz on your left for 400m. Turn left next to a large tree onto a small dirt path, and continue about 1km past a row of local-style houses to Chez Natalie.

Complexo de Contentores de Ilha Vumba   BUNGALOW $$
(☑82-311 4750; r small/large Mtc1420/2500; ⊛) This place, a temporary housing complex for oil and tourism project workers, has clean, air-con rooms in trailers. It also has Moçimboa's best **restaurant** (meals from Mtc180). It's along the road paralleling the beach.

Restaurante Estrelha   AFRICAN $
(Avenida Samora Machel; meals from Mtc150) Restaurante Estrelha is opposite the police station and on the right, just before the park. There's outdoor seating and, with luck, a choice of grilled chicken or fish.

ℹ Information

If you're travelling by dhow and enter or leave Mozambique here, have your passport stamped at the immigration office just back from the beach in the lower part of town. An immigration officer meets arriving international flights.

Barclays, Millennium BIM and BCI all have ATMs. Barclays changes US dollars cash. **Telecomunicações de Moçambique** (Avenida 7 de Março; per min Mtc1) has internet access.

ℹ Getting There & Away
Air
CFA Charters (☑82-575 2125; www.cfa.co.za) flies three times weekly between Moçimboa da Praia, Pemba and several of the Quirimbas islands, including Ibo, Matemo and Medjumbe, in coordination with Coastal Aviation flights from Dar es Salaam (Tanzania).

Bus & Pick-Up
The transport stand is near the market at the entrance to town, and near the large tree. Several pick-ups go daily to/from the Rovuma ('Namoto') via Palma (Mtc250, two hours). The road to Palma is being paved, and is in good shape. To Pemba, the Mecula bus departs daily at 5am (Mtc270, seven hours). Maning Nice departs daily by 3am. Several pick-ups also do the journey, departing by 7am from the main road in front of the market. Maning Nice goes daily between Moçimboa da Praia and Nampula (Mtc500, 13 hours), and several vehicles go daily to/from Mueda (Mtc150, two hours).

Palma

The large fishing village of Palma is nestled among the coconut groves about 45km south of the Tanzania border. It's a centre for basketry and mat weaving (although most of this is done in the outlying villages) and for boat making.

The immigration office is in the upper part of town. There's nowhere to change money, although changing meticais and Tanzanian shillings at the markets is no problem.

Pensão Managanha (r Mtc500) is in the upper part of town and has simple, clean rooms and a loud disco on weekends.

ℹ Getting There & Away
All transport leaves from the Boa Viagem roundabout at the town entrance. Some drivers continue down to the main market.

Chapas from Moçimboa da Praia en route to the Rovuma River pass Palma from about 6am (Mtc100 from Palma to the border). Transport from the Rovuma south to Moçimboa da Praia passes through Palma from about 10am, and there's at least one vehicle from Palma to Moçimboa da Praia each morning (Mtc150, one hour) along a good, graded road that will soon be paved.

UNDERSTAND MOZAMBIQUE

Mozambique Today

Since the signing of peace accords in 1992, and the first multiparty elections in 1994, Mozambique has been remarkably successful in moving beyond its history of war and transforming military conflict into political competition. In December 2004 Armando Guebuza, an insider in the ruling Frelimo political party, was elected to succeed long-serving former president Joaquim Chissano (also Frelimo), who had earlier announced his intent to step down. An easy re-election for Guebuza followed in 2009.

Thanks to these relatively smooth political transitions, Mozambique has won acclaim and donor funding over the past decade as a successful example of postwar reconciliation and democracy-building in Africa. It is also set to benefit economically from major coal and natural gas finds in the north of the country. Challenges include widespread corruption, rising organised crime and opposition party Renamo's ongoing struggles to prove itself as a viable political party.

History

From Bantu-speaking farmers and fishers to Arabic traders, Goan merchants and adventuring Europeans, Mozambique has long been a crossroads of cultures.

In the Beginning

The first Mozambicans were small, scattered clans of nomads, possibly distant cousins of the San, who were likely trekking through the bush as early as 10,000 years ago. They left few traces and little is known about this era.

About 3000 years ago, Bantu-speaking peoples from the Niger Delta in West Africa began moving through the Congo basin. Over a period of centuries they journeyed into East and Southern Africa, reaching present-day Mozambique sometime around the 1st century AD, where they made their living farming, fishing and raising livestock.

Early Kingdoms

Most of these early Mozambicans set themselves up in small chiefdoms, some of which gradually coalesced into larger states or kingdoms. These included the Karanga (Shona) in central Mozambique and the renowned kingdom of Monomotapa, south and west of present-day Tete.

Southern Mozambique, which was settled by the Nguni and various other groups, remained decentralised until the 19th century, when consolidation under the powerful kingdom of Gaza gave it at least nominal political cohesion.

Arrival of the Arabs

From around the 8th century AD sailors from Arabia began to arrive along the East African coast. Trade flourished and intermarriage with the indigenous Bantu-speakers gave birth to Swahili language and culture. By the 9th century several settlements had been established, including Kilwa island, in present-day Tanzania, which soon became the hub of Arab trade networks throughout southeastern Africa. Another was Sofala, near present-day Beira, which by the 15th century was the main link connecting Kilwa with the old Shona kingdoms and the inland goldfields. Other early coastal settlements included those at Mozambique Island, Quelimane and Ibo Island, all ruled by local sultans.

Portuguese Adventurers

In 1498 Vasco da Gama landed at Mozambique Island en route to India. Within a decade after da Gama's arrival, the Portuguese had established themselves on the island and gained control of numerous other Swahili-Arab trading posts – lured in part by their need for supply points on the sea route to the east and in part by their desire to control the gold trade with the interior.

Over the next 200 years the Portuguese set up trading enclaves and forts along the coast, making Mozambique Island the capital of what they called Portuguese East Africa. By the mid-16th century ivory had replaced gold as the main trading commodity and by the late 18th century slaves had been added to the list, with close to one million Africans sold into slavery through Mozambique's ports.

Portugal's Power Struggle

In the 17th century the Portuguese attempted to strengthen their control by setting up *prazos* (vast agricultural estates) on land granted by the Portuguese crown or by wresting control of it from local chiefs.

The next major effort by the Portuguese to consolidate their control came in the late 19th century with the establishment of charter companies, operated by private firms who were supposed to develop the land and natural resources within their boundaries. In reality these charter companies operated as independent fiefdoms, and did little to consolidate Portuguese control. With the onset of the 'Scramble for Africa' in the 1880s, Portugal was forced to strengthen its claims in the region. In 1891 a British-Portuguese treaty was signed formalising Portuguese control in the area.

Early 20th Century

One of the most significant events in early-20th-century Mozambique was the large-scale labour migration from the southern provinces to South Africa and Rhodesia (present-day Zimbabwe). This exodus was spurred by expansion of the Witwatersrand goldmines, and by passage of a new labour law in 1899 which divided the Mozambican population into nonindigenous (*não indígenas* or *assimilados*), who had full Portuguese citizenship rights, and indigenous (*indígenas*), who were subject to the provisions of colonial law and forced to work, to pay a poll tax and to adhere to passed laws.

Another major development was the growing economic importance of the southern part of the country. As ties with South Africa strengthened, Lourenço Marques (now Maputo) took on increasing importance as a major port and export channel and in the late 19th century the Portuguese transferred the capital here from Mozambique Island.

In the late 1920s António Salazar came to power in Portugal. He sealed off the colonies from non-Portuguese investment, abolished the remaining *prazos* and consolidated Portuguese control over Mozambique. Overall conditions for Mozambicans worsened considerably.

Mueda Massacre

Discontent with the situation grew and a nationalist consciousness developed. In June 1960, at Mueda in northern Mozambique, an official meeting was held by villagers protesting peacefully about taxes. Portuguese troops opened fire on the crowd, killing many demonstrators. Resentment at the 'massacre of Mueda' helped politicise the local Makonde people and became one of the sparks kindling the independence struggle. External support came from several sources, including Julius Nyerere's government in neighbouring Tanganyika (now Tanzania). In 1962, following a meeting of various political organisations working in exile for Mozambican independence, the Frente pela Libertação de Moçambique (Mozambique Liberation Front; Frelimo) was formed in Dar es Salaam, Tanzania, led by Eduardo Chivambu Mondlane.

Independence Struggle

Frelimo was plagued from the outset by internal divisions. However, under the leadership of the charismatic Mondlane and operating from bases in Tanzania, it succeeded in giving the liberation movement a structure and in defining a program of political and military action to support its aim of complete independence for Mozambique. On 25 September 1964 Mondlane proclaimed the beginning of the armed struggle for national independence.

In 1969 Mondlane was assassinated, and succeeded as president by Frelimo's military commander, Samora Moises Machel. Under Machel, Frelimo sought to extend its area of operations to the south. The Portuguese meanwhile attempted to eliminate rural support for Frelimo by implementing a scorched earth campaign and by resettling people in a series of *aldeamentos* (fortified village complexes).

However, struggles within Portugal's colonial empire and increasing international criticism sapped the government's resources. In 1974, at a ceremony in Lusaka (Zambia), Portugal agreed to hand over power to Frelimo and a transitional government was established. On 25 June 1975 the independent People's Republic of Mozambique was proclaimed with Samora Machel as president and Joaquim Chissano, a founding member of Frelimo's intellectual elite, as prime minister.

Early Years of Independence

The Portuguese pulled out virtually overnight, leaving the country in a state of chaos with few skilled professionals and virtually no infrastructure. Frelimo, which found itself suddenly faced with the task of running the country, threw itself headlong into a policy of radical social change.

However, Frelimo's socialist program proved unrealistic and by 1983 the country was almost bankrupt. Onto this scene came the Resistência Nacional de Moçambique (Mozambique National Resistance; Renamo), a ragtag group that had been established in the mid-1970s by Rhodesia (now Zimbabwe) as part of its destabilisation policy, and later kept alive with backing from the South African military and certain sectors in the West.

Ravages of War

Renamo, which had been created by external forces rather than by internal political motives, had no ideology of its own beyond the wholesale destruction of social and communications infrastructure within Mozambique, and the destabilisation of the government.

The drought and famine of 1983 crippled the country. Faced with this dire situation, Frelimo opened Mozambique to the West in return for Western aid.

In 1984 South Africa and Mozambique signed the Nkomati Accord, under which South Africa undertook to withdraw its support of Renamo, and Mozambique agreed to expel the ANC and open the country to South African investment. While Mozambique abided by the agreement, South Africa exploited the situation to the full and Renamo's activity did not diminish.

Samora Machel died in a plane crash in 1986 under questionable circumstances, and was succeeded by the more moderate Joaquim Chissano. The war between the Frelimo government and the Renamo rebels continued, but by the late 1980s political change was sweeping through the region. The collapse of the USSR altered the political balance, and the new president of South Africa, FW de Klerk, made it more difficult for right-wing factions to supply Renamo.

Peace

By the early 1990s Frelimo had disavowed its Marxist ideology. A ceasefire was arranged, followed by a formal peace agreement in October 1992 and a successful UN-monitored disarmament and demobilisation campaign.

People of Mozambique

There are 16 main ethnic groups, including the Makua (Cabo Delgado, Niassa, Nampula and parts of Zambézia), Makonde (Cabo Delgado), Sena (Sofala, Manica and Tete), and the Ronga and Shangaan (Gaza and Maputo). Smaller groups include the Lomwe and Chuabo (both Zambézia), Yao and Nyanja (Niassa), Mwani (Cabo Delgado), Nyungwe (Tete) and Tswa and Chopi (Inhambane).

About 1% of Mozambique's population is of Portuguese extraction, most of whom are at least second generation and consider themselves Mozambicans first.

The Arts

Dance

On Mozambique Island and along the northern coast, watch for *tufo,* a dance of Arabic origin. It is generally performed by women, wearing matching *capulanas* (sarongs) and scarves, and accompanied by special drums (some more like tambourines) known as *taware.*

A good place to get information on traditional dance performances are the *casas de cultura* (cultural centres), found in every provincial capital.

Literature

During the colonial era, local literature generally focused on nationalist themes. Two of the most famous poets of this period were Rui de Noronha and Noémia de Sousa.

In the late 1940s José Craveirinha (1922–2003) began to write poetry focusing on the social reality of the Mozambican people and calling for resistance and rebellion, which eventually led to his arrest. Today, he is honoured as Mozambique's greatest poet, and his work, including 'Poem of the Future Citizen', is recognised worldwide.

As the armed independence struggle gained strength, Frelimo freedom fighters began to write poems reflecting their life in the forest, their marches and the ambushes. One of the finest of these guerrilla poets was Marcelino dos Santos.

With Mozambican independence in 1975, writers and poets felt able to produce literature without interference. This newfound freedom was soon shattered by Frelimo's war against the Renamo rebels, but new writers emerged, including the internationally acclaimed Mia Couto, whose works include *Voices Made Night* and *The Last Flight of the Flamingo.* Contemporary female writers include Lilia Momple (*The Eyes of the Green Cobra*) and Paulina Chiziane (*Niketche – A Story of Polygamy*).

Music

The *timbila* orchestras of the Chopi people in southern Mozambique are one of the country's best-known musical traditions.

Modern music flourishes in the cities and the live-music scene in Maputo is excellent. *Marrabenta* is considered Mozambique's national music. It developed in the 1950s in the suburbs of Maputo (then Lourenço Marques) and has a light, upbeat style and distinctive beat inspired by the traditional rural *majika* rhythms of Gaza and Maputo provinces. It is often accompanied by a dance of the same name.

Sculpture & Painting

Mozambique is known for its woodcarvings, particularly for the sandalwood carvings found in the south and the ebony carvings of the Makonde.

The country's most famous painter is Malangatana, whose style is characterised by its dramatic figures and flamboyant yet restrained use of colour, and by its highly symbolic social and political commentary. Other internationally acclaimed artists include Bertina Lopes and Roberto Chichorro.

Food & Drink

Mozambique's cuisine blends African, Indian and Portuguese influences, and is especially noted for its seafood, and its use of coconut milk and *piri-piri* (chilli pepper).

Where to Eat

Roadside or market *barracas* (food stalls) serve plates of local food such as *xima* (maize- or casava-based staple) and sauce for about US$6 or less.

Most towns have a cafe, pastelaria (bakery and pastry shop) or *salão de chá* (tearoom) serving coffee, pastries and inexpensive snacks and light meals such as omelettes, *pregos* (thin steak sandwiches) or burgers.

CULINARY HIGHLIGHTS

Staples

xima or **upshwa** – a maize- or cassava-based staple or rice, served with a sauce of beans, vegetables or fish

frango grelhado (grilled chicken) – cheap and easy to find; usually served with chips or rice

Specialities

matapa (cassava leaves cooked in a peanut sauce, often with prawns or other additions) – in the south

galinha á Zambeziana (chicken with a sauce of lime juice, garlic, pepper and *piri-piri*) – in Quelimane and Zambézia provinces

caril (curry) dishes

chamusas (samosas – triangular wedges of fried pastry, filled with meat or vegetables) and **rissois de camarão** (similar to *chamusas*, but semicircular, and with a shrimp filling)

pão (bread) – freshly baked each morning, and best eaten warm

peixe & mariscos (fish and shellfish) – grilled prawns *(camarões) and* calamari *(lulas)* are some of the many seafood delicacies available along the coast

peixe grelhada (grilled fish) – delicious, served with rice or chips

prego – thin steak sandwich

Drinks

Bottled water *(água mineral)* is widely available, as are soft drinks *(refrescos* or 'sodas'). Beer (including the Manica, Laurentina and Dois M (2M) labels, plus South African and Namibian beers) is sold by the *garafa* (bottle) or *lata* (can). Portuguese and South African wines *(vinho)* are also widely available, as are nonsweetened fruit juices *(sumo)* from South Africa.

Restaurant prices and menu offerings are remarkably uniform throughout the country, ranging from about Mtc250 to Mtc400 for meals such as grilled fish or chicken served with rice or potatoes.

Markets in all larger towns sell an abundance of fresh tropical fruits along with a reasonably good selection of vegetables. High-quality meats from nearby South Africa are sold in delis and supermarkets.

Natural Environment

Mozambique has extensive coastal lowlands forming a broad plain 100km to 200km wide in the south and leaving it vulnerable to seasonal flooding. In the north, this plain narrows and the terrain rises to mountains and plateaus on the borders with Zimbabwe, Zambia and Malawi. In central Mozambique the predominant geographical feature is the Zambezi River valley and its wide delta plains. In many areas of the north, particularly in Nampula and Niassa provinces, towering granite outcrops or *inselbergs* dominate the landscape.

Wildlife

ANIMALS

While more than 200 types of mammals wander the interior, challenging access, dense vegetation and skittishness on the part of the animals can make spotting difficult, and Mozambique shouldn't be viewed as a Big Five destination. Work is proceeding in reviving several parks and reserves, especially Gorongosa National Park, which offers Mozambique's most accessible wildlife watching.

BIRDS

Of the approximately 900 bird species that have been identified in the Southern Africa region, close to 600 have been recorded in Mozambique. Among these are numerous aquatic species found primarily in the southern wetlands. Rare and unique species (most of which are found in isolated montane habitats such as the Chimanimani Mountains, Mt Gorongosa and Mt Namúli) include the dappled mountain robin, the chirinda apalis, Swynnerton's forest robin, the olive-headed weaver and the green-headed oriole.

MARINE LIFE

Coastal waters host populations of dolphins, including spinner, bottlenose, humpback and striped dolphins, plus loggerhead, leatherback, green, hawksbill and olive ridley marine turtles. The coast also serves as a winter breeding ground for the humpback whale, which occurs primarily between Ponta d'Ouro and Inhambane. Between July and October it's also common to see whales in the north, offshore from Pemba.

Dugongs have been sighted around Inhambane Bay, Mozambique Island, Nacala and the Quirimbas and Bazaruto Archipelagos.

National Parks & Reserves

Mozambique has six national parks: Gorongosa, Zinave, Banhine and Limpopo in the interior; Bazaruto National Park offshore; and Quirimbas National Park, encompassing both coastal and inland areas in Cabo Delgado province. Zinave and Banhine have no tourist infrastructure.

Wildlife reserves include Niassa, Marromeu, Pomene, Maputo and Gilé. The Chimanimani National Reserve has a network of rustic camps for hikers.

SURVIVAL GUIDE

Directory A–Z

Accommodation

Accommodation along the coast, especially in the south, fills during Christmas/New Year's, Easter and other South African school holidays (all of which are considered 'high season'; book accommodation in advance).

Always ask about low season (ie, during the February to April rainy months) and children's discounts.

When quoting prices, many establishments distinguish between a duplo (room with two twin beds) and a casal (double bed).

Rates are often quoted in US dollars or South African rand. Payment can almost always be made in meticais, dollars or rand.

SLEEPING PRICE RANGES

In this chapter, the following price ranges refer to a double room in high season.

$ less than Mtc1250
$$ Mtc1250–3750
$$$ more than Mtc3750

Backpacker lodges ('backpackers'), found mostly along the southern coast, offer dorm beds (average cost Mtc400), private rooms, cooking facilities and, sometimes, campsites.

There are many camping grounds. Carry a tent to save money, and for travel in rural areas. Per person prices: Mtc150 to Mtc250 per night. Where there is no established campsite, ask the local *régulo* (chief) for permission; you'll invariably be welcomed, and should reciprocate with a modest token of thanks (eg, what you would pay at an official camping ground or a bit less).

The cheapest hotels (*pensão*, singular, or *pensões*, plural) may have bucket bath, likely won't have air-conditioning and may or may not have electricity.

At the midrange level, expect private bathroom, hot running water, electricity, air-conditioning (sometimes) and a restaurant on the premises. Top-end hotels come with all the amenities, at a price.

Activities

BIRDWATCHING
Prime birding areas:

Bazaruto Archipelago

Gorongosa National Park (Parque Nacional de Gorongosa; 82-308 2252; www.gorongosa. net; adult/child/vehicle per day US$20/10/45; 6am-6pm Apr-Dec) and Mt Gorongosa.

Chimanimani Mountains

Mt Namúli

Maputo Special Reserve (adult/child/ vehicle Mtc200/100/200)

Area around Catapu, near Caia

Useful websites:

Avian Demography Unit (http://web.uct. ac.za/depts/stats/adu/p_mozat.htm)

Indicator Birding (www.birding.co.za)

Southern African Birding (www.sabirding. co.za)

African Bird Club (www.africanbirdclub.org)

DIVING & SNORKELLING
Attractions include the chance to sight whale sharks, dolphins, manta rays and dugongs; opportunities to discover new sites; the natural beauty of the Mozambican coast; seasonal humpback whale sighting; excellent fish diversity; and, a generally untouched array of hard and soft corals, especially in the north. You'll also have most spots almost to yourself.

Equipment, instruction and certification are available in Ponta d'Ouro, Tofo, Vilankulo, the Bazaruto Archipelago, Nacala, Pemba and the Quirimbas Archipelago. Prices are comparable to elsewhere in East Africa, although somewhat higher than in South Africa.

HIKING
Mountain climbs include Mt Gorongosa and Mt Namúli. For hiking, head to the Chimanimani Mountains, which also include Mt Binga, Mozambique's highest peak. The hills around Gurúè offer good walking.

SURFING & KITE SURFING
The best waves are at Ponta d'Ouro in the far south of the country and at Tofinho. Boards can be rented at both places.

For kite surfing, contact Pirate Kites (www.murrebue.com).

WILDLIFE WATCHING
The main wildlife-watching destination is Gorongosa National Park. Other possibilities include Niassa Reserve, Maputo Special Reserve and Limpopo National Park. Apart from Gorongosa, the chances of spotting significant wildlife are small, and Mozambique shouldn't be considered a Big Five destination.

Business Hours
Note that reviews don't list business hours unless they differ from these standard ones:

Banks 8am to 3pm Monday to Friday

Foreign Exchange Bureaus (*casas de câmbio*) 8.30am to 5pm Monday to Friday, 8.30am to noon Saturday

Government Offices 7.30am to 3.30pm Monday to Friday

Eating Breakfast 6am to 11am, lunch noon to 3pm, dinner 6pm to 10.30pm

Drinking 5pm to late

Shopping 8am to noon and 2pm to 6pm Monday to Friday, 8am to 1pm Saturday

Children
The beaches are ideal for visiting with young children. Many resorts also have swimming pools and most offer children's discounts.

In beach areas, be aware of the risk of hookworm infestation in populated areas, as well as the risk of bilharzia in lakes. Other things to watch out for: sea urchins at the beach (beach shoes are a good idea for children and adults) and thorns in the bush.

For malaria protection, bring mosquito nets from home for your children and ensure that they sleep under them. Also bring mosquito repellent from home, and check with your doctor regarding the use of malaria prophylactics. Long-sleeved shirts and trousers are the best protection at dawn and dusk.

PRACTICALITIES

Cots and spare beds Easily arranged; average cost Mtc500.

Child seats for hired cars Occasionally available; confirm in advance.

Restaurant high chairs Occasionally available.

Formula, disposable nappies & wet wipes Available in pharmacies, large supermarkets and markets in larger towns.

Child care Easy to arrange informally through your hotel.

Customs Regulations

It's illegal to export any endangered species or their products, including anything made from ivory or tortoiseshell.

'Reasonable' quantities of souvenirs for personal (rather than commercial) purposes can be exported without declaration.

Embassies & Consulates

The closest Australian representation is in South Africa. All of the following embassies and high commissions are in Maputo.

Canadian High Commission (☎21-492623; www.canadainternational.gc.ca/mozambique; 1138 Avenida Kenneth Kaunda)

French Embassy (☎21-484600; www.ambafrance-mz.org; 2361 Avenida Julius Nyerere)

German Embassy (☎21-482700; www.maputo.diplo.de; 506 Rua Damião de Gois)

Irish Embassy (☎21-491440; maputo embassy@dfa.ie; 3332 Avenida Julius Nyerere)

Malawi High Commission (☎21-492676; 75 Avenida Kenneth Kaundam)

Netherlands Embassy (☎21-484200; http://mozambique.nlembassy.org; 324 Avenida Kwame Nkrumah)

Portuguese Embassy (☎21-490316; www.embpormaputo.org.mz; 720 Avenida Julius Nyerere)

South African High Commission (☎21-243000; www.dfa.gov.za/foreign/sa_abroad/sam.htm; 41 Avenida Eduardo Mondlane)

Swaziland High Commission (☎21-491601; swazimoz@teledata.mz; 1271 Rua Luís Pasteur)

Tanzania High Commission (☎21-490110/3, 21-491051; ujamaa@zebra.uem.mz; 852 Avenida Mártires de Machava)

UK High Commission (☎82-313 8580; http://ukinmozambique.fco.gov.uk; 310 Avenida Vladimir Lenine)

US Embassy (☎21-492797; http://maputo.usembassy.gov; 193 Avenida Kenneth Kaunda)

Zambian High Commission (☎21-492452; 1286 Avenida Kenneth Kaunda)

Zimbabwe High Commission (☎21-486499, 21-490404; 1657 Avenida Mártires de Machava)

Food

The following price ranges are used for Eating reviews in this chapter.

$	Less than Mtc250 per meal
$$	Mtc250-500 per meal
$$$	More than Mtc500 per meal

Legal Matters

The use or possession of recreational drugs is illegal in Mozambique. If you're offered anything, it is often part of a setup, usually involving the police, and if you're caught, penalties are very stiff. At the least, expect to pay a large 'payment' to avoid arrest or imprisonment (which is a very real risk).

DOCUMENTS

All foreigners are required to carry a copy of their passport when out and about.

Rather than carrying the original, carry a notarised copy of the name and visa pages, plus notarised copies of your drivers licence and other essential documents. If you're stopped on the street or at a checkpoint and asked for any of these, always hand over the notarised copy, rather than parting with the original.

Notary facilities are available in Maputo and provincial capitals; see the town listings, or ask at your hotel for a recommendation. Some Mozambique embassies will also provide this service before you travel.

If you're arrested for more 'legitimate' reasons, you have the right to talk with someone from your embassy, as well as a lawyer, though don't expect this to help you out of your situation with any rapidity.

Driving on the beach, driving without a seatbelt (for all vehicle occupants), exceeding speed limits, driving while using your mobile phone, turning without using your indicator lights and driving without two red hazard triangles and a reflective vest in the boot are all illegal, and are common ways of attracting police attention and demands for a bribe or *multa* (fine).

Maps

Excellent Coopération Française maps cover Maputo, Beira, Quelimane, Nampula and Pemba; check at the local municipal council. The Reise Know-How *Mosambik & Malawi* and Globetrotter *Mozambique* maps are readily available, as are the following ones:

Tracks for Africa (www.tracks4africa.co.za) Downloadable GPS maps for self-drivers in the bush.

Instituto Nacional de Hidrografia e Navegação (Inahina; ☎21-429108, 21-429240; Rua Marques de Pombal, Maputo) Coastal and maritime maps *(cartas náuticas)* and tide tables *(tabelas de marés)*; at the *capitania*, behind the white Safmar building near the port.

Direcção Nacional de Geografia e Cadastro (Dinageca; ☎21-302555; 537 Avenida Josina Machel, Maputo) Detailed topographical maps.

Money

Mozambique's currency is the New Mozambique Metical (plural meticais, pronounced 'meticaish'), abbreviated here as Mtc, and sometimes also referred to as the 'metical nova família'. Note denominations include Mtc20, Mtc50, Mtc100, Mtc200, Mtc500 and Mtc1000, and coins include Mtc1, Mtc2, Mtc5 and Mtc10.

One metical is equivalent to 100 centavos (Ct), and there are also coins of Ct1, Ct5, Ct10, Ct20 and Ct50.

Visa card withdrawal from ATMs is the best way of accessing money.

Carry a standby mixture of US dollars (or South African rand, especially in the south) and meticais (including a good supply of small denomination notes, as nobody ever

has change) for times when an ATM is non-existent or not working.

ATMS

All larger and many smaller towns have ATMs for accessing cash meticais. Most (including Barclays, BCI and Standard Bank) accept Visa card only, Millennium BIM machines also accept MasterCard.

Many machines have a limit of Mtc3000 (US$120) per transaction. BCI's limit is Mtc5000 (US$200) and some Standard Bank machines dispense up to Mtc10,000 (US$400) per transaction.

CASH

US dollars are easily exchanged everywhere; together with South African rand (which are especially useful in southern Mozambique), they are the best currencies to carry.

Only new-design US dollar bills will be accepted. Euros are easy to change in major cities, but elsewhere you're likely to get a poor exchange rate.

Most banks don't charge commission for changing cash, and together with foreign exchange bureaus, these are the best places to change money. BCI branches are generally good. Many Millennium BIM branches will let you change cash only if you have an account.

Casas de câmbio (foreign exchange bureaus) usually give a rate equivalent to or slightly higher than the banks, and are open longer hours.

Changing money on the street isn't safe anywhere and is illegal; asking shopkeepers is a better bet.

CREDIT CARDS

Credit cards are accepted at most (but not all) top-end hotels, many midrange places, especially in the south, and at some car-hire agencies, but otherwise are of limited use in Mozambique.

Visa is by far the most useful, and is also the main (often only) card for accessing money from ATMs.

TRAVELLERS CHEQUES

Travellers cheques can only be exchanged with difficulty (try BCI) and with a high commission plus original purchase receipts. Nowhere accepts travellers cheques as direct payment.

Public Holidays

New Year's Day 1 January

Mozambican Heroes' Day 3 February

Women's Day 7 April

International Workers' Day 1 May

Independence Day 25 June

Lusaka Agreement/Victory Day 7 September

Revolution Day 25 September

Peace and Reconciliation Day 4 October

Christmas/Family Day 25 December

Safe Travel

Mozambique is a relatively safe place and most travellers shouldn't have any difficulties. That said, there are a few areas where caution is warranted.

CRIME

Petty theft and robbery are the main risks: watch your pockets or bag in markets; don't leave personal belongings unguarded on the beach or elsewhere; and minimise (or eliminate) trappings such as jewellery, watches, headsets and external money pouches.

If you leave your vehicle unguarded, don't be surprised if windscreen wipers and other accessories are gone when you return. Don't leave anything inside a parked vehicle.

When at stop lights or slowed in traffic, keep your windows up and doors locked, and don't leave anything on the seat next to you where it could be snatched.

In Maputo and southern Mozambique (due to the proximity of South African organised-crime rings) carjackings and more violent robberies do occur, although most incidents can be avoided by taking the usual precautions: avoid driving at night; keep the passenger windows up and the doors locked if you are in a vehicle (includ-

ing taxis) at any time during the day or night; don't wander around isolated or dark streets; avoid walking alone or in a group at dusk or at night, particularly in isolated areas or on isolated stretches of beach; and, avoid isolating situations in general. At all times of day, try to stick to busier areas of town, especially if you are alone, and don't walk alone along the beach away from hotel areas. If you're driving and your car is hijacked, hand over the keys immediately.

When riding on *chapas* or buses, keep your valuables well inside your clothes to avoid falling victim to unscrupulous entrepreneurs who take advantage of overcrowded conditions to pick their fellow passengers' pockets.

All this said, don't let these warnings deter you, simply be a savvy traveller. The vast majority of visitors travel through this beautiful country without incident.

HASSLES & BRIBES

More likely than violent crime are simple hassles with underpaid authorities in search of a bribe. The worst offenders here are regular (ie gray-uniformed nontraffic) police. If you get stopped you should not have any problem as long as your papers are in order. Being friendly, respectful and patient helps (you won't get anywhere otherwise), as does trying to give the impression that you know what you're doing and aren't new in the country. Sometimes the opposite tack is also helpful – feigning complete ignorance if you're told that you've violated some regulation, and apologising profusely. It's also worth remembering that only traffic police are authorised to stop you for traffic infractions. If stopped, you can request to wait until a traffic police officer arrives. Often this will diffuse the bribe attempt.

If you are asked to pay a *multa* (fine) for a trumped-up charge, playing the game a bit (asking to speak to the supervisor or *chefe*, and requesting a receipt) helps to counteract some of the more blatant attempts, as does insisting on going to the nearest *esquadrão* (police station); you should always do these things anyway.

LANDMINES

Thanks to a massive demining effort, many of the unexploded landmines littering Mozambique (a legacy of the country's long war) have been eliminated. However, mines are still a risk in a few areas.

To be on the safe side, stick to well-used paths, including on roadsides in rural areas, and don't free camp or go wandering off into the bush without first seeking local advice.

Areas that should always be avoided include the bases of bridges, old schools or abandoned buildings, and water tanks or other structures.

Telephone

Mobile phone numbers are seven digits, preceded by ☑82 for Mcel, ☑84 for Vodafone and ☑86 for Movitel.

Do not use an initial zero; seven-digit mobile numbers listed with zero at the outset are in South Africa, and must be preceded by the South Africa country code (☑27) when dialling.

All companies have outlets in all major towns where you can buy SIM-card starter packs (Mtc50), fill out the necessary registration form, and buy top-up cards.

TELEPHONE CODES

Country code ☑258

International dialling code ☑00

Landline area codes included with all numbers in this chapter; must be used whenever dialling long-distance. As with mobile numbers, there is no initial zero.

Time

Mozambique time is GMT/UTC plus two hours. There is no daylight savings.

Visas

Visas are required by all visitors except citizens of South Africa, Swaziland, Zambia, Tanzania, Botswana, Malawi, Mauritius and Zimbabwe.

Single-entry visas (only) are available at most land and air entry points (but not anywhere along the Tanzania border) for Mtc2085 (or the US dollar equivalent) for one month.

To avoid long visa lines at busy borders, or for a multiple-entry visa, arrange your visa in advance. If you're arriving in Maputo via bus from Johannesburg it's recommended (though not essential) to get your visa in advance.

Fees vary according to where you buy your visa and how quickly you need it. The maximum initial length of stay available is three months. Same-day visa service is available at several places including Johannes-burg and Nelspruit (South Africa), but at a price.

No matter where you get your visa, your passport must be valid for at least six months from the dates of intended travel, and have at least three blank pages.

For citizens of countries not requiring visas, visits are limited to 30 days from the date of entry, after which you'll need to exit Mozambique and re-enter.

The length of each stay for multiple-entry visas is determined when the visa is issued, and varies from embassy to embassy; only single-entry and transit visas are available at Mozambique's borders.

VISA EXTENSIONS

Visas can be extended at the *migração* (immigration office) in all provincial capitals provided you haven't exceeded the three-month maximum stay, at a cost of Mtc2085 for one month.

Processing takes from two days (with payment of an approximately Mtc200 supplemental express fee) to one week.

Don't wait until the visa has expired, as extensions are not granted automatically; hefty fines are levied for overstays.

Getting There & Away

Entering the Country

A valid passport and visa are required to enter, along with a yellow fever vaccination certificate if coming from an infected area.

Air

AIRPORTS

Maputo International (☑21-465827/8; www.aeroportos.co.mz) Mozambique's modern, main airport.

Vilankulo Regional flights.

Beira Regional flights.

Nampula Regional flights.

Moçimboa da Praia Regional flights.

Pemba Regional flights.

AIRLINES

Coastal Aviation (safari@coastal.co.tz) Dar es Salaam to Moçimboa da Praia, with connections to Pemba and the Quirimbas Archipelago.

Federal Air (www.fedair.com) Johannesburg to Vilankulo via Kruger Mpumalanga International Airport.

Kenya Airways (☎21-495483; www.kenya
-airways.com; 33/659 Avenida Barnabé Thawé,
Maputo) Nairobi to Maputo.

Linhas Aéreas de Moçambique (LAM;
www.lam.co.mz) Domestic routes plus flights
between Johannesburg, Maputo, Vilankulo
and Beira; Dar es Salaam, Pemba and
Nampula; Lisbon (Portugal) and Maputo.

SAAirlink (www.flyairlink.com) Johannesburg
to Beira, Nampula and Pemba; Durban to
Maputo.

South African Airways (www.flysaa.com)
Johannesburg to Maputo.

TAP Air Portugal (www.flytap.com) Lisbon
to Maputo.

Land
MALAWI

Border Crossings
Zóbuè On the Tete Corridor route linking
Blantyre (Malawi) and Harare (Zimba-
bwe); the busiest crossing

Dedza 85km southwest of Lilongwe

Melosa (Milange) 120km southeast of
Blantyre

Entre Lagos Southwest of Cuamba

Mandimba Northwest of Cuamba

Vila Nova da Fronteira At Malawi's
southern tip

Cóbuè On Lake Niassa

Metangula On Lake Niassa

To/From Blantyre
Via Zóbuè: vehicles go daily from Blantyre
to the border via Mwanza. Once in Mozambique (the border posts are separated by
about 5km of no man's land), *chapas* go daily to Tete (Mtc150, 1½ hours Zóbuè to Tete).

Via Vila Nova da Fronteira: daily minibuses go from Blantyre to Nsanje and on to
the border. Once across, there are *chapas*
to Mutarara, and from there to Sena and
on to Caia on the main north–south road.

Via Melosa (about 2km from Milange
town, and convenient for Quelimane and
Gurúè): buses go from Blantyre via Mulanje
to the border. Once across, several vehicles
go daily to Mocuba, from where there is
frequent transport south to Quelimane and
north to Nampevo junction (for Gurúè) and
Nampula.

Entre Lagos (for Cuamba and northern
Mozambique): possible with your own

4WD (allow about 1½ hours to cover the
80km from Entre Lagos to Cuamba), or
by *chapa* (about 2½ hours between the
border and Cuamba). On the Malawi side,
minibuses go from the border to Liwonde.
Another option: the weekly Malawi train
between the border and Liwonde (currently Thursday morning from Liwonde to Nayuchi on the border, and from Nayuchi back
to Liwonde that same afternoon). There is
basic accommodation at Entre Lagos if you
get stuck.

Via Mandimba: Malawian transport goes
frequently to Mangochi, where you can
get minibuses to Namwera, and on to the
border at Chiponde. Once in Mozambique
(moto-taxis bridge the approximately 1.5km
of no man's land for Mtc50, and then vehicles take you on to Mandimba town), several
vehicles daily go from Mandimba to both
Cuamba (three hours) and Lichinga.

To/From Lilongwe
The Dedza border is linked with the N103
to/from Tete by a scenic tarmac road. From
Tete, there's at least one *chapa* daily to Vila
Ulongwé and on to Dedza. Otherwise, go in
stages from Tete via Moatize and the junction about 15km southwest of Zóbuè. Once
across, it's easy to find transport for the final
85km to Lilongwe.

SOUTH AFRICA

Border Crossings
Lebombo–Ressano Garcia (6am to
10pm) Northwest of Maputo; very busy

Kosi Bay–Ponta d'Ouro (8am to 4pm)
11km south of Ponta d'Ouro

Pafuri (6am to 5.30pm) 11km east of
Pafuri Camp in Kruger National Park

Giriyondo (8am to 4pm October to
March, to 3pm April to September) 75km
west of Massingir town, 95km from
Kruger's Phalaborwa Gate

To/From Nelspruit & Johannesburg
Large 'luxury' buses do the Maputo to Johannesburg route daily (US$40 to US$50
one way, nine to 10 hours). All lines also
service Pretoria. It's best to organise your
Mozambique visa in advance, although
most of the companies will take you without a visa. The risk: if lines at the border
are long, the bus may not wait, in which
case you'll need to take a *chapa* the remaining 85km to Maputo.

Cheetah Express (☎84-444 3024, 21-486 3222; Av Eduardo Mondlane) Daily between Maputo and Nelspruit (Mtc1100 one way), departing Maputo at 7am from Avenida Eduardo Mondlane next to Mundo's, and departing Nelspruit at about 4pm from Mediclinic, Crossings and Riverside Mall.

Greyhound (☎in South Africa 083-915 9000; www.greyhound.co.za) Daily from Johannesburg's Park Station complex at 8am and 10pm, and from Maputo at 7am and 7pm.

Luciano Luxury Coach (☎84-860 2100, in South Africa 83-993 4897) Daily except Sunday from Johannesburg (Hotel Oribi, 24 Bezuidenhout Ave, Troyville) at 5pm; daily except Saturday from Maputo at 9pm.

Translux (☎in South Africa 011-774 3333; www.translux.co.za) Daily from Johannesburg at 8.45am; from Maputo at 7.45am.

To/From Kruger National Park
Neither the Pafuri nor the Giriyondo crossing is accessible via public transport. Visas are available on both sides of both borders. Officially, you're required to have a 4WD to cross both borders, and 4WD is essential for the Pafuri border, which crosses the Limpopo River near Mapai (for which there is a makeshift ferry during the rains). Allow two days between Pafuri and Vilankulo. Nhanfule Campsite (per person US$6) at Limpopo National Park's Mapai entry gate has hotwater showers.

Note that if you are entering/leaving South Africa via Giriyondo, you will be required to show proof of payment of one night's lodging within the Great Limpopo Transfrontier Park (ie either in Limpopo National Park or South Africa's Kruger park) to fulfil SANParks' requirement for one compulsory overnight within the transfrontier park for all visitors.

To/From Durban
Luciano Luxury Coach (☎84-860 2100, in South Africa 83-993 4897) goes between Maputo and Durban via Namaacha and Big Bend in Swaziland (Mtc1110, nine hours) departing Maputo at 6.30am Tuesday and Friday and Durban (Pavillion Hotel, North Beach) at 6.30am Wednesday and Sunday.

To/From Ponta d'Ouro
For travel via the Kosi Bay border post, see p183.

SWAZILAND
Border Crossings
Lomahasha–Namaacha (7am to 8pm) In Swaziland's extreme northeastern corner

Goba–Mhlumeni (7am to 8pm) Southwest of Maputo

To/From Manzini
While there are at least one or two direct *chapas* daily between Maputo and Manzini (about Mtc350), it's faster and cheaper to take a *chapa* between Maputo and Namaacha (Mtc70, 1½ hours), walk across the border, and then get Swaziland transport on the other side (about US$6 and three hours from the border to Manzini).

For self-drivers, the Namaacha border is notoriously slow on holiday weekends; the quiet border at Goba (Goba Fronteira), reached via a scenic, winding road from Maputo, is a good alternative. The road from Swaziland's Mananga border, connecting north to Lebombo-Ressano Garcia, is another option.

TANZANIA
Border Crossings
For all Mozambique–Tanzania posts, it is essential to arrange your Mozambique (or Tanzania) visa in advance.

Kilambo 130km north of Moçimboa da Praia, and called Namiranga or Namoto on the Mozambique side

Mtambaswala/Negomano Unity Bridge

Mtomoni Unity Bridge 2; 120km south of Songea (Tanzania)

Palma (Mozambique) Immigration and customs for those arriving by dhow

Moçimboa da Praia (Mozambique) Immigration and customs for those arriving by plane or dhow

To/From Mtwara
Vehicles go daily from 6am from Mtwara (Tanzania) to Kilambo (Tsh4000, one hour) and on to the Rovuma, which is crossed via a combination of walking and dugout canoe (Tsh5000, 10 minutes to over an hour, depending on water levels, and dangerous during heavy rains). The border is a rough one, and it's common for touts to demand up to 10 times the 'real' price for the boat crossing, and for boat captains to stop midriver and demand higher fees than those

that have already been agreed upon. Watch your belongings, especially when getting into and out of the boats, and keep up with the crowd.

Once in Mozambique, several pick-ups go daily to the Mozambique border post (4km further) and on to Moçimboa da Praia (Mtc250, two hours).

Depending on water levels, it is sometimes possible to arrange to take your vehicle across the Rovuma at Kilambo via dugout canoes strapped together by local entrepreneurs. This is obviously risky. And, it's potentially expensive (from US$100 to US$400 for the crossing depending on your negotiating skills).

To/From Masasi

The main vehicle crossing over the Rovuma is via the Unity Bridge at Negomano (⊙7.30am-4pm in Mozambique, 8.30am-5pm in Tanzania), near the confluence of the Lugenda River. From Masasi, go 35km southwest along the Tunduru road to Nangomba village, from where a good 68km track leads down to Masuguru village. The bridge is 10km further at Mtambaswala. Once over, there is 160km on a bush track with fine, deep, red dust (mud during the rains, and often blocked by lorries). This track continues through low land bordering the Rovuma before climbing up to Ngapa (shown as Moçimboa do Rovuma on some maps), where there is a customs and immigration checkpoint, as well as stunning views down over the Rovuma River basin. From Ngapa to Mueda is 40km further on a reasonable dirt road (four to six hours from the bridge to Mueda, longer during the rains).

Via public transport, there's a daily *chapa* from Masasi to Mtambaswala (Tsh5000) each morning. On the other side, a *chapa* leaves Negomano by about 1pm for Mueda (Mtc500). Going in the other direction, if you arrive at Mtambaswala after the *chapa* for Masasi has left (it doesn't always coordinate with the vehicle arriving from Mueda), there are some basic guesthouses for sleeping.

To/From Songea

One or two vehicles daily depart from Majengo C area in Songea (Tsh10,000, three to four hours) to Mtomoni village and the Unity Bridge 2. Once across, take Mozambique transport to Lichinga (Tsh25,000, five hours). Pay in stages, rather than paying the

entire Tsh35,000 Songea–Lichinga fare in Songea, as is sometimes requested.

ZAMBIA

Border Crossings

Cassacatiza (7am to 5pm) 290km northwest of Tete; main crossing

Zumbo (7am to 5pm) At the western end of Lake Cahora Bassa

To/From Zambia

The Cassacatiza–Chanida border is seldom used as most travellers combining Mozambique and Zambia go via Malawi. *Chapas* go daily from Tete to Matema, from where there's sporadic transport to the border. On the other side, there are daily vehicles to Katete (Zambia), and then on to Lusaka or Chipata.

The rarely used crossing at Zumbo is accessed with difficulty from Mozambique via Fíngoe and is of interest primarily to anglers and birdwatchers heading to the western reaches of Lake Cahora Bassa.

ZIMBABWE

Border Crossings

Nyamapanda On the Tete Corridor, linking Harare with Tete and Lilongwe (Malawi)

Machipanda On the Beira Corridor linking Harare with the sea

Espungabera In the Chimanimani Mountains

Mukumbura (7am to 5pm) West of Tete

To/From Harare

From Tete there are frequent vehicles to Changara and on to the border at Nyamapanda, where you can get transport to Harare. Through buses between Blantyre and Harare are another option.

From Chimoio there is frequent transport to Manica and from there to the border, from where you'll need to take a taxi 12km to Mutare, and then get Zimbabwe transport to Harare.

The seldom-used route via the orderly little border town of Espungabera is slow and scenic, and an interesting dry-season alternative for those with a 4WD.

Mukumbura (4WD) is of interest mainly to anglers heading to Cahora Bassa Dam. There is no public transport on the Mozambique side.

Lake

MALAWI

The *Ilala* ferry, which services several Mozambican ports on its way up and down Lake Niassa, was grounded for repairs at the time of research. Contact Malawi Lake Services (☎in Malawi 1-587221; ilala@malawi. net) for an update. Meanwhile, the journey between Cóbuè and Likoma Island (Malawi) can be done by local fishing boats (about US$7 one way), which wait each morning at both destinations for passengers.

There are immigration posts in Metangula and Cóbuè (and on Likoma Island and in Nkhata Bay, for Malawi). You can get a Mozambique visa at Cóbuè, but not at Metangula.

Getting Around

Air

AIRLINES IN MOZAMBIQUE

Linhas Aéreas de Moçambique (LAM; ☎21-468000; www.lam.co.mz) The national airline, with flights linking Maputo with Inhambane, Vilankulo, Beira, Chimoio, Quelimane, Tete, Nampula, Lichinga and Pemba. Always reconfirm your ticket, and check in early. Visa cards are accepted in most offices. Advance purchase tickets are significantly cheaper than last-minute fares. Sample one-way fares and flight frequencies: Maputo to Pemba (US$320, daily), Maputo to Vilankulo (US$180, daily), Maputo to Lichinga (US$225, four weekly).

CFA Charters (www.cfa.co.za) Scheduled and charter flights to the Bazaruto Archipelago, Quirimbas Archipelago and Gorongosa National Park.

Boat

On Lake Niassa there is passenger service between Metangula, Cóbuè and several other villages.

Bus

Direct services connect all major towns at least daily, although vehicle maintenance and driving standards leave much to be desired.

A large bus is called a *machibombo,* and sometimes also *autocarro.* The main companies include TCO, with comfortable buses

and constantly changing schedules; Maning Nice; Nagi Trans; and Grupo Mecula.

Most towns don't have central bus stations. Rather, transport usually leaves from the bus company garage, or from the start of the road towards the destination. Long-distance transport in general, and all transport in the north, leaves early – between 3am and 7am. Mozambican transport usually leaves quickly and close to the stated departure time.

Sample journey fares and times: Maputo to Vilanculos (Mtc750); Nampula to Pemba (Mtc350, seven hours); Maputo to Beira (Mtc1780, 16 hours); Pemba to Maputo (Mtc2500, three days).

There is no luggage fee for large buses. For smaller buses and *chapas*, if your bag is large enough that it needs to be stowed on the roof, you will be charged, with the amount varying depending on distance and size of the bag, and always negotiable.

Where there's a choice, always take buses rather than *chapas*.

RESERVATIONS

Book TCO buses in advance, as their routes fill quickly. Maning Nice and Grupo Mecula should be booked the afternoon before. Otherwise, showing up on the morning of travel (about an hour prior to departure) is usually enough to ensure a place.

If you are choosy about your seat (best is in front, on the shady side), get to the departure point earlier.

The more luggage on the roof, the slower the service.

Car & Motorcycle

A South African or international drivers licence is required to drive in Mozambique. Those staying longer than six months will need a Mozambique drivers licence.

Gasolina (petrol) is scarce off main roads, especially in the north. *Gasóleo* (diesel) supplies are more reliable. On bush journeys, always carry an extra jerry can and tank up whenever possible, as filling stations sometimes run out.

Temporary import permits (US$2) and third-party insurance (US$25 for 30 days) are available at most land borders, or in the nearest large town.

HIRE

There are rental agencies in Maputo, Vilankulo, Beira, Nampula, Tete and Pemba, most of which take credit cards. Elsewhere, you can usually arrange something with up-market hotels.

Rates start at about US$100 per day for 4WD, excluding fuel.

None of the major agencies offer unlimited kilometres, although some of the smaller ones do.

With the appropriate paperwork, rental cars from Mozambique can be taken into South Africa and Swaziland, but not into other neighbouring countries. Most South African rental agencies don't permit their vehicles to enter Mozambique.

INSURANCE
Private vehicles entering Mozambique must purchase third-party insurance at the border.

It's also advisable to take out insurance coverage at home or (for rental vehicles) with the rental agency to cover damage to the vehicle, yourself and your possessions.

Car-rental agencies in Mozambique have wildly differing policies (some offer no insurance at all, those that do often have high deductibles and most won't cover off-road driving); enquire before signing any agreements.

ROAD HAZARDS
Drunk driving is common, as are excessive speeds, and there are many road accidents. Throughout the country, travel as early in the day as possible, and avoid driving at night.

If you are not used to driving in Africa, watch out for pedestrians, children and animals on the road or running onto the road.

Tree branches on the road are the local version of flares or hazard lights, and mean there's a stopped vehicle, crater-sized pothole or similar calamity ahead.

ROAD RULES
In theory, traffic in Mozambique drives on the left.

Traffic in a roundabout has the right of way (again, in theory).

There's a seatbelt requirement for the driver and all passengers.

Other relevant provisions of Mozambique's traffic law include a prohibition on driving while using a mobile phone, a requirement to drive with the vehicle's insurance certificate, and a requirement to carry a reflector vest and two hazard triangles.

Speed limits (usually 100km/h on main roads, 80km/h on approaches to towns and 60km/h or less when passing through towns) are enforced by radar.

Fines for speeding and other traffic infringements vary, and should always be negotiated (in a polite, friendly way), keeping in mind that official speeding fines range from Mtc1000 up to Mtc24,000, depending on how much above the speed limit you are travelling and where the infringement occurs.

Driving on the beach is illegal.

Hitching
As anywhere in the world, hitching is never entirely safe, and we don't recommend it. This said, in parts of rural Mozambique, your only transport option will be hitching a lift. Payment is usually not expected, though clarify before getting in. A small token of thanks is always appreciated. If you do need to pay, it is usually equivalent to what you would pay on a bus or *chapa* for the same journey.

Throughout the country, the prevalence of drunk drivers makes it essential to try and assess the driver's condition before getting into a vehicle.

Local Transport
CHAPA
The main form of local transport is the *chapa*, the name given to any public transport that runs within a town or between towns, and isn't a bus or truck.

On longer routes, your only option may be a *camião* (truck). Many have open backs, and the sun and dust can be brutal unless you get a seat up front in the cab.

Chapas can be hailed anywhere, and prices are fixed. Intra-city fares average Mtc5; long-haul fares are usually slightly higher than the bus fare for the same route. The most comfortable seat is in the front, next to the window, though you'll have to make arrangements early and sometimes pay more.

Chapa drivers are notorious for their unsafe driving and there are many accidents. Where possible, bus is always a better option.

Like buses, long-haul *chapas* in Mozambique tend to depart early in the day and relatively promptly, although drivers will cruise for passengers before leaving town.

TAXI

Apart from airport arrivals, taxis don't cruise for business, so you'll need to seek them out. While several have functioning meters, usually you'll need to negotiate a price. Town trips cost from Mtc100.

☞ Tours

Dana Tours (www.danatours.net) Tours focusing on the coast, plus Mozambique–South Africa combination itineraries; midrange and upmarket.

Mozaic Travel (www.mozaictravel.com) A long-standing operator focusing on the coast and catering to all budgets.

Train

The only passenger train regularly used by tourists is the slow line between Nampula and Cuamba; see p215.

MOZAMBIQUE GETTING AROUND

Namibia

Best for Wildlife Watching

» Etosha National Park (p263)

» Waterberg Plateau (p259)

» Bwabwata National Park (p270)

» Khaudum National Park (p269)

» Mamili National Park (p273)

Best of the Outdoors

» Swakopmund (p281)

» Fish River Canyon (p304)

» Damaraland (p275)

» Kaokoveld (p277)

» Skeleton Coast (p280)

Why Go?

A journey through Southern Africa reveals its otherwordly face when you cross the border into the vast reaches of Namibia. The combination of space and landscapes ensures that a trip through this country is one of the great road adventures of the region. Natural wonders such as that mighty gash in the earth at Fish River Canyon and Etosha National Park enthrall, but it's the lonely desert roads cutting through swirling sands that will stay with you. Here, dunes in the world's oldest desert meet crashing rollers along the wild Atlantic coast, and amongst all this is a German legacy evident in the cuisine, art nouveau architecture and festivals.

Namibia is also the headquarters of adventure activities in Southern Africa, with myriad opportunities for skydiving, sandboarding or camel riding, to name but a few. However, whether your desert appreciation comes from behind an airconditioned window, or from hearing the crunch of earth under your boots, travel in Namibia will sear itself in your mind long after the desert vistas fade.

When to Go
Windhoek

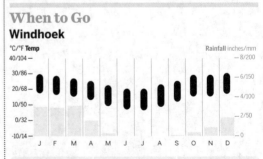

May–Oct Best for wildlife viewing, as animals congregate around the few remaining waterholes.

Jun–Aug Coastal towns of Swakopmund and Walvis Bay are subject to miserable sandstorm conditions.

Nov–Apr The low season as the wet gets into full swing: downpours from January to April.

WINDHOEK

☑061 / POP 340,000

Central Windhoek is a modern, well-groomed city where office workers lounge around Zoo Park at lunchtime, tourists funnel through Post St mall admiring African curios, and taxis whizz around honking at potential customers.

It's not a big city, making it eminently walkable; add to this a mixed population, a pedestrian-friendly city centre, a relaxed, relatively hassle-free pace and an utterly cosmopolitan outlook and Windhoek makes for very pleasant exploration indeed. Of course, that's only part of the story: a trip into Katutura, the once-ramshackle township on the outskirts of the city – now just another outer suburb – provides an insight into the reality of most people's lives within the boundaries of the capital.

Windhoek makes a great place to begin or break a journey through Namibia and Southern Africa. The accommodation choices, food variety, cultural sights, shopping and African urban buzz give it an edge not found anywhere else in Namibia.

History

Windhoek has only existed for just over a century. The modern name Windhoek, or 'windy corner', was corrupted from the original 'Winterhoek' during the German colonial occupation. At that time, it became the headquarters for the German Schutztruppe, which was ostensibly charged with brokering peace between the warring Herero and Nama peoples. For over 10 years around the turn of the 20th century, Windhoek served as the administrative capital of German South-West Africa.

◉ Sights & Activities

Windhoek is not really known for its tourist attractions, but if you're here for a few days and have time to kill it's an easy and interesting city for a stroll.

Zoo Park   PARK

(Map p250; ☺dawn-dusk) Although this leafy park served as a public zoo until 1962, today it functions primarily as a picnic spot and shady retreat for lunching office workers. Of course, 5000 years ago the park was the site of a Stone Age elephant hunt, as evidenced by the remains of two elephants and several quartz tools found here in the early 1960s. This prehistoric event is honoured by the park's prominent elephant column, designed by Namibian sculptor Dörthe Berner.

A rather anachronous mate to the elephant column is the Kriegerdenkmal (War Memorial), topped by a rather frightening golden imperial eagle, which was dedicated in 1987 to the memory of German Schutztruppe soldiers who died in the Nama wars of 1893–94.

Christuskirche   CHURCH

(Map p250; Fidel Castro St) Windhoek's best-recognised landmark, and something of an unofficial symbol of the city, this German Lutheran church stands on a traffic island and lords it over the city centre. This unusual building, constructed from local sandstone in 1907, was designed by architect Gottlieb Redecker in conflicting neo-Gothic and art-nouveau styles. The result looks strangely edible, and is somewhat reminiscent of a whimsical gingerbread house. The altarpiece, the *Resurrection of Lazarus*, is a copy of the renowned work by Rubens. To view the interior, pick up the key during business hours from the nearby church office on Peter Müller St.

✎ Tintenpalast   NOTABLE BUILDING

(Map p250; ☑288 9111; www.parliament.gov.na; admission free; ☺tours 9am-noon & 2-4pm Mon-Fri) The former administrative headquarters of German South West Africa have been given a new mandate as the Namibian parliament building. As a fitting homage to the bureaucracy of government, the name of the building means 'Ink Palace', in honour of all the ink spent on official paperwork.

The building is remarkable mainly for its construction from indigenous materials. The surrounding gardens, which were laid out in the 1930s, include an olive grove and a proper bowling green. In the front, have a look at Namibia's first post-independence monument, a bronze-cast statue of the Herero chief Hosea Kutako, who was best known for his vehement opposition to South African rule.

Turnhalle   HISTORICAL BUILDING

(Map p250; Bahnhof St) The Turnhalle was built in 1909 as a practise hall for the Windhoek Gymnastic Club, though in 1975 it was modernised and turned into a conference hall. On 1 September of that year, it served as the venue for the first Constitutional Conference on Independence for South West Africa, which subsequently came to be

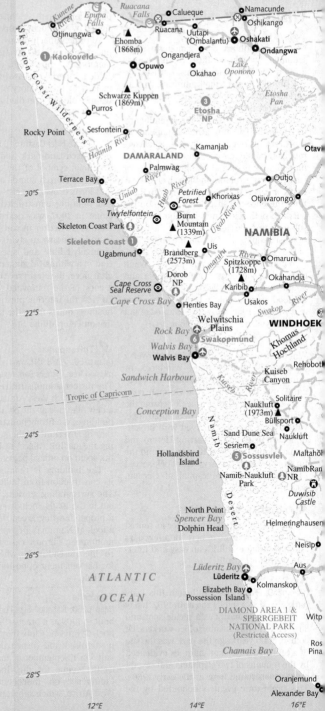

Namibia Highlights

1 Getting off the beaten track (and the tarred road) in the true African wilderness of the **Skeleton Coast** (p280) and **Kaokoveld** (p277)

2 Hiking through **Fish River Canyon** (p304), one of Africa's greatest natural wonders

3 Crouching by a waterhole in **Etosha National Park** (p263), one of the world's premier wildlife venues

4 Hiking to the top of the **Waterberg Plateau** (p259) for breathtaking views, keeping an eye out for rare sables and roans

5 Watching the sun rise from the fiery-coloured dunes of **Sossusvlei** (p296)

6 Getting your adrenaline fix at **Swakopmund** (p281), the extreme-sports capital of Namibia

called the Turnhalle Conference. During the 1980s, the building hosted several political summits and debates that paved the way for Namibian independence. It now houses a tribunal for the Southern African Development Community (SADC).

FREE **National Museum of Namibia** MUSEUM
(Map p250; Robert Mugabe Ave; ⊘9am-6pm Mon-Fri, 3-6pm Sat & Sun) There is an excellent display on Namibia's independence at the country's historical museum, which

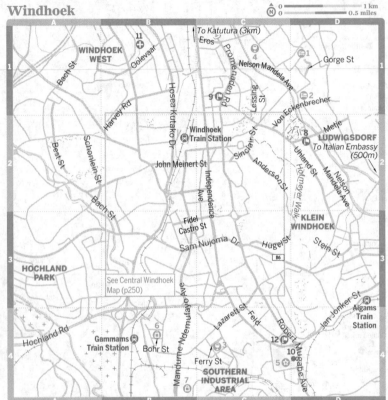

Windhoek

Sleeping
1	Hotel Thule	D1
2	Roof of Africa	D1

Drinking
3	Club London	C4
4	Joe's Beer House	C1

Entertainment
5	Ster Kinekor	C4

Shopping
	Cape Union Mart	(see 5)

6	Gräber's	B4
7	Safari Den	B4

Information
8	Botswanan Embassy	D2
9	French Embassy	C1
10	Maerua Park Centre	D4
11	Rhino Park Private Hospital	B1
12	South African High Commission	C4

KATUTURA – A PERMANENT PLACE?

In 1912, during the days of the South African mandate – and apartheid – the Windhoek town council set aside two 'locations', which were open to settlement by black Africans working in the city: the Main Location, which was west of the city centre, and Klein Windhoek, to the east. The following year, people were forcibly relocated to these areas, which effectively became haphazard settlements. In the early 1930s, streets were laid out in the Main Location and the area was divided into regions. Each subdivision within these regions was assigned to an ethnic group and referred to by that name (eg Herero, Nama, Owambo, Damara), followed by a numerical reference.

In the 1950s, the Windhoek municipal council, with encouragement from the South African government (which regarded Namibia as a province of South Africa), decided to 'take back' Klein Windhoek and consolidate all 'location' residents into a single settlement northwest of the main city. There was strong opposition to the move, and in early December 1959 a group of Herero women launched a protest march and boycott against the city government. On 10 December, unrest escalated into a confrontation with the police, resulting in 11 deaths and 44 serious injuries. Following this, the roughly 4000 residents of the Main Location moved to the new settlement, which was ultimately named 'Katutura'. In Herero the name means 'We Have No Permanent Place', though it can also be translated as 'The Place We Do Not Want to Settle'.

Today, in independent Namibia, Katutura is a vibrant Windhoek suburb – Namibia's Soweto – where poverty and affluence brush elbows. The town council has extended municipal water, power and telephone services to most areas of Katutura, and has also established the colourful and perpetually busy Soweto Market, where traders sell just about anything imaginable. Unlike its South African counterparts, Katutura is relatively safe by day – assuming, of course, that you find a trustworthy local who can act as a guide.

The tourist office can book township tours, but even better is **Katu Tours** (☑081-3032856; www.katuturatours.com; tours per person N$350), which offers guided tours by bike. You get a good taste of township life and the chance to meet plenty of locals; it also includes dropping into Penduka, where local women produce a range of handicrafts and textiles. Tours depart at 8am from Katutura and take 3½ hours.

NAMIBIA WINDHOEK

provides some enlightening context to the struggles of this young country. Probably the most interesting part of the museum, though, is the rock-art display, with some great reproductions – it would definitely be worth a nose around before you head to the Brandberg or Twyfontein.

The museum is housed in Windhoek's oldest surviving building, dating from the early 1890s, and originally served as the headquarters of the German Schutztruppe. Also on display are memorabilia and photos from the colonial period as well as indigenous artefacts.

Outside the museum, don't miss the somewhat incongruous collection of railway engines and coaches, which together formed one of the country's first narrow-gauge trains. This open-air exhibit is lorded over by a bronze statue known as the **Reiterdenkmal** (Rider's Memorial), which commemorates Schutztruppe soldiers killed during the Herero-Nama wars of 1904–08. History buffs should note that the statue was unveiled on 27 January 1912, which coincided with the birthday of Kaiser Wilhelm II.

FREE **Owela Museum** MUSEUM
(State Museum; Map p250; 4 Robert Mugabe Ave; ⊙9am-6pm Mon-Fri, 3-6pm Sat & Sun) The other half of the National Museum of Namibia, about 600m from the main building, is known as the Owela Museum. Exhibits focus on Namibia's natural and cultural history, and it has been popular with readers; note that it may sometimes close early.

Trans-Namib Transport Museum MUSEUM
(Map p250; ☑298 2186; admission N$5; ⊙8am-1pm & 2-5pm Mon-Fri) Windhoek's beautiful old Cape Dutch–style train station on Bahnhof St was constructed by the Germans in 1912, and was expanded in 1929 by the South African administration. Across the driveway from the entrance is the German steam locomotive 'Poor Old Joe', which was shipped to

Central Windhoek

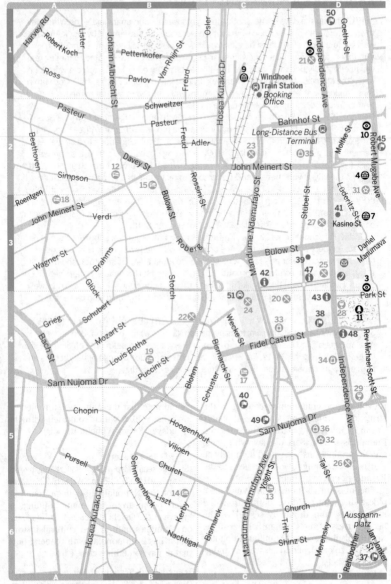

Swakopmund in 1899 and reassembled for the treacherous journey across the desert to Windhoek. Upstairs in the train station is the small but worthwhile Trans-Namib Transport Museum outlining Namibian transport history, particularly that of the railway.

National Art Gallery GALLERY
(Map p250; cnr Robert Mugabe Ave & John Meinert St; admission weekdays free, Sat N$20; ☉8am-

pict the liberation struggle from a religious and narrative perspective.

Wild Dog Safaris ADVENTURE TOUR
(☏257642; www.wilddog-safaris.com) This friendly operation runs weeklong northern or southern adventure tours, Etosha or Sossusvlei circuits, and longer participation camping safaris and accommodated excursions.

Magic Bus Safaris BUS TOUR
(☏259485; 081 129 8093; magicbus@iafrica.com.na) This small company runs budget trips from Windhoek to Sossusvlei, Etosha and other combinations.

★☆ Festivals & Events

Windhoek's annual cultural bash is September's **/Ae//Gams Festival**, which features colourful gatherings of dancers, musicians and people in ethnic dress. True to its partly Teutonic background, Windhoek also stages its own **Oktoberfest** in late October. Similarly, the German-style **Windhoek Karnival** (or WIKA) is held in late April and features a week of events.

🛏 Sleeping

Cardboard Box Backpackers BACKPACKERS **$**
(Map p250; ☏228994; www.cardboardbox.com.na; 15 Johann Albrecht St; campsites N$70, dm N$95, r from N$300; @🛜🏊) Hostels are hard to come by in this country, but 'The Box' has been doing it for years, with a rep as one of Windhoek's wildest backpackers. With a fully stocked bar and a swimming pool to cool off in, travellers have a tough time leaving this oasis of affordable luxury. If you do decide to motivate yourself, the city centre is just a short walk away. Rates include free coffee and pancakes in the morning, and there are free pickups from the Intercape bus stop.

Chameleon Backpackers Lodge & Guesthouse BACKPACKERS **$**
(Map p250; ☏244347; www.chameleonbackpackers.com; 5-7 Voight St; campsites N$80, dm from N$120, r from N$300; @🛜🏊) With a chilled vibe emanating from its considerable range of accommodation options, this well-matched rival to the Cardboard Box caters to a slightly more subdued crowd. It offers decent-sized, luxurious African-chic rooms and spick-and-span dorms at shoestring prices. There are also three self-catering flats if you're in town for an extended period. Rates include breakfast.

5pm Tue-Fri, 9am-2pm Sat) This art gallery contains a permanent collection of works reflecting Namibia's historical and natural heritage. The collection displays works by Muafangejo – Namibia's first black artist to gain international acclaim. His linocuts de-

Central Windhoek

TOP CHOICE **Guesthouse Tamboti** GUESTHOUSE **$$**
(Map p250; ☏235515; www.guesthouse-tamboti.
com; 9 Kerby St; s/d from N$415/620; ❋@🛜🏊)
Hands down our favourite place in Windhoek to stay, Tamboti is very well priced and has a great vibe. The terrific hosts will go out of their way to ensure that you're comfortable (such as driving you to the airport if you have a flight to catch). The rooms here are spacious and well set up. The guesthouse is situated on a small hill just above the city centre. Book ahead, as it's popular.

Hotel-Pension Steiner HOTEL **$$**
(Map p250; ☏222898; www.natron.net/tour/stein-
er/main.html; 11 Wecke St; s/d from N$540/850;
🛜🏊) Although it has an excellent city-centre location just a few minutes' walk from Independence Ave, this small hotel-pension is sheltered from the hustle and bustle of the street scene. Simple but comfortable rooms open to a thatched bar and swimming pool, where you can quickly unwind.

Vondelhof Guesthouse GUESTHOUSE **$$**
(Map p250; ☏248320; www.vondelhof.com; 2 Puccini St; s/d N$625/900; ❋@🏊) This very

friendly, rather grand-looking affair has great-size rooms, a good attitude towards hospitality and serves a decent breakfast. Ask to have a look at a few rooms, but we try to snare No 8, which is a beauty. Oh, and don't let the horrible green colour on the outside of the building put you off – the interior is far more palatable.

Rivendell Guest House
GUESTHOUSE $$

(Map p250; ☑250006; www.rivendellnamibia.com; 40 Beethoven St; s/d N$450/600, with shared bathroom from N$345/450; @☎) This homely set-up gets good reviews from travellers. It's a very relaxed guesthouse located in a shady suburb within easy walking distance of the city centre. Bright and airy rooms open to a lush garden and a sparkling pool. It's a good place to try if everywhere is full, as the owner will try to help with alternative accommodation. Rates do not include breakfast.

Roof of Africa
HOTEL $$

(Map p248; ☑254708; www.roofofafrica.com; 124-126 Nelson Mandela Ave; s N$660-1070, d N$860-1420; ✳@☎) A pleasant haven located about 30 minutes by foot from the city centre, Roof of Africa has a rustic barnyard feel, offering well-designed rooms of varying price and luxury that attract laid-back travellers looking for a quiet retreat from the city. It's worth shelling out a few more Namib dollars for a luxury room, which comes with far more space, sink-in-and-smile beds and modern bathrooms; ask to see a few, though, as they do vary.

Hotel Cela
HOTEL $$

(Map p250; ☑226295; info@hotelcela.com; Bulow St; s N$480-650, d N$660-850) This varied and well located set-up has a range of rooms to suit most tastes. The more expensive, renovated rooms are the best. It's a good place to try when everywhere else in the city is full.

Hotel Thule
HOTEL $$$

(Map p248; ☑371950; www.hotelthule.com; 1 Gorge St; s/d from N$1410/1960; ✳@☎) Perched on a towering hilltop in Eros Park, Hotel Thule commands some of the most impressive views of any hotel in the capital. Cavernous rooms with a touch of European elegance are complemented by a classy restaurant and wraparound sundowner bar where you can sip a cocktail while watching the twinkling lights of the city switch on for the night. Email the hotel for better rates than those listed above.

Hotel Heinitzburg
HOTEL $$$

(Map p250; ☑249597; www.heinitzburg.com; 22 Heinitzburg St; s/d from N$1530/2200; ✳@) This is Windhoek's most royal B&B option – quite literally, as it's located inside Heinitzburg Castle, which was commissioned in 1914. A member of the prestigious Relais & Chateaux hotel group, the Heinitzburg is far and away the most personable upmarket accommodation in Windhoek. Rooms have been updated for the 21st century with satellite TV and air-con, though the highlight of the hotel is the palatial dining room, which offers excellent gourmet cuisine and an extensive wine dungeon.

✖ Eating

Paul's
INTERNATIONAL $

(Map p250; ☑307176; Old Breweries Complex, Craft Market Inner Courtyard, cnr Garten & Tal Sts; mains N$30-60; ⊘8am-5pm Mon-Fri, to 2pm Sat) Mixing brasserie, coffee shop, and patisserie is this impressive eatery at the heart of Windhoek's craft market. Dining takes place in an industrial space made much more interesting for the modern African prints and decor. It's a quirky mix, as are the menu options, which include tapas in the evenings, salads, fresh-baked rolls or more substantial meals. Linking it all is a policy of low fat, no msg and the use of fresh ingredients.

Namibia Crafts Cafe
CAFE $

(Map p250; Old Breweries Complex, cnr Garten & Tal Sts; mains N$40-80; ⊘9am-6pm Mon-Fri, to 3.30pm Sat & Sun) This cafe-restaurant-bar is a great spot to perch yourself above Tal St, checking out the local action and taking in the breeze from the outside deck. The extensive drinks menu includes health shakes and freshly squeezed juices. Meals in the way of salads, large pitas, cold meat platters, open sandwiches and healthy (or just filling) breakfasts hit the spot.

Sardinia's Restaurant
ITALIAN $$

(Map p250; 39 Independence Ave; dishes N$60-100; ⊘lunch & dinner) An energetic restaurant that is a focal point for dining along the main drag. Always with a crowd, and understandably so, it churns out first-class pizzas and an impressive array of pasta dishes. And it doesn't stop there: chicken and beef dishes and salads are also offered (the baby chicken with herb and lemon is excellent).

O Pensador
ANGOLAN, SEAFOOD $$

(Map p250; ☑221223; cnr Mandume Ndemufayo Ave & John Meinert St; mains N$130-200; ⊘dinner)

A quality seafood restaurant with a twist of Angolan here and a hint of Portuguese there, the food may not be squirming on your plate, but our overall impression was one of freshness, tasty morsels and attentive service.

Gourmet INTERNATIONAL $$
(Map p250; ✆232360; Kaiserkrone Centre, Post St Mall; mains N$70-180; ⊗breakfast, lunch & dinner Mon-Sat) Tucked away in a lovely, peaceful courtyard just off Post St Mall, this alfresco bistro has one of the most comprehensive menus you've ever seen. The unifying trend is its adherence to using gourmet ingredients to create a blend of Namibian, German, French and Italian dishes that are as innovative as they are delicious. The carpaccio of ostrich is recommended, but ask them to go easy on the oil.

La Marmite WEST AFRICAN $$
(Map p250; Independence Ave; mains N$100; ⊗lunch & dinner) Commanding a veritable legion of devoted followers, this humble West African eatery deserves its long-garnered popularity. Here you can sample wonderful North and West African cuisine, including Algerian, Senegalese, Ivorian, Cameroonian (try the curry) and Nigerian dishes, all of which are prepared with the finesse of the finest French haute cuisine.

Nice INTERNATIONAL $$
(Map p250; ✆300710; cnr Mozart St & Hosea Kutako Dr; mains N$70-130; ⊗lunch Mon-Fri, dinner daily) The Namibian Institute of Culinary Education – or 'nice' for short – operates this wonderfully conceived 'living classroom' where apprentice chefs can field test their cooking skills. The restaurant itself is more akin to a stylish gallery (think white tablecloths and clinking wine glasses too); also here is a sushi and wine bar. Lunch dishes include tiger prawn and avocado salad, slow-cooked lamb shank and game meat such as oryx. The menu is short and targeted and service is very good.

Leo's INTERNATIONAL $$$
(Map p250; ✆249597; www.heinitzburg.com; 22 Heinitzburg St; mains N$250) Leo's takes its regal setting in Heinitzburg Castle to heart by welcoming diners into a banquet hall that previously served the likes of royalty. The formal settings of bone china and polished crystal glassware are almost as extravagant as the food itself, which spans cuisines and continents, land and sea.

Restaurant Gathemann NAMIBIAN $$$
(Map p250; ✆223853; 179 Independence Ave; mains N$120-240; ⊗dinner) Located in a prominent colonial building overlooking Independence Ave, this splash-out spot serves gourmet Namibian cuisine that fully utilises this country's unique list of ingredients. From Kalahari truffles and Owamboland legumes to tender cuts of game meat and Walvis Bay oysters, Restaurant Gathemann satisfies the pickiest of appetites.

🍷 Drinking

Joe's Beer House PUB
(Map p248; 160 Nelson Mandela Ave) True to its moniker, Joe's stocks a wide assortment of Namibian and German beers, and you can count on prolonged drinking here until early in the morning. It's the favoured drinking hole of Afrikaners.

El Cubano CLUB
(Map p250; cnr Sam Nujoma Dr & Independence St; ⊗Fri & Sat) Offering up a little bit of Havana, Namibian style, El Cubano reopened in 2012 in the basement of the Hilton hotel. It's the capital's most popular club, with a suave, modern interior, a mixed crowd and, of course, a Facebook page.

Café Balalaika BAR
(Map p250; Zoo Park, Independence Ave) This spot, cafe by day, bar by night, features a terrace with the capital's largest rubber tree. Live music and karaoke feature, as does a cool bar scene with some great beer on tap.

Club London CLUB
(Map p248; Southern Industrial Area, 4 Nasmith St; admission varies; ⊗Wed-Sat) Formerly La Dee Da's, this is another relocated club that has undergone a makeover. Check out its Facebook page to see whether it's a foam party, a glowstick event or some other inventive idea enticing patrons to show their moves. At other times you can dance to Angolan *kizomba* (fast-paced Portuguese-African music), hip-hop, rave, traditional African, rock and commercial pop accompanied by special effects.

Wine Bar BAR
(Map p250; ✆226514; 3 Garten St; ⊗4-11.30pm Mon-Thu, 3pm-midnight Fri, 5-10.30pm Sat) In a lovely historic mansion that used to store the town's water supply but now houses the city's premium wine selection; staff here have an excellent knowledge of their products. Playing off this ambience, your hosts

will satiate your palette with an admirable South African wine selection, paired with Mediterranean-style tapas and small snacks. It's a beautiful spot for a glass of wine and a fiery African sunset. There's a wine shop here too.

☆ Entertainment

National Theatre of Namibia   THEATRE
(Map p250; ☎234633; Robert Mugabe Ave) Located south of the National Art Gallery, the National Theatre stages infrequent theatrical performances; for information see the *Namibian* newspaper.

Ster Kinekor   CINEMA
(Map p248; ☎215912; Maerua Park Centre) Off Robert Mugabe Ave, this place shows recent films and has half-price admission on Tuesday.

Playhouse Theatre   THEATRE
(Map p250; ☎402253; Old South-West Brewery Bldg, 48 Tal St; admission varies) This place used to be a warehouse for the breweries but has been converted into a full-scale, state-of-the-art theatre. The industrial interior and versatility of its design makes the Playhouse ideal for staging live African and European music and theatre productions. There's also a permanent exhibition space and an internet cafe here.

🛍 Shopping

Mall culture is alive and well in Windhoek, and you'll find them scattered throughout the city centre and out in the 'burbs. Most of the stores are South African standards, which generally offer high-quality goods at a fraction of the price you're used to back home. Katutura's **Soweto Market** is more reminiscent of a traditional African market, though it's best to visit either with a local or as part of an organised tour.

Old Breweries Craft Market   CRAFT
(Map p250; cnr Garten & Tal Sts) This hive of tourist shopping euphoria contains a heap of small and large shops with a range of African arts and crafts on offer. A couple of our favourite shops are **Woven Arts of Africa**, with some wonderfully fine weavings in the form of wall hangings and rugs, and **Arti-San**, a small, pokey little shop with genuine San crafts.

Namibia Crafts Centre   CRAFT
(Map p250; ☎242222; Old Breweries Craft Market, 40 Tal St; ⊙9am-5.30pm Mon-Fri, to 3.30pm Sat &

Sun) This place is an outlet for heaps of wonderful Namibian inspiration – leatherwork, basketry, pottery, jewellery, needlework, hand-painted textiles and other material arts – and the artist and origin of each piece is documented. We like the root carvings.

House of Gems   GEMS
(Map p250; ☎225202; www.namrocks.com; 131 Werner List St) This is the most reputable shop in Windhoek for buying both raw and polished minerals and gemstones.

Penduka   CRAFT
(☎257210; www.penduka.com) Penduka, which means 'wake up', operates a nonprofit women's needlework project at Goreangab Dam, 8km northwest of the city centre. You can purchase needlework, baskets, carvings and fabric creations for fair prices and be assured that all proceeds go to the producers. To get there, take the Western Bypass north and turn left on Monte Cristo Rd, left on Otjomuise Rd, right on Eveline St and right again on Green Mountain Dam Rd. Then follow the signs to Goreangab Dam/Penduka.

Cymot Greensport   OUTDOOR EQUIPMENT
(Map p250; ☎234131; 60 Mandume Ndemufayo St) This is the place to go for supplies before you head off into the Namibian wilds – it's good for air compressors, a vital accessory. It is also a supplier of quality camping, hiking, cycling and vehicle-outfitting equipment.

Cape Union Mart   OUTDOOR EQUIPMENT
(Map p248; Maerua Park Centre) Good for quality equipment.

Safari Den   OUTDOOR EQUIPMENT
(Map p248; ☎290 9294; www.safariden.com; 20 Bessemer St) Gear for 4WD expeditions.

Gräber's   OUTDOOR EQUIPMENT
(Map p248; ☎222732; Bohr St) In the Southern Industrial Area.

ℹ Information

Emergency
Ambulance & Fire (☎211111)
City Police (☎290 2239; ⊙24hr)
National Police (☎10111)

Internet Access
Virtually all hotels and hostels now offer cheap and reliable internet access, with wireless becoming increasingly the norm. If you're out and about, internet cafes can be found in every mall in the city.

Medical Services

Rhino Park Private Hospital (Map p248; ☎225434; Sauer St) Provides excellent care and service, but patients must pay up front.

Mediclinic Windhoek (☎222687; Heliodoor St, Eros; ☺24hr) Has a 24-hour emergency centre and a range of medical services.

Money

Major banks and bureaus de change are concentrated around Independence Ave. All will change foreign currency and travellers cheques, and give credit-card advances. As a general rule, ATMs in Namibia handle Visa and MasterCard.

Post & Telephone

The modern **main post office** (Independence Ave) can readily handle overseas post. It also has telephone boxes in the lobby, and next door is the **Telecommunications Office**, where you can make international calls and send or receive faxes.

Safe Travel

Central Windhoek is actually quite relaxed and hassle free. As long as you stay alert, walk with confidence, keep a hand on your wallet and avoid wearing anything too flashy, you should encounter nothing worse than a few persistent touts and the odd con artist.

During the research for this book a popular con was for would-be thieves to play on the conscience of tourists and get their attention by posing the question, 'Why won't you talk to a black man?' Ignore this and keep walking. As an extra precaution, always travel by taxi at night, even in the wealthy suburbs. The streets are ominously quiet once the sun goes down, which sadly means that foreign tourists quickly become easy targets.

If you're driving, avoid parking on the street. Also, never leave your car doors unlocked, even if you're still in the car: a common ploy is for one guy to distract you while another opens one of the other doors, grabs a bag and does a runner. During the day, the safest and most convenient parking is the underground lot beneath the Wernhill Park Centre. At night, you should stay at accommodation that provides off-street secure parking.

Tourist Information

Namibia Wildlife Resorts (NWR; Map p250; ☎285 7200; www.nwr.com.na; Independence Ave) Books national-park accommodation and hikes.

Windhoek Information & Publicity Office (Main Office) (Map p250; ☎290 2092, 290 2596; www.cityofwindhoek.org.na; Independence Ave; ☺7.30am-4.30pm) This friendly office answers questions and distributes local publications and leaflets, including *What's On in Windhoek* and useful city maps. There's another branch (Map p250; Post St Mall; ☺7.30am-noon & 1-4.30pm) that is open the same hours but closed at lunchtime.

Travel Agencies

Cardboard Box Travel Shop (Map p250; ☎256580; www.namibian.org) Attached to the backpacker hostel of the same name, this recommended travel agency can arrange both budget and upmarket bookings all over the country.

Chameleon Safaris (Map p250; ☎247668; www.chameleonsafaris.com) This travel agency, although attached to a backpackers, is a great place to investigate and book all kinds of trips around Namibia, from safaris through Etosha to the sand dunes of the Namib-Naukluft Park. All budgets are covered.

❶ Getting There & Away

Air

Chief Hosea Kutako International Airport, which is about 40km east of the city centre, serves most international flights into and out of Windhoek. **Air Namibia** (☎299 6333; www.airnamibia.com.na) operates flights daily between Windhoek and Cape Town and Johannesburg (both in South Africa), as well as daily flights to/from Frankfurt (Germany). Several airlines also offer international services to/from Maun (Botswana) and Victoria Falls (Zimbabwe).

Eros airport, immediately south of the city centre, serves most domestic flights into and out of Windhoek. Air Namibia offers around three weekly flights to/from Katima Mulilo, Ondangwa, Rundu and Swakopmund/Walvis Bay.

Other airlines with flights into and out of Windhoek include **TAAG Angola** (☎226625; www.taag.com.br), **Lufthansa Airlines** (☎415 3747; www.lufthansa.com) and **South African Airways** (☎273340; www.flysaa.com).

Bus

From the main **long-distance bus terminal** (cnr Independence Ave & Bahnhof St), the Intercape Mainliner (p319) runs to/from Cape Town, Johannesburg, Victoria Falls and Swakopmund, serving a variety of local destinations along the way. Tickets can be purchased either through your accommodation, from the Intercape Mainliner Office or over the internet – given the popularity of these routes, advance reservations are recommended.

Local combis (minibuses) leave when full from the Rhino Park petrol station, Katutura (get there very early in the morning), and can take you to most urban centres in central and southern Namibia. For northern destinations such as Tsumeb, Grootfontein and Rundu you need to go to the local minibus station opposite the hospital on Independence Ave, Katutura.

Generally, combi routes do not serve the vast majority of Namibia's tourist destinations, which are located well beyond major population centres. Still, they're a fine way to travel if you want to visit some of the country's smaller towns and cities, and it's great fun to roll up your sleeves and jump into the bus with the locals.

Car & Motorcycle

Windhoek is literally the crossroads of Namibia – the point where the main north–south (the B1) and east–west routes (B2 and B6) cross – and all approaches to the city are extremely scenic, passing through beautiful desert hills. Roads are clearly signposted and those travelling between northern and southern Namibia can avoid the city centre by taking the Western Bypass.

Train

Windhoek train station has a **booking office** (⌨298 2175; ⌚7.30am-4pm Mon-Fri) where you are able to reserve seats on any of the country's public rail lines. Routes are varied, and include overnight trains to Keetmanshoop, Tsumeb and Swakopmund, though irregular schedules, lengthy travel times and far better bus connections make train travel of little interest for the majority of overseas travellers.

❶ Getting Around

Collective taxis from the main ranks at Wernhill Park Centre follow set routes to Khomasdal and Katutura, and if your destination is along the way, you'll pay around N$5 to N$15. With taxis from the main bus terminals or by radio dispatch, fares are either metered or are calculated on a per-kilometre basis, but you may be able to negotiate a set fare per journey. Plan on N$50 to anywhere around the city.

If you're arriving at Hosea Kutako International Airport, taxis typically wait outside the arrivals area. It's a long drive into the city, so you can expect to pay anywhere from N$270 to N$300 depending on your destination. From Eros airport, fares are much more modest at around N$50. In the city there are always reliable taxis that hang around the tourist office on Independence Ave. If you flag one down on the street just be aware that there are plenty of cowboys around and often not much English spoken.

NORTH-CENTRAL NAMIBIA

The tourist trail in North-Central Namibia leads directly to Etosha National Park, one of the world's pre-eminent wildlife areas.

Unlike in most safari parks in Africa, roads inside Etosha are 2WD accessible and open to private vehicles. This means that if you've been fortunate enough to rent your own vehicle, you're in for one of the most memorable safaris of your life. Anyone can tell their friends and family back home how quickly their guide spotted a leopard in a tree, but how many people can say they drove on the edges of a salt pan while spotting elephant herds in the distance?

Erongo Mountains (Erongoberg)

⌨064

The volcanic Erongo Mountains, often referred to as the Erongoberg, rise as a 2216m massif north of Karibib and Usakos. The site was occupied in prehistory by the San, who left behind a rich legacy of cave paintings and rock art that has weathered remarkably well throughout the ages.

The Erongo range is best known for its caves and rock paintings, particularly the 50m-deep Phillips Cave (day permit N$50). This cave, 3km off the road, contains the famous hump-backed white elephant painting. Superimposed on the elephant is a large hump-backed antelope (perhaps an eland), and around it frolic ostriches and giraffes.

Ameib Ranch (⌨684151; campsites per person N$130, s/d from N$600/1200; ❃) is a historic farmhouse that is adjacent to a landscaped pool, a *lapa* (a circular area with a firepit, used for socialising) and a well-maintained campsite. The ranch owns the concessions on Phillips Cave, and issues permits for the site in addition to providing guided hikes and day tours.

Erongo Wilderness Lodge (⌨570537; www.erongowilderness-namibia.com; tented bungalows per person with full board from N$1515; ❃@❃) is a highly acclaimed wilderness retreat that combines spectacular mountain scenery, wildlife viewing, birdwatching and environmentally sensitive architecture to create one of Namibia's most memorable lodges. To get to the lodge, go to Omaruru, turn west on the D2315 (off the Karibib road 1km south of town) and continue for 10km.

North of Ameib, the D1935 skirts the Erongo Mountains before heading into Damaraland. Alternatively, you can head east towards Omaruru on the D1937. This route virtually encircles the Erongo massif and provides access to minor 4WD roads into the heart of the mountains.

Omaruru

Omaruru's dry and dusty setting beside the shady Omaruru riverbed lends it a real outback feel. The town has a growing reputation as an arts and crafts centre and in recent years has become home to the Artist's Trail, an annual arts event involving painters, musicians, sculptors and jewellers. It runs for three days in September and you can pick up a free copy of the program of events around town. The town itself is a welcoming little oasis with some great accommodation options, good food and one of the very few wineries in the country.

☉ Sights

Kristall Kellerei Winery   WINERY
(☑570083; cheese & meat platters N$70; ☺8am-4.30pm Mon-Fri, to 12.30pm Sat) One of only three wineries in Namibia, this is a lovely spot to come for lunch. In the afternoon you can sit out in the art-filled garden and enjoy a light meal – cheese and cold-meat platters are available – while tasting the wines and other products. Apart from schnapps the winery produces Colombard (a white wine), and Paradise Flycatcher (a red blend of ruby

---

DON'T MISS

THE LIVING MUSEUM OF THE SAN PEOPLE

The **Living Museum** (☑064-571086; www.omandumba.de; Farm Omandumba) is a unique opportunity in Namibia to interact with, and learn about, the San people, one of the oldest traditional hunter-gatherer cultures in the world. Experiencing traditional San culture includes learning how to make arrows, jewellery and traditional medicine. Tourists can also go on bush walks and hunting trips and enjoy tribal song and dance. The museum features a typical San village and proceeds go towards a school, also here. Tours (N$200) to rock paintings in the area run from the museum, and there's **accommodation** in the way of campsites and simple rooms. The open-air museum is located 50km southwest of Omaruru on the D2315.

---

cabernet, cabernet sauvignon and tinta barocca). The winery is 4km east of town on the D2328.

🛏 Sleeping

River Guesthouse   GUESTHOUSE $$
(☑570274; Dr I Scheepers Dr; campsites N$90, s/d N$390/610; ⊛) The camping here is the best in town, with some great shady trees to pitch a tent under and excellent facilities including fireplaces and power outlets. You may just have four dogs keeping you company as well – they make a good blanket in winter. The rooms are fine and surround a shady courtyard well set up for relaxing.

Kashana Hotel   HOTEL $$$
(☑571434; www.kashana-namibia.com; Dr I Scheepers Dr; r per person from N$400; ⊛🖙⊛) Offering a swag of accommodation, upmarket Kashana has luxury bungalows and rooms set around a large, shady courtyard. In the main building is a bar and restaurant. Also based here is a goldsmith and a shop selling herbal products.

❶ Getting There & Away

If you have your own vehicle, follow the paved C33 through Omaruru; it provides the quickest route between Swakopmund and Etosha.

Otjiwarongo

☑067
Handy as a jumping-off point for Etosha, and particularly the Waterberg Plateau, Otjiwarongo is particularly pleasant in September and October when the town explodes with the vivid colours of blooming jacaranda and bougainvillea.

Otjiwarongo is home to Namibia's first **crocodile ranch** (cnr Zingel & Hospital Sts; admission N$25; ☺9am-5pm Mon-Fri, to 3pm Sat & Sun). This ranch produces skins for export, and you can do a worthwhile tour of the crocs. Try any number of croc delicacies at the restaurant.

Okonjima Lodge (☑687032; www.okonjima. com; s/d with half board from N$1500/2300), or 'the Place of Baboons' is home to the Afri-Cat Foundation, which sponsors a cheetah and leopard rehabilitation centre as well as a sanctuary for orphaned or problem lions, cheetahs and other cats. Guests are able to participate in cheetah- and leopard-tracking expeditions (including some on foot), in addition to more relaxing activities, including hiking, birdwatching and wildlife drives. Accommodation is in a variety of chalets, luxury tents and rooms with private bathrooms. To reach Okonjima, turn west onto the D2515, 49km south of Otjiwarongo; follow this road for 15km and then turn left onto the farm road for the last 10km.

The Out of Africa Town Lodge (☑302230; Long St; s/d from N$570/670; ✱✱) is an attractive whitewashed, colonial-style affair with lofty rooms that still retain their historical accents.

C'est Si Bon Hotel (☑301240; www.cestsibonhotel.com; Swembad Rd; s/d from N$570/670; ✱✱) is a charmer that takes its moniker (meaning 'it's so good') to heart, blending Namibian design with European flourishes.

The Intercape Mainliner service that departs Windhoek for Victoria Falls passes through Otjiwarongo (from N$300, 3½ hours, twice weekly), and minibuses travelling between Windhoek and the north stop at the Engen petrol station. All train services between Tsumeb and Windhoek or Walvis Bay (via Swakopmund) also pass through.

Outjo

☑067

Given the tourist traffic through this small town it has retained a surprisingly country, low-key feel. Although it's primarily a stopover with few attractions, its eating and accommodation options make it a good place to chill out for a day or two on the way to/from Etosha National Park. The 1899 military residence Franke House now houses the Outjo Museum (admission N$5; ◷8am-1pm & 2-5pm Mon-Fri).

Friendly and professionally run Etotongwe Lodge (☑313333; www.etotongwelodge.com; campsites per person N$90, s/d N$410/680), just outside town on the way to Etosha, feels like a little outpost. Rooms are fairly bare inside but have some nice African touches and are neat as a pin and very roomy. There's a bar and restaurant on site.

The Farmhouse (☑313444; www.thefarmhouse-outjo.com; mains N$50-80; ◷breakfast, lunch & dinner) is the centre of food and drink in town, serving meals all day every day. Its pleasant beer garden is a great spot to check your emails (N$30 per 30 minutes for wireless or terminals). Burgers, grills (including game such as kudu, eland and oryx), wraps, pizza and salads are on offer. The Farmhouse

also has a single and three double rooms, all at a very comfortable standard.

Just a short walk from the town centre, Etosha Garden Hotel (☑313130; www.etosha-garden-hotel.com; s/d incl breakfast N$360/580; ✱✱) features curio-filled rooms surrounding plush greenery and a swimming pool. It's looking a bit rundown these days and is pretty disorganised, but it's worth dropping in to see if they will give you a decent walkin rate.

Combis run between the OK supermarket in Outjo to towns and cities around North-Central Namibia, though there is no public transport leading up to Okaukuejo and the Andersson Gate of Etosha National Park. If you're driving, however, the paved route continues north as far as the park gate.

Waterberg Plateau Park

The wild Waterberg is highly recommended – there's else nothing quite like it in Namibia. The park (per person per day N$80, per vehicle N$10) takes in a 50km-long, 16km-wide sandstone plateau, looming 150m above the desert plains. It doesn't have the traditional big wildlife attractions, such as lions or elephants; instead it protects rarely seen, threatened species, and even here you have to be lucky to glimpse them, because they're skittish and the bush is very thick. Species living in the park include sable and roan antelopes, and white and black rhinos.

🏃 Activities

Wildlife Drive   WILDLIFE DRIVE

(incl breakfast pack N$450; ◷6am or 3pm) If you're not doing a hike, wildlife drives are the only way to get onto the plateau to spot the animals (self-drives are not allowed). The drive takes you to hides cleverly hidden around waterholes. Antelopes, including elands, sables, roans and red hartebeest are the ones you're most likely to spot. Leopards, cheetahs and brown hyenas are around but rarely seen.

Waterberg Wilderness Trail   HIKING

(per person N$220) From April to November the four-day, guided Waterberg Wilderness Trail operates every Thursday. The walks, led by armed guides, need a minimum of two people. They begin at 2pm from the visitor centre and end early on Sunday afternoon. Walks must be prebooked (well in advance) through NWR (p256) in Windhoek.

There's no set route, and the itinerary is left to the whim of the guide. Accommodation is in simple huts, but participants must carry their own food and sleeping bags.

Waterberg Unguided Hiking Trail   HIKING
(per person N$100) A four-day, 42km unguided hike around a figure-eight track begins at 9am every Wednesday from April to November. Groups are limited to between three and 10 people. Book well ahead through NWR (p256) in Windhoek.

Hikers stay in basic shelters along the course and don't need to carry a tent but must otherwise be self-sufficient (carry food, sleeping bag, torch etc). Shelters have drinking water, but you'll need to carry enough to last you between times – plan on drinking 3L to 4L per day, especially in the hot summer months.

The first day begins at the visitor centre (which is at the Waterberg Camp) and follows the escarpment for 13km to Otjozongombe shelter. The second day's walk to Otjomapenda shelter is just a three-hour, 7km walk. The third day consists of an 8km route that loops back to Otjomapenda for the third night. The fourth and final day is a six-hour, 14km return to the visitor centre.

🛏 Sleeping

The Waterberg Camp should be booked in advance through NWR (p256) in Windhoek, although walk-ins are accepted, subject to availability. The Waterberg Wilderness Lodge is privately owned and accepts walk-ins, though advance reservations are recommended given its popularity.

Waterberg Camp   CAMPGROUND, LODGE $$
(☎067-305001; 2-person campsites N$300, bush chalets N$1200) At Waterberg, campers can pitch a tent in any number of scattered sites around *braai* (barbecue) pits and picnic tables. Campsites benefit from space, views of the plateau and the plains beyond, and well-kept amenities. Campers can pick up firewood, alcohol, basic groceries and other supplies from the shop, while others can sink their teeth into a fine oryx steak at the restaurant and wash it down with a glass of South African pinotage from the bar. One word of warning, though: Waterberg is overrun with crafty baboons, so keep your tents zipped and your doors closed, and watch where you leave your food.

Waterberg Wilderness Lodge   LODGE $$$
(☎067-687018; www.waterberg-wilderness.com; campsites N$150, s/d with half board from N$1050/1800; ❄@☞) Waterberg Wilderness occupies a vast private concession within the park. The Rust family has painstakingly transformed the property (formerly a cattle farm) by repopulating game animals and allowing nature to return to its pregrazed state. The main lodge rests in a sun-drenched meadow at the end of a valley, where you'll find red-sandstone chalets adorned with rich hardwood furniture. Alternatively, you can choose from a handful of more secluded chalets perched high on a rock terrace deeper in the concession, or save a bit of money and pitch your own tent in the high-lying plateau campsite. To reach Waterberg Wilderness, take the D2512 gravel road 8km northeast of the park entrance.

❶ Getting There & Away

Waterberg Plateau Park is only accessible by private car – motorcycles are not permitted anywhere within the park boundaries. From Otjiwarongo it's about 90km to the park gate via the B1, the C22 and the gravel D512. While this route is passable to 2WD vehicles, go slow in the final stretches as the road can be in bad shape after the rainy season. An alternative route is the D2512, which runs between Waterberg and Grootfontein – this route is OK during winter but can be terrible during summer, the rainy season, when it requires a high-clearance 4WD.

Grootfontein
☎067

With a pronounced colonial feel, Grootfontein (Afrikaans for 'big spring') has an air of uprightness and respectability, with local limestone constructions and avenues of jacaranda trees that bloom in the autumn. The springboard for excursions out to Khaudum National Park and the San villages in Otjozondjupa, Grootfontein is the last town of any real significance before you head out into the deep, deep bush.

◉ Sights

German Fort & Museum   FORT, MUSEUM
(adult/child N$25/15; ⊙8.30am-4.30pm Mon-Fri) Historical settler history is depicted here through some fascinating black-and-white photos. The Himba, Kavango and Mbanderu collections of artefacts and photographs are also interesting, as is the history of research

Grootfontein

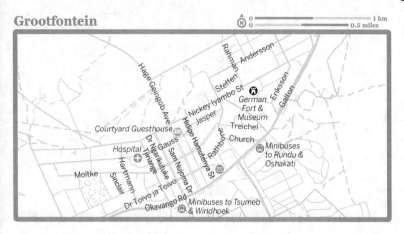

Ñ

0 _____ 1 km
0 _____ 0.5 miles

Rahman
Andersson
Hage Geingob Ave
Steffen
Nickey Iyambo St
Eriksson
Galton
German Fort & Museum
Jasper
Hidipo Hamutenya St
Treichel
Courtyard Guesthouse
Church
Hospital
Dr Ngarikutuke Tjiriange
Gauss
Sam Nujoma St
Rathbone
Minibuses to Rundu & Oshakati
Moltke
Hartmann
Sinclair
Dr Toivo ja Toivo
Okavango Rd
Minibuses to Tsumeb & Windhoek

into the area's rock paintings. It's a huge museum; put aside a couple of hours at least.

The 1896 fort that the museum is housed in was enlarged several times in the early 20th century and in 1922 a large limestone extension was added. Later the building served as a boarding school, but in 1968 it fell into disuse.

Hoba Meteorite   METEORITE
(adult/child N$20/10; ☉dawn-dusk) Near the Hoba Farm the world's largest meteorite was discovered in 1920 by hunter Jacobus Brits. No one knows when it fell to earth (it's thought to have been around 80,000 years ago), but since it weighs around 54,000kg, it must have made a hell of a thump. In 1955 the site was declared a national monument. There's now a visitor information board, a short nature trail and a shady picnic area.

From Grootfontein, follow the C42 towards Tsumeb. After 500m, turn west on the D2859 and continue 22km; then follow the clearly marked signs until you reach the complex.

🛏 Sleeping & Eating

Courtyard Guesthouse   GUESTHOUSE **$$**
(✆240027; 2 Gauss St; s/d N$430/660; ❀@🛜🏊) The top spot in Grootfontein is modest by any standard, but its truly enormous rooms (not all – ask to see a few) leave you plenty of space to unpack your bag and take stock of your gear. Probably the best place in town for food too. The **restaurant** (mains N$60 to N$80; open 7am to 10pm) dabbles in a bit of everything, serving fish, salads, pastas and grills.

Roy's Rest Camp   CAMP **$$**
(✆240302; www.roysrestcamp.com; campsites per person N$90, s/d N$700/1190; ❀) Accommodation at this recommended place looks like a fairy-tale illustration – the handmade wooden furnishings are all fabulously rustic, while the thatched bungalows sit tranquilly beneath towering trees. Activities are available. Roy's is located 55km from Grootfontein on the road towards Rundu, and it's a convenient stop if you're heading to Tsumkwe.

❶ Getting There & Away

Minibuses run frequently between Grootfontein and Tsumeb, Rundu, Katima Mulilo and Windhoek, departing when full from informal bus stops along Okavango Rd at the appropriate ends of town. The Intercape Mainliner (p319) bus that departs Windhoek for Victoria Falls also passes through Grootfontein (from N$350, six hours, twice weekly).

If you're heading out to Tsumkwe you'll need a private vehicle. The gravel road into town is accessible by 2WD if you take it slow, but you'll need a high-clearance vehicle to reach the various villages in Otjozondjupa, and a 4WD might be necessary in the rainy season. If you're heading to Khaudum, a sturdy 4WD is a requirement, as is travelling as part of a well-equipped convoy.

Tsumeb
✆067

Tsumeb is one Namibian town worth a poke around, especially if you're trying to get a feel for the country's urban side. The streets are very pleasant to wander, made more so by the plentiful shady trees; it's reasonably

Tsumeb

NAMIBIA TSUMEB

compact; and there's usually a smile or two drifting your way on the busy streets.

◉ Sights & Activities

Tsumeb Mining Museum MUSEUM
(cnr Main St & 8th Rd; adult/child N$30/5; ⊙9am-5pm Mon-Fri, to noon Sat) Tsumeb's history is told in this museum, which is housed in a 1915 colonial building that once served as both a school and a hospital for German troops. In addition to outstanding mineral displays (you've never seen anything like psitticinite!), the museum also houses mining machinery, stuffed birds, Himba and Herero artefacts, and weapons recovered from Lake Otjikoto. There is also a large collection of militaria, which was dumped here by German troops prior to their surrender to the South Africans in 1915.

Tsumeb Arts & Crafts Centre ARTS CENTRE
(☑220257; 18 Main St; ⊙9am-5pm Mon-Fri, to 1pm Sat) This craft centre markets Caprivian woodwork, San arts, Owambo basketry (also some great basketry from the San), European-Namibian leatherwork, karakul weavings, and other traditional northern Namibian arts and crafts. There's a very helpful lady overseeing what is a small but interesting selection.

Tsumeb Cultural Village CULTURAL VILLAGE
(☑220787; admission N$22; ⊙8am-4pm Mon-Fri, to 1pm Sat) This complex, located 3km outside the town on the road to Grootfontein, showcases examples of housing styles, cultural demonstrations and artefacts from all major Namibian traditions.

Muramba Bushman Trails CULTURAL TOUR
(☑067-220659; bushman@natron.net) This popular company, owned by Reinhard Friedrich in Tsumeb, provides a unique introduction to the Heikum San people.

🛏 Sleeping & Eating

**Mousebird Backpackers
& Safaris** BACKPACKERS $
(☑221777; 533 Pendukeni livula-Ithana St (4th St); campsites per person N$90, dm N$120, tw N$380; @) Tsumeb's longstanding backpacker spot continues to stay true to its roots, offering economical accommodation without sacrificing personality or character – there's a really good feel to this place. It's a small house-style set-up with decent communal areas including a kitchen. The best twin rooms share a bathroom inside the house,

but the twin outside does have its own bathroom. The four-bed dorm is also very good.

Travel North
Namibia Guesthouse   GUESTHOUSE **$$**
(✆220728;   http://natron.net/tnn/index.htm;
Sam Nujoma Dr; s/d N$365/480; ✷@🛜) This
budget guesthouse is a wonderful spot if
you're counting your Nam dollars. It's a
fantastically friendly place delivering good-
value accommodation. Rooms are a bit old-
fashioned and some of the decor wouldn't
look out of place at Grandma's, but it's well
kept and well run. The smallish beds still
have enough life left to ensure a good night's
snooze.

Makalani Hotel   HOTEL **$$**
(✆221051;   www.makalanihotel.com;   Ndilimani
Cultural Troupe St (3rd St); s/d from N$460/680;
✷🛜🏊) Situated in the town centre, the
upmarket Makalani Hotel is a rather garish-
looking place that markets itself as both a
small hotel and almost a mini resort complete with casino. But it can't have it both
ways and it sits uncomfortably between the
two. What it does have is excellent rooms.
If you prefer slightly more comfy hotel-like
options then this place is for you.

ℹ Information
Travel North Namibia Tourist Office
(✆220728; 1551 Sam Nujoma Dr; 🛜) Inside
the guesthouse of the same name. Provides
nationwide information, arranges accommodation, transport, car hire and Etosha bookings,
and has internet access. No maps available.

ℹ Getting There & Away
Bus
Intercape Mainliner (p319) buses make the trip
between Windhoek and Tsumeb (from N$310,
5½ hours, twice weekly). Book your tickets in
advance online as this service continues on to
Victoria Falls and fills up quickly.

Combis also run up and down the B1 with fairly
regular frequency, and a ride between Windhoek
and Tsumeb shouldn't cost more than N$220. If
you're continuing on to Etosha National Park, be
advised that there is no public transport serving
this route.

Car
Tsumeb is an easy day's drive from Windhoek
along paved roads, and serves as the jumping-off
point for Namutoni and the Von Lindequist gate
of Etosha National Park. The paved route continues north as far as the park gate.

Etosha National Park

Etosha National Park ranks as one of the
world's great wildlife-viewing venues. Its
unique nature is encapsulated by the vast
Etosha Pan – an immense, flat, saline desert
that, for a few days each year, is converted by
the rains into a shallow lagoon teeming with
flamingos and pelicans. In contrast, the surrounding bush and grasslands provide habitat for Etosha's diverse wildlife. Although it
may look barren, the landscape (covering an
area of more than 20,000 sq km) fringing the
pan is home to 114 mammal species as well
as 340 bird species, 16 reptile and amphib-
ian species, one fish species and countless
insects.

History
The first Europeans in Etosha were the
traders and explorers John Andersson and
Francis Galton, who arrived by wagon at
Namutoni in 1851. They were followed in
1876 by an American trader, G McKeirnan,
who observed: 'All the menageries in the
world turned loose would not compare to
the sight I saw that day'.

However, Etosha didn't attract the interest
of tourists or conservationists until after the
turn of the 20th century, when the governor
of German South-West Africa, Dr F von Lindequist, became concerned about diminishing
animal numbers and founded a 99,526-sq-
km reserve, which included Etosha Pan.

At the time, the land was still unfenced
and animals could follow their normal migration routes. In subsequent years, however, the park boundaries were altered a few
times, and by 1970 Etosha had been reduced
to its present size.

🏃 Activities
WILDLIFE WATCHING
Depending on the season, you may observe elephants, giraffes, Burchell's zebras,
springboks, red hartebeest, blue wildebeest,
gemsboks, elands, kudus, roan antelopes,
ostriches, jackals, hyenas, lions, and even
cheetahs and leopards. Among the endangered animal species are the black-faced
impala and the black rhinoceros.

The park's wildlife density varies with the
local ecology. As its Afrikaans name would
suggest, Oliphantsbad (near Okaukuejo) is
attractive to elephants, but for rhinos you
couldn't do better than the floodlit waterhole at Okaukuejo. In general, the further

NAMIBIA ETOSHA NATIONAL PARK

Etosha National Park

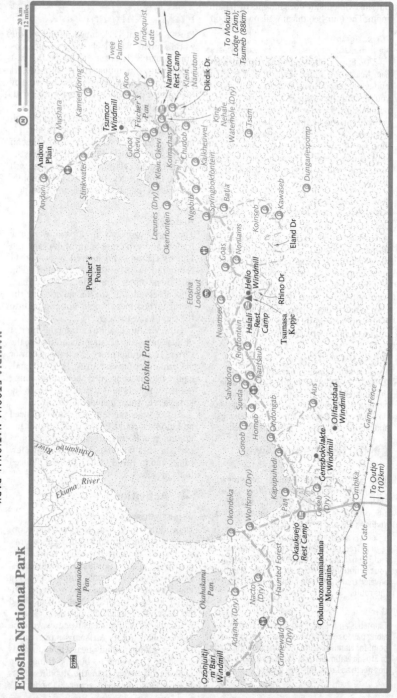

Etosha National Park

20 km
12 miles

To Mokuti
Lodge (2km);
Tsumeb (88km)

Von
Lindequist
Gate

Twee
Palms

Aroe

Namutoni
Rest Camp
Klein
Namutoni

Dikdik Dr

Mushara

Kameeldoring

Tsumcor
Windmill

Groot
Okevi

Klein Okevi

Fischer's
Pan

King
Nehale
Waterhole (Dry)

Kalkheuwel

Kalkheuwel

Tsam

Andoni

Andoni
Plain

Stinkwater

Leeunes (Dry)

Okerfontein

Ngobib

Springbokfontein

Batia

Kawaseb

Koinseb

Dungariespomp

Poacher's
Point

Goas

Nonjlams

Eland Dr

Etosha Pan

Etosha
Lookout

Nuamses

Helio
Windmill

Halali
Rest
Camp

Rhino Dr

Tsumasa
Kopje

Riedfontein

Charitsaub

Oshigambo River

Ekuma
River

Salvadora

Sueda

Gonob

Homob

Ondongab

Aus

Olifantsbad
Windmill

Game Fence

Okondeka

Wolfsnes (Dry)

Kapupuhedi
Pan

Casteb
(Dry)

Gemsbokvlakte
Windmill

Ombika

To Outjo
(102km)

Okaukuejo
Rest Camp

Andersson Gate

Natukanaoka
Pan

Okahakana
Pan

Haunted Forest

Nactoi
(Dry)

Adamax (Dry)

Grünewald
(Dry)

Ondundozonanandana
Mountains

Ozonjuitji
m'Bari
Windmill

east you go in the park, the more wildebeest, kudus and impalas join the springboks and gemsboks. The area around Namutoni is the best place to see black-faced impalas and Damara dik-diks, Africa's smallest antelopes. Etosha is also home to numerous smaller species, including both yellow and slender mongooses, honey badgers and leguaans.

In the dry winter season, wildlife clusters around waterholes, while in the hot, wet summer months, animals disperse and spend the days sheltering in the bush. In the afternoon, even in the dry season, look carefully for animals resting beneath the trees, especially prides of lions lazing about.

Bird life is also profuse. Yellow-billed hornbills are common, and on the ground you should look for the huge kori bustards, which weigh 15kg and seldom fly. You may also observe ostriches, korhaans, marabous, white-backed vultures and many smaller species.

The best time for wildlife drives is at first light and late in the evening, though visitors aren't permitted outside the camps after dark. While self-drivers should definitely wake up at twilight, when animals are most active, guided night drives (N$600 per person) can be booked through any of the main camps and are your best chance to see lions hunting as well as the various nocturnal species. Each of the camps also has a visitor register, which describes any recent sightings in the vicinity.

🛏 Sleeping & Eating

The main camps inside the park are open year-round and have restaurants, bars, shops, swimming pools, picnic sites, petrol stations, kiosks and floodlit waterholes that attract game throughout the night.

In the Park

Booking for the NWR-run camps is mandatory. Although it is sometimes possible to reserve a space at either of the park gates, it's best to contact the NWR (p256) office in Windhoek well in advance of your visit.

Okaukuejo Rest Camp   LODGE, CAMPGROUND **$$**
(campsites N$200, plus per person N$110, s/d from N$1020/1840, chalets from N$1100/2000; ❋ ❋) Pronounced 'o-ka-kui-yo', this is the site of the Etosha Research Station, and it functions as the official park headquarters and main visitor centre. The Okaukuejo waterhole is probably Etosha's best rhino-viewing venue, particularly at night, though you're almost guaranteed to spot zebras, wildebeest, jackals and even elephants virtually any time

of the day. Okaukuejo's campground can get very crowded, but the shared facilities are excellent, and include washing stations, *braai* pits, and bathroom and toilet facilities with hot water. The self-catering accommodation includes older but refurbished rooms alongside stand-alone chalets.

Halali Rest Camp   LODGE, CAMPGROUND **$$**
(campsites N$200, plus per person N$100, s/d from N$800/1400, chalets from N$1000/1700; ❋ ❋) Etosha's middle camp, Halali, nestles between several incongruous dolomite outcrops. The best feature of Halali is its floodlit waterhole, which is a 10-minute walk from the rest camp and is sheltered by a glen of trees with huge boulders strewn about. It's a wonderfully intimate setting where you can savour a glass of wine in peace, all the while scanning the bush for rhinos and lions, which frequently stop by to drink in the late evening hours. There is a very well-serviced campsite here, in addition to a fine collection of luxury chalets that make for a wonderfully relaxed night of sleep despite being deep in the African bush.

Namutoni Rest Camp   LODGE, CAMPGROUND **$$**
(campsites N$200, plus per person N$110, s/d from N$850/1500, chalets from N$1000/1800; ❋ ❋) Etosha's easternmost camp is defined by its landmark whitewashed German fort, a colonial relic that casts a surreal shadow over the rest of the camp. The floodlit King Nehale waterhole is filled with reed beds and some extremely vociferous frogs. The viewing benches are nice for lunch or watching the pleasant riverbank scene, but unfortunately the spot attracts surprisingly few thirsty animals. Namutoni also offers an immaculate campsite (the only campsite in the park with grass) in addition to a few luxury chalets on the edge of the bush.

Dolomite Camp   LODGE **$$$**
(s/d with half board from N$1250/2300; ❋ ❋) Recently opened in a previously restricted area of the park in western Etosha is Dolomite Camp, beautifully carved into its rocky surrounds. Accommodation is in thatched chalets (actually luxury tents) including a couple with their own plunge pool. The views of the surrounding plains are wonderful, and there's even a waterhole at the camp, so spotting the wildlife doesn't mean moving far from your bed. When you do get out and about, the wildlife viewing around here is superb as the area has been free from human activity for half a century.

OUTSIDE THE PARK

TOP CHOICE **Sachsenheim** CAMPING, CHALETS **$$**

(☑081 215 0100, 067-230011; campsites N$110, with private facilities N$150, s/d chalets N$500/900) This guest farm has some great options and is 3km north of the C38/B1 junction (off the B1). You can camp on grass under shady trees or stay in simply but beautifully decorated large-roomed stone chalets. The location gives this place a rather remote, harsh feel, which is softened by the grassed areas and plenty of shady trees. It's a very affordable spot close to Etosha. Meals available.

Taleni Etosha Village SAFARI TENTS **$$**

(☑067-687190; s/d self-catering N$900/1100; ❋ ❅) This little hideaway just a couple of kilometres outside Etosha has self-catering safari tents (half- and full-board options available) that are very well equipped and come with outdoor seating area, *braai*, wooden floors, power points and many little luxuries. The tents are nestled into bushland amongst mopani trees and the friendly staff can also organise food if you are self-catering. The internet is available for N$60 per hour and there's a restaurant and a great bar area. Walk-in rates are about half those listed above. Etosha Village is situated 2km before the Andersson Gate.

Mokuti Lodge **$$**

(☑067-229084; www.kempinski.com/mokuti; tw incl breakfast N$1300, chalets N$2300; ❋ @ ❅) This sprawling lodge, located just 2km from Von Lindequist Gate, has rooms, chalets and luxurious suites. The accommodation mixes contemporary fittings with African style, creating a funky blend. Chalets have sink-in-and-smile sofas and welcome platters. The lodge seeks to create an informal, relaxed atmosphere – there's a *boma* (sunken campfire circle) with firepit and nightly storytelling – which makes this a good choice if you're travelling with little ones.

❶ Information

Only the eastern two-thirds of Etosha are open to the general public; the western third is reserved exclusively for tour operators (with the exception of Dolomite Camp). Etosha's three main entry gates are Von Lindequist (Namutoni), west of Tsumeb; King Nehale, southeast of Ondangwa; and Andersson (Okaukuejo), north of Outjo.

Visitors are encouraged to check in at either Von Lindequist Gate or Andersson Gate (King Nehale Gate is frequently closed), where you then must purchase a permit costing N$80 per person plus N$10 per vehicle per day. The permits are to be presented at your reserved rest camp, where you pay any outstanding camping or accommodation fees.

❶ Getting There & Away

There's no public transport into or around the park, which means that you must visit either in a private vehicle or as part of an organised tour.

NORTHERN NAMIBIA

The country's most densely populated region, and undeniably its cultural heartland, northern Namibia is a place for some serious African adventure. It is where endless skies meet distant horizons in an expanse that will make you truly wonder whether this is your greatest road trip of all time. Northern Namibia takes form and identity from the Caprivi Strip, where alongside traditional villages there's a collection of national parks.

Ondangwa

☑065

The second-largest Owambo town is known as a minor transport hub, with combis fanning out from here to other cities and towns in the north. Its large number of warehouses provide stock to the 6000 tiny cuca shops (small bush shops named after the brand of Angolan beer they once sold) that serve the area's rural residents.

The main attraction in the area is Lake Oponono, a large wetland fed by the *culevai oshanas* (underground river channels). Also worthwhile is Nakambale House (admission N$5; ⊘8am-1pm & 2-5pm Mon-Fri, 8am-1pm Sat, noon-5pm Sun), which was built in the late 1870s by Finnish missionary Martti Rauttanen, and is believed to be the oldest building in northern Namibia. It now houses a small museum on Owambo history and culture.

⏢ Sleeping

Nakambale Campsite CAMPGROUND, HUT **$**

(☑245668; campsites N$50, huts per person N$100) Here's your opportunity to sleep in a basic hut that would have been used historically by an Owambo chief or one of his wives. Nakambale is located on the outskirts of Olukonda village, 20km south of Ondangwa on the D3629.

Protea Hotel Ondangwa　　　　HOTEL **$$**
(☑241900; www.proteahotels.com/protea-hotel-ondangwa.html; s/d from N$765/1050; ✴✳) This plush business hotel features bright rooms decorated with tasteful artwork as well as modern furnishings. The attached Chatters restaurant does decent Continental-inspired cuisine, and there's also a small espresso shop and takeaway in the lobby.

❶ Getting There & Away

Air

Air Namibia flies to and from Windhoek's Eros Airport daily. Note that the airstrip in Oshakati is for private charters only, which means that Ondangwa serves as the main access point in the north for airborne travellers.

Bus

Combis also run up and down the B1 with fairly regular frequency, and a ride between Windhoek and Ondangwa shouldn't cost more than N$160. From Ondangwa, a complex network of combi routes serve population centres throughout the north, with fares typically costing less than N$30 a ride.

Car

The B1 is paved all the way from Windhoek to Ondangwa and out to Oshakati.

The Oshikango border crossing to Santa Clara in Angola is 60km north of Ondangwa; to travel further north, you'll need an Angolan visa that allows overland travel.

Uutapi (Ombalantu)

Uutapi (also known as Ombalantu), which lies on the C46 between Oshakati and Ruacana, is home to a number of widely revered national heritage sites, and warrants a quick visit if you've got your own wheels and are passing through the area.

The most famous attraction in Uutapi is the former **South African Defence Force (SADF) base**, which is dominated by an enormous baobab tree. This tree, known locally as *omukwa*, was once used to shelter cattle from invaders, and later as a turret from which to ambush invading groups. It didn't work with the South African forces, however, who invaded and used the tree for everything from a chapel to a coffee shop. To reach the fort, turn left at the police station 350m south of the petrol station, and look for an obscure grassy track winding between desultory buildings towards the conspicuous baobab.

Another famous destination is the town of **Ongulumbashe**, which is regarded as the birthplace of modern Namibia. On 26 August 1966, the first shots of the war for Namibian independence were fired from this patch of scrubland. The site is also where the People's Liberation Army of Namibia enjoyed its first victory over the South African troops, who had been charged with rooting out and quelling potential guerrilla activities. From Uutapi, turn south on the D3612 to the village of Otsandi (Tsandi). At the eastern edge of the village, turn west down an unnumbered track and continue 20km to Ongulumbashe. Be advised that this area is considered politically sensitive – you will need permission to visit the site from the Swapo office in Uutapi.

Ongandjera, birthplace of independent Namibia's first president, Samuel Nujoma, lies on the D3612, 52km southeast of Uutapi near Okahao. It's also accessible via the C41 from Oshakati.

Ruacana

☑065

The tiny Kunene River town of Ruacana (from the Herero words *orua hakahana* – the rapids) is the jumping-off point for visiting the Ruacana Falls. Here, the Kunene River splits into several channels before plunging 85m over a dramatic escarpment and through a 2km-long gorge of its own making. The town was built as a company town to serve the 320-megawatt underground Ruacana hydroelectric project, which now supplies over half of Namibia's power requirements.

The dramatic 85m-high **Ruacana Falls** was once a great natural wonder, but thanks to Angola's Calueque Dam the water flows only during heavy rains, when the power station is satisfied and excess water is released over the dam. In wetter years, it's no exaggeration to say it rivals Victoria Falls – if you hear that it's flowing, you certainly won't regret a side trip to see it (and it may be the closest you ever get to Angola).

Hippo Pools Camp Site (☑270120; campsites per person N$50) is also known as Otjipahuriro, and this community-run campsite sits alongside the river and has a good measure of shade and privacy. Local community members can organise trips to Ruacana Falls or to nearby Himba villages for a small fee.

Ruacana Eha Lodge (☑271500; www.ruacanaehalodge.com.na; Springbom Ave; campsites per person N$70, huts per person N$220, s/d N$775/1080; ❄@≋) appeals to travellers of all budgets by offering manicured campsites and rustic A-frame huts alongside its polished rooms.

Ruacana is near the junction of roads between Opuwo, the Owambo country and the rough 4WD route along the Kunene River to Swartbooi's Drift. Note that mileage signs along the C46 confuse Ruacana town and the power plant, which are 15km apart. Both are signposted 'Ruacana' – don't let them throw you too badly.

For westbound travellers, the 24-hour petrol station is the last before the Atlantic; it's also the terminal for afternoon combis to and from Oshakati and Ondangwa, costing around N$30.

The Angolan border crossing is open to Namibians, though others need an Angolan visa that allows overland entry.

Rundu

☑066

Rundu, a sultry tropical outpost on the bluffs above the Okavango River, is a major centre of activity for Namibia's growing Angolan community. Although the town has little of specific interest for tourists, the area is home to a number of wonderful lodges where you

can laze along the riverside and spot crocs and hippos doing pretty much the same.

Take a stroll around the large **covered market**, which is one of Africa's most sophisticated informal sales outlets. From July to September, don't miss the fresh papayas, sold straight from the trees. Alternatively, head for the **Khemo Open Market** (⊙daily), located on Independence about 1km south of the intersection with Usivi Rd, where you can shop for both African staples and Kavango handicrafts.

Situated on the banks of the Okavango, about 20km from Rundu's town centre, is the **N'Kwazi Lodge** (☑081 242 4897; www.nkwazilodge.com; campsites per person N$120, r per person N$420), a tranquil and good-value riverside retreat. The lodge's owners, Valerie and Weynand Peyper, are active in the local community and have rebuilt a preschool that was washed away in the 2009 floods. They also have many other ongoing projects including supporting orphans in the area. You can visit the preschool and also local villages (N$50 for a village walk).

The laidback **Sarasungu River Lodge** (☑255161; www.sarasunguriverlodge.com; campsites per person N$70, s/d/tr N$530/750/1000; ❄🛜≋) is situated in a secluded riverine clearing 4km north of the town centre, off Sarasungu Rd. It has attractive thatched chalets that surround a landscaped pool and a decent-size grassed camping area with basic amenities and beautiful sunsets.

Hakusembe Lodge (☑257010; campsites per person N$100, chalets per person with half board from N$1100; ❄≋), located to the west of Rundu off the B10, has eight luxury chalets (one of which is floating) decked out in safari prints and locally crafted furniture.

ⓘ Getting There & Away

Bus

Several weekly Intercape Mainliner (p319) buses make the seven-hour trip between Windhoek and Rundu (fares from N$380). Book your tickets in advance online as this service continues on to Victoria Falls and fills up quickly.

Combis connect Windhoek and Rundu with fairly regular frequency, and a ride shouldn't cost more than N$250. From Rundu, routes fan out to various towns and cities in the north, with fares costing less than N$40 a ride. Both buses and combis depart and drop off at the Engen petrol station.

Car & Motorcycle

Drivers will need to be patient on the road (B8) to Rundu from Grootfontein. It's in good condi-

Rundu

△ N   0 ━━━━ 1 km
    0 ━━━━ 0.5 miles

Okavango River

Covered Market

Rundu Beach

Siwaronga St

Bank

Maria Mwengere St

Hospital

Main St

Nkarapamwe St

Kakakuru St

Rundu Stadium

Engen Petrol Station & Minibus Stop

B2

Rundu Airport

tion but passes by many schools where the speed limit drops suddenly - fertile ground for speed cameras.

Khaudum National Park

🚻066

Exploring the largely undeveloped 384,000-hectare Khaudum National Park is an intense wilderness challenge that is guaranteed not to disappoint. Meandering sand tracks lure you through pristine bush and across *omiramba* (fossil river valleys), which run parallel to the east–west Kalahari dunes. As there is virtually no signage, and navigation is largely based on GPS coordinates and topographic maps, few tourists make the effort to extend their safari experience beyond the secure confines of Etosha.

But that is precisely why Khaudum is worth exploring: as one of Namibia's most important game reserves, the park is home to one of only two protected populations of lions, and it's the only place in the country where African wild dogs can be spotted.

🏃 Activities

Wildlife watching is the primary activity in Khaudum. The park protects large populations of elephants, zebras, giraffes, wildebeest, kudus, oryxes and tsessebes, and there's a good chance you'll be able to spot large herds of roan antelopes here. If you're an avid birder, you'll be pleased to know that Khaudum supports 320 species, including summer migratory birds such as storks, crakes, bitterns, orioles, eagles and falcons.

Wildlife viewing is best from June to October, when herds congregate around the waterholes and along the *omiramba*. November to April is the richest time to visit for birdwatchers, though you'll have to be prepared for a difficult slog through muddy tracks.

🛏 Sleeping

NWR used to administer two official campsites in the park, but after one too many episodes of elephants gone wild, it decided to close up shop. These two sites have been neglected for a long time (although rumours of impending development persist); if you're planning to stay at either one, keep your expectations low.

Sikereti Camp ('Cigarette' camp) is located in a shady grove, though full appreciation of this place requires sensitivity to its subtle charms, namely isolation and silence; and

BORDER CROSSING: RUNDU TO ANGOLA

This border crossing has almost one-way traffic, with plenty of Angolans coming into Namibia to purchase goods from the shops, seek medical help and visit relatives. We have had reports from travellers that tourists crossing here are sometimes asked for a bribe or even arrested by Angolan authorities. Basic Portuguese language skills would be a huge bonus as English is not widely spoken. Getting an Angolan visa (US$100) in Windhoek is very difficult and you need time and patience (one traveller we heard about waited for months with no success). It may just depend on who you deal with at the Angolan embassy and of course your nationality. As part of your visa application, you will need a letter of invitation from somebody in Angola as well as a copy of that person's ID. At the time of writing, Oshakati was the best place in Namibia to lodge an Angolan visa application.

Khaudum Camp is somewhat akin to the Kalahari in miniature.

ℹ Information

In order to explore the reserve by private 4WD vehicle, you will have to be completely self-sufficient, as petrol and supplies are only available in towns along the Caprivi Strip. Water is available inside the reserve, though it must be boiled or treated prior to drinking.

Tracks in the reserve are mostly sand, though they deteriorate into mud slicks after the rains. As a result, NWR (p256) requires that parties travel in a convoy of at least two self-sufficient 4WDs, and are equipped with enough food, water and petrol to survive for at least three days. Caravans, trailers and motorcycles are prohibited.

ℹ Getting There & Away

From the north, take the sandy track from Katere on the B8 (signposted 'Khaudum'), 120km east of Rundu. After 45km you'll reach the Cwibadom Omuramba, where you should turn east into the park.

From the south, you can reach Sikereti Camp via Tsumkwe. From here, it's 20km to Groote Döbe and then another 15km to the Dorslandboom turning. It's then 25km north to Sikereti Camp.

Bwabwata National Park

☑066

Only recently recognised as a national park, Bwabwata was established to rehabilitate local wildlife populations. Prior to the 2002 Angolan ceasefire, this area saw almost no visitors, and wildlife populations had been virtually wiped out by rampant poaching instigated by ongoing conflict. Now that a decade of peace has returned, the animals are miraculously back again, and tourism is starting to pick up once more.

⊙ Sights

Bwabwata includes five main zones: the Divundu area, the West Caprivi Triangle, the Mahango Game Reserve, Popa Falls and the now-defunct West Caprivi Game Reserve. The Mahango Game Reserve presently has the largest concentrations of wildlife, and is resultantly the focus of most safaris in the area.

Mahango Game Reserve　　WILDLIFE RESERVE
(per person/vehicle N\$40/10; ⊙sunrise-sunset) This small but diverse 25,000-hectare park occupies a broad flood plain north of the Botswana border and west of the Okavango River. It attracts large concentrations of thirsty elephants and herd animals, particularly in the dry season.

With a 2WD vehicle, you can either zip through on the Mahango transit route or follow the Scenic Loop Dr past Kwetche picnic site, east of the main road. With a 4WD you can also explore the 20km Circular Drive Loop, which follows the *omiramba* and offers the best wildlife viewing. It's particularly nice to stop beside the river in the afternoon and watch the elephants swimming and drinking among hippos and crocodiles.

🛏 Sleeping

While private concessions here handle their own bookings, the campsite at Popa Falls is run by NWR (p256) and must be booked through its main office in Windhoek.

WESTERN SECTION

Ngepi Camp　　LODGE \$
(☑259903; www.ngepicamp.com; campsites per person N\$100, bush/tree huts per person N\$350/500) One of Namibia's top backpacker lodges that appeals beyond the budget market, Ngepi makes a great base for the area. Crash for the night in a bush or tree hut, or pitch a tent on grass right by the river's edge and let the sounds of hippos splashing about ease you into a restful sleep. There's

East Caprivi Strip

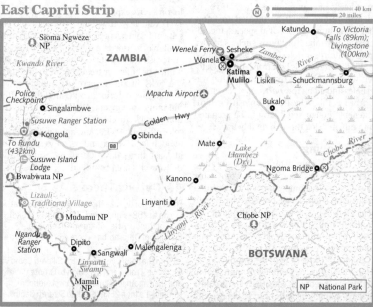

| NP | National Park |

BORDER CROSSING: MAHANGO TO MOHEMBO

About 12km before the Mahango–Mohembo border (open 6am to 6pm) with Botswana is the entry point to the Mahango Game Reserve. If you're transiting to the border there is no fee payable – just fill out the register at the entrance gate, indicating that you have entered the area. At the border, formalities are straightforward. On the Botswanan side fill in the registration book for your vehicle and the entry card, and get your passport stamped. Pay 110 pula (or N$160) for a road permit and insurance (payment is accepted in either currency). Exit into Botswana.

also a wide range of inexpensive excursions, including Mahango wildlife drives (N$420, three hours) and *mokoro* (traditional dugout canoe) trips (N$190, 2½ hours) in the Okavango Panhandle. Or try a local village walk for N$100. The camp is located 4km off the main road, though the sandy access can prove difficult without a high-clearance vehicle. Phone the lodge if you need a lift from Divundu.

Nunda Lodge   LODGE $$
(☑686070; www.nundalodge.com; campsites per person N$110, safari tents per person N$665, chalets N$760) This very welcoming lodge has an appealing aesthetic comprising stone buildings with thatched roofs and wooden decks on the river's edge. The campsites are excellent, with sites 6 and 7 the best; all have power, *braai* plates and bins. Safari tents are also on the riverbank with a small table and chairs on the deck out the front to enjoy the water views. Rates are often reduced if they're not busy.

Eastern Section

Nambwa Camp Site   CAMPGROUND $
(campsites per person N$60) Nambwa, 14km south of Kongola, is the only official camp in the park, and it provides easy access to the wildlife-rich oxbow lagoon, about 5km south. Book and pick up a permit at the Susuwe ranger station, about 4km north of Kongola (4WD access only) on the west bank of the river. To reach the camp, follow the 4WD track south along the western bank of the Kwando River.

Susuwe Island Lodge   LODGE $$$
(☑061-401047; www.islandsinafrica.com/susuwe-island-lodge; per person Jan-Apr from N$3220, Jun-Dec from N$5480; ❋@☀) This posh safari lodge is located on a remote island in the Kwando River and surrounded by a diverse habitat of savannah, woodland and wetland. Accommodation is in six stylish brick and thatch chalets adorned in soft earth tones. Susuwe is accessible only by charter flight or 4WD. Prebooking is mandatory.

ℹ Getting There & Away

The paved road between Rundu and Katima Mulilo is perfectly suited to 2WD vehicles, as is the gravel road between Divundu and Mohembo (on the Botswana border). Drivers may transit the park without charge, but you'll incur national-park entry fees to use the loop drive through the park.

Katima Mulilo

☑066

Out on a limb at the eastern end of the Caprivi Strip lies remote Katima Mulilo, which is as far from Windhoek (1200km) as you can get in Namibia. Once known for the elephants that marched through the village streets, Katima is devoid of wildlife these days – apart from the hippos and crocodiles in the Zambezi – though it continues to thrive as a border town and minor commercial centre.

🛏 Sleeping & Eating

Caprivi River Lodge   LODGE $$
(☑252288; www.capririverlodge.com; s N$415-1075, d N$620-1375; ❋☀) This diverse lodge offers options to suit travellers of all budgets, from rustic cabins with shared bathrooms to luxurious chalets facing the Zambezi River. It offers a decent variety of activities, including boating, fishing and wildlife drives in the various Caprivi parks. The lodge is located 5km from town along Ngoma Rd.

Mukusi Cabins   CABINS $$
(☑253255; Engen petrol station; campsites N$80, s/d from N$460/640; ❋) Although it lacks the riverside location of other properties in the area, this oasis behind the petrol station has a good range of accommodation, from simple rooms with fans to small but comfortable air-con cabins. The lovely bar-restaurant dishes up a range of unexpected options – including calamari, snails and kingklip – as well as steak and chicken standbys.

BORDER CROSSING: BOTSWANA & ZAMBIA

With a private vehicle, the Ngoma Bridge border crossing (open 8am to 6pm) enables you to access Chobe National Park (Botswana) and Kasane (Botswana) in just a couple of hours. If you stick to the Chobe National Park Transit Rte, you're excused from paying Botswana park fees.

The 1km-long Wenela bridge (open 7am to 6pm) spans the Zambezi between Katima Mulilo and Wenela, providing easy access to Livingstone and other destinations in Zambia. If you're heading to the falls, the road is tarred all the way to Livingstone, and is accessible by 2WD vehicle, even in the rainy season.

Protea Hotel Zambezi Lodge   LODGE $$$
(☑251500; www.proteahotels.com/katima-mulilo.html; campsites per person N$70, s/d from N$700/1050; ✳@☀) This stunning riverside lodge is perched on the banks of the Zambezi and features a floating bar where you can watch the crocs and hippos below. The campsite is amid a flowery garden, while accommodation is in well-equipped modern rooms that open up to small verandahs and ample views.

🛍 Shopping

Caprivi Arts Centre   ARTS & CRAFTS
(☺8am-5.30pm) Run by the Caprivi Art & Cultural Association, this centre is a good place to look for local curios and crafts, including elephant and hippo woodcarvings, baskets, bowls, kitchen implements, and traditional knives and spears.

ℹ Getting There & Away

Air
Air Namibia has several weekly departures between Windhoek's Eros Airport and Katima's Mpacha airport, located 18km southwest of town.

Bus & Minibus
Several weekly Intercape Mainliner (p319) buses make the 16-hour run between Windhoek and Katima Mulilo. Book your tickets (fares from N$460) in advance online as this service continues on to Victoria Falls and fills up quickly.

Combis connect Windhoek and Katima with fairly regular frequency, and a ride shouldn't

cost more than N$230. From Katima, routes fan out to various towns and cities in the north, with fares costing less than N$40 a ride.

Car
The paved Golden Hwy runs between Katima Mulilo and Rundu, and is accessible to all 2WD vehicles.

Mpalila Island
☑066

Mpalila (Impalila) Island, a wedge driven between the Chobe and Zambezi Rivers, represents Namibia's outer limits at the 'four-corners meeting' of Zimbabwe, Botswana, Namibia and Zambia. The island itself, which is within easy reach by boat of Chobe National Park, is home to a handful of exclusive lodges catering to upmarket tourists in search of luxurious isolation.

Booking for all accommodation on the island is essential. All lodges offer a variety of activities for guests including cruises on the Chobe River, guided game drives, fishing expeditions, island walks and *mokoro* trips. Rates include full board and transfers.

Overlooking the impressive Mombova rapids, the Impalila Island Lodge (☑061-401047; www.islandsinafrica.com/impalila-island-lodge; per person Jan-Apr N$2860, Jun-Dec N$4840; ✳☀) is a stylish retreat of eight luxury chalets built on elevated decks at the water's edge. The centrepiece of the lodge is a pair of ancient baobab trees, which tower majestically over the grounds.

The most famous spot on the island is the Chobe Savannah Lodge (☑in South Africa 021-4241037; www.desertdelta.co.za; per person Jan-Apr US$410, Jun-Dec US$650; ✳☀), which is renowned for its panoramic views of the game-rich Puku Flats. Each stylishly decorated room has a private verandah where you can spot wildlife without ever having to change out of your pyjamas.

Access to Mpalila Island is either by charter flight or by boat from Kasane (Botswana), though lodges will organise all transport for their booked guests.

Mudumu National Park
☑066

Mudumu National Park has a tragic history of environmental abuse and neglect. Although it was once one of Namibia's most stunning wildlife habitats, by the late 1980s the park had become an unofficial hunting concession gone mad. In under a decade, the wildlife was decimated by trophy hunters, which prompted the Ministry of Environment and Tourism (MET) to gazette Mudumu National Park in a last-ditch effort to rescue the area from total devastation. Mudumu's wildlife has begun to return, but it will take years of wise policy making and community awareness before the area approaches its former glory.

⊙ Sights

Lizauli Traditional Village   VILLAGE
(per person N$20; ⊘9am-5pm Mon-Sat) The culmination of a joint partnership between the owners of a one-time local lodge (Lianshulu, now closed), MET, private benefactors and the Lizauli community, the Lizauli Traditional Village was established to educate visitors about traditional Caprivian lifestyles, and to provide insight into the local diet, fishing and farming methods, village politics, music, games, traditional medicine, basketry and tool making.

The aforementioned partnership has also enabled the recruitment of Mudumu game scouts from Lizauli and other villages, and was given responsibility for community conservation and antipoaching education. Most importantly, the project provides a forum in which locals can interact with tourists, and benefit both economically and culturally from the adoption of a strict policy of environmental protection.

Mamili National Park

In years of good rains, this wild, seldom-visited national park (per person/vehicle N$40/10) becomes Namibia's equivalent of Botswana's Okavango Delta. Forested islands fringed by reed and papyrus marshes foster some of the country's richest birdwatching, with more than 430 recorded species to count. Poaching has taken a toll, though Mamili's wildlife, mainly semiaquatic species such as hippos, crocodiles, pukus, red lechwes, sitatungas and otters, will still impress.

Birding is best from December to March, though the vast majority of the park is inaccessible during this time. Wildlife viewing is best from June to August, and is especially good on Nkasa and Lupala Islands.

You must bring in everything, including your own water, and be prepared for extremely rough road conditions. Although there is generally a ranger to collect park fees at the entrance gate, you're all alone once inside, and it's highly recommended that you travel as part of a convoy.

There are two officially designated camping areas in the park: Liadura, beside the Kwando River, and Mparamura. Nkasa Lupala Lodge (✆081 147 7798; www.nkasa-lupalalodge.com; d per person N$1400) is just outside the entrance to Mamili and gets rave reviews from travellers.

Access to the park is by 4WD track from Malengalenga, northeast of the park, or from Sangwali village, which is due north.

Otjozondjupa

Otjozondjupa is commonly referred to as Bushmanland, a pejorative term that unfortunately seems to resist dying away. A largely flat landscape of scrub desert lying at the edge of the Kalahari, Otjozondjupa is part of the traditional homeland of the Ju/hoansi San, who were among the original inhabitants of Southern Africa. Following a spike in worldwide interest in Kalahari cultures, tourist traffic has increased throughout the region, though any expectations you might have of witnessing an entirely self-sufficient hunter-gatherer society will, sadly, not be met here.

For some people, witnessing the stark reality of the modern Ju/hoansi San lifestyle is a sobering experience fraught with disappointments. Hunting is forbidden throughout the region, and most communities have largely abandoned foraging in favour of cheap, high-calorie foods such as *pap* (corn meal) and rice, which are purchased in bulk from shops. Try to look beyond the dire realities of the San's economic situation, and attempt to use the experience as a rare chance to interact with the modern-day descendants of perhaps all of our ancestors.

TSUMKWE & AROUND
✆064

Tsumkwe is the only real permanent settlement in the whole of Otjozondjupa, though it's merely a wide spot in the sand with a few rust-covered buildings. Originally constructed as the regional headquarters of the SADF, Tsumkwe was then given a mandate as the administrative centre of the Ju/hoansi San community, and home to the Nyae Nyae Conservancy. While organised tourism in the region is still something of a work in progress, Tsumkwe is where you can arrange everything from bush walks to hunting

SAN INTERACTIONS

About 25km out of Tsumkwe, heading towards Khaudum National Park, is the **Living Hunter's Museum of the Ju/Hoansi** (D3315; ☉sunrise-sunset), which has been established for about 2½ years and is run and managed independently by the San. A lot of effort has gone into representing the old San hunter-gather culture as authentically as possible. Cultural interactions on offer include hunting trips (N$200 per person) with San hunters using traditional methods and equipment. There are also bush walks (N$100) and singing and dancing shows.

safaris, and inject some much-needed cash into the local community.

◉ Sights & Activities

Hunting and foraging trips are the highlight of any visit to Otjozondjupa. Much as they have for generations, the San still use traditional gear, namely a bow with poisoned arrows for men, and a digging stick and sling for women. In the past, men would be gone for several days at a time in pursuit of herds, so you shouldn't expect to take down any big game on an afternoon excursion. But it's fascinating to see trackers in pursuit of their quarry, and you're likely to come across spoor and maybe even an antelope or two.

Foraging is very likely to turn up edible roots and tubers, wild fruits and nuts, and even medicinal plants. At the end of your excursion, the women will be more than happy to slice up a bush potato for you, which tastes particularly wonderful when roasted over a bed of hot coals. Baobab fruit is also surprisingly sweet and tangy, while protein-rich nuts are an exotic yet nutritious desert treat.

While stereotypes of the San abound, from misleading Hollywood cinematic representations to misconstrued notions of a primitive people living in the bush, San society is extremely complex. Before visiting a San village, take some time to read up on their wonderfully rich cultural heritage – doing so will not only provide some context to your visit but also help you better engage with your hosts.

⨶ Sleeping & Eating

Nyae Nyae Conservancy Camp Sites CAMPGROUND $
(campsites per person from N$60) The Nyae Nyae Conservancy has several campsites, the most popular being the Holboom Baobab at Tjokwe, southeast of Tsumkwe; Makuri, a few kilometres east of that; and Khebi Pan, well out in the bush south of

Tsumkwe. Water is sometimes available in adjacent villages, but generally it's best to carry in all of your supplies and be entirely self-sufficient. Avoid building fires near the baobabs – it damages the trees' roots.

Omatako Valley Rest Camp CAMPGROUND $
(☏255977; campsites per person N$60) Outside the conservancy at the junction of the C44 and D3306, this community-run camp has solar power, a water pump, hot showers and a staff of local San. It offers both hunting and gathering trips as well as traditional music presentations.

Tsumkwe Country Lodge LODGE $$
(☏061-374750; www.namibialodges.com/tsumkwe_en.htm; campsites per person N$80, s/d from N$580/800; ❈◉☲) The only tourist lodge in Tsumkwe proper is an upmarket affair with a bar, restaurant, small shop and pool. Guests can base themselves here and visit surrounding villages as part of an organised tour.

Nhoma Safari Camp TENTED CAMP $$$
(☏081 273 4606; www.tsumkwel.iway.na; per person campsites N$150, luxury tents with full board from N$2200; ☲) The former owners of the Tsumkwe Country Lodge, Arno and Estelle, have lived in the area for much of their lives and are well respected by the local San communities. Their luxury tented camp is perched between a fossilised river valley and a verdant teak grove, though the main attraction continues to be their wonderful excursions into local San villages. The camp is located 280km east of Grootfontein and 80km west of Tsumkwe along the C44. You must book in advance to stay here – as mobile-phone reception at the camp is unreliable (there's no landline), it's best to email them.

❶ Information

If you're visiting the region as a tourist, you are required to stop by the office of the **Nyae Nyae Conservancy** (☏244011; ☉8am-5pm Mon-Fri) in central Tsumkwe. It's recommended that you book/get recommendations for activities through here rather than striking off on your own. This practice ensures that the money you spend ends up in the community fund rather than in the pockets of one or two individuals.

There are no officially posted prices for activities, though you can expect to be charged a reasonably modest amount for every person that accompanies you. English-speaking guides command the largest fee, generally in the realm of N$250 per day plus food, while hunters and foragers should be organised in the villages – ask in the office where to do this. It is also possible to arrange overnight stays in villages.

When visiting San villages, visitors are expected to either purchase or trade for beadwork, walking sticks, ostrich-shell necklaces, bow and arrow sets, and so on. Trading is a wonderful practice worth encouraging, and prized items include T-shirts, shoes, trousers, baseball caps and other useful items. People will also ask for sugar and tobacco – you'll have to decide whether to trade these products, given their attendant health risks. In any case, please trade fairly, avoid excessive payment and help keep local dignity intact by resisting the urge to hand out gifts for nothing.

❶ Getting There & Away

Note that you will need your own transport – a 4WD with good clearance is recommended. There are no sealed roads in the region, and only the C44 is passable to 2WD vehicles. Petrol is sometimes available at the Tsumkwe Country Lodge, though it's best to carry a few jerry cans with you. If you're planning to explore the bush around Tsumkwe, it is recommended that you hire a local guide and travel as part of a convoy.

The Dobe border crossing to Botswana requires a 4WD and extra fuel to reach the petrol stations at Maun or Etsha 6, which are accessed by a difficult sand track through northwestern Botswana.

NORTHWESTERN NAMIBIA

For those who like to take a walk (or even a drive) on the wild side, northwestern Namibia is a stark, desolate environment where some of the most incredible landscapes imaginable lie astride 4WD tracks. For 4WD explorers, Namibia is synonymous with the Skeleton Coast, a formidable desert coastline engulfed by icy breakers. Here, seemingly endless stretches of foggy beach are punctuated by rusting shipwrecks and flanked by wandering dunes. As you move inland, the sinister fogs give way to the won-drous desert wildernesses of Damaraland and the Kaokoveld. The former is sparsely populated by the Damara people, and is known for its unique geological features; the latter is known as one of the last great wildernesses in Southern Africa, as well as the home of the oft-photographed Himba people.

Damaraland

The territory between the Skeleton Coast and Namibia's central plateau has traditionally been known as Damaraland, after the people who make up much of its population. Although it's not an officially protected area, its wild open spaces are home to many desert-adapted species, including giraffes, zebras, lions, elephants and rhinos. In addition to its sense of freedom, the region is rich in both natural and cultural attractions, including Brandberg, Namibia's highest massif, and the rock engravings of Twyfelfontein.

THE SPITZKOPPE
♫064

The 1728m Spitzkoppe (Groot Spitzkoppe village; per person/car N$50/20; ☼sunrise-sunset), one of Namibia's most recognisable landmarks, rises miragelike above the dusty pro-Namib plains of southern Damaraland. Its dramatic shape has inspired its nickname, which is the Matterhorn of Africa, but similarities between this granite inselberg and the glaciated Swiss Alps begin and end with its sharp peak. Beside the Spitzkoppe rise the equally impressive Pondoks, another inselberg formation that comprises enormous granite domes.

Spitzkoppe Rest Camp (Groot Spitzkoppe village; campsites per person N$45, bungalows from N$120) is an excellent community-run camp that includes a number of sites dotted around the base of the Spitzkoppe and surrounding outcrops – most are set in magical rock hollows and provide a sense of real isolation.

Under normal dry conditions, a 2WD is sufficient to reach the mountain. Turn northwest off the B2 onto the D1918 towards Henties Bay. After 18km, turn north onto the D3716.

THE BRANDBERG
♫064

Driving around this massive pink-granite bulge, and marvelling at the ethereal light during sunset that appears to bounce off it, is a highlight of the region. But inside lies the real treasure – one of the finest remnants of prehistoric art on the African continent. The Brandberg (Fire Mountain) is Namibia's highest peak at 2573m.

Its best-known attraction, the gallery of rock art in Tsisab Ravine, features the White Lady of the Brandberg. The figure, which isn't necessarily a lady (it's still open to interpretation), stands about 40cm high, and is part of a larger painting that depicts a bizarre hunting procession. In one hand, the figure is carrying what appears to be a flower or possibly a feather. In the other, the figure is carrying a bow and arrows. The painting is distinct, however, because 'her' hair is straight and light-coloured – distinctly un-African – and the body is painted white from the chest down.

At the Brandberg White Lady Lodge (☑684004; www.brandbergwllodge.com; campsites per person N$80, twin luxury tents N$545, s/tw with half board N$775/1330) campers can pitch a tent along the riverine valley, all the while taking advantage of the lodge's upmarket facilities, while lovers of creature comforts can choose from rustic bungalows and chalets that are highlighted by their stone interiors and wraparound patios.

The Brandberg is a conservancy and the entry fee for admission is N$50 per person and N$20 per car. Note that this includes being allocated a compulsory guide – you cannot just walk around these fragile treasures by yourself. It's good to tip the guide afterwards if you're happy with their service.

To reach Tsisab Ravine from Uis, head 15km north, and turn west on the D2359, which leads 26km to the Tsisab car park. To reach Numas Ravine head 14km south of Uis, follow the D2342 for 55km, where you'll see a rough track turning eastward. After about 10km, you'll reach a fork; the 4WD track on the right leads to the Numas Ravine car park.

TWYFELFONTEIN & AROUND
☑067

Twyfelfontein (Doubtful Spring), at the head of the grassy Aba Huab Valley, is one of the most extensive rock-art galleries on the continent. The original name of this water source was /Ui-//Ais (Surrounded by Rocks), but in 1947 it was renamed by European settler D Levin, who deemed its daily output of 1 cu metre of water insufficient for survival. To date, over 2500 individual engravings

have been discovered, which led Twyfelfontein to become a national monument in 1952. In 2007 Twyfelfontein was declared a Unesco World Heritage site, the first such distinction in the whole of Namibia.

⊙ Sights

Rock Engravings ROCK ART
(per person/car N$50/20; ☺sunrise-sunset) Most dating back at least 6000 years to the early Stone Age, Twyfelfontein's rock engravings were probably the work of ancient San hunters, and were made by cutting through the hard patina covering the local sandstone. In time, this skin reformed over the engravings, protecting them from erosion. From colour differentiation and weathering, researchers have identified at least six distinct phases, but some are clearly the work of copycat artists and are thought to date from the 19th century. Guides are compulsory; note that tips are their only source of income.

**Burnt Mountain &
Organ Pipes** ROCK FORMATIONS
Southeast of Twyfelfontein rises a barren 12km-long volcanic ridge, at the foot of which lies the hill known as Burnt Mountain, an expanse of volcanic clinker that appears to have been literally exposed to fire. Virtually nothing grows in this eerie panorama of desolation. Burnt Mountain lies beside the D3254, 3km south of the Twyfelfontein turn-off. Over the road, you can follow an obvious path into a small gorge that contains a 100m stretch of unusual 4m-high dolerite (coarse-grained basalt) columns known as the Organ Pipes.

Petrified Forest FOREST
(per person/car N$40/20; ☺sunrise-sunset) The petrified forest is an area of open veld scattered with petrified tree trunks up to 34m long and 6m in circumference, which are estimated to be around 260 million years old. The original trees belonged to an ancient group of cone-bearing plants that are known as *Gymnospermae,* which includes such modern plants as conifers, cycads and welwitschias. Because of the lack of root or branch remnants, it's thought that the trunks were transported to the site in a flood.

About 50 individual trees are visible, some half buried in sandstone and many perfectly petrified in silica – complete with bark and tree rings. In 1950, after souvenir hunters had begun to take their toll, the site was declared a national monument, and it's now strictly forbidden to carry off even a small scrap of petrified wood. Guides are compulsory.

The Petrified Forest, signposted 'Versteende Woud', lies 40km west of Khorixas on the C39.

🍴 Sleeping & Eating

Campsites such as Aba Huab Camp beside a riverbed (immediately north of the Twyfelfontein turn-off) are worth trying if you're on a budget, although we've heard very mixed reports regarding this place, including that it's in a pretty bad state of disrepair. Otherwise, there are mainly luxury, upmarket options near the rock-art site.

Twyfelfontein Country Lodge   LODGE $$$
(☑374750; www.namibialodges.com; s/d from N$1324/1860; ✲@✈) Over the hill from Twyfelfontein, this architectural wonder is embedded in the red rock. On your way in, be sure not to miss the ancient rock engravings, as well as the swimming pool with its incongruous desert waterfall. The lodge boasts stylish rooms, an immense and airy elevated dining room, and a good variety of excursions throughout Damaraland. It's fairly well signposted from Twyfelfontein and easy to find.

Camp Kipwe   LODGE $$$
(☑232009, 687211; www.kipwe.com; r per person with half board N$1800; ✈) Brilliantly located amongst the boulders and rocks littered throughout its premises, Kipwe is languidly draped over the stunning landscape in large *rondavels* (traditional round huts) with thatched roofs that blend in beautifully with their surrounds. There are nine standard rooms and one honeymoon suite (rooms 3 and 4 are family rooms with kids' tents); all come with outdoor bathrooms so you can stargaze while you wash. The lodge also runs nature drives (N$540) and excursions to the rock art. The entrance to Kipwe is off the D2612.

ℹ Getting There & Away

There's no public transport in the area and little traffic. Turn off the C39, 73km west of Khorixas, turn south on the D3254 and continue 15km to a right turn signposted as Twyfelfontein. It's 5km to the petroglyph site.

SESFONTEIN

Damaraland's most northerly outpost is almost entirely encircled by the Kaokoveld

and is somewhat reminiscent of a remote oasis in the middle of the Sahara.

Ever fancy spending the night in a colonial fort out in the middle of the desert? At **Fort Sesfontein** (☑065-685034; www.fortsesfontein.com; r per person N$950; ✈), you and 63 other guests can live out all your Lawrence of Arabia fantasies! Accommodation is basic but incredibly atmospheric, and there's a good restaurant here that serves German-inspired dishes.

The road between Palmwag and Sesfontein is good gravel, and you'll only have problems if the Hoanib River is flowing. Unless it's been raining, the gravel road from Sesfontein to Opuwo is accessible to all vehicles.

Kaokoveld
☑065

Often described as one of the last true wildernesses in Southern Africa, the Kaokoveld is largely devoid of roads and is crossed only by sandy tracks laid down by the SADF decades ago. In this harsh wilderness of dry and arid conditions, wildlife has been forced to adapt in miraculous ways – consider the (now critically endangered) desert elephant, which has especially spindly legs suited for long walks in search of precious water. Beyond wildlife, the Kaokoveld is also home to the Himba, a group of nomadic pastoralists.

There's no public transport in the region and hitchhiking is near impossible, so the best way to explore the Kaokoveld is with a well-outfitted 4WD or an organised camping safari. In the dry season, the routes from Opuwo to Epupa Falls, Ruacana to Okongwati (via Swartbooi's Drift) and Sesfontein to Purros may be passable with high-clearance 2WD vehicles, but otherwise you'll need a 4WD.

OPUWO
☑064

In the Herero language, Opuwo means 'the end', which is certainly a fitting name for this dusty collection of concrete commercial buildings ringed by *rondavels* and huts. While first impressions are unlikely to be very positive, a visit to Opuwo is one of the cultural highlights of Namibia, particularly for anyone interested in interacting with the Himba people. As the unofficial capital of Himbaland, Opuwo serves as a convenient jumping-off point for excursions into the nearby villages, and there is a good assortment of lodges and campsites in the area to choose from.

Sights & Activities

People-watching is the primary thing to do in town. Tourism is booming in Himbaland, as evidenced by the paving of the road all the way up to Opuwo (but not to the border with Angola!), and the inauguration of the Opuwo Country Hotel by the Namibian president himself. Shots of Himba women appear on just about every Namibian tourism brochure, and busloads of tourists can be seen whizzing through Opuwo's dusty streets virtually every day.

Throughout Opuwo you will see Himba wherever you go – they will be walking the streets, shopping in the stores and even waiting in line behind you at the supermarket! However tempting it might be, please do not sneak a quick picture of them, as no one appreciates having a camera waved in front of their face without their permission.

Kaokohimba Safaris CULTURAL TOUR
(☎065-695106; www.kaoko-namibia.com) Organises cultural tours through Kaokoveld and Damaraland and wildlife-viewing trips in Etosha National Park. A highlight is Camp Syncro, in remote Marienflüss.

Sleeping

Ohakane Lodge LODGE $$
(☎273031; s/d N$520/900; ✴🐾) This well-established and centrally located lodge sits along the main drag in Opuwo and does good business with tour groups. Fairly standard but fully modern rooms are comfortable enough.

Opuwo Country Hotel HOTEL $$$
(☎061 374 750; www.namibialodges.com/opuwo_en.htm; campsites per person N$100, s/d from N$920/1320; ✴@✴🐾) Far and away the area's swankiest accommodation option, the hilltop Opuwo Country Hotel is an enormous thatched building (reportedly the largest in Namibia) that elegantly lords it over the town below. If the standard rooms are taken and you can't afford a luxury version, consider pitching a tent in the secluded campsite. The turn-off leading up to the hotel is a bit tricky to find, but there are signs posted throughout the town.

Shopping

Kunene Craft Centre ARTS & CRAFTS
(☺8am-5pm Mon-Fri, 9am-1pm Sat) Opuwo's brightly painted self-help curio shop sells local arts and crafts on consignment. You'll find all sorts of Himba adornments smeared with ochre: conch-shell pendants, wrist bands, chest pieces and even the headdresses worn by Himba brides. There's also a range of original jewellery, appliquéd pillowslips, Himba and Herero dolls, drums and wooden carvings.

Information

Kaoko Information Centre (☎273420; ☺8am-6pm) KK and Kemuu, the friendly guys at this information centre (look for the tiny, tiny yellow shack), can arrange visits to local Himba villages in addition to providing useful information for your trip through the Kaokoveld region.

Getting There & Away

The marvellously paved C41 runs from Outjo to Opuwo, which makes Himbaland accessible even to 2WD vehicles. Although there is a temptation to speed along this long and lonely highway, keep your foot off the pedal north of the veterinary-control fence, as herds of cattle commonly stray across the road. If you're heading deeper into the Kaokoveld, be advised that Opuwo is the last opportunity to buy petrol before Kamanjab, Ruacana or Sesfontein.

EPUPA FALLS

At Epupa, which means 'Falling Waters' in Herero, the Kunene River fans out into a vast flood plain, and is ushered through a 500m-wide series of parallel channels, dropping a total of 60m over 1.5km. The greatest single drop, an estimated 37m, is commonly identified as the Epupa Falls. Here the river tumbles into a dark, narrow, rainbow-wrapped cleft, which is a spectacular sight.

Sights & Activities

During periods of low water, the **pools** above the Epupa Falls make fabulous natural jacuzzis. You're safe from crocodiles in the eddies and rapids, but hang onto the rocks and keep away from the lip of the falls; once you're caught by the current, there's no way to prevent your being swept over. Every couple of years, some unfortunate locals and foreign tourists drown in the river, and it's difficult at best to retrieve their bodies. Swimming here is most definitely not suitable for children.

There's also excellent **hiking** along the river west of the falls, and plenty of mountains to climb, affording panoramic views along the river and far into Angola. Keen hikers can manage the route along the 'Namibian Riviera' from Swartbooi's Drift to Epupa Falls (93km, five days) or from Ruacana to Epupa Falls (150km, eight days). You're never far from water, but there are lots of crocodiles and, even in the winter, the heat can be oppressive and draining. It's wise to go by the full moon, when you can beat the heat by walking at night.

🛏 Sleeping

Epupa Camp   LODGE $$$
(☎061-232740; www.epupa.com.na; per person with full board N$1260; ✸) Located 800m upstream from the falls, this former engineering camp for a now-shelved hydroelectric project has been converted into beautifully situated accommodation among a grove of towering baobab trees. There are nine luxury tents filled to the brim with curios, and a slew of activities is on offer, including Himba visits, sundowner hikes, birdwatching walks, and trips to rock-art sites. Five campsites are also available.

Omarunga Lodge   LODGE $$$
(☎064-403096; www.natron.net/omarunga-camp/main.html; campsites per person N$100, single/double chalets with full board N$1600/2200) This German-run camp operates through a concession granted by a local chief, and has a well-groomed campsite with modern facilities as well as a dozen luxury chalets. It's a very attractive spot.

ⓘ Getting There & Away
The road from Okongwati is accessible to high-clearance 2WD vehicles, but it's still quite rough. The rugged 93km 4WD river route from Swartbooi's Drift may take several days, and it's far quicker to make the trip via Otjiveze/Epembe.

THE NORTHWEST CORNER
West of Epupa Falls is the Kaokoveld of travellers' dreams: stark, rugged desert peaks, vast landscapes, sparse scrubby vegetation, drought-resistant wildlife and nomadic bands of Himba people and their tiny settlements of beehive huts. This region, which is contiguous with the Skeleton Coast Wilderness, has now been designated the Kaokoveld Conservation Area.

◉ Sights
Otjinjange & Hartmann's Valleys   VALLEYS
Allow plenty of time to explore the wild and magical Otjinjange (better known as Marienflüss) and Hartmann's Valleys – broad sandy and grassy expanses descending gently to the Kunene River. Note that camping outside campsites is prohibited at both valleys.

Van Zyl's Pass   PASS
The beautiful but frightfully steep and challenging Van Zyl's Pass forms a dramatic transition between the Kaokoveld plateaus and the vast, grassy expanses of Otjijange Valley (Marienflüss). This winding 13km stretch isn't suitable for trailers and may only be passed from east to west, which means you'll have to return via Otjihaa Pass or through Purros.

🛏 Sleeping
Except for in Otjinjange and Hartmann's Valleys, unofficial bush camping is possible throughout the northwest corner.

Ngatutunge Pamwe
Camp Site   CAMPGROUND $
(campsites per person N$50; ✸) A community-run campsite, Ngatutunge is perched along the Hoarusib River in Purros, and surprisingly has hot showers, flush toilets, well-appointed bungalows, a communal kitchen and (believe it or not!) a swimming pool.

Elephant Song Camp   CAMPGROUND $
(☎064-403829; campsites per person N$80) Community run, Elephant Song is located in the Palmwag Concession, a very rough 25km down the Hoanib River from Sesfontein. This camp caters to outdoorsy types with great views, hiking, birdwatching and the chance to see rare desert elephants.

Okarohombo Camp Site   CAMPGROUND $
(campsites per person N$60) This community-run campsite is located at the mouth of the Otjinjange Valley. Facilities include flushable toilets, showers and a communal kitchen.

ⓘ Getting There & Away
From Okongwati, the westward route through Etengwa leads to either Van Zyl's Pass or Otjihaa Pass. From Okauwa (with a landmark broken windmill) to the road fork at Otjitanda – which is a Himba chief's *kraal* (fortified village of mud huts) – the journey is extremely rough and slow going. Along the way, stop for a swim at beautiful Ovivero Dam. From Otjitanda, you must decide whether you're heading west over Van Zyl's Pass (which may only be traversed from east to west!) into Otjinjange (Marienflüss) and Hartmann's Valleys, or south over the equally beautiful but much easier Otjihaa Pass towards Orupembe.

You can also access Otjinjange (Marienflüss) and Hartmann's Valleys without crossing Van Zyl's Pass by turning north at the three-way junction in the middle of the Onjuva Plains, 12km north of Orupembe. At the T-junction in Rooidrum (Red Drum), you can decide which valley you want. Turn right for Otjinjange (Marienflüss) and left for Hartmann's. West of this junction, 17km from Rooidrum, you can also turn south along the fairly good route to Orupembe, Purros (provided that the Hoarusib River isn't flowing) and on to Sesfontein.

Skeleton Coast

The term 'Skeleton Coast' is derived from the treacherous nature of the coast – a foggy region with rocky and sandy coastal shallows that has long been a graveyard for unwary ships and their crews. Early Portuguese sailors called it *As Areias do Inferno* (the Sands of Hell) as once a ship washed ashore, the fate of the crew was sealed.

Although it has been extrapolated to take in the entire Namib Desert coastline, the Skeleton Coast actually refers to the coastal stretch between the mouths of the Swakop and Kunene Rivers. For our purposes, it covers Dorob National Park and Skeleton Coast National Park (including the Skeleton Coast Wilderness). These protected areas stretch from just north of Swakopmund to the Kunene River, taking in nearly two million hectares of dunes and gravel plains to form one of the world's most inhospitable waterless areas.

DOROB NATIONAL PARK
⚡064

Declared in December 2010, Dorob National Park consumes the old National West Coast Tourist Recreation Area, and broadens out, especially to the south, beyond the borders of the old recreation area. Dorob extends beyond the Swakop River and down to Sandwich Harbour in the south, while its northern border is the Ugab River. This section focusses on the 200km-long, 25km-wide strip from Swakopmund to the Ugab River. It's extremely popular with anglers and wildlife watchers alike, and it's convenient to visit since you don't need to arrange a permit in advance, unlike for other destinations along the Skeleton Coast.

Most visitors head for the Cape Cross Seal Reserve (per person/car N$40/10; ⊙10am-5pm), where the seal population has grown large and fat by taking advantage of the rich concentrations of fish in the cold Benguela Current. The sight of more than 100,000 seals basking on the beach and frolicking in the surf is an impressive sight to behold, though you're going to have to contend with overwhelming piles (and piles) of stinky seal poo. There's a basic snack bar

with public toilets. No pets or motorcycles are permitted and visitors may not cross the low barrier between the seal-viewing area and the rocks where the colony lounges.

In Henties Bay Buck's Camping Lodge (⚡501039; Nickey Iyambo Rd; campsites N$230), near the police station in town, is expensive, but for the extra dollars you get a campsite with your own private bathroom. Look for the caravan sign just off the road.

The De Duine Country Hotel (⚡081 124 1181; www.deduinehotel.com; s/d N$400/600; ✳⚟), the most established hotel in Henties Bay, sits on the coast, though not a single room has a sea view – go figure! The German colonial–style property does feature rooms with swimming pool and garden views, though.

SKELETON COAST PARK

At Ugabmund, 110km north of Cape Cross, the salt road passes through the entry gate to Skeleton Coast Park, where rolling fogs and dusty sandstorms encapsulate its eerie, remote and wild feel. Despite the enduring fame of this coastline, surprisingly few travellers ever reach points north of Cape Cross.

In order to preserve this incredibly fragile environment, NWR imposes very strict regulations on individual travellers seeking to enter the park. Although this can be a deterrent for some, permits are easily obtainable if you do some planning. And, while you may have to sacrifice a bit of spontaneity to gain admittance to the park, the enigmatic Skeleton Coast really does live up to all the hype.

🏃 Activities

Ugab River Guided Hiking Route   HIKING
The 50km-long route is open to groups of between six and eight people on the second and fourth Thursday of each month from April to October. Hikes start at 9am from Ugabmund and finish on Saturday afternoon. Most hikers stay Wednesday night at the Mile 108 Camp Site, 40km south of Ugabmund, which allows you to arrive at Ugabmund in time for the hike. The hike must be booked through NWR (p256) in Windhoek – hikers must provide and carry their own food and camping equipment. The route begins by crossing the coastal plain, then climbs into the hills and follows a double loop through lichen fields and past caves, natural springs and unusual geological formations.

SKELETON COAST WILDERNESS AREA

The Skeleton Coast Wilderness Area, stretching between the Hoanib and Kunene Rivers, makes up the northern third of the Skeleton Coast and is part of Skeleton Coast Park. This section of coastline is among the most remote and inaccessible areas in Namibia, though it's here in the wilderness that you can truly live out your Skeleton Coast fantasies. Since the entire area is a private concession, you're going to have to part with some serious cash to visit. Up until late 2012, the sole accommodation here was at the Skeleton Coast Wilderness Camp, which was accessible only by charter flight. That camp was closed after being gutted by a fire, but it's rumoured that a new luxury operation, the Hoanib Skeleton Coast Camp, will open for business in the region in early to mid-2013.

Sleeping

All accommodation (with the exception of the Ugab River Camp Site) must be booked through NWR (p288) in Windhoek.

Ugab River Camp Site CAMPGROUND $
(www.rhino-trust.org.na; campsites per person N$60) Outside the Skeleton Coast Park, this campsite is administered by the Save the Rhino Trust. This remote landscape is truly intriguing, and those who've visited have only glowing comments. To get there, turn east onto the D2303, 40km north of Cape Cross; it's then 70km to the camp.

Torra Bay Camping Ground CAMPGROUND $
(per person N$125; ⊙Dec & Jan) This campsite, which is open to coincide with the Namibian school holidays, is flanked by a textbook field of barchan dunes. These dunes are actually the southernmost extension of a vast sand sea that stretches all the way to the Curoca River in Angola. Petrol, water, firewood and basic supplies are available, and campers may use the restaurant at Terrace Bay Resort. Torra Bay is located 215km north of Cape Cross.

Terrace Bay Resort CHALET $$$
(campsites per person N$125, s/d N$800/1600, 4- to 10-person beach chalets per person N$700) Open year-round, this resort is a luxurious alternative to camping at Torra Bay. Around the camp you may spot black-backed jackals or brown hyenas, and the scenery of sparse coastal vegetation and lonely dunes is the Skeleton Coast at its finest. The site has a restaurant, a shop and a petrol station. Terrace Bay is located 49km north of Torra Bay.

Information

The zone south of the Hoanib River is open to individual travellers, but you need a permit, which costs N$80 per person and N$10 per vehicle per day. These are available through NWR (p256) in Windhoek.

No day visits to the park are allowed, but you can obtain a transit permit to pass between Ugabmund and Springbokwater, which can be purchased at the gates. Note that transit permits aren't valid for Torra Bay or Terrace Bay.

Getting There & Away

Skeleton Coast Park is accessed via the salt road from Swakopmund, which ends 70km north of Terrace Bay. The park is also accessible via the C39 gravel road that runs between Khorixas and Torra Bay. Note that motorcycles are not permitted in the park. Hitchhikers may be discouraged by the bleak landscape, cold sea winds, fog, sandstorms and sparse traffic.

CENTRAL NAMIBIA

Central Namibia zeroes in on the tourist trade, but it does so Namibian style, offering epic road journeys, big skies and mesmerising landscapes. Though it's home to two large cities, the region is defined by the Namib Desert, a barren and desolate landscape of undulating apricot-coloured dunes interspersed with dry pans. Indeed, the Nama word 'Namib', which inspired the name of the entire country, rather prosaically means 'Vast Dry Plain'. Nowhere is this truer than at Sossusvlei, Namibia's most famous strip of sand, where gargantuan dunes tower more than 300m above the underlying strata.

Swakopmund

☑064

It can be an eerie feeling entering Swakop, especially out of tourist season when the city, sandwiched between Atlantic rollers and the Namib Desert, feels like a surreal colonial remnant. Some find it soothing, others weird – we have a foot in each camp. The

NAMIBIA SWAKOPMUND

Swakopmund

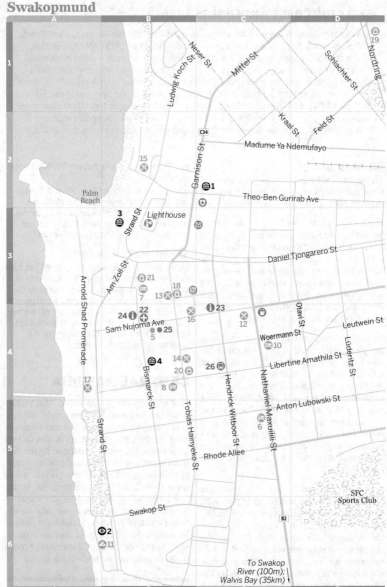

NAMIBIA SWAKOPMUND

people of Swakopmund are a quirky mix of German-Namibian residents and overseas German tourists, who feel right at home with the town's pervasive *Gemütlichkeit,* a distinctively German appreciation of comfort and hospitality. One thing Swakopmund isn't is boring. It's Namibia's most popular holiday destination, and there are myriad opportunities to enjoy the great climate, including surfing, fishing and lolling around on the beach. The city is also the adventure-sports capital of Namibia.

NAMIBIA SWAKOPMUND

⦿ Sights

Swakopmund Museum MUSEUM
(📞402046; Strand St; adults/students N\$20/10;
🕙10am-5pm) When ill winds blow, head for
this museum, at the foot of the lighthouse,
where you can hole up and learn about the
town's history. The museum occupies the
site of the old harbour warehouse, which
was destroyed in 1914 by a 'lucky' shot from
a British warship.

Displays include exhibits on Namibia's
history and ethnology, including information on local flora and fauna. Especially
good is the display on the !nara melon, a
fruit which was vital to the early Khoikhoi
people of the Namib region.

It also harbours a reconstructed colonial
home interior, Emil Kiewittand's apothecary
shop and an informative display on the

Rössing Mine. Military buffs will appreciate the stifling uniforms of the Camel Corps and the Shell furniture, so called because it was homemade from Depression-era petrol and paraffin tins.

National Marine Aquarium   AQUARIUM
(Strand St) This waterfront aquarium provides an excellent introduction to the cold offshore world in the South Atlantic Ocean. Most impressive is the tunnel through the largest aquarium, which allows close-up views of graceful rays, toothy sharks (you can literally count all the teeth!) and other little marine beasties found on Namibia's seafood platters. The place was getting a revamp when we passed through, so drop in to check out the admission price and opening hours.

Woermannhaus   HISTORIC BUILDING
(Bismarck St) From the shore, the delightful German-style Woermannhaus stands out above surrounding buildings. Built in 1905 as the main offices of the Damara & Namaqua Trading Company, it was taken over four years later by the Woermann & Brock Trading Company, which supplied the current name. In the 1920s it was used as a school dormitory, and later served as a merchant sailors' hostel. It eventually fell into disrepair, but it was declared a national monument and restored in 1976.

Kristall Galerie   GALLERY
(406080; cnr Garnison St & Theo-Ben Gurirab Ave; admission N$20; 9am-5pm Mon-Sat) This architecturally astute gallery features some of the planet's most incredible crystal formations, including the largest quartz crystal that has ever been found. The adjacent shop sells lovely mineral samples, crystal jewellery, and intriguing plates, cups and wine glasses that are carved from the local stone.

🏃 Activities

Swakopmund is Namibia's main beach resort, but even in summer the water is never warmer than around 15°C (remember: the Benguela Current sweeps upwards from Antarctica). Swimming in the sea is best in the lee of the Mole sea wall. North of town you can stroll along miles and miles of deserted beaches stretching towards the Skeleton Coast. The best surfing is at Nordstrand or 'Thick Lip' near Vineta Point.

Swakopmund is one of the top destinations in Southern Africa for extreme-sports enthusiasts. Although filling your days with adrenaline-soaked activities is certainly not cheap, there are few places in the world where you can climb up, race down and soar over towering sand dunes.

Most activity operators don't have offices in town, which means that you need to arrange all of your activities through either your accommodation or the Namib-i tourist information centre.

Alter Action   SANDBOARDING
(402737; www.alter-action.info; lie down/stand up US$40/55) Sandboarding with Alter Action is certain to increase your heart rate. If you have any experience snowboarding or surfing, it's highly recommended that you have a go at the stand-up option. You will be given a snowboard, gloves, goggles and enough polish to ensure a smooth ride. While you can't expect the same speeds as you would on the mountain, you can't beat the experience of carving a dune face, and falling on sand hurts a lot less than falling on ice! The lie-down option (which makes use of a greased-up sheet of masonite) requires much less finesse but is equally fun.

Ground Rush Adventures   SKYDIVING
(402841; www.skydiveswakop.com.na; tandem jumps N$1950, handycam/professional video N$450/850) Skydiving in Swakopmund is sweetened by the outstanding dune and ocean backdrop. The Ground Rush crew has an impeccable safety record, and they make even the most nervous participant feel comfortable about jumping out of a plane at 3000m and freefalling for 30 seconds at 220km/h. If you're having second thoughts about taking the plunge, know that your tandem master has been pulling the chord several times a day for years and years! Have a light breakfast – you'll thank us later.

Okakambe Trails   HORSE RIDING
(402799; www.okakambe.iway.na; prices variable) Meaning 'horse' in the local Herero and Oshivambo languages, Okakambe specialises in horseback riding and trekking through the desert. The German owner cares immensely for her horses, so you can be assured that they're well fed and looked after. Prices for a one-hour solo ride along the Swakop River to the Moon Landscape start at N$460, but discounts are available for larger groups and longer outings. More experienced riders can organise multiday treks with full board, as well as moonlight outings and jaunts along the beach and through the dunes.

☞ Tours

Possible tours include a sundowner on the dunes, the Cape Cross Seal Reserve, Rössing Mine gem tours, Welwitschia Dr, Walvis Bay Lagoon and various destinations in the Namib Desert and Naukluft Mountains.

The most popular operators are **Charly's Desert Tours** (☑404341; www.charlysdesert-tours.com; Sam Nujoma Ave), **Namib Tours & Safaris** (☑406038; www.namibia-tours-safaris.com) and **Turnstone Tours** (☑403123; www.turnstone-tours.com). With the exception of Charly's, many operators do not have central offices, so it's best to make arrangements through your accommodation.

If you're interested in arranging a visit to the Mondesa township, **Hafeni Cultural Tours** (☑400731; hafenictours@gmail.com; 4hr tour N$420) runs a variety of different excursions that provide insight into how the other half of Swakopmunders live.

Rössing Mine   MINE TOUR

(☑402046; mine tours per person N$50) This mine, 55km east of Swakopmund, is the world's largest open-cast uranium mine. Rössing, with 2500 employees, is currently a major player in Swakopmund's economy. Three-hour **mine tours** leave at 10am on the first and third Friday of each month; book at least one day in advance at the Swakopmund Museum (tours depart from here). You can also arrange a visit through most tour companies.

🛏 Sleeping

Tiger Reef Campsite   CAMPGROUND $

(☑081 380 6014; campsites N$200, plus per person N$75) This campsite sits right on the sand at the beach front, sheltered from the wind by lovely tamarisk trees. It's convenient to the city centre.

Desert Sky Backpackers   BACKPACKERS $

(☑402339; Anton Lubowski St; campsites per person N$70, dm/r N$80/200; @) This centrally located backpackers haunt is an excellent place to drop anchor in Swakopmund. The indoor lounge is simple and homey, while the outdoor picnic tables are a nice spot for a cold beer and conversation.

Swakop Lodge   BACKPACKERS $

(☑402030; 42 Nathaniel Maxuilili St; dm/s/d N$150/450/650; @) This backpacker-oriented hotel is the epicentre of the action in Swakopmund, especially since this is where many of the adrenaline activities depart from and return to, and where many of the videos are screened each night. The hotel is extremely popular with overland trucks, so it's a safe bet that the attached bar is probably bumping and grinding most nights of the week.

TOP CHOICE **Sea Breeze Guesthouse** GUESTHOUSE $$

(☑463348; www.seabreeze.com.na; Turmalin St; s/d incl breakfast N$700/1000; @) This upmarket guesthouse is right on the beach about 4.5km north of town, and is an excellent option if you're looking for a secluded retreat. Ask to see a few of the rooms as several of them have spectacular sea views; and there's a great family room for N$1050. There's plenty of advice available on what to see and do around town. Follow the Strand north and keep an eye out for signs.

Hotel-Pension d'Avignon   GUESTHOUSE $$

(☑405821; www.natron.net/tour/davignon/main.html; 25 Libertine Amathila St; s/d incl breakfast N$320/520; ☒) A great option close to town that won't break the budget, d'Avignon is a smart, well-run guesthouse that has been recommended by travellers. Triple rooms are also available and there's a TV lounge to collapse into in the evenings.

Hotel Pension Rapmund   GUESTHOUSE $$

(☑402035; www.hotelpensionrapmund.com; 6-8 Bismarck St; s/d N$585/770, luxury r N$1240) Overlooking the park promenade, this longstanding pension has light and airy rooms that are adorned with rich woods and plenty of African- and German-inspired flourishes to create an attractive accommodation spot. The location is on the money and some rooms have terrific views.

Sam's Giardino Hotel   HOTEL $$$

(☑403210; www.giardinonamibia.com; 89 Anton Lubowski St; s/d from N$650/1200; ☒☒) Sam's Giardino Hotel is a touch of luxury in the backstreets, emphasising superb wines, fine cigars and relaxing in the rose garden with a St Bernard named Ornelia. The rooms are tasteful and refined; they're cheaper at the walk-in rate if the hotel isn't busy.

✗ Eating

Garden Cafe   CAFE $$

(Tobias Hainyeko St; mains N$40-80; ⊙8am-6pm Mon-Fri, to 3pm Sat & Sun) Set in a nice little garden away from the main street, Garden Cafe has open-air tables and chairs, changing specials and freshly prepared cafe food including salads, wraps and burgers (desserts are yummy too). It's pleasantly topped off by friendly and efficient service. In winter the cafe is still in full swing, with patrons huddled around tables and basking in skinny shafts of sunlight.

Fish Deli
SEAFOOD $$

(Sam Nujoma Ave; dishes N$70-90; ⊘8.30am-5pm Mon, Tue, Thu & Fri, 8.30am-2pm Wed, 9am-1pm Sat) Recommended by locals as the best place for a seafood meal in town. It's a simple but clean set-up inside and, importantly, the fish comes straight from the water to your plate – no frozen stuff.

Lighthouse Pub & Cafe
PUB $$

(✆400894; The Mole, Main Beach; mains US$80-120) With a postcard-perfect view of the beach and crashing surf, the Lighthouse Pub & Cafe is an atmospheric choice for lovers of fine seafood. Depending on what the fishermen are catching in their nets, lines and pots, you'll find everything from kingklip and lobster to kabeljou and calamari. It also does some delicious pizza meals (half-price on Monday).

Swakopmund Brauhaus
GERMAN $$

(22 Sam Nujoma Ave; mains N$75-100; ⊘closed Sun) This excellent restaurant and boutique brewery offers one of Swakopmund's most sought-after commodities, namely authentic German-style beer. And, so as not to break with tradition, feel free to accompany your frothy brew with a plate of mixed sausages, piled sauerkraut and a healthy dollop of spicy mustard.

Tug
SEAFOOD $$$

(✆402356; mains US$80-140; ⊘lunch Sat-Sun, dinner daily) Housed in the beached tugboat *Danie Hugo* near the jetty, the Tug is something of an obligatory destination for any dinner-goer in Swakopmund. Regarded by many as the best restaurant in town, the Tug is an atmospheric, upmarket choice for meat and seafood, though a sundowner cocktail will do just fine. Due to its extreme popularity and small size, advance bookings are recommended.

🍷 Drinking & Entertainment

Swakopmund likes to party, and there are a few bars to find your favourite drink. The Tug and the Lighthouse have popular happy-hour spots to coincide with Swakop

sunsets. And both Kücki's Pub (✆402407; Tobias Hainyeko St; mains N$100-120) and Swakopmund Brauhaus are good places to prop up the bar. But if you really want to feel like you're in Africa, the beach bar at Tiger Reef (p285) is all the rage – and what better way to send off the day than to feel the sand between your toes while you enjoy a cold beer?

🛍 Shopping

Street stalls sell Zimbabwean crafts on the waterfront by the steps below Cafe Anton on Bismarck St.

Karakulia Weavers
CARPETS

(✆461415; www.karakulia.com.na; 2 Rakotoka St) This local carpet factory produces original and beautiful African rugs, carpets and wall hangings in karakul wool and offers tours of the spinning, dyeing and weaving processes.

Die Muschel Book & Art Shop
BOOKS

(✆402874; Hendrick Witbooi St; ⊘8.30am-6pm Mon-Fri, 8.30am-1pm & 4-6pm Sat, 10am-6pm Sun) German- and English-language books. Great for guides and maps. Esoteric works on art and local history are also available here.

Peter's Antiques
ANTIQUES

(✆405624; www.peters-antiques.com; 24 Tobias Hainyeko St) This place is an Ali Baba's cave of treasures, specialising in colonial relics, historic literature, West African art, politically incorrect German paraphernalia, and genuine West African fetishes and other artefacts from around the continent.

ℹ Information

Note that there is a continuing program of street-name changes (eg Lazarett St to Anton Lubowski Ave) around town, which can be confusing – where possible we've used new names (as signed in the town) or both in the text.

Dangers & Annoyances

Although the palm-fringed streets and cool sea breezes in Swakopmund are unlikely to make you tense, you should always keep your guard up in town. Regardless of how relaxed the ambience might be, petty crime unfortunately occurs.

If you have a private vehicle, be sure that you leave it all locked up with no possessions visible inside during the day. At night, you need to make sure you're parked in a gated parking lot and not on the street. Also, when you're choosing a hotel or hostel, be sure that the security precautions (ie an electric fence and/or a guard) are up to your standards. Finally, although Swakopmund

THE PATH TO BOTANICAL DISCOVERY

Among Namibia's many botanical curiosities, the extraordinary *Welwitschia mirabilis*, which exists only on the gravel plains of the northern Namib Desert from the Kuiseb River to southern Angola, is probably the strangest of all. It was first noted in 1859, when Austrian botanist and medical doctor Friedrich Welwitsch stumbled upon a large specimen east of Swakopmund.

Welwitschias

Despite their dishevelled appearance, welwitschias actually have only two long and leathery leaves, which grow from opposite sides of the corklike stem. Over the years, these leaves are darkened in the sun and torn by the wind into tattered strips, causing the plant to resemble a giant wilted lettuce. Pores in the leaves trap moisture, and longer leaves actually water the plant's own roots by channelling droplets onto the surrounding sand.

Welwitschias have a slow growth rate, and it's believed that the largest ones, whose tangled masses of leaf strips can measure up to 2m across, may have been growing for up to 2000 years! However, most midsized plants are less than 1000 years old. The plants don't even flower until they've been growing for at least 20 years. This longevity is probably only possible because they contain some compounds that are unpalatable to grazing animals, although black rhinos have been known to enjoy the odd plant.

The plants' most prominent inhabitant is the yellow and black pyrrhocorid bug, which lives by sucking sap from the plant. It's commonly called the push-me-pull-you bug, due to its almost continuous back-to-back mating.

Welwitschia Drive

This worthwhile excursion by vehicle or organised tour is recommended if you want to see one of Namibia's most unusual desert plants, the Welwitschia. Welwitschias reach their greatest concentrations on the Welwitschia Plains east of Swakopmund, near the confluence of the Khan and Swakop Rivers, where they're the dominant plant species.

In addition to this wilted wonder itself, Welwitschia Drive also takes in grey and black lichen fields, which were featured in the BBC production *The Private Life of Plants*. It was here that David Attenborough pointed out these delightful examples of plant-animal symbiosis, which burst into 'bloom' with the addition of fog droplets. If you're not visiting during a fog, sprinkle a few drops of water on them and watch the magic.

Further east is the Moon Landscape, a vista across eroded hills and valleys carved by the Swakop River. Here you may want to take a quick 12km return side-trip north to the farm and oasis of Goanikontes, which dates from 1848. It lies beside the Swakop River amid fabulous desert mountains, and serves as an excellent picnic site.

The Welwitschia Drive, which turns off the Bosua Pass route east of Swakopmund, lies inside the Dorob National Park. Most often visited as a day trip from Swakopmund, the drive can be completed in two hours, but allow more time to experience this otherworldly landscape.

---

is generally safe at night, it's best to stay in a group and, when possible, take a taxi to and from your accommodation.

Emergency
Ambulance (☎081 124 0019)
Fire (☎after-hours pager 405544, day 402411)
Police (☎402431, 10111)

Internet Access
Swakopmund Internet Cafe (Shop 1, Atlanta Cinema Building, Nedbank Arcade; per 30min N$20; ☺closed Sun morning) Down the mall opposite the Garden Cafe.

Medical Services
Bismarck Medical Centre (☎405000; cnr Bismarck St & Sam Nujoma Ave) For a doctor, see this recommended centre.

Money
There are plenty of banks with ATMs in the centre of town – try around the corner of Tobias Hainyeko St and Sam Nujoma Ave.

Post
Main Post Office (Garrison St) Also sells telephone cards and offers fax services.

Tourist Information

Namib-i (☎404827; www.natron.net/tour/swakop/infoe.htm; Sam Nujoma Ave; ◷8am-5pm Mon-Fri, 9am-5pm Sat, 9am-1pm Sun) A very helpful resource. In addition to helping you get your bearings, it can act as a booking agent for any activities and tours that take your fancy.

Namibia Wildlife Resorts Office (NWR; ☎402172; www.nwr.com.na; Woermannhaus, Bismarck St; ◷8am-1pm & 2-5pm Mon-Fri) Like its big brother in Windhoek, this office sells Namib-Naukluft Park and Skeleton Coast permits, and can also make reservations for other NWR-administered properties around the country.

❶ Getting There & Away

Air

Air Namibia (☎405123; www.airnamibia.com.na) has several flights a week between Windhoek's Eros Airport and Walvis Bay, from where you can easily catch a bus or taxi to Swakopmund.

Bus

There are several weekly buses between Windhoek and Swakopmund (around N$230, five hours) on the Intercape Mainliner (p319). You can easily book your tickets in advance online.

Also consider the **Town Hopper** (☎407223; www.namibiashuttle.com), which runs private shuttle buses between Windhoek and Swakopmund (N$270), and also offers door-to-door pick-up and drop-off service.

Finally, combis run this route fairly regularly, and a ride between Windhoek and Swakopmund shouldn't cost more than N$120. Swakopmund is also a minor public-transport hub, serving various regional destinations including Walvis Bay by combi, with fares averaging between N$20 and N$40.

Car

Swakopmund is about 400km west of Windhoek on the B2, the country's main east–west highway.

Train

Trans-Namib (☎061-298 1111) trains operate throughout the day and night (from N$100), though they're not very convenient or popular, especially given the ease of bus travel.

The plush **Desert Express** (☎061-298 2600; www.transnamib.com.na/desert-express.html) 'rail cruise' runs to and from Windhoek.

Walvis Bay

☎064 / POP 65,000

Walvis Bay is pleasant enough, particularly around the new waterfront development and along the esplanade. The town proper

Walvis Bay

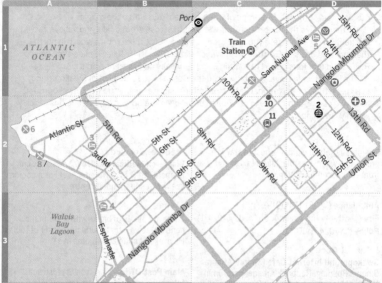

is not so compact and your own wheels will make life a lot easier. It's a good alternative to Swakopmund if that city is all a bit glitzy and urban for you – Walvis Bay has a far more relaxed feel to it. And the accommodation options and food choices are excellent.

Walvis Bay was snatched by the British years before the German colonists could get their hands on it. The town is architecturally uninspiring and lacks the old-world ambience of its northerly neighbour. In marked contrast, the area around Walvis Bay is home to a number of unique natural attractions, including one of the largest flocks of flamingos in the whole of Southern Africa.

◉ Sights

Dune 7   SAND DUNE
In the bleak expanse just off the C14, 6km by road from town, Dune 7 is popular with locals as a slope for sandboarding and skiing. The picnic site, which is now engulfed by sand, has several shady palm trees tucked away in the lee of the dune.

FREE **Walvis Bay Museum**   MUSEUM
(Nangolo Mbumba Dr; ⊙9am-5pm Mon-Thu, to 4.30pm Fri) The town museum is located in the library. It concentrates on the history and maritime background of Walvis Bay but also has archaeological exhibits, a mineral collection and natural-history displays on the Namib Desert and the Atlantic Coast.

Bird Island   NESTING SITE
Along the Swakopmund road, 10km north of Walvis Bay, take a look at the offshore wooden platform known as Bird Island. It was built to provide a roost and nesting site for sea birds and a source of guano for use as fertiliser. The annual yield is around 1000 tonnes, and the smell from the island is truly unforgettable.

Sandwich Harbour   HARBOUR
Sandwich Harbour, located 56km south of Walvis Bay in Dorob National Park, historically served as a commercial fishing and trading port. Some historians suggest that the name may be derived from an English whaler, the *Sandwich,* whose captain produced the first map of this coastline. Others contend that the name may also be a corruption of the German word *sandfische,* a type of shark often found here. History aside, at present the harbour is a total wilderness devoid of any human settlement.

Dunes up to 100m high slope into the Atlantic, which washes into the picturesque lagoon. Birdwatchers will have a field day, and **Sandwich Harbour 4x4** (📞207663; www.sandwich-harbour.com; Waterfront) facilitates full-/half-day (N$1050/850) trips down here.

To Swakopmund (35km)

11th St
16 12th St
6th Rd
18th Rd
14th St

B2

C14

To Rooikop Airport (10km)

Lookout

NAMIBIA WALVIS BAY

FLAMINGOS AT WALVIS BAY

Lesser and greater flamingos flock in large numbers to pools along the Namib Desert coast, particularly around Walvis Bay and Lüderitz. They're excellent fliers, and have been known to migrate up to 500km overnight in search of proliferations of algae and crustaceans.

The lesser flamingo filters algae and diatoms (microscopic organisms) from the water by sucking in, and vigorously expelling water from its bill. The minute particles are caught on fine hairlike protrusions that line the inside of the bird's mandibles. The suction is created by the thick fleshy tongue, which rests in a groove in the lower mandible and pumps back and forth like a piston. It has been estimated that a million lesser flamingos can consume over 180 tonnes of algae and diatoms daily.

While lesser flamingos obtain food by filtration, the greater flamingo supplements its algae diet with small molluscs, crustaceans and other organic particles from the mud. When feeding, it will rotate in a circle while stamping its feet in an effort to scare up a tasty potential meal.

The greater and lesser flamingos are best distinguished by their colouration. Greater flamingos are white to light pink, and their beaks are whitish with a black tip. Lesser flamingos are a deeper pink – often reddish – colour, with dark-red beaks.

Located near Walvis Bay are three diverse wetland areas, namely the lagoon, the salt works and the Bird Paradise at the sewage works. Together they form Southern Africa's single most important coastal wetland for migratory birds, with up to 150,000 transient avian visitors stopping by annually, including massive flocks of both lesser and greater flamingos. The three wetland areas are as follows:

The Lagoon This shallow and sheltered 45,000-hectare lagoon, southwest of Walvis Bay and west of the Kuiseb River mouth, attracts a range of coastal water birds in addition to enormous flocks of lesser and greater flamingos. It also supports chestnut banded plovers and curlew sandpipers, as well as the rare Damara tern.

The Salt Works Southwest of the lagoon is this 3500-hectare saltpan complex, which currently supplies over 90% of South Africa's salt. As with the one in Swakopmund, these pans concentrate salt from seawater with the aid of evaporation. They also act as a rich feeding ground for prawns and larval fish.

Bird Paradise Immediately east of town along the C14 at the municipal sewage-purification works is this nature sanctuary, which consists of a series of shallow artificial pools, fringed by reeds. An observation tower and a short nature walk afford excellent birdwatching.

🏃 Activities

Eco Marine Kayak Tours　　KAYAKING
(☎203144; www.emkayak.iway.na) Sea-kayaking trips around the beautiful Walvis Bay wetlands are conducted by this outfit. Note that there is no central office, though bookings can be made over the phone or through your accommodation.

Mola Mola Safaris　　BOATING
(☎205511; www.mola-namibia.com; Waterfront) This marine-safari company offers fully customisable boating trips around the Walvis Bay and Swakopmund coastal areas, where you can expect to see dolphins, seals and countless birds. Prices are dependent on your group size and length of voyage.

🛏 Sleeping

Remax　　ACCOMMODATION SERVICES $$
(☎212451; www.remax.co.za; Sam Nujoma Ave) Self-catering is a good option in Walvis Bay, with houses and apartments available both on the coast and in the city. A two-bedroom place can be found for around N$650.

Courtyard Hotel Garni　　HOTEL $$
(☎206252; 16 3rd Rd; r per person incl breakfast N$580; @🛜🌊) This low-rise place in a quiet neighbourhood near the water has generous rooms that are a bit beaten around the edges – it's comfortable enough and there are nice common areas, but it's probably a tad overpriced and the beds are quite small. The kitchenette is useful for self-caterers.

Lagoon Lodge

HOTEL $$$

(☎200850; www.lagoonlodge.com.na; 2 Nangolo Mbumba Dr; s/d N$600/1200; ☒) A garish yellow greets visitors to this French-run lodge, which commands a magnificent location next to the lagoon, and features individually decorated rooms with private terraces facing out towards the sand and sea. The location on the promenade is handy for an evening or early-morning walk along the waterfront.

Oyster Box Guesthouse

GUESTHOUSE $$$

(☎202247; www.oysterboxguesthouse.com; cnr Esplanade & 2nd St W; s/d N$750/1200; ❈🛜) More like a classy boutique hotel, this guesthouse is a stylish affair right on the waterfront. Rooms are very contemporary and bedding includes crisp sheets and fluffy pillows. Helpful staff can book activities for you around town and arrange transport.

✖ Eating & Drinking

The Waterfront area features a cluster of bar-restaurants right on the water overlooking the harbour and the big machinery of the port. There's a small but classy selection of places to sit outside on the water's edge and enjoy a cold drink and a meal.

Anchor

INTERNATIONAL $$

(Waterfront; breakfast N$45, mains N$70; ⊘breakfast, lunch & dinner) The food is OK at the Anchor, but the real attraction is the location overlooking the water. It makes a particularly lovely spot for breakfast, and if you're tired of eating stodgy food it does a pretty mean fruit salad. Sit at a table right on the water and watch the morning cruise boats slink out of the bay.

Raft

SEAFOOD $$

(☎204877; Esplanade; mains N$75-125; ⊘dinner) This Walvis Bay landmark sits on stilts offshore, and has a great front-row view of the ducks, pelicans and flamingos. It's the partner restaurant to the Tug in Swakopmund, and you can expect a similar offering of high-quality meats and seafood in addition to spectacular sunsets and ocean views. The seafood extravaganza is well worth the N$340 price tag.

Bon Aroma

INTERNATIONAL $$

(☎220226; Sam Nujoma Ave; starters N$50, mains N$70-120; ⊘lunch, dinner, closed Sun) A stylish restaurant with a sunny courtyard, Bon Aroma serves up a variety of dishes with a healthy bent toward seafood. Beef 'Gordon' Bleu also features, and you can sniff out pizzas, pastas, salads and grills on the menu. The sound system belts out good 'ole boy country tunes in the background and there's a decent wine list.

ℹ Information

Police (☎10111; cnr 11th St & 13th Rd)

Post Office (Sam Nujoma Ave) Provides public telephones and fax services.

Welwitschia Medical Centre (13th Rd; ⊘24hr) For medical services.

ℹ Getting There & Away

Air

Air Namibia (☎203102; www.airnamibia.com.na) has several flights a week between Windhoek's Eros Airport and Walvis Bay's Rooikop Airport, located 10km southeast of town on the C14.

Bus & Combi

All buses and combis to Walvis Bay run via Swakopmund. The Intercape Mainliner stop is the Spur Restaurant on Ben Gurirab St. There are also other private bus services running between Windhoek and Walvis Bay.

Namib-Naukluft Park

This is desert country and the swirling sand here is one of the highlights of a visit to Namibia. Nowhere else defines the country as do the much-photographed dunes: silent, constantly shifting and ageless.

The present boundaries of Namib-Naukluft Park, one of the world's largest national parks, were mostly established in 1978. However, the park's northern border was adjusted in December 2010 with the establishment of **Dorob National Park** (formerly the National West Coast Tourist Recreation Area), which stretches south as far as Sandwich Harbour.

The Namib-Naukluft Park takes in around 23,000 sq km of arid and semi-arid land, and protects various areas of vast ecological importance in the Namib and the Naukluft. The park also abuts the NamibRand Nature Reserve, the largest privately owned property in Southern Africa, forming a massive wildlife corridor that promotes migratory movement.

NAMIB SECTION

While most people associate the Namib solely with Sossusvlei, the desert sweeps across most of central Namibia, and is characterised by a large array of geological formations. Given the extremes of temperature

Namib-Naukluft Park

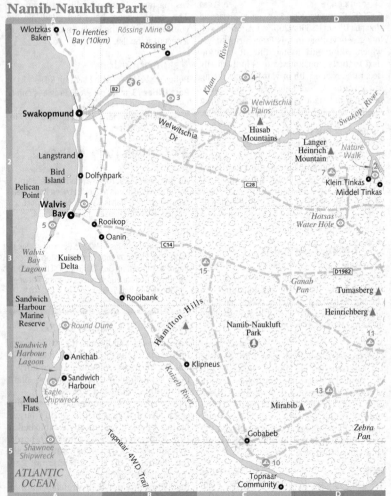

and environment, you will need a 4WD vehicle in addition to good navigation skills in order to properly explore the Namib. Truly this is one place where the journey itself is worth much more than the destination.

Sights

Kuiseb Canyon
CANYON

Located on the Gamsberg Pass route west of the Khomas Hochland, Kuiseb Canyon contains the ephemeral Kuiseb River, which is no more than a broad, sandy riverbed for most of the year. Although it may flow for two or three weeks during the rainy season,

it only gets as far as Gobabeb before seeping into the sand.

Hamilton Hills
HILLS

The limestone range known as the Hamilton Hills, south of Vogelfederberg campsite, rises 600m above the surrounding desert plains. It provides lovely desert hikes, and the fog-borne moisture supports an amazing range of succulents and other botanical wonders.

Sleeping

The Namib-Naukluft Park has eight exclusive camps, some of which have multiple but

you're coming from Swakopmund, they lie 55km northeast of the C28, along a sign-posted track. The northern sites may be accessed with 2WD, but they tend to be more crowded. The southern sites are quieter and more secluded but can be reached only by 4WD. The surrounding area offers some pleasant walking, and at Klein Tinkas, 5km east of Bloedkoppie, you'll see the ruins of a colonial police station (basically a ruined hut) and the graves of two German police officers dating back to 1895.

Ganab
CAMPGROUND $

Ganab is a dusty, exposed facility, translating to 'camelthorn acacia', that sits beside a shallow stream bed on the gravel plains. It's shaded by hardy acacia trees, and a nearby bore hole provides water for antelopes.

Groot Tinkas
CAMPGROUND $

Groot Tinkas must be accessed with 4WD, and rarely sees much traffic. It enjoys a lovely setting beneath shady rocks and the surroundings are super for nature walks. During rainy periods, the brackish water in the nearby dam attracts a variety of bird life.

Homeb
CAMPGROUND $

Homeb is located in a scenic spot upstream from the most accessible set of dunes in the Namib-Naukluft Park, and can accommodate several groups. Residents of the nearby

widely spaced campsites. Sites have tables, toilets and *braais*, but no washing facilities. Brackish water is available for cooking and washing but not drinking – be sure that you bring enough water. All sites must be booked through NWR in Windhoek (p256) or Swakopmund (p288). Camping costs N$110 per person (maximum of eight people) plus N$80/10 per person/car per day in park fees.

Bloedkoppie
CAMPGROUND $

(Blood Hill) These spots are among the most beautiful and popular sites in the park. If

NAMIBIA NAMIB-NAUKLUFT PARK

Topnaar Khoikhoi village dig wells in the Kuiseb riverbed to access water beneath the surface, and one of their dietary staples is the !nara melon, which obtains moisture from the water table through a long taproot. This hidden water also supports a good stand of trees, including camelthorn acacia and ebony.

Kriess-se-Rus   CAMPGROUND $

Kriess-se-Rus is a rather ordinary site in a dry stream bank on the gravel plains, 107km east of Walvis Bay on the Gamsberg Pass route. It is shaded, but isn't terribly prepossessing, and is best used simply as a convenient stop en route between Windhoek and Walvis Bay.

Kuiseb Canyon   CAMPGROUND $

Kuiseb Canyon is a shady site at the Kuiseb River crossing along the C14 and is also a convenient place to break up a trip between Windhoek and Walvis Bay. The location is scenic enough, but the dust and noise from passing vehicles make it less appealing than other campsites. There are pleasant short canyon walks, but during heavy rains in the mountains the site can be flooded; in the summer months, keep tabs on the weather.

Mirabib   CAMPGROUND $

Mirabib is a pleasant facility that accommodates two parties at separate sites, and is comfortably placed beneath rock overhangs along a large granite escarpment. There's evidence that these shelters were used by nomadic peoples as early as 9000 years ago, and also by nomadic shepherds in the 4th or 5th century.

Vogelfederberg   CAMPGROUND $

Vogelfederberg is a small facility, 2km south of the C14, and makes a convenient overnight camp. Located just 51km from Walvis Bay, it's more popular for picnics or short walks. It's worth looking at the intermittent pools on the summit, which shelter a species of brine prawn whose eggs hatch only when the pools are filled with rainwater. The only shade is provided by a small overhang, where there are two picnic tables and *braai* pits.

❶ Getting There & Away

The main park transit routes, the C28, C14, D1982 and D1998, are all open to 2WD traffic. However, the use of minor roads requires a park permit (N$80 per day plus N$10 per vehicle), which can either be picked up at any of the park gates or arranged in advance through NWR in Windhoek (p256) or Swakopmund (p288). While some minor roads in the park are accessible to high-clearance 2WD vehicles, a 4WD is highly recommended.

NAUKLUFT MOUNTAINS
🖉063 / ELEV 1973M

The Naukluft Mountains, which rise steeply from the gravel plains of the central Namib, are characterised by a high plateau bounded by gorges, caves and springs cut deeply from dolomite formations. The Tsondab, Tsams and Tsauchab Rivers all rise in the massif, and the relative abundance of water creates an ideal habitat for mountain zebras, kudus, leopards, springboks and klipspringers. In addition to wildlife watching, the Naukluft is home to a couple of challenging hikes that open up this largely inaccessible terrain.

◉ Sights & Activities

The lovely 17km Waterkloof Trail is a loop that takes about seven hours to complete, and begins at the Naukluft (Koedoesrus) campsite, 2km west of the park headquarters. It climbs the Naukluft River and goes past a series of pools, which offer cool and refreshing drinking and swimming. There are fabulous desert views shortly after the halfway mark, when the trail climbs steeply to a broad 1910m ridge.

The 11km Olive Trail, named for the wild olives that grow alongside it, begins at the car park 4km northeast of the park headquarters. The walk runs clockwise around the triangular loop and takes four to five hours.

Two big loops through the massif can be hiked in four and eight days. The four-day 60km loop is actually just the first third of the eight-day 120km loop, combined with a 22km cross-country jaunt across the plateau back to park headquarters. These straightforward hikes are marked by white footprints (except those sections that coincide with the Waterkloof Trail, which is marked with yellow footprints). In four places – Ubusis Canyon, above Tsams Ost, Die Valle and just beyond Tufa Shelter – hikers must negotiate dry waterfalls, boulder-blocked *kloofs* (ravines) and steep tufa formations with the aid of chains. Some people find this off-putting, so be sure you're up to it.

Naukluft Mountains

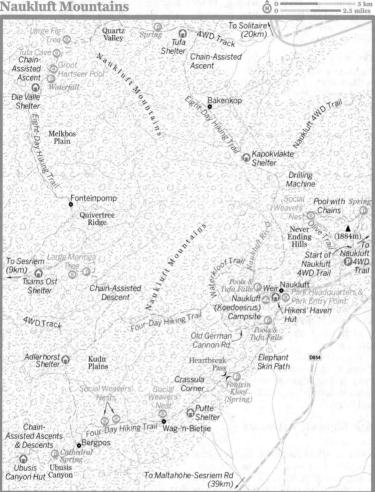

N
0 — 5 km
0 — 2.5 miles

Large Fig Tree
Quartz Valley
Spring
Tufa Shelter
4WD Track
To Solitaire (20km)
Tufa Cave
Chain-Assisted Ascent
Groot Hartseer Pool
Chain-Assisted Ascent
Waterfall
Die Valle Shelter
Naukluft Mountains
Bakenkop
Eight-Day Hiking Trail
Naukluft 4WD Trail
Melkbos Plain
Eight-Day Hiking Trail
Kapokvlakte Shelter
Drilling Machine
Fonteinpomp
Social Weavers' Nest
Pool with Chains
Spring
Quivertree Ridge
Olive Trail
Never Ending Hills
(1884m)
To Naukluft 4WD Trail
To Sesriem (9km)
Large Moringa Tree
Naukluft Mountains
Waterkloof Trail
Naukluft River
Start of Naukluft 4WD Trail
P 4WD Trail
Tsams Ost Shelter
Chain-Assisted Descent
Pools & Tufa Falls
Weir
Naukluft
Park Headquarters & Park Entry Point
4WD Track
Four-Day Hiking Trail
Naukluft (Koedoesrus) Campsite
Hikers' Haven Hut
Old German Cannon Rd
Pools & Tufa Falls
Adlerhorst Shelter
Kudu Plains
Heartbreak Pass
Elephant Skin Path
D854
Social Weavers' Nests
Social Weavers' Nest
Crassula Corner
Fontein Kloof (Spring)
Putte Shelter
Chain-Assisted Ascents & Descents
Four-Day Hiking Trail
Wag-'n-Bietjie
Bergpos
Cathedral Spring
Ubusis Canyon Hut
Ubusis Canyon
To Maltahöhe-Sesriem Rd (39km)

🛏 Sleeping

In addition to the unofficial campsites along the trails, there are several accommodation options outside the park.

Tsauchab River Camping   CAMPGROUND **$**
(📞293416; www.tsauchab.com; campsites N$150, plus per person N$100, single/double chalets N$760/1300) If you're an avid hiker (or just love excellent settings!), you're in for a treat. The scattered campsites here sit beside the Tsauchab riverbed – one occupies a huge hollow tree – and each has a private shower block, a sink and a *braai* area. The

6km Kudu Hiking Trail climbs to the summit of Rooikop. Beside a spring 11km away from the main site is the 4WD-exclusive site, which is the starting point for the wonderful 21km Mountain Zebra Hiking Trail.

Büllsport Guest Farm   FARMSTAY **$$**
(📞693371; www.buellsport.com/main.html; s/d with half board from N$840/1460) This scenic farm, owned by Ernst and Johanna Sauber, occupies a lovely, austere setting below the Naukluft Massif, and features a ruined colonial police station, the Bogenfels arch and several resident mountain zebras. A

highlight is the 4WD excursion up to the plateau and the hike back down the gorge, past several idyllic natural swimming pools.

ⓘ Getting There & Away

The Naukluft is best reached via the C24 from Rehoboth and the D1206 from Rietoog; petrol is available at Büllsport and Rietoog. From Sesriem, 100km away, the nearest access is via the dip-ridden D854.

Sesriem & Sossusvlei

✍063

Appropriate for this vast country with its epic landscapes is that its number-one tourist attraction, Sossusvlei, still manages to feel isolated. The dunes, appearing otherworldly at times, especially when the light hits them just so, are part of the 32,000-sq-km sand sea that covers much of the region. The dunes reach as high as 325m, and are part of one of the oldest and driest ecosystems on earth. However, the landscape here is constantly changing – wind forever alters the shape of the dunes, while colours shift with the changing light, reaching the peak of their brilliance just after sunrise.

The gateway to Sossusvlei is Sesriem (Six Thongs), which remains a lonely and far-flung outpost, home to little more than a petrol station and a handful of tourist hotels and lodges.

⊙ Sights & Activities

Sossusvlei   SAND DUNES

(round trip N$100) Sossusvlei, a large ephemeral pan, is set amid red sand dunes that tower up to 200m above the valley floor and more than 300m over the underlying strata. It rarely contains any water, but when the Tsauchab River has gathered enough volume and momentum to push beyond the thirsty plains to the sea sand, it's completely transformed. The normally cracked dry mud gives way to an ethereal blue-green lake, surrounded by greenery and attended by aquatic bird life, as well as the usual sand-loving gemsboks and ostriches.

At the end of the 65km 2WD road from Sesriem is the 2WD car park, and only 4WDs can drive the last 4km into the Sossusvlei Pan itself. Visitors with lesser vehicles park at the 2WD car park and walk, hitch or catch the shuttle to cover the remaining distance. If you choose to walk, which really is the best way to take in all the desert scenery, allot about 90 minutes, and carry enough water for a hot, sandy slog in the sun.

Dune 45   SAND DUNE

The most accessible of the large red dunes along the Sossusvlei road is Dune 45, so called because it's 45km from Sesriem. It rises over 150m above the surrounding plains, and is flanked by several scraggly and oft-photographed trees.

Elim Dune   SAND DUNE

This often visited red dune, 5km north of the Sesriem Camp Site, can be reached with 2WD vehicles but also makes a pleasant morning or afternoon walk.

Hidden Vlei   HIKING

The rewarding 4km return hike from the 2WD car park to Hidden Vlei, an unearthly dry *vlei* (low, open landscape) amid lonely dunes, makes a rewarding excursion. The route is marked by white-painted posts. It's most intriguing in the afternoon, when you're unlikely to see another person.

Dead Vlei   HIKING

The rugged 6km return walk from Sossusvlei to Dead Vlei is popular with those who think Hidden Vlei is becoming overly touristy. Despite the name, it's a lovely spot and is just as impressive as its more popular neighbour.

Namib Sky Balloon Safaris   HOT-AIR BALLOON

(✍683188; www.namibsky.com) For those who dream of looming over the dunes in a balloon, this company offers Namib Desert balloon flights. The early-morning flight departs before sunrise, when not a breath of wind is stirring.

🛏 Sleeping

Reservations are essential at most places, especially during the high season, school holidays and busy weekends.

Sesriem Camp Site   CAMPGROUND $$

(campsites per person N$130) With the exception of the upmarket Sossus Dune Lodge, this is the only accommodation inside the park gates; staying here guarantees that you will be able to arrive at Sossusvlei in time for sunrise. The campsite is rudimentary – sandy sites with bins, taps, and trees for shade – and expensive for what you get, but you pay for the location inside the park. A small shop at the office here sells snacks

Sesriem & Sossusvlei

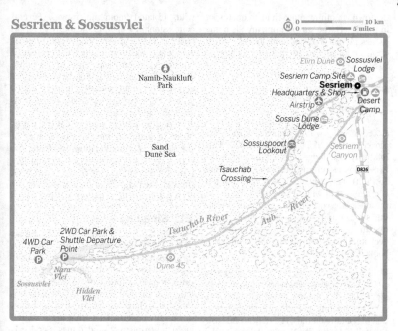

and cold drinks, and the campsite bar provides music and booze.

Sossusvlei Lodge   LODGE $$$
(📞293636; www.sossusvleilodge.com; campsites for 2 persons N$300, s/d from N$2330/3150; 🏊) People either love this curious place or hate it, but it does make a statement. Accommodation is in self-contained chalets with private verandahs, and guests can mingle with one another in the swimming pool, bar-restaurant and observatory. Walk-in rates are often cheaper. There's an adventure centre here that organises scenic flights, hot-air ballooning, quad biking and many other activities. The lodge also runs Sossus Oasis campsite, near the petrol station – an exposed site with good facilities.

Sossus Dune Lodge   LODGE $$$
(📞061-2857200; www.nwr.com.na/sossus_dune_lodge.html; single/double dune chalets with half board N$2400/4600; 🏊) Splash out at this ultra-exclusive lodge, which is administered by NWR, and is one of only two properties located inside the park gates. Constructed entirely of local materials, the lodge consists of elevated bungalows that run alongside a curving promenade, and face out towards the silent desert plains. In the morning you can roll out of your plush queen-size bed

and then be one of the first people to watch the morning light wash over Sossusvlei.

ℹ Information

Sesriem Canyon and Sossusvlei are open year-round between sunrise and sunset. All visitors headed for Sossusvlei must check in at the park office and secure a park entry permit. Namib-Naukluft **park entry** at Sossusvlei is N$80 per person, N$10 per car. There's an **internet cafe** at the petrol station near Sossus Oasis campsite (N$30 for half an hour).

ℹ Getting There & Away

Sesriem is reached via a signposted turn-off from the C14, and petrol is available in town. There is no public transport leading into the park, though hotels can arrange tours if you don't have your own vehicle.

The road leading from the park gate to the 2WD car park is paved, though the speed limit remains 60km/h. Although the road is conducive to higher speeds, there are oryxes and springboks dashing about, so drive with extreme care.

Solitaire & Around

Solitaire is a lonely and aptly named settlement of just a few buildings about 80km north of Sesriem along the A46. Although the town is nothing more than an open spot in the desert, the surrounding area is home to several guest farms and lodges, which serve as an alternative base for exploring Sossusvlei.

🛏 Sleeping

TOP CHOICE **Agama River Camp** LODGE, CAMPGROUND **$$**
(☎063-683245; www.agamarivercamp.com; per person campsites N$120, bungalows N$400) This relatively new lodge is in a handy spot between Sossusvlei and Sesriem (34km from Sesriem). The bungalows here have rooftop decks and staff will set up a sleeping kit on the deck for you, so you can sleep under the stars. Campsites have excellent facilities. In the main lodge there's a sundowner deck and lounge; meals are only available if booked well in advance.

Solitaire Guest Farm FARMSTAY **$$**
(☎062-682033; www.solitaireguestfarm.com; campsites N$120, s/d with half board from N$800/1440; ☎) This inviting guest farm, located 6km east of Solitaire on the C14, is a peaceful oasis situated between the Namib plains and the Naukluft massif. Bright rooms, home-cooked meals and relaxing surroundings make it a good choice.

Solitaire Country Lodge LODGE **$$**
(☎063-293621; www.namibialodges.com; campsites per person N$100, s/d N$495/805; @☎) Despite its relative youth, the property was designed to evoke images of a colonial-era farmhouse, albeit one with a large swimming pool in the backyard! Serviceable rooms are fairly sparse, a decent size and set around a large grassed square.

❶ Getting There & Away

Solitaire is connected to Sesriem by the unpaved C19, and petrol is available in town. When we visited there was a newish shuttle service from Solitaire petrol station to Sossusvlei for N$100 return; check with the station to see if it's still going and for the times the service runs.

NamibRand Nature Reserve

Boarding the Namib-Naukluft Park, this reserve is essentially a collection of private farms that together protect over 200,000 hectares of dunes, desert grasslands and wild, isolated mountain ranges. Several concessionaires operate on the reserve, offering a range of experiences amid one of Namibia's most stunning and colourful landscapes. A surprising amount of wildlife can be seen here, including large herds of gemsboks, springboks and zebras, as well as kudus, klipspringers, spotted hyenas, jackals, and Cape and bat-eared foxes.

Access by private vehicle is restricted in order to maintain the delicate balance of the reserve. Accommodation prices are also extremely high, which seeks to limit the tourist footprint. As a result, you must book through the lodges, and then arrange either a 4WD transfer or a chartered fly-in.

🛏 Sleeping

Wolwedans Dune Lodge LODGE **$$$**
(☎061-230616; www.wolwedans.com; chalets per person with full board & activities from N$4280; ✴☎) One of the more affordable (at this price bracket, affordable is a relative term) lodges in the NamibRand, Wolwedans features an architecturally arresting collection of raised wooden chalets that are scattered amid towering red sand dunes. Service is impeccable, and the atmosphere is overwhelmingly elegant, yet you can indulge in your wild side at any time with chauffeured 4WD dune drives and guided safaris.

SOUTHERN NAMIBIA

The deserts of southern Namibia sparkle beneath the sun – quite literally – as they're filled with millions of carats of diamonds. Since the Germans first unearthed vast treasure troves resting beneath the sands, much of the region has been dubbed the *Sperrgebeit* (Forbidden Area). Following the very recent declaration of Namibia's newest national park, this virtually pristine biodiversity hot spot is now open to the general public for the first time in more than a century.

While Sperrgebeit National Park has been grabbing all the headlines recently, the nearby port of Lüderitz has long been many a traveller's favourite. A surreal colonial relic that has been largely disregarded by the 21st century, Lüderitz clings fiercely to its European roots, astounding travellers with its traditional German architecture set against a backdrop of fiery sand dunes and deep blue seas.

Keetmanshoop

☑063

Keetmanshoop (kayt-mahns-hoo-up) sits at the main crossroads of southern Namibia, and this is why you may end up here. More of a place to overnight than one in which to spend any time, it's a friendly enough little town.

The town has a few examples of German colonial architecture, including the 1910 **Kaiserliches Postampt** (Imperial Post Office; cnr 5th Ave & Fenschel St), and the **town museum** (cnr Kaiser St & 7th Ave; admission free; ⊙7.30am-4.30pm Mon-Fri), housed in the 1895 Rhenish Mission Church, which itself is arguably more interesting than the contents of the museum inside. The ramshackle bits and pieces on display are good for killing an hour or so.

Although down a dirt road and without a street address, **Bernice B&B** (☑224851; bernicebeds@iway.na; s/d N$240/360) is extremely well signed from any direction from which you approach town. Just 14km east of town, the **Quivertree Forest Rest Camp** (☑683421; www.quivertreeforest.com; campsite per person N$100, s/d/tr/q bungalows from N$420/580/700/1000, day admission per person N$55) proudly boasts Namibia's largest *kokerboom* (quiver tree) stand.

❶ Getting There & Away

Intercape Mainliner (p319) runs buses between Windhoek and Keetmanshoop (from N$280, 5½ hours, four weekly). Book your tickets in advance online as this service continues on to Cape Town (South Africa) and fills up quickly.

Combis also run up and down the B1 with fairly regular frequency, and a ride between Windhoek to Keetmanshoop shouldn't cost more than N$100. Less regular combis connect Keetmanshoop to the township in Lüderitz, with fares averaging around N$175.

Trans-Namib (☑061-298 2175) operates a night train between Windhoek and Keetmanshoop (from N$90, 12 hours, daily except Saturday).

Duwisib Castle

☑063

A curious neo-baroque structure located about 70km south of Maltahöhe smack-dab in the middle of the barren desert, this European **castle** (admission N$60; ⊙8am-1pm & 2-5pm) is smaller than some grandiose descriptions suggest and really worth a stop only if you're passing by. The portraits and scant furniture certainly give it a European feel though, and the pleasant courtyard is a good place to relax in the shade of some majestic trees.

🛏 Sleeping

Duwisib Castle Rest Camp   CAMPGROUND $
(campsites per person N$90) This very amenable camp (with sparkling amenities block) occupies one corner of the castle grounds and is well set up with campsites containing bin, *braai* and bench seating. The adjoining kiosk sells snacks, coffee and cool drinks. Book through the NWR office (p256) in Windhoek.

Duwisib Guest Farm   GUESTHOUSE $$
(☑293344; www.farmduwisib.com; campsites per person N$90, s/d with half board N$760/1300) Located 300m from the castle, this pleasant guest farm has rooms with views of the main attraction, and self-catering family units that sleep up to eight people. While you're there, be sure to check out the historic blacksmith shop up the hill.

❶ Getting There & Away

There isn't any public transport to Duwisib Castle. If you're coming from Helmeringhausen, head north on the C14 for 62km and turn northwest onto the D831. Continue for 27km, then turn west onto the D826 and travel a further 15km to the castle.

Aus

☑063

A stop on the long drive west to Lüderitz, Aus is home to a former prison camp and, aside from the prison camp, also boasts two highly recommendable guest farms where you can slow down and spend some time soaking up the desolate beauty of the shifting sands.

Aus Information Centre (☑258151; ⊙ 8am-5pm Mon-Fri, to 2pm Sat & Sun), just off the B4, has a cafe, internet access and lots of information on nature, war and wild horses of the area. Ask here about the Aus Walking Trail, which begins at the info centre.

🛏 Sleeping

Klein-Aus Vista   LODGE $$
(☑258021; www.namibhorses.com; campsites per person N$90, cabins N$175, r/chalets per person

NAMIBIA KEETMANSHOOP

from N$780/1250; ❄ ❅) This 10,000-hectare ranch, 3km west of Aus, is a hiker's paradise, with six trails ranging from 4km to 20km. Meals are available at the main lodge. Accommodation is provided in the main lodge; in the dormitory hut Geister Schlucht, in a Shangri-La–like valley; or in the opulent Eagle's Nest complex, where several chalets are built right into the boulders. Apart from the wonderful hiking, activities include horse riding and 4WD tours of the ranch's vast desert concession.

🖉 **Namib Biosphere Reserve**   LODGE **$$$**
(🌐683055; www.namtib.net; campsites per person N$90, s/d N$800/1270) In the beautiful Tirasberge, this private reserve is run by ecologically conscious owners who've created a self-sustaining farm in a narrow valley, with distant views of the Namib plains and dune sea. There is an incredible wealth of nature on display here. To reach the reserve, take the C13 north of Aus for 55km, then turn west on the D707; after 48km turn east onto the 12km farm road to the lodge.

❶ Getting There & Away

Aus is 125km east of Lüderitz on the B4. Travel in this region typically requires a private vehicle.

Lüderitz
🌐063

Before travelling to Lüderitz, pause for a moment to study the country map, and you'll realise that the town is sandwiched between the barren Namib Desert and the windswept South Atlantic coast. And if Lüderitz's wholly unique geographical setting isn't impressive enough, its surreal German art nouveau architecture will seal the deal. Something of a colonial relic scarcely touched by the 21st century, Lüderitz might recall a Bavarian *dorfchen* (small village), with churches, bakeries and cafes.

❍ Sights

Lüderitz is chock-a-block with colonial buildings, and every view reveals something interesting. The curiously intriguing architecture, which mixes German imperial and art nouveau styles, makes this quirky little town appear even more otherworldly.

FREE **Felsenkirche**   CHURCH
(Kirche St; ⊗4-5pm Mon-Sat) The prominent Evangelical Lutheran church dominates Lüderitz from high on Diamond Hill. It was designed by Albert Bause, who implemented the Victorian influences he'd seen in the Cape. The brilliant stained-glass panel situated over the altar was donated by Kaiser Wilhelm II, while the Bible was a gift from his wife. Come for the views over the water and the town.

Lüderitz Museum   MUSEUM
(🌐202582; Diaz St; admission N$15; ⊗3.30-5pm Mon-Fri) This museum contains information on the town's history, including displays on natural history, local indigenous groups and the diamond-mining industry. Phone to arrange a visit outside standard opening hours.

Lüderitz Peninsula   PENINSULA
This peninsula, much of which lies outside the Sperrgebiet, makes an interesting half-day excursion from town.

Agate Bay, just north of Lüderitz, is made of tailings from the diamond work-

Lüderitz

ings. There aren't many agates these days, but you'll find fine sand partially consisting of tiny grey mica chips.

The picturesque bay **Sturmvogelbucht** is a pleasant place for a *braai*, though the water temperature would be amenable only

to a penguin or polar bear. The rusty ruin in the bay is the remains of a 1914 Norwegian whaling station; the salty pan just inland attracts flamingos and merits a quick stop.

At **Diaz Point**, 22km by road from Lüderitz, is a classic lighthouse and a replica of

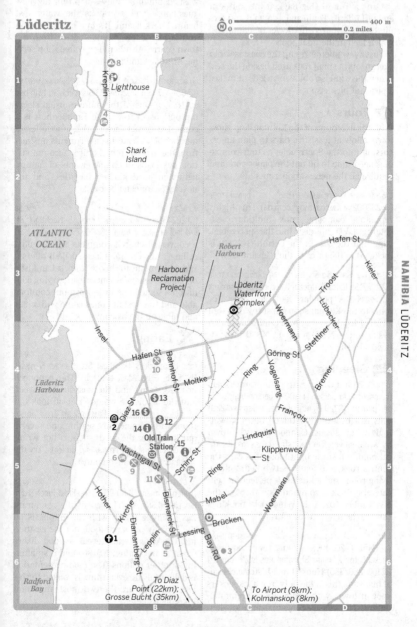

Lüderitz

the cross erected in July 1488 by Portuguese navigator Bartolomeu Dias on his return from the Cape of Good Hope.

Halifax Island, a short distance offshore south of Diaz Point, is home to Namibia's best-known jackass penguin colony.

Grosse Bucht (Big Bay), at the southern end of Lüderitz Peninsula, is a wild and scenic beach favoured by flocks of flamingos, which feed in the tidal pools.

Just a few kilometres up the coast is **Klein Bogenfels**, a small rock arch beside the sea. When the wind isn't blowing a gale, it makes a pleasant picnic spot.

☞ Tours

With the exception of the Kolmanskop ghost town, allow at least five days to plan an excursion into the Sperrgebiet as tour companies need time to fill out the paperwork and acquire all the necessary permits.

Coastway Tours Lüderitz DRIVING TOUR
(☎202002; www.coastways.com.na) This highly reputable company runs multiday self-catering 4WD trips deep into the Sperrgebiet. Note that the cost of the permit (N$250) is included in the price of the relevant tour.

Lüderitz Safaris & Tours ADVENTURE TOUR
(☎202719; ludsaf@africaonline.com.na; Bismarck St; ⊙daily) A popular booking agency for tours to the Kolmanskop ghost town as well as other local destinations. Conducts guided oyster tours (N$50 for tour, N$30 for tastings) as well.

🛏 Sleeping

Shark Island Camp Site CAMPGROUND $
(campsites per person N$100, 6-person bungalows per person N$220, lighthouse per person N$220) This is a beautifully situated but aggravatingly windy locale. Connected to the town by a causeway, Shark Island has as its focal point a historic lighthouse that caps the central rock, and features two bedrooms, a living room and a kitchen – perfect for self-caterers! Book accommodation through the NWR office (p256) in Windhoek; bookings can also be made at the entrance.

Lüderitz Backpackers BACKPACKERS $
(☎174513, 202000; www.namibweb.com/backpackers.htm; 7 Schinz St; campsites N$70, dm/d/f N$100/250/380) Housed in a historic colonial mansion, this is the only true backpackers spot in town, with rudimentary accommodation. The vibe is congenial and low-key,

and the friendly management is helpful in sorting out your onward travels.

Kairos B&B B&B $$
(☎081 650 5598; Shark Island; s/d N$400/520) This brand spanking new, cheerful white-washed building houses a promising new guesthouse and overlooks the water just before Shark Island. It's in a lovely location and is just a few minutes' drive from the town centre. Also here is a coffee shop serving breakfast and lunch.

Krabbenhoft une Lampe APARTMENT $$
(☎081 447 1151, 202674; 25 Bismarck St; twin-bed apt N$500) One of the more unusual sleeping options in town, the Krabbenhoft is a converted carpet factory that now offers a number of self-catering apartments upstairs from the Avis car-rental office. Accommodation has loads of character, lots of natural light and good kitchen facilities, and the novelty factor can't be beat.

Kratzplatz B&B $$
(☎202458; www.kratzplatz.com; 5 Nachtigal St; s/d incl breakfast from N$400/750) Housed in a converted church complete with vaulted ceilings, this centrally located B&B offers a variety of rooms to choose from, set amidst a patch of greenery. Rooms are in varying condition – some are a little worn but comfortable and the upstairs ones come with chair and table on the balcony.

✗ Eating

Diaz Coffee Shop CAFE $
(cnr Bismarck & Nachtigal Sts; snacks & meals N$25-45; ⊙breakfast & lunch) The cappuccinos are strong and the pastries are sweet, and the ambience wouldn't at all look out of place in Munich. Patrons sit in a large room with some comfy seating and receive quick service; the food, such as hot wraps and chicken schwarmas, is delicious. Try the specialty coffee…if you dare.

Bistro D'Cafe BISTRO $$
(Hafen St; mains N$60-90; ⊙breakfast, lunch & dinner, closed Sun; ☎) This cosy little restaurant has a simple set-up with the emphasis on the lovingly prepared food, not the aesthetics. The cute menus reveal seafood dishes (such as the platter, N$180) and a smattering of other options. The food presentation is delightful and everything is cooked fresh – love and time are the two most important ingredients here.

Barrels GERMAN $$

(☑202458; 5 Natchtigal St; mains N$45-100; ☺dinner Mon-Fri) A wonderfully festive bar-restaurant accented by occasional live music, Barrels offers rotating daily specials highlighting fresh seafood and German staples. Portions are hefty and the buffet (N$120) is great value. Bar opens at 6pm.

❶ Information

Stay well clear of the Sperrgebiet, unless you're part of an organised tour, as much of the area remains strictly off-limits despite its national-park status. The northern boundary is formed by the B4 and extends almost as far east as Aus. Trespassers will be prosecuted (or worse).

Several banks on Bismarck St change cash and travellers cheques.

Softcentre Computers (Waterfront Complex; per min N50c; ☺8am-5pm Mon-Fri, to 1pm Sat) Provides reliable internet access.

Lüderitz Safaris & Tours (☑202719; ludsaf@africaonline.com.na; Bismarck St; ☺daily) Provides useful tourist information, organises visitor permits for the Kolmanskop ghost town, and sells curios, books, stamps and phonecards.

❶ Getting There & Away

Air Namibia travels about three times a week between Windhoek and Lüderitz. The airport is 8km southeast of town.

Somewhat irregular combis connect Lüderitz to Keetmanshoop, with fares averaging around N$200. Buses depart from the southern edge of town at informal bus stops along Bismarck St.

Lüderitz and the scenery en route are worth the 334km trip from Keetmanshoop via the tarred B4.

Sperrgebiet National Park

Although it's been off-limits to the public for most of the last century, in 2008 Sperrgebiet was inaugurated as a national park. Known worldwide as the source of Namibia's exclusive diamonds, the Sperrgebiet (Forbidden Area) could become the gem of Namibia's protected spaces. Geographically speaking, the park encompasses the northern tip of the Succulent Karoo Biome, a 26,000-sq-km area of dunes and mountains that appear dramatically stark but represent one of 25 outstanding global 'hot spots' of unique biodiversity.

The Sperggebiet originally consisted of two private concessions: Diamond Area 1 and Diamond Area 2. The latter, home to the Kolmanskop ghost town and Elizabeth Bay, has been open to the public for some time now. Since 2004, parts of the former have also been opened up to specialist conservation groups, though, given the diamond industry's security concerns, access has been carefully controlled.

At the time of research, it appeared that disagreement between internal government departments was holding back further development and access for tourists in the park. Hopefully, once this has been resolved, more of this unique area will be open to visitors.

◉ Sights

Kolmanskop Ghost Town HISTORIC TOWN
(admission N$55) Given that permits can be arranged from Namdeb (Namdeb Diamond Corporation Limited, an organisation owned in equal shares by the government of Namibia and the De Beers Group) with relative ease, the most popular excursion from Lüderitz is the ghost town of Kolmanskop. Named after early Afrikaner trekker Jani Kolman, whose ox wagon became bogged in the sand here, Kolmanskop was originally constructed as the Consolidated Diamond Mines (CDM) headquarters. Although Kolmanskop once boasted a casino, a bowling alley and a theatre with fine acoustics, the slump in diamond sales after WWI and the discovery of richer pickings at Oranjemund ended its heyday. By 1956 the town was totally deserted, left to the mercy of the shifting desert sands. Today, Kolmanskop has been partially restored as a tourist attraction, and the sight of decrepit buildings being invaded by dunes is simply too surreal to describe.

You can turn up at any time, and you're not required to arrive as part of an organised tour, though you do need to purchase a permit in advance through either the NWR office (NWR; ☑202752; Schinz St; ☺7.30am-1pm & 2-4pm Mon-Fri) in Lüderitz or a local tour operator. Guided tours (in English and German; at 9.30am and 11am Monday to Friday, and 10am Sunday), which are included in the price of the permit, depart from the museum in Kolmanskop. After the tour, you can return to the museum, which contains relics and information on the history of Namibian diamond mining.

☞ Tours

One-third of the way down the Forbidden Coast between Lüderitz and Oranjemund is the 55m natural sea arch known as Bogenfels (Bow Rock). Bogenfels has only been opened to private tours for a few years, which also take in the mining ghost town of Pomona, the Maerchental Valley, the Bogenfels ghost town and a large cave near the arch itself. You must book this trip through tour operators in Lüderitz. Coastway Tours Lüderitz (p302) conducts daily sightseeing tours from Lüderitz out to Bogenfels (from N$1250 per person depending on numbers on tour), via Pomona, an old ghost mining town.

Elizabeth Bay   SCENIC TOUR

In 1986, CDM again began prospecting in the northern Sperrgebiet, and found bountiful diamond deposits around Elizabeth Bay, 30km south of Kolmanskop. The estimated 2.5 million carats weren't expected to last more than 10 years, but CDM installed a full-scale operation, and rather than duplicate its Lüderitz facilities here, it provided its workers with daily transport from the town. Half-day tours to Elizabeth Bay, which must be booked through tour operators in Lüderitz, also take in Kolmanskop and the Atlas Bay Cape fur seal colony.

🛏 Sleeping

There are no tourist lodges within the national park, and bush camping is strictly forbidden. It's likely that some form of accommodation will be constructed in the years to come; in the meantime your best option is to base yourself in Lüderitz.

ℹ Getting There & Away

Do not attempt to access the Sperrgebiet in a private vehicle as you will be inviting a whole mess of trouble. The only exception to this statement is Kolmanskop, which can be accessed if you have the necessary permits.

Fish River Canyon

🖉 063

Nowhere else in Africa will you find anything quite like Fish River Canyon: it's 160km long and up to 27km wide, and the dramatic inner canyon reaches a depth of 550m. Although these figures by themselves are impressive, it's difficult to get a sense of perspective without witnessing the canyon's enormous scope. In order to do this, you will need to embark on a monumental five-day hike that traverses half the length of the canyon, and tests the limits of your physical and mental endurance.

Your reward, however, will be the chance to tackle one of Namibia's – and indeed, one of Africa's – greatest natural wonders.

Fish River Canyon is part of the /Ai/Ais-Richtersveld Transfrontier Park, one of an increasing number of 'peace' or cross-border parks in Southern Africa. Straddling southern Namibia and South Africa (and measuring 6045 sq km), it boasts one of the most species-rich arid zones in the world. It also encompasses Richtersveld National Park (in South Africa) and the Orange River valley.

◉ Sights

Fish River Canyon   CANYON

From Hobas, it's 10km on a gravel road to the Main Viewpoint, which has probably the best – and most photographed – overall canyon view. Hikers' Viewpoint, a few kilometres north (at the start of the hiking route), is even more stunning. You can walk along the canyon rim between these two viewpoints and both vistas take in the sharp river bend known as Hell's Corner. Tracking the other way from the main viewpoint (ie turn left as you approach it) is a road to the Sunset Viewpoint, another well-located vantage point. A few kilometres before you reach the main viewpoint a 4WD-only track winds 13km out to other viewpoints, including Sulphur Springs and Eagle Rock.

Ai-Ais Hot Springs   SPRING

(per person N$15; ⊙9am-9pm) The hot springs at Ai-Ais (Nama for 'Scalding Hot') are beneath the towering peaks at the southern end of Fish River Canyon. They're rich in chloride, fluoride and sulphur, and are reputedly therapeutic for sufferers of rheumatism or nervous disorders. The hot water is piped to a series of baths and jacuzzis as well as an outdoor swimming pool.

🏃 Activities

Fish River Hiking Trail   HIKING

(per person N$250) The five-day hike from Hobas to Ai-Ais is Namibia's most popular long-distance walk, and with good reason. The magical 85km route, which follows the sandy riverbed past a series of ephemeral pools, begins at Hikers' Viewpoint, and ends at the hot-spring resort of Ai-Ais.

Due to flash flooding and heat in summer months, the route is open only from 15 April to 15 September. Groups of three to 30 people may begin the hike every day of the season, though you will have to book in advance as the trail is extremely popular. Reservations can be made at the NWR office (p256) in Windhoek.

Officials may need a doctor's certificate of fitness, issued fewer than 40 days before your hike, though if you look young and fit, they may not ask. Hikers must arrange their own transport to and from the start and finish as well as accommodation in Hobas and Ai-Ais.

Thanks to the typically warm, clear weather, you probably won't need a tent, but you must carry a sleeping bag and food. In Hobas, check on water availability in the canyon. In August and September, the last 15km of the walk can be completely dry and hikers will need several 2L water bottles to manage this hot, sandy stretch. Large plastic soft-drink bottles normally work just fine.

🛏 Sleeping

Accommodation inside the park must be prebooked through the NWR office in Windhoek.

Hobas Camp Site CAMPGROUND $
(campsites N$125; ☎) Administered by NWR, this pleasant and well-shaded campground near the park's northern end is about 10km from the main viewpoints. Facilities are clean, and there's a kiosk and a swimming pool, but no restaurant or petrol station.

Ai-Ais Hot Springs Spa RESORT $$
(campsites N$125, mountain-/river-view d N$900/1100; ☎) Also administered by NWR. Amenities include washing blocks, *braai* pits and the use of the resort facilities, including the hot springs. Family chalets are also available and there's an on-site restaurant and small grocery store.

Fish River Lodge LODGE $$$
(☎683005; www.fishriverlodge-namibia.com; s/d N$1500/2250) With 20 chalets located on the western rim of the canyon, this is a magical spot to enjoy the landscape. Activities include a five-night canyon hike (75km, April to September) and a day hike; both are in a private concession, so there's no need to book through NWR. Access to the lodge is from the D463, which links the B4 in the north and the C13 to the west.

ℹ Information

The main access points for Fish River Canyon are at Hobas, near the northern end of the park, and Ai-Ais, near the southern end. Both are administered by NWR. Daily park permits (N$80 per person and N$10 per vehicle) are valid for both Hobas and Ai-Ais.

The **Hobas Information Centre** (☎7.30am-noon & 2-5pm) at the northern end of the park is also the check-in point for the five-day canyon hike. Packaged snacks and cool drinks are available here, but little else.

ℹ Getting There & Away

There's no public transport to Hobas or Ai-Ais.

Gondwana Cañon Park

Founded in 1996, the 100,000-hectare Gondwana Cañon Park was created by amalgamating several former sheep farms and removing the fences to restore the wilderness country immediately northeast of /Ai/Ais-Richtersveld Transfrontier Park. Waterholes have been established and wildlife is returning to this wonderful, remote corner of Namibia. In the process, the park absorbed the former Augurabies-Steenbok Nature Reserve, which had been created earlier to protect not only steenboks but also Hartmann's mountain zebras, gemsboks and klipspringers.

🛏 Sleeping

Cañon Mountain Camp LODGE $
(☎061-230066; www.gondwana-collection.com; r per person from N$310; ☎) One of the more budget-orientated properties in the Cañon collection, this remote mountain camp occupies a high-altitude setting amid dolerite hills. Self-caterers can take advantage of the fully equipped kitchen, *braai* pits and communal lounges.

Cañon Roadhouse GUESTHOUSE $$
(☎061-230066; www.gondwana-collection.com; campsites per person N$100, s/d from N$815/1300; ☎) This wonderfully unique (and terribly kitsch) place attempts to recreate a roadhouse out on the wildest stretches of Route 66 – at least, as it exists in the collective imagination. Rooms (which are all the same) are brightly coloured with low-slung roofs and modern touches. The walk-in shower is a luxury and the cheapish furniture is offset by a Mediterranean feel. There are also 12 campsites with toilets and *braai* facilities.

TOP CHOICE Cañon Lodge LODGE $$$
(☎061-230066; www.gondwana-collection.com; s/d from N$1400/2240; ☎☎) This mountain

retreat is one of Namibia's most stunning accommodation options. The whole place, but especially the luxury stone bungalows, is sympathetically integrated into its boulder-strewn backdrop. The outlook is dramatic and the bungalows have great privacy. The restaurant, housed in a 1908 farmhouse, is tastefully decorated with historic farming implements and rambling gardens.

ⓘ Getting There & Away

Gondwana Cañon Park can be accessed via private vehicle along the C37.

Noordoewer

⊘063

Noordoewer sits astride the Orange River, which has its headwaters in the Drakensberg Mountains of Natal (South Africa) and forms much of the boundary between Namibia and South Africa. Although the town primarily exists as a border post and a centre for viticulture, it serves as a good base for organising a canoeing or rafting adventure on the Orange River.

🕴 Activities

Amanzi Trails   CANOEING
(⊘in South Africa 27-21-559 1573; www.amanzitrails.co.za) This well-established South African company is based in Abiqua Camp, and specialises in four-/five-day guided canoe trips down the Orange River costing N$2020/2360 per person. It also arranges shorter self-guided trips and longer excursions up Fish River for more experienced clients.

Felix Unite   CANOEING
(⊘in South Africa 27-21-702-9400; www.felixunite.com) Another highly reputable South African operator, Felix Unite is based in Camp Provenance, and specialises in four-/six-day guided canoe and rafting trips down the Orange River costing N$3175/3650 per person. It can also combine these excursions with lengthier trips around the Western Cape of South Africa.

🛏 Sleeping

Abiqua Camp   CAMPGROUND **$$**
(⊘297255; www.amanzitrails.co.za/abiqua_river_camp/abiqua_camp.html; campsites per person N$70, plus per vehicle N$30, chalets from N$350) This friendly and well-situated camp, 15km

down Orange River Rd, sits on the riverbank. It's the launching point for Amanzi Trails, so you can stock up on supplies, indulge in a hot meal and get a good night's rest before embarking on your canoe trip.

Camp Provenance   CAMPGROUND **$$**
(⊘in South Africa 27-21-702-9400; www.felixunite.com; campsites per person N$100, permanent twin tents N$600, twin cabanas N$800) Approximately 10km west of Noordoewer is this safari-chic river camp and launching point for Felix Unite. Purists can pitch their own tent on the grassy field, while lovers of creature comforts can bed down in a permanent tent or chalet, and stockpile their reserves for the paddling ahead.

ⓘ Getting There & Away

The town is just off the B1 near the South African border, and is only accessible by private transport.

UNDERSTAND NAMIBIA

Namibia Today

Namibia is one of the better-performing democracies in Africa, and scores comparatively well in world development indicators assessed by the World Bank. Although affected by the global recession in 2008-09, its economy rebounded as uranium and diamond prices recovered in 2010. In 2011 the government announced that it had discovered an estimated 11 billion barrels of offshore oil reserves.

With inflation topping 7% in late 2012, living costs are on the increase for most Namibians. Worryingly, food prices are part of the core reason for the increase. This increase in inflation was attributed to a weaker exchange rate, in part due to the recent labour unrest in South Africa, which resulted in the country's credit rating being downgraded.

Although Namibia is in relatively good shape as compared to the region, and for that matter the continent, poverty and disease are still enormous challenges for the government. The country also has one of the most unequal income distributions in the world.

With around 180,000 people living with AIDS (according to UNAIDS), and half that number women over the age of 15, it's still a massive problem for the country. Since 2008 the problem of coercion or forced sterilisations for women has come to light, although the government denies that forced sterilisations for HIV-positive women is government policy. Women living with HIV are subject to human-rights abuse due to the stigma, ignorance and prejudice brought about by the condition.

History

The Scramble for Africa

The Germans, under Chancellor Otto von Bismarck, were late entering the European scramble for Africa. Bismarck had always been against colonies; he considered them an expensive illusion, famously stating, 'My map of Africa is here in Europe'. But he was to be pushed into an ill-starred colonial venture by the actions of a Bremen merchant called Adolf Lüderitz.

Having already set up a trading station in Lagos (Nigeria) in 1881, Lüderitz convinced the Nama chief, Joseph Fredericks, to sell Angra Pequena, where he established his second station trading in guano (made from excrement, this manure was an effective fertiliser and gunpowder ingredient). He then petitioned the German chancellor for protection. Bismarck, still trying to stay out of Africa, politely requested the British at Walvis Bay to say whether they had any interest in the matter, but they never bothered to reply. Subsequently, in 1884, Lüderitz was officially declared part of the German Empire.

Between 1885 and 1890 the German colonial administration amounted to just three public administrators. German interests were served largely through a colonial company (along the lines of the British East India Company in India prior to the Raj), but the organisation couldn't maintain law and order.

So in the 1880s, due to renewed fighting between the Nama and the Herero, the German government dispatched Curt von François and 23 soldiers to restrict the supply of arms from British-administered Walvis Bay. This seemingly innocuous peacekeeping regiment slowly evolved into the more powerful Schutztruppe (Imperial Army), which constructed forts around the country to aid its efforts to put down opposition.

At this stage, Namibia became a fully fledged protectorate known as German South West Africa. The first German farmers arrived in 1892 to take up expropriated land on the central plateau, and were soon followed by merchants and other settlers. In the late 1890s, the Germans, the Portuguese in Angola and the British in Bechuanaland (now Botswana) agreed on Namibia's boundaries.

Colonial Atrocities

Once the Germans had completed their inventory of Namibia's natural resources, it is difficult to see how they could have avoided the stark picture that presented itself. Their new colony was a drought-afflicted land enveloped by desert, with a nonexistent transport network, highly restricted agricultural opportunities, unknown mineral resources and a sparse, well-armed indigenous population. It was hardly the stuff of empirical dreams. In fact, the only option that readily presented itself was to follow the example of the Herero and pursue a system of semi-nomadic pastoralism. The problem with this was that all the best land fell within the territories of either the Herero or the Nama and they weren't about to give it up without a fight.

In 1904 the paramount chief of the Herero invited his Nama, Baster and Owambo counterparts to join forces with him to resist the growing German presence. This was an unlikely alliance between traditional enemies, especially considering that warring between the Herero and the Nama had been a catalyst for increased involvement by the colonial powers. Driven almost all the way back to Windhoek, the German Schutztruppe brought in reinforcements and under the ruthless hand of General von Trotha went out in force to meet the Herero forces at their Waterberg camp.

On 11 August 1904 the Battle of Waterberg commenced. The general's plan was to surround the Herero position and with their massively superior firepower 'annihilate these masses with a simultaneous blow'. Although the casualties on the day were fairly light, Von Trotha ordered the pursuit and extermination of some 65,000 survivors over the following four weeks, only desisting when his troops began to die from exhaustion and typhoid, which they contracted from polluted waterholes littered with human bodies. In all, some

NAMIBIA HISTORY

80% of the entire Herero population was wiped out.

What may have been a minor episode in German colonial history was a cataclysm for the Herero nation. Demographic analysts suggest there would be 1.8 million Herero in Namibia today if it were not for the killings, making them the dominant ethnic group rather than the Owambo. In fact there are only about 120,000 Herero.

Reaping the Whirlwind

Meanwhile, in the south of the country, diamonds had been discovered at Grasplatz, east of Lüderitz, by a South African labourer, Zacharias Lewala. Despite the assessment of De Beers that the find probably wouldn't amount to much, prospectors flooded in to stake their claims. By 1910 the German authorities had branded the entire area between Lüderitz and the Orange River a *Sperrgebiet* (closed area), thrown out the prospectors and granted exclusive rights to Deutsche Diamanten Gesellschaft.

Despite their efforts to control the bounty, with dire consequences for the local populace, Germany was never to benefit from the diamond riches they found. The advent of WWI marked the end of German colonial rule in southwest Africa. By this time, though, the Germans had all but succeeded in devastating the Herero societal structures and taken over all Khoikhoi and Herero lands. The more fortunate Owambo, in the north, managed to avoid German conquest but were subsequently overrun during WWI by Portuguese forces fighting on the side of the Allies.

In 1914, at the beginning of WWI, Britain pressured South Africa into invading Namibia. Under the command of Prime Minister Louis Botha and General Jan Smuts, the South Africans pushed northwards, forcing the outnumbered Schutztruppe to retreat. In May 1915 the Germans faced their final defeat at Khorab, near Tsumeb, and a week later a South African administration was set up in Windhoek.

By 1920, many German farms had been sold to Afrikaans-speaking settlers, and the German diamond-mining interests in the south were handed over to the South Africa–based Consolidated Diamond Mines (CDM), which later gave way to the Namdeb Diamond Corporation Limited (Namdeb).

South African Occupation

Under the Treaty of Versailles in 1919, Germany was required to renounce all its colonial claims, and in 1921 the League of Nations granted South Africa a formal mandate to administer Namibia as part of the union.

The mandate was renewed by the UN following WWII. However, South Africa was more interested in annexing southwest Africa as a full province in the union and decided to scrap the terms of the mandate and rewrite the constitution. In response, the International Court of Justice determined that South Africa had overstepped its boundaries and the UN established the Committee on South-West Africa to enforce the original terms of the mandate. In 1956 the UN decided that South African control should be terminated.

Undeterred, the South African government tightened its grip on the territory, and in 1949 granted the white population parliamentary representation in Pretoria. The bulk of Namibia's viable farmland was parcelled into some 6000 farms for white settlers, while other ethnic groups were relegated to newly demarcated 'tribal homelands'. The official intent was ostensibly to 'channel economic development into predominantly poor rural areas'; however, the direct consequence of the policy was to maintain the majority of the country for white settlement and ranching.

As a result, a prominent line of demarcation appeared between the predominantly white ranching lands in the central and southern parts of the country, and the poorer but better-watered areas to the north. This arrangement was retained until Namibian independence in 1990, and to some extent continues up to the present day.

Swapo

Throughout the 1950s, despite mounting pressure from the UN, South Africa refused to release its grip on Namibia. This intransigence was based on its fears of having yet another antagonistic government on its doorstep and of losing the income that it derived from the mining operations there.

Forced labour had been the lot of most Namibians since German annexation, and was one of the main factors that led to mass demonstrations and the increasingly nationalist sentiments during the late 1950s. Among the parties was the Owamboland

MOVERS & SHAKERS: SAMUEL NUJOMA

Samuel Daniel Shafiishuna Nujoma was born on 12 May 1929 in the small village of On-gandjera in Owambo. His first rise to power was in the 1950s, when he assumed control of the Owamboland People's Organisation (OPO), which aimed to end the South African occupation of southwest Africa and to resist the implementation of apartheid. In 1960, OPO developed into the South West African People's Organisation (Swapo) and began its multi-decade campaign of guerrilla warfare under the helm of Nujoma and other Namibian leaders. During the struggle, Nujoma took the combat name 'Shafiishuna', which means 'lightning' in the Owambo language.

Following independence, Nujoma was unanimously declared president after Swapo's victory in a UN-supervised election in 1989, and he was sworn in by UN Secretary-General Javier Pérez de Cuéllar on 21 March 1990. Nujoma was re-elected in 1994 and in 1999 after changing the constitution of Namibia to allow a third five-year term. In 2005, he stepped down despite having an approval rating of over 75%, and hand-picked his successor, the current Namibian president, Hifikepunye Pohamba.

The defining issues of the Nujoma presidency were the Zimbabwe-style expropriation of a few dozen commercial farms, Namibia's HIV/AIDS crisis and a nascent secessionist movement in the Caprivi Strip. After retiring from public office, Nujoma stepped out of the limelight, and began pursuing a graduate degree in geology at the University of Windhoek in the hopes of improving Namibia's lucrative mining sector. At the time of research, Nujoma's portrait in a gown and mortarboard was splashed across every newspaper in the country, though it remains to be seen what his next move will be.

People's Congress, founded in Cape Town under the leadership of Samuel Daniel Shafiishuna Nujoma and Adimba Herman Toivo ja Toivo.

In 1959 the party's name was changed to the Owamboland People's Organisation and Nujoma took the issue of South African occupation to the UN in New York. By 1960 his party had gathered the support of several others and they eventually coalesced into the South West African People's Organisation (Swapo), with its headquarters in Dar es Salaam (Tanzania).

In 1966 Swapo took the issue of South African occupation to the International Court of Justice. The court upheld South Africa's right to govern southwest Africa, but the UN General Assembly voted to terminate South Africa's mandate and replace it with a Council for South-West Africa (renamed the Commission for Namibia in 1973) to administer the territory.

In response, on 26 August 1966 (now called Heroes' Day), Swapo launched its campaign of guerrilla warfare at Ongulumbashe in northern Namibia. The next year, one of Swapo's founders, Toivo ja Toivo, was convicted of terrorism and imprisoned in South Africa, where he would remain until 1984; Nujoma stayed in Tanzania. In 1972 the UN finally declared the South African

occupation of southwest Africa officially illegal and called for a withdrawal, proclaiming Swapo the legitimate representative of the Namibian people.

In 1975 the independence of Angola finally gave Swapo a safe base just across the border from the action in Namibia, which enabled them to step up their guerrilla campaign. South Africa responded by invading Angola in support of the opposition party Unita (National Union for the Total Independence of Angola). The attempt failed, and by March 1976 the troops had been withdrawn, although incursions continued well into the 1980s.

In the end, however, it was not the activities of Swapo alone or international sanctions that forced the South Africans to the negotiating table. People were growing tired of the war and the economy was suffering badly. South Africa's internal problems also had a significant effect. By 1985, the war was costing some R480 million (around US$250 million) per year and conscription was widespread. Mineral exports, which once provided around 88% of the country's GDP, had plummeted to just 27% by 1984.

Independence

In December 1988 a deal was finally struck between Cuba, Angola, South Africa and

Swapo that provided for the withdrawal of Cuban troops from Angola and South African troops from Namibia. It also stipulated that the transition to Namibian independence would formally begin on 1 April 1989, and would be followed by UN-monitored elections in November 1989 on the basis of universal suffrage. Although minor score-settling and unrest among some Swapo troops threatened to derail the whole process, the plan went ahead and, in September, Samuel Nujoma returned from his 30-year exile. In the elections, Swapo garnered two-thirds of the votes, but the numbers were insufficient to give the party the sole mandate to write the new constitution, an outcome that went some way to allaying fears that Namibia's minority groups would be excluded from the democratic process.

Following negotiations between the Constituent Assembly (which was soon to become the National Assembly) and international advisers, a constitution was drafted. The new constitution established a multiparty system and an impressive bill of rights, covering provisions for protection of the environment, the rights of families and children, freedom of religion, speech and the press, and a host of other matters. It also limited the presidential executive to two five-year terms. The new constitution was adopted in February 1990 and independence was granted a month later, with Samuel Nujoma being sworn in as Namibia's first president.

In 1999, Swapo won 76.8% of the vote, although concerns arose when President Nujoma amended the constitution to allow himself a third presidential term. Five years later, though, he announced that he would be stepping down in favour of his chosen successor, Hifikepunye Pohamba.

Like Sam Nujoma, Pohamba is a Swapo veteran, and swept to power with nearly 77% of the vote. In 2009 he was re-elected for a second term. He left behind the land ministry, where he presided over one of Namibia's most controversial schemes: the expropriation of land from white farmers. This 'poverty agenda', along with Namibia's HIV/AIDS crisis, the unequal distribution of incomes, managing the country's resource wealth fairly, and the challenge of raising living standards for Namibia's poor are the defining domestic issues of his presidency leading into 2013.

The Culture

The Namibian People

Namibia's population in 2012 was estimated at 2,165,828 people, with an annual population growth rate of 0.82%. This figure takes into account the effects of excess mortality due to AIDS, which became the leading cause of death in Namibia in 1996. At approximately two people per square kilometre, Namibia has one of Africa's lowest population densities.

The population comprises 12 major ethnic groups. The majority of people come from the Owambo tribe (50%), with other ethnic groups making up a relatively small percentage of the population: Kavango (9%), Herero/Himba (7%), Damara (7%), Caprivian (4%), Nama (5%), Afrikaner and German (6%), Baster (6.5%), San (1%) and Tswana (0.5%).

Like nearly all other sub-Saharan nations, Namibia is struggling to contain its HIV/AIDS epidemic, which is heavily affecting average life expectancy and population growth rates. Life expectancy in Namibia has dropped to 52 years, although some other estimates place it as low as 43. By 2021, it is estimated that up to a third of Namibia's children under the age of 15 could be orphaned.

Although Namibia is one of the world's least densely populated countries, its rich mix of ethnic groupings provides a wealth of social and cultural diversity. The indigenous people of Namibia, the Khoisan (comprised of San hunter-gatherers and Nama pastoralists), have inhabited the region from time immemorial. They were followed by Bantu-speaking herders, with the first Europeans trickling in during the 17th century.

The Namibian Way of LIfe

On the whole, Namibians are a conservative and God-fearing people – an estimated 80% to 90% of the country is Christian – so modesty in dress is important. Keeping up appearances extends to behaving modestly and respectfully to one's elders and social superiors, performing religious and social duties, and fulfilling all essential family obligations.

Education, too, is very important and the motivation to get a good education is high. But getting an education is by no means easy for everyone, and for families living in remote rural areas, it often means that very young children must be sent to schools far away, where they board in hostels. The literacy rate is 85%.

Most Namibians still live in homesteads in rural areas, and lead typical village lives. Villages tend to be family- and clan-based, and are presided over by an elected *elenga* (headman). The *elenga* is responsible for local affairs – everything from settling disputes to determining how communal lands are managed.

The sad reality is that life is a struggle for the vast majority of Namibians. Unemployment is high, and the economy remains dependent on the mining industry, and to a lesser extent on fishing and canning. In recent years, tourism has grown considerably throughout the country, though white Namibians still largely control the industry.

The Arts

Namibia is still in the process of developing a literary tradition, but its musical, visual and architectural arts are fairly well established. The country also enjoys a wealth of amateur talent in the production of material arts, including carvings, basketware and tapestry, along with simple but resourcefully designed and produced toys, clothing and household implements.

Music

Namibia's earliest musicians were the San, whose music probably emulated the sounds made by their animal neighbours, and was sung to accompany dances and storytelling. The early Nama, who had a more developed musical technique, used drums, flutes and basic stringed instruments, also to accompany dances. Some of these techniques were later adapted by Bantu peoples, who added marimbas, gourd rattles and animal-horn trumpets to the range. A prominent European contribution to Namibian music is the choir; the German colonists also introduced their traditional 'oom-pah-pah' bands, which feature mainly at German festivals.

If you need some music to keep you company on those long, lonely Namibian roads, check out the soulful tunes of Hishishi Papa, a storyteller musician, whose *Aantu Aantu* album is perfect driving music.

Architecture

The most obvious architectural contribution in Namibia was made by the German colo-

nists, who attempted to re-create late-19th-century Germany along the desert coast. In deference to the warmer climate, however, they added features such as shaded verandahs to provide a cool outdoor living space. The best examples can be seen in Lüderitz, Swakopmund and Windhoek. The most memorable structures were built in Wilhelminischer Stil and Jugendstil (art nouveau) styles.

Visual Arts

Most of Namibia's renowned modern painters and photographers are of European origin; they mainly interpret the country's colourful landscapes, bewitching light, native wildlife and diverse peoples. Artists include François de Mecker, Axel Eriksson, Fritz Krampe and Adolph Jentsch, as well as colonial landscape artists Carl Ossman and Ernst Vollbehr. Non-European rural Namibians, on the other hand, have generally concentrated on wood and stone sculpture. Township art, which develops sober themes in an expressive, colourful and generally light-hearted manner, first appeared in the townships of South Africa during the apartheid years and can be found at markets around Namibia.

Dance

Each Namibian group has its own dances, but common threads run through most of them. San dancing tends to mimic the animals they hunt. The Himba *ondjongo* dance is performed only by cattle owners, who dance to demonstrate their care and ownership of their animals. Herero dances feature the *outjina* for women and *otjipirangi* for men, in which dancers strap planks to one foot in order to deliver a hollow, rhythmic percussion. In the Kavango and Caprivi regions, traditional dancing involves rhythmic and exaggerated stamping and gyrating, accompanied by repetitive chanting and a pervasive drumbeat.

Namibian Cuisine

Food

Traditional Namibian food consists of a few staples, the most common of which is *oshifima*, a dough-like paste made from millet, and usually served with a stew of vegetables or meat. Other common dishes include *oshiwambo*, a rather tasty combination of spinach and beef, and *mealie pap*, an extremely basic porridge.

As a foreigner you'll rarely find such dishes on the menu. Most Namibian restaurants serve a variation on European-style foods, like Italian or French, alongside an abundance of seafood dishes. Such gourmet pretensions are confined to big towns like Windhoek, Swakopmund and Lüderitz; outside of these you'll rapidly become familiar with fried-food joints and pizza parlours.

More than anything else, you'll find German influences, including in Namibia's *konditoreien* (cake shops). Several places in Windhoek and Swakopmund are national institutions. You may also want to try Afrikaners' sticky-sweet *koeksesters* (small doughnuts dripping with honey) and *melktart* (milk tart).

Drinks

Namibia's dry heat means big sales for Namibia Breweries. The most popular drop is Windhoek Lager, a light and refreshing lager-style beer, but the brewery also produces Tafel Lager, the stronger and more bitter Windhoek Export and the slightly rough Windhoek Special. Windhoek Light (a tasty beer with just 2% alcohol) and the similarly light Das Pilsner are both drunk as soft drinks. The same brewery also produces a 7% stout known as Urbock.

Namibia Breweries' main competitor is Hansa. South African beers such as Lion, Castle and Black Label are widely available and you'll also find a range of refreshing spirit coolers and typically excellent and great-value South African wines.

In the rural areas – especially the Owambo regions – people socialise in tiny makeshift bars, enjoying such traditional local brews as *oshikundu* (millet beer), *mataku* (watermelon wine), *tambo* (fermented millet and sugar), *mushokolo* (a beer made from small seeds) and *walende,* which is distilled from the makalani palm and tastes similar to vodka. Apart from *walende,* all of these rural confections are brewed in the morning and drunk the same day, and they're all dirt cheap – around N$2 a glass.

Environment

The Land

The oldest desert in the world, the Namib is a garden of burned and blackened-red basalt that spilled out of the earth 130 million years ago in southwest Africa, hardening to form the driest country south of the Sahara. Precious little can grow or thrive in this merciless environment, with the exception of a few uniquely adapted animals and plants, which illustrate the sheer ingenuity of life on earth.

The Namib extends along the country's entire Atlantic coast, and is scored by a number of rivers, which rise in the central plateau but often run dry. Some, like the ephemeral Tsauchab, once reached the sea but now end in calcrete pans. Others flow only during the summer rainy season but, at some former stage, carried huge volumes of water, and carved out dramatic canyons like Fish River.

In wild contrast are the Kavango and Caprivi regions, which are nothing short of well-watered paradises. Bordering Angola, to the north, they are bounded by four great rivers – the Kunene, Okavango, Kwando/Mashi/Linyanti/Chobe and Zambezi – that flow year-round.

Wildlife

Etosha, Namibia's greatest wildlife park, contains a variety of antelope species, as well as other African ungulates, carnivores and

---

WILD HORSES

On the desert plains west of Aus live some of the world's only wild desert-dwelling horses. These horses, whose bony and scruffy appearance belies their probable high-bred ancestry and apparent adaptation to the harsh conditions, are protected inside Diamond Area 1. In years of good rain, they grow fat and their numbers increase to several hundred. Their only source of water is Garub Pan, which is fed by an artificial borehole. The horses may also be valuable for scientific purposes. For instance, they urinate less than domestic horses and are smaller than their supposed ancestors. The horses are also able to go without water for up to five days at a time. These adaptations may be valuable in helping scientists understand how animals cope with changing climatic conditions.

pachyderms. Damaraland, in the northwest, is home to antelopes and other ungulates, and also harbours desert rhinos, elephants and other species that have specially adapted to the arid climate. Hikers in the Naukluft massif may catch sight of elusive Hartmann's mountain zebras, and along the desert coast live jackass penguins, flamingos, Cape fur seals and the rare *Strandwolf* (brown hyena).

As Namibia is mostly arid, its typical vegetation features mainly scrubby bushveld and succulents such as *Euphorbia*. Some unique floral oddities include the *kokerboom* (quiver tree), which is a species of aloe, and the bizarre *Welwitschia mirabilis* (the welwitschia plant). Along the coastal plain around Swakopmund lie the world's most extensive and diverse lichen fields; in dry weather, they appear to be merely plant skeletons, but with the addition of water they burst into colourful bloom.

National Parks

Despite its harsh climate, Namibia has some of the world's grandest national parks, ranging from the world-famous wildlife-oriented Etosha National Park to the immense Namib-Naukluft Park, which protects vast dune fields, desert plains, wild mountains and unique flora. There are also the smaller reserves of the Caprivi region, the renowned Skeleton Coast and the awe-inspiring Fish River Canyon, in /Ai/Ais-Richtersveld Transfrontier Park, which ranks among Africa's most spectacular sights.

In addition to national parks, Namibia has a network of conservancies, which are individual farms supporting either tourist lodges or hunting opportunities. Examples of these are the 200,000-hectare NamibRand Nature Reserve and the 100,000-hectare Gondwana Cañon Park.

Access to most wildlife-oriented parks is limited to enclosed vehicles; no bicycles or motorcycles are allowed. For some parks, such as Etosha and Namib-Naukluft, a 2WD is sufficient, but you need a 4WD in Mamili National Park and Khaudum National Park.

Facilities in Namibian national parks are operated by the semiprivate Namibia Wildlife Resorts (p256), whose main office is in Windhoek. Bookings may be made up to 12 months in advance, and fees must be paid by credit card before the bookings will be confirmed. Parks also charge a daily admission fee per person and per vehicle, payable when you enter.

Booking is always advised for national parks. While you may be able to pick up accommodation at the last minute by just turning up at the park gates, it isn't recommended (especially for Etosha and Sossusvlei). Note that pets aren't permitted in any wildlife-oriented park.

SURVIVAL GUIDE

Directory A–Z

Accommodation

Namibia has an exhaustive (and growing) array of hotels, rest camps, camping grounds, caravan parks, guest farms, backpackers' hostels, B&Bs, guesthouses and safari lodges. It would take an enormous volume to mention everything that's available, so those included here are recommended and/or provide accommodation in areas with few options.

For further information, see the following annual publications, which are distributed at tourist offices: *Namibia: Where to Stay, Welcome to Namibia – Official Visitor's Guide* and the *Namibia B&B Guide*.

B&BS

Bed and breakfast (B&B) establishments are mushrooming all around the country. As they're in private homes, the standard, atmosphere and welcome tends to vary a great deal. Generally speaking, B&Bs are a pleasure to frequent, and can be one of the highlights of any trip to Namibia.

CAMPING

Namibia is campers' heaven, and wherever you go in the country you'll find a campsite nearby. These can vary from a patch of scrubland with basic facilities to well-kitted-out sites featuring concrete ablution blocks with hot and cold running water.

Most towns have caravan parks with bungalows or *rondavels* where you can stay

SLEEPING PRICE RANGES

The following price ranges refer to high-season rates for a double room.

$ less than N$400
$$ N$400-1000
$$$ more than N$1000

for very reasonable rates. On private land, you must secure permission from the landowner.

GUEST FARMS

A growing number of predominantly German-Namibian private farms welcome guests, and provide insight into the white rural lifestyle. Many of these farms have also established hiking routes and set aside areas as wildlife and hunting reserves. In all cases, bookings are essential.

HOSTELS

Backpacker hostels operate in Windhoek, Swakopmund, Walvis Bay, Outjo and Lüderitz. They provide dorm accommodation and cooking facilities. Most offer a very agreeable atmosphere, and are extremely popular with budget travellers.

HOTELS

Hotels in Namibia are much like hotels anywhere else, ranging from tired old has-beens to palaces of luxury and indulgence. Rarely, though, will you find a dirty or unsafe hotel in Namibia given the relatively strict classification system, which rates everything from small guesthouses to four-star hotels.

SAFARI LODGES

Most of Namibia's lodges offer luxury accommodation and superb international cuisine. Rates are very reasonable when compared with similar places in other countries in the region. Even around the popular Etosha National Park, you'll pay a third of what you'd pay for similar lodges in the Okavango Delta.

🏃 Activities

Hiking is a highlight in Namibia, and a growing number of private ranches have established wonderful hiking routes for their guests to enjoy. You'll also find superb routes in the national parks: Daan Viljoen, Namib-Naukluft, Fish River Canyon, Waterberg Plateau and the Ugab River area of the Skeleton Coast.

Sandboarding, which is commercially available in Swakopmund, is very popular. In the same area, operators offer horse and camel riding, quad biking, deep-sea fishing, sea kayaking, birdwatching and skydiving. A growing number of 4WD routes are opening up for a largely South African market, including several popular routes along remote sections of the Namib Desert. Whitewater rafting is available on the Kunene River, but it's extremely expensive; more down to earth is the whitewater canoeing along the Orange River, on the South African border.

Business Hours

Banks 8am or 9am to 3pm Monday to Friday, 8am to 12.30pm Saturday

Bars and clubs 5pm to close (midnight to 3am) Monday to Saturday

Petrol stations only a few open 24 hours; in outlying areas fuel is hard to find after hours and on Sunday

Post offices 8am to 4.30pm Monday to Friday, 8.30am to 11am Saturday

Restaurants and cafes breakfast 8am to 10am, lunch 11am to 3pm, dinner 6pm to

---

PRACTICALITIES

» Namibia uses the metric system for weights and measures.

» Plugs have three round pins (as in South Africa); the current is 220/240V, 50Hz.

» There are a decent number of commercial newspapers, of which the *Namibian* and the *Windhoek Advertiser* are probably the best. The *Windhoek Observer*, published on Saturday, is also good. The two main German-language newspapers are *Allgemeine Zeitung* and *Namibia Nachrichten*.

» The Namibian Broadcasting Corporation (NBC) operates a dozen or so radio stations broadcasting on different wavebands in nine languages. The two main stations in Windhoek are Radio Energy and Radio Kudu; the best pop station is Radio Wave, at 96.7FM in Windhoek.

» The NBC broadcasts government-vetted television programs in English and Afrikaans. News is broadcast at 10pm nightly. Most top-end hotels and lodges with televisions provide access to satellite-supported DSTV, which broadcasts NBC and a cocktail of cable channels.

10pm; some places open all day 8am to 10pm Monday to Saturday

Shops 8am or 9am to 5pm or 6pm Monday to Friday, 9am to 1pm or 5pm Saturday; to 9pm Thursday or Friday

Tourist information offices 8am or 9am to 5pm or 6pm Monday to Friday

Customs Regulations

Any item (except vehicles) from elsewhere in the Southern African Customs Union – Botswana, South Africa, Lesotho and Swaziland – may be imported duty free. From elsewhere, visitors can import duty free 400 cigarettes or 250g of tobacco, 2L of wine, 1L of spirits and 250mL of eau de cologne.

Embassies & Consulates

All of the following representations are in Windhoek (area code 061); opening hours are weekdays only:

Angolan Embassy (Map p250; ☎227535; 3 Dr Agostino Neto St; ⊙9am-3pm)

Botswanan Embassy (Map p248; ☎221941; 101 Nelson Mandela Ave; ⊙8am-1pm & 2-5pm)

French Embassy (Map p248; ☎276700; 1 Goethe St; ⊙9am-noon, afternoons by appointment Mon-Thu, 9am-noon Fri)

German Embassy (Map p250; ☎273100; 6th fl, Sanlam Centre, 154 Independence Ave; ⊙9am-noon Mon-Fri, plus 2-4pm Wed)

Malawian Embassy (Map p250; ☎221391; 56 Bismarck St, Windhoek West; ⊙8am-noon & 2-5pm Mon-Fri)

South African High Commission (Map p248; ☎205 7111; cnr Jan Jonker St & Nelson Mandela Dr, Klein Windhoek; ⊙8.15am-12.15pm)

UK High Commission (Map p250; ☎274800; 116 Robert Mugabe Ave; ⊙8am-1pm & 2-5pm Mon-Thu, 8am-noon Fri)

US Embassy (Map p250; ☎295 8500; 14 Lossen St; ⊙8.30am-noon Mon-Thu)

Zambian High Commission (Map p250; ☎237610; 22 Sam Nujoma Dr, cnr Mandume Ndemufeyo Ave; ⊙9am-1pm & 2-4pm)

Zimbabwean Embassy (Map p250; ☎228134; Gamsberg Bldg, cnr Independence Ave & Grimm St; ⊙8.30am-1pm & 2-4.45pm Mon-Thu, 8.30am-2pm Fri)

✯✯ Festivals & Events

A major local event is **Maherero Day**, on the weekend nearest 26 August, when the Red Flag Herero people gather in traditional dress at Okahandja for a memorial service for the chiefs killed in the German-Nama wars. A similar event, also at Okahandja, is staged by the Mbanderu (Green Flag Herero) on the weekend nearest 11 June. On the weekend nearest 10 October, the White Flag Herero gather in Omaruru to honour their chief, Zeraua.

Among the ethnic European community, events include the **Windhoek Karnival** (WIKA) in late April or early May; the **Küska** (Küste Karnival) at Swakopmund in late August or early September; the **Windhoek Agricultural Show** in late September; and the **Windhoek Oktoberfest** in late October.

Food

The following price ranges refer to a standard main course and are used for Eating reviews in this chapter.

$	less than N$60	
$$	N$60-200	
$$$	more than N$200	

Internet Access

Internet access is firmly established and widespread in Namibia. Most larger or tourist-oriented towns have at least one internet cafe. If you're travelling with a notebook or hand-held computer, more and more hotels, guesthouses and lodges are offering wi-fi connectability to their guests.

Language Courses

At independence in 1990, the official language of Namibia was designated as English, but the first language of most Namibians is either a Bantu language, which includes Owambo, Kavango, Herero and Caprivian languages; or a Khoisan language, including Khoikhoi (Nama/Damara) and San dialects. In addition, Afrikaans is used as a lingua franca, and is the first language of more than 100,000 Namibians of diverse ethnic backgrounds. German is also widely spoken but is the first language of only about 2% of the population. In the far north, Portuguese is the first language of an increasing number of Angolan immigrants.

Maps

Shell Roadmap – Namibia or *InfoMap Namibia* are the best references for remote routes. *InfoMap* contains GPS coordinates and both companies produce maps of

NAMIBIA DIRECTORY A–Z

remote areas such Namibia's far northwest and the Caprivi Strip.

For the average tourist (ie if you're not planning your own remote self-drive safari), these are too detailed. Much better is the *Namibia Map* endorsed by the Roads Authority, which shows major routes and lists accommodation. The *Globetrotter Namibia* map is easy to read and quite detailed.

Beautiful but generally outdated government-survey topographic sheets and aerial photos are available from the Office of the Surveyor General (Map p250; ☎245055; cnr Robert Mugabe Ave & Korn St) in Windhoek.

Money

The Namibian dollar (N$) equals 100 cents, and in Namibia it's pegged to the South African rand (in South Africa, it fetches only about R0.70), which is also legal tender at a rate of 1:1. This can be confusing, given that there are three sets of coins and notes in use, all with different sizes: old South African, new South African and Namibian. Namibian dollar notes come in denominations of N$10, N$20, N$50, N$100 and N$200, and coins in values of 5¢, 10¢, 20¢, 50¢, N$1 and N$5.

ATMS

ATMs are common in major cities and towns, and accept most major Western cards.

CREDIT/DEBIT CARDS

Most major credit cards (especially Visa and MasterCard) are accepted at shops, hotels and restaurants in the larger cities and towns.

TIPPING

Tipping is expected only in upmarket tourist establishments, but many places add a service charge as a matter of course. Tipping is officially prohibited in national parks and reserves, and bargaining is only acceptable when purchasing arts and handicrafts directly from the artist or artisan.

TRAVELLERS CHEQUES

Travellers cheques are falling into disuse in Namibia, though they can still be changed in large cities.

Post

Domestic post generally moves slowly; for example, it can take several weeks for a letter to travel from Windhoek to Lüderitz or Katima Mulilo. Overseas airmail post is normally more efficient, and is limited only by the time it takes the letter to get from where you post it to Windhoek.

Public Holidays

Resort areas are busiest over the Namibian and South African school holidays, which normally occur from mid-December to mid-January, around Easter, from late July to early August, and for two weeks in mid-October.

New Year's Day 1 January

Independence Day 21 March

Good Friday March or April

Easter Sunday March or April

Easter Monday March or April

Ascension Day April or May, 40 days after Easter

Workers' Day 1 May

Cassinga Day 4 May

Africa Day 25 May

Heroes' Day 26 August

Human Rights Day 10 December

Christmas 25 December

Family/Boxing Day 26 December

Safe Travel

Namibia is one of the safest countries in Africa. It's also a huge country with a very sparse population, and even Windhoek smacks more of a provincial town than an urban jungle. Unfortunately, however, crime is on the rise in the larger cities, particularly Windhoek, but a little street sense will go a long way here.

A scam, particularly prevalent in Walvis Bay, Swakopmund and Windhoek in 2012, is for one guy to distract a parked motorist while their accomplice opens a door and grabs your bags from the back seat or from the front passenger seat. So, always keep the doors of your vehicle locked, and be aware of distractions.

Telephone

Namibian area codes all have three digits and begin with 06. When phoning Namibia from abroad, dial the international access code (09 from South Africa, 011 from the US and 00 from most other places), then the country code (264), followed by the area code (without the leading zero) and the desired number.

To phone out of Namibia, dial 00 followed by the country code, area code and number.

Telecom Namibia phonecards are sold at post offices to the value of N$20, N$50 and N$100. They are also available at most shops and a number of hotels. Mobile coverage is usually fine in major towns and cities, and is sparse out on the open road.

Tourist Information

The level of service in Namibia's tourist offices is generally high, and everyone speaks impeccable English, German and Afrikaans.

Namibia's national tourist office, Namibia Tourism (Map p250; ☎290 6000; www. namibiatourism.com.na; 1st fl, Channel Life Towers, 39 Post St Mall), is in Windhoek, where you'll also find the local Windhoek Information & Publicity Office (p256), for more city-specific information.

Visas

All visitors require a passport from their home country that is valid for at least six months after their intended departure date from Namibia. You may also be asked for an onward plane, bus or rail ticket, although checks are rarely made. Nationals of many countries, including Australia, the EU, the USA and most Commonwealth countries do not need a visa to visit Namibia. Citizens of most Eastern European countries do require visas.

Tourists are granted an initial 90 days, which may be extended at the Ministry of Home Affairs (Map p250; ☎061-292 2111; www. mha.gov.na; cnr Kasino St & Independence Ave; ⊙8am-1pm Mon-Fri). For best results, be there when the office opens at 8am, and submit your application at the 3rd-floor offices (as opposed to the desk on the ground floor).

Women Travellers

On the whole Namibia is a safe destination for women travellers, and we receive few complaints about any sort of harassment. Having said that, Namibia is still a conservative society. Many bars are for men only (by either policy or convention), and even in places that welcome women, you may be more comfortable in a group or with a male companion. Note that accepting a drink from a local man is usually construed as a come-on.

The threat of sexual assault isn't any greater in Namibia than in Europe, but women should still avoid walking alone in parks and backstreets, especially at night. Hitching alone is not recommended. Also, never hitch at night and, if possible, find a companion for trips through sparsely populated areas.

In Windhoek and other urban areas, wearing shorts and sleeveless dresses or shirts is fine. However, if you're visiting rural areas, wear knee-length skirts or loose trousers and shirts with sleeves.

Getting There & Away

Entering Namibia

All visitors entering Namibia must hold a passport that is valid for at least six months. Also, allow a few empty pages for stamp-happy immigration officials, especially if you're crossing over to Zimbabwe and/or Zambia to see Victoria Falls.

Air

Most international flights into Namibia arrive at Windhoek's Chief Hosea Kutako International Airport (WDH; ☎061-299 6602; www.airports.com.na), 42km east of the capital. Shorter-haul international flights may also use Windhoek's in-town Eros Airport (ERS; ☎061-299 6500), although this airport mainly serves internal flights and light aircraft.

The main carrier is Air Namibia, which flies routes within Southern Africa as well as to Frankfurt (Germany). Most international airlines stop at Johannesburg or Cape Town in South Africa, where you'll typically switch to a South Africa Airlines (www.flysaa.com) flight for your final leg to Windhoek.

Book well in advance for flights from the following neighbouring countries:

Botswana Air Namibia runs several flights a week between Windhoek and Maun (Botswana).

Zimbabwe Air Namibia flies to Victoria Falls (Zimbabwe) a few times a week.

Zambia You will need to transit through Johannesburg (South Africa) for flights to Lusaka or Livingstone.

Border Crossings

Thanks to the Southern African Customs Union, you can drive through Namibia, Botswana, South Africa and Swaziland with a minimum of fuss. To travel further to the north needs serious consideration as it requires a *carnet de passage,* which can mean heavy expenditure.

If you're driving a hire car into Namibia you will need to present a letter of permission from the rental company saying the car is allowed to cross the border.

ANGOLA

To enter Namibia overland, you'll need an Angolan visa permitting overland entry. At Ruacana Falls, you can enter the border area temporarily without a visa to visit the falls by signing the immigration register.

BOTSWANA

The most commonly used crossing is at Buitepos/Mamuno, between Windhoek and Ghanzi, although the border post at Mohembo/Mahango is also popular. The only other real option is the crossing at Ngoma Bridge across the Chobe River. The Mpalila Island/Kasane border is only available to guests who have booked accommodation at upmarket lodges on the island.

Drivers crossing the border at Mahango must secure an entry permit for Mahango Game Reserve at Popa Falls. This is free if you're transiting, or US$3 per person per day plus US$3 per vehicle per day if you want to drive around the reserve (which is possible in a 2WD).

The public-transport options between Botswana and Namibia are few and far between. Monnakgotla Transport (☎067-350 0419; www.monnakgotla.co.bw) is your best bet: it runs a twice-weekly service between Windhoek and Gaborone on Friday and Sunday (N$440 one way). If you're travelling on to Ghanzi or Maun the bus connects with another service.

SOUTH AFRICA

The Intercape Mainliner (☎061-227847; www.intercape.co.za) bus service runs between Windhoek and Cape Town (South Africa). Students and seniors receive a 15% discount. Bus tickets can be easily booked by phone or via the internet.

ZAMBIA

A kilometre-long bridge (open from 7am to 6pm) spans the Zambezi between Katima Mulilo and Wenela, providing easy access to Livingstone and other destinations in Zambia. If you're heading to the falls, the road is now tarred all the way to Livingstone and is accessible by 2WD vehicle, even in the rainy season.

The Intercape Mainliner bus service runs between Windhoek and Livingstone.

ZIMBABWE

There's no direct border crossing between Namibia and Zimbabwe. To get there you must take the Chobe National Park transit route from Ngoma Bridge through northern Botswana to Kasane/Kazungula, and from there to Victoria Falls (Zimbabwe).

Bus

There's only really one main interregional bus service connecting cities in Namibia with Botswana and South Africa. Intercape Mainliner has services between Windhoek and Johannesburg and Cape Town (South Africa). They also travel northeast to Victoria Falls, and between larger towns within Namibia.

Car & Motorcycle

Crossing land borders with your own vehicle or hire car is generally straightforward as long as you have the necessary paperwork – the vehicle registration documents, proof of insurance and a letter from the hire company stating that you have permission to take the car over the border. You won't need a *carnet de passage* to drive around Namibia and other countries in the Southern African Customs Union (SACU), ie Lesotho, Botswana, South Africa and Swaziland, although if you're planning on travelling further north you will need to obtain one.

A vehicle registered outside Namibia can be driven around the country so long as you have proof of insurance and a letter from the hire-car agency giving you permission to cross the border with the car. Everyone entering Namibia with a foreign-registered car must pay a Cross Border Charge (CBC). Passenger vehicles carrying fewer than 25 passengers are charged N$140. Keep the receipt, because you may be asked to produce it at police roadblocks.

Getting Around

Air

Air Namibia has an extensive network of local flights operating out of Eros Airport. There are six flights per week to Rundu, Katima Mulilo and Ondangwa; and flights three times per week to Lüderitz and Oranjemund and daily to Walvis Bay.

Bicycle

Namibia is a desert country, and makes for a tough biking holiday. Distances are great and horizons are vast; the climate and landscapes are hot and very dry and the sun is intense; and, even along major routes, water is scarce and villages are widely spaced. If all this isn't enough of a deterrent, also bear in mind that bicycles are not permitted in any national parks.

Of course, loads of Namibians do get around by bicycle, and cycling around small cities and large towns is much easier than a cross-country excursion. With that said, be wary of cycling on dirt roads, as punctures from thorn trees are a major problem. Fortunately, however, many local people operate small repair shops, which are fairly common along populated roadsides.

Bus

Namibia's bus services aren't extensive. Luxury services are limited to the Intercape Mainliner (www.intercape.co.za), which has scheduled services from Windhoek to Swakopmund, Walvis Bay, Grootfontein, Rundu and Katima Mulilo.

There are also local combis, which depart when full and follow main routes around the country. They depart from Windhoek's Rhino Park petrol station for dozens of destinations.

Car

The easiest way to get around Namibia is in your own car, and an excellent system of sealed roads runs the length of the country from the South African border at Noordoewer to Ngoma Bridge on the Botswana border and Ruacana in the northwest. Similarly, sealed spur roads connect the main north-south routes to Buitepos, Lüderitz, Swakopmund and Walvis Bay. Elsewhere, towns and most sites of interest are accessible on good gravel roads. Most C-numbered highways are well maintained and passable to all vehicles, and D-numbered roads, although a bit rougher, are mostly (but not always) passable to 2WD vehicles. In the Kaokoveld, however, most D-numbered roads can only be negotiated with a 4WD.

Nearly all the main car-rental agencies have offices at Hosea Kutako Airport in Windhoek. Ideally, you'll want to hire a car for the duration of your holiday, but if cost is an issue you might consider a shorter hire from either Windhoek or Swakopmund. If you can muster a group of four, hiring a car will undoubtedly work out cheaper than an organised tour.

DRIVING LICENCE

Foreigners can drive in Namibia on their home driving licence for up to 90 days, and most (if not all) car-hire companies will accept foreign driving licences for car hire. If your home licence isn't written in English then you'd be better off getting yourself an International Driving Permit (IDP) before you arrive in Namibia.

FUEL & SPARE PARTS

The cost of fuel (petrol) is relatively expensive in Namibia, but prices vary according to the remoteness of the petrol station. Although the odd petrol station is occasionally open 24 hours, most are open from 7am to 7pm.

As a general rule you should never pass a petrol station without filling up, and it is advisable to carry an additional 100L of fuel (either in long-range tanks or jerry cans) if you're planning on driving in more remote areas.

Spare parts are readily available in most major towns, but not elsewhere. If you are planning on some 4WD driving it is advisable to carry the following: two spare tyres, jump leads, tow rope and cable, a few litres of oil, a wheel spanner and a complete tool kit.

HIRE

For a compact car, the least expensive companies charge N$340 to N$500 per day (the longer the hire period, the lower the daily rate) with unlimited kilometres. Hiring a 4WD vehicle opens up remote parts of the country, but it can get expensive at N$650 to N$920 per day.

Most companies include insurance and unlimited kilometres in their standard rates, but some require a minimum rental period before they allow unlimited kilometres. Most companies also require a N$1000 deposit, and won't hire to anyone under the age of 23 (although some go as low as 21).

It's cheaper to hire a car in South Africa and drive it into Namibia, but you need permission from the rental agency, as well as the appropriate paperwork to cross the borders. Most major international car-rental companies will allow you to take a vehicle to neighbouring South Africa, Botswana and Zimbabwe, but only if you clear it with the company beforehand so that they can sort out the paperwork. Rental companies are less happy about drivers going to Zambia, and will usually not allow you to go anywhere else in Africa.

Naturally, you should always check the paperwork carefully, and thoroughly examine the vehicle before accepting it. Car-rental agencies in Namibia have some very high excesses due to the general risks involved in driving on the country's gravel roads. You should also carefully check the condition of your car and never *ever* compromise if you don't feel totally happy with its state of repair.

Additional charges will be levied for the following: dropping off or picking up the car at your hotel (rather than the car-rental office); each additional driver; a 'cleaning fee' (which can amount to US$50!) may be incurred – at the discretion of the rental company; and a 'service fee' may be added.

Always give yourself plenty of time when dropping off your hire car to ensure that the vehicle can be checked over properly for damage etc. The car-rental firm should then issue you with your final invoice before you leave the office.

Avis (www.avis.com) Offices in Windhoek, Swakopmund, Tsumeb and Walvis Bay as well as at Hosea Kutako International Airport.

Budget (www.budget.co.za) Another big agency with offices in Windhoek and Walvis Bay as well as at Hosea Kutako International Airport.

INSURANCE
No matter who you hire your car from, make sure you understand what is included in the price (unlimited kilometres, tax, insurance, collision-waiver and so on) and what your liabilities are. Most local insurance policies do not include cover for damage to windscreens and tyres.

Third-party motor insurance is a minimum requirement in Namibia. However, it is also advisable to take Damage (Collision) Waiver, which costs around N$300 extra per day for a 2WD; and about US$40 per day for a 4WD. Loss (Theft) Waiver is also an extra that is worth having. For both types of insurance, the excess liability is about N$11,500 for a 2WD and N$23,000 for a 4WD. If you're only going for a short period of time it may be worth taking out the Super Collision Waiver, which covers absolutely everything, albeit at a price.

PURCHASE
Unless you're going to be staying in Namibia for several years, it's not worth purchasing a vehicle in-country. The best place to buy a vehicle is across the border in South Africa.

ROAD HAZARDS
In addition to its fantastic system of tarred roads, Namibia has everything from high-speed gravel roads to badly maintained main routes, farm roads, bush tracks, sand tracks and challenging 4WD routes. Driving under these conditions requires special techniques, appropriate vehicle preparation, a bit of practice and a heavy dose of caution.

ROAD RULES
To drive a car in Namibia, you must be at least 21 years old. As in most other Southern African countries, traffic keeps to the left side of the road. The national speed limit is 120km/h on paved roads, 80km/h on gravel roads and 40km/h in all national parks and reserves. When passing through towns and villages, assume a speed limit of 60km/h, even in the absence of any signs.

Highway police use radar and love to fine motorists (about N$75, plus an additional N$7.5 for every 10km you exceed the limit) for speeding. Sitting on the roof of a moving vehicle is illegal, and wearing seat belts (where installed) is compulsory in the front (but not back) seats. Drink-driving is also against the law, and your insurance policy will be invalid if you have an accident while drunk. Driving without a licence is also a serious offence.

If you have an accident causing injury, it must be reported to the authorities within 48 hours. If vehicles have sustained only minor damage and there are no injuries – and all parties agree – you can exchange names and addresses and sort it out later through your insurance companies.

Hitching
Hitching is possible in Namibia, but it's illegal in national parks, and even main highways see relatively little traffic. Truck drivers generally expect to be paid around N$11.50 per 100km, so agree on a price before climbing in. Your best options for lifts are Windhoek backpacker lodges, where you can post notices about rides wanted or offered.

Tours
Namibia's public-transport system will get you to population centres but not the

sites most visitors want to see: the Skeleton Coast, Damaraland, the Kaokoveld, the Kunene River, Fish River Canyon, Sossusvlei, the Naukluft and so on. Therefore, even those who would normally spurn organised tours may want to consider joining an inexpensive participation safari or a more luxurious option.

Train

Trans-Namib Railways (☎061-298 2032; www.transnamib.com.na) connects some major towns, but trains are extremely slow – as one reader remarked, moving 'at the pace of an energetic donkey cart'. In addition, passenger and freight cars are mixed on the same train, and trains tend to stop at every post, which means that rail travel isn't popular and services are rarely fully booked.

Windhoek is Namibia's rail hub, with services south to Keetmanshoop, north to Tsumeb, west to Swakopmund and east to Gobabis. Economy- and business-class seats are available,but, although most services operate overnight, sleepers are not available. Book at train stations or through the Windhoek booking office; tickets must be collected before 4pm on the day of departure.

South Africa

Best Places to Eat

» Bizerca Bistro (p343)
» Halfway House (p484)
» Narina Trogon (p446)
» Spice (p405)
» Tasting Room (p354)

Best Places to Stay

» Bulungula Backpackers (p394)
» Hobbit Boutique Hotel (p430)
» Palace of the Lost City (p480)
» POD (p342)

Why Go?

When Archbishop Desmond Tutu called South Africa the 'Rainbow Nation', his words described the very essence of what makes this country extraordinary. Certainly, the blend of peoples and cultures that his oft-used moniker referred to is instantly evident, but the country's diversity stretches far beyond its people.

Without straying beyond South Africa's borders you can sleep under the stars in a desert or hike to snow-capped peaks. The hills of Zululand and the Wild Coast provide a bucolic antidote to the bustle of large cities like Johannesburg and Durban. Wildlife watching ranges from remote safari walks to up-close encounters with waddling penguins.

Variety continues in the cuisine, with the delicate (West Coast seafood), the hearty (Karoo meat feasts), the fragrant (Cape Malay stews) and the spicy (Durban curries) all represented. And southwest of it all sits Cape Town, where gourmands, art lovers, thrill seekers and beach babes come together to sip, surf and sunbathe in beautiful surrounds.

When to Go

Cape Town

Apr-Aug Low season bargains; ideal wildlife-watching conditions; whales on the Western Cape coast.

Sep-Nov Spring flowers bloom; ideal weather for KwaZulu-Natal beaches and Karoo exploration.

Dec-Feb Coastal places fills up as South Africans escape the inland heat; busy but vibrant time.

CAPE TOWN

📞021 / POP 3.1 MILLION

Prepare to fall in love, as South Africa's 'Mother City' is an old pro at capturing people's hearts. And who wouldn't swoon at the sight of magnificent Table Mountain, its summit draped with cascading clouds, its flanks coated with unique flora and vineyards, its base fringed by golden beaches? Few cities can boast such a wonderful national park at their heart or provide the range of adventurous activities that take full advantage of it.

The World Design Capital 2014 is in the process of using design to transform the city and the quality of life of its population. From the brightly painted facades of the Bo-Kaap and the bathing chalets of Muizenberg to striking street art and the Afro-chic decor of countless guesthouses, this is one good-looking metropolis.

Above all it's a multicultural city where nearly everyone has a fascinating, sometimes heartbreaking, story to tell. When the time comes to leave, you may find your heart breaking too.

History

Long before the Dutch East India Company (Vereenigde Oost-Indische Compagnie; VOC) established a base here in 1652, the Cape Town area was settled by the San and Khoikhoi nomadic peoples, collectively known as the Khoisan. The indigenous people shunned the Dutch, so the VOC imported slaves from Madagascar, India, Ceylon, Malaya and Indonesia to deal with the colony's chronic labour shortage. In time the slaves intermixed with the Khoisan; the offspring of these unions formed the basis of sections of today's coloured population.

In the 150-odd years of Dutch rule, Kaapstad, as the Cape settlement became known, thrived and gained a wider reputation as the 'Tavern of the Seven Seas', a riotous port used by sailors travelling between Europe and the East. Following the British defeat of the Dutch in 1806 at Bloubergstrand, 25km north of Cape Town, the colony was ceded to the Crown. The slave trade was abolished in 1808, and all slaves were emancipated in 1833.

An outbreak of bubonic plague in 1901 was blamed on black African workers (although it actually came on boats from Argentina) and gave the government an excuse to introduce racial segregation. Blacks were moved to two locations; one near the docks and the other at Ndabeni on the eastern flank of Table Mountain. This was the start of what would later develop into the townships of the Cape Flats.

◉ Sights

CITY BOWL & SURROUNDS

The commercial heart of Cape Town, City Bowl is squeezed between Table Mountain, Signal Hill and the harbour. Immediately to the west is the Bo-Kaap, De Waterkant is to the north and Zonnebloem (once known as District Six) lies to the southeast.

District Six Museum   MUSEUM
(Map p330; 📞021-466 7200; www.districtsix.co.za; 25A Buitenkant St; adult/child R30/5, walking tour per person R120; ⊙9am-2pm Mon, 9am-4pm Tue-Sat) This moving museum is as much for the people of the now-vanished District Six as it is about them. Prior to the forced evictions of the 1960s and '70s, some 50,000 people of all races lived in the area. Many township tours stop here first to explain the history of the pass laws, which were designed to limit the movements of all non-white citizens.

Displays include a floor map of District Six on which former residents have labelled where their demolished homes and features of their neighbourhood once stood. Many of the staff, practically all displaced residents themselves, have heartbreaking stories to tell. The museum's annex in the nearby Sacks Futeran Building (Map p330; 15 Buitenkant St) houses permanent exhibitions related to soccer in the Cape.

Castle of Good Hope   MUSEUM
(Map p330; www.castleofgoodhope.co.za; entrance on Buitenkant St; adult/child R28/12; ⊙9am-4pm, guided tours 11am, noon & 2pm Mon-Sat; 🅿; 🚏St George's) Built by the Dutch between 1666 and 1679 to defend Cape Town, this stone-walled pentagonal castle remains the headquarters for the Western Cape military command. The Military Museum is interesting, as are the displays of antiques and decorative arts. Don't miss climbing up to the bastions for an elevated view of the castle's layout and across to Grand Pde.

Company's Gardens   GARDENS
(Map p330; ⊙7am-7pm; 🚏Dorp) These shady green gardens, which started as the vegetable patch for the Dutch East India Company, are a lovely place to relax. The squirrels that scamper here were imported to Cape Town from North America by Cecil Rhodes, whose

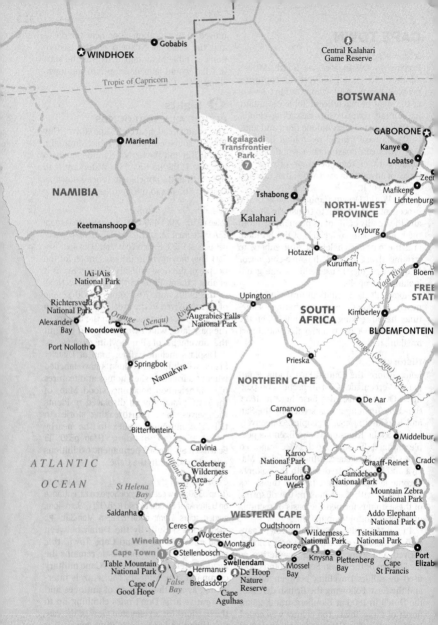

South Africa Highlights

❶ Tackling Table Mountain, paddling with penguins or just lazing on Atlantic beaches in **Cape Town** (p323)

❷ Joining rangers at **Kruger National Park** (p458) on a

safari of the most involving kind – on foot

❸ Hiking towards the peaks of the **Drakensberg** (p416) range for a view of

the Amphitheatre, an 8km mountain curtain

❹ Brushing up on recent history and learning about township life in bustling **Soweto** (p451)

ZIMBABWE

Mapungubwe NP · Musina
Banhine National Park

Louis Trichardt (Makhado) · Thohoyandou
Limpopo River
MOZAMBIQUE
Tropic of Capricorn

Great Limpopo Transfrontier Park
Ellisras · Polokwane (Pietersburg)
Limpopo National Park

LIMPOPO
Phalaborwa · Massingir
Inhambane

Marakele National Park
River
Blyde River Canyon Nature Reserve

Olifants

Pilanesberg National Park
un ity
Nelspruit
Sabie
Kruger National Park
Macia
Xai-Xai

PRETORIA · Middelburg
Pigg's Peak
Komatipoort

Rustenburg
Johannesburg
MAPUTO

Soweto
GAUTENG
MPUMALANGA
MBABANE

Potchefstroom
Vereeniging
Ermelo
Manzini

ksdorp
Standerton
SWAZILAND

Kroonstad
Golden Gate Highlands National Park
Piet Retief
Hlathikulu
Kosi Bay Nature Reserve

Welkom
Bohlakong
Volksrust
Golela
Sodwana Bay National Park

Senekal
Vryheid
iSimangaliso Wetland Park

Clarens
Harrismith
Hluhluwe-iMfolozi Park

haba Ichu
Drakensberg
Ladysmith
Dundee
Mtubatuba

MASERU
Estcourt
Zululand
Empangeni · Richards Bay

LESOTHO
uKhahlamba-Drakensberg Park
Pietermaritzburg
KWAZULU-NATAL

Mafeteng
Durban

Mohale's Hoek
Kokstad
Amanzimtoti

Aliwal North
Port Shepstone

EASTERN CAPE
Mkambati Nature Reserve

Mthatha
Port St Johns

Queenstown
Hluleka Nature Reserve
INDIAN

Great Kei River
Wild Coast
OCEAN

Dwesa Nature Reserve

Bhisho
hamstown · East London

Port Alfred

N 0 ——— 200 km
0 ——— 100 miles

⑤ Choosing between a hammock and the beach at one of the laid-back hostels along the **Wild Coast** (p391)

⑥ Sipping on world-class wines and enjoying posh nosh in the magnificent Cape Dutch surrounds of the **Winelands** (p349)

⑦ Watching a black-maned lion nap under a thorn tree in the crimson Kalahari wonderland of **Kgalagadi Transfrontier Park** (p486)

Cape Town & the Peninsula

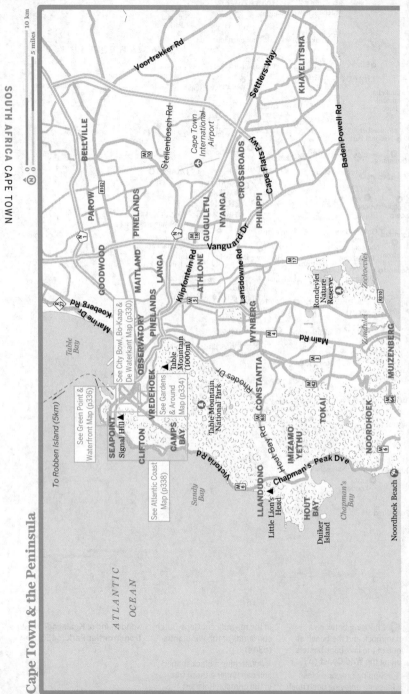

ATLANTIC OCEAN

To Robben Island (5km)

Table Bay

Sandy Bay

Chapman's Bay

Duiker Island

Noordhoek Beach

See Green Point & Waterfront Map (p336)

See City Bowl, Bo-Kaap & De Waterkant Map (p330)

See Gardens & Around Map (p334)

See Atlantic Coast Map (p338)

SEAPOINT

Signal Hill ▲

CLIFTON

CAMPS BAY

Table Mountain (1000m) ▲

VREDEHOEK

OBSERVATORY

PINELANDS

Marine Dr

Koeberg Rd

GOODWOOD

BELLVILLE

PAROW

R102

N1

Voortrekker Rd

Stellenbosch Rd

Cape Town International Airport

M10

Settlers Way

KHAYELITSHA

Baden Powell Rd

CROSSROADS

NYANGA

GUGULETU

M18

N2

Cape Flats Fwy

PHILIPPI

Vanguard Dr

LANGA

ATHLONE

Klipfontein Rd

M5

MAITLAND

PINELANDS

Lansdowne Rd

WYNBERG

M4

M17

Rondevlei Nature Reserve

R310

Zeekovlei

Zandvlei

MUIZENBERG

M64

M6

M3

M42

NOORDHOEK

TOKAI

M63

CONSTANTIA

Main Rd

Rhodes Dr

Table Mountain National Park

IMIZAMO YETHU

Hout Bay Rd

LLANDUDNO

Little Lion's Head ▲

Chapman's Peak Dve

HOUT BAY

Victoria Rd

M6

5 miles

10 km

0

0

N

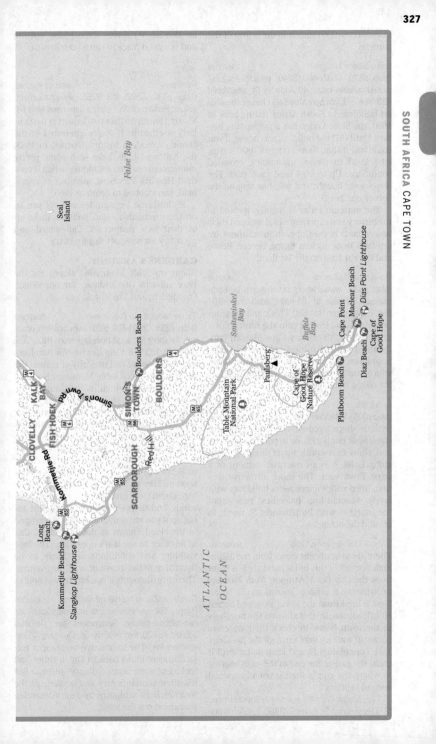

statue (Map p330) stands in the centre of the gardens.

Iziko Slave Lodge MUSEUM

(Map p330; ☎021-460 8240; www.iziko.org.za/museums/slave-lodge; 49 Adderley St; adult/child R20/free; ☺10am-5pm Mon-Sat) One of the oldest buildings in South Africa, dating back to 1660, the Slave Lodge has a fascinating history. Until 1811 the building was home, if you could call it that, to as many as 1000 slaves, who lived in damp, unsanitary, crowded conditions. Up to 20% died each year. The slaves were bought and sold just around the corner on Spin St.

The museum today is mainly devoted to the history and experience of slaves and their descendants in the Cape, although there are artefacts from ancient Egypt, Greece, Rome and the Far East on the 1st floor.

Bo-Kaap Museum MUSEUM

(Map p330; www.iziko.org.za/museums/bo-kaap-museum; 71 Wale St, Bo-Kaap; adult/child R10/free; ☺10am-5pm Mon-Sat) This small museum provides some insight into the lifestyle of a prosperous 19th-century Cape Muslim family, and a somewhat idealised view of Islamic practice in Cape Town. The house itself, which was built between 1763 and 1768, is the oldest in the area.

Long St NEIGHBOURHOOD

(Map p330) Whether you come to browse the antique shops, secondhand bookshops and streetwear boutiques, or to party at the bars and clubs that crank up at night, a stroll along Long St is an essential element of a Cape Town visit. The most attractive section, lined with Victorian-era buildings with lovely wrought-iron balconies, runs from the junction with Buitensingel St north to around the Strand.

Signal Hill & Noon Gun VIEWPOINT

There are magnificent views from the 350m-high summit of this hill separating Sea Point from the City Bowl. At noon from Monday to Saturday, a cannon known as the Noon Gun is fired from the lower slopes of Signal Hill. Traditionally this allowed the burghers in the town below to check their watches. It's a stiff walk up here through the Bo-Kaap. Take Longmarket St and keep going until it ends; the gate at the end of the path leading to where the gun is fired is usually opened around 11.30am.

The Noon Gun Tearoom & Restaurant (273 Longmarket St; mains R70-100; ☺lunch & din-

ner Mon-Sat; P) serves Cape Malay cuisine and is a good place to catch your breath.

FREE Houses of Parliament NOTABLE BUILDING

(Map p330; ☎021-403 2266; www.parliament.gov.za; Parliament St; ☺tours 9am-noon Mon-Fri) Visiting South Africa's parliament is particularly worthwhile if you're interested in the country's modern history. Opened in 1885, the hallowed halls have seen some pretty momentous events, including when President Hendrik Verwoerd, architect of apartheid, was stabbed to death in 1966.

Enthusiastic tour guides will fill you in on the mechanisms and political make-up of their new democracy. Call ahead and present your passport to gain entry.

GARDENS & AROUND

Rising up Table Mountain's slopes are the ritzy suburbs of Gardens, Tamboerskloof, Oranjezicht and Vredehoek.

Table Mountain Cableway VIEWPOINT

(Map p338; ☎021-424 8181; www.tablemountain.net; Tafelberg Rd; adult one-way/return R105/205, child R53/100; ☺8.30am-7pm Feb-Nov, 8am-10pm Dec & Jan) For the vast majority of visitors the main attraction of Table Mountain National Park is the 1086m-high mountain itself, the top of which can easily be accessed by the cableway; the views from the revolving car and the summit are phenomenal. At the top there are souvenir shops, a good cafe and some easy walks to follow. Departures are every 10 minutes in high season (December to February) and every 20 minutes in low season (May to September), but the cableway doesn't operate when it's dangerously windy, and there's obviously little point going up if you are simply going to be wrapped in the cloud known as the 'tablecloth'. Call in advance to see if it's operating. The best visibility and conditions are likely to be first thing in the morning or in the evening. There are discounts if you buy tickets online.

South African National Gallery GALLERY

(Map p334; www.iziko.org.za/museums/south-african-national-gallery; Government Ave, Gardens; adult/child R20/free; ☺10am-5pm Tue-Sun; ▣Government Ave) The impressive permanent collection here harks back to Dutch times and includes some extraordinary pieces. But it's often contemporary works, such as the *Butcher Boys* sculpture by Jane Alexander, that stand out the most.

South African Jewish Museum MUSEUM
(Map p334; www.sajewishmuseum.co.za; 88 Hatfield St, Gardens; adult/child R40/free; ☉10am-5pm Sun-Thu, 10am-2pm Fri; ℗; ⬚Government Ave) This imaginatively designed museum incorporates the beautifully restored Old Synagogue (1863). In the same complex, the Cape Town Holocaust Centre (Map p334; www.holocaust.org.za; admission free; ☉10am-5pm Sun-Thu, 10am-2pm Fri) is worth a visit. Although small, the centre packs a lot in with a considerable emotional punch. You need photo ID to enter the complex.

GREEN POINT & WATERFRONT

Robben Island & Nelson
Mandela Gateway MUSEUM
(☎021-413 4220; www.robben-island.org.za; adult/child R230/120; ☉ferries depart at 9am, 11am, 1pm & 3pm, weather permitting; ⬚Waterfront) Used as a prison from the early days of the VOC right up until 1996, this Unesco World Heritage Site is preserved as a memorial to those who spent many years incarcerated here, such as Nelson Mandela.

While we heartily recommend going to Robben Island, a visit here is not without its drawbacks. The first hurdle is getting a ticket – in peak times these often sell out days in advance. Reserve well in advance via the web, or book a ticket in conjunction with a township tour – many tour operators have access to blocks of tickets not available to the public. The packed guided tour allows a maximum of two hours on the island (plus a 30-minute boat ride in both directions). One of the former inmates will lead you around the prison.

The tours, which have set departure and return times, include a walk through the old prison (with the obligatory peek into Mandela's cell), as well as a 45-minute bus ride around the island with commentary on the various places of note. If you're lucky, you'll have about 10 minutes to wander around on your own.

Tours depart from the Nelson Mandela Gateway (Map p336; admission free; ☉9am-8.30pm) beside the clock tower at the Waterfront. Even if you don't plan a visit to the island, it's worth dropping by the museum here, with its focus on the struggle for equality. Also preserved as a small museum is the Waterfront's Jetty 1 (Map p336; admission free; ☉7am-9pm), the departure point for Robben Island when it was a prison.

V&A Waterfront NEIGHBOURHOOD
(www.waterfront.co.za; ℗; ⬚Waterfront) Commonly referred to as just the Waterfront, this historic working harbour has a spectacular setting and many tourist-oriented attractions, including masses of shops, restaurants, bars, cinemas and cruises. The Victoria and Alfred Basins date from 1860 and are named after Queen Victoria and her son. In the Alfred Basin you'll see ships under repair, and there are always seals splashing around or lazing on the giant tyres that line the docks.

Check out the statues of South Africa's four Nobel Prize winners – Nelson Mandela, Desmond Tutu, Albert Luthuli and FW de Klerk – at Nobel Square (Map p336). Nearby is the excellent Two Oceans Aquarium (Map p336; www.aquarium.co.za; Dock Rd; adult/child R112/55; ☉9.30am-6pm), home to denizens of the deep including ragged-tooth sharks, seals, penguins, turtles, an astounding kelp forest open to the sky, and pools in which kids can touch sea creatures. Qualified divers can get into the water for a closer look (R625, including dive gear). Try to coincide your visit with feeding time, either at the penguin exhibit (11.45am and 2.30pm daily) or the main aquarium (3pm daily, shark feeding Sunday only).

Cape Town Stadium STADIUM
(Map p336; ☎021-417 0101; Granger Bay Blvd, Green Point; tours adult/child R45.60/17.10; ☉tours 10am, noon & 2pm Tue-Sat; ℗; ⬚Stadium) The city's most striking piece of contemporary architecture cost R4.5 billion and seats 55,000. It's the home ground of the soccer team Ajax Cape Town and has been used for concerts by the likes of U2 and Lady Gaga. Hour-long tours take you behind the scenes into the VIP and press boxes as well as the teams' dressing rooms.

ATLANTIC COAST

Cape Town's Atlantic Coast is all about spectacular scenery and soft-sand beaches. Strong winds can be a downer and although it's possible to shelter from the summer southeasterlies at some beaches, the water at them all, flowing straight from the Antarctic, is freezing. From Sea Point (best visited for its excellent outdoor swimming pavilion), you can head down to Clifton and Camps Bay.

Clifton Beaches BEACHES
(Map p338) Giant granite boulders split the four linked beaches at Clifton, accessible by steps from Victoria Rd. Almost always

City Bowl, Bo-Kaap & De Waterkant

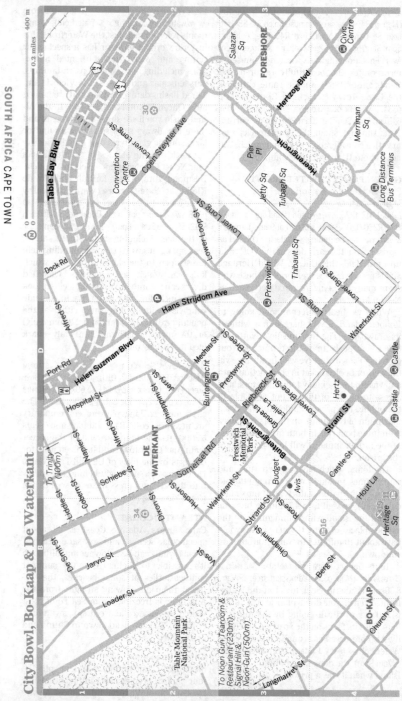

400 m

0.2 miles

FORESHORE

Salazar Sq

Civic Centre

Hertzog Blvd

Table Bay Blvd

Coen Steytler Ave

Convention Centre

Lower Long St

Merriman Sq

Pier Pl

Heerengracht

Jetty Sq

Tulbagh Sq

Long Distance Bus Terminus

Lower Loop St

Thibault Sq

Prestwich

Hans Strijdom Ave

Dock Rd

Long St

Lower Burg St

Alfred St

Port Rd

Waterkant St

Mechau St

Bree St

Prestwich St

Buitengracht

Jerry St

Waterkant St

Hertz

Strand St

Chiappini St

Hospital St

Alfred St

Lower Bree St

Riebeeck St

Grouse La

Leie La

Castle

Castle

DE WATERKANT

Napier St

Schiebe St

Somerset Rd

Buitengracht St

Prestwich Memorial Park

Budget

Castle St

Little St

Cobern St

Hudson St

Waterkant St

Avis

Dixon St

Hout La

Jarvis St

Chiappini St

Strand St

Rose St

Heritage Sq

Berg St

Vos St

Loader St

Table Mountain National Park

To Noon Gun Tearoom & Restaurant (230m); Signal Hill & Noon Gun (500m)

BO-KAAP

Church St

Longmarket St

To Trinity (100m)

De Smit St

Helen Suzman Blvd

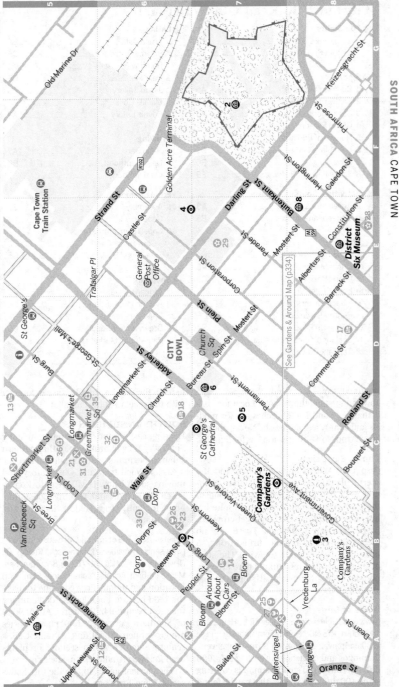

Old Marine Dr

Cape Town
Train Station

Golden Acre Terminal

Strand St

Castle St

Darling St

Buitenkant St

District
Six Museum

Keizersgracht St

Caledon St

Harrington St

Primrose St

Constitution St

Commercial St

Albertus St

Barrack St

Roeland St

Bouquet St

Dean St

Orange St

Itensingel

Buitensingel

Trafalgar Pl

General
Post
Office

Parade St

Corporation St

Mostert St

Plein St

Church
Sq

Spin St

Mostert St

Parliament St

CITY
BOWL

Adderley St

Bureau St

Church St

St George's
Cathedral

Longmarket St

St George's Mall

Burg St

St George's

Longmarket
Sq

Greenmarket
Sq

Wale St

Dorp

Keerom St

Queen Victoria St

Company's
Gardens

Government Ave

Company's
Gardens

Vredenburg La

Van Riebeeck
Sq

Shortmarket St

Longmarket St

Bree St

Loop St

Dorp St

Dorp

Leeuwen St

Long St

Pepper St

Bloem

Bloem St

Bloem

Around
About

Bloem Cars

Wale St

Buitengracht St

Upper Leeuwen St

Jordan St

Buiten St

See Gardens & Around Map (p334)

City Bowl, Bo-Kaap & De Waterkant

sheltered from the wind, these are Cape Town's top sunbathing spots. Local lore has it that No 1 and No 2 beaches are for models and confirmed narcissists, No 3 is the gay beach, and No 4 – the busiest – is for families.

Camps Bay Beach   BEACH
(Map p338) With soft white sand, and the spectacular Twelve Apostles of Table Mountain as a backdrop, Camps Bay is one of the city's most popular beaches despite being one of the windiest. It can get crowded, particularly on weekends. There are no lifeguards on duty and the surf is strong, so take care if you decide to swim. The strip of smart bars and restaurants here are very popular places for drinks at sunset or just general all-day lounging.

World of Birds   AVIARY
(www.worldofbirds.org.za; Valley Rd, Hout Bay; adult/child R75/40; ⊙9am-5pm, monkey jungle 11.30am-1pm & 2-3.30pm; P) Barbets, weavers, flamingos and ostriches are among the 3000 different birds and small mammals covering some 400 different species that can be found here. In the monkey jungle you can interact with the cheeky squirrel monkeys.

SOUTHERN SUBURBS

Heading east around Table Mountain along Sir Lowry Rd will bring you to the southern suburbs, beginning with the bohemian, edgy areas of Woodstock and Observatory and moving south below Devil's Peak to Rondebosch, Newlands and wealthy Constantia, home to South Africa's oldest vineyards and wine estates.

Kirstenbosch Botanical Gardens   GARDENS
(www.sanbi.org/gardens/kirstenbosch; Rhodes Dr, Newlands; adult/child R42/10; ⊙8am-7pm Sep-Mar, 8am-6pm Apr-Aug, conservatory 9am-5pm) Location and unique flora combine to make these 36-hectare botanical gardens among the most beautiful in the world. About 9000 of Southern Africa's 22,000 plant species are grown here. You'll find a Braille trail, a sculpture garden and a section for plants used for *muti* (traditional medicine).

The gardens are a stop on the City Sightseeing Cape Town bus.

Groot Constantia WINERY
(www.grootconstantia.co.za; Groot Constantia Rd, Constantia; tastings R30, museum adult/child R20/ free, cellar tours R40 incl tasting; ☉9am-5.30pm; **P**) Simon van der Stel's manor house, a superb example of Cape Dutch architecture, is maintained as a museum at Groot Constantia. Set in beautiful grounds, the estate can become busy with tour groups, but is big enough for you to escape the crowds. Cellar tours depart hourly from 10am to 4pm and there are walking tours of the vineyard daily at 2pm, weather permitting (R50 including tasting).

Other wineries in the Constantia area include Steenberg (www.steenberg-vineyards. co.za; Steenberg Rd, Steenberg; ☉10am-6pm), which has plush accommodation, two dining options and an 18-hole golf course, and Klein Constantia (www.kleinconstantia. com; Klein Constantia Rd, Constantia; tastings free; ☉tastings 9am-5pm Mon-Fri, 9am-3pm Sat), home to the sweet *vin de constance*, Napoleon's preferred tipple.

FREE Rhodes Memorial MONUMENT
(www.rhodesmemorial.co.za/memorial.aspx; off M3, below Devil's Peak, Groote Schuur Estate, Rondebosch; ☉7am-7pm; **P**) This impressive granite memorial to the mining magnate and former prime minister stands on the eastern slopes of Table Mountain.

There are sweeping views from the memorial to the Cape Flats and the mountain ranges beyond and a pleasant restaurant (Rhodes Memorial; ☉7am-5pm; **P**) specialising in Cape Malay dishes. The exit for the memorial is at the Princess Anne Interchange on the M3.

SOUTHERN PENINSULA

Cape of Good Hope NATURE RESERVE
(www.sanparks.org/parks/table_mountain; admission adult/child R90/40; ☉6am-6pm Oct-Mar, 7am-5pm Apr-Sep; **P**) Commonly called Cape Point, this 7750-hectare section of Table Mountain National Park includes awesome scenery, fantastic walks and often-deserted beaches. Some 250 species of birds live here, including cormorants and a family of ostriches that hangs out near the Cape of Good Hope, the southwestern-most point of the continent.

Many people visit on organised bus tours but, if you have the time, exploring the reserve on foot or by bicycle is much more rewarding. Bear in mind, though, that there is minimal shade and that the weather can change quickly.

It's not a hard walk uphill, but if you're feeling lazy the Flying Dutchman Funicular (www.capepoint.co.za; one-way/return adult R39/49, child R16/21; ☉9am-5.30pm) runs up from beside the restaurant to the souvenir kiosk next to the old lighthouse, dating from 1860.

Boulders PENGUIN COLONY
(www.sanparks.org/parks/table_mountain; adult/ child R45/20; ☉7am-7.30pm Dec & Jan, 8am-6.30pm Feb-May & Sep-Nov, 8am-5pm Jun-Aug) This picturesque area with a number of enormous boulders dividing sandy coves is home to a colony of African penguins. A boardwalk runs from the visitor centre at the Foxy Beach end of the protected area (another part of Table Mountain National Park) to Boulders Beach, where you can get down onto the sand and mingle with the waddling birds. The sea is calm and shallow in the coves, so Boulders is popular with families and can get extremely crowded, especially on holidays and at weekends.

Muizenberg Beach BEACH
(Beach Rd, Muizenberg; water slide 1hr/day pass R35/65; ☉water slide 9.30am-5.30pm Sat & Sun, daily in school holidays; ⓡKalk Bay) This surf beach, popular with families, is famous for its row of primary-colour-painted Victorian bathing chalets. Surfboards can be hired and lessons are available. The beach is very shallow at the shore and the sea is generally safer than elsewhere along the peninsula. At the eastern end of the promenade there's a water slide.

🏃 **Activities**

Abseiling & Kloofing

Abseil Africa ABSEILING
(Map p330; ☎021-424 4760; www.abseilafrica. co.za; 297 Long St; abseiling R650) The 112m drop off the top of Table Mountain with this long-established outfit is a guaranteed adrenaline rush. Abseil Africa also offers kloofing (canyoning) trips around Cape Town. The sport of clambering into and out of kloofs (cliffs or gorges) also entails abseiling, climbing, hiking, swimming and jumping.

Cycling

Downhill Adventures CYCLING, MOUNTAIN BIKING
(Map p334; ☎021-422 0388; www.downhilladventures.com; cnr Orange & Kloof Sts, Gardens; activities from R595; ⓑBuitensingel) This adrenaline-

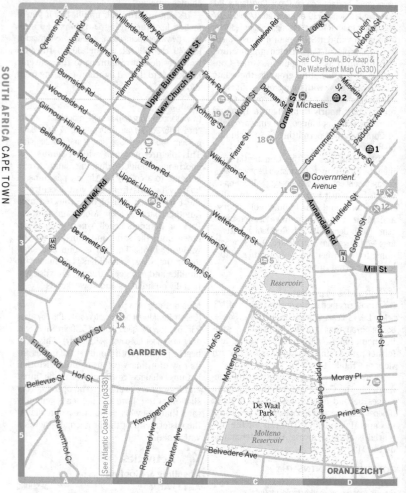

See City Bowl, Bo-Kaap &
De Waterkant Map (p330)

Michaelis

Government
Avenue

Reservoir

GARDENS

De Waal
Park

Molteno
Reservoir

Belvedere Ave

ORANJEZICHT

See Atlantic Coast Map (p338)

focused company offers a variety of cycling trips, including a thrilling mountain-bike ride down from the lower cable station on Table Mountain, mountain biking in the Tokai Forest, or a pedal through the Constantia Winelands and the Cape of Good Hope.

Diving

Table Bay Diving   DIVING
(Map p336; ☎021-419 8822; www.tablebaydiving.com; Quay 5, Shop 7, Waterfront; ☐Breakwater) This reputable operator is based at the Waterfront. Shore dives are R250, boat dives R300 and full equipment hire R300. Its

open-water PADI course is R3300 and it can also arrange shark-cage diving trips to Gansbaai.

In the Blue   DIVING
(Map p338; ☎021-434 3358; www.diveschoolcapetown.co.za; 88B Main Rd, Sea Point; open-water PADI courses from R3450, shore/boat dives R200/300, gear hire per day R380) Offers a number of excellent shore and boat dives.

Hiking & Rock Climbing

The mountainous spine of the Cape Peninsula is a hiker's and rock climber's paradise, but it's not without its dangers, chief

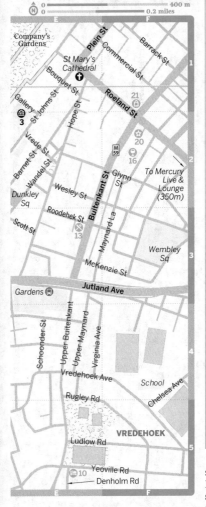

Gardens & Around

◎ Sights

	Cape Town Holocaust Centre	(see 1)
	Old Synagogue	(see 1)
1	South African Jewish Museum	D2
2	South African Museum	D1
3	South African National Gallery	E2

✪ Activities, Courses & Tours

4	Downhill Adventures	C1

🛏 Sleeping

5	Ashanti Gardens	C3
6	Backpack	C1
7	Cactusberry Lodge	D4
8	Cape Cadogan	B3
9	Hippo Boutique Hotel	C1
10	Mannabay	E5
11	Mount Nelson Hotel	C2

✪ Eating

12	Aubergine	D3
13	Dog's Bollocks	E3
14	Manna Epicure	B4
15	Maria's	D2

🍷 Drinking

16	Perseverance Tavern	F2
	Planet	(see 11)
17	Power & the Glory/Black Ram	B2

✪ Entertainment

18	Labia	C2
19	Labia on Kloof	C2
20	Mahogany Lounge	F2

🛍 Shopping

21	Book Lounge	F1

of which are the capricious weather conditions. **Venture Forth** (☎086 110 6548, 021-554 3225; www.ventureforth.co.za; 4 Drummond Rd, West Beach) offers excellent guided hikes and rock climbs with enthusiastic, savvy guides. Outings (around R500 per person) are tailored to individual requirements and aim to get you off the beaten track.

Kayaking & Surfing

**Boardroom Adventure
Centre**   KAYAKING, SURFING
(☎021-790 8132; www.theboardroomadventures. co.za; 37 Victoria Rd, Hout Bay; kayaking/surf les-

sons from R280) Kayaking out to Duiker Island or around Hout Bay and various surfing trips are offered by the guys at this surf-gear rental shop. It also has bikes for rent (per hour/day R50/160).

Sea Kayak Simon's Town   KAYAKING
(☎082 501 8930; www.kayakcapetown.co.za; 62 St Georges St, Simon's Town; ☒Simon's Town) Paddle out to the penguins at Boulders (R250) with this Simon's Town–based operation. It also offers a variety of other tours, including one to Cape Point (R950).

Gary's Surf School   SANDBOARDING, SURFING
(☎021-788 9839; www.garysurf.co.za; Beach Rd, Surfer's Corner, Muizenberg; ☺8.30am-5pm; ☒Muizenberg) If genial surfing coach Gary Kleynhans can't get you to stand on a board

Green Point & Waterfront

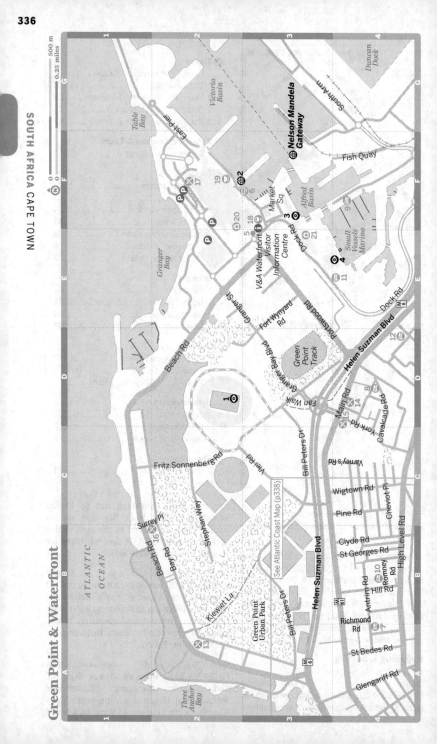

0   500 m
0   0.25 miles

ATLANTIC OCEAN

Three Anchor Bay

Table Bay

East Pier

Victoria Basin

Granger Bay

Duncan Dock

South Arm

Nelson Mandela Gateway

Fish Quay

Alfred Basin

Market Sq

Small Vessels Marina

V&A Waterfront Visitor Information Centre

Dock Rd

Portswood Rd

Fort Wynyard Rd

Granger St

Green Point Track

Beach Rd

Fan Walk

Grainger Bay Blvd

Vlei Rd

Helen Suzman Blvd

Main Rd

York Rd

Cavalcade Rd

Bill Peters Dr

Varney's Rd

Fritz Sonnenberg Rd

Stephan Way

Surrey Pl

Beach Rd

Bay Rd

Kiewiet La

Green Point Urban Park

Bill Peters Dr

Helen Suzman Blvd

See Atlantic Coast Map (p338)

Wigtown Rd

Pine Rd

Clyde Rd

St Georges Rd

Cheviot Pl

High Level Rd

Romney Rd

Antrim Rd

Hill Rd

Richmond Rd

St Bedes Rd

Glengariff Rd

Green Point & Waterfront

within a day, you don't pay for the two-hour lesson (R500). His shop hires out boards and wetsuits (per hour/day R100/300). It also runs sandboarding trips to the dunes at Kommetjie (R300).

☞ Tours

Cape Town Tourism (p347) should be your first stop to find out about the many tours on offer in and around the city.

City Sightseeing Cape Town   BUS TOUR
(☏021-511 6000; www.citysightseeing.co.za; adult/child 1 day R150/70, 2 day R250/150) These hop-on, hop-off buses, running two routes, are perfect for a quick orientation, with commentary available in 16 languages. The open-top double-deckers run at roughly half-hourly intervals between 9am and 4.30pm with extra services in peak season. City Sightseeing also offers a **canal cruise** (adult/child R30/10) with five stops between the Waterfront and the Cape Town International Convention Centre. There are discounts if you book online.

Coffeebeans Routes   CULTURAL TOUR
(Map p330; ☏021-424 3572; www.coffeebeansroutes.com; 70 Wale St; tours from R695) The concept – hooking up visitors with interesting local personalities, including musicians, artists and gardeners – is fantastic. Among innovative programs is its Friday-night reggae safari trip to Marcus Garvey, a Rastafarian settlement in Philippi.

Awol Tours   CYCLING TOUR
(☏021-418 3803, 083-234 6428; www.awoltours.co.za; Dock Rd, Information Centre, V&A Waterfront) Discover Cape Town's cycle lanes on this superb city bike tour (R350, three hours, daily) from Awol's Waterfront base. Other pedalling itineraries include the Winelands, Cape Point and the township of Masiphumelele – a great alternative to traditional township tours.

Uthando   TOWNSHIP TOUR
(☏021-683 8523; www.uthandosa.org; 9 Princes Rd, Harfield Village; R650) Half the tour fee goes towards the fantastic range of social upliftment projects that the tours visit. Usually four or so projects are visited and could be anything from an organic farm to an old folks' centre.

Andulela   CULTURAL TOUR
(☏021-790 2592; www.andulela.com; half-day tours from R495) Offers a variety of cultural, culinary and wildlife themed tours.

Hout Bay Harbour Tours   BOAT TOUR
(Harbour Rd, Hout Bay) **Circe Launches** (☏021-790 1040; www.circelaunches.co.za; adult/child R50/20), **Drumbeat Charters** (☏021-791 4441; www.drumbeatcharters.co.za; adult/child R65/25) and **Nauticat Charters** (☏021-790 7278; www.nauticatcharters.co.za; adult/child R70/35) run near-identical cruises to **Duiker Island** (also known as Seal Island because of its large colony of Cape fur seals, but not

Atlantic Coast

0 1 km
0 0.5 miles

ATLANTIC OCEAN

Rocklands Bay

Helen Suzman Blvd

Main Rd

Sea Point Promenade

High Level Rd

Rocklands Rd

Wisbeach Rd

See Green Point & Waterfront Map (p336)

Beach Rd

Albany Rd

Boat Bay

Main Rd

High Level Rd

St John's Rd

Signal Hill Rd

Beach Rd

Clarens Rd

Regent Rd

Hanover Rd

Disandt Ave

Kloof Rd

La Croix Ave

St Bartholomew Ave

Signal Hill

De Wet Rd

Ocean View Dr

Arcadia Rd

See Gardens & Around Map (p334)

3

Table Mountain National Park

Victoria Rd

Kloof Rd

2

Glen Country Club

Round House Rd

10

Kloof Rd

Lower Kloof Rd

11

Chilworth Rd

7

Glen Beach

Sedgemoor Rd

Shanklin Cr

Atholl Rd

Camps Bay Dr

Tafelberg Rd

Camps Bay

1

Argyle Rd

The Meadway

Central Dr

Geneva Dr

Woodford Rd

13

4

Lower Cableway Station

Victoria Rd

Camps Bay Dr

Bakoven Bay

Pipe Track

Table Mountain

Upper Cableway Station

Atlantic Coast

to be confused with the official Seal Island in False Bay). Trips last between 40 minutes and an hour.

Simon's Town Boat Company   BOAT TOUR
(☑083-257 7760; www.boatcompany.co.za; The Town Pier, Simon's Town; harbour cruise adult/child R50/20; ⏷Simon's Town) This company runs a popular cruise around Simon's Town harbour, as well as longer boat trips to Cape Point (adult/child R450/250) and Seal Island (adult/child R350/200). It also runs whale-watching trips in season (June to December).

🎊 Festivals & Events

Cape Town Minstrel Carnival   CULTURAL
(www.capetown-minstrels.co.za) Tweede Nuwe Jaar, on 2 January, is when the satin- and sequin-clad minstrel troupes traditionally march through the city for the Kaapse Klopse (Cape Minstrel Festival).

**Cape Argus Pick 'n' Pay
Cycle Tour**   SPORT
(www.cycletour.co.za) Held on a Saturday in the middle of March, this is the world's largest timed cycling event, attracting more than 30,000 contestants. Forget driving around town on the day.

**Cape Town International
Jazz Festival**   MUSIC
(www.capetownjazzfest.com) Cape Town's biggest jazz event is usually held at the Cape Town International Convention Centre at the end of March.

Obs Arts Festival   ARTS
(http://obsarts.org.za) South Africa's biggest street festival takes over the suburb of Observatory on the first weekend of December.

🛏 Sleeping

Whether you're into lively hostels, characterful guesthouses or unfettered luxury, Cape Town has it. If you have transport, then anywhere is OK, but inquire about parking and note that city-centre establishments often charge R30 to R70 per day for a bay.

Advance booking is recommended, especially during the school holidays from mid-December to the end of January and at Easter; prices can double and many places are fully booked.

Apartments & House Rentals

For longer-term stays or self-catering options a serviced apartment or villa can work out as a good deal. Cape Breaks (☑083-383 4888; http://capebreaks.co.za) offers a range of attractively decorated studios and apartments beside the Company's Gardens. Cape Stay (www.capestay.co.za) offers accommodation across the Cape, while Cape Town Budget Accommodation (☑021-4474398; www.capetownbudgetaccommodation.co.za) has units in Woodstock from R270 per night.

CITY BOWL & BO-KAAP

Scalabrini Guest House   HOSTEL $
(Map p330; ☑021-465 6433; www.scalabrini.org.za; 47 Commercial St; dm/s/d or tw R180/350/500; 🛜) Above a soup kitchen and social programs run by a charity, this pleasant guesthouse has 11 immaculately clean rooms with bathrooms, plus a great kitchen for self-catering in which you can also watch satellite TV.

Long Street Backpackers   HOSTEL $
(Map p330; ☑021-423 0615; www.longstreetback packers.co.za; 209 Long St; dm/s/d R120/220/330; 🛜; 🚌Bloem) Little has changed at this backpackers since it opened in 1993 (making it Long St's longest-running hostel). In a block

CLIMBING TABLE MOUNTAIN

Table Mountain National Park, stretching from flat-topped Table Mountain to Cape Point, is criss-crossed by myriad hiking routes, ranging from easy strolls to extreme rock climbing. Entrance fees have to be paid for the Boulders, Cape of Good Hope, Ouderkraal, Silvermine and Tokai sections of the park, but otherwise the routes are free. Signage is far from comprehensive and even with a map it's easy to get lost; tell someone where you're going and never hike alone.

Platteklip Gorge, the most straightforward route up the mountain, takes around two hours and is steep and fully exposed to the sun. Less of a slog is the **Pipe Track** but following it takes roughly double the time. Climbing **Lion's Head** and the walk from the upper cableway station to **Maclear's Beacon**, the highest point of the mountain, are both easily achievable in around an hour – the former is a popular night walk at full moon. There are two popular routes up the mountain from Kirstenbosch Botanical Gardens along either **Skeleton Gorge** (which involves negotiating some sections with chains) or **Nursery Ravine**. The trails are well marked, and steep in places, but the way to the gardens from the cableway and vice versa is not signposted.

Overnight hikes include the two-day, one-night, 33.8km **Cape of Good Hope Trail** and the five-day, four-night, 80km **Hoerikwaggo Trail** running the full length of the peninsula from Cape Point to the upper cableway station. The former has to be booked and includes accommodation; the latter can be done freely. Bookings for the tented camps along the trail can be made online (www.sanparks.org/parks/table_mountain/tourism/accommodation.php#tented) or by phone (☏021-422 2816).

of 14 small flats, with four beds and a bathroom in each, accommodation is arranged around a leafy courtyard.

Penthouse on Long HOSTEL $
(Map p330; ☏021-424 8356; www.penthouseon long.com; 6th fl, 112 Long St; dm/d without bathroom from R140/450, d R500; ❄@☎; ☐Dorp) High above Long St, this backpackers does amazing things with what was formerly office space. The cheapest dorm has 22 beds, while private rooms have colourful themes.

Dutch Manor BOUTIQUE HOTEL $$
TOP CHOICE
(Map p330; ☏021-422 4767; www.dutchmanor. co.za; 158 Buitengracht St; s/d incl breakfast R1200/1700; ❄☎; ☐Bloem) Four-poster beds, giant armoires and creaking floorboards lend terrific atmosphere to this property crafted from an 1812 building. Although it overlooks busy Buitengracht St the noise is largely kept at bay.

Cape Heritage Hotel BOUTIQUE HOTEL $$
(Map p330; ☏021-424 4646; www.capeherit age.co.za; 90 Bree St; d/ste incl breakfast from R2390/3310, parking R55; P❄@; ☐Longmarket) Each room at this elegant boutique hotel has its own character. Some have four-poster beds and all have modern conveniences such as satellite TV.

Grand Daddy Hotel BOUTIQUE HOTEL $$
(Map p330; ☏021-424 7247; www.granddaddy. co.za; 38 Long St; r or trailer incl breakfast from R1800, parking per day R30; P❄@☎; ☐Castle) The Grand Daddy's star attraction is its rooftop trailer park of penthouse suites made from vintage Airstream trailers decorated by different artists and designers. The regular rooms are also stylish.

Rouge On Rose BOUTIQUE HOTEL $$
(Map p330; ☏021-426 0298; www.rougeonrose. co.za; 25 Rose St; s/d incl breakfast R1000/1400; ❄☎; ☐Longmarket) Rustically chic rooms, including suites (for no extra charge) with kitchenettes and lounges. All rooms have luxurious open bathroom spaces with stand-alone tubs.

Taj Cape Town LUXURY HOTEL $$$
(Map p330; ☏021-819 2000; www.tajhotels.com; Wale St; s/d/ste incl breakfast R5000/5200/10,000; P❄@☎❋; ☐Dorp) Many of the chic, contemporary rooms here offer spectacular views of Table Mountain. Service and facilities are top grade. You can score huge savings if you book online a month or more in advance.

GARDENS & AROUND

Ashanti Gardens HOSTEL $
(Map p334; ☏021-423 8721; www.ashanti.co.za; 11 Hof St, Gardens; dm/s/d without bathroom

R160/350/500, d R700; **P ✱ @ ⊚ ✈**; ⬜Government Ave) One of Cape Town's slickest backpackers, with much of the action focused on its lively bar and deck, which overlooks Table Mountain. The beautiful old house holds the dorms and a lawn on which you can camp (R80 per person). There are excellent self-catering rooms with bathrooms in two separate heritage-listed houses around the corner.

TOP CHOICE Mannabay　　　BOUTIQUE HOTEL **$$**
(Map p334; ☑021-461 1094; www.mannabay.com; 1 Denholm Rd, Oranjezicht; r/ste incl breakfast from R1425/4000; **P ✱ @ ⊚ ✈**) This gorgeous luxury property offers seven guest rooms, each uniquely decorated with different themes. It's just far enough up the mountain to provide great views, but not so far that it's a slog home should you walk.

Backpack　　　HOSTEL **$$**
(Map p334; ☑021-423 4530; www.backpackers. co.za; 74 New Church St, Tamboerskloof; dm/s/d without bathroom R180/500/750, s/d R600/900, parking per day R20; **P @ ⊚ ✈**; ⬜Buitensingel) This 'boutique backpackers' offers affordable style, a buzzy vibe and fantastic staff. Its dorms may not be Cape Town's cheapest but they're among its nicest, while the private rooms are charmingly decorated.

Hippo Boutique Hotel　　　BOUTIQUE HOTEL **$$**
(Map p334; ☑021-423 2500; www.hippotique. co.za; 5-9 Park Rd, Gardens; d/ste incl breakfast R1400/1950; **P ✱ @ ⊚ ✈**; ⬜Michaelis) Brilliantly located and offering spacious, stylish rooms, each with a small kitchen for self-catering. Larger suites, with mezzanine-level bedrooms and arty themes, are worth the extra spend.

Cactusberry Lodge　　　B&B **$$**
(Map p334; ☑021-461 9787; www.cactusberry lodge.com; 30 Breda St, Oranjezicht; s/d incl breakfast from R700/1050; **P ⊚ ✈**) The rooms here sport striking contemporary design, mixing arty photography, African crafts and Euro style. Its sun deck overlooks Table Mountain and there's a tiny splash pool in the courtyard.

Mount Nelson Hotel　　　LUXURY HOTEL **$$$**
(Map p334; ☑021-483 1000; www.mountnelson. co.za; 76 Orange St, Gardens; r/ste incl breakfast from R3730/5890; **P ✱ @ ⊚ ✈**; ⬜Government Ave) The sugar-pink painted 'Nellie' recalls Cape Town's colonial era with its chintz de-

cor and doormen dressed in pith helmets. Recently renovated rooms sport elegant silver and mossy green decorations.

Cape Cadogan　　　BOUTIQUE HOTEL **$$$**
(Map p334; ☑021-480 8080; www.capecadogan. com; 5 Upper Union St, Gardens; s/d/apt incl breakfast R2100/2800/2670; **P ✱ @ ⊚ ✈**; ⬜Michaelis) This *Gone with the Wind*–style heritage-listed villa presents a very classy boutique operation with some rooms opening on to the secluded courtyard.

GREEN POINT, DE WATERKANT & WATERFRONT

Ashanti Green Point　　　HOSTEL **$**
(Map p336; ☑021-433 1619; www.ashanti.co.za; 23 Antrim Rd, Three Anchor Bay; dm/s/d without bathroom R160/350/500, d R700; **P @ ⊚ ✈**) More chilled than its original Gardens branch, this Ashanti has a breezy hillside position with sea views and is nicely decorated with old Cape Town photos.

Villa Zest　　　BOUTIQUE HOTEL **$$**
(Map p336; ☑021-433 1246; www.villazest.co.za; 2 Braemar Rd, Green Point; s/d/ste incl breakfast R1790/1990/2390; **P ✱ @ ✈**) This Bauhaus-style villa has been converted into a quirkily decorated boutique hotel that avoids the clichés of the genre. The seven guest rooms have bold retro-design furniture and wallpapered walls.

Cape Standard　　　BOUTIQUE HOTEL **$$**
(Map p336; ☑021-430 3060; www.capestandard. co.za; 3 Romney Rd, Green Point; s/d incl breakfast R1135/1490; **P @ ⊚ ✈**) This hidden gem offers whitewashed beach-house-style rooms downstairs or contemporary-style rooms upstairs. The mosaic-tiled bathrooms have showers big enough to dance in.

Atlantic Point Backpackers　　　HOSTEL **$$**
(Map p336; ☑021-433 1663; www.atlanticpoint. co.za; 2 Cavalcade Rd, Green Point; dm/d without bathroom from R145/550, d R700; **P @ ⊚**) This imaginatively designed, playful and well-run place is steps away from Green Point's main drag. Features include a big balcony and bar and the loft lounge is covered in astro turf. Rates include a basic breakfast, wi-fi and parking.

Cape Grace　　　LUXURY HOTEL **$$$**
(Map p336; ☑021-410 7100; www.capegrace. com; West Quay; s/d/ste incl breakfast from R5290/5450/12,155; **P ✱ @ ✈**; ⬜Breakwater) An arty decor combining antiques and crafts

PENINSULA SLEEPOVERS

If you have your own wheels and you'd like something quieter, leave the city for a while and hole up in the 'burbs.

In Newlands, the **Vineyard Hotel & Spa** (☎021-657 4500; www.vineyard.co.za; Colinton Rd, Newlands; s/d/ste incl breakfast from R1400/1850/5050; P❋@☎) is a luxurious option with views of Table Mountain. Those with a tighter budget can still enjoy superb accommodation within their means at **33 South Boutique Backpackers** (☎021-447 2423; www.33southbackpackers.com; 48 Trill Rd, Observatory; dm/s/d without bathroom from R130/300/410, s/d R350/470; @☎; ⊞Observatory).

Further south, **Boulders Beach Lodge** (☎021-786 1758; www.bouldersbeach.co.za; 4 Boulders Pl, Simon's Town; s/d/apt incl breakfast from R500/900/1875; P@☎; ⊞Simon's Town) is the spot for penguin lovers, provided you don't mind the sounds and smells associated with these comical birds. **Simon's Town Backpackers** (☎021-786 1964; www.capepax.co.za; 66 St George's St, Simon's Town; dm/s/d without bathroom R150/360/460, s/d R430/520; @; ⊞Simon's Town) has good views over the harbour.

provides a unique sense of place and Cape Town's history at this lovely luxury hotel. It also has a good spa and a private yacht should you wish to sail out into the bay.

One & Only Cape Town　　LUXURY HOTEL **$$$**
(Map p336; ☎021-431 5888; www.oneandonlycapetown.com; Dock Rd, V&A Waterfront; r/ste incl breakfast from R6650/12,500; P❋@☎; ⊞Breakwater) Take your pick between enormous, plush rooms in the main building (with panoramic views of Table Mountain) or the even more exclusive island beside the pool and spa.

ATLANTIC COAST

TOP CHOICE **POD**　　BOUTIQUE HOTEL **$$$**
(Map p338; ☎021-438 8550; www.pod.co.za; 3 Argyle Rd, Camps Bay; r/ste incl breakfast from R3900/8080; P❋@☎) Lovers of clean contemporary design will adore the slate- and wood-decorated POD. The cheapest rooms have mountain rather than sea views; luxury rooms have their own private plunge pools.

Camps Bay Retreat　　BOUTIQUE HOTEL **$$$**
(Map p338; ☎021-437 8300; www.campsbayretreat.com; 7 Chilworth Rd, The Glen; d/ste incl breakfast from R4380/12,240; P❋@☎) Set in a secluded nature reserve, there is a choice of 15 rooms in either the 1929 main house or the contemporary Deck House, reached by a rope bridge over a ravine. Take your pick of three pools, including one fed by a stream from Table Mountain.

Hout Bay Manor　　HOTEL **$$$**
(☎021-790 0116; www.houtbaymanor.co.za; Baviaanskloof Rd, Hout Bay; s/d incl breakfast from R2100/3200; P❋@☎) The 1871 Hout Bay Manor has been treated to a fab Afro-chic makeover. Tribal artefacts are mixed with brightly coloured contemporary furnishings and handicrafts in rooms that all contain the expected electronic conveniences.

✖ Eating

Dining in the Mother City is a pleasure offering everything from fresh seafood to traditional African and Cape Malay cuisine. There are places to suit practically everyone's taste and budget, with a particularly strong selection of cafes and eat-in delis.

Most restaurants are licensed but many allow you to bring your own wine for little or no corkage.

Self-caterers and picnickers can stock up at the major supermarkets Pick 'n' Pay and Woolworths, which have branches all over the city.

CITY BOWL & BO-KAAP

Long St has many great places to eat, plus fantastic street life. Head to the Bo-Kaap to sample authentic Cape Malay dishes in unpretentious surroundings.

Jason Bakery　　BAKERY, CAFE **$**
(Map p330; www.jasonbakery.com; 185 Bree St; mains R50; ☺7am-3.30pm Mon-Fri, 8am-2pm Sat (take-out and pavement tables only); ⊞Bloem) This super-popular street-corner cafe makes splendid breakfasts and sandwiches as well as serving decent coffee, craft beers and MCC (Methode Cap Classique) bubbles by the glass and bottle.

Masala Dosa INDIAN $

(Map p330; ☎021-424 6772; www.masaladosa. co.za; 167 Long St; mains R40-85; ◷lunch & dinner Mon-Sat; 🚇Dorp) Bollywood chic rules at this colourful South Indian cuisine outpost serving decent *dosas* (lentil pancakes) and *thalis* (set meals with a variety of curries). There are excellent Saturday-morning cooking classes (R390 per person).

TOP CHOICE Bizerca Bistro FRENCH $$

(Map p330; ☎021-423 8888; www.bizerca.com; 98 Shortmarket St; mains R110-150; ◷lunch & dinner Mon-Fri, dinner Sat; 🚇Longmarket) At this fantastic bistro the atmosphere is contemporary and relaxed, and the expertly prepared food is bursting with flavour.

Bombay Brasserie INDIAN $$

(Map p330; ☎021-819 2000; www.tajhotels.com; Wale St; mains R150, 4-course menu R395; ◷dinner Mon-Sat; P; 🚇Dorp) Far from your average curry house, the Taj Hotel's darkly luxurious restaurant, hung with glittering chandeliers and mirrors, is a winner. Chef Harpreet Kaur's cooking is creative and delicious and the service is spot on.

Africa Café AFRICAN $$

(Map p330; ☎021-422 0221; www.africacafe.co.za; 108 Shortmarket St; set banquet R245; ◷cafe 8am-4pm Mon-Fri, 10am-2pm Sat, restaurant 6.30-11pm Mon-Sat; 🚇Longmarket) Touristy, yes, but still one of the best places to sample African food. The set feast comprises some 15 dishes from across the continent, of which you can eat as much as you like. The cafe specialises in wheat-free baked goodies and a variety of tasty 'raw' foods, including salads and cassava.

Royale Eatery BURGERS $$

(Map p330; www.royaleeatery.com; 279 Long St; mains R60-70; ◷lunch & dinner Mon-Sat; 🚇Bloem) Gourmet burgers are grilled to perfection here; downstairs is casual and buzzy while upstairs is a restaurant where you can book a table. For something different try the Big Bird ostrich burger.

Dear Me DELI $$

(Map p330; ☎021-422 4920; www.dearme.co.za; 165 Longmarket St; mains R100, 9-course gourmet dinners R320; ◷7am-4pm Mon-Fri, 7-10pm Thu; 📶; 🚇Longmarket) High-quality ingredients, creatively combined and served by gracious staff in a pleasant playful space – what more could you wish for? There is a deli and bakery section, too. Book for the excellent Thursday-night gourmet dinners.

GARDENS & AROUND

Kloof St in Gardens has a high concentration of eateries and the street's two malls have pleasant cafes.

Dog's Bollocks BURGERS $

(Map p334; 6 Roodehek St, Gardens; burgers R50; ◷5-10pm Mon-Sat; 🚇Gardens) One-man-band Nigel Wood tosses just 30 premium patties per night in this alleyway operation, so get there early if you want to sample some of the best burgers in Cape Town.

Maria's GREEK $$

(Map p334; ☎021-461 3333; Barnet St, Dunkley Sq, Gardens; mains R50-90; ◷lunch & dinner Mon-Fri, dinner Sat; P; 🚇Government Ave) There are few places as romantic or relaxing for a meal than Maria's on a warm night when you can tuck into classic Greek meze and dishes such as moussaka on rustic tables beneath the trees in the square.

Manna Epicure BAKERY $$

(Map p334; ☎021-426 2413; www.mannaepicure. com; 151 Kloof St; mains R40-110; ◷8am-5pm Tue-Sun) Come for a deliciously simple breakfast or lunch or for late-afternoon cocktails and tapas on the verandah of this white-box cafe. It's worth dragging yourself up the hill just for the freshly baked bread.

Aubergine INTERNATIONAL $$$

(Map p334; www.aubergine.co.za; 39 Barnet St, Gardens; 2-course lunch R210, 3/4/5-course dinner R385/450/525; ◷noon-2pm Wed-Fri, 5-10pm Mon-Sat; 🚇Government Ave) Harald Bressel schmidt is one of Cape Town's most consistent chefs, producing creative yet unfussy dishes. Service and ambience are equally impeccable. It's a good pre-theatre option, as from 5pm to 7pm it serves drinks and a selection of smaller dishes from the dinner menu.

GREEN POINT, DE WATERKANT & WATERFRONT

The Waterfront's many restaurants and cafes have nice ocean views, although it's essentially a giant tourist trap. Better value and a less touristy dining experience are on offer a short walk away in Green Point and Mouille Point; closer to the city is De Waterkant's expanding Cape Quarter complex (Map p330; www.capequarter.co.za; 27 Somerset Rd; ◷9am-6pm Mon-Fri, 9am-4pm Sat, 10am-2pm Sun).

El Burro
MEXICAN $

(Map p336; ☑021-433 2364; www.elburro.co.za; 81 Main Rd, Green Point; mains R50-70; ☺noon-10.30pm; P; ☐Stadium) On the upper floor of the Exhibition Building, with a balcony overlooking Cape Town Stadium, this is one stylish donkey. Supplementing the usual tacos and enchiladas are trad dishes such as chicken mole poblano.

Café Neo
GREEK, CAFE $

(Map p336; 129 Beach Rd, Mouille Point; mains R50-70; ☺7am-7pm; ☎) This favourite seaside cafe has a relaxed vibe and views of the lighthouse.

Giovanni's Deli World
CAFE, DELI $

(Map p336; 103 Main Rd, Green Point; mains R20-40; ☺7.30am-8.30pm) Bursting with flavoursome products, Giovanni's can make any sandwich you fancy, which is ideal for a picnic if you're on your way to the beach. The pavement cafe is a popular hang-out.

Wakame
SEAFOOD, ASIAN $$

(Map p336; ☑021-433 2377; www.wakame.co.za; cnr Beach Rd & Surrey Pl, Mouille Point; mains R70-120; ☺lunch & dinner) Tucking into Wakame's salt and pepper squid or sushi platter while gazing at the glorious coastal view is Capetonian dining bliss. Wakame's second level specialises in Asian dumplings and sunset cocktails.

Willoughby & Co
SEAFOOD, JAPANESE $$

(Map p336; ☑021-418 6115; www.willoughbyandco.co.za; shop 6132, Victoria Wharf, Breakwater Blvd, Waterfront; mains R60-70; ☺deli 9.30am-8.30pm, restaurant noon-10.30pm; P; ☐Waterfront) Commonly acknowledged as one of the better places to eat at the Waterfront – with long queues to prove it. Huge servings of sushi

MARKET MUNCHING

Food markets, featuring organic produce, artisanal breads and homemade goodies, abound in Cape Town. The largest (and busiest) is the **Neighbourgoods Market** (www.neighbourgoodsmarket.co.za; 373-375 Albert Rd, Salt River; ☺9am-2pm Sat; ☐Salt River), held at the Old Biscuit Mill in Woodstock every Saturday morning.

are the standout from a good-value, fish-based menu.

ATLANTIC COAST

La Boheme
SPANISH $$

(Map p338; ☑021-434 8797; www.labohemebistro.co.za; 341 Main Rd, Sea Point; 2/3 courses R95/120; ☺9am-10.30pm Mon-Sat, noon-4pm Sun; ☎) With twinkling candles and fake Picassos on the walls, this superb-value wine bar and bistro is a lovely place to dine at night. At its daytime operation, La Bruixa, you can stoke up on espresso and delicious tapas.

TOP CHOICE Roundhouse
INTERNATIONAL $$$

(Map p338; ☑021-438 4347; http://theroundhouserestaurant.com; The Glen, Camps Bay; restaurant 4-/6-course menu R520/675, Rumbullion mains R70-95; ☺restaurant 6-10pm Tue-Sat year-round, noon-4pm Wed-Sat & noon-3pm Sun May-Sep, Rumbullion 9am-sunset Oct-Apr; P) This 18th-century building, in wooded grounds overlooking Camps Bay, houses an elegant restaurant. If it's full for dinner, then a relaxed breakfast (weekends only) or lunch on the lawns at its less formal offering, the Rumbullion, is a pleasure.

🍷 Drinking

Cape Town didn't become known as the 'Tavern of the Seven Seas' for nothing. Head out on a Friday or Saturday night to Long St, De Waterkant or Camps Bay for an eye-opening experience of how the locals like to party. Most bars open around 3pm and close after midnight, and much later on Friday and Saturday.

CITY BOWL

Waiting Room
BAR

(Map p330; 273 Long St; cover Fri & Sat R20; ☺6pm-2am Mon-Sat; ☐Bloem) Climb the narrow stairway beside the Royale Eatery to find this totally hip bar decorated in retro furniture, with DJs spinning funky tunes. The roof deck is the perfect spot from which to admire the city's glittering night lights.

Julep Bar
COCKTAIL BAR

(Map p330; Vredenburg Lane; ☺5pm-2am Tue-Sat; ☐Bloem) Occupying the ground floor of a former brothel, this hidden gem is a favourite with local hipsters.

Neighbourhood
BAR

(Map p330; www.goodinthehood.co.za; 163 Long St; ☐Dorp) At this relaxed bar and casual restaurant, styled after British gastropubs, the colour divide of Cape Town melts away. The long balcony is a good place to cool off or keep tabs on Long St.

GARDENS & AROUND

Planet   COCKTAIL BAR
(Map p334; ☑021-483 1864; Mount Nelson Hotel, 76 Orange St, Gardens; ☐Government Ave) Enjoy some 250 different bubblies and 50-odd alcoholic concoctions in the old Nellie's cool silver-coated champagne and cocktail bar.

Power & the Glory/Black Ram   CAFE, BAR
(Map p334; 13B Kloof Nek Rd, Tamboerskloof; ⊙cafe 8am-10pm, bar 5pm-late Mon-Sat) The coffee and food (pretzel hot dogs, crusty pies and other artisan munchies) are good but it's the smoky, cosy bar with its range of local craft beers that packs the hipsters in.

Perseverance Tavern   PUB
(Map p334; www.perseverancetavern.co.za; 83 Buitenkant St, Gardens; ⊙4pm-2am Mon, noon-2am Tue-Sat, 11am-8pm Sun) This convivial heritage-listed pub, which is affectionately known as Persies and has been around since 1808, was once Cecil Rhodes' local. There are beers on tap and you can order decent pub grub such as fish and chips (R45).

GREEN POINT, DE WATERKANT & WATERFRONT

Bascule   BAR
(Map p336; ☑021-410 7097; www.capegrace.com; West Quay Rd, Cape Grace, Waterfront; ⊙noon-2am) More than 450 varieties of whisky are served at the Grace's sophisticated bar, and there are still a few slugs of the 50-year-old Glenfiddich (just R18,000 a tot) left. Make a booking for one of the whisky tastings (R175 or R220).

W Tapas Bar   CAFE, WINE BAR
(Map p336; ☑021-415 3411; Woolworths, Victoria Wharf, Breakwater Blvd, Waterfront; ⊙9am-9pm; ☐Waterfront) Tucked away on the top floor of Woolworths is this modern, uncrowded wine bar where you can sample the best of the department store's selection of local drops along with tapas platters of charcuterie, seafood or vegetarian dips (R65 to R95).

Mitchell's Scottish Ale House & Brewery   PUB
(Map p336; www.mitchellsbreweries.co.za; East Pier Rd, Waterfront; ⊙11am-2am; ☐Breakwater) This unpretentious and perpetually packed pub serves the full range of Mitchell's beers, brewed at the country's oldest microbrewery

in Knysna. There's decent pub grub, including good wood-fired pizzas, and a range of other beers on tap as well.

ATLANTIC COAST

La Vie   BAR, CAFE
(Map p338; 205 Beach Rd; ⊙7.30am-midnight; ⊛) One of the very few places where you can have anything from breakfast to late-night cocktails within sight of Sea Point promenade. Lounge on the outdoor terrace and enjoy the thin-crust pizza (R40 to R90).

Bungalow   BAR
(Map p338; ☑021-438 2018; www.thebungalow.co.za; 1 Victoria Rd, Glen Country Club, Clifton; ⊙noon-2am) This Euro-chic restaurant and lounge bar is a great place for beers, cocktails or a boozy meal after which you can crash in the day-bed section or dangle your feet in the tiny bar-side splash pool. A DJ creates a more clubby atmosphere by night.

Dunes   BAR
(www.dunesrestaurant.co.za; 1 Beach Rd, Hout Bay; ⊙noon-11pm Mon-Fri, 9am-11pm Sat & Sun) You can hardly get closer to the beach than this – in fact, the front courtyard *is* the beach with a safe kids' play area. Up on the terrace or from inside the restaurant-bar there's a great view of Hout Bay to go with the decent pub grub and tapas.

☆ Entertainment

You can book seats for practically anything through **Webtickets** (www.webtickets.co.za) or **Computicket** (http://online.computicket.com/web), which has branches in numerous locations, including the Waterfront.

Cinemas

The big multiplexes can be found in Victoria Wharf at the Waterfront, Cavendish Sq and Canal Walk.

Labia   CINEMA
(Map p334; www.thelabia.co.za; 68 Orange St; tickets R35; ☐Michaelis) Along with **Labia on Kloof** (Map p334; ☑021-424 5727), in the Lifestyles on Kloof centre around the corner, this is Cape Town's best cinema in terms of price and programming.

Live Music

Cape Town City Hall   CLASSICAL MUSIC
(Map p330; www.cityhallsessions.co.za; Darling St, City Bowl; ☐St George's) One of several venues where the **Cape Philharmonic Orchestra** (www.cpo.org.za), South Africa's 'orchestra

for all seasons', plays concerts. Local choirs also take advantage of the auditorium's very good acoustics.

Zula Sound Bar   LIVE MUSIC, COMEDY
(Map p330; ☎021-424 2442; www.zulabar.co.za; 98 Long St, City Bowl; admission from R30; ☐Longmarket) Progress from the cafe and bar fronting the street to performance spaces upstairs and downstairs at the back. The line-up includes a range of hip local bands, DJs and comedy every Monday night.

Assembly   LIVE MUSIC, DJ
(Map p330; www.theassembly.co.za; 61 Harrington St, The Fringe; cover R30-50) In an old furniture-ssembly factory, this live-music and DJ performance space has made its mark with an exciting, eclectic line-up of both local and international artists.

Mercury Live & Lounge   LIVE MUSIC, DJ
(www.mercuryl.co.za; 43 De Villiers St, District Six; admission R30-50) A young, studenty crowd frequent Cape Town's premier rock venue, host to top South African bands and overseas acts.

Mahogany Lounge   JAZZ
(Map p334; ☎076 679 2697; www.themahog anyroom.com; 79 Buitenkant St, Gardens; 1/2 sets R60/100; ☺7pm-2am Wed-Sat) This tiny jazz club aims to recreate the atmosphere of Ronnie Scott's Jazz Club and New York's Village Vanguard. Bookings essential for the two sets starting at 8pm and 10pm.

Nightclubs
Trinity   CLUB
(www.trinitycapetown.co.za; 15 Bennett St, De Waterkant; cover R50-150) Occupying an enormous warehouse space, Trinity offers a state-of-the-art dance club as well as bars and an all-day restaurant serving sushi, pizza and burgers. Naturally, big-name DJs play here but you should also look out for other events, such as live jazz on Tuesday.

St Yves   CLUB
(Map p338; www.styves.co.za; Victoria Rd, The Promenade, Camps Bay) The latest incarnation of this slick Camps Bay nightspot has a groove going on with a class line-up of DJs and live acts (tickets available via Webtickets (p345)).

🛍 Shopping
There are craft shops all over town but few of the traditional African items come from the Cape Town area itself. Great buys include the local township-produced items,

such as beadwork dolls, toys made from recycled tin cans and wire sculptures.

Central markets include Pan African Market (Map p330; www.panafrican.co.za; 76 Long St; ☐Longmarket) and Greenmarket Square (Map p330; cnr Shortmarket & Berg Sts; ☺9am-5pm), which is in a great area for galleries and shops; a good one is African Image (Map p330; www.african-image.co.za; cnr Church & Burg Sts; ☐Longmarket), which stocks a range of ancient African artefacts and township crafts, as well as wildly patterned shirts.

Music lovers should head straight for Long Street's African Music Store (Map p330; www.africanmusicstore.co.za; 134 Long St; ☐Dorp), which stocks an unrivalled range of local music.

At the Waterfront there's Red Shed Craft Workshop (Map p336; ☎021-408 7847; Victoria Wharf; ☺9am-9pm Mon-Sat, 10am-9pm Sun) and Waterfront Craft Market (Map p336; Dock Rd, Waterfront; ☺9.30am-6pm; ☐Breakwater), also known as the Blue Shed.

For books, head to Book Lounge (Map p334; ☎021-462 2425; www.booklounge.co.za; 71 Roeland St, The Fringe; ☺9.30am-7.30pm Mon-Fri, 8.30am-6pm Sat, 10am-4pm Sun), close to the District Six Museum.

Although not as prominent as in Johannesburg, Cape Town does have some mega malls. Other than the Waterfront, there's Cavendish Square (www.cavendish.co.za; Cavendish Square Dreyer St, Claremont; ☺9am-7pm Mon-Sat, 10am-5pm Sun; ☐Claremont) in Claremont and Canal Walk (☎021-529 9699; www.canalwalk.co.za; Century Blvd, Century City; ☺9am-9pm), northeast of the city.

❶ Information

Emergency
In an emergency call ☎107, or ☎021-480 7700 if using a mobile phone. Other useful phone numbers:
Ambulance (☎10177)
Police (☎10111)
Sea Rescue (☎021-449 3500)

Internet Access
Cape Town is one of Africa's most wired cities. Most hotels and hostels offer internet facilities and you'll seldom have to hunt far for a wi-fi network or internet cafe. Rates are pretty uniform at R30 per hour.

Medical Services
Groote Schuur Hospital (☎021-404 9111; www.westerncape.gov.za/your_gov/5972; Main Rd, Observatory)

Netcare Christiaan Barnard Memorial Hospital (☑021-480 6111; www.netcare.co.za/live/netcare_content.php?Item_ID=5613; 181 Longmarket St, City Bowl)

Netcare Travel Clinic (☑021-419 3172; 58 Strand St, 11th fl, Picbal Arcade, City Bowl; ☺8am-4pm Mon-Fri) For vaccinations and travel-health advice.

Money

Money can be changed at the airport and there are ATMs all over town; be aware of scams.

Post

General Post Office (www.postoffice.co.za; Parliament St, City Bowl; ☺8am-4.30pm Mon-Fri, 8am-noon Sat) Has a poste-restante counter.

Safe Travel

Cape Town's relaxed vibe can instil a false sense of security. Thefts are most likely to happen when visitors do something foolish such as leaving their gear on a beach while they go swimming.

Paranoia is not required, but common sense is. There is tremendous poverty on the peninsula and the 'informal redistribution of wealth' is fairly common. The townships on the Cape Flats have an appalling crime rate; unless you have a trustworthy guide or are on a tour they are not places for a casual stroll.

While the city centre is generally safe to walk around, always listen to local advice on where not to go. There is safety in numbers.

Swimming at any of the Cape beaches is potentially hazardous, especially for those inexperienced in surf. Check for warning signs about rips and rocks and only swim in patrolled areas.

Tourist Information

At the head office of Cape Town Tourism (☑021-426 4260; www.capetown.travel; cnr Castle & Burg Sts; ☺8am-5.30pm Mon-Fri, 8.30am-2pm Sat, 9am-1pm Sun) there are advisers who can book accommodation, tours and car hire. You can also get information on national parks and reserves, safaris and overland tours.

Other Cape Town Tourism branches:

Kirstenbosch Visitor Information Centre (☑021-762 0687; Rhodes Dr, Kirstenbosch Botanical Gardens, main entrance, Newlands; ☺8am-5pm)

Muizenberg Visitor Information Centre (☑021-787 9140; Beach Rd, The Pavilion; ☺9am-5.30pm Mon-Fri, 9am-1pm Sat & Sun)

Simon's Town Visitor Information Centre (☑021-786 8440; 111 St George's St; ☺8.30am-5.30pm Mon-Fri, 9am-1pm Sat & Sun)

V&A Waterfront Visitor Information Centre (☑021-408 7600; Dock Rd; ☺9am-6pm)

❶ Getting There & Away

Air

Cape Town International Airport (☑021-937 1200; www.acsa.co.za/home.asp?pid=229) is 20km east of the city centre, approximately 20 minutes' drive depending on traffic.

Apart from South African Airways (☑021-936 1111; www.flysaa.com), two budget airlines connect Cape Town with the major South African cities: Kulula (☑0861 585 852; www.kulula.com) and Mango (☑0861 001 234, 021-815 4100; www.flymango.com). During the summer, you could pick up a one-way flight to Durban for a little over R1000; to Jo'burg for less than R900.

Bus

Interstate buses arrive at the bus terminus next to Cape Town Train Station, where you'll find the booking offices for the following bus companies, all open 6am to 6.30pm daily.

Greyhound (☑083 915 9000; www.greyhound.co.za)

Intercape Mainliner (☑0861 287 287; www.intercape.co.za)

SA Roadlink (☑083 918 3999; www.saroadlink.co.za)

Translux (☑0861 589 282; www.translux.co.za)

Sample fares include:

» Jo'burg (R550, 18 hours)

» Knysna (R265, eight hours)

» Port Elizabeth (R330, 12½ hours)

» Swellendam (R200, four hours)

» Windhoek (Namibia; R1350, 21½ hours)

Baz Bus (☑0861 229 287; www.bazbus.com) offers hop-on, hop-off fares and door-to-door service between Cape Town and Jo'burg/Pretoria (one way R2900) via the Northern Drakensberg, Durban and the Garden Route.

Train

Long-distance trains arrive at Cape Town Train Station (cnr Adderley & Strand Sts). There are services Wednesday, Friday and Sunday to and from Jo'burg (R560, 26 hours) via Kimberley (R380, 18 hours) on the Shosholoza Meyl (☑0860 008 888; www.shosholozameyl.co.za). These sleeper trains offer comfortable accommodation and dining cars, but if you require something more luxurious opt either for the elegant Blue Train (☑021-449 2672; www.bluetrain.co.za), which stops at Matjiesfontein on its way to Pretoria and Kimberley on the way back to Cape Town, or **Rovos Rail** (☎012-315 8242; www.rovos.com).

ⓘ Getting Around

To & From the Airport

MyCiTi (☎0800 656 463; www.capetown.gov. za/myciti) buses run every 20 minutes between 5am and 10pm to Civic Centre station (adult/ child R57/28.10). You cannot pay in cash on the buses; you need to buy a myconnect card and load it with credit at the ticket office.

Backpacker Bus (☎021-439 7600; www. backpackerbus.co.za) picks up from hostels and hotels in the city and offers airport transfers from R180 per person (R200 between 5pm and 8am).

Expect to pay around R200 for a nonshared taxi; the officially authorised airport taxi company is **Touch Down Taxis** (☎021-919 4659).

All the major car-hire companies have desks at the airport.

Bus

The MyCiTi network of commuter buses runs daily between 5am and 10pm. The main routes currently are from the airport to the city centre, from Table Bay to the city and Gardens to the Waterfront via the City Bowl. There are plans to extend routes along the Atlantic seaboard to Camps Bay and Hout Bay and east to Woodstock and Salt River. For most city-centre routes the fare is R5.30; to Table View it is R10.60 and to the airport R57. Fares have to be paid with a stored-value myconnect card.

Golden Arrow (☎0800 656 463; www.gabs. co.za) buses run from the **Golden Acre Terminal** (Grand Pde) and are most useful for getting along the Atlantic coast from the city centre to Hout Bay. Destinations and fares from the city include the Waterfront (R7), Sea Point (R8), Kloof Nek (R7), Camps Bay (R10) and Hout Bay (R18).

MYCONNECT CARDS

To travel on a **MyCiTi** bus, you must have a myconnect card. The card can be purchased from station kiosks and at a range of shops around the city – check the website for a complete list.

There is an issuing fee of R23: keep your receipt and you will be able to get this back if you return the card to a kiosk. You then need to charge the card with credit. A bank fee of 2.5% of the value loaded (with a minimum of R1.50) will be charged; so if you load the card with R200 you will have R195 in credit. You need cash to buy and top up the card – you can't do it with a debit or credit card.

The card, issued by ABSA, can also be used to pay for low-value transactions at shops and businesses displaying the MasterCard sign.

Car

Cape Town has an excellent road and freeway system that, outside the late-afternoon rush hour, carries surprisingly little traffic.

Car-hire companies:

Around About Cars (☎021-422 4022; www. aroundaboutcars.com; 20 Bloem St; ☉7.30am-7pm Mon-Fri, 7.30am-3pm Sat, 8am-1pm Sun)

Avis (☎021-424 1177; www.avis.co.za; 123 Strand St)

Budget (☎021-418-5232; www.budget.co.za; 120 Strand St)

Hertz (☎021-410 6800; www.hertz.co.za; 40 Loop St)

MinibusTaxi

In Cape Town (and South Africa in general) a minibus taxi means a shared taxi. These private services, which cover most of the city with an informal network of routes, are a cheap and fast way of getting around. On the downside they're usually crowded and some drivers can be reckless.

Useful routes are from Adderley St, opposite the Golden Acre Centre, to Sea Point along Main Rd and up Long St to Kloof Nek. The standard fare is R6.

The main rank is on the upper deck of Cape Town Train Station and is accessible from a walkway in the Golden Acre Centre or from stairways on Strand St. It's well organised, and finding the right stand is easy. Anywhere else, you just hail minibus taxis from the side of the road and ask the driver where they're going.

Rikkis

A cross between a taxi and a shared taxi are **Rikkis** (☎0861 745 547; www.rikkis.co.za). They offer shared rides most places around the City Bowl, and down the Atlantic coast to Camps Bay, for R15 to R30.

Although cheap, Rikkis are not the quickest way to get around, as there is usually a certain amount of meandering as passengers are dropped off, and they are notoriously slow to turn up to a booking.

Taxi

Consider taking a private taxi late at night or if you're in a group. Rates are about R10 per kilometre. Call **Excite Taxis** (☎021-448 4444; www.excitetaxis.co.za), **Marine Taxi** (☎021-913 6813, 0861 434 0434; www.marinetaxis.co.za) or **SA Cab** (☎0861 172 222; www.sacab.co.za).

Train

Cape Metro Rail (www.capemetrorail.co.za) trains are a handy way to get around, although there are few trains after 6.30pm on weekdays. Trains operate but are less frequent on weekends.

The difference between metro plus (1st-class) and metro (economy class) carriages in price and comfort is negligible, though economy class is more crowded. The most important line for visitors is the Simon's Town line, which runs through Observatory and around the back of Table Mountain through upper-income suburbs such as Newlands, on to Muizenberg and the False Bay coast. These trains run at least every hour from 5am to 7.30pm Monday to Friday (to 6pm on Saturday), and from 7.30am to 6.30pm on Sunday.

Metro trains also run out to Strand on the eastern side of False Bay, and into the Winelands to Stellenbosch and Paarl. They are the cheapest and easiest means of transport to these areas; security is best at peak times.

Some economy/1st-class fares are Observatory (R6/8), Muizenberg (R7.50/11), Simon's Town (R8.50/14), Paarl (R11/17) and Stellenbosch (R11/17).

WESTERN CAPE

The Western Cape is without a doubt one of the world's premier destinations, a place often so picture-perfect it's hard to describe without using clichés. The diversity of the landscape is unparalleled and the number of adventures to experience almost overwhelming. Dive with sharks, jump out of an aeroplane, surf some of Southern Africa's best breaks, cruise with whales, eat fresh crayfish at a beachside barbecue, stand at the southernmost tip of Africa and sample some of the world's finest wines.

The region is the country's most popular tourist destination, so at times you may feel a bit like a zebra in a herd travelling around here, particularly along the Garden Route. But it's a magical place, with ample opportunity to flee the crowds. Whichever way you go, there's no escaping the beauty of the Western Cape.

Winelands

The Boland, stretching inland and upwards from Cape Town, is not South Africa's only wine-growing region, but it's certainly the most famous. Its name means 'Upland', a reference to the dramatic mountain ranges that shoot up to over 1500m, on whose fertile slopes the vineyards form a patchwork.

With its centuries-long history of colonial settlement, there's a distinctly European feel to the Boland, particularly in French-themed culinary hotspot Franschhoek. Lively student-town Stellenbosch offers the most activities, while up-and-coming Paarl, long overshadowed, is now worth a longer look.

STELLENBOSCH
☑021 / POP 220,000

South Africa's second-oldest European settlement, established on the banks of the Eerste River in 1679, Stellenbosch wears many faces. At times it's a rowdy joint for Stellenbosch University students and at others it's a stately monument to colonial architectural splendour. But most times it's just plain busy, as Capetonians, vineyard workers and tourists descend on its museums, markets, quality hotels and varied eating and nightlife options.

◉ Sights & Activities

TOP
CHOICE Bergkelder   WINERY
(☑021-809 8025; www.bergkelder.co.za; ◷8am-5pm Mon-Fri, 9am-2pm Sat, tours 10am, 11am, 2pm & 3pm Mon-Fri, 10am, 11am & noon Sat) For wine lovers without wheels, this cellar a short walk from the town centre is ideal. Hourlong tours (R30) are followed by an atmospheric candlelit tasting in the cellar.

Village Museum   MUSEUM
(18 Ryneveld St; adult/child R25/5; ◷9am-5pm Mon-Sat, 10am-4pm Sun) A group of exquisitely restored and period-furnished houses dating from 1709 to 1850 make up this must-see museum, which occupies the entire city block bounded by Ryneveld, Plein, Drostdy and Church Sts.

Sasol Art Museum   GALLERY
(52 Ryneveld St; admission by donation; ◷9am-4.30pm Mon-Sat) Featuring one of the country's best selections of local art, both famous and emerging, this museum also contains African anthropological treasures.

Braak   SQUARE
At the north end of the Braak (Town Sq), an open stretch of grass, you'll find the neo-Gothic St Mary's on the Braak Church, completed in 1852. To the west is the VOC Kruithuis (Powder House; adult/child R5/2; ◷9am-2pm Mon-Fri, closed Jun-Aug), which was built in 1777 to store the town's weapons and gunpowder. On the northwest corner is Fick House (Burgerhuis), a fine example of Cape Dutch architecture.

Wineries   WINERIES
There are too many good wineries in the Stellenbosch area to list all of them, so it's

SOUTH AFRICA WINELANDS

SOUTH AFRICA WINELANDS

Western Cape

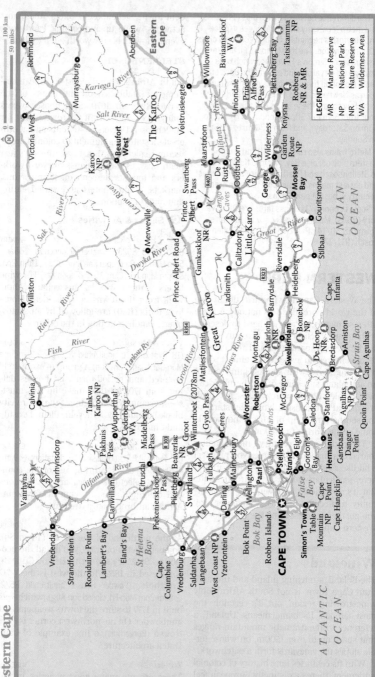

100 km
50 miles

LEGEND
MR Marine Reserve
NP National Park
NR Nature Reserve
WA Wilderness Area
MR & MR

Eastern Cape

Richmond

Aberdeen

Murraysburg

Willowmore

Baviaanskloof WA

Kariega River

Prince Alfred's Pass

Plettenberg Bay

Tsitsikamma NP

Salt River

The Karoo

Volstruisleegte

Uniondale

Robberg NR & MR

Victoria West

Klaarstroom

Olifants River

Garden Knysna

Leeuw River

Karoo NP

Beaufort West

Swartberg Pass

De Rust

Oudtshoorn

Wilderness

Garden Route NP

George

Mossel Bay

Lesuk River

Prince Albert

Cango Caves

Gouritsmond

Merweville

Prince Albert Road

Gamkaskloof NR

Little Karoo

Calitzdorp

Riversdale

Stilbaai

INDIAN OCEAN

Williston

Dwyka River

Ladismith

Groot River

Cape Infanta

Seak River

Riet River

Great Karoo

Matjiesfontein

Towns River

Barrydale

Heidelberg

Fish River

Calvinia

Montagu

Marloth NR

Swellendam

Bontebok NP

De Hoop NR

Bredasdorp

Arniston

Struis Bay

Cape Agulhas

River

Tankwa Karoo NP

Wuppertal

Cederberg WA

Middelberg Pass

Groot Winterhoek (2078m)

Gydo Pass

Ceres

Worcester

Robertson

McGregor

Caledon

Stanford

Agulhas NP

Quoin Point

Pakhuis Pass

Pakhuis Pass

Citrusdal

Clanwilliam

Piketberg

Beaverlac NR

Tulbagh

Malmesbury

Wellington

Paarl

Stellenbosch

Strand

Elgin

Gordon's Bay

Hermanus

Gansbaai

Danger Point

Vanrhyns Pass

Vanrhynsdorp

Olifants River

Piekenierskloof Pass

Darling

Cape Winelands

Vredendal

Strandfontein

Rooiduine Point

Lambert's Bay

Eland's Bay

St Helena Bay

Cape Columbine

Saldanha

Langebaan

West Coast NP

Yzerfontein

Bok Point

Robben Island

Wellington

False Bay

Cape Point

Bok Bay

CAPE TOWN

Simon's Town

Table Mountain NP

Cape Hangklip

ATLANTIC OCEAN

sometimes best to drive around and stop on a whim. We do, however, recommend a visit to Villiera (021-865 2002; www.villiera.com; tastings free; 9am-5pm Mon-Fri, 9am-3pm Sat), which produces excellent Méthode Cap Classique wines and a highly rated and very well-priced shiraz. Excellent two-hour wildlife drives (R150 per person) take in the various antelope, zebra and bird species on the farm.

The red wines at Warwick Estate (021-884 4410; www.warwickwine.com; tastings R25; 10am-5pm) are legendary, particularly its Bordeaux blends. The winery offers an informative 'Big Five' wine safari through the vineyards (think grape varieties, not large mammals) and picnics to enjoy on the lawns.

Thanks to a favourable microclimate, the Hartenberg Estate (021-865 2541; www.hartenbergestate.com; tastings free; 9am-5.15pm Mon-Fri, 9am-3pm Sat, 10am-3.30pm Sun (Dec only)) produces superlative reds. Lunch is served from noon to 2pm (bookings essential). Picnics are also available to take on a wetland walk through the estate.

Tours

If you need to walk off all that cheese and wine, explore with the brochure *Historical Stellenbosch on Foot* (R5), available at Stellenbosch Tourism (p352), or head to the same office to take the guided walk (per person R90; tours 11am & 3pm Mon-Fri), with a minimum of two people.

Easy Rider Wine Tours WINE TOURS
(021-886 4651; www.winetour.co.za; 12 Market St) A long-established company operating from the Stumble Inn with good-value day trips (R450 including lunch and all tastings).

Madiba CULTURAL TOUR
(083 479 2801; per person R120) Walking tours of Kayamandi township.

Vine Hopper WINE TOURS
(021-882 8112; www.vinehopper.co.za; 1-day pass R200) A hop-on, hop-off bus with two routes each covering six estates. The Hopper departs hourly from Stellenbosch Tourism, where you can buy tickets.

Sleeping

TOP
CHOICE **Banghoek Place** BACKPACKERS $
(021-887 0048; www.banghoek.co.za; 193 Banghoek Rd; dm/r R150/450; @) The owners of this stylish suburban hostel are keen to organise tours of the district. The recreation area has satellite TV and a pool table.

Ikhaya Backpackers BACKPACKERS $
(021-883 8550; www.stellenboschbackpackers.co.za; 56 Bird St; dm/d without bathroom from R100/310; @) The superb location means you're within easy stumbling distance of the bars. Rooms are in converted apartments, so there are kitchens and bathrooms galore.

Stumble Inn BACKPACKERS $
(021-887 4049; www.stumbleinnbackpackers.co.za; 12 Market St; campsites per person R55, dm R110, d with shared bathroom R330; @) Stellenbosch's undisputed party hostel is split over two old houses. Travellers have expressed concerns over security, so take extra care with your belongings.

Stellenbosch Hotel HOTEL $$
(021-887 3644; www.stellenboschhotel.co.za; 162 Dorp St; s/d incl breakfast from R835/1040; @) A comfortable country-style hotel with a variety of rooms, including some with self-catering facilities. A section dating from 1743 houses the Jan Cats Brasserie, a good spot for a drink.

De Oude Meul GUESTHOUSE $$
(021-887 7085; www.deoudemeul.com; 10A Mill St; s/d incl breakfast R595/850; @) Some rooms at this centrally located guesthouse have balconies and there's a good cafe downstairs. Rates are lower in winter.

Lanzerac Hotel LUXURY HOTEL $$$
(021-887 1132; www.lanzerac.co.za; Jonkershoek Valley; s/d/ste incl breakfast from R2560/3410/5780; @) This opulent place consists of a 300-year-old manor house and winery. Some suites have private pools and the views are stunning.

Eating

De Oude Bank DELI $
(www.paindevie.co.za; 7 Church St; platters R45-60; breakfast & lunch Tue-Sun) A vibrant bakery and deli priding itself on locally sourced ingredients. The menu changes weekly but always features meze-style platters, salads and sandwiches. If you're all wined out it also serves craft beer from a nearby brewery.

TOP
CHOICE **Apprentice@Institute of Culinary Arts** FUSION $$
(Andringa St; mains R55-130; breakfast & lunch Sun & Mon, breakfast, lunch & dinner Tue-Sat) This is a stylish restaurant with a small, inspired menu. The restaurant is operated by students attending the Institute of Culinary Arts and service is excellent.

Stellenbosch

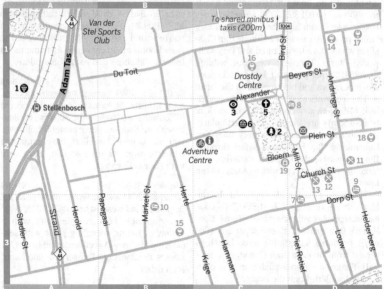

Brampton Wine Studio MEDITERRANEAN **$$**
(www.brampton.co.za; 11 Church St; mains R40-80;
⏰10am-7pm Mon-Sat) Play games and scribble on tables while munching on gourmet pizzas and sipping shiraz at this trendy pavement cafe that also serves as Brampton Winery's tasting room.

Rust en Vrede FUSION **$$$**
(☎021-881 3757; www.rustenvrede.com; Annandale Rd; ⏰dinner Tue-Sat) Chef John Shuttleworth prepares a four-course à la carte menu (R480) as well as a six-course tasting menu (with/without wines R880/585) with a contemporary take on the classics. Also a winery, it's at the end of Annandale Rd, off Rte 44 south of Stellenbosch.

96 Winery Road INTERNATIONAL **$$$**
(www.96wineryroad.co.za; Winery Rd, Zandberg Farm; mains R105-155; ⏰lunch & dinner Mon-Sat, lunch Sun) Off Rte 44 between Stellenbosch and Somerset West, it's one of the most respected restaurants in the area, known for its dry aged beef.

🍷 Drinking

Stellenbosch's nightlife scene is geared largely towards the interests of university students, but there are classier options.

Mystic Boer PUB
(3 Victoria St) Cool kids hang out here in surroundings that can perhaps best be described as posttransformation-era retro-Boer chic. Pizzas and steaks are on the menu.

Nu Bar BAR
(51 Plein St) This place has a nightclub feel, with a small dance floor beyond the long bar where the DJ pumps out hip hop and house.

Two classic student watering holes are **Bohemia** (cnr Andringa & Victoria Sts) and **De Akker** (90 Dorp St), both of which have live music. Lively bars are also found in the **Drostdy Centre** (off Bird St), north of the Braak.

ℹ Information

Snow Cafe (12 Mill St; per hr R25; ⏰8am-10pm Mon-Fri, 9am-6pm Sat & Sun) Internet access.
Stellenbosch Tourism (☎021-883 3584; www.stellenboschtourism.co.za; 36 Market St; ⏰8am-5pm Mon-Fri, 9am-2pm Sat & Sun)

ℹ Getting There & Away

Long-distance bus services charge high prices for the short sector to Cape Town. The cheapest operator is City to City (R125, one hour). The **Baz Bus** (☎0861 229 287; www.bazbus.com) (R160, 30 minutes) will pick you up from where you are staying.

Stellenbosch

◎ Top Sights
Village Museum.....................................E2

◎ Sights
1 Bergkelder A1
2 Braak C2
3 Fick House C2
4 Sasol Art Museum E1
5 St Mary's on the Braak Church..........C2
6 VOC Kruithuis....................................C2

◎ Activities, Courses & Tours
Easy Rider Wine Tours.............. (see 10)

◎ Sleeping
7 De Oude Meul D3
8 Ikhaya Backpackers D2
9 Stellenbosch Hotel D2
10 Stumble Inn B3

◎ Eating
11 Apprentice@Institute of
   Culinary Arts...................................D2
12 Brampton Wine Studio D2
13 De Oude Bank....................................D2

◎ Drinking
14 Bohemia... D1
15 De Akker...B3
16 Drostdy Centre................................. C1
17 Mystic Boer....................................... D1
18 Nu Bar D2

◎ Shopping
19 Craft Market C2

Minibus taxis to Paarl leave from the stand on Bird St (about R45, 45 minutes).

Metrorail (☏0800 656 463) trains run the 46km between Cape Town and Stellenbosch (1st/economy class R13/7.50, about one hour). For inquiries, call Metrorail. To be safe, travel in the middle of the day.

❶ Getting Around
Stellenbosch is navigable on foot and, being largely flat, this is good cycling territory. Bikes can be hired from the **Adventure Centre** (☏021-882 8112; per day R140) next to Stellenbosch Tourism.

For local trips in a private taxi call **Daksi Cab** (☏082 854 1541).

FRANSCHHOEK
☏021 / POP 13,000
The toughest decision you'll face in Franschhoek (French Corner), which bills itself as the country's gastronomic capital, is where to eat. It has a delightful setting and with a clutch of art galleries, wine farms and stylish guesthouses thrown in, it really is one of the loveliest towns in the Cape.

◎ Sights & Activities
Huguenot Memorial Museum MUSEUM
(www.museum.co.za; Lambrecht St; adult/child R10/2; ⊙9am-5pm Mon-Sat, 2-5pm Sun) This museum celebrates South Africa's Hugue-

nots and houses the genealogical records of their descendants. Behind the main complex is a pleasant cafe; in front is the Huguenot Monument (admission free; ⊙9am-5pm) and across the road is the annexe, which offers displays on the Anglo-Boer War and natural history.

Chamonix WINERY
(☏021-876 8426; www.chamonix.co.za; Uitkyk St; tastings R20; ⊙9.30am-5pm) As well as a range of exquisite wines, there's schnapps and grappa to sample and cellar tours are available (R30, bookings essential). The pretty, bistro-style restaurant, Mon Plaisir (mains R135-200; ⊙lunch Tue-Sun, dinner Wed-Sat), has a French menu.

Mont Rochelle WINERY
(www.montrochelle.co.za; Dassenberg Rd; tastings R20, tours R10; ⊙tastings 10am-7pm, tours 11am,

12.30pm & 3pm Mon-Fri) You can combine your wine tasting with a cheese platter (R75) here or enjoy lunch (mains R50 to R90) with a view of the town and the mountains beyond.

Grande Provence   WINERY
(www.grandeprovence.co.za; Main Rd; tastings R20, cellar tours R15; ⊙10am-6pm, cellar tours 11am and 3pm Mon-Fri) A beautifully revamped, 18th-century manor house that is home to a stylish restaurant and a splendid gallery.

Paradise Stables   HORSE RIDING
(☎021-876 2160; www.paradisestables.co.za; per hr R200; ⊙Mon-Sat) As well as hourly rides through Franschhoek's surrounds, there are four-hour trips taking in two vineyards (R650 including tastings).

Manic Cycles   CYCLING
(www.maniccycles.co.za; Fabriek St; half/full day R120/200) You can rent bikes or join a guided cycling tour visiting three different wine estates (R315).

🛏 Sleeping

Otter's Bend Lodge   BACKPACKERS $
(☎021-876 3200; www.ottersbendlodge.co.za; Dassenberg Rd; campsite R100, s/d R250/450) A delightful budget option in a town lacking in affordable accommodation. Double rooms lead on to a shared deck or there's space for a couple of tents on the lawn. It's a 15-minute walk from town and close to Mont Rochelle.

Chamonix Guest Cottages   CHALET $
(☎021-876 8406; www.chamonix.co.za; Uitkyk St; 2-person cottage from R700) Pleasant cottages sleeping up to four are set in the middle of the vineyards, a 20-minute walk uphill north of Huguenot St.

⌖ TOP CHOICE Reeden Lodge   CHALET $$
(☎021-876 3174; www.reedenlodge.co.za; Anne Marie St; cottage from R600; ⊛) A terrific option for families, with well-equipped, self-catering cottages sleeping up to eight people. Parents will love the peace and quiet and their kids will love the sheep, tree house and open space. It's about 10 minutes' walk from town.

Le Ballon Rouge   GUESTHOUSE $$
(☎021-876 2651; www.ballonrouge.co.za; 7 Reservoir St East; s/d incl breakfast R700/850; ⊛@⊛) A small guesthouse with good-quality rooms and stylish suites (with underfloor heating and stunning bathrooms) all opening onto a patio.

Le Quartier Français   BOUTIQUE HOTEL $$$
(☎021-876 2151; www.lequartier.co.za; 16 Huguenot St; d/ste from R3900/5900; ⊛⊛⊛) This is one of the swankiest places to stay in the Winelands, with huge, stylish rooms set around a leafy courtyard. It also boasts one of the country's top restaurants.

🍴 Eating

Common Room   AFRICAN $$
(☎021-876 2151; 16 Huguenot St; mains R45-85; ⊙breakfast, lunch & dinner) The revamped bistro option at Le Quartier Français offers South African ingredients such as wildebeest and crayfish in modern, original dishes. Also here is the Tasting Room (⊙dinner), consistently rated as one of the world's 50 top restaurants. If you're really serious about food, try the gourmet, nine-course menu at R770 (R1150 with wine pairings).

Kalfi's   SOUTH AFRICAN $$
(17 Huguenot St; mains R55-190; ⊙breakfast, lunch & dinner; ⊘) You can watch the world go by from the shady verandah of this family-oriented restaurant. There's a children's menu and a number of vegetarian options.

Haute Cabrière Cellar   FUSION $$$
(☎021-876 3688; Franschhoek Pass Rd; mains R75-145; ⊙lunch Tue-Sun, dinner Tue-Sat) As well as the delectable à la carte option offering imaginative dishes, there is a five-course set menu with accompanying wines (R495). Tastings are also available at the attached cellar.

La Petite Ferme   SOUTH AFRICAN $$$
(Franschhoek Pass Rd; mains R90-140; ⊙noon-4pm) In a stupendous setting overlooking the valley, this is a must for foodies. Sample the boutique wines and smoked, deboned salmon trout, the delicately flavoured signature dish. Charming rooms (from R600 per person) are available if you can't bear to leave.

Reuben's   FUSION $$$
(☎021-876 3772; 19 Huguenot St; mains R80-220; ⊙breakfast, lunch & dinner) The flagship restaurant for local celebrity chef Reuben Riffel has a deli-style eatery as well as a courtyard for breakfast and lunch. Dinner is served in the restaurant.

ⓘ Information
Franschhoek Wine Valley Tourism (☎021-876 2861; www.franschhoek.org.za; 62 Huguenot St; ⊙8am-6pm Mon-Fri, 9am-5pm Sat, 9am-4pm Sun) Staff here can provide you with a

map of the area's scenic walks and issue permits (R10) for walks in nearby forestry areas.

ⓘ Getting There & Away

The best way to reach Franschhoek is in your own vehicle. Some visitors choose to cycle the 32km from Stellenbosch, but the roads are winding and can be treacherous. Catching a minibus taxi from Stellenbosch (R20) or Paarl (R22) will likely involve a few changes. A private taxi operator is **Isak de Wet** (☎083 951 1733).

PAARL

☎021 / POP 165,000

Less touristy and more spread out than Stellenbosch, Paarl is a large commercial centre surrounded by mountains and vineyards. It's not really a town to tour on foot, because Main St is more than 11km long, but there is still quite a lot to see and do, including vineyards within the town limits. There are some great walks in the Paarl Mountain Nature Reserve, some excellent Cape Dutch architecture and some significant monuments to Afrikaner culture.

⊙ Sights & Activities

Paarl Museum   MUSEUM

(www.museums.org.za/paarlmuseum; 303 Main St; admission by donation of R5; ⊗9am-5pm Mon-Fri, 9am-1pm Sat) Housed in the Oude Pastorie (Old Parsonage), built in 1714, this museum has an interesting collection of Cape Dutch antiques.

Afrikaans Language Museum   MUSEUM

(www.taalmuseum.co.za; 11 Pastorie Ave; adult/child R15/5; ⊗9am-4pm Mon-Fri) Paarl is considered the wellspring of the Afrikaans language, a fact covered by this interesting museum.

Paarl Mountain Nature Reserve   PARK

The three giant granite domes that dominate this reserve glisten like pearls when washed by rain – hence the name 'Paarl'. The reserve has mountain *fynbos* ('fine bush', primarily proteas, heaths and ericas) and numerous walks with excellent views over the valley. A map showing walking trails is available from Paarl Tourism.

Nearby is the needlelike **Taal Monument** (adult/child R15/5; ⊗8am-5pm), commemorating the Afrikaans language (*taal* is Afrikaans for 'language').

Bainskloof Pass   SCENIC DRIVE

Bainskloof is one of the country's great mountain passes, with a superb caravan park halfway along. It's a magical drive which, if you have the lungs for it, would be even better experienced on a bicycle.

🛏 Sleeping

Berg River Resort   CAMPGROUND $

(☎021-863 1650; www.bergriverresort.co.za; campsites from R60, d chalets from R600; ☒) An attractive campground beside the Berg River, 5km from Paarl on the N45 towards Franschhoek. Facilities include canoes, trampolines and a cafe. It gets very crowded during school holidays and is best avoided then.

TOP CHOICE Oak Tree Lodge   GUESTHOUSE $$

(☎021-863 2631; www.oaktreelodge.co.za; 32 Main St; s/d incl breakfast from R570/790; ❄@☒)

WINE TASTING IN PAARL

As with other Winelands towns, Paarl has dozens of wineries worth a visit. Here are a few of our favourites.

If you're without your own wheels, **Laborie Cellar** (Taillefer St; tastings R15; ⊗9am-5pm Mon-Fri, 10am-5pm Sat) and **KWV** (www.kwvwineemporium.co.za; Kohler St; cellar tour with tastings R35; ⊗9am-4pm Mon-Sat, 11am-4pm Sun, cellar tours 10am, 10.30am & 2.15pm) are within easy walking distance of Paarl's train station.

Further afield, **Boschendal** (☎021-870 4210; www.boschendal.com; Rte 310, Groot Drakenstein; tastings R20, manor house R15; ⊗9am-5.30pm) is a quintessential Winelands estate, with lovely architecture, food and wine. **Fairview** (☎021-863 2450; www.fairview.co.za; wine & cheese tasting R25; ⊗9am-5pm) is a perennial favourite for its cheese tasting as well as its wide range of wines. **Backsberg** (☎021-875 5141; www.backsberg.co.za; tastings R15; ⊗8am-5pm Mon-Fri, 9.30am-4.30pm Sat, 10.30am-4.30pm Sun) and **Glen Carlou** (☎021-875 5528; www.glencarlou.co.za; Simondium Rd, Klapmuts; tastings R25-35; ⊗8.30am-5pm Mon-Fri, 10am-4pm Sat & Sun) both have good restaurants while **Solms-Delta** (☎021-874 3937; www.solms-delta.com; Delta Rd, off R45; tastings R10; ⊗9am-5pm Sun & Mon, 9am-6pm Tue-Sat) has an excellent museum, if you like your wine paired with a little local history.

Centrally located, this old house has comfortable, well-appointed rooms, some with balconies, as well as modern rooms and quieter suites at the back.

Mooikelder Manor House GUESTHOUSE $$
(021-869 8787; Main St, Noorder Paarl; s/d incl breakfast R470/840; @) Around 5km north of the town centre in an elegant homestead once occupied by Cecil John Rhodes, this is a lovely, quiet spot amid citrus orchards. There is plenty of antique atmosphere in the rooms.

Grande Roche Hotel LUXURY HOTEL $$$
(021-863 2727; www.granderoche.co.za; Plantasie St; ste from R3210; @) A superluxurious hotel set in a Cape Dutch manor house, offering wonderful mountain views, a heated swimming pool and the award-winning Bosman's Restaurant.

Eating

Several of the local vineyards have restaurants or do picnic lunches and are among the best places to eat.

TOP CHOICE **Bosman's Restaurant** INTERNATIONAL $$$
(021-863 2727; www.granderoche.co.za; Plantasie St; mains from R130; dinner Thu-Sun) This elegant spot within the Grande Roche Hotel is one of the country's top restaurants. It's best known for the eight-course tasting menu (R660) and the spectacular wine list, which runs to more than 40 pages. Bookings highly recommended.

TOP CHOICE **Harvest at Laborie** SOUTH AFRICAN $$$
(Taillefer St; mains R70-115; breakfast Sat, lunch daily, dinner Wed-Sat) Eat on a patio overlooking vines at this elegant wine estate a short walk from Main St. Local produce dominates the menu, including west coast mussels, Karoo lamb and seasonal game steaks.

Noop FUSION $$$
(www.noop.co.za; 127 Main St; mains R95-135; lunch & dinner Mon-Fri) Recommended by locals all over the Winelands, this restaurant and wine bar has a small but excellent menu and really fresh salads.

Information

Paarl Tourism (073 708 2835; www.paarl online.com; 216 Main St; 8am-5pm Mon-Fri, 10am-1pm Sat & Sun)

Getting There & Away

BUS

All the major long-distance bus companies offer services going through Paarl, making it easy to build into your itinerary. SA Roadlink (p511) has by far the cheapest service, with one-way fares from Cape Town starting from R50.

TRAIN

Metrorail (0800 656 463; www.capemetro rail.co.za) trains run roughly every hour (less frequently at weekends) between Cape Town and Paarl (1st/economy class R16/10, 1¼ hours). It's safer to travel on trains during the busy part of the day.

You can travel by train from Paarl to Stellenbosch: take a Cape Town–bound train and change at Muldersvlei.

The Overberg

Almost all roads heading east from Cape Town suddenly hit a rocky barrier, forcing drivers into the lower gears. Once you're up and over the top, you're 'over the mountain', the literal meaning of Overberg. The landscape here is quite different to the Cape Flats, with rolling wheat fields bordered by mountains, the Breede River and the coast.

Ballooning east from Cape Hangklip to the coastal De Hoop Nature Reserve and elegant Swellendam, the area is reached from Cape Town via the N2 over the scenic Sir Lowry's Pass or (slower) via Rte 44 from Strand, a breathtaking coastal drive.

This region's wealth of *fynbos* is unmatched; most species flower somewhere in the period between autumn and spring.

HERMANUS
028 / POP 45,000

Hermanus (hair-*maan*-es) was founded as a fishing village, and while it retains vestiges of its heritage, its proximity to Cape Town (122km) has made it a day-tripper's paradise, in part thanks to its status as the world's best land-based whale-watching destination. As a result, the town can get crowded, particularly during the Hermanus Whale Festival (www.whalefestival.co.za) in September and during school holidays in December and January.

Hermanus is highly recommended at quieter times of year; respite from whale-seeking hordes can also be found on the appealing beaches, on hikes in surrounding hills and along a largely undiscovered wine route in the Hemel-en-Aarde Valley.

◎ Sights & Activities

Between June and November, southern right whales come to Walker Bay to calve. There can be up to 70 whales in the bay at one time and humpback whales are also seen.

Whales often come very close to shore and there are some excellent vantage points from the cliff paths that run from one end of Hermanus to the other. The best places are Gearings Point and Kraal Rock.

The Cliff Path Walking Trail meanders for 10km from the new harbour, 2km west of town, along the sea to the mouth of the Klein River. Along the way you'll pass Kwaaiwater, a good whale-watching lookout, and Grotto Beach, the most popular beach with excellent facilities. The 1400-hectare Fernkloof Nature Reserve (http://fernkloof.com; Fir Ave; ◎9am-5pm) has some 1500 species of *fynbos* and trails lasting up to two hours.

🛏 Sleeping

Hermanus Backpackers BACKPACKERS $
(☑028-312 4293; www.hermanusbackpackers. co.za; 26 Flower St; dm/d R130/390, d with shared bathroom R360; @☲) This is a great place with upbeat decor, good facilities and clued-up staff who can help with activities. Free breakfast is served in the morning, and evening *braais* (barbecues) are R90.

TOP CHOICE Potting Shed GUESTHOUSE $$
(☑028-312 1712; www.thepottingshedguesthouse. co.za; 28 Albertyn St; s/d incl breakfast R525/700; @☲) An excellent-value guesthouse enjoyed by readers. The neat rooms are comfortable and have bright, imaginative decor. A self-catering unit (R950 for four people) is also available.

Auberge Burgundy GUESTHOUSE $$
(☑028-313 1201; www.auberge.co.za; 16 Harbour Rd; s/d incl breakfast from R840/1120; ☲) This wonderful place, built in the style of a Provençal villa, has just about the most perfect position – it's in the centre of town overlooking the sea.

Hermanus Esplanade APARTMENT $$
(☑028-312 3610; www.hermanusesplanade.com; 63 Marine Dr; sea-facing apt from R470) Some of these self-catering apartments overlook the sea. There are also simpler options catering to backpackers (R300 for two people).

PENGUIN COLONY

Stony Point African Penguin Colony (admission R10; ◎8am-5pm) is a much quieter place to watch the diminutive penguins than at the infinitely more famous Boulders Beach, across the other side of False Bay. It's at Betty's Bay, 50km west of Hermanus.

Marine LUXURY HOTEL $$$
(☑028-313 1000; www.marine-hermanus.co.za; Marine Dr; s/d incl breakfast from R2500/4000; ✳@☲) Right on the sea with immaculate grounds and amenities. The hotel has two seafront restaurants. The Pavilion (mains R95-175; ◎breakfast & dinner) serves contemporary South African cuisine, while the Seafood Restaurant (◎lunch & dinner) offers two-/three-course meals for R205/245.

✗ Eating & Drinking

TOP CHOICE Fisherman's Cottage SEAFOOD $$
(Lemm's Cnr; mains R55-120; ◎lunch & dinner Mon-Sat) The emphasis is on excellent seafood at this 1860s thatched cottage draped with fishing nets, though it also serves steaks and traditional meals.

Burgundy Restaurant SEAFOOD $$
(☑028-312 2800; www.burgundyrestaurant.co.za; Marine Dr; mains R60-140; ◎breakfast, lunch & dinner) Booking is recommended at this eatery, one of the most popular in the area. The menu is mostly seafood with a different vegetarian dish each day.

Annie se Kombuis SOUTH AFRICAN $$
(Warrington Pl, Annie's Kitchen; mains R65-130; ◎lunch & dinner Tue-Sun) If you're looking for traditional food, such as oxtail, *bobotie* (delicately flavoured curry with a topping of beaten egg baked to a crust) or game meat, this cosy place off Harbour Rd will fit the bill.

Gecko Bar BAR
(New Harbour; mains R45-75; ◎lunch & dinner) With wood-fired pizzas, beer from Birkenhead brewery in Stanford and a deck hanging over the ocean, this is a top spot for sundowners that turn into late-night drinks. There's live music on weekends.

❶ Information

Hermanus Tourism (☑028-312 2629; www. hermanustourism.info; Mitchell St, Old Station

SHARK-CAGE DIVING

It's a controversial activity, but climbing into a cage to see great whites up close is near the top of many visitors' to-do lists. The sleepy seaside town of Gansbaai is the base for shark-cage diving, though you can also organise a trip leaving from Cape Town or Hermanus. Operators include Shark Lady (028-313 2306; www.sharklady.co.za; R1350), which has scuba equipment available for qualified divers.

If you want to see sharks but prefer to avoid shark-cage diving, get in touch with an operator such as Simon's Town Boat Company (p339), which offers boat trips to view sharks feasting at Seal Island in False Bay.

Bldg; 8am-6pm Mon-Fri, 9am-5pm Sat, 11am-3pm Sun) North of the town centre.

Internet City (Main Rd, Waterkant Bldg; per hr R15; 8am-6pm Mon-Fri, 8.30am-3pm Sat, 9am-1pm Sun)

❶ Getting There & Away

Trevi's Tours (072 608 9213) offers daily shuttles to Gansbaai (two people R400, 30 minutes) and Cape Town (two people R700, 1½ hours).

All three hostels run a shuttle service to the Baz Bus drop-off point in Botrivier, 50km west of town; otherwise there are no regular bus services to Hermanus from Cape Town.

DE HOOP NATURE RESERVE

Covering 36,000 hectares, plus 5km out to sea, the De Hoop Nature Reserve (www. capenature.org.za; adult/child R40/20; 7am-6pm) is one of Cape Nature's best reserves. It includes a scenic coastline with stretches of beach, huge dunes and exceptional *fynbos*, plus a freshwater lake. Fauna includes the endangered Cape mountain zebra, various antelope and a wealth of birdlife, including the rare Cape vulture. The coast is a key breeding and calving area for the southern right whale.

Although there are numerous day walks, an overnight mountain-bike trail and good snorkelling along the coast, the reserve's most interesting feature is the five-day Whale Trail (per person R1550). Covering 55km, it offers excellent opportunities to see whales between June and December. Accommodation is in fully equipped self-catering cottages. The trail needs to be booked in advance, and only groups of six to 12 are accepted.

The wide variety of accommodation in the reserve is managed by De Hoop Collection (021-422 4522; www.dehoopcollection.co.za; campsites/rondavel for 2 with shared bathroom from R295/770, cottage per person from R595).

The reserve is about 260km from Cape Town. Access is via Wydgeleë on the road between Bredasdorp and Malgas. At Malgas a manually operated pont (river ferry) on the Breede River still operates (between dawn and dusk).

SWELLENDAM
028 / POP 23,000

Surrounded by the undulating wheat lands of the Overberg and protected by the Langeberge mountain range, Swellendam is perfectly positioned for exploring the Little Karoo and it makes a good stopover on the way further east to the Garden Route. One of the oldest towns in South Africa, it has beautiful Cape Dutch architecture and dates back to 1745.

◉ Sights

Drostdy Museum MUSEUM
(www.drostdymuseum.com; 18 Swellengrebel St; adult/child R20/5; 9am-4.45pm Mon-Fri, 10am-3pm Sat & Sun) The centrepiece of this excellent museum is the beautiful *drostdy* (residence of an official) itself, which dates from 1747. The museum ticket also covers entrance to the nearby old gaol, where you'll find part of the original administrative buildings and a watermill; and Mayville (Hermanus Steyn St), another residence dating back to 1853. On-site there's a shop selling stylish African curios.

Dutch Reformed Church CHURCH
(Voortrek St) Swellendam residents swear every visitor takes a photograph of this enormous church in the centre of town.

✦ Activities

Swellendam has adventures for all ages, budgets and tastes.

For day permits (adult/child R40/20) to walk in Marloth Nature Reserve in the Langeberge, 1.5km north of town, contact

the **Nature Conservation Department**
(☎028-514 1410) at the entrance to the reserve or Swellendam Backpackers Adventure Lodge. Trails include the demanding
Swellendam Hiking Trail (☎reservations
021-659 3500; www.capenature.co.za; admission
R38), regarded as one of South Africa's top
10 hikes.

Fynbus Tours   GUIDED TOUR
(☎028-514 3303; www.fynbus.co.za; 23 Swellengrebel St) This local company offers loads of
options, including trips to Cape Agulhas and
De Hoop Nature Reserve (both R495).

Two Feathers Horse Trails   HORSE RIDING
(☎082 494 8279; 5 Lichtenstein St, Swellendam
Backpackers Adventure Lodge; per hr R200) Both
inexperienced and experienced riders are
catered for. Advance booking is essential.

🛏 Sleeping

**Swellendam Backpackers
Adventure Lodge**   BACKPACKERS $
(☎028-514 2648; www.swellendambackpackers.
co.za; 5 Lichtenstein St; campsites per person R80,
dm R120, s/d with shared bathroom R200/260, s/d
R350/410) Set on a huge plot of land with its
own river and Marloth Nature Reserve next
door, this is an excellent hostel with enthusiastic management. Horse riding, permits
to the nature reserve and day trips to Cape
Agulhas (R450) can all be arranged.

TOP CHOICE Cypress Cottage   GUESTHOUSE $$
(☎028-514 3296; www.cypress-cottage.co.za; 3
Voortrek St; s/d R450/700; ❄@❄) There are
six individually decorated rooms in this
200-year-old house with a gorgeous garden
and a refreshing pool.

De Kloof   GUESTHOUSE $$$
(☎028-514 1303; www.dekloof.co.za; 8 Weltevrede
St; s/d incl champagne breakfast from R1195/1590;

❄@❄) One of Swellendam's swankiest options, this is a supremely stylish guesthouse
with a surprisingly personal touch. Set in a
large estate dating back to 1801, it offers a
library, cigar room, gym, putting green and
wonderful views.

Bloomestate   GUESTHOUSE $$$
(☎028-514 2984; www.bloomestate.com; 276
Voortrek St; s/d incl breakfast from R1200/1650;
❄@❄❄) A modern guesthouse set on a
beautiful 2.5-hectare property which offers
Zen-like privacy to go with the luxurious,
colourful rooms.

🍴 Eating

**TOP CHOICE Old Gaol on
Church Square**   SOUTH AFRICAN $
(www.oldgaolrestaurant.co.za; 8a Voortrekker St;
light meals R40-65; ❄breakfast & lunch) It might
not be in the old gaol anymore, but the food
at this empowerment venture is still just
as good. There's lots of seating outside under the trees where you can enjoy delicious
snacks, traditional breads and excellent
service.

La Belle Alliance   SOUTH AFRICAN $$
(1 Swellengrebel St; mains R35-100; ❄breakfast &
lunch) This appealing tearoom had the honour of serving Nelson Mandela in 1999. In
an old Masonic lodge with shaded outdoor
tables beside the river, it's a good spot for
lunch.

Koornlands Restaurant   SOUTH AFRICAN $$$
(☎082 430 8188; www.koornlandsrestaurant.co.za;
192 Voortrek St; mains R95-155; ❄lunch Wed-Sun,
dinner Wed-Mon) An eclectic menu of mostly
African meat is served in an intimate candlelit setting. It's generally considered the
top place in town. Try the crocodile sashimi
(R65) and kudu fillet.

WORTH A TRIP

CAPE AGULHAS

The Cape of Good Hope isn't Africa's southernmost point; it's actually Cape Agulhas,
which is part of **Agulhas National Park** (☎028-435 6078; www.sanparks.org.za; adult/
child R88/44). This rugged, windswept coastline, where the Atlantic and Indian Oceans
meet, has been a graveyard for many a ship. South Africa's second-oldest lighthouse
(1848) houses the **Lighthouse Museum** (☎028-435 6222; adult/child R15/7.50; ❄9am-
5pm).

The friendly tourism bureau, next to the lighthouse, can help with accommodation
and booking the various water sports, including kitesurfing. Most places to stay and eat
are found in the small town of **L'Agulhas**, just east of Cape Agulhas.

ℹ Information

Swellendam Tourism Bureau (☎028-514 2770; www.swellendamtourism.co.za; 22 Swellengrebel St; ⊙9am-5pm Mon-Fri, 10am-3pm Sat, 9am-2pm Sun) An exceptionally helpful office based in the Old Gaoler's Cottage.

ℹ Getting There & Away

Most of the major bus companies pass through Swellendam on their runs between Cape Town and Port Elizabeth, stopping opposite the Swellengrebel Hotel on Voortrek St. The Baz Bus stops at Swellendam Backpackers Adventure Lodge.

BONTEBOK NATIONAL PARK

Some 6km south of Swellendam is **Bontebok National Park** (☎028-514 2735; adult/child R60/30; ⊙7am-7pm Oct-Apr, 7am-6pm May-Sep), established in 1931 to save the remaining 30 bontebok. The project was successful, and bontebok as well as other antelopes and mountain zebras are found here. *Fynbos* (which flower in late winter and spring), rare *renosterveld* plants and an abundance of birdlife also feature. Swimming is possible in the Breede River.

A lot of thought has gone into the park's accommodation. Ten **chalets** (for 2 people R840), incorporating 'Touch the Earth Lightly' principles, include two geared towards people with special needs. **Campsites** (with/without electricity R205/170) are also available.

Route 62

This area, promoted as the longest wine route in the world, provides an excellent hinterland alternative to the N2 for travel between Cape Town and the Garden Route. Breathtaking mountain passes and intensively cultivated valleys, well-preserved towns and vast stretches of semi-arid plains dotted with ostriches provide eye candy, while delectable wine, country cafes and charming B&Bs enchant the palate and relax the body.

The Little (Klein) Karoo, east of the Breede River Valley, is more fertile and better watered than the harsher Great Karoo to the north.

MONTAGU

☎023 / POP 9500

Coming along Rte 62 from Robertson, the road passes through a narrow arch in the Cogmanskloof mountains, and suddenly the town of Montagu appears before you. Its wide streets are bordered by 24 restored

---

DON'T MISS

ROBERTSON'S WINERIES

Robertson's wineries are unpretentious and less crowded than their counterparts in Stellenbosch, Franschhoek and Paarl. Enjoy a picnic and a river cruise (adult/child R40/15) at **Viljoensdrift** (www.viljoensdrift.co.za; tasting free; ⊙9am-5pm Mon-Fri, 10am-3pm Sat), top-notch bubbly at **Graham Beck** (www.grahambeckwines.co.za; standard tasting free, other tasting options from R50; ⊙9am-5pm Mon-Fri, 10am-4pm Sat & Sun) or a walk through the tree-lined tropical gardens at **Van Loveren** (www.vanloveren.co.za; tastings with chocolate/cheese/charcuterie R40, bistro mains R55-75; ⊙8.30am-5pm Mon-Fri, 9.30am-3pm Sat, 11am-2pm Sun, bistro closed Tue).

---

national monuments, including some fine art-deco architecture. There's a wide range of activities, including hot springs, easy walks and more serious hikes, as well as excellent accommodation and restaurants.

◉ Sights & Activities

Montagu Museum & Joubert House   MUSEUM

Interesting displays and some good examples of antique furniture can be found at the **Montagu Museum** (41 Long St; adult/child R5/2; ⊙9am-5pm Mon-Fri, 10.30am-12.30pm Sat & Sun) in the old mission church. **Joubert House** (☎023-614 1774; 25 Long St; adult/child R5/2; ⊙9am-4.30pm Mon-Fri, 10.30am-12.30pm Sat & Sun), a short walk away, is the oldest house in Montagu (built in 1853) and has been restored to its Victorian glory.

TOP CHOICE **Tractor-Trailer Rides**   ECOTOUR

(☎023-614 3012; www.proteafarm.co.za; adult/child R90/45; ⊙tours 10am & 2pm Wed & Sat) Fun three-hour tractor-trailer rides are available on this farm 29km from Montagu. Enjoy a delicious lunch of *potjiekos* (traditional pot stew) with homemade bread for R100/70 per adult/child, and stay on at the farm accommodation (four-person cottage from R650).

Hot Springs   SWIMMING

(adult/child R60/40; ⊙8am-11pm) Water from the hot mineral springs finds its way into the swimming pools of the Avalon Springs

Hotel, about 3km from town by road. The water gushes from a rock face at a constant 43°C, and is renowned for its healing properties. Don't expect natural-looking pools – they're commercialised and can get unpleasantly busy on weekends and in school holidays. Try to visit off-peak.

A great way to get there is to hike along the 2.4km trail from the car park at the end of Tanner St. The route leads past Montagu's top rock-climbing spots. For guidance on climbing, abseiling and hiking in the area contact De Bos.

HIKING

The Bloupunt Trail (admission R20) is 15.6km long and can be walked in six to eight hours; it traverses ravines and mountain streams, and climbs to 1000m. The Cogmanskloof Trail (admission R20) is 12.1km and can be completed in four to six hours; it's not as steep as the Bloupunt Trail but is still fairly strenuous. Both trails start from the car park at the northern end of Tanner St. The tourism bureau handles bookings for basic overnight huts (per person R80) on the trails.

🛏 Sleeping

De Bos BACKPACKERS, CAMPGROUND **$**
(📞023-614 2532; www.debos.co.za; Bath St; campsites per person R50, dm/s/d R80/185/330; 🛜) There's a river, chickens and pecan-nut trees on this 7-hectare property, where colourful old workers' cottages have been converted into self-catering cottages (from R360). On weekends there is a two-night minimum stay, except for camping. Mountain bikes are available to hire.

Montagu Caravan Park CAMPGROUND **$**
(📞023-614 3034; Bath St; campsites per person R70, 4-person chalet from R480) This park is in a pleasant location with apricot trees and lots of shade and grass. The chalets come with cooking equipment and TVs. There are also hikers' cabins (for two R260).

TOP CHOICE 7 Church Street GUESTHOUSE **$$**
(📞023-614 1186; www.7churchstreet.co.za; 7 Church St; s/d incl breakfast from R650/1100; @🛜) A friendly, upmarket guesthouse in a charming Karoo building with traditional wrought-iron *broekie* (panty) lace trim. There are also luxury rooms in the manicured garden.

Mimosa Lodge HOTEL **$$**
(📞023-614 2351; www.mimosa.co.za; Church St; s/d incl breakfast from R710/1040; @🛜) A

delightful, upmarket lodge in a restored Edwardian landmark building with lovely gardens and a pool. The award-winning restaurant serves four-course dinners (R320) and is open to nonguests.

✕ Eating

TOP CHOICE Jessica's FUSION **$$**
(📞023-614 1805; www.jessicasrestaurant.co.za; 47 Bath St; mains R80-135; ⊗dinner Mon-Sat, closed Aug) Cosy Jessica's serves up inventive bistro dishes, many of them melding South African ingredients with Asian flavours.

Templeton's@Four Oaks FUSION **$$**
(46 Long St; mains R85-145; ⊗lunch & dinner Mon-Sat) Set in a lovely old house, the style is minimalist rather than the usual country decor and the food and service are excellent.

Die Stal INTERNATIONAL **$$**
(Touwsrivier Rd; mains R60-110; ⊗breakfast & lunch Tue-Sun) A countryside dining experience just 7km north of town off Rte 318, on a working citrus farm. The menu changes daily, but large country breakfasts are always on offer.

ℹ Information

Tourism Bureau (📞023-614 2471; www.montagu-ashton.info; 24 Bath St; ⊗8.30am-5pm Mon-Fri, 9am-5pm Sat, 9.30am-5pm Sun) Opening hours are slightly shorter between May and October.

ℹ Getting There & Around

Buses stop at Ashton, 9km from Montagu. **Translux** (www.translux.co.za) buses stop here on the run between Cape Town (R195, 2½ hours, daily) and Port Elizabeth (R305, eight hours, daily). Most accommodation establishments in town offer (prebooked) shuttles from Ashton to Montagu, but you can also jump in one of the minibus taxis (R15) that ply this route. They stop in Montagu at Foodzone (Bath St).

OUDTSHOORN
📞044 / POP 79,000

That Oudtshoorn bills itself as the ostrich capital of the world is no overstatement. The birds have been bred hereabouts since the 1860s, and at the turn of the 20th century fortunes were made from the fashion for ostrich feathers. Oudtshoorn boomed, and the so-called 'feather barons' built gracious homes and other grand edifices such as the sandstone building housing the CP Nel Museum.

The town still turns a pretty penny from breeding the birds for meat and leather. The ostriches also pay their way with tourists – you can buy ostrich eggs, feathers and *biltong* all over town – but more importantly Oudtshoorn is a great base for exploring the Little Karoo, the Garden Route (it's 55km to George along the N12) and the Great Karoo.

◉ Sights & Activities

TOP CHOICE Meerkat Adventures
WILDLIFE ENCOUNTERS

(☎084 772 9678; www.meerkatadventures.co.za; per person R550; ◉sunrise on sunny days) This unique wildlife encounter comes highly recommended by travellers and will likely be a trip highlight. Passionate conservationist Devey Glinister operates the sunrise experience on De Zeekoe Farm, 9km west of Oudtshoorn. At this pioneering conservation project, you will get to see up close how these curious, highly intelligent creatures communicate and live. Once you're at the meeting point (where Rte 62 and Rte 328 meet), sightings of the animals warming up in the morning sun are guaranteed since Devey seeks them out in their burrows each night. Little extras such as camping chairs, coffee and blankets make this a delightful way to start a day. No children under 10 years.

Cango Caves
CAVE

(☎044-272 7410; www.cangocaves.co.za; adult/child R75/35; ◉9am-4pm) Named after the Khoe-San word for 'a wet place', the Cango Caves are heavily commercialised but impressive. The one-hour tour gives you just a glimpse, while the 90-minute Adventure Tour (adult/child R95/55) lets you explore deeper into the caves. Advance booking for both tours is highly recommended. The caves are 30km north of Oudtshoorn.

CP Nel Museum
MUSEUM

(www.cpnelmuseum.co.za; 3 Baron van Rheede St; adult/child R15/5; ◉8am-5pm Mon-Fri, 9am-1pm Sat) Extensive displays about ostriches, as well as Karoo history, make up this large and interesting museum. Included in the ticket price is admission to Le Roux Townhouse (cnr Loop & High Sts; ◉9am-5pm Mon-Fri), decorated in authentic period furniture. It's as good an example of a 'feather palace' as you're likely to see.

Ostrich Farms
WILDLIFE ENCOUNTERS

There are three show farms offering guided tours (45 minutes to 1½ hours). There's little difference between them; we found the staff at Highgate Ostrich Show Farm (www.highgate.co.za; adult/child R70/32; ◉8am-5pm) very knowledgeable. It's 10km from Oudtshoorn en route to Mossel Bay. Nearby is Safari Ostrich Show Farm (www.safariostrich.co.za; adult/child R80/40; ◉8am-4pm). Cango Ostrich Show Farm (www.cangoostrich.co.za; Cango Caves Rd; adult/child R70/40; ◉8am-5pm) also receives good reviews.

Two Passes Route
SCENIC DRIVE

A wonderful day's excursion is the round trip from Oudtshoorn to Prince Albert taking in two magnificent passes. Head up the untarred Swartberg Pass to Prince Albert, then return via the Meiringspoort Pass. Halfway down the latter is a waterfall and small visitor centre. Ask at your accommodation or the tourism bureau for a route map.

You can also cycle the Swartberg Pass on a mountain-biking trip operated by Backpackers Paradise.

⊨ Sleeping

TOP CHOICE Backpackers Paradise
BACKPACKERS $

(☎044-272 3436; www.backpackersparadise.net; 148 Baron van Rheede St; campsites per person R60, dm/r/d R110/ 290/360; @⊠) In a large old house, this lively hostel has a bar, ostrich *braais* and free ostrich-egg breakfasts (in season, you'll be given an egg – cook it any way you please). It also offers discounts to attractions in the area and can arrange a host of activities.

Karoo Soul Travel Lodge
BACKPACKERS $

(☎044-272 0330; www.karoosoul.com; 170 Langenhoven Rd; campsites per person R60, dm R120, d with shared bathroom R320, d R380; @⊠) The gracious old house, with its luxury linens and comfortable surroundings, is proof that the backpacker has come of age. Try to get one of the west-facing doubles or ask about the garden cottages with bathroom (R420).

Kleinplaas Resort
CAMPGROUND $

(☎044-272 5811; www.kleinplaas.co.za; cnr North & Baron van Rheede Sts; campsites R280, 4-person chalet R660-900; ⊠) A terrific caravan park with a big pool. The restaurant is only open for breakfast.

La Pension
GUESTHOUSE $$

(☎044-279 2445; www.lapension.co.za; 169 Church St; s/d incl breakfast R650/940; ⊛@⊠) A reliable choice with spacious, stylish rooms and superb bathrooms, La Pension also has one self-catering cottage, plus a good-sized pool, sauna and large, immaculate garden.

Bisibee Guesthouse　　　GUESTHOUSE **$$**
(☏044-272 4784; www.bisibee.co.za; 171 Church St; s/d R275/540; @🌊) One of the original guest-houses in town, this is a friendly place offering excellent value and comfort.

✖ Eating

As you'd expect, most places serve ostrich in one form or another.

Bella Cibo　　　ITALIAN **$$**
(www.bellocibo.co.za; 145 Baron van Rheede St; mains R40-85; ⊗dinner Mon-Sat) Popular with locals and widely recommended around town, this Italian restaurant serves very well-priced pizza, pasta and seafood.

TOP
CHOICE **Jemima's**　　　SOUTH AFRICAN **$$$**
(www.jemimas.com; 94 Baron van Rheede St; mains R95-180; ⊗lunch & dinner) With a small menu specialising in traditional Cape fare, this restaurant is set in an attractive old house and garden.

Kalinka　　　FUSION **$$$**
(☏044-279 2596; www.kalinka.co.za; 93 Baron van Rheede St; mains R85-170; ⊗dinner Tue-Sun) This stylish, upmarket restaurant is a long-standing favourite that serves imaginative dishes featuring game meat with an Asian flair. The menu changes regularly, but is always excellent.

ⓘ Information

Cyber Ostrich Internet Café (37 Baron van Rheede St; per hr R35; ⊗8am-9pm Mon-Fri, 9am-6pm Sat & Sun)

Oudtshoorn Tourism Bureau (☏044-279 2532; www.oudtshoorn.com; cnr Baron van Rheede & Voortrekker Sts; ⊗8.30am-5pm Mon-Fri, 8.30am-1pm Sat) This helpful bureau is behind the CP Nel Museum.

ⓘ Getting There & Around

Buses stop in the Riverside Centre off Voortrekker St. **Intercape** (www.intercape.co.za) has services to Johannesburg (R650, 14½ hours, daily), Cape Town (R380, eight hours) and Mossel Bay (R250, two hours, daily).

The **Baz Bus** (☏0861 229 287; www.bazbus.com) stops at George, from where you can arrange a transfer to Oudtshoorn with Backpackers Paradise (R60 one way).

Minibus taxis leave from behind the Spar supermarket on Adderley St en route to George (R35, 30 minutes) or Cape Town (R200, three hours). The area east of Adderley St has a slightly dodgy feel to it, so be careful.

Garden Route

High on the must-see list of most visitors to South Africa is the Garden Route, and with good reason: you can't help but be seduced by the glorious natural beauty of the scenery. It's less than 300km from Mossel Bay in the west to just beyond Plettenberg Bay in the east, yet the range of topography, vegetation, wildlife and outdoor activity in this short space is breathtaking.

There are excellent beaches providing activities from boating to good surfing and fishing. Inland are picturesque lagoons and lakes, rolling hills and eventually the mountains of the Outeniqua and Tsitsikamma ranges that divide the Garden Route from the arid Little Karoo. The ancient indigenous forests that line the coast from Wilderness to Knysna offer adventure trails, hiking, birding, canoeing the rivers, sliding through the tree canopy or simply taking an easy walk between the trees.

Strong competition in the tourist industry has led to high standards in everything from activities to restaurants. The downside of this is the high volume of people in the most popular towns of Knysna and Plettenberg Bay. While they make good bases for exploring the area, they can get very crowded during December and January, when prices rise significantly. Book ahead if you're travelling at these times, or head for less-crowded Wilderness.

MOSSEL BAY
☏044 / POP 117,000

Once one of the jewels of the Garden Route, Mossel Bay was marred by rampant industrial sprawl in the 1980s. Today the town is enjoying a revival thanks to its historic buildings, excellent places to stay, plentiful activities, fine beaches and gnarly surf spots. Compared with the Garden Route's more developed spots, it's a pleasantly low-key place to wander in the footsteps of its original tourists, Portuguese explorers Bartholomeu Dias and Vasco da Gama.

◎ Sights & Activities

Mossel Bay is chock-full of activities. From the harbour, there are regular boat trips on both the **Romonza** (☏044-690 3101) and the **Seven Seas** (☏082 297 7165) to view the seal colony, birds and dolphins around Seal Island. One-hour trips cost R125. In late winter and spring the *Romonza* also runs whale-watching trips (R600, 2½ hours).

Garden Route

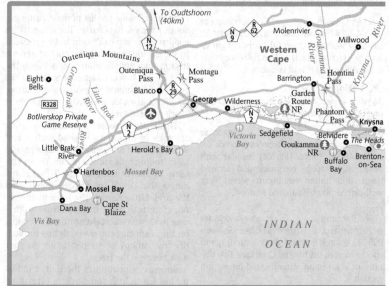

Adventurous travellers are well catered for: try scuba diving with **Electrodive** (☑082 561 1259; www.electrodive.co.za; 2 Field St; gear hire per day R200, shore- & boat-based dives R190-230), shark-cage diving with **White Shark Africa** (☑044-691 3796; www.whitesharkafrica.com; cnr Church & Bland Sts; dives R1350) or jumping out of a plane with **Skydive Mossel Bay** (☑082 824 8599; www.skydivemosselbay.com; Mossel Bay Airfield; from R1600). The **Oystercatcher Trail** (www.oystercatchertrail.co.za) is a superb four-day hiking route, or for something a little less energetic, try a cultural tour with **Back Road Safaris** (☑044-690 8150; www.backroad safaris.co.za).

TOP CHOICE Dias Museum Complex MUSEUM (www.diasmuseum.co.za; Market St; adult/child R20/5; ⊙9am-4.45pm Mon-Fri, 9am-3.45pm Sat & Sun) This excellent museum includes the **spring** where Dias watered the **postal tree**, the 1786 Dutch East India Company (Vereenigde Oost-Indische Compagnie; VOC) **granary**, a **shell museum** (with some interesting aquarium tanks) and a local **history museum**.

The highlight of the complex is the replica of the caravel that Dias used on his 1488 voyage of discovery. Boarding the caravel costs an extra R20.

🛌 Sleeping

There are three municipal **caravan parks** (☑044-690 3501; campsites from R190, chalet from R430) in town, all close to the ocean.

TOP CHOICE Park House Lodge & Travel Centre BACKPACKERS $ (☑044-691 1937; www.park-house.co.za; 121 High St; dm R160, d with/without bathroom from R600/400; @) This place, in a gracious old sandstone house next to the park, is friendly, smartly decorated and has beautiful gardens. Breakfast is R40.

Mossel Bay Backpackers BACKPACKERS $ (☑044-691 3182; www.mosselbayhostel.co.za; 1 Marsh St; dm R120, d without bathroom R340, d from R380; @🏊) Close to the beach at the Point and the bars on Marsh St, this long-established place is reliable and well run. It offers comfortable rooms, a pool and bar and an impressive fully equipped kitchen.

Santos Express BACKPACKERS $ (☑044-691 1995; www.santosexpress.co.za; Santos Beach; dm R100, s/d with shared bathroom & breakfast R210/400) The position of this converted train, right beside the beach, can't be beaten, but the compartments are undeniably cramped. The attached bar-restaurant has a large menu (mains R40 to R125).

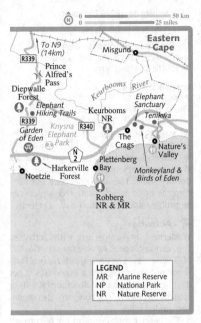

The map legend reads:

LEGEND
MR	Marine Reserve
NP	National Park
NR	Nature Reserve

Point Village Hotel
HOTEL **$$**

(☎044-690 3156; www.pointvillagehotel.co.za; 5 Point Rd; s/d R420/720; ☻) The quirky, fake lighthouse on this well-priced hotel's exterior is a sign of what's inside: a range of fun, funky, bright rooms and exceptionally friendly service. Rooms have a kitchenette and some have balconies.

Point Hotel
HOTEL **$$**

(☎044-691 3512; www.pointhotel.co.za; Point Rd; s/d R1075/1430, restaurant mains R55-110; ☻) This hotel boasts a spectacular location right above the wave-pounded rocks at the Point. There's a decent restaurant and the spacious rooms have balconies with ocean views.

✗ Eating

Marsh St and Point Rd are where it all happens in Mossel Bay.

TOP CHOICE Kaai 4
BARBECUE **$**

(www.kaai4.co.za; Mossel Bay Harbour; mains R25-60; ☻lunch & dinner) Boasting one of Mossel Bay's best locations, this low-key seafood spot has picnic tables on the sand overlooking the ocean. Food is cooked on massive fire pits and there's an all-you-can-eat option (R145).

Café Havana
INTERNATIONAL **$$**

(www.cafehavana.co.za; 38 Marsh St; mains R50-110; ☻lunch & dinner) About as Cuban as Mossel Bay can get, this restaurant and cocktail bar has a great vibe. The stews and steaks are a nice antidote to all the seafood in town – though of course there's plenty of that as well.

Kingfisher
SEAFOOD **$$**

(Point Rd; mains R45-120; ☻lunch & dinner) Locals love the seafood dishes and ocean views here. It also serve salads, meat, and has a children's menu.

ⓘ Getting There & Away

Mossel Bay is off the highway, so long-distance buses don't come into town; they drop you at the Voorbaai Shell petrol station, 8km away. The hostels can usually collect you if you give notice. The **Baz Bus** (☎0861 229 287; www.bazbus. com) will drop you in town.

Greyhound (www.greyhound.co.za), **Intercape** (www.intercape.co.za) and **City to City/Translux** (☎0861 589 282; www.translux.co.za) stop here on their Cape Town–Port Elizabeth runs. Sample fares:

» Cape Town (R330, six hours)

» Knysna (R235, two hours)

» Plettenberg Bay (R245, 2½ hours)

» Port Elizabeth (R320, six hours)

GEORGE
☎044 / POP 136,000

George, founded in 1811, is the largest town on the Garden Route yet remains little more than a commercial centre with not much to keep visitors for long. It has some attractive old buildings, including the tiny St Mark's Cathedral and the more imposing Dutch Reformed Mother Church, but it's 8km from the coast and for most people its chief draw is the range of championship golf courses.

⊙ Sights

George was the hub of the indigenous timber industry and thus the George Museum (Courtenay St; admission by donation; ☻9am-4pm Mon-Fri, 9am-12.30pm Sat) contains related artefacts, as well as exhibits covering other aspects of 19th-century life.

The George Transport Museum (☎044-801 8288; cnr Courtenay & York Sts; adult/child R10/5; ☻7.30am-6pm Mon-Sat) is worth a visit if you're interested in trains.

There is good surf at nearby Herold's Bay and Victoria Bay and some scenic drives in the mountains around George.

🛏 Sleeping & Eating

Outeniqua Travel Lodge   BACKPACKERS $
(☎082 316 7720; www.outeniqualodge.com; 70 Langenhoven St; dm/s/d R120/300/440; @) It's a way from the centre, but this is a great budget option in a quiet, residential area.

**TOP CHOICE ⟩ French Lodge
International**   GUESTHOUSE $$
(☎044-874 0345; www.frenchlodge.co.za; 29 York St; s/d incl breakfast from R550/800; ❄@☀) You can't miss this place with its mini Eiffel Tower in the garden. Rooms are in luxurious thatched-roof *rondavels* (round hut with a conical roof) or apartments set around the pool, with satellite TV and bathrooms with Jacuzzis.

Fancourt Hotel   LUXURY HOTEL $$$
(☎044-804 0000; www.fancourt.co.za; Montagu St, Blanco; d from R3200; ❄@☀) The area's most luxurious place is about 10km from the town centre. There's a range of top-notch accommodation options, a health spa, five restaurants and three 18-hole golf courses.

Old Townhouse   STEAKHOUSE $$
(Market St; mains R50-115; ⊘lunch & dinner Mon-Fri, dinner Sat) Situated in the one-time town administration building dating back to 1848, this long-standing restaurant is known for its excellent steaks and ever-changing game-meat options.

ℹ Information

George Tourism (☎044-801 9295; www.visitgeorge.co.za; 124 York St; ⊘7.45am-4.30pm Mon-Fri, 9am-1pm Sat) This office has a wealth of information for George and the surrounding area.

ℹ Getting There & Away

Kulula (www.kulula.com), **SAAirlink** (☎0861 606 606; www.flyairlink.com) and **SA Express** (www.flyexpress.aero) fly to **George airport** (☎044-876 9310), which is 7km west of town.

Greyhound (www.greyhound.co.za) bus services stop in St Mark's Sq behind the Spar supermarket on the main street, while **Intercape** (www.intercape.co.za) and **Translux** (www.translux.co.za) stop at the Sasol petrol station on the N2 just east of town.

Sample fares:
» Bloemfontein (R460, 10 hours)
» Cape Town (R340, seven hours)
» Jo'burg (R700, 15½ hours)
» Knysna (R260, 1½ hours)
» Plettenberg Bay (R270, two hours)
» Port Elizabeth (R310, 5½ hours)

The Baz Bus (p365) drops passengers off in town and you can call the hostels in Oudtshoorn for shuttle services there.

WILDERNESS
☎044

The name says it all: dense old-growth forests and steep hills run down to a beautiful stretch of coastline of rolling breakers, kilometres of white sand, bird-rich estuaries and sheltered lagoons. All this has made Wilderness very popular, but thankfully it doesn't show. The only drawback is everything is quite widely scattered, which can be problematic if you don't have a vehicle.

🏃 Activities

Wilderness is jam-packed with activities. You can try **Eden Adventures** (☎044-877 0179; www.eden.co.za; Garden Route National Park) if you're looking to rent a canoe (R350 per day) or try your hand at abseiling (R390) or canyoning (R495). The company also organises guided hikes.

The beach here is beautiful, but be warned: a strong rip means bathing is not advised.

🛏 Sleeping & Eating

Fairy Knowe Backpackers   BACKPACKERS $
(☎044-877 1285; www.wildernessbackpackers.com; Dumbleton Rd; dm R120, d with shared bathroom R350, d R450; @) Set in spacious, leafy grounds overlooking the Touws River, this 1874 farmhouse was the first in the area. The bar and cafe are in another building some distance away, so boozers won't keep you awake. The Baz Bus comes to the door.

Beach House Backpackers   BACKPACKERS $
(☎044-877 0549; www.wildernessbeachhouse.com; Wilderness Beach; dm from R130, d with shared bathroom from R450, r from R500; @☀) Southwest of town, this breezy hostel lives up to its name, providing prime beach views, accommodation ranging from dorms to a self-contained cottage, and a large pool for cooling off.

TOP CHOICE ⟩ Interlaken   GUESTHOUSE $$
(☎044-877 1374; www.interlaken.co.za; 713 North St; r per person incl breakfast from R500; @) Rave reviews from readers, and we can't argue: this is a well-run and very friendly guesthouse offering magnificent lagoon views. Delicious dinners are available on request.

Palms Wilderness Retreat &
Guesthouse   GUESTHOUSE $$$
(044-877 1420; www.palms-wilderness.com;
1 Owen Grant St; s/d incl breakfast R1350/1750;
✳@☀) This stylish place has African decor
in its luxurious rooms and it's a five-minute
walk from the beach.

TOP
CHOICE Zucchini   EUROPEAN $$
(www.zucchini.co.za; Timberlake Organic Village;
mains R60-115; ☼lunch & dinner; ✔) Stylish
decor combines with home-grown organic
produce, free-range meats and lots of vegetarian options at this delightful place.

Serendipity   SOUTH AFRICAN $$$
(044-877 0433; Freesia Ave; 5-course set menu
R350; ☼dinner Mon-Sat) Readers and locals
alike recommend this elegant restaurant
with a deck overlooking the lagoon. The
South African–inspired menu changes
monthly but always features original takes
on old classics.

ℹ Information
Wilderness Tourism Bureau (044-877
0045; George Rd, Milkwood Village; ☺7.45am-
4.30pm Mon-Fri, 9am-1pm Sat) This office is
just off the N2 as you pull into the village.

**GARDEN ROUTE NATIONAL PARK
(WILDERNESS SECTION)**
This national park (044-877 1197; adult/child
R88/44; ☺24hr), formerly called the Wilder-
ness National Park, covers a unique system
of lakes, rivers, wetlands and estuaries that
are vital for the survival of many species.
The rich bird life includes the beautiful Kny-
sna loerie and five species of kingfisher.

There are several nature trails taking in
the lakes, the beach and the indigenous for-
est. The lakes offer anglers, canoeists, wind-
surfers and sailors an ideal venue.

Two similar campgrounds (campsites
from R170, d rondavels with/without bathroom
R350/300, forest cabins R625, 4-person log cot-
tages from R1170) in the park offer basic but

comfortable accommodation with disabled
access. It's possible to walk to the park from
Wilderness, 5km west.

KNYSNA
044 / POP 65,000
Embracing an exquisitely beautiful lagoon
and surrounded by ancient forests, Knysna
(pronounced ny-znah) is the most important
town on the Garden Route.

With its serene setting, excellent places
to stay, eat and drink, and wide range of ac-
tivities, Knysna has plenty going for it. But
if you're after something quiet and undevel-
oped, you might like to look elsewhere, par-
ticularly in high season, when the numbers
of visitors threaten to overwhelm it.

There's an oyster festival (www.oysterfes
tival.co.za) in July, while in late April/early
May the town confirms its gay-friendly cre-
dentials with the Pink Loerie Festival (www.
pinkloerie.com).

👁 Sights & Activities
KNYSNA LAGOON
Although regulated by SAN Parks (044-302
5600; www.sanparks.org; Thesen Island), Knysna
Lagoon (13 sq km) is not a national park or
wilderness area. Much is still privately owned,
and the lagoon is used by industry and for
recreation. The lagoon opens up between two
sandstone cliffs, known as the Heads. There
are good views from a lookout on the eastern
head and the privately owned Featherbed Na-
ture Reserve on the western head.

The best way to appreciate the lagoon
is to take a cruise. The Featherbed Com-
pany (044-382 1693; www.featherbed.co.za;
Waterfront) has several vessels, including the
MV John Benn (adult/child R130/60; ☺departs
12.30pm & 5pm in winter, 12.30pm & 6pm in sum-
mer), which takes you to Featherbed Nature
Reserve.

TOWNSHIP TOURS & HOMESTAYS
Follow Gray St uphill and eventually you'll
emerge on the wooded slopes of the hills

WORTH A TRIP

BUFFALO BAY

Buffalo Bay, 20km southwest of Knysna, is distinctly un–Garden Route: a long, almost
deserted surf beach, only a tiny enclave of holiday homes, some self-catering accom-
modation and a nature reserve. That's about it, and it's more than enough.

The Goukamma Nature Reserve (www.capenature.co.za; adult/child R30/15; ☺8am-
6pm) protects 14km of rocky coastline, sandstone cliffs, dunes covered with coastal
fynbos and forest, and Groenvlei, a large freshwater lake. There are four day trails, ca-
noes for hire and a variety of accommodation (four-person bush camp from R800).

SOUTH AFRICA GARDEN ROUTE

Knysna

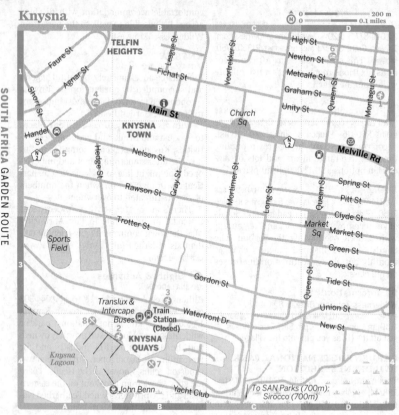

behind. On top are the sprawling Knysna townships, best visited on an excellent tour run by **Emzini Tours** (☎044-382 1087; www. emzinitours.co.za; adult/child R350/100). Township resident Ella leads the way as you visit a range of community projects. You can visit the Rastafarian community for an extra R100, and lunch in a township home (R150) is available if you prebook.

If you want to stay overnight in either the Rastafarian community or in the township, contact Knysna Tourism and ask for its brochure, *Living Local*.

OTHER ACTIVITIES

There are plenty of other activities available, including abseiling, kloofing, horse riding and kayaking.

Recommended operators:

» **Adventure Centre** (☎083 260 7198; www. theadventurecentre.co.za; 2 Graham St) Offers a wide range of activities.

» **Go Vertical** (☎082 731 4696; www. govertical.co.za) Rock climbing, abseiling and canoeing.
» **Liquid Grace** (☎044-343 3245; www. liquidgrace.co.za) Based in Sedgefield; specialises in water sports.

» **Knysna Cycle Works** (☎044-382 5152; www.knysnacycles.co.za; 20 Waterfront Dr; per day R170) Cycling trails and bike rental.

On the N2 to Plettenberg Bay, 22km east of Knysna, you'll find the **Knysna Elephant Park** (☎044-532 7732; www.knysnaelephantpark. co.za; 1hr tours adult/child R220/100; ⊙8.30am-4.30pm). Here, small groups of visitors go on walking tours with the elephants or take a short ride (adult/child R885/425). The tours might not be authentic wildlife encounters, but are guaranteed to bring out the child in any visitor.

🛏 Sleeping

Island Vibe BACKPACKERS $
(☎044-382 1728; www.islandvibe.co.za; 67 Main St; dm R120, d with shared bathroom R330, d R385; @🐕) A funky backpackers with excellent communal areas, cheery staff and nicely decorated rooms. There's a bar, free internet and a great view from the deck.

Knysna Backpackers BACKPACKERS $
(☎044-382 2554; www.knysnabackpackers. co.za; 42 Queen St; dm R120, d with shared bathroom R330, d R400) You'll find mainly double rooms at this large, spruce Victorian house on the hill a few blocks up from Main St. It tends to be quieter and more relaxing than other places and there's a free breakfast.

Woodbourne Resort CAMPGROUND $
(☎044-384 0316; www.gardenroute.co.za/woodbourne; George Rex Dr; campsites from R330, chalet from R900; 🐕) Here you'll find spacious, shaded camping and simple chalets with TVs. It's a quiet place a little way out of town. Follow signs to the Heads.

TOP CHOICE **Brenton Cottages** CHALET $$
(☎044-381 0082; www.brentononsea.net; 2-person cabin R890, 6-person cottage R1940; 🐕) On the seaward side of the lagoon, the *fynbos*-covered hills drop to Brenton-on-Sea, overlooking a magnificent 8km-long beach. The cottages here have a full kitchen while cabins have a kitchenette; some have ocean views.

Inyathi Guest Lodge GUESTHOUSE $$
(☎044-382 7768; www.inyathiguestlodge.co.za; 52 Main St; s/d from R500/800) Accommodation in this imaginatively designed place is in decorated timber lodges – some with Victorian bathtubs, others with stained-glass windows.

Phantom Forest Eco-Reserve LODGE $$$
(☎044-386 0046; www.phantomforest.com; s/d from R2375/3750; 🐕) This 137-hectare private ecoreserve, 6km west of Knysna along the Phantom Pass road, has elegantly decorated tree houses built with sustainable materials. If nothing else, visit for the award-winning six-course African dinner (R300) served in the Forest Boma daily; booking is essential.

🍴 Eating

Oystercatcher SEAFOOD $
(Knysna Quays; ⊙lunch & dinner) The Oystercatcher is a relaxed place serving four sizes of farmed oyster and other light dishes such as fish and chips in a great waterside setting.

TOP CHOICE **East Head Café** CAFE $$
(www.eastheadcafe.co.za; The Heads; mains R45-110; ⊙breakfast & lunch; 🐕) There's an outdoor deck overlooking the lagoon and ocean, and a good range of vegetarian dishes, plus wild oysters at R15 each.

Sirocco INTERNATIONAL $$
(www.sirocco.co.za; Thesen's Island; mains R50-130; ⊙lunch & dinner) Inside it's a stylish place to dine on steaks and seafood; outside it's a laid-back bar with wood-fired pizzas and the full range of Mitchell's beers.

34 South INTERNATIONAL $$
(www.34south.biz; Waterfront; mains R50-175; ⊙lunch & dinner) With outdoor tables overlooking the water, lavish salads, deli produce and seafood pâtés, this is a great place for lunch. The wine selection is one of the best in town.

Crab's Creek PUB $$
(www.crabscreek.co.za; mains R50-200; ⊙lunch & dinner; 🐕) This is a favourite local watering hole in a chilled-out setting right on the lagoon, off the N2. There's a buffet lunch (R65) on Sundays. Children will enjoy the sandpit and climbing frames.

❶ Information

Knysna Tourism (☎044-382 5510; www.visitknysna.co.za; 40 Main St; ⊙8am-5pm Mon-Fri, 8.30am-1pm Sat year-round, plus 9am-1pm Sun Dec, Jan & Jul) An excellent information office with very knowledgeable staff.

Motion Café (3 Gray St; per hr R30; ⊙8am-6pm Mon-Fri, 8am-3pm Sat & Sun) High-speed internet access. There's a coffee shop downstairs.

❶ Getting There & Away

BUS

Translux (www.translux.co.za) and **Intercape** (www.intercape.co.za) stop at the old train station at the Waterfront. **Greyhound** (www.greyhound.co.za) stops at the **Engen petrol station** (Main St); Baz Bus (p365) drops at all the hostels. For travel between nearby towns on the Garden Route, you're better looking for a minibus taxi than travelling with the major bus lines, which are expensive on short sectors.

Sample fares:

» Cape Town (R430, eight hours)

» George (R260, 1½ hours)

» Jo'burg (R650, 17½ hours)

» Mossel Bay (R260, two hours)

» Port Elizabeth (R300, 4½ hours)

MINIBUS TAXI

The main **minibus taxi stop** is at the Shell petrol station near the tourist office. Routes include Plettenberg Bay (R20, 30 minutes, daily) and Cape Town (R150, 7½ hours, daily).

PLETTENBERG BAY

☑044 / POP 34,000

Plettenberg Bay, or 'Plett' as it's more commonly known, is a resort town through and through, with mountains, white sand and crystal-blue water making it one of the country's top local tourist spots. As a result, things can get very busy and somewhat overpriced, but the town retains a relaxed, friendly atmosphere and has good-value hostels. The scenery to the east in particular is superb, with some of the best coast and indigenous forest in South Africa.

◉ Sights & Activities

Apart from lounging on the beaches or hiking on the Robberg Peninsula there's a lot to do in Plett. Albergo for Backpackers can organise most things, often at a discount.

Boat trips to view dolphins and whales in season are available with Ocean Blue (☑044-533 5083; www.oceanadventures.co.za; Hopewood St, Milkwood Centre) and Ocean Safaris (☑044-533 4963; www.oceansafaris.co.za; Hopewood St, Milkwood Centre; 1½hr trip R400). Regular two-hour trips cost R400; close encounters with whales cost R650.

Those wanting to try surfing can take a lesson through the Garden Route Surf Academy (☑082 436 6410; www.gardenroutesurfacademy.com; 2hr group lesson incl equipment R350), which caters to all levels of experience.

At the Crags, east of Knysna, you'll find four 'wildlife' parks in close proximity.

TOP CHOICE **Tenikwa**   WILDLIFE ENCOUNTERS
(☑044-534 8170; www.tenikwa.co.za; cheetah walk R550, Wild Cat Experience adult/child R165/85; ⊗9am-4.30pm) Tenikwa is a sanctuary and rehabilitation centre for injured or abandoned animals, mostly cats. The hour-long Wild Cat Experience visits all the lesser cats of South Africa, but it's the two-hour cheetah walks that have people sending postcards home. Bookings recommended.

Birds of Eden   WILDLIFE RESERVE
(www.birdsofeden.co.za; adult/child R150/75) This is the world's largest free-flight aviary with a 2-hectare dome over the forest. Combo tickets to Monkeyland and Birds of Eden cost R216/108 per adult/child.

Elephant Sanctuary   WILDLIFE ENCOUNTERS
(www.elephantsanctuary.co.za; tours adult/child from R325/175, rides adult/child over 8yr R435/220; ⊗8am-5pm) There are various tour and ride options allowing up-close encounters with pachyderms.

Monkeyland   WILDLIFE RESERVE
(www.monkeyland.co.za; 1hr tours adult/child R150/75; ⊗8am-5pm) This very popular attraction helps rehabilitate wild monkeys that have been in zoos or private homes. The walking safari through a dense forest and across a 128m-long rope bridge is recommended.

🛏 Sleeping

TOP CHOICE **Nothando Backpackers Hostel**   BACKPACKERS $
(☑044-533 0220; www.nothando.com; 5 Wilder St; dm R160, d with shared bathroom R420, d R500) This excellent, five-star budget option is owner-run and it shows. There's a great bar area with satellite TV, yet you can still find peace and quiet in the large grounds.

Abalone Beach House   BACKPACKERS $
(☑044-535 9602; www.abalonebeachhouse.co.za; 50 Milkwood Glen, Keurboomstrand; d with shared bathroom R420, d R500; @☀) This relaxing and extremely friendly backpackers is more like a budget guesthouse. A magnificent beach is two minutes away and surf and body boards are provided free. Follow Keurboomstrand signs from the N2 (about 6km east of Plett), then turn into Milkwood Glen.

Albergo for Backpackers BACKPACKERS $
(☑044-533 4434; www.albergo.co.za; 8 Church
St; campsites per person R90, dm R160, d with
shared bathroom R420, d R500; @) Well-run and
friendly, Albergo can organise just about any
activity in the area. The upstairs dorm has
huge windows and stellar ocean views from
the balcony.

Periwinkle Guest Lodge GUESTHOUSE $$
(☑044-533 1345; www.periwinkle.co.za; 75 Beachy
Head Dr; d incl breakfast R2230) This bright, col-
ourful beachfront guesthouse offers individ-
ually decorated rooms, all with great views
– you might even be able to spot whales and
dolphins.

Plettenberg LUXURY HOTEL $$$
(☑044-533 2030; www.plettenberg.com; 40
Church St; r incl breakfast from R3540; ❈@☎)
Built on a rocky headland with breathtaking
vistas, this five-star place is pure decadence.

✗ Eating

TOP CHOICE **Ristorante Enrico** SEAFOOD $$
(www.enricorestaurant.co.za; Main Beach, Keur-
boomstrand; mains R70-120; ☺lunch & dinner)
Highly recommended by readers, this is *the*
place for seafood in Plett. Enrico has his own
boat that, weather permitting, heads out
each morning. If you book ahead you can
join a fishing trip.

The Table ITALIAN $$
(www.thetable.co.za; 9 Main St; mains R60-105;
☺lunch & dinner) A funky, minimalist venue
with pizzas featuring an array of unusual top-
pings. At lunchtime there's a 'harvest table'
with ever-changing local produce.

Europa ITALIAN $$
(cnr Church & Main Sts; mains R42-120; ☺breakfast,
lunch & dinner) This large, snazzy restaurant-
bar has a great deck, a good range of salads
and plenty of Italian fare.

Lookout SEAFOOD $$
(☑044-533 1379; www.lookout.co.za; Lookout
Rocks; mains R60-130; ☺breakfast, lunch & dinner)
With a deck overlooking the beach, this is a
great place for a simple meal and perhaps
views of dolphins surfing the waves.

❶ Information
Internet Cafe (Main St, Melville's Corner Shopping Centre; per hr R60; ☺8am-5pm Mon-Fri,
9am-1pm Sat)
Plett Tourism (☑044-533 4065; www.pletten
bergbay.co.za; 5 Main St; ☺8.30am-5pm
Mon-Fri year-round, plus 9am-2pm Sat Apr-Oct)

DON'T MISS

ROBBERG NATURE & MARINE RESERVE

This **reserve** (☑044-533 2125; www.
capenature.org.za; adult/child R40/20;
☺7am-5pm Feb-Nov, 7am-8pm Dec & Jan),
9km southeast of Plettenberg Bay, protects a 4km-long peninsula with a rugged coastline of cliffs and rocks. There
are three circular walks of increasing
difficulty, with rich marine life and
coastal-dune *fynbos*, but it's very rocky
and not for the unfit or anyone with
knee problems! There's a hut (R1440,
half-price outside peak season) deep
in the reserve. To get here head along
Robberg Rd, off Piesang Valley Rd, until
you see the signs.

This office has useful information on accommodation and walks in the surrounding hills and
reserves.

❶ Getting There & Away
All the major buses stop at the Shell Ultra City on
the N2; the Baz Bus (p365) will come into town.
Sample fares:
» Bloemfontein (R530, 12 hours)
» Cape Town (R430, 9½ hours)
» George (R270, two hours)
» Graaff-Reinet (R380, 6½ hours)
» Jo'burg (R770, 18 hours)
» Port Elizabeth (R300, 3½ hours)

If you're heading to Knysna you're better off taking a minibus taxi (R20, 30 minutes) – services
leave from the corner of Kloof and High Sts.
Gecko (☑044-533 3705; www.geckotours.
co.za) provides transfers; for example George
airport to Plett is R600 for one passenger.

Central Karoo
The seemingly endless Karoo has a truly
magical feel. It's a vast, semi-arid plateau
(its name is a Khoisan word meaning 'land
of thirst') that features stunning sunsets and
starscapes. Inhabited for more than half a
million years, the region is rich in archaeological sites, fossils, San paintings, wildlife
and some 9000 plant species.

In this land of blazing summers and icy
winters, life is slow. Off the main highways
you can drive for hours without seeing

WORTH A TRIP

KAROO NATIONAL PARK

Just 5km north of Beaufort West, the Karoo National Park (☎023-415 2828/9; www.
sanparks.org; adult/child R120/60; ☉7am-7pm) covers 33,000 hectares of impressive
Karoo landscapes. The park has 61 species of mammal, the most common of which are
dassies (agile, rodentlike mammals, also called hyraxes) and bat-eared foxes. Mountain
zebras have been reintroduced, as has the odd black rhino, and there are a great many
reptiles and birds.

Facilities include a shop and restaurant. There are two short nature trails and an 11km
day walk. There are also vehicle routes and day or overnight 4WD guided trails.

Accommodation is at pleasant campsites (R205) or in Cape Dutch–style cottages
(2 people R1100).

You need your own transport to reach the park.

another car. If you need a break from the
crowds of the Garden Route, head over the
magnificent Swartberg Pass to unwind in
the quaint, peaceful villages and towns.

The region is often split into the Great
Karoo (north) and Little Karoo (south), but
it doesn't respect provincial boundaries; for
our purposes it's the Central Karoo here, and
Eastern Karoo in the Eastern Cape section
(p388).

Prince Albert & Around

☎023 / POP 2500

Prince Albert is a charming village dating
back to 1762 and dozing at the foot of the
Swartberg Pass. Despite being surrounded
by very harsh country, Prince Albert is green
and fertile (producing peaches, apricots,
grapes and olives), thanks to the run-off
from the mountain springs. There's an Olive
Festival each April.

☉ Sights & Activities

Prince Albert is a good base for exploring the
Karoo and hiking on the more than 100km
of trails in the Swartberg Nature Reserve.
Overnight walks have to be booked through
Cape Nature (☎021-659 3500; www.capena
ture.org.za).

The Two Passes Route links Prince Albert to Oudtshoorn via a pair of contrasting
but equally impressive roads: the winding
and untarred Swartberg Pass and the
Meiringspoort Pass.

Another worthy excursion is the drive to
Gamkaskloof Nature Reserve (☎044-203
6325; www.capenature.org.za; adult/child R40/20),
also known as Die Hel. This remote commu-

nity welcomes visitors; self-catering accommodation and meals are available. If you
don't fancy the vertiginous drive, opt for a
day trip with Dennehof Tours (☎023-5411
227; www.dennehof.co.za; day tour R850).

🛏 Sleeping & Eating

TOP CHOICE Bushman Valley CAMPGROUND $
(☎023-541 1322; www.bushmanvalley.com; Rte
407; campsite per person R60, dm R100, cottages
per person R250; ☒) Prince Albert's only real
budget option is just south of town and a
fantastic base for hiking in the Swartberg
mountains. The thatched cottages have decent kitchen facilities or you can camp in
the grounds (tents are available to hire for
R30).

Prince Albert of
Saxe-Coburg Lodge GUESTHOUSE $$
(☎023-541 1267; www.saxecoburg.co.za; 60 Church
St; s/d incl breakfast from R700/1040; ☒☒) This
place offers quality accommodation in lovely
garden rooms. Owners Dick and Regina are
a great source of information and offer guid-
ed hikes in the area.

TOP CHOICE Gallery FUSION $$
(57 Church St; mains R85-135; ☉lunch Mon-Sat,
dinner daily) Prince Albert's smartest dining
option has an ever-changing menu featuring
modern takes on local classics such as Karoo
lamb and game steaks as well as some vegetarian choices.

❶ Information

Prince Albert Tourism (☎023-541 1366; www.
patourism.co.za; Church St; ☉9am-5pm Mon-
Fri, 9am-1pm Sat)

DON'T MISS

!KHWA TTU

!Khwa ttu (www.khwattu.org; Rte 27, Yzerfontein; ⊗9am-5pm) is the only San-owned and operated culture centre in the Western Cape. Set within the ancestral lands of the San, !Khwa ttu is based on an 850-hectare nature reserve. Excellent tours (two hours, R250, 10am and 2pm) with a San guide involve a nature walk, a wildlife drive and learning about San culture. There's a good restaurant serving lunch and self-catering accommodation is available.

!Khwa ttu is off Rte 27 just south of Yzerfontein, 70km from Cape Town.

ℹ Getting There & Away

Most people visit by driving over one of the area's passes from Oudtshoorn, or from the N1 between Cape Town and Jo'burg. **Shosholoza Meyl** (☑0860 008 888; www.shosholozameyl.co.za) trains from Cape Town to Jo'burg stop at the Prince Albert Road station (tourist class R180, seven hours), 45km northwest of Prince Albert.

Long-distance buses, which are more expensive than the train (R345), also stop at Prince Albert Road. A taxi from there to Prince Albert costs R130, but most guesthouses will pick you up.

West Coast & Swartland

If you're keen to do the Western Cape the way locals do it, head north of Cape Town and explore the windswept coastline, rugged mountains and undulating hills of the West Coast and Swartland, a peaceful and undeveloped paradise. You'll come across quiet whitewashed fishing villages, unspoilt beaches, a lagoon and wetlands teeming with birds, fascinating country towns and one of the best hiking regions in the country.

WEST COAST NATIONAL PARK

Encompassing the clear, blue waters of the Langebaan Lagoon and home to an enormous number of birds is the West Coast National Park (www.sanparks.org; admission R48, Aug & Sep adult/child R96/48; ⊗7am-7.30pm). The park covers around 31,000 hectares and protects wetlands of international significance and important seabird breeding colonies. Wading birds flock here by the thousands in

summer. The offshore islands are home to colonies of African penguins.

The park is famous for its wildflower display, which is usually between August and October. It's about 120km from Cape Town, 7km south of Langebaan. The rainy season is between May and August.

The Geelbek Visitor's Centre & Restaurant (☑022-772 2134; West Coast National Park; mains R65-105; ⊗breakfast & lunch) has a wide menu specialising in traditional fare. The information centre can help with accommodation options, which include the chalets at Duinepos (☑022-707 9900; www.duinepos.co.za; 2-/4-person chalet from R685/915; ▣), two of which have disabled access, and the romantic lagoon houseboats (☑021-689 9718; www.houseboating.co.za; 4-person boat R1400) moored at Kraalbaai.

CEDERBERG WILDERNESS AREA

Bizarrely shaped, weathered sandstone formations, San rock art, craggy and rugged mountains and green valleys all make the desolate Cederberg a must-see. The peaks and valleys extend roughly north–south for 100km, between Citrusdal and Vanrhynsdorp. A good proportion is protected by the 83,000-hectare Cederberg Wilderness Area, which is administered by Cape Nature (www.capenature.org.za).

Spring is the best time to see the wildflowers, although there's plenty of interest at other times of the year. There are small populations of baboons, rheboks, klipspringers and grysboks; and predators such as caracals, Cape foxes and the elusive leopard.

The Cederberg is divided into three excellent hiking areas of around 24,000 hectares, each with a network of trails. Two of the most popular hikes are to the Maltese Cross and the Wolfberg Cracks and Arch.

ℹ **HIKING PERMITS**

Permits are required for all hikes. They vary in price and are obtainable from Cape Nature (☑021-426 0723; www.capenature.org.za) in Cape Town, Algeria (p374) or Dwarsrivier Farm (p374). At quiet times you can pick up a permit on the spot at Algeria or Dwarsrivier, but during school holidays it's best to book ahead as hiker numbers are limited. The maximum group size is 12 and, for safety, the minimum is two adults.

DON'T MISS

DWARSRIVIER FARM

Deep in the Cederberg, this is an excellent base for hiking – both the Wolfberg Arch and Maltese Cross hikes leave from this area. At **Sanddrif** (027-482 2825; www.cederbergwine.com/sanddrif; campsites R140, 4-person cottage from R680) there are shady campsites by the river or well-equipped cottages with patios gazing out at the mountains. Don't miss the **Cederberg Winery**, also on the premises. All of its wines are stupendous. There's an excellent **astronomical observatory** (www.cederbergobs.org.za) nearby, open on Saturday evenings, as well as the San art of the **Stadsaal Caves**.

To get here, follow the Algeria turn-off from the N7, 30km north of Citrusdal. From here a gravel road winds into the mountains; it's 46km to Dwarsrivier.

There is a buffer zone of conserved land between the wilderness area and the farmland, and here more intrusive activities such as mountain biking are allowed.

There are no eating places in the area so you will need to bring your own food.

Sleeping

See also Citrusdal (p375) and Clanwilliam for places to stay outside the Cederberg Wilderness Area.

Algeria   CAMPGROUND **$**
(027-482 2404; 6-person campsites R300, 4-person cottage from R1000) This is the main camping spot in the area, with exceptional grounds in a beautiful, shaded site alongside the Rondegat River. There is a swimming hole and lovely spots to picnic. It can get quite noisy at weekends and school holidays. Entrance to the campground closes at 4.30pm (9pm on Friday).

TOP CHOICE **Gecko Creek Wilderness Lodge**   LODGE **$$**
(027-482 1300; www.geckocreek.com; campsite/ tent/cabin per person R130/200/290; @☒) Highly recommended by readers, and rightly so. There are magnificent views, San rock art and hiking trails spread over 1000 hec-

tares. To find it, take the Algeria turn-off on the N7 and look out for the sign on the right.

Getting There & Away

The Cederberg range is about 200km from Cape Town, accessible from Citrusdal, Clanwilliam and the N7.

Public transport to Algeria is nonexistent. There are several roads to the campground, all offering magnificent views. It's not signposted from Clanwilliam, about 45 minutes away by car, but you just follow the road above the dam to the south. Algeria *is* signposted from the N7 and it's only 20 minutes from the main road.

CLANWILLIAM & AROUND

027 / POP 37,000

The adjacent dam and some adventurous dirt roads into the Cederberg make the compact town of Clanwilliam a popular weekend resort. Well-preserved examples of Cape Dutch architecture line the main street.

The **information centre** (027-482 2024; 8.30am-5pm Mon-Fri, 8.30am-12.30pm Sat) is at the top end of the main street, across from the old *tronk* (jail in Afrikaans), which doubles as the town's museum.

Clanwilliam is the centre of the rooibos (red bush) tea industry. Tours of the **Elandsberg Rooibos Estate** (027-482 2022; www.elandsberg.co.za; R125), 22km west of Clanwilliam, follow the process from planting to packaging.

A 150-year-old banyan tree looms over **Saint du Barrys Country Lodge** (027-482 1537; www.saintdubarrys.com; 13 Augsburg Dr; s/d incl breakfast R600/1000; ❉☒), a pleasant thatch-roofed guesthouse with a charming garden.

Intercape buses connect Clanwilliam with Cape Town (R290, three hours) and Windhoek, Namibia (R1000, 17 hours).

EASTERN CAPE

From uninhabited desert expanses to lush tropical forests, from seriously easygoing hammock time to adrenalin-pumping adventures, the Eastern Cape offers up a wide range of topography and experiences. Some of the finest hiking trails wind their way along stunning coastlines and through mountainous, waterfall-filled landscapes.Compared to the much wealthier and more developed Western Cape, it can feel like a different country and provides an opportunity to gain familiarity with Xhosa culture.

DON'T MISS

SCENIC SLEEPOVERS

Citrusdal is a pretty town, but it is the region around it that really merits a visit, particularly in flower season (August and September). Accommodation around Citrusdal is well-priced and much of it is in spectacular spots. Try the Baths (☏022-921 8026; www.thebaths.co.za; campsites per person R100, 2-person chalet from R620; ☒), a hot-water-springs resort about 18km from Citrusdal, or the hard-to-reach but unforgettable camping spot of Beaverlac (☏022-931 2945; www.beaverlac.co.za; Beaverlac Nature Reserve; admission per car R15, campsites per person R45, hut R200, 4-person cottage R280), between Citrusdal and Porterville.

Intercape buses link Citrusdal to Cape Town (R240, three hours), but you need your own transport to enjoy the area's more scenic sleepovers.

Private wildlife reserves and national and regional parks abound and the imposing mountains of the northeastern highlands are relatively unexplored. You'll find stillness and tranquillity in the semiarid Karoo; seriously good surfing up and down the coast; and history, including the legacy of some of the region's famous sons – Nelson Mandela, Oliver Tambo and Steve Biko.

Western Region

NATURE'S VALLEY
☏044

Nature's Valley is a small village nestled in yellowwood forest next to a magnificent beach in the west of the Tsitsikamma region of Garden Route National Park. The village itself lies in the Western Cape, but we've included it here because it's so much a part of exploring the Tsitsikamma area. This is where the Otter Trail ends and the Tsitsikamma Trail begins, but if you don't want to walk for that long, there are plenty of shorter hikes in the area.

A popular place to stay is Nature's Valley Rest Camp (☏in Pretoria 012-428 9111; www.sanparks.org; campsite/forest hut R190/450), on the edge of a river east of town.

There's no public transport to Nature's Valley, although the Baz Bus stops at the village.

TSITSIKAMMA (GARDEN ROUTE NATIONAL PARK)

Now incorporated into the Garden Route National Park, Tsitsikamma (adult/child R120/60) is an 80km stretch of coast between Plettenberg Bay and Humansdorp, including a marine protected area 5km out to sea. Located at the foot of the Tsitsikamma Range and cut by rivers that have carved deep ravines into the ancient forests, it's a spectacular area to walk through.

Elusive Cape clawless otters, after which the Otter Trail is named, inhabit this park; there are also baboons, monkeys, small antelopes and plentiful bird life.

Several short day walks give you a taste of the coastline. The Waterfall Trail (three hours) on the first part of the Otter Trail is recommended.

OTTER, TSITSIKAMMA & DOLPHIN TRAILS

The 42km Otter Trail (☏012-426 5111; www.sanparks.org; per person R925) is one of the country's most acclaimed hikes, hugging the coastline from Storms River Mouth to Nature's Valley. The walk, which lasts five days and four nights, involves fording a number of rivers and gives access to some superb stretches of coast. A good level of fitness is required.

The trail is usually booked up a year ahead, but there are often cancellations so it's always worth trying. Single hikers are not permitted.

Accommodation is in six-bed rest huts with mattresses but without bedding, cooking utensils or running water. Camping is not allowed.

The 60km Tsitsikamma Trail (☏042-281 1712; www.mtoecotourism.co.za; per day R110) commences at Nature's Valley and ends at Storms River, taking you inland through the forests and mountains. This hike takes up to six days and five nights, but you can opt for two, three, four or five days. Porterage is available as well as guided day walks and mountain-bike trails.

The Dolphin Trail (☏042-280 3588; www.dolphintrail.co.za; per person R4620) is ideal for hikers who don't want to carry heavy equipment or sleep in huts. Accommodation on this three-day, two-night hike, which runs from Storms River Mouth to Forest Fern, is in comfortable hotels, and luggage is carried

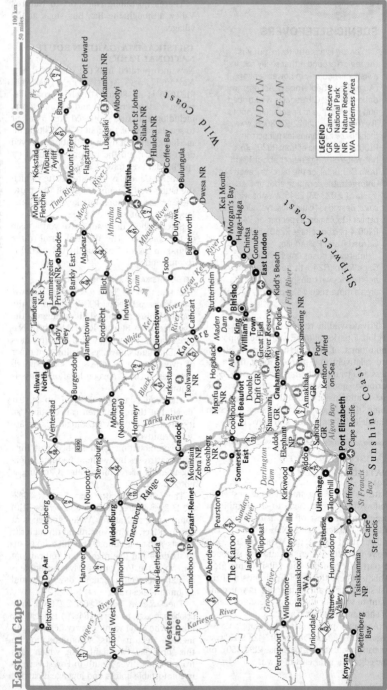

on vehicles. The price includes accommodation and meals, guides and a boat trip into the Storms River Gorge on the way back. Book at least a year in advance.

🛏 Sleeping & Eating

Bloukrans Backpackers Lodge
BACKPACKERS $
(☑042-281 1185; www.tsitsikamma.org.za; campsites 2 people R140, dm/d without bathroom R100/200, chalets 4/6 people R650/850; ☎) A functional backpackers with a well-equipped kitchen. It's next to a bungee-jump site and near the start of some shorter walking trails. You can also stay at the adjoining Bloukrans Chalets.

Storms River Mouth Camp Backpackers
BACKPACKERS $$
(☑in Pretoria 012-428 9111; www.sanparks.org; campsite R270, forest hut R465, family cottage R1405) This camp offers forest huts, chalets, cottages and 'oceanettes'; all except the forest huts are equipped with kitchens (including utensils), bedding and bathrooms. There are discounts from May to November.

Storms River Restaurant
INTERNATIONAL $$
(mains R55-135; ☺breakfast, lunch & dinner) At the reception complex to Tsitsikamma National Park, this place has a wide selection of meals at reasonable prices and superb views of the coast.

ℹ Information
The main information centre for the national park is Storms River Mouth Camp Backpackers. The park gate is 6km from the N2. It's 2km from the gate to the main camp, which is open 24 hours. You can also pay park entrance fees and get information at Nature's Valley Rest Camp (p375).

ℹ Getting There & Away
There is no public transport to either Nature's Valley Rest Camp or Storms River Mouth. **Greyhound** (☑083-915 9000; www.greyhound.co.za), **Intercape** (☑0861 287 287; www.intercape.co.za) and **Translux** (☑0861 589 282; www.translux.co.za) buses run along the N2, from where it's an 8km walk to Storms River Mouth.

STORMS RIVER
☑042
Tree-lined Storms River is a little hamlet with an excellent selection of accommodation options and a big tourism profile, in large part because of its proximity to Tsitsikamma. Don't confuse Storms River and the turn-off 4km to the west for Storms River Mouth (Stormsriviermond in Afrikaans), located in the park.

Storms River Information Centre (☑042-281 1098), just off the N2, can help with accommodation bookings.

The Fair Trade–accredited **Storms River Adventures** (☑042-281 1836; www.stormsriver.com; Darnell St, Storms River) arranges a variety of activities, including a tree-canopy slide (R450). **Blackwater Tubing** (☑079 636 8008; www.tubenaxe.co.za; cnr Darnell & Saffron Sts) runs tubing trips on the Storms River (R550).

The world's highest bridge **bungee jump** (216m) is at the **Bloukrans River Bridge** (☑042-281 1458; www.faceadrenalin.com; bungee jump R750, bridge walk R100; ☺9am-5pm), 21km west of Storms River.

If you're after a postbungee rest, try the jacuzzi on the upper deck at **Dijembe Backpackers** (☑042-281 1842; www.dijembebackpackers.com; cnr Formosa & Assegai Sts; campsites/dm/s/d R75/120/250/350; @☎), or **Armagh Country Lodge & Spa** (☑042-281 1512; www.thearmagh.com; s/d R850/1190; ☎🖥), which also has one of the best restaurants in town.

The **Baz Bus** stops at Storms River; otherwise buses and minibus taxis could drop you at Bloukrans River Bridge or Tsitsikamma Lodge, 5km away on the N2. A private service called **All Areas Shuttle** (☑072 226 4385) runs between Storms River and the area's main attractions.

JEFFREY'S BAY
☑042 / POP 25,000
Once just a sleepy seaside town, 'J-Bay' is now one of the world's top surfing destinations. Boardies from all over the planet flock here to ride waves such as the famous Supertubes, once described as 'the most perfect wave in the world'. June to September are the best months for experienced surfers, but novices can learn year-round. The biggest surf crowd comes to town every July for the Billabong Pro championship.

A number of operators offer surfing lessons. **Wavecrest Surf School** (☑073 509 0400; www.wavecrestsurfschool.co.za; Drommedaris St; 2hr lesson incl board & wetsuit R200) is a highly recommended long-running operation.

For nonsurfers, there's windsurfing and great birdwatching at Kabeljous Beach, horse riding, dolphin- and whale-watching from many of the surrounding beaches or sandboarding on nearby dunes.

⌂ Sleeping

Like many places in this part of Eastern Cape, J-Bay is chock-a-block with holiday-makers between mid-December and mid-January, so book way ahead for accommodation at this time.

Island Vibe   BACKPACKERS $

(☎042-293 1625; www.islandvibe.co.za; 10 Dageraad St; campsite R80, dm from R120, d with/without bathroom R460/340; @🛜) The most popular backpackers in town, Island Vibe is 500m south of the city centre. Activities include surf lessons (R200), horse riding and kite-surfing. For more privacy, the tastefully decorated beach house has double rooms with balconies. The bar can become raucous at night.

Beach Music   GUESTHOUSE $

(☎042-293 2291; www.beachmusic.co.za; 33 Flame Cres; s/d from R200/300; 🛜) This burnt-umber-coloured building overlooking Supertubes resembles a Mexican villa. The wonderfully airy 2nd-floor lounge and kitchen has superb ocean views, and some rooms share a kitchenette.

Dreamland   GUESTHOUSE $

(☎082 769 4060; www.jbaylocal.com; 29 Flame Cres; d from R350; 🛜) Next door to Beach Music and with equally privileged views is this thatch-roofed hand-crafted home with four individually designed units. Vegans are catered for and kids and dogs are welcomed.

African Ubuntu   BACKPACKERS $

(☎042-296 0376; www.jaybay.co.za; 8 Cherry St; campsites R85, dm/d without bathroom R120/300; @🛜) A suburban home transformed into an intimate and friendly backpackers. Rooms are small but well kept and the small garden, verandah and balcony are good places to chill. A simple breakfast is included.

African Perfection   B&B $$

(☎042-293 1401; www.africanperfection.co.za; 20 Pepper St; s/d incl breakfast from R600/1400, self-catering s/d from R600/880; ✳@🛜) Directly in front of Supertubes, this luxury option is perfect for surfing voyeurs. Every room comes with a private balcony offering stunning sea views. Smart budget accommodation is also available (d from R350).

✗ Eating

Die Walskipper   SEAFOOD $$

(☎042-292 0005; www.walskipper.co.za; mains R95; ⊙lunch & dinner Tue-Sat, lunch Sun) This alfresco restaurant is just metres from the lapping sea. It specialises in seafood, plus crocodile and ostrich steaks. At weekends, it's packed with visitors enjoying giant platters of oysters, calamari, crab and langoustine.

In Food   INTERNATIONAL $$

(cnr Schelde & Jeffrey Sts; mains R65; ⊙7am-5pm Mon-Sat, 9am-3pm Sun; 🛜) The sandwiches, burgers and other fare at this coffee shop-cum-bakery are far from ordinary. An attention to organic, locally sourced ingredients (such as Karoo *fynbos* honey) and wide-ranging culinary tastes make it a worthy foodie destination.

Kitchen Windows   SEAFOOD $$

(23 Ferreira St; mains R55-125; ⊙11am-late Mon-Sat, to 3pm Sun) Sea views and white stucco walls give this airy restaurant a Mediterranean island feel. Less-expensive fare like calamari burgers, Thai fish cakes and salads complement a sophisticated menu of creatively prepared fish, prawns and steaks.

ⓘ Information

Internet Café (Da Gama Rd; per hr R22)

Jeffrey's Bay Tourism (☎042-293 2923; www.jeffreysbaytourism.org; Da Gama Rd; ⊙9am-5pm Mon-Fri, to noon Sat)

ⓘ Getting There & Away

The **Baz Bus** (☎0861 229 287) stops daily at various backpackers. Travelling to Cape Town costs R1065 (12 hours); Port Elizabeth to Jeffrey's Bay costs R190 (one hour).

Minibus taxis depart from the corner of Goedehoop and St Francis Sts; it's R15 to Humansdorp (30 minutes) and R45 to Port Elizabeth (one hour).

Greyhound and Intercape long-distance buses plying the Cape Town–Port Elizabeth–Durban route arrive at and depart from the Caltex petrol station on St Francis St.

PORT ELIZABETH

☎041 / POP 1.5 MILLION

Port Elizabeth (PE for short) lies on the Sunshine Coast and certainly has good bathing beaches and surf spots. It's also a convenient gateway to worthy destinations in either direction along the coast, as well as to the Eastern Karoo. However, the downtown area, like many city centres throughout the country, is mostly run-down and full of fast-food chains and cheap stores. The more upmarket shops, chic bars and restaurants have moved out to the suburban shopping centres. PE, its industrial satellite towns of Uitenhage and Despatch, and the massive surrounding townships, are collectively referred to as Nelson Mandela Bay.

◎ Sights

FREE **South End Museum**   MUSEUM
(☑041-582 3325; www.southendmuseum.co.za; cnr Walmer Blvd & Humewood Rd; ◎9am-4pm Mon-Fri, 10am-3pm Sat & Sun) This small museum tells the history of South End, a vibrant multicultural district destroyed by apartheid bulldozers during forced removals between 1965 and 1975 (under the infamous Group Areas Act). The inhabitants were relocated to other parts of the city, designated by race.

Nelson Mandela Metropolitan Art Museum   GALLERY
(☑041-506 2000; www.artmuseum.co.za; 1 Park Dr, St George's Park; ◎9am-5pm Mon & Wed-Fri, 2-5pm Sat & Sun) The museum, housed in two handsome buildings at the entrance to St George's Park, has a small gallery of paintings and sculpture by contemporary South African artists and some older British and Eastern Cape works.

Bayworld   AQUARIUM, MUSEUM
(☑041-584 0650; www.bayworld.co.za; Beach Rd; adult/child R25/15; ◎9am-4.30pm) This ageing complex includes a small museum, an oceanarium and a snake park. Alongside the many stuffed and pickled marine mammals is some beautiful Xhosa beadwork incorporating modern materials, and a replica of the Algoasaurus dinosaur.

☆ Activities

The wide sandy beaches to the south of central Port Elizabeth make the town a major water-sports venue. Kings Beach stretches from the harbour to Humewood and there are more at Summerstrand that are all fairly sheltered.

Good diving sites around Port Elizabeth include some wrecks and the St Croix Islands, a marine reserve. Contact either Ocean Divers International (☑041-581 5121; www.odipe.co.za; 10 Albert Rd, Walmer) or Pro Dive (☑041-583 1144; www.prodive.co.za; Beach Rd, Shark Rock Pier, Summerstrand), which offer PADI diving courses.

Surfers are not left out either, with the best breaks between the harbour wall and Summerstrand, and at Pollok beach. The Surf Centre (☑041-585 6027; www.surf.co.za; Dolphins Leap; 2hr lesson R200) sells and hires

---

WORTH A TRIP

TOWNSHIP TRIP

If you'd like to visit the townships but don't fancy a tour, follow signs for the Red Location Museum (☑041-408 8400; www.freewebs.com/redlocation museum; cnr Singaphi & Olaf Palme Sts, New Brighton; adult/child R12/6; ◎9am-4pm Mon-Fri, 9am-3pm Sat). Sitting in the New Brighton township, east of Port Elizabeth, this gargantuan building houses an array of multimedia apartheid-related exhibits, some permanent and others temporary. It's an excellent project and well worth the drive.

---

surfboards and body boards. Its surf school will teach you how to use them.

☞ Tours

Calabash Tours (☑041-585 6162; www.calabashtours.co.za; 8 Dollery St, Central) runs local tours, including trips to Addo Elephant National Park (p382) (R800) and several cross-cultural township tours (from R500). The guides are locals who are proud of the Port Elizabeth townships' part in the anti-apartheid struggle.

Raggy Charters (☑073 152 2277; www.raggycharters.co.za) offers cruises led by a qualified marine biologist to St Croix, Jahleel and Benton Islands. You can see penguins, Cape fur seals, dolphins and whales on its half-day tour, which departs at 8.30am daily (R800).

🛏 Sleeping

Most of Port Elizabeth's accommodation choices are lined up along the beachfront, including dozens of self-catering flats.

Lungile Backpackers   BACKPACKERS $
(☑041-582 2042; www.lungilebackpackers.co.za; 12 La Roche Dr, Humewood; campsites/dm R80/120, d with/without bathroom R385/310; @🖙🏊) This well-managed operation is in a suburban neighbourhood, up a hill and minutes from the beachfront. The airy A-frame home's large entertainment area rocks most nights, and the dorms and tiny campsite can get full when the Baz Bus arrives.

99 Mile Lodge   LODGE $
(☑041-583 1256; www.99miles.co.za; 4 Jenvey Way; dm/s/d R120/270/385; 🖙🏊) Somewhere between a pleasant backpackers and a budget

Port Elizabeth

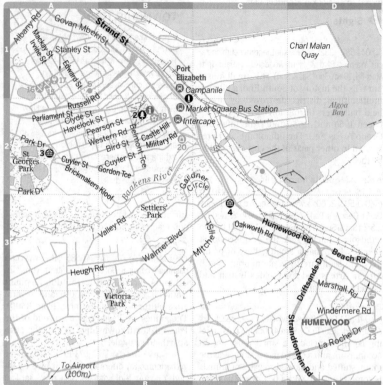

SOUTH AFRICA WESTERN REGION

guesthouse, this lodge is in a suburban neighbourhood only a few minutes' walk to Polo and Hobie beaches. There's a communal kitchen, a jacuzzi and a large pool with a big deck area.

Algoa Bay B&B   B&B $$
(☑041-582 5134; www.algoabay.co.za; 13 Ferndale Rd; s/d incl breakfast R550/900; ✳️☀️🛜🏊) Rooms are tastefully furnished and come with flat-screen TVs at this modern B&B; you can see King's Beach from the top-floor rooms. There's an outdoor deck and solar-heated swimming pool.

Chapman Hotel   HOTEL $$
(☑041-584 0678; www.chapman.co.za; 1 Lady Bea Cres, Brookes Hill Dr, Summerstrand; s/d incl breakfast R650/850; ✳️@🏊) The friendly, family-run Chapman, overlooking the sea next to Dolphin's Leap Centre, is a good midrange option with a rim-flow pool. Modern rooms have private balconies with sea views.

Beach Hotel   HOTEL $$$
(☑041-583 2161; www.thebeachhotel.co.za; Marine Dr, Summerstrand; s/d incl breakfast from R1325/1700; ✳️@🛜🏊) The friendly four-star Beach Hotel is beautifully positioned opposite Hobie Beach and next to the Boardwalk. Its Ginger restaurant (mains R90 to R110) faces the sea.

Windermere   BOUTIQUE HOTEL $$$
(☑041-582 2245; www.thewindermere.co.za; 35 Humewood Rd; d incl breakfast R1650; ✳️🛜🏊) Located on a quiet street only a block from the beach is this oasis of boutique-style luxury. There are plush and contemporary furnishings throughout and the rooms and bathrooms are large.

🍴 Eating

On **Stanley St**, between Glen and Mackay Sts in the Richmond Hill neighborhood, are more than half a dozen quality restaurants. The **Boardwalk Casino Complex** in Sum-

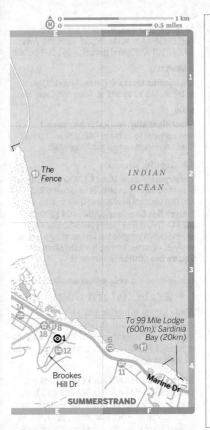

Port Elizabeth

⊙ Sights
1 Bayworld	E4
2 Donkin Reserve	B2
3 Nelson Mandela Metropolitan Art Museum	A2
4 South End Museum	C3

⊕ Activities, Courses & Tours
5 Calabash Tours	A1
6 Pro Dive	F4
7 Raggy Charters	C2
8 Surf Centre	E4
9 Surfing	F4

⊜ Sleeping
10 Algoa Bay B&B	D4
11 Beach Hotel	F4
12 Chapman Hotel	E4
13 Lungile Backpackers	D4
14 Windermere	E3

⊗ Eating
15 Deli Street Café	A1
16 Fushin	A1

⊜ Drinking
17 For the Love of Wine	A1

⊛ Entertainment
18 Gondwana Café	E4
19 Port Elizabeth Opera House	B2

⊜ Shopping
20 Wezandla Gallery & Craft Centre	B2

merstrand has several fast-food eateries, a good Chinese restaurant and a couple of cafes with outdoor patio seating.

Deli Street Café   SANDWICHES, SOUTH AFRICAN **$$**
(Stanley St; mains R60, sandwiches R45; ⊙7.30am-10pm; 🖘) This restaurant adheres to the farm-to-table theme in its menu and aesthetic. Diners munch on salads, burgers and 'build-your-own' sandwiches in an airy space with lofty ceilings and picnic tables.

Fushin   JAPANESE **$$**
(15 Stanley St; mains R70-100) Expect high-quality sushi and handmade Singapore-inspired noodle dishes as well as creative fare like stuffed giant squid. As with all Stanley St restaurants, you can opt to eat outside on the street.

Cubata   BARBECUE **$$**
(cnr Arthur & Stebonheath Sts, Sydenham; mains R65; ⊙Mon-Sat) In a large converted garage in a gritty neighborhood near the stadium, Cubata has a dedicated following of loyal locals who chow down on Portuguese-style barbecued prawns, ribs and chicken. BYOB.

🍷 Drinking & Entertainment

Stanley St has several bars, and its restaurants are great for after-dinner drinks. Half a dozen bars line nearby **Parliament St**, though it's considered a sketchy area at night.

[TOP CHOICE] For the Love of Wine   WINE BAR
(Stanley St, Richmond Hill; ⊙noon-10pm Mon-Sat) One of the few wine bars in PE, this owner-run friendly spot is above Yiayias Mediterranean Restaurant. There's a nice selection of reasonably priced wines (R25 per glass), and several Stanley St restaurants deliver food here.

Gondwana Café
BAR

(⊙9am-late Tue-Sun) There are DJs on Fridays and Saturdays and live jazz on Sundays from 5.30pm at this large cafe overlooking the ocean.

Port Elizabeth Opera House
OPERA

(☑041-586 2256; www.peoperahouse.co.za; Whites Rd) This opera house, the oldest in South Africa, hosts a wide range of concerts, ballets, plays and jazz recitals.

🛍 Shopping

Wezandla Gallery &
Craft Centre
HANDICRAFTS

(27 Baakens St) This brightly coloured arts-and-crafts centre has a huge array of artefacts made by local groups, and a small coffee shop.

ℹ Information

Nelson Mandela Bay Tourism (☑041-585 8884; www.nmbt.co.za; Donkin Reserve; ⊙8am-4.30pm Mon-Fri, 9.30am-3.30pm Sat & Sun) There's internet access here (R20 per hour) plus a decent cafe, and you can climb the lighthouse for good city views (adult/child R5/3). Other branches are at the Boardwalk (Summerstrand) and in front of Brooke's on the Bay Pavilion (Beach Rd, Humewood).

ℹ Getting There & Away

AIR

South African Airways (SAA; ☑041-507 1111; www.flysaa.com) and **Kulula** (☑0861 585 852; www.kulula.com) have daily flights between Port Elizabeth and Cape Town (from R1000, 1¼ hours), Durban (from R1000, 1¼ hours) and Jo'burg (from R850, 1¾ hours).

BUS

Greyhound (☑083 915 9000; www.greyhound.co.za) and **Translux** (Ring Rd, Ernst & Young Bldg, Greenacres Shopping Centre) buses depart from the Greenacres Shopping Centre, around 3km from Humewood. **Intercape** (☑0861 287 287; www.intercape.co.za; cnr Fleming & North Union Sts) departs from the bus stop on the corner of Fleming and North Union Sts, behind the old post office.

Sample fares:

» Cape Town (R330, 12 hours)

» Durban (R430, 14 hours)

» East London (R225, five hours)

» Grahamstown (R200, two hours)

» Jo'burg (R400, 15 hours)

The **Baz Bus** (☑0861 229 287) runs from Port Elizabeth to Cape Town (R1250 one way – hop-on, hop-off) and Durban (R1230).

CAR

All the big car-hire operators have offices in Port Elizabeth or at the airport, including **Avis** (☑041-501 7200) and **Hertz** (☑041-508 6600).

MINIBUS TAXI

The **minibus taxi rank** (Govan Mbeki St) services the local area as well as J-Bay and Cape Town.

TRAIN

Shosholoza Meyl (www.shosholozameyl.co.za) runs services to Jo'burg (R420, 20 hours) via Cradock, Bloemfontein and Kroonstad.

ℹ Getting Around

The **airport** (Allister Miller Rd, Walmer) is about 5km from the city centre. Taxis (around R65) and hire cars are available at the airport.

Algoa Bus Company (☑041-404 1200, 080 142 1444) runs most routes (R6.50 one way) around the city and to the surrounding suburbs every 25 minutes, leaving from the **Market Square bus station** on Strand St.

Central Eastern Cape

While this is something of an artificial geographic designation, it makes sense (from a traveller's perspective) to think of the area immediately east of Port Elizabeth as a self-contained region.

ADDO ELEPHANT NATIONAL PARK

This national park (☑042-233 8600; www.sanparks.org; adult/child R150/50; ⊙7am-7pm) is 72km north of Port Elizabeth, near the Zuurberg Range in the Sundays River Valley. Addo now encompasses five biomes over 180,000 hectares of malaria-free wildlife viewing, and there are plans to double its size and increase the marine reserve.

When Addo was proclaimed a national park in 1931, there were only 16 elephants left; today there are more than 450 in the park (their rehabilitation has been so successful that contraceptive measures are being considered), and you'd be unlucky not to see some. A day or two at Addo is a highlight of any visit to this part of the Eastern Cape, not only for the elephants but for the zebras, black rhinos, Cape buffaloes, leopards, lions, myriad birds and even the flightless dung beetles, endemic to Addo.

You can drive your own vehicle in the park, or guided wildlife drives are available (two hours, R240 per person). Horse riding is also popular in the park (two-hour ride R245).

🛏 Sleeping

Park accommodation can get booked up at busy periods, so always reserve in advance, if possible. There are a lot of B&Bs around the blink-and-you'll-miss-it town of Addo, just a few kilometres from the park gate.

Aardvark Guesthouse GUESTHOUSE $
(☎042-233 1244; www.theaardvarkbackpack ers.co.za; campsite per person R60, dm/s/d R120/300/440; ⊛) This handsome guesthouse is set around a manicured lawn 2.5km north of Addo village. There are *rondavels* with bathrooms in the yard, four-bed safari tents (R400) and a contemporary-design dormitory.

Addo Rest Camp CAMPGROUND, CABINS $$
(☎in Pretoria 012-428 9111; www.sanparks.org; campsites/safari tent R210/535, forest cabin R690, 4-person chalet R1125) Addo's main campsite at the main park headquarters is a great-value spot with various accommodation options, some of which overlook a waterhole where elephants come to slake their thirst.

TOP CHOICE Camp Figtree RESORT $$$
(☎082 611 3603; www.campfigtree.co.za; s/d incl breakfast from R1335/1780; ⊛☀) Tastefully appointed cottages share the grounds with a pool, library, lounge area and restaurant. There's emphasis on being environmentally friendly – electricity is limited and ingenious solar-powered jar lamps are used at night. Figtree is around 11km from the R335 turn-off towards the Zuurberg Pass.

ℹ Information

The park is closed if there has been heavy rain. There is a well-stocked **shop** (⊙8am-7pm) at the park headquarters.

GRAHAMSTOWN
☎046 / POP 120,000

The capital of Settler Country, Grahamstown has some fine examples of Victorian and early Edwardian building styles, with beautiful powder-blue and lemon-yellow shopfronts in the town centre. But Grahamstown's genteel conservatism and its English-style prettiness belie a bloody history. Visit the nearby townships for a glimpse into the culture of the Xhosa – once rulers of the region, they were defeated by British and Boer forces after a fierce struggle.

Socially, the students from Rhodes University dominate the town. But as established artists settle here and the population

ages, a more sophisticated side of Grahamstown is developing.

◉ Sights & Activities

Observatory Museum MUSEUM
(Bathurst St; adult/child R10/5; ⊙9am-4.30pm Mon-Fri) In this old house you'll find rare Victorian memorabilia and a truly wonderful camera obscura.

Albany History Museum MUSEUM
(www.am.org.za; Somerset St; adult/child R10/5; ⊙9am-4.30pm Mon-Fri) Dedicated to detailing the history and art of the peoples of the Eastern Cape.

FREE National English Literary Museum MUSEUM
(87 Beaufort St; ⊙8.30am-1pm & 2-4.30pm Mon-Fri) The collection here contains the first editions of just about every work by famous South African writers.

Victorian & Edwardian Storefronts HISTORIC BUILDINGS
The best examples of preserved Victorian and Edwardian storefronts are **Grocott's Mail** (Church Sq), still a working newspaper office, and **Birch's Gentlemen's Outfitters** (Church Sq).

🎉 Festivals & Events

Grahamstown bills itself as 'Africa's Festival Capital', with various events happening several times a year. The biggest is the hugely popular **National Arts Festival** (☎046-603 1103; www.nafest.co.za) and its associated **Fringe Festival**, which run for 10 days at the beginning of July. Accommodation at this time can be booked out a year in advance, and nights can be freezing.

🛏 Sleeping

Whethu Backpackers BACKPACKERS $
(☎046-636 1001; www.whethu.com; 6 George St; dm/d R120/450; ☎) The owner of the now-defunct Old Gaol backpackers has relocated to a decidedly less penal-like setting, though this converted suburban home does have small rooms.

Cock House GUESTHOUSE $$
(☎046-636 1287; www.cockhouse.co.za; 10 Market St; s/d incl breakfast R535/950, restaurant mains R75-100; ☎) This former settler home is now a national monument and a hugely popular guesthouse with old-fashioned furnishings and a pretty garden. There are also two

luxury, self-catering apartments and a highly regarded restaurant.

137 High Street
GUEST HOUSE $$

(☑046-622 3242; www.137highstreet.co.za; 137 High St; s/d incl breakfast R495/820; ☎) Well situated within walking distance of museums and shops, this guesthouse in a charming Georgian cottage also has a restaurant that locals claim makes the best cappuccino in town. Rooms are tiny, but well appointed and comfortable.

7 Worcester Street
GUESTHOUSE $$$

(☑046-622 2843; 7 Worcester St; s/d incl breakfast R1120/1790; ❄❄) This luxurious guesthouse is filled with artworks and sumptuous period furniture. A three-course dinner is available for R160.

✖ Eating & Drinking

Haricot's Deli & Bistro
DELI, MEDITERRANEAN $$

(www.haricots.co.za; 32 New St; mains R50-100; ⊙9am-late Mon-Sat, lunch Sun; ☎) Fill up a picnic basket with made-to-order sandwiches, enormous scones and delicious lemon meringue pie or sit down to a lamb and apricot tagine paired with a glass of wine from one of the city's best lists.

Calabash
SOUTH AFRICAN $$

(123 High St; mains R75) Traditional South African food, including specialities like Xhosa hotpots and *samp* (maize and beans), are served up in a warm, reed-ceilinged dining room.

Copper Kettle
BAR

(7 Bathurst St; ⊙7.30am-midnight Mon-Thu, 8am-2am Fri & Sat, 11am-midnight Sun) While many places come and go, Copper Kettle lives on. Largely operating as a bar, it also serves lunch (mains R50), and has live jazz on Sunday afternoons.

❶ Information

Makana Tourism (☑046-622 3241; www.grahamstown.co.za; 63 High St; ⊙8.30am-5pm Mon-Fri, 9am-noon Sat; ☎) Makana Tourism has lots of accommodation information available and sells Translux bus tickets. Offers free wi-fi and a computer with internet access.

❶ Getting There & Away

Greyhound and Translux buses depart from the terminus (cnr High & Bathurst Sts) on their daily runs to Cape Town (R400, 14 hours), Port Elizabeth (R200, two hours) and Durban (R375, 12½ hours). Mini-Lux (☑in Amalinda 043-741 3107)

runs to East London and Port Elizabeth from here. Check with the tourist office for prices and times.

You'll find minibus taxis on Raglan St, but most leave from Rhini township. Destinations include Port Elizabeth (R40, 2½ hours) and East London (R60, four hours).

PORT ALFRED
☑046 / POP 32,500

Known as 'the Kowie' for the picturesque canal-like river that flows through its centre, Port Alfred is blessed with beautiful beaches, some backed by massive sand dunes. Upscale, contemporary vacation homes line the canal and the hills surrounding town. It's quiet out of season except for Grahamstown students, but from mid-December to January it bustles with holidaymakers from elsewhere in South Africa. Because there's little budget accommodation it's not on the backpacker map.

🏃 Activities

For **surfers**, there are good right- and lefthand breaks at the river mouth. There's an 8km **walking trail** through the Kowie Nature Reserve – maps are available from the tourist office. You can climb the **Great Fish Point Lighthouse** (adult/child R16/8; ⊙10am-noon & 12.30-3pm), 25km east of Port Alfred. There's self-catering accommodation available here as well.

Outdoor Focus
CANOEING, DIVING

(☑046-624 4432; www.outdoorfocus.co.za; Beach Rd) A one-stop shop for diving (between May and August) and other outdoor activities. You can also book the two-day **Kowie Canoe Trail** (per person R150), a fairly easy 21km canoe trip upriver from Port Alfred with an overnight stay in a hut.

3 Sisters Horse Trails & Equestrian Centre
HORSE RIDING

(☑082 645 6345; www.threesistershorsetrails.co.za; R250) Offers horse rides of several hours on the beach, or overnight trips along a river valley.

🛌 Sleeping

Medolino Caravan Park
CAMPGROUND $

(☑046-624 1651; www.medolino.co.za; 23 Stewart St; campsites per person R130, 4-person chalet R850; ☎❄) This highly recommended tranquil, shaded park has two-bedroom chalets that are heavily discounted outside the high season.

Kelly's APARTMENT $$
(✆046-624 5439; www.kellys.co.za; 56 West Beach Dr; ste per person R420) These self-catering apartments, ideally located across the street from Kelly's Beach, are one of the best deals in town. Each is outfitted with a full kitchen, living room and spacious bedroom, as well as an outdoor deck.

4 Carnoustie GUESTHOUSE $$
(✆046-624 3306; www.4carnoustie.co.za; Carnoustie Ave; s/d incl breakfast R600/850; ❷❄) Located between the edge of the golf course and the beach, this house has chic, sunny rooms and a beautiful upstairs deck with a jacuzzi and magnificent sea views.

✗ Eating

TOP CHOICE **Zest Café** MEDITERRANEAN $$
(Van der Riet St; mains R60; ❂8am-5pm Mon-Fri, to 3pm Sat) As well as falafel and a variety of pizzas, try one of the more inventively prepared dishes like spicy seafood, red pepper and almond stew in the charming trellis-covered garden.

**Wharf Street
Brew Pub** INTERNATIONAL $$
(✆046-624 5705; 18 Wharf St; mains R55-125, brewery tours R30; ❂lunch & dinner Mon-Sat, lunch Sun) The handsome dining room of exposed stone and brick, wood floors and poster-sized photos overshadows a slightly uninspiring menu. The attached brewery offers tours (11am and 2.30pm Monday to Friday; reservations required).

Barmuda SOUTH AFRICAN $$
(23 Van der Riet St; mains R70; ❂10am-late) Worth a visit for its lovely setting overlooking the river. The menu features slightly elevated pub food like schnitzel, steaks and calamari.

❶ Information

Sunshine Coast Tourism Port Alfred
(✆046-624 1235; www.sunshinecoasttourism. co.za; Causeway Rd; ❂8am-4.30pm Mon-Fri, 8.30am-noon Sat) On the western bank of the Kowie River. Has brochures detailing accommodation, walks and canoe trails. Shares its building with Avis.

❶ Getting There & Away

The Baz Bus stops at Beavers Restaurant (Southwell Rd) on its run from Port Elizabeth (R175, two hours) to Durban (R1060, 13 hours).

The **minibus taxi rank** (Biscay Rd), outside the Heritage Mall, offers daily services to Port Elizabeth (R75), Grahamstown (R25) and East London (R75). Local daily services include Bathurst (R15).

Amathole Region

The stretch of coast and hinterland known as Amathole (pronounced 'ama-tawl-eh', from the Xhosa for 'calves') extends from the Great Fish River to the Great Kei River on the so-called Shipwreck Coast, and inland as far as Queenstown. It includes the enchanting mountain village of Hogsback, the surfside city of East London and little-visited nature reserves. A good part of this area was the former Xhosa homeland of Ciskei.

EAST LONDON
✆043 / POP 980,000

East London is the country's only river port, situated on a spectacular bay that curves round to huge sand hills. Much of the city centre is dilapidated, dotted with falling-to-pieces Victorian buildings and downright ugly 1960s and '70s monstrosities. Wealthy Queenstown Park (containing the zoo) is pretty, and the beaches and surf are excellent, but there's not a lot to keep you here. It's largely a transport hub for the Wild and Sunshine Coasts.

Its Khoisan name means 'Place of Buffalo', and the whole area is sometimes referred to as 'Buffalo City'.

The **East London Museum** (✆043-743 0686; www.elmuseum.za.org; 319 Oxford St; adult/ child R12/5; ❂9.30am-4.30pm Mon-Fri) is worth a visit. Its more unusual exhibits include a living beehive and a stuffed coelacanth – a fish thought to have become extinct over 50

DON'T MISS

HIKING THE SHIPWRECK COAST

As the graveyard for many errant ships, the coast between the Great Fish River and East London is deservedly known as the Shipwreck Coast. The 69km, six-day, five-night **Shipwreck Hiking & Canoe Trail** (per person R700) leads from Port Alfred to the Great Fish River Mouth. You are rewarded with wild, unspoiled sections of surf beach, rich coastal vegetation and beautiful estuaries. The trail can be booked through **Dave Marais** (✆082 391 0647; www. shipwreckhiking.co.za).

million years ago but rediscovered nearby in 1938.

The best **surfing** is at Nahoon Reef at the southern end of Nahoon Beach.

🛏 Sleeping

John Bailie Guest Lodge GUESTHOUSE **$**
(☏043-735 1058; www.johnbailieguestlodge.co.za; 9 John Bailie Rd, Bunkers Hill; s/d from R350/400; ❋🛜❋) Feel at home at this family-run guesthouse, near the golf course. There are a half-dozen carpeted rooms with TVs. Breakfast is an option and there's a nice garden pool area.

Hampton Court Guest Lodge HOTEL **$$**
(☏043-722 7924; www.hampton-court.co.za; 2 Marine Tce; s/d incl breakfast from R700/900; ❋🛜) This renovated 1920s landmark building with a waterfront location and contemporary furnishings is a good choice for the centre. Sea-facing rooms, while more expensive, have panoramic views.

White House GUESTHOUSE **$$**
(☏043-740 0344; www.thewhitehousebandb.co.za; 10 Whitthaus St, Gonubie; s/d incl breakfast R495/595; ❋🛜❋) Somewhat grand and a bit institutional-looking, the aptly named White House has panoramic views of cliffs and sea – watch for whales and dolphins while having breakfast. Some rooms have chintzy decor or feel under-furnished.

🍴 Eating

Café Neo MEDITERRANEAN **$$**
(Windmill Roadhouse; mains R65; 🛜) There are ocean views from the balcony of this stylish eatery. The large menu covers the gamut from healthy light wraps and grilled line-caught fish to steaks and decadent desserts. The bar stays open late.

Grazia Fine Food & Wine MEDITERRANEAN **$$**
(☏043-722 2009; www.graziafinefood.co.za; Upper Esplanade; mains R80-150; ◷noon-10.30pm) This stylish centrally located restaurant has sea

East London

views and an outdoor deck for dining. The sophisticated menu includes pasta, pizza, meat and seafood. Reservations recommended.

ℹ Getting There & Away

AIR

The airport is 10km from the centre. **SAA** (☎043-706 0247; www.flysaa.com) flies from East London daily to the following:

» Cape Town (R1500, 1½ hours)

» Durban (R1200, one hour)

» Jo'burg (R1000, 1½ hours)

» Port Elizabeth (R1400, 50 minutes)

BUS

Translux, City to City, Greyhound and Intercape all stop at the **Windmill Park Roadhouse** (cnr Moore St & Marine Tce). Among others, connections are available to the following:

» Cape Town (R440, 16 hours)

» Durban (R350, nine to 10 hours)

» Jo'burg/Pretoria (R350, 14 hours)

» Port Elizabeth (R230, three to four hours)

The Baz Bus stops at backpackers in East London on its runs between Port Elizabeth and Durban.

MINIBUS TAXI

On the corner of Buffalo and College Sts are long-distance minibus taxis to destinations north of East London. Nearby, on the corner of Caxton and Gillwell Sts, are minibus taxis for King William's Town (R18, one hour) and the local area.

Destinations include the following:

» Cape Town (R350, 18 hours)

» Jo'burg (R250, 15 hours)

» Mthatha (R70, five hours)

» Port Elizabeth (R100, six hours)

TRAIN

Shosholoza Meyl (☎0860 008 888; www.shosholozameyl.co.za) runs a tourist-class (with sleepers) train to Jo'burg (R390, 20 hours) every day except Saturday via Bloemfontein (R250, seven hours).

HOGSBACK
☎045 / POP 1500

There's something about Hogsback, improbably located 1300m up in the beautiful Amathole Mountains, that makes you half expect to meet a hobbit. Locals like to play on the Tolkien connection, but despite being born 500km away in Bloemfontein, it's doubtful

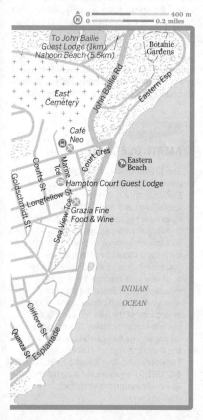

DON'T MISS

STRANDLOPER TRAIL

The **Strandloper Hiking Trail** (☎bookings 043-841 1046; www.strandlopertrails.org.za; per person R500, conservation fee R60) runs between Kei Mouth and Gonubie, just outside East London. The trail is fairly easy, but good fitness is required. Profits are channelled into environmental education for local children. The Strandlopers (meaning 'Beach Walkers') were a Khoisan ethnic group who lived on the coast but disappeared as a distinct group after white settlement.

There are three overnight huts and the cost of staying in these is included in the booking fee. Camping on the beach is prohibited, but most of the coastal hotels have campsites.

AMATHOLE MUSEUM

King William's Town was a colonial capital and an important military base in the interminable struggle with the Xhosa. The main reason for a visit is the excellent Amathole Museum (☑043-642 4506; www.museum.za.net; 3 Albert Rd; adult/child R5/free; ◎8am-4.30pm Mon-Fri), one of the finest in the region, with an excellent Xhosa Gallery featuring in-depth explanations of Xhosa culture, mysticism and history.

Hogsback inspired Tolkien's works – he left South Africa for good as a very young child.

Hogsback's artistic community, organic food and mind-boggling views of mountains and forested valleys in all directions make it an ecodestination par excellence. There are some great walks, bike rides and drives in the area (ask at the tourist office for a map), but be prepared for inclement weather – rainy and misty days can occur any time of year. Winter (June to August) sees occasional snowfall, with night-time temperatures dropping below freezing.

Sleeping & Eating

TOP CHOICE Away with the Fairies BACKPACKERS $
(☑045-962 1031; www.awaywiththefairies.co.za; Hydrangea Lane; campsites/dm R70/120, d with/without bathroom R350/290; @☎☀) Location isn't everything – but it's just one of the distinguishing features of this delightful backpackers. Horse riding (1½-hour trails R175) and a guided 16km mountain-biking trip (R250) taking in eight waterfalls are offered.

Edge Mountain Retreat LODGE $$
(☑082 603 5246; www.theedge-hogsback.co.za; Bluff End; self-catering cottage from R495; @☎) Tastefully decorated cottages and garden rooms are strung out along a mountain edge. The vibe here is peace, quiet and relaxation. The restaurant, Tea Thyme, is highly recommended.

❶ Information

Hogsback Information Centre (☑045-962 1245; www.hogsback.com; Main Rd; ◎10am-4pm Mon-Sat, 9am-3pm Sun)

❶ Getting There & Away

The easiest way to get to Hogsback without a car is by shuttle bus from East London (two hours,

R125 one way, daily) and from Buccaneers Lodge & Backpackers (p391) in Chintsa West (2½ hours, R150 one way) to Away with the Fairies.

Eastern Karoo

This is the southeastern extension of the vast semidesert that stretches across the great South African plateau, inland from the Cape coast. It's one of the region's most intriguing areas, with an overwhelming sense of space and peace that stands in sharp contrast to the cheery, sometimes overdeveloped coastline.

GRAAFF-REINET
☑049 / POP 44,317

Cradled in a curve of the Sundays River and within walking distance of the Camdeboo National Park, Graaff-Reinet is often referred to as the 'jewel of the Karoo'.

'Camdeboo', the Khoekhoen word for 'green valleys', is used to describe the hills surrounding the town, which is the fourth-oldest European town (established 1786) in South Africa. Graaff-Reinet has a superb architectural heritage, including Cape Dutch houses, flat-roofed Karoo cottages and ornate Victorian villas. Add in a small-town ambience, excellent accommodation and a few outstanding restaurants and you'll begin to understand why it aquired its moniker.

AMATHOLE TRAIL

The 121km, six-day Amathole Trail (per person per night R135) begins at the Maden Dam, 23km north of King William's Town, and ends at the Tyumie River near Hogsback. Accommodation is in huts. It ranks as one of South Africa's top mountain walks, but it's pretty tough and should be attempted only if you are reasonably experienced and fit.

Walkers are rewarded with great views, although about a third of the walk goes through dense forest. Shorter sections of the hike are available outside school holidays. Guides can be arranged. The trail can be booked with the Department of Water Affairs & Forestry (☑in King William's Town 043-642 2571; 2 Hargreaves Ave, King William's Town) or through the Hogsback Information Centre.

Graaff-Reinet

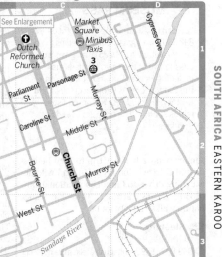

Sights

Old Library MUSEUM

(www.graaffreinetmuseums.co.za; cnr Church & Somerset Sts; adult/child R15/5; ⊙8am-1pm & 1.45-4.30pm Mon-Fri, 9am-1pm Sat & Sun) Houses a collection of historical artefacts, displays on Khoe-San rock paintings and fossils from the Karoo, and an exhibition telling the life story of Robert Mangaliso Sobukwe, the founder of the Pan African Congress (PAC).

Hester Rupert Art Museum MUSEUM

(☑049-892 2121; www.rupertartmuseum.co.za; Church St; adult/child R10/free; ⊙9am-noon & 2-5pm Mon-Fri, 9am-noon Sat & Sun) This museum's collection of paintings (and a few sculptures) from the 1960s were all donated by well-known South African artists.

Reinet House MUSEUM

(Murray St; adult/child R15/5; ⊙8am-4.30pm Mon-Fri, 9am-1pm Sat & Sun) This Dutch Reformed parsonage, built between 1806 and 1812, is a beautiful example of Cape Dutch architecture. The cobblestoned rear courtyard has a grapevine that was planted in 1870 and is now one of the largest in the world.

Tours

Ingomso Tours (☑083 559 1207; www.ingomso-tours.co.za; 2hr tours per person R100)

Graaff-Reinet

Sights
1 Hester Rupert Art Museum B3
2 Old Library B3
3 Reinet House C1

Activities, Courses & Tours
4 Karoo Connections A2

Sleeping
5 Aa 'Qtansisi B1
6 Buiten Verwagten B&B A3
7 Camdeboo Cottages A3
8 Drostdy Hotel A3
9 Le Jardin Backpackin' A1

Eating
10 Coldstream A2
11 Polka Café A3

take you to Umasizakhe, one of the oldest townships in the country and the birthplace of Robert Sobukwe, founder of the Pan African Congress. The tours provide insight into Xhosa culture and history and modern township life.

David McNaughton of **Karoo Connections** (☑049-892 3978; www.karooconnections.co.za; 7 Church St) organises tours to the Valley of Desolation at sunset (R375 including

MUSEUM PASS

You can buy a combined pass (☎049-892 3801; www.graaffreinetmuseums.co.za; adult/child R50/25) that gives access to five of the town's museums (not including Hester Rupert Art Museum) – the Old Residency, Urquhart House and Military History Museum aren't listed in this section. The pass isn't valid on Sundays.

sundowners), a half-day trip to Nieu Bethesda and the Owl House (R550), and wildlife-watching drives to Camdeboo National Park (R350). He also arranges township walks, nature walks and city tours.

🛏 Sleeping

Le Jardin Backpackin'　GUESTHOUSE $
(☎049-892 5890; nitagush@telkom.sa.net; cnr Donkin & Caledon Sts; s/d without bathroom R150/260; ✸) Hosts Terrence and Nita Gush share their time-capsule home – not a backpackers in the conventional sense – and knowledge about the area with enthusiasm. The small and homely rooms are worth considering for those short on rand. Bookings essential.

TOP CHOICE Aa 'Qtansisi　GUESTHOUSE $$
(☎049-891 0243; www.aaqtansisi.co.za; 69 Somerset St; s/d incl breakfast R650/950; ✸@🛜✸) Translating as 'We welcome you' in Khoe-San (when asking for directions, simply drop the 'Q', or ask for 69 Somerset), this lavishly designed guesthouse's rooms are evocative of an *Arabian Nights'* harem. A lovely trellis-covered backyard has a plunge pool and hammocks.

TOP CHOICE Camdeboo Cottages　GUESTHOUSE $$
(☎049-892 3180; www.camdeboocottages.co.za; 16 Parliament St; 2-/4-bed cottage R450/700; @🛜✸) Behind the classically restored facades of these Karoo-style cottages are contemporary creature comforts. There's a lovely pool and patio area – a much-needed refuge from the midday heat.

Buiten Verwagten B&B　B&B $$
(☎049-892 4504; www.buitenverwagten.co.za; 58 Bourke St; s/d incl breakfast R750/1000; ✸@🛜✸) Every aspect of this Victorian-era home is tastefully curated by its friendly and professional owners. There's a pool in the courtyard and a four-person self-catering cottage is also available (R800).

Drostdy Hotel　HOTEL $$
(☎049-892 2161; www.drostdy.co.za; 30 Church St; s/d R595/845; ✸@✸✸) Exuding old-world charm and nostalgia, this landmark hotel is in the beautifully restored *drostdy*. Guests stay in renovated mid-19th-century cottages, originally built for freed slaves along Stretch's Ct. It will be closed for renovations until the end of 2013.

🍴 Eating

TOP CHOICE Polka Café　DESSERTS, SOUTH AFRICAN $$
(www.polkacafe.co.za; 52 Somerset St; mains R75-130; ⏱7am-10pm Mon-Sat) Polka has an ambitious nouvelle cuisine menu that improves upon conventional fare – for example, springbok *bobotie* and kudu schnitzel. There's also a a bakery selling homemade cookies, frosting-heavy cupcakes and pastries.

Coldstream　SOUTH AFRICAN, STEAKHOUSE $$
(3 Church St; mains R95; ⏱Mon-Sat; 📞) Coldstream is an upscale dining option, delivering the juiciest and best-prepared steaks in town. The 'trio' platter of beef, ostrich and kudu or springbok will satiate the most ardent meat lover.

ℹ Information

Graaff-Reinet Tourism (☎049-892 4248; www.graaffreinet.co.za; 13A Church St; ⏱8am-5pm Mon-Fri, 9am-noon Sat)

Karoo Connections (www.karooconnections.co.za; Church St; per hr R30; ⏱8am-5pm Mon-Fri, 9am-noon Sat) Internet access and bookshop stocking South African titles.

ℹ Getting There & Away

Long-distance buses stop at **Kudu Motors** (Church St). Intercape and Translux service Cape Town (R320, 12 hours) and Jo'burg (R400, 11 hours); the latter also runs to East London (R260, five hours) and Port Elizabeth (R190, three hours). Tickets and info are available at the tourist office.

Minibus taxis leave from Market Sq. Major destinations are Port Elizabeth (R150) and Cape Town (R350).

CAMDEBOO NATIONAL PARK

Covering an area of 19,405 hectares, Camdeboo National Park (☎049-892 6128; www.sanparks.org; adult/child R70/35; ⏱6am-8pm) has plenty of animals, but the real draw is the spectacular geological formations and great views of Graaff-Reinet and the plains.

WORTH A TRIP

NIEU BETHESDA

Tucked away in the Karoo, the tiny, isolated village of Nieu Bethesda was once one of the most obscure places in South Africa. Interest surged when the extraordinary Owl House (☎049-841 1603; River St; admission R35; ⊙9am-5pm) was brought to light – the home of 'outsider' artist Helen Martins.

Nieu Bethesda makes a great day trip from Graaff-Reinet and there are a number of good lunch spots. The Brewery & Two Goats Deli (Pioneer St; mains R70; ⊙8am-5pm Mon-Sat, to 3pm Sun) serves platters of homemade bread, cheese and pickles, washed down with micro-brewed beer. Karoo Lamb (mains R80; ⊙7am-9pm; ☎) is a restaurant-cum-gift-shop serving hearty fare and offering tourist information.

If you do want to stay over, try Ganora Guest Farm (☎049-841 1302; www.ganora. co.za; s/d incl breakfast from R500/720; ☎), 7km out of town. As well as charming accommodation, it offers guided walks to rock-art sites.

There is no public transport to Nieu Bethesda, but it's a scenic hour-long drive from Graaff-Reinet. There are no petrol stations or ATMs in Nieu Bethesda.

The park is subdivided into three main sections: the wildlife-viewing area to the north of the dam; the western section with the Valley of Desolation, a hauntingly beautiful place with piled dolerite columns; and the eastern section, featuring various hiking trails.

You'll need to have your own vehicle to get around the reserve; otherwise, contact Karoo Connections in Graaff-Reinet for a tour. Highly recommended are two new accommodation options: Lakeview Tented Camp (R570) and the Nqweba Campsite (campsites R205); contact the Graaf-Reinet Tourism office for bookings.

Wild Coast

This shoreline rivals any in the country in terms of beauty, stretching for 350km from just east of Chintsa to Port Edward. Often referred to as the 'Transkei' (the name of the apartheid-era homeland the area once covered), the 'Wild Coast' is increasingly used to include inland areas as well: the pastoral landscapes where clusters of *rondavels* are scattered over rolling hills covered in short grass.

Whatever the name for the region, the Xhosa people are some of the friendliest you'll meet anywhere in South Africa, and chances are you'll be invited inside a home or, at the very least, a *shebeen* (pub). South of the Mbashe River live the Gcaleka people; Mpondomise live to the north. There are some absolutely amazing overnight hiking trails and far-flung river estuaries, plus backpackers accomodation that resembles

Xhosa settlements. Bird life, including fish eagles, egrets, cormorants and kingfishers, is abundant, especially in the parks, though, surprisingly, fishing is mostly subsistence level.

CHINTSA
☎043 / POP 2000

Heading up the N2, the sea spray starts to hit your face along an unspoilt stretch of white-sand beach called Chintsa (also spelt Cintsa), 38km from East London. Chintsa comprises two small, pretty villages – Chintsa East and Chintsa West. It's definitely the best place on this part of the coast to hang out for a few days (or weeks). Also in the area is the private, upmarket Inkwenkwezi Game Reserve (☎043-734 3234; www. inkwenkwezi.com; tented bush camp deluxe/luxury per person incl meals & activities R1800/2300), which contains all the Big Five (although the elephants are not wild). There are wildlife drives (from R495) and various elephant interaction activities (from R150).

🍴 Sleeping & Eating

TOP
CHOICE
Buccaneers Lodge & Backpackers   BACKPACKERS $$

(☎043-734 3012; www.cintsa.com; Chintsa West; campsites/dm/d R90/145/495; @☎) Sleeping options include comfortable dorms, contemporary rooms and cottages (R1200 for four people) with private sun decks. There's free use of canoes and boogie boards and surf classes (R185 per person). Tours include visits to Ngxingxolo village with Mama Tofu (☎073 148 7511), reputedly the oldest tour guide in South Africa. To get to Buccs, follow the Chintsa West turn-off for about 200m

The Wild Coast

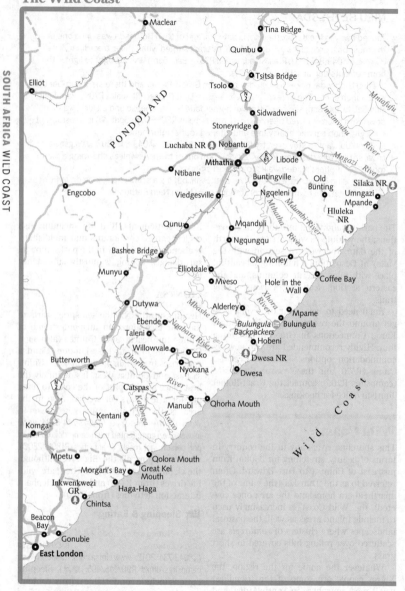

until you reach the entrance; it's a further 2km along the dirt road.

Prana Lodge　　　　　　RESORT **$$$**
(☎043-704 5100; www.pranalodge.co.za; Chintsa Dr, Chintsa East; ste incl breakfast from R2400; ❂@☎☯) Ideal for those seeking top-flight pampering, with suites boasting their own private plunge pool and enclosed garden courtyard. The property is hidden in a dune forest that's a short walk to the beach and includes an open-air dining area and luxurious spa facilities.

Flagstaff
Mtentu
Impisi
Mthamvuna River
Port Edward
Holy Cross Hospital
River
Mkambati NR
Palmerton
Msikaba
Lusikisiki
Port Grosvenor
River
Mbotyi
Mgoma
Mthambala
Gemvale
Port St Johns

INDIAN

OCEAN

LEGEND
NR Nature Reserve
GR Game Reserve

0 — 50 km
0 — 25 miles

tures creative burger combinations and local craft beer is available.

❶ Getting There & Away

To reach Chintsa from East London, take exit 26 (East Coast Resorts) off the N2. Go over the overpass and follow the road for 1km to the Chintsa East turn-off. The Chintsa West turn-off is another 16km further on.

COFFEE BAY
☏ 047 / POP 600

No one is sure how tiny Coffee Bay got its name, but there is a theory that a ship, wrecked here in 1863, deposited its cargo of coffee beans on the beach. These days, this once-remote hamlet is a commercialised backpackers' playground, with two busy hostels and a couple of more upmarket hotels jostling for space in the village centre. In between, a few hopeful locals hover, trying to sell *dagga* (marijuana), curios and day trips.

Coffee Bay itself is a fairly scruffy place, but the surrounding scenery is dramatic, with a beautiful kilometre-long beach set in front of towering cliffs. The backpackers hostels below run all sorts of day trips, including **horse riding** (2hr treks about R250), **guided hikes** (from R50), **cultural visits** (from R60) and **surfing trips** (R60).

🛏 Sleeping & Eating

Bomvu Paradise BACKPACKERS **$**
(☏ 047-575 2073; www.bomvubackpackers.com; campsites/dm R80/120, d with/without bathroom R350/280) Family-run Bomvu is a rambling complex of small buildings and gardens. It's a soulful place with organic food (dinner R55), yoga classes, fire poi performances and in-house band drumming sessions.

Coffee Shack BACKPACKERS **$**
(☏ 047-575 2048; www.coffeeshack.co.za; campsites/dm R70/120, d with/without bathroom R380/320; @) Coffee Shack caters to Baz Bus–loads of young travellers looking for a party. The rooms are fairly institutional (dorms can feel congested); however, there are *rondavels* across the river with more privacy. Camping is out back with river and ocean views.

Ocean View Hotel HOTEL **$$**
(☏ 047-575 2005; www.oceanview.co.za; s/d with full board R850/1500; ❄@☒) Typical holiday accommodation enviably located at the far end of the main beach. Chalet-style rooms have private decks and there's a pool and restaurant (set dinner R100).

Barefoot Café BURGERS, SOUTH AFRICAN **$$**
(Chintsa East; mains R60; ☎) What nightlife there is in Chintsa centers on this casual bar and restaurant where foreign volunteers, backpackers and locals mix. The menu fea-

WORTH A TRIP

MORGAN'S BAY & KEI MOUTH

North along the coast from Chintsa, and reached by turning off the N2 onto the R349, is the village of Morgan's Bay. It's a good place for some peace and quiet and for beachcombing and surfing. Prices skyrocket and places get booked solid between mid-December and mid-January.

Just after Morgan's Bay is the somewhat ramshackle Kei Mouth. It's reached by taking the pont (vehicle ferry; per car R60; ⊙7am-5.30pm) across the Great Kei River.

Light and airy Morgan Bay Hotel (☑043-841 1062; www.morganbayhotel.com; Beach Rd, Morgan Bay; s/d with full board R1230/1890; @🅿🏊) is perched directly over the beachfront and has an attached bar and restaurant with great outside seating. Yellowwood Forest (☑043-841 1598; www.yellowwoodforest.co.za; campsites R165, loft R195; 🅿), about 1km from Morgan's Bay beach, is a tranquil campsite surrounded by indigenous forest and frequented by birds and monkeys. There's a charming tea garden, craft shop and wood-fired pizzas on offer.

① Getting There & Away

If you're driving to Coffee Bay, take the sealed but dangerously potholed road that leaves the N2 at Viedgesville. A minibus taxi from Mthatha to Coffee Bay costs R25 and takes one hour. The backpacker shuttles (R60) meet the Baz Bus at the Shell Ultra City, 4km south of Mthatha.

PORT ST JOHNS
☑047 / POP 2100

Dramatically located at the mouth of the Umzimvubu River and framed by towering cliffs covered with dense tropical vegetation, the laid-back town of Port St Johns is the original Wild Coast journey's end. These days, there's something of a run-down quality to the town and it feels less out of the ordinary than more remotely situated spots elsewhere in the area.

Zambezi sharks calve upriver and, following six fatal attacks in the last half-dozen years, it's recommended that you do nothing more than wade off the town's beaches.

If sun-worshipping loses its lustre, take a walk in the lush surrounds of the coastal Silaka Nature Reserve (☑in East London 043-705 4400; www.ecparks.co.za; admission R20; ⊙6am-6pm). The path leaves from near Lodge on the Beach.

🛏 Sleeping & Eating

Amapondo Backpackers   BACKPACKERS $
(☑047-564 1344; www.amapondo.co.za; Second Beach Rd; campsites R80, dm/d without bathroom R120/350; 🅿) This mellow place has simple concrete-floored rooms, but the views of Second Beach compensate for the lack of decor. Activities offered include horse riding, boat trips, canoeing and surfing. There's a restaurant (mains R35) and bar, which can get lively with a mix of locals and travellers.

Delicious Monster Lodge   LODGE $$
(☑083 997 9856; www.deliciousmonsterpsj.co.za; Second Beach; r from R450; 🅿) This airy loft-style cottage has ocean views and is ideal for small groups. There's a restaurant here too (mains R70), with an eclectic menu that includes a meze platter, shwarma and line-caught fish.

Lodge on the Beach   LODGE $$
(☑047-564 1276; www.wildcoast.co.za/thelodge; Second Beach; r from R450) This well-kept thatched-roofed home has three rooms, each with an individual bathroom and its own small deck with unobstructed views of

DON'T MISS

BULUNGULA BACKPACKERS

Bulungula (☑047-577 8900; www.bulungula.com; campsites per person R70, dm/safari tent R130/300, d without bathroom R330) has legendary status on the Wild Coast for its community-based activities, ecofriendly ethos and stunning location. It's 40% owned by the local Xhosa community who run all the tours. There's an overall mellow vibe and beach parties take place well away from the main camp. All meals are offered (sandwiches R18, dinner R55). Self-caterers should bring their own supplies because there isn't much available nearby.

Bulungula is around two hours' drive from Coffee Bay. If you're coming in your own car, contact Bulungula in advance to get directions or to arrange pick-ups from Mthatha (R70).

RHODES

Sitting in the beautiful but scarcely visited North-Eastern Highlands, Rhodes has a spectacular mountain setting alongside the Bell River. The architecture remains as it was when the town was established in 1891.

Trout fishing is extremely popular throughout the whole district, and the Wild Trout Association (☑045-974 9292; www.wildtrout.co.za) headquarters is here. Dave Walker at the Walkerbouts Inn (☑045-974 9290; www.walkerbouts.co.za; per person with half board R525) is a local authority on fly-fishing. The inn has cosy, characterful rooms and there's a friendly bar serving good food.

The Rhodes Hotel (☑045-974 9305; www.rhodeshotel.co.za; Muller St; per person with half board R580; @) is in an atmospheric old complex with wood floors and well-appointed rooms. Horse riding can be arranged here.

The road to Rhodes from Barkly East (60km, 1½ hours), passing through gobsmacking scenery, is untarred but fine for 2WD cars. The route from Maclear is best undertaken in a 4WD vehicle.

Second Beach. Breakfast and dinner can be provided.

Wood 'n Spoon   SEAFOOD, SOUTH AFRICAN $
(Second Beach; mains R55; ⊙10.30am-9pm) A ramshackle restaurant with a chalkboard menu of fresh seafood and steaks.

❶ Information
Tourism Port St Johns (☑047-564 1187; www. portstjohns.org.za/tourism.htm) Located at the top of the roundabout when you enter Port St Johns.

❶ Getting There & Away
Most backpacker places will pick you up from the Shell Ultra City, 4km south of Mthatha (where the Baz Bus stops) for around R70, but it's essential to book ahead. There are also regular minibus taxis to Port St Johns from here (R40, two hours) that drop you at the roundabout.

KWAZULU-NATAL

Rough and ready, smart and sophisticated, rural and rustic, KwaZulu-Natal (KZN) is as eclectic as its cultures, people and landscapes. It has its metropolitan heart in the port of Durban and its nearby historic capital, Pietermaritzburg. The beaches along this coast attract local holidaymakers and visitors wishing to soak up the sand, sea, surf and sun. Head north and you enter Zululand, home to some of Africa's most evocative traditional settlements and cultural sites. The Elephant Coast (Maputaland) boasts the alluring iSimangaliso Wetland Park, encompassing remote wilderness areas.

Head northwest of Durban, and you enter another realm: the historic heartland where the province's history was thrashed out on the Battlefields during the Anglo-Zulu and Anglo-Boer Wars. On the province's western border, the heritage-listed uKhahlamba-Drakensberg Park features awesome peaks, unforgettable vistas and excellent hiking opportunities.

Durban
☑031 / POP 3.5 MILLION

Durban, a cosmopolitan queen, is sometimes passed over for her 'cooler' Capetonian cousin. But this isn't fair; there's a lot more to fun-loving Durbs (as she's affectionately known) than meets the eye. In preparation for the World Cup in 2010 the city had a major makeover and now offers a revamped beachfront, stylish cafes, wonderful cultural offerings and excellent shopping opportunities, much of which are clustered in fashionable areas within the suburbs.

South Africa's third-largest city (known as eThekweni in Zulu), Durban also claims to be the country's sporting capital. Thanks to its stadiums and venues, golf courses and a swath of butter-yellow sand, it's a great city for spectator sports and outdoor enthusiasts.

The downtown area – a buzzing, gritty grid comprising grandiose colonial buildings and fascinating art-deco architecture – throbs to a distinctly African beat. For beach lovers, the beachfront remains a city trademark for daytime activities.

Home to the largest concentration of people of Indian descent outside India, Durban also boasts a distinctive Asian twang, with

KwaZulu-Natal

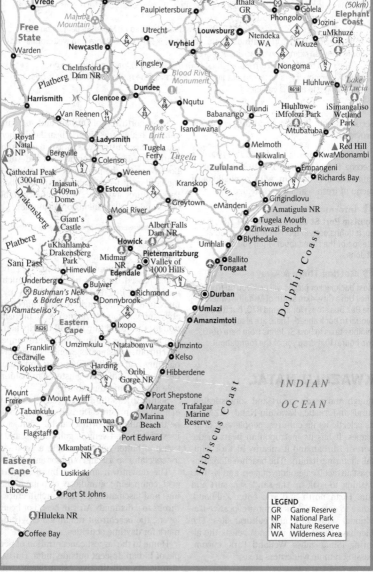
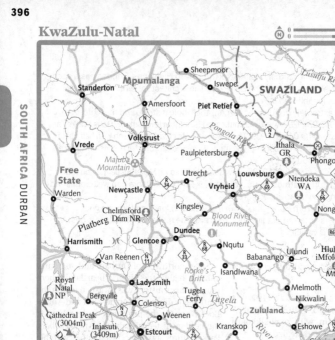

LEGEND
GR — Game Reserve
NP — National Park
NR — Nature Reserve
WA — Wilderness Area

the marketplaces and streets of the Indian area teeming with the sights, sounds and scents of the subcontinent.

History

Natal Bay, around which Durban is located, provided refuge for seafarers at least as early as 1685, and it's thought that Vasco da Gama anchored here in 1497.

In 1837 the Voortrekkers crossed the Drakensberg and founded Pietermaritzburg, 80km northwest of Durban. The next year, after Durban was evacuated during a Zulu raid, the Boers claimed control. It was reoccupied by a British force later that year, but the Boers stuck by their claim. The British sent troops to Durban and despite being defeated in 1842, Natal was soon annexed by the British and Durban began its growth as an important colonial port city.

In 1860 the first indentured Indian labourers arrived to work the cane fields. Despite the inequitable system – slave labour by another name – many more Indians arrived, including, in 1893, Mohandas Gandhi.

◎ Sights

BEACHFRONT

The beachfront has experienced a resurgence, thanks to the massive revamp that was completed prior to the World Cup in 2010. The new promenade – a pedestrian superhighway – runs behind the beaches, though it offers little shade. Both the beaches and promenade extend from the Blue Lagoon (at the mouth of the Umgeni River) to uShaka Marine World, a stretch known as the 'Golden Mile' although it's actually 6km long.

In summer, rickshaws ply their trade along the beachfront, many sporting exotic Zulu regalia. A 15-minute ride costs about R50 (plus R10 for a happy snap).

uShaka Marine World   AMUSEMENT PARK
(Map p402; ☑031-328 8000; www.ushakamarine world.co.za; uShaka Beach, the Point; Wet 'n' Wild or Sea World adult/child R125/95, combo ticket for both parks R165/125; ⊙9am-5pm) uShaka Marine World comprises Sea World, boasting one of the largest aquariums in the world, the biggest collection of sharks in the southern hemisphere, a seal stadium and a dolphinarium, and Wet 'n' Wild with enough freshwater rides to make you seasick. There's also a mock-up 1940s steamer wreck featuring two classy restaurants. The beach here is often slightly more sheltered than others along the 'Golden Mile'.

Moses Mabhida Stadium   STADIUM
(Map p398; ☑031-582 8222; www.mmstadium. com; Masabalala Yengwa Ave (NMR Ave); SkyCar adult/child R55/30, Adventure Walk per person R90, Big Swing per person R595; ⊙SkyCar 9am-6pm, Adventure Walk 10am, 1pm & 4pm Sat & Sun, Big Swing 9am-5pm) Constructed for the 2010 World Cup, the stadium seats over 56,000 people, and its arch was inspired by the 'Y' in the country's flag. Visitors can head up to the arch in a SkyCar, puff up on foot (550 steps) on an Adventure Walk or plunge off the 106m arch on the giant Big Swing. All options offer great views of Durban.

Sun Coast Casino   CASINO
(Map p398; ☑031-328 3000; www.suncoastcasino. co.za; OR Tambo Pde (Marine Pde)) The glitzy, art-deco-style casino is popular with locals and also features cinemas and some well attended restaurants. The beach in front of the casino – Suncoast Beach – is a safe and pleasant spot to lie.

CITY CENTRE

City Hall   NOTABLE BUILDING
(Map p402; Anton Lembede St (Smith St)) The opulent 1910 Edwardian neobaroque City Hall dominates the city centre. In front is Francis Farewell Square, where Henry Francis Fynn and Francis Farewell, founders of the Port Natal colony, made their camp in 1824.

FREE **Durban Art Gallery**   GALLERY
(Map p402; Anton Lembede St (Smith St), City Hall; ⊙8.30am-4pm Mon-Sat, 11am-4pm Sun) Houses an excellent collection of contemporary South African works, especially Zulu arts and crafts, and has temporary and rotating exhibitions.

FREE **Natural Science Museum**   MUSEUM
(Map p402; Anton Lembede St (Smith St), City Hall; ⊙8.30am-4pm Mon-Sat, 11am-4pm Sun) This museum boasts an impressive, if pleasantly retro' display of stuffed birds and insects, plus African animals. Check out the reconstructed dodo and the life-sized dinosaur model.

FREE **KwaMuhle Museum**   MUSEUM
(Map p402; 130 Bram Fischer Rd (Ordnance Rd); ⊙8.30am-4pm Mon-Sat) Based in the former Bantu Administration headquarters, this excellent museum has powerful displays on the 'Durban System', the blueprint of apartheid policy.

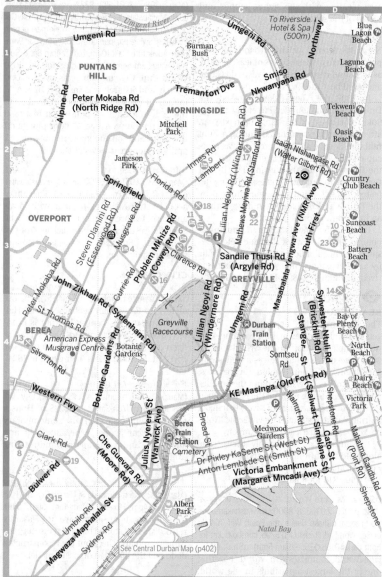

See Central Durban Map (p402)

FREE Old Courthouse Museum   MUSEUM
(Map p402; 77 Samora Machel St (Aliwal St);
⊙8.30am-4pm Mon-Fri, 8.30am-12.30pm Sat)
Found in the beautiful 1866 courthouse behind City Hall, this museum displays colonial items and corresponding Zulu objects.

MARGARET MNCADI AVE (VICTORIA EMBANKMENT)

Sugar Terminal   FACTORY
(Map p402; 51 Maydon Rd; adult/concession
R16/8; ⊙tours 8.30am, 10am, 11.30am & 2pm
Mon-Thu) Maydon Wharf, which runs along

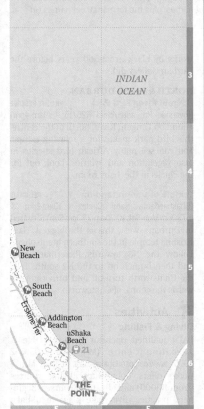

the southwestern side of the harbour and south of Margaret Mncadi Ave, is home to the Sugar Terminal, which offers an insight into the sugar trade. Three silos are still operating.

Wilson's Wharf   WATERFRONT
(Map p402; www.wilsonswharf.co.za) This is the best place to get a view of Durban's harbour – the busiest in Southern Africa (and ninth busiest in the world). The wharf has a clutch of eateries, boat-charter outfits, shops and a theatre.

Port Natal Maritime Museum   MUSEUM
(Map p402; Maritime Dr; adult/child R5/3; ⊙8.30am-3.30pm Mon-Sat, 11am-3.30pm Sun) On a service road running parallel to Margaret Mncadi Ave you can explore two former steam tugs and see the huge wicker basket once used for hoisting passengers onto ocean liners.

INDIAN AREA

Juma Mosque & Madrassa Arcade   MOSQUE
(Map p402; cnr Denis Hurley St (Queen St) & Dr Yusuf Dadoo (Grey St); ⊙9am-4pm Mon-Fri, to 11am Sat) The largest mosque in the southern

A PLACE BY ANY OTHER NAME...

Natal's original moniker came from Portuguese explorer Vasco da Gama, who sighted the coastline on Christmas Day 1497 and named it for the natal day of Jesus. Following the 1994 elections, Natal Province was renamed KwaZulu-Natal, in recognition of the fact that KwaZulu, the Zulu homeland, comprises a large part of the province.

Name changes have since been a recurring theme, particularly in Durban. Many of the city's streets were granted new monikers in 2007 and 2008 to reflect a 'new South Africa'. Debate continues to rage over the changes, with many locals annoyed about the huge cost involved in altering street signs, the identities of some of the names and, of course, the wider repercussions regarding familiarity and orientation.

Some of the changes were later declared illegal and – at the time of research – efforts were being made to have several changed back to their original names. Most locals (including businesses) often refer to the original street names. Many streets are now labelled twice, with a red line scored through the old name. For the purpose of this edition, we have provided the new street names, plus the former street names (in brackets).

hemisphere; call ahead for a guided tour. **Madrassa Arcade** is next to the mosque between Dr AB Xuma St (Commercial Rd) and Cathedral Rd, near the Catholic Emmanuel Cathedral.

Victoria St Market MARKET
(Map p402; ☎031-306 4021; www.victoriastreetmarket.co.za; Bertha Mkhize St (Victoria St); ◎6am-6pm Mon-Fri, 8am-2pm Sat & Sun) This is the hub of the Indian community. It offers a typically rip-roaring subcontinental shopping experience, with more than 160 stalls selling wares from across Asia. Watch your wallet and don't take valuables. Note: most shops run by Muslims close between noon and 2pm on Friday.

BEREA & AROUND

FREE **Durban Botanic Gardens** GARDENS
(Map p402; ☎031-309 1170; www.durbanbotanicgardens.org.za; John Zikhali Rd (Sydenham Rd); ◎7.30am-5.15pm 16 Apr–15 Sep, to 5.45pm 16 Sep–15 Apr) A 20-hectare garden featuring one of the rarest cycads, as well as many species of bromeliad. It's a lovely place to wander. The gardens play host to an annual concert series featuring the KwaZulu-Natal Philharmonic Orchestra.

Campbell Collections GALLERY
(Map p398; ☎031-207 3432; campbell.ukzn.ac.za; 220 Gladys Mazibuko Rd (Marriott Rd); admission R20; ◎by appointment only) Muckleneuk, a superb house designed by Sir Herbert Baker, holds the documents and artefacts collected by Dr Killie Campbell, who began collecting works by black artists 60 years before the Durban Gallery did.

NORTH & WEST DURBAN

Umgeni River Bird Park WILDLIFE RESERVE
(Riverside Rd; adult/child R25/15; ◎9am-4pm) Found on Umgeni River, north of the centre, this bird park makes for a relaxing escape. You can see many African bird species in lush vegetation and aviaries. Look out for the chicks in the 'baby room'.

Temple of Understanding RELIGIOUS
(Bhaktieedanta Sami Circle; ◎10am-1pm & 4-7.30pm Mon-Sat, 10.30am-7.30pm Sun) Situated in Durban's west, this is the biggest Hare Krishna temple in the southern hemisphere. Follow the N3 towards Pietermaritzburg and then branch off to the N2 south. Take the Chatsworth turn-off and turn right towards the centre of Chatsworth.

🏃 Activities

Diving & Fishing

PADI-qualified operator **Calypso Dive & Adventure Centre** (Map p402; ☎031-332 0905; www.calypsoushaka.co.za; uShaka Marine World) offers open-water diving courses (from R3000) and advanced courses. Beginners' practice dives take place in uShaka (p397)'s lagoon aquarium. Certified divers can also dive in uShaka's ocean aquarium (R450).

Casea Charters (☎031-561 7381; www.caseacharters.co.za; Grannies Pool, Main Beach, Umhlanga; 3/4hr trip R400/500) is a family-run fishing-charter business operating from

that the city centre shuts down (and is less safe) at night.

BEACHFRONT

Southern Sun Suncoast Hotel & Towers HOTEL $$$

(Map p398; ☑031-314 7878; www.southernsun. com; 20 Battery Beach Rd; r from R1550; [P][✳][☂][☒]) This hotel, adjacent to the casino, is a safe, if businesslike, bet. Some bathrooms are incorporated into the bedrooms themselves (read: little privacy among friends). Awesome vista from the top floor.

Protea Hotel Edward Durban BUSINESS HOTEL $$$

(Map p402; ☑031-337 3681; www.proteahotels. com/edwarddurban; 149 OR Tambo Pde (Marine Pde); s R865-1820, d R995-2060; [P][✳][@][☒]) King of the seafront hotels, this is classic and comfortable, with fresh-polish smells and full-on decor.

CITY CENTRE

Happy Hippo BACKPACKERS $

(Map p402; ☑031-368 7181; www.happy-hip po.info; 222 Mahatma Gandhi Rd (Point Rd); dm/d R150/470, dm/s/d without bathroom R140/330/370) Close to the beach, but in the dodgy part of town, is this spacious, well run, warehouse-style accommodation. Some travellers report it's noisy; rooms are off communal areas.

Durban Hilton International BUSINESS HOTEL $$$

(Map p402; ☑031-336 8100; www.hilton.com; 12 Walnut Rd; r incl breakfast from R1550; [P][✳][@][☂][☒]) Glitzy and chic, this modern behemoth offers a predictable hotel experience and attracts mainly business travellers. Ask about the specials.

BEREA & AROUND

Tekweni Backpackers BACKPACKERS $

(Map p398; ☑031-303 1433; www.tekwenibackpack ers.co.za; 169 Ninth Ave, Morningside; dm R125,

---

Umhlanga. Rods, tackle and bait are supplied, and you can keep your catch at no additional fee.

Surfing

For surfers, Durban has a multitude of good surfing beaches. **Ocean Adventures** (Map p402; ☑086 100 1138; www.surfandadven tures.co.za; lessons R150, board hire per hr/day R100/200; ⊙7am-4.30pm) can be found on uShaka Beach.

Kitesurfing is also popular in Durban. **Kitesports** (☑082 572 4163; www.kitesports. co.za; Umhlanga Rocks) offer lessons (two hours, R495).

Boat Cruises

The luxury yacht **African Queen** (Map p402; ☑032-943 1118; Durban Yacht Harbour; ⊙departs 10am & 1pm) cruises dolphin waters for three hours. Several other boat and charter trips can be arranged from Wilson's Wharf.

Ocean Safaris (Map p402; ☑084 565 5328; www.airandoceansafaris.co.za) is run by a marine scientist and offers one-/two-hour ocean tours (R250/400 per person) in an open, semirigid inflatable superduck. Trips depart from uShaka Marine World.

🛏 Sleeping

Despite the hotel-lined beachfront promenade, much of Durban's accommodation is in the western and northwestern suburbs. Unless you have come for the sun and sand alone, accommodation in the suburbs is better value than the beachfront options. Note

---

Central Durban

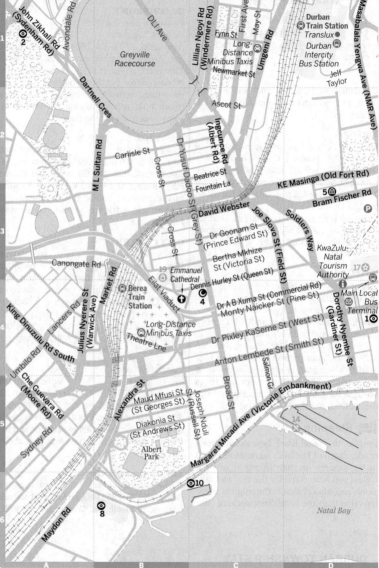

s/d/tr without bathroom from R350/400/480; P🐾🛜⊠) This old dog 'keeps on keeping on'; it's a slightly saggy place that nevertheless attracts the party animals who like raucous, gregarious surrounds.

TOP
CHOICE **Gibela Travellers Lodge**

BACKPACKERS **$$**

(Map p398; ☎031-303 6291; www.gibelabackpack ers.co.za; 119 Ninth Ave, Morningside; dm/s/d without bathroom incl breakfast R220/430/580; P@🛜⊠) If this hostel were a B&B, it

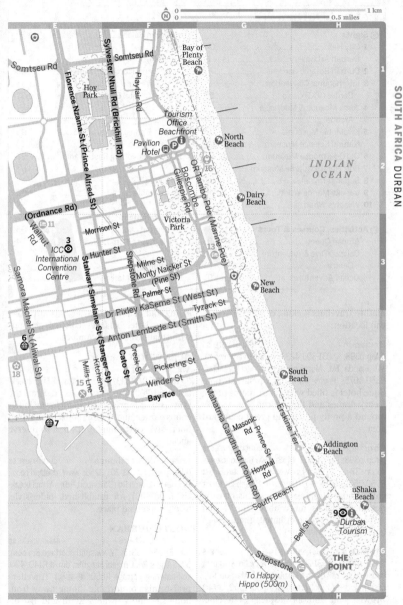

would be described as boutique. Rooms are neat enough to pass an army major's inspection. It even provides a continental breakfast. Helpful owner Elmar is the man-in-the-know about all things Durban and beyond.

Rosetta House B&B **$$**
(Map p398; ☑031-303 6180; www.rosettahouse.com; 126 Rosetta Rd, Morningside; s/d incl breakfast R675/950; P❋☎) This elegant place has a country-chic feel and is perfect for

Central Durban

Sights
1 City Hall ... D4
Durban Art Gallery ... (see 1)
2 Durban Botanic Gardens ... A1
3 International Convention Centre (ICC) ... E3
4 Juma Mosque & Madrassa Arcade ... C4
5 KwaMuhle Museum ... D3
Natural Science Museum ... (see 1)
6 Old Courthouse Museum ... E4
7 Port Natal Maritime Museum ... E5
8 Sugar Terminal ... B6
9 uShaka Marine World ... H6
10 Wilson's Wharf ... C6

Activities, Courses & Tours
African Queen ... (see 10)
Calypso Dive & Adventure Centre ... (see 9)
Ocean Adventures ... (see 9)
Ocean Safaris ... (see 9)

Sleeping
11 Durban Hilton International ... E3
12 Happy Hippo ... H6
13 Protea Hotel Edward Durban ... G3

Eating
14 Cafe Fish ... D5
Cargo Hold ... (see 9)
15 Roma Revolving Restaurant ... E4

Drinking
16 Joe Kool's ... G2

Entertainment
17 Computicket ... D3
18 Playhouse Company ... E4

Shopping
19 Victoria St Market ... B3

mature travellers seeking comfort in a central location.

Benjamin BOUTIQUE HOTEL **$$**
(Map p398; ☎031-303 4233; www.benjamin.co.za; 141 Florida Rd, Morningside; s/d incl breakfast R850/1075; P❄📶≋) This upmarket boutique hotel is filled with smart rooms of the 'heavy drapes and floral furnishing' variety around a pretty paved and green courtyard area.

Concierge BOUTIQUE HOTEL **$$$**
(Map p398; ☎031-309 4453; www.the-concierge.co.za; 37-43 St Mary's Ave; s/d incl breakfast R950/1500; P❄📶) One of Durbs' most cutting-edge sleeping options, this cleverly designed spot is more about the design (urban, funky, shape-oriented) than spaces (smallish, but adequate).

Brown's Bed & Breakfast B&B **$$$**
(Map p398; ☎031-208 7630; www.brownsguesthouse.co.za; 132 Gladys Mazibuko Rd (Marriott Rd), Essenwood; s/d incl breakfast R850/1500; P❄) Brown's chic interior attracts even chicer guests who enjoy the 'suites' – a choice of four spacious rooms, each with a small kitchen and smart living space.

Quarters BOUTIQUE HOTEL **$$$**
(Map p398; ☎031-303 5246; www.quarters.co.za; 101 Florida Rd; s/d incl breakfast from R1410/1992; P❄) Right in Durban's most fashionable eating and drinking quarter, this attractive boutique hotel balances colonial glamour with small-scale home comforts.

GLENWOOD

Mackaya Bella GUESTHOUSE **$$**
(☎031-205 8790; 137 Penzance Rd; s/d incl breakfast R660/900; P❄📶≋) Located near the university, this pretty spot has a lovely indigenous garden and stylish rooms in a relaxed home-style environment. It's best to reserve ahead.

Roseland Guesthouse GUESTHOUSE **$$**
(Map p398; ☎031-201 3256; www.roseland.co.za; 291 Helen Joseph Rd (Davenport Rd); s/d incl breakfast R700/900) An established, older-style, nicely appointed place.

NORTH DURBAN

Smith's Cottage BACKPACKERS **$$**
(☎031-564 6313; www.smithscottage.8m.com; 5 Mt Argus Rd, Umgeni Heights; dm/d R140/400, self-catering cottage R850; P📶≋) Travellers praise this comfortable 'home away from home'. Friendly owners Keith and Pat offer accommodation in all shapes and sizes with a laid-back atmosphere. It's within chirping distance of the Umgeni River Bird Park.

Riverside Hotel & Spa HOTEL **$$$**
(off Map p398; ☎031-563 0600; www.riversidehotel.co.za; 10 Northway, Durban North; s/d from

R1250/1640; P🛜🏊) Just over Umgeni River on the right-hand side, the rooms here offer all the comforts of an upmarket place.

🍴 Eating

Look out for the local Indian speciality, bunny chow (a half, quarter or full loaf of bread hollowed out and filled with curry). You'll find it in takeaways and hole-in-the-wall eateries throughout the city, particularly around the Victoria St Market.

BEACHFRONT

On the beachfront, you'll be hard pressed to find much more than eateries serving the usual spread of burgers, pizza and candy floss. You are better off heading to uShaka or the casino, both of which have some reasonable choices.

Cargo Hold SEAFOOD $$
(Map p402; ☑031-328 8065; uShaka Marina, the Point; mains R75-150; ☺lunch & dinner) A seafood encounter of the most novel kind; one wall of this restaurant is a giant window looking straight into uShaka's shark aquarium. Well known for serving some high-quality fish dishes with international flavours.

Cafe Jiran CAFE $$
(Map p398; ☑031-332 4485; 151 Snell Pde; mains R60-150; ☺6.30am-10pm) This funky space is the spot for a post-dip breakfast. Evening fine-dining options available from Tuesday to Saturday.

CITY CENTRE

Around Dr Yusuf Dadoo (Grey St) you'll find Indian takeaways (ask around). Otherwise, there are limited eating options in the centre.

Roma Revolving Restaurant INTERNATIONAL $$
(Map p402; ☑031-337 6707; www.roma.co.za; 32nd fl, John Ross House, Margaret Mncadi Ave (Victoria Embankment); mains R70-150; ☺lunch & dinner; ✺) One of the few central restaurants surviving in Durban, it offers stunning views over the city and generous helpings of largely Italian cuisine.

Cafe Fish SEAFOOD $$
(Map p402; ☑031-305 5062; www.cafefish.co.za; 31 Yacht Mole, Margaret Mncadi Ave (Victoria Embankment); mains R45-150; ☺lunch & dinner) This distinctive green-and-blue construction has seafood dishes that are as appealing as the

views. The best catch is the good-value set menu (four courses, R160 to R240).

BEREA & AROUND

Florida Rd and nearby Lilian Ngoyi (Windermere Rd) are the best places to forage for a meal. There is a wonderful cafe hub opposite Mitchell Park on Innes Rd.

The nondescript Avonmore Centre hides some other recommended eateries, including the friendly, highly regarded **9th Avenue Bistro** (Map p398; ☑031-312 9134; Ninth Ave, Avonmore Centre, Morningside; mains R120-140; ☺lunch & dinner Tue-Fri, dinner Mon & Sat) and unpretentious **Joop's Place** (Map p398; ☑031-312 9135; Ninth Ave, Avonmore Centre, Morningside; mains R80-165; ☺dinner Mon-Thu & Sat, lunch & dinner Fri), popular for its high-quality steaks.

TOP CHOICE Spice FUSION $$
(Map p398; ☑031-303 6375; 362 Lilian Ngoyi Rd (Windermere Rd), Morningside; mains R130-150; ☺lunch & dinner Tue-Sat, lunch Sun) Those in the cuisine scene rave about this place. Whether it's because the likes of Bill Gates and Bill Clinton have dined here or because the imaginative menu – South African and Indian fusion dishes – is so good, we'll leave for you to decide.

TOP CHOICE Market INTERNATIONAL $$
(Map p398; ☑031-309 8581; www.marketrestaurant.co.za; 40 Gladys Mazibuko Rd (Marriott Rd); mains R60-140; ☺breakfast & lunch Mon, breakfast, lunch & dinner Tue-Sat) All meals here – breakfasts, casual lunches and more formal dinners – are delectable. Imaginative dishes include the likes of calamari with quinoa and macadamia; produce is locally sourced, free range and organic, where possible.

Spiga D'oro ITALIAN $$
(Map p398; ☑031-303 9511; 200 Florida Rd; mains R45-80; ☺breakfast, lunch & dinner) Locals mention this in the 'of-course-you-already-know-about-Spiga-D'oro' tone. It looks like another typical cafe along this strip, yet serves up hearty helpings of Italian food, including good pasta dishes.

Cafe 1999 INTERNATIONAL $$
(Map p398; ☑031-202 3406; www.cafe1999.co.za; Silverton Rd, Silvervause Centre, Berea; mains R65-140; ☺lunch & dinner Sun-Fri, dinner Sat) This buzzing restaurant serves modern Mediterranean fusion food that comes in

'bitparts' – 'titbit' and 'bigbit'. Reservations are recommended in the evenings. The owners also run **Unity Brasserie & Bar** (www.unitybar.co.za; mains R55-115; ☺noon-late Mon-Sat) next door – think craft beers and gastro-pub fare.

GLENWOOD

Corner Cafe   CAFE $$
(Map p398; 197 Brand Rd; mains R30-70; ☺6am-5pm Mon-Fri, 8am-3pm Sat) This warehouse-style cafe is one of Durbs' best. It serves up home-baked pies and breads, great cakes, coffee and fresh juices.

🍷 Drinking

The best options are found in the suburbs. The casino also has some good spots. Night-clubs seem to set up and close down to their own very fast beat; it's best to ask around for the latest offerings.

Moyo uShaka Pier Bar   BAR
(Map p398; www.moyo.co.za; uShaka Marine World, the Point; drinks R45-55; ☺11am-late) Perched out on the edge of a pier in front of uShaka Marine World, this is Durban's top spot for a South African sundowner (a tipple at sunset) with fabulous views on every side.

Bean Green   CAFE
(Map p398; 147 Helen Joseph Rd (Davenport Rd); ☺8am-5pm Mon-Thu, 9am-1pm Sat; 🔊) Coffee snobs and wi-fi geeks: this is for you. This barely-larger-than-a-hole-in-the wall, award-winning roaster serves single-origin beans.

☆ Entertainment

Durban is a lively city with a vibrant cultural scene. Hundreds of events, from the Natal Sharks games and cricket matches to film festivals and theatre performances, can be booked through **Computicket** (Map p402; ☑083 915 8000; www.computicket.co.za).

Clubs

Billy the Bum's   CLUB
(Map p398; www.billythebums.co.za; 504 Lilian Ngoyi Rd (Windermere Rd), Morningside) Attracting a crowd of Durban's upwardly mobile (a sign even says 'elegantly wasted'), this suburban cocktail bar is reliably raucous.

Sasha's   CLUB
(Map p398; 17 Harvey Rd; ☺Fri) Beautifully decorated, this relaxed place has seven bars and several dance floors and is currently one of the 'it' places. Mainstream music.

Joe Kool's   CLUB
(Map p402; Lower OR Tambo Pde (Marine Pde, North Beach)) The inevitable finish line for any day on the beach, this venerable nightspot cooks up a cocktail of cold beer, big-screen TV, dance music and feisty crowds.

Live Music

KwaZulu-Natal
Philharmonic Orchestra   CLASSICAL MUSIC
(☑031-369 9438; www.kznpo.co.za) The orchestra has an interesting spring concert program with weekly performances in the City Hall. It also performs in the 'Botanic Gardens Music at the Lake' concert series.

Rainbow Restaurant & Jazz Club   JAZZ
(☑031-702 9161; www.therainbow.co.za; 23 Stanfield Lane, Pinetown) In Pinetown, 15km west of the centre, this was the first place in Natal to cater to blacks in a so-called 'white area' in the 1980s. It is renowned for its live jazz acts.

Theatre

Playhouse Company   THEATRE
(Map p402; ☑031-369 9555; www.playhousecompany.com; Anton Lembede St (Smith St)) Opposite City Hall, Durban's central theatre was recently renovated and is a stunning venue hosting dance, drama and music performances.

Barnyard Theatre   THEATRE
(☑031-566 3045; www.barnyardtheatre.co.za; Gateway Mall, Umhlanga Ridge) This popular place houses mainstream theatre productions. Audience members can take their own food (and buy drinks at the bar) or buy food at the takeaway outlets.

ⓘ Information

Emergency

Ambulance (☑10177)
General Emergency (☑031-361 0000)
Main Police Office ☑10111; Stalwart Simelane St (Stanger St)) North of the city centre.
Police OR Tambo Pde (Marine Pde)) Near Funworld on the beach.

Internet Access

Wi-fi access is available at Europa Cafes (Florida Rd, Morningside and Broadway, Durban North). Another option:
Cityzen (161 Gordon Rd, Morningside; per hr R20; ☺8am-midnight)

Medical Services

St Augustines (☏031-268 5000; 107 Chelmsford Rd, Berea) Good emergency department.

Umhlanga Hospital (☏031-560 5500; 323 Umhlanga Rocks Dr, Umhlanga) Handy for the North Coast and north Durban.

Money

There are banks with ATMs and change facilities across the city, including Standard Bank, FNB, Nedbank and ABSA.

American Express Musgrave Centre (☏031-202 8733; 151 Musgrave Rd, FNB House, Musgrave)

Post

Main Post Office (cnr Dr Pixley KaSeme St (West St) & Dorothy Nyembe St (Gardiner St); ⊙8am-5pm Mon-Fri, to 1pm Sat)

Safe Travel

As with elsewhere in South Africa, crime against tourists and locals can and does occur in Durban. You should be aware and careful, but not paranoid.

Muggings and pickpocketing, once a problem around the beach esplanade, have declined since that area's upgrade, but be careful here at night. Mahatma Gandhi Rd (Point Rd), south of Anton Lembede St (Smith St), should be avoided especially at night (take taxis to and from uShaka Marina). Extra care should also be taken around the Umgeni Rd side of the train station and the Warwick Triangle markets.

At night, with the exception of the casino and around the Playhouse theatre (if something is on), central Durban becomes a ghost town as people head to the suburbs for entertainment. Always catch a taxi to/from nightspots (and with others, if possible).

Tourist Information

You can pick up a free copy of the *Events Calendar* or the half-yearly *Destination Durban*.

Durban Tourism (www.durbanexperience. co.za) A useful information service on Durban and surrounds, with offices at uShaka Marine World (p407), **Morningside** (☏031-322 4164; 90 Florida Rd; ⊙8am-4.30pm Mon-Fri) and **Beachfront** (☏031-322 4205; Old Pavilion Site, OR Tambo Pde (Marine Pde); ⊙8am-5pm). It can help with general accommodation and arranges tours of Durban and beyond.

KwaZulu-Natal Tourism Authority (KZN Tourism; ☏031-366 7500; www.zulu.org.za; ground fl, Tourist Junction) Information office dealing with the whole province and offering a smorgasbord of reference and promotional brochures.

ⓘ Getting There & Away

Air

King Shaka International Airport (p507) is 40km north of the city.

South African Airways (SAA; www.flysaa. com) flies at least once daily to Jo'burg, Port Elizabeth, East London, Cape Town, George and Nelspruit. **Kulula** (www.kulula.com) flies to Jo'burg (one way from R700), Cape Town (from R860) and Port Elizabeth (from R1080). **Mango** (www.flymango.com) has one-way fares to Jo'burg/Cape Town from R800/1040.

Bus

The **Baz Bus** (www.bazbus.com) picks up and drops off at the city's many hostels.

Long-distance buses leave from the bus stations near Durban train station on Masabalala Yengwa Ave (NMR Ave). Enter the station from Masabalala Yengwa Ave (NMR Ave), not Umgeni Rd. **Greyhound** (☏083 915 9000; www.grey hound.co.za), **Intercape** (☏0861 287 287; www.intercape.co.za) and **Translux** (☏0861 589 282; www.translux.co.za) have their offices here.

Sample one-way fares:

» Cape Town (R590, 22 to 26 hours)

» Jo'burg (R230, seven hours)

» Pietermaritzburg (R185, two hours)

» Port Elizabeth (R435, 14 hours)

» Port Shepstone (R125, 1½ hours)

Tickets for all long-distance buses can be bought from Shoprite/Checkers shops and online from **Computicket** (www.computicket. com).

Margate Mini Coach (☏039-312 1406; www.margate.co.za/minicoach.htm) connects Durban with the South Coast (one-way fares to Margate/Port Shepstone R120). It operates from the Greyhound office.

A new service runs between Durban and Maputo, Mozambique, departing from the **Pavilion Hotel** (☏072 278 1 921, 073 427 8220; 15 K E Masinga Rd (Old Fort Rd)) at 6.30am on Wednesday and Sunday. (It departs Maputo for Durban every Tuesday and Saturday.) Tickets (R280) can be purchased on the day at the bus; arrive by 6am.

Car

Most major car-hire companies have offices at the airport, including the following:

Aroundabout Cars (☏086 0422 4022; www. aroundaboutcars.com)

Avis (☏0861 021 111, 032-436 7800; www. avis.co.za)

Budget (☏032-436 5500; www.budget.co.za)

Minibus Taxi

Some long-distance minibus taxis leave from stops in the streets opposite the Umgeni Rd entrance to Durban train station. Others running mainly to the South Coast and the Wild Coast region of Eastern Cape leave from around Berea train station. Check with your taxi driver; they usually know the departure points. Be alert in and around the minibus taxi ranks.

Train

Durban train station (Masabalala Yengwa Ave (NMR Ave)) is huge. The local inner-city or suburban trains are not recommended; even hardy travellers report feeling unsafe. However, mainline passenger long-distance services are efficient and arranged into separate male and female sleeper compartments. These are run by **Shosholoza Meyl** (☑031-361 7167; www. shosholozameyl.co.za) and include the Trans Natal, which leaves Durban daily except Saturday for Jo'burg (R290, 12½ hours) via Pietermaritzburg and Ladysmith.

The fully serviced luxury **Premier Classe** (☑031-361 7167; www.premierclasse.co.za) has Jo'burg to Durban departures on the last Friday of the month, returning Durban to Jo'burg the following Sunday. Tickets should be booked in advance (R990, 14 hours).

The **Rovos** (☑012-315 8242; www.rovosrail. co.za) is a luxury steam train on which, from a mere R13,000, you can enjoy old-world luxury on a three-day choof from Durban to Pretoria via the Battlefields and nature reserves.

ⓘ Getting Around

To & From the Airport

Some hostels run their own taxi shuttle services for clients at competitive prices. By taxi, the same trip should cost about R400. The King Shaka Airport Shuttle Bus runs hourly to hotels and key locations in Durban and the beachfront via Umhlanga Rocks. Costs start from R50 to Umhlanga to R80 and above for Durban suburbs.

Bus

The useful **Durban People Mover** (☑031-309 5942) operates along several routes within the city. Tickets (R15) can be purchased on the bus and allow you to get on and off the route as many times as you like within a day. Single-leg tickets cost R4. The service runs daily between 6.30am and 11pm.

Durban Transport (☑031-309 5942) runs the bus services Mynah and Aqualine. Mynah covers most of the city and local residential areas. Trips cost around R5 and there's a slight discount if you prepurchase 10 tickets. The larger Aqualine buses run through the outer-lying Durban metropolitan area.

Taxi

A taxi between the beach and Florida Rd, Morningside, costs about R50. **Mozzie Cabs** (☑0860 669 943) runs a reliable 24-hour service.

South of Durban

The South Coast is a 160km-long string of seaside resorts and suburbs running from Amanzimtoti to Port Edward, near the Eastern Cape border. There's a bit of a *Groundhog Day* feel about this mass of shoulder-to-shoulder getaways along the N2 and Rte 102, albeit a pleasant one. The region is a surfers' and divers' delight and the stunning Oribi Gorge Nature Reserve, inland from Port Shepstone, provides beautiful forest walks.

The first stop for information is **Amanzimtoti Tourism** (☑031-903 7498; 95 Beach Rd; ⊗8am-4pm Mon-Fri, 9am-2pm Sat) – look out for the useful brochure *Southern Explorer* (www.southernexplorer.co.za).

Warner Beach is less built-up and more relaxed than Amanzimtoti. Umkomaas and

---

SOUTH COAST DIVING

The highlight of this strip is the **Aliwal Shoal** – touted as one of the world's 10 best dive sites. The shoal's ledges, caves and pinnacles are home to wrecks, rays, turtles, 'raggies' (ragged-tooth sharks), tropical fish and soft corals.

Numerous operators along the South Coast offer day dives and four-day courses. Rates range from R2800 to R3500. Always speak to other travellers about their experiences, as safety standards vary.

Recommended operators include **2nd Breath** (☑039-317 2326; www.2ndbreath. co.za; cnr Bank St & Berea Rd, Margate), **Aliwal Dive Centre** (☑039-973 2233; www. aliwalshoal.co.za; 2 Moodie St, Umkomaas), **Shoal** (☑039-973 1777; www.theshoal.co.za; 21 Harvey St, Umkomaas) and **Oceanworx** (☑039-973 2578; www.oceanworx.co.za; 1 Maclean St, Umkomaas).

Scottburgh are good diving-off points for the Aliwal Shoal, while the bustling, industrial town of Port Shepstone is of little interest to tourists. You may prefer Ramsgate or Southbroom to nearby Margate, a claustrophobic holiday hub. The last main centre in the region is Port Edward, where the lush surrounds and some reasonable accommodation make a pleasant escape from the concrete jungle.

ORIBI GORGE NATURE RESERVE
🌐 039

This nature reserve (☎039-679 1644; www. kznwildlife.com; admission R10, campsites R65, 2-bed hut R320; ⊙6am-6pm summer, 7.30am-4.30pm winter) is inland from Port Shepstone, off the N2. The spectacular gorge, on the Umzimkulwana River, is one of the highlights of the South Coast with beautiful scenery, animals and birds. On the south side of the gorge are some delightful wooden chalets nestled in the forest.

Wild 5 Extreme Adventures (☎082 566 7424; www.wild5adventures.co.za) offers a 100m Wild Swing (free-fall jump and swing) off Lehr's Falls (R450), abseiling (R350), and white-water rafting (R495). It's 11km off the N2 along the Oribi Flats Rd.

Leopard Rock Lookout Chalets (☎039-687 0303; www.leopardrockc.co.za; Main Oribi Gorge Rd; s/d incl breakfast R750/1200; ⊙9am-4pm Wed-Sun) has accommodation in four pleasant chalets and a superb view of the uMzumkulu Gorge. Dinner (R40 to R80) is available on request.

RAMSGATE, SOUTHBROOM & AROUND
🌐 039 / POP 34,000

The tourist hub of Margate is a claustrophobic concrete jungle with a string of loud and lively bars. You're better off heading to Ramsgate, which has a nice little beach, or to the lush green confines of Southbroom, the posh neck of the woods, delightfully located within a bushbuck conservancy.

🛌 Sleeping & Eating

Southbroom

Backpackers Lodge   BACKPACKERS $
(☎039-316 8448; www.southbroomtravellerslodge.co.za; 11 Cliff Rd, Southbroom; dm/d R180/400; P🐾) A good-value place in this upmarket area, a beautiful neck of the (subtropical) woods that's a 10-minute walk from the beach. This comfortable, laid-back

place has light, airy rooms, a pool and a lovely garden.

Sunbirds   B&B $$
(☎039-316 8202; www.sunbirds.co.za; 643 Outlook Rd, Southbroom; s/d R750/1150; P🛜🐾) Welcoming hosts, wonderful breakfasts on the verandah (with good views), a smart, spacious lounge and homely ambience keep the guests coming here.

Trattoria La Terrazza   ITALIAN $$
(☎039-316 6162; www.trattoria.co.za; Southbroom; mains R75-115; ⊙lunch Fri-Sun, dinner Tue-Sat) Ask for a restaurant recommendation in the area and the answer is overwhelmingly this Italian option, serving meat, seafood and pasta. The setting, on an estuary, is gorgeous. Reservations recommended.

❶ Getting There & Away

The **Margate Mini Coach** (☎031-312 1406; www.margate.co.za) links Durban and Margate three times daily (one way R120). Book through **Hibiscus Coast Tourism** (☎039-312 2322; www.hibiscuscoast.kzn.org.za; Panorama Pde, Main Beach, Margate; ⊙8am-5pm Mon-Fri, to 1pm Sat, 9am-1pm Sun).

Intercity Express (☎031-305 9090; www.intercity.co.za) runs regular buses between Margate and Jo'burg (R330, 10 hours).

North of Durban

The stretch of coast from Umhlanga Rocks north to the Tugela River is a profusion of upmarket timeshare apartments and retirement villages with some pleasant beaches. The section from Zimbali, slightly north of Umhlanga, to the Tugela is known as the Dolphin Coast because of the bottlenose dolphins that favour the area.

Sangweni Tourism Centre (☎032-946 1997; www.thedolphincoast.co.za; cnr Ballito & Link Drs; ⊙7.45am-4.15pm Mon-Fri, 9am-1pm Sat), which lists accommodation in the area, is near the BP petrol station, where you leave the N2 to enter Ballito.

Metropolitan buses run between Durban and Umhlanga Rocks, and buses and minibus taxis also run between Durban and KwaDukuza (Stanger) and other inland towns.

UMHLANGA ROCKS
🌐 031

The buckle of Durban's chichi commuter belt, Umhlanga (the 'h' is pronounced something like a 'sh') is a cosmopolitan mix of upmarket beach resorts, moneyed suburbia and small malls.

◉ Sights & Activities

Natal Sharks Board ECOTOUR
(☎031-566 0400; www.shark.co.za; 1A Herrwood Dr, Umhlanga Rocks; audiovisual & dissection adult/child R35/20; ☺8am-4pm Mon-Fri) This research institute is dedicated to studying sharks, specifically in relation to their danger to humans. There are audiovisual presentations and shark dissections at 9am and 2pm Tuesday, Wednesday and Thursday. The public can accompany Sharks Board personnel on their boat trips from Durban (per person R250).

FREE **Umhlanga Lagoon Nature Reserve** NATURE RESERVE
(parking R5; ☺6am-9pm) Found on a river mouth just north of town, you'll see many bird species here. The trails lead through stunning dune forest, across the lagoon and onto the beach.

⌷ Sleeping & Eating

Umhlanga is crowded with holiday apartments and B&Bs, mostly close to the beach. Hotel prices are seasonal and vary enormously; expect fluctuations between seasons.

There are eating options galore and many pleasant pavement cafes, including the chic eatery Ile Maurice (☎031-561 7609; 9 McCausland Cres, Umhlanga Rocks; mains R90-270; ☺lunch & dinner Tue-Sun), for a special seaside splurge with a Gallic touch.

On the Beach Backpackers BACKPACKERS $$
(☎031-562 1591; www.durbanbackpackers.com; 17 The Promenade, Glenashley; dm/s/d R150/420/650; P⧆☎) Four kilometres south of Umhlanga is Glenashley, where you'll find this light and airy converted house-cum-

backpackers; it's the best budget beach option in this area.

Beverley Hills Sun Intercontinental HOTEL $$$
(☎031-561 2211; www.southernsun.com; Lighthouse Rd; s/d incl breakfast R3800/4000; P⧆☎☎) They didn't pull out all the stops on the exterior, but this top-notch classic is deliciously stylish on the inside.

Zululand

Evoking images of wild landscapes and tribal rhythms, this beautiful swath of KwaZulu-Natal offers fine coastline, mist-clad hills and traditional settlements. Dominated by the Zulu ethnic group, the region offers a fascinating historical and contemporary insight into one of the country's most enigmatic and best-known cultures. Intense poverty and all the social problems that come with it are still commonplace.

The region is most visited for the spectacular Hluhluwe-Imfolozi Park and its many traditional Zulu villages.

Zululand's transport hub is **Richard's Bay**, otherwise a nondescript industrial town. **Greyhound** (☎083-915 9000; www.greyhound.co.za) buses connect Richard's Bay with Durban (R215, 2½ hours) and Johannesburg (R310, 9½ hours) and from here you can catch minibus taxis to the surrounding towns. Renting a car is the best way to explore Zululand.

ESHOWE
☎035 / POP 14,700
Situated around a beautiful indigenous forest and surrounded by green rolling hills, Eshowe typifies idiosyncratic Zululand. The centre has a rural, rough-and-tumble atmos-

---

WORTH A TRIP

SHAKALAND

Created as a set for the telemovie *Shaka Zulu*, the slightly Disney-fied **Shakaland** (☎035-460 0912; www.shakaland.com; Nandi Experience R275; ☺display 11am & noon) beats up a touristy, but entertaining, blend of perma-grin performance and informative authenticity. The **Nandi Experience** (Nandi was Shaka's mother) is a display of Zulu culture and customs (including lunch); the **Zulu dance performance** is said to be the best in the country. You can also stay overnight in luxury beehive huts at the four-star **hotel** (Shaka Experience cultural programme & s/d with full board R1125/1688).

Shakaland is at Norman Hurst Farm, Nikwalini, 3km off Rte 66 and 14km north of Eshowe.

LEGENDARY KING SHAKA

Whether fact or mythology, the enigmatic and controversial King Shaka is frequently portrayed as either a vicious and bloodthirsty tyrant or a military genius.

By the 1820s Shaka had created one of the most powerful kingdoms in the subcontinent. Violence was one of his weapons, both against his enemy and his own warriors. (On the death of his mother it is said that he killed many Zulus, whom he believed weren't grieving enough.)

In 1828 Shaka's life came to an unpleasant end – he was murdered by his half-brothers Dingaan and Mhlangane (who was later toppled by Dingaan). Contemporary Zulus are incredibly proud of their 'warrior king'. Shaka Day is celebrated annually on 24 September at the Shaka Memorial Gardens in KwaDukuza. Thousands of Zulus wearing traditional dress and carrying shields, spears and dancing sticks descend upon the gardens.

---

phere, but the suburbs are leafy and quiet. It is well placed for exploring the wider region and there are decent attractions and accommodation options on offer.

◉ Sights & Activities

Fort Nongqayi Museum Village   MUSEUM
(Nongqayi Rd; adult/child R25/5; ⊙7.30am-4pm Mon-Fri, 9am-4pm Sat & Sun) Based around three-turreted Fort Nonqqayi, the entrance fee includes access to the Zululand Historical Museum, with artefacts and Victoriana and the excellent Vukani Museum with a Zulu basketry collection.

There is also a **butterfly house** (per person R35) with indigenous vegetation and hundreds of African butterfly species.

From the museum you can walk to Mpushini Falls (40 minutes return), but note that bilharzia (a type of parasitic infection) has been reported here in the past.

FREE **Dlinza Forest Reserve**   NATURE RESERVE
(⊙6am-6pm Sep-Apr, 8am-5pm May-Aug) When war approached, King Shaka is said to have hidden his wives in the thick swath of forest that now makes up the 200-hectare Dlinza Forest Reserve. There is prolific bird life – look out for crowned eagles – as well as a few walking trails. Within the reserve, 125m-long **Dlinza Forest Aerial Boardwalk** (adult/child R25/5) offers some great views of the canopy and bird life.

🛏 Sleeping

Eshowe Guesthouse   B&B $$
(☎035-474 2362; dlinza@telkomsa.net; 3 Oftebro St; s/d R450/600; P※◙) This place has a top setting, backing onto the bird-filled Dlinza Forest. Rooms are spotless, stylish,

airy and spacious. Follow the signs to the Dlinza Forest Reserve; the guesthouse is just beyond the entrance. Reservations recommended.

Dlinza Forest Accommodation   CABIN $$
(☎035-474 2377; dlinza@zulucom.net; 2 Oftebro St; s/d R400/500) These four self-catering log cabins are neat, modern, clean and spacious. Breakfast costs R50.

❶ Getting There & Away

Minibus taxis leave from the bus and taxi rank (downhill from KFC near the Osborne/Main Sts roundabout; go across the bridge and to the right) to Empangeni (R45, one hour), the best place to catch taxis deeper into Zululand, and Durban (R90, 1½ hours).

ULUNDI & AROUND
☑035 / POP 15,200

Formerly the hub of the powerful Zulu empire, Ulundi is an unattractive, merely functional place, but for Zulu fanatics, there are plenty of historic sites to explore in the immediate area.

Established as Cetshwayo's capital in 1873, **Ondini** (High Place; ☎035-870 2050; adult/child R20/10; ⊙8am-4pm Mon-Fri, 9am-4pm Sat & Sun) was razed by British troops after the Battle of Ulundi. The royal *kraal* (fortified village) section of the site has been rebuilt and you can see where archaeological digs have uncovered the floors of identifiable buildings.

The **KwaZulu Cultural-Historical Museum** (included in Ondini admission; ⊙8am-4pm Mon-Fri, 9am-4pm Sat & Sun), part of the site, has good exhibits on Zulu history and culture, including a superb collection of beadwork.

WORTH A TRIP

ITHALA GAME RESERVE

This **game reserve** (☎034-983 2540, 033-845 1000; www.kznwildlife.com; adult/child/vehicle R40/20/30; ⏰5am-7pm Nov-Feb, 6am-6pm Mar-Oct) is severely underrated. It has all the assets of a private wildlife reserve but at much lower prices and is less crowded than Hluhluwe-iMfolozi. Animals include black and white rhinos, elephants, tsessebis, buffaloes, giraffes and rare bird species. Guided walks (R170 per person) and wildlife drives (R190 per person) are available. Accommodation is in **bush camps** (☎033-845 1000; www.kznwildlife.com; campsites per person R120) and **cabins** (☎033-845 1000; www.kznwildlife.com; self-catering 2-bed chalet per person R735, 2-bed nonself-catering unit per person R675; ✱).

Ithala is reached from Louwsburg, about 55km northeast of Vryheid on R69, and about the same distance southwest of Phongolo via R66 and R69. Louwsburg is much smaller than many maps indicate.

Ulundi lies within the Valley of the Kings, the name of which is officially promoted as **Emakhosini Ophathe Heritage Park** (Valley of the Kings; admission free). The area is of great significance to the Zulu. The great *makhosi* (chiefs) Nkhosinkulu, Senzangakhona (father of Shaka, Dingaan and Mpande) and Dinizulu are buried here. A monument, the **Spirit of eMakhosini** (⏰8am-4pm Mon-Fri, 9am-4pm Sat & Sun), sits on a hill.

The minibus taxi rank is opposite the Southern Sun Garden Court, with services to destinations including Vryheid (R70, 1½ hours) and Eshowe (R65, 1½ hours).

The Elephant Coast

Up there with the world's great ecotourist destinations, the Elephant Coast is a must-see stretch of natural beauty, with a fabulously diverse mix of environments and wildlife. Incorporating the northern region known as Maputaland, it's bound in the south by the Imfolozi River just below the St Lucia Estuary, and to the northwest by the Lebombo Mountains.

HLUHLUWE-IMFOLOZI PARK
☑035

Hluhluwe-iMfolozi Park (☎035-550 8476; www.kznwildlife.com; adult/child R110/55; ⏰5am-7pm Nov-Feb, 6am-6pm Mar-Oct) is one of South Africa's best-known, most evocative parks. It covers 96,000 hectares (around one-20th the size of Kruger National Park) and there's plenty of wildlife, including lions, elephants, rhinos (black and white), leopards, giraffes, buffaloes and African wild dogs.

Hluhluwe-iMfolozi can be visited at any time of year; there's always something happening and plenty to see. In summer (wet season) it's beautifully lush and animals range widely. Winter (dry season) visits can also be very rewarding, especially in the open savannah country areas; animals often congregate at water sources.

⦿ Sights & Activities

The **Centenary Centre** (⏰8am-4pm), a wildlife-holding centre with an attached museum and information centre, is in the eastern section of iMfolozi. It incorporates rhino enclosures and antelope pens, and was established to allow visitors to view animals in transit to their new homes.

The **wildlife drives** (adult/child R300/150) are very popular. **Hilltop Camp** offers morning and evening drives, while **Mpila Camp** does evening drives only. The drives are open to guests of these camps.

One of iMfolozi's main attractions is its (seasonal) wilderness trail system, in a special 24,000-hectare wilderness area. The **Base Trail** (three nights/four days, R3592) is, as the name suggests, at a base camp.

The **Short Wilderness Trail** (two nights/three days, R2180) is at satellite camps, which have no amenities (bucket shower only) but are fully catered. Similar is the **Extended Wilderness Trail** (three nights/four days, R3200) but guests must carry their gear for 7km into camp. On the **Primitive Trail** (four nights/five days, R2220), you carry equipment, help prepare the food (provided) and sit up in 1½-hour watches during the night.

🛏 Sleeping & Eating

You must book accommodation in advance through **KZN Wildlife** (📞 033-845 1000; www. kznwildlife.com) in Pietermaritzburg. Last-minute bookings (those made 48 hours ahead) should be made directly with the camps. As well as Hilltop Camp (p413) and Mpila Camp (p413), there's a range of fabulous lodges, but minimum charges apply; they cater for six to eight guests.

Hilltop Camp   CABIN $$

(📞035-562 0848; 2-person rondavel/chalet R640/1280) The signature resort on the Hluhluwe side of Hluhluwe-iMfolozi Park, with stupendous views, a restaurant and a much-needed bar (it gets very hot here). The drawback is that it's the most popular destination for tour buses and is generally quite busy.

Mpila Camp   TENTED CAMP, CABIN $$

(2-bed safari camp d R750, d chalet R750) The main accommodation centre on the iMfolozi side of Hluhluwe-iMfolozi Park is a spectacular and peaceful camp perched on top of a hill. The safari tents are the most fun, but self-contained cabins (called 'chalets') are available, too. Note: there's an electric fence but wildlife (lions, hyena, wild dogs) can still wander through.

❶ Getting There & Away

The main entrance, Memorial Gate, is about 15km west of the N2, about 50km north of Mtubatuba. The second entrance, the Nyalazi Gate, is accessed by turning left off the N2 onto Rte 618 just after Mtubatuba towards Nongoma. The third, Cengeni Gate, on iMfolozi's western

---

DON'T MISS

HLUHLUWE RIVER LODGE

If you don't want to stay inside Hluhluwe-iMfolozi Park, or can't secure a booking, this lodge (📞035-562 0246; www.hluhluwe.co.za; s/d with half board R2250/3200) is a superb option. Set in its own piece of bush, each chalet is stylish, airy and spacious. The communal area features a stunning indoor-outdoor living room with terrace, and the lodge's chef serves up top-notch fare. The indigenous forest has a delightful 'duiker walk', and a range of other activities are on offer.

---

side, is accessible by road (tarred for 30km) from Ulundi.

ISIMANGALISO WETLAND PARK
📞035

This Unesco World Heritage Site stretches for 220 glorious kilometres, from the Mozambican border to Maphelana, at the southern end of Lake St Lucia. With the Indian Ocean on one side, and a series of lakes on the other (including Lake St Lucia), the 328,000-hectare park protects five distinct ecosystems, offering everything from off-shore reefs and beaches to lakes, wetlands, woodlands and coastal forests. The wildlife ranges from dolphins to zebras and the ocean beaches pull big crowds during the holiday season.

Lake St Lucia is Africa's largest estuary. Despite its past healthy water levels, it is currently at its lowest level for 55 years, due to a severe drought. The estuary mouth is currently closed; controversy surrounds a long-term solution to the management of the lake, with both animal and plant species being affected by changing ecological factors.

Unless otherwise specified, all Ezemvelo KZN Wildlife accommodation must be booked at **Ezemvelo KZN Wildlife** (📞in Durban 031-304 4934, in Pietermaritzburg 033-845 1000; www.kznwildlife.com) with 48 hours' notice. Less than 48 hours before, try your luck directly with the lodges and campsites.

ST LUCIA

Although not officially within the iSimangaliso Wetland Park, the pleasant village of St Lucia is a useful base to explore the park's southern sections. In high season, the village is a hotbed of activity as the population swells from 600 to the thousands. Hippos sometimes amble down the quieter streets (that's not cute, just dangerous).

🕱 Activities & Tours

As part of the iSimangaliso Wetland Park Authority's responsible tourism practices, every few years an ecotour operator must officially reapply for a permit to operate activity tours. Go to www.iSimangaliso.com for a list of current companies and organisations; tour operators listed may have changed by the time you read this.

The following is a selection of operators based in and around iSimangaliso Wetland Park.

BIRDWATCHING

Birdwatching is a delight in St Lucia and beyond. Recommended companies include Themba's Birding & Eco Tours (☎071 413 3243; www.zulubirding.com; St Lucia; per person from R200, minimum 2 people). Other guides can be found on the Zululand Birding Route (www.zbr.co.za) website.

BOAT TOURS & WHALE-WATCHING

In season, there's a high chance of spotting whales here, as well as dolphins and other sea creatures. Trips cost around R170 per person. Advantage Tours (☎035-590 1259; www.advantagetours.co.za) and Ocean Experience (☎035-590 1555; www.stlucia.co.za) run daily tours between June and September, weather permitting. You can also head upriver on boat tours to view hippos and crocodiles. Sodwana Bay also offers whale watching through Sodwana Bay Lodge.

KAYAK SAFARIS

St Lucia Kayak Safaris (☎035-590 1233; www.kayaksafaris.co.za; per person R290) runs tours in Greater St Lucia Wetland Park.

TURTLE-WATCHING

Fascinating night turtle tours operate from Cape Vidal. Euro Zulu Safaris (☎035-590 1635; www.eurozulu.com; per person incl dinner & drinks R850) is highly recommended.

WILDLIFE WATCHING

There are a number of operators offering excellent day and night trips on the Eastern and Western Shores. Operators are listed on www.iSimangaliso.com; Shakabarker Tours (☎035-590 1162; www.shakabarker.co.za; 43 Hornbill St) comes highly recommended.

🛏 Sleeping & Eating

Sugarloaf Campsite   CAMPGROUND $
(☎033-845 1000; www.kznwildlife.com; Pelican St; campsites per person R85) This pretty campground on the estuary is within snorting distance of hippos, monkeys and crocodiles.

Hornbill House   B&B $$
(☎035-590 1162; www.hornbillhouse.com; 43 Hornbill St; s/d incl breakfast R550/900; ✳@✳) Homey B&B comforts and a small pool make this a very pleasant place. Knowledgeable owner Kian runs a tour company offering a range of ecofriendly trips.

Sunset Lodge   CABIN $$
(☎035-590 1197; www.sunsetstlucia.co.za; 54 McKenzie St; d R695-950; P✳🛜) These well-maintained, self-catering log cabins afford a lovely view overlooking the estuary – you

can watch the hippos, mongooses and monkeys wander onto the lawn.

St Lucia Deep Sea Angling Club   INTERNATIONAL $$
(Ski Club; mains R40-90; ⏰lunch & dinner) This friendly, casual spot, popular with locals, whips up hearty servings of pasta, meat and fish. And it's not often that you can watch hippos and birds from an outdoor bench table.

🛈 Getting There & Away

Minibus taxis connect Durban and Mtubatuba (R110); the latter is 25km from St Lucia, and it's from where you must catch a connecting minibus taxi to St Lucia. Alternatively, buses run between St Lucia, Richards Bay and Mtubatuba; you must change at each point. If you're not doing tours out of St Lucia Estuary, the only way of getting around is to have your own wheels.

EASTERN SHORES

One of the most accessible areas from St Lucia, the Eastern Shores (☎035-590 1631; www.isimangaliso.com; adult/child/vehicle R30/20/40; ⏰5am-7pm Nov-Mar, 6am-6pm Apr-Oct) have a range of scenic routes, taking in the area's various ecosystems, including grassland, *vlei* (marshland), pans and coastal dune forest. About 14km north of the entrance is Mission Rocks, a rugged and rock-covered shoreline where, at low tide, you can view a fabulous array of sea life in the rock pools (you cannot swim here). About 4km before Mission Rocks, the Mission Rocks lookout (signed) provides a wonderful view of Lake St Lucia and the Indian Ocean.

About 20km north of Mission Rocks (30km from St Lucia), taking in the land between Lake Bhangazi and the ocean, is Cape Vidal. Some of the forested sand dunes are 150m high and the beaches are excellent for swimming. There is accommodation at the pretty Cape Vidal Camp (☎033-845 1000; www.kznwildlife.com; campsites R400, 5-bed log cabin minimum R930), near the shores of Lake Bhangazi.

WESTERN SHORES & FALSE BAY

The region northwest of St Lucia Estuary is called the Western Shores, and comprises two stunning lakeside spots known as Fani's Island (at the time of research this was closed to visitors due to the drought) and Charters Creek (entrance is off the N2, 18km north of Mtubatuba and 32km south of Hluhluwe), an area of dense coastal forest and grasslands. A newly constructed road provides direct access between St Lucia and

Charter's Creek, and will offer excellent leisurely wildlife-drive opportunities up the western side of Lake St Lucia (check status on arrival; it had yet to open at the time of research).

To access the Western Shores from the town of St Lucia, leave town on the road to Mtubatuba, and after 2km turn right at the Dukuduku Gate.

UMKHUZE GAME RESERVE & AROUND

A possible trip highlight is the uMkhuze Game Reserve (☑573 9001, 031-845 1000; www.kznwildlife.com; adult/child/vehicle R30/20/40; ⏰5am-7pm Nov-Mar, 6am-6pm Apr-Oct), covering 36,000 spectacular hectares of dense scrub and open acacia plains. It may lack lions, but just about every other sought-after animal is represented, as well as 400-plus bird species. Better still, the reserve has hides at waterholes, which offer some of the best wildlife viewing in the country. Evening wildlife drives (R200) are available and there's a wonderful escorted walk across multilevel walkways (per person R180). The reserve is 15km from Mkuze town.

Ezemvelo KZN Wildlife runs a fabulous bush lodge at Nhlonhlela (8-bed lodge R2280) and various accommodation options at Mantuma (2-bed safari camp R680, d chalets R945).

SODWANA BAY

☑035

Spectacular Sodwana Bay (adult/child R25/20; ⏰24hr) is bordered by lush forest on one side and glittering sands on another. Popular activities include guided walking and birding trails, especially along the 5km Mgobozeleni Trail, which features coastal forest and grassland. Serious deep-sea fishing also occurs here, but it's best known for its scuba diving. The diversity of underwater seascapes and marine flora and fauna makes it one of South Africa's diving capitals.

Avoid visiting during the summer holidays, when thousands throng here to take the plunge – literally. At all other times it's a peaceful place.

There is an ATM in the general store (⏰8.30am-4.30pm Mon-Fri, to 11.30am Sat) at the park entrance; otherwise you'll need to head to Mbazwana, 14km west.

🛏 Sleeping

Ezemvelo KZN Wildlife   CAMPGROUND **$$**
(☑033-845 1000; www.kznwildlife.com; campsites from R400, 4-bed cabin R1155) Has hundreds of well-organised campsites and cabins set within the park's coastal forest. Minimum charges apply.

Sodwana Bay Lodge   LODGE **$$**
(☑035-571 6015; www.sodwanabaylodge.co.za; s/d with half board R860/1560) This resort has neat boardwalks, banana palms and pine-filled, slightly dated rooms. It's on the main road on the approach to the park. Sodwana Bay Lodge Scuba Centre (☑035-571 0117; www.sodwanadiving.co.za) is on the premises; dive and accommodation packages are available.

Coral Divers   LODGE **$$**
(☑033-345 6531; www.coraldivers.co.za; Sodwana Bay; d tent R380, d cabin with/without bathroom from R770/640; @🐾) Inside the Sodwana Bay park proper, this factory-style operation continues to 'net the shoals' with its diving packages and other activities. There's something for all budgets, from tents to upmarket cabins with their own patch of lawn.

❶ Getting There & Away

Turn off the N2 at Hluhluwe village heading to Mbazwana, and continue about 20km to the park. Minibus taxis ply this route.

COASTAL FOREST & LAKE SIBAYA

Remote grassland plains, lush forests and pristine beaches are the main features of the Ezemvelo KZN Wildlife–administered Coastal Forest, a magical area accessible by 4WD (along the coastal sandy track between Kosi Bay and Sodwana Bay or from KwaNgwanase). Highlights include Black Rock, a rugged rocky peninsula reached by climbing over sand dunes, and Lala Nek, a beautiful and seemingly never-ending stretch of sand.

Further south sits Lake Sibaya, South Africa's largest freshwater lake, with hippos, crocs and more than 280 bird species. Canoeing trips can arranged through the luxurious beachside Thonga Beach Lodge (☑035-474 1473; www.isibindiafrica.co.za; d with full board R5980-6880; ❄🐾) which transfers guests from the main road.

KOSI BAY

The jewel of iSimangaliso Wetland Park, Kosi Bay (☑035-845 1000; adult/child/vehicle R25/15/20; ⏰6am-6pm Apr-Oct, 5am-7pm Nov-Mar) features a string of four lakes starting from an estuary lined with some of South Africa's most untouched beaches. Within the estuary mouth, there's excellent snorkelling. There are hippos, Zambezi sharks and some crocs in the lake system, and the rare palmnut vulture is one of 250-plus species that have been identified here.

There are two entrances to the reserve: Kosi Bay Camp (7km north of KwaNgwanase, the nearest service centre) and Kosi Bay Mouth (adult/child/vehicle R20/10/15), 19km north of KwaNgwanase. You'll need a 4WD and permit to visit Kosi Bay Mouth – these must be arranged one day in advance by calling ☑035-592 0236, or through your lodgings.

🛏 Sleeping & Eating

Most lodge accommodation is dispersed around the region's sandy dunes several kilometres from KwaNgwanase. In many cases 4WDs are needed to negotiate the sandy tracks.

Utshwayelo Campsite　CAMPGROUND, CHALET **$$**
(☑074 587 1574; www.kosimouth.co.za; campsites R350, chalets R740) This lovely community-run camp offers basic but neat bamboo-lined chalets with a communal kitchen. It's right by the entrance to the park at the Kosi Bay Mouth access road. Issues car-entry permits to Kosi Bay Mouth.

Ezemvelo KZN Wildlife　CAMPGROUND, CABIN **$$**
(☑033-845 1000; www.kznwildlife.com; campsites R385, 2-/5-/6-bed cabin R500/1320/1320) Offers camping and fully equipped, pleasant cabin accommodation within lush forest surrounds on the western shore of Lake Nhlange.

Maputaland Lodge　CHALET **$$**
(☑035-592 0654; www.maputalandlodge.co.za; KwaNgwanase; s/d R500/700; ❉❉) These 23 simple, yet pleasant, self-catering chalets in KwaNgwanase have all the mod cons, including DSTV, a bar and a restaurant. A good option in a creature-free zone.

❶ Getting There & Away

A 4WD is required to access both Kosi Bay Mouth and Kosi Bay Camp, but some lodges in other areas organise trips here.

If you are driving, Rte 22 runs north to Kosi Bay from Hluhluwe and the N2. If heading from Sodwana Bay, continue up Rte 22; if you have a 4WD, the sandy coastal route is not to be missed.

TEMBE ELEPHANT PARK
☑035

South Africa's last free-ranging elephants are protected in the sandveld (dry, sandy belt) forests of Tembe Elephant Park (☑035-592 0001; www.tembe.co.za; adult/child/vehicle R30/15/35; ☉6am-6pm), straddling the

South Africa–Mozambique border. There are about 230 elephants in its 30,000 hectares, plus the rest of the Big Five (buffalo, rhino, lion and leopard) and more than 300 bird species.

Tembe Lodge (☑031-267 0144; www.tembe.co.za; with full board & activities per person R800-1250; ❉) offers accommodation in delightful, secluded safari tents (with bathrooms) built on wooden platforms.

To reach the park, head westwards along a dirt road to the N2 from Kosi Bay. There's a sealed road to the park entrance, but only 4WD vehicles are allowed to drive inside the park itself; secure parking is available and visitors are collected in open safari vehicles.

NDUMO GAME RESERVE
☑035

The Ndumo Game Reserve (☑591 0004, 035-845 1000; www.kznwildlife.com; adult/child/vehicle R40/20/35; ☉5am-7pm Oct-Mar, 6am-6pm Apr-Sep) is beside the Mozambique border and close to the Swaziland border, about 100km north of Mkuze. On some 10,000 hectares, there are black and white rhinos, hippos, crocodiles and antelope species, but it is the bird life on the Phongola and Usutu Rivers that attracts visitors. The reserve is known locally as a 'mini Okavango'.

Wildlife viewing and birdwatching, guided walks (R110) and vehicle tours (R220) are available.

Fuel and limited supplies are usually available 2km outside the park gate. Camping and rest huts are offered by Ezemvelo KZN Wildlife (☑033-845 1000; www.kznwildlife.com; campsites per person R110, 2-bed rest hut R660).

Drakensberg

If any landscape lives up to its airbrushed, publicity-shot alter ego, it is the jagged tabletop peaks of the Drakensberg range. This range forms the boundary between South Africa and the mountain kingdom of Lesotho, and offers some of the country's most awe-inspiring landscapes.

Within the area is the uKhahlamba-Drakensberg Park, a vast 243,000-hectare sweep of basalt summits and buttresses that was granted World Heritage status in November 2000.

Drakensberg means 'Dragon Mountains'; the Zulu named it Quathlamba, meaning 'Battlement of Spears'. The Zulu word is a more accurate description of the sheer escarpment but the Afrikaans name captures something of the Drakensberg's otherworldly atmosphere. People have lived here for thousands of years – this is evidenced by the many San rock-art sites – yet many of the peaks were first climbed little more than 50 years ago.

Climate

The frosts come in winter, but the rain falls in summer, and snow has been recorded on the summits every month of the year. While the summer weather forecasts often make bleak reading for those hoping for blue skies and sunshine, you can often bet on clear, dry mornings, with the thunderheads only rolling in during the afternoon. Whenever you visit, always carry wet-weather gear, and be prepared for icy conditions and snowfalls.

Hiking

The Drakensberg range is one of Africa's best hiking destinations and there is something for walkers of all levels, though only experienced climbers should attempt peaks. There are gentle day walks, moderate half-day hikes, strenuous 10- to 12-hour hikes, and multiday hikes for more serious and experienced hikers.

Make sure you obtain the relevant 1:50,000 scale maps and seek advice on the current status of any trail. You must always fill in a register; permits, needed on all hikes within the park, can be organised through Ezemvelo KZN Wildlife offices at the trailheads. The only trail accommodation is at Giant's Castle; in some areas walkers can use caves, but always carry a tent. Hikers are not allowed to light fires, so you'll need to bring a stove. Arranging to rent camping equipment is borderline impossible, so you need to come prepared.

Ezemvelo KZN Wildlife cautions hikers not to walk alone, and it recommends a minimum of four people for overnight hikes. Registered guides can be organised for short walks (R100 per person), longer hikes (R200 per person) or overnight hikes (around R700 per person per night), depending on numbers. Hiking guides need to be booked through the relevant section of the park and reservations should be made well in advance.

April to July are good months for hiking. Summer hiking can be made frustrating, and even dangerous, by rain and flooding rivers. In winter, frost is the main hazard; snow occurs occasionally.

Wildlife

With plentiful water, a range of up to 3000m in altitude and distinct areas such as plateaus, cliffs and valleys, it isn't surprising that the uKhahlamba-Drakensberg Park's flora and fauna are extremely varied. The park is home to hundreds of bird species and about 60 mammal species, including several species of antelope (such as elands, oribis and klipspringer), baboons, rare ice rats, bearded vultures, and black eagles. Various hides throughout the park allow for closer viewing.

🛈 Getting There & Around

There is little public transport to and within the Drakensberg, although there is a lot of tourist traffic and the occasional minibus taxi ferrying resort staff. The main jumping-off points are on or near the N3. The Baz Bus drops off and picks up passengers at a couple of hostels in the area. Through hostels in Durban you can arrange a shuttle to the hostels near Sani Pass and Himeville. To explore in any great depth, a car is strongly recommended.

NORTHERN BERG
📖 036

An ideal stopover on the journey between Durban and Jo'burg, the Northern Berg is

---

🛈 'DOING' THE BERG

Be aware that the area is deceptive – it's not easy to cover the whole of Drakensberg (the Berg) – whether outside or inside the park. There is no single road linking all the main areas of interest – you have to exit and reenter each region of the park from the N3, R103 or R74. You are better off basing yourself in one spot (Northern, Central or Southern Berg) and exploring the immediate area, otherwise you'll end up spending most of your time behind a wheel driving between hikes and sites.

Each section of the park essentially operates as its own self-contained reserve, with entry fees payable each time you enter and all information and maps pertaining only to the section you're in. You need to allow at least an hour to drive from one section of the uKhahlamba-Drakensberg Park to the next. There are no unattractive parts of the Berg, so whichever area you choose is bound to delight.

Drakensberg

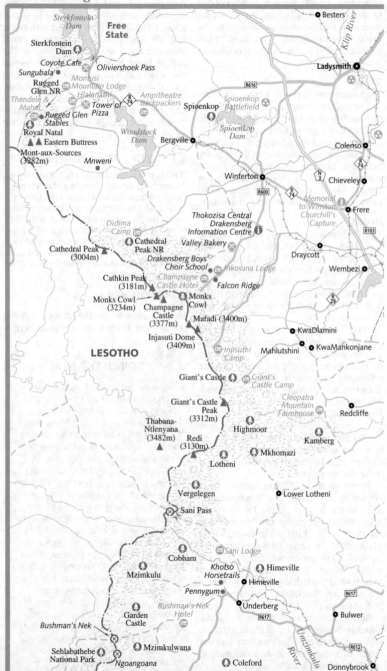

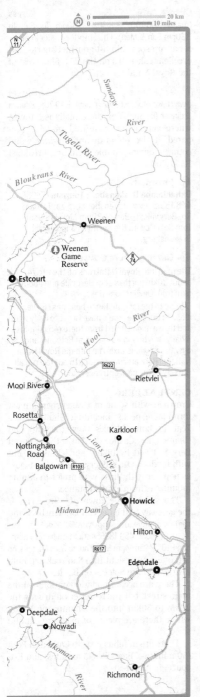

crowned with the beautiful Royal Natal National Park, with some excellent day walks and wonderfully empty spaces.

The nearest town, Bergville, is small and rough around the edges, but is nevertheless a useful stocking-up and jumping-off point for the Northern Drakensberg. The minibus taxi rank is behind the tourist office.

ROYAL NATAL NATIONAL PARK

Spanning out from some of the range's loftiest summits, the 8000-hectare Royal Natal National Park (☏036-438 6310; www.kznwildlife.com; adult/child R30/20; ☺5am-7pm summer, 6am-6pm winter) has a presence that far outstrips its relatively meagre size, with many of the surrounding peaks rising as high into the air as the park stretches across. With some of the Drakensberg's most dramatic and accessible scenery, the park is crowned by the sublime Amphitheatre, an 8km wall of cliff and canyon, which is spectacular from below or from up on high. Here the Tugela Falls drop 850m in five stages.

Other notable peaks in the area are the Devil's Tooth, the Eastern Buttress and the Sentinel. Rugged Glen Nature Reserve adjoins the park on the northeastern side.

The park's visitors centre (☺8am-4.30pm) is about 1km in from the main gate. There's also a shop selling basic provisions.

⊙ Sights & Activities
ROCK ART

There are several San rock-art sites within the park, but only one is open to visitors. Look for the 'San Rock Art' sign near the first bridge after entry – here, community guides are waiting to take you on a guided walk (adult/child R20/10; ☺10am-3.30pm). The return trip takes about one hour, including time to chat about flora, fauna and Zulu culture as well as the paintings themselves. If no one is there, they'll be off guiding another party – it's worth waiting for them to return.

HIKING

Day walks are explained in a map provided at the visitor centre. Guides are available for both day and overnight hikes – contact Elijah Mbonane (☏073 137 4690; elijahmbonane@yahoo.com) for advance bookings. A well-known trail taking in the Amphitheatre is the Tugela Falls. This trip can be done in a day on your own, but with great care (eight to nine hours return for fit hikers). To get there, drive to the Sentinel car park in Qwa Qwa (via Phutadijaba in the Free State) and hike on to the escarpment above the Amphitheatre. The hike involves climbing chain ladders. In winter there is no water in the falls; also, avoid cloudy days in summer.

HORSE RIDING

Just outside the park gates, Rugged Glen Stables ([☎]036-438 6422; 1-/2-hr rides R120/160) organises a wide range of horse-riding activities, including two-day trails.

🛏 Sleeping & Eating

INSIDE THE PARK

Thendele   CHALET $$
([☎]033-845 1000; www.kznwildlife.com; 2-person chalet R875-995, 4-person chalet R1525-1735) The park's fabulous main camp has two- and four-bed chalets as well as cottages and a lodge for larger groups. All chalets have in-your-face views of the peaks opposite. It's a great walking base.

Rustic camping is also available at Mahai (campsites per person R90), which is a beautiful campground approximately 1km from the visitors centre, and at Rugged Glen Nature Reserve (campsites per person R90), a more basic experience.

OUTSIDE THE PARK

Amphitheatre Backpackers   BACKPACKERS $
([☎]036-438 6675; www.amphibackpackers.co.za; campsites per person from R75, dm R125, d R280-520; [P🛜🏊]) Facing the Amphitheatre, this is an in-your-face experience with a selection of sleeping options. Some travellers report feeling pressured to do the backpackers' organised trips, while others enjoy the rolled-out convenience. Found 21km north of Bergville on R74.

Hlalanathi   RESORT $$
([☎]036-438 6308; www.hlalanathi.co.za; campsites per person R140, 2-/4-bed chalet R700/1350; 🏊) With a location lifted straight from an African chocolate-box lid, this pretty, unpretentious resort offers camping and excellent accommodation in thatched chalets overlooking the Tugela River. Prices are substantially cheaper outside high season.

TOP CHOICE Montusi Mountain Lodge   LODGE $$$
([☎]036-438 6243; www.montusi.co.za; s/d with half board R1500/2600; 🛜🏊) With oodles of bush-lodge exclusivity, this opulent place blends a thatch-and-fireplace homeliness with plenty of luxury comforts in very swish chalets. The turn-off is just after the Tower of Pizza.

Coyote Cafe   CAFE $$
(mains R60-100; ⊗8.30am-5.30pm Tue-Sat, to 3.30pm Sun & Mon) This modern, sleek place serves up some almost-gourmet snacks and excellent cakes. It's on the R74, 8km west of the Royal Natal turn-off.

Tower of Pizza   ITALIAN $$
(www.towerofpizza.co.za; mains R40-70; ⊗lunch & dinner Tue-Sun) Yep, there really is a tower, where very good oven-fired pizza is prepared. It also offers quaint rondavels and cottages (single/double including breakfast R550/800).

ℹ Information

Okhahlamba Drakensberg Tourism ([☎]036-448 1557; www.drakensberg.org.za; Tatham Rd, Bergville; ⊗9am-4.30pm Mon-Fri, 9am-1pm Sat) Covers the northern and central Drakensberg.

ℹ Getting There & Away

The road into Royal Natal runs off the Rte 74, about 30km northwest of Bergville and about 5km from Oliviershoek Pass.

None of the long-distance bus lines run very close to Bergville. You'll have to get to Ladysmith and take a minibus taxi from there (45 minutes). A daily Greyhound bus stops at Estcourt and Ladysmith. Minibus taxis run into the Royal Natal National Park area for about R15 but few run all the way to the park entrance.

CENTRAL BERG

Crowned with some of Drakensberg's most formidable peaks, including Giant's Castle Peak (3312m), Monk's Cowl (3234m) and Champagne Castle (3377m), the Central Berg is loved by hikers and climbers. But with its dramatic scenery, this region is just as popular with those who prefer to admire mountains from a safe distance.

The sedate little town of Winterton is the gateway to the Central Drakensberg and makes a pleasant stopover. Winterton Museum ([☎]036-488 1885; Kerk St; minimum donation R10; ⊗9am-4pm Mon-Thu, to 3pm Fri, to noon Sat) offers an insight into San rock art, Zulu history and the Spioenkop battle.

There are accommodation options on the main street, but you're better off driving the 20km to 30km into the Champagne Valley, where there are plenty of places to eat and sleep.

There are minibus taxis to Cathedral Peak (30 minutes), Bergville (15 minutes) and Estcourt (45 minutes).

CATHEDRAL PEAK NATURE RESERVE
☑036

A beautifully photogenic area in the shadow of the ramparts of Cathedral Peak, Cathedral Peak Nature Reserve (☑036-488 8000; www.kznwildlife.com; adult/child R30/15; ☺6am-6pm) backs up against a colossal escarpment of peaks, with the Bell (2930m), the Horns (3005m) and Cleft Peak (3281m) on the horizon.

The park office (☑036-488 8000; www.kzn wildlife.com), in Didima Camp, sells permits for the scenic drive (4WD only) up Mike's Pass and arranges guides. At the time of research the pass was closed due to the poor conditions; check on its status. You can also get hiking infomation here.

The Didima Rock Art Centre (☑036-488 1332; adult/child R50/25; ☺8am-4pm), at Didima Camp 1km into the park, offers a good insight into San rock art, though the multimedia display was out of action when we visited.

You can camp near the main gate or at Didima Camp (☑033-845 1000; www.kznwildlife. com; campsites R90, 2-person chalet R1000; ☒), one of Ezemvelo KZN Wildlife's swankiest offerings, with huge views, a restaurant, tennis courts and excellent self-catering chalets.

MONK'S COWL
☑036

Within uKhahlamba-Drakensberg Park, Monk's Cowl (☑036-468 1103; www.kznwildlife. com; adult/child R35/18; ☺6am-6pm), another stunning slice of the Drakensberg range, offers superb hiking and rock climbing. Within the reserve are the three peaks, Monk's Cowl, Champagne Castle and Cathkin Peak.

The park office (☑036-468 1103; campsites 2-person minimum R190) is 3km beyond Champagne Castle Hotel, which is at the end of the R600 running southwest from Winterton. Overnight hiking (adult/child R45/22) is also possible but the shelter caves must be booked in advance. The area en route to the park is known as Champagne Valley. This is full of cafes, pleasant accommodation options and enough (non-hiking) tourist activities to keep you busy for days.

Just off Dragon Peaks Rd are South Africa's singing ambassadors, the Drakensberg Boys' Choir School (☑036-468 1012; www. dbchoir.co.za). There are public performances at 3.30pm on Wednesday during school terms.

Horse trail rides are available through Ushaka Horse Trails (☑072 664 2993; www. monkscowl.com; 4 Bell Park Dam Rd; 2hr R180, full day R550).

Drakensberg Canopy Tour (☑036-468 1981; www.drakensbergcanopytour.co.za; per person R450; ☺7.30am-2.30pm) is the Berg's latest adrenaline-filled activity. You 'fly' on a series of 12 slides above the beautiful canopy of an ancient indigenous forest.

🛏 Sleeping & Eating

TOP CHOICE Inkosana Lodge — BACKPACKERS $$

(☑036-468 1202; www.inkosana.co.za; campsites R100, dm/d without bathroom R150/450, 2-person thatched rondavel with/without bathroom R600/450; P☒) This Drakensberg delight's indigenous garden, clean rooms and lovely *rondavels* make it one of the best spots around. Although promoted as a 'backpacker lodge', its range of rooms would suit any discerning traveller. Former mountaineer and welcoming owner Ed can give expert advice on hikes. It's on the R600, en route to Champagne Castle.

Champagne Castle Hotel — RESORT $$$

(☑036-468 1063; www.champagnecastle.co.za; s/d with full board from R1830/2440) The reliable and predictably 'nice' Champagne Castle is one of the best-known resorts, conveniently located in the mountains at the end of the road to Monk's Cowl (on the R600).

Valley Bakery — BAKERY $

(snacks R25-40; ☺8am-5pm Mon-Fri, 7am-2pm Sat) Baguettes, croissants and a range of delicious items are baked on the premises (the owners even grow and grind their wheat).

❶ Information

Central Drakensberg Information Centre

(☑036-488 1207; www.cdic.co.za; ☺8.30am-5pm) Based in the Thokozisa complex, 13km outside Winterton on the R600.

GIANT'S CASTLE & INJISUTHI
☑036

Rising up to Injasuti Dome (3409m), Giant's Castle (☑033-845 1000, 036-353 3718; www.kzn-wildlife.com; adult/child R30/15; ☺5am-10pm Oct-Mar, 6am-10pm Apr-Sep, reception 8am-4.30pm) is one of the Drakensberg's loftiest sections – even its lowest point sits at 1300m above sea level. Established in 1904, mainly to protect the eland, it is a rugged, remote and popular destination, with huge forest reserves to the north and south and Lesotho's barren plateau over the escarpment to the west.

The office at Giant's Castle Camp gives out a basic map of the hiking trails (distances not stated). Here, too, is a shop selling basic provisions, and fuel is available.

Injisuthi, on the northern side of Giant's Castle, is another 'wow' spot of the Berg. It's a secluded and extraordinarily beautiful place with a terrific view of the Monk's Cowl peak. Injisuthi features the Drakensberg's highest points, Mafadi (3400m) and Injisuthi (3300m). Please note: these peaks cannot be done in a day.

◉ Sights & Activities
WILDLIFE

The rare lammergeier, or bearded vulture, which is found only in the Drakensberg, nests in the reserve. Reserve staff sometimes give guests bones to put out to encourage the birds to feed here. The **Lammergeyer Hide** (☑036-353 3718; giants@kznwildlife.com; per person R215, minimum R645), the best place to see the vultures, is extremely popular so it's necessary to book in advance.

ROCK ART

The area is rich in San rock art, with at least 26 sites. It is thought that the last San lived here at the beginning of the 20th century.

To see the paintings, you can visit **Main Cave** (adult/child R30/15; ⊗9am-3pm), 2.3km south of Giant's Camp (a 30-minute walk). You can walk by yourself, but make sure you time it well – the cave is only unlocked on the hour, when a guide conducts an explanatory tour.

Injisuthi is the departure point for the guided hike to the extraordinary **Battle Cave**, a massive rock overhang featuring remarkable San bushmen's paintings. This is a six-hour round-trip guided hike. Walks must be reserved in advance (☑036 431 9000; around R100 per person, minimum two people).

🛏 Sleeping

Injisuthi Camp   CAMPGROUND, CHALET **$**
(☑033-845 1000; campsites per person R75; 2-person safari camp R290, 4-person chalet R980) As well as campsites and self-contained cabins, the area has caves for overnight hikers (however, check on their state before departing).

Giant's Castle Camp   CHALET **$$**
(☑033-845 1000; www.kznwildlife.com; trail hut per person R45, 2-person chalet from R960) The main, very pretty camp has two-, four- and six-bed chalets with fireplace, kitchenette,

floor-to-ceiling windows, TV and thatched verandahs, and eight-bed mountain huts.

ℹ Getting There & Away

The roads from both Mooi River and Estcourt are sealed – do not take the unsealed back roads as they can become impassable.

Infrequent minibus taxis run from Estcourt to villages near the main entrance (KwaDlamini, Mahlutshini and KwaMankonjane), but these are still several kilometres from Giant's Castle Camp.

SOUTHERN BERG

Best accessed from the pleasant towns of Himeville and Underberg, the Southern Berg boasts one of the region's highlights: the journey up to Lesotho over the Sani Pass. It is renowned as a serious hiking area, offering a smorgasbord of wilderness areas and some great walks, including the fabulous Giant's Cup Trail.

◉ Sights & Activities

Highmoor Nature Reserve   NATURE RESERVE
(☑033-845 1000; www.kznwildlife.com; adult/child R50/25, campsites per person R110, cave camping R45; ⊗6am-6pm) Although more exposed and less dramatic than some of the Drakensberg region, the undulating hills of Highmoor Nature Reserve make for pleasant walks. It's also one of the few places where you're driving 'on top of' the foothills. There are two caves – Aasvoel Cave and Caracal Cave – both 2.5km from the main office, and Fultons Rock, which has rock paintings (an easy 4km walk), plus caves for overnight hikers. Access is via the towns of Nottingham Road or Rosetta.

DON'T MISS

SPLURGE

The **Cleopatra Mountain Farmhouse** (☑033-267 7243; www.cleo-mountain.com; Balgowan; per person from R1795) is a luxury retreat owned by chef Richard Poynton. Guests enjoy a nightly six-course menu of quality produce prepared innovatively. Each of the 11 rooms is decked out in a theme and features quirky touches, such as a picket-fence bedhead and Boer memorabilia. The experience comes at a price, but this is one place where it's worth forgetting the budget...and the calorie count.

GIANT'S CUP TRAIL

Without doubt, the Giant's Cup Trail (68km, five days and five nights), running from Sani Pass to Bushman's Nek, is one of the nation's great walks. Any reasonably fit person can walk it. Early booking, through Ezemvelo KZN Wildlife (☏033-845 1000; www. kznwildlife.com), is advisable in local holiday seasons. Fees are based on the composition of the hiking party.

Highlights include the Bathplug Cave with San rock art and the breathtaking mountain scenery on day four. Accommodation is in limited shared huts (adult/child per trail R65/50). No firewood is available so you'll need a stove and fuel. Sani Lodge, which sells maps (R45), is almost at the head of the trail.

Kamberg Nature Reserve & Rock Art Centre
NATURE RESERVE

(☏033-267 7251; www.kznwildlife.com; adult/child R30/15, rock-art walks per person R50, documentaries R20; ⊙5am-7pm Oct-Mar, 6am-6pm Apr-Sep) Southeast of Giant's Castle, Kamberg Nature Reserve has a number of antelope species. The rock-art centre, run by the local community, is well worth visiting. From there you can join a 3.5km guided walk to the impressive Game Pass Shelter, known as the 'Rosetta Stone of San rock art'.

Two documentaries are shown in a purpose-built multimedia centre: the first is about the San people, and the other is a visual tour of the actual walk, aimed at those who are unable to walk to the site.

For accommodation within the park, Ezemvelo KZN Wildlife (☏033-267 7251; www.kznwildlife.com; 2-bed chalet R570) has well equipped chalets in a quaint garden setting.

You can get here from Nottingham Road or Rosetta, off the N3 south of Mooi River.

UNDERBERG & HIMEVILLE
☏033 / POP 1500

Clustered in the foothills of the southern Drakensberg, the small farming town of Underberg fills up in summer, when Durbanites head to the peaks for a breath of the fresh stuff. It has good infrastructure, and is the place to go for money and shopping and to organise activities in the region. Only a few kilometres from Underberg, Himeville is a pretty, if sedate town. It has a characteristic old pub, a cluster of reasonable B&Bs and the excellent Himeville Museum (admission by donation; ⊙8.30am-12.30pm Tue-Sun) which contains an incredible array of bric-a-brac.

🛏 Sleeping & Eating

Tumble In
B&B $$

(☏033-7011 556; www.tumble-in-bnb.co.za; Underberg; r incl breakfast per person R330, self-catering per person R280) This unpretentious place of-fers spacious, homely rooms. It's 2.5km from Underberg on the Himeville Rd.

Yellowwood Cottage B&B
B&B $$

(☏033-702 1065; 8 Mackenzie St, Himeville; s/d incl breakfast R440/680; 🅿🛜) An enjoyable homely experience: four cosy, frilly rooms in a pretty house with views of Hodgson's Peaks.

Pucketty Farm 🏆 TOP CHOICE
DELI $

(☏033-701 1035; ⊙8am-5pm) There's more to this extraordinary cute-cum-gourmet mix than meets the eye, with a huge selection of great-value gourmet products, plus an art gallery and small cafe. The farm is 1.5km east from the Himeville turn-off.

ℹ Information

Southern Berg Escape (☏033-701 1471; www. drakensberg.org; Old Main Rd, Clocktower Centre, Underberg; ⊙8am-4pm Mon-Fri, 9am-1pm Sat & Sun) Has the useful *Southern Drakensberg Pocket Guide*.

ℹ Getting There & Away

NUD Express (☏079 696 7018, 033-701 2750; www.underbergexpress.co.za) operates shuttle-bus services between Underberg and central Durban (from R350), Durban's King Shaka International Airport (R450) and Pietermaritzburg (R250). You must book these services; they are not known for their reliability for sticking to times.

Underberg Metered Taxi Association (☏076 719 2451, 076 199 5823, 072 016 5809) can take up to four passengers to Durban (R1200), Pietermaritzburg (R700), and Kokstad (R550).

SANI PASS

The drive up the Sani Pass is a spectacular ride around hairpin bends into the clouds to the kingdom of Lesotho. At 2865m, this is the highest pass in the country and the vistas (on a clear day!) are magical. There are hikes in almost every direction and inexpensive horse rides are available. Amazingly, this is also the only road link between Lesotho and KwaZulu-Natal.

Descending from Lesotho requires great brakes and nerves of steel – if you lack either, lots of companies in Himeville and Underberg offer day tours, including Sani Lodge (☎033-702 0330; www.sanilodge.co.za; campsites R70, dm/d without bathroom R110/320, 2-bed rondavel R400, self-catering cottage per person from R230). At the bottom of the pass, the lodge tops the pops in the local-knowledge stakes, offering a range of fabulous tours and activities and insider tips about the region.

You need a passport to cross into Lesotho. The border is open from 6am to 6pm daily, but check beforehand; times alter.

BUSHMAN'S NEK

This is a South Africa–Lesotho border crossing (no vehicles!). From here there are hiking trails up into the escarpment, including to Lesotho's Sehlabathebe National Park. You can trot through the border and into Lesotho on horseback with Khotso Horsetrails (☎033-701 1502; www.khotsotrails.co.za).

Accommodation options include the Silverstreams Caravan Park (☎033-701 1249; www.silverstreams.co.za; campsites R400, cottage R1000, cheaper on weekdays), right next to the border, and Bushman's Nek Hotel (☎033-701 1460; www.bushmansnek.co.za; r R902; ☒), a full-on resort about 2km east of the border crossing.

The Midlands

The Midlands run northwest from Pietermaritzburg, KwaZulu-Natal's capital, to Estcourt, skirting the Battlefields to the northeast. West of Pietermaritzburg is picturesque, hilly country, originally settled by English farmers. The region is promoted as the Midlands Meander, a slightly contrived concoction of craft shops, artistic endeavours, teashops and B&Bs winding along and around the R103 west of the N3.

PIETERMARITZBURG
☎033 / POP 457,000

Billed as the heritage city, Pietermaritzburg's (usually known as PMB) grand historic buildings hark back to an age of pith helmets and midday martinis. Today, they proudly house museums and refurbished hotels. By day, KZN's administrative and legislative capital is vibrant: its large Zulu community sets a colourful flavour and the

Indian community brings echoes of the subcontinent to its busy streets. A large student population adds to the city's vitality.

◉ Sights & Activities

One of the city's finest sights is the Tatham Art Gallery (Map p425; www.tatham.org.za; Chief Albert Luthuli St; admission free; ⊘10am-5pm Tue-Sun), a fine collection of French and English 19th- and early 20th-century works housed in the beautiful Old Supreme Court. The nearby, colonial-era City Hall (cnr Langalibalele St & Chief Albert Luthuli St) is the largest load-bearing red-brick building in the southern hemisphere.

The Msunduzi Museum (www.voortrekker museum.co.za; 351 Langalibalele St; adult/student R8/5; ⊘9am-4pm Mon-Fri, to 1pm Sat) incorporates Voortrekker, Zulu and Indian displays as well as buildings including the Church of the Vow (1841), built to fulfil the Voortrekkers' promise to God at the Battle of Blood River.

Three Hindu temples (Langalibalele St) grace the northern end of Langalibalele St and the main mosque (East St) is nearby. A statue of Gandhi (Church St), who was famously ejected from a 1st-class carriage at Pietermaritzburg station, stands defiant opposite the old colonial buildings on Church St.

⌂ Sleeping

Sleepy Hollow
Adventure Backpackers   BACKPACKERS $
(☎082 455 8325; www.sleepyhollowbackpack ers.com; 80 Leinster Rd; campsite R90, dm/d/f R130/330/495) A rambling 1940s abode in the heart of the student precinct with a preloved feel; well-worn carpets and furniture, and a communal kitchen.

Heritage Guest House   GUESTHOUSE $$
(☎033-394 4364; 45 Miller St; s/d incl breakfast R475/650, f ste R1200; ☒) This place has six small units of varying shapes and sizes surrounding a small pretty garden and pool. It can get booked out by long-term business travellers.

Smith Grove   B&B $$
(☎033-345 3963; www.smithgrove.co.za; 37 Howick Rd; s/d incl breakfast R420/620) This pleasant, renovated Victorian home offers English-style B&B comforts with spacious, individually styled rooms, each in a different colour.

Pietermaritzburg

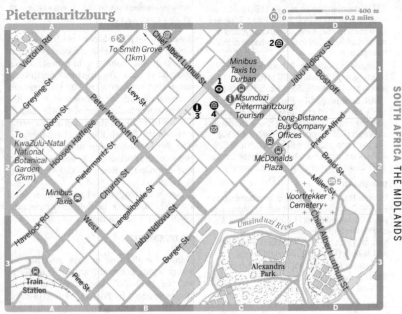

SOUTH AFRICA THE MIDLANDS

✗ Eating

Rosehurst INTERNATIONAL **$$**
(239 Boom St; mains R60-75; ⊙8.30am-4.30pm
Mon-Fri, to 2pm Sat) This delightful oasis, in
a lovely Victorian house, is a quintessential
English garden in the middle of 'Maritz-
burg. Relax under blossoms while supping
on fresh and very tasty salads, sandwiches
and pastries. There are excellent break-
fasts, too.

Traffords INTERNATIONAL **$$**
(43 Miller St; lunch mains R40-70, dinner mains
R75-120; ⊙lunch Wed-Fri, dinner Wed-Sat; ⊘) This
place offers oxtail, slow-roasted lamb shanks
and homemade gnocchi. Lunches include
more salad-based offerings. Vegetarians are
well catered for.

❶ Information

Ezemvelo KZN Wildlife Headquarters (⊘033-
845 1000; www.kznwildlife.com; Peter Brown
Dr, Queen Elizabeth Park; ⊙reception 8am-
4.30pm Mon-Fri, reservations 8am-5.30pm
Mon-Thu, to 4.30pm Fri, to 12.30pm Sat)
Provides information and accommodation
bookings for all Ezemvelo KZN Wildlife parks
and reserves – at least 48 hours' notice is
required for bookings.
Msunduzi Pietermaritzburg Tourism (⊘033-
345 1348; www.pmbtourism.co.za; 117 Chief

Pietermaritzburg

Albert Luthuli St, Publicity House; ⊙8am-5pm
Mon-Fri, to 1pm Sat)
Orange Ring (⊘033-342 9254; 31 Chief Albert
Luthuli St; ⊙7am-9pm) Internet cafe.

❶ Getting There & Away

AIR

SAAirlink (⊘033-3869 2861; www.flyairlink.
com), with an office at the airport, flies to
Jo'burg daily (from R1300). The airport is 4km
south of the city centre.

BUS

The head offices of most bus companies, including **Greyhound** (⊘083 915 9000; www.
greyhound.co.za) and **Intercape** (⊘0861 287

287; www.intercape.co.za), are in Burger St, or directly opposite in McDonalds Plaza. **Translux** (☎0861 589 282; www.translux.co.za) and its no-frills affiliate, City to City, are based at the train station.

Sample fares include: Jo'burg (R300 to R375, seven hours), Pretoria (R300 to R350, eight hours) and Durban (R185 to R255, 1½ hours).

NUD Express (☎079 696 7108, 033-701 2750; www.underbergexpress.co.za) offers a daily service to Durban's King Shaka International Airport (R350) and Durban Central (R250). You must pre-book. The **Baz Bus** (☎0861 229 287; www.bazbus.com) travels between Durban and Pietermaritzburg three times a week.

MINIBUS TAXI

Minibus taxis to Durban leave from behind City Hall (R60, one hour), while those to Underberg (R65, 2½ hours) depart from the corner of West and Pietermaritz Sts. Destinations from this stop also include Ladysmith (R80, 2½ hours) and Jo'burg (R160 to R200, eight hours).

Those for Estcourt (R55, 1¾ hours) depart from the rank on the corner of Retief and Hoosen Haffejee Sts; this is not a safe part of town.

TRAIN

Shosholoza Meyl (☎0860 008 888; www.shosholozameyl.co.za) runs daily (except Saturday) to Jo'burg (tourist class R250, 10 hours) via Ladysmith, and to Durban (economy class R50, 2¼ hours).

Battlefields

KwaZulu-Natal's history is intrinsically linked to its Battlefields, the stage on which many of the country's bloodiest scenes were played out. The province's northwestern region is where some 500 Voortrekkers avenged the murder of their leader Piet Retief by defeating a force of 12,000 Zulu at the Battle of Blood River, and a Zulu army crushed the British Empire at Isandlwana. The Brits subsequently staged the heroic defence of Rorke's Drift, and slogged it out against the Boers at Ladysmith and Spioenkop.

See www.battlefields.kzn.org.za or pick up KZN Tourism's Battlefields Route brochure from KZN Tourism.

LADYSMITH
☑036

Named for the wife of Cape governor Sir Harry Smith, Ladysmith achieved fame during the 1899–1902 Anglo-Boer War, when it was besieged by Boer forces for 118 days. The famous vocal group Ladysmith Black Mambazo has its roots here. Apart from the historical aspect, Ladysmith is a reasonable base for the area's Battlefield tours.

BATTLING IT OUT

Roughly following the N11 and R33 roads and occupying an area that stretches north from Estcourt to the Free State and Mpumalanga borders, the Battlefields are a crusade to get to without a car. Even with a car, they are isolated and can be a challenge to find.

Guides

The best way to tackle the Battlefields is with a guide – that way, you won't feel as though you're traipsing through a string of empty fields peppered with memorials. With a knowledgeable person at hand, and with a bit of swotting up beforehand, the Battlefields Route can be extremely rewarding.

Guides generally charge between R800 and R1500 for a one-day tour of sites, including Rorke's Drift and Isandlwana. Note: some guides quote these rates per person, others per group; rates are cheaper in your own vehicle.

For those on a budget and happy to share the tour with others, **BushBaby Safaris** (☎082 415 4359; www.bushbaby.co.za) offers a daily shuttle bus with a guide to Isandlwana and Rorke's Drift (R490 per person, minimum two people). Pick-ups from Dundee or Talana Heritage Park.

Other (but by no means all) recommended guides:

Bethuel Manyathi (☎083 531 0061) Nqutu, near Dundee.

Thulani Khuzwayo (☎072 872 9782; thulani.khuzwayo@gmail.com; group tours R640, minimum 2 people) Rorke's Drift.

Ken Gillings (☎083 654 5880; ken.gillings@mweb.co.za) Durban.

Liz Spiret (☎072 262 9669) Ladysmith.

SPIOENKOP NATURE RESERVE

The 6000-hectare Spioenkop Nature Reserve (☑036-488 1578; www.kznwildlife.com; admission R20; ☺5am-7pm Oct-Mar, 6am-6pm Apr-Sep) is based on the Spioenkop Dam on the Tugela River. The reserve is handy for most of the area's Battlefield sites and not far from the Drakensberg. Animals include white rhinos, giraffes, various antelope species and 270-plus bird species. There's horse riding, a vulture hide and guided walks.

Inside the reserve in a valley, iPika (www.kznwildlife.com; campsites/bush camp per person R65/205) offers campsites and one four-bed tented bush camp.

Three Trees at Spioenkop (☑036-448 1171; threetreehill.co.za; s/d with full board R2540/3900) is an upmarket ecofriendly house with a beautiful setting and views. Horse riding and battlefield tours are available. It's between Ladysmith and Bergville off the R616.

The reserve is northeast of Bergville but the entrance is on the eastern side, 13km from Winterton off Rte 600. You will need a car to get here.

⊙ Sights

Outside the town hall are two guns, Castor and Pollux, used by the British in defence of Ladysmith. Nearby is a replica of Long Tom, a Boer gun capable of heaving a shell 10km.

Siege Museum   MUSEUM
(Murchison St; adult/child R11/5; ☺9am-4pm Mon-Fri, to 1pm Sat) The excellent museum, next to the town hall in the old Market House (built in 1884), was used to store rations during the siege. It has displays about the Anglo-Boer War and can provide a list of battlefield tour guides.

Emnambithi Cultural Centre   MUSEUM
(316 Murchison St; ☺9am-4pm Mon-Fri) Comprises the Cultural Museum and a tribute to Ladysmith Black Mambazo. The centre offers the Black Mambazo Beat Tour, showing the important sites and significance of the musical group.

⊨ Sleeping & Eating

Buller's Rest Lodge   B&B $$
(☑036-637 6154; www.bullersrestlodge.co.za; 61 Cove Cres; s/d incl breakfast R575/770; ☜▦) This smart thatched abode has the snug 'Boer War' pub, scrumptious home cooking (R155 for three courses) and views from the attractive sundeck-cum-bar area. Turn right at Francis Rd off Harrismith (Poort) Rd, and follow the signs.

Budleigh Guesthouse   B&B $$
(☑036-635 7700; 12 Berea Rd; s/d incl breakfast R480/680; ☜▦) This mansion, with its verandahs and stunning garden, has a range of neat and smart rooms with wooden bedsteads and faux antiques, set around trimmed lawns and flower beds.

Sonia's Pizza & Coffee Shop   ITALIAN $$
(☑036-631 2895; San Marco Centre; mains R20-130; ☺7am-7pm Mon-Sat, 8am-1.30pm Sun) The troops would have killed for this authentic Italian grub; this little place has a reputation around town for its delectable pizzas.

⊙ Getting There & Away

BUS

Bus tickets can be purchased from Shoprite/ Checkers in the Oval Shopping Centre. Buses depart from the Guinea Fowl petrol station on Murchison Rd, and run to Durban (R275, 3½ hours), Jo'burg (R320, 6½ hours) and Cape Town (R555, 19 hours).

MINIBUS TAXI

The main taxi rank is east of the town centre near the corner of Queen and Lyell Sts. Destinations include Pietermaritzburg (1½ hours) and Durban (2½ hours). Taxis bound for Jo'burg (five hours) are nearby on Alexandra St.

TRAIN

Shosholoza Meyl (☑0860 008 888; www.shosholozameyl.co.za) trains stop here as they travel between Durban (R140, 5½ hours) and Jo'burg (R180, seven hours).

ISANDLWANA & RORKE'S DRIFT
☑034

If you have seen *Zulu,* the film that made Michael Caine a star, you will have doubt-less heard of Rorke's Drift, a victory of the misty-eyed variety, where on 22–23 January 1879, 139 British soldiers successfully defended a small mission station from around 4000 Zulu warriors. Queen Victoria lavished

DON'T MISS

TALANA HERITAGE PARK & BATTLEFIELD

Talana means 'the shelf where precious items are stored', which is strangely appropriate for this excellent battlefield site–cum–heritage park (☎034-212 2654; www.talana.co.za; adult/child R25/2; ⊗8am-4.30pm Mon-Fri, 9am-4.30pm Sat & Sun). There are memorials, cairns and 27 historic buildings relating to the 1899 Anglo-Boer Battle of Talana. Curator Pam McFadden is Talana's knowledge guru.

It's on the Vryheid road, 1.5km out of Dundee.

Victoria Crosses on the survivors and the battle was assured its dramatic place in British military history.

For the full picture, however, you must travel 15km across the plain to Isandlwana, the precursor of Rorke's Drift, where only hours earlier the Zulu dealt the Empire one of its great battlefield disasters by annihilating the main body of the British force in devastating style. Tellingly, *Zulu Dawn* (1979), the film made about the Battle of Isandlwana, never became the cult classic *Zulu* (1964) is now.

Ideally, the two battlefields should be visited together. Start at the Isandlwana Visitors Centre (adult/child R25/12; ⊗8am-4pm Mon-Fri, 9am-4pm Sat & Sun), where there is a small museum. The battlefield itself is extremely evocative, with white cairns and memorials marking the spots where British soldiers fell.

Zulu was filmed in the Drakensberg, but the scenery around Rorke's Drift is nonetheless beautifully rugged, and the Rorke's Drift Orientation Centre (☎034-642 1687; adult/child R25/12; ⊗8am-4pm Mon-Fri, 9am-4pm Sat & Sun), on the site of the original mission station, is excellent. The Zulu know this site as Shiyane, their name for the hill at the back of the village.

Thulani Khuzwayo (p426) gives an in-depth tour of the area, providing details of battles from a Zulu perspective.

🛏 Sleeping

Isandalwana Lodge   LODGE $$$
(☎034-271 8301; www.isandlwana.co.za; s/d with full board R2850/3800; ☎☒) This modern lodge ingeniously blends into the landscape, and its stunning rooms have expansive views over Mt Isandlwana, the Anglo-Zulu battle site.

Rorke's Drift Hotel   LODGE $$$
(☎034-642 1760; www.rorkesdrifthotel.com; s/d with half board R1185/1760) The common areas and restaurant of this giant rotunda promise big things – a wide expanse with massive sofas and an enormous central fireplace. The rooms have less appealing decor, though it's pleasant enough. The restaurant is a popular snack spot for day trippers.

❶ Getting There & Away

The battle sites are both southeast of Dundee (Isandlwana is 70km southeast and Rorke's Drift is 42km) and accessible from Rte 68. The roads to both can be dusty and rough, and a dirt road connects the two sites.

BLOOD RIVER & NCOME MONUMENTS
☎034

On 16 December 1838, some 500 Voortrekkers avenged the massacre of Piet Retief's diplomatic party by crushing a 12,000-strong Zulu army. More than 3000 Zulu died – the Ncome River ran red with their blood – while the Voortrekkers sustained barely a few casualties. The Battle of Blood River became a seminal event in Afrikaner history, seen as proof that the trekkers had a divine mandate to conquer and 'civilise' Southern Africa. Afrikaners still visit the site on 16 December, but the former 'Day of the Vow' is now the 'Day of Reconciliation'.

The battle site is marked by a full-scale bronze re-creation of the Voortrekkers' 64-wagon *laager* (wagon circle). The monument and the nearby Blood River Museum (☎034-632 1695; adult/child R25/10; ⊗8am-4.30pm) are 20km southeast of Rte 33; the turn-off is 27km from Dundee and 45km from Vryheid.

The interesting Ncome Museum (☎034-271 8121; www.ncomemuseum.co.za; admission by donation; ⊗8am-4.30pm), on the other side of the river, gives the Zulu perspective of events.

FREE STATE

In this rural province, farmers in floppy hats and overalls drive rusty *bakkies* (pick-up trucks) full of sheep down empty roads, and brightly painted Sotho houses languish by vast fields of sunflowers. The Free State may not boast many not-to-be-missed attractions, but it has a subtle country charm that's easy to fall for.

In this conservative bastion, the colour divide remains stark, and dreams of an Afrikaner Arcadia live on. But the news isn't all bad. Though the province is a long way from racial nirvana, progress is happening; even in the smallest rural enclaves, the colour barrier is slowly starting to dissolve.

Bloemfontein

📞 051 / POP 645,000

Bloemfontein is a refreshing change from other South African cities. Despite being a double capital (it's the Free State's capital and the judicial capital of South Africa), 'Bloem' feels more like a small country village than a big, imposing city. The central business district, though a little scruffy, is safe and easily walkable, and when the university is in session, the place has a buzzing atmosphere.

The city is also a central crash pad for travellers on the move. While there is no reason to go out of your way to visit Bloemfontein (most of the tourism here is business oriented), the city's location, smack in the middle of the country and at the intersection of a few major highways, means you'll likely pass through at some point.

History

Originally called Mangaung (Place of Cheetahs) by the Setswana people who inhabited it, Bloemfontein's Afrikaans name translates to 'Fountain of Flowers'. Today, the greater metropolitan area is once again called Manguang.

Bloem became the capital of the newly minted Orange Free State in 1854. At the time it was a struggling frontier village in constant danger of being wiped out by the soldiers of Sotho king Moshoeshoe. By the end of Johannes Brand's 25-year term as president in 1888, however, Bloemfontein had grown into a wealthy city with imposing buildings and rail links to the coast.

🔘 Sights & Activities

Manguang Township   TOWNSHIP TOUR

The African National Congress (ANC) party was born in a shanty town 5km outside Bloemfontein in 1912. Today, you can experience township life, and learn some important history, on a guided tour of Manguang Township.

After dark, guided tours hit the township's buzzing *shebeens* (unlicensed bars), where you can sample home brews and dance to a jazz quartet. Both day and night tours are informal, and cost about R400. Obtain a list of tour operators from the tourist information centre.

FREE **Oliewenhuis Art Museum**   GALLERY

(16 Harry Smith St; ⏰8am-5pm Mon-Fri, 10am-5pm Sat, 1-5pm Sun) One of South Africa's most striking art galleries, the Oliewenhuis Art Museum is housed in an exquisite 1935 mansion that's set in beautiful gardens.

Anglo-Boer War Museum &
National Women's Monument   MUSEUM

(www.anglo-boer.co.za; Monument Rd; adult/child R10/5; ⏰8am-4.30pm Mon-Fri, 11am-5pm Sat & Sun) The Anglo-Boer War Museum has some interesting displays, including photos from concentration camps in South Africa and elsewhere. The large paintings depicting battle scenes are striking.

In front of the museum is the National Women's Monument, commemorating the 26,000 women and children who died in British concentration camps during the 1899–1902 Anglo-Boer War.

FREE **Naval Hill**   PARK

(⏰Franklin Game Reserve 8am-5pm) This was the site of the British naval-gun emplacements during the Anglo-Boer War. On the eastern side of the hill is a large white horse (akin to a Wiltshire Horse) that served as a landmark for British cavalry during the war.

There are good views from the top of the hill, which is also home to the Franklin Game Reserve. Walking is permitted and you might spot zebras, giraffes or antelopes.

National Museum   MUSEUM

(www.nasmus.co.za; 36 Aliwal St; admission R5; ⏰8am-5pm Mon-Fri, 10am-5pm Sat, noon-5.30pm Sun) A great re-creation of a 19th-century street, complete with sound effects, is the most interesting display at this museum. There is also a shop and a cafe here.

🛏 Sleeping

Odessa Guesthouse   GUESTHOUSE $

(📞081 966 0200; 4 Gannie Viljoen St; s/d from R320/440; @🏊) This multilingual (Russian and Ukrainian are spoken along with English) guesthouse has a good rep for its home-away-from-home vibe and friendly hosts.

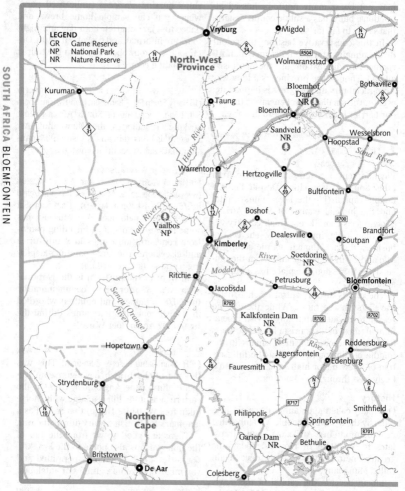

LEGEND
GR   Game Reserve
NP   National Park
NR   Nature Reserve

Rooms are simple but spotless and homely. Breakfast in bed can be arranged.

Reyneke Caravan Park CARAVAN PARK $
(☏051-523 3888; www.reynekepark.co.za; Brendar Rd; campsites R200, r & chalets R350-750; ☒) Two kilometres out of town (take the N8 towards Kimberley), this well-organised park has a swimming pool, a trampoline and a basketball court.

TOP CHOICE Hobbit Boutique Hotel BOUTIQUE HOTEL $$
(☏051-447 0663; www.hobbit.co.za; 19 President Steyn Ave; r incl breakfast from R950; ❋@☒) The local Tolkien society meets at this charming Victorian guesthouse, comprising two 1921 houses. The cottage-style bedrooms have painted bathtubs, plus a couple of teddy bears apiece. Check out the pub and lovely outdoor patio.

Urban Hotel HOTEL $$
(☏051-444 3142; www.urbanhotel.co.za; cnr Parfitt Ave & Henry St; r R750; ❋☎) Rooms are comfortable, good value and have excellent bathrooms. The location is also superb as you can walk to restaurants, bars and Loch Logan.

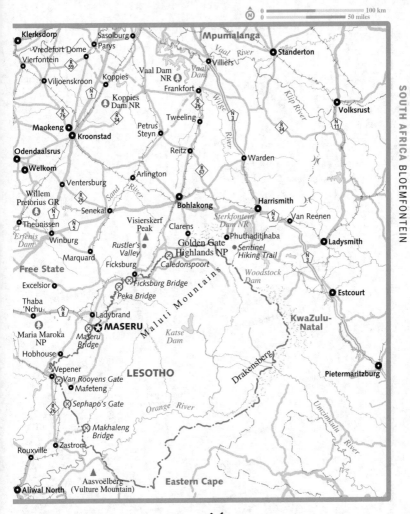

De Akker Guest House GUESTHOUSE **$$**
(📞051-444 2010; www.de-akker.co.za; 25 Parfitt
Ave; s/d R400/500; 🛜) This stylish offering
in a central location is very friendly and is
popular with visiting cricket teams, so book
ahead in summer.

Protea Hotel Willow Lake HOTEL **$$**
(📞051-412 5400; www.proteahotels.com/protea
-hotel-willow-lake.html; 101 Henry St; r from R1200;
❄@🛜🏊) Very stylish rooms and a big move
up from other midrange choices in the city.
A genuine touch of luxury close to Loch Logan, and overlooking the zoo.

✖ Eating

On a small lake is the Loch Logan Waterfront, modelled after Cape Town's waterfront. You'll find the usual South African
chains here and at Mimosa Mall. The main
eating street is 2nd Ave.

Picnic CAFE **$**
(Loch Logan Waterfront; dishes R40-65; tapas R12-24;
⏰8am-5pm Mon-Fri, until 4pm Sat, until 3pm Sun) A
cool place with a great outlook over the water.
The service is excellent and so is the food, especially the salads and sandwiches.

Bloemfontein

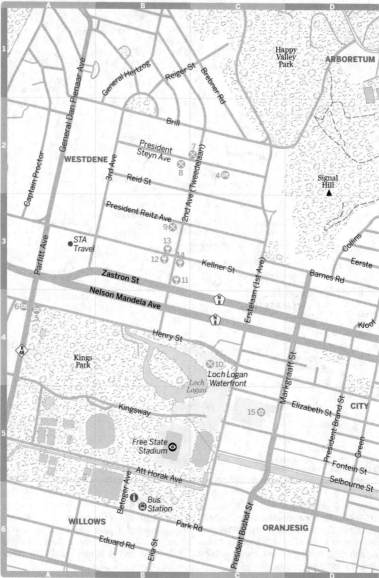

Avanti INTERNATIONAL **$$**
(☎447 4198; www.avantirestaurant.co.za; 53 2nd Ave; mains R60-130; ☺breakfast, lunch & dinner Mon-Sat, breakfast & lunch Sun) This popular spot has an extensive SA wine list and the usual Bloem offerings, including pizza, pasta, steaks and seafood.

Cubana LATIN AMERICAN **$$**
(cnr 2nd Ave & President Reitz St; mains R40-90; ☺9am-late) Part of a national chain, this

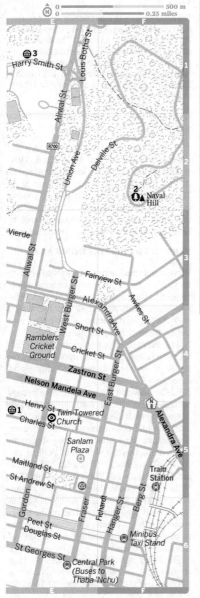

Bloemfontein

Bella Casa Trattoria   ITALIAN $$

(☎051-448 9573; 31 President Steyn Ave; mains R60-130; ⊗Mon-Sat; 🖶) This efficient Italian trattoria serves lots of pasta choices, along with pizzas and salads. The thin-crust Naples-style pizzas are recommended.

🍷 Drinking & Entertainment

As a university town, Bloemfontein has a good range of places to drink, party and listen to live music. Particularly around Kellner St, 2nd Ave bustles with revellers in the evening and competes for the nightlife scene with the Waterfront. There are cinemas in the Mimosa Mall and at the Waterfront.

Mystic Boer   PUB

(84 Kellner St; 🕿) Bloem's most popular long-standing pub and live-music venue provides an eccentric twist to Afrikaner culture – check out the psychedelic pictures of long-bearded Boers on the walls. There are regular gigs by unsigned rock and hip-hop outfits.

Karma   BAR

(Kellner St) There's a downmarket menu here in a very pleasant upmarket chandelier-and-white-tablecloth setting. In the evening it's

popular 'Latino social cafe' is in the heart of the 2nd Ave scene. The lengthy food menu offers lots of chicken and beef dishes with tasty but not-quite-authentic Cuban sauces.

a great outdoors place for a cocktail among the well-heeled.

Barba's Café BAR
(16 2nd Ave; ⊙7.30am-2am Mon-Thu, to 4am Fri) An extensive cocktail list, live music and weekend DJs make this a staple on a 2nd Ave pub crawl. The cafe also serves Greek specialities.

Oolong Lounge LOUNGE
(16B 2nd Ave; ⊙Tue-Sat) This stylish little number attracts a young crowd of movers and shakers.

❶ Information

3@1 Bloemfontein (cnr 2nd & President Reitz Aves; per hr R30) Fast internet connections and wi-fi.

Tourist Information Centre (☏051-405 8489; www.bloemfontein.co.za; 60 Park Rd; ⊙8am-4.15pm Mon-Fri, 8am-noon Sat)

❶ Getting There & Around

Air

Regular flights with **South African Airways** (☏086 160 6606; www.flysaa.com) connect Bloemfontein and Jo'burg (R1200), Cape Town (from R900) and Durban (R2200). **Mango** (☏086 100 1234; www.flymango.com) also flies between Bloem and Cape Town (from R800). Book online or with **STA Travel** (☏051-444 6062; bloemfontein@statravel.co.za; Mimosa Mall).

A taxi from the airport (there's often only one available) to the city centre is a standard R180.

Bus & Minibus Taxi

Long-distance buses leave from the tourist centre on Park Rd. **Translux** (☏0861 589 282; www.translux.co.za), **Greyhound** (☏083 915 9000; www.greyhound.co.za) and **Intercape** (☏0861 287 287; www.intercape.co.za) run daily buses to the following:

» Cape Town (R475, 12½ hours)

» East London (R320, eight hours)

» Jo'burg/Pretoria (R275, 5½ hours)

» Port Elizabeth (R325, nine hours)

Greyhound also has a daily service to Durban (R410, 9½ hours).

Most minibus taxis leave from opposite the train station and head to Maseru, Lesotho (R80, three hours), Kimberley (R90, four hours) and Jo'burg (R150, six hours). There's usually at least one daily, but times vary.

A new multimillion-rand minibus-taxi stand was due to open in 2012 but protests from taxi drivers about its accessibility meant that it wasn't in use at the time of research.

Train

The *Algoa* runs three times weekly via Bloemfontein between Jo'burg (R250, seven hours) and Port Elizabeth (R260, 13 hours). The *Amatola* runs three times weekly via Bloemfontein on the run between Jo'burg and East London (R250, 13 hours). See **Shosholoza Meyl** (☏011-774 4555, 0860 008 888; www.shosholozameyl.co.za) for more details.

Northern Free State

The area around Parys in the far north is the most interesting part of this region. Here you'll find the Vredefort Dome, one of South Africa's seven Unesco World Heritage Sites. The pretty area of rolling hills offers a growing number of hiking, mountain-biking and fishing opportunities. The small towns around here are decidedly un-touristy, rural enclaves.

PARYS & VREDEFORT DOME AREA
☏056 / POP 44,000
Parys is is a small, vibrant town that's handy for visiting Vredefort Dome, an area of hills created by the impact of a gigantic meteorite two billion years ago. Vredefort, measuring over 200km in diameter, is the oldest and largest meteorite impact site on earth.

The Parys area is a growing adventure-sport hub and there are opportunities to try white-water rafting, fly-fishing and mountain biking. Otter's Haunt (☏056-818 1814; www.otters.co.za; self-catering cottage per person from R280; @☎🐕) can arrange all of the above. It also has accommodation available just out of town, either in rustic bush cabins or a spacious, three-bedroom self-catering house with its own pool.

O's Restaurant (☏056-811 3683; www.osrestaurant.co.za; 1 de Villiers St; mains R60-120; ⊙11am-10pm Wed-Sat, 11am-3pm Sun) is a long-running favourite, set in a gorgeous garden locale right by the river. The menu offers something for everyone – from vegie pastas to mussel fettuccine and a fine selection of tender beef steaks.

For other activities and places to stay, contact the helpful Parys Info Centre (☏056-811 4000; www.parys.info; 30 Water St; ⊙8am-5pm Mon-Fri, 9am-1pm Sat & Sun). You need your own wheels to reach Parys.

Eastern Highlands

Bumped up against the wild and rugged mountains that guard Lesotho's border, this is the most beautiful portion of the Free

DON'T MISS

SENTINEL HIKING TRAIL

The most famous of the hiking trails in the area is the 10km Sentinel Hiking Trail (⌨ bookings 083 956 0325; admission R25), which commences in Free State and ends in KwaZulu-Natal. The trail starts at the Sentinel car park, at an altitude of 2540m, and runs for 4km to the top of the Drakensberg plateau, where the average height is 3000m. It's about a two-hour ascent that makes use of a chain ladder running up over a set of sheer rocks. Those who find the ladder frightening can take the route up The Gully, which emerges at Beacon Buttress. The reward for the steep ascent is majestic mountain scenery and the opportunity to climb Mont-aux-Sources (3282m).

State and well worth exploring. The region boasts sandstone monoliths towering above undulating golden fields, the fantastic Golden Gate Highlands National Park and South Africa's coolest country-village art destination, trendy Clarens.

GOLDEN GATE HIGHLANDS NATIONAL PARK

Right before the darkness erases the remaining flecks of colour from the sky, something magical happens in Golden Gate Highlands National Park (⌨ 058-255 0000; www.sanparks.org/parks/golden_gate; adult/child R120/60). The jagged sandstone outcroppings fronting the foothills of the wild, maroon-hued Maluti Mountains glow golden in the dying light; lemon-yellow rays silhouette a lone kudu standing still in a sea of mint-green grasses before the sky explodes in a fiery collision of purple and red.

The park might not boast any of the Big Five, but it does feature fantastic nightly sunsets. There are quite a few animals in the park, including grey rheboks, blesboks, elands, oribis, Burchell's zebras, jackals, baboons and numerous bird species. The park is popular with hikers on long treks, but there are also shorter walking trails. You can buy entry permits at the park reception.

The main road through the park is a public road and entrance fees do not apply if you're just driving through.

◉ Sights & Activities

Basotho Cultural Village CULTURAL VILLAGE
(tours R30; ◷ 8am-4.30pm Mon-Fri, 8am-5pm Sat & Sun) Within the park you'll find the small Basotho Cultural Village. It's essentially an open-air museum, peopled by actors depicting various aspects of traditional Sotho life. A two-hour guided hiking trail (R60 per person) explores medicinal and other plants, and a rock-art site. You can stay in two-person, self-catering *rondavels* (R700), but bring your own food. To get a truer feel for how most Sotho live, cross the border into Lesotho.

Rhebok Hiking Trail HIKING
This circular, 33km trail (R135 per person) is a two-day trek and offers a great way to see the park. The trail starts at the Glen Reenen Rest Camp and on the second day the track climbs up to the park's highest point (2732m). The trail is limited to 18 people and must be booked through the park board in advance.

⌂ Sleeping

Glen Reenen Rest Camp CAMPGROUND $$
(⌨ 058-255 1000; 2-person campsites R180, 2-person rondavel from R740) This place is conveniently located on the main road, and has well-maintained chalets and campsites by the river. A shop sells basic supplies.

Golden Gate Hotel HOTEL $$
(⌨ 058-255 0000; r from R1025, 2-person chalet from R980) In the heart of the park, this stately old lodge offers self-catering chalets and upmarket rooms. It recently underwent an extensive renovation that added more rooms and modern interiors. There is a restaurant, bar and coffee shop.

ℹ Getting There & Away

Rte 712, a sealed road, crosses the park. Minibus taxis running between Bethlehem and Harrismith, via Clarens and Phuthaditjhaba, travel through the park.

CLARENS
⌨ 058 / POP 4500
The jewel of the Free State, Clarens is one of those places you stumble upon expecting little, then find yourself talking about long after you depart. Set against a backdrop of craggy limestone rocks, green hills, spun-gold fields and the magnificent Maluti Mountains, this town of whitewashed buildings, art galleries and quiet shady streets is a bucolic country retreat.

RUSTLER'S VALLEY

To journey into the wildly beautiful heart of nowhere, ditch the pavement and head down brown, dusty byways to random oases scattered amid this rough-and-ready countryside. The remote Rustler's Valley is located off Rte 26 between Fouriesburg and Ficksburg and is home to the enchanting Franshoek Mountain Lodge (☑051-933 2828; www.franshoek.co.za; r per person with half board R580; @☎). A working farm with comfortable sandstone cottages in its garden, an African steam hut and great views of the valley, it emits a lovely country charm.

Clarens Xtreme (☑082 563 6242; www. clarensxtreme.co.za; Sias Oosthuizen St) is a one-stop shop for all things outdoors. Popular activities include quad-biking, white-water rafting (R450/650 half/full day) and mountain biking (trails R50 to R100).

The town's best budget accommodation option, Clarens Inn & Backpackers (☑082 377 3621; www.clarensinn.com; 93 Van Reenan St; campsites R80, teepee R100, dm R120, self-catering cottage per person from R180), offers single-sex dorms and basic doubles in a tranquil locale, pushed up against a mountain.

Patcham Place (☑058-256 1017; www.pat champlace.co.za; 262 Church St; s/d with breakfast from R550/880, reduced rates on weekdays) is a good central option offering better value in this range than competitors around town. Its airy rooms have giant windows and fab views from the balconies.

Valley Cats (Market St; mains R35-50) serves wraps, salads and excellent breakfasts under a shady tree overlooking the main square.

Clarens Tourism Centre (☑082 963 3398, 058-256 1542; www.clarenstourism.co.za; Market St; ☺8am-5pm Mon-Thu, 8am-6pm Fri, 8am-4pm Sat & Sun) can help arrange activities and accommodation. Guesthouses get booked up way in advance for the annual Clarens Craft Beer Festival, held in the Village Sq over the last weekend in February.

There are sporadic minibus taxis to Bethlehem and Harrismith from Clarens, and no set departure point; head towards the outskirts of town and ask around.

FOURIESBURG
☑058
Entirely surrounded by wild, craggy mountains, Fouriesburg occupies a magnificent spot just 12km north of the Caledonspoort border crossing to Lesotho. Two nearby peaks, Snijmanshoek and Visierskerf, are the highest in the Free State. You'll also find the largest sandstone overhang in the southern hemisphere, Salpeterkrans, around here. An eerie example of wind erosion, the area is considered sacred and used by local tribes for ancestral worship.

About 11km outside Fouriesburg, and just 800m from the Lesotho border, Camelroc Guest Farm (☑058-223 0368; www. camelroc.co.za; campsites R170, s/d with breakfast R400/600, chalets from R660) sits in a spectacular location against a camel-shaped sandstone outcrop with mountain views. It's a great rustic retreat, offering a variety of sleeping options.

FICKSBURG
☑051
Nestled against the purple-hued Maluti Mountains on the banks of the Caledon River, Ficksburg is particularly spectacular in winter when dollops of snow cover the craggy peaks.

The village is the centre of the Free State's cherry industry. There's a Cherry Festival (www.cherryfestival.co.za) in November but September and October are the best times to see the trees in bloom.

African-flavoured Imperani Guest House & Coffee Shop (☑051-933 3606; www.imperan iguesthouse.co.za; 53 McCabe Rd; s/d with breakfast from R395/595; ☎) has a country-cottage vibe, with spotless, modern rooms in expansive, beautifully maintained grassy grounds scattered with cherry trees and fountains.

GAUTENG

Gauteng, formerly the Boer Republic of Transvaal, remains the pulse of the South African nation.

Johannesburg (Jo'burg) is the country's largest and most happening city, where gold was discovered in the late 19th century and where fortunes are still made and lost. Gauteng's provincial capital is still riding on the back of the World Cup in 2010, and the creative and inventive spirit is alive in the cafes, galleries and clubs popping up across the rejuvenated city streets. The wealth divide is stark, though, and it can be difficult to reconcile the glistening wealth with the sprawling townships.

The political centre of Pretoria, a short drive north, is decidedly less urbane but is somewhat grander with its stately buildings and jacaranda-lined streets.

In the World Heritage–listed Cradle of Humankind, in a vast valley full of caves and fossils, you can ponder three million years of humanity's existence.

Johannesburg

📞 011 / POP 5.7 MILLION

Johannesburg, more commonly known as Jo'burg or Jozi, is a rapidly changing city and the vibrant heart of South Africa. The city is flourishing. Its centre is smartening up and new loft apartments and office developments are being constructed at a rapid pace. The cultural district of Newtown, with its theatres, restaurants, museums and jazz clubs, is livelier than ever. Other inner-city suburbs like Braamfontein and Doornfontein have continued to gentrify since Jo'burg hosted the World Cup in 2010 and now house the coolest clubs, bars and cultural spaces.

A thriving black middle class has risen from the ashes of apartheid, both in the suburbs and in the famous township of Soweto. However, the wealth divide remains stark. The affluenza of Rosebank and Sandton breeds discontent in desperately poor, neighbouring townships such as Alexandra and Diepsloot. Politicians stagnate while crime continues to disrupt daily life.

Still, Jo'burg is an incredibly friendly, unstuffy city and there's a lot to see here, from sobering reminders of the country's recent past at the Apartheid Museum to the progressive streets of Melville.

The most-visited areas are Newtown to the south and university-oriented Braamfontein to the north. While the city centre is OK during the day, it pays to keep your wits about you when you're out and about.

History

It all started in 1886 when traces of gold were discovered on the Witwatersrand. Mining quickly took hold and within three years Jo'burg had become Southern Africa's metropolis. It was a boisterous city where fortune-seekers of all colours lived it up in the city's bars and brothels. The Boers, the Transvaal government and the president, Paul Kruger, regarded these multicultural fortune-seekers with deep distrust. Laws were passed to effectively ensure that only Boers had the right to vote, and laws were also passed to control the movement of blacks.

Under increasing pressure in the countryside, thousands of blacks moved to the city in search of jobs and from the 1930s onwards, vast squatter camps developed around the outskirts of Jo'burg. These camps became well-organised cities, later becoming known as townships. Since the end of apartheid, the black townships have been integrated into the municipal government system, the city centre is alive with hawkers and street stalls, and the suburbs are becoming increasingly multiracial.

⊙ Sights & Activities

CITY CENTRE

Walk around Jo'burg's concrete downtown streets and you'd hardly guess that the city was once an art-deco showpiece, because so few good examples remain. Sights aside, the energy generated by the thousands of hawkers, hair-braiders and pungent street food give the centre an urban atmosphere that you won't find in the northern suburbs, and that alone makes it worth a visit.

There are plenty of colonial-era buildings that are worth a look: the defunct Rissik St Post Office (Map p444; Rissik St) and City Hall (Map p444; cnr Rissik & Market Sts), now a sometime concert venue, are among the finest. The Mandela & Tambo Law Offices

---

DON'T MISS

LILIESLEAF FARM

The secret headquarters of the ANC (African National Congress) during the 1960s, Liliesleaf (Map p440; 📞 011-803 7882/3/4; www.liliesleaf.co.za; 7 George Ave, Rivonia; 2hr guided tour adult/child R60/35; ☺ 8.30am-5pm Mon-Fri, 9am-4pm Sat-Sun) reopened as an excellent museum in 2008. Sitting in the northern suburbs, it tells the story of South Africa's liberation struggle through a series of high-tech, interactive exhibits.

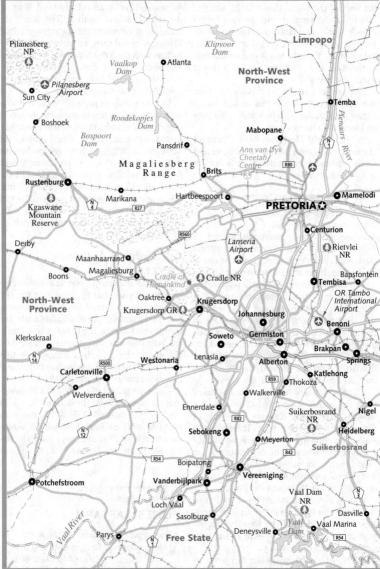

(Map p444; 25 Fox St, Chancellor House) offer a slice of more recent history.

Johannesburg Art Gallery (Map p444; ☎011-725 3130; Joubert Park; ☺10am-5pm Tue-Sun) regularly rotates its large collection, which includes European and South African

paintings and traditional African objects. It's on the Noord St side of Joubert Park (the park itself a no-go area).

For a view of Jo'burg from on high, take the lift to the **Top of Africa** (Map p444; ☎011-308 1331; 50th fl, Carlton Centre, 152 Commissioner

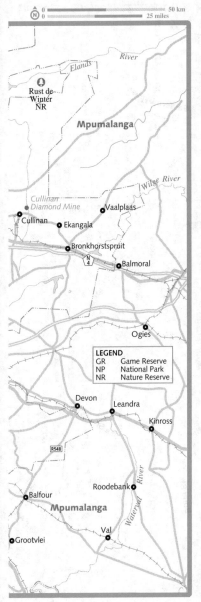

p444; Jeppe St) (named after South Africa's first female trade unionist), bordered by the Jazz Walk of Fame, a Hollywood Boulevard–style walkway that pays tribute to South Africa's most influential jazz musicians.

FREE **Museum Africa** MUSEUM
(Map p444; ☎011-833 5624; museumafrica@ joburg.org.za; 121 Bree St; ⓢ9am-5pm Tue-Sun) This museum is housed in the impressive old Bree St fruit market, next to the Market Theatre complex. The thoughtful curatorship features exhibitions on the Treason Trials of 1956–61, the development of South African music and the history of housing in the city.

SAB World of Beer MUSEUM
(Map p444; ☎011-836 4900; www.worldofbeer. co.za; 15 President St; admission & tour R55; ⓢ10am-6pm Tue-Sat) Take a 1½-hour jaunt through the history of beer. Taste traditional sorghum beer, sample a cheeky half-pint at a re-created Victorian pub, then nail two free pints in the bar afterwards. You even get a World of Beer glass keepsake.

Nelson Mandela Bridge BRIDGE
(Map p444) Opened two days after Mandela's 85th birthday in 2003, this cable-stayed bridge is an icon of the rejuvenated city centre.

CONSTITUTION HILL & AROUND
Inspiring Constitution Hill (Map p444; ☎011-381 3100; www.constitutionhill.org.za; Kotze St; tours adult/child R50/20; ⓢ9am-5pm Mon-Fri, to 3pm Sat) is one of the city's most important attractions. Tours explore various exhibits within the ramparts of the Old Fort, largely focusing on Number Four, the notorious apartheid prison that once held Mandela, and the Women's Gaol. A more cheerful section of the tour visits the Constitutional Court, a very real symbol of the changing South Africa with cases heard in all 11 official languages.

The nearby Hillbrow neighbourhood, dominated by the 269m Telkom Tower (Map p440; Goldreich St), was the nation's first 'Grey Area' – a zone where blacks and whites could live side by side. Today, the area has a reputation for lawlessness and violent crime and is best avoided unless you're with an extremely savvy guide.

Located in the east of the city, Maboneng Precinct (☎010-007 0080; www.mabonengpre cinct.com; Fox St) is worth a visit, primarily for

St; adult/child R20/10; ⓢ9am-6pm Mon-Sat, 9am-2pm Sun).

NEWTOWN
Rejuvenation has made Newtown the most appealing section of the downtown area. The centrepiece is Mary Fitzgerald Square (Map

Johannesburg

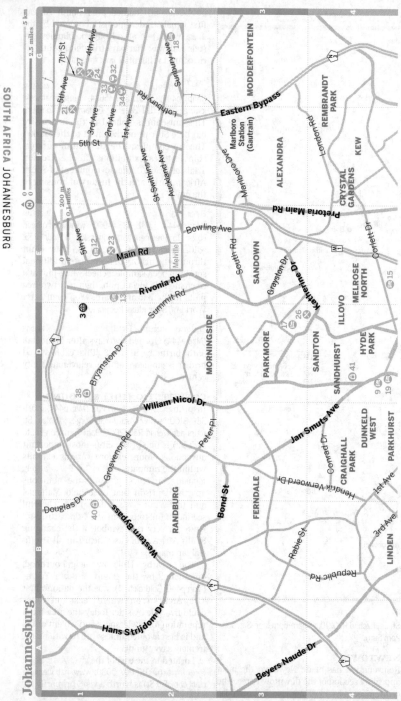

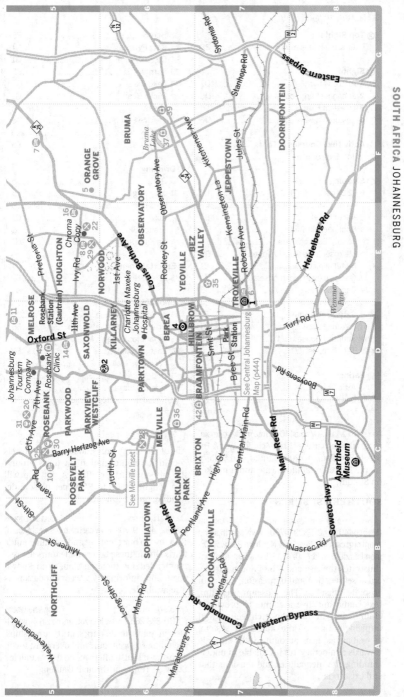

Johannesburg

Arts on Main (Map p440; http://marketonmain.co.za; admission free; ☺10am-4pm Tue, Wed & Fri-Sun, to 8pm Thu), a retail, studio and gallery space. There's a fabulous cafe and a market on Sunday.

SOUTHERN SUBURBS

TOP CHOICE / **Apartheid Museum**   MUSEUM
(Map p440; ☎011-309 4700; www.apartheidmuseum.org; cnr Gold Reef Rd & Northern Parkway, Ormonde; adult/child R60/45; ☺9am-5pm Tue-Sun) Illustrates the rise and fall of South Africa's era of segregation and oppression, and is an absolute must-see. The museum uses film, text, audio and live accounts to provide a chilling insight into the architecture and implementation of the apartheid system, as well as inspiring accounts of the struggle towards democracy. It's invaluable in understanding the inequalities and tensions that still exist today.

☞ Tours

All of Jo'burg's guesthouses and hostels should have information on tours around the city and further afield. A day trip will cost roughly R500 to R800 per person, depending on the itinerary.

Cashan Tours   CULTURAL TOURS
(☎082 491 9370; www.cashantours.weebly.com) Run by Jo'burg native and wildlife guide Chris Green, these tailor-made tours are recommended for their passion, deep knowledge and informality. Accommodation is also available.

Imbizo Tours   TOWNSHIP TOURS
(☎011-838 2667; www.imbizotours.co.za) Specialises in tours to Jo'burg's gritty townships, including *shebeen* tours and overnight township stays. It also offers a one-day Mandela's Struggle Trail tour through Gauteng.

Jozi Experience   CITY TOURS
(Map p440; ☎011-022 8397; www.joziexperience.
co.za; 27 10th Ave, Orange Grove) Offers a one-
on-one, personalised way to see the city.
Tours include an afternoon walk through
downtown Jo'burg, or a night out at the
city's coolest bars and most obscure shopping spots.

🛏 Sleeping

Most of the tourist accommodation is concentrated in the northern suburbs. Melville and
Norwood provide the best options if you like
to walk to bars and restaurants. Places in the
northern suburbs tend to be quite spread out,
with no entertainment or shopping options
on their doorstep. The city centre is slowly
improving its tourist infrastructure, but there
is still only a handful of decent options.

CITY CENTRE & NEWTOWN
If you do decide to stay in the city centre,
be mindful that it's not a good idea to walk
around at night.

TOP CHOICE 12 Decades Hotel   BOUTIQUE HOTEL $$
(Map p440; ☎011-026 5601; www.12decadeshotel.
co.za; 286 Fox St, Doornfontein; s/d from R620/820;
P🅿🌢@) This terrific concept hotel in the
heart of the Maboneng Precinct has a dozen
7th-floor rooms (the rest are residential),
each one inspired by an era in the city's his-
tory. Sunday nights see neighbourhood par-
ties on the rooftop.

Hotel Lamunu   BOUTIQUE HOTEL $$
(Map p444; ☎011-242 8600; www.lamunu.co.za; 90
De Korte St, Braamfontein; r from R650; P🌢🛜)
This boutique business hotel has 60 citrus-
coloured rooms with bathrooms. The loca-
tion is spot-on – across the road from Narina
Trogon (p446).

MELVILLE & NORWOOD
Sunbury House   GUESTHOUSE $
(Map p440; ☎011-726 1114; www.sunburyhouse.
com; 24 Sunbury Ave; s/d incl breakfast from
R250/315; P@🌢) The best-value budget accommodation in Melville has a variety of
rooms, all with quirky furniture, wooden
floorboards and bright colour schemes. The
owners also have a cheap backpacker place
(singles/doubles R150/250) in nearby West-
dene.

TOP CHOICE Motel Mipichi   BOUTIQUE HOTEL $$
(Map p440; ☎011-726 8844; www.motelmipichi.
co.za; 35 4th Ave; s/d incl breakfast from R520/780;

P@) An alternative to the traditional
Melville guesthouse experience, Mipichi is a
minimalist delight, its four calming rooms
sporting walk-through showers adjoining
private courtyards.

Ascot Hotel   BOUTIQUE HOTEL $$
(Map p440; ☎011-483 3371; www.ascothotel.co.za;
59 Grant Ave; r incl breakfast from R860; P🅿@)
The Ascot has successfully filled Norwood's
'High Street' hotel vacuum. It's a stylish bou-
tique business hotel with an adjacent day
spa offering generous discounts for guests.
Rooms are smallish, but well presented.

NORTHERN SUBURBS
Backpackers Ritz   BACKPACKERS $
(Map p440; ☎011-325 7125; www.backpackers-ritz.
co.za; 1A North Rd, Dunkeld West; dm/s/d without
bathroom R125/250/375; P@🌢) The rooms
are decent enough at the most authoritative
of the city's hostels, aside from the pokey
dorms and the odd dampish 'cave' room.
There are excellent shared facilities, a vibrant social scene and beautiful views.

Joburg Backpackers   BACKPACKERS $
(Map p440; ☎011-888 4742; www.joburgbackpack
ers.com; 14 Umgwezi Rd, Emmerentia; dm R110, r
with/without bathroom R440/330, f R660; P🅿@)
This new hostel in the leafy streets of Emmerentia has a range of well-appointed
rooms and a relaxed country feel. Greenside's
eateries and bars are a 10-minute stroll away.

TOP CHOICE Oasis Luxury
Guesthouse   GUESTHOUSE $$
(Map p440; ☎011-807 4351; www.oasisguesthouse.
co.za; 29 Homestead Rd, Rivonia; s/d incl breakfast
from R950/1150; P🅿@🌢) The lush gardens
at this delightful suburban hideaway feature
a good-sized pool. Rooms vary in size and
price, but all are stylish and furnished with
art from different periods.

Melrose Place Guest Lodge   GUESTHOUSE $$
(Map p440; ☎011-442 5231; 12A North St, Melrose;
s/d incl breakfast R1150/1300; P🅿@🌢) This
very quiet and secluded country-style home
is perfect for those who crave space and is
well located between Rosebank and Sandton.

Peech Hotel   BOUTIQUE HOTEL $$$
(Map p440; ☎011-537 9797; www.thepeech.co.za;
61 North St, Melrose; r incl breakfast from R2250;
P🅿@🌢) This converted duplex apartment
block is an exercise in African minimalism,
with 16 large rooms sporting one-off sculp-
tures and furnishings. There's a decent gym

Central Johannesburg

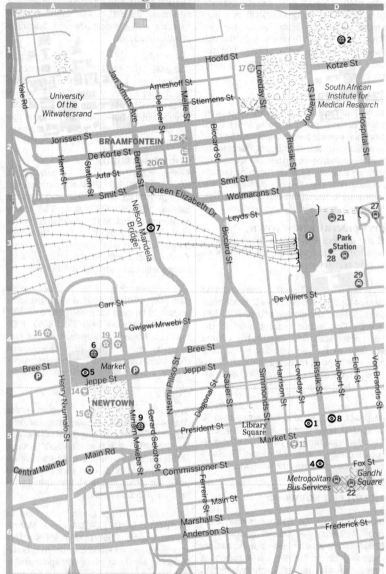

next door and the restaurant boasts an excellent international menu.

Parkwood　BOUTIQUE HOTEL **$$$**
(Map p440; ☑011-880 1748; www.theparkwood.
com; 72 Worcester Rd, Parkwood; r incl breakfast
from R1550; [P][❄][@][☎]) The Parkwood is a

series of separate, narrow, self-contained
buildings. The rooms are all class, thanks to
the interior-designer owner.

Ten Bompas　BOUTIQUE HOTEL **$$$**
(Map p440; ☑011-341 0282; www.tenbompas.com;
10 Bompas Rd, Dunkeld West; ste incl breakfast

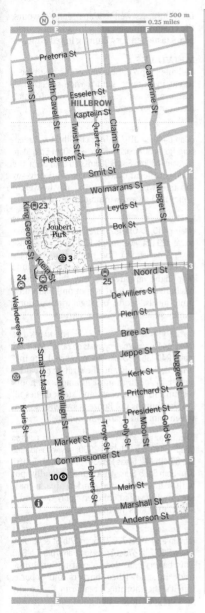

Central Johannesburg

◎ Sights
1	City Hall	D5
2	Constitution Hill	D1
3	Johannesburg Art Gallery	E3
4	Mandela & Tambo Law Offices	D5
5	Mary Fitzgerald Square	A4
6	Museum Africa	A4
7	Nelson Mandela Bridge	B3
8	Rissik St Post Office	D5
9	SAB World of Beer	B5
10	Top of Africa	E5

⊟ Sleeping
11	Hotel Lamunu	B2

⊗ Eating
	Gramadoela's	(see 19)
12	Narina Trogon	B2

⊖ Drinking
13	Guildhall Bar & Restaurant	D5
14	Sophiatown Bar Lounge	A5

✿ Entertainment
15	Bassline	A5
16	Carfax	A4
17	Joburg Theatre	C1
18	Kippies Jazz International	B4
19	Market Theatre	B4

⊜ Shopping
20	Neighbour Goods Market	B2

⊕ Transport
21	Long-Distance Buses Booking Offices	D3
	Metro	(see 28)
22	Metrobus Terminal	D5
23	Minibus Taxis to Bulawayo, Zimbabwe	E2
24	Minibus Taxis to Durban	E3
25	Minibus Taxis to Lesotho, Bloemfontein, Free State	F3
26	Minibus Taxis to Pretoria	E3
27	Minibus Taxis to Upington, Kimberley & Cape Town	D3
28	Shosholoza Meyl	D3
29	Taxis	D3

R3250; P❄@☎) More centrally located than some other top Johannesburg hotels, 'Ten Rooms' is also a pioneer of the boutique tag. Dark wood and savannah hues colour an exquisite private collection of African art. The restaurant is a destination in its own right.

Saxon　　　　　　　　　　　　　HOTEL $$$
(Map p440; ☏011-292 6000; www.thesaxon.com; 36 Saxon Rd, Sandhurst; r incl breakfast from R7500; P❄@☎) The pride of Sandhurst is a palatial suite hotel where Mandela edited his famed memoir. Private elevators, personal attendants and the finest day spa in

the country make the Saxon an otherworldly experience for the 99%.

EASTERN SUBURBS

Mbizi Backpackers   HOSTEL $

(☎011-892 0421; www.mbizi.com; 288 Trichardt Rd; campsites R100, dm R130, d with/without bathroom R350/300; P@☎) Mbizi is a self-contained backpacker joint that's handy for the airport. Simple, colourful dorms and spartan double rooms are on offer.

44 on Livingston Guesthouse   GUESTHOUSE $$

(Map p440; ☎011-485 1156; www.44onlivingston. com; 5 Sandler Rd, Linksfield; s/d incl breakfast from R410/820; P☀@☎) This lovely, small guesthouse near the Johannesburg Golf Course is a good option – it has a beautiful pool and seven tasteful, immaculate rooms.

TOP CHOICE Satyagraha House   GUESTHOUSE $$$

(Map p440; ☎011-485 5928; www.satyagraha house.com; 15 Pine Rd, Orchards; r incl breakfast from R1650; P@) The former home of Mahatma Gandhi, who lived here between 1907 and 1908, has been restored into a serene, innovative guesthouse and museum. Meals are vegetarian.

✖ Eating

Jo'burg is a fabulous city for foodies, especially at the top end. The northern suburbs have the most options, but you'll need wheels to get around. All of Jo'burg's shopping centres have big supermarkets for self-caterers.

NEWTOWN

TOP CHOICE Narina Trogon   AFRICAN $$

(Map p444; ☎011-339 6645; www.narinatrogon. com; 81 De Korte St, Braamfontein; mains R70-140; ⊙ breakfast & lunch Mon, breakfast, lunch & dinner Tue-Sat) Narina Trogon is an inner-city eatery that sources both local produce and local designers to sustain its fine sense of taste. Expect dishes along the lines of grilled steak with camembert and polenta or butternut and sweet potato curry.

Gramadoela's   AFRICAN $$

(Map p444; ☎011-838 6960; www.gramadoelas. co.za; Bree St, Newtown; mains R70-130; ⊙dinner Mon, lunch & dinner Tue-Sat; ✲) Grama's is a hit with the glitterati and visiting dignitaries, and makes a perfect all-in-one night out

in Jo'burg. As well as Cape Malay flavours, the creamy mussels are a hit and, of course, pears taste better swimming in red wine.

MELVILLE

Melville's hip 7th St is one of the best places to eat in Jo'burg, with a wide selection of restaurants and cafes, almost all of which have outdoor seating.

Service Station   CAFE $

(Map p440; ☎011-726 1701; cnr 9th St & Rustenburg Rd; light meals R45-65; ⊙7.30am-6pm Mon-Fri, 8am-4.30pm Sat, 8.30am-3pm Sun) Join the queues of local office workers and drive-by hipsters who swear by the pay-by-weight policy and award-winning coffee here.

Lucky Bean   AFRICAN $$

(Map p440; ☎011-482 5572; www.luckybeantree. co.za; 129 1st Ave; mains R60-130; ⊙breakfast, lunch & dinner; ✎) The restaurant formerly known as Soulsa may have a different name (copyright, apparently) but the recipe is unchanged. The food is spot on – light anytime meals, loads of vegetarian options, gamey stews, and creative starters.

Catz Pyjamas   INTERNATIONAL $$

(Map p440; www.catzpyjamas.co.za; 12 Main Rd; mains R40-130; ⊙24hr) The nocturnal, the inebriated, the shady and the strange all eat together in Jo'burg's most infamous all-hours restaurant. Pizza, pasta and steak dishes all get the thumbs up. Booze is switched off between 4am and 10am – an outrage!

Bambanani   TAPAS $$

(Map p440; ☎011-482 2900; www.bambanini. biz; 85 4th Ave; tapas R25-30; ⊙9am-8pm Tue-Fri, 8am-8pm Sat & Sun; ✋) A family-friendly spot with a huge deck and garden area, a massive, multilevelled children's play den and a superlative kids' menu.

De La Creme   CAFE $$

(Map p440; ☎011-726 7716; cnr 7th St & 4th Ave; mains R60-70; ⊙7am-5pm Mon, 7am-7pm Tue-Sat) This bakery-cafe does a roaring lunchtime trade in sandwiches, burgers and bobotie, but it's the morning bread run that really gets up your nose – in a good way.

Nuno's   PUB $$

(Map p440; ☎011-482 6990; 4 7th St; mains R50-100; ⊙8am-late) Less about the food – including decent-enough steak and chips or grilled fish – and more about the beer-sodden carpet, fiery banter, surly staff and kick-arse location at the left-leaning ventricle of 7th St.

NORWOOD

Zahava's   MIDDLE EASTERN $
(Map p440; ☐011-728 6511; 47A Grant Ave; snacks R15-30; ☺breakfast & lunch; ✦) There's good live 'world' music on weekends, strong coffee and fragrant hookahs at this Middle Eastern hang-out, which serves ethnic staples and snack-size *zivas* (flatbread) and *latkes* (potato fritters).

Barrio   KOSHER $$
(Map p440; ☐011-728 2577; 80 Grant Ave; mains R90-170; ☺lunch & dinner Sun-Thu, lunch Fri, dinner Sat; ✦) Rub shoulders with rabbis and Jewish families in this welcoming kosher restaurant, which fills up quickly most evenings.

ShahiKhana   INDIAN $$
(Map p440; ☐011-728 8157; 80 Grant Ave; mains R55-70; ☺lunch & dinner; ✦🖊) Super tasty and fiery North Indian cuisine, with plenty of vegetarian and fish dishes on offer.

NORTHERN SUBURBS
The many eating options in these affluent suburbs are centred on the huge shopping malls that form the core of northern-suburbs society.

Not far from Melville, around the junction of Gleneagles and Greenway Rds in Greenside, is a variety of restaurants and trendy bars.

Attic   INTERNATIONAL $$
(Map p440; ☐011-880 6102; 24 4th Ave, Parkhurst; mains R70-130; ☺lunch & dinner) Patrons at this quality corner restaurant happily spill from the homely interiors onto the street seats. Try dishes like crab fettuccini and sparkling wine and pea risotto. There's an attached tapas and cocktail bar, while the same crew also runs the Office, a cool speakeasy around the corner in Greenside.

Karma   INDIAN $$
(Map p440; ☐011-646 8555; cnr Barry Hertzog Ave & Gleneagles Rd, Greenside; mains R60-90; ☺dinner Mon, lunch & dinner Tue-Sat, lunch Sun; 🖊) Regularly voted best this and top that, Karma's interior feels like New Age Indian with a Hollywood makeover. The mostly north Indian offerings are flavoursome and generously proportioned, with loads of interesting vegie options.

Lekgotla   AFRICAN $$$
(Map p440; ☐011-884 9555; www.lekgotla.com; Nelson Mandela Sq, Sandton; mains R90-160; ☺lunch & dinner; ✦) Set beneath traditional huts on the edge of Nelson Mandela Sq, the 'Meeting Place' provides a good sample of the diversity of the continent's cuisine, including Ethiopian coffee steak, Nile crocodile curry and South African staples like mealie pap (cornmeal porridge) and *chakalaka* (a spicy relish).

🍷 Drinking

Jo'burg has an ever-evolving bar scene, with options including Bohemian haunts, chic cocktail lounges and conservative wine bars. Newtown has a few lively places, but much of the action is in the northern suburbs, particularly around Melville, Greenside and Rosebank.

CITY CENTRE & NEWTOWN

Guildhall Bar & Restaurant   PUB
(Map p444; ☐011-833 1770; 88 Market St, Marshalltown; mains R45-70; ☺lunch & dinner) City of Gold fortunes have been squandered in Jo'burg's oldest bar, established c 1888. This is one of the CBD's best meeting places and it's completely unpretentious. DJs perform most weekends and Portuguese-style pub food is available.

Sophiatown Bar Lounge   BAR
(Map p444; ☐011-836 5999; www.sophiatownbar lounge.co.za; 1 Central Pl, cnr Jeppe & Henry Nxumalo Sts, Newtown; ☺8.30am-11.30pm Sun-Thu, to 2am Fri & Sat) Sophiatown's township spirit is celebrated in one of Newtown's most enjoyable venues. There's live music (mostly jazz) on Wednesday and Saturday nights and hearty food is served. There's another site on 7th St, Melville.

MELVILLE

Six   COCKTAIL BAR
(Map p440; ☐011-482 8306; 7th St) Fabulous artwork, a soft orange and red colour scheme, iconic reggae, and soul and house music at a level conducive to hearing key questions: want another drink?

XaiXai Lounge   PUB
(Map p440; ☐011-482 6990; 7th St, shop 7 Melville Gardens) Air your grievances loudly and proudly in this left-leaning Mozambican pub that has the busiest tables on the street, all day and night long. A half-kilo of prawns is R120.

Ratz Bar
COCKTAIL BAR

(Map p440; 9B 7th St) Ratz is a tiny cocktail bar that cranks the '80s rock and cheesy pop. There's always a crowd for cheap cocktails.

Trance Sky
BAR

(Map p440; 77th St) A Durban-style open-front music bar that plays deep, dark coastal breaks and grimy, oily techno. Wash down good bar snacks with cheap cocktails.

NORTHERN SUBURBS

Gin
COCKTAIL BAR

(Map p440; ☑011-486 2404; 12 Gleneagles Rd, Greenside) Cocktails are the pièce de résistance here, and house and hip hop keep the very young crowd happy.

Jolly Roger Pub
PUB

(Map p440; ☑011-442 3954; 10 4th Ave, Parkhurst; pizza R50-80; ☺11am-midnight) This two-storey English-style pub on the edge of burgeoning 4th Ave is very good. Upstairs is our favourite pizza in the city and a fabulous view of the busy street below.

☆ Entertainment

The best entertainment guide is in Friday's *Mail & Guardian*. 'Tonight' in the daily *Star* is also good. For bookings by credit card, contact Computicket (☑011-915 8000; www. computicket.com), which has a booth at Park Station.

Cinemas

Huge cinemas are found across Jo'burg, with one in almost every shopping centre.

Ster-Kinekor
CINEMA

(☑central bookings 082 16789; www.sterkinekor. co.za) Has the widest distribution of multiplexes, with screens in the Fourways, Westgate, Eastgate, Sandton and Rosebank malls.

Live Music & Nightclubs

The city is home to a thriving live-music scene, especially across the jazz-tipped and electronic spectrum.

Johannesburg Philharmonic Orchestra
CLASSICAL

(☑011-789 2733; www.jpo.co.za) The city's orchestra stages a regular circuit of concerts at venues such as Wits University and City Hall. Call, or check its website, for the latest program.

Kippies Jazz International
JAZZ

(Map p444; ☑011-833 3316; Margaret Mcingana St, Newtown; ☺Thu-Sat) Once known as the 'sad man of jazz', Kippies Moeketsi would have a smile on his face if he could see what the city authorities have done to his classic jazz haunt. Look for Kippies' bronze statue out the front.

Bassline
LIVE MUSIC

(Map p444; ☑011-838 9145; http://bassline.co.za; 10 Henry Nxumalo St, Newtown; admission R60-170; ☺6pm-late) This is still the most respected live-music venue in Jo'burg, covering the full range of international musicianship and more popular reggae, rock and hip-hop styles.

Carfax
CLUB

(Map p444; 39 Pim St, Newtown; admission R70; ☺9pm-late) They still roll up to this Newtown beat factory for progressive/deep house and hip-hop parties, and the more interesting international acts.

Theatres

Market Theatre
THEATRE

(Map p444; ☑011-832 1641; www.markettheatre. co.za; Margaret Mcingana St, Newtown) This venue has three live-theatre spaces (Main, Laager and Barney Simon Theatres) as well as galleries and a cafe. There is always some interesting theatre, from sharply critical contemporary plays to musicals and stand-up comedy – check the program in the *Mail & Guardian* entertainment section.

Joburg Theatre
THEATRE

(Map p444; ☑011-877 6800; www.joburgthe atre.com; Loveday St, Braamfontein) This leading theatre hosts mainstream local and international acts.

🛍 Shopping
Arts & Crafts

TOP CHOICE Neighbour Goods Market
MARKET

(Map www.neighbourgoodsmarket.co.za; cnr Juta & de Beer Sts, Braamfontein; ☺9am-3pm Sat) Cape Town's acclaimed community market has come to Braamfontein, with artisan purveyors and their foodie fans scoffing on healthy brunches, craft beer and stiff coffee.

Rosebank Rooftop Market
CRAFTS

(Map p440; www.craft.co.za; Cradock Ave, Rosebank; ☺9am-5pm Sun) This is a favourite place to shop for traditional carvings, beadwork, jewellery, books and fertility dolls.

It's held in Rosebank Mall's multilevel car park.

Bryanston Organic Market   MARKET
(Map p440; www.bryanstonorganicmarket.co.za; Culross Rd, Bryanston; ☺9am-3pm Thu & Sat) Arts and crafts are on offer here but the main attraction is the splendid organic produce.

Bruma Lake Market World   CRAFTS
(Map p440; ☎011-622 9648; Observatory Rd, Bruma) By Bruma Lake, this place sells a wide range of crafts and cheap electronics, and loads of kitsch.

Malls
Jo'burg prides itself on its malls jammed with Western consumer goods. They are as much a wealthy white habitat as a place to go shopping.

44 Stanley Avenue   MALL
(Map p440; ☎011-482 1082; www.44stanley.co.za; Stanley Ave, Milpark) 44 Stanley is the antithesis of consumer tack and is a blueprint for future mall development. It's in a previously disused building and features only local designers and interesting restaurants.

Oriental Plaza   MALL
(Map p440; ☎011-838 6752; www.orientalplaza. co.za; Bree St, Fordsburg; ☺9am-5pm Mon-Fri, 8.30am-3pm Sat; ☎) A bustling collection of mostly Indian-owned stores selling everything from spices to cheap watches to cookware. If you get peckish, there are plenty of stalls selling samosas, sweets and other goodies.

ⓘ Information

Emergency
AIDS Line (☎0800 012 322)
Fire (☎10111)
Police (☎10111; Main Rd, Headquarters)

Internet Access
Chroma Copy (☎011-483 2320; per hr R30; ☺8.30am-6pm Mon-Thu, to 5pm Fri, to 1pm Sat)

Medical Services
Charlotte Maxeke Johannesburg Hospital (☎011-488 4911; M1/Jubilee Rd, Parktown) Jo'burg's main public hospital.
Rosebank Clinic (☎011-328 0500; 14 Sturdee Ave, Rosebank; ☺7am-10pm) A private hospital in the northern suburbs, with casualty, GP and specialist services.

Money
There are banks with ATMs and exchange facilities at every commercial centre. American Express and Rennies Travel (an agent for Thomas Cook) have branches at the airport and in major malls.

Post
Main Post Office (Jeppe St; ☺8.30am-4.30pm Mon-Fri, to noon Sat) Has a poste restante service.

Safe travel
Pay careful attention to your personal security in Jo'burg. Daylight muggings in the city centre and other inner suburbs, notably Hillbrow, do happen and you must be on your guard. We've also heard of incidents in the suburban underpasses leading out of Park Station. Don't walk around central Jo'burg at night – if you arrive after dark and don't have a car, catch a taxi.

Crime is a problem, but it is important to put things in perspective: remember that most travellers come and go without incident and that much of the crime afflicts parts of the city you would have little reason to stray into. Take care when using ATMs.

The secret to success is simple: seek local advice, listen to it and remain aware of what's going on around you.

Tourist Information
Gauteng Tourism Authority (☎011-085 2500; www.gauteng.net; 124 Main St; ☺8am-5pm Mon-Fri) You can pick up a copy of the monthly *Go Gauteng* magazine here.
Johannesburg Tourism Company (☎011-214 0700; www.joburgtourism.com; 195 Jan Smuts Ave, ground fl, Grosvenor Cnr, Parktown North; ☺8am-5pm Mon-Fri) There's also an office at Park Station.

ⓘ Getting There & Away

Air
South Africa's major international and domestic airport is **OR Tambo International Airport** (Ortia; ☎011-921 6262; www.airports.co.za).

For regular flights to national and regional destinations try **South African Airways** (SAA; ☎0861 359 722; www.flysaa.com), **SAAirlink** (SAAirlink; ☎0861 606 606; www.flyairlink. com) and **SA Express** (☎011-978 5577; www. saexpress.co.za). All flights can be booked through SAA, which has offices in the airport's domestic and international terminals.

Smaller budget airlines, including **Kulula. com** (www.kulula.com) and **Mango** (☎086 100 1234; www.flymango.com), also link Jo'burg with major destinations and often offer the cheapest fares.

Bus

A number of international bus services leave Jo'burg from the Park Station complex for Botswana, Mozambique and Zimbabwe. The main long-distance bus lines (national and international) also depart from and arrive at the Park Station transit centre, in the northwest corner of the site, where you will also find the booking offices.

Translux/City to City (☎0861 589 282; www.translux.co.za), **Greyhound** (☎083 915 9000; www.greyhound.co.za), **SA Roadlink** (☎011-333 2223; www.saroadlink.co.za) and **Intercape** (☎0861 287 287; www.intercape. co.za) all offer a range of services to/from Jo'burg.

Except for City to City buses, which start in Jo'burg, all services not heading north commence in Pretoria.

The following routes are offered by all the main operators:

» Bloemfontein (R225, six hours)

» Cape Town (R550, 19 hours)

» Durban (R300, eight hours)

» East London (R350, 14 hours)

» Kimberley (R250, 6½ hours)

» Knysna (R585, 17 hours)

» Nelspruit (R255, five hours)

» Port Elizabeth (R350, 16 hours)

City to City runs to Polokwane (R145, 4¼ hours) and Phalaborwa (R255, 7¼ hours).

The **Baz Bus** (☎0861 229 287; www.bazbus. com) connects Jo'burg with the most popular destinations, including Durban, Garden Route and Cape Town. It stops at most of the city's backpackers hostels.

International services Intercape has daily buses to Gaborone, Botswana (R240, seven hours) and Harare (R580, 17 hours). All of the major operators have several daily services to Maputo (R320, nine hours).

Car

All the major car-hire operators have counters at OR Tambo International Airport and at various locations around the city, including Park Station. A satellite navigation device is a recommended investment for tackling Jo'burg's roads; you can rent them at the airport (but nowhere else in the city).

Minibus Taxi

Most minibus taxis use the road-transport interchange in Park Station, over the tracks between the Metro Concourse and Wanderers St. Because of the risk of mugging, it isn't a good idea to go searching for a taxi while carrying your luggage. Store your bags, go down and collect the information, then retrieve your luggage and return in a taxi.

You can also find minibus taxis going towards Cape Town and the Northern Cape on Wanderers St; Bulawayo taxis at the northern end of King George St; Pretoria, Lesotho and Free State destinations on Noord St; and Durban taxis near the corner of Wanderers and Noord Sts. Take extreme care waiting in these areas; you should ideally be accompanied by a local.

Train

Shosholoza Meyl (Map p444; ☎0860 008 888; www.shosholozameyl.co.za) trains run to destinations including the following:

» Bloemfontein (R260, seven hours)

» Cape Town (R560, 25 hours)

» Durban (R290, 13 hours)

» Kimberley (R370, eight hours)

» Komatipoort (economy class R150, 12 hours)

» Musina, on the Zimbabwean border (economy R140, 16 hours)

» Nelspruit (economy class R120, 10 hours)

» Polokwane (economy class R110, nine hours)

» Port Elizabeth (R420, 20 hours)

① Getting Around

When you arrive in Jo'burg, most hostels offer free or cheap pick-up from the airport or Park Station. Guesthouses and hotels will also arrange pick-ups but you'll be charged about the same as a taxi.

To & From the Airport

OR Tambo International Airport is about 25km northeast of central Johannesburg in Kempton Park. The 24-hour **Airport Shuttle** (☎0861 748 8853; www.airportshuttle.co.za) charges

---

GAUTRAIN

The rapid transit **Gautrain** (www. gautrain.co.za) connects the airport, Park Station, Sandton, Rosebank and Pretoria. Trains depart every 15 minutes at peak times (7am to 7pm daily) and every 30 minutes thereafter. If you're travelling in peak periods, or staying near a station, it's a fast, state-of-the-art and cost-effective way to enter/exit the city.

R370 (one to three passengers) for most destinations in Jo'burg, but book a day in advance if possible.

The Gautrain operates from 5.30am to 8.30pm, connecting the airport with Sandton (R115), Park Station (R125) and Pretoria (R135).

Bus

Metropolitan Bus Services (Metrobus; ☑0860 562 874; Gandhi Sq) runs services throughout greater Jo'burg. The main bus terminal is at Gandhi Sq, two blocks west of the Carlton Centre, and fares work on a zonal system ranging from Zone 1 (R7.90) to Zone 8 (R19.30). Travellers buy tags from the bus terminal or at Computicket outlets. You can still pay for journeys with cash, but Metrobus does its best to discourage this.

Rea Vaya (☑0860 562 874; www.reavaya.org.za) buses were introduced in the build-up to the 2010 World Cup as a way of addressing the lack of safe, reliable public transport between Soweto (and other townships) and the Johannesburg CBD. An inner-city circular route costs R4.50 (green line), while a full trip from the feeder routes to the CBD (blue line) costs R12.

Minibus Taxi

R5 will get you around the inner suburbs and the city centre and R9 will get you almost anywhere. If you take a minibus taxi into central Jo'burg, be sure to get off before it reaches the end of the route, and avoid the taxi rank – it's a mugging zone.

Getting a minibus taxi home from the city is a more difficult proposition. There's a complex system of hand/finger signals to tell a passing taxi where you want to go, so it's best to look as though you know where you're going and raise a confident index finger (drivers will stop if they're going the same way).

Taxi

Taxis are a relatively expensive but necessary evil in this city. They operate meters if they work, but it's wise to ask a local the likely price and agree on a fare at the outset. From the taxi rank at Park Station a trip to Rosebank should cost around R100, and significantly more to Sandton. **Maxi Taxi Cabs** (☑011-648 1212) and **Rose's Radio Taxis** (☑011-403 9625) are reputable firms.

Train

For inquiries about **Metro** (Map p444; ☑011-773 5878) services, call or visit the information office in Park Station. The Metro system is not recommended as it has a reputation for violent crime, particularly its lines connecting with the townships. The Jo'burg–Pretoria Metro line should also be avoided; take the **Gautrain** instead.

Soweto

☑011 / POP 2.3 MILLION

No township in South Africa has as much political and historical resonance as Soweto, created in 1904 to move nonwhites out of the city while keeping them close enough to use as workers.

The 'South West Townships' have since evolved from an area of forced habitation to an address of pride and social prestige. Mirroring much of South Africa, the rising middle class lives here alongside shack dwellers and the mass unemployed, yet all are equally buoyed by the history of Soweto as an icon of the struggle. The townships are the heart of the nation and none beats louder than Soweto.

Soweto is by far the most visited township in the country, so don't feel that coming here as a tourist is either unsafe or inappropriate. Travellers come to witness the welcoming township life and to visit the excellent museums. A stroll down laid-back Vilakazi St offers an insight into modern African sensibilities, while the addition of Soccer City and the Soweto Bungee provide quality, concrete experiences in a place of great political abstraction.

Most visitors still come on a tour, but the infrastructure is now such that a self-guided tour is not out of the question. If you choose to do this, heed local advice and stick to the area around Vilakazi St (where two Nobel Peace Prize winners, Nelson Mandela and Archbishop Desmond Tutu, once lived) and Hector Pieterson Sq (where the Soweto Uprising began in 1976).

◉ Sights & Activities

Mandela House Museum MUSEUM
(☑011-936 7754; www.mandelahouse.com; 8115 Orlando West; admission R60; ◷9am-5pm) Nelson Mandela lived with his first wife, Evelyn, and later with his second wife, Winnie, in this house, just off Vilakazi St. The museum includes interactive exhibits on the history of the house and some interesting family photos. Just down Vilakazi St, by Sakhumzi Restaurant, is the home of Archbishop Desmond Tutu.

Hector Pieterson Museum MUSEUM
(☎011-536 0611; cnr Khumalo & Pela Sts; adult/child R30/10; ⏱10am-5pm) This powerful museum illuminates the role of Sowetan life in the history of the independence struggle. It follows the tragic incidents of 16 June 1976, when a peaceful student protest against the introduction of Afrikaans as a language of instruction was violently quelled by police. In the resulting chaos police opened fire and a 13-year-old boy, Hector Pieterson, was shot dead. The ensuing hours and days saw students fight running battles with the security forces in what would become known as the Soweto uprising.

TOP CHOICE **Orlando Towers** BUNGEE JUMPING
(☎071 674-4343; www.orlandotowers.co.za; cnr Khumalo & Pela Sts; viewing platform/bungee jumping R60/480; ⏱10am-sunset Fri-Sun) Built originally for Orlando's Power Station, the towers host one of the world's more incongruous bungee jumps. Once painted a drab white, one tower is now decorated with a colourful mural, the largest in South Africa, depicting, among others, Nelson Mandela. There is a range of other activities on offer, including abseiling (R260).

Tours

Soweto Bicycle Tours BICYCLE TOUR
(☎011-936 3444; www.sowetobicycletours.com; 2hr/full-day tour R350/550) Soweto's clay paths and grassy nooks make for fabulous cycling terrain. The company also owns Soweto Backpackers, which offers tour discounts for guests.

Sleeping & Eating

Soweto Backpackers BACKPACKERS $
(☎011-936 3444; www.sowetobackpackers.co.za; 10823 A Pooe St, Orlando West; dm/s/d without bathroom R130/210/325) Lebo is the host of Soweto's original hostel. It's a healthy walk from the Vilakazi St action, but guests love the shaded beer garden, restaurant and pool table. Dorms are neat and clean and the double rooms are excellent value. The friendly staff encourage interactivity and all kinds of tours are available.

Nthateng's B&B GUESTHOUSE $$
(☎011-936 2676; 6991 Inhlwathi St, Orlando West; s/d incl breakfast R450/650) Nthateng is an animated host who insists on top-shelf personal tours, delicious breakfasts and a *mi casa su casa* state of mind. It's in an ideal location near the museum.

Soweto Hotel HOTEL $$
(☎011-527 7300; www.sowetohotel.co.za; Walter Sisulu Sq of Dedication, cnr Union Ave & Main Rd, Kliptown; s/d incl breakfast from R980/1110; P@) Mostly an above-average business hotel, with a smattering of celebrity guests. The rooms here are modern and hip, with a jazz design that continues in the restaurant and bar.

Nambitha SOUTH AFRICAN $$
(☎082 785 7190; www.nambitharestaurant.co.za; 6877 Vilakazi St, Orlando West; mains R50-95; ⏱breakfast, lunch & dinner) This stylish, open-fronted bar and restaurant is popular with Soweto's bright young 20-somethings, and serves a whole range of food from toasted sandwiches to steaks to *mogodu* (tripe).

Western Gauteng

The area to the northwest of Jo'burg, a World Heritage Site, is thought of as one of the world's most important palaeontological zones, focused around the Sterkfontein hominid fossil fields. The area is part of the **Cradle of Humankind**, and at 47,000 hectares it can be difficult knowing where to visit first. Most Jo'burg-based tour operators offer full- and half-day tours of the area.

Off Rte 563 and on the way to Hekpoort, **Maropeng** (☎014-577 9000; www.maropeng.co.za; adult/child R125/70, with Sterkfontein Caves entry R200/120; ⏱9am-5pm) is a good place to start. Interactive exhibits, including a boat ride 'back in time', show how the human race has progressed since its beginnings.

Your next stop should be the visitors centre at the **Sterkfontein Caves** (☎011-577 9000; Sterkfontein Caves Rd; adult/child R130/75; ⏱9am-5pm). Tours down into the caves, one of the world's most significant archaeological sites, leave every 30 minutes.

There are also a number of nature reserves and wildlife parks in the area.

Pretoria

☎012 / POP 1.65 MILLION

Though only 50km away from Jo'burg, Pretoria, South Africa's administrative centre, lacks its sister city's rough-and-tumble vibrancy. It's slower and more old-fashioned, and many travellers feel safer here than they do in Jo'burg. It's also a handsome city, home to gracious old buildings in the city centre, the stately Union Buildings, leafy

CHANGING NAMES

As with other cities in South Africa, name changes are in vogue in Pretoria and in 2012 a number of roads received new titles. Where relevant we have listed the new name, followed by the former name (in brackets). Most people still use the old names and both appear on road signs (with the former names struck through with a red line).

suburbs, and wide streets that are lined with a purple haze of jacarandas in October and November.

Culturally, Pretoria feels more like an Afrikaner-dominated country town than a capital city, and its bars and restaurants are less cosmopolitan than Jo'burg's. It was once at the heart of the apartheid regime, and its very name was a symbol of oppression, but today it's home to a growing number of black civil servants and foreign embassy workers who are infusing the city with a new sense of multiculturalism.

History

The British granted independence to the Zuid-Afrikaansche Republiek (ZAR) in the early 1850s. In 1853 two farms on the Apies River were bought as the site for the republic's capital.

Pretoria, which was named after Andries Pretorius (a 19th-century Boer leader), was nothing more than a tiny frontier village with a grandiose title, but the servants of the British Empire were watching it with growing misgivings and in 1877 they annexed the republic. The Boers went to war and won back their independence, but the discovery of gold on the Witwatersrand in the late 1880s would change everything. Within 20 years the Boers would again be at war with the British.

Self-government was again granted to the Transvaal in 1906, and Pretoria was made the country's administrative capital following the Union of South Africa in 1910. Attempts have been made to change the city's name and it is sometimes called Tshwane.

◎ Sights

**Voortrekker Monument
& Nature Reserve**   MONUMENT

(☏012-326 6770; www.voortrekkermon.org.za; Eeufees Rd; adult/child R45/25; ◷8am-6pm Sep-Apr, to 5pm May-Aug) The imposing Voor-

trekker Monument is a place of pilgrimage for many Afrikaners. It was constructed between 1938 and 1949 – a time of great Afrikaner nationalism – to honour the journey of the Voortrekkers.

The edifice is surrounded by a stone wall carved with 64 wagons in a traditional defensive *laager* (circle). The building itself is a huge stone cube and each corner bears the face of an Afrikaner hero. A staircase and elevator lead to the roof and a great panoramic view of Pretoria and the highveld.

The monument is surrounded by a 340-hectare nature reserve full of zebras, wildebeests, bucks and other small mammals.

Church Square   SQUARE

At the heart of Pretoria, imposing public buildings surround Church Sq. These include the Palace of Justice, where the Rivonia Trial that sentenced Nelson Mandela to life imprisonment was held, on the northern side; the Ou Raadsaal (Old Government) building on the southern side; the Old Capitol Theatre in the northwestern corner and First National Bank in the northeast.

Old Lion (Paul Kruger) takes pride of place in the centre, surveying his miniature kingdom.

Melrose House   HISTORIC BUILDING

(☏012-322 2805; 275 Jeff Masemola St (Jacob Maré St); adult/child R20/5; ◷10am-5pm Tue-Sun) During the 1899–1902 Anglo-Boer War, Lords Roberts and Kitchener (both British commanders) lived in this splendid mansion. On 31 May 1902 the Treaty of Vereeniging, which marked the end of the war, was signed in the dining room.

DON'T MISS

FREEDOM PARK

The remarkable memorial at Freedom Park (☏012-361 0021, 012-470 7400; www.freedompark.co.za; Koch St, Salvokop; adult/child R45/25; ◷8am-4.30pm, tours 9am, noon & 3pm) adopts an integrated approach to South Africa's war history and is a place of architectural imagination and collective healing. Located across the *kopjie* (rocky hill) from the austere Voortrekker Monument, Freedom Park is a legacy of the Mandela government and honours all fallen South Africans in all major conflicts.

Central Pretoria

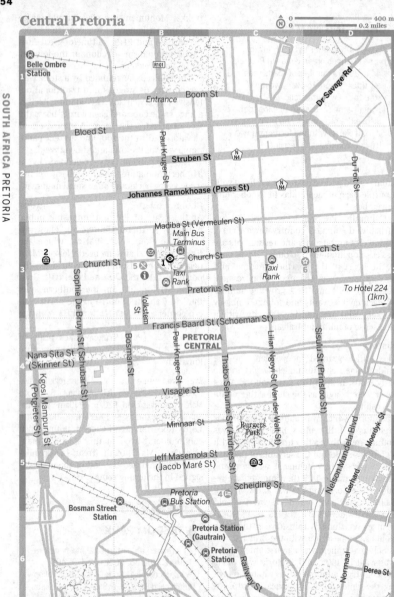

Kruger Museum   MUSEUM
(☏012-000 0010; www.ditsong.org.za; 60 Church St; adult/child R25/10; ☺8.30am-4.30pm Mon-Fri, 9am-4.30pm Sat & Sun) A short walk west from Church Sq is the former residence of Paul Kruger (president of the South African Republic from 1883 to 1900). Guarded by two stone lions, the house, built in 1884, contains period furniture and a random collection of personal knick-knacks belonging to Kruger.

Union Buildings　　　　　　　　BUILDING
These sweeping sandstone buildings are the headquarters of government and home to the presidential offices. The buildings, designed by Sir Herbert Baker, are about a 2km walk from the city centre. There are no tours here, and the buildings themselves aren't open to the public, but the grounds are open seven days a week.

🛏 Sleeping

1322 Backpackers
International　　　　　　BACKPACKERS $
(☑012-362 3905; www.1322backpackers.com; 1322 Arcadia St, Hatfield; dm/s/d without bathroom from R135/195/305; ℗@🛜🏊) This is our favourite hostel for miles around, with a huge backyard pool and a buzzing little anteroom bar. You can stay in neat, clean dorms, or cosy, converted wood and brick sheds at the bottom of the garden. Tours are available.

TOP CHOICE Crane's Nest
Guesthouse　　　　　　GUESTHOUSE $$
(☑012-460 7223; www.cranesnest.co.za; 212 Boshoff St, New Muckleneuk; s/d R675/880; ℗✳@🏊) The Crane (along with its two nearby sister properties) is our favourite place to stay in Pretoria, with easy access to the bird sanctuary across the road. The large white house is modern and stylish, with a full-time reception area and hotelier touches like minibars and wine lists.

TOP CHOICE Manhattan Hotel　　HOTEL $$
(☑012-392 0000; www.manhattanhotel.co.za; 247 Scheiding St, City Centre; s/d from R920/1070; ℗✳🛜🏊) A thorough renovation has lifted this mid-level city hotel into a whole new category. There's five-star service, complimentary wi-fi and shuttles to Gautrain sta-

tions, extensive dining options and well-appointed rooms. The area is not ideal for an evening amble, but the in-room amenities more than compensate.

That's It　　　　　　　　GUESTHOUSE $$
(☑012-344 3404; www.thatsit.co.za; 5 Brecher St, Clydesdale; s/d incl breakfast R495/690; ℗✳@🏊) Professionally run and competitively priced. The plain-ish rooms face out towards a sofa-filled *lapa* and the owners are quick to attend to guests' needs. There's also a family unit in the garden that sleeps four.

Hotel 224　　　　　　　　　　HOTEL $$
(☑012-440 5281; www.hotel224.com; cnr Francis Baard (Schoeman) & Leyds Sts, Arcadia; s/d incl breakfast R650/755; ℗✳) A smart, serviceable option if you need to be close to the city, and a good choice if you tire of the guesthouse banter.

Brooklyn Guesthouses　　GUESTHOUSE $$
(☑012-362 1728; www.brooklynguesthouses.co.za; 128 Murray St, Brooklyn; s/d incl breakfast R515/740; ℗✳@🏊) This 'urban village' of 30-odd rooms (with bathrooms) draws savvy conference-goers and travellers in search of respite. The gardens and swimming pool are immaculately presented.

B' Guest House　　　　　　GUESTHOUSE $$
(☑012-344 0524; www.bguesthouse.co.za; 751 Park St, Arcadia; s/d incl breakfast R675/850; ℗✳@🛜🏊) There's a smashing pool here, set in gardens that can be viewed from private patios. The cuisine comes highly recommended.

🍴 Eating
CITY CENTRE
Café Riche　　　　　　　　　　　PUB $
(☑012-328 3173; www.caferiche.co.za; 2 Church St; mains R35-70; ☺6am-6pm) This historic, early-20th-century bistro in the heart of Church Sq is the ideal place to sip beer and watch the South African capital roll through the day.

HATFIELD & ARCADIA
Harrie's Pancakes　　　　　PANCAKES $
(☑012-342 3613; Eastwood Village Centre, cnr Eastwood & Pretorius Sts, Arcadia; mains R30-75; ☺breakfast, lunch & dinner) With a range of sweet and savoury pancakes, Harrie's is equally adept at curing hangovers or feeding a fussy family's hunger. The breakfast is decent, too, and the service is friendly and efficient.

DON'T MISS

PRETORIA BOEREMARK

Held at the Pioneer Museum in Silverton, this superb farmers' market (Pioneer Park; ⊙6-9am Sat) is full of stalls selling all kinds of artisanal foodstuffs, from cheeses to cakes to preserves. It's a great place to sample some traditional South African fare, but you need to make a very early start – the good stuff sells out quickly.

The museum is also worth a look. Based in an early farmhouse, it showcases Pretoria life in the late 19th century. The demonstrations of traditional farming practices are a highlight.

TOP CHOICE **Pappa's** SOUTH AFRICAN, INTERNATIONAL **$$**
(☎012-362 2224; Duncan Yard, cnr Jan Shoba (Duncan) & Prospect Sts, Hatfield; mains R60-95; ⊙7am-10pm Mon-Sat, 7am-4pm Sun; ⊛) Pappa's is located inside a mini antiques market and serves various South African faves, including steaming *potjiekos* (meat and vegetables cooked in a cast-iron pot over an open fire). Try the parma ham omelette (R55) washed down with the city's best coffee.

Hombaze AFRICAN **$$**
(☎012-342 7753; www.hombazeafricacuisine.co.za; Eastwood Village Centre, cnr Eastwood & Pretorius Sts, Arcadia; mains R45-90; ⊙breakfast, lunch & dinner; ☞) This small franchise serves African staples in a family environment. Lots of meaty dishes and fried sides plus one of the longest vegetarian menus in the city.

Café 41 MEDITERRANEAN **$$**
(☎012-342 8914; www.cafe41.co.za; Eastwood Village Centre, cnr Eastwood & Pretorius Sts, Arcadia; mains R50-110; ⊙breakfast, lunch & dinner) A huge menu and a plethora of seating options make this one of Pretoria's more enjoyable lunch spots. The pasta dishes and sandwiches are good deals, as are the meze platters.

BROOKLYN & NEW MUCKLENEUK

TOP CHOICE **Kream** INTERNATIONAL **$$**
(☎012-346 4642; www.kream.co.za; 570 Fehrsen St, Brooklyn Bridge; mains R80-160; ⊙noon-late Mon-Sat, lunch Sun; ⊛) A bold concept in a conservative city, Kream, in many ways, *is* the crop. The ubertrendy menu features exotic starters and the usual grilled suspects for main course.

Blue Crane SOUTH AFRICAN **$$**
(☎012-460 7615; www.bluecranerestaurant.co.za; Melk St, New Muckleneuk; mains R40-80; ⊙breakfast & lunch Sun & Mon, lunch & dinner Tue-Sat; ⊛) As part of the Austin Roberts Bird Sanctuary, Blue Crane is famed among ornithologists worldwide (and anyone else who enjoys a Castle beer at sunset). The menu is a bastion of Afrikaner favourites.

Geet INDIAN **$$**
(☎012-460 3199; www.geetindianrestaurant.com; 541 Fehrsen St, Brooklyn; mains R90; ⊙11.30am-10.30pm; ⊛☞) The huge menu emphasises North Indian delights, and vegetarians can feast. The whisky lounge is a treat.

Cynthia's Indigo Moon BISTRO **$$$**
(☎012-346 8926; www.cynthiasindigomoon.co.za; 283 Dey St, Brooklyn; mains R70-155; ⊙lunch & dinner Mon-Fri, dinner Sat; ⊛) An effortless familiarity is achieved at Cynthia's, with nods to Paris and New York. Steaks are consumed en masse on dimly lit corner tables. The chicken couscous salad (R50) is a hit.

🍷 Drinking

Hatfield is the best place for a night out with bars, restaurants and clubs catering for all types. Hatfield Sq is a university-student stronghold after dark.

Tings an' Times BAR
(☎012-430 3176; 1065 Arcadia St) This bohemian bar attracts an eclectic crowd to chill out to a reggae soundtrack, punctuated by regular live performances. If you get the munchies, the speciality is pitas (R28 to R50).

TriBeCa Lounge COCKTAIL BAR
(☎012-460 3068; Veale St, Brooklyn Sq, Brooklyn) Laid-back and stylish, this trendy cafe is the perfect place to chill out with a latte and browse the magazines for a few hours, or join the beautiful people in sipping exquisite cocktails on weekend nights.

Eastwood's PUB
(☎012-344 0243; cnr Eastwood & Park Sts, Arcadia; ⊙8am-late) This hugely popular pub has won the 'best pub in Pretoria' award several times and has good-value steak-and-beer deals, such as a 500g T-bone and a Castle beer for R49.

☆ Entertainment

Cinemas

There are several large cinema complexes in Pretoria, including Ster Kinekor (☎0860

300 222; Fehrson St, Brooklyn Mall, Brooklyn; tickets R38) at the Brooklyn Mall. The *Pretoria News* lists screenings daily.

Live Music & Shebeens

Despite being home to a large student population, Pretoria's live-music scene can be a bit uninspiring. Check out the *Pretoria News* for listings or just head to Hatfield.

The surrounding townships, especially Mamelodi and Atteridgeville, have plenty of *shebeens,* best visited with a local resident or as part of a tour.

Theatres

Most shows can be booked through **Computicket** (☏in Johannesburg 011-915 8000; www.computicket.com; Burnett St, Hatfield Plaza; ⊙8.30am-4.30pm Mon-Sat).

State Theatre   THEATRE
(☏012-392 4000; www.statetheatre.co.za; cnr Sisulu (Prinsloo) & Church Sts) This theatre complex hosts productions (including opera, music, ballet and theatre) in its five theatres: the Arena, Studio, Opera, Drama and Momentum.

❶ Information

Dangers & Annoyances

Pretoria is certainly safer and more relaxed than Jo'burg. That said, crime is a problem, particularly in the city centre and Sunnyside, with restaurants and other businesses mostly found in the safer Hatfield and Brooklyn areas. Avoid the centre after dark and be on guard at the weekend when there are fewer people about.

Emergency

Fire (☏10111)
Metro Emergency Rescue Service (☏10177)
Police (☏10111) There are police stations on Railway St and on the corner of Leyds and Robert Sobukwe (Esselen) Sts.

Internet Access

Most accommodation offers internet facilities and wi-fi; **4 in Love Internet Café** (⊙9am-7pm Mon-Fri, to 6pm Sat, 10am-5pm Sun) is a cheaper alternative.

Medical Services

Hatfield Clinic (☏012-362 7180; 454 Hilda St)
Tshwane District Hospital (☏012-354 5958; Dr Savage Rd) The place to head in a medical emergency.

Money

There are banks with ATMs and change facilities across town.

American Express (☏012-346 2599; Brooklyn Mall; ⊙9am-5pm)

Post

Main Post Office (cnr Church St & Church Sq; ⊙8am-4.30pm Mon-Fri, to noon Sat)

Tourist Information

SAN Parks (☏011-428 9111; www.sanparks. org; 643 Leyds St, Muckleneuk; ⊙offices 7.45am-3.45pm Mon-Fri, call centre 7.30am-5pm Mon-Fri, 8am-1pm Sat)
Tourist Information Centre (☏012-358 1430; www.tshwane.gov.za; Old Nederlandsche Bank Bldg, Church Sq; ⊙7.30am-4pm Mon-Fri) Fairly unhelpful for the common traveller; better off asking your hotel or locals for advice.

❶ Getting There & Away

Air

OR Tambo International Airport (p449) is South Africa's international hub, with flights from across the globe.

Bus

Pretoria Bus Station (Railway St) is next to Pretoria's train station. You will also find booking and information offices here.

Most **Translux/City to City** (☏0861 589 282; www.translux.co.za), **Intercape** (☏0861 287 287; www.intercape.co.za), **Greyhound** (☏083 915 9000; www.greyhound.co.za) and **SA Roadlink** (☏012-323 5105; www.saroadlink.co.za) services running from Jo'burg to Durban, the south coast and Cape Town originate in Pretoria. Services running north up the N1 also stop here.

Translux, Greyhound and Intercape fares from Pretoria are identical to those from Jo'burg (see p450). If you only want to go between the two cities, it will cost about R150.

The **Baz Bus** (☏0861 229 287; www.bazbus. com) picks up and drops off at Pretoria hostels.

Car

Many large local and international car-hire companies are represented in Pretoria.

Metro & Gautrain

Because of high incidence of crime, we don't recommend travelling between Pretoria and Jo'burg by Metro. The **Gautrain** (☏0800 4288 7246; www.gautrain.co.za) is a safer, faster option, connecting Pretoria and Hatfield to OR Tambo (R135) and Jo'burg (around R50).

Minibus Taxis

Minibus taxis go from the main terminal by the train station and travel to a host of destinations, including Jo'burg (R45, one hour), but this is not the place to be wandering around with lots of luggage or after dark.

Train

Shosholoza Meyl (☎0860 008 888; www.sho holoza meyl.co.za) has economy class services to the following:

» Komatipoort (R120, 11½ hours)

» Musina (R130, 16 hours)

» Nelspruit (R110, nine hours)

» Polokwane (R120, nine hours)

The luxury **Blue Train** (www.bluetrain.co.za), which links Pretoria, Jo'burg and Cape Town, originates here.

Pretoria train station is about a 20-minute walk from the city centre. Buses run along Paul Kruger St to Church Sq, the main local bus station.

ⓘ Getting Around

To & From the Airport

If you call ahead, most hostels, and many hotels, offer free pick up.

Get You There Transfers (☎012-346 3175; www.getyouthere transfers.co.za) operates shuttle buses between OR Tambo International Airport (Jo'burg) and Pretoria for about R400, the same price as a taxi.

Bus & Minibus Taxi

There's an extensive network of local buses. A booklet of timetables and route maps is available from the inquiry office in the main **bus station** (☎012-308 0839; Church Sq) or from pharmacies. Fares range from R5 to R10. Handy services include buses 5 and 8, which run between Church Sq and Brooklyn via Burnett St in Hatfield.

Minibus taxis run pretty much everywhere and the standard fare is about R5.

Taxi

There are taxi ranks on the corner of Church and Lilian Ngoyi (Van der Walt) Sts, and on the corner of Pretorius and Paul Kruger Sts. Or you can get a metered taxi (around R10 per kilometre) from **Rixi Taxis** (☎012-362 6262).

Around Pretoria

National Botanical Garden   GARDENS
(☎012-843 5172; Cussonia Ave, Brummeria; adult/child R24/10; ◷6am-6pm) Around 9km east of the city centre, these gardens cover 77 hectares and are planted with indigenous flora from around the country. Garden picnic concerts are held from May to September.

Smuts House Museum   MUSEUM
(☎012-667 1941; www.smutshouse.co.za; Nelmapius Rd, Irene; adult/child R10/5; picnic garden per car R5; ◷9.30am-4.30pm Mon-Fri, to 5pm Sat & Sun) Former prime minister Jan Smuts' home for over 40 years has been turned into an interesting museum. Surrounded by a wide verandah and shaded by trees, it has a family atmosphere and gives a vivid insight into Smuts' life.

**Ann van Dyk
Cheetah Centre**   WILDLIFE ENCOUNTERS
(☎012-504 9906; www.dewildt.co.za; R513 Pretoria North Rd, Farm 22; tour only R270, cheetah run & guided tour R380; ◷tours 8.30am & 1.30pm Mon, Wed & Fri, 1.30pm only Tue, Thu, Sat & Sun, cheetah runs 8am Tue, Thu, Sat & Sun) Just past Hartbeespoort, about 50km northwest of Pretoria, is this highly impressive centre famous for its breeding success of rare and endangered animals.

MPUMALANGA

Apart from Kruger National Park, Mpumalanga's major draw is the Blyde River Canyon, which carves its way spectacularly through the Drakensberg Escarpment. Surrounding it are mountains, rivers, waterfalls and thick tracts of pine forest – which make the region a prime target for outdoor enthusiasts.

Those not into death-defying pursuits can soak up gold-mining history in Baberton or the living museum of Pilgrim's Rest. The dry, hot lowveld surrounding Kruger is home to Mpumalanga's answer to the big smoke, Nelspruit.

Many travellers zip through the province en route to Kruger, but it's worth setting aside a few days to explore the area.

Eastern Lowveld

The hot and dry Eastern Lowveld lacks the obvious appeal of the Drakensberg Escarpment and is mostly used as a staging post on the way into and out of Kruger National Park. However, the region has its attractions. You can learn about the history of the gold rush in laid-back Barberton, get your big-city fix in Nelspruit and whet your appetite for the mighty Kruger in country lodges.

KRUGER NATIONAL PARK

Kruger is one of South Africa's national symbols, and for many visitors, the park is *the* 'must-see' wildlife destination in the country. Little wonder: in an area the size of Wales, enough elephants wander around to populate a major city, giraffes nibble on acacia trees, hippos wallow in the rivers, leopards prowl through the night and a multitude of birds sing, fly and roost.

Kruger is one of the world's most famed protected areas – known for its size, conservation history, wildlife diversity and ease of access. It's a place where the drama of life and death plays out on a daily basis. One morning you may spot lions feasting on a kill, the next a newborn impala struggling to take its first steps.

The park has an extensive network of sealed roads and comfortable camps, but if you prefer to keep it rough, there are also 4WD tracks and hiking trails. Even when you stick to the tarmac, the sounds and scents of the bush are never far away.

Southern Kruger is the most popular section, with the highest animal concentrations and easiest access. The park is at its best in the far north, around Punda Maria and Pafuri Gates. Here, although animal concentrations are somewhat lower, the bush setting and wilderness atmosphere are all-enveloping.

Activities

Although it's possible to get a sense of Kruger in a day, the park merits at least four to five days, and ideally a week. The closer you get to the bush, and the more time you devote to becoming acquainted with its sounds, smells and rhythms, the more rewarding your experience will be. Activities need to be booked in advance, except short bush walks and wildlife drives, which can be booked at the gates and camps.

4WD TRAILS

Kruger's longest 4WD trail is the five-day Lebombo Motorised Eco Trail (per vehicle incl maximum of 4 people R8600), a rough, rugged 500km route along the eastern boundary of the park. You'll need to provide your own vehicle, food and drink.

There are also four shorter 'adventure trails' (from R500 per vehicle plus a R100 refundable deposit, about four hours, 50km).

BUSH WALKS

Recommended guided morning and afternoon bush walks (per person R300-460) are possible at most camps. Accompanied by two armed rangers, the excellent walks both get you into the bush and offer the chance of up-close encounters with animals.

WILDERNESS TRAILS

Kruger's seven wilderness walking trails are one of the park's highlights, offering a superb opportunity for an intimate experience of the bush. The three-day walks, done in small groups (maximum eight people) with highly knowledgeable armed guides, are not particularly strenuous, covering about 20km per day at a modest pace.

Trails cost R3900 per person, including accommodation in rustic huts, plus food and equipment, and depart on Wednesday and Sunday afternoon. All are extremely popular, and should be booked well in advance through central reservations (p461). No children under 12 are allowed.

WILDLIFE DRIVES

Dawn (three hours), mid-morning (two hours), sunset (three hours) and night (two hours) wildlife drives in 10- or 20-seat vehicles are available at most rest camps, and offer good chances to maximise your safari experience. They cost between R200 and R340 per person, depending on time and vehicle size.

Tours

At the budget level, the best places to contact are the backpacker lodges in Hazyview, Nelspruit and Graskop, most of which organise tours into Kruger from about R1000 per day, plus entry fees and meals.

At the upper end of the spectrum, or if you're on a tight schedule, eHolidaysTours (www.airlinktours.com) runs flight and accommodation packages between Jo'burg and central Kruger. Other operators include Wildlife Safaris (☎011-791 4238; www.wildlifesafaris.com), which has four-day panorama tours taking in the Blyde River and Kruger for R7900 per person, including half board.

Sleeping & Eating

Most visitors stay in one of the park's 12 main rest camps. These offer camping, plus a range of huts, bungalows and cottages (self-catering or sharing cooking facilities), as well as shops, restaurants and other facilities. Several of the rest camps have satellite camps, which are set a few kilometres away, and are much more rustic, with only an ablutions block, kitchen and *braai* area.

Huts (2 people from around R410) are the cheapest noncamping option, with shared ablutions and communal cooking facilities; bungalows (2 people from around R865) range from simple to luxurious, and generally have

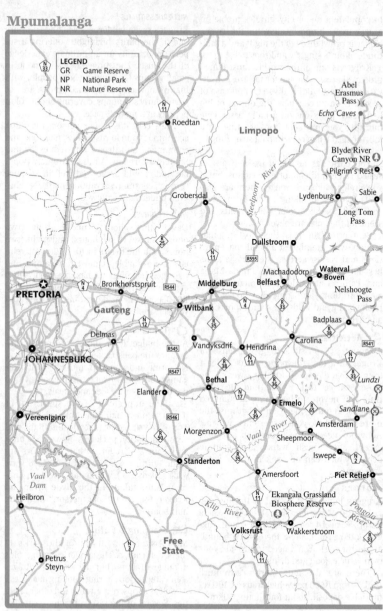

LEGEND
GR   Game Reserve
NP   National Park
NR   Nature Reserve

bathrooms; **cottages** (up to 4 people around R1590), the next step up in comfort and price, usually have a living area.

Some camps also offer **safari tents** (from R435), all of which are furnished and have a refrigerator and fan.

For those with tents or caravans, **camping** (per campsite for 1-2 people R200, per additional adult/child up to 6 maximum R62/31) is available at many rest camps. As with other types of accommodation, book in advance during the high season.

the wilderness, and must be booked in their entirety by a single group.

At the opposite end of the spectrum, there's luxurious accommodation in the private reserves bordering Kruger to the west. Another possibility is to stay outside the park. For budget travellers, the best places for this are Hazyview and Nelspruit.

ⓘ Information

Kruger is a long, narrow wedge (about 65km across, and 350km long), bordered by Zimbabwe to the north, Limpopo to the west, Mpumalanga to the west and south, and Mozambique to the east. Rimming the park to the west, and sharing the same unfenced terrain, is a chain of private wildlife reserves.

There are nine South African *heks* (entry gates). It is also possible to enter Kruger from Mozambique at the Giriyondo and Pafuri Gates, which double as international border crossings (visas are available on both sides).

BOOKINGS

Accommodation can be booked through central reservations **SAN Parks** (www.sanparks.org), which has offices in Pretoria and Durban, and **Lowveld Tourism** (www.lowveldtourism.com), which has offices in Nelspruit and Cape Town.

Except in the high season (school holidays, Christmas and Easter) and at weekends, bookings are advisable but not essential.

ENTRY

Day or overnight entry to the park costs R204/102 per adult/child, with significant discounts available for South African citizens and residents, and for South African Development Community (SADC) nationals.

Bicycles and motorcycles are not permitted to enter the park. During school holidays you can stay in the park for a maximum of 10 days, and at any one rest camp for five days (10 days if you're camping). Park authorities restrict the total number of visitors, so in the high season it pays to arrive early if you don't have a booking.

Entry-gate opening times vary slightly according to the season, and are currently as follows:

MONTH	GATES/CAMPS OPEN (AM)	GATES/CAMPS CLOSE (PM)
Jan	5.30/4.30	6.30
Feb	5.30	6.30
Mar	5.30	6
Apr	6	6
May-Jul	6	5.30
Aug & Sep	6	6
Oct	5.30	6
Nov & Dec	5.30/4.30	6.30

There are also five **bushveld camps** (cottages for up to 4 people R1320-1910) – smaller, more remote clusters of self-catering cottages without shops or restaurants – and two **bush lodges** (lodges for 4/8 people R2465/5100), which are set in the middle of

Kruger National Park

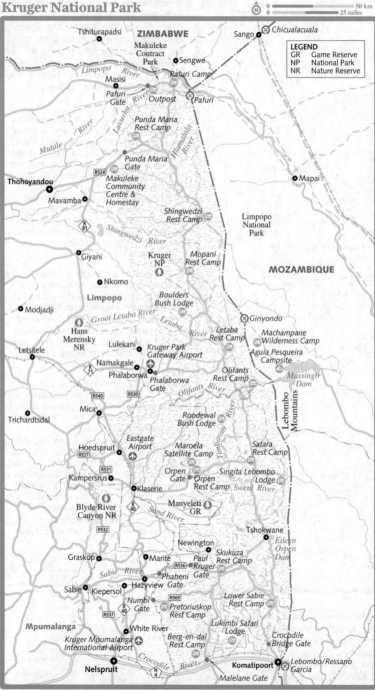

N
0   50 km
0   25 miles

LEGEND
GR   Game Reserve
NP   National Park
NR   Nature Reserve

Tshiturapadsi
ZIMBABWE
Sango
Chicualacuala

Makuleke
Contract
Park
Sengwe
Rafuri Camp
Limpopo River

Masisi
Pafuri
Gate
Outpost
Pafuri
Luvuvhu River
Mutale River

Punda Maria
Rest Camp

Hlamalala River

Mapai

Thohoyandou
R524
Punda Maria
Gate
Mavamba
Makuleke
Community
Centre &
Homestay
Shingwedzi
Rest Camp

Limpopo
National
Park

R81
Shingwedzi River

Giyani
Kruger
NP
Mopani
Rest Camp

MOZAMBIQUE

Nkomo
Limpopo

Modjadji
Boulders
Bush Lodge
Groot Letaba River
Letaba River
Giriyondo

Hans
Merensky
NR
Lulekani
Kruger Park
Gateway Airport
Letaba
Rest Camp
Machampane
Wilderness Camp

Letsitele
R71
Namakgale
Phalaborwa
Phalaborwa
Gate
Aguia Pesqueira
Campsite
Olifants
Rest Camp
*Massingir
Dam*

R540   R530
Olifants River

Mica
Roodewal
Bush Lodge
Timbavati River

**Lebombo
Mountains**

Trichardtsdal

Eastgate
Airport
Maroela
Satellite Camp
Satara
Rest Camp

Hoedspruit
R527

R531
Orpen
Gate
Orpen
Rest Camp
Singita Lebombo
Lodge
Sweni River

Kampersrus
Klaserie
R40
Manyeleti
GR

Blyde River
Canyon NR
Sand River

R532
Tshokwane
*Eileen
Orpen
Dam*

Newington
Skukuza
Rest Camp

Graskop
Marite
Paul
Kruger
Gate
Sabie River
R536
Phabeni
Gate

Sabie
Kiepersol
Hazyview
Numbi
Gate
R569
Pretoriuskop
Rest Camp
Lower Sabie
Rest Camp

R40
R537
White River
Lukimbi Safari
Lodge
Crocodile
Bridge Gate

Mpumalanga
Kruger Mpumalanga
International Airport
Berg-en-dal
Rest Camp

Nelspruit
N4
Crocodile River
Komatipoort
Lebombo/Ressano
Garcia
Malelane Gate

WILDLIFE WHEREABOUTS

Impalas, buffaloes, Burchell's zebras, blue wildebeests, kudus, waterbucks, baboons, vervet monkeys, cheetahs, leopards and other smaller predators are all widespread in Kruger National Park. Bird life is prolific along the rivers and north of the Luvuvhu River.

In the southern section of the park, where rainfall is highest (700mm a year), the grasslands and thick woods attract white rhinos, zebras and buffaloes. Antelope – and therefore predators – are not as abundant.

The central eastern sections of the park – to the south of the Olifants River, on the plains around Satara rest camp and south to the Crocodile River – host large populations of impalas, zebras, wildebeests, giraffes and black rhinos. Joining them are predators, particularly lions and cheetahs.

North of the Olifants River, the rainfall drops below 500mm and the dominant tree is mopane (mopani), a favoured food of elephants – which are common around Olifants and Letaba rest camps. The mopaneveld also attracts *tsessebes*, elands, roans and sables.

Perhaps the most interesting area is in the far north around Punda Maria and Pafuri, which lies completely in the tropics and has a higher rainfall (close to 700mm at Punda Maria) than the mopaneveld. Baobabs abound, elephants, lions and leopards are encountered, and there's an exceptional array of birds.

Note that even outside the park borders there are areas that support wildlife, such as along the Olifants River to the south of Phalaborwa.

It's an offence to arrive late at a camp and you can be fined for doing so (the camps are fenced). There are strictly enforced speed limits of 50km/h on sealed roads and 40km/h on dirt roads.

ⓘ Getting There & Around

AIR

South African Airways (☎0861 359 722; www.flysaa.com) has daily flights linking both Jo'burg and Cape Town with Kruger Mpumalanga International Airport (MQP) near Nelspruit (for Numbi, Malelane and Crocodile Bridge Gates), Kruger Park Gateway Airport in Phalaborwa (2km from Phalaborwa Gate) and Hoedspruit Eastgate Airport (for Orpen Gate).

Sample one-way fares from Jo'burg:

» Hoedspruit (from R1160)

» MQP (from R950, one hour)

» Phalaborwa (from R1720, one hour)

One-way fares from Cape Town to MQP are about R2540 (2¼ hours).

Flights are operated by SAA, SA Express and Airlink.

BUS & MINIBUS TAXI

For most visitors, Nelspruit is the most convenient large town near Kruger, and it's well served by buses and minibus taxis to and from Jo'burg. Numbi Gate is about 50km away, and Malelane Gate about 65km away. Phalaborwa (for Phalaborwa Gate) and, to a lesser extent, Hoedspruit (70km from Orpen Gate) are connected to Polokwane, Pretoria and Jo'burg by bus.

CAR

Skukuza is 500km from Jo'burg (six hours) and Punda Maria about 620km (eight hours). **Avis** (☎in Johannesburg 011-923 3600, in Skukuza 013-735 5651; www.avis.co.za) has a branch at Skukuza, and there is car hire from the Nelspruit, Hoedspruit and Phalaborwa airports.

Most visitors drive themselves around the park, and this is the best way to experience Kruger.

TRAIN

An economy-class-only **Shosholoza Meyl** (☎0860 008 888; www.shosholozameyl.co.za) service runs from Jo'burg via Nelspruit to Komatipoort (R150, 12 hours), about 12km from Kruger's Crocodile Bridge Gate, but you would need to arrange vehicle hire or a tour to visit the park.

PRIVATE WILDLIFE RESERVES

Spreading over a vast lowveld area just west of Kruger is a string of private reserves that offer comparable wildlife watching to what you'll experience in the park. The main reserves – Sabi Sand, Manyeleti and Timbavati – directly border Kruger (with no fences), and the same Big Five populations that roam the park are also at home here.

There are around 200 lodges and camps in the private reserves and most are expensive. However, together with the private concessions within the park, the private reserves offer among Africa's best opportunities for safari connoisseurs, and are the place to go for those who want to experience the bush in the lap of luxury.

Prices tend to be seasonal, so it's best to have a look at the websites for the most accurate costs. Note that many of these places like to call themselves 'game reserves'. They're not. They are simply lodges inside a designated wildlife reserve.

The best known, most luxurious options are found within the large Sabi Sand Reserve (www.sabisand.co.za), including Nkorho Bush Lodge (☑013-735 5367; www.nkorho.com; s/d all-inclusive R3585/5520; ☀), one of the more moderately priced lodges, and top-end favourite Singita (☑021-683 3424; www.singita.com; all-inclusive per person from R9250; ☀@☀).

NELSPRUIT
☑013 / POP 235,000

Nelspruit is Mpumalanga's largest town and the provincial capital. While not unpleasant, it's more of a place to get things done than a worthwhile destination for tourists. There are, however, good accommodation options and a couple of excellent restaurants, so it makes a good-enough breathing point on the way elsewhere.

Nelspruit has officially changed its name to Mbombela and, while the new moniker is scarcely used, you might see it on the occasional map.

◉ Sights

Lowveld National Botanical Garden GARDENS
(www.sanbi.org; adult/child R22/12; ⊗8am-6pm) Out of town, the 150-hectare botanical garden is home to tropical African rainforest and is a nice place for a stroll. It's on Rte 40 about 2km north of the junction with the N4.

Chimpanzee Eden WILDLIFE ENCOUNTERS
(☑013-737 8191; www.janegoodall.co.za; adult/child R120/60) This chimp centre, 12km south of Nelspruit on Rte 40, acts as a sanctuary for rescued chimpanzees. The entry fee includes a guided tour (10am, noon and 2pm).

⌕ Sleeping

Funky Monkey Backpackers BACKPACKERS $
(☑013-744 1310; www.funkymonkeys.co.za; 102 Van Wijk St; campsites per person R80, dm R130, s/d without bathroom R200/380; @☀) While a little out of town, this is an excellent backpackers, with clean dorms and doubles, a spacious garden and a pool area that sees some great parties. Take Ferreira St east, then turn right

Nelspruit

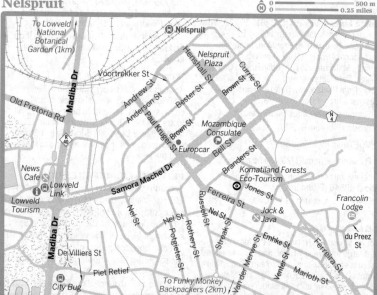

onto Van der Merwe St, which becomes Van Wijk St.

TOP CHOICE Utopia in Africa GUESTHOUSE $$

(☑013-745 7714; www.utopiainafrica.co.za; 6 Daleen St; s/d incl breakfast from R675/990; ❀☒) Rooms here are beautifully furnished and come with balconies overlooking the nearby nature reserve. Head south on Madiba Dr, turn left onto Dr Enos Mabuza Dr, and left onto Halssnoer St – Utopia is signposted off this road.

Francolin Lodge GUESTHOUSE $$

(☑013-744 1251; www.francolinlodge.co.za; 4 du Preez St; s/d incl breakfast R950/1500; @☒) This top Nelspruit guesthouse has rooms with private patios and corner bathrooms with views. It also owns the equally lovely Loerie's Call next door. The lodge also has an excellent, upmarket restaurant.

✖ Eating

TOP CHOICE Jock & Java PUB $$

(www.jockandjava.co.za; Ferreira St; mains R60-110, breakfast R30; ⊙breakfast, lunch & dinner Mon-Sat; ☑) This rambling 'outback-style' pub and separate tearoom set in large grassy lawns has a great selection of steaks, salads, wood-fired pizzas and some decent vegetarian options. Very popular spot for locals, despite the at-times-terrible service.

News Cafe CAFE $$

(Nelspruit Crossing Mall; mains R50-70; ⊙breakfast, lunch & dinner; ☎) A good bet for breakfast or lunch in particular, serving cooked breakfasts, muesli, fresh fruit salads, burgers and wraps.

ⓘ Information

Lowveld Tourism (☑013-755 1988; www.lowveldtourism.com; cnr Madiba & Samora Machel Drs; ⊙7am-6pm Mon-Fri, 8am-1.30pm Sat) This helpful office at Nelspruit Crossing Mall takes bookings for all national parks and can help arrange accommodation and tours.

Mozambique Consulate (☑013-752 7396; 32 Bell St; ⊙8am-3pm Mon-Fri) Does same-day, single-entry visa processing for R650 to R800. Drop visa applications in before noon and pick up visas from 2pm.

ⓘ Getting There & Around

AIR

Kruger Mpumalanga International Airport (MKIA; ☑013-753 7500; www.mceglobal.net) is the closest commercial airport. There are daily flights with **SAAirlink** (☑0861 606 606; www.

flyairlink.com) to Jo'burg (one way from R950, one hour), Cape Town (from R2600, 2¾ hours) and Durban (from R1900, 1½ hours).

BUS

Intercape (☑0861 287 287; www.intercape.co.za), **Greyhound** (☑083-915 9000; www.greyhound.co.za) and **Translux** (☑0861 589 282; www.translux.co.za) all run daily to Jo'burg/Pretoria (R245, five hours) and Maputo, Mozambique (R230, five hours).Ticket offices for all three companies are on Samora Machel Dr, opposite the Promenade Center.

CAR

Avis airport (☑013-750 1015); downtown (☑013-757 0911; Riverside Auto Centre, Mystic River Cres)

Europcar airport (☑013-750 2871); downtown (☑013-741 1805; Orion Promenade Hotel)

First (☑013-750 2538)

MINIBUS TAXI

The local bus and minibus-taxi rank is behind Nelspruit Plaza. Minibus taxi destinations include the following:

» Barberton (R25, 40 minutes)

» Graskop (R30, 1½ hours)

» Hazyview (R30, one hour)

» Jo'burg (R120, five hours)

City Bug (☑086-133 4433; www.citybug.co.za) operates a shuttle from Sonpark BP petrol station to Durban (R590 per person one way, nine hours, twice weekly), Pretoria (R320, 3½ to five hours, daily) and OR Tambo International Airport (R370, four to 5½ hours, daily).

Lowveld Link (☑013-750 1174; www.lowveldlink.com) operates a convenient daily shuttle service from Lowveld Tourism to Pretoria, OR Tambo International Airport and Sandton, Jo'burg (R350, 4¾ hours).

TRAIN

Shosholoza Meyl (☑0860 008 888; www.shosholozameyl.co.za) runs a seat-only service daily except Saturday between Jo'burg (R120, 10 hours) and Komatipoort (R70, 2½ hours) via Nelspruit.

HAZYVIEW
☑013 / POP 20,000

Strung out along Rte 40, the town of Hazyview acts as a service centre and gateway for nearby Kruger National Park. There are good facilities and a few activities but generally it's little more than an overnight stop before the early-morning dash to the Phabeni (12km), Numbi (15km) or Paul Kruger (47km) Gates.

If you do have some time to spare, consider a visit to the Elephant Sanctuary (☎013-737 6609; www.elephantsanctuary.co.za; tours adult/child from R495/250; ⊘tours from 7.15am), which offers a range of interactive pachyderm experiences. You could also drop in at the Shangana Cultural Village (☎013-737 5804; www.shangana.co.za; ⊘9am-4pm), 5km north of town along Rte 535. It's very touristy but offers some insight into Shangaan culture. Day tours cost R120. There's a craft market here too.

🛏 Sleeping & Eating

Bushpackers BACKPACKERS $
(☎013-737 8140; campsites R60, dm R100, d R300-400; ⾵) This basic set-up has clean, roomy dorms and a choice of en suite or shared-facility twin rooms. There's a great bar, home-cooked meals and lots of outdoor activities. It's located 3km from Hazyview, just off Rte 536 (the Sabie Rd).

TOP CHOICE Idle & Wild GUESTHOUSE $$
(☎013-737 8173; www.idleandwild.com; s/d rondavels incl breakfast R550/840; ⓟ) These roomy *rondavels* each have a kitchenette and are set in a wonderful tropical garden. All have beautiful garden outlooks and outside table and chairs to enjoy them. It's 5km from Hazyview on Rte 536 to Sabie.

Summerfields Kitchen FUSION $$
(☎013-737 6500; mains R105; ⊘lunch & dinner) For something romantic, head to Summerfields, some 5km out of town on Rte 536. The food is generally on the rich side, including meats with creamy sauces, buttery trout and sinful desserts.

❶ Information

Big 5 Country Tourist Office (☎013-737 7414; www.big5country.co.za; ⊘8am-5pm Mon-Fri, to 2pm Sat) This helpful office is in the Rendezvous Tourism Centre, as you come into Hazyview from the south.

❶ Getting There & Away

City to City has a daily bus to/from Jo'burg (R165, six hours). It stops at the Shell petrol station. Minibus taxis go daily to Nelspruit (R30, one hour) and Sabie (R30, one hour).

BARBERTON
☎013 / POP 29,500
The splendid town of Barberton dates to the gold-rush days of the late 19th century, when it was a boom town and home to South Africa's first stock exchange. Its prominence later declined, leaving quiet, leafy streets and beautifully preserved old buildings, against a backdrop of green and purple mountains.

You can pick up a Heritage Walk map and leaflet at the tourist information centre. It's a self-guided tour that takes in the restored houses as well as other sights.

🛏 Sleeping

Barberton Chalets & Caravan Park CAMPGROUND $
(☎013-712 3323; www.barbertonchalets.co.za; General St; campsites per person R50, caravan sites R70, s/d/tr cottages R300/400/500; ⾵) This caravan park, in large grassy, shady grounds, is conveniently close to the town centre. The 1970s-style chalets sleep four, but two would be more comfortable.

Kloof House GUESTHOUSE $$
(☎013-712 4268; www.kloofhuis.co.za; 1 Kloof St; s/d incl breakfast R400/600; @🛜) A lovely old hillside Victorian house with grand views from the wrap-around verandah onto which the comfortable guest rooms open out. Rooms are simple but appealingly large and with homespun comforts. There is also a self-catering chalet.

🍴 Eating

Victorian Tea Garden & Restaurant CAFE $
(Crown St, Market Sq; light meals R25-40; ⊘8am-5pm Mon-Fri, to 1pm Sat; 🛜) Here you can munch on sandwiches, cakes and more substantial offerings while watching the world

---

INTO MOZAMBIQUE

Komatipoort is convenient stop if you're travelling to/from Mozambique. The border town sits at the foot of the Lebombo Mountains only 10km from Kruger National Park's Crocodile Bridge Gate.

If you're staying over, Trees Too (☎013-793 8262; www.treestoo.com; s/d incl breakfast R460/720; 🛜⾵) is a standout.

Minibus taxis leave from just off Rissik St near the Score supermarket, and regularly run between Komatipoort and Maputo (Mozambique; R80, two hours). Exit procedures are fairly swift.

go by. It's next to the tourist information office, and it's also a wi-fi hotspot.

Papa's MEDITERRANEAN $

(18 Judge St; mains R30-50; ⊘breakfast, lunch & dinner; 🖬) Family friendly and with a large garden courtyard, this pseudo-Mediterranean establishment serves pizzas, pastas, the odd burger and even *shwarmas*. It's also an exceedingly pleasant place for a beer.

ⓘ Information

Tourist Information Centre (⌨013-712 2880; www.barberton.co.za; Crown St, Market Sq; ⊘7.30am-4.30pm Mon-Fri, 9am-2pm Sat) This helpful office in the town centre can assist with accommodation, tours of historic sites and day hikes in the area.

ⓘ Getting There & Away

A few minibus taxis stop in town near Shoprite, but it's best to go to the minibus-taxi rank near Emjindini (3km from town on the Nelspruit road). The fare to Nelspruit is R25 (40 minutes). Most departures are in the early morning.

Drakensberg Escarpment

The Drakensberg Escarpment marks the point where the highveld plunges over 1000m before spilling out onto the eastern lowveld. Here it forms a dramatic knot of soaring cliffs, canyons, sweeping hillsides and cool valleys thick with pine trees – an apt backdrop for the myriad adventure activities that are on offer here. While it's possible to get around via minibus taxi, the going is slow; car hire is the best option.

BLYDE RIVER CANYON

The Blyde River's spectacular canyon is nearly 30km long and one of South Africa's most impressive natural features. Much of it is rimmed by the 26,000-hectare Blyde River Canyon Nature Reserve (per person/car R25/5), which snakes north from Graskop, following the escarpment and meeting the Blyde River as it carves its way down to the lowveld. Most visitors drive along the edge of the canyon, with stops at the many wonderful viewpoints, but if you have the time, it's well worth exploring on foot.

Heading north from Graskop, look first for the Pinnacle, a striking skyscraperlike rock formation; lock up your vehicle here. Just to the north along Rte 534 (a loop off Rte 532) are God's Window and Wonder View – two viewpoints with amazing vistas and batteries of craft stalls. At God's Window take the trail up to the rainforest (300 steps).

Back on Rte 532, take a short detour 2km south to the impressive Lisbon Falls (or if you are coming back to Graskop, catch it in the afternoon).

The Blyde River Canyon starts north of here, near Bourke's Luck Potholes. These bizarre cylindrical holes were carved into the rock by whirlpools near the confluence of the Blyde and Treur Rivers.

Continuing north past Bourke's Luck Potholes and into the heart of the nature reserve, you'll reach a viewpoint overlooking the Three Rondavels – huge cylinders of rock with hutlike pointed 'roofs' rising out of the canyon. There are a number of short walks in the surrounding area.

West of here, outside the reserve and off Rte 36, are the Echo Caves (admission & guided tour adult/child R50/20), where Stone Age relics have been found. The caves get their name from dripstone formations that echo when tapped.

🏃 Activities

The main hiking route is the popular and scenic 2½-day Blyde River Canyon Hiking Trail (⌨013-759 5432; mpbinfo@cis.co.za; Rte 60), which begins at Paradise Camp and finishes at Bourke's Luck Potholes. Bookings can be made at the Bourke's Luck Potholes visitors centre. You'll need to sort out onward transport from the end of the trail.

The short but reasonably strenuous Belvedere Day Walk (R5, five hours) takes you in a circular route to the Belvedere hydroelectric power station at Bourke's Luck Potholes; turn left at the guesthouse down a path to some beautiful waterfalls and rock pools. Bookings should be made at Potholes.

🛏 Sleeping

It's easy to explore the canyon by car as a day jaunt from Graskop, Sabie or Pilgrim's Rest. If you're continuing further north, a good alternative is to stay in or around the nature reserve.

Forever Blyde Canyon RESORT $$

(⌨0861 226 966; www.foreverblydecanyon.co.za; campsites per person R120, 2-/4-person self-catering chalets R725/1040, 2-/4-person deluxe chalets from R820/1550; 🖳🛏) This rambling resort has a wide choice of accommodation. For jaw-dropping views of the Three Rondavels ask for chalet Nos 89 to 96. The solid brick chalets are very well set up, and the pricier ones are worth it for the views and extra space.

Thaba Tsweni Lodge   CHALET $$
(☎013-767 1380; www.blyderivercanyonaccommo dation.com; d from R600, breakfast R75) Beautifully located just a short walk from Berlin Falls in the heart of the panorama route are several self-catering chalets, with kitchens, private garden areas with *braai* facilities and beautiful views. It's just off Rte 352.

GRASKOP
☎013 / POP 2000 / ELEV 1450M
A useful base for exploring the Blyde River Canyon, compact little Graskop is one of the area's most appealing towns. The nearby views over the edge of the Drakensberg Escarpment are magnificent. There's good **hiking** and **mountain biking** in the area. Those seeking something more adventurous should try the **Big Swing** (☎013-737 8191; single/tandem jump R320/R480, foefie slide only R70).

🛏 Sleeping

TOP CHOICE Graskop Valley View
Backpackers   BACKPACKERS $
(☎013-767 1112; www.yebo-afrika.nl; 47 de Lange St; campsites per person R70, dm R100, tw R240-290; ❉⊠) This friendly backpackers has a variety

Drakensberg Escarpment & Eastern Lowveld

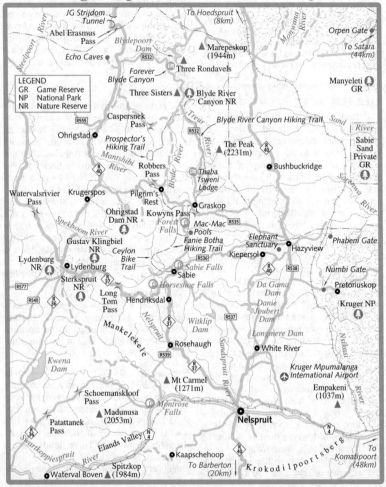

of rooms plus *rondavels* and a self-catering flat. The owners can organise adventure tours and rent out mountain bikes (R200 per day).

Graskop Hotel HOTEL **$$**
(☎013-767 1244; www.graskophotel.co.za; cnr Hoof & Louis Trichardt Sts; s/d incl breakfast R550/800; 🛜🖭) Rooms here are slick, stylish and individual, several featuring art and design by contemporary South African artists. Rooms out the back are little country cottages with doll's-house-like furniture (but are extremely comfortable).

Autumn Breath B&B **$$**
(☎082 877 2811; www.autumnbreath.co.za; Louis Trichardt St; r per person incl breakfast R275-365) This quaint B&B has three modern rooms. There's a restaurant downstairs, set in a lawn under cheerful yellow awnings, serving sandwiches, homemade pies and home-brewed ginger beer.

✖ Eating

Harrie's Pancakes PANCAKES **$**
(Louis Trichardt St; pancakes R45-65; ⊗8am-7pm) You won't find breakfast-style pancakes here, but mostly savoury and exotic fillings, as well as some sweet offerings. Its reputation perhaps outdoes what it delivers, but it's a nice spot.

Canimambo PORTUGUESE **$$**
(☎013-767 1868; cnr Hoof & Louis Trichardt Sts; dishes R70-120; ⊗breakfast, lunch & dinner; 🛜) A Portuguese and Mozambican joint serving up spicy stews and grills as well as some excellent seafood dishes. Try the bean stew with chorizo or smoked chicken. Alternatively, Canimambo does some wonderful things with prawns.

ℹ Information

Tourist Information Office (☎013-767 1833; Pilgrim St; ⊗8.30am-5pm Mon-Sat) Inside Spar supermarket.

ℹ Getting There & Away

The **minibus-taxi stand** (Hoof St) is at the southern end of town, with daily morning departures to Pilgrim's Rest (R10, 30 minutes), Sabie (R20, 40 minutes) and Hazyview (R22, one hour).

SABIE

☎013 / POP 12,000 / ELEV 1100M
While Sabie itself is nothing special, the town's surroundings are lovely – roads lined with pine plantations, and green mountains hiding waterfalls, streams and walking trails – and it makes an excellent base for a couple of days.

◉ Sights & Activities

Waterfalls WATERFALL
(admission to each R5-10) The local waterfalls include the 70m Bridal Veil Falls and the 68m Lone Creek Falls, both northwest of Sabie off Old Lydenburg Rd. The popular Mac-Mac Falls is about 12km north of Sabie off Rte 532 to Graskop. About 3km southeast of the falls are the Mac-Mac Pools, where you can swim.

Sabie Xtreme Adventures ADVENTURE SPORTS
(☎013-764 2118; www.sabiextreme.co.za) This outfit can organise kloofing, candlelight caving, rafting, tours of Blyde River Canyon and more.

🛏 Sleeping

Artists' Café & Guest House TOP CHOICE GUESTHOUSE **$$**
(☎078 876 9293; r per person R250) Wonderfully quirky place in Hendriksdal, about 15km south of Sabie along Rte 37. Accommodation is in old train-station buildings that have been converted into rooms, retaining lots of the old signs and quirks.

Sabie Townhouse B&B **$$**
(☎013-764 2292; www.sabietownhouse.co.za; Power St; s/d R425/800; 🖭) This is a pretty stone house, with a pool and terrace, and fabulous views over the hills. You'll get no wi-fi or fancy gadgets here, but you will get space, simplicity and birdsong.

✖ Eating

Wild Fig Tree TOP CHOICE SOUTH AFRICAN **$$**
(☎013-764 2239; cnr Main & Louis Trichardt Sts; light meals R35-60, mains R90-120; ⊗breakfast, lunch & dinner) There's a meat-driven menu and a warm atmosphere here. For dinner try the SA meze, which includes ostrich medallions and crocodile kebabs. With seating on a breezy balcony, it's a very pleasant place to while away an afternoon.

Woodsman GREEK **$$**
(☎013-764 2204; Main St; mains R60-100) Half pub, half restaurant, the Woodsman has fine offerings with a Greek twist: souvlaki, grilled calamari, mezethes and other dishes mix with such local fare as pan-fried trout and ostrich in red wine.

WORTH A TRIP

PILGRIM'S REST

Tiny Pilgrim's Rest appears frozen in time – a perfectly preserved gold-rush town with wood and corrugated-iron houses lining a pretty, manicured main street. Tourists come here by the coachload and the town can feel a little Disney-fied during the height of the day. Come early in the morning, or even stay the night – when you'll be able to soak up the ghosts of the past.

The **information centre** (☎013-768 1060; Main St, Uptown; ☺9am-12.45pm & 1.15-4.30pm) sells tickets for the town's **museums** (total admission R12; ☺all 9am-12.45pm & 1.45-4pm), which include a printing shop, a restored Victorian home and a general store. Historic **Alanglade** (☎013-768 1060; admission R20; ☺tours 11am & 2pm daily) is a former mine manager's residence, furnished with period objects from the 1920s. Just east of town along the Graskop road is the open-air **Diggings Museum** (guided tours adult/child R12/6; ☺tours 10am, 11am, noon, 2pm & 3pm), where you can see how gold was panned. Tours are arranged through the information centre.

It's worth spending the night at the **Royal Hotel** (☎013-768 1100; www.royal-hotel. co.za; s/d incl breakfast from R550/800; ❆). Rooms have Victorian baths, brass beds and other period features. The Church Bar, adjoining, is a good spot for a drink.

There are sporadic minibus taxis between Pilgrim's Rest and Graskop (R20, 30 minutes), but the best way to get here is in your own vehicle.

❶ Information
Tourist Information Office (☎082 736 8253; Main St; ☺8am-5pm Mon-Fri, to 1pm Sat) Next to Engen petrol station. Very helpful; hours can be erratic.

❶ Getting There & Away
There are daily buses from Jo'burg to Nelspruit, from where you can get minibus taxis to Sabie (R30, one hour). Minibus taxis also run frequently to/from Hazyview (R30, one hour). Minibus taxis stop next to the Engen petrol station.

LIMPOPO

Limpopo is a rambling province characterised by traditional culture, wildlife and vast open spaces. With icons ranging from Mapungubwe's gold-plated rhino figurine to 'Breaker' Morant, the second Anglo-Boer War folk hero, Limpopo is an extraordinarily diverse province.

The subtropical area includes mysterious Modjadji, home of rain-summoning queens; and the Venda region, a traditional area where a python god is believed to live in Lake Fundudzi, and artists produce highly original work.

The province also contains national parks featuring the Big Five, ancient and striking landscapes and the remains of a millennium-old civilisation. And if you feel the need to get away from it all, the Waterberg Biosphere Reserve offers endless skies and a distinctly South African beauty.

Capricorn

The Capricorn region includes little more than Polokwane (Pietersburg), the provincial capital. The Tropic of Capricorn crosses the N1 halfway between Polokwane and Louis Trichardt (Makhado), marked by an anticlimactic monument and a few aloe trees.

POLOKWANE (PIETERSBURG)
☎015 / POP 140,000

Although not unpleasant, Polokwane is a provincial capital without a definable character. It's a mishmash of lively, semi-organised African chaos and security fences sheltering clipped lawns in the prim-and-proper eastern suburbs. Geographically, it's handy for visitors to use as a stopover, with plenty of decent guesthouses, two good information centres and a few interesting attractions in and around town.

❂ Sights & Activities
Polokwane Game Reserve   WILDLIFE RESERVE
(☎015-290 2331; adult/child/vehicle R17/13/25; ☺7am-5.30pm, last entry 3.30pm May-Sep, to 6.30pm, last entry 4.30pm Oct-Apr) Less than 5km south of Polokwane, you can go on safari at this 3250-hectare reserve, home to zebras, giraffes and white rhinos, among others.

Bakone Malapa Open-Air Museum   MUSEUM

(☑015-295 2432; adult/child R7.50/5; ⊗9am-3.30pm Mon-Sat) Located 9km south of Polokwane on Rte 37 to Chuniespoort, this museum features a recreated village showcasing the customs of the Northern Sotho people who lived here 300 years ago.

FREE **Hugh Exton**

Photographic Museum   MUSEUM

(☑015-290 2186; Civic Sq; ⊗9am-3.30pm Mon-Fri) Set in a restored 19th-century church, Hugh Exton covers Polokwane's first half-century and the second Anglo-Boer War through the work of the prolific photographer.

🍽 Sleeping & Eating

TOP CHOICE **Plumtree Lodge**   GUESTHOUSE $$

(☑015-295 6153; www.plumtree.co.za; 138 Marshall St; s/d incl breakfast R620/790; ❀🐾🛜) This German-run guesthouse's bungalow rooms are some of the most spacious and appealing in town. Standard features are high ceilings, lounge areas, minibars and DSTV. Rates are cheaper on weekends.

Rustic Rest   GUESTHOUSE $$

(☑015-295 7402; www.rusticrest.co.za; 36 Rabe St; s/d incl breakfast R630/840; ❀) Family-run Rustic Rest is one of the best deals in Polokwane, offering DSTV, minibars and friendly service.

TOP CHOICE **Cafe Pavilion**   CAFE $$

(Kerk St, Sterkloop Garden Pavilion; mains R55-90; ⊗8am-5pm Mon-Sat, to 2pm Sun) Overlooking a garden centre, the Pavilion is Polokwane's venue of choice for long, leisurely meals. Food has the usual focus on meat feasts prepared in a variety of styles, with a couple of salads thrown in for good measure.

ℹ Information

Limpopo Tourism & Parks Board (☑015-293 3600; www.golimpopo.com; N1; ⊗8am-4.30pm Mon-Fri) On the N1, approaching town from the south, this office covers the whole province.

Polokwane Municipality Local Development Office (☑015-290 2010; www.polokwane.gov. za; Landdros Mare St, Civic Sq; ⊗7.45am-5pm Mon-Fri) A better source of Polokwane information; has brochures and a list of accommodation.

ℹ Getting There & Away

AIR

SAAirlink (☑0861 606 606; www.flyairlink. com), with offices at the airport, flies daily to/

from Jo'burg (around R1150 one way). **Polokwane airport** (☑015-288 0122) is 5km north of town.

BUS

Citiliner and Eagle Liner have daily departures to Harare (from R365, 12 hours).

Translux (☑0861 589 282; www.translux. co.za; cnr Joubert & Thabo Mbeki Sts) runs services to Jo'burg (R185, 4½ hours) via Pretoria (R185, 3½ hours). There are also cheaper City to City buses (R145).

CAR

Located at the airport:

Avis (☑015-288 0171)

Budget (☑015-288 0169)

First (☑015-291 4819)

MINIBUS TAXI

Minibus taxis run to destinations including Louis Trichardt (R50, 1½ hours) and Thohoyandou (R65, 2½ hours) from the rank at the Indian Centre, on the corner of Kerk and Excelsior Sts. For Jo'burg and Pretoria, head to the main rank, on the corner of Kerk and Devenish Sts (prices are similar to those for the bus, which is faster and safer).

TRAIN

Economy-class Shosholoza Meyl trains stop in Polokwane as they travel between Jo'burg (R70, nine hours) and Musina (R90, 3½ hours).

Bushveld

MOKOPANE (POTGIETERSRUS) & AROUND

☑015 / POP 120,000

Mokopane is a tough Bushveld town. The main attractions for visitors are Makapan's Caves – a fossil trove of world significance and the site of the Ndebele people's resistance to the advancing Voortrekkers. The area forms part of a mineral-rich region the size of Ireland. Over the weekend, accommodation empties as mine workers flood home.

A drive through the 1300-hectare Game Breeding Centre (☑015-491 4314; Thabo Mbeki Dr; adult/child R20/12, feeding tours R35;

WHAT'S IN A NAME?

Many town names in Limpopo have changed in recent years. Where possible, we'll list the new name, followed by the old moniker. Many locals still use the former names and some old road signs still exist.

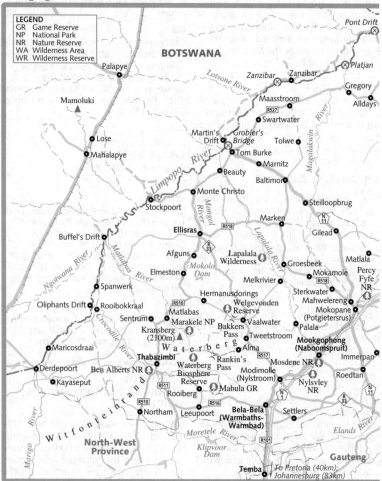

⏱8am-4pm Mon-Fri, to 6pm Sat & Sun) yields sightings of gibbons, wild dogs and lions. It's the breeding centre for the National Zoo in Pretoria. Accommodation (R230/300 for singles/doubles) is available.

Makapan's Caves (☎079 515 6491; adult/student R25/15), 23km northeast of Mokopane, was declared a World Heritage Site for its palaeontological significance, having yielded the skull of a 3.3-million-year-old humanoid. Chief Makapan and 1000-plus followers were besieged here for a month in 1854 by the Voortrekkers. You must prebook visits.

BELA-BELA (WARMBATHS)
☎014 / POP 37,200

The small, soporific town of Bela-Bela has grown on the back of the hot springs discovered by the Setswana in the early 19th century. Around 22,000L of the warm stuff bubbles out of the earth every hour and there's no shortage of folk from the big cities to soak it up.

At the **hydro spa** (☎014-736 8500; www.aventura.co.za; Chris Hani Dr; day/evening R90/100; ⏱7am-4pm & 5-10pm), children head to the pools with slides, while those who prefer a more relaxing experience can wallow in 52°C water. There's also a range of

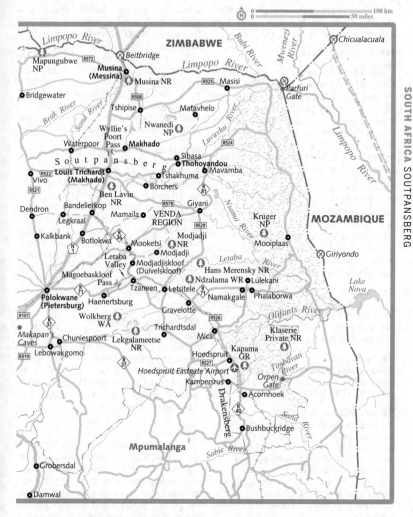

accommodation here (campsites from R250, rooms from R1650).

There are restaurants at the Waterfront, including good breakfasts and lunches at **Greenfields** (Old Pretoria Rd, The Waterfront; mains R30-60; ⏲breakfast & lunch).

Soutpansberg

LOUIS TRICHARDT (MAKHADO)
☑015 / POP 90,000

Spunky Louis Trichardt has a very busy centre with streets of booming retail chain outlets and hordes of shoppers. The outlying streets, however, reveal verdant parkland, wide roads and shady jacarandas, giving the place a very pleasant feel.

There's not much to do here, but it's a great base, especially if you have wheels – 10km north and south of town are some superb places to stay. The nearby spectacular Soutpansberg mountains boast an extraordinary diversity of flora and fauna, with one of the continent's highest concentrations of the African leopard and more tree species than you'll spot in the whole of Canada.

Louis Trichardt changed its name to Makhado, reverted to its original moniker and is now amid a dispute over whether it should be renamed Makhado again. Both names feature on maps and road signs.

🛏 Sleeping & Eating

TOP CHOICE **Ultimate Guest House**   GUESTHOUSE **$$**
(☎015-517 7005; www.ultimategh.co.za; s/d incl breakfast R555/730; ⊠) After a long day on the N1, this quirky guesthouse's name seems a fair description. It has a bar-restaurant (mains R90) with a verandah overlooking a lush valley. It's 10km from the centre; turn left 100m after Mountain Inn, head 1.6km along the dirt track and it'll be on your right.

Madi a Thavha   LODGE **$$**
(☎015-516 0220; www.madiathavha.com; campsites per person R90, s/d incl breakfast R625/1030; ⊠) This Fair Trade–accredited farm lodge offers colourful little cottages with Venda bedspreads and cushions, tea-light candles aplenty and kitchenettes. It's some 10km west of Louis Trichardt, off Rte 522.

Casa Café   INTERNATIONAL **$**
(129 Krogh St; mains R50-60; ⊘breakfast, lunch & dinner Mon-Sat, lunch Sun) Opening onto a garden, this place serves seafood dishes, loads of burger variations, salads and pastas.

ℹ Information

Soutpansberg Tourist Office (☎015-516 3415; www.soutpansberg-tourism.co.za; Songozwi Rd; ⊘8am-4.30pm Mon-Sat)

ℹ Getting There & Away

The **Louis Trichardt Travel Agency** (☎015-516 5042; ⊘8am-1pm & 2-4.30pm Mon-Fri, 9-11am Sat), down an alley off Krogh St (opposite Louis Trichardt Stationers), is the local agent for Greyhound and Translux buses.

Most buses to Jo'burg (R225, 6½ hours) and Harare, Zimbabwe (R395, 11 hours) stop by the Caltex petrol station on the corner of the N1 and Baobab St.

The minibus-taxi rank is in the Shoprite supermarket car park off Burger St. Destinations from Louis Trichardt include Musina (R40, 1½ hours) and Polokwane (R50, 1½ hours).

The train station, at the southwestern end of Kruger St, is served by the Bosvelder train.

AROUND LOUIS TRICHARDT (MAKHADO)

SOUTPANSBERG MOUNTAINS

Beginning on the outskirts of town, the two-day, 20.5km **Hanglip Trail** (☎013-754 2724; www.komatiecotourism.co.za) climbs through indigenous forest to a 1719m peak. Take precautions against malaria, bilharzia and ticks. Overnight accommodation is in huts (per person R105); alternatively, a 2½-hour walk begins in the same location.

There are a number of Soutpansberg hideaways off Rte 522 to Vivo, including Fair Trade–accredited **Leshiba Wilderness** (☎015-593 0076; www.leshiba.co.za; 2-person chalets R420, s/d incl full board & an activity R1925/3200; @⊠), a dreamy resort perched in the clouds and based on a Venda village.

MUSINA (MESSINA)
☎015 / POP 20,000

Some 18km south of the Beitbridge border crossing with Zimbabwe, Musina hums with typical border-town tension. The cars, many visiting from Zimbabwe, never seem to stop blowing their horns; and groups of economic refugees from the defunct state trudge along the N1, hiking south in search of work.

The **Musina Nature Reserve** (☎015-534 3235; admission free; ⊘7.30am-6.30pm daily), 5km south of town, is a good spot to admire the giant baobab trees that characterise this region.

🛏 Sleeping & Eating

Backpackers Lodge   BACKPACKERS **$**
(☎082 401 2939; 23 Bachman Ave; r R200) This excellent budget option, set up in a suburban home, is great value. Beds are firm, the place is clean, rooms have TV and the cooking facilities are well equipped. Located off Rte 508 next to the police station.

TOP CHOICE **Ilala Country Lodge**   LODGE **$$**
(☎076 138 0699; ilala@vodamail.co.za; Rte 572; s/d incl breakfast R500/700; ⊠) You'll find sweeping views of the Limpopo River Valley and outstanding accommodation here. As well as rooms, there are huge chalets with lounge area, *braai* facilities and separate kitchen. It's 8km northwest of town, on the way to Mapungubwe.

Tikva Coffee Shop   CAFE **$**
(14 Paul Mills Ave; light meals R50) With an outdoor terrace overlooking a quiet suburban street, Tikva is a great local spot to chow down on freshly prepared wraps, paninis and pancakes.

ℹ Information

Musina Tourism (☎015-534 3500; www.golimpopo.com; National Rd) In a thatched hut on the way into town on the N1 from Polokwane. Keeps erratic hours; always shut when we passed by.

WORTH A TRIP

NYLSVLEY NATURE RESERVE

The 4000-hectare Nylsvley Nature Reserve (www.nylsvley.co.za; adult/child/vehicle R15/10/25; ⊘6am-6pm), on the Nyl River flood plain, is one of the country's best places to see birds (380 species are listed).

The Nylsvley Wildlife Resort (☑014-743 6925; campsites per person R30, 2-person chalets R480) is birding central and offers well-organised accommodation in the reserve. Nylsvley is 20km south of Mookgophong (Naboomspruit), signposted from Rte 101.

The Waterberg

The 150km-long Waterberg range, which makes up part of the Bushveld region, stretches northeast from Thabazimbi in southern Limpopo. Protected by a Unesco biosphere reserve the size of the Okavango Delta, it's a wild and inspirational place etched by rivers.

If you fancy exploring the rolling terrain of the Waterberg on horseback, several operators near Vaalwater can set you up with a steed. Horizon Horseback Adventures (☑0834 191 929; www.ridinginafrica.com) offers intrepid options.

The mountainous Marakele National Park (☑014-777 6928; www.sanparks.org/parks/marakele; adult/child R120/60; ⊘6am-5.30pm May-Aug, to 6pm Sep-Apr) is at the southwestern end of the Waterberg Biosphere Reserve. As well as elephants, rhinos and other large wildlife species, you can see one of the world's largest colonies of the endangered Cape vulture.

Regular cars can access much of the park, including the sky-high vulture-viewing point, as well as the hard-dirt Bakkers Pass Rd, which runs alongside the mountains from Vaalwater and offers spectacular views.

The park offers tent sites (2-person campsites R205, extra adult/child R68/34) and, at Tlopi Tent Camp (tents R1065), 15km from reception, furnished tents with bathroom and open-air kitchen.

Look out for the *Waterberg Meander* leaflet in local tourist offices. The 350km route links 13 community projects and sites of interest.

---

❶ Getting There & Away

The Zimbabwe border at Beitbridge is open 24 hours. If you are coming from Zimbabwe, there is a large taxi rank on the South African side of the border. If you want to take a minibus taxi further south than Musina, catch one here as there are many more than Musina.

Daily Eagle Liner buses go from Beitbridge to Harare (R400, eight hours) and Bulawayo (R350, 4½ hours), picking up at the Beitbridge Hotel.

Taxis between the border and Musina cost R35 (20 minutes).

Car hire is available at Avis (☑015-534 2220; 10 Hans van der Merwe Ave, Lifestyle Corner; ⊘8am-5pm Mon-Fri).

MAPUNGUBWE NATIONAL PARK

A Unesco World Heritage Site, Mapungubwe National Park (☑015-534 7923; www.sanparks.org/parks/mapungubwe; adult/child R120/60; ⊘6am-6.30pm) contains South Africa's most significant Iron Age site, as well as animals ranging from white and black rhinos to the rare Pel's fishing owl to meerkats.

The park will realise its full potential when plans to incorporate it into an 800,000-hectare transfrontier conservation area, which will stretch into Botswana and Zimbabwe, are implemented by respective governments.

The impressive interpretative centre (adult/child R40/20) has plenty of information on the Mapungubwe cultural landscape, including finds from archaeological digs. Keep an eye out for the exquisite beadwork and the replica of the famous gold rhino. Guided tours are obligatory.

Self-catering accommodation ranges from camping (campsites from R205) to forest tents at Limpopo Forest Camp (luxury tents R950) and the chalets at Leokwe Camp (chalets from R1100; ❄️🍽️).

Be aware that there is no shop or restaurant here.

Mapungubwe is a 60km drive from Musina on Rte 572 to Pont Drift.

Venda Region

The most enigmatic section of the Soutpansberg region, this is the traditional home of

DON'T MISS

LAKE FUNDUDZI

Lake Fundudzi is a sacred site that emerges spectacularly from forested hills, a turquoise gem on a bed of green velvet. The python god, who holds an important place in the rites of the Venda's matriarchal culture, is believed to live in the lake.

You can't visit the lake, 35km northwest of Thohoyandou, without permission from its custodians, the Netshiavha people. The easiest way to get permission is to hire a guide in Thohoyandou, Elim or Louis Trichardt. Remember that when you approach the lake you must do so with proper respect; turn your back to it, bend over, and view it from between your legs.

Basic accommodation is available at the community-run **Funduzi African Ivory Route Camp** (☏072 778 3252; www.africanivoryroute.co.za; per person R475).

the Venda people, who moved to the area from modern-day Zimbabwe in the early 18th century. The last 'homeland' created by the apartheid regime, the Venda region is a world away from the South Africa of uptown Jo'burg; here even a short diversion from the freeway takes you through an Africa of mist-clad hilltops, dusty streets and mud huts, a land where myth and legend continue to play a major role in everyday life.

ELIM & AROUND

The tiny township of Elim, some 25km southeast of Louis Trichardt, is closer to the N1 than the Venda capital Thohoyandou and makes a more convenient, and pleasanter, base for touring the Venda and Tsonga-Shangaan art-and-craft studios.

There are also some worthwhile cooperatives, including the **Twananani weavers** and the **Mukhondeni Pottery Factory**. The **Ribolla Tourism Association** (☏015-556 4262; www.openafrica.org; Old Khoja Bldg, Elim) produces a useful brochure and can help to source local guides.

Set among verdant greenery on the shores of Albasini Dam, **Shiluvari Lakeside Lodge** (☏015-556 3406; www.shiluvari.com; s/d incl breakfast R550/900; ❄) is immersed in

the local culture and countryside. Thatched chalets, standard rooms and a family suite, reached on walkways lined with sculptures, are adorned with local craftwork that can be purchased in the on-site shop. A country restaurant and pub are also here.

Translux buses serve Jo'burg (R200, seven hours) and Sibasa (R90, one hour).

Valley of the Olifants

These days, the Valley of the Olifants may be largely devoid of pachyderms, but the subtropical area feels exotic in places. The region is culturally rich, being the traditional home of the Tsonga-Shangaan and Lobedu peoples. Phalaborwa, a popular entry point to the Kruger National Park, is the start of the 'Kruger to Beach' trail to the Mozambican coast. The main town of Tzaneen and the pretty village of Haenertsburg make pleasant bases for trips to the scenic Modjadji and Magoebaskloof areas.

LETABA VALLEY

The Letaba Valley, east of Polokwane, is lush, with tea plantations and fruit farms overlooked by forested hills. At Haenertsburg, known locally as 'The Mountain', Rte 71 climbs northeast over the steep **Magoebaskloof Pass**. A less scenic route to Tzaneen is Rte 528, which runs along the gentler George's Valley. With a great pub and a couple of upmarket restaurants, **Haenertsburg** makes an excellent alternative base to Tzaneen.

Magoebaskloof is the escarpment on the edge of the highveld, and Rte 71 careers down to Tzaneen and the lowveld, winding through plantations and tracts of thick indigenous forest.

There are a number of waterfalls in the area, including the glorious **Debengeni Falls** (De Hoek State Forest; adult R10; ⊙8am-5pm). Turn left off Rte 71 just after the sign saying 'Tzaneen 15km'.

There are 10 **walking trails** (☏013-754 2724; www.komatiecotourism.co.za) in the area, and six huts, including some above Debengeni Falls. A recommended option is the three-night, 40km **Dokolewa Waterfall Trail**.

Magoebaskloof Adventures (☏0838 661 546; www.thabametsi.com) runs adventure trips in the area, including kloofing (canyoning), tubing, fly-fishing, mountain biking, horse riding and canopy tours.

Off Rte 71, near the junction of Rte 36, **Pekoe View Tea Garden** (⊙10am-5pm) is on the estate where Magoebaskloof tea is grown.

TZANEEN & AROUND
☏015 / POP 81,000

An affluent town with a chaotic street layout, Tzaneen makes a very pleasant place to base yourself for a few days on your way to Kruger, the Blyde River Canyon or deeper into Limpopo's arts-and-crafts territory further north. The Letaba Valley's largest town has personality – not a description we'd bestow on many other Limpopo towns. The pace of life is slow, but you can shake off the stupor at some cool hideaways and quirky sights in the surrounding hills.

◎ Sights & Activities

Tzaneen Museum　　　　　　　MUSEUM
(Agatha St; donation welcome; ⊙9am-4pm Mon-Fri, to noon Sat) The town museum is particularly interesting if you're visiting Modjadji or the Venda region.

Kings Walden　　　　　　　　GARDENS
(www.kingswalden.co.za; Agatha; ⊙daylight) This formal English garden sits at 1050m and offers sweeping Drakensberg views. Decadent picnics are available (R100 per person).

Modjadji Nature Reserve　　NATURE RESERVE
(adult/vehicle R15/25; ⊙7.30am-6pm) Covering 305 hectares, Modjadji Nature Reserve protects forests of the ancient Modjadji cycad. **Modjadji African Ivory Route Camp** (☏015-781 0690) offers basic *rondavels* and hiking trails among the 800-year-old plant species.

Take the Modjadji turn-off from Rte 36 about 10km north of Modjadjiskloof (Duivelskloof); after 10km, turn left at the signpost to the reserve, then right at the signpost 12km further on, and continue for 5km.

Sunland Nursery　　　　　　GARDENS
(www.bigbaobab.co.za; Sunland Nursery; adult/child R15/free; ⊙9am-5pm) On the road to Modjadji, look out for signs to the 22m-high Sunland Boabab. It takes 40 tree-huggers with outstretched arms to encircle its 47m circumference. The bar no longer occupies the two cavities that it used to inside the tree, but you can still take a peek.

⏚ Sleeping & Eating

TOP CHOICE **Kings Walden**　　　　　　HOTEL $$
(☏015-307 3262; www.kingswalden.co.za; Old Coach Rd, Agatha; s/d incl breakfast R950/1450;

☎🅿) The sizeable rooms are as dreamy as the gardens and mountains they overlook, with fireplaces, antiquated prints everywhere, and bathrooms you could get lost in.

Silver Palms Lodge　　　　　HOTEL $$
(☏015-307 3092; Monument St; r economy/luxury incl breakfast R550/800; ❄🅿) This good-value hotel is cheaper on weekends. The luxury rooms here are newer and in better shape. The big plus to staying here is the sunken swimming pool, which backs onto a bar...

TOP CHOICE **Market Cafe**　　　　　　　CAFE $
(Tzaneen Lifestyle Centre; mains R30-40) A small operation delivering quality breakfasts, light lunches (salads and wraps) and even more substantial meals such as steaks and pizzas.

❶ Getting There & Away

Checkers (Letaba Blvd shopping centre) sells tickets for the daily Translux buses to Phalaborwa (R125, one hour), Jo'burg (R255,6½ hours) and Polokwane (R155, two hours).

Most minibus taxis depart from the rank behind the Tzaneng Mall.

PHALABORWA
☏015 / POP 109,000

Phalaborwa is a stretch of suburban tidiness on the edge of Kruger, with a green belt in the centre and the occasional warthog grazing on a lawn. There's a range of sleeping options thanks to the town's proximity to the park.

Phalaborwa makes an ideal starting point if you're intending to explore central and northern Kruger. For people with limited time in South Africa, it is possible to visit Kruger by flying from Jo'burg to Phalaborwa (or Hoedspruit) and hiring a car at the airport. **Africa Unlimited** (☏015-781 7466; www.africaunltd.co.za) offers activities including astronomy safaris, river cruises, bush walks and Kruger trips.

Phalaborwa is also a gateway to Mozambique, as it's possible to drive across Kruger and into Mozambique via the **Giriyondo Gate** (☏013-735 8919) in a car with good clearance.

Hans Merensky Estate (☏015-781 3931; www.hansmerensky.com; 3 Copper Rd; 9-/18-hole round R240/435) is an 18-hole championship golf course with a difference: here you have to hold your shot while wildlife from the adjoining Kruger crosses the fairways.

🛏 Sleeping & Eating

Elephant Walk   BACKPACKERS $
(☎015-781 5860; elephant.walk@nix.co.za; 30 Anna Scheepers Ave; campsites R90, dm/s/tw without bathroom R110/210/320, B&B s/d R310/520; ❄) Close enough to Kruger to hear the lions roar, this is a great spot to plan your foray into the park. The rooms with en suite are more like a guesthouse.

Daan & Zena's   BACKPACKERS $
(☎015-781 6049; www.daanzena.co.za; 15 Birkenhead St; s/d from R300/350; ❄@🖳) Bridging the gap between a backpackers and a B&B, Daan & Zena's is brought to life by lashings of colour and a friendly atmosphere. A good spot if you're looking for a comfy bed and a youthful vibe.

Kaia Tani   GUESTHOUSE $$
(☎015-781 1358; www.kaiatani.com; 29 Boekenhout St; r per person incl breakfast R620; ❄🖳🏊) The six rooms at this reader-recommended guesthouse have flourishes such as rope-lined wooden walls, and a thatched restaurant-bar overlooking the rock swimming pool.

Buffalo Pub & Grill   PUB $$
(1 Lekkerbreek St; mains R70-90; ❄) If you've emerged from Kruger feeling like a hungry lion, stop here for some pub grub. There's a terrace for al fresco dining and African trimmings aplenty. Best of all, locals recommend the place.

ℹ Information

Bollanoto Tourism Centre (☎015-769 5090; www.phalaborwa.co.za; cnr Hendrick van Eck & Pres Steyn Sts) The centre kept very unpredictable opening hours when we dropped by – try your luck.

ℹ Getting There & Away

AIR

SAAirlink (☎015-781 5823; www.flyairlink. com), with an office at the airport, flies daily to Jo'burg (from R1700). The airport is 2km north of town.

SA Express (☎0861 729 227; www.flyexpress. aero) flies daily out of Hoedspruit Eastgate airport (Rte 40) to Jo'burg (from R1350).

BUS

Sure Turn Key Travel (☎015-781 7760; Sealene St) is the local agent for Translux/City to City. Translux connects Phalaborwa with Jo'burg (R255, eight hours) via Tzaneen, Polokwane and Pretoria; City to City travels to Jo'burg (R205, 9½ hours) via Middelburg.

CAR

Hiring a car is often the cheapest way of seeing Kruger. **Avis** (☎015-781 3169) and **Hertz** (☎015-781 3565) have offices at the airport.

MINIBUS TAXI

There aren't many minibus taxis in this area, and most run from the township of Namakgale (R7, 20 minutes).

NORTH-WEST PROVINCE

This stretch of bushveld between Pretoria and the Kalahari is famous for Sun City, the southern hemisphere's answer to Las Vegas. The slot machines and kitsch edifices are grotesquely fascinating, but you may prefer a different kind of gambling in nearby Pilanesberg National Park. Wager that lions and rhinos will wander to the waterhole you have staked out; sightings on self-drive safaris come with a serendipitous thrill.

Alternatively, improve your odds of spotting elusive predators, in Pilanesberg and Madikwe Game Reserve, by joining a guided drive or walk. For that once-in-a-lifetime, romantic *Out of Africa*–style experience, a night in the bush at Madikwe's exclusive lodges can't be beat.

Conveniently, these opportunities to encounter big cats and one-armed bandits are all within four hours' drive of Jo'burg.

Rustenburg

Sitting on the edge of the Magaliesberg mountains, Rustenburg is a big country town with an urban grittiness to its crowded central business district.

Sitting just 40km southeast of Sun City and Pilanesberg National Park, it makes a good budget base for travellers wishing to visit these major attractions without paying high accommodation rates. Just south of town are **Bushwillows B&B** (☎014-537 2333; wjmcgill@lantic.net; r per person incl breakfast R250; ❄), a quaint country retreat with basic rooms, and **Hodge Podge Lodge** (☎0846 980 417; www.hodgepodgebackpackers. co.za; Plot 66, Kommiesdrift; campsites R50, dm R150, r per person R300; ❄), which has dinky en suite cabins, a pool and a range of tours on offer.

Rustenburg is not well serviced by public transport and you really need to hire a car to get here.

North-West Province

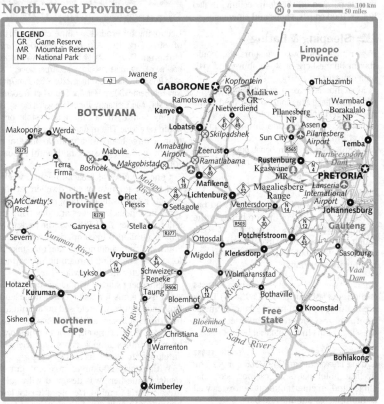

Sun City

☑014

Welcome to Sin City, South African style. At Sun City, the legendary creation of entrepreneur Sol Kerzer, Disneyland collides with ancient Egypt in Africa's version of Vegas. Filled with artificial beaches, 1200 hotel rooms and line upon line of clinking slot machines, it serves no other purpose than to entertain. Yet even though there's no question this gambling-centric resort is almost grotesquely gaudy, a visit here can also be pretty damn fun.

Although it was started as an apartheid-era haven for wealthy whites, these days one of Sun City's best features is the mix of black, white and Asian people who flock here. Losers at the tables can console themselves with the thought that they are helping to pay more than 7000 salaries.

If you're travelling with children or on a budget, Sun City is a good bargain. The admission fee covers all the main attractions, and you'll be given R30 in 'Sunbucks', which can be spent at the various restaurants, shops or slot machines. If you've got the cash to splash out, this place boasts one of the world's most luxurious hotels.

❂ Sights & Activities

The best part of Sun City is **Lost City**, entered over a bridge flanked by life-size fake elephants. The African-themed mega-amusement park mostly consists of **Valley of the Waves** (adult/child R120/70, overnight guests free; ⊘9am-6pm Sep-Apr, 10am-5pm May-Aug), a pool with a large wave-making machine, a sandy beach, water slides and various rides. It's good, kitsch fun.

You'll find separate smoking and nonsmoking casinos in the **entertainment centre**. Done up in a jungle theme with animal murals painted on the dome ceiling, it also houses food courts, shops and cinemas.

🛏 Sleeping & Eating

If you have your own transport, you could stay in Pilanesberg or Rustenburg and visit on a day trip.

Most hotels have a selection of restaurants and there are plenty of fast-food joints in the entertainment centre.

Bookings can be made through Sun International central reservations (☏011-780 7810; www.suninternational.com), though you can usually find a better rate using an online booking engine.

Palace of the Lost City   LUXURY HOTEL $$$
(s/d incl breakfast from R5200/5460; ❀❄) Consistently ranked one of the top hotels in the world, this place does a good job at redefining the fantasy of luxury. The rooms are done up with bold-coloured carpets and hand-painted ceilings.

Cascades   LUXURY HOTEL $$$
(s/d incl breakfast from R3580/3750; ❀❄) There are multiple pools, al fresco island dining at Santorini restaurant, and luxuries such as dressing rooms in the palatial bedrooms.

Sun City Hotel   CASINO HOTEL $$$
(s/d incl breakfast from R3490/3660; ❀❄) The liveliest hotel packs in casinos, slot machines and an entertainment centre, as well as multiple restaurants and bars.

Sun City Cabanas   RESORT $$$
(r incl breakfast from R2625; ❀❄) Sun City's most informal and affordable option is the best choice for families, with facilities and activities for children. Family rooms with a fold-out sofa and up to eight beds are available.

ℹ Information

Welcome Centre (☏014-557 1544; ⏲8am-7pm Mon-Thu, to 10pm Sat & Sun) At the entrance to the Entertainment Centre. There's a Computicket branch here too.

ℹ Getting There & Away

From Jo'burg it's less than a three-hour drive. The most straightforward route is via Rustenburg and Boshoek on Rte 565.

Ingelosi Shuttles (☏014-552 3260; www.ingelositours.co.za; Welcome Centre, Entertainment Complex) runs daily air-conditioned shuttles to/from Jo'burg, Pretoria and OR Tambo International Airport (R400).

Pilanesberg National Park

Occupying an eroded alkaline crater north of Sun City, the 550-sq-km Pilanesberg National Park (☏014-555 1600; www.parksnorthwest.co.za/pilanesberg; adult/pensioner & child R65/20, vehicle R20, map R20; ⏲5.30am-7pm Nov-Feb, 6am-6.30pm Mar, Apr, Sep & Oct, 6.30am-6pm May-Aug, last entry 1hr before gates close) is among South Africa's most accessible big-game reserves. The malaria-free park is less than a three-hour drive from Jo'burg, and its two southern gates are both within about 10km of Sun City.

Conceptualised as a back-to-nature weekend escape for nearby city dwellers at the end of the 1970s, Pilanesberg remains a haven where lions, buffaloes and day trippers still roam today. And although the park may appear developed in comparison with some South African wildernesses, don't mistake it for a zoo. The animals roaming the extinct volcano crater are 100% wild.

Pilanesberg started with Operation Genesis in 1979, a mission that reclaimed the land from agriculture and released 6000 animals into the area. Today, all the Big Five are here, as are cheetahs, caracals, African wild dogs, hyenas, giraffes, hippos, zebras, a variety of antelopes and 300-plus bird species.

With nearly 200km of excellent gravel roads, Pilanesberg was designed with self-drive safaris in mind. Devote at least a few hours to camping out with a cooler of Castles and a pair of binoculars in one of the many public hides, which have been constructed next to the water sources that attract thirsty animals.

Gametrackers Outdoor Adventures (☏014-552 5020; www.gametrac.co.za; wildlife drives adult/child R370/195), in Sun City and at Bakgatla and Manyane Gates, offers a dizzying range of organised activities, and **Mankwe Safaris** (☏014-555 7056; www.mankwesafaris.co.za; Heritage Game Drive adult/child under 16yr/child under 10yr R395/230/145) combines looking for wildlife with Setswana cultural lessons.

🛏 Sleeping & Eating

Manyane   CAMPGROUND, RESORT $$
(☏014-555 1000; www.goldenleopardresorts.co.za; campsites R260, safari tent s/d incl breakfast R950/1050, chalet s/d incl breakfast R1530/1630; ❀❄) The thatched African chalets are comfortable and facilities include a reasonable

shop, a poolside restaurant and grassy *braai* areas.

TOP
CHOICE **Bakubung** LODGE $$$

(☎014-552 6000; www.legacyhotels.co.za; s/d with half board R3025/4280; ❄🛜🏊) The thatched chalets are well kitted out and the lodge is attractively arranged, its terrace and lawn overlooking a waterhole. The Marula Grill *lapa* (large, thatched common area) restaurant is one of Pilanesberg's smartest.

Kwa Maritane LODGE $$$

(☎014-552 5100; www.legacyhotels.co.za; s/d half board R3025/4280; ❄🛜🏊) Kwa Maritane's smart thatched rooms encircle its pool, and the restaurant verandah has a bird's-eye view of bush-covered hills and rocky cliffs.

❶ Getting There & Away

There are four gates into Pilanesberg. Driving, the route described to Sun City is sensible for Bakubung and Kwa Maritane Gates. For Manyane and Bakgatla Gates, you may prefer to take Rte 510, which runs between Rustenburg and Thabazimbi.

Madikwe Game Reserve

South Africa's fourth-largest game reserve (☎018-350 9931; www.parksnorthwest.co.za; adult/child R150/60) is vastly underrated. It comprises 760 sq km of bushveld, savannah grassland and riverine forest on the edge of the Kalahari Desert. Closer to Jo'burg than Kruger, it offers Big Five wildlife viewing and dreamy lodging in striking (and malaria-free) red-sand and thorn-bush environs.

🛏 Sleeping & Eating

Madikwe is not open to day visitors, so to visit you'll have to book into one of the lodges within the park. Any rates quoted are usually per person per day, based on double occupancy, and include meals, wildlife drives and evening sundowners.

TOP
CHOICE **Mosetlha Bush Camp** LODGE $$$

(☎011-444 9345; www.thebushcamp.com; Abjaterskop Gate; s/d with full board & activities R2295/3590) The reserve's only non-five-star option has donkey boilers, bucket showers and VIP toilets (ventilation-improved pit). With nine open-fronted cabins around the campfire, Mosetlha is truly off the grid. There's no electricity or running water.

Tau Game Lodge LODGE $$$

(☎011-314 4350; www.taugamelodge.com; Tau Gate; per person with full board R3300; ❄🛜) The cosy thatched chalets have giant bathtubs, massive outdoor bush showers, huge beds, and private decks for watching the waterhole action. The Tau Foundation seeks to benefit the local people, and guests can visit schools and community schemes.

❶ Getting There & Away

Madikwe is next to the Kopfontein/Tlokweng Gate border crossing with Botswana, about 400km northwest of J'burg and Pretoria via the N4 and Rte 47/49 (the road is referred to by both numbers). If you don't have your own transport, you can organise a transfer through your lodge or take a Gaborone (Botswana) bus and arrange for your lodge to pick you up from the Kopfontein border crossing, where the bus will stop.

Mafikeng

The excellent **Mafikeng Museum** (☎018-381 0773; cnr Carrington & Martin Sts; admission by donation; ⊙8am-4pm Mon-Fri, 10am-12.30pm Sat) has reams of quirky regional information, including an exhibit charting the rise of the Boy Scout Movement and a room dedicated to the famous 217-day siege. It occupies the former town hall (built 1904). There's a **tourist information** desk here too.

Mafikeng also comprises Mmabatho, built as the capital of the 'independent' homeland of Bophuthatswana, and famous for the monumental and absurd buildings erected by corrupt Bophuthatswana president Lucas Mangope. Today Mafikeng is a friendly and relaxed town with a large middle-class black population.

If you want to stay over, **Ferns Country House** (☎018-381 5971; 12 Cooke St; s/d from R590/690; @🏊) is a quiet option with two pools, secure parking and a variety of rooms. The bar-restaurant (mains R75) serves good food, although service can be slow.

NORTHERN CAPE

With just a million people inhabiting its 373,000 sq km, the Northern Cape is South Africa's last great frontier. The scattered towns are hundreds of kilometres apart, connected by empty roads across the wildernesses of Namakwa, the Kalahari and Upper Karoo. In these sublime, surreal expanses,

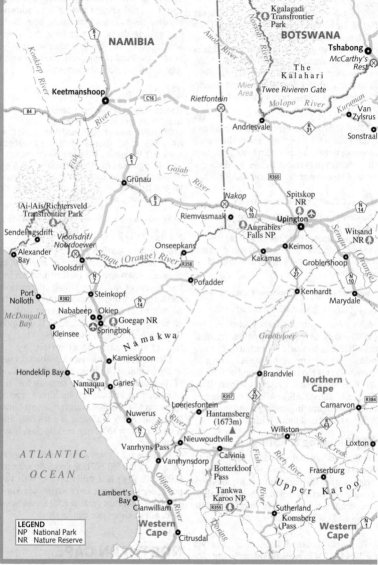

reality disappears faster than a meerkat into its burrow. Under the remorseless sun, vehicles share park roads with lions, dune boards swish down roaring sands, and Kimberley's pubs serve as they have done since the 19th-century diamond rush.

It's a raw, elemental land, where gnarly camel-thorn, quiver and Halfmens trees break the boundless horizons. Yet some of nature's greatest tricks here are the instances of rejuvenating beauty. The Senqu (Orange) River waters this dry region, creating

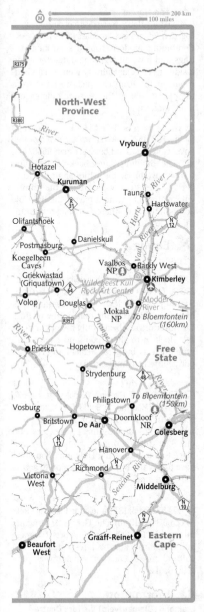

Kimberley

053 / POP 170,500

Whether you are drinking in raucous saloons dating back to the diamond rush, surveying the world's largest hand-dug hole, or on a ghost tour, learning about the folk who lived, mined and died here, Kimberley is an excellent place to get stuck into South Africa's eventful history.

The last earth was shovelled at the landmark Big Hole back in 1914, but the Northern Cape's capital remains synonymous with diamonds. Step inside an atmospheric old pub, with dark interiors, scarred wooden tables and last century's liquor ads, and you'll feel you've been transported to Kimberley's rough-and-ready mining heyday.

The Northern Cape's only real city is also home to fantastic museums, some wonderful accommodation and Galeshewe, a township with plenty of its own history.

⊙ Sights

Big Hole Complex MUSEUM
(053-830 4417; www.thebighole.co.za; West Circular Rd; adult/child R75/45; ⊗8am-5pm, tours on the hour Mon-Fri, weekends 9am, 11am, 1pm & 3pm) Although the R50 million that turned the Big Hole into a world-class tourist destination came from De Beers Consolidated Mines, touring the world's largest hand-dug hole gives an honest impression of the mining industry's chequered past in Kimberley. Whether you join a free guided tour or wander round by yourself, visits start with a film about mining conditions in late-19th-century Kimberley, followed by a walk along the viewing platform for a vertigo-inducing view of the water filling all but the last 175m of the Big Hole.

A lift takes you down a shaft for the simulated mine experience, where audio and visual effects give an idea of how bad life was for the black diamond miners.

Outside, and entered for free, is a perfect partial reconstruction of Kimberley's 1880s mining settlement. Try your luck panning for diamonds and hitting skittles in the bowling alley.

William Humphreys Art Gallery GALLERY
(053-831 1724; www.whag.co.za; 1 Cullinan Cres, Civic Centre; adult/child R5/2; ⊗8am-4.45pm Mon-Fri, 10am-4.45pm Sat, 9am-noon Sun) One of the country's best public galleries, with changing exhibitions of contemporary South African work, as well as a surprisingly good

the Green Kalahari with its vineyards and epic Augrabies Falls. Following the rains, red Kalahari sands shimmer with grasses, and Namakwa's spring bloom carpets rocky hills and plains with wildflowers.

collection of European masters. There's a cafe and an auditorium.

Wildebeest Kuil Rock Art Centre
ARCHAEOLOGICAL SITE

(☑053-833 7069; www.wildebeestkuil.itgo.com; Rte 31; adult/child R24/12; ☺9am-4pm Mon-Fri, 10am-4pm Sat & Sun) On a site owned by the !Xun and Khwe San people, this small sacred hill has 400-plus rock engravings dating back millennia. The guided tour leads to the mound along an 800m walkway with information boards covering the site and its Khoe-San heritage.

The centre is 16km northwest of town, en route to Barkly West. A shared minibus taxi costs R25; a private taxi costs R300 return, including waiting time.

☞ Tours

A quirky way to explore Kimberley is on a ghost tour (☑0837 323 189; per person R140; ☺6.30pm) with local historian Steve Lunderstedt. Tours last four hours and visit six sites. Slightly shorter tours (three hours, four stops) are available with Jaco Powell (☑0825 720 065; per person R120).

Tours of the Galeshewe Township (☑078 069 5104; bphirisi@yahoo.com; half-day R250) take in the Mayibuye Uprising Memorial and Robert Sobukwe's practice, where the Pan Africanist Congress (PAC) founder worked while under house arrest. To visit a home or artist's studio, ask in advance.

Pick up a copy of the *Kimberley Meander* at the Diamond Visitors Centre; it details a number of themed walking and driving tours.

▥ Sleeping

Ekhaya Guest House
GUESTHOUSE $

(☑053-874 3795; ekhayag@telkomsa.net; cnr Hulana & Montshiwa Sts, Galeshewe; s R360, d from R440, breakfast R65; ❋▥) The thatched cottages are comfortable and stylish, and rooms are a notch above backpacker standards, with tea, coffee and a large TV. Next to Galeshewe municipal centre.

Kimberley Club
TOP CHOICE
BOUTIQUE HOTEL $$

(☑053-832 4224; www.kimberleyclub.co.za; 72 Du Toitspan Rd; s/d from R945/1225, breakfast R85; ❋☢) Founded by Rhodes as a private club in 1881, the reputedly haunted hotel was renovated 10 years ago. It exudes history and rooms are period elegant. There's a good restaurant here too, recommended for a light lunch.

Edgerton House
GUESTHOUSE $$

(☑053-831 1150; www.edgertonhouse.co.za; 5 Edgerton Rd; s/d incl breakfast R595/750; ❋▥) Combining modern comforts, original fittings and a warm welcome, Edgerton is on a side street near Halfway House. The bedrooms at the front can pick up noise from the pub; rooms at the rear are quieter and more modern.

Australian Arms Guest House
HOTEL $$

(☑053-832 1526; www.australianarms.co.za; Big Hole Complex; s/d incl breakfast from R580/700; ❋) The building dates back to 1873 and rooms have black-and-white photos of Kimberley. Guests can walk around the mining village at night (without paying the Big Hole admission) and there's a bar-restaurant (mains R55).

✖ Eating

Halfway House
TOP CHOICE
PUB $$

(☑053-831 6324; www.halfwayhousehotel.co.za; 229 Du Toitspan Rd; mains R70; ☺lunch & dinner) Soak up Kimberley's diamonds-and-drink history in this watering hole dating to 1872. The interiors are beautifully historic and locals flock in to shoot pool and chomp pub grub such as burgers, steaks and crumbed pork chops (recommended).

Occidental Grill Bar
PUB $$

(☑053-830 4418; Big Hole Complex; mains R60; ☺9am-7pm Mon-Thu, to 9pm Fri, to 6pm Sat, to 5pm Sun) With a long bar and black-and-white photos of old-time prospectors and quaffers, this Victorian-era saloon is a fun place to pause on a Big Hole tour. You don't have to pay the Big Hole admission to access the Occidental.

George & Dragon
PUB $$

(☑053-833 2075; 187 Du Toitspan Rd; mains R60; ☺food 9.30am-10pm) The George & Dragon's mix of old English charm, sports coverage and rock music attracts a respectable multicultural crowd. Look out for midweek pubgrub deals.

❶ Information

Diamond (Diamantveld) Visitors Centre (☑053-832 7298; www.northerncape.org.za; 121 Bultfontein Rd; ☺8am-5pm Mon-Fri, to noon Sat)

Small World Net Café (☑053-831 3484; 42 Sidney St; per hr R30; ☺8am-5pm Mon-Fri) Slow internet access.

ℹ Getting There & Away

Air

SA Express (☏053-838 3337; www.flyexpress. aero) connects Kimberley with Jo'burg (one way from R1340, 1½ hours) and Cape Town (one way from 1170, 1¾ hours).

Kimberley airport is about 7km south of the city centre.

Bus

Translux (www.translux.co.za), **City to City**, **Intercape** (www.intercape.co.za) and **Greyhound** (www.greyhound.co.za) all stop in Kimberley daily en route to Jo'burg/Pretoria (R195 to R450, seven hours) and Cape Town (R350 to R500, 12 hours).

Train

Kimberley is an important junction for **Shosholoza Meyl** (www.shosholozameyl.co.za) tourist-class trains travelling between Cape Town (R380, 17 hours) and Jo'burg (R200, nine hours). The Blue Train and Rovos Rail stop here and tour the mine.

Mokala National Park

This 28,000-hectare park (☏053-204 0158; www.sanparks.org/parks/mokala; adult/child R96/ 48; ⊙6.30am-6.30pm Apr, May & Sep–mid-Oct, 7am-6pm Jun & Aug, 6am-7pm mid-Oct–Mar) about 40km southwest of Kimberley is home to animals including black and white rhinos, roan antelopes, Cape buffaloes, giraffes and kudus. Organised activities include wildlife drives, rock engraving and bush *braais*.

Accommodation ranges from campsites (R290) to the upmarket Mosu Lodge (r from R540; ✳✿). Rustic self-catering accommodation is also available at Haak-en-Steek Camp (1-4 people R875) and Lilydale Rest Camp (r from R575; ✳).

To enter the park, head southwest from Kimberley along the N12, then turn right at the 'Mokala Mosu' sign and follow the dirt road for 21km. It's possible to cross the park and exit by the Lilydale Gate, then follow a dirt road for 16km and meet the N12.

Upington

☏054 / POP 53,000

On the banks of the Senqu (Orange) River, orderly and prosperous Upington is a good place to catch your breath at either end of a long Kalahari slog. Wide boulevards slightly cluttered with supermarkets and chain stores fill the centre of town, but on the side streets, lazy river views and endless rows of date palms create a calm and quiet atmosphere perfect for an afternoon stroll (if the heat is not too stifling).

The town's star attraction is the Senqu (Orange) River, with much of Upington's accommodation clinging to the riverbanks. Sunset cruises on the Sakkie se Arkie (☏082 564 5447; www.arkie.co.za; Park St; adult/ child R80/50; ⊙6pm Fri-Sun, daily during holidays) are a great way to see the river.

Upington's central location makes it a good place to organise a remote desert adventure. Reader-recommended Kalahari Safaris (☏054-332 5653; www.kalaharisafaris. co.za; 3 Orange St) runs small-group trips to Kgalagadi Transfrontier Park (three days R5900), Augrabies Falls National Park and Witsand Nature Reserve.

🛏 Sleeping & Eating

TOP CHOICE **Le Must River Residence**   BOUTIQUE HOTEL $$

(☏054-332 3971; www.lemustupington.com; 14 Budler St; s/d incl breakfast from R890/1180; ✳✿) This elegant riverside getaway has sumptuous, African-themed rooms with antique furnishings and crisp white linen. Nearby, Le Must's River Manor (singles/doubles from R495/730) boasts the same professional service.

A Riviera Garden B&B   B&B $$

(☏054-332 6554; 16 Budler St; r R640; ✿) The gardens at this friendly lodge with two cosy rooms are a fairy-tale creation, and run all the way down to the river.

Die Eiland Holiday Resort   CAMPGROUND $$

(☏054-334 0287; www.kharahais.gov.za/eiland. html; campsites from R105, chalets from R660; ✿) A palm-lined avenue leads to 'The Island', in a wonderful natural setting on the river's southeastern bank. The basic self-catering chalets have kitchenettes with hob and microwave, and tiny bathrooms with shower.

O'Hagan's   INTERNATIONAL, PUB $$

(☏054-331 2005; 20 Schröder St; mains R85) For sundowners or an early-evening meal, you can't beat this chain Irish bar's patio overlooking the river. The menu features pizzas, a few salads and plenty of meat; the funghi pasta is a good vegetarian option.

ℹ Information

@lantic Internet Cafe (☏054-331 2689; 58 Le Roux St; per hr R30)

Upington Tourist Office (☏054-338 7151; www.northerncape.org.za; Mutual St, Town Library Bldg; ☉7.30am-4.30pm Mon-Fri, 9am-noon Sat)

❶ Getting There & Away

Air

The airport is 6.5km from town. SA Express operates daily flights to Cape Town (one way from R1780) and Johannesburg (one way from R1895).

Bus

Intercape (☏0861 287 287; www.intercape. co.za; Lutz St) has services to the following:

» Bloemfontein (R400, 7½ hours, Thursday and Saturday)

» Cape Town (R530, 12 hours, Sunday to Friday nights)

» Jo'burg (R740, 11 hours, daily)

» Windhoek (Namibia; R550, 12 hours, Tuesday, Thursday, Friday and Sunday)

Ca

Major agencies, including Avis, Europcar and Budget, have their offices at the airport. Book well in advance if you want a 4WD.

Minibus Taxi

You'll find minibus taxis near the Checkers supermarket near the corner of Mark and Basson Sts. Destinations include Springbok (R190, four hours).

Kgalagadi Transfrontier Park

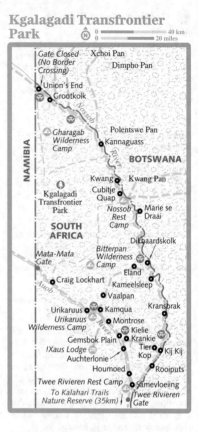

A long, hot road leads between crimson dunes from Upington to the magical Kgalagadi Transfrontier Park (☏054-561 2000; www. sanparks.org/parks/kgalagadi; adult/child R204/102), one of the world's last great, unspoilt ecosystems. The Kgalagadi is a wild land of harsh extremes and frequent droughts, where shifting red and white sands meet thorn trees and dry riverbeds.

The semiarid countryside (with around 250mm of rainfall a year) is richer than it appears, and supports large populations of birds, reptiles, rodents, small mammals and antelopes. These in turn support the large population of predators. There are some 1775 species of predator here, including around 200 cheetahs, 450 lions and 150 leopards. It's one of the best places in the world to spot big cats, especially cheetahs. Most of the animals are remarkably tolerant of vehicles, allowing you to get extraordinarily close.

Add in those giant, orange-ball sunsets and the black-velvet night skies studded with twinkling stars, and you'll feel like you've entered the Africa of storybooks.

The best time to visit is in June and July, when the days are coolest (below freezing at night) and the animals have been drawn to the bores along the dry riverbeds. September to October is the wet season, and if it rains many of the animals scatter out across the plain to take advantage of the fresh pastures.

☞ Tours

Sunrise, sunset, night and full-morning wildlife drives (adult/child from R170/85) and three-hour morning walks depart from the rest camps. We recommend trying a drive; you have a better chance of spotting predators when accompanied by a trained ranger.

At least two people are needed for tours to depart.

🛏 Sleeping & Eating

Inside the park are three rest camps and seven luxury wilderness camps, which fill up during the December-January school holidays and can be booked through SAN Parks (☎012-428 9111; www.sanparks.org).

All of the rest camps have campsites with shared ablutions facilities. The camps also have a range of huts, bungalows and cottages equipped with bedding, towels, utensils, and with kitchens and bathrooms.

Twee Rivieren Rest Camp (☎054-561 2000; 2-person cottages from R890; ▨), the closest camp to the park's entrance and the one with the most facilities, is the only rest camp with a swimming pool and air-con, hence the higher-than-average rates. This is also the site of the park's only restaurant (mains R85; ⊙7.30-10am & 6-9pm).

The wilderness camps give you the opportunity to really get off the beaten path. None is fenced, which means animals are able to wander in at will, although a ranger is on duty at all times. Stock up on petrol and drinking water before visiting.

The focus at !Xaus Lodge (☎021-701 7860; www.xauslodge.co.za; s/d with full board R4030/6200), which is owned by the Khomani San (Bushmen) and Mier people, is on interaction, from wildlife walks to campfire chats. Blending beautifully into the red-sand environs and overlooking an enormous salt pan, accommodation is in creatively decorated chalets with decks facing a waterhole.

There are dozens of places to stay on Rte 360 from Upington to Twee Rivieren Gate. If you arrive late in the afternoon, you may want to spend the night outside the park to avoid paying that day's fees. Try Kalahari Trails (☎054-511 0900; www.kalahari-trails.co.za; Rte 360; campsites R50, s/d R300/500), a private reserve, 35km south of Twee Rivieren.

❶ Information

Gates open between 5.30am and 7.30am and shut between 6pm and 7.30pm. Times change between seasons but generally follow the rising and setting sun.

At Twee Rivieren Gate are the South Africa National (SAN) Parks reception and South African immigration (open 7.30am to 4pm), police and border police; Botswana Wildlife and the Botswanan immigration and police are also found here.

Twee Rivieren has public telephones and mobile-phone access. All the rest camps have displays covering Kgalagadi's wildlife.

If you want to venture into the Botswanan side of the park, this is only possible on 4WD trails. Accommodation is in unfenced camps, and campsites at the two Botswanan gates, Mabuasehube and Kaa. Book in advance through **Botswana Wildlife** (☎267-653 0226; dwnp@gov.bw; Gaborone). If you want to exit the park via Mabuasehube or Kaa, you must carry out border-crossing formalities at Twee Rivieren and spend at least two nights in the park.

If you want to enter Namibia through Kgalagadi's Mata-Mata Gate, you must spend at least two nights in the park. Present your passport to South African immigration at Twee Rivieren, and to Namibian immigration at Mata-Mata.

❶ Getting There & Around

Twee Rivieren Gate is 270km northwest of Upington on the tarred Rte 360.

In the park, visitors are restricted to four gravel/sand roads: two leading up the dried beds of the Nossob and Auob Rivers, and two linking these. The roads are passable in a normal car, though renting a 4WD in Upington gives you peace of mind, a little more height for wildlife viewing and the possibility of tackling one of the 4WD-only routes. There is an extra fee for these routes and they should be booked in advance.

Upington to Namakwa

The N14 southwest of Upington follows the course of the Senqu (Orange) River, passing through an area that produces 10% of the country's wines. Try Bezalel (☎054-491 1325; www.bezalel.co.za), 25km west of Upington, or Die Mas van Kakamas (☎054-431 0245; www.diemasvankakamas.co.za) in Kakamas for cellar tours and unpretentious tastings.

Kakamas, surrounded by cotton fields and vineyards, isn't a bad place to spend a night. The Kalahari Gateway Hotel (☎054-431 0838; www.kalaharigateway.co.za; s/d from R520/760; ❄▨) has slightly worn but spacious rooms and a bar-restaurant (mains from R40; ⊙dinner) that boasts a sushi bar alongside its meaty menu – not a common sight in the Northern Cape.

AUGRABIES FALLS NATIONAL PARK
☎054

When the waterfall for which this park is named is fat with rainy-season run-off, its thunderous roar is nothing short of spectacular. The Khoisan people called it 'Aukoerbis', meaning place of great noise. It's the world's sixth-tallest waterfall, formed when the Senqu (Orange) River thunders into an 18km-long ravine with 200m-high cliffs. The main falls drop 56m, while the adjoining Bridal Veil Falls plunge 75m. It's a short walk from the visitor centre to the six viewing platforms.

The three-hour, 5km Dassie Trail is well worth doing, particularly if your time is short. It involves clambering over rocks through some magical landscape. The popular three-day, 36km Klipspringer Hiking Trail (per person R190; ☺Apr–mid-Oct) runs along the southern bank of the Senqu (Orange) River and the Gariep 3-in-1 Route (adult/child R180/90) includes canoeing, walking and mountain biking.

Kalahari Outventures (☎082 476 8213; www.kalahari-adventures.co.za; Augrabies; Augrabies Rush per person R350) offer rafting trips on the Senqu (Orange) River (four-hour trip R315 per person).

Accommodation in the park can be booked through SAN Parks (www.sanparks. org; campsites R195, chalets from R795, cottages from R1585; ☺restaurant 7am-8pm; ❋❋). There are also accommodation options on the road to the park, including Augrabies Falls Lodge & Camp (☎054-451 7203; www.augfallslodge.co.za; Rte 359; s/d R365/530, breakfast R35, restaurant mains R70; ❋).

The park is 38km northwest of Kakamas and 120km from Upington.

Namakwa

In the Northern Cape's rugged northwestern corner the roads stretch on forever, the stars seem bigger and brighter than they do anywhere else and you can tumble off the map without anyone noticing. From exploring the misty shipwrecked diamond coastline on the country's far western edge to 4WDing through an otherworldly mountain desert in remote /Ai/Ais-Richtersveld Transfrontier Park, experiences pile up fast here. Every spring, Namakwa's sunbaked desert sprouts a multihued wildflower blanket so spectacular you'll leave believing miracles do happen.

SPRINGBOK
☎027 / POP 11,000

Springbok sits in a valley surrounded by harsh rocky hills that explode with colour in flower season. When the flowers aren't blooming, there's little to see or do, although the town's desolate landscape and 300-plus days of sunshine are alluring. After dark, with little light pollution, the stars are brilliantly bright and nights are dramatically quiet and still.

From an edgy frontier town, Springbok has been transformed into a busy service centre for the copper and diamond mines in the region.

The Goegap Nature Reserve (☎027-718 9906; admission R15, campsites R30, huts R100; ☺7am-4pm), 15km east of town, is famous for its extraordinary display of spring flowers and is also home to 45 mammal species and 94 types of bird. There is a 13km circuit for cars and circular 4km and 7km hiking trails.

🛏 Sleeping

Cat Nap Accommodation   HOSTEL $
(☎027-718 1905; richtersveld.challen@kingsley. co.za; Voortrekker St; dm R130, s/d R280/420; ❋) Rooms here are cosy African-themed affairs and there are dorm beds in the barn, although it gets hot in summer.

WORTH A TRIP

NAMAQUA NATIONAL PARK

For most of the year it's a forgotten region of shrubland and boulder-strewn hills, but in spring (August and September) the Namaqua National Park (☎027-672 1948; www. sanparks.org/parks/namaqua; admission R48; ☺8am-5pm) bursts into flower. Their clarity and prevalence often surpass that of all other areas in the region, making this one of the best places to photograph the flowers.

In terms of accommodation, there are coastal campsites (from R75) and the Skilpad Rest Camp (self-catering chalets from R650) in the park. A temporary tented beach camp (per person incl brunch, high tea & dinner from R2105) operates from mid-August to mid-September – book well in advance.

The park is about 18km southwest of Kamieskroon – you'll need your own transport to reach it.

Annie's Cottage
GUESTHOUSE $$

(☑027-712 1451; www.springbokinfo.com; 4 King St; s/d incl breakfast R1240/1490; ❄🅿🐾) With a verandah overlooking a fountain, ferns and fronds in the leafy garden, Annie's is one of Springbok's few options that feels like a place to linger. The attic and Afro-themed rooms are fun choices.

Mountain View
GUESTHOUSE $$

(☑027-712 1438; www.mountview.co.za; 2 Overberg Ave; s/d incl breakfast from R990/1100; ❄🛜🐾) Perching in a tranquil location up against the hills, some of the four-star rooms open onto a garden leading to the pool, which has wonderful views.

Old Mill Lodge
GUESTHOUSE $$

(☑027-718 1705; www.oldmilllodge.com; 69 Van Riebeeck St; s/d incl breakfast R650/800; ❄@🐾) Pleasantly situated in a peaceful garden on a quiet side street. The 11 comfortable rooms are decorated with modern art. Flower-season tours can be arranged.

✖ Eating

Melkboschkuil Plaaskombuis
SOUTH AFRICAN $$

(☑0832 557 689; Voortrekker St; mains R75; ⊙8am-9pm Sun-Fri, to 1pm Sat) This *plaaskombuis* (farm kitchen) serves hearty food, such as *braaivleis* (barbequed meat), *potjiekos* (slow-cooked stew), steaks, burgers and salads, in traditional surrounds.

⃣TOP CHOICE Tauren Steak Ranch
STEAKHOUSE $$$

(☑027-712 2717; 2 Hospital St; mains R100; ⊙6pm-late Mon-Sat) Meat lovers, rejoice: Tauren serves steaks weighing up to 1kg with delectable toppings such as blue cheese and *biltong*. There are a few vegetarian choices and the pizza schnitzel is a local tip.

❶ Information
Tourist Office (☑027-712 8035; www.northerncape.org.za; Voortrekker St; ⊙7.30am-4.15pm Mon-Fri)

❶ Getting There & Away
Intercape (www.intercape.co.za) has buses to Cape Town (R340, 7½ hours) and Windhoek, Namibia (R970, 13 hours), that depart four times weekly from opposite the Springbok Lodge.

For 4WD hire, contact Cat Nap Accommodation or the tourism information office. Rental starts at about R1000 per day; online consolidators usually offer cheaper rates.

Minibus taxis depart from the rank opposite the First National Bank near the *kopje*. Destinations include Cape Town (R270, 8½ hours, daily), Upington (R190, four hours) and Port Nolloth (R80, 2½ hours).

/AI/AIS-RICHTERSVELD TRANSFRONTIER PARK
A seemingly barren wilderness of lava rocks and sandy moonscapes studded with semi-precious stones, the /Ai/Ais-Richtersveld Transfrontier Park (☑027-831 1506; www.sanparks.org/parks/richtersveld; adult/child R140/70; ⊙6am-8pm, office 8am-6pm) is South Africa's final wild frontier. The 6000 sq km of surreal mountain desert joins South Africa's Richtersveld National Park with Namibia's Ai-Ais Hot Springs Game Park. It's most beautiful during the spring flower season, when the park turns into a technicolour wonderland. The three hiking trails (42km, 23km and 15km) are challenging but spectacular, traversing jagged peaks, grotesque rock formations, deep ravines and gorges.

Sendelingsdrift rest camp (campsites R195, 2-person chalets R715; ❄🐾) is surprisingly comfortable for such a remote area. There are also two remote wilderness camps (2-person cabin R710), where you must bring your own water, and four camping areas (per 2 people R195). All should be booked in advance with SAN Parks (☑012-428 9111; www.sanparks.org).

The park is only accessible by 4WD, so the easiest way to visit is on a tour, which should be booked in advance – try Richtersveld Tours (☑082 335 1399; www.richtersveldtours.com; 4-night tours R5800).

Because the park is so remote and slow to travel around, a trip of at least a few days is recommended.

UNDERSTAND SOUTH AFRICA

South Africa Today

Two decades after the end of apartheid, life in South Africa remains dominated by social inequality. Cape Town's mountain and beach communities, for example, contrast with the townships sprawling across the Cape Flats, lining the N2 with shacks and portaloos. Seeing first-world wealth alongside African poverty is confronting for first-time visitors. Yet what makes South Africa an uplifting and intriguing place to visit is the dissolution of divisions. Projects aim to empower inhabitants of the townships and former homelands; to provide work in a country with one of the world's worst unemployment rates (about 25%).

South Africa is grappling with both apartheid's legacy – Archbishop Tutu has blamed violent crime and aggressive driving on psychological scars left by the regime – and pan-African problems. Economic refugees continue to arrive from neighbouring countries, intensifying pressure on infrastructure and competition for jobs.

Also reflecting pan-African issues, South Africa has the world's largest population of people with HIV/AIDS. Educational efforts face numerous taboos: *sangomas* (traditional healers) preach superstitious lore and, every day, funerals commemorate supposed tuberculosis victims.

South Africa's record on gender issues exemplifies the country's contradictions. Its constitution is the world's most progressive, promoting the rights of women and gay people (same-sex marriage is legal) among others. Yet street-level reality is far harsher, with one of the world's highest reported incidences of rape, including 'corrective' rape of lesbians.

Crime and corruption will be hot topics at the 2014 elections, when Helen Zille is likely to shrink the gap between her opposition Democratic Alliance party, which already governs the Western Cape, and the African National Congress (ANC).

History

South Africa's history extends back to around 40,000 BC when the San people first settled Southern Africa. By AD 500, Bantu-speaking peoples had arrived from West Africa's Niger Delta. Competing colonial European powers began settling here in small numbers from the 17th century, mostly in the Cape. Widespread colonial settlement of South Africa began in the 19th century.

The Great Trek

From 1836, groups of Boers dissatisfied with British rule in the Cape Colony trekked off into the interior in search of freedom. In a decade of migration known as the Great Trek, increasing numbers of Voortrekkers (pioneers) abandoned their farms and crossed the Senqu (Orange) River. Reports from early missions told of vast, uninhabited – or at least poorly defended – grazing lands.

Tensions between the Boers and the government had been building for some time, but the reason given by many trekkers for leaving was the 1833 act banning slavery.

The Great Trek coincided with the *difaqane* (forced migration) and the Boers mistakenly believed that what they found – deserted pasture lands, disorganised bands of refugees and tales of brutality – was the normal state of affairs. This gave rise to the Afrikaner myths that the Voortrekkers moved into unoccupied territory or arrived at much the same time as black Africans.

The Voortrekkers Meet the Zulu

The Great Trek's first halt was at Thaba 'Nchu, near present-day Bloemfontein, where a republic was established. Following disagreements among their leadership, the various Voortrekker groups split, with most crossing the Drakensberg into Natal to try to establish a republic there. As this was Zulu territory, the Voortrekker leader, Piet Retief, paid a visit to King Dingaan, and was promptly massacred by the suspicious Zulu. This massacre triggered others, as well as a revenge attack by the Boers. The culmination came at the Battle of Blood River (1838) in Natal. While the Boers sustained some injuries, more than 3000 Zulu were killed, reportedly causing the Ncome River to run red.

After this victory (the result of vastly superior weapons), the Boers felt their expansion really did have that long-suspected stamp of divine approval. The 16 December victory was celebrated as the Day of the Vow until 1994, when it was renamed the Day of Reconciliation.

The Boer Republics

Several short-lived Boer republics sprang up, but soon the only serious contenders were the Orange Free State and the Transvaal. The republics' financial position was always precarious and their economies depended entirely on cattle. Just when it seemed that the republics, with their thinly spread population of fiercely independent Boers, were beginning to settle into stable states, diamonds were discovered near Kimberley in 1869. Britain stepped in quickly and annexed the area.

The Boers were disturbed by the foreigners, both black and white, who poured in following the discovery and were angry that their impoverished republics were missing out on the money the mines brought in.

Anglo-Boer Wars

Longstanding Boer resentment became a full-blown rebellion in the Transvaal and the first Anglo-Boer War, known by Afrikaners as the War of Independence, broke out. It was over almost as soon as it began, with a crushing Boer victory at the Battle of Majuba Hill in 1881, and the republic regained its independence as the Zuid-Afrikaansche Republiek (ZAR; South African Republic).

With the discovery of a huge reef of gold in the Witwatersrand (the area around Johannesburg) in 1886 and the ensuing explosive growth of Jo'burg itself, the ZAR was suddenly host to thousands of *uitlanders* (foreigners), black and white.

This only intensified the Boers' grievances that had begun during the earlier diamond rush. In 1899 the British demanded voting rights for the 60,000 foreign whites on the Witwatersrand. Paul Kruger (ZAR president 1883–1900) refused, and demanded that British troops be withdrawn from the republic's borders, leading to the second Anglo-Boer War.

The conflict was more protracted than its predecessor, as the British were better prepared. By mid-1900, Pretoria, the last of the major Boer towns, had surrendered. Yet resistance by Boer *bittereinders* (bitter enders) continued for two more years with guerrilla-style battles, which in turn were met by scorched-earth tactics by the British. In May 1902, the Treaty of Vereeniging brought a superficial peace. Under its terms, the Boer republics acknowledged British sovereignty.

British Rule

The British response after their victory was a mixture of appeasement and insensitive imperialism. The nonwhites were scarcely considered, other than as potential labour, despite the fact that they constituted more than 75% of the combined population of the provinces.

Political awareness was growing, however. Mohandas (later Mahatma) Gandhi was working with the Indian populations of the Natal and Transvaal, and men such as John Jabavu, Walter Rubusana and Abdullah Abdurahman laid the foundations for new nontribal black political groups.

Afrikaners found themselves in the position of being poor farmers in a country where big mining ventures and foreign capital rendered them irrelevant. Afrikaans came to be seen as the *volkstaal* (people's language) and a symbol of Afrikaner nationhood.

The former Boer republics were given representative government in 1906–07, and moves towards union began almost immediately.

Union of South Africa

The Union of South Africa was established in 1910. The British High Commission Territories of Basotholand (now Lesotho), Bechuanaland (now Botswana), Swaziland and Rhodesia (now Zimbabwe) continued to be ruled directly by Britain.

English and Dutch became the official languages – Afrikaans was not recognised as an official language until 1925.

The first government of the new union was the South African National Party (later known as the South African Party, or SAP). A diverse coalition of Boer groups under General Louis Botha, with General Jan Smuts as his deputy, the party followed a generally pro-British, white-unity line.

General Barry Hertzog raised divisive issues, championing Afrikaner interests, advocating separate development for the two white groups and independence from Britain. He and his supporters formed the National Party (NP).

Soon after the union was established a barrage of repressive legislation was passed. It became illegal for black workers to strike; skilled jobs were reserved for whites; blacks were barred from military service; and pass laws, restricting black freedom of movement, were tightened.

In 1912, Pixley ka Isaka Seme formed a national democratic organisation to represent blacks. It was initially called the South African Native Congress, but from 1923 it was known as the African National Congress (ANC).

In 1913 the Natives Land Act set aside 8% of South Africa's land for black occupancy. Blacks were not allowed to buy, rent or even become sharecroppers outside their designated areas. Thousands of squatters were evicted from farms and forced into increasingly overcrowded reserves, or into the cities.

In 1914 South Africa, as a part of the British Empire, was drawn into war with Germany and saddled with the responsibility of dealing with German South West Africa (now Namibia). After the war, South West Africa became part of South Africa under a 'mandate' from the League of Nations.

Coalitions

In 1924 Hertzog and the NP came to power in a coalition government, and Afrikaner nationalism gained a greater hold. The dominant issue of the 1929 election was the *swaart gevaar* (black threat).

Hertzog joined briefly in a coalition with the more moderate Jan Smuts in the mid-1930s, after which Smuts took the reins. However, any hopes of turning the tide of Afrikaner nationalism were dashed by the rise of DF Malan and the Purified National Party, which quickly became the dominant force in Afrikaner political life. The Afrikaner Broederbond, a secret ultranationalistic Afrikaner brotherhood, became an extraordinarily influential force behind the NP.

Due to the booming WWII economy, black labour became increasingly important to the mining and manufacturing industries, and the black urban population nearly doubled. Enormous squatter camps grew up on the outskirts of Johannesburg and, to a lesser extent, other major cities.

Apartheid

The NP, led by DF Malan in a coalition with the Afrikaner Party (AP), won the 1948 election on a platform of establishing apartheid (literally, the state of being apart). With the help of creative electoral boundaries the NP held power right up to the first democratic election in 1994.

Mixed marriages were prohibited and interracial sex was made illegal. Every individual was classified by race. The Group Areas Act enforcing the physical separation of residential areas was promulgated. The Separate Amenities Act created separate public facilities – separate beaches, separate buses, separate toilets and separate schools. The pass laws were further strengthened and blacks were compelled to carry identity documents at all times and were prohibited from remaining in towns, or even visiting them, without specific permission.

Black Action

In 1949 the ANC for the first time advocated open resistance in the form of strikes, acts of public disobedience and protest marches. These continued intermittently throughout the 1950s, with occasional violent clashes.

In June 1955, at a congress held at Kliptown near Johannesburg, a number of organisations, including the Indian Congress and the ANC, adopted a Freedom Charter setting out a vision of a nonracial democratic state.

In 1960 the Pan African Congress (PAC), a breakaway group from the ANC, called for nationwide protests against the hated pass laws. When demonstrators surrounded a police station in Sharpeville, police opened fire, killing at least 67 people and wounding 186. To onlookers in South Africa and the rest of the world, the struggle had now crossed a crucial line – there were no longer any doubts about the nature of the white regime.

Soon after, the PAC and ANC were banned and the security forces were given the right to detain people indefinitely without trial. Prime Minister Verwoerd announced a referendum on whether the country should become a republic. A slim majority of white voters gave their approval to the change and in May 1961 the Republic of South Africa came into existence.

Nelson Mandela became the leader of the underground ANC and Oliver Tambo went abroad to establish the organisation in exile. As more black activists were arrested, the ANC and PAC began a campaign of sabotage through the armed wings of their organisations, respectively Umkonto We Sizwe (Spear of the Nation; usually known as MK) and Poqo (Pure). In 1963 Nelson Mandela, along with a number of other ANC and communist leaders, was arrested, charged with fomenting violent revolution and later sentenced to life imprisonment.

The Homelands

Verwoerd was assassinated in parliament in 1966 and was succeeded by BJ Vorster, who was followed in 1978 by PW Botha. Both men continued to pursue the dream of separate black homelands and a white South Africa.

The plan was to restrict blacks to homelands that were, according to the propaganda, to become self-sufficient, self-governing states on the traditional lands of particular ethnic groups. In reality, they had little infrastructure and no industry and were therefore incapable of producing sufficient food for the expanding black population. Under the plan, 14% of the country's total land area was to be home to some 80% of the population.

Intense and widespread suffering was the result, as blacks could not even leave their homeland without a pass and permission. The situation was further worsened by internal political strife. In an effort to garner more power for themselves, some homeland leaders became collaborators with the government, accepting 'independence' while crushing all resistance to their rule and to the South African government.

Decades of Darkness

As international opinion turned decisively against the white regime, the government (and most of the white population) increasingly saw the country as a bastion besieged by communism, atheism and black anarchy. Considerable effort was put into circumventing international sanctions, and the government even developed nuclear weapons (since destroyed).

On 16 June 1976 the Soweto Students' Representative Council protested against the use of Afrikaans (considered the language of the oppressor) in black schools. Police opened fire on a student march, sparking nationwide demonstrations, strikes, mass arrests and riots that, over the following 12 months, took more than 1000 lives.

Steve Biko, the charismatic leader of the Black Consciousness movement, which stressed the need for psychological liberation and black pride, was killed in 1977. The security police beat him until he lapsed into a coma – he went without medical treatment for three days and finally died in Pretoria. At the subsequent inquest, the magistrate found that no one was to blame.

South Africa was never the same again – a generation of young blacks committed themselves to a revolutionary struggle against apartheid, and black communities were politicised.

President PW Botha, telling white South Africans to 'adapt or die', instituted numerous reforms, including repeal of the pass laws. But he stopped well short of full reform, and many blacks (as well as the international community) felt that the changes were only cosmetic. International pressures increased as economic sanctions began to dig in harder, and the value of the rand collapsed. In 1985 the government declared a state of emergency that was to stay in force for the next five years. The media wasstrictly censored and, by 1988, 30,000 people had been detained without trial. Thousands were tortured.

Reform

In late 1989, FW de Klerk succeeded a physically ailing Botha. At his opening address to the parliament in February 1990 De Klerk announced that he would repeal discriminatory laws and legalise the ANC, PAC and Communist Party. Media restrictions were lifted, and political prisoners not guilty of common-law crimes were released. On 11 February, Nelson Mandela was freed after 27 years in jail. During 1990 and 1991 virtually all the old apartheid regulations were repealed.

In December 1991 the Convention for a Democratic South Africa (Codesa) began negotiations on the formation of a multiracial transitional government and a new constitution extending political rights to all groups. Months of wrangling produced a compromise and an election date, although at considerable human cost. Political violence exploded across the country during this time, particularly in the wake of the assassination of Chris Hani, the popular leader of the South African Communist Party.

Free Elections

Finally, at midnight on 26–27 April 1994, the old national anthem 'Die Stem' (The Call) was sung across the country and the old flag was lowered. Then the new rainbow flag was raised and the new anthem, 'Nkosi Sikelele Afrika' (God Bless Africa), was sung.

In the country's first democratic elections, the ANC won 62.7% of the vote, less than the 66.7% that would have enabled it to rewrite the interim constitution. As well as deciding the national government, the election also decided the provincial governments, and the ANC won in all but two of the provinces. The NP captured most of the white and coloured (mixed race) vote and became the official opposition party.

Truth & Reconciliation

After the elections, focus turned to the Truth and Reconciliation Commission (1994–99), which worked to expose crimes of the apartheid era. It proceeded under the dictum of Archbishop Desmond Tutu: 'Without forgiveness there is no future, but without confession there can be no forgiveness'. Many stories of horrific brutality and injustice were heard by the commission, offering some catharsis to people and communities shattered by their past.

The commission operated by allowing victims to tell their stories and perpetrators to confess their guilt, with amnesty on offer to those who made a clean breast of it.

MOVERS & SHAKERS: NELSON MANDELA

Nelson Rolihlahla Mandela is without doubt one of the global leaders of the millennium. Once vilified by South Africa's ruling whites and sentenced to life imprisonment, he emerged from 27 years of incarceration calling for reconciliation and forgiveness, and was able to rally together all South Africans at the most crucial of times.

Mandela, son of a Xhosa chief, was born on 18 July 1918 in the village of Mveso on the Mbashe River. When he was young the family moved to Qunu, south of Mthata in what is now Eastern Cape. He grew up living a typical rural life, while being groomed for a future position in the ethnic leadership. After attending the University College of Fort Hare, Mandela headed to Johannesburg, where he soon became immersed in politics. He finished his law degree and, together with Oliver Tambo, opened South Africa's first black law firm.

Meanwhile, in 1944, together with Tambo and Walter Sisulu, Mandela formed the Youth League of the ANC, which worked to turn the party into a nationwide grass-roots movement. During the 1950s, Mandela was at the forefront of the ANC's civil-disobedience campaigns. Various arrests and detention followed.

After the ANC was banned in the wake of the Sharpeville massacre (p492), Mandela advocated establishing its underground military wing, Umkhonto we Sizwe. In 1964, he stood trial for sabotage and fomenting revolution in the widely publicised Rivonia Trial. After brilliantly arguing his own defence, he was sentenced to life imprisonment, and spent the next 18 years in the infamous Robben Island prison, before moving to jails on the mainland.

Throughout his incarceration, Mandela repeatedly refused to compromise his political beliefs in exchange for freedom, saying that only free men can negotiate. He rejected offers of release in exchange for recognising the independence of the Transkei (and thereby giving tacit approval of the legitimacy of the apartheid regime).

On 18 February 1990, Mandela was released and in 1991 he was elected president of the ANC. From this position, he continued the negotiations (which had started secretly while he was in prison) to demolish apartheid and bring an end to minority rule. In 1993, Mandela shared the Nobel Peace Prize with FW de Klerk and, in the country's first democratic elections the following year, was elected president of South Africa. In his much-quoted speech, 'Free at Last!', made after winning the 1994 elections, he focused the nation's attention on the future, declaring, 'This is the time to heal the old wounds and build a new South Africa'.

Mandela – or Madiba, his traditional Xhosa name – stepped down as ANC president in 1997, although he continues to be revered as an elder statesman.

Those who chose not to appear before the commission would face criminal prosecution if their guilt could be proven. Yet, while some soldiers, police and 'ordinary' citizens confessed their crimes, many who gave the orders and dictated the policies failed to present themselves (PW Botha is one famous no-show).

South Africa Recently

In 1999 South Africa held its second democratic elections. Two years previously Mandela had handed over the ANC leadership to his deputy, Thabo Mbeki, and the ANC's share of the vote increased to put the party within one seat of the two-thirds majority that would allow it to alter the constitution.

The Democratic Party (DP) – traditionally a stronghold of liberal whites, with new support from conservatives disenchanted with the NP and from some middle-class blacks – won official opposition status.

By any account, Mbeki had huge shoes to fill as president, although how close he came to doing so is the subject of sharply divided debate, and his years in office can only be characterised as a roller-coaster ride. In the early days of his presidency, Mbeki's effective denial of the HIV/AIDS crisis invited global criticism, and his conspicuous failure to condemn the forced reclamation of white-owned farms in neighbouring Zimbabwe and to speak out publicly against his long-time comrade, Zimbabwean president Robert Mugabe, unnerved both South African landowners and foreign investors.

In 2005 Mbeki dismissed his deputy president Jacob Zuma in the wake of corruption charges against Zuma, setting off a ruthless internal ANC power struggle that Zuma won. In September 2008, Mbeki was asked to step down as president in an unprecedented move by the party.

Corruption charges against Zuma were dropped and, as widely expected, the ANC won the 2009 election, with Jacob Zuma declared president. Since assuming leadership, Zuma has managed to balance out considerable domestic and international criticism with his approachable personality and strong grass-roots popularity. There is a widely held view, however, that well into his term as president he has demonstrated weak leadership and failed to fulfil promises to create jobs and alleviate poverty.

The ability of the opposition parties to pressure the government to tackle South Africa's problems will be an important test of South Africa's political maturity in the coming years. Corruption, crime, economic inequality and HIV/AIDS all loom as major challenges.

Reading newspaper headlines presents a mixed picture, but it's likely that most South Africans would agree that the country today is an immeasurably more optimistic and relaxed place than it was in 1990, despite the massive problems that it still confronts.

The Culture

Dubbed the 'Rainbow Nation' by Archbishop Desmond Tutu in 1991, South Africa has become more homogeneous in the almost 20 years since the country's first democratic elections. There's still a long way to go, perhaps even a generation or two, and there are flare-ups that increase racial tension, such as the hate-speech perpetrated by the likes of Julius Malema, the controversial Black Economic Empowerment and affirmative action, government corruption and the disparity between rich and poor. However, people tend to live and work much more harmoniously these days; the nation is divided less by colour than by class.

While crime continues to undermine South Africa's reputation as a tourism destination, it's important to keep it in perspective. South Africa is one of the most inspiring and hope-filled places on the continent. Visiting provides a rare chance to experience a nation that is rebuilding itself after profound change. As a backdrop to all this is the magnificent natural scenery, and the remarkbly deep bond – perhaps best expressed in the country's literature – that most South Africans feel for their land.

Population & People

During the apartheid era, the government attempted to categorise everyone into one of four major groups – easily enough said, perhaps, but disastrous to implement. The classifications – black (at various times also called African, 'native' and 'Bantu'), coloured, Asian or white – were often arbitrary and highly contentious. They were used to regulate where and how people could live and work, and became the basis for institutionalised inequality and intolerance.

These times are fading into history, although discrimination based on wealth is threatening to replace racial discrimination. While the apartheid-era classification terms continue to be used, they work only to a certain extent; within each of the four major categories are dozens of subgroups that are even more subjective and less clearly defined.

Most of the 'coloured' population, descended from mixed ancestors as diverse as Afrikaners and Khoisan peoples, lives in Northern Cape and Western Cape. A major subgroup is the Cape Malays, who are mostly Muslim and can trace their roots to places as widely dispersed as India, Indonesia and parts of East Africa. Most South Africans of Indian descent live in KwaZulu-Natal.

Rural provinces such as Limpopo and the Free State are the Afrikaner heartlands. People of British descent are concentrated in KwaZulu-Natal, Western Cape and Eastern Cape.

The Zulu have maintained the highest-profile ethnic identity and about 24% of South Africans speak Zulu as a first language. The second-largest group, the Xhosa, has traditionally formed the heart of the black professional class and been influential in politics (numerous figures in the apartheid struggle, including Mandela, were Xhosa). About 18% of the population uses Xhosa as a first language. Other major groups include the Basotho, the Setswana, and the distinct Ndebele and Venda peoples.

South Africa's Gauteng province, which includes Jo'burg and Pretoria, is the most densely populated and urbanised province. At the other end of the scale is the rural and underdeveloped Limpopo, where more than 30% of adults are illiterate.

Millions of immigrants from across the continent make their way to South Africa to take advantage of its powerhouse economy. Many of those who are considered illegal live in Jo'burg's impoverished inner city, causing resentment among some South Africans who accuse the outsiders of taking jobs and housing.

South Africa has the highest incidence of reported rape in the world, with approximately 55,000 cases reported to the police annually. Some women's groups say the real figures are much worse, because many women are too afraid to report the crime.

Women are statistically more likely than men to be infected with HIV, and many women become infected at an early age because they are having sex with older men. Worsening the situation is the threat of sexual violence, which often undermines the ability of young women to ensure that their partner is wearing a condom.

Religion

Religion plays a central role in the lives of most South Africans, more than 75% of whom identify themselves as Christians. Major denominations include the Dutch Reformed Churches, which have a national congregation of more than 3.5 million people and 1200-plus churches nationwide; and the flamboyant Zion Christian Church (ZCC), with more than four million followers.

Despite their large social influence in some cities, Muslims, Hindus and Jews combined make up less than 6% of the population. About 15% are atheist and agnostic, and some 2% follow traditional African beliefs.

Up to two-thirds of South Africa's Indians have retained their Hindu faith, and Islam has a small but growing following, particularly in the Cape. The Jewish community is estimated to number around 70,000, mostly in Jo'burg and the Cape.

Traditional African beliefs and practices have a significant influence on the cultural fabric and life of the region. The use of *muti* (traditional medicine) is widespread, even among those who practise Christianity.

Arts

Literature

Many of the first black South African writers were missionary-educated, including Solomon Tshekisho Plaatje, who was also the first Secretary-General of the ANC. In 1930, his epic romance, *Mhudi,* became one of the first books published in English by a black South African.

In 1948, Alan Paton's *Cry, the Beloved Country* became an international bestseller. This beautifully crafted, lyrical tale of a black priest who comes to Jo'burg to find his son is still one of the country's most widely recognised titles.

In the 1960s, future Nobel laureate Nadine Gordimer published her first books; her most famous novel, *July's People* (1981), depicts the collapse of white rule.

It was also in the 1960s and into the '70s that Afrikaner writers such as Breyten Breytenbach and André Brink began to gain prominence as powerful voices for the opposition. Brink's classic novel, *A Dry White Season,* portrays the lonely struggles of a white South African who discovered the truth about a black friend who died in police custody.

SPORT – ALMOST A RELIGION

South Africans are sports fanatics, with club sports generating passionate loyalties. Football (soccer) is the most popular spectator sport, followed by rugby and cricket. The majority of football fans are black; while cricket and rugby attracted predominately white crowds, this is now changing.

Hosting the 2010 World Cup was a historic event for South Africa. The action took place at 10 venues from Cape Town to Polokwane (Pietersburg), and the country spent more than US$1 billion on building new stadiums and renovating existing ones.

The second most popular sport, rugby, has benefited from development programs across the colour divides. South African fans adore their beloved 'Boks', ranked in the top three teams in the world by the International Rugby Board.

The South African cricket team, known as the Proteas, is up there with the top cricket-playing nations around the world, and fans enjoy friendly rivalry with England, India, Australia, New Zealand and Pakistan.

The 1970s also gave rise to several influential black poets, including Mongane Wally Serote, a veteran of the liberation struggle. His work, including the moving epic poem 'No Baby Must Weep', served as a rallying force for those living under apartheid.

JM Coetzee gained international acclaim with his novel *Disgrace* (1999), which won him his second Booker Prize. Coetzee was awarded the Nobel Prize for Literature in 2003.

One of the most prominent contemporary authors is Zakes Mda. He published the acclaimed *Ways of Dying* in 1995.

Visual Arts

South African art had its beginnings with the San, who left their distinctive designs on rock faces and cave walls throughout the region. When European painters arrived, many of their early works centred on depictions of Africa for colonial enthusiasts back home, although with time, a more South Africa–centred focus developed.

Black artists were sidelined for many decades. Gerard Sekoto was one of the first to break through the barriers. Contemporary art ranges from the vibrant crafts sold in the Venda region, or on the side of the road in cities and tourist areas, to high-priced paintings that hang in trendy galleries. Innovative artists are using 'found' materials such as telephone wire, safety pins, beads, plastic bags and tin cans to create their works.

Theatre & Dance

After the colonial era, home-grown playwrights, performers and directors gradually emerged. Writer and director Athol Fugard was a major influence in the 1950s in developing black talent. He is still active today, with his Fugard Theatre in Cape Town.

Actor and playwright John Kani is another major name in South African theatre.

The First National Bank Dance Umbrella festival of dance and choreography, held in February and March, brings together local and international artists and provides a stage for new work.

Environment

The Land

South Africa occupies over 1.23 million sq km – it's five times the size of the UK – and is Africa's ninth-largest and fifth-most populous country. On three sides it's edged by a windswept and stunningly beautiful coastline, winding down the Atlantic seaboard in the west, and up into the warmer Indian Ocean waters to the east.

Much of the country consists of the highveld, a vast plateau averaging 1500m in height. To the east is the lowveld, while to the northwest is the low-lying Kalahari basin. The dramatic Drakensberg Escarpment marks the point where the highveld plummets down towards the eastern lowlands.

Wildlife

ANIMALS

South Africa boasts some of the most accessible wildlife viewing on the continent; you probably have a better chance of seeing the Big Five (rhinos, buffaloes, elephants, leopards and lions) here than anywhere else. On even a short visit to the country's parks you are almost guaranteed to see dozens of creatures, and the chance to spot the big cats and great herd animals is one of the region's prime attractions.

The best time for wildlife watching is the cooler, dry winter months (June to September), when foliage is less dense and animals congregate at waterholes. Summer (late November to March) is rainy and hot, with the animals more widely dispersed and often difficult to see, although the landscape turns beautiful shades of green.

South Africa's 800-plus bird species include the world's largest bird (the ostrich), the heaviest flying bird (the Kori bustard) and the smallest raptor (the pygmy falcon). Birdwatching is good year-round, with spring (September to November) and summer the best times.

PLANTS

More than 20,000 plant species sprout from South Africa's soil – an amazing 10% of the world's total, although the country constitutes only 1% of the earth's land surface.

Dozens of flowers that are domesticated elsewhere grow wild here, including gladioli, proteas, birds of paradise and African lilies. South Africa is also the only country with one of the world's six floral kingdoms within its borders.

In the drier northwest, there are succulents (dominated by euphorbias and aloes) and annuals, which flower brilliantly after the spring rains.

South Africa has few natural forests, though. They were never extensive, and today only remnants remain. Temperate forests occur on the southern coastal strip between George and Humansdorp, in the KwaZulu-Natal Drakensberg and in Mpumalanga. Subtropical forests are found northeast of Port Elizabeth in areas just inland from the Wild Coast, and in KwaZulu-Natal.

In the north are large savannah areas, dotted with acacias and thorn trees.

National Parks & Reserves

South Africa has close to 600 national parks and reserves, many featuring wildlife, while others are primarily wilderness sanctuaries or hiking areas. Oversight bodies:

» CapeNature (021-426 0723; www.capenature.org.za) Promotes nature conservation in the Western Cape, and is responsible for permits and bookings for Western Cape reserves.
» Ezemvelo KZN Wildlife (033-845 1000; www.kznwildlife.com) Responsible for wildlife parks in KwaZulu-Natal.
» Komatiland Forests Eco-Tourism (013-754 2724; www.komatiecotourism.co.za) Oversees forest areas, promotes ecotourism and manages hiking trails around Mpumalanga.
» South African National (SAN) Parks Board (012-426 5000; www.sanparkis.org) Oversees most larger wildlife parks, except for those in KwaZulu-Natal.

All national parks charge a daily conservation fee, discounted for South African residents and nationals of Southern African Development Community (SADC) countries; see park listings for amounts.

In addition to its national parks, South Africa is party to several transfrontier conservation areas. These include the still-in-process Greater Mapungubwe Transfrontier

---

i WILD CARD

All South African national parks charge a daily entry ('conservation') fee. One way to save is to purchase a Wild Card (www.wildinafrica.com) online. The version of the card for foreign tourists, which is valid for a year, gives you unlimited entry into any of the parks and reserves in the Wild Card system. It's an excellent deal if you're a frequent parkgoer, or even if you're just planning more than five days in one of the more expensive parks such as Kruger.

ENDANGERED SPECIES

Endangered species include the black rhino (sometimes spotted in Addo National Park, uMkhuze Game Reserve and Hluhluwe-iMfolozi Park); the riverine rabbit (found only near rivers in the central Karoo); the wild dog (Hluhluwe-iMfolozi Park and Kruger National Park); and the roan antelope.

Endangered bird species include the wattled crane and the blue swallow; the African penguin and the Cape vulture are threatened.

Conservation Area linking South Africa, Zimbabwe and Botswana; Kgalagadi Transfrontier Park, combining the Northern Cape's former Kalahari Gemsbok National Park with Botswana's Gemsbok National Park; the Maloti-Drakensberg Peace Park, which links Sehlabathebe National Park and other areas of the Lesotho Drakensberg with their South African counterparts in uKhahlamba-Drakensberg; and the Great Limpopo Transfrontier Park, which spans the borders of South Africa, Mozambique and Zimbabwe.

Private wildlife reserves also abound. In total, just under 3% of South African land has national-park status, with an estimated 4% to 5% more enjoying other types of protective status. The government has started teaming up with private landowners to bring private conservation land under government protection, with the goal of increasing the amount of conservation land to over 10%.

Environmental Issues

South Africa is the world's third most biologically diverse country. It's also one of Africa's most urbanised, with over 50% of the population living in towns and cities. Major challenges for the government include managing increasing urbanisation while protecting the environment. The picture is complicated by a distorted rural-urban settlement pattern – a legacy of the apartheid era – with huge population concentrations in townships that generally lack adequate utilities and infrastructure.

Land degradation is one of the most serious problems, with about 25% of South Africa's land considered to be severely degraded. In former homeland areas, years of overgrazing and overcropping have resulted in massive soil depletion. This, plus poor overall conditions, is pushing people to the cities, further increasing urban pressures.

South Africa receives an average of only 500mm of rainfall annually, and droughts are common. To meet demand, all major South African rivers have been dammed or modified. While this has improved water supplies to many areas, it has also disrupted local ecosystems and caused increased silting.

South Africa has long been at the forefront of African countries in conservation of its fauna. However, funding is tight (and SAN Parks' ability to counter an increase in rhino poaching is very worrying), and will likely remain so as long as many South Africans still lack access to basic amenities. Potential solutions include public–private sector conservation partnerships, and

TOP PARKS & RESERVES

LOCATION (PARK)	FEATURES	ACTIVITIES	BEST TIME TO VISIT
Cape Peninsula (Table Mountain NP)	rocky headlands, seascapes; waterbirds, bonteboks, elands, African penguins	hiking, mountain biking	year-round
Western Cape (Cederberg WA)	mountainous & rugged formations, abundant plant life, San rock art, bizarre sandstone	hiking	year-round
Mpumalanga/ Limpopo (Blyde River Canyon NR)	canyon, caves, river, stunning vistas	hiking, kloofing (canyoning)	year-round
(Kruger NP)	savannah, woodlands, thornveld; the Big Five & many more	vehicle safaris, guided wildlife walks	year-round
Northern Cape (/Ai/Ais-Richtersveld Transfrontier Park)	mountainous desert, haunting beauty; klipspringers, jackals, zebras, plants, birds	hiking	Apr-Sep
(Augrabies Falls NP)	desert, river, waterfalls, striking scenery; klipspringers, rock dassies	hiking, canoeing, rafting	Apr-Sep
Eastern Cape (Addo Elephant NP)	dense bush, coastal grasslands, forested kloofs (ravines); elephants, black rhinos, buffaloes	vehicle safaris, walking trails, horse riding	year-round
(Tsitsikamma NP)	coast, cliffs, rivers, ravines, forests; Cape clawless otters, baboons, monkeys, bird life	hiking	year-round
KwaZulu-Natal (Hluhluwe-iMfolozi Park)	lush, subtropical vegetation, rolling savannah; rhinos, giraffes, lions, elephants, lots of birds	wildlife watching, wilderness walks	May-Oct
(iSimangaliso Wetland Park)	wetlands, coastal grasslands; elephants, birds, hippos	wilderness walks, vehicle/boat safaris	Mar-Nov
(uKhahlamba-Drakensberg Park)	awe-inspiring Drakensberg Escarpment, fantastic scenery & wilderness areas	hiking	year-round
(uMkhuze GR)	savannah, woodlands, swamp; rhinos & almost everything else, hundreds of bird species	guided walks, bird walks, vehicle safaris	year-round
Free State (Golden Gate Highlands NP)	spectacular sandstone cliffs & outcrops; zebras, jackals, rheboks, elands, birds	hiking	year-round

increased contributions from private donors and international conservation bodies such as World Wide Fund for Nature (WWF).

Food & Drink

It's only since the dismantling of apartheid that anyone has talked of South African cuisine as a unified whole. Earlier, the Africans had their mealie pap (maize porridge), the Afrikaners their *boerewors* (spicy farmers sausages), and the Indians and Cape Malays their curries.

Today, along with divisions in other aspects of life, the culinary barriers are starting to fall. Now, a simmering *potjie* (pot) of culinary influences awaits the visiting gastronome – once described by foodie writer Lannice Snyman as 'a bit of black magic, a dash of Dutch heartiness, a pinch of Indian spice and a smidgen of Malay mystery'.

Perhaps more than anything else, it's the *braai* (barbecue) – an Afrikaner institution that has broken across race lines - that defines South African cuisine. It's as much a social event as a form of cooking, with the essential elements being meat, corncobs and beer. The Winelands and Cape Town remain the best places to eat well.

Food

BILTONG & BOEREWORS

The Afrikaner history of trekking led to their developing portable food: hence the traditional *biltong* (dried strips of salted meat); rusks (hard biscuits) for dunking; and *boerewors,* a well-seasoned sausage, also found dried *(droëwors).*

CAPE CUISINE

Cape cuisine is a fusion of Malay influence on Dutch staples, so you'll find dishes such as *bobotie* (curried-mince pie topped with savoury egg custard, served on yellow rice with chutney) and *waterblommetjie bredie* (lamb stew with Cape Pondweed flowers, lemon juice and sorrel). Puddings can be the delicious *malva* sponge dessert or *melktert* (rich, custardlike tart), usually brightened up with a sprinkling of cinnamon.

CURRIES

South African Indian cuisine includes delicious curries and *breyanis* (similar to biryanis), and fuses with Malay cooking; you'll get hotter curries in Durban and milder ones in Cape Town. In Durban, fill up on bunny chow (a half, quarter or full loaf of bread hollowed out and filled with curry).

MEALIE PAP

The most widely eaten food in South Africa, mealie pap is thinner or stiffer depending on where you eat it, and is completely bland. However, it's ideal if you want something filling and economical, and can be quite satisfying served with a good sauce or stew.

Drink

BEER

Beer is the national beverage. It comes in bottles (or cans) at around R10, and bars serve draught from around R20. South Africa is home to the world's second-largest brewer, SAB Miller, so there's no shortage of brands, with Black Label the favourite. Craft beer has taken off in a big way, with close to 50 boutique breweries across the country.

WATER

Tap water is generally safe in South Africa's cities. However, in rural areas (or anywhere that local conditions indicate that water sources may be contaminated), use bottled water and purify stream water.

WINE

Since it made its debut in 1659, South African wine has had time to age to perfection, and is both of a high standard and reasonably priced. Dry whites are particularly good – try sauvignon blanc, chardonnay and chenin blanc – while popular reds include cabernet sauvignon, pinotage (a local cross of pinot and cinsaut, which was known as hermitage) and shiraz.

Wine prices average from around R50 in a bottle store, twice that in a restaurant. Wine by the glass is often available from around R25.

SURVIVAL GUIDE

Directory A–Z

Accommodation

South Africa offers a range of good-value accommodation. You'll generally find high standards, often for significantly less than you would pay in Europe or North America.

Rates rise steeply during the summer school break (early December to mid-January) and the Easter break (late March

SLEEPING PRICE RANGES

The rates quoted in this chapter are for a high-season double room with private bathroom.

$ Less than R450

$$ R450–1500

$$$ More than R1500

In Cape Town and the Garden Route, price ranges are higher:

$ Less than R650

$$ R650–2500

$$$ More than R2500

to mid-April). Room prices often double and minimum stays are imposed; advance bookings are essential. The other school holidays are also often classified as high season. You can get excellent deals during the winter low season, which is also the best time for wildlife watching.

Discounts Discounted midweek rates are common, so always ask. Occasionally, in towns geared towards business travellers rather than tourists, such as mining centres, midweek rates can be more expensive.

Budget accommodation The main budget options are campsites, backpacker hostels, self-catering cottages and community-run offerings, including homestays. Campsites are fairly ubiquitous, but other budget options are often scarce outside tourist areas.

Midrange This category is particularly good value, and includes guesthouses, B&Bs and many self-catering options in national parks.

Top end South Africa boasts some of Africa's best wildlife lodges, as well as superb guesthouses and hotels. Prices at this level are similar to, or slightly less than, those in Europe or North America.

🏃 Activities

Thanks to South Africa's diverse terrain and favourable climate, almost anything is possible – from coastal hikes to the world's highest bridge bungee jump. Good facilities and instruction mean that most activities are accessible to all, whatever their experience level.

There are dozens of operators. Ask other travellers and at hostels.

AERIAL PURSUITS

Ideal weather conditions and an abundance of high points to launch yourself from make South Africa a fine destination for aerial pursuits. A helpful contact for getting started is the Aero Club of South Africa (☎011-082 1100; www.aeroclub.org.za).

South Africa is one of the world's best destinations for paragliding, particularly Table Mountain. South African Hang Gliding & Paragliding Association (☎074-152 2505; www.sahpa.co.za) can provide names of operators, and numerous schools offer courses for beginners.

BIRDWATCHING

With its enormous diversity of habitats, South Africa is a paradise for birdwatchers.

Cape Peninsula & West Coast Cape of Good Hope, within Table Mountain National Park, is excellent for seabird watching, as is West Coast National Park, about 120km to the north.

Kruger National Park One of the continent's best areas for birdwatching, especially the south and the far north; known for its raptors and migratory species.

Northern KwaZulu-Natal uMkhuze Game Reserve hosts more than 400 species; iSimangaliso Wetland Park protects one of Southern Africa's most significant waterbird breeding grounds.

Soutpansberg The mountain range attracts some 540 feathered species (55% of South Africa's species).

CANOEING, KAYAKING & RAFTING

South Africa has few major rivers, but the ones that do flow year-round offer rewarding canoeing and rafting. Popular ones include the Blyde and Sabie Rivers, both in Mpumalanga; the waterways around Wilderness National Park in the Western Cape; and the Senqu (Orange) River, especially through Augrabies Falls National Park. There's some serene canoeing at the iSimangaliso Wetland Park.

Rafting is highly rain-dependent, with the best months in most areas from December-January to April. Good contacts:

Felix Unite (☎021-670 1300; www.felixunite.com)

Hardy Ventures (www.iafrica.com)

Intrapid (☎072-900 0348; www.rafts.a.co.za)

For sea kayaking, try the Sea Kayaking Association of South Africa (www.doorway.co.za/kayak/recskasa).

DIVING

Strong currents and often windy conditions mean advanced divers can find challenges all along the coast. Sodwana Bay on KwaZulu-Natal's Elephant Coast is good for beginners.

Conditions These vary widely. The best time to dive the KwaZulu-Natal shoreline is from May to September, when visibility tends to be highest. In the west, along the Atlantic seaboard, the water is cold year-round but is at its most diveable, with many days of high visibility, between November and January-February.

Costs Prices are generally lower in South Africa than elsewhere in the region. Expect to pay over R3000 for a three- or four-day open-water certification course, and over R300 per day for equipment rental.

Equipment Coastal towns where diving is possible have dive outfitters. With the exception of Sodwana Bay during the warmer months (when a 3mm wetsuit will suffice), you'll need at least a 5mm wetsuit for many sites, and a drysuit for sites to the south and west.

HIKING

South Africa is wonderful for hiking, with an excellent system of well-marked trails varied enough to suit every ability.

Accommodation Some trails have accommodation, from camping to simple huts with electricity and running water, and all must be booked well in advance.

Regulations Most longer routes and wilderness areas require hikers to be in a group of at least three or four.

Resources Ezemvelo KZN Wildlife (p498) controls most trails in KwaZulu-Natal. Elsewhere, most trails are administered by SAN Parks (☎012-426 5000; www.sanparks. org) or the various Forest Region authorities. To find out about local hiking clubs, contact Hiking South Africa (☎083-535 4538; www.hiking-south-africa.info).

Seasons Hiking is possible year-round, although you'll need to be prepared in summer for extremes of wet and heat. The best time is March to October.

KLOOFING (CANYONING)

Kloofing is a mix of climbing, hiking, swimming and some serious jumping. There's an element of risk to the sport, so check operators' credentials carefully before signing up.

MOUNTAIN BIKING

There are trails almost everywhere in South Africa. Some suggestions to get you started: the ride up (and down) Sani Pass, on the South Africa–Lesotho border; Cederberg Wilderness Area; and Knysna and the surrounding area. Cape Town is an unofficial national hub for the activity.

Useful sources of information include Mountain Bike South Africa (www.mtbsa. co.za) and the bimonthly *Ride* (www.ride. co.za), South Africa's main mountain-biking magazine.

ROCK CLIMBING

The Cederberg and the Drakensberg are two favourite spots for climbers.

South African Climbing Info Network (www.saclimb.co.za) Has listings and photos of many climbing and bouldering sites.

Mountain Club of South Africa (☎021-465 3412; http://mcsacapetown.co.za; 97 Hatfield St; ☐Government Ave, Cape Town) Information on regional clubs.

Roc-n-Rope (☎013-257 0363; www.rocrope. com) Runs climbing trips and courses.

SURFING

The best time of the year for surfing the southern and eastern coasts is autumn and early winter (from about April to July). Boards and gear can be bought in most of the big coastal cities. New boards typically cost about R3000. Resources:

Wavescape (www.wavescape.co.za)

Zig Zag (www.zigzag.co.za) South Africa's main surf magazine.

WHALE WATCHING

» South Africa is considered one of the world's best spots to sight whales without boarding a boat.
» Southern right and humpback whales are regularly seen offshore between June-July and November, with occasional spottings of Bryde's and killer whales.
» Hermanus, where southern right whales come to calve, is the country's whale-watching capital.
» Whale-watching spots dot the southern and eastern coastlines, from False Bay to iSimangaliso Wetland Park.

WILDLIFE WATCHING

South Africa's populations of large animals are one of its biggest attractions. In comparison with some nearby countries, such as Botswana and Zambia, wildlife watching here tends to be very accessible, with good roads and accommodation for all categories of traveller. It is also comparatively inexpensive, although there are plenty of pricier choices for those seeking a luxury experience in the bush.

Business Hours

Usual business hours are as follows. Exceptions are noted in listings.

Banks 9am to 3.30pm Monday to Friday, 9am to 11am Saturday; many foreign exchange bureaus have longer hours.

Bars 4pm to 2am.

Businesses and shopping 8.30am to 5pm Monday to Friday, 8.30am to 1pm Saturday; many supermarkets also open 9am to noon Sunday; shopping centres to 9pm.

Cafes breakfast 7am to noon, lunch noon to 5pm.

Government offices 8am to 4.30pm Monday to Friday.

Post offices 8.30am to 4.30pm Monday to Friday, 8.30am to noon Saturday.

Restaurants lunch 11.30am to 3pm, dinner 7pm to 10pm (last orders); many open 3pm to 7pm.

Customs Regulations

» You're permitted to bring 1L of spirits, 2L of wine, 200 cigarettes and up to R3000 worth of goods into South Africa without paying duties.

» The import and export of protected animal products such as ivory is not permitted.

» Visit www.southafrica.info/travel/advice/redtape.htm for more information.

Embassies & Consulates

Most countries have their main embassy in Pretoria, with an office or consulate in Cape Town (which becomes the official embassy during Cape Town's parliamentary sessions).

Most open for visa services and consular matters on weekday mornings, between about 9am and noon.

For more listings, see www.dfa.gov.za/consular/index.html.

Australian Embassy (☑012-423 6000; www.southafrica.embassy.gov.au; 292 Orient St, Arcadia) High commission in Pretoria.

Botswanan Embassy (www.botswana consulate.co.za) high commission in Pretoria (☑012-430 9640; www.mofaic.gov.bw; 24 Amos St, Colbyn); Cape Town (☑021-421 1045; www.mofaic.gov.bw; 7 Coen Steyler Ave, 13th fl, Metropolitan Life Bldg, City Bowl); Jo'burg (☑011-403 3748; 122 De Korte St, 2nd fl, Future Bank Bldg, Braamfontein)

Canadian Embassy (☑012-422 3000; 1103 Arcadia St, Pretoria)

Dutch Embassy (www.dutchembassy.co.za) embassy in Pretoria (☑012-425 4500; www.dutch embassy.co.za; 210 Queen Wilhelmina Ave, New Muckleneuk); Cape Town (☑021-421 5660; www.dutchembassy.co.za; 100 Strand St, City Bowl)

French Embassy (www.ambafrance-rsa.org) Pretoria (☑012-425 1600; www.ambafrance-rsa. org; 250 Melk St, New Muckleneuk); Cape Town (☑021-423 1575; www.consulfrance-lecap.org; 78 Queen Victoria St, Gardens); Jo'burg (☑011-778 5600; 191 Jan Smuts Ave, Rosebank)

German Embassy (www.southafrica.diplo.de) embassy in Pretoria (☑012-427 8900; www.pretoria.diplo.de; 180 Blackwood St, Arcadia); Cape Town (☑021-405 3000; www.southafrica.diplo.de; 22 Riebeeck St, 19th fl, Triangle Hse, City Bowl)

Irish Embassy (☎012-452 1000; www.embas syoflireland.org.za; 570 Fehrsen St, 2nd fl, Parkdev Bldg, Brooklyn Bridge Office Park, Brooklyn, Pretoria)

Lesotho Embassy high commission in Pre-toria (☎012-460 7648; 391 Anderson St, Menlo Park); Durban (☎031-307 2168; 2nd fl, Westguard House, cnr Dr Pixley KaSeme/West St & Dorothy Nyembe/Gardiner St); Jo'burg (☎011-339 3653; 76 Juta St, Indent House, Braamfontein)

Mozambican Embassy (www.embamoc. co.za) high commission in Pretoria (☎012-401 0300; www.embamoc.co.za; 529 Edmond St, Arcadia); Cape Town (☎021-426 2944; www. minec.gov.mz; 8 Burg St, 11th fl, Pinnacle Bldg, City Bowl); Durban (☎031-304 0200; 320 Dr Pixley KaSeme/West St, room 520); Jo'burg (☎011-336 1819; 18 Hurlingham Rd, Illovo); Nelspruit (☎013-752 7396; 43 Brown St)

Namibian Embassy (☎012-481 9100; www. namibia.org.za; 197 Blackwood St, Arcadia) High commission in Pretoria.

New Zealand Embassy (☎012-435 9000; www.nzembassy.com/south-africa; 125 Middel St, New Muckleneuk) Embassy in Pretoria.

Swazi Embassy (www.swazihighcom.co.za) high commission in Pretoria (☎012-344 1910; www.swazihighcom.co.za; 715 Government Ave, Arcadia); Jo'burg (☎011-403 2036, 011-403 7372; 23 Jorissen St, 6th fl, Braamfontein Centre)

UK Embassy (www.ukinsouthafrica.fco.gov. uk) high commission in Pretoria (☎012-421 7500; 255 Hill St, Arcadia, consular section 256 Glyn St, Hatfield); Cape Town (☎021-405 2400; 8 Rie-beeck St, 15th fl, Norton Rose House, City Bowl); Durban (☎031-572 7259; 86 Armstrong Rd, FWJK Court, La Lucia Ridge)

US Embassy Cape Town (☎021-702 7300; southafrica.usembassy.gov; 2 Reddam Ave, Westlake); embassy in Pretoria (☎012-431 4000; http://southafrica.usembassy.gov; 877 Pretorius St, Arcadia) Also has missions in Durban and Jo'burg.

Zimbabwean Embassy (www.zimfa.gov.zw) high commission in Pretoria (☎012-342 5125; zimpret@lantic.net) Also has a consulate in Jo'burg.

Food

Dining in South Africa is pleasurable and good value. Sit-down meals in restaurants (not haute cuisine) average between R70 and R90 per person (less in pubs), and fresh produce everywhere is good value.

The following price ranges are used for Eating reviews in this chapter.

$	Less than R60 per main
$$	R60-150 per main
$$$	More than R150 per main

Internet Access

» Internet access is widely available in South Africa.
» Accommodation options often offer access and there are internet cafes in major towns and some smaller places.
» Costs average R30 to R40 per hour.
» Many accommodation options, cafes and eateries have wi-fi, often for free. Branches of PostNet, found nationwide, normally have a few terminals.

Language Courses

There are numerous language schools for learning Xhosa, Zulu, Sotho, Afrikaans and English, including the following:

Inlingua (www.inlingua.co.za) Afrikaans, English.

Language Teaching Centre (www.lang uageteachingcentre.co.za; City Bowl, Cape Town) Xhosa, Zulu, Afrikaans, English.

Phaphama Initiatives (www.phaphama.org; Soweto, Gauteng) Organises immersive tours and homestays offering opportunities to learn languages outside a classroom.

University of the Witwatersrand (www. witslanguageschool.com/aae.aspx; Braamfontein, Jo'burg) Zulu, Sotho, Afrikaans.

Maps

Maps are widely available at bookshops and tourist offices. Map Studio (www.mapstudio. co.za) sells maps from road atlases to pock-et maps, with branches in Cape Town and Jo'burg.

Money

Foreign currencies The best currencies to bring are US dollars, euros or British pounds in a mixture of cash and travellers cheques, plus a Visa or MasterCard for withdrawing money from ATMs.

South Africa South Africa's currency is the rand (R), which is divided into 100 cents. The coins are one, two, five, 10, 20 and 50 cents, and R1, R2 and R5. The notes are R10, R20, R50, R100 and R200. The rand remains weak against Western currencies, making travelling in South Africa less expensive than travelling in Europe and North America.

ATMS

ATMs are widespread, both in the cities and beyond, but stash some cash if visiting rural areas.

CREDIT CARDS

Because South Africa has a reputation for scams, many banks abroad automatically prevent transactions in the country. Particularly if you plan to use a credit card in South Africa, contact your bank before leaving home and inform it of your travel plans.

» MasterCard and Visa are widely accepted.

» Credit and debit cards can be used at many ATMs.

» If you get a failed transaction or anything irregular happens while making a payment with a card or using an ATM, retrieve your card as quickly as possible and do not try the procedure again.

MONEYCHANGERS

» Cash is readily exchanged at banks and foreign-exchange bureaus in all major cities.

» Most banks change travellers cheques in major currencies with varying commissions.

» Thomas Cook has travellers cheques in rand, though it works out best in the end to buy US-dollar cheques.

» The Thomas Cook agent in South Africa is the Rennies Travel chain of travel agencies, and there are American Express offices in major cities. Neither charges a commission for its own travellers cheques, though you'll usually get a higher rate of exchange from a bank.

» Keep at least some of your exchange receipts as you'll need these to reconvert leftover rand when you leave.

TAXES & REFUNDS

» South Africa has a value-added tax (VAT) of 14%, but departing foreign visitors can reclaim much of this on goods being taken out of the country.

» To make a claim, the goods' total value must exceed R250.

» Visit www.taxrefunds.co.za for more information.

TIPPING

» Wages are low, and tipping is expected; around 10% to 15% is usual.

» The usual tip for a car guard or petrol-station attendant is R2 to R5.

Post

For mailing anything of value consider using a private mail service such as PostNet.

Public Holidays

New Year's Day 1 January

Human Rights Day 21 March

Good Friday March or April

Family Day March or April (Easter Monday)

Freedom Day 27 April

Workers' Day 1 May

Youth Day 16 June

National Women's Day 9 August

Heritage Day 24 September

Day of Reconciliation 16 December

Christmas Day 25 December

Day of Goodwill 26 December

SCHOOL HOLIDAYS

School holiday periods are approximately from: late March to mid-April (varying, depending on when Easter is); late June to mid-July; late September to early October; and early December to mid-January.

» The inland provinces (Free State, Gauteng, Mpumalanga, North-West Province and Limpopo) and coastal provinces (Eastern Cape, KwaZulu-Natal, Northern Cape and Western Cape) stagger their school holidays.

» For exact dates, see the calendars at www.saschools.co.za.

Safe Travel

Crime is the national obsession and, apart from car accidents, it's the major risk that you'll face in South Africa. However, try to keep things in perspective, and remember that despite the statistics and newspaper headlines, the majority of travellers visit the country without incident.

The risks are highest in Jo'burg, followed by some townships and other urban centres.

You can minimise the risks by following basic safety precautions:

» If arriving at OR Tambo International Airport (Jo'burg) keep valuables in your hand luggage and/or vacuum-wrap your baggage, as items are sometimes pilfered from bags before they reach the carousel.

» One of the greatest dangers during muggings or carjackings, especially in Jo'burg, is that your assailants will assume you are armed, and that you will kill them if you get a chance. Stay calm, and don't resist or give them any reason to think you will fight back.

» Listen to local advice on unsafe areas.

» Avoid deserted areas day and night, and especially avoid the commercial business district areas of larger cities at night and weekends.

» If you're going to visit a township, go with a trusted guide or as part of a tour.

Telephone

South Africa has good telephone facilities.

» Telkom (www.telkom.co.za) phonecards and, for international calls, Worldcall cards are widely available.

» Local phone calls cost R0.47 per minute.

» Domestic long-distance calls cost about R0.90 per minute.

» There are private phone centres where you can pay cash for your call, but at high rates.

PHONE CODES

Telephone numbers in South Africa are 10 digits, including the local area code, which must always be dialled.

In South Africa, there are several four-digit nationwide prefixes, followed by six-digit numbers. These include:

» 080 (usually 0800; toll free).

» 0860 (charged as a local call).

» 0861 (flat-rate calls).

MOBILE PHONES

» The mobile-phone network covers most of the country.

» There are GSM and 3G digital networks.

» The major mobile networks are Vodacom (www.vodacom.co.za), MTN (www.mtn.co.za), Cell C (www.cellc.co.za) and Virgin Mobile (www.virginmobile.co.za).

» You can hire a mobile phone through your car-rental provider.

» A cheaper alternative is to bring your own phone (check ahead that it's compatible) and insert a local SIM card.

» SIM cards and credit (known as 'airtime') are widely available.

» You need ID and proof of a South African address (an accommodation receipt) to buy and 'RICA' (register) a SIM card.

Tourist Information

Almost every town in the country has a tourist office. These are often private entities, which will only recommend member organisations and may add commissions to bookings they make on your behalf. They are worth visiting, but you may have to push to find out about all the possible options.

In state-run offices, staff are often badly informed and lethargic; asking for assistance at your accommodation may prove more useful. South African Tourism (☏083-123 6789, 011-895 3000; www.southafrica.net) has a helpful website, with practical information and inspirational features.

Eastern Cape Tourism Board (☏043-701 9600; www.ectourism.co.za)

Free State Tourism Board (☏051-447 1362; www.dteea.fs.gov.za)

Gauteng Tourism Authority (☏011-639 1600; www.gauteng.net)

KwaZulu-Natal Tourism Authority (KZN Tourism; ☏031-366 7500; www.zulu.org.za; ground fl, Tourist Junction)

Limpopo Tourism Board (☏0860 730 730, 015-290 7300; www.golimpopo.com)

Mpumalanga Tourism Authority (☏013-759 5300; www.mpumalanga.com)

Northern Cape Tourism Authority (☏053-832 2657; www.northerncape.org.za)

North-West Province Parks & Tourism Board (www.tourismnorthwest.co.za)

Western Cape Tourism Board (☏021-426 5639; www.thewesterncape.co.za)

Travellers with Disabilities

» South Africa is one of the best destinations on the continent for disabled travellers, with an ever-expanding network of facilities catering to those who are mobility impaired or blind.

» SAN Parks (p502) has a detailed and inspirational overview of accommodation and trail accessibility for the mobility impaired at all its parks.

» A helpful initial contact is the National Council for Persons with Physical Disabilities in South Africa (☏011-726 8040; www.ncppdsa.org.za).

Visas

» Travellers from most Commonwealth countries (including Australia and the UK), most Western European countries, Japan and the USA are issued with a free 90-day visitor's permit on arrival.

» Your passport must be valid for at least 30 days after the end of your intended visit.

» If you aren't entitled to an entry permit, you'll need to get a visa (R425 or equivalent) before you arrive.

» Visas aren't issued at the borders.

» For more information, visit the Department of Home Affairs (www.home-affairs.gov.za).

VISA EXTENSIONS

» Applications for extensions to visas or entry permits should be made at the Department of Home Affairs in Cape Town, Durban, Jo'burg and Pretoria.

» Extensions normally allow for another 30 days in South Africa.

» Apply with plenty of time – extensions can take several weeks to process.

Volunteering

» Volunteer work is possible, especially if you're interested in teaching or wildlife conservation.

» To work on an unpaid voluntary basis, a visitor's permit or visa suffices.

» A good starting point is Volunteer Abroad (www.volunteerabroad.com), with extensive listings of opportunities in the country.

Getting There & Away

Entering South Africa

Once you have an entry permit or visa, entering South Africa is straightforward and hassle-free. Travellers arriving by air are sometimes required to show an onward ticket – preferably an air ticket, though an overland ticket also seems to be acceptable.

If you're coming to South Africa after travelling through a yellow-fever zone, you must have an international vaccination certificate against yellow fever. No other vaccinations are mandatory, although there are some you should consider (see p718).

Air

AIRPORTS & AIRLINES

The major air hub for South Africa, and for the surrounding region, is Jo'burg's OR Tambo International Airport (ORTIA; ☎011-921 6911; www.airports.co.za).

The other principal international airports:

Cape Town International Airport. (CPT; ☎021-937 1200; www.airports.co.za)

King Shaka International Airport (☎032-436 6585) Durban.

National airline South African Airways has an excellent route network and safety record. In addition to its international routes, it operates regional flights together with its subsidiaries SAAirlink and SA Express.

Some other international carriers flying to/from Jo'burg (except as noted):

Air France (www.airfrance.co.za)

Air Mauritius (www.airmauritius.com) Also serves Cape Town and Durban.

British Airways (www.britishairways.com) Also serves Cape Town.

Cathay Pacific (www.cathaypacific.com)

Egyptair (www.egyptair.com)

Emirates (www.emirates.com) Also serves Cape Town and Durban.

Kenya Airways (www.kenya-airways.com)

KLM (www.klm.com) Also serves Cape Town.

Lufthansa (www.lufthansa.com) Also serves Cape Town.

Qantas (www.qantas.com.au)

Qatar Airways (www.qatarairways.com) Also serves Cape Town.

Singapore Airlines (www.singaporeair.com) Also serves Cape Town.

Turkish Airlines (www.turkishairlines.com) Also serves Cape Town.

Virgin Atlantic (www.virgin-atlantic.com) Also serves Cape Town.

Bicycle

There are no restrictions on bringing your own bicycle into South Africa. Sources of information:

Cycling SA (http://cms.cyclingsa.com)

International Bicycle Fund (www.ibike.org)

Border Crossings

BOTSWANA

There are 18 official South Africa–Botswana border posts, open at least between 8am and 4pm.

Some of the more remote crossings are impassable to 2WD vehicles and may be closed during periods of high water. Otherwise, the crossings are hassle-free.

Grobler's Bridge/Martin's Drift (8am to 10pm) Northwest of Polokwane (Pietersburg).

Kopfontein/Tlokweng Gate (6am to 10pm) Next to Madikwe Game Reserve; a main border crossing.

Pont Drift (8am to 4pm) Convenient for Mapungubwe National Park (Limpopo) and Tuli Block (Botswana).

Ramatlabama (6am to 8pm) North of Mafikeng; a main border crossing.

Skilpadshek/Pioneer Gate (6am to 10pm) Northwest of Zeerust; a main border crossing.

By Bus

Intercape (☑0861 287 287; www.intercape.co.za) runs daily between Gaborone (Botswana) and Pretoria (from R240, eight hours).

Minibuses (less safe and comfortable than buses) run between Jo'burg and Gaborone via Mafikeng (North-West Province).

You can also pick up minibuses over the border from Mafikeng to Lobatse (1½ hours) and Gaborone (2½ hours).

Another route from Jo'burg is to/from Palapye (Botswana) via Grobler's Bridge/Martin's Drift (eight hours).

LESOTHO

All of Lesotho's borders are with South Africa and are straightforward to cross.

The main crossing is at Maseru Bridge, east of Bloemfontein; queues here are often very long exiting Lesotho and, on some weekend evenings, coming into Lesotho.

By Bus

Minibus taxis connect Jo'burg and Maseru.

It's quicker and easier to catch a bus to Bloemfontein, then continue by minibus taxi to Maseru (three hours), changing in Botshabelo (Mtabelo) or Ladybrand.

Bus services also run to Ladybrand.

Leaving Maseru, long-distance minibus taxis leave from the rank at the Maseru Bridge crossing.

Other routes:

» Mokhotlong (Lesotho) to/from Underberg (KwaZulu-Natal) via Sani Pass.
» Qacha's Nek (Lesotho) to/from Matatiele (Eastern Cape).
» Maputsoe Bridge crossing, 6km southeast of Ficksburg (Free State), to/from Butha-Buthe and northern Lesotho.
» Jo'burg to/from Butha-Buthe via Fouriesburg (Free State) and the Caledonspoort crossing.

By Car & Motorcycle

» The easiest entry points for car and motorcycle are on the northern and western sides of the country.
» Most of the entry points to the south and east are unpaved, though most are passable in a 2WD.
» A sealed road runs westwards from Qacha's Nek.
» You'll need a 4WD to enter and exit Lesotho via Sani Pass.

MOZAMBIQUE

There are four main South Africa–Mozambique border crossings.

Giriyondo (8am to 4pm October to March, to 3pm April to September) Between Kruger National Park's Phalaborwa Gate and Massingir (Mozambique).

Kosi Bay/Ponta d'Ouro (8am to 4pm) On the coast, well north of Durban.

Lebombo/Ressano Garcia (6am to midnight) Main crossing, east of Nelspruit.

Pafuri (8am to 4pm) In Kruger National Park's northeastern corner.

By Bus

Bus companies including Greyhound (p511), Intercape (p511) and Translux (p511) run daily 'luxury' coaches between Jo'burg/Pretoria and Maputo (Mozambique) via Nelspruit and Komatipoort (R330, nine hours).

The above route can be tackled in minibus taxis.

Taxis run between Maputo and the Namaacha/Lomahasha post on the Swazi border (1¾ hours); some continue to Manzini (3¼ hours).

By Car & Motorcycle

Kosi Bay/Ponta d'Ouro Travelling to/from Mozambique via this border, you'll need your own vehicle (4WD on the Mozambique side). Accommodation options in Ponta d'Ouro (Mozambique) offer transfers.

Lebombo The N4 and EN4 freeways connect Jo'burg/Pretoria with Maputo via this border post, with six tolls on the South African side (two via the N12 from Jo'burg) and one on the Mozambique side.

By Train

You can travel from Jo'burg/Pretoria on a domestic Shosholoza Meyl (☑011-774 4555, 0860 008 888; www.shosholozameyl.co.za) train to Komatipoort, then cross the border on foot and continue to Maputo on a Caminhos de Ferro do Moçambique (CFM) train.

NAMIBIA

South Africa–Namibia border posts include the following:

Alexander Bay/Oranjemund (6am to 10pm) On the Atlantic coast; public access sometimes not permitted.

Nakop/Ariamsvlei (24 hours) West of Upington.

Rietfontein/Aroab (8am to 4.30pm) Just south of Kgalagadi Transfrontier Park.

Vioolsdrif/Noordoewer (24 hours) North of Springbok, en route to/from Cape Town.

By Bus

Intercape (p508) runs between Cape Town and Windhoek, Namibia (from R680, 21 hours) via Springbok on Tuesday, Thursday, Friday and Sunday.

SWAZILAND

There are 11 South Africa–Swaziland border crossings, all of which are hassle-free. Note that small posts close at 4pm.

Golela/Lavumisa (7am to 10pm) En route between Durban and Swaziland's Ezulwini Valley.

Josefsdal/Bulembu (8am to 4pm) Between Piggs Peak and Barberton (Mpumalanga); can be tricky in wet weather.

Mahamba (7am to 10pm) The best crossing to use from Piet Retief (Mpumalanga).

Mananga (7am to 6pm) Southwest of Komatipoort (Mpumalanga).

Matsamo/Jeppe's Reef (7am to 8pm) Southwest of Malelane (Mpumalanga) and a possible route to Kruger National Park.

Onverwacht/Salitje (7am to 6pm) North of Pongola (KwaZulu-Natal).

Oshoek/Ngwenya (7am to 10pm) The busiest crossing, approximately 360km southeast of Pretoria.

By Bus

A daily shuttle runs between Jo'burg and Mbabane.

Minibus-taxi routes:

» Jo'burg to/from Manzini (four hours) via Mbabane.
» Durban to/from Manzini (eight hours).
» Manzini to/from Maputo (3¼ hours).

ZIMBABWE

Situated on the Limpopo River, Beitbridge (24 hours) is the only border post between Zimbabwe and South Africa. There is lots of smuggling, so searches are very thorough and the queues are often long.

The closest South African town to the border is Musina (15km south), where you can change money.

Ignore touts on the Zimbabwean side trying to 'help' you through Zimbabwean immigration and customs; there is no charge for the government forms needed for immigration.

By Bus

Greyhound (p511) and Intercape (p511) services operate daily buses between Jo'burg and Harare (16½ hours, R600), and between Jo'burg and Bulawayo (14 hours, R440), via Pretoria and Limpopo.

Minibus taxis run south from Beitbridge to Musina and beyond.

Bus & Minibus Taxi

BUS

» Numerous buses cross the borders between South Africa and all of its neighbours.
» It's the most efficient way to travel overland, unless you have your own vehicle.
» Sometimes-lengthy queues are usually the only hassle.
» You'll need to disembark to take care of visa formalities, then reboard your bus and carry on.
» Some bus lines offer student discounts, upon presentation of a student ID.

MINIBUS TAXI

» You can travel to/from all of South Africa's neighbours by local minibus taxi.
» It's often necessary to walk across the border and pick up onward transport on the other side.

Car & Motorcycle

» If you hire a car in South Africa and plan to take it across an international border, you'll need a permission letter from the hire company.
» If you're arriving in South Africa by car or motorcycle, you'll need the vehicle's registration papers, liability insurance and your driving licence or international permit.
» You'll also need a *carnet de passage en douane,* which acts as a temporary waiver of import duty; arrange for this through your local automobile association.
» Cars registered in South Africa, Lesotho, Swaziland, Botswana and Namibia don't

need a *carnet* to visit the other countries in this group.

☞ Tours

Dozens of tour and safari companies organise package tours to South Africa, including for various special interests (birdwatching etc).

AUSTRALIA

Adventure World (www.adventureworld.com. au) A range of tours and safaris in South Africa and the region.

Peregrine Adventures (www.peregrine-adventures.com) Itineraries range from trans-continental missions to two-week safaris.

FRANCE

Makila Voyages (☎01 42 96 80 00; www. makila.fr) Upper-end tailored tours in South Africa and its neighbours.

UK

Dragoman (www.dragoman.com) Overland tours.

Exodus Travels (www.exodustravels.co.uk) A variety of tours, including overland trips and walking, cycling and wildlife itineraries, covering South Africa and surrounds.

USA

Adventure Center (www.adventurecenter. com) Adventure tours and activity-focused trips, covering South Africa, Swaziland and Lesotho.

Africa Adventure Company (www.africa-adventure.com) Upper-end wildlife safaris, including the private reserves around Kruger National Park, plus itineraries in and around Cape Town.

Getting Around

Air

National airline South African Airways (☎0861 359 722; www.flysaa.com) is the main domestic carrier, with an extensive network of routes.

Its subsidiaries, SAAirlink (☎0861 606 606; www.flyairlink.com) and SA Express (☎0861 729 227; www.flyexpress.aero), also serve domestic routes and share SAA's excellent safety record.

Domestic fares aren't cheap; one way to save is to book online months before travelling.

Comair (☎0860 435 922; www.comair.co.za) Operates British Airways flights in Southern Africa, and has flights linking Cape Town, Durban, Jo'burg and Port Elizabeth.

Kulula.com (☎0861 585 852; www.kulula. com) No-frills flights linking Jo'burg, Cape Town, Durban, George, East London and Port Elizabeth.

Mango (☎0861 001 234; www.flymango.com) No-frills flights linking Jo'burg, Cape Town, Durban, Port Elizabeth and Bloemfontein.

Bicycle

South Africa offers some rewarding cycling.

Good areas The Cape Peninsula and the Winelands of the Western Cape are excellent; the Wild Coast is beautiful and challenging; the northern lowveld offers wide plains.

Public transport Trains can carry bikes, but most bus lines don't want bicycles in their luggage holds, and minibuses don't carry luggage on the roof.

Safety It's illegal to cycle on highways, and roads near urban areas are too busy for comfort. Bring a good lock with you.

Weather Much of the country (except for the Western Cape and the west coast) gets most of its rain in summer (late November to March), often in the form of violent thunderstorms. When it isn't raining, summer days can be unpleasantly hot, especially in the lowveld.

Bus

A good network of buses, of varying reliability and comfort, links the major cities.

Classes There are no class tiers on the bus lines, although major companies generally offer a 'luxury' service, with features such as air-con, a toilet and films.

Discounts The major bus lines offer student, backpacker and senior-citizen discounts, as well as specials; check their websites for details. Inquire about travel passes if you'll be taking several bus journeys.

Fares Roughly calculated by distance, although short runs are disproportionately expensive. Prices rise during school holidays.

Safety Apart from where noted, the lines listed in this chapter are generally safe.

Note, however, that many long-distance services run through the night. On overnight journeys, travellers should take care of their valuables and women might feel more comfortable sitting near the front of the bus.

Ticket purchase For the main lines, purchase tickets at least 24 hours in advance, and as far in advance as possible for travel during peak periods. Tickets can be bought through bus offices, Computicket (www.computicket.co.za) and Shoprite/Checkers supermarkets.

BUS LINES
Greyhound and Translux are considered the premium lines.

City to City (☎0861 589 282, 011-774 3333; www.translux.co.za) In partnership with Translux, it operates a no-frills service along the routes that once carried people between the homelands under apartheid. It is less expensive than the other lines, and serves many off-the-beaten-track places, including townships and mining towns. Destinations include Mthatha, Nelspruit, Hazyview, Beitbridge (for Zimbabwe) and various towns in KwaZulu-Natal.

Greyhound (☎0839 159 000; www.greyhound. co.za) An extensive network of comfortable buses. Operates other lines, including the cheaper Citiliner buses.

Intercape (☎0861 287 287; www.intercape. co.za) An extensive network stretching from Cape Town to Limpopo and beyond. For longer hauls (including Cape Town to Windhoek, Namibia, and Mossel Bay to Jo'burg), it's worth paying extra for a reclining seat on an overnight Sleepliner bus.

SA Roadlink (☎011-333 2223; www.saroadlink. co.za) Links Jo'burg/Pretoria with Bloemfontein, Port Elizabeth, East London, Mthatha, Durban, Cape Town, Polokwane and points in between. A smaller network than the others, but prices are reasonable – generally just above City to City fares.

Translux (☎0861 589 282; www.translux.co.za) The main long-distance operator, with a comprehensive list of destinations.

Car & Motorcycle

South Africa is ideal for driving, and away from the main bus and train routes, having your own wheels is the best way to get around. If you're in a group, it's also often the most economical.

Most major roads are in excellent condition, and off the main routes there are interesting back roads to explore. Toll roads are marked by a black 'T' in a yellow circle; there's always an alternative route, marked by a black 'A' in a yellow circle. On alternative routes, signposting is sparse, generally only giving route numbers or directing you to the nearby towns, rather than the next large city.

Smaller roads are numbered (eg R44 or Rte 44), and when giving directions most people will refer to these numbers rather than destinations, so it pays to have a good road map.

FUEL
» Unleaded petrol costs about R12 per litre.
» An attendant will always fill up your tank and clean your windows – tip R2.
» If they check your oil, water or tyres, tip R5.

BAZ BUS

A convenient alternative to standard bus lines, Baz Bus (p365) caters almost exclusively to backpackers and travellers. It offers hop-on, hop-off fares and door-to-door service between Cape Town and Jo'burg via the Garden Route, Port Elizabeth, Durban and Northern Drakensberg.

Baz Bus drops off and picks up at hostels, and has transfer arrangements with those off its route in areas such as the Wild Coast. You can book directly with Baz Bus or at most hostels.

Point-to-point fares are more expensive than on the major bus lines, but it can work out economically if you take advantage of the hop-on, hop-off feature.

Sample one-way hop-on, hop-off fares to Cape Town: from Jo'burg/Pretoria R2900; from Durban R2430; from Port Elizabeth R1250.

One-/two-/three-week travel passes cost R1200/2100/2600.

HIRE

» Car hire is relatively inexpensive in South Africa compared with Europe and North America.

» Most companies have a minimum age requirement of 21 years.

» All accept major credit cards, and most do not accept debit cards.

» Rates start below R200 per day, including insurance and 200km free per day (unlimited mileage in some cases).

» Rental of a 4WD starts at around R900 per day.

» As well as the companies below, check the budget domestic airlines and backpacker hostels; many can arrange good deals.

» Hiring a camper van is another option, although one-way hire is not always possible.

» Some camper-van rentals include camping gear.

» *Bakkie* campers, which sleep two in the back of a canopied pick-up, are cheaper.

» Two places to try are African Leisure Travel (☎011-475 2902; www.africanleisure.co.za) (Jo'burg; 4WD and campervans) and Britz 4x4 Rentals (☎011-396 1860; www.brit z.co.za) (Cape Town and Jo'burg; 4WD).

» For motorcycle rental, good contacts include Motozulu (www.motozu.lu.ms) in Port Shepstone (KwaZulu-Natal), and LDV Biking (☎083 528 0897; www.ldvbiking.co.za) in Cape Town.

Car-hire companies:

Argus (www.arguscarhire.co.za) Online consolidator generally offering excellent rates.

Around About Cars (www.aroundaboutcars. com) A recommended budget agent based in Cape Town but operating nationwide.

Avis (www.avis.co.za)

Budget (www.budget.co.za)

Europcar (www.europcar.co.za)

First (www.firstcarrental.co.za)

Hertz (www.hertz.co.za)

Tempest (www.tempestcarhire.co.za)

INSURANCE

» Insurance for third-party damage, and damage to or loss of your vehicle, is highly recommended, though not legally required.

» The Automobile Association of South Africa (AASA; ☎011-799 1000, emergencies 0838 43 22; www.aasa.co.za) is a good contact.

» Insurance agencies include Sansure (☎0860 786 847, 021-914 3488; www.sansure. com) in Cape Town.

ROAD HAZARDS

» South Africa has a horrific road-accident record, with an annual death toll of about 14,000.

» Notably dangerous stretches of road: N1 between Cape Town and Beaufort West; N2 between Cape Town and Somerset West; N2 between East London and Kokstad; N1 between Mokopane (Potgietersrus) and Polokwane; and N2 between Durban and Tongaat.

» The main hazards are your fellow drivers. Be particularly wary of minibus taxi drivers, who operate under pressure on little sleep in shoddy vehicles.

» On freeways, drivers coming up behind you will expect you to move into the hard shoulder to let them pass, even if you are approaching a corner and regardless of what is happening in the hard shoulder. Motorists often remain hard on your tail until you move over.

» Drivers on little-used rural roads often speed and assume that there is no other traffic.

» Despite road blocks and alcohol breath-testing, particularly in urban areas, drink driving is widespread.

» Farm animals, wildlife (particularly baboons) and pedestrians stray onto the roads, especially in rural areas. If you hit an animal in an area where you're uncertain of your safety, continue to the nearest police station and report it there.

» During the rainy season, thick fog can slow you to a crawl, especially in higher areas of KwaZulu-Natal.

ROAD RULES

» Driving is on the left-hand side of the road.

» Seatbelts are mandatory for the driver and front-seat passenger.

» The main local idiosyncrasy is the 'four-way stop' (crossroad), found even on major roads. All vehicles are required to stop, with

---

ℹ️ DRIVING LICENCE

» You can use your driving licence from your home country if it is in English (or you have a certified translation) and it carries your photo.

» Otherwise you'll need an international driving permit.

CARJACKING

In Jo'burg, and to a lesser extent in the other big cities, carjacking is a danger. It's more likely if you're driving something flash rather than a standard hire car. Stay alert, keep your taste in cars modest, and avoid driving in urban areas at night; if you have to do so, keep windows wound up and doors locked.

   If you're waiting at a red light and notice anything suspicious, it's standard practice to check that the junction is clear, and jump the light. If you do get carjacked, don't resist; just hand over the keys immediately. The carjackers are almost always armed, and people have been killed for their cars.

those arriving first the first to go (even if they're on a minor cross street).

» On freeways, faster drivers will expect you to move into the emergency lane to let them pass, and will probably flash their hazard lights as thanks.

» If you are parking in the street or a car park in larger towns and cities, you will often be approached by a 'car guard'. They will keep an eye on your motor for R2 to R5; they may also offer to wash it for an extra charge.

Hitching

Hitchhiking and picking up hitchers is inadvisable. If you're strapped for cash, you could look into share drives. Hostel noticeboards often have details of free or shared-cost lifts.

Local Transport

For getting around within a city or town, the main options are city buses, minibus taxis and regular taxis.

BUS

» Cape Town, Jo'burg, Pretoria and several other urban areas have city bus systems.

» Fares are cheap.

» Routes, which are signboarded, are extensive.

» Services usually stop running early in the evening, and there aren't many buses on weekends.

MINIBUS TAXI

Minibus taxis run almost everywhere – within cities, to the suburbs and to neighbouring towns.

» They leave when full.

» 'Full' in South Africa isn't as packed in as many African countries.

» Most accommodate 14 to 16 people.

» Away from train and main bus routes, minibus taxis may be the only choice of public transport.

» They're also a good way to get insights into local life.

Security

Money saved by taking minibus taxis is outweighed by safety considerations.

» Overall, taking minibus taxis is not recommended.

» Driving standards and vehicle conditions are poor.

» There are frequent accidents.

» Minibus-taxi stops are often unsafe.

» Muggings, pickpocketing, sexual harrassment and other incidents are common.

» If you want to try one, don't ride at night; seek local advice on areas to avoid.

» In a few areas, notably central Cape Town, they're a handy and popular way to get around during daylight hours.

» Most minibus taxis don't carry luggage on the roof, and stowing backpacks can be a hassle.

PRIVATE TAXI

» Larger cities have private taxi services.

» There are taxi stands in popular areas.

» Phoning for a cab is often safer than hailing one on the street.

» Prices average about R10 per kilometre.

☞ Tours

There are dozens of tours run by local companies, ranging from budget-oriented overland truck tours to exclusive luxury safaris.

   The best way to get information on budget tours is from the nationwide network of backpacker hostels; many have travellers' bulletin boards, and some are affiliated with tour operators.

Bird-Watch Cape (www.birdwatch.co.za) Small, Cape Town–based outfit for avid twitchers.

Bok Bus (www.bokbus.com) Budget-oriented tours along the Garden Route and around.

Cape Gourmet Adventure Tours (http://gourmet.cape-town.info) Mouth-watering tours of Cape Town and the Western Cape.

Signature Tours (www.signaturetours.co.za) Tours focused on topics including botany, birding and the environment.

Springbok-Atlas (www.springbokatlas.com) Coach tours nationwide.

Thompsons Africa (www.thompsonsafrica.com) Midrange and top-end package tours and safaris.

Wilderness Safaris (www.wilderness-safaris.com) Upscale, conservation-focused operator offering high-end safaris and special-interest trips.

Wildlife Safaris (www.wildlifesaf.co.za) Midrange safaris from Jo'burg to Kruger and Pilanesberg National Parks.

Train

South Africa's **Shosholoza Meyl** (☎011-774 4555, 0860 008 888; www.shosholozameyl.co.za) offers regular services connecting major cities.

For an overview and valuable advice, consult the **Man in Seat 61** (www.seat61.com/SouthAfrica.htm).

CLASSES
Tourist and economy classes are affordable options. Unlike on long-distance buses, fares on short sectors are not inflated.

Premier class A luxurious experience, offering a more affordable alternative to the Blue Train. Cars can be transported for a surcharge.

Tourist class Recommended: scenic and safe, albeit sometimes slow, way to travel. On overnight journeys, tourist-class fares include a sleeping berth (with a small additional charge for bedding hire). Couples are normally given two-berth coupés and single travellers and larger groups are put in four-berth compartments. If you are travelling alone and you want a coupé to yourself, you could buy two tickets. Meals and drinks are available in the dining car, or in your compartment.

Economy class Does not have sleeping compartments and is not a comfortable or secure option for overnight travel.

TICKETS & FARES
» Unless otherwise stated, all fares quoted in this chapter are for tourist class.
» Tickets must be booked at least 24 hours in advance (you can book up to three months in advance).
» Bookings can be done at train stations, through the website or by phone.
» If booking telephonically you must pay in person at a station or deposit the money in Shosholoza Meyl's bank account and send the company proof of payment.

ROUTES
Jo'burg–Cape Town Via Kimberley and Beaufort West; 27 hours; premier (twice weekly), tourist (Wednesday, Friday and Sunday) and economy (daily).

Jo'burg–Durban Via Ladysmith and Pietermaritzburg; 13 hours; premier (weekly), tourist and economy (Wednesday, Friday and Sunday).

Jo'burg–East London Via Bloemfontein; 20 hours; economy (three times weekly).

Jo'burg–Port Elizabeth Via Kroonstad, Bloemfontein and Cradock; 21 hours; tourist and economy (Wednesday, Friday and Sunday).

Jo'burg–Musina Via Pretoria and Louis Trichardt (Makhado); 17 hours; economy (twice weekly).

Jo'burg–Komatipoort Via Pretoria and Nelspruit; 13 hours; economy (three times weekly).

Luxurious special lines include the famous Blue Train (p347), which runs weekly between Pretoria and Cape Town (one way per person sharing from R13,485, including meals and drinks); and Rovos Rail (p348), which has regular trips including Pretoria–Cape Town, stopping at Kimberley and Matjiesfontein, and Pretoria–Durban.

METRO TRAINS
Cape Metro Rail (p348) Services from Cape Town to either Simon's Town or the Winelands are quite safe during the day.

Gautrain (www.gautrain.co.za) connects Jo'burg with Pretoria and OR Tambo International Airport. Other metro trains in Jo'burg and Pretoria are not recommended, for security reasons.

Swaziland

Includes »

Best Wildlife Experiences

» Mkhaya Game Reserve (p524)

» Hlane Royal National Park (p524)

Best Places to Stay

» Malandela's B&B (p521)

» Mkhaya Game Reserve (p525)

» Mlilwane Wildlife Sanctuary (p520)

» Bulembu (p523)

Why Go?

In short: big things come in small packages. The intriguing kingdom of Swaziland is diminutive, but boasts a huge checklist for any visitor. Rewarding wildlife watching? Tick. Adrenalin-boosting activities such as rafting and mountain biking? Tick. Lively and colourful local culture, with celebrations and ceremonies still common practice? Tick. Plus there are superb walking trails, stunning mountain and flatland scenery, and excellent, high-quality handicrafts.

Presiding over this is King Mswati III, the last remaining absolute monarch in Africa, who, despite his critics, is is the source of national pride, and local culture is flourishing. This is exemplified in its national festivals – the Incwala ceremony and the Umhlanga (Reed) dance.

The excellent road system makes Swaziland a pleasure to navigate. Accommodation ranges from hostels to family-friendly hotels, wilderness lodges and upmarket retreats. Many travellers make a flying visit on their way to Kruger National Park, but it's well worth lingering here if you can.

When to Go
Mbabane

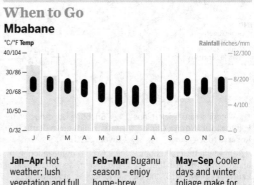

Jan–Apr Hot weather; lush vegetation and full rivers provide perfect photographic backdrops

Feb–Mar Buganu season – enjoy home-brew marula wine in rural Swaziland

May–Sep Cooler days and winter foliage make for wonderful wildlife viewing in the lowveld

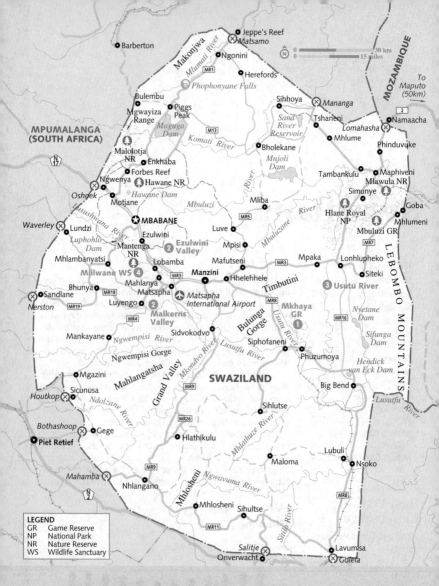

Swaziland Highlights

① Watching rare black rhinos in the wild at **Mkhaya Game Reserve** (p524)

② Browsing the craft shops and royal heartland in the **Ezulwini Valley** (p518) and the **Malkerns Valley** (p521)

③ Shooting wondrous white-water rapids down **Usutu River** (p520)

④ Cycling or meandering in the wilderness, and relaxing in its lodges, at **Mlilwane Wildlife Sanctuary** (p518)

⑤ Digging in for the night in a community-run hut and experiencing the best of **local culture** (p524)

MBABANE

POP 100,000 / ELEV 1243M

Swaziland's capital, Mbabane (pronounced mba-*baa*-nee), is pretty nondescript and there isn't that much to see or do here. It's in a pleasant setting in the Dlangeni Hills. These make Mbabane cooler than Manzini, one reason why the British moved their administrative centre here from Manzini in 1902. The adjacent Ezulwini and Malkerns Valleys have plenty of attractions.

⊙ Sights & Activities

Eight kilometres northeast of Mbabane is Sibebe Rock (admission E30), a massive, sheer granite dome hulking over the surrounding countryside; the area is managed by the local community through Swazi Trails (📞2416 2180; www.swazitrails.co.sz) in Ezulwini Valley. The company takes half-day nontechnical climbs up the rock (per person E580, including transport, entry and refreshments; guide only per person E295, minimum two people).

The Ezulwini and Malkerns Valleys are where most people go for sightseeing, activities and crafts.

🛏 Sleeping

Brackenhill Lodge   GUESTHOUSE **$$**
(📞2404 2887; www.brackenhillswazi.com; Mountain Dr; s/d incl breakfast from E640/840; ⓟⓢ⌕) Located 4.5km north of Mbabane, this attractive place has a range of comfortable and airy, if dated (but not unpleasantly so), rooms. Lovely staff; evening meals on request. Ring for directions.

Foresters Arms   LODGE **$$**
(📞2467 4177; www.forestersarms.co.za; s/d incl breakfast E620/960; ⓟⓢⓦ⌕) Penelope Keith, star of *To the Manor Born*, would enjoy the cream teas and the cosy, British-style interiors here. Situated 27km southwest of Mbabane in the hills around Mhlambanyatsi.

Kapola Boutique Hotel   BOUTIQUE HOTEL **$$**
(📞2404 0906; www.safarinow.com/go/KapolaBoutiqueHotel; s/d incl breakfast E800/1100) About 5km from Mbabane, this recently built hotel boasts plush, stylish decor in its eight rooms. A major downside is that it's on, and exposed to, the busy and noisy MR3.

Mountain Inn   INN **$$**
(📞2404 2781; www.mountaininn.sz; s/d incl breakfast from E795/696; ⓟ✳ⓦ⌕) It's not five-star

luxury, but this sprawling inn is friendly, unpretentious and a safe bet. There's a pool, library, lawns and panoramas looking over the valley from the inviting Friar Tuck's restaurant, which is open for breakfast, lunch and dinner.

🍴 Eating

Ramblas   INTERNATIONAL **$$**
(mains E40-100; ⊙8am-late Mon-Sat; ⓟ) Mbabane's top choice for good cuisine and a buzzing ambience; located within the Serendipity Health complex. It's worth the drive for its great salads, meat dishes and good breakfasts.

Plaza Tandoori Restaurant   INDIAN **$$**
(Swazi Plaza; mains E45-80; ⊙lunch & dinner) It's not the size of the Taj Mahal, but it's certainly got the atmosphere. As well as great-value

curries, the usual grills and burgers add a touch of the international.

Indingilizi Gallery & Restaurant CAFE $$
(📞2404 6213; www.africanoriginal.com; 112 Dzeli-we St; light meals E40-80; ⊙8am-5pm Mon-Fri, 8.30am-1pm Sat) This longstanding place – a gallery with a small outdoor cafe – offers snacks and light lunches.

ⓘ Information

Dangers & Annoyances
Mbabane can be unsafe at night, so don't walk around by yourself away from the main streets. Take precautions in the streets even during the day – muggings are on the increase.

Emergency
Fire (📞933, 2404 3333)
Police (📞999, 2404 2221)

Internet Access
There are internet centres at **Swazi.net Internet Cafe** (⊙8am-6pm Mon-Fri, 8am-2pm Sat), located upstairs at Swazi Plaza, and in the Mall, near Pick 'n Pay. Internet access starts from E30 per hour.

Medical Services
Mbabane Clinic (📞2404 2423; St Michael's Rd, Mbabane) For emergencies try this clinic in the southwest corner of town just off the bypass road.
Medi-Sun Clinic (📞2416 2800; Ezulwini Valley) Behind Gables Shopping Complex.

Money
Banks with ATMs include **First National Bank**, **Nedbank** and **Standard Bank**; these are located in Swazi Plaza.

Post & Telephone
Post Office (Msunduza St) You can also make international (though not reverse-charge) calls here.

Tourist Information
Tourist Information Office (📞2404 2531; www.welcometoswaziland.com; Cooper Centre, Sozisa Road; ⊙8am-4.45pm Mon-Thu, 8am-4pm Fri, 9am-1pm Sat) Offers a fee map of Mbabane, Manzini and Swaziland. Pick up copies of *What's Happening in Swaziland* and *What's On in Swaziland*.

ⓘ Getting There & Away

Minibus taxis to South Africa (mostly north-bound) leave from the taxi rank near Swazi Plaza; otherwise your best bet is to catch one from Manzini.

ⓘ Getting Around

To/From the Airport
A taxi from Mbabane to Matsapha International Airport costs around E150. Buses and minibuses from Mbabane to Manzini go past the turn-off to the airport, from where it's a long walk to the terminal.

Bus & Minibus Taxi
The main **bus and minibus taxi rank** is near Swazi Plaza. Vehicles heading towards Manzini (E15, 35 minutes) and points east pass through the Ezulwini Valley, though most take the highways, bypassing the valley itself. There are several minibus taxis daily to Piggs Peak (E25, one hour), Ngwenya and the Oshoek border post (E10, 50 minutes), and Malkerns Valley (E10.50, 45 minutes).

Taxi
Nonshared taxis congregate near the bus station by Swazi Plaza. Nonshared taxis to the Ezulwini Valley cost from E70, more to the far end of the valley (from E100), and still more at night.

EZULWINI VALLEY

This pretty valley (also known as Royal Valley) begins just outside Mbabane and extends down past Lobamba village, 18km away. The area boasts good accommodation and craft shopping. The Ezulwini tourist information office (📞2416 2180; www.swazi.travel; Mantenga Craft Centre, Ezulwini Valley), run out of the Swazi Trails (p517) office, is useful. The Mbabane Medi-Sun Clinic is located in Ezulwini.

◉ Sights & Activities

Mlilwane Wildlife Sanctuary PARK
(Map p519; 📞2528 3943; www.biggameparks.org; admission E35; ⊙6.30am-5.30pm summer, 6am-6pm winter) This beautiful and tranquil private reserve near Lobamba was Swaziland's first protected area, created in the 1950s by conservationist Ted Reilly. Reilly later opened Mkhaya Game Reserve and supervised the establishment of Hlane Royal National Park. Mlilwane means 'Little Fire', named after the many fires started by lightning strikes here.

While it doesn't have the drama or vastness of some of the South African parks, the reserve is easily accessible and worth a visit. Its terrain is dominated by the precipitous Nyonyane (Little Bird) peak, and there are some fine walks in the area. Animals include zebras, giraffes, warthogs, antelope species, crocodiles, hippos and a variety of birds, including black eagles.

There are horse rides (one to three hours E135, fully catered overnight trips E1190), mountain biking (per hour from E105) and wildlife walks (per hour from E75).

🛏 Sleeping

The Ezulwini Valley has both budget digs and upmarket choices. The Sun group's hotels (www.suninternational.com) offer the most opulent accommodation in the country: **Royal Swazi Spa** (Map p519; ☎2416 5000; www.suninternational.com; s/d E2945/3100;

Ezulwini & Malkerns Valleys

Ezulwini & Malkerns Valleys

◎ Sights
1 Mantenga Nature Reserve	A2
2 Mlilwane Wildlife Sanctuary	B2
3 National Museum	B2

🛏 Sleeping
4 Ezulwini Sun Hotel	B1
5 Legends Backpackers Lodge	B2
Lidwala Backpacker Lodge	(see 5)
6 Lugogo Sun Hotel	A1
7 Malandela's B&B	B3
Mantenga Nature Reserve	(see 1)
8 Mlilwane Wildlife Sanctuary Main Camp	B3
9 Reilly's Rock Hilltop Lodge	A2
10 Royal Swazi Spa	A1
11 Sondzela Backpackers (IYHF) Lodge	B3

🍴 Eating
12 Calabash	A1
Khazimula's Restaurant	(see 5)
13 Lihawu Restaurant	B1
Malandela's Restaurant	(see 7)

🎭 Entertainment
House on Fire	(see 7)

🛍 Shopping
Baobab Batik	(see 16)
14 Ezulwini Craft Market	B1
15 Gables Shopping Centre	B2
Gone Rural	(see 7)
Mantenga Craft Centre	(see 5)
16 Swazi Candles Craft Centre	C3

ℹ Information
Swazi Trails	(see 5)

❀🛜🏊), which has a golf course and casino; **Lugogo Sun** (Map p519; ☎2416 4500; www.sun international.com; s/d E1885/2010; ❀🛜🏊), and **Ezulwini Sun** (Map p519; ☎2416 6500; www.sun international.com; s/d E2065/2190; ❀🛜🏊), which is across the road from the other two.

There is a variety of excellent accommodation options in Milwane Wildlife Sanctuary. This must be booked via telephone or email and paid in advance through Big Game Parks (p527).

Mantenga Nature Reserve HUTS **$**
(Map p519; ☎2416 1178, 2416 1151; www.sntc.org.za; beehives E100, cottages incl breakfast per person E700) Located in a nature reserve within the valley, these cottages provide soft 'safari' adventure: the appealing rooms are set in lush bushland and offer all the creature comforts and stylish decor. Visitors don't pay entry to the nature reserve.

Legends Backpackers Lodge BACKPACKERS **$**
(Map p519; ☎2416 1870; www.legends.co.sz; campsites per person E50, dm E100, d without bathroom E300; 🅿🛜) This mellow place offers a straightforward stay in Ezulwini Valley, behind the Gables Shopping Centre. You'll sleep well in any case, especially if you've just spun out on an activity organised by Swazi Trails, the lodge's sister company.

Lidwala Backpacker Lodge BACKPACKERS **$**
(Map p519; ☎2550 4951; www.lidwala.co.sz; camping spot R80, dm & safari tents per person E120, d E330; 🅿@🛜🏊) A laid-back, friendly spot with dorms, safari tents and campsites set within a pretty garden.

Reilly's Rock Hilltop Lodge LODGE **$$**
(Map p519; ☎2528 3943/4; www.biggameparks. org; s/d with half board E1190/1700; 🅿) Located in the Mlilwane Wildlife Sanctuary, this is a delightfully tranquil, old-world and nonfussy luxury experience with striking views of the valley and Mdzimba Mountains.

Sondzela Backpackers (IYHF) Lodge BACKPACKERS **$$**
(Map p519; ☎2528 3117; www.biggameparks.org; campsites per person E75, dm E100, s/d without bathroom E190/260, rondavel s/d E190/290; 🏊) The hilltop perch in Mlilwane Wildlife Sanctuary provides one of the best backpackers' settings in Southern Africa. There is a daily shuttle between Malandea's B&B and Sondzela's (30 minutes).

Mlilwane Wildlife Sanctuary Main Camp CAMPSITE, HUTS **$$**
(Map p519; ☎2528 3943/4; www.biggameparks. org; campsites per person E84, huts s/d E400/570; 🅿🏊) This homely camp within Mlilwane is set in a scenic wooded location, complete with simple huts (including two-person traditional beehive huts), a restaurant and a great pool.

🍴 Eating

There is a supermarket located in the Gables Shopping Centre as well as several other good restaurants.

GO WILD!

Wildlife Drives

For wildlife drives, the Big Game Parks reserves organise good-value tours. Mkhaya offers Land Rover day trips (E620, minimum two people, includes lunch). These trips must be pre-booked through Big Game Parks (p527). Set arrival and departure times are 10am and 4pm. Hlane has a two-hour sunrise/sunset drive (E295, minimum two people); Mlilwane offers a shorter game drive (E210, minimum two people). Check the website for the latest activities on offer, as these do change.

White-Water Rafting & Caving

One of Swaziland's highlights is white-water rafting on the Usutu River. You'll encounter Grade IV rapids, which aren't for the faint-hearted, although first-timers with a sense of adventure should handle the day easily. Swazi Trails (Map p519; ☎2416 2180; www. swazitrails.co.sz; Mantenga Craft Centre) offers full-/half-day trips (E750/650 per person, including lunch and transport, minimum two people). Trips run from the Ezulwini Valley.

For an off-the-scale challenge rating, the company also offers adventure caving trips in the vast Gobholo Cave (from E595).

WORTH A TRIP

LOBAMBA

Lobamba is the heart of Swaziland's Royal Valley. The British-built royal palace, the Embo State Palace, isn't open to visitors, and photos aren't allowed. Swazi kings now live in the Lozitha State House, about 10km from Lobamba.

You can see the monarchy in action at the Royal Kraal in Lobamba during the Incwala ceremony and the Umhlanga (Reed) dance.

The National Museum (Map p519; adult/child E25/15; ⊙8am-4.30pm Mon-Fri, 10am-4pm Sat & Sun) has some interesting displays on Swazi culture. The ticket price also allows you to enter the memorial to King Sobhuza II, the most revered of Swazi kings. Next to the museum is the parliament, which is sometimes open to visitors.

All Out Africa (✆2550 4951; www.alloutafrica.com) runs a fascinating half-day cultural tour through Lobamba, including an unscripted 'what-you-see-is-what-you-get' wander through the local village (per person R250; no minimum numbers).

Not far from Lobamba is the Mantenga Nature Reserve (Map p519; admission E150; ⊙8am-6pm), where you can visit a 'living' Swazi Cultural Village, watch a sibhaca dance and see the Mantega Falls.

Khazimula's Restaurant   ITALIAN $$
(Map p519; mains E50-80; ⊙10am-10pm Tue-Sun; P) This modest little place in the Mantenga Craft Centre is said to serve the best pizza in Swaziland.

Lihawu Restaurant   FUSION $$$
(Map p519; www.lihawu.co.sz; Royal Villas; mains E78-120; ⊙breakfast, lunch & dinner; P) Within the swish Royal Villa resort nestles this elegant eatery that serves Afro-fusion dishes.

Calabash   GERMAN $$$
(Map p519; mains E110-180; ⊙lunch & dinner) Specialises in German and Austrian-Swiss cuisine.

🛍 Shopping

The best crafts are to be found at the Ezulwini Craft Market (Map p519), in a slightly obscured location opposite the Zeemans Filling Station on the corner of MR103 and Mpumalanga Loop Rd (look for the blue tin roofs). Also in Ezulwini, the Mantenga Craft Centre (Map p519; ✆2416 1136) has a variety of artistic and craft offerings. The modern Gables Shopping Centre (Map p519; ⊙8am-5pm Mon-Fri, to 1pm Sat) has a supermarket and ATMs.

❶ Getting There & Away

During the day you could get on a Manzini-bound minibus, but make sure the driver knows that you want to alight in Ezulwini Valley, as many aren't keen on stopping.

Nonshared taxis from Mbabane cost E80 to E130, depending on how far down the valley you go.

If you're driving from either Mbabane or Manzini, take the Ezulwini Valley/Lobamba exit off the highway (this puts you on the MR103).

MALKERNS VALLEY

About 7km south of Lobamba/Ezulwini Valley on the MR103 is the turn-off to the fertile Malkerns Valley, known for its arts and crafts outlets, and offering a scenic and fun drive.

There's internet access and tourist information at Malandela's Tourist Information & Internet Cafe (per hr E45; ⊙8am-5pm Mon-Sat, 9am-5pm Sun) at the Malandela's complex.

🛏 Sleeping & Eating

Malandela's B&B   B&B $$
TOP CHOICE
(Map p519; ✆2528 3448, 2528 3339; www.malandelas.com; s/d incl breakfast E400/550; 🛜🏊) Along the MR27, Malandela's has fabulously creative and stylish rooms with a touch of ethnic Africa. Reservations are advised; it's understandably popular.

Umdoni   B&B $$
(✆2528 3009; www.umdoni.com; s/d incl breakfast E460/800; 🛁🏊) An upmarket experience in the heart of the Malkerns Valley. Think chic and stylish rooms in two cottages.

Rainbird Chalets B&B CHALET $$
(☑7603 7273; rainbird@swazi.net; s/d incl breakfast E510/880; ❄@☒) Six chalets – three log, and three brick A-frames – are set in a manicured, rose-filled private garden near the owners' house.

Malandela's Restaurant INTERNATIONAL $$
(Map p519; mains E50-90; ☺lunch & dinner Mon-Sun; P☎) Part of the Malandela complex, this is one of the best restaurants in the region. A bar serves pub grub as well.

☆ Entertainment

House on Fire MUSIC
(Map p519; ☑2528 2001; www.house-on-fire.com) Part of the Malandela's complex, this well-known venue hosts everything from African theatre, music and films to rave partys. Since 2007 it has hosted the annual Bush Fire Festival, featuring music, poetry, theatre and any wacky thing you can think of.

🔒 Shopping

Gone Rural ARTS & CRAFTS
(Map p519; www.goneruralswazi.com; ☺8am-5pm Mon-Sat, 9am-5pm Sun) Located at Malandela's, this is the place to go for good quality produce – baskets, mats and traditional clay pots – made by groups of local women.

Swazi Candles Craft Centre HANDICRAFTS
(Map p519; ☑2528 3219; www.swazicandles.com; ☺7am-5pm) This craft centre, 7km south of the MR103 turn-off for Malkerns, houses Swazi Candles itself, where you can wax lyrical about these creative pigment-coloured candles, and Baobab Batik (Map p519; ☑2528 3219; www.baobab-batik.com; ☺8am-5pm), the place to head if you're dye-ing for a wall

hanging. You can also pop into its onsite workshop west of Malandela's.

Manzini

Manzini, Swaziland's largest town and the country's industrial centre, was the administrative centre for the squabbling British and Boers from 1890 to 1902. During the Anglo-Boer War a renegade Boer commando burnt it down.

Today Manzini is an active commercial and industrial hub. There is a slight hint of menace – watch out for pickpockets and be careful as crime (including muggings) is more common here than elsewhere in Swaziland.

Manzini's main drawcard is its colourful handicrafts market (cnr Mhlakuvane & Mancishane Sts; ☺closed Sun). This aside, you can happily move on.

🛏 Sleeping & Eating

Takeaways abound in Bhunu Mall and on Ngwane St.

George Hotel HOTEL $$
(☑2505 2260; www.tgh.sz; cnr Ngwane & du Toit Sts; s/d incl breakfast from E680/890; ❄☒) Manzini's fanciest hotel attempts an international atmosphere, and caters for the conference crowd. It has a pool bar and stylish restaurants.

TOP CHOICE Gil Vincente Restaurant INTERNATIONAL $$
(Ngwane St, Mkhaya Centre; mains R70-100; ☺lunch & dinner Tue-Sun) This elegant choice has smart decor and high-quality Italian and

---

SWAZI CEREMONIES

Incwala
The Incwala (sometimes Ncwala) is the most sacred Swazi ceremony. During this 'first fruits' ceremony the king gives his people permission to eat the first crops of the new year. Preparation for the Incwala begins some weeks in advance.

Umhlanga
Not as sacred as the Incwala, the Umhlanga (Reed) dance serves a similar function in drawing the nation together and reminding the people of their relationship to the king. It is something like a week-long debutante ball for marriageable young Swazi women and a showcase of potential wives for the king.

On the sixth day young women perform the Umhlanga dance and carry their reeds to the queen mother. They repeat the dance the next day. Princesses wear red feathers in their hair.

CULTURAL EXPERIENCES

Woza Nawe Tours (☑7642 6780; www.swaziculturaltours.com), headed by local Swazi Myxo Mdluli, runs highly recommended village visits (day tour E1150) and overnight stays (adult/child E1250/625) to Kaphunga, 55km southeast of Manzini. The fee includes transport, meals and a guide. Guests join in on whatever activities are going on in the village – including cooking, planting, and harvesting.

international cuisine. It's in the Makhaya Centre, down from George Hotel.

ℹ Getting There & Away

The main bus and minibus taxi rank is at the northern end of Louw St, where you can also find some nonshared taxis. A minibus taxi trip up the Ezulwini Valley to Mbabane costs E15 (35 minutes). A nonshared taxi to Matsapha International Airport costs around E80. Minibus taxis to Mozambique leave from the car park next to KFC up the hill.

NORTHWESTERN SWAZILAND

Lush hills, plantations and woodlands, streams and waterfalls and plunging ravines are the main features of Swaziland's beautiful north, along with some excellent hiking and accommodation options. Be-

ware the heavy mists that roll in during the summer months – they can limit visibility to almost zero.

Ngwenya

Tiny Ngwenya (Crocodile) is 5km east of the Oshoek border crossing on the road to Mbabane. At Ngwenya Glass Factory (☑2442 4142; www.ngwenyaglass.co.sz; ⊙8am-4.30pm Mon-Fri, 8am-4pm Sat & Sun) recycled glass is used to create African animals and birds as well as vases and tableware.

Also near here is the Ngwenya iron ore mine (admission E28; ⊙8am-4pm), dating from around 40,000 BC and one of the world's oldest known mines.

Hawane Resort (☑2444 1744; www.hawane. co.sz; dm E115, chalet s/d incl breakfast E550/840; @⊠) offers stylish chalets that are a blend of traditional Swazi materials and glass with ethnic African interiors. Backpackers are stabled in a converted barn. It's about 5km up the Piggs Peak road from the junction of the MR1 and MR3, and 1.5km off the main road.

Malolotja Nature Reserve

This beautiful middleveld/highveld nature reserve (☑7613 3990, 2444 1744; adult/child E28/14; ⊙6am-6pm) is a true wilderness area, rugged and for the most part unspoiled. The terrain ranges from mountainous and high-altitude grassland to forest and lower-lying bushveld, all with streams and cut by three rivers, including the Komati River.

WORTH A TRIP

BULEMBU

An interesting detour from Piggs Peak is to wind your way 20km through scenic plantation country to the historic town of Bulembu, built in 1936 for the former Havelock asbestos mine. Following its closure, the 10,000 workers left and by 2003 Bulembu was a ghost town with around 100 residents. Several years ago the town's new investors started a community tourism project (based on Christian principles), bringing the town back to life. Thousands of deserted corrugated iron houses and many art deco buildings which nestle on a pretty hilly landscape are being renovated. There's even a former cableway. Stunning hikes include the highest mountain in Swaziland, Emlembe Peak (1863m). Note: asbestos dumps exist around the village.

Accommodation is available in the main Bulembu Lodge (☑7602 1593; www.bulembu.org; per person from E456), in the former general manager's residence, or stylish directors' cottages, all renovated. Alternatively, you can choose a spacious and delightfully converted house, known as 'village stays' (E342). Basic meals are served in the lodge's dining room (breakfast E75-95, lunch/dinner E75/125).

It's an excellent walking destination, and an ornithologist's paradise, with over 280 species of birds. Wildflowers and rare plants are added attractions; several are found only in this part of Africa.

Basic brochures outlining hiking trails are available for free at the restaurant/reception. These days, many visit the park for the Malolotja Canopy Tour (☎7613 3990; www.malolotjacanopytour.com; per person R450; ☼7am-4pm summer, 8am-3pm winter). You can 'slide' your way across Malalotja's stunning, lush tree canopy on 11 slides (12 platforms).

Accommodation consists of camping (per person at main camp/on trails E70/50), either at the well-equipped (but infrequently used) main site, with ablutions and braai (barbecue) area, or along the overnight trails (no facilities). Self-catering wooden cabins (per person E250, minimum E400, children half-price) sleep a maximum of five people. Reservations are made through Hawane Resort (p523).

The entrance gate for Malolotja is about 35km northwest of Mbabane, along the Piggs Peak road (MR1); minibus taxis will drop you here (E15, 45 minutes).

EASTERN SWAZILAND

The hot, northeastern corner of Swaziland is a major sugar-producing area. The arid foothills of the Lebombo Mountains epitomise what most people think of as 'Africa'.

This area's notable parks and reserves are Hlane, Mlawula and Mkhaya.

Hlane Royal National Park

This national park (☎2528 3943; www.biggameparks.org; admission E35; ☼6am-6pm) in Swaziland's northeast is near the former royal hunting grounds and offers wonderfully low-key wildlife watching (white rhinos, antelope species, elephants and lions). There are guided walking trails (per person E155), two-hour wildlife day drives (per person E235, minimum two people), a cultural village tour (per person E70, minimum four people) and mountain-bike rentals (per two hours E175). Minibus taxis to Simunye will drop you at the entrance to Hlane (E5; 7km from Simunye).

Ndlovu Camp (campsites per person E40, rondavel s/d from E295/410, 8-person cottages per person E220) is a pleasant and rustic fenced-off camp, with no electricity, a communal area and a restaurant.

Book through the Big Game Parks office (☎2528 3943/4; www.biggameparks.org).

Mlawula Nature Reserve

This tranquil reserve (☎2383 8885; www.sntc.org.sz; adult/child E25/12; ☼6am-6pm), where the lowveld plains meet the Lebombo Mountains, boasts antelope species, hyenas and crocodiles, plus rewarding birdwatching. Walking (from two- to nine-hour hikes) along plateaus, or to caves and a waterfall is a highlight here.

You can pitch your own tent at Siphiso camping ground (campsites per person E60). Mapelepele Cottage (up to 7 people, per person E150, minimum E500) is self-catering.

Mkhaya Game Reserve

This top-notch private reserve (☎2528 3943; www.biggameparks.org), off the Manzini–Big Bend road near the hamlet of Phuzumoya, was established in 1979 to

COMMUNITY CONCERNS

Several excellent community-owned tourism projects operate in Swaziland. Shewula Mountain Camp (☎7605 1160, 7603 1931; www.shewulacamp.com; dm/r E100/260), a camp northeast of Simunye in the Lebombo Mountains, is 36km by dirt road. You can camp or stay in basic rondavels, with shared ablutions and self-catering facilities. The newer Mahamba Gorge Lodge (☎2237 0100, 7617 9880; Mahamba; s/d E285/400), near Nhlangano, has clean, modern stone chalets and wonderful guided walks (per person E50) through the nearby gorge, where there are nesting eagles. Ngwempisi Hiking Trail (☎7625 6004) is a community-run 33km trail with the atmospheric Khopho Hut (also known as Rock Lodge). It's located 30km south of the Malkerns Valley in the Ntfungula Hills that are on the Mankayane-Vlelzizweni road. Ezulwini Tourist Information Office (p518) and All Out Africa (p521) also take bookings as a community service on their behalf.

save the pure Nguni breed of cattle from extinction. Its focus expanded to antelopes, elephants, and white and black rhinos. The reserve's name comes from the *mkhaya* (or knobthorn) tree, which abounds here.

You can't visit or stay in the reserve without booking in advance, and even then you can't drive in alone; you'll be met at Phuzumoya at a specified pick-up time, usually 10am or 4pm. While day tours can be arranged, it's ideal to stay for at least one night.

Stone Camp (☎2528 3943; www.biggame parks.org; s/d with full board E2210/3320) has a smart, slightly colonial feel; it's well worth the stopover. Accommodation is in rustic and luxurious semi-open stone and thatch cottages (a proper loo with a view). The price includes wildlife drives, walking safaris, park entry and meals; it's excellent value compared with many of the private reserves near Kruger National Park in South Africa.

UNDERSTAND SWAZILAND

Swaziland Today

King Mswati III currently rules Swaziland as Africa's last remaining absolute monarch. However, he has his critics.

There is widespread dissatisfaction with the lack of progress in Swaziland's current socio-economic climate, as well as the perceived disintegration in family life and morals, as reflected in the devastating effects of HIV/AIDS. Swazi critics and women's rights advocates rally against the current system, which stifles individual autonomy and rights, especially those of women.

Furthermore, attempts by unions and opposition groups to press for democratic change have met with legislation to curb their activities. Yet, despite these political tensions and increasing popular dissatisfaction with royalty, reformers call for modification of the monarchy, demanding a constitutional instead of absolute monarchy, not its complete abandonment. It's a complex situation – as the symbolic head of the Swazi family, the king is, despite his critics, largely respected.

Swaziland has one of the world's highest HIV infection rates, although in recent years it has stabilised; around 26% of the adult population is HIV positive, and the average life expectancy is currently 37.

History

The area that is now Swaziland has been inhabited for a long time – in eastern Swaziland archaeologists have discovered human remains dating back 110,000 years – but the Swazi people arrived relatively recently.

During the great Bantu migrations into Southern Africa, one group, the Nguni, moved down the east coast. A clan settled in the area near what is now Maputo in Mozambique, and a dynasty was founded by the Dlamini family.

In the mid-18th century increasing pressure from other Nguni clans forced King Ngwane III to lead his people south to lands by the Pongola River, in what is now southern Swaziland. Today, Swazis consider Ngwane III to have been the first king of Swaziland.

Clan encroachment continued, and the next king, Sobhuza I, also came under pressure from the Zulus. He withdrew to the Ezulwini Valley, which remains the centre of Swazi royalty and ritual today. Trouble with the Zulus continued, though the next king, Mswati, managed to unify the whole kingdom and, by the time he died in 1868, a Swazi nation was secure. Mswati's subjects called themselves people of Mswati, or Swazis.

European Interference

During the same period the Zulus were coming under pressure from both the British and the Boers, creating frequent respites for the Swazis. However, from the mid-19th century the arrival of increasing numbers of Europeans brought new problems. Mswati's successor, Mbandzeni, inherited a kingdom rife with European carpetbaggers – hunters, traders, missionaries and farmers, many of whom leased large expanses of land.

The Boers' South African Republic (ZAR) decided to extend its control to Maputo along with Swaziland, which was in the way. Before this could happen, however, the British annexed the ZAR itself in 1877.

The Pretoria Convention of 1881 guaranteed Swaziland's 'independence', but also defined its borders, and Swaziland lost large chunks of territory. 'Independence' in fact meant that both the British and the Boers had responsibility for administering their various interests in Swaziland, and the result was chaos. The Boer administration collapsed with the 1899–1902 Anglo-Boer War, and afterwards the British took control of Swaziland as a protectorate.

During this troubled time, King Sobhuza II was only a young child, but Labotsibeni, his mother, acted ably as regent until her son took over in 1921. Throughout the regency and for most of Sobhuza's long reign, the Swazis sought to regain their land, a large portion of which was owned by foreign interests. Labotsibeni encouraged Swazis to buy the land back, and many sought work in the Witwatersrand mines (near Johannesburg) to raise money. By the time of independence in 1968, about two-thirds of the kingdom was again under Swazi control.

Independence

In 1960 King Sobhuza II proposed the creation of a legislative council, composed of elected Europeans, and a national council formed in accordance with Swazi culture. One of the Swazi political parties formed at this time was the Mbokodvo (Grindstone) National Movement, which pledged to maintain traditional Swazi culture, but also to eschew racial discrimination. When the British finally agreed to elections in 1964, Mbokodvo won a majority and, at the next elections in 1967, won all the seats. Independence was achieved on 6 September 1968.

The country's constitution was largely the work of the British. In 1973 the king suspended it on the grounds that it did not accord with Swazi culture. Four years later, the parliament reconvened under a new constitution that vested all power in the king. Sobhuza II, then the world's longest-reigning monarch, died in 1982.

The young Mswati III ascended the throne in 1986 and continues to rule as the country's monarch.

The Culture

Daily Life

Ancient traditions are vital to and inherent in everyday life – business may be conducted in *emahiya* (traditional Swazi dress, often complemented with a shield and knobkerrie) or Western suits – and cultural festivals are followed closely.

As in other parts of Africa, the extended family is integral to a person's life. While polygamy is permitted and exists, it is not always practised. Traditional marriage allows for the husband to take a number of wives, although many Swazis also follow Western marriage conventions, rejecting polygamy but permitting divorce.

Many people in rural areas continue to live in the traditional beehive huts, while others, particularly in the cities, live in Western-style houses.

Schooling is not compulsory. The roll-out of free primary school education has somewhat counteracted the impact of the increased numbers of orphans due to the HIV/AIDS epidemic and ensured that schools are full to capacity.

Population

The ancestors of modern-day Swazis were part of the general, gradual migration of Bantu-language speakers from central Africa who broke from the main group and settled in Mozambique, finally moving in the mid-18th century into what became known as Swaziland. Today, Swazis still share a close cultural and linguistic heritage with other Southern African peoples including the Zulu and the Ndebele. Almost all people here are Swazi. The rest are Zulu, Tsonga (Shangaan) and European.

The population, which was about 85,000 in 1904, today hovers at around a million people.

Religion

Around 40% of the population is African Zionist, a mix of Christianity and traditional indigenous worship, with Roman Catholics, Anglicans and Methodists making up the balance. Muslims, Baha'i and Jewish faiths have small followings also.

Arts & Crafts

Music & Dance

Traditional music is integral to Swazi festivals and dancing, most prominently the Incwala and Umhlanga festivals. Music and rhythm also play an important role in other festivals, such as harvest and marriage. Traditional instruments include the calabash, kudu horn, rattle and reed flute.

Dance is an integral part of Swazi cultural festivals. The energetic sibhaca dance is a vigorous, foot-stamping dance performed by teams of males, usually at festivals and formal occasions.

Architecture

The architecture of Swaziland ranges from the traditional round beehive huts of the rural areas to the more Western-style houses in the suburbs and larger towns. The beehive huts are thatched with dry grass and often surrounded by reed fences.

The traditional *umuti* (homestead) is important to the Swazi social unit. In a polygamous homestead, each wife has her own huts, plus a yard surrounded by reed fences for privacy. Larger homesteads have huts for bachelors' quarters and guest housing. The cattle byre, a circular area enclosed by logs and branches, is central to the traditional homestead. This area has an important ritualistic and practical significance, reflecting both wealth and prestige. The hut opposite the cattle byre is occupied by the mother of the headman. Nowadays, while many construct square houses from cement blocks and corrugated iron, they still maintain the layout of the traditional homestead.

Handicrafts

Swaziland's handicrafts include pottery, jewellery, weapons and implements. Woven grasswares such as *liqhaga* (grassware 'bottles') and mats are popular, as are wooden items, ranging from bowls to knobkerries.

Environment

The Land

Swaziland, although tiny, has a wide range of ecological zones, from montane forest in the northwest to savanna scrub in the east.

The western edge of the country is highveld, consisting mainly of short, sharp mountains where there are large plantations of pine and eucalyptus. The mountains dwindle to middleveld in the heavily populated centre of the country. The eastern half is scrubby lowveld, lightly populated, but now home to sugar estates. To the east, the harsh Lebombo Mountains form the border with Mozambique.

Wildlife

ANIMALS

Swaziland has about 121 species of mammals, representing a third of nonmarine mammal species in Southern Africa. These days the larger animals are restricted to the nature reserves and private wildlife reserves dotted around the country. Many species (such as elephants, warthogs, rhinos and lions) have been reintroduced to nature reserves. Mongooses and large-spotted genets are common throughout the country, while hyenas and jackals are found in the reserves. Poaching is an ongoing problem in some parks.

PLANTS

Although small in size, Swaziland is rich in flora and accounts for 14% of the recorded plant life in Southern Africa. The remoteness of parts of the countryside means there are probably species that have not yet been brought to the attention of botanists. Nature reserves help to conserve indigenous plants.

National Parks

Swaziland's nature reserves reflect the country's geographical diversity. Easiest to get to is Mlilwane Wildlife Sanctuary in the Ezulwini Valley. Hlane Royal National Park and Mkhaya Game Reserve are also well worth visiting. These three reserves are privately run as part of the Big Game Parks (☑2528 3943/4; www.biggameparks.org).

Mantenga, Hawane, Malolotja and Mlawula Nature Reserves are under the jurisdiction of the Swaziland National Trust Commission (p529), based at the National Museum in Lobamba (Ezulwini Valley). Bookings can also be made through the Ezulwini Tourist Information Office (p518).

Malolotja is a rugged highlands reserve with some very good hiking trails. Mlawula is in harsh lowveld country near the Mozambican border.

Environmental Issues

The overgrazing of cattle has caused soil erosion. The use of and reliance on natural medicinal plants has led to the loss of certain indigenous plants. Poverty is a major cause of land degradation; land-management issues focused on sustainability are simply not on the agendas of individuals struggling to eke out a living or dealing with the impact of HIV/AIDS. Poaching is an ongoing problem in some parks.

Food & Drink

Although it's not exactly a gourmet's paradise, you won't eat badly in Swaziland. There's a good range of places to eat in Mbabane and the tourist areas of the Malkerns and Ezulwini Valleys. Portuguese

SWAZILAND ENVIRONMENT

cuisine, including seafood, can be found. In more remote areas, African staples such as stew and *pap* (also known as mealie meal) are common.

SURVIVAL GUIDE

Directory A–Z

Accommodation

You'll find hostels and budget accommodation in Mbabane, Manzini and Ezulwini Valley. Many of the country's hotels are expensive, but there are some good midrange B&B options available.

Books & Films

Wild Swaziland – Common Animals and Plants by Boycott, Forrester, Loffler and Monadjem and *Mammals of Swaziland* by Ara Monadjem are useful for nature lovers.

The film *Wah-Wah*, the account of actor Richard E Grant's childhood in Swaziland, is worth seeing.

Business Hours

Shops are open 8am to 7pm and offices 8am to 5pm Monday to Friday. Bank hours are 8.30am to 3.30pm Monday to Friday, and 8.30am to 11.30am on Saturday.

Children

Travelling with little 'uns should be hassle-free in Swaziland. Most accommodation options, especially the more upmarket establishments, cater to young visitors. Many hotels have pools and entertainment facilities. Elsewhere, national parks are good to visit with kids. Stock up on baby food before heading to remote areas.

Customs Regulations

You're permitted to import 200 cigarettes and 20 cigars and 250g of tobacco; 1L of

---

SLEEPING PRICE RANGES

The following price ranges refer to a double room with bathroom in high season.

$ less than E500
$$ E500 to E1000
$$$ more than E1000

---

spirits, 2L of wine; and 50mL of perfume per person. The import and export of protected animal products such as ivory is not permitted.

Embassies & Consulates

American Embassy (☑404 6441; swaziland. usembassy.gov; Mhlokohla St, 7th fl, Central Bank Bldg) Note that hours for visas are limited.

Mozambican High Commission (☑404 1296; Princess Drive Rd, Highlands View)

South African High Commission (☑404 4651; www.dfa.gov.za; Dr Sishayi Rd, 2nd fl, the New Mall)

★ Festivals & Events

Swaziland's most important cultural events are the Incwala ceremony (December/January), and the Umhlanga (Reed) dance (August or September). Photography and sound recording are not allowed (permits can be organised in advance). Sibhaca dancing competitions are held – ask the Mbabane tourist office for details. You can see performances in the Mantenga Nature Reserve.

Food

The following price ranges are used for Eating reviews in this chapter.

$	Less than E40 per main
$$	E40-100 per main
$$$	More than E100 per main

Gay & Lesbian Travellers

Gay sexual relationships are culturally taboo and officially illegal in (conservative) Swaziland – imprisonment and fines apply. Public displays of affection are generally frowned upon whatever your gender or orientation.

Health

Beware of both schistosomiasis (bilharzia) and malaria. Malaria is a risk in the northeast near Mozambique; you'll be at highest risk from November to April.

Holidays

Public holidays observed in Swaziland:

New Year's Day 1 January

Easter (March/April) Good Friday, Holy Saturday and Easter Monday

King Mswati III's Birthday 19 April

National Flag Day 25 April

PRACTICALITIES

» The *Times* (www.times.co.sz), a virtual mouthpiece for royalty and a would-be lurid tabloid, is a fascinating read as much for what it doesn't say as what it does.

» The *Swazi Observer* is a daily publication.

» The electricity supply in Swaziland is 220V. Plugs have three large round pins as used in South Africa.

» Swaziland uses the metric system.

King Sobhuza II's Birthday 22 July

Umhlanga (Reed) Dance August/September

Somhlolo Day (Independence) 6 September

Christmas Day 25 December

Boxing Day 26 December

Incwala Ceremony December/January (dates vary each year)

Internet Access

Internet facilities are scarce outside Mbabane, Manzini and the Ezulwini and Malkerns Valleys.

Internet Resources

Discover Swaziland (www.welcometoswazi land.com) Commercial, but most thorough site.

Swaziland National Trust Commission (www.sntc.org.sz) Helpful site with information about Swaziland's cultural heritage.

Language

The official languages are Swati and English, and English is the official written language.

Maps

The main tourist information office hands out a free map of Swaziland. Topographical maps are available from the Ministry of Public Works.

Money

The unit of currency is the lilangeni (plural emalangeni – E), which is fixed at a value equal to the South African rand. Rand are accepted everywhere, but Emalangeni are difficult to change for other currencies outside Swaziland.

Most ATMs accept international credit or debit cards. NedBank and First National Bank change cash and travellers cheques (show receipt of purchase).

The normal practice for tipping in rural parts of Swaziland is to round up a bill. In smarter tourist establishments, 5% to 10% is usual.

Photography & Video

It is prohibited to photograph or sound record the Incwala ceremony. Always ask permission before taking a photo of anyone, particularly in ethnic villages.

Post

Post offices are open from 8.30am to 4pm weekdays, and until 11am Saturday.

Telephone

Swaziland has a reasonable telephone network. The international country code is 268; there are no area codes. Mobile SIM cards are available, as are public phone cards.

Tourist Information

Swaziland's main tourist information office (☎2404 2531; www.welcometoswaziland. com; Cooper Centre access road, Sozisa Rd; ⊗8am-4.45pm Mon-Thu, 8am-4pm Fri, 9am-1pm Sat) is in Mbabane. The websites of Swaziland National Trust (www.sntc.org.sz) and Big Game Parks (p527) offer useful parks information. Privately run by Swazi Trails, the Ezulwini Tourist Information Office (p518) also supplies tourist information.

Visas

Most people don't need a visa to visit Swaziland. Those who do, need to obtain them in advance from the Swaziland High Commission (☎in South Africa 012-344 1910; 715 Government Avenue, Arcadia) in Pretoria. Anyone staying for more than 30 days must apply for an extension of stay. If staying for longer than 60 days you must apply for a temporary residence permit from the Chief Immigration Officer (☎2404 2941; PO Box 372, Mbabane), whose offices are in the Ministry of Home Affairs.

Getting There & Away

Entering Swaziland

Most travellers enter Swaziland overland from South Africa, although it's also possible to fly in from Johannesburg and Mozambique. A passport is required for entering Swaziland and entry is usually hassle-free. No vaccination certificates are required unless you have recently been in a yellow-fever area.

Air

Swaziland Airlink (☎2518 6155; www.flyswazi land.com) operates out of Matsapha airport, north of Manzini. It flies daily between Swaziland and Johannesburg.

Border Crossings

SOUTH AFRICA

There are 13 South Africa–Swaziland border crossings, including the following:

Golela–Lavumisa (open 7am to 10pm)

Houtkop–Sicunusa (8am to 6pm)

Josefsdal–Bulembu (8am to 4pm)

Mahamba (7am to 10pm)

Matsamo–Jeppe's Reef (7am to 10pm)

Oshoek–Ngwenya (7am to midnight)

To/From Durban & Johannesburg

A daily luxury shuttle service, TransMagnific (☎2404 9977; www.goswaziland.co.sz), runs between Jo'burg and Swaziland and costs E500.

Minibus taxis run daily between Jo'burg (Park Station), Mbabane and Manzini (four hours) and between Manzini and Durban (eight hours). For many routes, you'll need to change minibuses at the border. Most long-distance taxis leave early in the morning.

MOZAMBIQUE

Swaziland shares two border crossings with Mozambique: Lomahasha–Namaacha (7am to 10pm) in the extreme northeast of the country, and Goba–Mhlumeni (24 hours). Check border times as these can change.

To/From Maputo

Minibuses between Maputo (Mozambique) and Manzini depart throughout the day as soon as seats are filled. They travel via the Goba–Mhlumeni border (E90, 3½ hours). Extra charges for large luggage.

DEPARTURE TAX

An E50 departure tax is levied at Matsapha airport.

Car & Motorcycle

If you're arriving or departing Swaziland via car or motorcycle you'll need the vehicle's registration and insurance papers and your licence. If carrying any expensive spare parts, such as a gearbox (or any item with a serial number), officially, you are meant to declare them for importation. Border posts generally don't have petrol stations or repair shops.

Getting Around

Bus & Minibus Taxi

There are infrequent (but cheap) domestic buses; most depart and terminate at the main stop in the centre of Mbabane. Minibus taxis leave when full; these are plentiful, run almost everywhere and stop often. There are also nonshared taxis in some of the larger towns.

Car & Motorcycle

DRIVING LICENCE

A domestic (with photo ID) or international driving licence is compulsory.

FUEL & SPARE PARTS

Many petrol stations are open 24 hours, and the price of petrol is similar to that of South Africa.

HIRE

Hiring a car will allow you to cover much of the country in a few days. Note: if you have hired your car in South Africa, ensure that you have the written agreement from the rental company to enter Swaziland. There's a small road tax payable on entry.

Car hire in Swaziland is available from Avis (☎2518 6222; www.avis.co.za) at Matsapha International Airport and Europcar (☎Matsapha Airport 2518 4393, Mbabane 2404 0459; www.europcar.com/airport-swaziland-car-rental.html) at Matsapha International Airport or Engen Auto Plaza, Mbabane. You have to be 23 years old to hire cars from most companies.

INSURANCE

Insurance for third-party damage and damage to or loss of your vehicle is highly recommended.

ROAD CONDITIONS & ROAD HAZARDS

Swaziland has good sealed roads and highways. The main one from east to west is the MR3. There are some rough back roads through the bush; beware slippery and boggy conditions when wet. The other main dangers are people and animals on the road, plus the odd kamikaze minibus driver.

ROAD RULES

In Swaziland, vehicles are driven on the left-hand side. Wearing seat belts is compulsory. Always pull over and stop for official motorcades or road stops. The speed limit on highways is 120km/h, on national roads 80km/h and in built-up areas 60km/h.

Hitching

Hitching is easier here than in South Africa, but hitching alone is foolhardy, especially for women. Hitchhikers might wait a long time for a car on back roads, and there's keen competition from locals.

☞ Tours

Swazi Trails (☏2416 2180; www.swazitrails. co.sz) Specialises in one-day and half-day tours around the country, including whitewater rafting and caving tours, cultural tours, and hiking.

Bundu Bus (☏in South Africa 011-675 0767; www.bundusafaris.co.za; 1735 Gauteng, PO Box 697, Wilgeheuwel, South Africa) A South African operator that runs a seven-day around South Africa tour that includes one day in Swaziland.

Victoria Falls

Best Places to Eat

» Cafe Zambezi (p542)

» In Da Belly (p546)

» Olga's Italian Corner
(p542)

» Mama Africa (p547)

Best Places to Stay

» Victoria Falls Hotel (p545)

» Elephant Camp (p546)

» Jollyboys Backpackers
(p539)

» Stanley Safari Lodge
(p541)

Why Go?

Taking its place alongside the Pyramids and the Serengeti, Victoria Falls (*Mosi-oa-Tunya* – the 'smoke that thunders') is one of Africa's original blockbusters. And although Zimbabwe and Zambia share it, Victoria Falls is a place all of its own.

As a magnet for tourists of all descriptions – backpackers, tour groups, thrill seekers, families, honeymooners – Vic Falls is one of the earth's great spectacles. View it directly as a raging mile-long curtain of water, in all its glory, from a helicopter ride or peek precariously over its edge from Devil's Pools; the sheer power and force of the falls is something that simply does not disappoint.

Whether you're here purely to take in the sight of a natural wonder of the world, or for a serious hit of adrenaline via rafting or bungee jumping into the Zambezi, Victoria Falls is a place where you're sure to tick off numerous items from that bucket list.

When to Go

There are two main reasons to go to Victoria Falls – to view the falls and to experience the outdoor activities – and each has its season.

July to December is the season for white-water rafting, especially August for hardcore rapids.

From February to June don't forget your raincoat as you'll experience the falls at their full force.

From July to September You'll get the best views of the falls, combined with lovely weather and all activities to keep you busy.

Victoria Falls

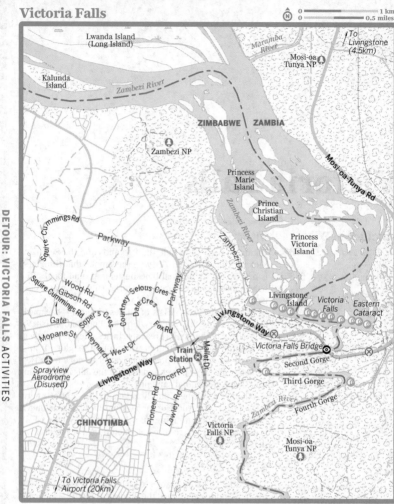

Seventh Natural Wonder of the World

Victoria Falls is the largest, most beautiful and most majestic waterfall on the planet, and is the Seventh Natural Wonder of the World as well as being a UNESCO World Heritage Site. A trip to Southern Africa would not be complete without visiting this unforgettable place.

One million litres of water fall – per second – down a 108m drop along a 1.7km wide strip in the Zambezi Gorge; an awesome sight. Victoria Falls can be seen, heard, tast-ed and touched: it is a treat that few other places in the world can offer, a 'must see before you die' spot.

Victoria Falls is spectacular at any time of year, yet varies in the experiences it offers.

🏃 Activities

While of course it's the spectacular sight of Vic Falls that lures travellers to the region, the astonishing amount of activities to do here is what makes them hang around. White-water rafting, bungee jumping, tak-ing a chopper ride over the falls, walking with rhinos: Vic Falls is well and truly established as one of the world's premier adventure destinations.

To get the best value out of your time here, look into packages which combine various adrenaline leaps, slides and swings for around US$125. Confirm any extra costs such as park or visa fees at the time of booking.

Costs are fairly standard across the board and activities can be organised through accommodation providers and tour operators.

Abseiling

Strap on a helmet, grab a rope and spend the day rappelling down the 54m sheer-drop cliff face for US$40.

Birdwatching

Twitchers will want to bring binoculars to check out 470 species of birds that inhabit the region, including Schalow's turaco, the African finfoot and half-collared kingfisher. Spot them on foot in the parks or on a canoe trip along the Zambezi.

Bungee Jumping & Swings

The third-highest bungee in the world (111m), this famous jump is from atop the iconic Victoria Falls bridge. It's a long way down, but man, it's a lot of fun. It costs US$125 per person.

Otherwise there's the bridge swing where you jump feet first, and free fall for four seconds; you'll end up swinging the right way up, not upside down. There are two main spots, one right off the Victoria Falls Bridge, and the other a bit further along the Batoka Gorge. Costs for single/tandem are US$125/195.

Combine bungee with a bridge swing and bridge slide, and it'll cost US$160.

Canoeing & Kayaking

On the Zambian side, take on the Zambezi's raging rapids in an inflatable kayak on a full-day trip (US$155), or learn to eskimo roll by signing up for half-/one-/three-day courses for US$82/145/412.

Otherwise there are peaceful canoe trips along the Upper Zambezi River on two-person inflatable canoes for US$125 or even more relaxed three-hour guided sunset trips for US$60 including wine and beer. Overnight jaunts cost US$200, with longer trips available.

Cultural Activities

Spend an evening by a campfire drumming under the Southern African sky, which includes a traditional meal, for US$25 for the hour. You can arrange to watch and participate in traditional dance for US$40.

Fishing

Grab a rod and cruise out to the Zambezi for the opportunity to reel in a mighty tiger fish, for around US$125 for a half day, and

THE FALLS VIEWING SEASON

Though spectacular at any time of year, the falls has a wet and dry season and each brings a distinct experience.

When the river is higher and the falls fuller it's the Wet, and when the river is lower and the falls aren't smothered in spray it's the Dry. Broadly speaking, you can expect the following conditions during the year:

January to April The beginning of the rainy season sees the falls begin their transitional period from low to high water, which should give you decent views, combined with experiencing its famous spray.

May to June Don't forget your raincoat, as you're gonna get drenched! While the falls will be hard to see through the mist, it'll give you a true sense of its power as 500 million litres of water plummets over the edge. The mist during this time can be seen from 50kms away. If you want views, don't despair, this is the best time for aerial views with a chopper flight taking you up and over this incredible sight.

July to October The most popular time to visit, as the mist dissipates to unveil the best views and photography options from directly across the falls, while the volume maintains its rage to give you an idea of its sheer force.

November to January The least popular time to visit, as temperatures rise and the falls are at their lowest flow. But they're still impressive nevertheless, as the curtain of water divides into sections. The advantage of this time of year is you're able to swim right up to the edge of Devil's Pool on the Zambian side.

US$255 for a full day, which includes beer, fuel and transfers. Get in touch with Angle Zambia (☏327489; www.zambezifishing.com) for more info.

Horse Riding
Indulge in a bit of wildlife spotting from horseback along the Zambezi. Rides for 2½ hours cost around $US90, and full-day trips for experienced riders are US$145.

Jet Boats
Power straight into whirlpools! This hair-raising trip costs US$97, and is combined with a cable-car ride down into the Batoka Gorge.

Quad biking
Discover the spectacular landscape around Livingstone, Zambia and the Batoka Gorge, spotting wildlife as you go on all-terrain quad bikes. Trips vary from ecotrail riding at Batoka Land to longer-range cultural trips in the African bush. Trips are 1 hour (US$80) or 2½ hours (US$150).

Rafting
This is one of the best white-water rafting destinations in the world, both for experienced rafters and newbies. Rafting can be done on either side of the Zambezi, in Zim or Zam, and fills up between mid-February and July, high-water season. In the river below Vic Falls you'll find Grade 5 rapids – very long with huge drops and big kicks, and not for the faint-hearted. In high-water season, day trips move downstream from rapids 11 to 24, covering a distance of around 18km.

Low-water (open) season is between July and mid-February and is considered the best time for rafting. Day trips run between rapids 1 and 19, covering a distance of around 25km. The river will usually close for its 'off season' around April/May, depending on the rain pattern for the year.

Half-/full-day trips cost about US$120/130. Overnight and multiday jaunts can also be arranged.

Other options include **riverboarding**, which is basically lying on a boogie board and careering down the rapids for US$135/150 for a half/full day. The best time of year for riverboarding is February to June. A rafting/riverboarding combo is available, US$165.

River Cruises
River cruises along the Zambezi range from civilised jaunts on the grand *African Queen* to all-you-can-drink sunset booze cruises. Prices range from US$30 to US$60. Great for spotting wildlife, though some tourists get just as much enjoyment out of the bottomless drinks. Highly recommended.

Scenic Flights
Just when you thought the falls couldn't get any more spectacular, discover the 'flight of angels' helicopter ride that flies you right by the drama for the undisputed best views available. Rides aren't cheap, but it's worth it. Zambezi Helicopter Company (www.shearwatervictoriafalls.com/helicopters; flights 13/25 mins US$130/250, plus US$10 park entry fee) in Zimbabwe and United Air Charter (☏213

323095; www.uaczam.com; Baobab Ridge, Livingstone) in Zambia both offer flights.

Another option is motorised hang-gliders, which also offer fabulous aerial views, and the pilot will take pictures for you with a camera fixed to the wing. It costs US$140 for 15 minutes over the falls.

Steam-train Journeys

To take in the romance of yesteryear, book yourself a ride on a historical steam train. On the Zimbabwe side there is the 1953 class 14A Garratt steam train through Victoria Falls Steam Train Co (☎13 42912; www.steamtraincompany.com; incl drinks US$40, incl dinner from US$75), that will take you over the iconic bridge at sunset or through the Zambezi National Park with either a full dinner or gourmet canapes and unlimited drinks. Even if you're not booked on a trip it's worth getting along to the station to watch the incredible drama of its departure. There are also daily vintage tram trips (one way/return US$15/30) that head over the bridge and which also have a drinks and canapes option (US$40).

In Zambia the Royal Livingstone Express (☎213 323232; www.royal-livingstone-express.com; Mosi-oa-Tunya Rd, Livingstone; incl dinner & drinks US$170; ⏲Wed & Sat) takes you on a 3½-hour ride including five-course dinner and drinks on a 1922 10th-class steam engine that will chug you through Mosi-oa-Tunya National Park on plush leather couches.

Wildlife Safaris

There are plenty of options for wildlife watching in the area, both in the nearby national parks and private game reserves, or further afield. Both guided walks and jeep safaris are available in the parks on both sides of the border. At Mosi-oa-Tunya Game Park (wildlife sanctuary admission US$10; ⏲wildlife sanctuary 6am-6pm) in Zambia, there's a chance to see white rhinos, while the Zambezi National Park in Zimbabwe has a small population of lions. Walks cost around US$70, and drives US$50 to US$90. There are also dusk, dawn or night wildlife drives (US$50 to US$90). River safaris (US$30) along the Zambezi River are another popular way to see various wildlife including elephants, hippos and plenty of birdlife.

Another convenient option, only 15km from Victoria Falls town, is the Victoria Falls Private Game Reserve (☎44471;

www.shearwatervictoriafalls.com/safaris), a 4000-hectare private reserve run by Shearwaters. Here you can track the Big Five on a game drive (US$90), where apparently you stand a 97% (to be precise) chance of encountering a black rhino.

You can travel further afield, with operators arranging day trips to Chobe National Park (see p54) in Botswana for US$170 (excluding visas). It's only a one-hour drive from Victoria Falls, and includes a breakfast boat cruise, a game drive in Chobe National Park, lunch and transfer back to Victoria Falls by 5pm. Wildlife viewing is excellent: lions, elephants, wild dogs, cheetahs, buffaloes and plenty of antelopes.

Hwange National Park (admission per day US$15; ⏲about 6am-6pm) in Zimbabwe is the other option, with one of the largest number of elephants in the world. A day trip will cost around US$250.

Zipline & Slides

Glide at 106km/h along a zipline (single/tandem US$66/105), or soar like a superhero from one country to another (from Zim to Zam) on the 'bridge slide' as you whiz over Batoka Gorge (single/tandem US$35/50). Other similar options are flying-fox rides (US$40).

❶ Information

Tourist Information

Hands down the best independent advice is from Backpackers Bazaar (p548) in the town of Victoria Falls, run by the passionate owner, Joy, who is a wealth of all info and advice for Vic Falls and beyond. In Livingstone, the folks at Jollyboys Backpackers (p539) are also extremely knowledgeable on all the latest happenings. Both are good places to book activities and onward travel.

Travel & Adventure Companies

With activities and prices standardised across the board, all bookings can conveniently be arranged through backpacker accommodation and big hotels.

You can also go directly to the tour operators. The main ones in Zimbabwe are **Wild Horizons** (☎0712-213721, 13 42013; www.wildhorizons.co.za; 310 Parkway Dr) and **Shearwater** (☎13 44471; www.shearwatervictoriafalls.com; Parkway Dr). In Zambia try **Safari Par Excellence** (☎213 320606; www.safpar.net) and **Livingstone's Adventure** (☎213 323587; www.livingstonesadventure.com) both in Livingstone. All cover activities on either side.

VISAS

You will need a visa to cross sides between Zim and Zam. These are available at the border crossings, open from around 7am to 10pm. Note that you can't get multi-entry visas at these crossing; in most cases you need to apply at the embassy in your home country before travelling.

Crossing into Zambia, a day visit costs US$20 for 24 hours, a single-entry visa costs US$50 and double entry is US$80.

Crossing into Zimbabwe, a single-entry visa costs US$30 for most nationalities (US$55 for British/Irish, US$75 for Canadian). Double entry is US$45 for most nationalities (US$75 for British/Irish, and unavailable for Canadians).

ZAMBIA

☑ 260

As Zambia continues to ride the wave of tourism generated by the falls, it manages to keep itself grounded, offering a wonderfully low-key destination that has been recognised as such; it's co-host of the 2013 United Nations World Tourism Assembly. The waterfront straddling the falls continues its rapid development and is fast becoming one of the most exclusive destinations in Southern Africa.

Livingstone & Around

☑ 0213

Set 11km away from Victoria Falls, the relaxed town of Livingstone has taken on the role of a backpacking mecca. It attracts travellers not only to experience the falls, but to tackle the thrilling adventure scene. The town is not much to look at, but it is a safe, lively place with some fantastic restaurants. Those looking for a more scenic and luxurious experience can treat themselves to the natural setting along the Zambezi River at any number of plush lodges with river and wildlife views.

The town centres itself around one main road, Mosi-oa-Tunya Rd, 11km from the entrance to the falls. Several establishments are set right on the Zambezi River, but most of the action is set a bit back from the waterfront.

◎ Sights & Activities

TOP
CHOICE Victoria Falls World Heritage National Monument Site   WATERFALL

(admission ZMW103.5; ☺6am-6pm) This is what you're here for, the mighty Victoria Falls. It's a part of the Mosi-oa-Tunya National Park, 11km outside town before the Zambia border crossing; a path here leads to the visitor information centre, which has modest displays on local fauna, geology and culture.

From the centre, a network of paths leads through thick vegetation to various viewpoints. You can walk upstream along a path free of fences – and warning notices (so take care!) – to watch the Zambezi waters glide smoothly through rocks and little islands towards the lip of the falls.

For close-up views of the **Eastern Cataract**, nothing beats the hair-raising (and hair-wetting) walk across the footbridge, through swirling clouds of mist, to a sheer buttress called the **Knife Edge**. If the water is low, or the wind is favourable, you'll be treated to a magnificent view of the falls as well as the yawning abyss below. Otherwise, your vision (and your clothes) will be drenched by spray. Then you can walk down a steep track to the banks of the great Zambezi to see the huge whirlpool called the **Boiling Pot**. Watch out for cheeky baboons.

The park is open again in the evenings during (and just before and after) a full moon in order to see the amazing lunar rainbow. The tickets cost an extra ZMW51 – hours of operation vary, so inquire through your accommodation.

TOP
CHOICE Livingstone Island   VIEWPOINT

One of the most thrilling experiences not only at the falls, but in Africa, is the hair-raising journey to Livingstone Island. Here you will bathe in **Devil's Pool** – nature's ultimate infinity pool, set directly on the edge of the raging drama of Victoria Falls. You can leap into the pool and then poke your head over the edge to get an extraordinary view of the 100m drop.

Livingstone Island is in the middle of the Zambezi River, located at the top of the falls, and here you'll see a plaque marking the spot where David Livingstone first sighted the falls. The island is accessed via boat, and prices include either breakfast (ZMW333), lunch (ZMW615) or high tea (ZMW486). When the water is low, you're able to access it via walking or swimming across, but a guide is compulsory. Note that access to the island is closed from around March to May when the water levels are too high.

Mosi-oa-Tunya Game Park   WILDLIFE RESERVE
(admission US$10; ⊘6am-6pm) The other part of the Mosi-oa-Tunya National Park is up-river from the falls, and only 3km southwest of Livingstone. The tiny wildlife sanctuary has a surprising range of animals including rhinos, zebras, giraffes, buffaloes, elephants and antelopes. It's most famous for tracking white rhinos on foot. Walks cost ZMW435 per person, for groups of up to eight.

Livingstone Museum   MUSEUM
(Mosi-oa-Tunya Rd; admission ZMW25; ⊘9am-4.30pm) The excellent Livingstone Museum is divided into five sections covering archaeology, history, ethnography, natural history and art, and is highlighted by Tonga ritual artefacts, a life-sized model African village, a collection of David Livingstone memorabilia and historic maps dating back to 1690.

🛏 Sleeping

TOWN CENTRE

TOP CHOICE **Jollyboys Backpackers**   BACKPACKERS $
(☑324229; www.backpackzambia.com; 34 Kanyanta Rd; campsite/dm/r ZMW40/50/205; @🛱🛋) The British and Canadian owners of Jollyboys know exactly what backpackers want, and it is wildly popular for a good reason. They have kept the needs of independent travellers at the forefront, from the sunken lounge and excellent coffee to the sparkling pool, cheap restaurant-bar and clean bright rooms. Things can get a bit hectic in the evenings, so they've

LIVINGSTONE – THE MAN, THE MYTH, THE LEGEND

David Livingstone is one of a few European explorers who is still revered by modern-day Africans. His legendary exploits on the continent border the realm of fiction, though his life's mission to end the slave trade was very real (and ultimately very successful).

Born into rural poverty in the south of Scotland on 19 March 1813, Livingstone worked in London for several years before being ordained as a missionary in 1840. The following year he arrived in Bechuanaland (now Botswana) and began travelling inland, looking for converts and seeking to end the slave trade.

As early as 1842 Livingstone had already become the first European to penetrate the northern reaches of the Kalahari. For the next several years he explored the African interior with the purpose of opening up trade routes and establishing missions. In 1854 Livingstone discovered a route to the Atlantic coast, and arrived in present-day Luanda. However, his most famous discovery occurred in 1855 when he first set eyes on Victoria Falls during his epic boat journey down the Zambezi River. Livingstone returned to Britain a national hero, and recounted his travels in the 1857 publication *Missionary Travels and Researches in South Africa*.

In 1858 Livingstone returned to Africa as the head of the 'Zambezi Expedition', a government-funded venture that aimed to identify natural resource reserves in the region. Unfortunately, the expedition ended when a previously unexplored section of the Zambezi turned out to be unnavigable.

In 1869 Livingstone reached Lake Tanganyika despite failing health, though several of his followers abandoned the expedition en route. These desertions were headline news in Britain, sparking rumours regarding Livingstone's health and sanity. In response to the growing mystery surrounding Livingstone's whereabouts, the *New York Herald* arranged a publicity stunt by sending journalist Henry Morton Stanley to find Livingstone.

After arriving in Zanzibar and setting out with nearly 200 porters, Stanley finally found Livingstone on 10 November 1871 in Ujiji near Lake Tanganyika and famously greeted him with the line 'Dr Livingstone, I presume?'.

Although Stanley urged him to leave the continent, Livingstone was determined to find the source of the Nile, and penetrated deeper into the continent than any European prior. On 1 May 1873 Livingstone died from malaria and dysentery near Lake Bangweula in present-day Zambia. His body was carried for thousands of kilometres by his attendants, and now lies in the ground at Westminster Abbey in London.

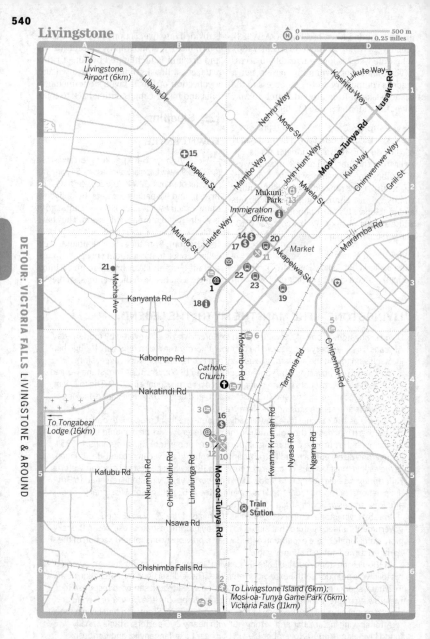

opened up the quieter **Jollyboys Camp** (Chipembi Rd) guesthouse nearby, in Chipembi Rd, to suit couples and families.

Fawlty Towers   BACKPACKERS, LODGE **$$**
(☏323432; www.adventure-africa.com; 216 Mosi-oa-Tunya Rd; campsite/dm/tr ZMW40/76/215, d

with/without bathroom ZMW307/205; ❋@ 🛜 ⊠)
Once a backpacker institution, things have been spruced up here into a guesthouse full of upmarket touches: free internet and wi-fi, shady lawns, a great pool and some of the nicest and most spacious dorms we've seen. No Basil or Manuel in sight.

Livingstone

DETOUR: VICTORIA FALLS LIVINGSTONE & AROUND

ZigZag GUESTHOUSE $$
(☎322814; www.zigzagzambia.com; off Mosi-oa-Tunya Rd; s/d ZMW280/410; P🅿❄@🛜🏊) Don't be deceived by the motel-meets-caravan-park exterior; the rooms here are more boutique B&B with loving touches throughout. Run by a friendly Scottish and Namibian couple, the lovely swimming pool, great restaurant and playground for kids give it a classic holiday feel.

Olga's Guesthouse GUESTHOUSE $$
(☎324160; www.olgasproject.com; cnr Mosi-oa-Tunya & Nakatindi Rds; s/d/f ZMW256/358/460; ❄🛜) If you need a lie down after gorging at Olga's Italian Corner restaurant, Olga's has it covered. Clean, spacious rooms with cool tiled floors, teak furniture and slick bathrooms are just a few feet away. Profits go towards helping an organisation supporting local youth.

Livingstone Backpackers BACKPACKERS $
(☎324730; www.livingstonebackpackers.com; 559 Mokambo Rd; campsite/dm ZMW40/50; 🛜🏊) Resembling the *Big Brother* household, this place can be a bit 'party central', particularly when the Gen Y volunteer brigade is on holiday. You'll find them lounging by the pool or in the sandy outdoor cabana, swinging in hammocks or tackling the rock-climbing wall! There is also a hot tub, open-air kitchen and living room.

ZAMBEZI RIVERFRONT
Most prices include meals and transfers from Livingstone and reservations are recommended.

TOP CHOICE **Stanley Safari Lodge** LODGE $$$
(☎in South Africa 27-72-170 8879; www.stanleysafaris.com; per person with full board and activities from ZMW2,203; @🛜🏊) Intimate and indulgent, Stanley is a 10km drive from the falls in a peaceful spot surrounded by mopane forest. Rooms are as plush as can be expected at these prices; the standouts are the open-air suites where you can soak up nature from your own private plunge pool. When you tire of that, curl up by the fire in the open-air lounge. Rates are all-inclusive.

David Livingstone LODGE $$$
(☎324601; www.thedavidlivingstone.com; River Side Dr, Mosi-oa-Tunya National Park; s/d incl breakfast & activities ZMW1,745/2,675; 🛜🏊) The newest addition to Livingstone's luxury hotels: all rooms have river views, Rhodesian teak furniture, concertina doors, four-poster beds and stand-alone bathtubs looking out to the water. It's set within the national park, hippos honk around at night, and the decking and bar around the riverfront infinity pool is a wonderful spot for a sundowner. It's located halfway between Livingstone and the falls.

Jungle Junction
Bovu Island
LODGE, CAMPGROUND $

(☏0978-725282, 323708; www.junglejunction.
info; campsite per person ZMW50, hut per person
ZMW128–179; ☷) Hippos, hammocks and
harmony. On a lush island in the middle of
the Zambezi River, around 50km from Livingstone, Jungle Junction attracts travellers
who just want to lounge beneath palm trees,
or engage in some fishing (ZMW77 including equipment and guide). Meals are available (ZMW36 to ZMW60).

Zambezi Waterfront
LODGE $$$

(☏320606; www.safpar.net/waterfront.html; camp-
site per person ZMW50, s/d tent ZMW155/200,
s/d incl breakfast from ZMW640/920; ❄🛜🏊)
Another waterfront lodge, things feel more
rustic here with a wilderness charm, as crocs
inhabit a small creek on the property. Ac-
commodation ranges from luxury tents and
riverside chalets to executive rooms or family
suites. The riverside open-air beer garden is
unsurprisingly popular at sunset. It's located
4km south of Livingstone, and a handy free
shuttle service takes you to the falls and
town.

Zambezi Sun
RESORT $

(☏321122; www.suninternational.com; s/d incl break-
fast from ZMW2,355/2,510, f ZMW2,550; ❄@🛜🏊)
Only a 10-minute walk from the falls, this
sprawling resort provides a great base for ex-
ploring the area. The North African kasbah-
inspired rooms are vibrant while plenty of
pools and a playground are perfect for fami-
lies. It's within the perimeter of the national
park, so expect to see grazing zebras but keep
your distance. Rates include falls entry.

Tongabezi Lodge
LODGE $$$

(☏323235; www.tongabezi.com; cottage/house per
person ZMW2,200/2,710; ❄☷) Here you'll find
sumptuous spacious cottages and open-
faced 'treehouses' and private dining decks.
Guests are invited to spend an evening on
nearby Sindabezi Island (per person per
night US$350), selected by the *Sunday
Times* as the best remote place to stay in the
world.

✖ Eating & Drinking

Livingstone is home to a number of high-
quality restaurants, including a batch of
excellent newcomers. Enjoy a sundowner
at any of the the Zambezi riverfront resorts
that allow nonguests to pop in for a drink
and a stellar sunset.

⬛TOP CHOICE Cafe Zambezi
AFRICAN $$

(☏0978-978578; 217 Mosi-oa-Tunya Rd; mains
ZMW30-48; ☺9am-midnight; 🛜🍴) Bursting
with local flavour; vibrant decor flows from
the indoor dining room to the outdoor
courtyard, sunny by day and candlelit by
night. The broad menu covers local *braai*
(barbecue) favourites of goat meat and mo-
pane caterpillars or an international twist
of roasted veg with feta, served with *sadza*
(maize porridge). Authentic wood-fired
pizzas are a winner or sink your teeth into
crocodile or eggplant-and-haloumi burgers.

⬛TOP CHOICE Olga's Italian Corner
ITALIAN $$

(www.olgasproject.con; cnr Mosi-oa-Tunya & Nakatindi
Rds; pizza & pasta from ZMW40; ☺7am-10pm; 🛜🍴)
Olga's does authentic wood-fired thin-crust
pizzas, as well as delicious homemade pasta
classics all served under a large thatched roof.
Great options for vegetarians, include the la-
sagna with its crispy blackened edge served in
the dish. All profits go to a community centre
to help disadvantaged youth.

ZigZag
CAFE $$

(off Mosi-oa-Tunya Rd; mains from ZMW25; ☺7am-
9pm; 🛜) Another string to Livingstone's bow
of culinary choices, ZigZag has a drool-
inducing menu of homemade muffins (such
as cranberry and white chocolate), smooth-
ies using fresh fruit from the garden, and a
changing small menu of comfort food.

Spot
CAFE $

(Mosi-oa-Tunya Rd; mains from ZMW40; ☺10am-
10pm) Promising 'forkin good food', this at-
tractive little outdoor eatery with picnic tables
delivers with its mix of local and international
dishes, including a mean chicken schnitzel.

Wonderbake
CAFE, BAKERY $

(Mosi-oa-Tunga Rd; ☺8am-9pm; 🛜) There's
nothing fancy about this bakery cafeteria,
but it has a good local flavour, sells cheap
pies and has free wi-fi.

Fez Bar
BAR

(Mosi-oa-Tunya Rd) This open-air bar set under
a garage tin roof is a popular place to kick on
to with its drinking games, pool tables and
menu of soft-shell tacos.

🛍 Shopping

Mukuni Crafts
CRAFTS

(Mosi-oa-Tunya Rd) The craft stalls in the south-
ern corner of Mukuni Park are a pleasant,
and hassle-free place to browse for souvenirs.

ℹ️ Information

Dangers & Annoyances

Don't walk from town to the falls as there have been a number of muggings along this stretch of road – even tourists on bicycles have been attacked. It's a long and not terribly interesting walk anyway, and simply not worth the risk. Take a minivan for under ZMW5 or a blue taxi for ZMW40.

Emergency
Police (☎320116; Maramba Rd)

Internet Access
Computer Centre (216 Mosi-oa-Tunya Rd; internet per hr US$2; ⊙8am-8pm) Also offers international phone calls and faxes. All the hostels now have wi-fi or at least internet access.

Medical Services
Livingstone General Hospital (☎321475; Akapelwa St)

Money
Barclays Bank (cnr Mosi-oa-Tunya Rd & Akapelwa St) and **Standard Charted Bank** (Mosi-oa-Tunya Rd) both accept Visa cards, while **Stanbic** (Mosi-oa-Tunya Rd) accepts MasterCard.

Post
Post Office (Mosi-oa-Tunya Rd) Has a *poste restante* and fax service.

Tourist Information
Tourist Centre (☎321404; www.zambia tourism.com; Mosi-oa-Tunya Rd; ⊙8am-5pm Mon-Fri) Mildly useful and can help with booking tours and accommodation, but Jollyboys and Fawlty Towers have all the information you need.

ℹ️ Getting There & Away

Air
South African Airways (☎0212-612207; www.flysaa.com) and **British Airways** (www.britishairways.com) have daily flights to and from Johannesburg. **1Time** (☎322744; www.1time.aero) flies three times a week. The cheapest economy fare starts at around US$400 return. **Proflight Zambia** (☎0211-845944; www.proflight-zambia.com) flies daily from Livingstone to Lusaka.

Bus & Combi (Minibus)
The Zambian side of the falls is 11km south of Livingstone and along the main road to the border with Zimbabwe. Plenty of minibuses and shared taxis ply the route from the minibus terminal along Senanga Rd in Livingstone. As muggings have been reported, it is best to take a taxi.

TO LUSAKA
CR Holdings (☎0977-861063; cnr Mosi-oa-Tunya Rd & Akapelwa St) Runs four services a day to Lusaka (ZMW80, seven hours).
Mazhandu Family Bus (☎0975-805064) Seven daily buses to Lusaka (ZMW80 to ZMW115) from 6am till 10.30pm.
Shalom Bus (☎0977-747013; Mutelo St) Eight buses a day travelling to Lusaka (ZMW75, six hours), from 5.30am till 10pm, as well as to many other parts of Zambia

TO NAMIBIA
For travelling to Namibia, and crossing the Zambia–Namibia border at Katima Mulilo, see p597.

TO BOTSWANA
Buses to Shesheke (ZMW60, two hours) depart with Mazhandu Family Bus at 5am and 2pm. Otherwise there are buses to Sesheke (ZMW50) departing when full from Mingongo bus station next to the Catholic church at Dambwa village, 3km west of the town centre. To get to Mongu from Livingstone, it's best to head to Sesheke or Lusaka, and then transfer to a Mongu bus.

Combis (minibuses) to the Botswana border at Kazungula depart when they are full from Mingongo bus station and cost ZMW30. Shared taxis can be taken from the taxi rank by Shoprite and cost ZMW40.

For information about travelling to Botswana, and crossing the Zambia–Botswana border at Kazungula, see p597.

Car & Motorcycle
If you're driving a rented car or motorcycle, be sure to carefully check all info regarding insurance, and that you have all the necessary papers for checks and border crossings such as 'owners' and 'permission to drive' documents, insurance papers and a copy of carbon tax receipt. Expect to pay around $US55 in various fees when crossing the border into Zimbabwe.

Train
While the bus is a much quicker way to get around, the *Zambezi Express* is more for lovers of slow travel or trains. It leaves Livingstone for Lusaka (economy/1st class/sleeper ZMW30/45/45, 15 hours), via Choma, on Tuesday and Friday at 8pm. Reservations are available at the **train station** (☎320001), which is signed off Mosi-oa-Tunya Rd.

ℹ️ Getting Around

To/From the Airport
Livingstone Airport is located 6km northwest of town, and is easily accessible by taxi (ZMW50 each way).

Combis & Taxis

Combis run regularly along Mosi-oa-Tunya Rd to Victoria Falls and the Zambian border, 11km south of Livingstone (ZMW5, 15 minutes). Blue taxis cost ZMW40 to ZMW50 from the border to Livingstone. Coming from the border, combis are parked just over from the waiting taxis, and depart when full.

Car Hire

Hemingways (☑ 320996; www.hemingways zambia.com; Mosi-oa-Tunya Rd) in Livingstone has new Toyota Hi-Lux 4WDs for around US$210 per day. Prices include cooking and camping equipment. Drivers must be over 25.

ZIMBABWE

☑ 263

There may still be a long way to go, but finally things seem to be looking up for Zimbabwe. All the bad news that has kept it in the glare of the spotlight – rampant land reform, hyper inflation and food shortages – fortunately now seem to be a thing of the past. In reality, safety has never been a concern for travellers here and, even during the worst of it, tourists were never targets for political violence. Word of this seems to have spread, as tourists stream back to the Zim side of the falls.

Victoria Falls

☑ 013

Having temporarily lost its mantle to Livingstone as the falls' premier tourist town, the town of Victoria Falls has reclaimed what's historically theirs as tourists return across the border in numbers.

Unlike Livingstone, the town was built for tourism. It is right upon the falls with neat, walkable streets (though not at dark, because of the wild animals) lined with hotels, bars and some of the best crafts you'll find in Southern Africa. While for a few years it felt like a resort in off-season, there's

Victoria Falls

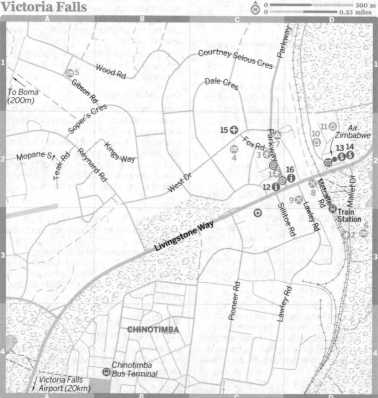

no mistake about it now – it's officially reopened for business.

☉ Sights & Activities

TOP CHOICE Victoria Falls National Park WATERFALL
(admission US$30; ☉6am-6pm) Located just before the border crossing and about 1km from the town centre, here on the Zim side of the falls you're in for a real treat. The walk is along the top of the gorge on a path, with various viewing points opening up to the extraordinary front-on panoramas of these world-famous falls. One of the most dramatic spots is the westernmost point known as **Cataract View**. Another track leads to the aptly named **Danger Point**, where a sheer, unfenced 100m drop-off will rattle your nerves. From there, you can follow a side track for a view of the **Victoria Falls Bridge**.

Hire a raincoat and umbrella just inside the gates if you go in April, or you may as well walk in your swimsuit – you will get soaked! The park is open again in the evenings during (and just before and after) a full moon, in order to see the amazing lunar rainbow (tickets cost an extra US$10).

Zambezi National Park   WILDLIFE RESERVE
(admission US$15; ☉6am-6.30pm) Consisting of 40km of Zambezi River frontage and a spread of wildlife-rich mopane forest and savannah, this national park is best known for its herds of sable antelopes, but it is also home to giraffes, elephants and an occasional lion. The entrance to the park is only 5km northwest of the Victoria Falls town centre, and is easily accessible by private vehicle. Tour operators on both sides of the border offer wildlife drives, guided hikes and fishing expeditions.

FREE Jafuta Heritage
Centre   CULTURAL CENTRE
(www.elephantswalk.com/heritage;   Elephant's Walk Shopping Village, off Adam Stander Dr; ☉8am-6pm) This worthwhile collection details the cultural heritage of local ethnic groups, from Shona, Ndebele, Tonga and Lozi people.

🛏 Sleeping

TOP CHOICE Victoria Falls Hotel   LUXURY HOTEL $$$
(☏44751; www.victoria-falls-hotels.net; 2 Mallet Dr; s/d incl breakfast from US$312/336; ❄🛜🏊) Built in 1904, this historic hotel (the oldest in Zimbabwe) oozes elegance and sophistication, and occupies an impossibly scenic location. Looking across manicured lawns (with roaming warthogs) to the gorge and bridge, you can't see the falls as such but you do see the spray from some rooms. High tea here at Stanley's Terrace is an institution.

Shoestrings Backpackers   BACKPACKERS $
(☏40167; 12 West Dr; campsite per person US$6, dm/d US$9/35; @🛜🏊) A perennial favourite

---

Victoria Falls

◉ Sights
Jafuta Heritage Centre..................(see 11)

◉ Activities, Courses & Tours
1 Shearwater Victoria Falls.....................C2
2 Victoria Falls Steam Train Co...............D3
3 Wild Horizons C2

◉ Sleeping
4 Shoestrings Backpackers....................C2
5 Victoria Falls Backpackers A1
6 Victoria Falls Hotel...............................D3
7 Victoria Falls Restcamp &
   Lodges...C2

◉ Eating
Africa Cafe ....(see 11)
In Da Belly Restaurant....................(see 7)
8 Lola's Tapas & Bar................................ D2
9 Mama Africa D2

◉ Drinking
Shoestrings Backpackers..............(see 4)
Stanley's Terrace ....(see 6)

◉ Shopping
10 Curio Shops...D2
11 Elephant's Walk Shopping &
    Artist Village.......................................D2
Jairos Jiri Crafts.............................(see 11)
Matsimela...(see 11)
Ndau Collection ....(see 11)
Prime Art Gallery...........................(see 11)

ℹ Information
12 Backpackers Bazaar...............................C2
13 Barclays Bank...D2
14 Standard Chartered Bank.....................D2
15 Victoria Falls Surgery............................C2
16 Zimbabwe Tourism Authority...............D2

Victoria Falls & Mosi-oa-Tunya National Parks

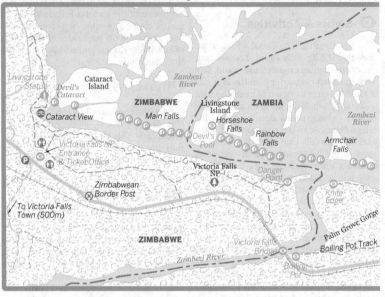

for backpackers, both the overland truck crowd and independent variety, who are here for its laid-back ambience, swimming pool and social bar (things gets very rowdy here on weekends). Rooms are a mix of dorms or privates, or pitch a tent. They also book all activities.

Elephant Camp LUXURY LODGE **$$$**
(www.theelephantcamp.com; s/d full board US$350/700; @🛜🛏) One of the best spots to splash out; the luxurious 'tents' have a classic lodge feel and are set on a private game reserve looking out to the mopane woodland savannah. Each room has its own outdoor private plunge pool and balcony decking to spot grazing animals or the spray of the falls. You might get to meet Sylvester, the resident cheetah.

Victoria Falls
Restcamp & Lodges CAMPSITE, LODGE **$**
(☑40509; www.vicfallsrestcamp.com; cnr Parkway & West Dr; campsite/dm/fitted dome tents US$10/11/20, s/d chalets without bathroom US$25/34, cottages US$67; 🛜🛏) A great alternative for budget travellers wanting to avoid the party atmosphere of other backpackers. Rooms are basic no-frills lodge-style and tented camps. There's a lovely pool and fantastic

open-air restaurant, In Da Belly. Rooms are basic, but spotless.

Victoria Falls Backpackers BACKPACKERS **$**
(☑42209; www.victoriafallsbackpackers.com; 357 Gibson Rd; campsite per person US$4, dm US$8, s/d without bathroom US$10/20; @🛜) Slightly rough around the edges, and a bit further away from the centre of town, it nevertheless remains a very good choice for budget travellers wanting a more laid-back environment.

Bengula Cottages GUESTHOUSE **$$**
(☑45945, 0778-173286; www.bengulacottages.com/; 645 Mahogany Rd; s/d/f low season US$60/100/120, high season $US100/160/220; 🛏) In the leafy suburbs, these attractive units are a solid midrange choice set around a shady pool with paper lanterns strung up and a relaxed atmosphere. The communal kitchen comes well equipped.

✖ Eating

In Da Belly
Restaurant AFRICAN, INTERNATIONAL **$**
(☑332077; Victoria Falls Restcamp & Lodges; meals US$5-15; ⏰7am-9.30pm) Under a large thatched hut, looking out to a sparkling pool, this relaxed open-air eatery has a menu of warthog schnitzel, crocodile curry and impala burgers, as well as one of the

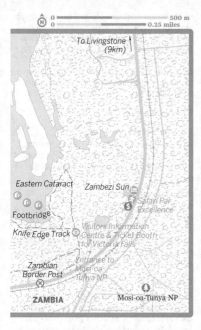

Lodge; buffet US$40; ⊙dinner 7pm) While it may be a bit of a tourist trap, Boma manages to be more genuine than tacky. Enjoy a taste of Africa at this buffet restaurant set under a massive thatched roof. Dine on smoked guinea-fowl starter, impala-knuckle terrine or spit-roast warthog. There's also traditional dancing, interactive drumming and fortune telling by a witch doctor.

🍷 Drinking

⬆TOP CHOICE Stanley's Terrace RESTAURANT
(Mallet Dr, Victoria Falls Hotel; high tea for 2 people US$30; ⊙high tea 3-6pm; 🛜) The Terrace at the stately Victoria Falls Hotel just brims with English colonial ambience. High tea is served with a postcard-perfect backdrop of the gardens and Vic Falls Bridge, with polished silverware, decadent cakes and three-tiered trays of finger sandwiches (cucumber? why yes, of course). Jugs of Pimms are perfect on a summer day at US$22. The only thing missing is the croquet.

Shoestrings Backpackers BAR
(12 West Dr) It's fairly laid back during the week, while weekends often feel like a house party as the dance floor gets a lot of action.

🛍 Shopping

A good selection of craft shops are located along Adam Stander Dr, with a quality items such as Shona sculpture and pieces made from recycled materials.

⬆TOP CHOICE Elephant's Walk Shopping & Artist Village SHOPPING CENTRE
(📞0772-254552; www.elephantswalk.com; Adam Stander Dr) A must for those in the market for quality Zimbabwean and African craft, this shopping village is home to boutique stores and galleries owned by a collective that aims to promote and set up local artists.

Prime Art Gallery ART
(📞342783; www.primeart-gallery.com; Elephant's Walk Shopping & Arts Village) Sells original pieces by Dominic Benhura, Zimbabwe's most prominent current-day Shona sculptor whose worked has been exhibited around the world.

Matsimela BEAUTY
(www.matsimela.co.za; Elephant's Walk Shopping & Arts Village; ⊙8am-5pm) South African body-care brand Matsimela has set up store here with an enticing aroma of natural scented soaps and body scrubs such as rose and

---

best breakfast menus in town. The name is a play on Ndebele, one of the two major population tribes in Zimbabwe.

Africa Cafe CAFE $
(www.elephantswalk.com/africa_cafe.htm; Elephant's Walk Shopping & Art Village; ⊙8am-5pm; 🖋) This appealing outdoor cafe at the Elephant's Walk Shopping & Artist Village, with smiley staff, is a great place to refuel with quality coffee, delicious breakfast, burgers and vegetarian food.

Lola's Tapas & Bar SPANISH $$
(📞42994; 8B Landela Complex; tapas US$2-9; ⊙8am-10pm; 🛜) Tapas such as *patatas bravas* and *calamares a la Romana* served by a welcoming couple from Barcelona. Dine outdoors or in the more intimate indoor area. Jugs of sangria available (US$15).

Mama Africa AFRICAN $$
(📞41725; www.mamaafricaeatinghouse.com; meals US$5-8; ⊙10am-10pm) This long-time tourist haunt behind the Landela Centre specialises in local dishes, steaks and game meats. Also has regular live music and traditional dance performances.

Boma AFRICAN $$
(off Map p544; 📞43211; www.thebomarestaurant.com; Squire Cummings Rd, Victoria Falls Safari

lychee and baobab-seed oil. Also has a branch at Doon Estate in Harare.

Jairos Jiri Crafts
CRAFTS

(Victoria Falls Curio Village; ⊘8am-5pm Mon-Fri, 8.30am-4.30pm Sat, 8.30am-1pm Sun) Good range of Shona arts and crafts, with proceeds assisting disadvantaged locals.

Ndau Collection
JEWELLERY

(☑386221; www.ndaujewelry.com) Watch local artisans hand-make individually pieced silver bracelets, rings and necklaces at this store-workshop. They also sell exquisite antique African trade beads to be incorporated into custom-made jewellery.

ⓘ Information

Dangers & Annoyances

Mugging is not such a problem anymore, but at dawn and dusk wild animals such as elephants and warthogs do roam the streets away from the town centre, so take taxis at these times. Although it's perfectly safe to walk to and from the falls, it's advisable to stick to the more touristed areas.

Emergency

Medical Air Rescue Service (MARS; ☑44764)
Police (☑44206; Livingstone Way)
Victoria Falls Surgery (☑43356; West Dr)

Internet Access

Econet (Park Way; per 30min/1hr US$1/2; ⊘8am-5pm Mon-Fri, to 1pm Sat & Sun)
Telco (☑43441; Phumula Centre; per hr US$1; ⊘8am-6pm)

Money

Barclays Bank (off Livingstone Way)
Standard Chartered Bank (off Livingstone Way)

Post

Post Office (off Livingstone Way)

Tourist Information

Backpackers Bazaar (☑013-45828; www.backpackersbazaarvicfalls.com; off Parkway; ⊘8am-5pm Mon-Fri, 9am-4pm Sat & Sun) Definitive place for all tourist info and bookings.
Zimbabwe Tourism Authority (☑44202; zta@vicfalls.ztazim.co.zw; 258 Adam Stander Dr; ⊘8am-5pm Mon-Fri, 8am-1pm Sat) A few brochures, but not very useful.

ⓘ Getting There & Away

Air

Check out www.flightsite.co.za or www.travelstart.co.za, where you can search all the airlines including low-cost carriers (and car-hire companies) for the cheapest flights and book yourself.
South African Airways (☑011-808678; www.flysaa.com) and **British Airways** (www.british airways.com) fly every day to Johannesburg from around US$320 return. **Air Namibia** (www.airnamibia.com) flies to Windhoek for around US$530 return.

Bus & Minibus

TO JOHANNESBURG

By road the easiest option is Pathfinder from VicFalls to Bulawayo (arrives 1pm) then connect with Intercaper Greyhound at 4pm to Johannesbur.

TO BULAWAYO/HWANGE

Pathfinder has a daily service to Bulawayo (US$30, six hours) en route to Harare (US$60, 12 hours), stopping outside Hwange National Park on the way. Bravo Tours also plies the route for similar prices. Otherwise combis (US$20) and local buses (US$15) head to Bulawayo.

Car & Motorcycle

If you're driving a rented vehicle into Zambia, you need to make sure you have insurance and carbon tax papers, as well original owner documents. When you enter Zambia you are issued with a Temporary Import Permit, valid for while you are in the country. This must be returned to immigration for them to acquit the vehicle.

Train

A popular way of getting to/from Vic Falls is by the overnight Mosi-oa-Tunya train that leaves Victoria Falls daily at 7pm for Bulawayo, Zimbabwe (economy/2nd/1st class US$8/10/12, 12 hours). First class is the only way to go. Make reservations at the **ticket office** (☑44392; ⊘7am-10am & 2.30-6.45pm Mon-Fri, 9-10am & 4.30-6.45pm Sat & Sun) inside the train station.

ⓘ Getting Around

To/From the Airport

Victoria Falls Airport is located 20km southeast of town, and is easily accessible by taxi (US$30 each way). Another option is to book a transfer with one of the companies through your hostel or travel agent in Vic Falls. Transfers are US$15 per person one way.

Car & Motorcycle

At the time of research, petrol was readily available in petrol stations. Avis and Europcar both have offices at the Vic Falls airport.

Taxis

A taxi around town costs about US$10, slightly more after dark.

Zambia

Best Off the Beaten Path

» Shiwa Ng'andu (p581)

» Liuwa Plain National Park (p576)

» Lake Bangweulu (p580)

» Chimfunshi Wildlife Orphanage (p585)

Best Places to Stay

» Busanga Plains Camp (p573)

» South Luangwa bushcamps (p564)

» Chongwe River Camp (p573)

» Ndole Bay Lodge (p573)

» Kapishya Hot Springs Lodge (p573)

Why Go?

Get out into the bush where animals, both predators and prey, wander through unfenced camps, where night-time means swapping stories around the fire and where the human footprint is nowhere to be seen. The rewards of travelling in Zambia are those of exploring remote, mesmerising wilderness as full of an astonishing diversity of wildlife as any part of Southern Africa. The geography is similarly varied: one day you canoe down a wide, placid river, and the next raft through raging rapids near world-famous Victoria Falls.

Though the country is landlocked, three great rivers, the Kafue, the Luangwa and the Zambezi, flow through Zambia, defining both its geography and the rhythms of life for many of its people. For the independent traveller, however, Zambia is a logistical challenge because of its sheer size, dilapidated road network and upmarket facilities. For those who do venture here, though, the relative lack of crowds means an even more satisfying journey.

When to Go

Lusaka

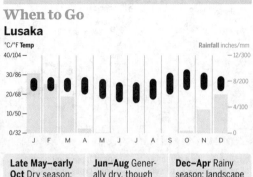

Late May–early Oct Dry season; prime wildlife-viewing time; October can be brutally hot.	**Jun–Aug** Generally dry, though temperatures are cooler; can get downright frosty at night.	**Dec–Apr** Rainy season; landscape vibrant, though wildlife difficult to spot; many lodges closed.

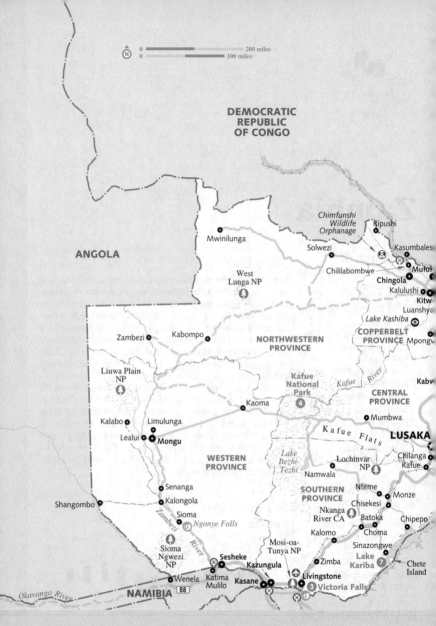

N
0 — 200 miles
0 — 100 miles

DEMOCRATIC REPUBLIC OF CONGO

ANGOLA

Chimfunshi Wildlife Orphanage
Kipushi
Solwezi
Kasumbalesa
Muful
Chililabombwe
Chingola
Kalulushi
Mwinilunga
West Lunga NP
Kitw
Luanshya
Lake Kashiba
COPPERBELT PROVINCE Mpongv
Zambezi
Kabompo
NORTHWESTERN PROVINCE
Kafue National Park
Kafue River
Liuwa Plain NP
Kaoma
CENTRAL PROVINCE
Kabv
Kalabo
Limulunga
Mumbwa
Lealui
Mongu
Lake Itezhi-Tezhi
K a f u e *Flats*
LUSAKA
Lochinvar NP
Chilanga
Kafue
Namwala
WESTERN PROVINCE
Senanga
Kalongola
Sioma
Ngonye Falls
Shangombo
SOUTHERN PROVINCE
Nteme
Monze
Chisekesi
Nkanga River CA
Batoka
Chipepo
Sioma Ngwezi NP
Kalomo
Choma
Sinazongwe
Lake Kariba
Mosi-oa-Tunya NP
Sesheke
Kazungula
Zimba
Chete Island
Wenela
Katima Mulilo
Kasane
Livingstone
Victoria Falls
NAMIBIA B8
Okavango River
Zambezi River

Zambia Highlights

① Walking like a detective following the tracks of wild animals in **South Luangwa National Park** (p561)

② Paddling a canoe down the **Zambezi River** (p567) past

pods of hippos, menacing-looking crocs and thirsty elephants

③ Rafting, bungee jumping or getting your adrenaline going in any one

of the adventures available at **Victoria Falls** (p534)

④ Spotting leopards in **Kafue National Park** (p572), a behemoth wilderness area

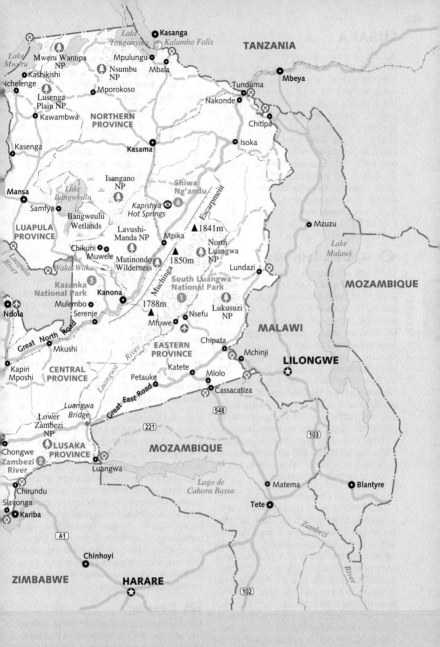

where wildlife dreams unfold amid stunning landscapes

⑤ Spying on elusive, semi-aquatic sitatungas (swamp-dwelling antelopes) from a tree hide in **Kasanka National Park** (p578)

⑥ Taking a step back in time and a leap to another continent at **Shiwa Ng'andu** (p581), a remarkably well preserved English manor estate

⑦ Kicking back at **Lake Kariba** (p569) and watching a storm roll in over the Zimbabwean peaks across the waters

LUSAKA

📞0211 / POP 1.4 MILLION / ELEV 1300M

All roads lead to Lusaka, the geographic, commercial and metaphorical heart of the country. Zambia's capital and largest urban zone is a mishmash of dusty tree-lined streets, bustling African markets, modern commerce and Soviet-looking high-rise blocks. The city doesn't easily justify exploration by the casual visitor, as there are no real attractions: no grand monuments to drool over, no historical treasures to unearth. However, for some, the city's genuine African feel, cosmopolitan populace, and quality restaurants and accommodation – at least as far as top-end hotels go – is reason enough to spend a night or two.

◎ Sights & Activities

The main commercial thoroughfare, or at least that of the 'old' central business district is Cairo Rd, lined with basic shops, fast-food outlets, banks and offices. To the north and south are major traffic roundabouts. West of Cairo Rd are small shops selling everything from maize meal to auto parts and then the crowded and chaotic city markets. East of Cairo Rd, across the railway line and near the train station, is the Inter-City Bus Station. Further east are the wide jacaranda-lined streets of the smarter residential suburbs and the area officially called Embassy Triangle (not surprisingly, home to many embassies and high commissions). Further east and north, around Manda Hill and Arcades Shopping Centres, is where many visitors end up spending the bulk of their time.

Munda Wanga Environmental Park   ZOO
(📞0211-278614; www.mundawanga.com; Kafue Rd, Chilanga; adult/child ZMW25/15; ⊙8am-5pm Mon-Thu, to 6pm Fri-Sun) Munda Wanga Environmental Park rehabilitates all sorts of animals for re-entry into the wild, including rarely seen pangolins and owls used for black magic. The park features plenty of regional fauna, including cheetahs, lions and wild dogs; feeding time is 2pm Friday to Sunday. The park is shabby in parts with slightly dilapidated enclosures, but the animals seem well cared for and it's perhaps the first and only exposure to wildlife for Zambians in Lusaka. But the lovely botanical gardens, with nearly 500 species of plants and one of the few places in the city suitable for a picnic, is at least as much of a reason to visit.

Munda Wanga is about 16km south of central Lusaka and accessible by any minibus heading towards Chilanga or Kafue from the Kalima Towers Bus Station or South End Roundabout (near the downtown Spar supermarket).

Lusaka City Market   MARKET
(Los Angeles Rd, New City Market; ⊙7am-7pm) Fronted by the chaotic and congested eponymously named bus station as well as a veritable Maginot line of sidewalk vendors, the Lusaka City Market can be a challenge to reach. Unfortunately, while the place is large, lively and packed to the rafters, the clothing and housewares sold in the warren of stalls aren't of much interest to the average traveler.

Soweto Market   MARKET
(New City Market) Soweto is the largest market in Lusaka (and Zambia). The sheer scale of the place, essentially a densely packed shanty town spilling out into the surrounding streets in a haphazard fashion, the amount of goods on offer and the number of people buzzing around can be overwhelming – consider a visit on a Sunday when things are a little quieter. Immediately to the west of the market is the New Soweto Market, a dull and only partly occupied building with numbered stalls under a covered roof.

National Museum   MUSEUM
(Nasser Rd; adult/child ZMW20/12; ⊙9am-4.30pm) This big square box of a building resembling a Soviet-era Moscow ministry is not much more than a shell of a museum. The decade-long plan to renovate the upstairs galleries to include exhibitions on urban culture and Zambian history seems to be in a permanent state of suspension, leaving a rather decrepit hodgepodge of cultural, ethnographic and archaeological artifacts. Some of the textual descriptions related to witchcraft and initiation ceremonies are interesting at least. Contemporary Zambian paintings and sculpture are displayed downstairs.

🛏 Sleeping

Lusaka's sleeping options are pretty spread out, although if you're looking for a backpackers there are several within a few blocks of one another. In central Lusaka midrange and top-end options are clustered around Rhodes Park and Embassy Triangle; in Greater Lusaka most accommodation tends to be in the east, off Great East Rd, in the direction of the airport. An important factor to keep in mind is proximity to restaurants; often this means the closer to a mall the better.

Lusaka Backpackers
BACKPACKERS $

(☑0977 805483; www.lusakabackpackers.com; 161 Mulombwa Cl; dm ZMW75, r with/without bathroom ZMW250/150; @ 🛜 🖃) With few alternatives, this deservedly popular place (formerly Chachacha) is the obvious choice for those on a budget in Lusaka. The centrepiece of activity is the patio area out front, with a small pool and bar that can get lively and loud, especially on weekends. The backyard accommodation options are better all around than those up front: a mixed dorm is nicer and quieter than the smaller and barer ones up front; and two basic safari tents, the simply furnished A-frame double and 'log cabin', all in the backyard, are the most pleasant accommodation. Other facilities include a restaurant (serving basic meals); a tub for doing laundry; a communal, dilapidated kitchen and baggage storage. Organises overnight safari trips to national parks and Livingstone.

Zamcom Lodge
HOTEL $

(☑0211-253503; doreen@zamcom.ac.zm; Church Rd; r ZMW250; 🕸 🛜) Though it looks like a school built in the '70s or earlier, this small motel-style complex has simple spick-and-span rooms. There's a shady courtyard–car park with resident turkeys strutting their stuff out the front. Conferences and wedding receptions aren't uncommon on weekends, so it's best to check with reception beforehand as these can be loud and raucous affairs.

Stay Easy Lusaka
HOTEL $$

(☑0211-372000; www.tsogosunhotels.com; cnr Church & Kabalenga Rds, Levy Junction; r incl breakfast ZMW500; 🕸 @ 🛜 🖃) Only in Lusaka would a mall parking lot be considered an ideal location for a hotel. But not only is this smart boutique-style property, part of a South African hotel group along with the Southern Sun, within shouting distance of Levy Junction's restaurants, banks and cinema but also it's a short walk to Inter-City Bus Station and Cairo Rd. Rooms are small – as are the wall-mounted flat-screen TVs – but comfortable, and you can always decamp to the backyard patio pool area or breakfast dining room for more elbow room during the day. Free wi-fi is a bonus.

Bongwe Barn
GUESTHOUSE $$

(☑0977 762096; www.bongwesafaris.com; 305 Ngwezi Rd, Roma; s/d with shared bathroom ZMW175/250, with private bathroom ZMW250/350; 🛜 🖃) In a quiet suburban neighborhood, Bongwe's seven rooms offer a secure and social – if you're so inclined – refuge. Simply furnished rooms line a single hallway with a stocked kitchen (coffee, toast and scones for breakfast) and a living room at one end. Out the back is a small pool and members-only bar (guests of course are considered members) with a TV tuned to international sporting events, a pool table and a menu of hearty steaks and other fare. It's 2.5km north (and just slightly west) of Arcades Shopping Centre.

Pioneer Camp
CAMPGROUND, CHALET $$

(☑0966 432700; www.pioneercampzambia.com; Palabana Rd, off Great East Rd; r ZMW300, campsites per person ZMW35; 🛜 🖃) An isolated 25-acre camp, surrounded by bird-rich woodland, Pioneer is the accommodation of choice for many expats living outside Lusaka. Most of the widely dispersed and simply furnished thatch-roofed chalets have flagstone floors, small verandahs and large bathrooms. The well-kept facilities for campers are up the front next to the comfortable bar, lounge and restaurant (mains ZMW70) area (which has a small plunge pool), where the free wi-fi reception works best. The campground's signposted 5km south of Great East Rd; If you don't have a car, a transfer from the airport or city centre should run around ZMW150.

Wayside Bed & Breakfast
GUESTHOUSE $$$

(☑0211-273439; www.wayside-guesthouse.com; 39 Makeni Rd, Makeni; s/d incl breakfast ZMW500/ 550; 🛜 🖃) This upmarket and peaceful guesthouse is one of the best in Lusaka, with only a handful of snug, en suite rooms. It used to be a farm and today the sizeable grounds are devoted to the owners' love of gardening, and really are magnificent (and ever growing); this is a place where you can wander well away from other guests. Three rooms in a separate cottage have air conditioning and there's a lounge with TV and comfortable couches. Located around 4.5km southwest of the South End Roundabout on Cairo Rd.

Kilimanjaro Country Lodge
LODGE $$$

(☑0211-255830; www.kilimanjarozambia.com; Leopards Hill Rd; s/d incl breakfast ZMW540/648; 🛜) A good out-of-town option – especially for groups and families – around 7.5km east

Lusaka

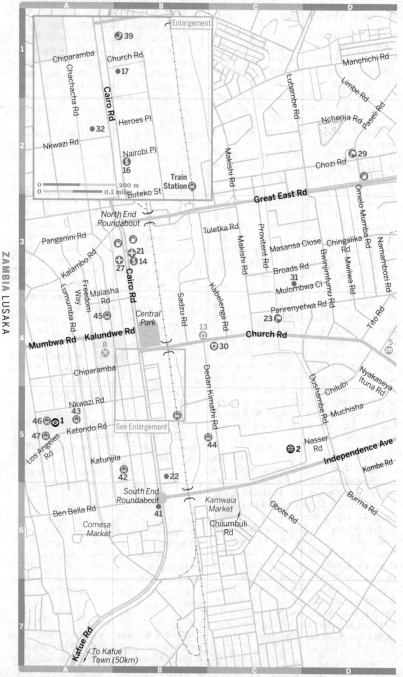

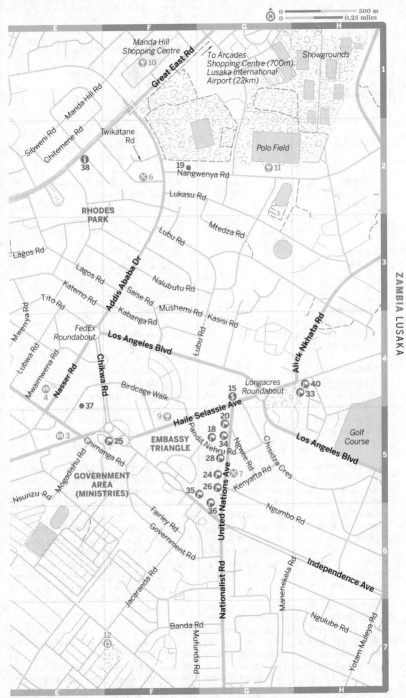

Lusaka

of the city centre, Kilimanjaro consists of several well-kept low-slung buildings on a manicured lawn. The 10 rooms are spacious and simply furnished and management is responsive to any requests. Another eight rooms and a pool were in the works at the time of our visit. The curio-filled garden restaurant here has a large menu (mains ZMW45) and a mouth-watering selection of desserts; there's a playground for children and mini pony rides as well.

Southern Sun Ridgeway HOTEL **$$$**
(☏0211-251666; www.southernsun.com; cnr Church Rd & Independence Ave; s/d incl breakfast ZMW1445/1602; ❄️🛜🏊) Deservedly popular with in-the-know expats and a coterie of international business and government types, the Southern Sun is a no-brainer for those seeking an affordable low-key, comfort-

able city-centre option. Rooms are tastefully done in muted tones – those in the 'weaver' block wing are the most newly renovated (all are due to be refurbished by the summer of 2013). Past the foyer is an inviting outdoor sitting area surrounding a fish pond and **Musuku**, a restaurant serving possibly the best breakfast and dinner buffet in the city. A pub, small gym, large outdoor pool area and free wi-fi round out the offerings. Conveniently on the premises are a Barclays Bank and offices for South African Airways and Proflight.

Taj Pamodzi Hotel HOTEL **$$$**
(☏0211-254455; www.tajhotels.com; Church Rd; s/d incl breakfast from US$300/325; ❄️@🛜🏊) An oasis of luxury and tranquility with fastidiously trained staff, the Taj is a welcoming cushion for travellers transitioning between

the bush and home. Featuring plush bedding and top-quality amenities, from slippers to skincare products, rooms at the Taj are a step up from others in a similar category in Lusaka. Views from the top-floor balconies of the sprawling city below are incomparable. A lavish breakfast buffet is served in one of the hotel's restaurants – the other, Steaks & Grills, does candlelit dinner outside with live music most nights – and drinks can be had at the bar, accompanied by the tinkling of a piano. Guests have access to the full-service gym – racquetball, anyone? – and spa out the back next to a lovely pool and patio area.

✗ Eating

The better places tend to congregate either inside or fairly close to the three main shopping centres: Arcades (Great East Rd), Levy Junction (cnr Church & Kabalenga Rds) or Manda Hill (Great East Rd), where you'll find massive and modern grocery stores, a handful of quality independent restaurants and a wide range of mostly South African fast-food and chain ones (Manda Hill probably has the best selection). Other options are scattered around the suburbs, especially around Embassy Triangle and Rhodes Park.

For local meals, the food stalls at the Town Centre Market (Chachacha Rd) serve cheap local food, but the scavenging dogs roaming the piles of rubbish are not a sight for the squeamish. Sausages and steaks are grilled before your eyes and served with a generous portion of veg and *nshima* (maize porridge) for around ZMW10. Other food stalls are scattered elsewhere around the city.

Deli CAFE, BAKERY $
(Lunzua Rd, Rhodes Park; mains ZMW25; ☺7am-6pm Mon-Fri, 9am-2pm Sat; 🛜) With an enviable garden setting and excellent coffee, the Deli is a good place to plant yourself for a few hours. The sophisticated kitchen turns out all-day breakfasts such as eggs and French toast, speciality sandwiches like Asian-pork meatballs and classics like pastrami, wood-fired pizzas and homemade ice cream.

Design House Cafe INTERNATIONAL, ORGANIC $$
(Leopards Hill Rd, Sugarbush Farm; mains ZMW35-60; ☺8am-5pm Tue-Sat, 9am-4pm Sun) This picture-postcard idyllic cafe is worth every kwacha of the journey it takes to get here. Chill out for an afternoon at one of the picnic tables munching on homemade bread

and pastries, salads made with vegetables from the organic garden and expertly prepared sandwiches, pasta and meat dishes as well as a glass of wine. It's southeast of the city centre on the same premises as the also highly recommended shop Jackal & Hide.

Chicago's STEAKHOUSE $$
(Manda Hill Shopping Centre, Great East Rd; mains ZMW45-115; ☺lunch & dinner) This theme restaurant – think Al Capone and gangsters, not meat-packing plants and 'duh Bears – located on the mall's 2nd floor is a nighttime haunt of Lusaka's young, prosperous and stylish. The large menu specialises in steaks and seafood, though the quality is akin to, well, a theme restaurant.

Oriental Garden Restaurant CHINESE, INDIAN $$
(United Nations Ave; mains ZMW25-65; ☺lunch & dinner; 🖥) Forget the Chinese and grill dishes at the back of the menu and stick to the speciality: Indian. There's a small bar terrace area (with a pool, for diners in need of a refreshing dip?) and a spacious indoor dining room, offering excellent service. Good veggie options are on the menu, such as a tasty masala kofta.

Rhapsody's INTERNATIONAL $$$
(Arcades Shopping Centre, Great East Rd; mains ZMW55-110; 🖥) Despite the views of the shopping-centre car park, this is one of the best places to eat in Lusaka. The international menu does everything from steaks to Thai chicken, salads and even nasi goreng. There are also lots of seafood dishes, but try the chicken Espetada, a delicious Portuguese-inspired chicken dish whose presentation will have you playing hangman in minutes.

Plates Restaurant &
Wine Bar INTERNATIONAL $$$
(🖥0211-841015; Acacia Park, Great East Rd; mains ZMW60-95; ☺noon-10pm Mon-Thu, to midnight Fri & Sat) In a modern office park with nice outdoor seating next to Arcades Shopping Centre, Plates is quickly becoming regarded as one of the city's best restaurants. A Culinary Institute of America–trained chef prepares sophisticated dishes like almond-crusted bream, Kansas barbeque-style ribs, plus good burgers and wraps. The menu changes monthly.

🍷 Drinking & Entertainment

Bars and restaurants aren't allowed to sell alcohol after 11pm, nightclubs 2am; it's prohibited everywhere on Sunday.

ZAMBIA LUSAKA

Lusaka nightclubs play internationally familiar house music on weekends. The pub at the **InterContinental Hotel** (☎0211-250000; www.ichotelsgroup.com; Haile Selassie Ave; 🛜) is good for watching English Premier League and rugby on the telly, as is O'Hagan's, though it's less conveniently located in Kabulonga. Most of the hotels, from backpackers to top-end places, have their own bars. Levy Junction and Manda Hill Shopping Centres have stylish and state-of-the-art Fresh View Cinemas, and Ster-Kinekor is at Arcades (tickets from ZMW16). The busy casino at Arcades Shopping Centre is one of the most popular in the city, especially with Chinese businessmen and visitors.

Polo Grill
BAR

(2374 Nangwenya Rd; ⊗8am-midnight) A large, open-air bar under an enormous thatched roof overlooking a huge, well-kept polo field (where you can occasionally catch a live match); it's all rather incongruous for Lusaka, but it's an exceedingly pleasant place to knock back a few Mosi's and catch some live music.

O'Hagans
PUB

(Manda Hill Shopping Centre, Great East Road) This South African chain pub, popular with South Africans and Brits, is ideal if you like fake Irish pubs and a more Western drinking experience. There are decent beers and a great outdoor terrace, even if it does overlook a car park.

🛍 Shopping

Sunday Market
MARKET

(Arcades Shopping Centre, Great East Rd; ⊗9am-6pm Sun) This weekly market in the car park at the Arcades Shopping Centre features Lusaka's best range of handicrafts, especially wood carvings, curios made from malachite and African prints. Bargaining is expected, though it's a relaxing, low-pressure affair.

Jackal & Hide
ACCESSORIES

(www.jackalandhide.net; Leopards Hill Rd) For extremely high-quality leather goods, especially purses, travel bags and accessories, head to this spot that shares an idyllic location with a highly recommended cafe on Sugarbush Farm east of Kabulonga, around 15km from the city centre.

Kabwata Cultural Village
HANDICRAFTS

(Burma Rd; ⊗9am-5pm) You'll find a scruffy collection of thatch-roofed huts and stalls selling carvings, baskets, masks, drums, fabrics and more at this place southeast of the city centre. Prices are cheap, however, because you can buy directly from the workers who live here.

ℹ Information

Emergency
Ambulance (☎994)

Police (☎991; Church Rd)

Specialty Emergency Services (☎0211-273302; www.ses-zambia.com) For evacuations. Has bases in Lusaka, Livingstone and Kitwe but operates throughout the country. Also has ambulances and in-patient care.

Internet Access
Wireless internet is available all over Lusaka now – at many cafes, restaurants and hotels. Look for the 'I Spot' sign. All three of the large malls have internet cafes and there are a couple along Cairo Rd; however, these seem to come and go with some frequency.

I-Zone Internet (Arcades Shopping Centre, Great East Rd; per 30min ZMW6; ⊗9am-9pm) Reliable, fast internet access, plus wireless facility.

Medical Services
Corpmed (☎0211-222612; Cairo Rd; ⊗24hr) Behind Barclays Bank. Has a doctor on duty 24 hours and is probably the city's best-equipped facility. Also runs its own ambulance service.

Greenwood Pharmacy (☎0211-227811; 680 Cairo Rd)

Money
Banks (Barclays Bank, FNB, Indo-Zambian Bank, Standard Chartered Bank and Zanaco) with ATMs and bureaus de change are located in Arcades, Levy Junction and Manda Hill Shopping Centres, along Cairo Rd and elsewhere in Lusaka, such as on Haile Selassie Ave.

Safe Travel
As in most African cities, pickpockets take advantage of crowds, so be alert in the markets and bus stations and along the busy streets immediately west of Cairo Rd. At night, most streets are dark and often empty, so even if you're on a tight budget, take a taxi. It would be foolish to wander the streets after dark, especially in and around Cairo Rd.

Lumumba Rd, parallel to and just west of Cairo Rd, has a bad reputation for robbery, especially from cars at a standstill in traffic jams, and especially from foreigners. Keep your windows up and doors locked if driving down this road.

Telephone & Fax
A dozen telephone booths (using tokens and phonecards) can be found outside the post

office. 'Phone shops' and 'fax bureaus' are dotted along Cairo Rd.

Zamtel (cnr Cairo & Church Rds) International calls can be made and faxes sent at the telephone office upstairs from the main post office.

Tourist Information

Zambia National Tourist Board (☑0211-229087; www.zambiatourism.com; 1st fl, Petroda House, Great East Rd; ⊗8am-1pm & 2-5pm Mon-Fri, 9am-noon Sat) Information and maps of Lusaka are limited.

Travel Agencies

Bimm Travel Agency (☑0211-234372; www.bimmtourszambia.com; shop 3, Luangwa House, Cairo Rd) Just south of the post office, Bimm is reliable and locally run. It can also arrange car hire.

Bush Buzz (☑0211-256992; www.bush-buzz.com) Organises trips to Kafue, Lower Zambezi and South Luangwa National Parks and Livingstone.

Steve Blagus Travel (☑0211-227739; www.sbltravel.com; 24 Nkwazi Rd; ⊗8am-4pm Mon-Fri, to 11.30am Sat) The agency for Amex and a dozen upmarket lodges and camps; also organises regional and domestic tours.

Voyagers (☑0211-253064; www.voyagerszambia.com; Suez Rd) Perhaps the most popular agency in Zambia (it has other offices in Ndola, Chingola and Kitwe), it arranges flights and hotel reservations and partners with Europcar for car hire.

❶ Getting There & Away

Air

There's a departure tax of ZMW156 per person applicable to all international flights. Before you make your way to the relevant counter to pay, check with your airline, as it's often included in the price of your ticket. You *will* have to pay the ZMW58 tax at the counter (just outside and to the right of the entrance of the domestic lounge) for all domestic departures.

The humble international airport has slim pickings as far as services are concerned. There's a coffee stand in the main hall, or make your way upstairs to the Copper Chimney Restaurant. Once you're through security for international flights the only eating option is a very basic bar selling reheated burgers, hot dogs and pies (ZMW25); a couple of shops sell a poor selection of overpriced curios. Several ATMs, a bureau de change, Europcar and Avis rental-car offices and Airtel and MTN mobile-phone company offices are in the hallway immediately outside the arrivals area.

For further information on air travel in Zambia, see p597.

Bus & Minibus

DOMESTIC

From in front of the massive and chaotic **Lusaka City Market Bus Station** (Lumumba Rd) buses and minibuses leave for nearby towns such as Kafue (ZMW25, one hour, 10 to 15 daily), Chirundu (ZMW30, 2½ hours, five to seven daily) and Siavonga (ZMW70, three hours, three to five daily).

Public transport to nearby towns, especially minibuses, also leaves from the **Soweto Market Bus Station** (Los Angeles Rd), but here nothing is signposted and you're better off avoiding it.

To add to the confusion, minibuses to places not far south of Lusaka also leave from the **City Bus Station** (Kulima Towers Bus Station; off Chachacha Rd), so it's possible to get to Kafue, Chirundu and Siavonga from here too.

Minibuses heading to the north (eg to Manda Hill Shopping Centre) depart from the **Millennium Bus Station** (Malasha Rd).

All long-distance public buses (and most private ones) use the larger though still somewhat confusing and disorderly **Lusaka Inter-City Bus Station** (Dedan Kimathi Rd), where there is a left-luggage office and inquiries counter. A range of buses from different companies cover most tourist destinations (all leaving from this bus station unless otherwise stated) – we've quoted the highest prices because they represent the best companies, with the most comfortable buses (two-storey with reclining seats) and are generally only between ZMW10 and ZMW20 higher in price (and well worth the extra). It's certainly worth double-checking the schedules and booking your tickets one or two days before you leave.

Heading southwest, as you'd expect, there are plenty of buses to Livingstone (ordinary/business class ZMW90/115, six to seven hours, at least seven daily), but we'd recommend traveling business class (one or two morning departures) with either **Mazahandu Family** (☑0978 05064) or Shalom bus services.

Travelling east, many companies operate services to Chipata, the road link for South Luangwa or Malawi (ZMW130, seven hours); Johabie, with departures at around 5am, 6am, 7am and 2pm, is the most recommended.

Heading west, catch an 8am Juldan or Shalom bus through Kafue National Park and on to Mongu (ZMW160, seven hours); for Kafue camps just off the highway it's ZMW100 and three hours.

Juldan, Power Tools and Mazandhu Family buses, among others, go to Copperbelt destinations such as Ndola (ZMW65, four hours, five daily), Kitwe (ZMW70, five hours, five daily), Solwezi (ZMW110, two daily) and Kapiri Mposhi (ZMW50, 2½ hours, five daily).

Tracking northeast, Germins and Juldan are two of the better companies, making a beeline for Kasama (ZMW130, 14 hours, four daily) and Mpulungu (ZMW150, 18 hours, four daily).

INTERNATIONAL

All buses mentioned here (unless stated otherwise) leave from the Lusaka Inter-City Bus Station.

To Botswana, Zambia-Botswana has buses to Gaborone (ZMW180, 22 hours, three weekly) via Kasane and Francistown; Mazandhu Family has a 5am departure for the border at Kazngula.

For South Africa, Intercape (ZMW400, 6am and noon daily) and Shalom (ZMW380, 6am Tuesday and Wednesday) have buses that head to Johannesburg (18 hours more or less) via Livingstone, Harare, Masvingo and Pretoria.

To Zimbabwe, take any bus going to South Africa, or Pioneer, Zupco or First Class buses go directly to Harare (ZMW120, nine hours, one daily per company).

For Malawi, there's no direct service to Blantyre, but there are three services a week to Lilongwe (ZMW150, 12 hours, 5am), where you can change buses; try Kobs Transport.

Zambia-Tanzania and Takwa Bus Services both make the run to Dar es Salaam (Tanzania; ZMW250, 27 hours, six weekly), but services can be haphazard (and the train is a more interesting and adventurous experience).

Train

The Zambezi Express travelling to Livingstone (economy class ZMW40, 14 hours), via Choma, leaves Lusaka at 11.50pm on Monday and Friday but has no 1st or sleeper class. Tickets are available from the reservations office inside the **train station** (btwn Cairo & Dedan Kimathi Rds). Get there early and be prepared for hustle and bustle. Slow, 'ordinary' trains to Ndola (standard class ZMW25, 12 hours), via Kapiri Mposhi (ZMW17, eight hours) depart Tuesday and Saturday at 1.20pm.

The Tazara train runs between Kapiri Mposhi and Dar es Salaam (Tanzania).

ⓘ Getting Around

To/From the Airport

The international airport is about 20km northeast of the city centre. Taxis to and from the airport to central Lusaka cost anywhere from ZMW110 to ZMW150. There's no airport bus, but the upmarket hotels send minibuses (usually for a fee) to meet international flights, so you may be able to arrange a ride into town with the minibus driver (for a negotiable fee).

Bus & Minibus

Local minibuses run along Lusaka's main roads, but there are no route numbers or destination signs, so the system is difficult to work out. There is a confusing array of bus and minibus stations. The standard fare is ZMW2 to ZMW3.

Car & Motorcycle

The roads can get extremely clogged around Lusaka at peak traffic times, and you should always be alert on the road as accidents are not infrequent. Speed limits are enforced in and around the city. Do not park your vehicle on the streets unless you have someone to keep an eye on it for you. If you drive around at night you significantly increase the risk of an accident or carjacking – after dark leave the car at your hotel and take a taxi.

Several international car-rental companies have counters at the airport, such as Avis (p600) and Europcar/Voyagers (p600). **Benmark Transways & Car Hire** (✆0211-292192) – bookings can be made through Lusaka Backpackers – rents cars for use within Lusaka for ZMW300 per day and for use outside Lusaka for ZMW400 to ZMW500 per day.

If you want a car and driver to help get you around Lusaka, you're better off hiring a taxi for the day, although travel agencies do offer this service. One of the official blue taxis should charge around ZMW300 to ZMW350 for a day, but an unofficial taxi would be cheaper.

Taxi

Official taxis can be identified by the numbers painted on the doors and their colour – light blue – but hundreds of unofficial taxis also cruise the streets. Generally they'll be ZMW5 to ZMW10 cheaper for a single journey within the city.

Official taxis can be hailed along the street or found at ranks near the main hotels and markets. Fares are negotiable, but, as a guide, ZMW30 will get you between Cairo Rd and Manda Hill Shopping Centre during the day – always agree on the fare before setting out.

EASTERN ZAMBIA

This part of the country contains one of Zambia's finest attractions: South Luangwa National Park, often considered one of the greatest parks in Africa for the density and variety of its game and for the beauty of its landscape. Sitting further north is wild North Luangwa, more difficult to access than its southern cousin and far less developed but also notable for its density of game.

Eastern Zambia covers the Great East Rd – and sections around it – extending east of Lusaka to the border with Malawi. There are several buses a day up to Chipata and through to Malawi and frequent flights between Lusaka and South Luangwa National Park.

Great East Road: From Lusaka to Chipata

The Great East Rd crosses the Luangwa River on a large suspension bridge about halfway between Lusaka and Chipata; there's a permanent security checkpoint manned by the army. In the nearby settlement of Luangwa Bridge, about 3km south of the main road on the western side of the muddy river, is the Bridge Camp (☎0977 197456; www.bridgecampzambia.com; Feira Rd; campsites ZMW40, per person chalets ZMW85-205; ☒), with comfortable, simple stone chalets.

About 90km from Chipata and 500km from Lusaka, Katete is a small town just south of the Great East Rd. On the main road 4km west of town, Tikondane Community Centre (☎0216-252122; tikoeducation@gmail.com; campsites per person ZMW25, dm ZMW30, s/d from ZMW60/75), next to St Francis Hospital, is a grass-roots initiative that works with local villages. Among its many activities, it focuses on adult and child education and agricultural initiatives, and trains home-based carers for AIDS victims. Tikondane also accepts volunteers to work at its centre and on its projects (there's a minimum two-week commitment). Contact volunteer director Elke Kroeger-Radcliffe for more details.

If you're interested in experiencing village life or just want a break from the road, consider a stay at the friendly Community Centre's Guest House. The rooms are small and simple; meals, such as chicken and *nshima* (ZMW30), are provided and internet access is available. You can visit the school, hospital and community projects, take a guided walk up a nearby mountain or see a traditional dance performed.

Chipata

The primary commercial and urban centre in this district, Chipata is a traffic-clogged town in a valley surrounded by a fertile agricultural region. For travellers it's simply a stop on the way to South Luangwa National Park or Malawi, only 30km away. There are a few decent accommodation options, petrol stations, banks with ATMs and a large Spar supermarket to stock up on food and other supplies.

Mama Rula's (☎0977 790226; www.mamarulas.com; campsites per person ZMW35, s/d incl breakfast ZMW248/315; @☒) is a long-running operation in a leafy compound around 4km out of Chipata along the road to Mfuwe. Simply furnished rooms with mosquito nets are in a low-slung building by the pool; out the back is a huge, grassy garden campground and nearby are small but clean cheaper rooms with shared bathroom facilities. Meals (ZMW90) can be served in the informal bar festooned with pennants and flags.

Another good option, perched at the top of a hill with great views of the valley below, is Deans Hill View Lodge (☎0216-221673; www.deanshillview.com; campsites per person ZMW25, r without bathroom per person ZMW50), run by a friendly British expat. There's little to distinguish the rooms, which are very simple, and the shared ablutions are generally kept clean; camping is out on a nice, big sloping garden.

ℹ Getting There & Away

Of the handful of bus companies offering service to Lusaka, Johabie (ZMW130, seven hours, 5am, 6am, 8am and 2pm) is easily the most recommended. The main bus station, also the departure point for minibuses to Mfuwe (around ZMW150, 3½ hours, 11pm) for South Luangwa National Park, is located about 1.5km north of the town centre. A taxi, official or otherwise, to Mfuwe (ZMW450, at least three hours) is a better option, especially as the minibuses arrive in Mfuwe around 3.30am.

Minibuses for the Malawi border depart from the BP petrol station on the main drag in town; otherwise a taxi should run around ZMW80 (30 minutes).

South Luangwa National Park

☎0216

For scenery, variety and density of animals, accessibility and choice of accommodation, South Luangwa (per person US$25, vehicle Zambian-registered/non-Zambian-registered ZMW15/US$15; ☉6am-6pm) is the best park in Zambia and one of the most majestic in Africa. Impalas, pukus, waterbucks, giraffes and buffaloes wander on the wide-open plains; leopards, of which there are many in the park, hunt in the dense woodlands; herds of elephants wade through the marshes; and hippos munch serenely on Nile cabbage in the Luangwa River. The bird life is also

South Luangwa NP

South Luangwa NP

◎ Activities, Courses & Tours
Bush-Spa .... (see 5)

🛏 Sleeping
1 Croc Valley..A1
2 Flatdogs Camp.....................................A1
3 Kapani Lodge..A1
4 Kawaza Village B2
5 Mfuwe Lodge..A1
6 Track & Trail River Camp....................A1
7 Wildlife Camp A1

🛍 Shopping
8 Tribal Textiles.......................................B2

tremendous: about 400 species have been recorded – large birds like snake eagles, bateleurs and ground hornbills are normally easy to spot. The quality of the park is reflected in the quality of its guides – the highest in Zambia.

The focal point is Mfuwe, an uninspiring though more prosperous than average village, with shops, petrol station and market. Around 1.8km further along is **Mfuwe Gate**, the main entrance to the park, where a bridge crosses the Luangwa River. A little before the gate are turn-off signs for a hand-

ful of lodges and camps. The area around the gate can get quite busy with vehicles in the high season, but only because it probably has the highest concentration of wildlife in the park.

Away from Mfuwe, in the northern and southern parts of the park, the camps and lodges enjoy a quieter and more exclusive atmosphere. The animals may be less used to vehicles and slightly harder to find, but there are fewer visitors in these areas and watching the wildlife here is immensely rewarding.

Much of the park is inaccessible because of rains between November and April (especially February and March), so many lodges close at this time.

If you're in either Zambia or Malawi, on a budget and looking for ways to see South Luangwa without breaking the bank, consider organising an all-inclusive safari, which will also sort out those challenging transport logistics. Recommended budget operators with accommodation in tents are: **River Safari Company** (www.riversafari company.com; 161 Mulombwa Cl, Lusaka; 3-/4-day safari per person US$545/695) (run out of Lusaka Backpackers) and **Jackalberry Safaris** (www.jackalberrysafaris.net; 3-/4-/5-day safari per person US$425/545/645) in Zambia, and **Land & Lake Safaris** (www.landlake.net) and **Kiboko Safaris** (www.kiboko-safaris.com; 4-day safari per person US$515), both of which operate from Lilongwe (Malawi).

FLORA & FAUNA
The wide Luangwa River is the lifeblood of the park. It rises in the far northeast of Zambia, near the border with Malawi, and flows southward for 800km through the broad Luangwa Valley – an offshoot of the Great Rift Valley, which cuts through East and Southern Africa. It flows all year, and gets very shallow in the dry season (May to October), when vast midstream sandbanks are exposed – usually covered in groups of hippos or crocodiles basking in the sun. Steep exposed banks mean animals prefer to drink at the park's numerous oxbow lagoons, formed as the river continually changes its course.

Vegetation ranges from open grassy plains to the strips of woodland along the riverbank, dominated by large trees including ebony, mahogany, leadwood and winterthorn, sometimes growing in beautiful groves. As you move away from the river onto higher ground, the woodland gets denser and finding animals takes more patience.

Not that you'll ever be disappointed by Luangwa's wildlife. The park is famous for its herds of buffaloes, and elephant numbers are also very healthy, even though ivory poaching in the 1980s had a dramatic effect on the population. This park is also a great place to see lions and leopards (especially on night drives), and local specialities include Cookson's wildebeest (an unusual light-coloured subspecies) and the endemic Thornicroft's giraffe, distinguished from other giraffes by a dark neck pattern.

There's a stunning variety of 'plains game'; the numerous antelope species include bushbuck, waterbuck, kudu, impala and puku. Roan antelopes, hartebeest and reedbucks are all here, but they're encountered less often.

Luangwa's population of wild dogs, one of the rarest animals in Zambia (and Africa), seems to be on the increase, especially around the Mfuwe area from November to January; there has been a resurgence in numbers around the Nsefu sector as well.

The bird life in South Luangwa is also tremendous. As small lagoons dry out, fish writhe in the shallows and birds mass together as 'fishing parties'. Pelicans and yellow-billed storks stuff themselves silly and herons, spoonbills and marabou storks join the fun, while grasses and seeds around the lagoons attract a moving coloured carpet of queleas and Lilian's lovebirds. Other ornithological highlights are the stately crowned cranes and the unfeasibly colourful carmine bee-eaters, whose migration here every August is one of the world's great wildlife spectacles.

🏃 Activities

All lodges/camps run excellent day or night wildlife drives (called 'game drives' in Zambia) and most have walking safaris (June to November). These activities are included in the rates charged by the upmarket places, while the cheaper lodges and camps can organise things with little notice. A three-hour morning or evening wildlife drive normally costs around ZMW210. You also have to pay park fees (ZMW156) on top of this, but only once every 24 hours, so you can have an evening drive on one day and a morning drive on the next. A walking safari (ZMW260) is perhaps the best way of all to experience the park; expect most attention

to be paid to animal tracks, what animal dung reveals and the medicinal uses of various plants.

You can visit the office of the South Luangwa Conservation Society (SLCS; ☎0216-246069; www.slcszambia.org), which supports and works closely with the Zambian Wildlife Authority spearheading anti-poaching and anti-snaring initiatives.

For an absolutely decadent experience of relief, head to the Bush-Spa (☎0216-246123; www.bush-spa.com; 1hr massage ZMW380; ⊗8am-4.30pm daily), a beautifully designed Balinese-style spa built over a hippo pond on the grounds of Mfuwe Lodge. Massages are of the highest quality and house calls to area lodges can be arranged.

🛏 Sleeping & Eating

All of the lodges and camps deep in the park are all-inclusive and at the very top end in terms of price (the park fee for these camps, ZMW309 per person per night, is also included). Some companies offer walking safaris for a few days from one bushcamp to the next, as well as what's often referred to as 'fly camping': camping out under the stars with nothing more than a mosquito net.

Most travellers will end up choosing from the places just outside the park boundary. These range from budget camping to top-end lodges; however, you don't pay admission fees until you actually enter the park. Note that some lodges and camps open only in the high season (April to November), but those in and around Mfuwe are open all year. Places that open in the low (or 'green' or 'emerald') season offer substantial discounts.

Any rates listed here are per person during the high season; single supplements usually cost 30% more. None of the lodges or camps described here are fenced, which means loud grunting hippos and their like might disturb your sleep and you may require an escort at night.

All the lodges, camps and camping grounds provide meals – from simple snacks, to creative haute cuisine at the top-end places. Flatdogs Camp probably has the best food of the 'drop-in' lodge restaurants. Highly recommended by area expats and one of the few places to eat in the village is friendly Dophil Restaurant (mains ZMW25; ⊗5am-10pm). If you're coming from the airport it's on the left-hand side of the road just after the Matizye Bridge.

Around Mfuwe Gate

Croc Valley
CAMPGROUND $

(📞0216-246074; www.crocvalley.com; campsites per person ZMW52, r without bathroom ZMW78, safari tents from ZMW180; ⊠) This sprawling, continually expanding compound is set under a tangle of trees lining the riverbank. The campground is popular with independent travellers; 'backpacker rooms' with shared, clean toilets and showers are quite a good deal; safari tents of varying levels of luxury and cost run the gamut. There's a big bar and restaurant with nightly three-course meals on offer for those paying full board, not to mention plenty of hammocks and shaded chill-out spots. Wildlife drives and walking safaris can be arranged.

Wildlife Camp
CAMPGROUND $

(📞0216-246026; www.wildlifecamp-zambia. com; campsites ZMW52, safari tents/chalets ZMW211/317; ⊠) This spacious, secluded spot about 5km southwest of Mfuwe village is popular with both overland groups and independent travelers. There are nine simple stone and thatch chalets (two with basic kitchenettes), five airy tented ones and a big, open area for campers with its own bar and pool area perfect sundowner views. A restaurant serves up standard international fare (mains ZMW80). Wildlife drives and walks are available in the park and in the area around the camp, which is rich in wildlife.

Flatdogs Camp
TENTED CAMP $$

(📞0216-246038; www.flatdogscamp.com; safari tents from ZMW240, chalets ZMW405; @⊠) This large, leafy property along a kilometre of riverfront is one of the best of the midrange options. Eleven safari tents of varying features – all are well kept and have outdoor showers – are at the end of snaking pathways. Groups of four can consider the 'tree house', which has two open-air bedrooms overlooking a floodplain frequented by all manner of wildlife. Four enormous chalets are good for families. Flatdogs bar is a welcoming spot and the restaurant, one of the only places with an à la carte menu open to nonguests, has a variety of Zambian and international fare (mains ZMW60). Wildlife drives and walking safaris are offered at affordable rates.

Track & Trail River Camp
CHALET, CAMPGROUND $$$

(📞in Lusaka 0211-246020; www.trackandtrail-rivercamp.com; campsites per person ZMW53, all-inclusive chalets & safari tents from ZMW1610; ⊠) Set on a riverfront property about 400m east of Mfuwe Gate are four fairly luxurious chalets sleeping up to four, each with a deck overlooking the river. There are also five large safari tents raised on concrete platforms with open-air bathrooms, some a bit further back in the bush. The camping grounds, shaded by a giant African fig, are just lovely. An above-ground pool has an elevated deck with lounge chairs overlooking

---

BUSHCAMP COMPANIES

Only a handful of companies offer lodging within the park proper, primarily in what are generally referred to as 'bushcamps'. Despite the misleading name, these are very comfortable, ranging from simple thatch-roofed chalets to stylishly furnished tents with gold-plated faucets and plunge pools. Most have only three to five rooms and offer customised itineraries that take guests to multiple camps by vehicle or on foot.

There are three major companies, all with 'base lodges' near the Mfuwe Gate. Sophisticated and expertly managed by its founder, Andy Hogg, **Bushcamp Company** (www.bushcampcompany.com) operates six uniquely designed camps (Bilimungwe, Chamilandu, Chindeni, Kapamba, Kuyenda and Zungulila), all in the southern section of the park, as well as its base, Mfuwe Lodge. **Norman Carr Safaris** (📞0216-246015; www.normancarrsafaris.com) operates five somewhat more rustic camps (Kakuli, Kapani, Luwi, Mchenja and Nsolo), all in the northern section of the park, as well as its base at Kapani. **Robin Pope Safaris** (www.robinpopesafaris.net) has its base at Nkwali, not far south of Mfuwe Gate, and operates three camps (Luangwa River Camp, Nsefu and Tena Tena).

The other companies in the park are the highly recommended **Remote Africa** (www.remoteafrica.com; Chikoko, Crocodile and Tafika camps) in the northern section, run by John and Carol Coppinger; **Sanctuary Retreats** (www.sanctuarylodges.com; Chichele, Puku Ridge and Zebra Plains camps); **Shenton Safaris** (www.kaingo.com; Mwamba and Kaingo camps); and **Wilderness Safaris** (www.wilderness-safaris.com; Kalamu Lagoon camp).

KAWAZA VILLAGE

This enterprise (www.kawazavillage.co.uk; day visits ZMW181, s with full board ZMW362) run by the local Kunda people gives tourists the opportunity to visit a real rural Zambian village while helping the local community. Four *rondavels* (round huts; each sleeps two) with open-air reed showers and long-drop toilets are reserved for visitors, who are encouraged to take part in village life, such as learning how to cook *nshima*, attending local church services and visiting local schools. Other activities include visits to the local healer or to the chief's palace, and bush walking. Evenings are filled with traditionally cooked meals, dancing, drumming and storytelling around the fire. Transfers can be arranged from camps around Mfuwe village.

the river. Built around a lime tree, the bar-restaurant offers excellent food.

Mfuwe Lodge BUSHCAMP $$$
(☏0216-245041; www.bushcampcompany.com; per person per night all-inclusive US$450; ☉year-round; ☎☒) Laid out along an enviable stretch of a well-trafficked oxbow lagoon only 2km from the Mfuwe Gate, this lodge, one of the largest, is also certainly one of the nicest and best run. The 18 separate cottages are imaginatively designed with private ve-randahs and colourful bathrooms. From the back porch of the suites or from the huge outdoor deck with a restaurant, bar and swimmming pool, it's like having front-row seats to, well, *The Lion King*. Besides operating as the base for its own six bushcamps in the southern section of the park, it's also the site of the recommended Bush-Spa.

Kapani Lodge LODGE $$$
(☏0216-246015; www.normancarrsafaris.com; all-inclusive per person US$325) Known as one of the camps Norman Carr built and inter-twined with this pioneer's reputation, Ka-pani is set about 4km southwest of Mfuwe Gate overlooking a beautiful oxbow lagoon. The 10 fairly ordinary thatch and stucco cot-tages are simply furnished and meals are taken on a large wooden deck that hangs over the river. The majority of guests spend only a night or two here, choosing to shuttle between the company's four smaller rustic bushcamps in the north of the park.

🛍 Shopping

Tribal Textiles HANDICRAFTS
(☏0216-245137; www.tribaltextiles.co.zm; ☉7am-4.30pm) Along the road between Mfuwe village and the airport is a large enterprise that employs a team of local artists to pro-duce, among other things, bags, wall hang-ings, bed linen and sarongs, much of which are sold abroad. It's quite a refined place to shop or take a short (free) tour around the factory.

ℹ Getting There & Away

Air

Most people reach South Luangwa by air. Mfuwe airport is about 20km southeast of Mfuwe Gate and served by **Proflight** (☏0211-271032; www. proflight-zambia.com), with several daily flights from Lusaka (ZMW810 to ZMW1500 one way). **Bush & Lake Aviation** (www.bla.mw) flies from Lilongwe (Malawi) to Mfuwe. There's a bureau de change in the little terminal, a Barclay's Bank and Zanaco ATMs. Most every lodge meets clients at the airport. Otherwise, a taxi to loca-tions near the Mfuwe Gate should run around ZMW80.

Car

To get to Mfuwe Gate and the surrounding camps from Chipata you should have a 4WD, high-clearance vehicle. In the dry season the dirt road is poor and the drive takes about three hours. In the wet season, however, the drive can take all day (or be impassable). Check locally before you make the trip.

Minibus & Private Vehicle

Several crowded minibuses leave from the BP petrol station in Mfuwe village for Chipata (around ZMW150, luggage supplement ZMW10 to ZMW20, 3½ hours). Unfortunately, they depart around 7.30pm, meaning a late-night arrival.

A shared taxi (around ZMW450 for the entire taxi, around ZMW250 for the front seat for solo travelers) is a more convenient though pricier alternative. If you arrive at the BP station early in the morning, say before 7am, you have a good chance of joining a carload of Zambians or pos-sibly other travellers.

A taxi from Mfuwe village to one of the lodges near the gate only a few kilometres away will cost anywhere from ZMW30 to ZMW100.

North Luangwa National Park

This **park** (admission US$20, vehicle US$15; ⊙6am-6pm) is large, wild and spectacular, but nowhere *near* as developed or set up for tourism as its southern counterpart. The big draw of North Luangwa is its walking safaris, where you can get up close to the wildlife in a truly remote wilderness.

It's important to note that most of the southern part of the park has been set aside as a wilderness area. There are not many roads and only a few smallish camps, which mainly run walking safaris.

Located in the south of the park, **Buffalo Camp** (📞0976 970444; www.shiwasafaris.com; all-inclusive per person ZMW1700) is a quiet, secluded place run by Mark Harvey, grandson of Stewart Gore Browne of Shiwa Ng'andu, where he was raised. The six traditional-style thatch-roofed chalets overlook the river. Book ahead for the 'self-catering rates' (ZMW500 per person excluding park rates and bed levy), normally only available when there's a paucity of guests on the all-inclusive package.

Mwaleshi Camp (📞0216-246185; www.remoteafrica.com; all-inclusive per person ZMW2900) is a top-notch operation, at once luxurious and relaxed with accommodation in four charmingly simple chalets made from reeds and thatch with open-roofed bathrooms. Walking is the main activity and that's a fortunate thing once you've tasted the excellent food.

There is no public transport to the park. Most guests fly in and out on expensive charter flights arranged by their lodge (the typical price per person from Mfuwe to one of the airstrips is ZMW1000 one way); the result is that only several hundred people a year visit the park.

If you are coming into the park independently, remember that you need to be well set up with a fully equipped high-clearance 4WD, and your accommodation prebooked. Also, get advice regarding the state of the roads into the park and make sure you've got maps (and GPS) that cover the area.

SOUTHERN ZAMBIA

This region is a real highlight of Zambia, with some wonderful natural attractions. The most popular and highly regarded of these is the Lower Zambezi Valley, with its wildlife (especially elephants), scenic landscape and canoe safaris. Then there are massive Lake Kariba and Siavonga's sandy beaches; if you're lucky enough to see a storm roll in over the steely waters from Zimbabwe, it'll be an experience you'll long remember. (The Zambian side of of the lake isn't nearly as developed or popular as the eastern shores in Zimbabwe.) The area is also home to the remote Lochinvar National Park, a World Heritage Wetland Site with pristine wetlands – it's worth a visit by those with their own vehicle.

Chirundu

📞0211

This dusty and bedraggled border town is on the main road between Lusaka and Harare. The only reason to stay here is if you're going on to Zimbabwe or planning to explore the Lower Zambezi Valley. Other than a few shops and bars, as well as a Barclays Bank with ATM and a number of moneychangers (no petrol station), there's little else to note.

🛏 Sleeping

Zambezi Breezers CAMPGROUND $$
(📞0979 279468; zambezibreezers@gmail.com; campsites per person ZMW50, r without bathroom ZMW190, s/d chalets incl breakfast ZMW375/650; ☀) Especially popular with backpackers and overland trucks, Breezers, only 6km from Chirundu, can take on a party atmosphere when busy. There's a variety of accommodation options, including a wide lawn for camping, six simple and clean tented chalets and 'budget' rooms (really nothing more than concrete boxes with beds). A pool table, basic but cavernous bar area, riverside deck and restaurant (mains ZMW60) encourage socialising. Other activities on offer are boat trips, and River Horse Safaris (which operates out of Breezers) can organise recommended overnight canoeing trips on the Zambezi.

Gwabi Lodge CAMPGROUND, CHALET $$
(📞0211-515078; www.gwabiriverlodge.com; campsites per person ZMW50, s/d chalets incl breakfast ZMW425/660; @🛜☀) This long-running lodge, which sees mostly weekending Lusakans, is set on large leafy grounds 12km east of Chirundu. There's a well-equipped campground (tents can be rented) and nine solid chalets (with four new ones in the works). With a lovely elevated outlook over

the Kafue River, 6km from the confluence with the Zambezi, the decking in front of the à la carte restaurant is a great spot. Fishing, boating and overnight canoe safaris can be arranged.

❶ Getting There & Away

Minibuses leave regularly for Chirundu from Lusaka (ZMW30, 3½ hours, five to seven daily). To reach Siavonga (on Lake Kariba) from Chirundu, catch a minibus towards Lusaka, get off at the obvious turn-off to Siavonga and wait for something else to come along. You can also get to Zimbabwe from Chirundu.

Lower Zambezi Valley

One of the country's premier wildlife-viewing areas includes the Chiawa Game Management Area (GMA) as well as the Lower Zambezi National Park, covering 4200 sq km along the northwestern bank of the Zambezi River. Several smaller rivers flow through the park itself, which is centered on a beautiful floodplain alongside the Zambezi, dotted with acacias and other large trees, and flanked by a steep escarpment on the northern side, covered with thick *miombo* woodland.

On the Zambezi are several islands. Some are large rocky outcrops covered in old trees, which feature in the writings of explorers such as Livingstone and Selous. Others are nothing more than temporary sandbanks with grass and low bush. Along the riverside grow the largest trees – jackleberry, mahogany and winterthorn. On the opposite bank, in Zimbabwe, is Mana Pools National Park, and together the parks constitute one of Africa's finest wildlife areas.

The best wildlife viewing is on the floodplain and along the river itself, so boat rides (about ZMW150) are a major feature of all camps and lodges. The elephant population, ravaged by poaching until the early 1990s, is making a strong comeback thanks to the efforts of Conservation Lower Zambezi (www.conservationlowerzambezi.org), an organisation funded by the area's lodges and private grants.

Other mammal species include puku, impala, zebra, buffalo, bushbuck, leopard, lion and cheetah, and more than 400 bird species have been recorded, including the unusual African skimmer and narina trogon. Seeing elephants swim across the river, or hundreds of colourful bee-eaters nesting in the steep sandy banks, could be the highlight of your trip. The best time to visit is May to October; however, temps average around 40°C – and have been recorded as high as 55°C – in the latter half of October.

The main entrance to the park is at Chongwe Gate along the southwestern boundary (park fee ZMW132). The southwestern sector of the park is the easiest to reach and the most scenic, and has excellent wildlife viewing, so as you might expect it's a popular area. As you go further into the central part of the park the surroundings become wilder and more open and there's more chance of having the place to yourself. Although the park is technically open all year, access is impossible in the rainy season and most lodges are closed down from at least mid-December to the end of February.

Lower Zambezi National Park

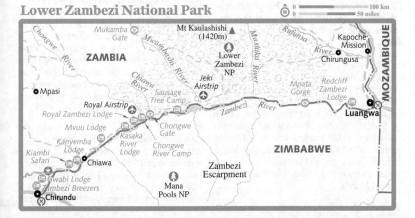

🏃 Activities

One of the best ways to see the Lower Zambezi is by canoe safari. Drifting silently past the riverbank, you can get surprisingly close to birds and animals without disturbing them. Most of the camps and lodges have canoes, so you can go out with a river guide for a few hours; longer safaris are even more enjoyable.

The best time for tiger fishing (strictly catch and release) is September to December but still possible in other months. Rods, reels and bait can be supplied by all the lodges and camps.

🛏 Sleeping

There is a line of lodges running through the Chiawa GMA before the Chongwe Gate (this is where all of the properties reviewed here are located), a few in the park itself (all at the very, very top end in terms of price) and one to the east of the park boundary (only really accesssible to self-drivers).

Rates listed are usually per person during the high season (April to October) staying in twins/doubles unless mentioned otherwise. Also, add on transfers if you haven't got your own wheels. Most lodges offer wildlife-viewing activities by boat or 4WD and are not fenced. Keep in mind, however, that while this is theoretically on offer, most of the lodges in the GMA, especially those closer to Chirundu than to Chongwe Gate, don't take their wildlife drives in the park proper.

Kiambi Safari   CAMPGROUND $$

(📞0977 186106; www.kiambi.co.za; campsites per person ZMW52, chalets per person with full board from ZMW420; ❄️📶🏊) This well-run operation at the confluence of the Zambezi and Kafue Rivers has a smattering of different, relatively affordable accommodation options. Wood-floored tented chalets are comfy with attached outdoor bathrooms; the spacious air-con chalets are good if the humidity is getting a bit much, and well-equipped self-catering cottages can sleep six. Campers get their own fire pit, swimming pool, a separate bar and upstairs viewing platform (Kiambi provides tents and bedding for an extra ZMW42). In addition to the usual river activities, Kiambi offers three-night canoe safaris (ZMW820 per person per day including all meals, tent and bedding). It's open all year; enquire about discounts from December to March.

Chongwe River Camp   TENTED CAMP $$$

TOP CHOICE

(📞0211-286 808; www.chongwe.com; s/d all-inclusive US$900/1400; ☀️Apr-Nov; 📶🏊) This camp has an enviable position right on the Chongwe River that marks the boundary between the GMA and the national park. The river's confluence with the Zambezi is within view and a menagerie of wildlife grazes on a spit of grassland with the park's escarpment in the background. The tented chalets, well spaced along the edge of the river, have plush bedding, shaded verandahs and charming open-air bathrooms. It's a laid-back place with a small fenced-in pool, nightly bonfires and large lantern-lit communal dining table.

Tsika Island is Chongwe's very rustic adobe-and-thatch bushcamp further up-river; hot water for showers is supplied by buckets suspended high above on poles to catch sunlight.

Royal Zambezi Lodge   CHALET $$$

(📞0211-840682; www.royalzambezilodge.com; per person all-inclusive US$650; ☀️year-round; 📶🏊) The epitome of luxury bush mixed with a colonial-era vibe, Royal is only a short drive to the airstrip as well as Chongwe Gate. Despite its understated opulence – think brass fixtures, claw-footed tubs and private day beds on decks overlooking the river – it's unpretentious and friendly. In addition, there's a full-service spa (the only one on the Zambezi) and a bar built around the trunk of a sausage tree next to a small pool.

Kanyemba Lodge   CHALET $$$

(📞0977 755720; www.kanyemba.com; chalets with full board around US$330; 🏊) This lodge has phenomenal river views and proximity to big wildlife, as well as authentic, homemade Italian food and cappuccinos. The spacious round chalets are stylishly furnished and stone-floored bathrooms have rainwater showers. In an attic-like space above the open-air dining area is a charming little library and lounge and the pool with river-front deck is ideal for those long between-activities afternoons. Take a guided canoeing safari, try your luck at tiger fishing or down G&Ts on a sundowner cruise.

Mvuu Lodge   CAMPGROUND $$$

(📞in South Africa 012-660 5369; www.mvuulodge.com; campsites per person ZMW115, safari tents per person from ZMW1155) A large, leafy property with an informal vibe, Mvuu is built on the edge of the tree-lined riverbank. Comfortable, elevated safari tents with balconies are on either side of a casual lounge and dining area. The communal campfire encourages guests to share their tales of leopard and lion sightings. Each site in the campground, the furthest one into the GMA, has its own outdoor stone shower and toilet, fire pit (firewood is provided), concrete cooking table and sink; self-caterers can use the lodge kitchen's refrigerator.

Kasaka River Lodge   TENTED CAMP $$$
(☑0211-256202; www.kasakariverlodge.com; safari tents all-inclusive per person ZMW2090) Kasaka is perched high above the Zambezi only 4km from the park entrance. On one side are eight fairly luxurious tented chalets with charming outdoor bathrooms set on a manicured lawn with a small pool. On the other, 'bush' side is the honeymoon suite, with Ottoman-style bed, or a group-oriented two-bedroom thatch-roofed home with its own viewing deck and fire pit. In between, built under several large trees, is the dining and bar area; just below is another small 'library' deck, best used for kicking back and watching the river flow by.

❶ Getting There & Away

There's no public transport to Chongwe Gate, nor anything to the eastern and northern boundaries, and hitching is very difficult. Most people visit the park on an organised tour and/or stay at a lodge that offers wildlife drives and boat rides as part of the deal. The lodges also arrange transfers from Lusaka – generally a minivan to Chirundu and then a boat to the lodge (rates and travel times vary depending on the distance from Chirundu).

Uncomfortable minibuses run from the City Bus Station in Lusaka to Chirundu; departures are throughout the morning, but you have to sort out transport from town to your accommodation.

If you have your own vehicle (you'll need a high-clearance 4WD), head down to Chirundu. As you enter the town, you are looking for a left-hand turn to Gwabi Lodge and from there into the GMA and on to the Chongwe Gate into the Lower Zambezi.

For budget travellers, ask at Bongwe Barn (p553) and Lusaka Backpackers (p553) in Lusaka or Jollyboys (p600) in Livingstone for deals on budget safaris into the Lower Zambezi.

Air

Proflight (p598) has twice-daily flights (in high season) between Lusaka and Royal Airstrip (30 minutes; in the GMA just a few kilometres west of Chongwe Gate) and Jeki Airstrip (40 min-utes; in the heart of the park); both are around ZMW820 one way. Royal is very convenient for the lodges near Chongwe Gate.

❶ Getting Around

Not far from Gwabi Lodge in the GMA is a pontoon (operational 6am to 6pm), which you'll need to take to cross a river; it costs ZMW40 for a Zambian-registered vehicle, ZMW100 for a non-Zambian registered vehicle, and foot passengers go free.

Remember that you'll need a well-equipped 4WD to access and get around the park. You must drive slowly in the GMA area and the park itself. There are several loops inside the park for wildlife viewing, but these change from year to year, so pick up a guide at any of the gates.

Siavonga
☑0211

Siavonga, the main town and resort along the Zambian side of Lake Kariba, has a location to be envied. Set among hills and verdant greenery, just a few kilometres from the massive Kariba Dam, the town has some stunning lake views. Built up primarily in the 1960s and '70s, though, it gives the impression that no architects, builders or designers have visited it since. Set up primarily for the conference-business market and wealthy urban Zambians, the town is a challenge to get to for independent travellers without their own wheels. The accommodation, though relatively affordable, is spread out, with just a market, a few shops, a bakery, a Zanaco bank with ATM, a post office and little else. But it is the closest 'beach vacation' to Lusaka and you can kick back or experience water activities such as canoeing through the Zambezi Gorge or a sunset cruise to the dam wall. Just don't think of putting your big toe in the water – crocs lurk around the lakeshore.

🏃 Activities

The lodges organise activities in and around the lake, including boat trips to the dam wall (price depends on boat size and ranges from ZMW135 to ZMW530), sunset cruises (per person ZMW75), fishing trips, longer-distance motoring around to Lottery Bay (ZMW1550) and one-day to four-night canoe safaris on the Zambezi where you'll canoe through the gorgeous Zambezi Gorge (these must be booked in advance and average around ZMW500 per person per day).

🛏 Sleeping & Eating

Eagles Rest CAMPGROUND, CHALET **$$**
(☑0211-511168; www.eaglesrestresort.com; campsites per person ZMW50, s/d incl breakfast ZMW400/550; ❋❄) With its own sandy area (swimming not recommended, of course), pool and the only campsite around town, Eagles Rest is easily the best set up for independent travellers. Large, spacious chalets overlook the lake, and the campground is well landscaped; tents (ZMW50) and mattresses (ZMW25) are available for rent. Everything from wakeboarding, tubing, fishing and canoeing can be arranged; the houseboat *Bateuleur* (sleeps 12) is available for rental March to November.

Lake Kariba Inns HOTEL **$$**
(☑0211-253768; www.karibainns.com; s/d from ZMW305/420; ❋@❂❄) Lush gardens, great lake views and relatively luxurious rooms – that is, at least an attempt to bring the decor into the modern era – make this a good choice for those who don't mind sharing space with conference attendees (the upside is a good gym and, for those who have spent too much time in the bush, a hair salon). The restaurant is a grandiose affair, overlooking the pool area, which is itself perched high above the lake.

Lake Safari Lodge LODGE **$$**
(☑0211-511148; www.lake-safari.com; s/d incl breakfast from ZMW400/500; ❋@❂❄) Slightly upmarket and nicely situated with an elevated position on the shore, Lake Safari is the longest-standing lodge in town. The large rooms come with cable TV and bland stylings. There are lovely landscaped grounds, including a nice pool area, giving the whole set-up a tropical vibe.

Sinazongwe
☑0213

Near the southwestern end of Lake Kariba and far from its cousin on the water at the other end of the lake, Sinazongwe is used

---

THE CURSE OF KARIBA

Beyond Victoria Falls, the Zambezi River flows through the Batoka Gorge then enters the waters of Lake Kariba, with the silhouettes of jagged Zimbabwean peaks far across its shimmering waters. Formed behind the massive Kariba Dam, this is one of the largest artificial lakes in Africa. When the local Tonga people learnt that the new lake would flood a huge rock buttress called Kariba, which they believe is the home of their river god, the fish-headed and serpent-tailed Nyaminyami, they were understandably angry. But when they found out that their own homes and ancestral lands would also be submerged it was the last straw, and they called on their god to step in and destroy the interference.

Did the god deliver? Oh, yes. In July 1957, about a year into the dam's construction, a torrential storm on the Upper Zambezi sent floodwaters roaring through the work site, breaching the temporary coffer dam and damaging equipment. The following March, there was an even greater flood – the sort expected only once in a thousand years, and never two years running – again destroying the coffer dam and causing major damage, as well as washing away a bridge that had been constructed downstream.

The engineers may have had a grudging respect for Nyaminyami by this time (they did increase the number of spillway gates from four to six), but the building continued and the dam was officially opened in 1960. Meanwhile, the justifiably disgruntled Tonga were forced to leave their homeland.

But Nyaminyami still had a final trick up his sleeve. No sooner had the lake begun to fill than a destructive floating weed called *Salvinia molesta* began choking the lake's surface. As the weed is native to South America, its arrival in Kariba remains a mystery. At one stage, a third of the lake was covered in a green carpet, rendering boating impossible and threatening to block the dam's outflow.

Finally, for reasons still not fully understood, the weed started to disappear, but other problems continued: in the early 1990s, a drought caused water levels to drop so low that there wasn't water enough to generate power. The rains returned and through 2000 and 2001 the lake was mostly full again. However, with rumours of earth tremors and cracks in the concrete, and concern over the dam's long-term strength and design – not to mention that another dam has been proposed at Batoka Gorge, below Victoria Falls – it remains to be seen whether Nyaminyami will rise in wrath again.

by *kapenta* fisherman as an outpost. The centre of the small town is actually up on a hill away from the lake's edge and the whole area has little tourism footprint.

A kilometre from town and easy to find is Lakeview Lodge (☑0976 667752; www. lakeview-zambia.com; campsites per person ZMW50, s/d incl breakfast ZMW250/470; ✿), where simple chalets with ceiling fans have a secluded terrace overlooking the lake and verdant grounds. There's also a pool, a small beach area and a *braai* (barbecue). Meals are ZMW40. You can hire a boat to Chikanka or Chete island.

A lot further away (60km from Sinazongwe), but with an excellent array of accommodation options, is Kariba Bush Club (☑0979 493980; www.karibabushclub.com; campsites per person ZMW50, dm ZMW110, r ZMW192; ✿). Traditional buildings have dorm accommodation as well as very tastefully furnished double, twin and family rooms and thatch-roofed chalets, and there are two wonderfully comfortable guesthouses for groups. Activities include walking safaris on the club's private islands (you can camp or stay in a safari tent on Maaze Island, 20 minutes away by speedboat). To get to the club, take the road to Maamba from Batoka on the main Lusaka–Livingstone Hwy; about 2km before Maamba take the dirt road to the left and follow the signs.

Ask in Choma for minibuses that can take you to Sinazongwe. By car, head to Batoka, just north of Choma. From here take the turn-off to Maamba. After about 50km look for the turn-off to Sinazongwe; the town is a short distance down this dirt road.

Choma

☑0213

This busy market town, the capital of the Southern Province, is strung out along the highway 188km northeast of Livingstone. Most people zip through, but Choma is a convenient stopover or staging post for trips to Lake Kariba and even to the southern section of Kafue National Park. Other than the museum there's not much to distinguish the town, though it has all of the facilities and services travellers need.

For anyone interested in regional history, Choma Museum (adult/child ZMW10/5; ⊙9am-5pm), about 1.5km east of the town centre, is worth a visit. Displays focus on the traditional practices of the Tonga people,

most of whom were forcibly displaced when the Kariba Dam was built, including possession dances, and some lovely beadwork.

Kozo Lodge & Lituwa Fast Foods (☑0977 619665; www.kozolodge.co.zm; s/d ZMW200/300) is about 7km south of Choma. Out the front, the large fast-food outlet is a common stop for tour groups; around the back is the lodge, which has chalets with fridges, fans and somewhat limited satellite TV. Being this far south of town, they're quiet and convenient for getting on the road the next morning.

Despite the two enormous stone carved lions out the front, Leon's Lodge (☑0978 666008; r ZMW180-200, chalets ZMW250-350), just off the main street (clearly signposted), is welcoming rather than grandiose. The large, clean rooms come with satellite TV and fridge; the thatch-roofed chalets are a step up in luxury.

All daily buses and trains between Livingstone and Lusaka stop at Choma. The bus to either Lusaka or Livingstone is ZMW65 or ZMW50 and there are many departures every day.

Lochinvar National Park

This small (410 sq km) park (admission US$10, vehicle US$15; ⊙6am-6pm), northwest of Monze, consists of grassland, low, wooded hills and the seasonally flooded Chunga Lagoon – all part of a huge World Heritage Wetland Site called the Kafue Flats. You may see buffaloes, wildebeest, zebras, kudus and some of the 30,000 Kafue lechwes residing in the park. Bushbucks, oribis, hippos, jackals, reedbucks and common waterbucks are also here. Lochinvar is a haven for bird life, with more than 400 species recorded. An excellent selection of wetland birds (including wattled cranes) occurs near the ranger post along the edge of Chunga Lagoon.

For history and geology fans, Gwisho Hot Springs is the site of a Stone Age settlement, today surrounded by palms and lush vegetation with steaming water far too hot to swim in.

Lochinvar was virtually abandoned in the 1980s; since then various developers have come and gone. Provided you bring all your own gear, you should be able to camp – ask the scouts at the gate for the latest on viable campsites within the park.

The best option for sleeping in the area with one of the nicer campgrounds in Zambia is Moorings Campsite (☎0977 521352; www.mooringscampsite.com; campsites ZMW35, s/d chalets ZMW175/250), located on an old farm 11km north of Monze. It's a lovely, secluded spot with plenty of grass and open-walled thatch huts with *braais*. Simple meals are available and day visitors can picnic here (ZMW5/2.50 per adult/child); proceeds are used to support an on-site clinic and the Malambo Women's Centre.

The network of tracks around the park is still mostly overgrown, with only the track from the gate to Chunga Lagoon reliably open. A 4WD with high clearance is recommended for getting to and around the park, though you may get stuck if you don't also have a winch.

WESTERN ZAMBIA

The little-visited western area, dominated by two huge rivers, the Kafue and the upper waters of the Zambezi, is home to the magnificent Kafue National Park, the biggest single park in Africa. Kafue has all the big mammals, marvellous birdwatching and a thousand different landscapes that include river systems offering the chance to float past a leopard stretched out on the shore.

Other highlights are thundering waterfalls and tremendous views of floodplains; a chance to experience even more remote wilderness areas, such as Liuwa Plain National Park, which sees few visitors but is a majestic patch of Africa; an exploration of Barotseland, home of the Lozi people and site of the colourful Kuomboka, Zambia's best-known traditional ceremony; and easy access to Botswana and Namibia, with world-class national parks such as Chobe to explore.

Kafue National Park

This stunning park (per person/vehicle US$15/15; ☉6am-6pm), about 200km west of Lusaka, is a highlight of Zambia. Covering more than 22,500 sq km (nearly the size of Belgium), it's the largest park in the country and one of the biggest in the world (ZAWA has only one scout for every 400 sq km). This is the only major park in Zambia that's easily accessible by car, with a handful of camps just off the highway.

The main road between Lusaka and Mongu runs through the park, dividing it into northern and southern sectors. (You don't pay the park fee of ZMW79 per person per day if in transit; self-drivers pay another ZMW79 per vehicle per day). There's an incredible number of animals to be seen just from the main road – wildlife watching doesn't get much easier than this! There are several gates, but three main ones: Nalusanga Gate, along the eastern boundary, for the northern sector; Musa Gate for the southern sector; and Tateyoyo Gate for either sector if you're coming from the west.

To the far north is Kafue's top highlight, the Busanga Plains, a vast tract of Serengeti-style grassland, covered by huge herds of near-endemic red lechwes and more solitary grazers such as roan antelopes and oribis. (Note that this area is accessible only between mid-July and November.) Attracted by rich pickings, lions (which climb the local sycamore figs – to keep cool and away from the flies – and swim through deep pools in the swamps during the wet season) and hyenas are plentiful, and during the dry season there are buffaloes, zebras, wildebeest herds and even a handful of wild dogs.

In the little-visited southern sector of the park, the vegetation is more dense, and early in the season the grass is very high, making animals harder to locate, although the thick woodland around Ngoma is the best place to see elephants. Lake Itezhi-Tezhi, a vast expanse of water, is both tranquil and beautiful, especially at sunset. In the far south, the Nanzhila Plains support an abundance of red lechwes, while other species include oribis, roan and sable antelopes, hartebeest, wildebeest and pukus.

🛏 Sleeping

Several lodges and camps are just outside the park boundaries, which means that you don't have to pay admission fees until you actually visit the park. An additional 'bed levy' (ZMW53) charged to tourists is usually included in the rates for the upmarket lodges, but elsewhere the levy is added to your accommodation bill (unless you're just camping).

Just Off the Lusaka–Mongu Highway

Mayukuyuku   CAMPGROUND, BUSHCAMP **$$**
(www.kafuecamps.com; campsites per person ZMW78, with full board ZMW802) A rustic bushcamp, small and personal, in a gorgeous spot on the river with a well-landscaped camping area and four tastefully furnished thatch-roofed safari tents. If you don't have

Kafue National Park

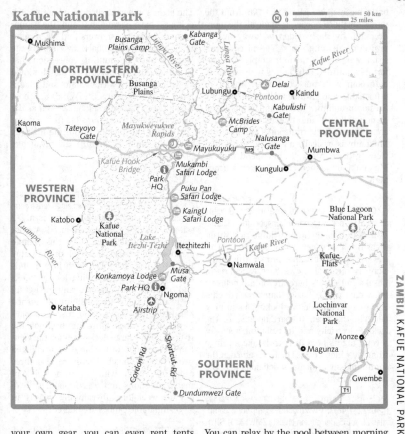

your own gear, you can even rent tents (ZMW78/130 per small/large tent). It's possible to self-cater, to have meals prepared with advance notice (dinner is ZMW150) or to stay with full board. Mayukuyuku is only 5km off the main highway on decent gravel; the camp does pick-ups (ZMW160 per vehicle) from the nearby bus stop (jump off any Lusaka–Mongu bus or minibus) or transfers from Lusaka (round trip ZMW2650).

TOP CHOICE **Mukambi Safari Lodge** CHALET **$$$**
(☏0974 424013; www.mukambi.com; per person with full board ZMW1422; ☎☑) Easily the most accessible of the Kafue lodges and easy to reach from Lusaka, Mukambi makes for a great base to explore the park. Tastefully designed *rondavels* (round huts) are set back from the riverfront and a few luxurious 'tents' (reserved for Busanga Plains Camp guests) have private back decks overlooking the river with their own outdoor claw-footed tubs!

You can relax by the pool between morning and afternoon activities. The beautifully designed dining area has a 2nd-floor lounge, a great spot for contemplating sunsets – that is, if you're not out on a sunset cruise on the motorised pontoon boat that covers a placid stretch of the river. Ask about camping, soon to be available nearby.

Northern Sector

Other than one highly recommended property, Wilderness Safari Company has a monopoly on accommodation in the Busanga Plains. Several other lodges and camps are in the centre and northeastern section and one, Delai, is outside the park proper in the Mushingashi Conservancy, a GMA/hunting concession with thriving wildlife.

TOP CHOICE **Busanga Plains Camp** TENTED CAMP **$$$**
(www.mukambi.com; all-inclusive per person ZMW 3409; ☉Jul-Oct) The approach to this bucolic

oasis, basically an island just 7km from the park's northern border, is made all the more dramatic by the wooden walkway over a prairie of 'floating grass'. The pièce de résistance of each of the four simply but comfortably outfitted safari tents is the outdoor bathroom with bucket shower. An air of informality and intimacy is encouraged by fireside pre-dinner drinks and meals taken communally in the thatch-roofed lounge area. The six-hour transport (160km) from Mukambi is basically an extended wildlife-viewing drive. Most visitors spend time at Mukambi on either end of their journey here.

Delai BUSHCAMP **$$$**
(☏0977 762096; www.bongwesafaris.com; 3 nights all-inclusive per person incl transport from Lusaka ZMW5800) Located in the wildlife-rich Mushingashi Conservancy just outside the north-eastern border of Kafue proper, this rustic camp is run by Bongwe Barn & Safaris in Lusaka (all guests here are on all-inclusive multi-day trips). Basic thatch-roofed chalets are on a hillside overlooking a stunning bend in the river. In part because of the lack of electricity and its isolation, a stay of several nights here feels truly like a refuge from the wider world. The food served at the communal-style meals is delicious and the portions are huge.

McBrides Camp CHALET, CAMPGROUND **$$$**
(☏0977 414871; www.mcbridescamp.com; campsites ZMW155, per person chalets ZMW1200) Situated at the confluence of the Mushingashi and Kafue Rivers, this genuine bushcamp is cleverly built around wildlife paths, assuring the regular presence of wild visitors. The seven chalets are spacious and simple, built of thatch and wood. The simple, shady campsite is the budget alternative and has two clean ablution blocks. Chris, one of the owners, has written three books on lions and is a font of knowledge.

Southern Sector

Contact lodges for driving directions from the Lusaka–Mongu highway. Charter flights can land at Chunga, the nearby airstrip.

Puku Pan Safari Lodge CAMPGROUND, CHALET **$$**
(☏in Lusaka 0211-266927; www.pukupansafari lodge.com; campsites per person ZMW156, chalets with full board & 1 activity per person ZMW1090; ☺year-round) A low-key, no-frills Zambian-managed compound beautifully situated overlooking the hippo- and croc-filled river.

The eight somewhat rustic mud-and-thatch cottages have verandahs, and the camp-grounds have hot showers and clean ablutions blocks. Out the back, overlooking the swamps and the hunting concession that surrounds the property, is a thatch-roofed viewing area with wicker chairs and a hammock. Walking safaris (ZMW106) and boat trips (ZMW132) are available as well as the usual wildlife drives. Transfers from Lusaka (ZMW260) and pick-ups from the highway near Mukambi (ZMW518) are available; prices are per vehicle.

TOP CHOICE **KaingU**

Safari Lodge CAMPGROUND, CHALET **$$$**
(☏in Lusaka 0211-256992; www.kaingu-lodge.com; campsites per person ZMW127, with full board & 2 activities ZMW1905; 🛜) Experienced African travellers especially will love this remote camp set on a magical stretch of the Kafue River – broad, but filled with lush islands among the rapids providing lots of nooks and crannies to explore, and delightful birdwatching. The four tastefully furnished Meru-style tents raised on rosewood platforms with stone bathrooms overlook the river and have large decks to enjoy the view. Families can opt for the large high-ceilinged two-bedroom chalet. There are also three campsites, each with its own well-kept thatch ablutions and *braai* facilities. Two-day to week-long fly-camping safaris in large, inflatable canoes are offered.

Konkamoya Lodge CHALET **$$$**
(www.konkamoya.com; all-inclusive per person ZMW1820; ☺mid-Jun–mid-Nov) Easily the best accommodation on the southern shores of Lake Itezhi-Tezhi, Konkamoya has five enormous and luxurious safari tents raised on wooden platforms with stunning lake-facing views. Morning and afternoon walks and wildlife drives are part of the daily schedule.

❶ Getting There & Away

Most guests of the top-end lodges and camps fly in on chartered planes. Transfers from the airstrip to the lodges and camps are often included in the rates.

For drivers, the main route into Kafue National Park is along the road between Lusaka and Mongu. It's about 200km from Lusaka to Nalusanga Gate; 30km west of Nalusanga Gate a road leads southwest towards Lake Itezhi-Tezhi. The road is in very bad condition, with only a small part graded; the rest is terrible – it's only accessible by a 4WD with high clearance. Note that the tsetse flies are bad down here. Just past Itezhitezhi village is Musa Gate, from where the road crosses Lake Itezhi-Tezhi.

For Mukambi Safari Lodge, continue west along the main road from Lusaka until about 10km before Kafue Hook Bridge and look for the signposted turn-off to the south. On the western side of the bridge, a main track leads into the northern sector of the park.

There's no public transport in the park, but you could easily catch a Mongu-bound Juldan or Shalom bus from Lusaka (ZMW100, three hours, 8am) to the highway stop near Mukambi Safari Lodge or Mayukuyuku. For a ride back to Lusaka, wait out by Hook Bridge or the stop by Mukambi between 11am and 11.30am.

Mongu
☏ 0217

The largest town in Barotseland, and the capital of the Western Province, is on high ground overlooking the flat and seemingly endless Liuwa Plain. There's plenty of activity on Mongu's streets but little to draw travellers apart from the spectacular panoramic views over the floodplains and the annual Kuomboka ceremony, when thousands flock here and room prices skyrocket. The town is quite spread out with no real centre; from a harbour on the southwestern outskirts, an 8km canal runs westwards to meet a tributary of the Zambezi. The river port is a settlement of reed and thatch buildings, where local fishermen sell their catch, and it's a good spot for people watching as longboats glide down the river transporting people and goods to nearby villages.

There are a few internet cafes around town.

🛏 Sleeping

Country Lodge   LODGE $
(☏ 0977 427777; countrylodge@iconnect.zm; 3066 Independence Ave; r incl breakfast ZMW175; ✳ 🛜)
Close to the centre of town, this modern and well-run place sees its fair share of conferences, weddings and the like. The rooms are plainly decorated, though they come with amenities like satellite TV and nice modern bathrooms; there's a bar and restaurant on site.

ⓘ Getting There & Away

The public bus station is on the southeastern edge of town, behind the Catholic church. Juldan and Shalom are the most recommended bus companies servicing the Lusaka to Mongu route (ZMW150, eight hours).

A daily bus operates between Livingstone and Mongu (ZMW125, 10 hours) via Sesheke, Kalongola and Senanga, but you might want to break up the journey in Senanga; minibuses and pick-ups leave on a fill-up-and-go basis from here (ZMW25, 2½ hours).

VISITING THE PALACES

The village of Limulunga is 15km north of Mongu. Here you can see the palace of the *litunga* – the king of the Lozi. It's a large traditional house, occupied by the *litunga* from around April to June, when his main residence at Lealui is flooded. You cannot go inside, and photos are not allowed. Of more interest is the Nayuma Museum (admission ZMW5; ⊙8am-5pm daily), with its colony of bats in the roof, and exhibits about the Lozi, the *litunga* and the Kuomboka, including a large model of the *nalikwanda* boat used in the ceremony. Minibuses run between Mongu and Limulunga throughout the day.

The village of Lealui, on the floodplain 15km northwest of Mongu, is the site of the *litunga*'s main palace; he lives here for most of the year (July to March), when the waters are low. The palace is a large single-storey Lozi house, built with traditional materials (wood, reeds, mud and thatch) and meticulously maintained. Around the palace are smaller houses for the *litunga*'s wives and family, and a tall reed fence surrounds the whole compound. It's not easy to reach, but the journey by boat (along a canal from Mongu to a branch of the Zambezi, then upstream to Lealui) is interesting, passing local villages and plenty of bird life. Avoid visiting at weekends, when the *litunga*'s *kotu* (court) is closed, because you need permission from his *indunas* (advisers) and the *kotu* is only open from Monday to Friday.

Public longboats between Mongu harbour and Lealui (ZMW10, one hour) leave once or twice a day. Alternatively, charter a boat to Lealui for about ZMW500 return (for up to six people). Make enquiries at the shed on the left as you enter the harbour. Buses do the trip in the latter months of the dry season.

Liuwa Plain National Park

About 100km northwest of Mongu, **Liuwa Plain National Park** (☎0977 158733; liuwa@africanparks.co.zm; per person per day US$40, campsites per person US$10, scout per day US$10) is 3600 sq km of true wilderness on the Angolan border. A remote and rarely visited wild grassland area, it's where vast numbers of wildebeest and other grazing species such as lechwes, zebras, tsessebes and buffaloes gather at the beginning of the wet season (November). Although their gathering is often called a migration, it's more of a meander, but the wall-to-wall herds are nonetheless spectacular. Roan antelopes, wild dogs, cheetahs and especially big and well-fed hyenas in particularly large numbers can be found in the park. Birdwatching is also a highlight; there are waterbirds such as wattled and crowned cranes, marabous, saddle-billed storks, herons, pelicans and egrets, among others.

Although it became a national park in 1972, for years the park was in decline with no government funds to rehabilitate it. However, an organisation called **African Parks** (www.african-parks.org), which assists African governments in funding conservation projects, signed a lease agreement in 2004, and now manages the welfare and facilities of the park.

Liuwa Plain is accessible from June to December, but the best time to go is November, just after the rains start (the later the better). Make sure you leave before the floodwaters rise, however, or you'll be stuck for months.

There are three campsites in the park, **Kwale**, **Lyangu** and **Katoyana**, that are open to independent travellers. Remember that you must be totally self-sufficient, including bringing all food for yourself and your guide.

Getting here independently, via the park headquarters at Kalabo, is restricted to well-equipped and completely self-contained vehicles and is a real expedition, hence the small visitor numbers (only 25 vehicles are allowed in at any one time; and a GPS is advisable). One of the only companies to offer all-inclusive organised trips is the highly recommended **Robin Pope Safaris** (www.robinpopesafaris.net); a trip out to Liuwa Plains will cost about ZMW17,200 for four nights.

KUOMBOKA CEREMONY

The Kuomboka (literally, 'to move to dry ground') is probably one of the last great Southern African ceremonies. It is celebrated by the Lozi people of western Zambia, and marks the ceremonial journey of the *litunga* (the Lozi king) from his dry-season palace at Lealui, near Mongu, to his wet-season palace on higher ground at Limulunga. It usually takes place in late March or early April, and sometimes ties in with Easter. The dates are not fixed, however; they're dependent on the rains. In fact the Kuomboka does not happen every year and is not infrequently cancelled because of insufficient floodwaters; the 2012 ceremony was called off because it's against Lozi tradition to hold the Kuomboka under a full moon.

The palace at Limulunga was built in 1933 by Litunga Yeta III. Although the Kuomboka was already a long-standing tradition, it was Yeta III who first made the move from Lealui to Limulunga a major ceremony.

Central to the ceremony is the royal barge – the *nalikwanda*, a huge wooden canoe, painted with black-and-white stripes, that carries the *litunga*. It is considered a great honour to be one of the hundred or so paddlers on the *nalikwanda*, and each paddler wears a headdress of a scarlet beret with a piece of lion's mane and a knee-length skirt of animal skins. Drums also play a leading role in the ceremony. The most important are the three royal war drums, *kanaona*, *munanga* and *mundili*, each more than 1m wide and said to be at least 170 years old.

The journey from Lealui to Limulanga takes about six hours. The *litunga* begins the day in traditional dress but during the journey changes into the full uniform of a British admiral, complete with all regalia including an ostrich-plume hat. The uniform was presented to the *litunga* in 1902 by King Edward VII, in recognition of the treaties signed between the Lozi and Queen Victoria.

Senanga

☏ 0217

If you're coming from Lusaka, Senanga has a real 'end of the line' feel – although the main street can be surprisingly lively, especially in the evening, and the views of the Zambezi are beautiful. It is the best place to break up a journey between Mongu and Ngonye (Sioma) Falls or Sesheke.

The best accommodation option is **Senanga Safaris** (☏ 0217-230156; campsites per person ZMW30, d incl breakfast ZMW321). It offers comfortable *rondavels* with splendid views over the Zambezi plains – spoilt only by the giant satellite TV dish in the garden. The bar sells cold beer and the restaurant serves expensive meals. Be warned that you may have difficulty getting accommodation when it hosts an annual fishing competition over a few days in the dry season.

Minibuses and pick-ups run between Senanga and Mongu (ZMW25, 2½ hours) several times a day. About 30km south of Senanga, the pontoon ferry (passengers free, 2/4WD vehicles ZMW100/150) across the Zambezi to the tiny settlement of Kalongola (marked as Sitoti on some maps, but this is a separate village about 5km south of Kalongola) on the west bank of the river is being replaced by a bridge. From here, a recently tarred road continues south towards Sesheke and Namibia.

Sioma & Ngonye Falls

☏ 0217

The village of Sioma is about 60km southeast of Kalongola. It has a large mission and a row of shops, and that's about it. The only reason to come here is **Ngonye Falls** (Sioma Falls; ⏱ 24hr) – a 1km-wide chain of waterfalls, rapids and rocky islands cutting across the Zambezi River. It's beautiful and very impressive and would be a major attraction if it weren't so difficult to reach.

If you can, stop at the National Parks & Wildlife Service office near the falls, which can advise on the best way to visit the falls and point out a local **campsite** (campsites US$10). You should be able to engage an official guide here.

Situated 8km south of Ngonye Falls, **Maziba Bay Lodge** (☏ 0927 11 234 1747; www.mutemwa.com/maziba.htm; all-inclusive per person US$320) has large wooden chalets with bathrooms and comfortable furnishings, and overlooks an idyllic sandy beach on the Zambezi.

The falls are less than 1km east of the main road, about 10km south of Sioma. For drivers, access is not difficult.

Sesheke

☏ 0211

Sesheke, 200km upstream from Livingstone (virtually opposite the Namibian town of Katima Mulilo), consists of two towns on either side of the Zambezi River linked by a new bridge. The major part of town is on the eastern side of the river, before you cross the bridge. There's not much to see or do here, it's really just a transit point between Zambia and Namibia. The smaller section of town, on the western side of the river, is centred on the Zambian border post, with the Namibian border a few hundred metres down the road.

Friendly **Brenda's Best & Baobab Bar** (☏ 0979 011917; campsites per person ZMW30, chalets ZMW150-250) is the best place to stay in Sesheke. It offers airy thatch-roofed chalets and a lovely campsite with a popular bar built around a massive baobab. The entrance to Brenda's is 200m beyond the western side of the church on the main street, down an unmarked road towards the river.

Small buses link Sesheke with Natakindi Rd in Livingstone (ZMW55, two hours, two daily), usually in the morning, and minibuses also make the run. Occasional minibuses also link Sesheke with Katima Mulilo.

NORTHERN ZAMBIA

Those with a spirit of adventure who love wild, open spaces will be at home in Zambia's untamed north. True, it can be difficult to get around, as the distances are vast and the tracks often rough, but this is all part of the experience.

Topping the list of attractions are Kasanka National Park, where you can camp by the side of a river and watch sitatungas splashing in the swamps at dawn from high up in a mahogany tree; Mutinondo Wilderness, a vast area of whaleback hills, rivers and valleys so untouched you feel almost transported to a prehistoric era; and striking Shiwa Ng'andu, a grand English mansion buried deep in the Zambian bush with a relaxing hot spring to enjoy.

Northern Zambia starts after the 'Pedicle', the slice of DR Congo territory that juts sharply into Zambia, almost splitting it in two. From here onwards the old Great North Rd shoots its way straight up to Tanzania, passing national parks, vast wilderness areas and waterfalls.

Serenje

📞 0215

Serenje is a relatively uninspiring town, spread out around the Great North Rd. The only reason for travellers to pass through is as a convenient refuelling stop (both petrol and food wise) on the way to more exciting destinations. There are two main hubs: the turn-off at the junction, which has a petrol station, a couple of shops and a few basic restaurants, and the town centre, 3km north of the Great North Rd, which has a bank, a market, a bus station and a couple of places to stay.

Mapontela Inn (📞 0215-382026; r ZMW175-235), with its leafy courtyard and bright, homey rooms, is the lodging of choice in town. The attached restaurant (meals ZMW15 to ZMW25) has a patio overlooking the street and serves tasty staples.

The basic Siga Siga Resthouse (📞 0215-382362; d with shared bathroom ZMW60) is a useful option for bus travel as it's right by the junction with the Great North Rd. There are a couple of restaurants nearby, including the guesthouse's own.

All buses between Lusaka (ZMW80, five hours) and Kasama (ZMW90, five hours) pass through Serenje. Most of the big buses stop beside the petrol station at the junction with the Great North Rd, while minibuses stop in town.

Kasanka National Park

One of Zambia's least known wilderness areas and a real highlight of a visit to this part of the country is the privately managed Kasanka National Park (www.kasanka.com; admission US$10; ☉ 6am-6pm). At just 390 sq km, it's pretty small compared with most African parks, doesn't have a huge range of facilities and sees few visitors, and this is what makes it special: you'll discover great tracts of *miombo* woodland, evergreen thicket, open grassland and rivers fringed with emerald forest, all by yourself.

Kasanka is perhaps most famous for its swampland, though, and this is the terrain in which to see the park's shy and retiring star, the sitatunga, a semi-aquatic antelope distinguished by its long, splayed hooves and oily coat. Between July and October you'll most likely see sable antelopes and hartebeest, and may also be treated to a glimpse of roan antelopes. Hippos and crocodiles inhabit the lakes and rivers here and there's a small population of elephants. During the months of November and December, this park is home to more than eight *million* migratory fruit bats – the biggest mammal gathering anywhere in the world – which can blanket the sky for several minutes at dusk. Bird spotters will also love Kasanka: 463 species have been recorded here.

👁 Sights & Activities

A trip to Kasanka isn't complete without viewing the park from the heights of the Fibwe Hide, a 15-minute drive from Wasa Lodge. Ascend 20m up an old mahogany tree via a rickety wooden ladder to a platform where you can sit and watch the swamps below. Come at dawn and dusk for the best chance of spotting sitatungas.

Game drives can be arranged at the main lodge for wildlife viewing in comfort. Drives cost ZMW140 per person (minimum two people). The lodge also arranges walking safaris – anything from a one-hour jaunt near the camp to a five-day extravaganza with an armed ranger, camping out in the bush.

Finally, gliding along the Luwombwa River in a canoe (per person ZMW40) or a motorboat (per person ZMW140) surrounded by bustling forest on either side is a wonderful way to get a different look at the park; fishing on the river can also be arranged.

🛏 Sleeping

There are two campsites in Kasanka, where you'll be surrounded by the stars, the noise of animals, and little else. The Pontoon Campsite (per person US$10) and the Kabwe Campsite (per person US$10) both look out over the Kasanka River. Both are 10km to 12km from the main Wasa Lodge and come equipped with long-drop toilets and bucket showers.

Wasa Lodge   LODGE $$$
(📞 873 76 2067957; www.kasanka.com; per person self-catering chalets ZMW267, with full board incl all activities ZMW1920) This lodge overlooking

Lake Wasa doubles as the park headquarters. Accommodation consists of thatched bungalows in two sizes; the larger chalets are airy and cool with wide balconies. There are several vantage points, including stone benches on the lakeshore, a small hide in the trees and the deck of the large bar and dining area. If you don't want the full-board option you bring your own supplies and the camp staff will cook for you.

ℹ Getting There & Away

From Lusaka, take a bus (ZMW110) in the direction of Mansa, or take any bus from Lusaka to Serenje and change to a minibus (ZMW35) for Mansa. After turning off the Great North Rd, ask the driver to drop you at Kasanka National Park (near Mulembo village), not at Kasanka village, which is much further away. From the gate to Wasa Lodge is 12km; you can radio Wasa Lodge for a lift. It is also possible to charter a taxi from Serenje directly to Wasa Lodge (ZMW150 to ZMW200).

If you have your own vehicle, continue north along the Great North Rd from Serenje for 36km, then turn left onto the road towards Mansa. It's then 55km on a good road to the Kasanka entrance gate, clearly signposted on the left. There is no fuel available in the park, so stock up at Serenje.

Around Kasanka

Drivers with 4WD and high clearance may like to take the 'back route' from Kasanka direct to the Great North Rd, which winds past several attractions.

History buffs can go in search of the David Livingstone Memorial – a simple stone memorial topped with a cross – which honours the famous explorer, who died here in 1873 whilst searching for the source of the Nile. The local villagers buried Livingstone's heart under a mupundu tree before his body was sent home to the mother country; the memorial marks that spot, though the tree is no longer there. To get here, pass the Kasanka National Park gate and continue 11km to the Livingstone Memorial turn-off, which will be on your right. Take the first left, from where it's another 25km to the memorial. However, the road is pretty bad, so it is really only for dedicated Livingstone buffs.

This route also winds past beautiful little Lake Waka-Waka, with glassy, croc-free waters (though always check the situation locally before jumping in) encircled by *miombo* woodland. Accommodation is in the form of a small community campsite (per person US$5) with basic bucket showers, barbecues and long-drop toilets. Local villagers will collect clean water for you and prepare fires. To get here, pass the Kasanka gates and take the turn-off to the Livingstone Memorial, but this time continue straight on for 35km, leaving the Livingstone Memorial road on your left.

In between Kasanka National Park and the Bangweulu Wetlands is the Nakapalayo Tourism Project (www.kasanka.com; campsites US$20, huts per person incl village tour & entertainment US$40), a community initiative that allows tourists to experience life in a real Zambian village. Visitors can camp, or stay in specially made huts with double beds and nets. Activities revolve around village life and include learning how to pound cassava, meeting local healers, and bush walks where you're taught about traditional uses for plants and trees. Meals (US$20 per person per day) are local fare, eaten with the villagers. Day visits are also available for ZMW106 per person. To get here, continue just past Lake Waka-Waka, where the road will fork. Take the left-hand fork and continue on for 35km to Chiundaponde, where you'll find the project.

Bangweulu Wetlands

The Bangweulu Wetlands is a watery wilderness of lakes, seasonally flooded grasslands, swamp and unspoilt miombo woodland that lies 50km to the north of Kasanka. This rarely visited part of Zambia is the only place in Africa to see major numbers of black lechwes (antelopes with long, curved antlers). There are estimated to be some 100,000 here, enough to rival the great wildebeest migrations of the Serengeti. The wetlands are also home to the swamp-dwelling sitatunga and many other antelope species. Attracted by rich pickings, jackals are often seen and hyenas often heard at night, and, when the floodwaters have receded, herds of elephants and buffaloes venture here.

Bangweulu is also known for its birds. Some 400 species have been noted, and a particular highlight for twitchers is the strange and rare shoebill stork. Other birds found here include crowned hornbills, swamp flycatchers, Denham's bustards, herons, ibises and storks, plus 15% of the world's wattled cranes.

The best time to see the lechwe herds is June to July, as the waters have begun receding, leaving vast plains of fresh green grass. September to November is great for general birdwatching, though you may not see shoebills at this time (March to April is best for these).

🛏 Sleeping

Nsobe Camp   CAMPGROUND $

(www.african-parks.org; campsites per person ZMW53) This is a basic campground with *braai* area, bucket showers, long-drop toilets and a couple of thatched cooking shelters. It is now under the management of African Parks.

Shoebill Island Camp   CAMPGROUND $$$

(www.kasanka.com; per person tents US$50, incl meals & activities US$360) This camp rests in the heart of the wetlands and is splendidly positioned on a tiny permanent island with only birds, hippos, lechwes and the occasional passing fisher for company. Guests stay in safari tents and there's a dining area and lookout point. Most activities revolve around dugout canoes, but drives and guided walks are also on offer. The camp is sometimes inaccessible from January to April.

❶ Getting There & Away

The only way into the wetlands is by vehicle and chartered plane. Dirt roads lead here from Kasanka via Lake Waka-Waka and the Nakapalayo Tourism Project. The Chikuni ranger post and Nsobe Camp are 65km on from Nakapalayo, and from here it's another 10km to Shoebill Island Camp if it's dry. When it's wet, you have to travel this last stretch by boat. You will definitely need a fully equipped 4WD to attempt this trip as the going is tough.

There's an airstrip 3km from Shoebill Island Camp and charters from Lusaka are available.

Samfya

Perched on the western shore of Lake Bangweulu, about 10km east of the main road between Mansa and Serenje, is Samfya, a small and dusty trading centre with little going for it except for its excellent location. Just outside town is a long strip of blinding white beach bathed by startlingly blue waters. Don't jump in here, though, unless you fancy being a crocodile's dinner.

Located on the shores of the lake, the **Bangweulu Bay Lodge** (☑in Lusaka 0211-266927; www.bangweulubaylodge.com; r per person US$150-180) offers three smart guest chalets with views over the beach and blue waters beyond. Activities on tap include hobie-cat sailing, boat trips and wildlife spotting in the area.

Samfya Beach Hotel (campsites per person ZMW50, r ZMW150) has a pretty good location sitting on Cabana Beach, though the rooms are small and the bathrooms basic. Camping is an affordable option for those with a tent. Take the first turning on the left in town and it's about 2km north of the centre.

Samfya is regularly served by minibuses from Serenje (ZMW70, four to five hours). Buses from Lusaka (ZMW120, 10 hours) may drop you into town or at the junction 10km away, from where local pick-ups shuttle passengers to and fro.

Mutinondo Wilderness

This is one of the most stunning places in northern Zambia. Mutinondo is a beautiful 10,000-hectare wilderness littered with whaleback hills or inselbergs: huge, sweeping hulks of stone in varying shades of black, purple, green and brown. The landscape here feels unspoilt and somehow ancient. Scramble to the top of one of those great granite beasts and it is easy to imagine a time when Stone Age hunters wandered the endless valleys, woodland and rivers below.

Mammal sightings are rare here, although there are plenty of tree squirrels, klipspringers and other antelopes (roan, sable, reedbuck and bushbuck) lurking around out of sight. Mutinondo is an important birding destination and there are about 320 species here, including plenty of rare specimens. Notable are the Ross's turaco, the Anchieta's sunbird and the bar-winged weaver.

Other than hiking and taking in the views, you can canoe and swim in the river, ride horses and, during the mushroom-friendly rainy season, go in search of the largest edible mushroom in the world.

🛏 Sleeping

TOP CHOICE Mayense Camp   LODGE $$$

(www.mutinodozambia.com; s/d per person incl meals & activities from ZMW600/550) Built into the hillside are a handful of individually designed chalets, which, while not luxurious, are beautiful in their simplicity and blend in seamlessly with their natural environment. All have outstanding views and the majority are open to the elements; the camp uses a number of alternative energy sources and the kitchen uses as much locally sourced produce as possible. Campers at other sites can enjoy hearty home-cooked meals (a three-course dinner is ZMW120).

ℹ Getting There & Away

The turn-off to Mutinondo is 164km past Serenje heading north on the Great North Rd. It's signposted to the right; Mutinondo is 25km down a 2WD-friendly track.

Travelling by bus from Lusaka, ask for a ticket to Kalonje Railway Station (ZMW110, six hours). Road transfers for a maximum of five people can be arranged from the Great North Rd turn-off (ZMW180). There's also an airstrip for charters.

Shiwa Ng'andu

Deep in the northern Zambian wilderness sits Shiwa Ng'andu (www.shiwangandu.com; tours US$20; ⊕9-11am Mon-Sat, closed to nonguests Sun), a grand country estate and the labour of love of eccentric British aristocrat Sir Stewart Gore-Brown. The estate's crowning glory is Shiwa Ng'andu Manor House, a glorious brick mansion. Driving up to the house through farm buildings, settlements and workers houses, it almost feels like an old feudal domain. Today Gore-Brown's grandchildren live on and manage the estate, which is a working farm.

Shiwa House, full of old family heirlooms, photographs and stories, is the main draw and visitors can go on guided tours. Standing on the perfectly tended lawns, you could almost forget that you're in Southern Africa and imagine instead that you're at a 1920s garden party on an English summer's day.

Guided tours of the estate (home to 27 species of mammal and 380 species of bird), in a car or on foot, are possible, though you are also free to wander.

About 20km west of Shiwa House, but still on the Shiwa Ng'andu estate, is Kapishya Hot Springs (guests/nonguests of Kapishya Lodge free/ZMW26). The setting is marvellous – a blue-green, steaming lagoon of hot water surrounded by palms. From the lodge, walking, fishing and canoeing trips are also offered.

🛏 Sleeping

TOP CHOICE **Kapishya Hot Springs Lodge**　　　LODGE $$
(☑0211-229261; www.shiwasafaris.com; campsites US$10, per person chalets US$60, d incl breakfast & dinner US$110; 🕱🏊) Light and spacious chalets have wide wooden decks complete with fireplaces and views over the river and gardens; also has a lovely campground with free firewood, hot showers and barbecue areas. Excellent meals (full breakfast ZMW100, packed lunch ZMW50, three-course dinner ZMW150) are available. The owners have recently added a spa on the banks of the river.

Shiwa House　　　HISTORIC HOTEL $$$
(☑0211-229261; www.shiwasafaris.com; d per person with full board from US$350) This old place is suitably attired for a grand English manor, with fireplaces, four-poster beds, oil paintings and big roll-top baths. There's a glorious guest sitting room looking out onto the front lawn, lit by candles and a crackling fire at night. Tasty dinners are taken in the rather splendid dining room. The hosts (the grandchildren of Sir Stewart Gore-Brown) are happy to chat and to give you tours of the house. Guests can browse the Gore-Brown archives, a fascinating collection of Sir Stewart's journals, letters and photographs.

ℹ Getting There and Away

To reach Shiwa House, head along the highway by bus (or car) from Mpika for about 90km towards Chisoso. Look for the signpost to the west, from where a 20km dirt road leads to the house. Kapishya Hot Springs and the lodge are a further 20km along this track. You can also get to Shiwa from the Mpika-to-Kasama road; this time look for the signpost pointing east and it's then 42km down the dirt track to Kapishya. There is no public transport along this last section, but vehicle transfers are available from the Great North Rd turn-off for ZMW212 per vehicle (maximum four people). Transfers are also available between Kapishya and Shiwa House for ZMW159 per vehicle.

Kasama
☑0214

Kasama is the capital of the Northern Province and the cultural centre of the Bemba people, and with its wide, leafy streets and handsome old tin-roofed colonial houses, it is the most appealing of the northern towns.

Thorn Tree Guesthouse (☑0214-221615; www.thorntreesafaris.com; 612 Zambia Rd; s/d

THE SHIWA STORY

In 1914 Stewart Gore-Brown, a young British colonial officer, was helping establish the border between Rhodesia and the Belgian Congo when he stumbled across a lake that the local Bemba people called Shiwa Ng'andu, or the place of the royal crocodiles. For years he'd harboured dreams of his own kingdom in Africa, and with characteristic verve he decided this was the ideal spot, swiftly buying about 10,000 hectares from the local chief and returning after the end of WWI to build his little piece of England in the bush.

The heart of the estate was the great mansion of Shiwa House, made from materials found locally, or transported on foot by porters from the nearest town of Ndola, a 300km, three-week walk away. Essentials such as grand pianos and fine wines were shipped from London. The house sat overlooking the lake, complete with manicured lawns and servants clad in white gloves and pillbox hats. Around the house grew an estate, which included houses for 2000 employees, schools and a post office.

All of this upkeep was expensive and Gore-Brown tried many money-making schemes, including growing flowers from which to extract and export oils for perfume, but none ultimately succeeded, and Shiwa was continually bankrolled by his wealthy aunt in Britain.

Gore-Brown was a stickler for discipline in his attempts to create a utopian fiefdom, and his violent temper was legendary. But, unusually for the time, he believed in African independence and became a well-known figure in Northern Rhodesia and in Britain. He was knighted by George VI and was close friends with early nationalists, including Kenneth Kaunda, Zambia's first president. When he died in 1967 he was, uniquely for a white colonist, given a full state funeral and is buried on the hill overlooking the lake at Shiwa.

Through the 1980s, Gore-Brown's daughter and son-in-law continued struggling to run the estate, and were actively involved in the campaign against poachers, especially in nearby North Luangwa National Park. In 1992 they were mysteriously murdered. Shiwa House stood empty for several years, and rapidly disintegrated, but in 2001 Gore-Brown's grandsons began a major renovation and opened the house to visitors again.

Stewart Gore-Brown's story is described (or perhaps romanticised) in *The Africa House* by Christina Lamb.

ZMW230/290, f from ZMW350; 🕾), well sign-posted from the centre of town, is family run, homely and very popular – you should definitely book before turning up. There's a bar and a restaurant serving fresh farm produce and it can organise tours of little-visited parts of the northern region.

The JB Hotel (Golf Rd; mains ZMW20-40) has a good restaurant at the rear that serves local dishes such as *nshima* and chicken as well as sea-bream curry and chicken schnitzel.

Buses and minibuses leave for Lusaka (ZMW130, 10 hours) daily. Buses go via Mpika (ZMW75, two hours) and Serenje (ZMW95, four hours). Northbound buses go to Mbala (ZMW35, two hours) and Mpulungu (ZMW40, three hours). The Tazara train station is 6km south of the town centre.

Mbala

This sleepy town sits on the periphery of the Great Rift Valley, from where the road drops over 1000m down to Lake Tanganyika. It was once a colonial centre called Abercorn, and today the only reason to visit is the local museum, or as a way station en route to Kalambo Falls. Moto Moto Museum (admission ZMW15; ⊘9am-4.45pm), about 3km from the town centre, is a huge and fascinating collection of artefacts based on the cultural life of the Bemba people. Particularly noteworthy is an exhibition detailing how young Bemba women were traditionally initiated into adulthood.

The most atmospheric and welcoming place to stay in Mbala is Lake Chila Lodge (📞0977 795241; lakechilalodge@yahoo.com; Lake Chila; r ZMW150), located on the lakeshore about 2km from town. Rooms are set in spacious chalets with hot showers and satellite TV. The lodge includes a lively bar-restaurant (mains ZMW20 to ZMW40), which makes for a good rest stop on a road trip.

Minibuses run a couple of times a day to Kasama (ZMW35, two hours) and Mpulungu (ZMW15, 50 minutes), leaving from the main street.

Kalambo Falls

About 40km northwest of Mbala, along the border between Zambia and Tanzania, is the 221m-high Kalambo Falls (adult/child/car US$15/7/15, campsites US$10). Twice as high (but nowhere near as expansive) as Victoria Falls, Kalambo is the second-highest single-drop waterfall in Africa (the highest being Tugela Falls in South Africa). From spectacular viewpoints near the top of the falls, you can see the Kalambo River plummeting off a steep V-shaped cliff cut into the Rift Valley escarpment down into a deep valley, which then winds towards Lake Tanganyika. There is a very basic campground here, with stunning views out over the Great Rift Valley.

The best way for travellers without a car to get here is from Mpulungu. A thrice-weekly taxi-boat service (ZMW25) stops at villages east of Mpulungu. It moves quite slowly and makes plenty of stops, so just getting to the base of the falls can take all day. Avoid arriving in the dark, as it's two to three hours' walking uphill to the viewpoint near the top of the falls (and the campsite). It's also possible to hire a private boat from Mpulungu harbour, which will cost around ZMW700 a day, including fuel.

Another alternative is to stay in one of the lakeshore lodges near the falls, from where you could hike to the falls or visit on an organised boat trip.

Travel by road is possible, but only with a 4WD, as the road is in very poor condition, with plenty of deep, sandy stretches.

Mpulungu

☑0214

Resting at the foot of mighty Lake Tanganyika, Mpulungu is a crossroads between Eastern, Central and Southern Africa and the terminal for the ferry across the lake to Tanzania. The streets are fairly lively and busy, especially at night, but there is no real reason to come here unless you're travelling north to Nsumbu National Park and Ndole Bay or northeast to Tanzania.

Nkupi Lodge (☑0214-455166; nkupilodge@ hotmail.com; campsites per person ZMW40, dm ZMW75, rondavels from ZMW125), a short walk out of town near the lake, is the best place for independent travellers. It has plenty of space for tents as well as a number of spacious *rondavels* and there's a self-catering kitchen and a bar, or food can be prepared with notice.

Long-distance buses link Mpulungu with Kasama (ZMW40, three hours) and Mpika (ZMW100, six hours). Minibuses also depart from near the BP petrol station for Mbala (ZMW15, 40 minutes).

Nsumbu (Sumbu) National Park

Hugging the southern shores of Lake Tanganyika, little-visited Nsumbu (admission US$10; ⊙6am-6pm) is a beautiful 2020 sq km of hilly grassland and escarpment, interrupted by rivers and wetlands. Like other remote parks in Zambia, Nsumbu was virtually abandoned in the 1980s and 1990s, and poaching seriously affected wildlife stocks here. Conditions have improved over the past decade, though. Poaching has come under control, and animal numbers have increased, in part thanks to a buffer zone created by two game management areas that adjoin the park.

Herds of elephants and buffaloes are seen here once again, often coming to the lake to drink. There are also plenty of antelopes, including roan and sable antelopes, waterbucks and sitatungas. All of these animals attract predators, and these days lions and hyenas can often be heard at night. In the lake itself are hippos as well as some of the largest crocodiles in Africa. For anglers, Lake Tanganyika offers top-class sport: Nile perch, tigerfish and *nkupi* (yellow belly) are plentiful, while golden perch and giant tigerfish all exist in the waters.

🛏 Sleeping

TOP CHOICE **Ndole Bay Lodge**　　　　　LODGE $$

(☑088-2165 2077; www.ndolebaylodge.com; campsites US$11, per person chalets with full board from US$100; ☀) Set on a pretty beach just outside Nsumbu National Park, this lodge has several spacious chalets made from natural local materials – the newest ones include a huge attached bathroom with Balinese-style outdoor showers. There is also a campground under the trees on the sandy beach. Fresh Lake Tanganyika fish is on the menu at the restaurant. All kinds of activities are on offer here, including snorkelling, waterskiing, bush walks, fishing trips and even scuba diving. Or try a sailing trip up Lake Tanganyika in a wooden dhow, including fishing and diving on the side and rainforest and water-fall walking safaris.

Nkamba Bay Lodge
LODGE $$$

(☑027 73 690 2992; www.nkambabaylodge.com; per person with full board & activities US$180-400; ✖) This exclusive private lodge set in a gorgeous, pristine cove is the only accommodation operating within the park itself. Nine luxurious and spacious chalets are decorated with Africana and the bathrooms and balconies overlook either the lake or the bush. There's also a small swimming pool (you can't swim in the lake here because of crocodiles and hippos), and the food is excellent and plentiful. Game drives, birdwatching and fishing are the main activities, but canoe trips or walks in the surrounding rainforest are also available.

❶ Getting There & Away

Each lodge will arrange transfers for guests from the airstrip in the national park, or across the lake from Mpulungu. **Proflight** (☑0211-271032; www.proflight-zambia.com) offers charter flights to Kasaba Bay on a five-seater plane.

Slow local passenger boats (ZMW60 one way) chug up and down the lake heading north to Nsumbu on Thursday and Friday and heading south to Mpulungu on Monday and Wednesday. Boat charters to either lodge start from ZMW1318 one way for a slow boat.

Hardy overlanders can drive, but aim to come from the southwest, where the roads are in better condition. A new road is nearing completion from Mbala direct to Nsumbu – check with the lodges for up-to-date information.

THE COPPERBELT

Not on the radar for most visitors unless they happen to be mining consultants, the Copperbelt Province is the industrial heartland of Zambia and the main population centre outside of Lusaka. The region is home to the unique attraction of Chimfunshi Wildlife Orphanage, the largest chimpanzee sanctuary in the world.

The world copper market slumped during the 1970s, so vast opencast mines cut back production, creating high unemployment in the area. The cost of copper and cobalt went through the roof in the early 21st century and has once more seen the region prosper as Zambia records impressive economic growth.

Kapiri Mposhi

☑0215

This uninspiring transit town, about 200km north of Lusaka, is at the southern end of the Tazara railway from Dar es Salaam (Tanzania) and at the fork in the roads to Lusaka, the Copperbelt and northern Zambia.

Coming from Tanzania, there's a passport check before exiting the station, then from outside the station there's a mad rush for buses to Lusaka and elsewhere. Thieves and pickpockets thrive in the crowds and confusion, so stay alert.

Buses and minibuses from Lusaka (ZMW50, three hours) leave regularly and are a quicker and more convenient option than the irregular local trains.

Ndola

☑0212 / POP 500,000

Ndola, the capital of the Copperbelt Province, is a peaceful, prosperous little city that provides relief from the pace, pollution and chaos of its larger cousin, Lusaka. However, other than the Copperbelt Museum (☑0212-617450; Buteko Ave; adult/child ZMW25/10; ⊙9am-4.30pm), which showcases the local industry as well as artefacts of traditional culture in the area, there are few genuine attractions for the average visitor.

While the New Savoy Hotel (☑0212-611097; savoy@zamnet.zm; Buteko Ave; r incl breakfast ZMW500-1100; ❋@✖) is a bit of a hulking concrete block from the outside, inside it's upholding standards well: old-fashioned, true, but not without a certain charm.

'New' is rather optimistic given the creaky state of the corridors of the New Ambassador Hotel (☑0212-374396; President Ave; r ZMW140-550), but the spacious rooms are of reasonable value.

The dining destination in Ndola is Michelangelo (☑0212-620325; 126 Broadway; mains ZMW35-65; ⊙breakfast, lunch & dinner; ❋🛈), which does impressively authentic pizza and homemade pasta and ground coffee. There's also a small boutique hotel attached.

Ndola is about 325km north of Lusaka. Proflight (☑0211-271032; www.proflight-zambia.com) flies daily to Lusaka (from ZMW316 one way); South African Airlink (☑0211-254350; www.saairlink.co.za) has daily flights to Johannesburg from US$400 one way and

Kenya Airways (☏0212-620709; www.kenya-airways.com) has daily flights to Nairobi from US$600 one way. The airport is 3.5km south of the public bus station.

From the public bus station, at the southern end of Chimwemwe Rd, three blocks south of Buteko Ave, minibuses and buses run every few minutes to Kitwe (bus ZMW15, 45 minutes). Long-distance buses depart from the stand next to the Broadway–Maina Soko roundabout and run to Lusaka (ZMW65, four hours, around 10 buses daily). The train station is 700m north of the museum, but trains to Lusaka (ZMW25, Monday and Friday) are infrequent and slow.

Avis (☏0212-620741) and Voyagers (☏0212-620604) both have offices at the airport.

Kitwe

☏0212 / POP 700,000

Zambia's second-largest city and the centre of the country's mining industry, Kitwe seems far larger than quiet Ndola. Business travellers (read: mining consultants) stop here for the good selection of accommodation and eating places.

Mukwa Lodge (☏0212-224266; www.mukwalodge.co.zm; 26 Mpezeni Ave; s/d incl breakfast ZMW585/690) has gorgeous, beautifully furnished rooms with stone floors – the bathrooms are as good as you'll find in Zambia. Its well-laid-out restaurant, the Courtyard Cafe (☏0212-224266; 26 Mpezeni Ave; mains ZMW55-75; ⊙10am-2.30pm & 6-10pm), is a soothing dining sensation, especially with the sound of trickling water in the courtyard garden.

Dazi Lodge (☏0955 460487; Pamo Ave; r ZMW200-350; ﹡) has a wonderful kitschy air about it. Some rooms have private bathrooms, others come with shared facilities, and all are spick and span.

Formerly Arabian Nights, Heer (☏0212-229530; 11 Mushita Cl; mains ZMW60-95; ⊙noon-2.30pm & 6-10.30pm; ﹡🛜) is one of the top restaurants in the region, featuring subcontinental curries, European dishes and sizeable cuts of meat.

Kitwe is about 60km northwest of Ndola. The public bus station is situated 500m west of Independence Ave, and the train station (☏0212-223078) is at the southern end of Independence Ave. Frequent minibuses and buses run to Lusaka (ZMW70, five hours), Ndola (ZMW15, 45 minutes) and Chingola (ZMW15, 30 minutes).

Voyagers (☏0212-617062; Enos Chomba Ave) is very helpful and can organise car hire and other travel arrangements.

Chingola

☏0212

Chingola is basically a huge mine with a settlement wrapped around it. The reason to come here is because it's the closest town to Chimfunshi and has a decent range of accommodation. Traditional bed and breakfast is served up at homely English-style New Hibiscus Guest House (☏0212-313635; hibiscus@copperbeltlodging.com; 33 Katutwa Rd; r per person incl breakfast US$70, with full board US$100; @🛜﹡), or try the Protea (☏0212-310624; www.proteahotels.com; Kabundi St; s/d US$149/165; ﹡@🛜﹡), sparkling with modern amenities and featuring a pool. Chingola is 50km northwest of Kitwe. The bus station (13th St) is in the centre of town. There are frequent buses and minibuses to Kitwe (ZMW15, 30 minutes).

Chimfunshi Wildlife Orphanage

On a farm deep in the African bush, about 70km northwest of Chingola, this chimpanzee sanctuary (www.chimfunshi.org.za; day visit adult/child project area ZMW50/25; ⊙9am-3pm) is home to around 120 adult and young chimps, most of which have been confiscated from poachers and traders in neighbouring Congo or other parts of Africa. It's the largest sanctuary of its kind in the world. This is not a natural wildlife experience, but it's still a unique and fascinating opportunity to observe the chimps as they feed, play and socialise. It is undoubtedly the standout highlight in the Copperbelt region.

Entry fees go directly towards helping the sanctuary remain financially viable. Ensure that you do not come if you're sick; the chimps can easily die of a simple disease like the flu. The best time to visit is for the 1.30pm feed, when the chimps are out in the open (not in the concrete blocks they enter for their morning feed). A very special way to experience this place is to do a chimpanzee bush walk (ZMW520) with some of the younger chimps. Volunteering opportunities are available too.

It is possible to stay overnight at the campground (per person ZMW75) or in the self-catering cottage (adult/child ZMW150/75) at the education centre, which has 10 beds and linen.

By car, there's a new, well-signposted road that starts about 55km from Chingola. It's about 20km off the main road straight to the project area. Contact the sanctuary in advance and staff can arrange a one-way transfer for ZMW100 to coincide with a supply run. Although buses between Chingola and Solwezi can drop passengers at the turnoff, it's generally easier to visit with a private vehicle.

UNDERSTAND ZAMBIA

Zambia Today

In September 2011 Michael Sata, nicknamed 'King Cobra', and his party, the Patriotic Front (PF), won national elections. This made Sata only the fifth president in Zambia's post-independence history. The tables have turned on the two major opposition parties, the Movement for Multiparty Democracy (MMD; the party of Frederick Chiluba, Levy Mwanawasa and Rupiah Banda) and the United National Independence Party (UNIP; the party of Kenneth Kuanda), which now face a familiar strain of authoritarianism in the form of the PF's 'mild' hostility to a free press and a series of laws passed with little consultation.

There's an undercurrent of worry that Sata's rhetoric and some of his decisions, as well as his continued support of Robert Mugabe in Zimbabwe, augur a move towards a more centralised economy and less democratic government. After Sata's inauguration, he sacked and replaced all of the Supreme Court judges with new handpicked ones. In a highly publicised move, he snubbed former US president George W Bush and his wife, Laura, when they visited Zambia in July 2012 promoting health and anti-poverty initiatives. In a disturbing move in the eyes of conservationists, he ordered the release of hundreds of prisoners, including many doing time for illegal poaching.

However, observers claim that the populist strain in Sata's rhetoric and policy, including the revaluing of the country's currency, motivated more by symbolism than economics, also indicates a sincere focus on redirecting the country's wealth to the majority of Zambians who are poor. To this end, Sata announced a significant increase in the minimum wage in September 2012 and his administration continues to encourage Zambian participation and ownership in the tourism industry.

Almost half of all Zambians live in urban centres, crowding into housing compounds, where water shortages and overstretched sewerage systems cause all sorts of health problems. Most unskilled city labourers work six to seven days per week, with their families sometimes living on less than US$1 per day. Still, a small middle class and expats frequent high-end shops and cinemas in Lusaka's malls and the music industry is thriving, in part because ordinary Zambians can listen to and share music on their Bluetooth mobile phones. Life hasn't changed much in rural Zambia: subsistence farmers still eke out a living at the whim of crop success or failure, and traditional religions mixed with Christian beliefs and village hierarchies are the mainstays. (Ironically, the production of Christian-themed music videos, usually with a chorus of 'church ladies,' is big business in Lusaka.)

Two of the more pressing contemporary issues are the impact on Zambia of rebounding tourism in Zimbabwe, and the influence of Chinese investment in the mining sector. During Sata's presidential campaign he argued against such investment, worried about workers' rights and pay. Perhaps unsurprisingly, his administration has since been more welcoming. Conflict has sporadically spilled over into violence, and tensions over the business practices and benefits of China's influence continue to press on the government.

History

The first of the 'modern' (ie still found today) ethnic groups of Zambia to arrive were the Tonga and Ila peoples (sometimes combined as the Tonga-Ila), who migrated from the Congo area in the late 15th century. Next to arrive were the Chewa. Between the 14th and 16th centuries they followed a long and circuitous route via Lakes Mweru, Tanganyika and Malawi before founding a powerful kingdom covering much of present-day eastern Zambia, as well as parts of Malawi and Mozambique.

The Bemba had migrated from Congo by crossing the Luapula River into northern Zambia by around 1700. Meanwhile, the Lamba people migrated to the area of the

Copperbelt in about 1650. At around the same time, the related Lala settled in the region around Serenje.

Meanwhile, in western Zambia, the Lozi people established a dynasty and the basis of a solid political entity that still exists. The Lozi's ancestors may have migrated from what is now Angola as early as AD 450.

Early 19th Century

In the early 19th century, the fearsome reputation of the newly powerful and highly disciplined warrior army under the command of Shaka Zulu in Kwa-Zulu Natal (South Africa) led to a domino effect of groups living in his path fleeing elsewhere and in turn displacing other groups. This included the Ngoni, who fled to Malawi and Zambia, and the Makololo, who moved into southern Zambia, around the towns of Kalomo and Monze, and eventually were forced further west into southwest Zambia, where they displaced more Tonga people.

Also around this time, the slave trade – which had existed for many centuries – increased considerably. Swahili-Arabs, who dominated the trade on the east coast of Africa, pushed into the interior; many people from Zambia were captured and taken across Lake Malawi and through Mozambique or Tanzania to be sold in the slave markets of Zanzibar.

Colonial Era

David Livingstone, the Scottish explorer, journeyed through large swaths of Zambia, including the lower Zambezi, where he came upon a magnificent waterfall never before seen by a European, naming it Victoria Falls in homage to royalty back home. On a subsequent trip, Livingstone died while searching for the source of the Nile in northern Zambia. His heart was buried under a tree near the spot where he died, in Chief Chitambo's village, southeast of Lake Bangweulu.

In 1885 claims over African territory by European powers were settled at the Berlin Conference and the continent was split into colonies and spheres of influence – Britain claimed Rhodesia (Zambia and Zimbabwe) and Malawi.

This 'new' territory did not escape the notice of entrepreneur Cecil John Rhodes, who was already establishing mines and a vast business empire in South Africa. Rhodes' British South Africa Company (BSAC) laid claim to the area in the early 1890s and was backed by the British government in 1895 to help combat slavery and prevent further Portuguese expansion in the region.

Two separate territories were initially created – North-Western Rhodesia and North-Eastern Rhodesia – but these were combined in 1911 to become Northern Rhodesia. In 1907, Livingstone became the capital. At around the same time, vast deposits of copper were discovered in the area now called the Copperbelt.

In 1924 the colony was put under direct British control and in 1935 the capital was moved to Lusaka. To make them less dependent on colonial rule, settlers soon pushed for closer ties with Southern Rhodesia and Nyasaland (Malawi), but various interruptions (such as WWII) meant that the Federation of Rhodesia and Nyasaland did not come about until 1953.

Independence & Kaunda

In Zambia the United National Independence Party (UNIP) was founded in the late 1950s by Dr Kenneth Kaunda, who spoke out against the federation on the grounds that it promoted the rights of white settlers to the detriment of the indigenous African population. As other African countries gained independence, Zambian nationalists opposed colonial forces through civil disobedience and a small but decisive conflict called the Chachacha Rebellion.

Northern Rhodesia became independent a year after the federation was dissolved and changed its name to Zambia. While the British government had profited enormously from Northern Rhodesia, the colonialists chose to spend a large portion of this wealth on the development of Southern Rhodesia (now Zimbabwe).

After gaining independence, Zambia inherited a British-style multiparty political system. Kaunda, as leader of the majority UNIP, became the new republic's first president. The other main party was the African National Congress (ANC), led by Harry Nkumbula. But Kaunda disliked opposition. In one swift move during 1972, he disbanded the Zambian ANC, created the 'second republic', declared UNIP the sole legal party and made himself the only presidential candidate.

Consequently, Kaunda remained in power for the next 27 years. His rule was based upon 'humanism' – his own mix of Marxism and traditional African values. The civil

ZAMBIA HISTORY

service was increased, and nearly all private businesses (including the copper mines) were nationalised. But corruption and mismanagement, exacerbated by a fall in world copper prices, doomed Zambia to become one of the poorest countries in the world by the end of the 1970s. The economy continued to flounder, and Zambia's trade routes to the coast through neighbouring countries (such as Zimbabwe and Mozambique) were closed in retaliation for Kaunda's support for several liberation movements in the region.

By the early 1980s Rhodesia gained independence (and had become Zimbabwe), which allowed Kaunda to take his country off a war footing; and the Tazara railway to Dar es Salaam (Tanzania) was completed, giving Zambia unencumbered access to the coast. Yet the economy remained on the brink of collapse: foreign-exchange reserves were almost exhausted, serious shortages of food, fuel and other basic commodities were common, and unemployment and crime rates rose sharply.

In 1986 an attempt was made to diversify the economy and improve the country's balance of payments. Zambia received economic aid from the International Monetary Fund (IMF), but the IMF conditions were severe and included cutting basic food subsidies. Subsequent price rises led to countrywide riots in which many people lost their lives. Kaunda was forced to restore subsidies.

The winds of change blowing through Africa during the late 1980s, coupled with Zambia's disastrous domestic situation, meant that something had to give. Following another round of violent street protests against increased food prices in 1990, which quickly transformed into a general demand for the return of multiparty politics, Kaunda was forced to accede to public opinion.

He announced a snap referendum in late 1990 but, as protests grew more vocal, he was forced to legalise opposition parties and announce full presidential and parliamentary elections for October 1991. Not surprisingly, UNIP (and Kaunda) were resoundingly defeated by the Movement for Multiparty Democracy (MMD), led by Frederick Chiluba, a former trade-union leader. Kaunda admirably stepped down without complaint, which may have saved Zambia from descending into anarchy.

The 1990s

President Chiluba moved quickly to encourage loans and investment from the IMF and World Bank. Exchange controls were liberalised to attract investors, particularly from South Africa, but tough austerity measures were also introduced. Once again, food prices soared. The civil service was rationalised, state industries were privatised or simply closed, and thousands of people lost their jobs.

By the mid-1990s, the lack of visible change in Zambia allowed Kaunda to confidently re-enter the political arena. He attracted strong support and soon became the UNIP leader. Leading up to the 1996 elections, the MMD panicked and passed a law forbidding anyone with foreign parents to enter politics (Kaunda's parents were from Malawi). Despite intercessions from Western aid donors and world leaders like Nelson Mandela – not to mention accusations that Chiluba's parents were from the Democratic Republic of the Congo (Zaïre) – the law was not repealed. The UNIP withdrew all its candidates in protest and many voters boycotted the election. Consequently, Chiluba and the MMD easily won, and the result was grudgingly accepted by most Zambians.

In the 21st Century

The political shenanigans continued unabated at the start of the new millennium: in mid-2001 Vice-President Christon Tembo was expelled from parliament by Chiluba, so he formed an opposition party – the Forum for Democratic Development (FDD). Later, Paul Tembo, a former MMD national secretary, joined the FDD but was assassinated the day before he was due to front a tribunal about alleged MMD corruption.

Chiluba was thwarted from changing the constitution and running for a third presidential term by parliamentary threats of impeachment and growing public unrest. He anointed his former vice-president, Levy Mwanawasa, as his successor, but Mwanawasa only just beat a coalition of opposition parties known as the United Party for National Development (UPND). Again, allegations from international observers about the MMD rigging the results and buying votes fell on deaf ears. To Chiluba's horror, Mwanawasa stripped his predecessor of immunity from prosecution and proceeded to launch an anti-corruption drive, which targeted the former president. In August

2009, after a long-running trial, Chiluba was cleared of embezzling US$500,000 by Zambia's High Court. His wife, however, was given a jail term earlier in the year for receiving stolen funds while her husband was in office. In a separate case, the High Court in Britain ruled that Chiluba and four of his aides conspired to rob Zambia of about US$46 million, but it remains to be seen whether this judgement will be enforced within Zambia.

Though Zambia is still a poor country, its economy experienced strong growth in the early part of the 21st century, with GDP growth at around 6%. However, the country is still very dependant on world prices for its minerals (copper and cobalt). Knocking Zambia off its feet in the early '70s, the whim of the market then brought about huge gains in wealth early in the new millennium as world copper prices rose steadily. However, with the global economic slump of 2008-09, and with the price of minerals such as copper falling rapidly, Zambia is on the same merry-go-round. There has been large foreign investment in the mines (especially from China), and South African-owned businesses are exploding in towns across the country, as there is finally local demand for them.

In 2005, under the Highly Indebted Poor Country Initiative, Zambia qualified for debt relief to the tune of US$6 billion.

People

The population of Zambia is made up of between 70 and 80 ethnic groups. The final count varies according to your definition of ethnicity, but the Zambian government officially recognises 73 groups.

There is considerable homogeneity among the tribes of Zambia. This is partly due to a long history of people moving around the country, settling new areas or looking for work, and also because after independence President Kaunda fostered national unity, while still recognising the country's disparate languages and cultures. Intermarriage among the officially recognised groups is also common, and Zambia is justifiably proud of its relative lack of ethnic problems.

The Bemba, whose traditional homeland is in northern Zambia around Kasama and Lake Bangweulu, are the largest ethnic group, forming about 20% of the population. All together, speakers of Tonga as a first

language make up about 15% and Nyanja speakers another 15% (the term Nyanja is used more to describe a language than a particular people); the Chewa people make up about a third of the Nyanja speakers in Zambia. The Ngoni, descendants of Zulus who migrated here in the early 19th century, make up about 6% and are found in southeast Zambia around the town of Chipata. The Lozi, who have their own distinct nation called Barotseland, which takes up a significant part of Zambia's Western Province and the vast Zambezi floodplain, number about 650,000 and make up roughly 6% of the population.

The vast majority (99%) of Zambians are indigenous Africans. The final 1% are people of Indian or European origin (mostly involved in business, commerce, farming and the tourist industry). These are Zambian citizens; many white and Asian families have lived here for generations – although race relations are still sometimes a little strained.

Relative newcomers to the country include South African business people and Zimbabwean farmers who lost their land due to the policies of Robert Mugabe's government. There are also many Europeans and North Americans. Some (such as mining consultants) have lived in Zambia for decades; others (such as aid workers) stay for only a few years before moving on.

Around 75% of Zambians are Christians, the majority members of one of the hundreds of Protestant churches; in addition, there are some Catholics and those who follow indigenous Christian faiths, including large branches of the African Zion churches. Many of these people also follow traditional animist-based belief systems. There is also a significant Muslim population.

Environment

The Land

Landlocked Zambia is one of Africa's most eccentric legacies of colonialism. Shaped like a mangled butterfly, its borders don't correspond to any tribal or linguistic area. And Zambia is huge. At some 752,000 sq km, it's about the size of France, England and the Republic of Ireland combined.

The country is chock full of rivers. The Luangwa, the Kafue and the mighty Zambezi dominate western, southern and eastern Zambia, flowing through a beautiful mix of floodplains, forests and farmland. In the north, the main rivers are the Chambeshi and the Luapula – sources of the Congo River. Northern Zambia has many smaller rivers too, and the broken landscape helps create stunning scenery of lakes, rapids and waterfalls.

Of course, Zambia's most famous waterfall is Victoria Falls, where the Zambezi plunges over a mile-wide cliff before thundering down the long, zigzagging Batoka Gorge. The Zambezi flows into Lake Kariba, created by a dam but still one of the largest lakes in Africa. In northern Zambia is the even larger Lake Tanganyika – 675km long, second deepest in the world, and holding one-sixth of the earth's fresh water.

In the south and east, Zambia is cut by deep valleys – some of them branches of the Great Rift Valley. The Zambezi Valley is the largest, and defines the country's southern border, while the 700km-long Luangwa Valley is lined by the steep and spectacular Muchinga Escarpment.

Even the flat places can be stunning: the endless grassy Busanga Plains in Kafue National Park attract fantastic wildlife, while the Liuwa Plain – part of the even larger Upper Zambezi floodplain that makes up much of western Zambia – is home to Africa's second-largest wildebeest migration.

Wildlife

Because of Zambia's diverse landscape, plentiful water supplies, and position between Eastern, Southern and Central Africa, the diversity of animal species is huge. The rivers, of course, support large populations of hippos and crocs, and the associated grasslands provide plenty of fodder for herds of zebras, impalas and pukus.

Huge herds of rare black lechwes live near Lake Bangweulu, and endemic Kafue lechwes settle in the area around the Kafue River. Kasanka National Park is one of the best places on the continent to see the rare, water-loving antelopes called sitatungas. South Luangwa and Lower Zambezi National Parks are good places to see tall and stunningly graceful giraffes, and Zambia has its own subspecies – Thornicroft's giraffe. South Luangwa has its very own subspecies of wildebeest too – the light-coloured Cookson's wildebeest – but the best place to see these creatures is the Liuwa Plain, a remote grassland area in western Zambia where thousands converge every year.

These animals naturally attract predators, so most parks contain lions, leopards, hyenas and cheetahs. Wild dogs were once very rare but are now encountered more frequently. Elephants are also found in huge herds in South Luangwa, Lower Zambezi and some other national parks. Zambia's herds of black rhinos were destroyed by poachers in the 1970s and 1980s, but reintroduction programs have seen rhinos transported to North Luangwa National Park.

Bird lovers will love Zambia, where about 750 bird species have been recorded. Most notable are the endangered shoebill storks (found in the Bangweulu Wetlands); fish eagles (Zambia's national bird); and endemic Chaplin's barbets (mostly around Monze).

Plants

About 65% of Zambia, mainly plateau areas and escarpments, is covered in *miombo*

ZAMBIA'S MOST IMPORTANT NATIONAL PARKS

PARK	FEATURES
Bangweulu Wetlands	floodplain; black lechwes, shoebills, waterbirds
Kafue National Park	*miombo* woodland, open grasslands, Kafue River; red lechwes, leopards, cheetahs, lions
Kasanka National Park	woodlands, plains, rivers, swamps; sitatungas, wattled cranes, hippos, blue monkeys, bats (migration Oct-Dec)
Lower Zambezi National Park	Zambezi River, sandy flats, mopane woodland; crocs, hippos, elephants, buffaloes, lions
North Luangwa National Park	Luangwa River, *miombo* woodland, plains; buffaloes, elephants, hippos, Thornicroft's giraffes, leopards, lions
South Luangwa National Park	mopane & *miombo* woodland, grasslands; Thornicroft's giraffes, Cookson's wildebeest, lions, leopards, elephants, pukus

woodland, which consists mainly of broad-leaved deciduous trees. Some areas are thickly wooded, others are more open, but the trees never form a continuous canopy, allowing grass and other plants to grow between them. In the dryer, hotter valleys and best-known national parks like South Luangwa and Lower Zambezi, much of the vegetation is mopane woodland.

With its many rivers and lakes, Zambia has some of the most extensive wetlands in Southern Africa. These include the Bang-weulu Wetlands, along the southern and eastern shores of Lake Bangweulu; and the vast plains of the Kafue Flats downstream from Kafue National Park, which is dotted with seasonally flooded marshes, lagoons and oxbow lakes.

Most grassland in Zambia is low, flat and flooded for part of the year – with hardly a tree in sight. The largest floodplain area is west of the Upper Zambezi – including Liuwa Plain National Park – where thousands of square kilometres are inundated every year. Another is the Busanga Plains in Kafue National Park.

Along many of Zambia's rivers are riverine forests. Tourists will see a lot of this type of landscape as national-park camps are often built on riverbanks, under the shade of huge trees such as ebony, winterthorn and the unmistakable 'sausage tree' (*Kigelia africana*).

Evergreen forest, the 'jungle' of Tarzan films, is found only in isolated pockets in northwestern Zambia – a remnant of the larger forests over the border in Angola and the Democratic Republic of Congo.

National Parks

Zambia boasts 20 national parks and reserves (and 34 GMAs), and some 30% of the land is protected, but after decades of poaching, clearing and general bad management, many are just lines on the map that no longer protect (or even contain) much wildlife. However, some national parks accommodate extremely healthy stocks of wildlife and are among the best in Southern Africa. Privately funded conservation organisations have done much to rehabiliate the condition of some of these.

Admission fees to the parks vary. Each ticket is valid for 24 hours from the time you enter the park, but if you're staying inside the park at official accommodation this admission fee is valid for seven days.

Environmental Issues & Conservation

Although the population is growing rapidly, it's still relatively sparse, so Zambia doesn't suffer some of the environmental problems its neighbours have – or at least to the same extent. That being said, the country faces the daunting challenge of deforestation and consequent soil erosion and loss of productivity. Poachers set fire to ambush animals, land is regularly burned and cleared for agricultural purposes, local people chop down wood for charcoal, and illegal logging and timber smuggling continues, now primarily to meet the demand for wood from China.

Hunting has greatly damaged Zambia's wildlife. The '70s were a devastating time when other countries' civil wars

ACTIVITIES	SIZE	BEST TIME TO VISIT
walking, canoe trips, birdwatching	9800 sq km	Dec-Mar
game drives, birdwatching, fishing	22,400 sq km	May-Oct
boat trips, walking, game drives	390 sq km	Jul-Nov
canoeing, boating, birdwatching, game drives	4092 sq km	Jun-Sep
walking safaris	4636 sq km	May-Oct
day & night game drives, walking safaris	9050 sq km	Apr-Oct

were funded with ivory coming out of the parks. In 1960 North Luangwa had 70,000 elephants; an estimated 5000 remained by 1986. Under pressure from international organisations, however, the government introduced serious anti-poaching and development measures. Despite successes in some parks, poaching and poor management remain major problems.

In the past, people moved into some protected areas, chopped down trees, grew crops or hunted the animals. They were poor, and good land and food were scarce elsewhere. Animals were a source of protein, since in areas with tsetse flies raising livestock isn't an option. Even outside the parks, on areas of land shared by people and animals, there was conflict. The same is still true today. To a poor rural subsistence farmer, wildlife is nothing but a problem: lions will kill cattle, and an elephant takes an hour to polish off a field of crops that took all year to grow.

With this inevitable tension in mind, all of the national parks are surrounded by a ring of game management areas (GMAs), a good portion of which are earmarked as hunting concessions. To many, this might at first seem like a compromise of conservationist ideals, but it's argued that if there was no hunting there'd be indiscriminate and unregulated slaughter.

Arguably, the biggest problem is indiscriminate snaring for commercial bushmeat. Sold 'underground' in the back of shops or door to door to trusted customers, it's the middle and upper class, mostly in Lusaka, who are driving the bushmeat market. After all, widely available buffalo, warthog and antelope is on average 50% more expensive than beef.

As might be expected, there's considerable tension between environmental preservation and conservation and Zambia's underground wealth. Many worry that it's only a matter of time before the profits to be wrung from the region's mineral resources will be too seductive to deny.

One of the most important developments regarding conservation in recent years is the Kavango Zambezi Transfrontier Park (KAZA), a multinational effort to link the historic and instinctual migratory patterns of elephants and other wildlife between Zambia, Botswana, Namibia and Angola.

SURVIVAL GUIDE

Directory A–Z

Accommodation

We list accommodation prices based on 'international rates'. Often, lodges offer resident rates that can be half as much. Some lodges and camps close in the wet season (November to April); if they're open, discounts of up to 50% are common.

It should be noted that accommodation in the national parks (there is some variety in terms of cost just outside park boundaries) is even more skewed towards the way, way top end: rates average around ZMW2000 per person. These privately operated lodges and 'camps' (a confusing term often used to describe expensive lodges) in the parks offer the same sort of luxury and exclusivity as other lodges and camps in Southern and East Africa. Rates usually include all meals, drinks, park fees and activities, such as wildlife drives, but not transfers by road, air and/or boat.

A real treat of travel here are the open-air toilets and showers; most bushcamps and many lodges have them.

Most cities and larger towns have campgrounds where you can pitch your tent, but most are way out in the suburbs (wood and charcoal is usually for sale). Camping is also possible at privately run campgrounds just outside national-park boundaries (you don't pay admission fees until you actually want to visit the park). Some lodges around national parks have multiple types of accommodation, everything from safari tents to chalets as well as campsites – this can be a great deal as you have access to the lodge's facilities while paying a pittance for accommodation (in these cases we've placed them in the budget category in terms of room rates).

SLEEPING PRICE RANGES

The following price ranges refer to accommodation rates per person in high season (April-May to September-October).

$ less than ZMW250

$$ ZMW250–500

$$$ more than ZMW500

The better budget hotels charge by the room, so two, three or even four people travelling together can get some real (if crowded) bargains. Single travellers are often charged a 'supplement'; negotiation is usually possible.

🏃 Activities

Companies in Livingstone (and Victoria Falls town in Zimbabwe) offer a bewildering array of activities, such as white-water rafting in the gorge below the falls or river boarding and canoeing on the quieter waters above the falls. Those with plenty of nerve and money can try bungee jumping or abseiling, or take a ride in a microlight or helicopter. The less intrepid may want to try hiking and horse riding.

Canoeing, either for a few hours or a few days, is a great way to explore the Zambezi River and can be arranged at lodges in the Lower Zambezi Valley and Siavonga. Fishing along the Zambezi, and at several lakes in northern Zambia, is also popular; the tiger fish provide a tough contest for anglers. Fishing and boating are also possible on Lakes Kariba, Bangweulu and Tanganyika.

Most national parks, such as Kafue, Kasanka, Lower Zambezi and South Luangwa, have activities for visitors, with wildlife drives and walks the main focus of these places, and the main drawcard for visitors to Zambia. Expect early mornings in the bush as morning drives and walks depart around 6am; night drives typically last from 4pm to 8pm.

'Fly camping' – trips that involve walking or boating during the day and informal bush camping at night – is becoming more popular, especially in South Luangwa, Kafue and Liuwa National Parks.

Business Hours

Government offices are open from 8am or 9am to 4pm or 5pm Monday to Friday, with an hour for lunch sometime between noon and 2pm. Shops keep the same hours but also open on Saturday. Supermarkets are normally open from 8am to 8pm Monday to Friday, 8am to 6pm Saturday and 9am to 1pm Sunday (although some are open 8am to 10pm daily at the big shopping centres in Lusaka). Banks operate weekdays from 8am to 3.30pm (or 5pm), and from 8am to 11am (or noon) on Saturday. Post offices open from 8am or 9am to 4pm or 4.30pm weekdays. Restaurants are normally open for lunch between 11.30am and 2.30pm and dinner between 6pm and 10.30pm, though bar-restaurants in Lusaka are often open until 11pm on Friday and Saturday.

Embassies & Consulates

The British high commission looks after the interests of Aussies and Kiwis. Most consulates are open from 8.30am to 5pm Monday to Thursday and from 8.30am to 12.30pm Friday, though visas are usually only dealt with in the mornings.

Botswanan High Commission (☏0211-250555; 5201 Pandit Nehru Rd, Lusaka)

Canadian High Commission (☏0211-250833; 5119 United Nations Ave, Lusaka)

DRC Embassy (☏0211-235679; 1124 Parirenyetwa Rd, Lusaka)

Dutch Embassy (☏0211-253819; 5208 United Nations Ave, Lusaka)

French Embassy (☏0211-251322; 74 Independence Ave, Cathedral Hill)

German Embassy (☏0211-250644; 5209 United Nations Ave, Lusaka)

Irish Embassy (☏0211-291298; 6663 Katima Mulilo Rd, Lusaka)

Kenyan High Commission (☏0211-250722; 5207 United Nations Ave, Lusaka)

Malawian High Comission (☏0211-265768; 31 Bishops Rd, Kabulonga)

Mozambican Embassy (☏0211-220333; 9592 Kacha Rd, off Paseli Rd, Northmead)

Namibian High Comission (☏0211-260407; 30B Mutende Rd, Woodlands)

South African High Comission (☏0211-260999; 26D Cheetah Rd, Kabulonga)

Swedish Embassy (☏0211-251711; Haile Selassie Ave, Lusaka)

Tanzanian High Commission (☏0211-253323; 5200 United Nations Ave, Lusaka)

UK High Commission (☏0211-423200; http://ukinzambia.fco.gov.uk/en; 5210 Independence Ave, Lusaka)

US Embassy (☏0211-250955; http://zambia.usembassy.gov; cnr Independence & United Nations Aves, Lusaka)

Zimbabwean High Commission (☏0211-254006; 11058 Haile Selassie Ave, Lusaka)

✨ Festivals & Events

One remarkable festival to look out for is **Kusefya Pangwena**, practised by the Bem-

PRACTICALITIES

» The *Daily Times* (www.times.co.zm) and *Daily Mail* (www.daily-mail.co.zm) are government-controlled newspapers. The *Post* (www.postzambia.com) is independent. Published in the UK but printed in South Africa, the *Weekly Telegraph*, the *Guardian Weekly* and the *Economist* are available in Lusaka and Livingstone.

» Both of the Zambian National Broadcasting Corporation (ZNBC) radio stations can be heard nationwide; they play Western and African music, as well as news and chat shows in English. Radio Phoenix (89.5FM) has a call-in show called 'Let the People Talk' on Tuesday and Friday from 9am to 11am. MUVI TV is independently owned, while ZNBC also runs the solitary government-controlled TV station, but anyone who can afford it will subscribe to South African satellite TV. The BBC World Service can be heard in Lusaka (88.2FM) and Kitwe (89.1FM); Radio France Internationale (RFI) can also be heard in Lusaka.

» Televisions use the PAL system.

» Electricity supply is 220V to 240V/50Hz and plugs are of the British three-prong variety.

» The metric system is used in Zambia.

ba people of northern Zambia. This program of music, drama and dance, which is held near Kasama over four days in August, commemorates the victory of the Bemba over the Ngoni in the 1830s.

N'cwala is a Ngoni festival held near Chipata in eastern Zambia on 24 February. At this time, food, dance and music are all enjoyed by participants who celebrate the end of the rainy season and pray for a successful harvest.

The remarkable **Kuomboka Ceremony** is one of Southern Africa's last great festivals.

Information about these and other festivals are on the official Zambian tourism website: www.zambiatourism.com.

Food & Drink

The staple diet for Zambians is unquestionably *nshima*, a thick, doughy maize porridge that's bland but filling. It's eaten with your hands and always accompanied by beans or vegetables and a hot relish, and sometimes meat or fish.

Although food is generally not a highlight of travel in Zambia, lodges and camps in and around the national parks usually offer the highest standards of culinary options. Perhaps the opportunity to taste local game (kudu is very good) is the standout.

The local beer is Mosi, but you may come across discarded plastic sachets of *tujilijili*, a strong home-brewed alcohol, the manufacturing and importation of

which was declared illegal in 2012. Nevertheless, a thriving business in Malawi supplies Zambian drinkers.

The following price ranges are used for Eating reviews in this chapter. Remember that this is a guide only and prices will be considerably more in many lodges and camps in national parks.

$	Less than ZWM30 per main
$$	ZMW30-70 per main
$$$	More than ZMW70 per main

Internet Access

Zamnet is the country's largest internet service provider. Internet centres are in Lusaka, Livingstone and the bigger towns, such as Mongu and Ndola, and are spreading. Access at internet centres is cheap – about ZMW0.12 to ZMW0.20 per minute – and the speed and reliability of connections vary.

Wi-fi is becoming more common, so travelling with a laptop that has wireless connectivity can be useful, even in remote towns. In Lusaka look for 'I Spot' zones, which can be found at accommodation and eating places, but the quality of these connections varies. When we've used the wi-fi symbol in sleeping reviews, it can mean either that wi-fi is free or that guests pay a fee for it. In addition, wi-fi is likely only available in a small area around the lobby and usually not in rooms.

Maps

The German *Zambia Road Map* by Ilona Hupe Verlag is currently the best available map for touring around Zambia – it shows petrol stations and important wildlife areas. Also easy to find is Globetrotter's *Zambia and Victoria Falls* map, which includes regional and national-park insets, and *Street Guide Lusaka and Livingstone*, which is a book-form collection of blow-ups of the two cities. All are available at bookshops in Lusaka. Self-drivers should check out *Tracks4Africa* (www.tracks4africa.com), a highly detailed downloadable GPS system.

Money

President Sata passed legislation in 2012 that revalued Zambia's currency and prohibited any other currency from being accepted as a form of payment. This means that as of 1 January 2013 three zeros were removed from every banknote denomination and the unit of currency changed from ZMK (or ZK) to ZMW: eg ZMK90,000 is now ZMW90. Every single bank and ATM was to change over to the new system on that date.

While tourist-oriented places might still quote prices in US dollars on websites and in promotional materials, you must by law pay in kwacha (except for international airfares, some organised tours and visas). This includes national parks, domestic flights, restaurants and so on.

CASH & ATMS

In the cities and larger towns, you can easily change cash (no commission; photo ID required) at branches of Barclays Bank, FNB, Standard Chartered Bank and Zanaco. We've received reports that many banks, including at least one at the airport, won't accept US dollars issued before 2000. You can obtain cash (kwacha) at ATMs at Barclays Bank, Stanbic and Standard Chartered banks in the cities and larger towns.

CREDIT CARDS

Some shops, restaurants and better hotels and lodges accept major credit cards, though Visa is the most readily recognised (MasterCard less so and Amex still less). A surcharge of 4% to 7% may be added to your bill if you pay with a credit card, so you might be better off using it to draw cash and paying with that.

Note that payment by credit card requires a PIN to authorise the transaction.

MONEYCHANGERS

The best currencies to take to Zambia (in order of preference) are US dollars, UK pounds, South African rands and euros; the currencies of most neighbouring countries are worthless in Zambia, except at the relevant borders. The exception is Botswanan pula, which can also be exchanged in Lusaka.

Foreign-exchange offices – almost always called bureaus de change – are easy to find in all cities and larger towns. Their rates aren't significantly better than those of banks.

There is no black market. You might get a few kwacha more by changing money on the street, but it's illegal and there is a chance that you'll be ripped off, robbed or set up for some sort of scam.

TIPPING

While most restaurants add a 10% service charge, rarely does it actually get into the pockets of waiters. Therefore, you may choose to tip the waiter directly. The top-end lodges and camps often provide separate envelopes for staff and guides if guests wish to tip.

Public Holidays

During public holidays, most businesses and government offices are closed.

New Year's Day 1 January

Youth Day Second Monday in March

Easter March or April

Labour/Workers' Day 1 May

Africa (Freedom) Day 25 May

Heroes' Day First Monday in July

Unity Day First Tuesday in July

Farmers' Day First Monday in August

Independence Day 24 October

Christmas Day 25 December

Boxing Day 26 December

Safe Travel

Generally, Zambia is very safe, though in the cities and tourist areas there is always a chance of being targeted by muggers or con artists. As always, you can reduce the risk considerably by being sensible. In Zambia, thieves are known as *kabwalalas* universally.

For as long as the seemingly endless civil strife continues in the Democratic Republic of the Congo (Zaïre), avoid any areas along the Zambia–Congo (Zaïre) border, especially around Lake Mweru. Foreign embassies in Zambia warn of landmines (left over from the Rhodesian civil war) in the Sinazongwe area on the shores of Lake Kariba. Avoid trekking off the beaten track in this area.

The possession, use and trade of recreational drugs is illegal in Zambia and penalties are harsh.

Telephone

Every landline in Zambia has an area code; you only have to dial it if you are calling from outside the area code.

Public phones operated by Zamtel, the government monopoly, use tokens, which are available from post offices (for ZMW0.50) or local boys (for ZMW1) hanging around phone booths. These tokens last three minutes but are only good for calls within Zambia. Phone booths operated by Zamtel use phonecards (ZMW5, ZMW10, ZMW20 or ZMW50) available from post offices and grocery shops. These phonecards can be used for international calls, but it's often easier to find a 'phone shop' or 'fax bureau', from where all international calls cost about ZMW12 per minute.

International services are generally good, but reverse-charge (collect) and toll-free calls are not possible. The international access code for dialling outside Zambia is 00, followed by the relevant country code. If you're calling Zambia from another country, the country code is 260, but drop the initial zero of the area code.

MOBILE PHONES

MTN and Airtel offer mobile (cell) phone networks. It's almost impossible to rent mobile phones in Zambia, though if you own a GSM phone, you can buy a SIM card for only around ZMW3 without a problem (this is easy to do at Lusaka airport). You can then purchase credits – from the same company from which you bought your SIM – in whatever denominations you need; scratch cards range from ZMW1 to ZMW100. In Lusaka the best place to buy a cheap mobile phone is around Kalima Towers (at the corner of Chachacha Rd and Katunjila Rd); a basic model is about ZMW80 to ZMW100.

Numbers starting with 09 plus another two numbers (for example 0977) are mobile phone numbers.

Mobile-phone reception is getting better all the time; generally it's very good in urban areas, surprisingly good in some rural parts of the country and patchy or nonexistent in others.

Visas

Tourist visas are available at major borders, airports and ports, but it's important to note that you should have a Zambian visa *before* arrival if you're travelling by train or boat from Tanzania.

All foreign visitors – other than South African Development Community (SADC) passport holders, who are issued visas free of charge – pay US$50 for single entry (up to one month) and US$80 for double entry (up to three months; good if you plan on venturing into one of the bordering countries). Applications for multiple-entry visas (US$80; different from double-entry visas) must be made in advance at a Zambian embassy or high commission. If you're staying less than 24 hours – for example, visiting Livingstone from Zimbabwe – you pay only US$20.

Payment can be made in US dollars, and sometimes UK pounds, although other currencies such as euros, South African rand, Botswanan pula or Namibian dollars, may be accepted at borders, but don't count on it.

Most visas for travel to neighbouring countries are available at border crossings. However, your chances of obtaining a visa for Democratic Republic of Congo (Zaïre) or Angola are extremely remote at borders or in Lusaka, so make arrangements for these before you arrive in Zambia.

VISA EXTENSIONS

Extensions for all types of tourist visa are possible at any Department of Immigration office in any main town in Zambia, though you're likely to be more successful in **Lusaka** and **Livingstone** (Mosi-oa-Tunya Rd). The Lusaka office is an efficient operation: there's generally no queue and no fee for an additional 30 days. It's possible to seek an extension twice for a total of 90 days a year. Be aware of the expiration date of the visa; if it's a Saturday or Sunday it's best to go in on a weekday beforehand.

If for some reason you overstay your visa, humility and politeness go a long way in dealing with Zambian authorities.

Getting There & Away

The main way to get to Zambia is by land or air. Overland, travellers might enter Zambia from Malawi, Botswana, Namibia, Zimbabwe or Tanzania.

Entering Zambia

Visas are generally issued upon arrival.

A yellow-fever certificate is not required before entering Zambia, but it *is* often requested by Zambian immigration officials if you have come from a country with yellow fever. It is required if you're travelling from Zambia to South Africa (and, possibly, Zimbabwe) – it's worth checking on this since negotiations with South Africa to drop this requirement were ongoing in late 2012. It's also worth noting that the Centers for Disease Control in the US do not recommend the vaccination for travellers to Zambia.

Air

Zambia's main international airport is in Lusaka, though some international airlines fly to the airports at Livingstone (for Victoria Falls), Mfuwe (for South Luangwa National Park) and Ndola.

The country is increasingly well connected, with direct flights to destinations outside Africa. British Airways (www.britishairways.com) has thrice-weekly flights from London, KLM/Air France (www.klm.com) from Amsterdam and Emirates (www.emirates.com; Acacia Park, Arcades Shopping Centre, Great East Rd, Lusaka) from Dubai.

For North Americans who don't want to fly first to London or Amsterdam, South African Airways (www.flysaa.com) has daily direct flights from New York City to Johannesburg (South Africa). From here there are regular flights to Lusaka, Ndola and Livingstone.

Zambia is also well connected to Southern Africa. Zambezi Airlines (☎0211-250342; www.flyzambezi.com) flies to regional destinations such as Johannesburg (from Lusaka and Ndola) and Dar es Salaam (Tanzania).

Air Malawi (☎0211-228120; www.flyairmalawi.com; COMESA Centre, Zone B, ground fl, Ben Bella Rd) connects Lusaka with Lilongwe and Blantyre (both in Malawi), while Air Zimbabwe (www.airzimbabwe.com) flies to Harare (Zimbabwe). Air Botswana (☎0211-255024; www.airbotswana.co.bw; InterContinental Hotel, Lusaka) connects Lusaka and Gaborone (Botswana) and Air Namibia (☎0211-258370; www.airnamibia.co.na; Manda Hill Shopping Centre, Lusaka) flies between Lusaka, Livingstone and Windhoek (Namibia).

It's also easy to find a flight from Nairobi (Kenya) on Kenya Airways (☎0211-228886; www.kenya-airways.com; 3rd fl, Maanu Centre, Chikwa Rd, Lusaka), and Ethiopian Airlines (☎0211-236402/3; www.flyethiopian.com) has daily flights between Addis Ababa (Ethiopia) and Lusaka.

There is also an increasing number of flights to Livingstone for Victoria Falls: South African Airways, British Airways and discount airline Kulula (www.kulula.com) fly there from Johannesburg (and increasingly from Cape Town and Durban).

The departure tax for all international flights is ZMW156. This tax is often included in the price of your airline ticket, but if not, must be paid at the airport (in Zambian kwacha only).

Border Crossings

Zambia shares borders with eight countries, so there are a huge number of crossing points. Most are open daily from 6am to 6pm, though the border closes at 8pm at Victoria Falls and at 7pm at Chirundu. Before you leave the Zambian side ensure that you have enough currency of whatever country you're travelling to, or South African rand, to pay for your visa (if you require one).

If you are crossing borders in your own vehicle (be sure to inform your rental-car company to guarantee that you have all the required documents in order), you need a free Temporary Export Permit (TEP), obtained at the border. You'll likely need to purchase insurance, sometimes called COMESA and bought either at the Zambian border posts or just after you've gone through formalities on the other country's side (for Zimbabwe it'll cost around ZMW150). For Zim you also need an Interpol Certificate (good for three months) obtained from the police in Zambia and a typed 'Permission to Drive' document, which states that the vehicle's owner knows you're driving their car.

You also need to request and complete a Temporary Import Permit (TIP), and of course pay for it (retain the document and payment receipt for when you re-enter Zambia).

Heading back into Zambia you might get hassled by Zambians trying to sell you insurance – you don't need this if you're in a Zambian-registered vehicle.

Note also that Zambia charges a carbon tax for non-Zambian-registered vehicles; it's usually about ZMW150 to ZMW200 per vehicle.

The following borders issue visas to foreigners on arrival:

Botswana Zambia and Botswana share what is probably the world's shortest international boundary: 750m across the Zambezi River at Kazungula. The pontoon ferry (ZMW40 for foot passengers, ZMW30 for an ordinary Zambian-registered vehicle) across the Zambezi is 65km west of Livingstone and 11km south of the main road between Livingstone and Sesheke. There are one or two buses (ZMW20, 35 minutes) here daily from Livingstone, departing from Nakatindi Rd in the morning.

Note that US dollars and other currencies are not accepted at the Botswanan border post.

A quicker and more comfortable (but more expensive) way to reach Botswana from Zambia is to cross from Livingstone to Victoria Falls (in Zimbabwe), from where shuttle buses head to Kasane.

Buses to Gaborone, via Kasane and Francistown, leave several days a week from Lusaka.

Democratic Republic of Congo (DRC, Zaïre) DRC visas are only available to Zambian residents and this rule is strictly enforced unless you can get a letter of invitation from the Congolese government. The most convenient border to use connects Chingola in the Copperbelt with Lubumbashi in Katanga Province, via the border towns of Chililabombwe (Zambia) and Kasumbalesa (DRC).

Malawi Most foreigners use the border at Mchinji, 30km southeast of Chipata, because it's along the road between Lusaka and Lilongwe. Note that visas into Malawi are free for most nationalities.

Mozambique The main border is between Mlolo (Zambia) and fairly remote Cassacatiza (Mozambique), but most travellers choose to reach Mozambique through Malawi. There is no public transport between the two countries.

Namibia The only border is at Sesheke (Zambia), on the northern and southern bank of the Zambezi, while the Namibian border is at Wenela near Katima Mulilo. There are bus services to Sesheke from

Lusaka and Livingstone respectively; it's 200km west of the latter.

Alternatively, cross from Livingstone to Victoria Falls (in Zimbabwe) and travel onwards from there.

South Africa There is no border between Zambia and South Africa, but several buses travel daily between Johannesburg and Lusaka via Harare and Masvingo in Zimbabwe. Make sure you have a Zimbabwean visa (if you need one before arrival) and a yellow-fever certificate for entering South Africa (and, possibly, Zimbabwe).

Tanzania The main border by road, and the only crossing by train, is between Nakonde (Zambia) and Tunduma (Tanzania). Bus services run from Lusaka to Nakonde (ZMW140, 15 hours, 3pm) and on to Dar es Salaam.

Zimbabwe There are three easy crossings: at Chirundu, along the road between Lusaka and Harare; between Siavonga (Zambia) and Kariba (Zimbabwe), about 50km upstream from Chirundu; and easiest and most common of all, between Livingstone (Zambia) and Victoria Falls town (Zimbabwe). Plenty of buses travel every day between Lusaka and Harare via Chirundu.

Getting Around

Air

The main domestic airports are at Lusaka, Livingstone, Ndola, Kitwe, Mfuwe, Kasama and Kasaba Bay, though dozens of minor airstrips, most notably those in the Lower Zambezi National Park (Proflight flies here regularly) and North Luangwa National Park, cater for chartered planes.

The departure tax for domestic flights is ZMW58. It is not included in the price of airline tickets and must be paid at the airport in Zambian kwacha. An additional 'infrastructure' tax applied to every ticket was passed and then subsequently cancelled in October 2012. It may be reinstataed in the future.

AIRLINES IN ZAMBIA

Proflight (www.proflight-zambia.com) is the only domestic airline offering regularly scheduled flights connecting Lusaka to Chipata, Livingstone (for Victoria Falls), Lower Zambezi (Jeki and Royal Airstrips), Mfuwe (for South Luangwa National Park),

Ndola (also flies direct from here to Kasama) and Solwezi. The fare class with the most flexibility (in case of change of travel plans) is the most expensive. A one-way ticket from Lusaka to Mfuwe (one hour 20 minutes) ranges from ZMW810 to ZMW1500; to Jeki, from ZMW470 to ZMW1000; to Livingstone, from ZMW750 to ZMW1400. Visa, Master-Card, Amex and Paypal are accepted for on-line payments.

On the Livingstone and Ndola routes, which use larger planes, passengers can check one or two bags totalling 23kg; on all other flights the limit is only 15kg (additional fees are applied for excess weight). Carry-on baggage on all flights is limited to 5kg.

There are plenty of charter-flight companies (Proflight also does charters) catering primarily for guests staying at upmarket lodges and camps in national parks. Flights only leave with a minimum number of prebooked passengers and fares are always high, but it's sometimes worth looking around for a last-minute stand-by flight.

Pro Charter (☎0974 250110; www.avocet
-charters.com)

Royal Air Charters (☎0971 251493; www.
royalaircharters.com)

Bus & Minibus

Distances are long, buses are often slow and many roads are badly potholed, so travelling around Zambia by bus and minibus can exhaust even the hardiest of travellers.

All main routes are served by ordinary public buses, which either run on a fill-up-and-go basis or have fixed departures (these are called 'time buses'). 'Express buses' are faster – often terrifyingly so – and stop less but cost about 15% more. In addition, several private companies run comfortable European-style express buses along the major routes, eg between Lusaka and Livingstone, Lusaka and Chipata, and Lusaka and the Copperbelt region. These fares cost about 25% more than the ordinary bus fares and are well worth the extra kwacha. Tickets for these buses can often be bought the day before. There are also express buses zipping around the country.

Many routes are also served by minibuses, which only leave when full – so full that you might lose all feeling in one butt cheek. Their fares can be more or less the same as ordinary buses. In remote areas the only public transport is often a truck or pick-up.

Car & Motorcycle

BRING YOUR OWN VEHICLE

If you're driving into Zambia in a rented or privately owned car or motorcycle, you will need a carnet; if you don't have one, a free Customs Importation Permit will be issued to you at major borders instead. You'll also be charged a carbon tax if it's a non-Zambian-registered vehicle, which just means a bit more paperwork and about ZMW200 at the border depending on the size of your car.

Compulsory third-party insurance for Zambia is available at major borders (or the nearest large towns); however, it is strongly advised that you carry insurance from your own country on top of your Zambian policy.

While it is certainly possible to get around Zambia by car or motorbike, many sealed roads are in bad condition and the dirt roads can range from shocking to completely impassable, particularly after the rains. We strongly recommend that you hire a 4WD if driving anywhere outside Lusaka, and certainly if you're heading to any of the national parks or other wilderness areas. Wearing a seat belt in the front seat is compulsory.

Self-drivers should seriously consider purchasing the in-car GPS navigation system Tracks for Africa (www.tracks4africa. co.za); even petrol stations come up.

DRIVING LICENCE

Foreign licences are fine as long as they are in English, and it doesn't hurt to carry an international driver's licence (also in English).

FUEL & SPARE PARTS

Diesel costs around ZMW8 per litre, petrol ZMW8.15. Distances between towns with filling stations are great and fuel is not always available, so fill the tank at every opportunity.

It is advisable to carry at least one spare wheel, as well as a filled jerrycan. If you need spare parts, the easiest (and cheapest) vehicle parts to find are those of Toyota and Nissan.

HIRE

Cars can be hired from international and Zambian-owned companies in Lusaka, Livingstone, Kitwe and Ndola, but renting is

ZAMBIA GETTING AROUND

very expensive. Avis (☏airport 0211-271303; www.avis.com) and Europcar/Voyagers (☏0212-620314; www.europcarzambia.com) are at Lusaka airport.

Europcar/Voyagers charges from ZMW365 per day for the smallest vehicle, plus ZMW2 per kilometre, and this doesn't include 16% VAT, petrol or insurance. Other companies, such as Hemingways (☏0213-320996; www.hemingwayszambia.com; Mosi-oa-Tunya Rd), 4x4 Hire Africa (☏in South Africa 721-791 3904; www.4x4hire.co.za) and Limo Car Hire (☏0211-278628; www.limohire-zambia.com) rent out Toyota Hiluxes and old-school Land Rover vehicles respectively, unequipped or fully decked out with everything you would need for a trip to the bush (including unlimited kilometres and the ability to take them across borders), with the price for an unequipped vehicle starting at about ZMW680 per day.

Most companies insist that drivers are at least 23 years old and have held a licence for at least five years.

INSURANCE
Compulsory third-party insurance for Zambia is available at major borders (or the nearest large towns) and costs about ZMW63 per month. However, it is strongly advised that you carry insurance from your own country on top of your Zambian policy.

ROAD CONDITIONS
While many main stretches of sealed road are OK, beware of the occasional pothole. Sections of main highway can be in a pretty bad way, with gaping potholes, ridges, dips and very narrow sections that drop steeply off the side into loose gravel. Be wary and alert at all times, and seek out information about road conditions. Gravel roads vary a lot from pretty good to pretty terrible. Road conditions are probably at their worst soon after the end of the wet season (April to June) when many dirt and gravel roads have been washed away or seriously damaged – this is especially the case in and around national parks.

ROAD RULES
Speed limits in and around cities are enforced, though on the open road buses and Land Cruisers fly at speeds of 140km/h to 160km/h. If you break down, you must place an orange triangle about 6m in front of and behind the vehicle. At police checkposts (which are very common), smile, say good morning/afternoon, be very polite and

take off your sunglasses. A little respect will make a huge difference to the way you are treated. Mostly you'll be met with a smile, perhaps asked curiously where you're from, and waved through without a problem.

Hitching

Despite the general warning, hitching is a common way to get around Zambia. Some drivers, particularly expats, may offer you free lifts, but you should expect to pay for rides with local drivers (normally about the same as the bus fare, depending on the comfort of the vehicle). In such cases, agree on a price beforehand.

Taxis

Often the most convenient and comfortable way of getting around, especially in the cities. They have no meters, so rates are negotiable.

🤝 Tours

Tours and safaris around Zambia invariably focus on the national parks. Since many of these parks are hard to visit without a vehicle, joining a tour might be your only option anyway. Budget-priced operators run scheduled trips, or arrange things on the spot (with enough passengers), and can often be booked through a backpackers – try Lusaka Backpackers (p553), or Jollyboys (p539) in Livingstone. Upmarket companies prefer to take bookings in advance, directly or through an agent in Zambia, South Africa or your home country.

Most Zambian tour operators are based in Lusaka and Livingstone. Several companies in Lilongwe (Malawi) may also offer tours to South Luangwa National Park. There are travel agents in Lusaka who can often organise tours of South Luangwa and other parks.

Train

The Tazara trains between Kapiri Mposhi and Dar es Salaam (Tanzania) can also be used for travel to/from northern Zambia. While the Lusaka–Kitwe service does stop at Kapiri Mposhi, the Lusaka–Kitwe and Tazara trains are not timed to connect with each other, and the domestic and international train stations are 2km apart.

Zambia's only other railway services are the 'ordinary trains' between Lusaka and Kitwe, via Kapiri Mposhi and Ndola, and the 'express trains' between Lusaka and Livingstone.

Domestic trains are unreliable and slow, so buses are always better. Conditions on domestic trains generally range from slightly dilapidated to ready for scrap. Most compartments have no lights or locks, so take a torch and something to secure the door at night.

Tickets for all classes on domestic trains (but not the Tazara service) can be bought up to 30 days in advance.

Zimbabwe

Includes »

Best Places to Eat

» Amanzi (p606)

» Governors' Restaurant (p627)

» Garwe (p605)

» 26 on Park (p627)

Best Places to Stay

» Camp Amalinda (p629)

» Jacana Gardens Guest Lodge (p605)

» National Parks Lodges Mana Pools (p616)

» Rhino Island Safari Camp (p615)

Why Go?

After a decade of political ruin, violence and economic disaster, finally some good news is coming out of Zimbabwe – tourism is back. Visitors are returning in numbers not seen since the turmoil began, to spot the Big Five strut their stuff around spectacular parks, discover World Heritage–listed archaeological sites and stand in awe of the natural wonder of the world, Victoria Falls.

A journey here will take you through an attractive patchwork of landscapes, from central highveld, balancing boulders and flaming *msasa* trees, to laidback towns, lush Eastern Highlands mountains and a network of lifeblood rivers up north. Along the way you'll receive a friendly welcome from locals, famous for their politeness and resilience in the face of hardship.

While there may be a long way to go, sure signs of recovery continue in Zimbabwe, giving hope to this embattled nation that a new dawn will soon rise.

When to Go
Harare

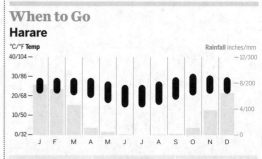

Apr–Oct Best time seasonally, with sunny days and cold, clear nights.

Nov–Apr The rainy season is beautiful, with only sporadic rain and dramatic electrical storms.

Jul–Sep Peak season; prime wildlife viewing, white-water rafting and canoeing the Zambezi.

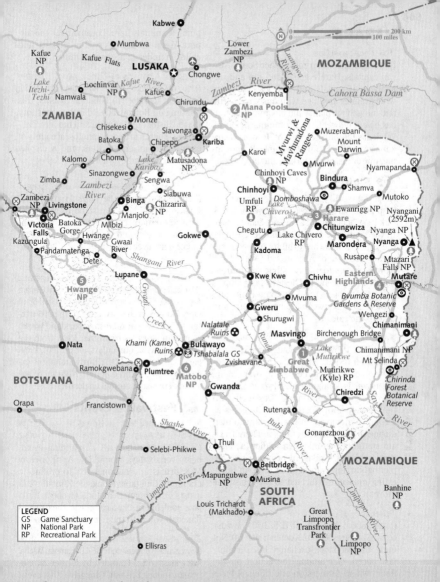

Zimbabwe Highlights

1 Exploring the atmospheric 11th-century stone ruins of **Great Zimbabwe** (p622)

2 Visiting **Mana Pools National Park** (p615), Africa's only park (with lions) that allows unguided walking safaris

3 Shopping for crafts in the capital city and going to HIFA – **Harare's International Festival of the Arts** (p604)

4 Exchanging arid highveld for cool, lush mountain air in the **Eastern Highlands** (p617)

5 Going on safari in **Hwange** (p629), Zimbabwe's largest national park and home to Africa's biggest elephant population

6 Finding the spiritual heart of Zimbabwe, packed with balancing rocks and birdlife in **Matobo National Park** (p628)

HARARE

⊘04 / POP 1.8 MILLION

More attractive than most other South African capitals, Harare gets a bad rap and unjustly so. It's a safe and laidback city where wide avenues are lined with dusty red earth, and indigenous plants and blooming jacarandas give it a lovely African summertime feel. While it's tempting to rush off to your safari, hang around in Harare to sample its fine dining, museums, craft markets and hip bars.

◎ Sights

National Gallery of Zimbabwe   GALLERY
(Map p610; ⊘704666; cnr Julius Nyerere Way & Park Lane; admission US$1; ⊙9am-5pm Tue-Sun) In the southeast corner of Harare Gardens, the gallery's monthly exhibits mix contemporary local and African art. You'll find paintings, photography, stone sculptures, masks and carvings. The attached shop is an excellent place to stock up on crafts and books on Zimbabwean art, before coffee and cake in the cafe.

National Heroes' Acre   MONUMENT
(Map p606; ⊘277965; 107 Rotten Row; admission to museum US$10; ⊙8am-4.30pm) The grandiose obelisk of Heroes' Acre, overlooking the town, is straight outta Pyongyang, yet lies just 7km from Harare. Designed with the assistance of North Korea, it serves as a somber memorial to the forces who died during the Second Chimurenga. There's a giant statue of the unknown soldier (actually three soldiers), flanked by bronze friezes depicting stirring war victories, and an interesting museum dedicated to the resistance movement.

Tobacco Floor   AUCTION HOUSE
(Map p606; ⊘621621, 0773-523170; www.tsf.co.zw; Gleneagles Rd; ⊙7.30am-1pm Mon-Fri) Not quite the NY stock exchange but certainly fast paced. Get among the action on the floors where farmers on one side sell bales of tobacco to brokers on the other. Tobacco used to be one of Zimbabwe's major foreign-exchange earners and the country produced the best leaf in the world. Auctions only take place from around February to August.

Wild is Life   WILDLIFE SANCTUARY
(⊘0779-949821; www.wildislife.com; adult/teenager US$70/50; ⊙3.30-6.30pm) A wildlife sanctuary with a difference – sip on afternoon tea and champagne while getting a hands-on experience with the injured, rescued or orphaned animals here. Located near the airport. You need to book well in advance and children under 12 are not permitted.

National Archives of Zimbabwe   MUSEUM
(Map p606; Ruth Taylor Rd; admission US$1; ⊙8.30am-4pm Mon-Fri) Founded in 1935, this building off Borrowdale Rd is the repository for the history of Rhodesia and modern Zimbabwe. There's artefacts, photos, accounts of early explorers and settlers, and a display about the Second Chimurenga.

FREE Harare Gardens   GARDENS
(Map p610) This is the city's largest park. Look for the island-like stand of rainforest with its miniature Victoria Falls (often minus the water) and Zambezi Gorge. Don't linger here after dusk.

Mukuvisi Woodlands Environmental Centre   WILDLIFE RESERVE
(Map p606; ⊘747111; mukwa@zol.co.zw; cnr Glenara Ave & Hillside Rd; adult/child US$4/3; ⊙8am-5pm) Only 7km from the city, most of the 265 hectares here are natural *msasa* parkland where zebras and giraffes roam free. View from the platform (bring binoculars) or on foot, bicycle or horse safari ($12). Birdwatching is excellent ($20 for three hours). Note there are some depressing animal enclosures.

✷✷ Festivals & Events

HIFA – Harare International Festival of Arts   MUSIC
(⊘300119; www.hifa.co.zw) *The* annual event, held over six days around late April or early May, brings international acts to produce a crammed timetable alongside Zimbabwean artists. Performances include Afrobeat, funk, jazz, soul, opera, classical music, theatre and dance. If you're in the region, don't miss it.

Zimbabwe Fashion Week   FASHION
(www.zimfashionweek.com; 16-20 Samora Machel Ave; admission $5) Founded by former Zimbabwean model Priscilla Chigariro, this event held from 30 August to 1 September showcases the latest in African designers and is a buzz on the social calendar.

⌂ Sleeping

TOP CHOICE It's a Small World Backpackers Lodge   BACKPACKERS $
(Map p606; ⊘335176; www.smallworldlodge.com; 25 Ridge Rd, Avondale; camping US$5; dm from US$11, s/d without bathroom from $15/30, d from $40; ❄☞◨) Single-handedly flying the flag

for backpackers in Harare, this old faithful knows what backpackers want – a safe neighbourhood, clean and affordable rooms, communal kitchen, wi-fi and a sociable, low-key bar. Bikes are also available for hire (US$5 per day). You may get transferred to their other place on the corner of 9th and Fife St if rooms are full here.

Jacana Gardens Guest Lodge B&B $$

(Map p606; ☑0779-715297; www.jacana-gardens. com; 14 Jacana Dr, Borrowdale; s/d incl breakfast US$95/130; ❋🛜🌊) Raising the bar to lofty heights, this guesthouse is as boutique as they come yet the best value in town. The tasteful interior, designed by the friendly Dutch owners, incorporates Zimbabwean antiques and colourful local paintings. Renowned architect Mick Pearce designed the award-winning house, which has natural light pouring into open spaces. Other clinchers here are free wi-fi, an alluring pool and trees full of birdlife.

Sunshine Guesthouse GUESTHOUSE $$

(Map p606; ☑497265; www.sunshineguesthouse. net; 91 Enterprise Rd, Highlands; r incl breakfast from $75; ❋🛜🌊) Lacks atmosphere, but the friendly owners, pool, jacuzzi, attractive lawns, soft beds and free wi-fi make it a good deal. Airport pick-up can be arranged for $12 per person.

Bronte HOTEL $$$

(Map p610; ☑796631; www.brontehotel.com; 132 Baines Ave; s/d from US$125/155; ❋🛜🌊) Located on the eastern edge of town, Bronte is sprawled out over peaceful gardens and features colonial style rooms, which are comfortable but a bit dated. It's a popular choice with NGOs – always a good sign.

York Lodge LODGE $$$

(Map p606; ☑776239; www.yorklodge.com; 1 York Ave, Newlands; s/d incl breakfast US$160/200; 🛜🌊) Journey back to Rhodesia at this colonial-style lodge – the kind of place you expect stories of hunting expeditions to be shared around the fireplace. The peaceful suburban location and dainty rooms with claw-foot baths lend a quaint atmosphere.

Amanzi Lodges LODGE $$$

(Map p606; ☑480880, 499257; www.amanzi. co.zw; 1 Masasa Lane, Kambanji; s/d US$185/280; ❋🛜🌊) Set over a tropical garden, the 12 luxury lodges here are each individually styled after different African countries, with mixed results ranging from stunning to gaudy. It offers intimate, five-star service.

Meikles HOTEL $$$

(Map p610; ☑795655; www.meikles.com; cnr Jason Moyo Ave & Third St; r incl breakfast US$275; ❋🛜🌊) Looks dated these days, but it's still the fanciest hotel in town. Sister of the Victoria Falls Hotel, it has fine dining, a smart bar, gym and rooftop pool.

🍴 Eating

Most supermarkets have inexpensive ready-to-eat meals such as *sadza* (maize meal porridge) and meat dishes.

St Elmo's PIZZERIA $

(Map p606; Avondale Shopping Centre; pizzas from US$9; ⏱11am-9pm Mon, Wed & Thu, to 10pm Fri-Sun) Popular family pizza parlour with cheap red wine and unpretentious pizzas, the type you ate when you were a kid.

Garwe AFRICAN $$

(Map p606; 18637 Donald McDonald Rd, Eastlea; mains US$8-20; ⏱noon-9pm Mon-Sat, to 4pm Sun; 🍴) Highly recommended by locals, this restaurant has traditional Zimbabwean cuisine served under a thatched roof around a large roaring fire. Lunch draws a busy crowd filling up on *sadza* and dishes including goat and guinea fowl. Vegetarians are catered for with tasty leaf vegetable dishes.

Shop Café CAFE $$

(Map p606; 1 Harrow Rd, Doon Estate, Msasa; buffet $10; ⏱9am-3pm Tue-Sat; 🛜🍴) In a land of carnivores, this vegetarian cafe is a welcome peculiarity. It bakes its own bread, grows herbs and serves coffee from the Eastern Highlands. But it's all about the vegetarian buffet (Tuesday to Friday).

Chang Thai THAI $$

(Map p606; 1 Harrow Rd, Doon Estate; mains US$7-15) With a Thai owner and chef team, it's no wonder this place has locals salivating – and perspiring – at the mention of its name. This is the real deal, with the green, red and massaman curries some of the most authentic you'll find outside Bangkok.

Millers Kitchen CAFE $$

(Map p606; Sam Levy's Village; mains US$10-20) Upmarket cafe with *sarmies* (toasted open sandwiches) served with thick-cut chips. There's sports on the TV and an outdoor patio.

40 Cork Road CAFE $$

(Map p606; ☑253585; 40 Cork Rd, Belgravia; lunch from US$10, coffee $US3; ⏱8.30am-4pm Mon-Sat; 🛜) House-turned-restaurant with a relaxed atmosphere serving quality breakfasts and

Harare

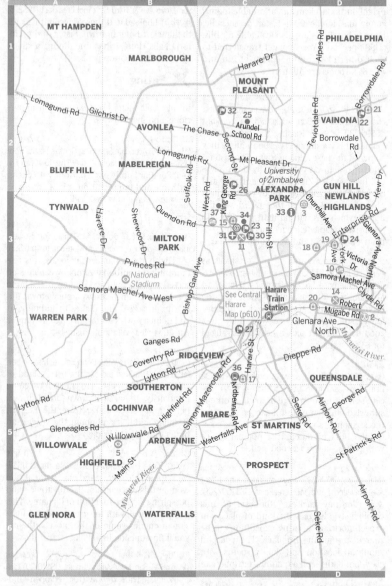

lunches, and a strong Chipinge coffee. Also has an excellent gelato shop.

Pointe Restaurant PORTUGUESE **$$**
(Map p610; Third St; mains $10-15; ◷noon-10pm) Ignore the run-down facade – it opens up to a character-filled dining room busy with

regulars eating charcoal meats and classic Portuguese dishes. Friday nights and Sunday lunch is karaoke time.

TOP CHOICE Amanzi FUSION **$$$**
(Map p606; ☑497768; www.amanzi.co.zw; 158 Enterprise Rd, Highlands; mains $15-25; ◷noon-

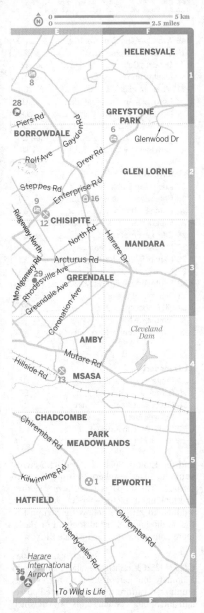

nearby garden waterfall and crackling fire brazier. Bookings essential.

Butchers Kitchen　　　STEAKHOUSE $$$
(Map p606; Sam Levy's Village; steak from US$20; ⊙8am-5pm Mon, Tue, Thu, Sat & Sun, to 9pm Wed & Fri) Enticing aromas from charcoal-grilled meats thicken the air at this winning combo of buzzing restaurant, butcher and deli. The Butchers Kitchen knows what the typical Zimbabwean craves – meat, and lots of it. Choose yours from the display, hand it to the chef and tear into a juicy steak cooked to your liking.

L'Ô de Vie　　　BELGIAN $$$
(Map p606; Newlands Shopping Centre; mains $14-25; ⊙noon-3pm & 6-10pm Tue-Fri, 7-9.30pm Sat, noon-3pm Mon) Suave Belgian restaurant with zebra-print walls that serves up creamy rabbit stew, frog legs imported from France and grilled crayfish from the waters of Kariba. Also stocks Belgian beers.

🍷 Drinking

Red Bar　　　BAR
(Map p606; www.redbar.co.zw; Enterprise Rd; ⊙closed Mon & Tue) On a mission to bring nightlife back to Harare, the recently repatriated owner here is doing a fine job. The best place for Zimbabwe's hip and mixed-race crowd. DJs play pumping tunes and the decor is industrial minimalist. Watch for pickpockets; leave your valuables in the safety deposit box or at your hotel.

Maiden Public House　　　PUB
(Map p610; ☑700037; Harare Sports Club; ⊙9am-11pm) Looking out to Harare's international cricket ground, this cheerful pub, behind the bowler's arm, is the ultimate spot to watch a game. Other times it pulls a lively crowd of sports fans glued to the TV screens with beer in hand while chowing down on pub classics (mains US$15).

★ Entertainment
Live Music
Never walk to or from any of these (or any other) late-night spots after dark; take a taxi.

TOP
CHOICE ⬧ **Book Café**　　　LIVE MUSIC
(Map p610; cnr 139 Samora Machel Ave & 6th St; ⊙10am-late Mon-Sat) No-frills but still the place for live music, with a changing roster of bands and genres every night except Sunday. Look for notices around town about events, otherwise visit the Book Café Facebook page. It also does woodfired pizzas.

2.30pm & 6.30-9.30pm) Don some nice threads as Amanzi is a class act and still *the* special night out. In a stunning colonial house with African decor, local art (for sale) and an amazing garden, it serves delicious international food with a great vibe. The outdoor patio is ridiculously atmospheric with

Harare

Jazz 105   JAZZ

(Map p610; ☏722516; cnr Second St & Robson Manyika Ave; ◷live shows from 6pm) A local haunt with live Afro jazz on Sunday and Wednesday evenings.

Sport

Harare Sports Ground   CRICKET

(Map p610; www.zimcricket.org; international games \$US5) With Zimbabwe regaining its status as a test-playing nation, cricket fans should try to make it to this scenic ground. See the website for the schedule.

🔒 Shopping

TOP
CHOICE Patrick Mavros   JEWELLERY
(☏0772-414414, 860131; www.patrickmavros.com; ◷Mon-Fri 8am-5pm, Sat till 1pm) His clients may include Bruce Springsteen, Kate Middleton

and the King of Spain, but Patrick Mavros' stunning silver jewellery is surprisingly affordable. The shop has a picture-setting, overlooking a picture-perfect valley with wildlife. To get here, follow the signpost to the studio and gallery at the end of Haslemere Lane, 1km off Umwinsidale Rd.

Kikis   ARTS & CRAFTS, HOMEWARES

(☏0774-125363; esther@iwayafrica.com) Set in a homely loungeroom, this showroom has stunning furniture, art, hand-painted porcelain and Shona wooden stools, 90% of which is produced by local artists. It's located a few doors down from Patrick Mavros.

Dendera Gallery   ARTS & CRAFTS

(Map p606; ☏0772-114731; dendera@mweb. co.zw; 1 Harrow Rd, Doon Estate; ◷9am-4.30pm Mon-Sat) This fantastic gallery has the best of Zimbabwean and African craft, many of which are antiques, as well as masks, jewellery, baskets, textiles, wooden carvings and paintings.

Newlands Art & Craft Market
ARTS & CRAFTS, SOUVENIRS

(Map p606; Enterprise Rd) Spread out along the side of the road, this market is a top spot for souvenirs with plenty of metal and stone Shona sculpture.

Avondale Flea Market
MARKET

(Map p606; Avondale Shopping Centre, King George Rd) On top of the old car park at the back of Avondale Shopping Centre, this daily flea market predominantly sells clothing but is also worth a browse for local music, crafts and secondhand books.

Mbare Market
MARKET

(Map p606) Harare, sleepy? Not in the hectic Mbare area where this infamous market has a heady mix of fresh produce and random goods. It's the curios that bring most tourists here – there's a big collection of Shona sculpture, wooden crafts and basketry. It's in a poor part of town and pickpockets are rife, so leave your valuables at home. It's best to travel here in a group, with safety better in numbers.

Ros Byrne
HOMEWARES

(Map p606; ☎487118; www.rosbyrne.co.zw; 1 Harrow Rd, Doon Estate; ⊙8am-4.30pm Mon-Fri, to 2pm Sat) Sells hand-printed fabrics, including cushion covers and bed linen, and beautiful hand-painted pottery.

KwaMambo
ARTS & CRAFTS

(Map p606; 40 Cork Rd; ⊙8.30am-4pm Mon-Sat) Excellent crafts by local artists, from metal sculptures to hand-painted ceramics and original paintings.

OK Mart
OUTDOOR EQUIPMENT

(Map p606; 30 Chiremba Rd, Hillside) The best option for tents and other camping supplies.

ℹ️ Information

Emergency
Medical Air Rescue Service (MARS; ☎706034, 771221; www.mars.co.zw) For serious medical issues, this is the best private medical care and evacuation rescue service via air and road.

Police (☎733033; cnr Inez Tce & Kenneth Kaunda Ave) Police station.

Internet Access
The town centre, radiating out from First St, has many internet centres. All charge US$1 to US$2 per hour. There is also wi-fi internet access at most hotels, restaurants and cafes for a similar cost.

Internet Cafe (Avondale Shopping Centre) Reliable internet located above Nandos.

Net Access (⊙8am-7pm Mon-Fri, to 4pm Sat) Outside Miekles Hotel.

One Stop Internet Café (60 Speke Ave)

Medical Services
Avenues Clinic (Map p610; ☎251199, 251180; www.avenuesclinic.co.zw; cnr Mazowe St & Baines Ave) Recommended hospital by expats.

Trauma Centre (Map p606; ☎700815, 700666; Lanark Rd, Belgravia) Also recommended by expats.

Post
Main Post Office (Inez Tce; ⊙8am-4pm Mon-Fri, to 11.30am Sat) Stamp sales and poste restante facilities are in the arcade, while the parcel office is downstairs.

Safe Travel
Harare is generally a safe city, but you'll need to be careful as robberies occasionally occur. Take a cab in the evenings and watch for bag snatching and pickpocketing in markets, parks and bus stations. While in no way comparable to South Africa, carjacking is on the rise, so take precautions by always keeping your windows up and your bags in the boot or, if not possible, safely wedged under your feet.

Take care when photographing certain areas in the city centre, particularly Robert Mugabe's government buildings, offices and residential areas. Keep an eye out for street signs stating 'no photography' and avoid snapping anywhere with armed soldiers. Take heed if you're asked to move along as it's not unheard of for tourists clutching cameras to be detained for questioning.

Tourist Information
Department of Immigration Control (Map p610; ☎791913; 1st fl, Linquenda House, cnr Nelson Mandela Ave & First St; ⊙8am-4pm Mon-Fri) To extend your visa, contact this office.

Harare Publicity Association (Map p610; ☎2504701; cnr Sam Nujoma (Second St) & Jason Moyo Ave, Africa Unity Sq) Supplies a free Harare city map and a few brochures.

Zimbabwe National Parks & Wildlife Central Reservations Office (NPWZ; Map p606; ☎7076259; www.zimparks.org; cnr Borrowdale Rd & Sandringham Dr, Harare; ⊙8am-4pm Mon-Fri) A good source of information and

Central Harare

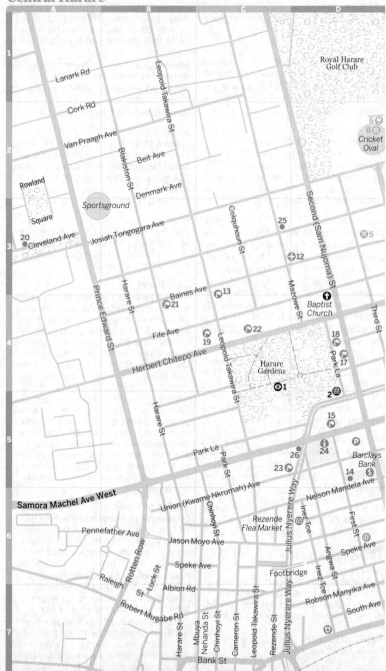

Royal Harare
Golf Club

Cricket
Oval

Lanark Rd
Cork Rd
Van Praagh Ave
Leopold Takawira St
Beit Ave
Blakiston St
Denmark Ave
Rowland
Square
Sportsground
Cleveland Ave
Josiah Tongogara Ave
Colquhoun St
Second (Sam Nujoma) St
Mazowe St
Third St
Harare St
Prince Edward St
Baines Ave
Fife Ave
Herbert Chitepo Ave
Leopold Takawira St
Harare Gardens
Baptist Church
Park La
Harare St
Park La
Park St
Samora Machel Ave West
Union (Kwame Nkrumah) Ave
Pennefather Ave
Chinhoyi St
Jason Moyo Ave
Rotten Row
Lucck St
Speke Ave
Raleigh
St
Albion Rd
Robert Mugabe Rd
Harare St
Mbuya
Nehanda St
Chinhoyi St
Cameron St
Leopold Takawira St
Rezende St
Julius Nyerere Way
Bank St
Rezende Flea Market
Footbridge
Inez Tce
Inez Tce
Angwa St
Speke Ave
Robson Manyika Ave
South Ave
Nelson Mandela Ave
First St
Barclays Bank

accommodation-booking assistance for those planning to head into the national parks.

Zimbabwe Tourism Authority (Map p610; ☏758712; www.zimbabwetourism.net; 55 Samora Machel Ave; ⊙8am-5pm Mon-Fri) Has a few brochures (but don't expect too much) and an excellent website.

Travel Agencies

Experience Africa Safaris (Map p606; ☏369185; www.xafricasafaris.com; Shop 37, Arundel Village, Quorn Ave, Mount Pleasant) Books tours around Zimbabwe and Southern Africa.

Nyati Travel (Map p606; ☏495804; www.nyati-travel.com; 29 Rhodesville Ave, Greendale) Experienced Dutch-owned company specialising in group and tailor-made tours.

Premier Travel & Tours (Map p610; ☏7047817; www.premier.co.zw; 24 Cleveland Ave, Milton Park) Recommended travel agent.

❶ Getting There & Away

Air

All international and domestic airlines use **Harare International Airport**, 15km southeast of the city centre.

Air Zimbabwe (Map p610; ☏253752, 253751; Eastgate Centre) operates flights to/from Bulawayo (one-way/return US$176/342, 45 minutes) and Victoria Falls (one-way/return US$215/421).

For details about international flights to and from Harare, see p640.

Bus

INTERNATIONAL

Companies servicing international destinations depart from **Road Port Terminal** (Map p610; cnr Robert Mugabe & Fifth Sts); see p641 for details of bus departures across borders.

DOMESTIC

The best way of getting to/from Harare is via its growing fleet of luxury buses. Otherwise you'll need to brave the chaotic **Mbare Musika bus terminal** (Map p606; Ardbennie Rd) for local 'chicken' buses. There are no schedules, and buses depart when full. Be alert for pickpockets here. The other option popular with intrepid travellers are combis (minibuses), an inexpensive option, but which have a poor safety record.

Train

The train station has departures to Bulawayo (sleeper US$12, nine hours) on Tuesdays, Fridays and Sundays at 8pm, and Mutare (US$7, 8½ hours) at 9.30pm on Wednesdays, Fridays and Sundays. Call ahead to confirm departure dates.

ZIMBABWE HARARE

Central Harare

ⓘ Getting Around

To/From the Airport

Airport taxis from Harare International cost US$25 to US$30 to town.

Car

Car-rental companies in Harare include **Avis** (Map p610; ☏796409; www.avis.co.zw; Third St) and **Europcar** (Map p606; ☏575592; www.europcar.co.zw; Harare International Airport), but mileage makes it pricey once outside Harare. Both have branches at the airport.

At the time of writing, fuel was freely available at a cost of around US$1.60 per litre for petrol and US$1.40 per litre for diesel.

Taxi

Official services include **Rixi Taxi** (☏753080), **AA Taxi** (☏704222) and **AI Taxi** (☏703334). Count on around US$50 for day-hire touring Harare.

Around Harare

Most places around Harare can be visited on day trips from the capital, but avoid travelling after dusk.

Epworth Balancing Rocks (Map p606; admission with guided tour US$10; ☺6am-6pm) are probably the most famous (and convenient) balancing rocks found in Zimbabwe, located 13km southeast of Harare, off Chiremba Rd.

Located 105km east of Harare, Imire Safari Lodge (☏2222094, 0772-522201; www.imiresafariranch.com) was built on a farm where indigenous wildlife – including black rhinos and elephants – were once hunted to clear land for farming. It now contributes enormously to the conservation of Zimbabwean wildlife. It is renowned for breeding and releasing black rhinos into Matusadona National Park and for providing orphan elephants a home. There is a student volunteer program, and accommodation in lodges or camping. Travel 70km on the Mutare road; 3km before Marondera you will see an Imire signpost – turn right here. Drive for 2.5km, turn left at the Imire sign, drive for 40km.

NORTHERN ZIMBABWE

Often overlooked by foreign travellers without their own transport, the major attractions in this part of the country are Lake Kariba and Mana Pools National Park.

HARARE DOMESTIC BUS INFORMATION

DESTINATION	COMPANY	FARE (US$)	SCHEDULE	TIME (HR)
Bulawayo	Pathfinder	30-40	departs 7.30am	5½
	Bravo	25-35	departs 2pm	
	Citylink	30-35	departs 7.30am & 2pm	
	Local buses from Mbare terminal	15	times vary	
Vic Falls	Pathfinder	60-80	departs 7.30am	12
	Citylink	55	departs 7.30am	
Hwange	Pathfinder	60	departs 7.30am	9.5
Masvingo (for Great Zimbabwe)	Local buses and mini-buses from Mbare	8-12	from 6.30am to early afternoon	3.5
Mutare (for Eastern Highlands)	local buses from Mbare	8	times vary	4
	combis outside Road Port Terminal	5-8	regularly	
Kariba	local buses	12	times vary	5-6

Lake Kariba

Lake Kariba is the nation's Riviera where it's all about houseboats, beer, fishing and amazing sunsets. It's one of the world's largest artificial lakes, covering an area of more than 5000 sq km and holding 180 billion tonnes of water. Its location adjoining the Matusadona National Park means it's home to plenty of wildlife, including the Big Five. Yet it sees few overseas visitors due to perceived high costs and difficulty of public transport access. Rest assured, it's only a five-hour bus journey from Harare, and there are backpacker options to match the luxury lodges. It also provides a good alternative route into Zambia, as well as Victoria Falls if you have a double-entry visa.

There's no better way to experience the peacefulness and beauty of Lake Kariba than by renting a houseboat, which is best arranged in Kariba town.

The climate here is much hotter than in other parts of the country, so try to avoid the summer months (October to December), when the humidity is stifling. Also take precautions against mosquitoes, as malaria is present in the area. Swimming in the lake isn't possible due to big crocs and reported bilharzia.

A good source of information covering the region is *Wild Zambezi* (www.wildzambezi. com), which has a comprehensive listing of houseboats, accommodation and activities in the area.

Kariba Town

061 / POP 27,500

The small, sprawling lakeside settlement of Kariba is spread out along the steep lakeshore. There are lovely lake views and elephants often come through town.

🏃 Activities

Houseboating

Renting a houseboat allows you to have the whole of beautiful Lake Kariba to yourself while getting close to wildlife and enjoying stellar sunsets over cold drinks.

Most boats here are large vessels that come with a crew, and sleep anywhere from 12 to 40 people, making them more suitable for larger groups. Boats cost from US$300 to US$1000.

The best option for budget travellers is to hire a houseboat that sleeps six and costs

TENGENENGE SHONA SCULPTURE VILLAGE

While the surrounding hills in the Great Dyke region are scarred by years of heavy mining, there's a whole different kind of rock chipping going on at Tengenenge Art Community (☏0774-747138, 582418; www.tengenengeartcommunity.com). Founded in 1966 by former tobacco farmer Tom Bloefield, this harmonious arts village has defied the odds to survive through the hard times and is now home to a population of 120 sculptors, representing three generations.

In a country famous for its sculpture, Tengenenge is the pick of the places to visit, being one large open-air gallery where you'll meet and see the artists at work, several of whom have exhibited their works overseas. Each has their own plot of land where they both exhibit and work away using serpentine and spring stone, producing world-class, yet affordable, pieces. The village is currently run by Dominic Benhura, arguably Zimbabwe's most successful current-day Shona sculptor. Around 65% of sales goes directly into the hands of the artist.

Most visitors are day trippers, but it's worth staying overnight in the attractive and well-maintained traditional mud huts (per person full board US$35), to give you a very off-the-beaten track feel. Visitors are also able to help out at Tengenenge's delightful preschool if they wish. Donations such as kids books and crayons are accepted.

The village is located about 150km north of Harare, and is around a two-hour drive. Getting here by public transport is more of a challenge, but it can be done. Catch a bus from Mbare station to Guruve, from where you can get dropped off at Ruyamuro and prearrange a pick-up from the village's pick-up truck (US$3).

US$150 per night through Warthogs Bush Camp. Otherwise, get in touch with Rhino Rendezvous (☏0772-220831, 04-490124; www.houseboatsonkariba.com) and Marineland Harbour (☏2845; www.marineland.co.zw).

Fishing

Reel in one of the lake's famous residents, whether it be a tiger fish, Kariba bream or giant vundu. Warthogs can arrange half-/full-day fishing trips for US$60/80 (excluding fuel).

🛏 Sleeping & Eating

TOP CHOICE Warthogs Bush Camp   LODGE $
(☏0775-068406; www.warthogs.co.zw; Kariba; campsite per person US$5, tented camps s/d US$10/15, lodges d US$40, 6-person chalet US$70; 🛜) On the lake, this bush camp is the only place catering to budget travellers – thankfully it does a fantastic job. The A-frame huts, tented camps and thatched cabins are basic but it's the liveliest spot in Kariba with a 24-hour bar, good pub grub, houseboats for hire and fishing trips, too. There are also plenty of animal visitors, from hippos and elephants to zebra – keep your distance!

Cutty Sark   HOTEL $$
(☏0772-151668; www.cuttysarkhotel.com; Nzou Dr; s/d incl breakfast from US$45/70, full board

US$115; ❄@🛜🏊) In a region dominated by wildlife lodges, here's an affordable hotel right on the lake with fantastic views and a lovely pool to lounge around in.

Hornbill Lodge   LODGE $$
(Mica Point; r per person with full board US$130-150; 🏊) A prime spot overlooking the lake, with thatched *rondavels* (round traditional-style huts) set among landscaped gardens and a small plunge pool. Rates include alcoholic beverages.

❶ Getting There & Away

Local buses run to Harare daily (US$12, five hours).

Taxis are the best way to get to Zambia (via Kariba border), 10km from Kariba. Expect to pay US$5 to US$7 for the 10-minute trip.

Kariba Ferries runs a service between Kariba and Mlibizi (adult/child incl meals US$160/80, sedan US$120, 4WD US$180), departing 9am and arriving 7am the next day.

Matusadona National Park

Situated on the southern shore of Lake Kariba, the beautiful Matusadona National Park (☏0772-143506; entry fee US$15 per person) is home to the Big Five, including the endangered black rhino. Ghostly dead trees act as roosting places for fish eagles, cormorants and darters. The best time for wildlife viewing is between July and November.

The only downside to the park is a combination of limited budget accommodation and difficult access via public transport.

🏃 Activities

You can safari in the area by houseboat, 4WD, canoe or on foot. These activities are included as part of the package offered by lodges.

🛏 Sleeping

Other than the Tashinga campsite, all the following rates include meals and activities, but not park fees or transfers.

Tashinga   CAMPGROUND **$**
(campsite per person US$15) Run by the national park and located 1km from the main office, this campsite overlooks the Ume River and has basic facilities. It's only accessible via 4WD, and bookings should be arranged in the central office (p609) in Harare.

TOP CHOICE **Rhino Island Safari Camp**   LODGE **$$$**
(📞0772-400021, 0772-205000; www.rhinosafaricamp.com; r per person US$295) One of the best camps in the country, this is remote, wild and everything you want from a safari experience. Lodging is in thatched, stilted chalets, and the staff is friendly and passionate. There's no electricity, but there are paraffin and solar lamps, and camera batteries can be charged. It's located on a peninsula at Elephant Point, and black rhinos, lions and elephants are often spotted.

Musango Safari Camp   LODGE **$$$**
(📞0772-307875; www.musangosafaricamp.com; per person US$260-300) Just outside the national park, Musango is one of the most popular (permanent) 'tented' camps in Lake Kariba because of its location and abundant wildlife. It's run by former warden of the park and expert guide Steve Edwards, who has more than 35 years' experience.

Bumi Hills Safari Lodge   LODGE **$$$**
(📞0772-135665, 04-307087; www.bumihills.com; s/d with full board from US$400/650; 🛜🏊) Sitting on the shoreline up in the hills, Bumi Hills has 20 lodges, all with balconies and views of the lake and plenty of wildlife to see. It has an infinity pool, and its own airstrip and airline (BumiAir) for high-flyers.

Spurwing Island   LODGE **$$$**
(www.spurwingisland.com; s/d with full board from US$163/244; 🛜🏊) On an island in the middle of the lake, Spurwing has a range of accommodation including tented camping, cabins and chalets. It's a good lodge for kids as it has a fenced swimming pool and babysitting services. It's about 45 minutes by boat from Kariba town. Wi-fi is available for US$10 per day.

ℹ Getting There & Away

Transfers to the lodges are additional to nightly rates, and cost around US$60 to US$100.

You can fly to Matusadona National Park from Harare or Victoria Falls for around US$500 per person via BumiAir at Bumi Hills Safari Lodge. You don't have to be a guest there to do so. For more information on chartered flights, see p642.

Mana Pools National Park

This magnificent 2200-sq-km **national park** (📞63512, 63513; admission adult/child US$30/15; ⊙6am-6pm) is a Unesco World Heritage–listed site, and its magic stems from its remoteness and pervading sense of the wild and natural. This is one park in Zimbabwe where you're guaranteed to see plenty of hippos, crocs, zebras and elephants, and *almost* guaranteed to see lions and possibly wild (painted) dogs.

What sets Mana Pools apart from just about any other park in the world is that it's all unfenced, so there can be elephants strolling by while you have your breakfast. You're also allowed to walk around without a guide, as you can see for miles around. But be aware, this is about personal responsibility: wild animals are incredibly dangerous – and fast. Hence walking with a guide is highly advised.

🏃 Activities

Fishing and canoeing on the Zambezi River provide breathtaking (read: heart in mouth) experiences. Also for the brave at heart: book a side trip to the famous Chitake Springs; these isolated springs have prearranged camping only, and are known for the number of lions that roam around there.

The **Mana Pools Game Count**, which is held over the weekend of the first full moon in September, offers an interesting opportunity. It's open to Wildlife & Environment Zimbabwe members, which is gained through a US$50 annual subscription payable to the Department of National Parks & Wildlife Management office (p609) in Harare. Admission to the park is free for the weekend only, but volunteers pay all their own expenses and bring all their own supplies. In brief, you count animals during the day and enjoy a *braai* (barbecue) and 'much merriment' at night. For more information or to register, contact Jane and Kelvin Hein on bushpig@mango.zw.

See p613 for information on hiring houseboats.

🛏 Sleeping

Other than the national parks accommodation, rates include meals and activities.

TOP CHOICE **National Parks Lodges** CAMPGROUND $$
(☑04-706077; national-parks@gta.gov.zw; campsite per person US$20, lodges from US$100) The only budget option in Mana Pools, these well-equipped lodges and campsites along the Zambezi River offer prime animal viewing. Lodges book out during July to October, so you'll need to make reservations well in advance (accepted one year ahead) and can be done through the Harare office (☑04-706077; national-parks@gta.gov.zw; cnr Borrowdale Rd & Sandringham Dr, Harare; ⊗8am-4pm Mon-Fri) by phone or email.

Chikwenya Safari Lodge LODGE $$$
(☑0772-470065; www.chikwenyasafaris.com; s/d with full board & activities US$475/750; ⊗Apr-Dec; ✳🎖☒) Tented rooms are nestled into the bush and huge gauze windows look out across the Sapi River mouth to acacia flood plains, the Zambezi River and Chikwenya Island, with the Zambian escarpment as the awesome backdrop. Sleep to the honking of hippos. Open from April to December.

Kanga Bush Camp TENTED CAMP $$$
(☑9234307; www.africanbushcamps.com; per person US$440; ☒) Very private, permanent but seasonal camp (closed mid-November to April), Kanga Bush Camp has six luxury tents with ensuite bathrooms built around the Kanga pan, the only permanent water source in its area, so it heaves with wildlife and good predator sightings. Rates include alcohol.

Ruckomechi TENTED CAMP $$$
(☑43371, 0772-247155; www.wilderness-safaris.com; per person from US$600; ☒) An amazing luxury tented camp. Each tent overlooks the Zambezi, and has indoor and outdoor showers – great for animal watching. Closed from mid-November to April.

❶ Getting There & Away

Mana Pools National Park is only accessible via 4WD, so it's limited to self-drive or those on all-inclusive packages. Wet season (November to April) is best avoided as dirt roads turn to sludge and no assisting car service is available. If self-driving, take note you need to register at the gate before 3pm. Charter flights are the other option to get here; for more information, see p642.

MIDDLE ZAMBEZI CANOE SAFARIS

Adventurers describe canoe trips down this awesome wilderness route as one of the best things they've ever done. Several companies run trips between Kariba and Kanyemba (on the river junction with Zimbabwe, Zambia and Mozambique).

The trip is normally done in stages: Kariba to Chirundu (three days), Chirundu to Mana Pools National Park (three to four days) and Mana Pools to Kanyemba (four to five days). Any combination is possible, but if you can do only one, Chirundu to Mana Pools offers the best scenery and diversity of wildlife.

Most canoe safaris run from April/May to October/November, but some operate year-round. November, during the dry season, is the best time for game viewing on the lower Zambezi.

For classic tented-camp safaris through to hiking or canoe trails, try **Natureways Safaris** (☑0772-335038; www.natureways.com; Stand 473, Andora Harbour, Kariba) based in Kariba. On the 'shoreline canoe trails', you get a fully licensed guide to do safari walks inland and a team to go ahead and set up camp downriver each night – guests are generally flown in for these. Natureways can also organise less expensive 'participating' canoe trips, where all your kit goes with you in the canoe (tents, cooking, equipment, clothes) and you have a guide.

Mavuradonha Wilderness

Little known to visitors, Mavuradonha is home to some of Zimbabwe's most pristine wilderness, a rugged blend of grey granite with the red soils of Zimbabwe's Great Dyke Complex. It's the escarpment of the Zambezi Valley, where deep valleys bisect towering rock faces and grass-covered mountains.

Those looking to get deep into the true wilderness should look into the horseback safaris run by Varden Safaris (✆04-861766; www.vardensafaris.com; all-inclusive horseback safaris US$290). Trips run anywhere from weekend journeys to week-long adventures, where you stay in rustic bush camps and eat fresh bush cuisine.

Wilderness Eco Lodge (huts s/d US$10/15, s/d US$20/30) is another base for exploring the area, and offers nature walks as well as visits and homestays in local villages.

The wilderness area is funded by the Campfire project, which supports local rural communities. A significant portion of its revenues are generated by hunting concessions in the region, a contentious topic that divides conservationists. See the boxed text, p691.

EASTERN HIGHLANDS

This narrow strip of mountain country that makes up Manicaland isn't the Africa that normally crops up in armchair travellers' fantasies. It's a land of mountains, national parks, pine forests, botanical gardens, rivers, dams and secluded getaways.

Mutare

✆020 / POP 188, 750

Mutare is set in a pretty valley surrounded by hills. Zimbabwe's third-largest city, it has a relaxed rural-town atmosphere. Its real value, though, is its proximity to both Mozambique and the Bvumba region and Nyanga National Park. It's a nice enough place to break up your trip.

◎ Sights

Mutare Museum MUSEUM
(✆63630; Aerodrome Rd; admission US$10; ⊙9am-5pm) Definitely worth popping your head in to to see what exhibit is showing at the time. The museum also has a permanent collection of vintage cars, artefacts, and displays on anthropology and zoology.

🛏 Sleeping & Eating

Ann Bruce Backpackers BACKPACKERS $
(✆0772-249089; annbruce@zol.co.zw; cnr Fourth St & Sixth Ave; dm/s/d US$15/15/30; 🛜) Kudos to this long-established backpackers for staying open through the dark times. Run by a friendly owner, it has a homely feel with a garden gazebo and a mix of dorms and private rooms, but only some have bathrooms. Ann is a great source of info on the Eastern Highlands.

Homestead Guest House GUESTHOUSE $$
(✆65870; homestead@mweb.co.zw; 52 Park Rd; d/tr without bathroom US$30/45, d US$40; ▨) This renovated late-19th-century home is set in a pretty garden with a pool. It has clean and comfortable rooms with wooden floorboards. Dinner costs US$5 a head.

The Green Coucal CAFE $$
(111 Second St; ⊙8am-5pm Mon-Sat; 🛜) With its inviting open-air deck and outdoor garden, this is a great place to while away a morning or afternoon. It's run by an ultrafriendly Irishman and his wife, who use coffee beans from the Eastern Highlands and serve up hearty fare.

ℹ Information

Manicaland Publicity Bureau (✆64711; www.manicalandpublicity.co.zw; cnr Herbert Chitepo St & Robert Mugabe Rd; ⊙8.30am-12.45pm & 2-4pm Mon-Fri) has basic tourist info available, but head to Ann Bruce Backpackers to get up-to-date travel info.

Try **Internet Cyber Cafe** (✆67939; 67 Fourth St; per hr US$2.50) if you want to get online.

ℹ Getting There & Away

Regular 'local' and express buses head to Harare (US$6 to US$8, four hours) from either the town bus terminal, long-distance bus terminal (Railway Ave) or central bus stand (Masvingo Rd, Sakubva Musica) 3km south of town. Pathfinder was due to start operating here, too.

Regular combis (US$1) head to the Mozambique border (from 6am to 8pm), which is 8km from Mutare. A taxi will cost US$10.

To get to Bvumba, catch a combi (US$3) from the start of Bvumba Rd; they leave when full. Alternatively, Ann Bruce Backpackers offer a private transfer option and tour ($US50).

Mutare

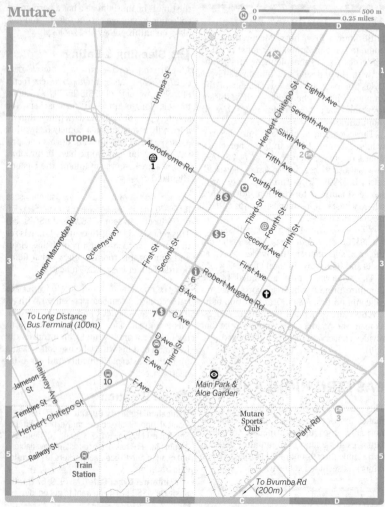

Bvumba Mountains

📷 020

Just 28km southeast of Mutare, the Bvumba (pronounced Vumba) Mountains are characterised by cool, forested highlands and deep, misty valleys. In the language of the Manyika Shona people, Bvumba means 'drizzle' and you'll probably see why. With its meadows, apple orchards, country gardens and teahouses, the area seems akin to the British countryside. While it's beautiful year-round, things can get hazy during August when forest fires commonly burn in the hills.

◉ Sights & Activities

Seldomseen BIRDWATCHING

(📷68482, 0714-516743; per person per hour US$5) Twitchers can do a two-hour bird-life walk with Seldomseen Farm. There are 250 birds that are spotted in the area, including buff-spotted fluff tail or striped-cheek green bulbul.

Leopard Rock Golf Club GOLF

(9/18 holes US$30/50, club hire US$25; ⊘8am-5.30pm) Even if you can't tell a putter from a wedge, don't miss out on a round of golf at the PGA-ranked course at Leopard Rock

Mutare

◉ Sights
1 Mutare Museum..B2

🛏 Sleeping
2 Ann Bruce Backpackers D2
3 Homestead Guest House D5

✕ Eating
4 The Green Coucal C1

ℹ Information
5 Barclays C3
6 Manicaland Publicity Bureau B3
7 Stanbic...B4
8 Standard Chartered Bank C2

ℹ Transport
9 Combis to Mozambique Border B4
   Taxi Stand.....................................(see 6)
10 Town Bus Terminal..............................B4

Hotel. It features breathtaking vistas, including over Mozambique from the 17th.

🛏 Sleeping & Eating

TOP CHOICE **It's a Small World**

Lodge Vumba   GUESTHOUSE $
(☏0912-612319; www.smallworldlodge.com; Lot 1 Cloudlands Arusha Estate; d from US$40, cottages weekday/weekend US$50/90) An attractive guesthouse set in a colonial-style holiday home with an English garden and views to the valley. Rooms are large and comfy, and the homely lounge with roaring fireplace is a social place to gather in the evenings. Also has a kitchen for self-caterers, and self-contained cottages up the hill. Bikes are available for hire.

Hivu   GUESTHOUSE $
(☏0773-246873; campsite per person US$8, r per person US$15, cottage per person US$20) An attractive country house with homely rooms, calm pastoral setting and kitchen for self-catering. There's horse riding (US$15 per person), and transport from Mutare available for US$3. Rates increase slightly on weekends.

Eden Lodge   LODGE $$
(☏0736-038390; Freshwater Rd, Bvumba; r from US$120) Cosy red-brick cottages with dated decor, but the fireplaces, valley views and manicured lawns make up for it. There's also a British-style pub, horse riding and

free bike hire. Rates include free pick-up from Mutare. Downhill from the main road.

Leopard Rock Hotel   HOTEL $$$
(☏60192; www.lonrhohotels.com/content/leopard-rock-hotel; s/d US$150/250; ☒) Once a favourite of English royalty, Leopard Rock is still the poshest place in the region – yet rooms are in need of refurbishment. It backs on to the famous golf course.

Tony's Coffee House   DESSERTS $$
(Bvumba Rd; coffee from US$5, slice of cake US$9-12; ◷10am-5pm Wed-Sun) Yes, $10 is expensive for a slice of cake but Tony's can justify it. White-chocolate cheese cake with edible flowers is divine. Enjoy it indoors by the fire or on the lawn looking out to fruit orchards. If you're lucky, you'll spot simango monkeys.

ℹ Getting There & Away

Getting here from Mutare isn't an issue – combis and taxis (US$2 to US$3) depart when full – but getting back is trickier. Your lodge should be able to assist with arranging transport, otherwise hitching (while never entirely safe) is an option.

Nyanga National Park
☏029

The 47,000-hectare **Nyanga National Park** (☏8274, 0773-500398; www.nyangapark.com; admission US$10; ◷6am-6pm) is a geographically and scenically distinct enclave in the Eastern Highlands. Nyanga is famous not for its wildlife (though it does have antelopes and zebras) but rather for its verdant, mountainous scenery, crystal-clear streams, and Zimbabwe's highest mountain and waterfall. It's also reknowned for trout fly-fishing.

The main gate is a few kilometres from Nyanga town, close to the Rhodes Nyanga Hotel.

◉ Sights & Activities

Nyanga Historical Exhibition   MUSEUM
(Rhodes Museum; admission US$2; ◷9am-1pm & 2.30-5.30pm Thu-Tue) The Nyanga Historical Exhibition is housed in Cecil Rhodes' former stables in the grounds next door to the Rhodes Nyanga Hotel.

World's View   ARCHAEOLOGICAL SITE
(admission US$4) World's View is perched atop the Troutbeck Massif. This National Trust site affords broad views of northern Zimbabwe. It's 11km up a winding, steep road from Troutbeck – follow the signposts.

The flat-topped and myth-shrouded Nyangani (2592m) is Zimbabwe's highest mountain. From the car park 14km east of Nyanga Dam, the climb to the summit takes two to three hours. Note that the weather can change abruptly, and when the mists drop the view becomes irrelevant.

It's also famous for Mtazari Falls, Zim's highest waterfall. Falling from a height of 479m, it trumps Victoria Falls by 300m, and is number two in Africa. It's at its peak from February to May.

🛏 Sleeping & Eating

National Park Lodge CAMPGROUND **$**
(✆0773-500398, 8274; campsite per person US$8, d from US$80) Set over three different locations within Nyanga. Choose from self-catering lodges and campsites at Rhodes Dam near the main gate, Udu Dam on the western side of the park, or Mare Dam, 10km from the main gate.

Rhodes Nyanga Hotel HOTEL **$$**
(✆0779-478645; www.rhodesnyangahotel.com; s/d incl breakfast from US$80/90) At the park's entrance, this is the former holiday home of Cecil Rhodes. Converted into a hotel in 1933, it features tropical verandahs and English gardens overlooking the Nyanga Dam. It has *rondavels* as well as rooms, some which have furniture used by the man himself.

Inn on Rupurara INN **$$$**
(✆3021; rupurara@bsatt.com; s/d incl breakfast & activities US$136/218; ☀) A beautifully appointed hotel of African-style bungalows with verandahs, overlooking the valley to Rupurara Mountain (or Bald Man's Head).

❶ Information

The **Nyanga Tourist Association** (✆0712-218440) is housed in Pine Tree Inn, Juliasdale, and has good local info and maps of the region.

❶ Getting There & Away

Regular combis run the 106km leg between Nyanga and Mutare for US$4.

Chimanimani

✆026 / POP 2700

Chimanimani village, 150km south of Mutare, is enclosed by green hills on three sides, and opens on the fourth side to the dramatic wall of the Chimanimani Mountains.

🛏 Sleeping & Eating

TOP CHOICE **Frog & Fern** LODGE **$**
(✆0774-659789; www.thefrogandfern.com; campsite US$15, r US$40-50; @) Backing on to the Pork Pie Eland sanctuary, accommodation here is in *rondavel* cottages or stone cabins, all with cooking facilities, fireplaces and garden views. The owners here are an excellent source of trekking and local info, and can arrange cultural tours.

Farmhouse LODGE **$**
(✆0772-101283; www.chimanifarmhouse.com; r US$10) This restored colonial farmhouse, with cheap rooms and inspiring views of the surrounding hills, is a good option for backpackers. It's also a good place to arrange your trek, and kids will love the farm animals here. Horse riding is also possible.

Heaven Lodge LODGE **$**
(✆2701; www.heavenlodge.com; campsite US$5, r US$10) One of the original backpackers, this lodge fell on hard times during the turmoil, yet it was in the process of a facelift at the time of research.

Msasa Café CAFE **$**
(mains US$10; ⏰8am-5pm Mon-Sat) Best spot in the village for eating out. Serves a wide

Chimanimani & Around

variety of meals; try the *sadza*, chicken and gravy.

ℹ️ Information

There's a **Chimanimani Tourist Association** (touristassociationchimanimani@gmail.com) in town, and the website for the Frog & Fern lodge has good info.

ℹ️ Getting There & Away

Transport to Chimanimani is via local buses and combis from either Mutare (US$6, three hours) or Masvingo (from US$7, four hours).

Chimanimani National Park

With its pristine wilderness, Chimanimani National Park (hiking US$10; ⏲️6am-6pm) is a hiker's paradise. The northern end of the park, Corner, is still very wild and un-spoiled, but the road there is not good. The park shares a border with Mozambique.

For hiking in Chimanimani National Park, 19km from Chimanimani village, you must sign in and pay park fees at Mutekeswane Base Camp. The road ends here and the park is then only accessible on foot. Mountain biking is also popular.

From base camp, Bailey's Folly is the shortest and most popular route to the mountain hut (around three hours). Another option is the gentler Banana Grove Track. From the mountain hut, it's an easy 40-minute walk to Skeleton Pass, a former guerrilla route between Zimbabwe and Mozambique. Go in the late afternoon for an unsurpassed view into Wizard Valley in Mozambique.

The highest point in the Chimanimani Range is the 2437m-high Mt Binga on the Mozambican border, a stiff three-hour climb from the hut. Carry plenty of water.

Hadange River Track is a good but challenging exit route that emerges near

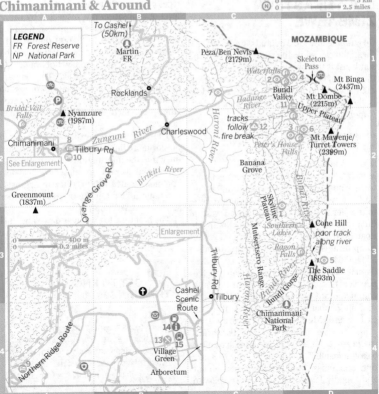

Chimanimani & Around

0——5 km
0——2.5 miles

LEGEND
FR Forest Reserve
NP National Park

To Cashel (50km)

Martin FR

MOZAMBIQUE

Peza/Ben Nevis (2179m)

Skeleton Pass

Mt Binga (2437m)

Waterfalls

Rocklands

Hadange River

Bundi Valley

Mt Dombe (2215m)

Upper Plateau

Bridal Veil Falls

Nyamzure (1987m)

tracks follow fire break

Mt Mawenje/ Turret Towers (2399m)

Chimanimani

Tilbury Rd

Zunguni River

Charleswood

Haroni River

Petri's House Falls

Banana Grove

See Enlargement

Birikiti River

Greenmount (1837m)

Orange Grove Rd

Skyline Plateau

Southern Lakes

Cone Hill poor track along river

Enlargement

Bundi River

0——400 m
0——0.2 miles

Matsetsero Range

Ragon Falls

The Saddle (1893m)

Northern Ridge Route

Tilbury Rd

Haroni River

Cashel Scenic Route

Tilbury

Bundi Gorge

Village Green

Chimanimani National Park

Arboretum

ZIMBABWE CHIMANIMANI NATIONAL PARK

the Outward Bound School and Tessa's Pool, a lovely swimming hole. If you exit this way, you'll need to walk back along the road to sign out at base camp. The Bundi Valley is riddled with caves and rock overhangs, ideal (free) campsites. The most accessible caves lie near the valley's northern end. North Cave, a 30-minute walk north of the mountain hut, overlooks a waterfall and opens onto views of the highest peaks. Above the waterfall is a pool, perfect for a teeth-chattering dip if you need some refreshment. Red Wall Cave lies 10 minutes further on.

Camping is free in the park, but it's advised to camp at either Mutekeswane Base Camp (campsite per person US$8) or stay in the mountain hut (per person US$8), which at an elevation of 1630m is a long and steep half-day walk from the base camp. Bit grubby but has running water and cooking facilities.

THE MIDLANDS & SOUTHEASTERN ZIMBABWE

Geographically, the Midlands are known as the high-veld, while the warmer, lower-lying southeast is the low-veld. At the transition of the regions is Masvingo and nearby is Great Zimbabwe. The low-veld's finest attraction is the beautiful, often-ignored Gonarezhou National Park.

Masvingo

039 / POP 73,000

Masvingo is a classic crossroads country town. Though pleasant enough, it offers little for travellers and most people are here to transfer to Great Zimbabwe, head west to Bulawayo or, further south, to the South African border. Stock up on food here if you're camping at Great Zimbabwe campgrounds.

The Church of St Francis of Assisi (Italian Chapel; 8am-6pm) was constructed between 1942 and 1946 by Italian POWs to commemorate 71 of their compatriots who died in Zimbabwe during WWII. It's 4km east towards Mutare from the caravan park.

Backpackers Rest (63960; Josiah Tongogara Ave; dm US$20, s/d without bathroom incl breakfast from US$36/48) has rooms that are dim and noisy, but it's cheap, convenient and friendly. It's located upstairs and easy to

miss so keep your eyes peeled. The entrance is along Robertson St.

The folks at Masvingo Publicity Association (0773-998028; mapepetah@gmail.com; Robert Mugabe St; 8am-4:30pm Mon-Fri) can help with general information and assistance with accommodation in Masvingo and Great Zimbabwe.

Regular buses and combis run the gauntlet between Masvingo and Harare (US$8 to US$12, 3½ hours). It's one of the country's most treacherous stretches of road, used 24/7 by cargo trucks heading to South Africa, so avoid after late afternoon.

Great Zimbabwe

039

The greatest medieval city in sub-Saharan Africa, the World Heritage–listed Great Zimbabwe (admission adult/child US$15/8, guide $US3; 6am-6pm) is one of the nation's most treasured sights. So much so, that it was named after it! This mysterious site provides evidence that ancient Africa reached a level of civilisation not suspected by earlier scholars. As a religious and political capital, this city of 10,000 to 20,000 dominated a realm that stretched across eastern Zimbabwe and into modern-day Botswana, Mozambique and South Africa. The name is believed to come from one of two possible Shona origins: *dzimba dza mabwe* (great stone houses) or *dzimba woye* (esteemed houses).

The site is easily explored by yourself, but for more info, maps and the best routes, duck into the information centre at the site's checkpoint to pick up one of the booklets. For more in-depth info, you can arrange a two-hour guided tour (about US$12 per person) at the checkpoint.

The best time to explore is dawn and dusk when the sunrise, or sunset, enhances what is already a stunning site and means you

---

ZIMBABWE MASVINGO

GET TO KNOW THE RUINS

Head to the Great Zimbabwe Museum (9am-5pm) before you start exploring the site to prep yourself and gain some insight through the informative displays there. It's located a short walk within the entry, across from the kiosk.

Great Zimbabwe

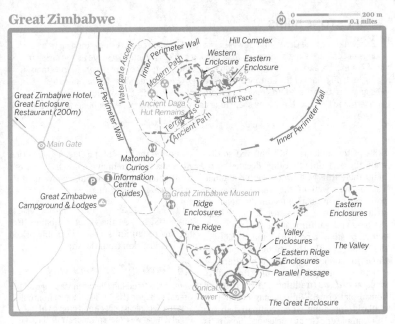

beat the heat. Allow at least three hours to explore.

History

Great Zimbabwe was first occupied in the 11th century. The settlers probably comprised several scattered groups that recognised the safety of numbers. Construction of the Hill Complex commenced in the 13th century, while the remainder was built over the next 100 years.

Fuelled by the Swahili gold trade, the city grew into a powerful religious and political capital, and became the heart of Rozwi culture. Royal herds increased and coffers overflowed. But eventually Great Zimbabwe likely became a victim of its own success: by the 15th century the growing human and bovine population, and their associated environmental impacts, had depleted local resources, necessitating emigration to more productive lands. Great Zimbabwe declined rapidly, and when the Portuguese arrived in the 16th century the city was virtually deserted.

☉ Sights

The site is divided into several major ruins with three main areas – the Hill Complex, the Valley and the Great Enclosure.

Most likely the first of the Great Zimbabwe structures to be completed, the Hill Complex is a maze of enclosures with spectacular views over the ruins. These ruins were a series of royal and ritual enclosures and at the top is the most salient feature, the Western Enclosure. It can be reached by two paths: the Ancient Path and the Modern Path, both signposted near the start. The Ancient Path is a steeper, rocky climb where you squeeze through narrow crevices of ruins and boulders. Choose one to go up and the other to come back down.

The Great Enclosure, thought to have served as a royal compound, is the structure most identified with Great Zimbabwe. Nearly 100m wide and 255m in circumference, it's the largest ancient structure in sub-Saharan Africa. The mortarless walls rise 11m and, in places, are 5m thick. The greatest source of speculation is the 10m-high Conical Tower, a solid and ceremonial structure that perhaps had phallic significance for fertility, but it's not known for sure.

Leading north from the Conical Tower is the narrow 70m-long Parallel Passage. It may have been a means of moving from the northern entrance to the Conical Tower without being detected by those within the enclosure. It may also have been that the

SOAPSTONE BIRDS

Excavations of the Great Zimbabwe ruins in the late 19th century unearthed eight carvings of soapstone birds (believed to be fishing eagles), which now serve as the emblem of Zimbabwe, and are immortalised on the national flag. Six of them were found standing high on pillars at the entrance of the Eastern Enclosure in the Hill Complex. It's suggested that these birds may have represented the ancestors of Great Zimbabwe's rulers. You'll see several of the soapstone carved birds in the Great Zimbabwe Museum here.

skills of the builders had improved so dramatically over time that they decided to rebuild the entire wall in a superior manner. The outside wall of the Parallel Passage, perhaps the most architecturally advanced structure in Great Zimbabwe, is 6m thick at the base and 4m thick at the top, with each course of stone tapering to add stability to the 11m-high wall. This stretch is capped by three rings of decorative chevron patterns.

The Valley is a series of 13th-century walls and *daga* (traditional African round house) platforms. While it may not be particularly appealing when compared to the Hill Complex or Great Enclosure, the area is a significant architectural area which yielded metal tools as well as some of the soapstone bird carvings that became the national symbol of Zimbabwe.

🛏 Sleeping & Eating

Great Zimbabwe

Campground & Lodges   CAMPGROUND $
(✆0773-456622; campsite/dm/rondavel per person US$5/5/15, r/ste US$30/50) Inside the main gate and within sight of the Hill Complex, dorms, lodges, campsite and *rondavels* are spread out over a stretch of around 500m. *Rondavels* are spacious with shared bathroom blocks but, like the campsite, can feel a bit isolated. Suite lodges are good value for couples and come with bathroom, kitchen and TV. *Braais* and firewood (US$2) are provided for self-caterers, and the Great Enclosure Restaurant is a short walk away.

Peter's Lodge   GUESTHOUSE $
(✆0775-377101; r from US$30) On the road between Great Zimbabwe and Masvingo, Peter's has simple homely rooms set in lovely gardens with shared bathrooms and an attached restaurant.

Great Zimbabwe Hotel   HOTEL $$$
(✆262274; r from US$140) Built in 1905 this hotel is certainly past its prime, when Room 29 hosted the likes of the Queen and Nelson Mandela (hard to imagine now). Overpriced for the mediocre rooms but a convenient location close to the ruins.

Great Enclosure Restaurant   INTERNATIONAL $$
(mains US$8-15) At the Great Zimbabwe Hotel, this restaurant serves reasonably priced cuisine, just 1km from the site.

❶ Getting There & Away

Combis run frequently between Masvingo and Great Zimbabwe (US$2, 30 minutes) from outside the Technical College and drop off at the Great Zimbabwe Hotel entrance. Walk through the grounds to reach the Great Zimbabwe main gate – about 800m.

Gonarezhou National Park

Bordering Mozambique, Gonarezhou National Park (admission US$15; ☉6am-6pm May-Oct) is virtually an extension of South Africa's Kruger National Park. So, in late 2002, the relevant authorities in Zimbabwe, South Africa and Mozambique created the Great Limpopo Transfrontier Park, a 35,000-sq-km park straddling all three countries (with no boundaries).

🛏 Sleeping

National Park Lodge   CAMPGROUND $
(campsite per person US$15-25, chalets 2/4 people US$75/100) Book at National Parks & Wildlife Zimbabwe in Harare (p609) for the chalets or campsites here.

Pamushana   LODGE $$$
(✆0772-292056, in South Africa 27 21-683 3424; www.singita.com; s/d with full board $US950; 🐾) Zimbabwe's uberluxurious lodge (Michael Douglas and Catherine Zeta-Jones are two past guests) has bungalows perched upon a cliff among the trees, some overlooking a hippo-laden lake. Each has a private sun deck, infinity pool and outdoor rock shower.

It is nonprofit and dedicated to protecting and saving endangered species of wildlife.

❶ Getting There & Away

You'll need a 4WD, and there's no access to the national park camps from November to April. Pamushana has its own airstrip for those who want to arrange a chartered flight.

WESTERN ZIMBABWE

With three of the country's major attractions – Victoria Falls, Hwange National Park and Matobo National Park – western Zimbabwe is a place worth allocating a good portion of your travel time.

Bulawayo

⏱09 / POP 1 MILLION

Wide tree-lined avenues, parks and charming colonial architecture make Bulawayo, Zimbabwe's second city, an attractive one. It has a lovely historic feel to it, and it's worth spending a night or two. It's also a popular base for trips to the nearby Khami Ruins and Matobo National Park, and an ideal staging point for Hwange National Park, on the way to Victoria Falls.

◉ Sights & Activities

Wandering about the city centre, you'll spot excellent examples of its art deco, Victorian and Edwardian colonial-heritage buildings.

National Art Gallery GALLERY
(☑70721; www.nationalgallerybyo.com; cnr Main St & Leopold Takawira Ave; admission US$5; ◉9am-5pm Tue-Sat) Set in a beautiful 100-year-old classical Edwardian building, the National Art Gallery has temporary and permanent exhibitions of contemporary Zimbabwean sculpture and paintings. There's also a gallery shop with local literature, arts and craft, a lovely cafe and studios where you can see artists at work.

Natural History Museum MUSEUM
(Centenary Park; adult/child US$10/5; ◉8am-5pm) Explore the country's natural, anthropological and geological history, set over three floors at Zimbabwe's largest and best museum. The impressive collection of gemstones shows the country's astounding wealth of natural resources. Also has a good taxidermy display.

Prospector's Pub Crawl WALKING TOUR
(resman@amalindacollection.co.zw; half-day min 4 people US$70, full day min 2 people US$140) A pub crawl and history lesson rolled into one. Archaeologist and historian Paul Hubbard shows you Bulawayo's architectural and pioneer gems, including the oldest pub in Zimbabwe. Tours are flexible; book two weeks in advance. No cameras.

☞ Tours

There are several Bulawayo-based tour operators for Matobo, Khami Ruins, Hwange and surrounds.

African Wanderer TOUR
(☑72736; www.african-wanderer.com) Offers fully qualified and passionate guides.

Zulu Safaris TOUR
(☑0779-711644; www.zulusafaris.co.zw; 104 Robert Mugabe Way) Tours to Matobo (half-/full-day US$70/90) for minimum of two persons. Can also arrange trips to Khami Ruins.

WORTH A TRIP

KHAMI RUINS

Just 22km from Bulawayo, the UNESCO World Heritage listed Khami Ruins (Kame, Kami; US$10; ◉gates close at 4:30pm) may not have the grandeur of Great Zimbabwe, but it's an impressive archaeological site. The second largest stone monument built in Zimbabwe, Khami was developed between 1450 and 1650 (after Great Zimbabwe) and is spread over a 2km site in a peaceful natural setting overlooking the Khami Dam. The complex series of walled structures generally follows the same aspects of Great Zimbabwe, but possesses its own features and expressions in the patterns and elaborate decorations. It also has the longest decorated wall in the entire sub-region.

Archaeological remains of Spanish and Ming porcelain found at the ruins provide evidence of an historic trade link; some are on display at Bulawayo's Natural History Museum. Tour operators run day trips from Bulawayo, or alternatively take a taxi (US$20 one way).

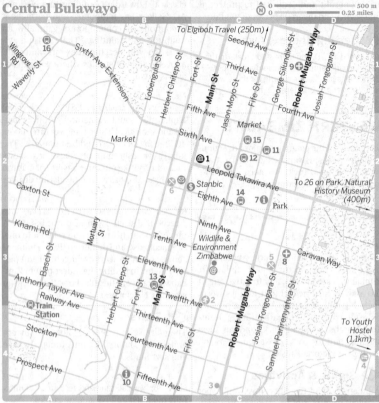

Central Bulawayo

Eco Logical Africa TOUR
(☎61189; www.ecologicalafrica.com) Around 30
years of professional wilderness guiding.

Elgiboh Travel TOUR
(☎886497; www.elgibohtravel.com; 71 Fife St)
Runs tours to the Matopos (half-day/full day
US$75/100 excl entry fees) and Khami Ruins.

🛏 Sleeping

Packer's Paradise GUESTHOUSE $
(☎251110; 1 Oak Ave, Suburbs; campsites per
person US$10, dm US$15, s/d without bathroom
US$40/50; @) The overpriced dorms means
it's definitely not a backpacker's paradise,
but it does have decent private rooms and a
homely kitchen. Enter off Twelfth Ave.

Burke's Paradise BACKPACKERS $
(☎246481; www.burkes-paradise.com; 11 Inver-
leith Drive, Burnside; campsite per person/dm/d
US$5/10/15) Set on 15 acres of bushland in
the outskirts of town, Burke's caters primarily to the overland crowd, but is a good
choice for independent travellers, too. Try
the cosy dorms near the main house, which
are less isolated. Pick-up service available
($US1) from town.

Youth Hostel HOSTEL $
(☎256488; cnr Townsend Rd & Third Sts, Suburbs;
dm/s/d without bathroom US$10/15/25) Run by
an elderly lady, the rooms here are good
value, but the downside is an unreliable
supply of hot water and electricity, and a
9.30pm curfew. Has a kitchen and common
lounge.

TOP CHOICE Traveller's Guest House GUESTHOUSE $$$
(☎246059; www.travellerszim.net; 2 Banff Rd, Hill-
side; s/d US$47/65; 🤝🖥️) Charm just oozes
from this guesthouse where recently reno-
vated rooms (ask for one of these) come with
blond-wood floors, stainless-steel bathroom

Central Bulawayo

fittings and African art. The communal de-signer kitchen is well equipped, while the garden and pool setting provides a nice spot to kick back in.

✖ Eating

Dickies   AFRICAN **$**
(Tenth Ave; mains from US$5) Try a traditional Zimbabwean meal at this cheery eatery. Follow the locals and plunge your fingers into tasty fish and sticky meat dishes sopped up with filling piles of *sadza*. There are a few branches throughout town. BYO alcohol.

TOP
CHOICE ⟩ **26 on Park**   INTERNATIONAL **$$**
(www.26onpark.com; 26 Park Rd; mains US$11-17; ⊙breakfast, lunch & dinner; 🛜) Housed in a colonial building with sprawling lawns and a big patio. Well-trained chefs serve up great dishes any time of the day. Fill up on eggs benedict for brekky, grilled calamari for lunch or game options such as kudu carpaccio or ostrich steaks for dinner. It's just across from the Natural History Museum. The cocktail bar is a lively spot for a drink.

Governors' Restaurant   INTERNATIONAL **$$**
(Cnr Eighth Ave and Fort St; mains from US$12; ⊙lunch & dinner Mon-Sat) Chandeliers, zebra skin rugs and silverware might have you thinking you need to dust off your blazer. Not to worry chaps, the Bulawayo Club's dining-room surrounds may be fit for royalty but the dress code is smart casual with prices to match. The fish and chips are their speciality.

ℹ Information

Dangers & Annoyances
As with most African cities, avoid walking at night and instead call a cab.

Emergency
Main Police Station (📞72516; cnr Leopold Takawira Ave & Fife St)
Medical Air Rescue Service (MARS; 📞60351; 42 Robert Mugabe Way) For ambulance services.

Medical Services
Galen House Casualty (📞881051; galen@gatorzw.co.uk; cnr Josiah Tongogara St & Ninth Ave) This privately run clinic is better than the central hospital.

Post
Main Post Office (📞62535; Main St) Between Leopold Takawira & Eighth Aves.

Tourist Information
Bulawayo & District Publicity Association
(📞60867; www.bulawayopublicity.com; btwn Eighth & Takawira Aves; ⊙8.30am-4.45pm Mon-Fri, to noon Sat) In the City Hall car park, this is an excellent source of information on accommodation, transport, tours and activities in Bulawayo and around.
National Parks & Wildlife Zimbabwe
(📞63646-7; Fifteenth Ave, btwn Fort & Main Sts; ⊙8am-4pm Mon-Fri) Takes accommodation bookings for Matobo National Park.

ℹ Getting There & Away

Bus
TO HARARE
Luxury buses do trips to Harare in 6 hours:
Bravo Tours (📞0772-873438; www.bravotours.co.zw) Departs 7.30am (1st/2nd class US$35/25)
Pathfinder (📞2936907-8; www.pathfinderlx.com) Daily departure at 7.30am & 2pm (US$30).
For buses to South Africa, see p641.

TO VICTORIA FALLS & HWANGE NATIONAL PARK
Pathfinder (departs 1.30pm, US$30) and Bravo Tours (departs 10am, US$15) run daily luxury buses to Vic Falls in 6 hours. Pathfinder stops en

route at Hwange Safari Lodge, around 5km from the Hwange main camp entrance, departing around 11am.

Train

TO VICTORIA FALLS

A nightly train leaves from Bulawayo to Victoria Falls at 7.30pm (1st class $15). Arrives around 9.30am.

TO SOUTH AFRICA

A train to Beitbridge runs Thursdays and Sundays (2nd class US$11), departing 6pm.

TO BOTSWANA

The train to Francistown runs Mondays and Fridays (around US$4), departing 9am.

❶ Getting Around

The city central is fairly walkable during the day.

Mike's Bike Shop (☑0775-195174; Twelfth Ave; per day US$15) rents mountain bikes, ideal for getting around. Leave a US$300 security deposit or ID.

A taxi or combi is the best way for the outer limits, and take a taxi for travelling anywhere at night. Try **Proline Taxis** (☑886686); agree on a price before setting out.

Matobo National Park (The Matopos)

Home to some of the most majestic granite scenery in the world, the Matobo National Park (Matopos; admission US$15, car US$10; ⊘main gate 24 hr, game park 6am-6pm) is one of the unsung highlights of Zimbabwe. This Unesco World Heritage site is a stunning and otherworldly landscape of balancing *kopjes* – giant boulders unfeasibly teetering on top of one another. When you see it, it's easy to understand why Matobo is considered the spiritual home of Zimbabwe.

The national park is essentially separated into two sections – the recreational park and the game park. The recreational park includes World's View and the rock art caves. The game park may not have the most prolific wildlife in Zimbabwe – it's been hard hit by poaching – but it remains one of the best places to see both black and white rhinos. It also has the highest density of leopards in Zimbabwe, but you'll be extremely lucky to spot one. Matobo is home to one-third of the world's species of eagle, so you may see black eagles, African hawk eagles or rare Cape eagle owls.

◉ Sights & Activities

World's View
(Malindidzimu Hill) HISTORIC SITE
(Matobo National Park; adult/child US$10/5) One of Zimbabwe's most breathtaking sites, the aptly named World's View takes in epic 360-degree views of the park. The peacefulness up here is immense, taking on a spiritual quality that makes it clear why it's so sacred to the Ndebele people. It's also the burial spot of Rhodesia's founder, Cecil Rhodes, whose grave sits, somewhat controversially, atop between two boulders. The landscape up here is surreal with giant boulders covered in multicoloured lichen, clumps of hair-like grass and rainbow-striped lizards flitting between the rocks, all of which make it feel like another planet.

Downhill from Rhodes' grave is the Shangani River Memorial. Erected in 1904, it pays tribute to Allan Wilson and his soldiers who were wiped out by General Mtjaan and his 30,000 Ndebele warriors when attempting to take over the territory.

The entry fee also gains you access to the Pomongwe and Nswatugi rock art caves.

Rock Art Caves ARCHAEOLOGICAL SITE
Dotted around the 425-sq-km Matopo National park are 3000 officially registered rock-art sites, including one of the best collections in the world of San paintings (estimated to be anywhere from 6000 to 10,000 years old). White Rhino Shelter, Bambata Cave, Pomongwe Cave and Nswatugi Cave have some fine examples.

Game Drive DRIVING TOUR
The game park at Matobo National Park is a good spot to try your luck at spying both black and white rhinos. Guides can be arranged at the park if you have your own vehicle, otherwise sign up for a tour.

🛏 Sleeping & Eating

The Farmhouse GUESTHOUSE $$
(☑60867; cozim@coz.co.zw; campsite US$10, cottage per person incl breakfast US$55, all-inclusive US$120) Another family-run lodge owned by recent repatriates, the Farmhouse is just outside the park at the private Granite Ridge Lodge. Thatched-roof cottages are quaintly decked out, each with an outdoor *braai*. There's a deep plunge pool and a roaming resident zebra. Rock climbing and abseiling can be arranged, along with safaris.

ZIMBABWE MATOBO NATIONAL PARK (THE MATOPOS)

Maleme Rest Camp
CAMPGROUND **$$**

(☑0383257; www.zimparks.org; campsites per person US$8, chalet US$35-75, lodge US$75-100) Set around boulders and candelabra cacti, this national parks accommodation offers the best option for budget travellers. While a bit on the shabby side, lodges come with kitchens and bathrooms, while camping is down near the dam. There's no restaurant, but it has a kiosk with basic items.

TOP CHOICE Camp Amalinda
LODGE **$$$**

(☑11-438162, 243954; www.campamalinda.com; per person US$255) Tucked away in the granite of the Matobo Hills, 10 thatched chalets are carved into the boulders, blending seamlessly, and have bulging rocks as an in-room feature. Each room is unique, some with open bathroom, clawfoot outdoor bath and even a swing bridge to a private sundeck (Room 10). End the day with a sundowner at the stunning lagoon-style pool and bar.

Big Cave Camp
LODGE **$$$**

(☑in South Africa 27 21-914 0966; reservations@ bigcave.co.za; per person incl breakfast & dinner US$140; 🛜🏊) Seven thatched cottages are built into the spectacular granite boulders for a luxurious Flintstones feel. The honeymoon suite has the best views for the same price.

ℹ Information

Maps of the park are available from the main (northern) gate; or from **Wildlife & Environment Zimbabwe** (☑77309; 105 Fife St) or the Bulawayo & District Publicity Association (p627).

ℹ Getting There & Away

Just 33km from Bulawayo, the Matopos can be done as a day trip (see p625), although it's recommended to stay at least one night in this beautiful area. If you don't have transfers prearranged by your accommodation, take a taxi (around $US40).

Hwange National Park

One of the 10 largest national parks in Africa, and the largest in Zimbabwe, at 14,651 sq km Hwange (entry fee national-parks accommodation guests US$20, per day nonguests US$20; ☺main gate 6am-6pm) has a ridiculous amount of wildlife. Some 400 species of bird and 107 types of animal can be found in the park, including lions, giraffes, leopards, cheetahs, hyenas and wild (painted) dogs. But the elephant is what really defines Hwange ('Wang-ee'), being home to one of the world's largest populations of around 40,000 tuskers.

The best time for wildlife viewing is July to October, when animals congregate around the 60 waterholes or 'pans' (most of which are artificially filled) and the forest is stripped of its greenery.

The park is situated on the road from Bulawayo to Vic Falls, making it the most accessible and convenient park for many visitors. Access is possible in any sturdy vehicle between May and October, but you'll need a 4WD during the wet season. Consult a ranger (at any of the three camps) about road conditions before heading off too far into the park.

Maps and information about the park are available at the rangers' offices at Hwange Main Camp (Map p630), Sinamatella Camp (Map p630) and Robins Camp (Map p630).

◉ Sights & Activities

If you're self-driving, most visitors make a few loops starting near the main camp. Nyamandhlovu Pan, featuring the high-rise Nyamandhlovu Viewing Platform, overlooks a popular waterhole. On the way from the main camp, check for wildlife hanging around Dom Pan. South of the main camp is Ngwethla Loop, accessible to any vehicle. It passes the magnificent Kennedy Pans, popular with elephants, though the greatest variety of wildlife can be found at the Ngwethla Picnic Site.

If you stay at Hwange Main Camp, you can book guided safaris in vehicles or walks (US$10 to $45) at the main office. At Sinamatella and Robins camps the only options available are guided walks with the national parks rangers (US$10 per person) – so for

> ℹ **DRIVING BETWEEN HWANGE'S CAMPS**
>
> There's no private driving after 6pm, so you must leave Robins Camp by 3pm to reach Sinamatella (and vice versa). Robins is 150km west of Hwange Main Camp, so to get there you must depart Robins by noon (and vice versa). Similarly, Sinamatella is 125km northwest of Hwange Main Camp, so you must leave Sinamatella by 2pm (and vice versa).

ZIMBABWE HWANGE NATIONAL PARK

Hwange National Park

ZIMBABWE HWANGE NATIONAL PARK

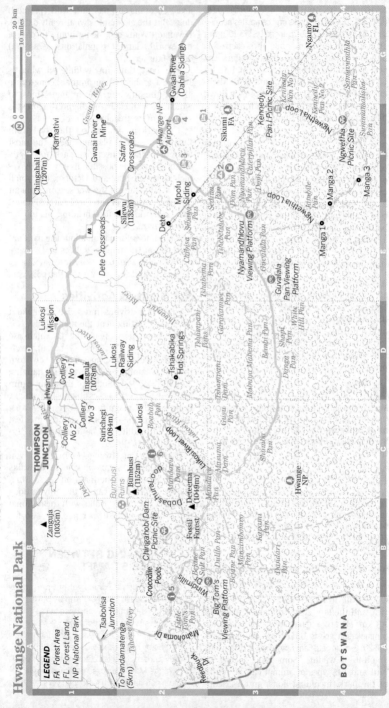

LEGEND
FA Forest Area
FL Forest Land
NP National Park

Hwange National Park

😴 Sleeping

1 Hide Safari Lodge	F2
2 Hwange Main Camp	F3
3 Hwange Safari Lodge	F2
4 Ivory Safari Lodge	F2

ℹ️ Information

Hwange Main Camp Rangers Office	(see 2)
5 Robins Camp Rangers Office	B2
6 Sinamatella Camp Rangers Office	C2

excursions further afield you'll need your own vehicle.

🛏️ Sleeping

Hwange Main Camp CAMPGROUND **$**
(Map p630; ☎014-706077; campsites per person US$15, chalet/cottage/lodge d US$35/60/75; ⏰office 6am-6pm) At the main park entrance, this attractive camp offers most services – safari vehicles, grocery shop, petrol station and a restaurant where you can watch the chef fire it up in the thatched *boma*. Accommodation ranges from self-catering lodges, cottages with communal kitchen, chalets (without bathroom) and campsites. It also has grazing wildlife and all the sounds of predators at night.

There are also decent national park lodges at **Sinamatella** and **Robins Camp**, the former has stunning panoramic views over open plains.

Ivory Safari Lodge LODGE **$$**
(Map p630; ☎09-64868; www.ivorysafarilodge.com; campsite per person US$15, per person with full board US$255) Take in the sweeping view overlooking a waterhole from your treehouse suite at this intimate lodge, just outside the park's border in Sikumi forest. You'll see loads of elephants and have the chance of spotting lions, leopards and buffaloes. The electric fence keeps you safe unless you opt for more adventure in the unfenced camping area. The stilted-huts with bathtubs overlooking the waterhole are superb. Cheaper safari tents (without bathroom) are also available. It's located down a sandy track 1km off the Bulawayo–Vic Falls road.

Hwange Safari Lodge LODGE **$$**
(Map p630; ☎021-8550395; s/d incl breakfast US$81/137; 🛜🏊) On a massive private estate

within the Sikumi Forest Area just outside the park, this looks more like a motel than a lodge. Bright, clean rooms overlook a distant waterhole popular with wildlife. The lodge can arrange game drives (US$35) even if you're not staying here – a good way of getting to Hwange Main Camp if you've come by bus.

Hide Safari Camp TENTED CAMP **$$$**
(Map p630; ☎04-498835; www.thehide.com; per person all-inclusive from US$460) One of the best safari camps in the country, the spectacular luxury tents are situated inside the park on the eastern boundary overlooking a waterhole. Named after the underground hiding points built to view elephants close up, the Hide has great guides and excellent food.

ℹ️ Getting There & Away

The park is between Bulawayo and Victoria Falls, 300km and 180km away respectively.

The Pathfinder bus stops at Hwange Safari Lodge at 10am when coming from Vic Falls or 5pm when leaving Bulawayo. You'll need to arrange transport from here to the Main Camp, approximately 10km.

UNDERSTAND ZIMBABWE

Zimbabwe Today

Zimbabwe continues to dip in and out of international headlines, often creating an unclear but daunting vibe for prospective visitors. Tourists have never been the targets for internal politics and violence, but always check with your embassy or consulate for the latest travel advice.

Compared to prior years, the last few have been relatively stable for Zimbabwe. Dollarisation in 2009 instantly put an end to hyperinflation, and the booming mining industry has seen marked improvements to the economy. While issues of water shortages and power blackouts continue to hamper parts of the country, living conditions have generally improved.

Leading into the 2013 elections, Zimbabwe once again finds itself at a crossroads, as the world waits with bated breath to see whether elections will be free, and minus the violence and alleged vote rigging that's plagued previous elections. Reports of land grabs and voter intimidation continue, while reports from the diamond-watchdog Partnership Africa Canada alleging that Mugabe's ruling Zanu-PF party has misappropriated profits from the lucrative diamond industry for its campaign have many concerned. Furthermore, in early 2013 the finance minister announced a paltry US$217 was all that was left in government accounts, casting doubts about whether indeed the nation can afford to hold elections.

At the time of research a new constitution was being drafted that would see presidential stints limited to two five-year terms, which would start following the 2013 elections. This would mean it's unlikely to interfere with 89-year-old Mugabe's ambition to be president for life.

History

The Shona Kingdoms & the Portuguese

In the 11th century, the city of Great Zimbabwe was wealthy and powerful from trading gold and ivory for glass, porcelain and cloth from Asia with Swahili traders. By the 15th century, however, its influence was in decline because of overpopulation, overgrazing, political fragmentation and uprisings.

During this twilight period, Shona dynasties fractured into autonomous states. In the 16th century Portuguese traders arrived in search of riches and golden cities in the vast empire of Mwene Mutapa (or 'Monomatapa' to the Europeans). They hoped to find King Solomon's mines and the mysterious land of Ophir.

A new alliance of Shona was formed – the Rozwi State – which covered over half of present-day Zimbabwe, until 1834 when Ndebele (Those Who Carry Long Shields) raiders, under the command of Mzilikazi, invaded from what is now South Africa. They assassinated the Rozwi leader. Upon reaching the Matobo Hills, Mzilikazi established a Ndebele state. After Mzilikazi's death in 1870, his son, Lobengula, ascended the throne and relocated the Ndebele capital to Bulawayo.

Lobengula soon came face to face with the British South African Company (BSAC). In 1888 Cecil Rhodes, the founder of the company, urged him to sign the Rudd Concession, which granted foreigners mineral rights in exchange for 10,000 rifles, 100,000 rounds of ammunition, a gun-boat and £100 each month.

But a series of misunderstandings followed. Lobengula sent a group of Ndebele raiders to Fort Victoria (near Masvingo) to stop Shona interference between the British and the Ndebele. The British mistook this as aggression and launched an attack on Matabeleland. Lobengula's *kraals* (hut villages) were destroyed and Bulawayo was burned. A peace offering of gold sent by Lobengula to the BSAC was commandeered by company employees. Ignorant of this gesture, the vengeful British sent the Shangani River Patrol to track down the missing king and finish him off. In the end, Lobengula died in exile of smallpox.

Without their king, the Ndebele continued to resist the BSAC and foreign rule. In the early 1890s they allied themselves with the Shona, and guerrilla warfare broke out against the BSAC in the Matobo Hills. When Rhodes suggested a negotiated settlement, the Ndebele, with their depleted numbers, couldn't refuse.

Meanwhile, finding little gold, the colonists appropriated farmlands on the Mashonaland Plateau. By 1895 the new country was being called Rhodesia, after its founder, and a white legislature was set up. European immigration began in earnest: by 1904 there were some 12,000 settlers in the country, and seven years later the figure had doubled.

Beginnings of Nationalism

Conflicts between blacks and whites came into sharp focus after the 1922 referendum, in which the whites chose to become a self-governing colony rather than join the Union of South Africa. Although Rhodesia's constitution was, in theory, nonracial, suffrage was based on British citizenship and annual income, so few blacks qualified. In 1930 white supremacy was legislated in the form of the Land Apportionment Act, which disallowed black Africans from ownership of the best farmland, and a labour law that excluded them from skilled trades and professions.

Poor wages and conditions eventually led to a rebellion, and by the time Southern Rhodesia, Northern Rhodesia and Nyasaland were federated, in 1953, mining and industrial concerns favoured a more racially mixed middle class as a counterweight to the radical elements in the labour force.

Two African parties soon emerged – the Zimbabwe African Peoples' Union (ZAPU) under Joshua Nkomo, and the Zimbabwe

African National Union (ZANU), a break-away group under Ndabaningi Sithole. Following the federation's break-up in 1963 and independence for Northern Rhodesia (Zambia) and Nyasaland (Malawi) – ZAPU and ZANU were banned and their leaders imprisoned.

Ian Smith & the War for Independence

In 1964 Ian Smith took over the Rhodesian presidency and began pressing for independence. British prime minister Harold Wilson argued for co nditions to be met before Britain would agree: guarantee of racial equality, course towards majority rule, and majority desire for independence. Smith realised the whites would never agree, so in 1965 he made a Unilateral Declaration of Independence.

Britain responded by declaring Smith's action illegal and imposed economic sanctions, which were also adopted by the UN in 1968 (in reality, though, sanctions were ignored by most Western countries and even by some British companies). Meanwhile, ZANU and ZAPU opted for guerrilla warfare. Their raids struck deeper into the country with increasing ferocity, and whites, most of whom had been born in Africa and knew no other home, abandoned their properties.

On 11 December 1974, South Africa's John Vorster and Zambia's Kenneth Kaunda persuaded Smith to call a ceasefire and release high-ranking nationalists (namely ZANU and ZAPU party leaders, including Robert Mugabe, who were imprisoned in 1964 during their struggle for majority black rule), and to begin peace negotiations. The talks, however, broke down; ZANU split and Mugabe fled to Mozambique. The following year, ZANU chairman Herbert Chitepo was assassinated in Lusaka by Rhodesian intelligence.

The nationalist groups fragmented and re-formed. ZANU and ZAPU created an alliance known as the Patriotic Front (PF), and their military arms – Zipra and Zanla – combined to form the Zimbabwe People's Army.

Smith, facing wholesale white emigration and a collapsing economy, was forced to try an 'internal settlement': Sithole, and the leader of the African National Congress (ANC), Abel Muzorewa, joined a so-called 'transitional government' in which whites were guaranteed 28 out of the 100 parlia-mentary seats; veto over all legislation for 10 years; guarantee of their property and pension rights; and control of the armed forces, police, judiciary and civil service. An amnesty was declared for PF guerrillas.

The effort was a dismal failure. Indeed, the only result was an escalation of the war. To salvage the settlement, Smith entered into secret negotiations with Nkomo, offering to ditch both Sithole and Muzorewa, but Nkomo proved to be intransigent. Finally, Smith was forced to call a general, nonracial election and hand over leadership to Muzorewa, but on much the same conditions as the 'internal settlement'.

Independence

On 10 September 1979, delegations met at Lancaster House, London, to draw up a constitution favourable to both the PF of Nkomo and Mugabe, and the Zimbabwean Rhodesian government of Muzorewa and Smith. Mugabe, who wanted ultimate power, initially refused to make any concessions, but after 14 weeks the Lancaster House Agreement was reached. It guaranteed whites (then 3% of the population) 20 of the 100 parliamentary seats.

In the carefully monitored election of 4 March 1980, Mugabe prevailed by a wide margin, and Zimbabwe and its majority-rule government joined the ranks of Africa's independent nations.

Soon after, the economy soared, wages increased, and basic social programs – notably education and health care – were initiated. However, the initial euphoria, unity and optimism quickly faded: a resurgence of rivalry between ZANU (run mostly by Shona people) and ZAPU (mostly by Ndebele) escalated into armed conflict, and the ZAPU leader, Nkomo, was accused of plotting against the government. Guerrilla activity resumed in ZAPU areas of Mata-beleland, and Mugabe deployed the North Korean-trained Fifth Brigade in early 1983 to quell the disturbances. Villagers were gunned down and prominent members of ZAPU were eliminated in order to root out 'dissidents'. The result was massacres in which tens of thousands of civilians, sometimes entire villages, were slaughtered. A world that was eager to revere Mr Mugabe closed its eyes.

Nkomo, meanwhile, fled to England until Mugabe, as strife threatened to erupt into civil war, publicly relented and guaranteed his safe return. Talks resulted in a ZAPU and ZANU confederation (called ZANU-PF) and amnesty for the dissidents, thereby masterfully sweeping the matter – but not the underlying discontent – under the rug. Zimbabwe's one-party state had begun.

Life as the Opposition

In 1999 thousands attended a Zimbabwe Congress of Trade Unions (ZCTU) rally to launch the Movement for Democratic Change (MDC). Morgan Tsvangirai, the secretary general, stated he would lead a social democratic party fighting for workers' interests. The arrival of the MDC brought waves of new hope and real opportunity for the end of Mugabe's era.

In 2000 Mugabe's chief propaganda architect, Jonathan Moyo, led the president's campaign for a new constitution. Three months later – and despite the full weight of state media and Treasury – the president's constitution was given the thumbs down by the people. It was Mugabe's first defeat and it notified him of MDC's very real strength at the ballot box. A parliamentary election was due later that year. Ironically, the MDC's greatest success would soon lead to a nasty defeat.

Mugabe responded to the threat of defeat with waves of violence, voter intimidation, and a destructive and controversial land-reform program that saw many white farmers lose their land. Despite this, and the election being damned by the US and EU as 'neither free nor fair', the MDC lost by a mere four seats. Two years later Mugabe's rule was under even greater threat during the country's presidential elections. Again, an election marred by violence and intimidation, backed by a new set of repressive laws, with no independent monitors and huge numbers of voters turned away, was won by Mugabe.

The next parliamentary election – in 2005 – was not so close. Mugabe and his security and propaganda networks had had five years since 2000 to readjust the playing field. Newspapers were closed (bombed in one case); the state dominated print, radio and TV; voters were offered food (and threatened with no food); the leader of the opposition, Morgan Tsvangirai, went through two treason trials; and up to one million ghost voters were created on the role. Mugabe won the elections.

Mugabe's toughest ever electoral challenges came in 2008 in the presidential and parliamentary elections. Although the MDC led by Morgan Tsvangirai had been able to campaign in rural areas that were closed to it in previous elections, the 2008 election was again seen as deeply flawed, with areas where the number of votes cast exceeded the number of enrolled voters.

Following election day, with growing signs that Mugabe had lost, Mugabe's men took more than a month to 'count' votes. When they were finally announced, Tsvangirai won 47.9% against Mugabe's 43.2%. With neither man having attained 50%, a second round of voting was needed, before which Mugabe's ruling ZANU-PF unleashed waves of violence across the countryside. MDC supporters who had shown their allegiance to the party before the first round of voting were now easily identified. Scores – perhaps hundreds – were killed, many more tortured, and thousands fled. In an attempt to stop some of the violence against his supporters, Tsvangirai withdrew from the second round a week before it was scheduled to take place. The second round went ahead

MONEY MATTERS – THE SWITCH TO AMERICAN DOLLARS

From the end of 2007 to the end of 2008, the real rate of inflation in Zimbabwe was seven sextillion per cent. Then the economy finally collapsed, as supermarket shelves became empty and many were forced to relocate to South Africa or the UK. The country has now switched from Zimbabwean dollars to US dollars. At first, costs quadrupled in real terms because Zimbabwean retailers, used to hyperinflation, knew only how to jack their prices right up, but they soon realised they could stabilise prices. The use of US dollars was a crime until the end of 2008, and the government claimed the only reason for finally allowing US dollars was to accustom the population to dealing with the said currency in time for the 2010 World Cup, when an influx of tourists was expected. Officially, the country is a 'multicurrency' economy where sterling, pula, rand and US dollars are accepted.

anyway, and led to yet another victory for Mugabe.

But while South Africa under the then-president Thabo Mbeki continued to support Mugabe, pressure from other areas was growing. The economy had officially collapsed, Mugabe could not pay his army or civil service, and then came cholera.

In February 2009, Morgan Tsvangirai signed a coalition deal with Zanu-PF, a mutual promise to restore the rule of law and to 'ensure security of tenure to all land holders'. Nonetheless, violence and land grabs continued. At the time of writing, MDC was in government with Mugabe's party, but largely impotent, and leading into the 2013 elections, Tsvangirai conceded the two-party experiment government was unlikely to continue.

Culture

The People of Zimbabwe

Most Zimbabweans are of Bantu origin; 9.8 million belong to various Shona groups and about 2.3 million are Ndebele. The remainder are divided between the Tonga (or Batonga) people of the upper Kariba area, the Shangaan (or Hlengwe) of the low-veld, and the Venda of the far south. Europeans (18,000), Asians (10,000), and mixed Europeans and Africans (25,000) are scattered around the country.

About 65% of the population lives in rural areas, while around 40% of the population is under 18 years old. The average life expectancy is about 40 years.

The official language of Zimbabwe is English. It's used in government, legal and business proceedings, but is the first language for only about 2% of the population. Most Zimbabweans speak Shona (mainly in the north and east) or Ndebele (in the centre and west). Another dialect, Chilapalapa, is a pidgin version of Ndebele, English, Shona and Afrikaans, and isn't overly laden with niceties, so most people prefer you sticking to English.

Way of Life

No matter what their race, Zimbabweans have a stoicism reminiscent of bygone eras. In Zimbabwe, the Southern African expression to 'make a plan' can be defined as: 'If it's broke, fix it. If you can't fix it, live with it, or, change your life' (overnight if need be). This kind of mental strength and generosity,

combined with a deep love of Zimbabwe, is the key to their survival.

Unfortunately, many of Zimbabwe's great gains made since independence – life expectancy, education, health – have been threatened since 1998 (due to gross mismanagement, corruption, and HIV/AIDS).

Certainly, many Zimbabweans, for whom basics such as water and electricity are hardly available, experience major difficulties in their day-to-day lives.

Dollarisation, however, at the beginning of 2009, solved many problems for those with access to cash. Diaspora funding has always buoyed the economy, which avoided collapse for years longer than it should have. It is estimated that 60% of Zimbabweans have someone from the diaspora sending them money. Those who do not – and are in rural areas – remain dangerously below the poverty line.

Somehow, despite the immense hardship for everyday Zimbabweans, crime remains relatively low.

Sport

For a long time Zimbabwe punched well above its weight in football (soccer), constantly upset heavyweights in cricket, produced some great tennis and golf players, and won Olympic gold. Unfortunately, however, Zimbabwe's sporting teams have followed the same trajectory as the country's economy.

Good news for cricket fans is that Zimbabwe was rehanded test status in 2012, but it has a long way to go before it's competitive.

Religion

The majority of Zimbabweans are Christian, although traditional spiritual beliefs and customs are still practised, especially in rural areas, where merciless economic times have led to an increase in faith.

The Arts

Zimbabwe's festivals, fairs and streetside stalls, live music and poetry, dance, art and sculpture are great expressions of its people, and a wonderful way for visitors to meet the locals and learn about their lives. Most Zimbabweans are creative in some way: whether they bead, embroider, weave, sculpt or carve.

Sculpture

The word 'Zimbabwe' means 'great stone house', so it is fitting that stone sculpture – also referred to as Shona sculpture – is the art form that most represents the people of Zimbabwe. The exuberance of the work, the vast varieties of stone, and the great skill and imagination of the sculptors has led to many major, critically acclaimed exhibitions worldwide over the years.

Books

LITERATURE

Zimbabwe has produced some of the finest African writers. The most contemporary, *Mukiwa* (A White Boy in Africa) and its sequel, *When a Crocodile Eats the Sun,* by Peter Godwin, are engrossing memoirs. Likewise, *Don't Let's Go to the Dogs Tonight – An African Childhood,* by Alexandra Fuller, is about nature and loss, and the unbreakable bond some people have with Africa.

Since independence, Zimbabwean literature has focused on the struggle to build a new society. *Harvest of Thorns,* by Shimmer Chinodya, on the Second War for Independence, won the 1992 Commonwealth Prize for Literature. Another internationally renowned writer, Chenjerai Hove, wrote the war-inspired *Bones,* the tragic *Shadows* and the humorous *Shebeen Tales.*

The country's most famous female writer is the late Yvonne Vera, known for her courageous writing on challenging issues: rape, incest and gender inequality. She won the Commonwealth Prize in 1997 for *Under the Tongue,* and the Macmillan book prize for her acclaimed 2002 novel, *The Stone Virgins.*

BOOKS ABOUT ZIMBABWE

For those keen to learn about the country, its people, arts and landscape, there are some great reads available. *Journey from the Depths of Zimbabwe: The Stone Sculptures,* by Vivienne Prince, is a stunning book that captures the ever-important sculpture work of Zimbabwean artists. Peter Garlake's *Great Zimbabwe Described & Explained* attempts to sort out the history, purpose and architecture of the ancient ruins, while his book *The Painted Caves – An Introduction to the Prehistoric Art of Zimbabwe* is a detailed guide uncovering major prehistoric rock-art sites in Zimbabwe. Still in the art vein, *The Painted Hills – Rock Art of the Matopos,* by Nick Walker, explores the revealing and interesting rock art of the Matopos, and *A Resource Guide to Zimbabwe Craft,* by Jane Lee and Jane Stillwell, is a must for anyone keen on Shona art, as it offers tips on the best places to buy.

To brush up on Zimbabwean history and politics, check out *Where We Have Hope,* by Andrew Meldrum, which gives a good overview of post-independence Zimbabwe, up to 2003. *Mugabe,* by Colin Simpson and David Smith, is a biography of the Zimbabwean president tracing his controversial rise to power, while Ian Smith has penned *The Great Betrayal,* an autobiography by colonial Rhodesia's most controversial leader. David Martin and Phyllis Johnson's *The Struggle for Zimbabwe* is a popular history of the Second Chimurenga.

Environment

The Land

Landlocked Zimbabwe is roughly three times the size of England. It lies within both tropics and consists of middle-veld and high-veld plateaus, 900m to 1700m above sea level. A low ridge, running northeast to southwest across the country, marks the divide between the Zambezi and Limpopo–Save River systems.

The northwest is characterised by bush-veld dotted with rocky hills. The hot, dry low-veld of southern Zimbabwe slopes gradually towards the Limpopo River.

In the mountainous region to the east, which straddles the border with Mozambique, Zimbabwe's highest peak, Nyangani, rises to 2592m.

Wildlife

ANIMALS

The Big Five (that is, lions, leopards, buffaloes, elephants and rhinos) are found in Zimbabwe. The number of elephants is almost at plague proportions, with Hwange having the most out of any park in the world.

There are hundreds of bird species found all over the country, including vultures, storks and herons, and Matobo National Park is home to one-third of the world's eagle species.

PLANTS

The ubiquitous *msasa* tree is the mascot for Zimbabwe, but in the town centres a multitude of jacarandas and fire trees bloom between September and November. Thanks to the English and their love of gardens, ubiquitous roses and stunning gardens remain one of the happiest colonial legacies.

The Zimbabwean high-veld is dominated by *miombo* woodland and is particularly beautiful in the spring (August to October). Perhaps the most charismatic low-veld species is the baobab, instantly recognisable by its enormous bulbous trunk and frequently leafless branches.

National Parks

Most of Zimbabwe's national parks are – or contain – Unesco World Heritage Sites. Close to 20% of Zimbabwe's surface area is protected, or semiprotected, in national parks, privately protected game parks, nature conservancies and recreational parks.

Park entry fees range from US$5 to US$20 per day. Never enter without paying the fee (which constitutes a permit), as national parks are zealously guarded against poaching.

There are different rates for vehicles – none are free – and an average entry fee for a four-seater vehicle is US$5, but exact rates should be confirmed when booking. Go to www.zimparks.com for the latest figures.

Environmental Issues

Zimbabwe is dry for at least nine months of the year and many areas suffer from long-term drought. Poaching, hunting and the destruction of the land has caused serious stress on flora, fauna and the land. Lakes and rivers have also been overfished. These factors then have an impact on those whose lives depend on a properly functioning environment.

To learn more about Zimbabwe's ecological situation, contact Wildlife & Environment Zimbabwe (www.zimwild.org).

Food & Drink

Food

The staple for locals is *sadza*, a white maize meal made into either porridge or something resembling mashed potato, which is eaten with your fingers, and served with tomato-based relishes, meat and/or gravy.

Zimbabwe, once one of the world's great beef producers, still has good beef widely available. Popular fish include trout from rivers or dams in the Eastern Highlands, and bream or the whitebait-like dried *kap-*

enta, another staple, both plentiful in Lake Kariba.

The cities and bigger towns offer a variety of cosmopolitan restaurants. In Harare they are mostly in converted houses with beautiful gardens. All tourist hotels serve European and vegetarian dishes. Generally the restaurants are good, and a meal will cost US$10 to US$30.

Drinks

The tap water in Zimbabwe is not safe to drink, but bottled mineral water, fruit juices and soft drinks are widely available.

Tea and coffee are grown in the Eastern Highlands. Cafes and restaurants in the cities serve espresso coffee from either local or imported beans.

The religious majority aren't big drinkers, but *chibuku* (also known as scuds), sold in large brown plastic containers, is popular with men. It's a kind of beer made from fermented yeast and sold in bottle shops (sometimes grandly called 'cocktail bars') and township beer halls. The beer you will more commonly see is lager. The domestically brewed lagers – Zambezi and Castle – are really good.

Imported and local spirits and wine are both widely available in supermarkets and very well priced.

SURVIVAL GUIDE

Directory A–Z

Accommodation

Zimbabwe generally has a good standard of accommodation that will suit most traveller's needs, whether roughing it in US$10 dorms or lapping it up in US$700 luxury lodges.

Backpackers usually have a choice of one or two options in each town, which have dorms, private rooms, wi-fi access and

---

SLEEPING PRICE RANGES

The following price ranges refer to a double room with bathroom in high season.

$ less than US$50

$$ US$50–US$150

$$$ more than US$150

kitchen facilities for cooking meals. Camping is an option, with budget lodges allowing you to pitch a tent for around US$10, and use their facilities. Having your own tent is handy for national parks, too.

In cities, you can opt for comfortable four- to five-star hotels or boutique B&Bs, all of which are reasonably priced around the US$100 to US$200 mark.

Upmarket lodges in national parks are stunning and built in close harmony with nature. Most are in the middle of the action, allowing you to enjoy wildlife among your luxurious surrounds of teak furniture, poster bed and verandahs. Prices are high, but rates include activities such as wildlife drives, food and alcohol. Many have 'tented camp' accommodation, which are pre-erected walk-in tents with comfortable beds and flooring, which range from fairly basic to luxurious.

National parks also have affordable lodges run by the **Zimbabwe National Parks & Wildlife Management Authority** (NPWZ; Map p606; ☏7076259; www.zimparks.org; cnr Borrowdale Rd & Sandringham Dr, Harare; ⏰8am-4pm Mon-Fri), which offer a good choice of lodges (from US$35) and campsites (from US$8). A few have restaurants, but mostly you will have to rely on self-catering. The main office in Harare is the best place to book in person: booking by phone and email are also theoretically possible, but less reliable.

🏃 Activities

Victoria Falls is the epicentre of activities in Southern Africa. The adventurous can get their adrenalin pumping with white-water rafting, helicopter rides, gorge swings and bungee jumping. There and elsewhere, it's all about natural features in Zimbabwe: river cruises, walks along the falls, classic driving safaris, hiking in the cool Eastern Highlands, horse riding and wildlife viewing in national parks, canoeing safaris on the Zambezi River, houseboating on Lake Kariba, and fishing or golfing almost anywhere.

Business Hours

Shops and restaurants are generally open from 8am to 1pm and 2pm to 5pm Monday to Friday, and 8am to noon on Saturday. Very little is open on Sunday.

Children

Zimbabwe is a great place to travel with kids. Wildlife spotting in the national parks and kid-friendly activities in Victoria Falls, such as canoeing and elephant rides, are likely to be the most popular choices. Take note, however, that some lodges in the parks have age limits for safety reasons, so be sure to confirm before booking.

Customs Regulations

Visitors may import a maximum of US$350 in items not for trade, excluding personal effects. Travellers over 18 years of age can also import up to 3L of alcohol, including 1L of spirits.

Embassies & Consulates

The following embassies and high commissions are based in Harare.

For any embassies or websites not listed here, go to www.embassiesabroad.com/embassies-in/Zimbabwe to find addresses and contact details.

Angolan Embassy (Map p610; ☏04-770075; www.projectvisa.com; 26 Speke Ave, Doncaster House)

Australian Embassy (Map p606; ☏04-870566; www.zimbabwe.embassy.gov.au; 1 Green Close, Borrowdale; ⏰8am-5pm Mon-Thu, to 1.30pm Fri)

Botswanan Embassy (Map p606; ☏04-794645; www.embassiesabroad.com/embassies-of/Botswana; 22 Phillips Ave; ⏰visas 8am-12.30pm Mon, Wed & Fri)

PRACTICALITIES

» The government's control over media has resulted in much self-censorship and bland press.

» The only surviving dailies (the *Herald* and the *Standard*) are both state-run. Friday's *Independent* and *The Zimbabwean,* which is produced out of London, offer the week's only dose of propaganda-free political reporting.

» The government controls all TV and radio, though most hotels and many lodges have great DSTV satellite TV.

» Zimbabwe uses the metric system.

Canadian Embassy (Map p610; ☑04-252181; www.harare.gc.ca; 45 Baines Ave; ⊙8am-1pm Mon-Thu)

French Embassy (Map p610; ☑04-703216; www.ambafrance-zw.org; First Bank Bldg, 74-76 Samora Machel Ave, Greendale; ⊙9am-1pm & 2-5pm)

German Embassy (Map p606; ☑04-308655; www.harare.diplo.de; 30 Ceres Rd , Avondale; ⊙7.30-5pm Mon, to 4.20 Tue-Thu, to 3pm Fri)

Japanese Embassy (Map p610; ☑04-250025; www.zw.emb-japan.go.jp; 4th Fl Social Security Centre, cnr Julius Nyerere Way & Sam Nujoma St; ⊙8am-12.45pm & 1.45-5pm Mon-Fri)

Kenyan Embassy (Map p610; ☑04-704820; kenhicom@africaonline.co.zw; 95 Park Lane; ⊙8.30am-4.30pm Mon-Thu, to 1pm Fri)

Malawian High Commission (Map p606; ☑04-798584; malahigh@africaonline.co.zw; 9/11 Duthie Rd, Alexandra Park; ⊙visas 9am-noon Mon-Thu)

Mozambican Embassy (Map p610; ☑04-253871; 152 Herbert Chitepo Ave; ⊙visas 8am-noon Mon-Fri)

Namibian Embassy (Map p606; ☑04-885841; 69 Borrowdale Rd)

Dutch Embassy (Map p606; ☑04-776701; www.zimbabwe.nlembassy.org; 2 Arden Rd, Newlands; ⊙8am-5pm Mon-Thu, to 2pm Fri)

South African Embassy (Map p606; ☑04-753147; dhacon@mweb.co.zw; 7 Elcombe Ave)

Tanzanian Embassy (Map p610; ☑04-721870; tanrep@icon.co.zw; Ujamaa House, 23 Baines Ave)

UK Embassy (Map p606; ☑04-85855200; www.ukinzimbabwe.fco.gov.uk/en; 3 Norfolk Rd, Mount Pleasant; ⊙8am-4.30 Mon-Thu, to 1pm Fri)

US Embassy (Map p610; ☑04-250593; http://harare.usembassy.gov/; Arax House, 172 Herbert Chitepo Ave; ⊙7.30am-5pm Mon-Thu, to 12.30pm Fri)

Zambian Embassy (Map p610; ☑04-773777; zambians@africaonline.com; 6th fl, Zambia House, 48 Kwame Nkrumah Ave (Union Ave); ⊙9am-1pm)

Food

The following price ranges are used for Eating reviews in this chapter.

$	Less than US$10 per main
$$	US$10-20 per main
$$$	More than US$20 per main

Gay & Lesbian Travellers

Homosexual activities for men are illegal and officially punishable by up to five years in jail (although penalties are invariably not nearly as severe), yet lesbianism is not illegal.

Contact Gays & Lesbians of Zimbabwe (☑04-740614, 04-741736; www.galz.co.zw; 35 Colenbrander Rd, Milton Park, Harare) for information about LGBT clubs and meeting places in Zimbabwe.

Health

Vaccination for yellow fever is not required for entry to Zimbabwe unless you have recently been to an infected area. For all sorts of reasons, however, get a jab before you come to Southern Africa and carry a certificate to prove it.

Internet Access

There are internet centres in all the main cities and towns that charge around US$2 per hour.

Wi-fi access is pretty prevalent these days, but it's slow; you can find it in many hotels and cafes in the bigger cities for around $2 to $3 an hour.

Another option is mobile internet using USB prepaid internet on your phone or laptop. Econet and Telecel both have branches at Harare's airport and in town. The USB dongle costs around US$50. Connections are patchy at best.

Legal Matters

There are several things to keep in mind if you're travelling to Zimbabwe while Robert Mugabe is still in power. It is illegal to criticise the government or the president (best to avoid talking about the government at all, and avoid taking photographs of 'sensitive' sites, such as government buildings).

Money

Since 2009, US dollars are the most commonly used currency in Zimbabwe, while the rand is used to a lesser extent. Change for cash is a big problem, so make sure you have plenty of small notes.

ATMS

At the time of writing, ATMs were common across Zimbabwe, but the larger towns are the most reliable. Barclays, Standard Charter and Stanbic are the main banks accepting MasterCard, Visa and Cirrus.

CREDIT CARDS

Credit cards are accepted in top hotels and some upmarket restaurants and shops.

TIPPING

Some restaurants automatically add a 10% service charge to the bill; if so, no tip is required. Otherwise, any tip is hugely appreciated.

Post

Sending letters and postcards by surface mail to Europe and the UK costs US$0.80, and US$1.10 to the rest of the world.

Public Holidays

Most government offices and other businesses are closed during public holidays.

New Year's Day 1 January

Independence Day 18 April

Workers' Day 1 May

Africa Day 25 May

Heroes' Day 11 August

Defence Forces' Day 12 August

National Unity Day 22 December

Christmas Day 25 December

Boxing Day 26 December

Safe Travel

Zimbabwe is nowhere near as dangerous as foreign media makes out, but crime is on the rise. Although the number of incidents and degree of violence are a far cry from that in South Africa, it is a reality. Don't walk around at night; the best option is to take a taxi, which is safe. Drivers should take the following precautions: lock all doors, lock all valuables in the boot, keep windows up and avoid stopping at traffic lights at night if it's safe to do so.

Telephone

If calling from overseas, the country code for Zimbabwe is ☏263, but drop the initial zero for area codes. The international access code from within Zimbabwe is ☏00. International calls can be made from your hotel or lodge.

MOBILE PHONES

Easily the best option for making calls is to purchase a prepaid SIM card (US$1) on arrival, which are cheap and easy to arrange. Econet and Telecel are the main operators, and have branches throughout the main towns, as well as at Harare airport. Be aware that your phone needs to be unlocked to activate the Sim. Credit or 'airtime' is widely available from street vendors.

Mobile numbers are recognised by the ☏07- prefix.

Visas

With a few exceptions, visas are required by nationals of all countries. They can be obtained at your point of entry. Single-/double-entry visas cost US$30/45 (and can be issued upon arrival) and multiple-entry visas (valid for six months) cost US$55, but are only issued at Zimbabwean diplomatic missions. British and Irish citizens pay US$55/70 for single/double entry.

For visa extensions, contact the **Department of Immigration Control** (Map p610; ☏791913; 1st fl, Linquenda House, cnr Nelson Mandela Ave & First St; ◷8am-4pm Mon-Fri).

For more information on visas, see p706.

Getting There & Away

Air

A sure sign that Zimbabwe is back on the tourist radar is the return of international airlines such as Emirates and KLM flying into Harare.

International flights link Harare to Johannesburg (one-way/return US$230/442, 1¾ hours), Gaborone (US$265/432, two hours), Windhoek (US$425/592, two hours), Maputo (US$468/767, 1½ hours), Lilongwe and Blantyre (US$395/582, 1½ hours), Lusaka (US$450/295, 50 minutes), Dar es Salaam (US$1154/1888, 2½ hours) and Nairobi (US$1070/1274, 3½ hours).

International flights also arrive at Vic Falls from Johannesburg (one-way/return US$340/750) and Windhoek (US$300/650).

The only way by air from Harare or Vic Falls to Kariba is to charter, which is very expensive. Companies include **HAC** (Halsteds Aviation Corporation; ☏0778-750086; www.flyhac.com) and **Altair Charters** (☏0772-515852; giles@altaircharters.com), and **BumiAir** (☏04-307087; www.bumihills.com) in Matusadona.

Airlines with services to/from Zimbabwe:

Air Botswana (Map p610; ☏04-793229, 04-793228, 04-707131; www.airbotswana.co.bw; Travel Plaza, Harare)

Air Malawi (Map p610; ☏04-752563; www.airmalawi.com; 9th fl, Throgmorton House, cnr Julius Nyerere Way & Samora Marhel)

Air Namibia (Map p610; ☎0736-688568, 0779-758869, in Victoria Falls 1345825; www.airnamibia.com.na; Joina City, Harare)

Air Zimbabwe (Map p610; ☎04-253751, at airport 04-575111; www.airzimbabwe.aero; cnr Speke Ave & 3rd St)

Emirates (Map p606; ☎04-799999; www.emirates.com; 18 Wakefield Rd, Avondale)

KLM (☎04-731070; www.klm.com)

Precision Air (www.precisionairtz.com)

South African Airways (Map p606; ☎04-794512, 04-794511; 1st fl, Pa Sangano, 20 King George Rd, Avondale)

Land

BORDER CROSSINGS

Travelling between Zimbabwe's neighbouring Southern African countries by land is fairly hassle-free, with visas on arrival issued to many nationalities (but be sure to check this out before you leave and see p706 for further details).

Botswana

The most popular border crossing into Botswana is from Kazangula near Vic Falls, which links it to Chobe National Park. The other crossing is at Plumtree, 94km from Bulawayo, heading to Francistown in Botswana. The border posts at Plumtree and Kazangula are open 6am to 6pm.

The following run buses from Harare (Road Port Terminal) to Francistown:

Zupco (Map p610; ☎0772-666530, 750571; Road Port Terminal) Depart 6.30am Tuesdays, Thursdays and Fridays ($15).

PCJ Coaches Depart every day at 6pm ($60).

Malawi

The most direct route between Malawi and Zimbabwe is via Mozambique's Tete Corridor. You'll need a transit visa (US$25) for Mozambique if travelling through Mozambique to Malawi, which you can arrange in Harare. Alternatively, you'll have to fork out for a visa at the border; enquire with the Mozambique embassy before setting out.

Buses from Harare (Road Port Terminal) to Blantyre (Malawi):

Zupco (Map p610; ☎0772-666530, 750571; Road Port Terminal) Depart Tuesdays, Thursdays and Sundays at 7.30am (US$25, 12 hours).

Munorurama (Map p610; ☎0772-361296) Daily at 8am.

Mozambique

There are two border crossings into Mozambique (open from 6am to 8pm). Easily the most popular is from Mutare, which links up to Beira. The other is at Nyamapanda, northeast from Harare, used to get to Malawi.

South Africa

Beitbridge is the somewhat infamous border crossing into South Africa. It's open 24 hours, but always fairly hectic.

Numerous luxury and semiluxury buses ply the route between Harare or Bulawayo to Johannesburg (16 to 17 hours), departing from Road Port Terminal in Harare. It's best to call ahead for departure times.

Buses from Harare:

Greyhound (Map p610; ☎720801; Road Port Terminal) Has an overnight bus departing 8pm Monday to Saturday, and 1pm on Sundays (US$52).

Pioneer (Map p606; ☎790531, 795863; Road Port Terminal) Has two daily departures at 1pm and 7pm (US$42).

Buses from Bulawayo:

Intercape (☎27-21-3804400; www.intercape.co.za) Departs 4pm (US$55).

Citiliner (www.citiliner.co.za) Departs 2pm (US$42).

Greyhound (www.greyhound.co.za) Departs 4pm (US$50).

Eagle Liner (www.eagleliner.co.za; 5th Ave, George Silundika) Departs 2.30pm (US$40).

Trains are once again running between Zimbabwe and South Africa. **Rovos Rail** (☎+27-123158242; www.rovos.com) runs a three-day/two-night luxury-train journey from Pretoria to Victoria Falls travelling through Zimbabwe via Bulawayo. Prices start from around US$1850 per person, inclusive of meals, alcoholic drinks and excursions.

Zambia

Zimbabwe has three border crossings into Zambia, with Victoria Falls (open from 6am to 10pm) by far the most popular. You can also cross via Kariba and Chirundu (Zambia), which is open 6am to 6pm.

From Harare (Road Port Terminal):

Zupco (Map p610; ☎0772-666530, 750571; Road Port Terminal) Two daily buses depart for Lusaka (US$15, nine hours) at 7.30am and a slower bus at 7.30pm.

Tenda Luxury (Map p610; ☎0773-817602; Road Port terminal; US$20) has a bus to Lusaka (15 hours) at 6.30pm.

Tenda also has a bus to Lusaka departing from Mutare (US$28) at 10am.

Getting Around

Air

Air Zimbabwe (Map p610; ☎04-253751, at airport 04-575111; www.airzimbabwe.aero; cnr Speke Ave & 3rd St) has one flight per day between Harare and Bulawayo (one-way/return US$176/342, 45 minutes) and Harare and Victoria Falls (one-way/return US$215/421). There's a domestic departure tax of US$10.

The only way by air from Harare or Vic Falls to Kariba is to charter, which is very expensive. The following can arrange charter flights, which will seat four to six people, to Kariba, Mana Pools and Matusadona National Park from Harare or Vic Falls:

HAC (Halsteds Aviation Corporation; ☎0778-750086; www.flyhac.com)

Altair Charters (☎0772-515852; giles@altaircharters.com)

BumiAir (☎04-307087; www.bumihills.com) In Matusadona.

Boat

Kariba Ferries (☎0772-236330, 04-614162; www.karibaferries.com; Andora Harbour, Kariba) runs a ferry service between Kariba at the eastern end of the lake and Mlibizi at the western end.

Bus

The express or 'luxury' buses operate according to published timetables. Check carefully, however, as most bus companies have both local ('chicken buses') and luxury coaches. For example, Pioneer and Zupco have both luxury and chicken buses.

Pathfinder (Map p610; ☎36907, 0778-888880; www.pathfinderlx.com; cnr 115 Nelson Mandela Ave & 5th St) This luxury '7-star' (it claims to have wi-fi) bus service has started up a daily service linking Harare to Vic Falls, Bulawayo and even Hwange. It has plans for services to Mutare and Kariba.

Bravo (Map p610; ☎0772-873438; www.bravotours.co.zw; 88 George Sulindka Ave) Plys the route Harare–Bulawayo–Vic Falls.

For details on buses departing Harare, see the boxed text, p613.

Car & Motorcyle

DRIVING LICENCES

Visitors can use their driving licence from their home country for up to 90 days in Zimbabwe as long as it's written in English. Given the growing possibility of police trying to elicit bribes, however, it's best to ensure you also have an international driving licence.

FUEL

The cost of petrol was US$1.60 a litre at the time of research.

CAR HIRE

» The minimum driving age required by rental companies varies, but it is usually between 23 and 25 years. The maximum age is normally about 65 years.

» It's important to note that most collision damage waiver (CDW) insurance policies do not cover 2WD vehicles travelling on rough roads in national parks.

» Be sure you have all the relevant papers and your car is fitted with the legally required fire extinguisher, warning triangles and reflectors.

» Due to the high costs of car rental in Zimbabwe, many DIY travellers opt to arrange a 4WD in South Africa and drive across the border.

ROAD HAZARDS

Many residents make a rule of not driving outside the major towns after dark. Police roadblocks are another inevitable part of driving in Zim, and you can expect to be waved down multiple times for long journeys. As long as you have all the correct papers and safety equipment, a smile and being courteous should see you waved through without any problems.

Local Transport

Taxis are safe and reliable, and can be booked through your hotel front desk. Most are metered, charging around $2.50 for 1km at the time of writing. Taxis in cities travel within a 40km radius of the city. Always take a taxi at night.

Train

Connecting Harare, Bulawayo, Mutare and Victoria Falls, all major train services travel at night. The most popular route is from Vic Falls to Bulawayo. Definitely opt for first-class, which is good value and comfortable, and gets you a sleeping compartment.

Understand
Southern
Africa

❯

population per sq km

SOUTH AFRICA   BOTSWANA   ZIMBABWE

≈ 4 people

Southern Africa Today

Southern Africa constitutes a loose grouping of nations, each with a distinct heritage but who share many common attributes. Some of these attributes, such as poverty, inequality, food insecurity and the spread of HIV/AIDS remain real challenges.

Many countries in Southern Africa felt the ramifications of the 2008–09 economic downturn. By early 2013, though, things were looking brighter. The R40 billion South Africa pumped into hosting the 2010 World Cup was seen as a sound investment, propelled by around 350,000 new arrivals specifically for the event. Tourism revenue for neighbouring countries was not such a star performer, however, with only 5% of World Cup tourists visiting other Southern African countries.

Crime and corruption will be hot topics at the South African 2014 elections, when Helen Zille will likely shrink the gap between her opposition Democratic Alliance party and the governing African National Congress (ANC). Failure of key government service delivery and the whiff of corruption in official circles have dogged the ANC. Crime continues to grab headlines, too, and undermine South Africa's reputation as a tourism destination despite its boost from the World Cup.

Elections were held in Lesotho in 2012, resulting in 72-year-old Thomas Thabane, leader of the All Basotho Convention (ABC), taking office as the new prime minister. He takes over from Bethuel Pakalitha Mosisili, who held power for 14 years. The rate of HIV/AIDS and the King, who represents the slow pace of political reform, are issues in Swaziland but the reality is that locals are busy getting on with their lives (ie surviving).

Botswana and Namibia continue to be beacons of political stability in the region. The subject of diamonds, and when they'll run out, is an issue in both countries, however, as is the fate of the San, an ancient nomadic hunter-gatherer group that has been relocated from its ancestral lands

> » If you're offered a gift, don't feel guilty about accepting it.
>
> » To receive a gift, accept with both hands and bow slightly.

Top Movies

The Gentleman (Dir Joe Njagu, 2011)
District 9 (Dir Neill Blomkamp, 2009)
Wah-Wah (Dir Richard E Grant, 2005)
Tsotsi (Dir Gavin Hood, 2006)
In My Country (Dir John Boorman, 2005)

Top Books

Mukiwa (Peter Goodwin) Story of a young Rhodesian boy witnessing a neighbour's murder.
Lost World of the Kalahari (Laurens van der Post) An account of the San during colonial rule.

Interaction

» Learn local words for 'hello' and 'goodbye' and use unsparingly

» Emphasis is placed on handshakes all over the region

» Always treat elders with the utmost courtesy

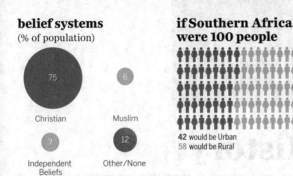

belief systems
(% of population)

75 — Christian

6 — Muslim

7 — Independent Beliefs

12 — Other/None

if Southern Africa were 100 people

42 would be Urban
58 would be Rural

into government-sponsored settlements in the Central Kalahari. The issue remains highly contentious, especially in Botswana.

Mozambique wins acclaim (and donor funding) as a successful example of postwar reconciliation and democracy-building in Africa. It's also set to benefit economically from major coal and natural gas finds in the north of the country. This is in the face of challenges such as widespread corruption and rising organised crime.

The chat in Malawi is all about Joyce Banda, the new premier who came into office in April 2012. She has international funding flowing again, is a prominent figure on the world stage and has made headway into resolving the debilitating fuel crisis. Hope for the first time in years is strong. She's also trying to lift the ban on homosexuality.

In Zimbabwe there is finally hope that things may be improving. There was a lot of optimism around the tourism sector in 2012; expats were even returning and setting up businesses. The presidential elections in 2013 loom large, however. Land grabs and voter intimidation continues, although on a lesser scale than previous elections. In early 2013, Morgan Tsvangirai's Movement for Democratic Change (MDC) party was still in a government with Robert Mugabe's Zimbabwe African National Union–Patriotic Front (ZANU-PF), but was largely impotent, and the two-party experiment government is unlikely to continue.

In September 2011, Michael Sata, nicknamed 'King Cobra', and his party the Patriotic Front (PF) won national elections in Zambia. Sata's rhetoric and actions so far, and continued support of Robert Mugabe in Zimbabwe, may mean a shift towards a more centralised economy and a less democratic government. It appears, however, he has a sincere focus on redirecting the country's wealth to the majority of poor Zambians. He announced a significant increase in the minimum wage in September 2012.

Be aware of the source of your seafood; overfishing and inappropriate fishing methods mean that many species are over-exploited, and some stocks are running dangerously low. For lists on what to avoid, check out www.wwfsassi.co.za.

Travel Hints

» Don't drive 4WDs off-road or on sand dunes, and especially don't drive on beaches in Mozambique

» Save water; it's a precious resource

» Always ask permission before photographing people

» Support local enterprise and buy locally made souvenirs; avoid skins and ivory

» If you want to help local kids, consider seeking out the village school or medical facility and making a donation there, rather than to individuals

HIV/AIDS

Botswana 300,000 people
Lesotho 320,000 people
Malawi 910,000 people
Mozambique 1.4 million people
Namibia 190,000 people
South Africa 5.6 million people
Swaziland 190,000 people
Zambia 970,000 people
Zimbabwe 1.2 million people

History

The precolonial history of Southern Africa is a compelling, interwoven web of peoples on the move throughout this vast region – the original travellers on our planet. It's also a story of technology and its impact on our early ancestors. Although Southern Africa's history stretches far back into the mists of time, the only records today are intriguing fossil remains and an extraordinary human diary of Stone Age rock art.

Here we give an overview of this history up until colonial times; the story of each individual country is then picked up in the On the Road chapters.

The Mists of Time

The region has revealed many archaeological records of the world's earliest human inhabitants. It's generally agreed among scientists that the first hominids (upright-walking human-like creatures) became established in the savannahs of East and Southern Africa nearly four million years ago, although hominid remains dating to between six and seven million years old have been found further north in Chad.

Sterkfontein in South Africa is regarded as one of the richest places on the planet for early human remains and is a World Heritage Site. In Malawi, archaeologists have found remains thought to date back as far as 2.5 million years.

It is surmised that about two million years ago several hominid species evolved, with Homo erectus developing basic tool-making abilities and eventually becoming dominant. Later evolving into Homo sapiens (modern humans), these early Africans are believed to have trekked to other parts of the world, where local factors determined the racial characteristics of each group.

Today, remains of temporary camps and stone tools are found throughout Southern Africa, and one site in Namibia suggests that 750,000 years ago these early people were hunting elephants and cutting up carcasses

TIMELINE	c 3.5 million BC	c 2 million BC	c 100,000 BC
	Evidence of early hominid fossils dating back millions of years has been discovered at the Sterkfontein Caves in Gauteng, northwest of Johannesburg, South Africa.	Homo erectus becomes the dominant hominid species, later evolving into what we now define as modern humans; sub-Saharan Africa is considered the birthplace of humanity.	Zambia's most celebrated early inhabitant, Broken Hill Man, lives and dies. Evidence unearthed by archaeologists suggests Early Stone Age settlements existed along the shore of Lake Malawi at this time.

with large stone axes. By 150,000 years ago, people were using lighter spear heads, knives, saws and other tools. Archaeologists classify this period of tool-making as the Stone Age, subdivided into the Early, Middle and Late stages, although the term applies to the people's level of technological development, rather than to a specific period.

Early Khoisan Inhabitants

Thousands of years ago, humans in Southern Africa developed an organised hunting and gathering society. Use of fire was universal, tools became more sophisticated (made from wood and animal products as well as stone), and make-up (natural pigments used for personal adornment) was in fashion. These Boskop people (named after the site in South Africa where their remains were discovered) are believed to be the ancestors of the San people, who still exist in isolated pockets today.

Eventually, tools became smaller and better designed, which increased hunting efficiency and allowed time for further innovation, artistic pursuits and admiring the fiery African sunsets. This stage is called the Microlithic Revolution because it was characterised by the working of small stones. The remains of microliths are often found alongside clear evidence of food gathering, shellfish remains and the working of wood, bone and ostrich eggshell.

The artistic traditions of the San are evidenced by pottery and especially by the wonderful paintings that can be seen today in rock shelters and caves all over Southern Africa. The better examples capture the elegance and movement of African wildlife with astonishing clarity. More recent paintings even depict white farmers.

Despite these artistic and technical developments, the San had no knowledge of metal working, and thus remain classified as Stone Age people.

The San and another group called the Khoikhoi (of Khoi-Khoi) are thought to share a common ancestry. Differences between the peoples were slight, based more on habitat and lifestyle than on significant physiological features. The Khoikhoi kept cattle, which were a source of food and transport, and were even trained to charge the enemy in warfare. These two groups also shared a language group, characterised by distinctive 'click' sounds. Today these two peoples are regarded as one, termed Khoisan or Khoi-San, and are mostly found in remote parts of Namibia and Botswana.

In recent times the San have been controversially relocated from their ancestral lands to new government settlements such as New Xade in the central Kalahari in Botswana.

Click onto www.h-net.org/~safrica, and join in with this electronic discussion group on all things pertaining to the history and culture of Southern Africa.

To learn more about the San, including current issues for survival, see www.kalaharipeoples.org, created by a nonprofit organisation involved with the people of the Kalahari.

c 30,000 BC	c 20,000 BC	c 8000 BC	c 2000–500 BC
Evidence suggests that the peoples of Southern Africa had developed an organised hunting and gathering lifestyle, made possible by more sophisticated tools and weapons.	The San had made significant technological progress by this time, although it was restricted to stone. This meant increased time for leisure and artistic pursuits, which included rock art.	The San likely began producing pottery around this time, supporting the notion that their progress allowed them increased time away from hunting and gathering food.	Iron-skilled Bantu migrate from West Africa through the Congo basin into present-day Zambia and Malawi. Over the centuries they spread into other parts of East and Southern Africa.

The Bantu Migration

While the Khoisan were developing, in West Africa another group with larger body types and darker skin was emerging: the Bantu.

Their advanced skills led to improved farming methods and the ability to make unwanted guests of themselves on their neighbours' lands. Over

ANCIENT ROCK ART

The magnificent rock art sprinkled around Southern Africa is like a remarkable human diary left by an ancient people, and it's a major highlight for many visitors. There's much speculation about the origins of ancient rock paintings and engravings. Evidence such as tools and animal remains left around major sites, and the kinds of scenes depicted, suggest the artists were the early San people.

A tantalising sliver of Stone Age existence, these sites provide a snapshot of the way the San lived and hunted, and insight into their spirituality. Unlike works in a museum, rock art remains where it was created, which means you may catch a glimpse of the inspiration that went into these paintings. Although rock art is found all over Southern Africa, the best examples are in Matobo National Park, and in Domboshawa and Ngomakurira, all in Zimbabwe; the Tsodilo Hills in Botswana; Twyfelfontein in Namibia; and Giant's Castle in South Africa.

Most rock paintings reflect a relationship with nature. Some are stylised representations of the region's people and animals, but the majority are realistic portrayals of hunters, giraffes, elephants, rhino, lions, antelopes and so on, in rich red, yellow, brown and ochre. Common themes include the roles of men and women, hunting scenes and natural medicine. Examples of the last include trance dancing and spiritual healing using the San life force, known as *nxum*, which was invoked to control aspects of the natural world, including climate and disease. All these elements still feature in San tradition.

Although climatic onslaught means the earliest works have long faded, flaked and eroded into oblivion, the dry climate and sheltered granite overhangs have preserved many of the more recent paintings. Three distinct periods have been identified: the earliest paintings seem to reflect a period of gentle nomadism, during which people were occupied primarily with the hunt; later works, which revealed great artistic improvement, suggest peaceful arrivals by outside groups, perhaps Bantu or Khoikhoi; the final stage indicates a decline in the standard of the paintings – or they may be imitations of earlier works by more recently arrived peoples.

Red pigments were ground mainly from iron oxides, powdered and mixed with animal fat to form an adhesive paste. Whites came from silica, powdered quartz and white clays, and were less adhesive than the red pigments. For this reason, white paintings survive only in sheltered locations. Both pigments were applied to the rock using fingers, sticks and brushes made of animal hair. While admiring rock art, please keep in mind the fragility of the paintings.

AD 500–1000	13th Century	1498
Gokomere people and subsequent groups in what is now Zimbabwe develop gold-mining techniques and produce progressively finer-quality ceramics, jewellery, textiles and soapstone carvings.	Construction of Great Zimbabwe commences – the city grows into a powerful religious and political capital, becoming the heart of Rozwi culture and the greatest medieval city in sub-Saharan Africa.	Portuguese explorer Vasco da Gama lands at Mozambique Island. Over the next 200 years, the Portuguese establish coastal trading enclaves and settlements in the interior along the Zambezi Valley.

DAVID WALL PHOTO/GETTY IMAGES©

» Great Zimbabwe (p622)

2000 years ago the Bantu moved into the Congo basin and, over the next thousand years, spread across present-day Uganda, Kenya and Tanzania and migrated south into Zambia, Malawi, Mozambique and other parts of Southern Africa. The term 'migration' here refers to a sporadic spread over many hundreds of years. Typically, a group would move from valley to valley or from one water source to the next. This process inevitably had a knock-on effect, as weaker ethnic groups were constantly being 'moved on' by invaders from other areas.

At first, the Bantu in Southern Africa apparently lived in relative harmony with the original Khoisan inhabitants, trading goods, language and culture. As Bantu numbers increased, however, some Khoisan were conquered or absorbed by this more advanced group of peoples, while the remainder were pushed further and further into inhospitable lands.

History of South-
ern Africa, by JD
Omer-Cooper,
provides an
excellent, highly
readable account
of the early peo-
ples of Southern
Africa, includ-
ing fascinating
cultural detail
that differenti-
ates the many
Bantu-speaking
groups.

Bantu Culture & Early Kingdoms

A feature of Bantu culture was its strong social system, based on extended family or clan loyalties and dependencies, generally centred on the rule of a chief. Some chiefdoms developed into powerful kingdoms, uniting many disparate ethnic groups and covering large geographical areas.

Cattle played an essential role in the lives of Southern Africa's Bantu population. Apart from providing food, skins and a form of capital, cattle were also most essential when it came to bride wealth. Marriage involved the transfer of a woman to the household of her husband. In turn, the cattle from the husband's family were reassigned to the family of the bride's father. A man who had many daughters would one day end up with many cattle.

One of the earliest Bantu kingdoms was Gokomere, in the uplands of Zimbabwe. The Gokomere people are thought to be the first occupants of the Great Zimbabwe site, near present-day Masvingo.

Early Traders

Meanwhile, from the latter half of the 1st millennium, Arabs from the lands around the Red Sea were sailing southwards along the eastern

---

THE BANTU

The Bantu peoples could more accurately be called 'Bantu-speaking peoples', since the word 'Bantu' actually refers to a language group rather than a specific race. Nevertheless, it has become a convenient term of reference for the black African peoples of southern and eastern Africa, even though the grouping is as ill-defined as 'American' or 'Asian'. The Bantu ethnic group comprises many subgroups, each with their own language, customs and traditions.

1616	**17th century**	**mid-17th century**	**1750**
Portuguese explorer Gaspar Bocarro journeys from Tete (on the Zambezi River) through the Shire Valley to Lake Chilwa, then through the south of Tanzania and back into Mozambique.	Competing European powers begin settling in South Africa, mostly in the Cape. This signals the eventual change of life for the peoples of Southern Africa brought about by colonialism.	European colonists come into conflict with the San. The early Boers' campaign of land seizures and forced migrations lasts for 200 years and results in the death of up to 200,000 people.	Dutch elephant hunter Jacobus Coetsee becomes the first European to cross the Orange River, followed by a series of traders, hunters and missionaries.

seaboard of Africa. They traded with the local Bantu inhabitants, who by this time had reached the coast, and bought ivory, gold and slaves to take back to Arabia.

Between AD 1000 and 1500 the Arab-influenced Bantu founded several major settlements along the coast, from Mogadishu (in present-day Somalia) to Kilwa (in southern Tanzania), including Lamu (Kenya) and Zanzibar (Tanzania). In Kenya and Tanzania particularly, the Bantu people were influenced by the Arabs, and a certain degree of intermarriage occurred, so that gradually a mixed language and culture was created, called Swahili, which remains intact today.

From southern Tanzania the Swahili-Arabs traded along the coast of present-day Mozambique, establishing bases at Quelimane and Mozambique Island.

From the coast the Swahili-Arabs pushed into the interior, and developed a network of trade routes across much of East and Southern Africa. Ivory and gold continued to be sought-after, but the demand for slaves grew considerably, and reached its zenith in the early-19th century when the Swahili-Arabs and dominant local ethnic groups are reckoned to have either killed or sold into slavery 80,000 to 100,000 Africans per year.

An Introduction to the History of Central Africa – Zambia, Malawi and Zimbabwe, by AJ Wills, provides a comprehensive work on the region and is considered one of the best around.

Later Bantu Kingdoms & People

As early as the 11th century, the inhabitants of Great Zimbabwe had come into contact with Arab-Swahili traders from the coast. Great Zimbabwe became the capital of the wealthiest and most powerful society in Southern Africa – its people the ancestors of today's Shona people – and reached the zenith of its powers around the 14th century, becoming the greatest medieval city in sub-Saharan Africa.

From around the 11th century it appears that more advanced Bantu-speaking Iron Age people migrated to the area, absorbing the earlier immigrants. As they settled they branched out into a number of cultural groups. One of these groups, the Nguni, was distinguished from its neighbours by strict matrimony rules – marriage was forbidden to a partner that could be traced to a common ancestor. The Xhosa were the southernmost of these people. Covering large areas of present-day South Africa, Botswana and Lesotho were the Sotho-Setswana, who encouraged intercousin marriage. The Venda, who have a matriarchal culture and are thought to be related to the Shona people of Zimbabwe, occupied the north of Limpopo province in South Africa.

Further north, between the 14th and 16th centuries, another Bantu group called the Maravi (of whom the Chewa became the dominant ethnic group) arrived in Southern Africa from the Congo Basin and founded a powerful kingdom covering southern Malawi and parts of present-day

19th century	1836	1884
The difaqane (forced migration) sees waves of Southern Africa's peoples displaced as the powerful warrior army of Shaka Zulu uproots ethnic groups in its path, forcing them to flee to new territory.	Groups of Boers, dissatisfied with British rule in the Cape Colony, begin a decade of migration known as the Great Trek; increasing numbers abandon their farms and cross the Senqu (Orange) River.	Otto von Bismarck invites other dominant European powers to participate in the Berlin Conference, which officially begins the 'Scramble for Africa', and marks Germany's emergence as an imperial power.

BRITISH LIBRARY/ROBANA VIA GETTY IMAGES ©

» Zulu warrior

Mozambique and Zambia. Masks made by a men's secret society called Nyau were an integral part of ceremonies for this group. As well as representing cultural ideals with themes such as wisdom, sickness, death and ancestors, masks also caricatured undesirables such as slave-traders, invaders and colonial figures.

At about the same time the Tumbuka and the Phoka groups migrated into the north of Malawi. The Tumbuka are known for their healing practices, which combine traditional medicine and music.

During the 16th and 17th centuries, another Bantu group, called the Herero, migrated from the Zambezi Valley into present-day Namibia, where they came into conflict with the San and competed with the Khoikhoi for the best grazing lands. Eventually, most indigenous groups submitted to the Herero. Only the Nama people, thought to be descended from early Khoikhoi groups, held out. One of Africa's most traditional cultures, the Himba people in Namibia, are descended from the Herero.

The power of the Bantu kingdoms started to falter in the late 18th and early 19th centuries due to a major dispersal of indigenous ethnic groups called the *difaqane,* and a rapid increase in the number of European settlers.

Today's Herero women are distinguished by their extravagant neck to ankle Victorian dresses, petticoats and large hats – a by-product of contact with German missionaries.

The Difaqane

The *difaqane* (meaning 'forced migration' in Sotho, or *mfeqane,* 'the crushing', in Zulu) was a period of immense upheaval and suffering for the indigenous peoples of Southern Africa. It originated in the early 19th century when the Nguni ethnic groups in modern KwaZulu-Natal (South Africa) changed rapidly from loosely organised collections of chiefdoms to the more centralised Zulu Nation. Based on a highly disciplined and powerful warrior army, the process began under Chief Dingiswayo, and reached its peak under the military commander Shaka Zulu.

Shaka was a ruthless conqueror and his reputation preceded him. Not surprisingly, ethnic groups living in his path chose to flee, in turn displacing neighbours and causing disruption and terror across Southern Africa. Ethnic groups displaced from Zululand include the Matabele, who settled in present-day Zimbabwe, and the Ngoni, who fled to Malawi and Zambia. Notable survivors were the Swazi and Basotho, who forged powerful kingdoms that became Swaziland and Lesotho.

The Makololo were uprooted from Zululand during the *difaqane* and moved into southwest Zambia, where they displaced the Tonga people. To this day the dominant language of much of western Zambia remains Makololo.

European Colonisation & Settlement

Although there had been a European presence in Southern Africa for several hundred years, in 1820 the British Cape Colony saw a major influx of settlers. Around 5000 were brought from Britain on the promise of fertile farmland around the Great Fish River, near the Shipwreck Coast, Eastern Cape. In reality, the settlers were brought in to form a

19th century	1989	2006	2006
The face of Southern Africa changes significantly as the earlier trickle of European settlers to South Africa becomes widespread colonial settlement, filtering through to many parts of the region.	One of Africa's youngest countries, second only to Eritrea, Namibia officially becomes independent on 1 April after a multiparty peace deal is brokered between Cuba, Angola, South Africa and Swapo.	Botswana's government is reprimanded by the UN's Committee on the Elimination of Racial Discrimination for its resettlement program relocating San from their ancestral lands.	In a highly publicised act mirroring neighbouring Zimbabwe, the Namibian government commences the expropriation of white-owned farms as part of a hotly contested land-reform program.

buffer between the Boers (historic name for the Afrikaner people); to the west of the river and the Xhosa (amaXhosa), to the east, who competed for territory.

From this point, European settlement rapidly spread from the Cape Colony to Natal and later to the Transvaal – especially after the discovery of gold and diamonds. In many cases Europeans were able to occupy land abandoned by African people following the *difaqane*.

From the 1830s groups of Boers fed up with British rule in the Cape Colony trekked off into the wilds of what is now South Africa, to carve out a living free from British interference. These early trekkers, or Voortrekkers as they were known, went on what is referred to as The Great Trek during a decade of migration.

Over the next 100 to 150 years, an ever-increasing number of Europeans from South Africa settled in areas that became the colonies of Swaziland, Nyasaland (Malawi), Northern and Southern Rhodesia (Zambia and Zimbabwe), Bechuanaland (Botswana), Basotholand (Lesotho), German South West Africa (Namibia) and Portuguese East Africa (Mozambique). With this change, Southern Africans would never again be permitted to follow entirely traditional ways.

For the colonial and modern history of the individual countries, see the relevant country chapters.

The Scramble for Africa: White Man's Conquest of the Dark Continent from 1876 to 1912, by Thomas Pakenham, details the colonial history of Southern Africa and the continent in well-written and entertaining prose.

2008	**2010**	**2010–11**	**2013**
Long simmering social discontent boils over and xenophobic rioting breaks out in South Africa, with migrants from neighbouring countries (such as Zimbabwe) targeted; there are more than 60 deaths.	After spending billions upgrading infrastructure, giving a major boost to local employment, South Africa hosts the 2010 FIFA World Cup, which sees new arrivals pour into the region.	The region recorded very heavy rains with flooding causing loss of life in South Africa, Mozambique and Zimbabwe, with other countries in the area also affected.	The Southern African Development Community (SADC) begins to flex its regional muscle, sending troops into eastern Democratic Republic of Congo (DRC) to oppose rebel forces backed by Rwanda.

Wildlife

by David Lukas

Southern Africa encompasses diverse habitats ranging from verdant forests to stony deserts and soaring mountains, from lush grasslands to classic African savannahs. It is home to penguins and hippos, great white sharks and elephants, and many more animals that will surprise and amaze visitors. Approximately 15% of the region receives some sort of formal protection. Kruger National Park and Kgalagadi Transfrontier Park include some of the region's largest and most significant protected areas.

Meerkats standing in the sun, Botswana

OCEAN/CORBIS©

Cats

With their excellent vision and keen hearing, the seven cats found in Southern Africa are superb hunters. Experience unforgettable feline scenes, such as the big cats making their kills or the small cats performing incredible leaps to snatch birds out of the air.

Lion

1 *Weight 120–150kg (female), 150–225kg (male); length 210–275cm (female), 240–350cm (male)*
Lions are Africa's most feared predators, with teeth that tear through bone and tendon. Each group of adults (a pride) is based around generations of females that do all the hunting; males fight among themselves and eat what the females catch.

Cheetah

2 *Weight 40–60kg; length 200–220cm* A world-class sprinter reaching speeds of 112km/h, the cheetah runs out of steam after 300m and must cool down for 30 minutes before hunting again.

Leopard

3 *Weight 30–60kg (female), 40–90kg (male); length 170–300cm* More common than you realise, the leopard relies on expert camouflage to stay hidden. During the day you might only spot one reclining in a tree after it twitches its tail, but at night there is no mistaking their bone-chilling groans.

Caracal

4 *Weight 8–19kg; length 80–120cm* The caracal is a tawny cat with long, pointy ears. This African version of the European lynx has jacked up hind legs, enabling it to make vertical leaps of 3m and swat birds out of the air.

Black-Footed Cat

5 *Weight 1–2kg; length 40–60cm* This pint-sized predator is one of the smallest cats in the world. Though only 25cm high, this nocturnal cat is a fearsome hunter that can leap six times its height.

Primates

While East Africa is the evolutionary cradle of primate diversity, Southern Africa is a relative newcomer on the scene and home to a mere half-dozen or so species. These versatile, intelligent animals, however, have many fascinating behaviours and complex social systems that can provide hours of entertainment.

Vervet Monkey

1 *Weight 4–8kg; length 90–140cm* Found in well-wooded areas, the vervet spends a lot of time on the ground, but always near to trees where it can escape from predators. Each troop is composed of females, while males fight each other for access to females.

Chacma Baboon

2 *Weight 12–30kg (female), 25–45kg (male); length 100–200cm* Common enough to be overlooked, the Chacma baboon is worth watching because it has complex social dynamics. See if you can spot signs of friendship, deception or dealmaking within a troop.

Greater Galago

3 *Weight 550g–2kg; length 55–100cm* A cat-sized nocturnal creature with doglike face, the greater galago (commonly called 'bushbaby') has changed little in 60 million years. They communicate with each other through scent and sound and are rarely seen, except at some safari-lodge feeding stations.

Samango Monkey

4 *Weight 3.5–5.5kg (female), 5.5–12kg (male); length 100–160cm* The Samango monkey is part of a large group of African primates called gentle or blue monkeys. Found exclusively in forests, it lives in peaceful female-based groups.

Cud-Chewing Mammals

Many of Africa's ungulates – hoofed mammals – live in groups to protect themselves from the continent's formidable predators. The subgroup of ungulates that ruminate (chew their cud) and have horns are called bovines. Among this family, antelopes are particularly numerous, with more than 20 species in Southern Africa.

Wildebeest

1 *Weight 140–290kg; length 230–340cm* Most wildebeest of Southern Africa are rather sedentary creatures, moving only as the seasons fluctuate. Because it favours expansive views, the wildebeest is in turn easily viewed itself.

Klipspringer

2 *Weight 8–18kg; length 80–125cm* Perpetually walking on tiptoes, the klipspringer finds safety on rocky outcrops in the mountains of central Namibia. Pairs establish permanent territories and communicate with each other by whistling.

African Buffalo

3 *Weight 250–850kg; length 220–420cm* Imagine a cow on steroids, then add a fearsome set of curling horns, and you get the African buffalo. Fortunately it's usually docile, because an angry or injured buffalo is extremely dangerous.

Impala

4 *Weight 40–80kg; length 150–200cm* With a prodigious capacity to reproduce, impalas can reach great numbers quickly, outstripping predators' ability to eat them all.

Sitatunga

5 *Weight 40–80kg (female), 80–120kg (male); length 150cm* The shy aquatic sitatunga antelope will submerge itself in the face of danger, making it hard to find. Listen for its loud barking at night.

Hoofed Mammals

Other than the giraffe, these ungulates are not ruminants and can be seen over a much broader range of habitats than bovines. At home in Africa for millions of years, they are among the most successful mammals to have ever wandered the continent.

Giraffe

1 *Weight 450–1200kg (female), 1800–2000kg (male); height 3.5–5.2m* The 5m-tall giraffe does such a good job reaching up to high branches that stretching down to get a simple drink of water is difficult. Though it strolls along casually, it can outrun any predator.

African Elephant

2 *Weight 2200–3500kg (female), 4000–6300kg (male); height 2.4–3.4m (female), 3–4m (male)* Widespread throughout Southern Africa, up to 55,000 elephants congregate in the lush wetlands of Chobe National Park. There are also the unique desert-loving elephants of Namibia.

Black Rhinoceros

3 *Weight 700–1400kg; length 350–450cm* Once widespread and abundant, the slow-moving rhino has been poached to the brink of extinction for having a horn worth more than gold.

Mountain Zebra

4 *Weight 230–380kg; length 260–300cm* The unique mountain zebra of central Namibia and South Africa differs from its savannah relatives in having an unstriped belly and a rusty muzzle.

Hippopotamus

5 *Weight 510–3200kg; length 320–400cm* Designed like a big grey floating sack with tiny legs, the 3000kg hippo spends all its time in or very near water. Hippos display a tremendous ferocity and strength when provoked.

Carnivores

In addition to seven types of cats, Southern Africa is home to a couple of dozen other carnivores, ranging from slinky mongooses to highly social hunting dogs. All are linked in having 'carnassial' (shearing) teeth, and superb hunting prowess.

Bat-Eared Fox

1 *Weight 3–5kg; length 70–100cm* This animal has huge ears which swivel in all directions to pick up the sounds of subterranean food items such as termites. Monogamous pairs of these social foxes will often mingle with others when hunting for food.

Spotted Hyena

2 *Weight 40–90kg; length 125–215cm* The spotted hyena is one of Southern Africa's most unusual animals. Living in packs ruled by females, this savage fighter uses its bone-crushing jaws to disembowel prey or to do battle with lions.

Cape Fur Seal

3 *Weight 80kg (female), 350kg (male); length 120–200cm* Several giant breeding colonies of seals can be found along the coastlines of Southern Africa. Forced to gather in dense numbers as protection against marauding hyenas, these colonies are turbulent, noisy and exciting to watch.

Meerkat

4 *Weight 0.5–1kg; length 50cm* The area's several species of mongoose may be best represented by the meerkat (also known as a suricate). If threatened, they all spit and jump up and down together.

Hunting Dog

5 *Weight 20–35kg; length 100–150cm* Uniquely patterned, hunting dogs run in packs of 20 to 60. Organised in complex hierarchies, these highly social but endangered canids are incredibly efficient hunters.

Birds of Prey

Southern Africa is home to about 70 species of hawk, eagle, vulture and owl, meaning that you are likely to see an incredible variety of birds of prey. Look for them in trees, soaring high overhead or gathered around a carcass.

Secretary Bird

1 *Length 100cm* With the body of an eagle and the legs of a crane, the secretary bird towers 1.3m tall and walks up to 20km a day across the savannah in search of vipers, cobras and other snakes that it kills with lightning speed and agility.

Pale Chanting Goshawk

2 *Length 55cm* This grey raptor with red beak and legs is seen perched low on bushes. Look closely because it is probably following some other small hunter, such as a honey badger.

Bearded Vulture

3 *Length 110cm* Around the cliffs of the Drakensberg you may spot one of the world's most sought-after birds of prey – known for its habit of dropping bones onto rocks from great heights to expose the marrow.

Bateleur

4 *Length 60cm* French for 'tightrope walker', the name refers to this bird's low-flying aerial acrobatics. In flight, look for its white wings and tailless appearance; up close look for the bold colour pattern and scarlet face.

African Fish Eagle

5 *Length 75cm* With a wingspan over 2m, this eagle hunts for fish, but it is most familiar for its loud ringing vocalisations that have become known as 'the voice of Africa'.

Lappet-Faced Vulture

6 *Length 115cm* Vultures mingle with predators around carcasses, competing for scraps of flesh and bone. The monstrous lappet-faced vulture gets its fill before other vultures move in.

Other Birds

Come to Southern Africa prepared to see an astounding number of birds in every shape and colour imaginable. You may find them a pleasant diversion after a couple of days staring at sleeping lions.

Jackass Penguin

1 *Length 60cm* The Jackass penguin is actually named for its donkey-like call, part of the courtship displays given by the males.

Hamerkop

2 *Length 60cm* The hamerkop is a stork relative with an oddly crested, woodpecker-like head. Nicknamed the 'hammerhead', it hunts frogs and fish at the water's edge. Look for its massive 2m-wide nests in nearby trees.

Ostrich

3 *Length 200–270cm* Standing 2.7m tall and weighing upwards of 130kg, this ancient flightless bird escapes predators by running away at 70km/h or lying flat on the ground to resemble a pile of dirt.

Cape Gannet

4 *Length 85cm* This crisply marked seabird gathers by the thousands to catch fish with high-speed dives into the waves.

Lesser Flamingo

5 *Length 100cm* Gathering by the hundreds of thousands on shimmering salt lakes, the rose-pink lesser flamingo creates one of Africa's most dramatic wildlife spectacles.

Lilac-Breasted Roller

6 *Length 40cm* Related to kingfishers, the gorgeously coloured lilac-breasted roller gets its name from the tendency to 'roll' from side to side in flight as a way of showing off its iridescent blues, purples and greens.

Culture

Peoples of Southern Africa

Southern Africa's population is made up of Bantu-speaking people (the majority) who migrated from the north and west of the African continent; later-arriving Europeans (including Dutch, British, Portuguese and Germans); Indians (who arrived with the British, brought over to the Cape Colony as labourers); and pockets of the Khoisan (an ancient Stone Age people who survive in small numbers, mainly in Botswana and Namibia). 'Bantu' refers to a convenient language-grouping, not a race, and in reality the Bantu ethnic group comprises many subgroups or tribes, each with its own language, customs and traditions, living all over the region.

Broadly speaking, two societies and cultures (Western and African) run in parallel, and they rarely cross. As you might expect, in a Western situation social customs are similar to those in Europe, although often a touch more formal – but at the same time more friendly – than in other parts of the Western world. For example, Afrikaners will often shake hands and say their name, even if you're only meeting them briefly. While you'll meet locals of European origin and 'Europeanised' black Africans all over the region, the societies and cultures are predominantly African.

Southern Africa is very multicultural and surprisingly peaceful given the extraordinary number of ethnic groups. Integrating European and African populations has been a source of tension though for many years in the region, exacerbated by colonial rule, apartheid governments and, in Zimbabwe, a policy of reclaiming white-owned farms in recent years. Disharmony stretches much further back, however, with the destruction and dispersal of the *difaqane* (p651), which led to tribal affiliations being disrupted among various Bantu groups in the region. This was exacerbated in South Africa by the Great Trek and the Voortrekkers (see p651), who settled into areas they believed were 'vacant'.

Migration from the poorer countries to the wealthier countries in the region has also brought about tensions and hostility. South Africa for example has far more job opportunities than other countries in the region, and this has led to a great number of migrant workers (many illegal) drifting there. Africans who look different or don't speak the local language are often harassed by officialdom and the police. Locals are often suspicious of migrants, too, as there is a perception that they take jobs away from locals and are responsible for crime.

A migrant's money makes a big difference to the local economy back home – Lesotho is a good example, with many travelling to South Africa until the late 1990s to work in mines and sending money back home to their families. It is widely agreed, however, that this type of migration has also contributed to the spread of HIV/AIDS.

ETHNIC DIVERSITY

Many countries within Southern Africa are incredibly ethnically diverse. This is exemplified in South Africa, which has 11 official languages.

Daily Life

Distribution of Wealth

Southern Africa covers an enormous geographical area with an incredibly diverse population, and there is stark wealth differentiation between and within the countries of the region. Therefore, giving a precise impression of daily life for Southern Africans is virtually impossible. Nevertheless, there are some generalisations able to be made that represent very real trends in the region.

Life varies considerably between the 'haves' and the 'have-nots'. Middle-class and wealthy families live in homes reflecting that wealth, and many leafy, wealthy neighbourhoods look just like anywhere else in the Western world. Leisure time is often defined by time spent at upmarket (and in the case of South Africa, heavily guarded) shopping centres, which provide alfresco dining, plenty of retail therapy and a place 'to be seen'.

For the millions of Southern Africans (in fact, the vast majority of the population) who still live in great poverty, however, life is about survival. Simple huts or enclosures house large extended families, and obtaining and preparing food is the focus of daily life.

Major Challenges

There are two major plights affecting the households of the majority of Southern Africa's population. Firstly, the food insecurity that afflicts the region is a distressing problem and seems to have no end in sight. Dependent on the rains, the region is caught up in a merciless cycle of drought (and in some cases floods) that, when combined with other factors, leads to regular food shortages.

The second, and largest, problem facing the people of Southern Africa, though, is HIV/AIDS. The sub-Saharan region is the worst-affected region in Africa and, while the statistics are simply dreadful, the socio-economic effects are overwhelming. In 2011 an estimated 23.5 million people in sub-Saharan Africa were living with HIV – this represents 69% of the world HIV population. South Africa has the world's largest HIV-positive population (5.6 million people), and national adult HIV prevalence is above 18% in that country and around the same level in Botswana, Lesotho, Namibia, Zambia and Zimbabwe. Swaziland has an HIV prevalence rate of around 26% – the highest ever documented in a country anywhere in the world. It should be noted that both Botswana and Zimbabwe have made progress in recording drops in HIV infection rates, proving that through education change is possible.

Unlike diseases that attack the weak, HIV/AIDS predominantly hits the productive members of a household – young adults. It's particularly rife among those who are highly educated, and have relatively high earn-

Masters of Illusion: The World Bank and the Poverty of Nations, by Catherine Caufield, discusses the influence that the global development lending agency has had on poor countries around the world.

FAMINE & FLOOD

Food shortages and hunger remain critically serious problems in Southern Africa. The region suffers from a seemingly endless cycle of food insecurity.

The simple reason for the food shortage is prolonged dry spells, which lead to crop failure. The reasons behind the region's continued problems in feeding itself, however, are more complex and deeply rooted. There is a multitude of causes including inadequate agricultural policies, the ripping away of a generation of workers through the HIV/AIDS epidemic, a lack of employment opportunities, bad governance and environmental degradation.

In addition to these problems, floods also wreak havoc, especially in western Zambia, and northern Namibia and Botswana.

ings and mobility. This has an enormous impact on household incomes, with the region facing the loss of a large proportion of a generation in the prime of its life. This has also meant a sharp increase in the number of orphans, of grandparents being pressured into assuming parenting roles of young children, and of children pulled out of school to care for the sick, grow food or earn money. There's still a lot of stigma attached to HIV/AIDS, too, and many locals won't admit to the cause of a loved one's death.

HIV/AIDS has led to a sharp decrease in life expectancy in Southern Africa. Recent projections have put life expectancy at around 50 years across the region – between 1990 and 1995 it peaked at just over 60 years. This fall has hopefully now bottomed out, with new treatments bringing a slight rise in recent years.

Attitudes to Sexuality

All the countries in Southern Africa are conservative in their attitudes towards gay men and lesbians. In traditional African societies, gay sexual relationships are a cultural taboo. In practice, rights for gay citizens contrast strongly between countries. South Africa's progressive constitution, for example, outlaws discrimination on the basis of sexual orientation, and gay couples have won many rights. On the other hand, Namibia and Zimbabwe have strongly condemned homosexuality, with President Mugabe describing homosexuals as 'worse than pigs and dogs'. At the time of writing, Malawi's government was attempting to lift the ban on homosexuality in that country, an unpopular move among many conservatively minded Malawians.

South Africa has one of the highest incidences of rape in the world and, as many are too afraid to report the crime, the true extent of the problem is likely much worse than official figures would suggest. Another tragic issue in the region is sexual abuse of girls in schools by their teachers; and as a result, many girls are reluctant to attend school.

Religion
Christianity

Most people in Southern Africa follow Christianity or traditional religion, often combining aspects of both. South Africa, Malawi, Botswana and Namibia have very high Christian populations (between 70% and 80% of the general population), while Mozambique has the lowest (around 35%). All the Western-style Christian churches are represented (Catholic, Protestant, Baptist, Adventist etc), most of which were introduced in colonial times by European missionaries. Their spread across the region reflects their colonial roots – the dominant Christian sect in Namibia is German Lutheranism, while Malawi is dominated by Protestant churches, founded by British missionaries. Mozambique's Portuguese heritage means Roman Catholicism is favoured among that country's Christians.

The influence of missionaries has been beneficial in education, campaigning against the slave trade, and in trying to raise the standard of living in Southern Africa; however, benefits have been tempered by the search for ideological control and disruption to traditional cultures. Missionaries were certainly influential in Malawi, where the country's history and existence was shaped by figures such as Dr Livingstone. He was a famous missionary and explorer whose intrepid travels on foot through the continent opened up much of Southern Africa to the traders and settlers who followed in his footsteps.

Although Christian denominations in Southern Africa are generally conservative, many churches actively participate in the fight against HIV/AIDS. Organisations such as Churches United Against HIV/AIDS

CULTURE RELIGION

Working to end violence against women and supporting victims of rape, Rape Crisis is based in Cape Town, South Africa. Click onto www.rapecrisis. org.za if you'd like to learn more about its work.

Christianity in Southern Africa is known for its conservatism. Roman Catholic bishops in the region have controversially condemned the use of condoms in the fight against HIV/AIDS.

WITCHCRAFT

Within many traditional African religions, there is a belief in spells and magic (usually called witchcraft or, in some places, *mutu*). In brief simplistic terms it goes like this: physical or mental illnesses are often ascribed to a spell or curse having been put on the sufferer. Often, a relative or villager is suspected of being the 'witch' who placed the curse, often for reasons of spite or jealousy. A traditional doctor, also called a diviner or witchdoctor, is then required to hunt out the witch and cure the victim. This is done in different ways in various parts of the region, and may involve the use of herbs, divining implements, prayers, chanting, dance or placing the spell in a bottle and casting it into a remote spot (if you find such a bottle in the bush, don't touch it).

Services do not come free of charge, however, and many witchdoctors demand high payments – up to US$20, in countries where an average month's earnings may be little more than this. The 'witches' who are unearthed are frequently those who cannot defend themselves – the sick, the old or the very poorest members of society. There are even reports of very young children being accused by witchdoctors of harbouring evil spirits.

(CUAHA) work with local churches to support families, care for those afflicted by the disease and reduce the stigma associated with HIV/AIDS.

Many indigenous Christian faiths have also been established, ranging from a small congregation meeting in a simple hut to vast organisations with millions of followers, such as the Zion and Apostolic churches in Zimbabwe and South Africa. In South Africa alone the Zion Church claims four million followers (the largest in the country).

Islam, Hinduism & Judaism

South Africa's Archbishop Desmond Tutu said, 'When the missionaries came to Africa they had the Bible and we had the land. They said, "Let us pray." We closed our eyes. When we opened them we had the Bible and they had the land.'

Islam is also followed in some areas, predominantly in the north of Malawi and along its lakeshore, and in the northern provinces of Mozambique, where 35% of the population attest to the Islamic faith, the highest percentage in Southern Africa. There are also Hindus and Jews, particularly in South Africa, but their numbers are small.

Traditional

There are many traditional religions in Southern Africa, but no great temples or written scriptures. For outsiders, beliefs can be complex (and to the Western mind, illogical), as can the rituals and ceremonies that surround them. Most traditional religions are animist – based on the attribution of life or consciousness to natural objects or phenomena – and many accept the existence of a Supreme Being, with whom communication is possible through the intercession of ancestors. Thus, ancestors play a particularly strong role. Their principal function is to protect the tribe or family, and they may on occasion show their pleasure (such as through a good harvest) or displeasure (such as a member of the family becoming sick).

Arts

The countries and indigenous peoples of Southern Africa all have their own artistic traditions, often interwoven with culture and beliefs.

Rock art created by the San people since time immemorial is the one artistic tradition that unifies the region, and can still be seen today in many Southern African countries. See p648 for details.

When travelling around the region, the more popular handicrafts you're likely to see (and be able to purchase) include San crafts (particularly in Namibia and Botswana), such as jewellery and leatherwork, bows and arrows, and ostrich shell beads; mohair products such as tapestries and ponchos, especially in Lesotho and South Africa; exquisite palm-woven and African-themed baskets, particularly renowned in Botswana and Zambia; pottery, often highly decorative and of course very practical; Shona sculpture (Zimbabwean), renowned worldwide, with recurring themes such as the metamorphosis of man into beast, and Makonde sculpture (Mozambican); glassware and candles (Swazi) in the shape of regional wildlife, and in the case of the former often made from recyclable material. You'll also find wooden carvings, particularly in places where tourists are likely to wander – wildlife carvings such as huge giraffes are popular, and you'll even find earthmovers, aeroplanes and helicopters.

If you've developed a taste for wonderful Shona sculpture, but had no room in your bag to bring some home, see www.shonaart.co.za to order online.

Township art is found throughout the region, and has developed sober themes in an expressive, colourful and usually light-hearted manner. Ranging from complex wire-work toys to prints and paintings, deceptively naive images in township art can embody messages far from simple.

In South Africa, the woodcarvers of Limpopo's Venda region have gained international recognition.

Galleries display works from Southern African artists, and include more traditional sculpture and paintings. Painters often interpret the landscape, wildlife and the diverse peoples of the region – Namibia, South Africa, Mozambique and Zambia in particular have galleries that display work from local artists.

Literature

Southern Africa has a strong tradition of oral literature among the various Bantu groups. Traditions and stories were preserved and passed on from generation to generation. In many parts of the region, written language was introduced only by Christian missionaries and assumed more importance in the 20th century. Common forms of literature that have developed include short stories, novels and poetry.

Although writers have focused on themes usually concerning their own country, there are common threads. Nationalism, white minority rule, the struggle for independence and life after colonialism are all themes explored by Southern African writers. In Malawi, oppression and abuse of power were common themes through the Banda years, after independence; Samson Kambalu is a contemporary author who writes about growing up in 1970s and '80s Malawi. Guerrilla poets such as Marcelino dos Santos from Mozambique make fascinating reading. In many countries the growth of literature has paralleled the struggle for independence and freedom.

The Penguin Book of Southern African Stories, edited by Stephen Gray, features stories (some thousands of years old) from the region, showing similarities and common threads in various literary traditions.

Works by authors such as Bessie Head from Botswana address African village life and landscape, and Zimbabwean writers include precolonial traditions, myths and folk tales in their writings.

Stephen Gill has written several historical books on Lesotho and, thanks to him, archives were established and much local history saved.

White South African writers have had much overseas success, with literary giants such as Nadine Gordimer and JM Coetzee both awarded Nobel prizes for literature. If you want to get a sense of where South Africa has come from and where it's going, delving into its literary roots is a good place to start. Local literature takes you back into the days of apartheid (from both a black and a white perspective) and the realities of building the rainbow nation.

Architecture

The greatest indigenous architectural legacy is in the past – in Zimbabwe the ruins of great stone cities such as Great Zimbabwe and Khami are rare examples of medieval African architecture in the region.

Mapungubwe in South Africa also contains excellent examples of ancient historical roots from a forgotten kingdom.

Architecturally, the colonial legacy in Southern Africa is dominated by European designs, with South Africa containing by far the best examples. Pretoria's stately Union Building has won much acclaim, while art deco design sprang up in Durban and Cape Town after building booms in the early 20th century. Unique Cape Dutch buildings, especially town houses, can be seen throughout Cape Town. Examples of 19th- and 20th-century English architecture (especially Victorian) can be seen in many parts of the region, and at times in the most unlikely of places (such as Livingstonia in Malawi and Shiwa Ngandu in Zambia). In Namibia, Germany has left a colonial legacy of late-19th-century-designed places, including art nouveau design. Mozambique Island is an architectural treasure trove and includes the oldest European building in the southern hemisphere.

Safari lodges, such as those in Zimbabwe, can be a mix of an English sensibility with African design pieces and environment.

Dance

Dance, along with music, in Southern Africa is often closely linked with, and plays an important role in, social function rather than being mere entertainment. Movement is regarded as an important type of communication in traditional African societies, and dance can be associated with contact between spirits and the living; traditional healers often performed curative dances to rid patients of sickness. Symbolic gestures, mime, props, masks, costumes and body painting can all play a part. If you have the chance to see traditional song and dance while you're in Southern Africa, try not to miss out.

Dance also helps to define culture and, in Swaziland, for example, the Umhlanga (reed) dance plays a very important role in society, drawing the nation together and reinforcing Swazi culture. Mozambicans are on the whole excellent dancers, and Arabic influence is evident in their slow, swaying rhythms – check out the Mozambique National Company of Song & Dance (National Company of Song & Dance; http://myspace.com/cnc dmoz; 2182 Av 24 de Julho, Cine Teatro África; ⊙rehearsals 8am-3pm Mon-Fri).

Food & Drink

The business of eating tends to be all about survival for most of the population, and much of the day's activity is associated with the preparation of meals. In a region racked by famine, with many countries not able to consistently produce enough food to feed their own population, food is about functionality, not creativity.

Although food is not a real highlight of Southern Africa, the variety and quality of food for visitors and well-to-do locals is improving all the time. Certainly an urban setting will usually mean more variety for visitors, and the colonial legacy in some countries does mean some intriguing culinary combinations.

South Africa is the best place to eat and certainly has the most variety, an inheritance of its varied African, European and Asian population. Here you'll find a fusion of influences, from the curry and coriander that wafted over the Indian Ocean to Afrikaner favourites such as steaks the size of half a cow and *boerewors* (a tasty Afrikaner sausage), and Cape Malay cuisine, an exotic mix of spices and local produce.

Seafood is popular in places that have a coastline (be it lake or ocean), both with locals and travellers. In Swaziland you'll readily find prawns on menus, courtesy of Mozambique, which itself blends a variety of in-

SAN ART

Images of Power, by D Lewis-Williams and T Dowson, is a fascinating study of the art of the San people, utilising modern scientific techniques and rediscovered records of discussions between the San and early European settlers.

FOOD ETIQUETTE

Most travellers will have the opportunity to share an African meal sometime during their stay, and will normally be given royal treatment and a seat of honour. Although concessions are sometimes made for foreigners, to avoid offence be aware that table manners are probably different to those you're accustomed to. The African staple, maize or sorghum meal, is the centre of nearly every meal. It is normally taken with the right hand from a communal pot, rolled into balls, dipped in some sort of *relish* – meat, beans or vegetables – and eaten. As in most societies, it is considered impolite to scoff food, or to hoard it or be stingy with it. If you do, your host may feel that he or she hasn't provided enough. Similarly, if you can't finish your food, don't worry; the host will be pleased that you have been satisfied. Often, containers of water or home-brew beer may be passed around from person to person. It is not customary to share coffee, tea or bottled soft drinks.

fluences (African, Indian and Portuguese) into its delectable seafood offerings. In Malawi, eating *chambo* (fried fish) by the lake is a highlight. Around the Cape and Winelands of South Africa, look for lightly spiced fish stews, *snoekbraai* (grilled snoek), mussels, oysters and even lobster.

A favourite for many visitors to Southern Africa is the fruit, and depending on the season you'll find bananas, pineapples, pawpaws (papayas), mangoes and avocados in plentiful supply.

Staples & Specialities

In parts of Southern Africa, especially in South Africa, Namibia and Botswana, meat features as a staple, and anything that can be grilled is grilled – including ostrich, crocodile, warthog and kudu. Meat also features in local celebrations.

Takeaway snack food found on the street may include bits of grilled meat, deep-fried potato or cassava chips, roasted corn cobs, boiled eggs, peanuts (called ground nuts locally), biscuits, cakes, fried dough balls (which approximate doughnuts) and miniature green bananas. Prices are always dirt cheap (unfortunately, often with the emphasis on dirt).

For something more substantial, but still inexpensive, the most common meal is the regional staple, boiled maize meal, which is called *mealie pap* in South Africa and Namibia, *sadza* in Zimbabwe, and *nshima* or *nsima* in countries further north. In Botswana, the staple is known as *bogobe,* in which sorghum replaces the maize. When fresh and well cooked, all varieties are both tasty and filling, and are usually eaten with a *relish* (sauce or stew), which is either very simple (eg boiled vegetable leaves) or something more substantial, such as a stew of beef, fish, beans or chicken.

The main meal is at noon, so most cheap eateries are closed in the evening. In the morning you can buy coffee or tea (with or without milk – the latter is cheaper) and bread, sometimes with margarine, or maybe a slightly sweetened breadlike cake.

Up a notch, and popular with tourists, are traditional meals of *mielies* (cobs of maize) and relish, or Western dishes, such as beef or chicken served with rice or chips (fries). More elaborate options, such as steaks, pies, fish dishes, pasta and something that resembles curry over rice are worth trying for a change.

Most cities also have speciality restaurants serving genuine (or at least pretty close to it) Indian, Thai, Chinese, Lebanese, Mexican or ethnic African (such as Ethiopian or West African) cuisine.

The San eat *hoodia,* a prickly, cucumber-like plant, to suppress their appetite on long hunting treks – in the West *hoodia* is used in one of the most popular weight-loss drugs on the market.

TRAVEL YOUR TASTEBUDS

If you're not squeamish about watching wildlife during the day and then sampling it in the evening, meat lovers can try some (nonendangered) local produce: dishes such as warthog stew, buffalo steak and impala sausages go down a treat. They can be hard to find, but wildlife lodges and upmarket restaurants are usually the best bet.

Bunny chow is a South African favourite, also popular in Swaziland. It's basically curry inside a hollowed-out loaf, messy to eat but quite delicious.

African bush tucker varies across the region among Southern Africa's indigenous groups – for example, the San still eat many desert creatures including caterpillar-like mopane worms, prepared in many different ways, such as deep-fried, or just eaten raw.

Drinks

You can buy tea and coffee in many places, from top-end hotels and restaurants to humble local eating houses.

In bars, hotels and bottle stores you can buy beer and spirits, either imported international brands or locally brewed drinks. South African and Namibian beers (Windhoek is excellent) are available throughout the region, and in many areas they dominate local markets. Wonderful South African wines are widely available, as is a growing range of extremely popular spirit coolers.

Traditional beer of the region is made from maize, brewed in the villages and drunk from communal pots with great ceremony on special occasions, and with less ado in everyday situations. This product, known as chibuku (or *shake-shake*), is commercially brewed in many countries and sold in large blue paper cartons, or by the bucketful. It's definitely an acquired taste, and it does pack a punch.

Cooking the Southern African Way, by Kari Cornell, includes authentic ethnic foods (even vegetarian) from across the region, including a section on holiday and festival food.

Vegetarians & Vegans

Vegetarianism isn't widely understood in Africa, and many locals think a meal is incomplete unless at least half of it once lived and breathed. That said, if you're not worried about variety or taste, finding inexpensive vegetarian options isn't that difficult. In the cheapest places, you may have to stick to the *mielies* and greens. A step above that would be eggs and chips (which may be fried in animal fat) with whatever vegetables may be available. Those who eat fish should have even more luck, but note that many places will even serve chicken as a vegetarian dish, on the notion that it's not really meat. Nearly all midrange and upmarket restaurants offer some sort of genuine vegetarian dish, even if it's just a vegetable omelette or pasta and sauce. In larger cities and towns, a growing number of places specialise in light vegetarian cuisine – especially at lunchtime – and of course, Lebanese, Indian and Italian restaurants usually offer various interesting meat-free choices.

Music in Southern Africa

Jane Cornwell

Long before there were borders, there was music. Thousands of years ago, right across the handful of countries we now loosely term Southern Africa, a host of cultures were singing, dancing and creating rhythms to accompany their lives. Arguably it is music, more than any other aspect of culture, that has best survived the onslaught of Western influences. Not always untarnished, though: while some traditions persist, others have merged, shape-shifted and formed new genres. South Africa alone has the greatest range of musical styles on the African continent, helped along by its gargantuan recording industry. Some of these styles have spilled over into neighbouring countries, all of which have styles of their own.

Music still marks the important stages of a Southern African person's life. It still enlightens, heals, invokes spirits. It still makes people dance, sing, holler. It does all this regardless of the instrument – whose form can change according to ethnicity, geography, gender of the player and, sometimes, whatever objects are lying around. Expressing oneself through music isn't always easy: think of long-suffering, government-censored Zimbabwe; or Namibia, whose music industry lacks distribution networks and major record labels and is only now slowly addressing the fact; or Mozambique, where most artists don't receive royalties, and promoters frequently don't pay. Regardless, music still pulses in the region like a heartbeat. So remember: just because you can't buy it – or even see or hear it – doesn't mean that it isn't there.

A Potted History

Early Origins

It's better, initially, to think ethnicity rather than country. Southern Africa is one of the world's oldest inhabited regions, after all. It's so old, in fact, that its earliest music can be traced back some 4000 years to the Stone Age, when groups of hunter-gatherer San played basic flutes and rattles and sang in their unique click language. Today's San still sound wonderfully ethereal, their singing, clapping trance-dance the stuff of ritual, tourist haunts and left-field record labels. But it's the glorious vocal polyphony of the Bantu-speaking people – the Zulu, Xhosa and Sotho of the present day – that has come to characterise the region; this is the music that attracted Paul Simon before he recorded his seminal 1988 album *Graceland*.

Long before the Christian missionaries and colonialists arrived in the 19th century, there were kingdoms. In Zambia, each king had his own royal musician, just as each kingdom had its own music. Singing often

Radio Chikuni (www.chikuni radio.org) is a community radio station broadcasting from Zambia's Chikuni Mission Station. It is dedicated to preserving the music and culture of the Batonga people for whom music is a means of personal expression and communication and, of course, of spreading the word.

accompanied instrumental music played on horns, percussion, drums and the stringed *babatone* – the inspiration for the contemporary Zambian-style *kalindula*. Elsewhere, herders used flutes and other instruments to help control the movement of cattle. (Oh, and the first major style of South African popular music? None other than penny-whistle jive, later known as *kwela*.) The Bantu of Namibia played gourds, horn trumpets and marimbas, while the various ethnic groups of Malawi travelled widely, spreading musical influences from the Zulu of South Africa and the Islamic Yao people of Tanzania.

Music Industry Online (www.mio.co.za) is the largest music-industry portal in South Africa, providing news, articles, podcasts and more to thousands of visitors.

European Influence

Colonial rule altered everything. The folk forms of Mozambique, a former Portuguese colony, bear hallmarks of colonial rule – though its main style, *marrabenta*, flourished after independence. Mozambican bands began to play a roots style similar to that heard in Tanzania and Zambia, while musicians in the heart of the country played a style like that of Zimbabwe. The music of southern Mozambique was altered by the influx of workers returning from the South African mines (revolutionary lyrics were delivered over regional melodies), just as the workers who have migrated from Lesotho to the mines and cities of neighbouring South Africa have developed a rich genre of sung oral poetry – or word music – that focuses on the experiences of migrant life. African folk music also became popular in Zambia, as troubadours entertained exhausted miners. In South Africa, Dutch farmers brought a European folk music that became what is known today as *boeremusiek*.

The Mozambique Music Video Chart (www.africatv24.com/music_video/mozambique) offers clips by popular artists and lets you search for your favourites.

It's no wonder, then, that the banjo, violin, concertina and electric guitar have all had a profound influence on Southern African music. Malawian banjo-and-guitar duos were huge in the 1950s and '60s, after which South African *kwela* took over. The influence of guitar-based *rumba* from Zaïre (now the Democratic Republic of Congo, DRC) was felt right across the region (political upheaval saw many Congolese musicians relocate to Southern Africa); its upstart cousin, *soukous*, has made its presence felt in everything from Zambian *kalindula* to Malawian *kwasa kwasa*. The gospel mega-genre has evolved from the teachings of 19th-century Christian missionaries, which were customised accordingly. Reckon those chord sequences in south African songs are familiar? Blame the Church.

A Political Voice

Numerous musical styles have been born out of oppression, too. Ladysmith Black Mambazo's 'tiptoe' *isicathimiya* music, with its high-kicking, soft-stepping dance, has its origins in the all-male miners' hostels in

TOP 10 SOUTHERN AFRICAN ALBUMS

» *Senzo* (Sunny Side Records), Abdullah Ibrahim
» *Home is Where the Music Is* (Decca), Hugh Masekela
» *Best of Miriam Makeba and the Skylarks* (BMG), Miriam Makeba
» *Shaka Zulu* (Warner), Ladysmith Black Mambazo
» *Indestructible Beat of Soweto Volume One* (Earthworks), various artists
» *Zambush Vol 2: Zambian Hits from the '60s & '70s* (SWP Records), various artists
» *Loliwe* (TS Records), Zahara
» *Rising Tide* (Igloo/Discovery Records), Makoomba
» *Father Creeper* (Sub Pop), Spoek Mathambo
» *Deception* (Mashaso Productions), The Dog

South Africa's Natal Province (now KwaZulu-Natal) in the 1930s, when workers were at pains not to wake their bosses. *Kwela* music, like most modern South African styles, came out of the townships; *kwela*, meaning 'jump up', was the instruction given to those about to be thrown into police vans during raids. Thomas Mapfumo's *chimurenga* is once again the music of resistance in Zimbabwe, even if – for the majority of Zimbabwean musicians – outspokenness is just not the Zimbabwean way. Even the prolific Oliver 'Tuku' Mtukudzi (whose infectious dance pop, informed by the country's jit-jive and tsava rhythms, is known simply as 'Tuku music') has never done more than express his 'great disappointment'. Rising stars Mokoomba – six Tonga musicians from Victoria Falls – are looking forward with energy and dynamism, their multilingual lyrics rooted in home reality.

In Malawi the intentionally controversial songs of politician and reggae giant Lucius 'Soldier of the Poor Man' Banda has spawned a slew of similarly antsy reggae outfits; there is also a softer reggae led by Black Missionaries and other Malawian Rastafarians. In postapartheid South Africa, freedom of expression is pretty much expected: rap, hip hop and their indigenous sibling *kwaito* are as socially concerned as they are lacking political correctness, depending on who you're listening to. South African jazz remains some of the best in the world; the international success of the likes of Afro-soul/jazz chanteuse Thandiswa and Afro-fusion outfit Freshlyground has new audiences in new countries taking notice.

The popular music of Southern Africa has created itself by mingling local ideas and forms with those from outside the region. And while every country has its own distinctive and constantly evolving array of styles supported by local audiences, that doesn't mean you won't be in one place and hear something from somewhere else.

Musical Instruments

As with most traditional African instruments, the membranophones (drums), chordophones (stringed instruments), aerophones (wind instruments) and idiophones (percussion) of Southern Africa tend to be found in rural areas. Local materials and found objects are often used to musical effect. In Namibia and Zimbabwe dry cocoons are tied together and strapped to dancers' ankles and waists; in Swaziland and South Africa, ankles rattle with dried fruit. Right across the region, everything from seeds, sticks and stalks to horsehair, oryx horns and goat skins are being shaken and blown, plucked and beaten. Some people in Namibia customise their drums by carving human faces into them.

The MaNyungwe people of northeastern Zimbabwe and northwestern Mozambique play *nyanga* music on panpipes, using different interlocking parts and quick bursts of singing in a sort of highly melodic musical round called *hocketting*. The Tonga people of Zambia do a similar thing with animal horns known as *nyele*. Variations on musical themes abound. The people of Sesfontein, Namibia, play reed pipes made from papaya stems. Basotho herding boys fashion their *lekolulo* flutes from sticks, cords and reeds. Everywhere, too, there is men's music and women's music, just as there are men's dances and women's dances. In Lesotho men use their mouths to play the stringed *setolo-tolo*. Namibian women play the scraped mouth-resonated bow.

Oh, and then there's the voice. Be they roaring Zulu choirs or clicking San, four-part Nama harmonies or ululating Zambian church-goers, the people of Southern Africa really do sing up some glorious polyphonic storms. Keep an ear out.

Featuring big-name UK and African live acts and DJs, the award-winning three-day Lake of Stars Malawi Music Festival is held on the palm-fringed shores of Lake Malawi each October. It attracts around 1500 locals and travellers; proceeds go to charity. (www.lakeofstars.org)

With winners announced each May, the Namibian Music Awards (www.nama.com.na/) is an annual gong-fest run by the Namibian Broadcasting Corporation, intended to highlight and promote Namibian musicians and music producers.

Drums

There is a huge variety of drums (*ngoma* is the general term in the Bantu language). Stick-struck and hand-struck. Square, goblet-shaped and round. Small cowhide-covered ones for Zulu children. Khetebu 'bushtom' drums beloved by the South African Tsonga. Namalwa 'lion-drums' of Zambia, played by inserting a stick through the drum head and rubbing. High-pitched talking drums (which are more commonly found in West Africa), held tight under the armpit and beaten with hook-shaped sticks; the Chewa people of Zambia call theirs the *vimbuza*. Drum families – mother, father, son, played in sets of three – like the conical drums of the northeast of Namibia. Drums to accompany reed ensembles, a cappella groups and, more often than not, ankle-rattling dances.

Held each July in Selebi-Phikwe, between Gaborone and Francistown, Botswana's National Music Eisteddfod showcases traditional dances and music from around the country, courtesy of its schools, colleges and choirs.

Bows

If drums are the region's collective heartbeat, then the bow is its lonely soul. Southern Africa has several kinds of musical bow, many resembling the Brazilian *berimbau*; braced, mouth and/or gourd-resonated bows. There are large hunting bows used as mouth bows; two-stringed bows, played while simultaneously singing and resonating; multiple bows with multiple strings; mouth bows that use palm leaves instead of strings. String instruments abound: the lute (both strummed and bowed) is present in several forms. The Setswana of Botswana sing and strum the violin-like *segaba* (which is a single string attached to a tin). The dance of the Nama of Namibia uses flutes, drums and strings to emulate animal sounds.

Set in the eponymous colourful township, *Katutura* is a film made by Namibians for Namibians. Due for release in late 2013 or early 2014, it will underline the importance of respecting women, children and elders as it celebrates the country's vibrant heritage. Including, of course, its music.

Keyboard Percussion

The xylophone is also prevalent, and the xylophone music of southern Malawi has influenced contemporary music in both East and Southern Africa. Mallet instruments with wooden keys are the main instrument of the Lozi and Nkoya of western Zambia, who place slats of wood over a long platform and gourds in descending size; up to four people play simultaneously. The marimbas of South Africa feed into the mbaqanga (township jive) style. It's an entirely different sound from that of the *mbila* (plural *timbila*) played by the Chopi people of coastal Mozambique, which features resonators made from gourds and a buzzing tone created via a sheet of plastic (formerly an animal skin) over a hole in the ground. The master of *timbila* is the great Venancio Mbande, who still rehearses regularly with his large orchestra at his homestead in Chopiland.

Mbiras

But perhaps no instrument is as distinctively Southern African as the *mbira*, a hand-held instrument with small metal keys attached to an amplifying wooden box or calabash; attached shells and/or bottle tops distort and fuzz its sound. There are many traditions of these 'thumb pianos', each with a different name according to its size and origin – for instance, they're called *kankobela* by the Tonga of Zambia. But it is Zimbabwe with which the *mbira* is generally identified: central to the Shona people's marathon religious trance ceremonies known as *bira*, interlocking *mbira* patterns are considered both healing and spiritual. Since independence the *mbira* has been adapted to modern styles, such as the *chimurenga* guitar bands.

A group of musicians in Botswana is campaigning to have Botswanan music featured on the country's radio stations, which tend to overlook local talent in favour of international artists.

Musical Styles

A rich network of musical styles has developed in Southern Africa. And although those of South Africa are probably the best known, the entire region is humming with musical traditions, expressions and textures. In most countries there are polyphonic, repetitive patterns and call-and-response singing. There are styles that reflect ethnic diversity and geography. Cities are dominated by pop, rock, jazz and urban music, much of which combines core African principles with Western influences. Electric guitars fuel genres such as *afroma* in Malawi, *jit*-jive in South Africa

INTERVIEW WITH HUGH MASEKELA

Two-time Grammy winner, jazz musician Hugh Ramopolo Masekela has taken his place as the elder statesman of South African music.

'I don't want to boast,' says Masekela, puffing out his chest, 'but the only musicians I know who can play any style of music are South African.'

He jerks his thumb over his shoulder at two of the musicians from his band: bassist Fana Zulu, 53, and 68-year-old percussionist Francis Maneh Fuster. 'These guys grew up around music, just like I did.' Masekela's gaze is direct. 'Traditional music, children's songs and migrant labour music; gospel, township jive, big bands and combos.'

And of course, jazz: 'Everybody had a gramophone. Our greatest mirror was African America. We meshed what they were doing with our own interpretations week by week.'

The band's remaining three musicians are all in their twenties. 'About three years ago I decided that since I was playing live so much I had better get a leaner band together. Those older guys have been with me for 22 years on and off. But those young guys!', he exclaims. 'We've gelled into a great piece of synergy.'

At 70-plus years of age, Masekela is busier than he's ever been. Back home in Johannesburg, where he returned in 1990 after 26 years of exile in countries including Botswana and England, Masekela is immersed in establishing an infrastructure aimed at preserving and nurturing the 'unfathomable' amount of music that exists in his homeland.

'I want to see music and heritage in Africa come back into African life,' he says animatedly. 'I want Africans to develop and form their own African market, especially in rural ethnic areas. I want tourists to come to South Africa for the music as well as for the geography and the animals.'

As progressive and experimental as he always was – this, after all, is the man who fused jazz, pop, Latin and African influences into a style all his own – Masekela has been rediscovering his own musical roots as well. 'I'm going backwards,' he quips.

His 33rd studio album, *Jabulani* (2012), is a tribute to the township weddings he attended as a youth, around the time when he saw Kirk Douglas play an American jazz trumpeter in the film *Young Man With a Horn* and decided to chuck in the piano in favour of the trumpet, which he sensed was the instrument for him.

After being given his first trumpet aged 14 by the anti-apartheid campaigner Archbishop Trevor Huddleston, he went on to join jazz groups including the Jazz Epistles with pianist Dollar Brand (later known as Abdullah Ibrahim) and played in the orchestra of the successful musical *King Kong,* which starred his future wife Miriam Makeba, the late, great Mama Africa.

Following the Sharpeville Massacre of 1960 – after which gatherings of more than 10 people were banned – Masekela left South Africa to study music in London, then in New York. His tales of that city's buzzing jazz scene are peppered with heroic names: Dizzy Gillespie, John Coltrane, Charlie Mingus.

'It was the golden age,' he says. 'Dizzy introduced me to everybody. I thought maybe I could join the Jazz Messengers with Art Blakey but everyone said, "You're from Africa. Form your own group. Use what you know and stand out."'

So he did. In 1968 he recorded the catchy instrumental pop tune 'Grazing in the Grass', which gave him a surprise number one hit and sent him on his way to household name status. 'I remember performing that tune on the Johnny Cash TV show, which was very exciting at the time because I loved country and western music.'

Masekela has no truck with the increasingly unfashionable 'world music' label. Never has: 'World music is a marketing term that came up in the 1980s and neutralised African music. What we play is *music.*'

and Zam-rock in Zambia. Local sounds keep migrating, metamorphosing. New genres keep forming. The following is a by no means definitive round-up of what is being listened to.

Chimurenga

In Zimbabwe in the late 1970s the musician Thomas Mapfumo and the Blacks Unlimited transferred traditional Shona *mbira* patterns to the electric guitar. They sang songs of resistance, using bright, harmonised vocals, against the white-controlled Rhodesian government. *Chimurenga,* meaning 'struggle', became a tool of social activism and, with lyrics in Shona, a secret means of communication. Banned by Zimbabwean state radio then, much of today's *chimurenga* bubbles away underground, and no wonder: high-profile artist and prominent government critic Raymond Majongwe has been denied international travel visas, and has said that he fears for his life. Apolitical, good-time *sungura* guitar music (the current industry's favoured genre) and bland Shona impersonations of hip hop and ragga (a dance-oriented style of reggae) abound.

Gospel

Gospel music is huge everywhere. In Malawi spiritual songs are sung in church, at school assemblies and political functions, and during everyday tasks. Many of Zambia's Christian churches boast US-style gospel synthesisers and guitars. The effects of popular influences on church music can be heard in top-sellers Adonai Pentecostal Singers and Emphraim Sekeleti Mutalange. In Botswana, traditional music is present in church singing. Zimbabwe's lucrative gospel market is dominated by Pastor Charles Charamba and his *sungura*-based songs (gospel singers in Zimbabwe are as big as the biggest popular music stars). South Africa is the really commercial holy roller: a mega-selling amalgam of European, American, Zulu and other African traditions, neatly divided into traditional and modern styles. Look out for Rebecca Malope, South African Gospel Singers and the 2010 Grammy-winning Soweto Gospel Choir.

Jazz

What Malawi calls 'jazz' began in the late 1960s when, inspired by South African *kwela* music, bands such as Chimvu Jazz featured semirural musicians on acoustic instruments – a tradition that continues today. In Botswana most popular music tends to be labelled 'jazz', but it is probably *gumba-gumba* ('party-party') music – modernised Zulu and Setswana music mixed with traditional jazz – that comes closest to it. Zambia's Zam-rock has its jazzy elements. But if you're after jazz that is structurally, harmonically and melodically distinctive – and is, unequivocally, jazz – then head to South Africa. What was famously an expatriate music representing the suffering of a people is now a thriving, progressive force. The likes of Lira, Thandiswa and the legendary Hugh Masekela are at the vanguard.

Kalindula

The urban dance style known as *kalindula* has its roots in the Bemba traditions of northern Zambia's Luapula Province – where a stringed instrument called the *babatone* swings like a double bass. Inspired (like many Southern African genres) by Congolese rumba, *kalindula* took hold in the mid-1970s in the wake of the presidential decree that 95% of broadcast music should be Zambian. Most *kalindula* bands broke up following the country's economic collapse in the 1990s. Artists such

For information on music and censorship in Zimbabwe, go to freemuse.org and musicfreedomday.org

Featuring music and interviews by Abdullah Ibrahim, Hugh Masekela and Miriam Makeba among others, Lee Hirsch's documentary *Amandla! A Revolution in Four Part Harmony* (2002) explores the role of music in the fight against apartheid. Made over nine years, this is a deeply affecting film.

Taking place annually on the first Sunday in September, Jazz on the Lake is a free daytime concert and a Jo'burg institution (www.joburg.org.za).

as the Glorious Band tried to revive *kalindula* with moderate success; Kabukulu Mwamba Chimo, whose *kalindula* includes traces of rumba, *sinjonjo* (an upbeat song and type of dance popular in copper belt mining areas in Zambia and Zimbabwe) and traditional Lamba music, is currently enjoying popularity.

Kwaito

Post 1994, *kwaito* (*kway*-to, meaning hot or angry) exploded onto South Africa's dance floors. A rowdy mix of bubblegum, hip hop, R&B, ragga, *mbaqanga*, traditional, jazz, and British and American house music, *kwaito* remains a lifestyle even if its bubble has arguably burst. Chanted or sung in township slang (usually over programmed beats), *kwaito*'s lyrics range from the anodyne to the fiercely political. Given an international lease of life as the soundtrack for the feature film *Tsotsi* (which bagged the 2006 Oscar for Best Foreign Film, and saw *kwaito* star Zola playing a gangster), *kwaito* remains huge across the Southern African region. It's still Lesotho's favourite music style. If you're in Namibia, look out for EES, The Dogg and Gazza. In Zambia, try the *kwaito*-house of Ma Africa. If you're in South Africa, take your pick.

Yfm (www.yfm.co.za) is South Africa's most popular youth station, with an emphasis on live podcasting and blogging and a 50% self-imposed local music quota.

MUSIC IN SOUTHERN AFRICA MUSICAL STYLES

MOKOOMBA

In 2012 everyone was talking about Mokoomba (www.mokoomba.com), a young six-piece made up of friends from Victoria Falls in the north of Zimbabwe, all of whom come from the country's tiny Tonga minority.

After bursting onto the international scene in 2012 with *Rising Tide,* a sizzling debut album that blends local Tonga rhythms with global influences such as funk and rap, Mokoomba went on to prove its worth with a series of energetic live shows from South Africa to Europe. Critics hailed them as the bright new hopes of African music.

'We are proudly Tonga of the Zambezi Valley,' says bass player Abundance Mutori, 'and our traditional rhythms come from instruments like the *kankobela* (Tonga thumb piano), antelope horns and an array of Tonga drums.'

'Mokoomba play these rhythms on modern instruments; of utmost importance to us are our lyrics, which come from our strong oral tradition.'

Frontman Mathias Muzaza sings in no less than six Southern African languages in a voice both keening and edgy, and with guitarist/singer Trustworth Samende writes most of the band's songs. Songs include 'Njoka', a mash-up of warm riffs and beat boxing; 'Misozi', a Congolese-style pop excursion; and 'Nimukonda', a party track that's part reggae, part dancehall.

Message-driven lyrics variously ask for guidance from ancestors, encourage young people to heed the advice of elders and examine the conflicting emotions surrounding moving from the country to the city.

'As young children living in a small border town' – Victoria Falls borders Zambia, Botswana and Namibia and is close to Angola – 'we grew up exposed to everything from the traditional music of different rural areas to the British and American chart music we heard on the radio,' says Mutori. 'While our sound is very pan-African, our goal has been to open the world to the cultural and musical diversity that exists in Zimbabwe and share the music and message of our Tonga culture. Our repertoire is very broad.'

Mokoomba's overseas success has raised their profile in their beleaguered Zimbabwe, a country where music piracy is rampant, internet access is limited (as is free speech) and music promoters are unwilling to take risks.

'Our goal is to open the world to the cultural and musical diversity that exists in Zimbabwe by sharing and promoting the music and story of the Tonga people,' says Mutori, flashing a grin. 'We want to show the world a different face of Zimbabwe: positive, optimistic, full of joy and promise.'

Kwasa Kwasa

Film-maker and musician Kenny Gilmore's 55-minute documentary *Deep Roots Malawi* showcases the country's musical traditions and takes the viewer into the heart of Malawian music culture; his band Sangalala fuses pop, reggae, jazz and blues with Malawian rhythms. For more, see www.myspace.com/sangalala.

Beginning in Zaïre (now DRC) in the mid-1980s and spreading quickly to surrounding areas, *kwasa kwasa* (from the French street slang, *Quoi ca?* – 'What's this?') took its cue from Congolese rumba and soukous. Characterised by an all-important lead guitar and lighter background drumming, *kwasa kwasa* songs typically let guitar and drums set the pace before the vocals enter, with an intricate guitar solo somewhere in the middle. Arguments rage over whether *kwasa kwasa* is actually just rumba; for others it's simply a dance style. Everyone from politicians to street vendors knows how to do the *kwasa kwasa*: booties wildly gyrating – à la American hip hop – while legs and torsos are kept still.

Marrabenta

Sounding a little like salsa or merengue, *marrabenta* is the best-known urban dance music in Mozambique, and one created from a fusion of imported European music played on improvised materials: oil cans, wooden stakes and fishing lines. Taking its name from the Portuguese word 'to break' (hard-playing musos frequently snap their guitar strings), *marrabenta's* local-language songs of love and social criticism were banned by Portuguese colonialists – ensuring its popularity postindependence. Stalwart *marrabenta* band Ghorwane uses horns, guitars, percussion and strong vocal harmonies; *marrabenta*-meets-dance-music diva Neyma is a megacelebrity.

Rap & Hip-Hop

Focus: Music of South Africa (Routledge, 2008), by Carol Ann Muller, is an impressive, scholarly and highly readable tome that takes an in-depth look at the full spectrum of South African music from past to present.

The genre that was born in New York more than three decades ago now has another home in (or has come back to) Africa. In Namibia, writer and skateboarder Ruusa Namupala is mixing township sounds with hip hop. In Botswana, Game 'Zeus' Bantsi is flying the flag for home-grown rap. Young Swaziland rap groups – and indeed, rap groups across Southern Africa – are using the medium to educate listeners about HIV/AIDS. South Africa's rappers are exploring uncharted territory: look out for emerging genres such as Afro-Futurism and township house, and sonic explorers Simphiwe Dana and Spoek Mathambo. Look out, too, for the sounds of the city: 'I feel that I am Johannesburg,' says Spoek Mathambo. 'An amalgamation of influences from the streets to the churches, from the taxi ranks to the traditional medicine markets, the clubs and bars, shebeens and taverns...to the entertainment industry of Johannesburg. I am Jozi.'

The Natural Environment

Southern Africa's environment is as fragile as elsewhere on the continent, with exploitation and mismanagement the cause of many long-term problems.

The Land

Southern Africa consists of a plateau rising from 1000m to 2000m, with escarpments on either side. Below the escarpments lies a coastal plain, which is narrowest in Namibia and widest in southern Mozambique.

The most prominent break in the Southern African plateau is the Great Rift Valley – a 6500km-long fissure where tectonic forces have attempted to rip the continent of Africa in two. This enormous fault runs from the earth's crust runs from the Jordan Valley (between Israel and Jordan) in the north, southward through the Red Sea, where it enters Ethiopia's Danakil Depression. At this point, it heads south across Kenya, Tanzania and Malawi, dividing in two at one stage, to form the great lakes of East Africa. Lake Malawi is the third-largest lake in Africa and lies in a trough formed by the valley. This feature has created unique fish life. The lake has more fish species than any inland body of water in the world – there are more than 500, and 350 of these are endemic to the lake. This spreading zone ends at the present site of Lake Kariba, between Zimbabwe and Zambia.

The highest part of the region is Lesotho (often called the Kingdom in the Sky) and the neighbouring Drakensberg area, where many peaks rise above 3000m, including Thabana-Ntlenyana (3482m), which is the highest point in Southern Africa. Other highland areas include the Nyika Plateau (in northern Malawi and northeastern Zambia), Mt Mulanje (in southern Malawi), the Eastern Highlands (between Zimbabwe and Mozambique) and the Khomas Hochland (Central Namibia).

These highlands provide jaw-dropping scenery, as well as some of the best-preserved and most distinctive plants, wildlife and ancient rock art in the region. Hiking, climbing and mountain biking are just some of the myriad activities on offer in these often wonderfully preserved patches of African wilderness.

Lower and more isolated hills include the characteristic inselbergs of Namibia and South Africa's Karoo, and the lush Zomba Plateau in central Malawi.

Wildlife

Southern Africa contains some of the most accessible and varied wildlife found anywhere on the continent, and it's the major attraction of the area. Countries all over the region provide opportunities for wildlife watching, and each has its highlights. Even the smaller countries such

Good safari companions: Chris and Tilde Stuart's *Field Guide to Mammals of Southern Africa* and *A Field Guide to the Tracks and Signs of Southern and East African Wildlife*, and Richard Estes' *The Safari Companion: A Guide to Watching African Mammals*.

CLOSE ENCOUNTERS OF THE WILD KIND

Although you'll hear plenty of horror stories, the threat of attack by wild animals in Africa is largely exaggerated and problems are extremely rare. That said, it is important to remember that most African animals are *wild* and that wherever you go on safari, particularly on foot, there is always an element of danger.

On organised safaris you should always get advice from your guide. If you're on a self-drive safari, ask authorities of the park you are entering. Some of the advice you will receive – such as not getting between a hippo and its water; and that black rhino are skittish, as are lone animals such as male elephants and buffaloes – holds true across the region, and you will pick it up easily enough. And a good rule of thumb is, if you're not sure, just don't get too close.

Wildlife viewing requires a bit of common sense, and by following a few simple guidelines you're sure to have a trouble-free experience. Remember that viewing wildlife in its natural habitat may present dangers not found in a zoo, but it's a large part of what makes a visit to Southern Africa so special, and is incomparable to seeing an animal in a cage.

as Swaziland have magnificent wildlife viewing, which can offer great alternatives to better-known parks, but for sheer variety and numbers South Africa and Botswana top the list.

The best times of day for wildlife viewing are early in the morning and in the late afternoon or evening, when many animals are looking for their next meal. Planting yourself at a waterhole at these times can be very rewarding. Night safaris provide wonderful wildlife-viewing opportunities, especially to see many nocturnal animals such as genets and bush babies (look in the trees, not just on the ground).

> Rhino aren't named for their colour, but for their lip shape: 'white' comes from *wijde* (wide) – the Boers' term for the fatter-lipped white rhino.

Happily, southern African parks are some of the best managed in Africa, and the development of the massive transfrontier parks in the region, which link national parks and wildlife migration routes in different countries, should open up even more opportunities for wildlife viewing.

Animals

Nowhere else on the planet is there such a variety and quantity of large mammal species. Southern Africa boasts the world's largest land mammal (the African elephant), as well as the second largest (white rhino) and the third largest (hippopotamus). It's also home to the tallest (giraffe), fastest (cheetah) and smallest (pygmy shrew). You stand a great chance of seeing the Big Five – black rhino, Cape buffaloes, elephants, leopards and lions – but the region also supports a wonderful array of birds, reptiles, amphibians and even insects (often in less-welcomed quantities). The longer you spend in Southern Africa, the more you'll appreciate the subtleties of the region, including the delight of spotting some of the less-famous species. If you're up for a challenge, the lesser-known Little Five are the rhinoceros beetle, buffalo weaver, elephant shrew, leopard tortoise and ant lion.

> For information on campaigns to save elephants, and the fight against the illegal international trade in wildlife, visit the website of the International Fund for Animal Welfare (www.ifaw.org).

ENDANGERED SPECIES

The result of years of poaching, the black rhino is the highest-profile entry on Southern Africa's endangered species list, considered to be critically endangered. Good places to spot these animals include Hluhluwe-iMfolozi Park, in South Africa; Etosha National Park, in Namibia; and Mkhaya Game Reserve, in Swaziland. The beautiful African wild dog, which lives in a matriarchal system, is listed as endangered, and with luck can be seen in the Okavango Delta, Botswana; Hluhluwe-iMfolozi Park; and South Luangwa National Park, Zambia. The riverine rabbit is one of Southern Africa's most endangered mammals, and the mountain zebra, hippopotamus and African lion are considered vulnerable in the wider region. Turtles don't fare well, either, with both the loggerhead and green turtle listed as endangered, while the hawksbill turtle is considered critically endangered.

BIRDS

Birds rate highly among the many attractions of southern Africa. For sheer abundance and variety, few parts of the world offer as much for the birdwatcher, whether expert or beginner. Southern Africa is host to nearly 10% of the world's bird species – more than 900 species have been recorded in the region. More than 130 are endemic to southern Africa or are near-endemic, being found also only in adjoining territories to the north.

All the region's national parks and reserves are home to a great range of bird life, especially Mana Pools, Victoria Falls and Hwange National Parks in Zimbabwe; Etosha, Mudumu and Mamili National Parks in

The lure of riches to be made from ivory is staggering. By the late 1980s the price of 1kg of ivory (US$300) was three times the *annual* income of more than 60% of Africa's population.

IVORY & ELEPHANT CULLING CONTROVERSY

All over Southern Africa elephant conservation is a major issue. The local African sentiment maintains that the elephant must justify its existence on long-term economic grounds for the benefit of local people, or for the country as a whole.

From the 1970s various factors (especially the value of ivory) led to an increase in elephant poaching in many parts of Africa. The real money was made not by poachers – often villagers who were paid a pittance for the valuable tusks – but by dealers. The number of elephants in Africa went from 1.3 million to 625,000 between 1979 and 1989, and in East Africa and some Southern African countries – notably Zambia – elephant populations were reduced by up to 90% in about 15 years. In other Southern African countries, where parks and reserves were well managed, in particular South Africa, Botswana and Namibia, elephant populations were relatively unaffected.

In 1989, in response to the illegal trade and diminishing numbers of elephants, a world body called the Convention on International Trade in Endangered Species (CITES) internationally banned the import and export of ivory. It also increased funding for antipoaching measures. When the ban was established, world raw ivory prices plummeted by 90%, and the market for poaching and smuggling was radically reduced.

Ironically, in recent years, park authorities across the region are facing elephant overpopulation. Botswana, parts of Namibia's Caprivi region, Zimbabwe and South Africa's Kruger National Park are particularly affected. Proposed solutions include relocation (whereby herds are permanently transplanted to other areas) and contraception. In Kruger in 2005, park authorities recommended culling to return the elephant population to a manageable 7500 (down from 12,500). South Africa's announcement to reverse a ban on elephant culling from 1 May 2008 – although culling would only happen as a last resort once other options had been exhausted – caused outrage among many conservation groups, as culling has been banned for 15 years in South African parks.

Some Southern African countries have large ivory stockpiles due to natural attrition and through the seizure of illegal ivory hauls. In late 2008 CITES approved a one-off sale of ivory from South Africa, Botswana, Namibia and Zimbabwe. One hundred and one tonnes was auctioned to buyers from China and Japan for about US$15 million. These countries are now in a 'resting period' and CITES will not consider any further ivory sales for the following nine years. However there is still much dispute about whether controlled ivory sales, such as an annual export allowance, should be permitted, with Southern African countries with excessive elephant populations and large ivory stockpiles pushing hard for a further relaxation of the ban. Some argue that Southern Africa is paying for the inability of other African countries to manage and protect their wildlife, and that the ban on the ivory trade is an unfair punishment.

It remains to be seen whether the ban will be lifted. Meanwhile debate about the ivory trade, and the culling solution to overpopulation, rages on.

Namibia; and Chobe National Park and virtually any part of the Okavango Delta in Botswana. Mozambique has more than half of all bird species identified in southern Africa; on Inhaca Island alone, about 300 bird species have been recorded.

Highlights in the region include the world's largest bird (the ostrich) and heaviest flying bird (the kori bustard). Also in abundance are weavers, which share their huge city-like nests (often attached to telephone poles) with pygmy falcons, the world's smallest raptors. Also keep an eye out for majestic birds of prey such as the African fish eagle, bateleur (a serpent eagle), martial eagle, red-necked falcon and chanting goshawk, as well as secretary birds, rollers, vividly coloured bee-eaters, sunbirds and rainbow-flecked kingfishers.

Birdwatching is good all year round, with spring (August to November) and summer the best.

REPTILES

Ian Sinclair's *Field Guide to the Birds of Southern Africa* is a comprehensive work with colour plates of all avian species in the region. The abridged *Illustrated Guide to the Birds of Southern Africa* concentrates on commonly observed species.

Southern Africa's most notable reptile is the Nile crocodile. Once abundant in lakes and rivers across the region, its numbers have been greatly reduced by hunting and habitat destruction. Female crocs lay up to 80 eggs at a time, depositing them in sandy areas above the high-water line. After three months' incubation in the hot sand, the young emerge. Many live up to 70 years.

Southern Africa has a complement of both venomous and harmless snakes, but most of them fear humans and you'll be lucky to even see one. The largest snake – generally harmless to humans – is the python, which grows to more than 5m in length. The puff adder is one of the deadliest and most widespread snakes on the African continent. It inhabits mainly mountain and desert areas, and grows to about 1m long. It's very slow but highly aggressive. Stepping on one, resulting in being bitten, would potentially mean death. The bite of a puff adder is usually a long, slow breakdown of the body if you have no medical attention and is hard to reverse.

Seriously dangerous snakes include the fat and lazy gaboon viper; the black mamba; the boomslang, which lives in trees; the spitting cobra, which needs no introduction; and the zebra snake, which is one of the world's most aggressive serpentine sorts. If you're tramping in snake country, be sure to watch your step.

Lizards are ubiquitous from the hot and dusty Kaokoveld in Namibia to the cool highlands of the Nyika Plateau in Malawi, and from the bathroom ceiling to the kitchen sink. The largest of these is the water monitor, a docile creature that reaches more than 2m in length and is often seen lying around waterholes, perhaps dreaming of being a crocodile. Two others frequently seen are chameleons and geckos – the latter often in hotel rooms; they are quite harmless and help to control the bug population.

Plants

The following rundown of major vegetation zones (arranged roughly south to north, and from the coasts to the inland areas) is greatly simplified, but provides a useful overview.

Southern Africa's distinctive *fynbos* (literally 'fine bush'; primarily proteas, heaths and ericas) zone occurs around the Cape Peninsula and along the south coast of South Africa, interspersed with pockets of temperate forest, where you'll find trees such as the large yellowwood, with its characteristic 'peeling' bark.

The west coast of Southern Africa consists largely of desert, which receives less than 100mm of precipitation per year. Vegetation consists of tough grasses, shrubs and euphorbias, plus local specialities, includ-

INTRODUCED PLANT SPECIES

Introduced plant species present a real threat to Southern African ecosystems. For example, Australian wattle trees and Mexican mesquite flourish by sinking their roots deeper into the soil than indigenous trees, causing the latter to suffer from lack of nourishment. The Australian hakea shrub was introduced to serve as a hedge, and is now rampant, displacing native trees and killing off smaller plants. Areas such as South Africa's unique Cape *fynbos* (literally 'fine bush'; primarily proteas, heaths and ericas) floral kingdom are threatened by Australian acacias, which were introduced for their timber products and to stabilise sand dunes.

ing the bizarre welwitschia (a miniature conifer) and *kokerboom* (a type of aloe).

Along the east coast of Southern Africa, the natural vegetation is coastal bush, a mixture of light woodland and dune forest; high rainfall has also created pockets of subtropical forest.

In South Africa's Karoo, typical vegetation includes grasses, bushes and succulents that bloom colourfully after the rains. Much original Karoo vegetation has been destroyed since the introduction of grazing animals and alien plants.

To the east lie the temperate grasslands of the high-veld and to the north, a vast arid savannah, characterised by acacia scrub, which takes in most of central Namibia, much of Botswana and the northern parts of South Africa.

To the north and east is the woodland savannah, consisting of mainly broadleaf deciduous trees. Dry woodland, dominated by mopane trees, covers northern Namibia, northern Botswana, the Zimbabwean low-veld and the Zambezi Valley. In wetter areas – central Zimbabwe, northern Mozambique and most of Zambia and Malawi – the dominant vegetation is moist woodland, or *miombo*. A mix of the two, which occurs in northeastern South Africa and central Mozambique, is known as mixed woodland, or 'bush-veld'.

Small pockets of high ground all over the region have a vegetation zone termed afro-montane, which occurs in highland areas where open grasslands are interspersed with heathland and isolated forests.

There are more than 700 alien plant species in the region, and about 10% of these are classed as invasive aliens – that is, they thrive to the detriment of endemic species.

National Parks

The term 'national park' is often used in Southern Africa as a catch-all term to include wildlife reserves, forest parks or any government conservation area; there are also several privately owned reserves.

The beauty of the parks and reserves is that they all have an individual identity – a unique character born from the varied landscapes, wildlife and vistas. Happily, this means you can spend a lot of time visiting parks and never get bored!

Most parks in Southern Africa conserve habitats and wildlife species and provide recreational facilities for visitors. South African parks are among the best managed in the world, and most of the rest are very good, although Zimbabwean parks have declined, some of Zambia's parks are still recovering from years of neglect, and those in Mozambique are still being developed, with parks such as Gorongosa leading the way.

In most parks and reserves harbouring large (and potentially dangerous) animals, visitors must travel in vehicles or on an organised safari, but several do allow hiking or walking with a ranger or safari guide.

Nearly all parks charge an entrance fee, and in almost all cases foreigners pay substantially more than local residents or citizens. This may rankle some visitors – and some parks are seriously overpriced – but the

Trees of Southern Africa, by Keith Coates Palgrave, provides the most thorough coverage of the subcontinent's arboreal richness, illustrated with colour photos and paintings.

NATIONAL PARK ACCOMMODATION

Most parks and reserves contain accommodation, so you can stay overnight and take wildlife drives in the early morning and evening. Accommodation ranges from simple campsites to luxury lodges run by companies that have concessions inside the parks. Prices vary to match the quality of facilities. In some countries you can just turn up and find a place to camp or stay; in other countries reservations are advised (or are essential at busy times).

idea is that residents and citizens pay taxes to the governments that support the parks, and therefore are entitled to discounts.

Park facilities, geography and wildlife-viewing opportunities vary considerably across the region. World-famous national parks such as Kruger, Etosha, South Luangwa and Chobe offer excellent wildlife viewing, and usually a dazzling array of accommodation options, while lesser-known gems such as Swaziland's Hlane Royal National Park and Mkhaya Game Reserve, are smaller and quieter than their famous counterparts.

Botswana

Central Kalahari Botswana's largest park, with the widest horizons you'll ever see.

Chobe A large and varied park with both a wildlife-rich riverfront and broad savannah plains. It's particularly known for its large elephant herds.

Makgadikgadi & Nxai Pan Vast and remote, this is the site of Southern Africa's last great wildlife migrations.

Moremi This beautiful park takes in a portion of the stunning Okavango Delta.

Lesotho

Sehlabathebe National Park A mountain wilderness offering wonderful isolation, rheboks, baboons and bearded vultures.

Malawi

Earthlife Africa (www.earthlife.org.za) is an active environmental group operating in South Africa and Namibia. It's a good contact for anyone wanting to get involved.

Lengwe This lovely park in southern Malawi protects a range of antelopes (including the rare *nyala*), as well as diverse bird species.

Liwonde A magical lowland park with wonderful, varied bird life, including a stunning rainbow-flecked kingfisher population, and excellent elephant and hippo viewing.

Mt Mulanje The 'island in the sky', with sheer peaks and excellent hiking.

Nyika Unique montane grassland area, with endless views and splendid horse riding.

Mozambique

Gorongosa This park is being rehabilitated with international backing and the wildlife is making a real comeback. The community development element is a highlight.

Namibia

Etosha This vast park is one of Africa's most renowned wildlife-viewing venues – and deservedly so. It features an enormous pan and numerous waterholes, and is one of the best places in the region to see black rhino.

Namib-Naukluft One of the world's largest national parks, this stunning and magical wilderness takes in world-famous sand dunes and wild desert mountains, with excellent hiking.
Sperrgebiet In this country's famous diamond fields, the country's newest (2008) national park is set to become the gem of Namibia's protected spaces.

South Africa
Drakensberg This mountain region may be low on the Big Five, but it's high on awe-inspiring mountain scenery and rock art, and has extensive hiking opportunities.
Hluhluwe-iMfolozi Near the Zulu heartland, this bushland park is best known for its rhino populations.
iSimangaliso Wetland Park This coastal wetland in a remote part of the country presents a unique ecosystem of global significance.

HUNTING: ANIMAL WELFARE VERSUS ECONOMICS

In some parts of Southern Africa, areas of land are set aside for hunting, and hunters are charged 'trophy fees' to shoot animals.

On the one hand it is argued that trophy or sport hunting is a form of tourism that stimulates local economies and thereby fosters 'conservation-minded' attitudes. For people who lack other resources, the trophy fees are large (thousands of US dollars for animals such as elephants or lions) and an invaluable source of income. Paradoxically, the financial benefit of hunting tourism encourages the management and protection of these animals and their environment. Hunting, it is argued, provides an enticement to landowners to maintain the natural habitats that provide a home for the hunted animals.

On the other hand, killing an animal for sport is simply morally and ethically wrong to many people, a belief that is often accentuated once the beauty, grace and intelligence of various African animals is witnessed in the wild.

Can killing for sport ever be justified in a modern society? Hunters claim that killing is not the purpose of hunting; instead, it's all about outwitting and learning behavioural patterns of their prey. Their respondents answer: then why not take a camera instead of a rifle? It is also argued that slaughtering wildlife in order to raise conservation funds to save it is an illogical way of thinking. Further, improperly managed trophy hunting can have seriously detrimental effects on wildlife, especially threatened and endangered species.

Although conservation organisations do not agree on policy towards hunting, the World Wildlife Fund (WWF) has a pragmatic attitude, stating that 'for endangered species, trophy hunting should only be considered when all other options have been explored…and that trophy hunting, where it is scientifically based and properly managed, has proven to be an effective conservation and management method in some countries and for certain species'.

In 2004 the Convention on International Trade in Endangered Species (CITES) lifted a ban on hunting the black rhino, once a potent symbol of endangered African animals, allowing an annual hunt quota of five each for South Africa and Namibia. Conservationists opposed to the move say that the rhino is still a target for poachers, with its horn being highly valued in Asia and the Middle East. It is claimed that hunting quotas would make it far easier to cover up the illegal trade of rhino horns from poached animals. Also, the black rhino remains critically endangered in most countries outside Southern Africa. Namibia and South Africa have pledged to spend the substantial revenues from the allowed quota to improve conservation in their countries.

The practice of 'canned hunting', in which wildlife bred in captivity are killed by tourists in sealed reserves for sport, is highly controversial in Southern Africa. In South Africa where canned hunting of lions in particular is popular, recent legislative attempts by the government to end this practice have thus far failed.

Kruger South Africa's most popular national park covers an enormous area and offers the classic wildlife experience, while boasting top-notch facilities.

Pilanesberg This park protects an unusual complex of extinct volcanoes with towering rocky outcrops and an impressive variety and number of wildlife, including wild dogs.

Tsitsikamma A lovely coastal park with forests, *fynbos*, beaches, rocky headlands and a world-renowned hiking trail.

Swaziland

Hlane Royal National Park The country's largest protected area is home to elephants, lions, cheetahs and leopards, and offers excellent low-key wildlife watching.

Mkhaya Game Reserve One of the best places in Southern Africa to spot black rhino in the wild. Also great for bird-watching.

Zambia

Kafue Massive and genuinely wild, with an impressive range of habitats and wildlife.

Kasanka A pioneering, privately managed park, noted for sightings of the rare sitatunga antelope.

Lower Zambezi Spectacular setting, escarpments and plains, plus the great river itself. It's best appreciated on multiday canoe trips.

South Luangwa This wild and pristine wildlife park is growing more popular, but many still consider it to be Africa's best-kept secret.

Zimbabwe

Hwange Zimbabwe's best-known wildlife park holds one of the most dense wildlife populations in Africa. It's conveniently close to Victoria Falls.

Mana Pools Combines the Zambezi Escarpment, a swath of bushland and beautiful riverine scenery to create a varied wildlife experience. Canoe safaris are popular.

Matusadona With both lakefront and mountain habitats south of Lake Kariba, this rewarding wildlife park is known for its enormous buffalo herds and lion population.

Nyanga, Bvumba and Chimanimani These three parks in the misty Eastern Highlands offer mountain retreats and excellent hiking opportunities.

Some national parks and protected areas are rehabilitated by funding from overseas. In some cases the funder is in partnership with the local wildlife authority – examples include Gile Reserve in Mozambique and Liuwa Plain National Park in Zambia.

Transfrontier Peace Parks

In addition to national parks there are several transfrontier conservation areas at various stages of completion. These mammoth ventures cross national borders and are flagship conservation projects designed to re-establish age-old migration routes.

Malawi and Zambia are setting up the first transfrontier park outside South Africa and secured funding for its establishment in 2012. The area combines the Nyika Plateau on both sides of the border, Malawi's Vwaza Marsh Wildlife Reserve and Kasungu National Park, with Zambian forest reserves, Musalangu Game Management Area and Lukusuzi National Park.

/Ai/Ais-Richtersveld Transfrontier Park Africa's grand Fish River Canyon presents one of the most scenic scenes on the continent and Namibia's most popular hiking track.

Great Limpopo Transfrontier Park This spreads nearly 100,000 sq km (larger than Portugal) across the borders of South Africa (Kruger

See www.peace parks.org for all the latest news on the transfrontier parks in the region, including progress reports and maps of all the parks.

National Park), Mozambique (Limpopo National Park) and Zimbabwe (Gonarezhou National Park).

Greater Mapungubwe Transfrontier Conservation Area A conservation area in progress straddling the borders of South Africa, Botswana and Zimbabwe.

Kavango-Zambezi Transfrontier Conservation Area A work in progress situated around the border convergence of Angola, Botswana, Namibia, Zambia and Zimbabwe, and set to become the world's biggest conservation area, taking in the Caprivi Strip in Namibia, Chobe National Park and the Okavango Delta in Botswana, and Victoria Falls in Zambia.

Kgalagadi Transfrontier Park This park combines Northern Cape's old Kalahari Gemsbok National Park (South Africa) with Botswana's Gemsbok National Park.

Maloti-Drakensberg Transfrontier Project A project that protects the natural and cultural heritage of the Maloti-Drakensberg Mountains in South Africa and Lesotho.

Survival Guide

Directory A–Z

Accommodation

Accommodation in Southern Africa encompasses a wide variety of definitions from a patch of turf at a basic campground to opulent lodges that defy any star rating. Although prices vary immensely from country to country, budget travellers can generally get a night's sleep for under US$50. Midrange options cost from US$50 to US$100 (although this can be up to US$150 in parts of the region, such as Mozambique). Top-end options charge upwards of US$100. For a more accurate indication of price ranges check individual country Directories for the relevant budget breakdown. Sleeping reviews in this book are ordered by budget order ($, $$ and $$$) then author preference within each budget.

B&Bs & Guesthouses

B&Bs and guesthouses are interchangeable terms in much of Southern Africa. They range from a simple room in someone's house to well-established B&Bs with five-star ratings and deluxe accommodation. B&Bs and guesthouses are most prevalent in South Africa, where the standards are high and features such as antique furniture, private verandahs, landscaped gardens and a pool are common. Indeed some of the finest accommodation on the continent is found in B&Bs along the Garden Route. Breakfast is usually included and almost always involves gut-busting quantities of eggs, bacon, toast and other cooked goodies.

Camping & Camps

Camping is also popular, especially in national parks, in coastal and lakeshore areas, and in more expensive destinations, such as Botswana. Some camping grounds are quite basic, while others have a range of facilities, including hot showers and security fences. 'Wild' or free camping (ie not at an official site) is another option, but security can be a problem and wild animals are always a concern, so choose your tent site with care.

In the national parks and wildlife reserves, there's a wide choice of accommodation, ranging from simple camping grounds to cabins, chalets, bungalows and luxurious camps and lodges. It's important to note that 'camp' doesn't necessarily denote a campsite (although it may). A camp is usually a well-appointed, upmarket option run by a private company. Accommodation is usually in tents or chalets made from natural materials. The contact number for these places will be at their office in a larger town and are for bookings and inquiries only, not for direct contact with the lodge or camp.

In upmarket lodges and camps the rates will typically include accommodation plus full board, activities (wildlife drives, boat trips etc) and perhaps even house wine and beer. It may also include laundry and transfers by air or 4WD (although these are usually extra).

Hostels

Many towns and cities on the main tourist trail have at least one hostel, and in some places, such as South Africa's Garden Route, you'll have a wide choice. The hostels generally mirror small hostels anywhere else in the world and offer camping space, dorms and a few private doubles. Many also have a travel desk where you can book tours and safaris.

Another budget option, albeit dwindling but still avail-

BOOK YOUR STAY ONLINE

For more accommodation reviews by Lonely Planet authors, check out http://hotels.lonelyplanet.com. You'll find independent reviews, as well as recommendations on the best places to stay. Best of all, you can book online.

PRACTICALITIES

» News magazines that cover the continent include *Africa Today, Business Africa* and *New African*. All are available from newsagents in South Africa and bookshops in capital cities elsewhere. *Getaway* magazine, a South African publication, covers travel in Southern Africa, with articles ranging from epic 4WD trips to active and not-so-active tours all over the region.

» The beautiful *Africa Geographic,* published bimonthly, should be considered an essential subscription for every Africa buff. Birdwatchers will also want to read the excellent bimonthly *Africa Birds & Birding*. For subscriptions to these magazines contact Africa Geographic (www.africageographic.com).

» Most countries in Southern Africa use the metric system.

» Electricity in Southern Africa is generated at 220V to 240V AC. Most plugs have three prongs (or pins), either round or rectangular ('square') in section. In South Africa, round-pin plugs are used. Outside South Africa, British-style square three-pin plugs are common. A voltage adaptor is needed for US appliances.

able in Malawi and Zambia, are resthouses run by local governments or district councils. These are peppered throughout the region, and many date from colonial times. Some are very cheap and less than appealing; others are well kept and good value.

Hotels

In towns and cities, top-end hotels generally offer clean, air-conditioned rooms with private bathrooms, while midrange hotels typically offer fans instead of air-con. At the budget end, rooms aren't always clean (and may be downright filthy), and bathrooms are usually shared and may well be in an appalling state. Often, your only source of air will be a hole in the window. Many cheap hotels double as brothels, so if this is your budget level don't be surprised if there's a lot of coming and going during the night. Some countries, including Malawi and Botswana, offer little in the way of hotels between budget and top end.

Many hotels offer self-catering facilities, which may mean anything from a fridge and a hotplate in the corner to a full kitchen in every unit. In some cases, guests will have to supply their own cooking implements – and perhaps even water and firewood.

Throughout the region you'll probably encounter hotels and lodges that charge in tiers. That is, overseas visitors are charged international rates (full price), visitors from other Southern African countries pay a regional rate (say around 30% less) and locals get resident rates (often less than half the full rate). Most places also give discounts in the low season. Where possible we quoted the international high-season rates, including the value-added tax (VAT), which ranges from 10% to 30%.

Activities

Southern Africa's climate and landscape make the region ideal for numerous outdoor activities – from peaceful and relaxing to energetic and downright terrifying. The following list is not exhaustive, but provides some tantalising options.

Adrenaline Activities

Southern Africa is something of a gathering place for adrenaline nuts, and a range of weird and wonderful activities keep them happily crazed. The top spots for extreme sports are Victoria Falls and Livingstone, where white-water rafting in the Zambezi and bungee jumping off the Victoria Falls bridge are hourly occurrences. The highest bridge bungee jump in the world (allegedly) can be found in South Africa at Bloukrans River Bridge, but if you're only half-nuts you can try any number of smaller ones.

» Swakopmund is the adventure capital of Namibia; sandboarding, skydiving and quad biking through the dunes are popular.

» In Malawi you can try abseiling around Manchewe Falls near Livingstonia.

» In Mozambique kite surfing is popular at Murrebue (near Pemba).

» Finances and infrastructure make South Africa the easiest destination to scare yourself silly. South Africa is also one of the world's top destinations for paragliding, particularly at Cape Town's Table Mountain. The strongest thermals are from November to April.

» There is excellent and challenging climbing on the close-to-sheer faces of the KwaZulu-Natal Drakensberg in South Africa.

Canoeing, Kayaking & White-Water Rafting

In South Africa canoeing and white-water rafting are popular pursuits on the waterways around Wilderness National Park in the Western Cape, and the Senqu (Orange)

River, particularly through Augrabies Falls National Park. There's also some serene canoeing at the iSimangaliso Wetland Park.

» In Swaziland, the classic rafting destination is the Great Usutu River.

» The Zambezi River lures white-water rafters from around the globe to tackle its angry churn, and there are plenty of operators in Zimbabwe and Livingstone, Zambia; canoeing is also popular.

» Gorongosa National Park and Niassa Reserve in Mozambique both offer canoeing opportunities in wonderful wilderness areas.

» Rafting is highly rain-dependent, and the best months usually fall between December/January and April.

» Sea kayaking is popular in sporadic locations along the coast, and best experienced in Malawi at Cape Maclear and Nkhata Bay.

» In Mozambique you can try a live-aboard dhow safari, in custom-built traditional wooden dhows.

Diving & Snorkelling

The best diving and snorkelling in the region is along the coast of Mozambique, particularly the Bazaruto Archipelago and Vilankulo, Ponta D'Ouro, Tofo, Pemba, Nacala and the Quirimbas Archipelago. Quality equipment, instruction and certification are readily available at most of these locations.

» In South Africa the Cape Peninsula offers superb wreck diving and giant kelp forests.

» The east coast of South Africa is home to good coral formations and there is excellent warm-water diving on the KwaZulu-Natal north coast, particularly around Sodwana Bay.

» For a freshwater flutter, Lake Malawi offers some of the best snorkelling and diving in the world. There are

---

RESPONSIBLE DIVING

Please consider the following tips when diving and help preserve the ecology and beauty of reefs:

» Never use anchors on the reef, and take care not to ground boats on coral.

» Avoid touching or standing on living marine organisms or dragging equipment across the reef. Polyps can be damaged by even the gentlest contact. If you must hold on to the reef, touch only exposed rock or dead coral.

» Be conscious of your fins. Even without contact, the surge from fin strokes near the reef can damage delicate organisms. Take care not to kick up clouds of sand, which can smother organisms.

» Practise and maintain proper buoyancy control. Major damage can be done by divers descending too quickly and colliding with the reef.

» Take great care in underwater caves. Spend as little time within them as possible as your air bubbles may be caught within the roof and thereby leave organisms high and dry. Take turns to inspect the interior of a small cave.

» Resist the temptation to collect or buy corals or shells or to loot marine archaeological sites (mainly shipwrecks).

» Ensure that you take home all your rubbish and any litter you may find as well. Plastics in particular are a serious threat to marine life.

» Do not feed fish.

» Minimise your disturbance of marine animals. *Never* ride on the back of turtles.

---

good outfits in Nkhata Bay and Cape Maclear.

Fishing

Southern Africa's wild and varied coastline and wealth of rivers and lakes make for profitable fishing expeditions.

» Cape Maclear is a good launching pad for fishing trips along Lake Malawi; and you can fish for trout on the Zomba Plateau and at Nyika National Park.

» In Zambia the tigerfish of the Lower Zambezi River give a good fight, but not as good as the vundu, a catfish weighing upwards of 45kg.

» In South African parks and reserves, anglers fish for introduced trout; there are some particularly good

highland streams in the Drakensberg.

» Lesotho is an insider's tip among trout anglers. The nearest fishing area to Maseru is the Makhaleng River. Other places to fish are the Malibamat'so River near Oxbow; the Mokhotlong River in the northeast; and the Thaba-Tseka main dam.

» Mozambique's coast is legendary among anglers, particularly in the south between Ponta d'Ouro and Inhassoro. Species you are likely to encounter include marlin, kingfish, tuna, sailfish and more.

Hiking

Across Southern Africa there are many excellent opportunities for hiking, and this is one of the most popular activities in the region.

» Namibia's Fish River Canyon is one of Africa's most spectacular hikes, but proper gear, food, water and experience are musts.

» In Malawi you can trek the scenic peaks of Mt Mulanje, the Zomba Plateau and the Nyika Plateau.

» Mozambique boasts beautiful vantage points to trek to but little infrastructure so you'll likely be on your own. A good place to start is the beautiful Chimanimani Mountains, with lovely scenery, a handful of basic campsites and an excellent new eco-camp.

» South Africa's undulating topography offers superb hiking opportunities. Among the best walks are the Hoerikwaggo hiking trails of Table Mountain National Park, the five-day Whale Route in De Hoop Nature Reserve and the celebrated Otter Trail, a five-day journey along the Garden Route that needs to be booked months in advance.

» Some other notable South African hikes include the Tsitsikamma Trail, which runs parallel to the Otter Trail, KwaZulu-Natal's Giant's Cup Trail – up to five days in the southern Drakensberg – and Mpumalanga's Blyde River Canyon Hiking Trail.

Horse Riding

In South Africa it's easy to find rides for all experience levels. Particularly good areas include the iSimangaliso Wetland Park and Limpopo's Waterberg range. Riding is also an option in Zimbabwe's national parks.

Mountain Biking

It goes without saying that a region so rich in hiking opportunities will have equally rewarding mountain-biking possibilities. Outside South Africa and the main tourist areas in the region, it's relatively difficult to hire bikes, so you'll need to bring your own.

You can also hire local-style sit-up-and-beg steel roadsters. These are good for getting around towns (especially flat ones) or exploring rural areas at a leisurely pace.

» South Africa is littered with excellent biking trails; among the best are those in De Hoop Nature Reserve, with overnight and day trails, and Citrusdal, with a network of trails. Then there's Cape Town, which is something of an unofficial national hub.

» In Malawi great mountain-biking areas include Nyika National Park and the Viphya Plateau.

Surfing

Any surfer worth their wax is familiar with the legendary waves at J-Bay, better known to nonconverts as Jeffrey's Bay. Situated on the Garden Route, the town's choppy surf lures experts and amateurs from around the globe. South Africa also offers a myriad of less-celebrated alternatives, particularly along the Eastern Cape coast from Port Alfred northwards.

» Although undeveloped for surfers, Namibia's Skeleton Coast is famous for rough waves and unspoilt beaches. This stretch is only for the seriously experienced and brave, though, with savage rips, icy water temperatures and the odd great white.

» Mozambique's best waves are at Ponta d'Ouro in the far south of the country and (for skilled surfers) at Tofinho – Mozambique's unofficial surfing capital, just south of Tofo.

Books

This section lists publications covering most of Southern Africa. Note that many books have different publishers in different countries, and that a hardcover rarity in one country may be a readily available paperback in another, so we haven't included publishers in this list (unless relevant).

Field Guides

Southern Africa's incredible floral and faunal diversity has inspired a large number of field guides for visitors and wildlife enthusiasts. In the UK, an excellent source for wildlife and nature titles is Subbuteo Natural History Books Ltd. International mail orders are welcome. In Australia, check out Andrew Isles Natural History Books.

» *Field Guide to the Snakes and Other Reptiles of Southern Africa* by Bill Branch

» *Field Guide to the Mammals of Southern Africa* by Chris and Mathilde Stuart

» *Newman's Birds of Southern Africa* by Kenneth Newman

» *Complete Guide to Freshwater Fishes of Southern Africa* by Paul Skelton

» *Medicinal Plants of South Africa*; available from Briza Publications in South Africa.

General

» *The Fate of Africa* by Martin Meredith

» *At the Hand of Man* by Raymond Bonner; conservation issues and the destruction of African wildlife.

» *Zambezi: Journey of a River* by Michael Main

» *Kakuli* by Norman Carr; the author spent a lifetime working with animals and people in the South Luangwa National Park.

» *Dead Aid* by Dambisa Moyo; challenges traditional thinking regarding aid in Africa.

Guidebooks

If you're looking for more in-depth guidebook coverage, Lonely Planet also publishes *South Africa, Lesotho & Swaziland; Botswana & Namibia;* and *Zambia, Malawi & Mozambique* guides. If you're travelling the entire continent, you may want to check out *Africa on a Shoestring*. Lonely Planet also publishes guidebooks to a number of other African countries, as well as *Trekking in East*

RESPONSIBLE HIKING

To help preserve the ecology and beauty of Southern Africa, consider the following tips when hiking.

Rubbish

» Carry out *all* your rubbish. Don't overlook easily forgotten items, such as orange peel. Empty packaging should be stored in a dedicated rubbish bag. Carry out rubbish left by others.

» Never bury your rubbish: digging disturbs soil and ground cover and encourages erosion. Buried rubbish will likely be dug up by animals, who may be injured or poisoned by it. It may also take years to decompose.

» Minimise waste by taking minimal packaging and no more food than you will need. Take reusable containers.

» Sanitary napkins, tampons, condoms and toilet paper should be carried out despite the inconvenience. They burn and decompose poorly.

Human Waste Disposal

» Contamination of water sources by human faeces can lead to the transmission of all sorts of nasties. If there is no toilet, bury your waste. Dig a small hole 15cm deep and at least 100m from any watercourse. Cover the waste with soil and a rock. In snow, dig down to the soil.

Washing

» Don't use detergents or toothpaste in or near watercourses, even if they are biodegradable.

» For personal washing, use biodegradable soap and a water container at least 50m away from the watercourse. Disperse the waste water widely to allow the soil to filter it fully.

» Wash cooking utensils 50m from watercourses using a scourer, sand or snow instead of detergent.

Erosion

» Hillsides and mountain slopes, especially at high altitudes, are prone to erosion. Stick to existing trails and avoid short cuts.

Africa, which includes routes in Malawi.

» *Hiking Trails of Southern Africa* by Willie and Sandra Olivier

» *Complete Guide to Hiking Trails in Southern Africa* by Jaynee Levy

» *Adventure Motorbiking Handbook* by Chris Scott

» *Ilustrated Guide to Southern Africa* (Readers Digest)

» *Secret Southern Africa* (AA of South Africa)

History & Politics

» *Africa* by Phyllis Martin and Patrick O'Meara

» *Africa: Dispatches from a Fragile Continent* by Blaine Harden

» *Banana Sunday – Datelines from Africa* by Chris Munion

» *Blood on the Tracks* by Miles Bredin

» *Southern Africa: Old Treacheries & New Deceits* by Stephen Chan

Business Hours

Standard opening hours vary from country to country; specifics can be found in the Directory of each country.

Children

Southern Africa presents few problems specific to children, and while health concerns are always an issue, food and lodging are mostly quite familiar and manageable. What's more, foreigners with children are usually treated with great kindness, and a widespread local affection for the younger set opens up all sorts of social interaction for travelling families.

In South Africa, away from the coast, many resorts, hotels and national-park lodges and camping grounds have a wide range of facilities for children. Many families hire campervans in South Africa to tour the region. There are fewer child-oriented facilities in the other countries, but here the attractions usually provide entertainment

» If a well-used trail passes through a mud patch, walk through the mud so as not to increase the size of the patch.

» Avoid removing plant life, which keeps topsoil in place.

Fires & Low-Impact Cooking

» Don't depend on open fires for cooking. The cutting of wood for fires in popular hiking areas can cause rapid deforestation. Cook on a lightweight kerosene, alcohol or Shellite (white gas) stove, and avoid those powered by disposable butane-gas canisters.

» If you are trekking in highland areas, ensure you have enough clothing so that fires are not a necessity for warmth.

» If you use local accommodation, select those places that do not use wood fires to heat water or cook food.

» Fires may be acceptable below the treeline in areas that get very few visitors. If you light a fire, use an existing fireplace. Don't surround fires with rocks. Use only dead, fallen wood. Remember the adage 'the bigger the fool, the bigger the fire'. Use minimal wood, just what you need for cooking. In huts, leave wood for the next person.

» Ensure that you fully extinguish a fire; spread the embers and flood them with water.

Wildlife Conservation

» Don't buy items made from endangered species.

» Don't attempt to exterminate animals in huts. In wild places, they are likely to be protected native animals.

» Discourage the presence of wildlife by not leaving food scraps behind you. Place gear out of reach and tie packs to rafters or trees.

» Do not feed the wildlife as this can lead to animals becoming dependent on handouts, to unbalanced populations and to diseases.

Camping

» Always seek permission to camp from landowners.

---

enough: large wild animals in the national parks are a major draw, and even bored teenagers have been known to enjoy Vic Falls and its adrenaline activities. Namibia also lends itself to family travel by campervan, and the attractions – such as the wildlife of Etosha National Park, or the world's biggest sandbox at Sossusvlei – are entertainment in themselves. Lake Malawi has plenty of child-friendly lodges and the highland areas of Malawi such as the Viphya and Zomba Plateaus are also good for families.

In tourist hotels and lodges, family rooms and chalets are normally available for only slightly more than doubles. Otherwise, it's normally easy to arrange more beds in a standard adult double for a minimal extra charge. On public transport children are expected to pay for their seats unless they spend the entire journey on their parents' laps.

In Southern Africa, compared with some other parts of the world, there are few nasty diseases to worry about, and good (if expensive) medical services are almost always within reach.

Outside cities and major towns in South Africa, do not plan on finding pasteurised milk, formula or disposable nappies. They may be avail-able sporadically (especially in Mozambique), but this is the exception rather than the rule. Breastfeeding in public is fairly common for locals, but in rural areas it's likely to attract significant unwanted attention for visitors.

For more advice and anecdotes, see Lonely Planet's *Travel with Children*.

Customs Regulations

Customs information varies from country to country in the region – see the relevant country Directory.

Electricity

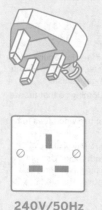

240V/50Hz

230V/50Hz

Embassies & Consulates

Embassies are most plentiful in South Africa, where whole suburbs of Pretoria are a who's who of global representation. Where home countries have no embassy, often a consul is appointed, who is not a full-time diplomat but has certain diplomatic responsibilities. Australia, Canada and New Zealand have few embassies in Southern Africa, but there is limited emergency assistance available from the British High Commission.

It's important to realise what your own embassy can and can't do to help you if you get into trouble. Generally speaking, it won't be much help if whatever trouble you're in is remotely your own fault. Remember that you are bound by the laws of the country you are in. In genuine emergencies you might get some assistance, but only if other channels have been exhausted. If you have all your money and documents stolen, your embassy might assist with getting a new passport, but that's about it.

Food

The type and quality of food varies across the region although local game meats such as kudu and springbok can be found in most places, as can a variety of fruit and vegetables. South Africa has the greatest variety of cuisine, although even here it is mainly restricted to cities and larger towns. For a guide to pricing see the individual country Directories, and for more information on food across Southern Africa see p674.

Gay & Lesbian Travellers

Countries in the region are conservative in their attitudes towards gay men and lesbians, and homosexuality is rarely discussed in public. In traditional African societies, gay sexual relationships are a cultural taboo. In 2001, President Sam Nujoma of Namibia famously said, "In Namibia we don't allow lesbianism or homosexuality... We will combat this with vigour... Police are ordered to arrest you and deport you and imprison you... Those who are practising homosexuality in Namibia are destroying the nation. Homosexuals must be condemned and rejected in our society."

While this may seem both alarming and deluded, observers see it – along with Zimbabwean president Robert Mugabe's vociferous diatribes against homosexuals – as a way of deflecting attention from greater governmental problems.

Officially, homosexual activity is illegal in all Southern Africa, except in South Africa and Lesotho. Lesbian activities are ignored in some countries because officials aren't really aware of them.

South Africa's constitution is one of the few in the world that explicitly prohibits discrimination on the grounds of sexual orientation, and there are active gay and lesbian communities and scenes in Cape Town, Jo'burg, Pretoria and Durban. Cape Town is without doubt the focal point, and the most openly gay city on the continent.

Open displays of affection are generally frowned upon in Southern Africa, whatever your orientation. Please be sensitive to local sensibilities.

Resources

South African resources:

» **Exit** (www.exit.co.za) South Africa's longest-running gay newspaper.

» **Gay Pages** (www.gay pagessa.co.za) Bimonthly glossy magazine.

» *OUTright* For gay males; available at CNA and other chain bookstores nationwide.

» **South Africa tourism** (www.southafrica.net) Lists gay and lesbian events.

Insurance

As a rule all travellers need a travel insurance policy, which will provide some sense of security in the case of a medical emergency or the loss or theft of money or belongings. Travel health insurance policies can usually be extended to include baggage, flight-departure insurance and a range of other options.

Claims on your travel insurance must be accompanied by proof of the value of any items lost or stolen (purchase receipts are the best, so if you buy a new camera for your trip, for example, hang onto the receipt). In the case of medical claims, you'll need detailed medical reports and receipts. If you're claiming on a trip cancelled by circumstances beyond your control (illness, airline bankruptcy, industrial action etc), you'll have to produce all flight tickets purchased, tour-agency receipts and itinerary, and proof of whatever glitch caused your trip to be cancelled.

Worldwide travel insurance is available at www.lonelyplanet.com/travel_services. You can buy, extend and claim online anytime – even if you're already on the road.

Internet Access

Most capital cities (and some large towns) in the region have at least one internet cafe, and many hotels and backpackers hostels also offer these services. Speed, reliability and hourly rates vary greatly (between about US$1 and US$5). South Africa and Zimbabwe in particular offer plenty of opportunities to get wired. Wireless access is becoming more common everywhere, making a small laptop a handy addition in your luggage. Rural areas in all countries are essentially devoid of internet access, although some small towns may have an internet centre, and lodges and camps in and around national parks increasingly have wireless services.

Maps

The Automobile Association (AA) of South Africa pro-

duces a useful map of South Africa (as well as numerous South African area maps), plus others covering Botswana and Namibia. The maps are available from any AA shop in South Africa.

For a useful overview of the region, pick up a copy of Map Studio's *Southern & Central Africa*, which shows all the countries in this guide.

Money

Note that the US dollar is the official currency of Zimbabwe.

In all countries it's wise to rely on a variety of methods to fund your trip. Local currency, US dollars, travellers cheques and a credit card will cover all bases.

ATMs

ATMs are readily available throughout South Africa and in cities and main urban centres in the rest of the region. If you're planning to travel for lengthy periods of time in rural areas, however, plan ahead as ATMs are still a foreign concept. There are a few ATM scams to be aware of, operating particularly in South Africa and Zimbabwe.

Black Market

In some parts of the world, artificially fixed exchange rates in the bank mean you can get more local money for your hard currency by changing on the so-called black market. Not only is this illegal, it's also potentially dangerous. In most of the region, currency deregulation has eliminated the black market. If someone approaches you anywhere in the region offering a lot more than the bank rate, they almost certainly have a well-formulated plan for separating you from your money.

Cash

Most travellers carry a mix of cash and travellers cheques, although cash is more convenient. The best currencies

to bring are US dollars or British pounds, preferably in a mixture. The South African rand is also widely recognised throughout the region, but it's not worth changing your currency into rand before converting it to kwacha, pula or whatever.

It's always wise to have at least an emergency US$20 note tucked somewhere safe in case you find yourself suddenly devoid of all other possessions. Due to counterfeiting, few places accept US$100 notes unless they have a light machine to check validity.

Credit Cards

Most credit and debit cards can be used in ATMs, which are found all over South Africa, Malawi, Botswana and Namibia. In other countries, they're found only in capital cities and larger towns, and may not be reliable.

Credit cards work for purchases all over South Africa, Namibia and Botswana, and in tourist establishments in other countries. You can also use credit cards to draw cash advances (but even in South Africa this can take several hours).

Whatever card you choose to use, it isn't wise to rely totally on plastic, as computer or telephone breakdowns can leave you stranded. Always have some cash or travellers cheques as backup.

Moneychangers

Throughout the region, you can exchange currency at banks and foreign exchange bureaus, which are normally found near borders, in larger cities and in tourist areas. You can also change money at some shops and hotels (which almost always give very poor rates).

The easiest currencies to exchange are US dollars, euros or British pounds. At border crossings where there is no bank, unofficial moneychangers are usually tolerated by the authorities. It's always important to be alert, though, as these guys can pull all sorts of stunts with poor exchange rates, folded notes and clipped newspaper sandwiched between legitimate notes.

Tipping

When it comes to tipping, every country is different. Generally, it isn't necessary in small local establishments, midrange restaurants, backpackers lodges, hotels or fast-food places, but in any upmarket restaurant that doesn't automatically include a service charge (which isn't obligatory if the service has been poor), it may be appropriate. There is a grey area between midrange and upmarket restaurants, because tipping is rarely expected from locals but may be expected of foreigners. On the other hand, wealthier Africans may sometimes tip even at smaller restaurants, not because it's expected, but as a show of status.

» At safari lodges and on tours, everyone is expected to leave a blanket tip to be divided among the staff.

» Safari guides expect a separate tip from other staff.

» Taxi drivers aren't normally tipped, but may expect about 10% from well-heeled travellers (which includes backpackers in larger cities).

» If you're driving – especially in cities – you are expected to tip parking guards, who'll watch your car while you're away (in a few cases, this is a protection racket, but they're mostly legitimate).

» There's no need to tip the guys who wave you into the parking space you were going to take anyway.

Travellers Cheques

It's wise to purchase a range of travellers cheque denominations so you don't have to exchange US$100 in a country where you need only half that. When exchanging travellers cheques, many places want to check your

purchase receipts (the ones the travellers cheque company told you to always keep separate), but carry them with you only when you want to change money. Just be sure to have photocopies of them, along with the international numbers to call in case of loss or theft. Be aware that it can be difficult to change travellers cheques in Zambia and Malawi; some banks don't recognise modern purchase receipts (or perhaps don't want to), although US dollars cash in the same institutions is welcomed with open arms.

Photography

In South Africa, and to a lesser degree, Namibia, cameras and accessories are readily available in large towns. The best advice is to carry any special requirements from home.

» Some African airports may have old X-ray machines, so it's always wise to request a hand check of any film and camera equipment.

» Travellers coming from the US should carry any film and camera equipment in their hand luggage, as anti-terrorism X-ray machines for checked baggage are not safe.

» In all countries, be careful about taking photos of soldiers, police, airports, defence installations and government buildings.

» You should always ask permission before taking a photo of anyone, but particularly so if you're in a village.

» Transfer of digital images to CD is becoming increasingly common in Southern African cities, particularly in internet cafes and at photography shops.

» For more information, check out Lonely Planet's *Travel Photography*.

Safe Travel

It is very important not to make sweeping statements about personal safety in Southern Africa. While some areas are undeniably risky, most places are completely safe. Essentially, violent robbery is much more prevalent in cities and towns than in rural or wilderness areas. But even towns can differ; there's more of a danger in those frequented by foreigners than in places off the usual tourist track.

The main annoyances you'll come across in Southern Africa are the various hustlers, touts, con artists

WILDLIFE PHOTOGRAPHY

To score some excellent wildlife photos, a good lightweight 35mm SLR automatic camera with a lens between 210mm and 300mm – and a modicum of skill – should do the trick. Video cameras with a zoom facility may be able to get closer and digital cameras will perform all sorts of magic. If your subject is nothing but a speck in the distance, resist wasting film but keep the camera ready. An early start is advisable because most wildlife is active during the cooler hours. When photographing animals, take light readings on the subject and not the brilliant African background or your shots will be underexposed. The best times to take photos on sunny days are the first two hours after sunrise and the last two before sunset, both of which take advantage of the low sun's colour-enhancing rays. Filters (eg ultraviolet, polarising or skylight) can also produce good results; ask for advice in a good camera shop.

and scam merchants who recognise tourists as easy prey. Although these characters aren't always dangerous, they can part you from your valuables.

Popular scams include young people carrying sign-up sheets, requesting sponsorship for their school, sports team, youth club, grandmother's liver transplant or other apparently worthwhile causes. The sheets will invariably include the names of 'generous' foreigners who have donated US$100 or more. These are almost invariably a scam; ignore them and politely take your leave. Another scam to look out for is people selling bogus bus tickets in and around bus stations. Always purchase your tickets from official sources, even if that's a hole in the wall with a penned sign above it.

In the major cities of Zimbabwe, South Africa and Mozambique it's advisable to keep your wits about you when using an ATM. There are dozens of scams that involve stealing your cash, your card or your personal identification number (PIN) – usually all three. The ATM scam you're most likely to encounter involves the thief tampering with the machine so your card becomes jammed. By the time you realise this you've entered your PIN. The thief will have seen this, and when you go inside to report that your card has been swallowed, he will take the card and leave your account significantly lighter.

A popular scam in Namibia is when one guy distracts the driver out of the car while another opens up the passenger side grabbing whatever is lying around and does a runner. Keep your stuff stashed out of sight in the car and be vigilant if someone wanders up to your car window and starts a conversation.

Safety Tips

Some simple precautions will hopefully ensure that you have a trouble-free journey. Travellers who exercise due caution rarely have problems. The precautions suggested in this section are particularly relevant to Johannesburg and parts of Cape Town, but it's worth reading them if you're travelling in other main urban centres as well.

» Be discreet with your belongings when on the street. Consider leaving your daypack and camera in your hotel room if the room is safe.

» Don't wear jewellery or watches, however inexpensive they may be. Use a separate wallet for day-to-day purchases, and keep the bulk of your cash out of sight, preferably hidden in a pouch under loose-fitting clothing.

» Walk confidently, but not aggressively. Never look like you're lost (even if you are!). Don't obviously refer to a guidebook. Tear out the pages you need, or duck into a shop to have a look at the map to get your bearings.

» At night get off the streets and take a taxi – a couple of dollars for the fare could save you a lot of pain and trouble.

» Don't fall into the trap of thinking all robbers are on the street. Although most hotels are reputable, some travellers have left money in a safe, only to find that less reputable staff members with a spare key have helped themselves. Often this trick involves taking just a few notes, in the hope that you won't notice. To avoid this, store any valuables in a safe inside a pouch with a lockable zip, or in an envelope you can seal.

Solo Travellers

Solo travel in Southern Africa, whether you're male or female, is straightforward. While you may be a minor curiosity in rural areas, especially solo women travellers, it's likely that in most places nobody will even bat an eye. Times when you'd likely want to find a group to join would be for a safari (to cut costs), on hiking trails (many in South Africa have a three-person minimum for safety reasons) and at night. Solo women should always exercise extreme caution at night and avoid isolating situations. If you're hitting the pubs and bars in a major city it's much wiser and safer to go with a group.

Telephone

South Africa in general, and major cities elsewhere in the region, has good telephone facilities. Although local calls are relatively inexpensive, long-distance calls and international calls can be pricey. Aside from public phones, there are also private phone centres where you can pay cash for your call, but at double the rate of public phones.

Mobile Phones

In Southern Africa mobile phones are very popular due, in no small part, to the often dismal state of national landline service providers. Reception varies from country to country. Airports in some countries often have a counter where you can rent a mobile phone for the duration of your stay.

Time

In the southern summer, Southern Africa is two hours ahead of UTC (Universal Time Coordinate, formerly called GMT, or Greenwich Mean Time). The only Southern African country with daylight-saving time is Namibia, which turns its clocks forward one hour in September, and back one hour in April.

In the southern winter, however, the region is on the same time as British Summer Time (daylight-saving time).

Toilets

There are two main types of toilet in Africa: the Western style, with a toilet bowl and seat; and the African style, which is a squat toilet with a hole in the floor.

» Standards of both types of toilet vary tremendously from pristine to nauseating.

» In rural areas, long-drop squat toilets are built over a deep hole in the ground, where waste matter decomposes naturally as long as people avoid depositing rubbish (including tampons or sanitary pads, which should be disposed of separately).

» There's also a bizarre hybrid, in which an unplumbed Western toilet is perched over a long-drop hole. As you can imagine, the lack of running water can turn these into an unspeakable horror.

Tourist Information

All countries in Southern Africa have national tourist boards, but their efficiency and benefit range from excellent to little more than a friendly smile. South Africa's tourist information centres are prolific and fabulous. Usually staffed by devoted locals, they are a great source of microscopic information for travellers. In Zimbabwe, Mozambique, Malawi and Zambia the tourist boards' websites are useful for preplanning, but the offices themselves don't provide very much enlightenment.

Travellers with Disabilities

People with mobility limitations will not have an easy time in Southern Africa. Even though there are more disabled people per head of population here than in the West, facilities are few. South Africa stands out from its neighbours with regard to

its disabled organisations. In South Africa and the capitals of some other countries, some official buildings have ramps and lifts, but these are probably not the sort of places you want to visit!

For the imaginative, Zambezi raft trips, *mokoro* (dugout canoe) trips in the Okavango Delta (where at least one mobility-disabled person works as a *mokoro* poler), wildlife drives and cruises, lie-down sandboarding in the Namib dunes (if you can reach the top on a quad bike), and other activities won't be inaccessible. In almost all cases, safari companies – including budget operators – are happy to accommodate travellers with special needs.

In South Africa, the South African National Parks' website (www.sanparks.org) has a detailed and inspirational overview of accommodation and trail accessibility for the mobility impaired at all its parks, including Kruger.

Most wheelchair users find travel easier with an able-bodied companion, and happily, travel in Southern Africa does offer a few advantages compared with other parts of the developing world: footpaths and public areas are often surfaced with tar or concrete, rather than with sand, mud or gravel; many buildings (including safari lodges and national-park cabins) are single storey; and assistance is usually available on domestic and regional flights. Car hire is easy in South Africa, Namibia and Botswana and, with permission, vehicles can be taken to neighbouring countries.

Organisations

» **Mobility International** (www.miusa.org), in the US, advises disabled travellers on mobility issues; it primarily runs educational exchange programs, and some include African travel.

» **Society for Accessible Travel & Hospitality** (www.sath.org), in the US; assistance and advice.

» **Royal Association for Disability & Rehabilitation** (www.radar.org.uk), in the UK.
» **Access-Able Travel Source** (www.access-able.com) is a US-based site providing information on disabled-friendly tours and hotels in South Africa.

Visas

Visa requirements change according to your nationality. More details about who needs what can be found on Lonely Planet's website (www.lonelyplanet.com), which also has links to other visa sites.

In general, travellers from North America, Commonwealth countries and most of Western Europe don't require visas for much of the region. To visit Mozambique, however, almost everyone needs a visa, either purchased at most points of entry (except when coming from Tanzania – arrange in advance) or pre-issued from a Mozambican embassy or consulate. The other exceptions are Zimbabwe and Zambia, where just about everyone requires a visa, but these can be purchased at most points of entry (except when coming from Tanzania into Zambia).

If you're from Asia, Africa, Eastern Europe or Latin America, you should check with the local embassies of the countries you intend to visit, as some may accept only visas issued in your home country. This may also apply to travellers of Asian descent (even those with a Western passport), who may require visas even though their black or white compatriots don't. Note also that some visas have limited validity – that is, in some cases you're required to enter the country in question within a specified time period.

Please note that at some time in the future (perhaps by the time you read this?) visa conditions may have changed. The Southern Africa Development Community

USEFUL DOCUMENTATION

Depending on which countries you're visiting, you may need the following: a vaccination certificate to show you have had all the right jabs; a driver's licence, and perhaps an International Driving Permit (for the rare occasions when it may be required to hire a vehicle, or for insurance purposes if you're buying a vehicle); as well as a youth hostel card and a student or youth identity card (such as ISIC), which may be good for accessing discounts on flights, long-distance buses and visits to sites of interest (especially museums).

(SADC) is moving towards a univisa system, albeit slowly, to be theoretically introduced when all countries are up to speed on the required technical and security arrangements. Basically it will enable tourists to obtain a single visa for all countries within Southern Africa. In late 2012 the stumbling block was Botswana, which refused to endorse the scheme, citing security concerns.

Volunteering

Unemployment in Southern Africa is high and finding work is difficult. Volunteer work is a more likely possibility, especially if you are interested in teaching or wildlife conservation. A good initial contact is Volunteer Abroad (www.goabroad.com/volunteer-abroad), which has extensive listings of volunteer opportunities in the region.

There are some excellent local, grassroots opportunities for travellers wanting to volunteer – see the country chapters for listings. The following agencies are also useful for long-term paid or volunteer work:

Australian Volunteers International (☑03-9279 1788; www.australianvolunteers.com) Places qualified Australian residents on mainly two-year contracts.

Earthwatch (www.earthwatch.org) Places paying volunteers in short-term environmental projects around the globe.

UN Volunteers (☑228-815 2000; www.unv.org; Postfach 260 111 D-53153 Bonn, Germany) Places volunteers with qualifications and experience in a range of fields.

Voluntary Service Overseas (VSO) Canada (☑1-888-434 2876; www.vsocanada.org); Netherlands (www.vso.nl); UK (☑020-8780 7500; www.vso.org.uk) Places qualified and experienced volunteers for up to two years.

Volunteer Service Abroad (☑04 472 5759; www.vsa.org.nz) Organises professional contracts for New Zealanders.

Women Travellers

Compared with North Africa and the Middle East, South America and many Western countries, Southern Africa is relatively safe and unthreatening for women travellers, whether solo or in small groups.

Attitudes towards foreign women travellers tend to be fairly liberal, and if travelling solo there are plenty of opportunities to meet people along the way. Southern Africa is one of the few places in the developing world where women can meet and communicate freely with local men – of any race – without automatically being misconstrued. You'll still get questions about what you're doing, and where your husband and children are, but reactions are usually matter-of-fact.

When it comes to nightlife, both black and white societies in Southern Africa are very much conservative, traditional and male-dominated. Many bars are male only (by law of the establishment, or by law of tradition), and even where women are 'allowed', cultural conventions often dictate that women don't enter without a male companion. To avoid attracting unwanted attention, it's best to seek out and follow local female advice on which places are acceptable.

Stay safe with a bit of common sense and keep your wits about you, ie don't wander around alone anywhere at night, and during the daytime, avoid anywhere that's isolated, including streets, beaches and parks. If you go out at night, it's best to go in a group. Additionally, many budget hotels double as brothels, and are best avoided if you're travelling solo.

Never forget that in Africa, HIV/AIDS presents a threat that's unimaginable in the West. Throughout the region, local sex workers are almost always infected. This also means local men may see a foreign woman as a safe alternative.

Tampons and sanitary napkins are sold in pharmacies and supermarkets in major towns, although you're best off bringing your own preferred supply from home. It's also a good idea to pack anti-thrush medication, UTI antibiotics and any other medication you might need.

Female travellers may like to contact the global organisation called **Women Welcome Women World Wide** (www.womenwelcomewomen.org.uk), which fosters international friendship by enabling women of different countries to visit one another.

Transport

GETTING THERE & AWAY

This section describes access possibilities to Southern Africa from other parts of the world. Regional access is described in the Getting Around section. Details on travel between and around individual countries are provided in their respective countries.

Flights, tours and train tickets can be booked online at www.lonelyplanet.com/travel_services.

Entering Southern Africa

Visitors require a valid passport to enter every country in Southern Africa. To accommodate visas and border stamps, you'll need at least one or two empty pages per country you intend to visit, especially if your itinerary calls for multiple border crossings. If your passport is close to full, get a new one or pick up an insert – but apply for it well in advance. If your passport is due to expire, replace it before you leave home, as some officials won't admit you unless your passport is valid at least three (or even six) months beyond the end of your stay.

Air

Most flights into Southern Africa arrive at Johannesburg (South Africa) and this is usually the cheapest access point for the region. Although not the most salubrious city to kick-start your travels, it is the heart of the new South Africa and change – be it good or bad – is in your face. The airport itself is in between Jo'burg and Pretoria, so it's easy enough to catch a bus in the other direction and stay in a more relaxing city.

Airports & Airlines
AIRPORTS
The major air hub for Southern Africa is **OTR Tambo International Airport** (☎011-921 6262; www.worldairportguides.com/johannesburg-jnb) in Johannesburg, which has had a major upgrade. It is now a world-class airport with a full range of shops, restaurants, internet access, ATMs, foreign-exchange bureaus, and mobile-phone and car-rental outlets. Other useful airports

for visitors are Cape Town, Windhoek (Namibia), Lusaka (Zambia) and Lilongwe (Malawi). Gaborone (Botswana) is a pricey access point. The town of Victoria Falls is best accessed via Harare or Johannesburg; however, Livingstone (Zambia) has become a more popular access point for Victoria Falls in the last few years since the troubles in Zimbabwe.

You can fly to any major city in Southern Africa from anywhere in the world, but some routes are more popular (and therefore usually cheaper) than others.

» From Europe most flights go through London, from where you can fly into most major Southern African cities.

» The main European continental hubs are Amsterdam and Frankfurt.

» From America, Atlanta and New York have direct flights to Jo'burg.

» From Australia, Sydney and Perth are hubs for flights to Jo'burg.

» From Asia there are direct flights from Singapore, Hong Kong and Kuala Lumpur (Malaysia).

» From Africa there are good links between major cities such as Nairobi (Kenya) and Jo'burg: other easy links include Dar es Salaam (Tanzania) and Lilongwe (Malawi), and Addis Ababa (Ethiopia) and Lilongwe, or Lusaka (Zambia).

Remember that your access point need not necessarily be the nearest point to your intended destination. For example, it's often cheaper to fly into South Africa, from where you can take a short hop to Harare, Windhoek or Lusaka for less than the price of a direct flight. On the other hand, bargain deals to Namibia, Zimbabwe or Zambia may be cheaper than a direct flight to South Africa.

AIRLINES
Most major European airlines serve Southern Africa

including British Airways, KLM-Royal Dutch Airlines, Lufthansa Airlines, Swiss, Air France, Virgin and TAP Air Portugal. Additionally, Emirates, Kenya Airways, South African Airways and Air Namibia fly between Europe and the region, and lesser-known carriers such as Ethiopian Airlines often offer good-value services between Europe and many parts of Africa.

Although several airlines fly between the USA (Atlanta) and Southern Africa, many prospective visitors find it less convenient, but considerably cheaper, to fly via Europe. From Australia, Qantas has regular services from Sydney and Perth to Johannesburg. Note that there has been an increase in the number of airlines servicing Zimbabwe since the troubles in that country vastly reduced international air services – they include Emirates and KLM.

Tickets

When buying your air ticket, you may want to check out 'open-jaw' deals – ie flying into one country and out of another. Sometimes though, even if you want to do a linear trip (starting in Cape Town and finishing in Lusaka, for example), it may be easier and cheaper to get a standard return (eg in and out of Cape Town) and a one-way regional flight (Lusaka to Cape Town) at the end of your trip.

Note that fares quoted in this book for international flights are full-fare economy. Always ask about seasonal and advance purchase discounts, and other special rates. Some useful online ticket sellers:

» www.cheaptickets.com
» www.flightcentre.com
» www.lowestfare.com
» www.onetravel.com
» www.priceline.com
» www.travel.yahoo.com
» www.travelocity.com

Jo'burg and Cape Town are the most popular Southern African stops on a round-the-world (RTW) itinerary, and this usually means flying into one city and out of the other. Travel agents can also put together 'alternative' RTW tickets, which are more expensive, but more flexible, than standard RTW itineraries.

Africa

Many travellers on trans-Africa trips fly some sections, either because time is short or simply because the routes are virtually impassable.

The overland route between East Africa and Southern Africa is extremely popular, but it's also easy to find a flight between Nairobi and cities in the region such as Jo'burg or Lusaka. Alternatively, it's a short hop between Dar es Salaam and Lilongwe, which avoids a gruelling overland stretch. Coming from Cairo (Egypt) or Ethiopia, most flights

to Southern Africa go via Nairobi.

If you're travelling from West Africa, you have to fly as the overland route is blocked by turmoil in the Democratic Republic of Congo (DRC, formerly Zaïre). Travellers also tend to avoid Nigeria and Congo-Brazzaville. Options include flying from Accra (Ghana) or Dakar (Senegal) to Jo'burg. Flying from Abidjan (Côte d'Ivoire) to Jo'burg is also possible but less popular.

A recommended airline for getting to Mozambique is Coastal Aviation (www.coastal.cc), which flies thrice weekly from Dar es Salaam to Moçimboa da Praia (Mozambique), with connections on to Pemba and the Quirimbas Archipelago.

Australia & New Zealand

Airlines flying from Australia to Southern Africa include Qantas and South African Airways (SAA). There are direct flights from Sydney and Perth on Qantas, and from Perth on SAA, to Jo'burg (flying time about 14 hours from Sydney, 10½ hours from Perth). If flying between New Zealand and Southern Africa you must go via Australia. One of the best places to start looking for cheap deals is the ads in major weekend newspapers.

The following agencies specialise in Africa travel:
The Africa Safari Co (☑02 9541 4199; www.africasafarico.com.au) Uses small lodges

---

CLIMATE CHANGE & TRAVEL

Every form of transport that relies on carbon-based fuel generates CO_2, the main cause of human-induced climate change. Modern travel is dependent on aeroplanes, which might use less fuel per kilometre per person than most cars but travel much greater distances. The altitude at which aircraft emit gases (including CO_2) and particles also contributes to their climate-change impact. Many websites offer 'carbon calculators' that allow people to estimate the carbon emissions generated by their journey and, for those who wish to do so, to offset the impact of the greenhouse gases emitted with contributions to portfolios of climate-friendly initiatives throughout the world. Lonely Planet offsets the carbon footprint of all staff and author travel.

and tented camps when planning Southern African itineraries. These include routes such as Cape Town to Vic Falls.

African Wildlife Safaris (☑03-9249 3777, 1300 363 302; www.africanwildlife safaris.com.au) Co-ordinates custom tours to the entire region with a focus on wildlife safaris.

Continental Europe

You can fly to Southern Africa from any European capital, but the main hubs are Amsterdam and Frankfurt, and to a lesser extent Zurich and Lisbon (for Maputo, Mozambique). The most popular routes are generally the cheapest, which means that Jo'burg or Cape Town will normally be destinations of choice. Specialist travel agencies advertise in newspapers and travel magazines.

There are bucket shops by the dozen in cities such as Paris, Amsterdam, Brussels and Frankfurt. Many travel agents in Europe have ties with STA Travel, where you'll find cheap tickets. STA Travel and other discount outlets in major transport hubs include the following:

Barcelo Viajes (☑902 200 400; www.barceloviajes.com) Spain

CTS Viaggi (☑06 462 0431; www.cts.it; ☑) Italy; specialises in student and youth travel.

STA Travel (☑01805 456 422; www.statravel.de) Germany

STA Travel (☑0900 450 402; www.statravel.ch) Switzerland

UK & Ireland

Numerous airlines fly between Britain and Southern Africa, and you'll occasionally find excellent rates. The least expensive point of arrival will probably be Jo'burg, although an increasing number of flights arrive in Cape Town, which is a safer introduction to Africa.

London is normally the best place to buy a ticket, but specialist agencies elsewhere in the UK can provide comparable value. Also check the ads in the travel pages of the weekend broadsheet newspapers, in *Time Out*, the *Evening Standard,* in the free online magazine TNT (www.tntmagazine.com) and in the free *SA Times,* which is aimed at South Africans in the UK.

Some tour companies also sell flights, and some of the agents listed here also sell tours and safaris.

Africa Travel Centre (☑020 7387 1211; www.africatravel.co.uk)

North-South Travel (☑01245-608291; www.northsouthtravel.co.uk) Profits at this experienced agency support development projects overseas.

STA Travel (☑0333 321 0099; www.statravel.co.uk) STA Travel has branches in London, Manchester, Bristol and most large university towns.

Trailfinders (☑020 7628 7628; www.trailfinders.co.uk) This popular company has several offices in London, as well as Manchester, Bristol and several other cities.

Travel Bag (☑0871-703 4698; www.travelbag.co.uk)

Travel Mood (☑01 4331040; www.travelmood.com) Ireland

USA & Canada

SAA flies direct from New York to Jo'burg (17½ hours), while Delta flies direct from Atlanta (15 hours) and this is generally one of the least expensive routings. To reach one of the other capitals, such as Lusaka, Lilongwe or Maputo, you can get a connection from Jo'burg. It may be cheaper to fly on an economy hop from the USA to London (on British Airways or Virgin Atlantic) or Amsterdam (on KLM), and then buy a discount ticket from there to Southern Africa. Canadians also will probably find

the best deals travelling via Atlanta or London.

North Americans won't get the great deals that are available in London, but discount agencies to watch out for include the following:

Air Brokers (☑415-836 8718, 800-883 3273; www.airbrokers.com) A consolidator that can come up with good rates on complicated itineraries.

STA Travel (☑800 781 4040; www.statravel.com) Not limited to students and with offices all over the USA.

Travel Cuts (☑866-246 9762, 1 800 667 2887; www.travelcuts.com) The Canadian student travel association.

Land

However you travel (by car, bike or public transport), if you're planning to reach Southern Africa overland, your first decision should be which of the main routes through Africa you want to take.

Bicycle

Cycling is a cheap, convenient, healthy, environmentally sound and, above all, fun way to travel. It can also be addictive. It's quite straightforward to take your bike onto a plane and use the bike to get around on the ground. For air travel, you can dismantle the bike and box it up. Bike boxes are available at airports and most bike shops. If you're willing to risk damage to your bike, it's also possible to deflate the tyres, remove the pedals and turn the handlebars sideways, then just wheel the bike up to the check-in desk (if your bike doesn't hold up to baggage handlers, it probably won't survive Africa!). Some airlines don't charge to carry a bike, and don't even include it in the weight allowance; others charge an extra handling fee of around US$50.

Outside South Africa, you'll have difficulty buying hi-tech European or American spares, so bring anything essential along with you, and know how to make your own repairs. Plan for frequent punctures, and take lots of spare inner tubes. Because automobile tyres are constantly being repaired, patches and glue are available almost everywhere. However, it may be worth carrying a spare tyre, in case of a really devastating blowout.

Border Crossings

The most frequented routes into Southern Africa are from Tanzania into Malawi at Songwe and from Tanzania into Zambia at Nakonde.

The crossing points from Tanzania into Mozambique provide an excellent introduction to the region, but they are off the beaten track and for intrepid travellers only. From Tanzania, the main border post for travellers using public transport is at Kilambo (Namiranga or Namoto on the Mozambique side). Further west, it's also possible to cross now at Negomane, across the new Unity Bridge; arrange visas for both sides in advance. Continuing westwards, there is a new bridge open south of Songea (crossing over to Segundo Congresso in Mozambique) that also has an immigration post, and which makes a handy, albeit adventurous, entry to the Lake Niassa and Lichinga areas. Back on the coast, there are Mozambique border and customs officials at Palma and Moçimboa da Praia for those arriving in the country from Tanzania by dhow.

Other countries bordering the Southern African region include Angola and the troubled DRC. From DRC, the main border crossing is at Chilabombwe into Zambia. Due to safety issues, though, few travellers use this option.

The situation has improved in Angola since the end of the 27-year war in 2002. Some travellers are crossing in from Namibia, and independent travel is possible although it's recommended only for the intrepid; you need to arrange your visa in advance before entering, and this can take a long time through Angolan embassies in Namibia, as well as ultimately being a frustrating experience. From Angola, the main border crossings into Namibia are at Ruacana, Oshikango and Rundu. A few intrepid travellers are also crossing the border between Angola and Zambia, but this is a very remote crossing and you should research this in advance.

Car & Motorcycle

Driving from Europe to Southern Africa is a major undertaking. The main points to emphasise:

» Incredibly long distances.

» The appalling nature of most roads and the constant challenge of dealing with police and/or border officials.

» Drivers will have to be mechanically competent and carry a good collection of spares.

» You'll need vehicle registration papers, liability insurance, a driver's licence and International Driving Permit, as well as a *carnet de passage*, effectively a passport for the vehicle and temporary waiver of import duty, designed to prevent car-import rackets.

» Your home liability insurance won't be valid in many countries, and some require international drivers to purchase expensive (and effectively useless) insurance when crossing borders. In most cases, this is just a racket, and no matter what you spend on local insurance, you'll effectively be travelling uninsured.

» Check the website www.sahara-overland.com for information about crossing the Sahara.

East Africa

From Nairobi the most popular route runs via Mombasa (Kenya) or Arusha (Tanzania) to Dar es Salaam (Tanzania). From here, drivers follow the Great North Rd, and those without wheels take the Tanzania–Zambia railway (Tazara); both lead to Kapiri Mposhi (Zambia), which is within easy reach of Lusaka, Livingstone and Victoria Falls. Alternatively, get off at Mbeya (in southern Tanzania) and enter northern Malawi at Songwe. Another option from Dar es Salaam takes you across the country to Kigoma on Lake Tanganyika, then by steamer to Mpulungu (Zambia), from where you can continue overland to Lusaka and beyond.

Other possibilities from Nairobi include travelling through Uganda, Rwanda and Burundi (however, although this country has stabilised, banditry is still a problem so travel through Burundi is not currently recommended; in late 2012 Western governments were strongly advising against travel to the provinces of Bujumbura Rural, Bubanza and Cibitoke in particular because of the risk of banditry and armed clashes between FNL and the Burundi government), catching the Lake Tanganyika steamer from Bujumbura (Burundi; if it's running), and connecting with the previously outlined route at Mpulungu (Zambia). When the troubles have ended, this route will be a rewarding option.

North & West Africa

The threat of terrorism and kidnappings makes travel to Algeria dangerous, particularly in rural areas, and most trans-Sahara travellers still use the Morocco and Mauritania route into Senegal and the rest of West Africa. Due to unrest, the route from Algeria into Mali (currently experiencing enormous problems with armed rebel groups taking over a large swath of the country) and Niger is still not recommended. Once through West Africa, your route to Southern Africa will next be blocked by more unrest in DRC. This means a flight – probably from Accra (Ghana) or Lagos (Nigeria) to Nairobi, from where you can follow the route outlined under East Africa.

Northeast Africa

The Nile Route through northeast Africa starts in Egypt, and goes into Sudan (either via Lake Nasser or via the Red Sea from Suez or Hurghada); note, however, that these days travel through Sudan is not advised, especially outside of Khartoum and even here civil unrest is an issue with protestors attacking the US, British and German embassies in September 2012. Most people fly from Cairo (Egypt) or Khartoum (Sudan) to Kampala (Uganda) or Nairobi, where again you can follow the route outlined under East Africa.

Sea

For most people, reaching Southern Africa by sea is not a viable option. The days of working your passage on commercial boats have vanished, although a few travellers do manage to hitch rides on private yachts along the east coast of Africa from Mombasa (Kenya) to Mozambique or South Africa.

Alternatively, several cargo-shipping companies sail between Europe and South Africa, with comfortable cabins for public passengers. The voyage between London and Cape Town takes about 16 days.

Tours

When deciding upon your preferred method of travel, the same thing about overland tours can very much be applied to tours around Southern Africa. If you feel inexperienced, are unsure of travelling by yourself or just a sucker for

constant company, then tours can be a very good option. However, many find the experience quite suffocating and restrictive.

» Hedge your bets and take a shorter tour – this gives you the option of either taking another tour or striking out on your own with the benefit of having visited some of the places you may like to spend more time in.

» In Europe it's becoming increasingly popular to look for late bookings, which may be advertised in travel sections of weekend newspapers, or even at special late-bookings counters in some international airports.

» One of the best places to begin looking for reputable agencies is weekend newspapers or travel magazines, such as *Wanderlust* in the UK and *Outside* or *National Geographic Adventure* in the US.

» Speciality magazines for flower, birdwatching, wildlife-viewing, railway and other buffs may also include advertising for tours focusing on their own areas of interest.

AUSTRALIA

Adventure World (www.adventureworld.com.au) A range of tours and safaris in South Africa and the region.

African Wildlife Safaris (www.africanwildlifesafaris.

com.au) Customised wildlife safaris in South Africa and neighbouring countries.

Peregrine Adventures (☏1300 791 485; www.peregrineadventures.com) This Africa specialist offers all types of adventures, for all budgets.

FRANCE

Makila Voyages (www.makila.fr) Upper-end tailored tours and safaris in South Africa and its neighbours.

UK

Explore Worldwide Ltd (☏0845 291 4541; www.exploreworldwide.com) Organises group tours throughout the region, focusing on adventure and wildlife safaris.

In the Saddle (☏01299-272 997; www.inthesaddle.com) Appeals specifically to horse aficionados, and includes a range of adventurous horse-riding routes.

Naturetrek (☏01962-733051; www.naturetrek.co.uk) This company's aim is to get you to where the animals are. It offers specialised wildlife-viewing itineraries.

Temple World (☏020-8940 4114; www.templeworld.co.uk) This sophisticated and recommended company organises middle- to upper-range tours to the best of the region.

OVERLANDING

Although overlanding across Africa from Europe or the Middle East has become quite difficult due to the various 'roadblocks' imposed by unrest, some overland tour operators still take up the challenge. Some begin in Morocco and head down through Mauritania, Mali, Niger and onward as far as possible. Others take the easier option and begin in Kenya. While these trips are popular, they're designed mainly for inexperienced travellers who feel uncomfortable striking out on their own, or for those who prefer guaranteed social interaction to the uncertainties of the road. If you have the slightest inclination towards independence or would feel confined travelling with the same group of 25 or so people for most of the trip (although quite a few normally drop out along the way), think twice before booking an overland trip.

USA
Adventure Center (☑800 228 8747, 510-654 1879; www. adventurecenter.com) A travel specialist that organises budget to midrange tours and is the US agent for several overland operators, including Guerba, Dragoman and Karibu.

Africa Adventure Company (☑954-491 8877, 800 882 9453; www.africa-adventure.com) This top safari specialist can organise any sort of Southern Africa itinerary.

Born Free Safaris (www. safaris2africa.com) Itineraries covering areas from the Cape to Swaziland and further north in Southern Africa.

Bushtracks (☑800 995 8689; www.bushtracks.com) Luxury safaris and private air charters.

Mountain Travel Sobek (☑888-831 7526; www. mtsobek.com) Offers package trips to Botswana and throughout Southern Africa, including Zambia and Zimbabwe.

Premier Tours & Travel (☑800 545 1910; www. premiertours.com) Premier specialises in detailed, customised itineraries all over Southern Africa; including accommodating special interests.

Voyagers (☑800 234 9620; www.voyagers.com) Specialises in photographic and wildlife-viewing safaris.

Wilderness Travel (☑510-558 2488, 800 368 2794; www. wildernesstravel.com) Offers guided group tours with an emphasis on down-to-earth touring, including hikes and other hands-on pursuits.

GETTING AROUND

Air

Distances are great in Africa and, if time is short, regional flights can considerably widen your options. For example, after touring South Africa for a while you could fly from Cape Town to Victoria Falls and then tour Zimbabwe or southern Zambia. Alternatively, fly to Lilongwe, which is a good staging point for trips around Malawi or eastern Zambia, or to Windhoek, which opens up all the wonders of Namibia.

Even within a country, tight schedules can be accommodated with short hops by air. Both domestic and regional flights are usually operated by both state airlines and private carriers and, except in Botswana and Zambia, the competition generally keeps prices down to reasonable levels.

Sometimes the only practical way into remote national parks, reserves and lodges is by air, and charter flights provide easy access. Although these are normally for travellers on less restricted budgets, access to the best of the Okavango Delta is possible only by charter flight.

Airlines in Southern Africa
The following list includes regional airlines with domestic and intra–Southern Africa routes.

Airlink (☑27-11-978 1111; www.flyairlink.com) Flights throughout the region, connecting South Africa with most other countries, including Swaziland.

Air Botswana (☑267-390 5500; www.airbotswana.co.bw)

Air Malawi (☑265-1-620811; www.airmalawi.com) Connects Lusaka to Lilongwe.

Air Namibia (☑264-61-299 6111; www.airnamibia.com.na)

Air Zimbabwe (www.airzimbabwe.com)

British Airways Comair (☑27-11-921 0111; www.comair.co.za)

Kulula (www.kulula.com) Flies to many cities in the region, and Livingstone (Vic Falls), from its base at Johannesburg.

Linhas Aereas de Moçambique (☑258-1-426001; www. lam.co.mz/en)

Proflight Zambia (☑260-211 845 944; www.proflight -zambia.com) Regular flights around Zambia and between Zambia and Jo'burg.

SA Express (☑27-11-978 9905; www.flyexpress.aero)

Air Passes
The Star Alliance Africa Airpass allows flexible travel around sub-Saharan Africa, including all the countries in Southern Africa except Swaziland and Lesotho. It covers more than 30 airports in 23 different countries, and you can buy between three and 10 coupons (each coupon representing a single trip, ie Jo'burg to Windhoek). The Airpass allows for substantial savings, and flights are operated by Ethiopian Airlines, South African Airways and EgyptAir – see www.staralliance.com for more.

Bicycle
On a bicycle travellers will often be on an equal footing with locals and will have plenty of opportunities to meet and visit people in small towns and villages along the way. Be aware that cyclists are usually regarded as second-class road users so always be on high alert for cars and trucks.

Aim to travel in cool, dry periods, and carry at least 4L of drinking water. Bikes can easily be carried on buses or trucks – although you'll need to pay an extra luggage fee, and be prepared for some rough handling.

A good source of information may be your national cycling organisation. In Britain, the Cyclists' Touring Club (www.ctc.org.uk) provides cycling advice. In the USA, the International Bicycle Fund (www.ibike.org) organises socially conscious tours and provides information.

You'll normally be able to hire a bike locally, especially

in tourist areas. Otherwise, local people in villages and towns are often willing to rent their bikes for the day. Ask at your hotel or track down a bicycle repair shop (every town market has one).

Boat

Boat types and services in the region vary greatly from large ferries and cargo ships to traditional dhows plying the coastline of Mozambique and *mokoros* (dugout canoes) skimming along the Okavango Delta.

Based in South Africa, Tall Ships (www.tallships.co.za) has cargo ships between Durban and various Mozambican ports that sometimes take passengers; and Starlight Lines (www.starlight. co.za) is a good contact for connections to Mozambique, Madagascar and Mauritius.

The Ilala ([📞]01-587311; ilala@malawi.net) ferry chugs passengers and cargo up and down Lake Malawi. Stops include Monkey Bay, Nkhotakota, Nkhata Bay and Likoma Island in Malawi; and Metangula on the Mozambique side of the lake.

There is a ferry crossing between Zambia and Botswana, departing from Kazungula, Botswana, which takes vehicles.

Bus

Long-distance buses operate regularly between most Southern African countries. Most routes are covered by fairly basic, cheap and often slow services. From Cape Town and Jo'burg, larger and more comfortable buses run to many destinations in the region, including Maseru (Lesotho), Mbabane (Swaziland), Maputo (Mozambique) and Windhoek (Namibia).

For bus travellers, border crossings can be tedious while customs officials search through huge amounts of luggage. Minibus services may be more efficient, as fewer passengers will mean less time at the border.

There are also several international bus services especially designed for backpackers and other tourists. These companies normally have pick-ups/drop-offs at main tourist centres and backpackers' hostels. Among these is the Baz Bus ([📞]021-439 2323; www.bazbus.com), which links Cape Town, Jo'burg, Pretoria and Durban with Manzini (Swaziland), from where you can get a minibus taxi to Maputo (Mozambique).

Greyhound ([📞]083 915 9000; www.greyhound.co.za) Jo'burg, Cape Town, Harare, Bulawayo and Maputo.

The following are major bus companies operating throughout the region. They are generally safe and reliable, and standard facilities usually include air-con, video, sound system, reclining seats and on-board toilet:

Intercape Mainliner ([📞]021-380 4400, 0861 287 287; www.intercape.co.za) Extensive services with destinations including Jo'burg, Cape Town, Maputo, Windhoek, Victoria Falls and Gaborone.

Panthera Azul ([📞]011 618 8813; www.pantheraazul.co.za) Jo'burg, Durban, Nelspruit, Maputo.

Pathfinder (http://path finderlx.com) This luxury bus service has a daily service linking Harare to Vic Falls, Bulawayo and even Hwange.

Translux ([📞]0861 589 282; www.translux.co.za) Jo'burg, Pretoria, Maputo, Blantyre, Lusaka.

Buying Tickets

In general it's always better to buy tickets in advance, over the phone, on the internet or by dropping into an office in person, although sometimes it may not be necessary. Sample fares include approximately US$35 for Jo'burg to Gaborone, and US$100 for Cape Town to Windhoek; both one-way.

Car & Motorcycle

Fuel & Spare Parts

Fuel and spare parts are available across the region, although both have recently been scarce in Zimbabwe. If you're driving in remote areas, such as Zambia, careful planning is required to ensure you have enough fuel until you reach the next petrol station.

Hire

Car rental isn't cheap, but can be a very convenient way to travel, especially if you're short of time or want to visit national parks and other out-

---

AN ALTERNATIVE TO THE BUS – OVERLAND TRUCKS

Lots of companies run overland camping tours in trucks converted to carry passengers. Sometimes the trucks finish a tour, then run straight back to base to start the next one and drivers are often happy to carry 'transit' passengers on their way back. This is not a tour, as such, but can be a comfortable way of transiting between Vic Falls and Jo'burg, or Harare and Nairobi (Kenya), for around US$30 per day, plus food-kitty contributions. Those looking for rides should check around truck stops in well-known tourist areas, such as Cape Town, Jo'burg, Harare, Victoria Falls, Windhoek or Lilongwe or visit backpackers' hostels (where these companies invariably leave stacks of brochures).

of-the-way places. Costs can be mitigated by mustering a group to share the rental and petrol, and will open up all sorts of opportunities. In Southern Africa, to hire a vehicle you must be at least 21 years old (in some cases as old as 25).

» Check whether you're able to cross borders with a rental vehicle. This is usually allowed by South African companies, into Namibia, Botswana, Lesotho and Swaziland, as well as Zimbabwe (but not Mozambique), with payment of an additional cross-border fee (usually around US$100).

» Check for an unlimited-mileage deal. Also, check on the fees for other items such as tax, excess and insurance.

» Generally, South Africa is the cheapest place to hire a car (under US$30 per day), although Namibia and Botswana are also pretty good (around US$40 to US$50 per day) and Malawi isn't too bad. Zimbabwe is ridiculously expensive and in Zambia and Mozambique you're looking at a minimum of US$100 per day to take a 2WD out of the city.

» In South Africa and Namibia you can hire campervans (RVs) that accommodate two to six people. With additional payment, these come with as much equipment as you may need for demanding safaris.

» In most countries, you can also opt for a 4WD vehicle, which will typically cost from around US$150 per day (from about US$100 in South Africa), with unlimited mileage. These can also come supplied with comprehensive camping/safari equipment.

Insurance

When hiring a car always check the insurance provisions and any excess that you may be liable to pay in the event of an accident. It's also worth checking if the insurance covers driving into other Southern African countries (depending on where you intend going) and driving on dirt roads for 2WDs.

Purchase

For visitors, South Africa is the best place to buy a car (other countries place restrictions on foreign ownership, have stiff tax laws, or simply don't have the choice of vehicles). Also, South African-registered vehicles don't need a *carnet de passage* to visit any of the countries in the region. Travelling through Botswana, Lesotho, Namibia and Swaziland is easy, while for Malawi, Mozambique, Zimbabwe and Zambia you'll easily get temporary import permits at the border.

It's usually cheaper to buy privately, but for tourists it is often more convenient to go to a dealer. The weekly Cape Ads (www.junkmail.co.za/cape-town) is the best place to look for a private sale. Also try Auto Trader (www.autotrader.co.za), which advertises thousands of cars around the country.

Although prices tend to be cheaper in Jo'burg, most people do their buying in Cape Town – a much nicer place to spend the week or two that it will likely take for the process. Cape Town's main congregation of used-car dealers is on Voortrekker Rd between Maitland and Belleville metro train stations.

Some dealers might agree to a buy-back arrangement – if you don't trash the car, you can reasonably expect to get a decent percentage of your purchase price back after a three-month trip, but you need to check all aspects of the contract to be sure this deal will stick.

A recommended contact in Cape Town is Graham Duncan Smith (☎021 797 3048), who's a Land Rover expert offering consultation, repairs and sales.

No matter who you buy from, make sure that the car details correspond accurately with the ownership (registration) papers, that there is a current licence disc on the windscreen and that the vehicle has been checked by the police clearance department. Check the owner's name against their identity document, and check the car's engine and chassis numbers. Consider getting the car tested by a garage.

Cheap cars will often be sold without a roadworthy certificate – required when you register the change-of-ownership form (RLV) and pay tax for a licence disc. Some private garages are now allowed to issue them (a few hundred rand), and some will overlook minor faults.

In 2011 one reader reported paying approximately US$14,000 for a four-year-old Nissan 2.4 4WD *bakkie* (pick-up truck) with a canopy and 135,000km on the clock. Of course cheaper, older cars are also available.

Registering your car is a bureaucratic headache and will likely take a couple of weeks. **City of Capetown** (www.capetown.gov.za/en/rev/pages/motorvehicleregistration.aspx) has details of vehicle-registration offices around the city; and **Enatis** (www.enatis.com) has information on registering a used vehicle. The forms you need should be available at vehicle-registration offices, dealers or through some websites (listed in this section). They include the following:

» RLV/NCO5 (notification of change of ownership/sale of motor vehicle).

» ANR8 (application and notice in respect of traffic register number).

Next, present yourself at a vehicle-registration office along with the following:

» Your passport and a photocopy.

» A copy of the seller's ID.

» The registration certificate (in the seller's name).

» Proof of purchase.

» Proof of address (a letter from your accommodation should suffice).

» A valid licence.

» Your money.

It will help if the seller comes with you and brings their ID. Call ahead to check how much cash you'll need. Charges are currently about R400/800 for a small car/4WD.

Insurance against theft or damage is highly recommended, though not legally required for private-vehicle owners. It can be difficult to arrange by the month. The Automobile Association of South Africa (www.aasa. co.za) is a good contact, and may be willing to negotiate payment for a year's worth of insurance with a pro-rata refund when you sell the car. Insurance agencies include Sansure (www.sansure.com) in Cape Town.

Road Conditions

The good news is that most main roads in Southern Africa are in fair to excellent condition, and are passable for even small compact cars. In Malawi, Zambia and Mozambique, however, you may be slowed down considerably by sealed roads that haven't seen any maintenance for many years and are plagued with bone-crunching and tyre-bursting potholes. On lesser roads, standards vary considerably, from relatively smooth highways to dirt tracks.

Road Hazards

Whatever vehicle you drive, prepare to deal with some of the world's worst, fastest and most arrogant and aggressive drivers. Also be aware of the following:

» Tree branches on the road are the local version of warning triangles.

» If you come up behind someone on a bicycle, hoot the horn as a warning and offer a friendly wave as you pass.

» On rural highways, always be on the lookout for children playing, people selling goods, seeds drying or animals wandering around on the loose.

» Livestock is always a concern, and hitting even a small animal can cause vehicle damage, while hitting something large – like a cow or a kudu – can be fatal (for both the driver and the animal).

» If you see kids with red flags on the road, it means they're leading a herd of cows.

» Potential hazards become much harder to deal with in the dark and many vehicles have faulty lights – or none at all – so avoid driving at night.

Road Rules

Traffic officially drives on the left – but that may not always be obvious, so be especially prepared on blind corners and hills.

Hitching

Hitching is a way of life in Southern Africa, and visitors may well have the opportunity to join the throng of locals looking for lifts. While this is a good way to get around places without public transport (or even with public transport), there is a protocol involved. As a visitor, you're likely to take precedence over locals (especially with white drivers), but if other people are hitching, it's still polite to stand further along the road so they'll have the first crack (that is, unless there's a designated hitching spot where everyone waits).

Another option is to wait around petrol stations and try to arrange lifts from drivers who may be going your way. If you do get a lift, be sure to determine what sort of payment is expected before you climb aboard. In most cases, plan on paying just a bit less than the equivalent bus fare.

As in any other part of the world, hitching is never entirely safe, and we therefore don't recommend it. Travellers who hitch should understand that they are taking a small but potentially serious risk.

Local Transport

Within individual countries, public bus services range from basic to luxurious.

» As well as typically spluttering big buses, many countries also have minibuses.

» Minibuses are faster, run more frequently and perhaps are even more dangerous due to their speed.

» Minibuses or combis in Zimbabwe are not recom-

TO GO OR NOT TO GO?

A dangerous traffic quirk in Southern Africa concerns the use and significance of indicator lights. When a car comes up behind a slow vehicle, wanting to overtake, the driver of the slower vehicle will often flash one indicator to let the other driver know whether or not it's safe to overtake. Logically, the left indicator would mean 'go' (that is, it may potentially be turning left, and the way is clear) and the right would mean 'don't go' (it may potentially be turning right, indicating that the way is not clear). Unfortunately, quite a few confused drivers get this backwards, creating a potentially disastrous situation for a trusting driver in the vehicle behind. The moral is, ignore the well-intentioned signals and never overtake unless you can see that the road ahead is completely clear.

mended to travellers – they break down and constantly have lethal accidents.

» In Southern Africa, there's a lack of long-distance shared service taxis (such as the seven-seat Peugeots that are so popular in other parts of Africa).

» In rural areas, the frequency of bus services drops dramatically.

» Public transport may be limited to the back of a pick-up truck (ute) in rural regions. Everyone pays a fare to the driver, which is normally comparable to the bus fare for a similar distance.

Tours

Travellers are faced with a boggling array of organised tour options in Southern Africa, and the only problem will be making your selection. In addition to the very convenient hop-on, hop-off bus services in South Africa, there are plenty of budget tours and safaris available to take you to the regional highlights. You'll have the most options in Cape Town, Jo'burg, Victoria Falls, Livingstone, Maun, Windhoek and other places frequented by tourists. As with all tours, the range of options is enormous: they can last from two days to three weeks and can involve camping and mucking-in to luxury shuttles between five-star lodges. Vehicles may be private aircraft, Kombi vans, no-frills safari trucks or comfort-

able buses with air-con and chilled wine in the fridge.

Some questions to ask when deciding on which company to choose:

» Is the itinerary exactly what you want? Do you understand the planning and what is expected for each stage of the tour?

» Will you be staying in, or near, the park you want to visit?

» Is accommodation in a large lodge or an intimate, private camp?

» Does the operator have a commitment to responsible tourism? Do they give back to local communities and respect cultures?

» What are the numbers like on the tour – how many people will be in your group?

» Does the operator have a good reputation? Ask around.

Barefoot Safaris (☎0211-707 346; www.barefoot -safaris.com) Small group safaris, self-drive, trekking and sailing; covers Zambia, Malawi and surrounding countries.

Dana Tours (☎258-21-497 483; www.danatours.net) Combined Mozambique–South Africa–Swaziland itineraries. Offices in Maputo and Nelspruit.

Kiboko Safaris (☎in Mfuwe 0216-246111; www.kiboko -safaris.com) Excellent budget camping and lodge safaris in Malawi and South Luangwa, Zambia. Also luxury safaris in Malawi.

Wilderness Safaris (www. wilderness-safaris.com) Offers a range of tours in all Southern African countries, including Zambia and Malawi. In addition to the standard luxury-lodge-based tours in remote areas, it offers fly-in safaris and activity-based trips.

Train

Rail travel around Southern Africa focuses on the South African network and its offshoots into Botswana, Mozambique, Namibia, Swaziland, Zimbabwe and Zambia. For example, for train services between Mozambique and South Africa, the only current route is Maputo–Komatipoort, where you need to disembark at the border and change trains. Trains on the Mozambique side, however, are very bad and slow. It's much better to travel via train on the South Africa side, and then bus or *chapa* (minivan) for the Mozambique stretch (Ressano Garcia to Maputo).

Currently the only cross-border train services are the Tazara line between Zambia and Tanzania and the **Trans-Namib** (☎Namibia 061-298 2175; www.transnamib.com.na) 'StarLine' between Windhoek and Upington, South Africa (25 hours).

Travelling by train within the various countries is still a decent option – and it's almost always fun – but can be a slow way to go.

Health

As long as you stay up to date with your vaccinations and take basic preventive measures, you're unlikely to succumb to most health hazards. While countries in Southern Africa have an impressive selection of tropical diseases on offer, it's more likely you'll get a bout of diarrhoea or a cold than a more exotic malady. The main exception to this is malaria, which is a widespread risk in Southern Africa, and precautions should be taken.

BEFORE YOU GO

A little predeparture planning will save you trouble later. Get a check-up from your dentist and your doctor if you have any regular medication or chronic illness, eg high blood pressure or asthma. You should also organise spare contact lenses and glasses (and take your prescription with you); get a first-aid and medical kit together; and arrange necessary vaccinations.

Travellers can register with the International Association for Medical Assistance to Travellers (www.iamat.org), which provides directories of certified doctors. If you'll be spending much time in remote areas, consider doing a first-aid course (contact the Red Cross or St John's Ambulance), or attending a remote medicine first-aid course, such as that offered by Wilderness Medical Training (http://wildernessmedicaltraining.co.uk).

If you are bringing medications with you, carry them in their original containers, clearly labelled. A signed and dated letter from your physician describing all medical conditions and medications, including generic names, is also a good idea. If carrying syringes or needles, be sure to have a physician's letter documenting their medical necessity.

Insurance

Find out in advance whether your insurance plan will make payments directly to providers, or will reimburse you later for overseas health expenditures. In most countries in Southern Africa, doctors expect payment upfront in cash. It's vital to ensure that your travel insurance will cover any emergency transport required to get you to a hospital in a major city, or all the way home, by air and with a medical attendant if necessary. Not all insurance covers this, so check the contract carefully. If you need medical assistance, your insurance company might be able to help locate the nearest hospital or clinic, or you can ask at your hotel. In an emergency, contact your embassy or consulate.

Recommended Vaccinations

The World Health Organization (WHO) recommends that all travellers be covered for diphtheria, tetanus, measles, mumps, rubella and polio, as well as for hepatitis B, regardless of their destination. The consequences of these diseases can be severe, and outbreaks do occur.

According to the **Centers for Disease Control & Prevention** (www.cdc.gov), the following vaccinations may be recommended for travel in Southern African countries: hepatitis A, hepatitis B, rabies and typhoid, and boosters for tetanus, diphtheria and measles. Yellow fever is not a risk in the region, but the certificate is an entry requirement if you're travelling from an infected region. Consult your medical practitioner for the most up-to-date information.

Medical Checklist

It's a very good idea to carry a medical and first-aid kit with you, to help yourself in the case of minor illness or injury. Following is a list of items to consider packing.

» antibiotics (prescription only), eg ciprofloxacin (Ciproxin) or norfloxacin (Utinor)
» antidiarrhoeal drugs (eg loperamide)

» acetaminophen (paracetamol) or aspirin

» anti-inflammatory drugs (eg ibuprofen)

» antihistamines (for hay fever and allergic reactions)

» antibacterial ointment (eg Bactroban) for cuts and abrasions (prescription only)

» antimalaria pills, if you'll be in malarial areas

» bandages, gauze

» scissors, safety pins, tweezers, pocket knife

» insect repellent containing DEET for the skin

» insect spray containing permethrin for clothing, tents and bed nets

» sun block

» oral rehydration salts

» iodine tablets (for water purification)

» sterile needles, syringes and fluids if travelling to remote areas

Websites

There is a wealth of travel health advice on the internet. The Lonely Planet website at www.lonelyplanet.com is a good place to start. WHO publishes the helpful *International Travel and Health*, available free at www.who.int/ith. Another useful website is **MD Travel Health** (www.mdtravelhealth.com).

Some official government travel health websites:

Australia www.smartraveller.gov.au/tips/travelwell.html

Canada www.hc-sc.gc.ca/index_e.html

UK www.fitfortravel.nhs.uk

USA www.cdc.gov/travel

Further Reading

» *A Comprehensive Guide to Wilderness and Travel Medicine* (1998) Eric A Weiss

» *Essential Guide to Travel Health: Don't Let Bugs, Bites and Bowels Spoil Your Trip* (2009) Jane Wilson-Howarth

» *Healthy Travel Africa* (2008) Dr Isabelle Young and Dr Tony Gherardin

» *How to Stay Healthy Abroad* (2002) Richard Dawood

» *Travel in Health* (2001) Graham Fry and Dr Vincent Kenny

» *Travel with Children* (2009) Brigitte Barta

IN TRANSIT

Deep Vein Thrombosis

Prolonged immobility during flights can cause deep vein thrombosis (DVT) – the formation of blood clots in the legs. The longer the flight, the greater the risk. Although most blood clots are reabsorbed uneventfully, some might break off and travel through the blood vessels to the lungs, where they could cause life-threatening complications.

The chief symptom is swelling or pain of the foot, ankle or calf, usually but not always on just one side. When a blood clot travels to the lungs, it may cause chest pain and breathing difficulty. Travellers with any of these symptoms should immediately seek medical attention. To prevent DVT, walk about the cabin, perform isometric compressions of the leg muscles (ie contract the leg muscles while sitting), drink plenty of fluids and avoid alcohol.

Jet Lag

If you're crossing more than five time zones you could suffer jet lag, resulting in insomnia, fatigue, malaise or nausea. To avoid jet lag try drinking plenty of fluids (nonalcoholic) and eating light meals. Upon arrival, get exposure to natural sunlight and readjust your schedule (for meals, sleep etc) as soon as possible.

IN SOUTHERN AFRICA

Availability & Cost of Health Care

Good-quality health care is available in the urban areas of many countries in Southern Africa, and private hospitals are generally of a good standard. Public hospitals by contrast are often underfunded and overcrowded; in off-the-beaten-track areas, reliable medical facilities are rare.

Prescriptions are required in most countries in Southern Africa. Drugs for chronic diseases should be brought from home. In many countries there is a high risk of contracting HIV from infected blood transfusions. The BloodCare Foundation (www.bloodcare.org.uk) is a useful source of safe, screened blood, which can be transported to any part of the world within 24 hours.

Infectious Diseases

With a few basic preventive measures, it's unlikely that you'll succumb to any of the diseases that are found in Southern Africa.

Cholera

Cholera is caused by a bacteria, and spread via contaminated drinking water. In South Africa, the risk to travellers is very low; you're likely to encounter it only in eastern rural areas, where you should avoid tap water and unpeeled or uncooked fruits and vegetables. The main symptom is profuse watery diarrhoea, which causes debilitation if fluids are not replaced quickly.

An oral cholera vaccine is available in the USA, but it is not particularly effective. Most cases of cholera can be avoided by close attention to drinking water and by avoiding potentially contaminated food. Treatment is by fluid replacement (orally or via a drip), but sometimes antibiotics are needed. Self-treatment is not advised.

Dengue Fever (Break-Bone Fever)

Dengue fever, spread through the bite of mosquitos, causes a feverish illness with headache and muscle pains similar to those experienced with a bad, prolonged attack of influenza. There might be a rash. Mosquito bites should be avoided whenever possible. Self-treatment: paracetamol and rest. In rare cases in Africa this becomes Severe Dengue Fever, with worsening symptoms including vomiting, rapid breathing and abdominal pain. Seek medical help as this can be fatal.

Filariasis

Filariasis is caused by tiny worms migrating in the lymphatic system, and is spread by the bite from an infected mosquito. Symptoms include localised itching and swelling of the legs and/or genitalia. Treatment is available. Self-treatment: none.

Hepatitis A

Hepatitis A is spread through contaminated food (particularly shellfish) and water. It causes jaundice and, although it is rarely fatal, it can cause prolonged lethargy and delayed recovery. If you've had hepatitis A, you shouldn't drink alcohol for up to six months afterwards, but once you've recovered, there won't be any long-term problems. The first symptoms include dark urine and a yellow colour to the whites of the eyes. Sometimes a fever and abdominal pain might be present. Hepatitis A vaccine (Avaxim, VAQTA, Havrix) is given as an injection: a single

dose will give protection for up to a year, and a booster after a year gives 10-year protection. Hepatitis A and typhoid vaccines can also be given as a single-dose vaccine (hepatyrix or viatim). Self-treatment: none.

Hepatitis B

Hepatitis B is spread through infected blood, contaminated needles and sexual intercourse. It can also be spread from an infected mother to the baby during childbirth. It affects the liver, causing jaundice and occasionally liver failure. Most people recover completely, but some people might be chronic carriers of the virus, which could lead eventually to cirrhosis or liver cancer. Those visiting high-risk areas for long periods or those with increased social or occupational risk should be immunised. Many countries now routinely give hepatitis B as part of the childhood vaccination program. It is given singly or can be given at the same time as hepatitis A (hepatyrix).

A course will give protection for at least five years. It can be given over four weeks or six months. Self-treatment: none.

HIV

HIV, the virus that causes AIDS, is an enormous problem across Southern Africa, with a devastating impact on local health systems and community structures. The virus is spread through infected blood and blood products, by sexual intercourse with an infected partner, and from an infected mother to her baby during childbirth and breastfeeding. It can be spread through 'blood to blood' contacts, such as with contaminated instruments during medical, dental, acupuncture and other body-piercing procedures, and through sharing used intravenous needles. At present there is no cure; medication that might keep the disease under control is

available, but these drugs are too expensive, or unavailable, for the overwhelming majority of those living in Southern Africa. If you think you might have been infected with HIV, a blood test is necessary; a three-month gap after exposure and before testing is required to allow antibodies to appear in the blood. Self-treatment: none.

Malaria

Malaria is a widespread risk in Southern Africa. Apart from road accidents, it is probably the only major health risk that you face travelling in this area, and precautions should be taken. The disease is caused by a parasite in the bloodstream spread via the bite of the female anopheles mosquito. There are several types of malaria; falciparum malaria is the most dangerous type and the predominant form in South Africa. Infection rates vary with season and climate, so check out the situation before departure. Several different drugs are used to prevent malaria, and new ones are in the pipeline. Up-to-date advice from a travel health clinic is essential as some medication is more suitable for some travellers than others (eg people with epilepsy should avoid mefloquine, and doxycycline should not be taken by pregnant women or children aged under 12).

The early stages of malaria include headaches, fevers, generalised aches and pains, and malaise, which could be mistaken for the flu. Other symptoms can include abdominal pain, diarrhoea and a cough. Anyone who develops a fever in a malarial area should assume malarial infection until a blood test proves negative, even if you have been taking antimalarial medication. If not treated, the next stage could develop within 24 hours, particularly if falciparum malaria is the parasite: jaundice, then reduced consciousness and coma (also known as cerebral malaria) followed by death. Treatment in hospital is essential, and the death rate might still be as high as 10% even in the best intensive-care facilities.

Many travellers think that malaria is a mild illness, and that taking antimalarial drugs causes more illness through side effects than actually getting malaria. This is unfortunately not true. If you decide against taking antimalarial drugs, you must understand the risks, and be obsessive about avoiding mosquito bites. Use nets and insect repellent, and report any fever or flulike symptoms to a doctor as soon as possible. Some people advocate homeopathic preparations against malaria, such as Demal200, but as yet there is no conclusive evidence that this is effective, and many homeopaths do not recommend their use.

Malaria in pregnancy frequently results in miscarriage or premature labour, and the risks to both mother and foetus during pregnancy are considerable. Travel throughout the region when pregnant should be carefully considered. Adults who have survived childhood malaria have developed immunity and usually only develop mild cases of malaria; most Western travellers have no immunity at all. Immunity wanes after 18 months of nonexposure, so even if you have had malaria in the past and used to live in a malaria-prone area, you might no longer be immune.

Rabies

Rabies is spread by receiving bites or licks from an infected animal on broken skin. Few human cases are reported in Southern Africa, with the risks highest in rural areas. It is always fatal once the clinical symptoms start (which might be up to several months after an infected bite), so postbite vaccination should be given as soon as

possible. Postbite vaccination (whether or not you've been vaccinated before the bite) prevents the virus from spreading to the central nervous system. Animal handlers should be vaccinated, as should those travelling to remote areas where a reliable source of postbite vaccine is not available within 24 hours. Three preventive injections are needed over a month. If you have not been vaccinated you'll need a course of five injections starting within 24 hours or as soon as possible after the injury. If you have been vaccinated, you'll need fewer postbite injections, and have more time to seek medical help. Self-treatment: none.

Schistosomiasis (Bilharzia)

This disease is a risk when swimming in freshwater lakes and slow-running rivers – always seek local advice before venturing in. It's spread by flukes (minute worms) that are carried by a species of freshwater snail, which then

sheds them into slow-moving or still water. The parasites penetrate human skin during swimming and then migrate to the bladder or bowel. They are excreted via stool or urine and could contaminate fresh water, where the cycle starts again. Swimming in suspect freshwater lakes or slow-running rivers should be avoided. Symptoms range from none to transient fever and rash, and advanced cases might have blood in the stool or in the urine. A blood test can detect antibodies if you might have been exposed, and treatment is readily available. If not treated, the infection can cause kidney failure or permanent bowel damage. It's not possible for you to infect others. Self-treatment: none.

Tuberculosis

Tuberculosis (TB) is spread through close respiratory contact and occasionally through infected milk or milk products. BCG vaccination is recommended if you'll be mixing closely with the local

ANTIMALARIAL A TO D

» A – Awareness of the risk. No medication is totally effective, but protection of up to 95% is achievable with most drugs, as long as other measures have been taken.

» B – Bites, to be avoided at all costs. Sleep in a screened room, use a mosquito spray or coils, sleep under a permethrin-impregnated net at night. Cover up at night with long trousers and long sleeves, preferably with permethrin-treated clothing. Apply appropriate repellent to all areas of exposed skin in the evenings.

» C – Chemical prevention (ie antimalarial drugs) is usually needed in malarial areas. Expert advice is needed as resistance patterns can change, and new drugs are in development. Not all antimalarial drugs are suitable for everyone. Most antimalarial drugs need to be started at least a week before exposure and be continued for four weeks after the last possible exposure to malaria.

» D – Diagnosis. If you have a fever or flulike illness within a year of travel to a malarial area, malaria is a possibility, and immediate medical attention is necessary.

population, especially on long-term stays, although it gives only moderate protection against the disease. TB can be asymptomatic, being picked up only on a routine chest X-ray. Alternatively, it can cause a cough, weight loss or fever, sometimes occurring months or even years after exposure. Self-treatment: none.

Typhoid

This is spread through food or water contaminated by infected human faeces. The first symptom is usually a fever or a pink rash on the abdomen. Sometimes septicaemia (blood poisoning) can occur. A typhoid vaccine (typhim Vi, typherix) will give protection for three years. In some countries, the oral vaccine Vivotif is also available. Antibiotics are usually given as treatment, and death is rare unless septicaemia occurs. Self-treatment: none.

Yellow Fever

Although not a problem within Southern Africa, you'll need to carry a certificate of vaccination if you'll be arriving from an infected country. For a list of infected countries see **WHO** (WHO; www.who.int/wer/) or **Centers for Disease Control & Prevention** (www.cdc.gov).

Travellers' Diarrhoea

This is a common travel-related illness, sometimes simply due to dietary changes. It's possible that you'll succumb, especially if you're spending a lot of time in rural areas or eating at inexpensive local food stalls. To avoid diarrhoea, eat only fresh fruits or vegetables that have been cooked or peeled, and be wary of dairy products that might contain unpasteurised milk. Although freshly cooked food can often be a safe option, plates or serving utensils might be dirty, so be selective when eating food from street vendors (make sure that cooked food is piping hot all the way through). If you develop diarrhoea, be sure to drink plenty of fluids, preferably an oral rehydration solution containing lots of water and some salt and sugar. A few loose stools don't require treatment but, if you start having more than four or five stools a day, you should start taking an antibiotic (usually a quinoline drug, such as ciprofloxacin or norfloxacin) and an antidiarrhoeal agent (such as loperamide) if you're not within easy reach of a toilet. If diarrhoea is bloody, persists for more than 72 hours or is accompanied by fever, shaking chills or severe abdominal pain, you should seek medical attention.

Amoebic Dysentery

Contracted by eating contaminated food and water, amoebic dysentery causes blood and mucus in the faeces. It can be relatively mild and tends to come on gradually, but seek medical advice if you think you have the illness as it won't clear up without treatment (which is with specific antibiotics).

Giardiasis

This, like amoebic dysentery, is also caused by ingesting contaminated food and water. The illness usually appears a week or more after you have been exposed to the offending parasite. Giardiasis might cause only a short-lived bout of typical travellers' diarrhoea, but it can also cause persistent diarrhoea. Ideally, seek medical advice if you suspect you have giardiasis, but if you are in a remote area you could start a course of antibiotics.

Environmental Hazards

Heat Exhaustion

This condition occurs following heavy sweating and excessive fluid loss with inadequate replacement of fluids and salt, and is primarily a risk in hot climates when taking unaccustomed exercise before full acclimatisation. Symptoms include headache, dizziness and tiredness. Dehydration is already happening by the time you feel thirsty – aim to drink sufficient water to produce pale, diluted urine. Self-treatment: fluid replacement with water and/or fruit juice, and cooling by cold water and fans. The treatment of the salt-loss component consists of consuming salty fluids as in soup, and adding a little more table salt to foods than usual.

Heatstroke

Heat exhaustion is a precursor to the much more serious condition of heatstroke. In this case there is damage to the sweating mechanism, with an excessive rise in body temperature, irrational and hyperactive behaviour, and eventually loss of consciousness and death. Rapid cooling by spraying the body with water and fanning is ideal. Emergency fluid and electrolyte replacement is usually also required by intravenous drip.

Insect Bites & Stings

Mosquitoes might not always carry malaria or dengue fever, but they (and other insects) can cause irritation and infected bites. To avoid these, take the same precautions as you would for avoiding malaria. Bee and wasp stings cause real problems only to those who have a severe allergy to the stings (anaphylaxis), in which case, carry an adrenaline (epinephrine) injection.

Scorpions are found in arid areas. They can cause a painful bite that is sometimes life-threatening. If bitten by a scorpion, take a painkiller. Medical treatment should be sought if collapse occurs.

Ticks are always a risk away from urban areas. If

you get bitten, press down around the tick's head with tweezers, grab the head and gently pull upwards. Avoid pulling the rear of the body as this may squeeze the tick's gut contents through the attached mouth parts into the skin, increasing the risk of infection and disease. Smearing chemicals on the tick will not make it let go and is not recommended.

Snake Bites

Basically, avoid getting bitten! Don't walk barefoot, or stick your hand into holes or cracks. Half of those bitten by venomous snakes are not actually injected with poison (envenomed). If bitten by a snake, do not panic. Immobilise the bitten limb with a splint (such as a stick) and apply a bandage over the site with firm pressure, similar to bandaging a sprain. Do not apply a tourniquet, or cut or suck the bite. Get medical help as soon as possible.

Water

In most areas of Southern Africa you should stick to bottled water rather than drinking water from the tap, and purify stream water before drinking it.

Language

WANT MORE?

For in-depth language information and handy phrases, check out Lonely Planet's *Africa Phrasebook*. You'll find it at **shop.lonelyplanet.com**, or you can buy Lonely Planet's iPhone phrasebooks at the Apple App Store.

English is an official language in every Southern African country except Mozambique (where it's Portuguese). Afrikaans is widely used in the region and is the first language of millions of people of diverse ethnic backgrounds. It's also used as a lingua franca in both South Africa and Namibia.

As a first language, most Southern Africans speak either a Bantu or a Khoisan language. Due to common roots, a number of Bantu varieties in the region, including Zulu and Ndebele, as well as Sotho and Tswana, are mutually intelligible. Many native Khoisan speakers also speak at least one Bantu and one other language, usually Afrikaans.

In Mozambique and parts of northern Namibia along the Angola border, Portuguese is the European language of choice. In parts of Namibia, German is also widely spoken, but is the first language of only about 2% of Namibians.

AFRIKAANS

Afrikaans developed from the dialect spoken by the Dutch settlers in South Africa from the 17th century. Until the late 19th century it was considered a Dutch dialect (known as 'Cape Dutch'), and in 1925 it became one of the official languages of South Africa. Today, it has about six million speakers.

If you read our coloured pronunciation guides as if they were English, you should be understood. Note that aw is pronounced as in 'law', eu as the 'u' in 'nurse', ew as the 'ee' in 'see' with rounded lips, oh as the 'o' in 'cold', uh as the 'a' in 'ago', kh as the 'ch' in the Scottish *loch*, zh as the 's' in 'pleasure', and r is trilled. The stressed syllables are in italics.

Basics

Hello.	*Hallo.*	ha·*loh*
Goodbye.	*Totsiens.*	tot·*seens*
Yes.	*Ja.*	yaa
No.	*Nee.*	ney
Please.	*Asseblief.*	a·si·*bleef*
Thank you.	*Dankie.*	*dang*·kee
Sorry.	*Jammer.*	*ya*·min

How are you?
Hoe gaan dit? hu khaan dit

Fine, and you?
Goed dankie, en jy? khut *dang*·kee en yay

What's your name?
Wat's jou naam? vats yoh naam

My name is ...
My naam is ... may naam is ...

Do you speak English?
Praat jy Engels? praat yay *eng*·ils

I don't understand.
Ek verstaan nie. ek vir·*staan* nee

Eating & Drinking

Can you recommend a ...?	*Kan jy 'n ... aanbeveel?*	kan yay i ... *aan*·bi·feyl
bar	*kroeg*	krukh
dish	*gereg*	khi·*rekh*
place to eat	*eetplek*	*eyt*·plek

I'd like ..., please.	Ek wil asseblief ... hê.	ek vil a·si·bleef ... he
a table for two	'n tafel vir twee	i taa·fil fir twey
that dish	daardie gereg	daar·dee khi·rekh
the bill	die rekening	dee rey·ki·ning
the menu	die spyskaart	dee spays·kaart

Emergencies

Help!	Help!	help
Call a doctor!	Kry 'n dokter!	kray i dok·tir
Call the police!	Kry die polisie!	kray dee pu·lee·see

I'm lost.
Ek is verdwaal.   ek is fir·dwaal

Where are the toilets?
Waar is die toilette?   vaar is dee toy·le·ti

I need a doctor.
Ek het 'n dokter nodig.   ek het i dok·tir noo·dikh

Shopping & Services

I'm looking for ...
Ek soek na ...   ek suk naa ...

How much is it?
Hoeveel kos dit?   hu·fil kos dit

What's your lowest price?
Wat is jou laagste prys?   vat is yoh laakh·sti prays

I want to buy a phonecard.
Ek wil asseblief   ek vil a·si·bleef
'n foonkaart koop.   i foon·kaart koop

I'd like to change money.
Ek wil asseblief geld ruil.   ek vil a·si·bleef khelt rayl

I want to use the internet.
Ek wil asseblief die   ek vil a·si·bleef dee
Internet gebruik.   in·tir·net khi·brayk

Transport & Directions

A ... ticket, please.	Een ... kaartjie, asseblief.	eyn ... kaar·kee a·si·bleef
one-way	eenrigting	eyn·rikh·ting
return	retoer	ri·tur

How much is it to ...?
Hoeveel kos dit na ...?   hu·fil kos dit naa ...

Please take me to (this address).
Neem my asseblief na   neym may a·si·bleef naa
(hierdie adres).   (heer·dee a·dres)

Where's the (nearest) ...?
Waar's die (naaste) ...?   vaars dee (naas·ti) ...

Can you show me (on the map)?
Kan jy my   kan yay may
(op die kaart) wys?   (op dee kaart) vays

What's the address?
Wat is die adres?   vat is dee a·dres

CHEWA

Chewa (Chichewa), a Bantu language, is the national language of Malawi and is also a very close relative of Nyanja, spoken in Zambia – the two are mutually intelligible.

Bambo, literally meaning 'father', is a polite way to address any Malawian man. The female equivalent is *amai* or *mai*. *Mazungu* means 'white person', but isn't derogatory.

Chichewa speakers will normally use English for numbers and prices. Similarly, time is nearly always expressed in English.

Hello.	Moni.
Hello, anybody in?	Odi. (when knocking on door or calling at gate)
Come in./Welcome.	Lowani.
Goodbye. (if leaving)	Tsala bwino. (lit: 'stay well')
Goodbye. (if staying)	Pitani bwino. (lit: 'go well')
Good night.	Gonani bwino.
Please.	Chonde.
Thank you./ Excuse me.	Zikomo.
Thank you very much.	Zikomo kwambile/ kwambiri.
Yes.	Inde.
No.	Iyayi.
How are you?	Muli bwanji?
I'm fine.	Ndili bwino.
And you?	Kaya-iwe? (to one person) Kaya inu? (to several people)
Good./Fine./OK.	Chabwino.

DAMARA/NAMA

The Damara and Nama peoples' languages belong to the Khoisan group and, like other Khoisan varieties, they feature several 'click' sounds. The clicks are made by a sucking motion with the tongue against different parts of the mouth to produce different sounds. The clicks represented by ! are a hollow tone, like that when pulling a cork from a bottle. The click represented by / is like the 'tsk!' in English used to indicate disapproval. The sideways click sound, like the sound made when encouraging a horse, is represented by //. However, you'll be forgiven if you just render all the clicks as a 'k' sound.

Good morning.	!Gai//oas.
How are you?	Matisa?
Thank you.	Eio.
Pardon.	Mati.
Yes.	Ii.
Goodbye.	!Gaise hare. (if leaving) !Gure. (if staying)
Do you speak English?	Engelsa !goa idu ra?
What's your name?	Mati du/onha?
My name is ...	Ti/ons ge a ...
I'm from ...	Tita ge a ...
How much is this?	Ne xu e matigo marie ni gan?
Where is the ...?	Maha ... ha?

1	/gui
2	/gam
3	!nona
4	haga
5	goro
6	!nani
7	hu
8	//khaisa
9	khoese
10	disi

HERERO/HIMBA

Herero and Himba, both Bantu languages, are quite similar, and will be especially useful when travelling around Kaokoland and remote areas of north central Namibia, where Afrikaans remains the lingua franca.

Hello.	Tjike.
Good morning, sir.	Wa penduka, mutengua.
Good afternoon, madam.	Wa uhara, serekaze.
Good evening.	Wa tokerua.

Good night.	Ongurova ombua.
Please.	Arikana.
Thank you.	Okuhepa.
How are you?	Kora?
Fine.	Naua.
Well, thank you.	Mbiri naua, okuhepa.
Pardon.	Makuvi.
Yes./No.	Ii./Kako.
Where are you from?	Ove ua za pi?
Do you speak English?	U hungira Otjingirisa?

daughters	ovanatje ovakazona
father	tate
husband	omurumendu ngua kupa
mother	mama
older sibling	erumbi
sons	ovanatje ovazandu
wife	omukazendu ngua kupua
younger sibling	omuangu

caravan park	omasuviro uo zo karavana
game reserve	orumbo ro vipuka
(long/short) hiking trail	okaira ko makaendero uo pehi (okare/okasupi)
river (channel)	omuramba
road	ondjiira
rooms	omatuuo

1	iimue
2	imbari
3	indatu
4	iine
5	indano
6	hamboumue
7	hambomabari
8	hambondatu
9	imuvyu
10	omurongo

!KUNG SAN

The Khoisan languages in Namibia and Botswana are characterised by click sounds. Perhaps the most useful dialect is that of the !Kung people, who are concentrated in eastern Bushmanland in Namibia and around northwestern Botswana.

To simplify matters, in the following phrases all clicks are represented by !k.

Hello.	!Kao.
Good morning.	Tuwa.

Goodbye, go well.	!King se !kau.
What's your name?	!Kang ya tsedia/tsidia? (to a man/woman)
How are you?	!Ka tseya/tsiya? (to a man/woman)
My name is ...	!Kang ya tse/tsi ... (m/f)
Thank you.	!Ka.
Thank you very much.	!Kin!ka.

LOZI

Lozi, a Bantu language, is spoken throughout much of western Zambia and in the Caprivi region of Namibia.

Hello.	Eeni, sha./Lumela.
Good morning.	U zuhile.
Good afternoon/ evening.	Ki manzibuana.
Good night.	Ki busihu.
Goodbye.	Siala foo./Siala hande.
How are you?	U cwang'./W'a pila./ W'a zuha?
I'm fine.	N'i teng'./N'a pila./ N'a zuha.
And you?	Wen'a bo?/Wena u cwang'?
Good./Fine.	Ki hande.
OK.	Ku lukile.
Excuse me.	Ni swalele. (inf) Mu ni swalele. (pol)
Please.	Sha. (only said to people of higher social standing)
Thank you.	N'itumezi.
Thank you very much.	N'i tumezi hahulu.
Yes./No.	Ee./Awa.
Do you speak English?	Wa bulela sikuwa?
How much?	Ki bukai?

1	il'ingw'i
2	z'e peli or bubeli
3	z'e t'alu or bulalu
4	z'e ne or bune
5	z'e keta-lizoho
6	z'e keta-lizoho ka ka li kang'wi
7	supile
10	lishumi
20	mashumi a mabeli likiti

NDEBELE

The language of Zimbabwe's Ndebele people is spoken primarily in Matabeleland in the western and southwestern parts of the country.

It's a Bantu language related to Zulu and is not mutually intelligible with Shona.

The Ndebele of Zimbabwe and that of South Africa (also known as Southern Ndebele) are quite distinct languages.

Hello.	Sawubona./Salibonani.
Hello. (reply)	Yebo.
Good morning.	Livukenjani.
Good afternoon.	Litshonile.
Good evening.	Litshone njani.
How are you?	Linjani?/Kunjani?
I'm well.	Sikona.
Goodbye.	Lisale kuhle. (if staying) Uhambe kuhle. (if leaving)
Yes.	Yebo.
No.	Hayi.
Please.	Uxolo.
Thank you.	Siyabonga kakulu.
What's your name?	Ibizo lakho ngubani?
My name is ...	Elami igama ngingu ...
I'm from ...	Ngivela e ...
sir/madam	umnimzana/inkosikazi
How much?	Yimalini?
Where's the (station)?	Singapi (isiteshi)?

1	okukodwa
2	okubili
3	okutathu
4	okune
5	okuyisihlanu
6	okuyisithupha
7	okuyisikhombisa
8	okuyisitshiyangalo mbila
9	okuyisitshiyangalo lunye
10	okuli tshumi

NORTHERN SOTHO

Northern Sotho (Sepedi) is a Bantu language spoken in South Africa's northeastern provinces.

Hello.	Thobela.
Goodbye.	Sala gabotse.
Yes./No.	Ee./Aowa.
Please.	Ke kgopela.
Thank you.	Ke ya leboga.
What's your name?	Ke mang lebitso la gago?
My name is ...	Lebitso laka ke ...
I come from ...	Ke bowa kwa ...

OWAMBO

A Bantu language, Owambo (Oshiwambo), specifically the Kwanyama dialect, is the first tongue of more Namibians than any other language. It's also spoken as a second or third language by many non-Owambo Namibians of both Bantu and Khoisan origin.

Good morning.	Wa lalapo.
Good evening.	Wa tokelwapo.
How are you?	Owu li po ngiini?
I'm fine.	Ondi li nawa.
Thank you.	Tangi.
Please.	Ombili.
Yes./No.	Eeno./Aawe.
Maybe.	Andiya manga.
Excuse me.	Ombili manga.
I'm sorry.	Onde shi panda.
I don't know.	Ombili mwaa sho.
Do you speak English?	Oho popi Oshiingilisa?
How much is this?	Ingapi tashi kotha?
Can you please help me?	Eto vuluwu pukulule ndje?
I'm lost.	Ombili, onda puka.

Where is the ...?	Openi pu na ...?
bank	ombaanga
hospital	oshipangelo
pharmacy	oaputeka
police station	opolisi
post office	opoosa
telephone	ngodhi
toilet	kandjugo

1	yimwe
2	mbali
3	ndatu
4	ne
5	ntano
6	hamano
7	heyali
8	hetatu
9	omugoyi
10	omulongo

PORTUGUESE

Portuguese is spoken in Mozambique and in parts of northern Namibia. It has nasal vowels (represented in our pronunciation guides by ng after the vowel), which are pronounced 'through the nose', as well as a strongly rolled r (rr in our pronunciation guides). Also note that the symbol zh sounds like the 's' in 'pleasure'. The stressed syllables are in italics.

Basics

Hello.	Olá.	o·laa
Goodbye.	Adeus.	a·de·oosh
How are you?	Como está?	ko·moo shtaa
Fine, and you?	Bem, e você?	beng e vo·se
Excuse me.	Faz favor.	faash fa·vor
Sorry.	Desculpe.	desh·kool·pe
Yes./No.	Sim./Não.	seeng/nowng
Please.	Por favor.	poor fa·vor
Thank you.	Obrigado.	o·bree·gaa·doo (m)
	Obrigada.	o·bree·gaa·da (f)
You're welcome.	De nada.	de naa·da

What's your name?
Qual é o seu nome? — kwaal e oo se·oo no·me

My name is ...
O meu nome é ... — oo me·oo no·me e ...

Do you speak English?
Fala inglês? — faa·la eeng·glesh

I don't understand.
Não entendo. — nowng eng·teng·doo

Eating & Drinking

What would you recommend?
O que é que recomenda? — oo ke e ke rre·koo·meng·da

I don't eat ...
Eu não como ... — e·oo nowng ko·moo ...

I'd like (the menu).
Queria (um menu). — ke·ree·a (oong me·noo)

Cheers!
Saúde! — sa·oo·de

That was delicious.
Isto estava delicioso. — eesh·too shtaa·va de·lee·see·o·zoo

Please bring the bill.
Pode-me trazer a conta. — po·de·me tra·zer a kong·ta

Emergencies

Help!	Socorro!	soo·ko·rroo
Go away!	Vá-se embora!	vaa·se eng·bo·ra
Call ...!	Chame ...!	shaa·me ...
a doctor	um médico	oong me·dee·koo
the police	a polícia	a poo·lee·sya

Numbers – Portuguese

1	*um*	oong
2	*dois*	doysh
3	*três*	tresh
4	*quatro*	kwaa·troo
5	*cinco*	seeng·koo
6	*seis*	saysh
7	*sete*	se·te
8	*oito*	oy·too
9	*nove*	no·ve
10	*dez*	desh

I'm lost.
Estou perdido.   shtoh per·dee·doo (m)
Estou perdida.   shtoh per·dee·da (f)

I'm ill.
Estou doente.   shtoh doo·eng·te

Where is the toilet?
Onde é a casa de   ong·de e a kaa·za de
banho?   ba·nyoo

Shopping & Services

I'd like to buy ...
Queria comprar ...   ke·ree·a kong·praar ...

How much is it?
Quanto custa?   kwang·too koosh·ta

It's too expensive.
Está muito caro.   shtaa mweeng·too kaa·roo

There's a mistake in the bill.
Há um erro na conta.   aa oong e·rroo na kong·ta

Transport & Directions

boat	*barco*	baar·koo
bus	*autocarro*	ow·to·kaa·roo
plane	*avião*	a·vee·owng
train	*comboio*	kong·boy·oo

... ticket	*um bilhete*	oong bee·lye·te
	de ...	de ...
one-way	*ida*	ee·da
return	*ida e volta*	ee·da ee vol·ta

I want to go to ...
Queria ir a ...   ke·ree·a eer a ...

What time does it leave/arrive?
A que horas sai/chega?   a ke o·rash sai/she·ga

Where's (the station)?
Onde é (a estação)?   ong·de e (a shta·sowng)

What's the address?
Qual é o endereço?   kwaal e oo eng·de·re·soo

Could you please write it down?
Podia escrever   poo·dee·a shkre·ver
isso, por favor?   ee·soo poor fa·vor

Can you show me (on the map)?
Pode-me mostrar   po·de·me moosh·traar
(no mapa)?   (noo maa·pa)

SHONA

Shona, a Bantu language, is spoken almost universally in the central and eastern parts of Zimbabwe. The 'high' dialect, used in broadcasts and other media, is Zezuru, which is indigenous to the Harare area.

Where two translations are given for the following phrases, the first is used when speaking to one person; the second, to more than one. Note that *dya* is pronounced 'jga' (as near to one syllable as possible); *tya* as 'chka' (said quickly); *sv* as 's' with the tongue near the roof of your mouth; *zv* like the 'sv' sound in 'is very'; and that *m/n* before consonants at the start of a word are pronounced as a light 'm' or 'n' humming sound.

Hello.	*Mhoro./Mhoroi.*
Hello. (reply)	*Ahoi.*
Welcome.	*Titambire.*
How are you?	*Makadii?/Makadi-ni?*
I'm well.	*Ndiripo.*
Good morning.	*Mangwanani.*
Good afternoon.	*Masikati.*
Good evening.	*Manheru.*
Goodbye.	*Chisarai zvakanaka.* (if staying) *Fambai zvakanaka.* (if leaving)
Please.	*Ndapota.*
Thank you.	*Ndatenda./Masvita.*
Yes./No.	*Ehe./Aiw.*
What's your name?	*Unonzi ani zita rako?*
My name is ...	*Ndini ...*
I'm from ...	*Ndinobva ku ...*
How much?	*I marii?*

1	*potsi*
2	*piri*
3	*tatu*
4	*ina*
5	*shanu*
6	*tanhatu*
7	*nomwe*
8	*tsere*
9	*pfumbamwe*
10	*gumi*

SOUTHERN SOTHO

Southern Sotho (Sesotho), a Bantu language, is the official language in Lesotho (along with English). It is also spoken by the Basotho people in the Free State, North West and Gauteng provinces in South Africa.

Hello.	Dumela.
Greetings, father.	Lumela ntate.
Greetings, mother.	Lumela 'me.
Greetings, brother.	Lumela abuti.
Greetings, sister.	Lumela ausi.

There are three commonly used ways of saying 'How are you?' (followed by suitable responses). Note that these questions and answers are quite interchangeable.

How are you?	O/Le kae? (sg/pl)
How do you live?	O/Le phela joang? (sg/pl)
How did you get up?	O/Le tsohele joang? (sg/pl)
I'm here.	Ke/Re teng. (sg/pl)
I live well.	Ke/Re phela hantle. (sg/pl)
I got up well.	Ke/Re tsohile hantle. (sg/pl)

When trekking, people always ask Lea kae? or O tsoa kae? (Where are you going?), or the plural Le tsoa kae? (Where have you come from?). When parting, use these expressions:

Stay well.	Sala hantle. (sg)
	Salang hantle. (pl)
Go well.	Tsamaea hantle. (sg)
	Tsamaeang hantle. (pl)

'Thank you' is kea leboha (pronounced 'ke-ya le-bo-wa'). The herd boys often ask for chelete (money) or lipompong (sweets, pronounced 'dee-pom-pong'). To say 'I don't have any', use ha dio.

SWATI

Swati (siSwati) is the official language in Swaziland (along with English). A Bantu language, it's very similar to Zulu, and they are mutually intelligible.

It's the custom to greet everyone you meet. Yebo is often said as a casual greeting. Often you will be asked U ya phi? (Where are you going?).

Hello.	Sawubona. (to one person)
	Sanibona.
	(to more than one person)
How are you?	Kunjani?
I'm fine.	Kulungile.

Goodbye.	Sala kahle. (if leaving)
	Hamba kahle. (if staying)
Please.	Ngicela.
I thank you.	Ngiyabonga.
We thank you.	Siyabonga.
Yes.	Yebo. (also an all-purpose greeting)
No.	Cha.
Sorry.	Lucolo.
What's your name?	Ngubani libito lakho?
My name is ...	Libitolami ningu ...
I'm from ...	Ngingewekubuya e ...
How much?	Malini?

TSONGA

Tsonga (Xitsonga), a Bantu language, is spoken in South Africa (north of Hluhluwe in KwaZulu-Natal) and in parts of Mozambique.

Hello.	Avusheni. (morning)
	Inhelekani. (afternoon)
	Riperile. (evening)
Goodbye.	Salani kahle.
Yes.	Hi swona.
No.	A hi swona.
Please.	Nakombela.
Thank you.	I nkomu.
What's your name?	U mani vito ra wena?
My name is ...	Vito ra mina i ...
I come from ...	Ndzihuma e ...

TSWANA

Tswana (Setswana), a Bantu language, is widely spoken throughout Botswana and in some parts of South Africa (in the eastern areas of Northern Cape, in North West and in western Free State). There are similarities in vocabulary between Tswana and the two Sotho languages, and the speakers of each can generally understand one another.

The letter g is pronounced as the 'ch' in Scottish 'loch'; th is pronounced as a slightly aspirated 't', ie with a puff of air.

The greetings dumela mma, dumela rra and dumelang are considered compliments and Batswana people appreciate their liberal usage. Another useful phrase (usually placed at the end of a sentence or conversation) is go siame, meaning 'all right, no problem'.

Hello.	Dumela mma/rra.
	(to a woman/man)
	Dumelang. (to a group)
Hello!	Ko ko! (on arrival at a gate or house)

Goodbye.	Tsamaya sentle. (if staying)
	Sala sentle. (if leaving)
Yes.	Ee.
No.	Nnyaa.
Please.	Tsweetswee.
Thank you.	Kea leboga.
Excuse me./Sorry.	Intshwarele.
Pardon me.	Ke kopa tsela.
OK./No problem.	Go siame.
How are you?	A o tsogile? (morning)
	O tlhotse jang?
	(afternoon/evening)
Do you speak	A o bua Sekgoa?
English?	
I don't understand.	Ga ke tlhaloganye.
How much is it?	Ke bokae?
Where is a/the ...?	E ko kae ...?

I'm looking for a/the ...	Ke batla ...
bank	ntlo ya polokelo
guesthouse	matlo a baeng
hotel	hotele
market	mmaraka
post office	poso
public toilet	matlwana a boitiketso
tourist office	ntlo ya bajanala

1	bongwe
2	bobedi
3	borara
4	bone
5	botlhano
6	borataro
7	bosupa
8	boroba bobedi
9	boroba bongwe
10	lesome

VENDA

Venda (Tshivenda), a Bantu language, is spoken in the northeastern region of South Africa's Limpopo province.

Hello.	Ndi matseloni. (morning)
	Ndi masiari. (afternoon)
	Ndi madekwana. (evening)
Goodbye.	Kha vha sale zwavhudi.
Yes.	Ndi zwone.
No.	A si zwone.
Please.	Ndikho u humbela.
Thank you.	Ndo livhuwa.

What's your name?	Zina lavho ndi nnyi?
My name is ...	Zina langa ndi ...
I come from ...	Ndi bva ...

XHOSA

Xhosa (isiXhosa) is the language of the people of the same name. A Bantu language, it's the dominant indigenous variety in Eastern Cape in South Africa, although you'll meet Xhosa speakers throughout the region.

Note that *Bawo* is a term of respect used when addressing an older man.

Hello.	Molo.
Goodbye.	Sala kakuhle.
Goodnight.	Rhonanai.
Please.	Nceda.
Thank you.	Enkosi.
Are you well?	Uphilile na namhlanje?
Yes, I'm well.	Ewe, ndiphilile kanye.
Yes.	Ewe.
No.	Hayi.
Do you speak	Uyakwazi ukuthetha
English?	siNgesi?
Where are you from?	Uvela phi na okanye
	ngaphi na?
I'm from ...	Ndivela ...
I'm lost.	Ndilahlekile.
Is this the road to ...?	Yindlela eya ... yini le?
How much is it?	Idla ntoni na?

ZULU

Zulu (isiZulu), a Bantu language, is spoken in South Africa by the people of the same name. As with several other Nguni languages, Zulu uses a variety of clicks. To ask a question, add -na to the end of a sentence.

Hello.	Sawubona.
Goodbye.	Sala kahle.
Please.	Jabulisa.
Thank you.	Ngiyabonga.
Yes./No.	Yebo./Cha.
Where does this	Iqondaphi lendlela na?
road go?	
Which is the road	Iphi indlela yokuya ku ...?
to ...?	
Is it far?	Kukude yini?
left	ekhohlo
right	ekumene
food	ukudla
water	amanzi

GLOSSARY

Although English is widely spoken in most Southern African countries, native speakers from Australasia, North America and the UK will notice that many words have developed different meanings locally. There are also many unusual terms that have been borrowed from Afrikaans, Portuguese or indigenous languages. This glossary includes some of these particular 'Afro-English' words, as well as some other general terms and abbreviations that may not be understood.

In African English, repetition for emphasis is common: something that burnt you would be 'hot hot'; fields after the rains are 'green green'; a crowded minibus with no more room is 'full full', and so on.

4WD – four-wheel drive; locally called 4x4

apartheid – literally, the state of being apart; a political system in which peoples were officially segregated according to their race

asimilados – Mozambican term for Africans who assimilated to European ways

assegais – spears; used against the colonialists in Zimbabwe

bakkie – pronounced 'bucky'; utility or pick-up truck

barchan dunes – migrating crescent-shaped sand dunes

Basarwa – Batswana name for the San people

Batswana – citizens of Botswana

bemanti – learned Swazi men

Big Five – elephant, lion, rhino, leopard, buffalo

biltong – chewy dried meat that can be anything from beef to kudu or ostrich

bobotie – traditional Malay dish; delicately flavoured curry with a topping of beaten egg baked to a crust, served with stewed fruits and chutney

Boer – farmer in Afrikaans; historic name for the Afrikaner people

boerewors – sausage of varying quality made by Afrikaner farmers

bogobe – sorghum porridge, a staple in Botswana

bojalwa – inexpensive sorghum beer drunk in Botswana that is also brewed commercially

boma – in Zambia, Malawi and some other countries, this is a local word for 'town'; in East Africa the same word means 'fortified stockade'; in Zimbabwe, Botswana, Namibia and much of South Africa, it's normally just a sunken campfire circle; it may be derived from the colonial term BOMA (British Overseas Military Administration), applied to any government building, such as offices or forts

boomslang – dangerous 2m-long tree snake

braai – barbecue; a Southern African institution, particularly among whites

bushveld – flat, grassy plain covered in thorn scrub

camarões – Mozambican term for prawns

camião – truck in Mozambique

campeamento principal – Mozambican term for main entrance

capulanas – colourful sarongs worn by Mozambican women around their waist

capuzinio – mission in Mozambique

casal – room with a double bed, for married couples, in Mozambique

cascata – Mozambican term for waterfall

chapa – word for converted passenger truck or minivan in Mozambique or Malawi

chibuku – local style mass-produced beer, stored in tanks and served in buckets, or available in takeaway cartons (mostly in Zimbabwe and Malawi) and plastic bottles known as *scuds;* it's good for a quick euphoria and a debilitating babalass (hangover)

chiperone – damp misty weather that affects southern Malawi

concession – communal land area designated by the government for use by a given commercial entity for a set amount of time – usually five years; a popular concept in both Namibia and Botswana

coupé – two-person compartment on a train

cuca shops – small shops in northern Namibia; named after the Angolan beer once sold in them

daga hut – traditional African round house consisting of a wooden frame, mud and straw walls, and a thatched roof (mainly in Zimbabwe)

dagga – pronounced da-kha; Southern African term for marijuana

dassies – herbivorous gopherlike mammals of two species: *Procavia capensis*, also called the rock hyrax, and *Dendrohyrax arborea* or tree hyrax; they're in fact not rodents, but are thought to be the closest living relatives of the elephant

dhow – Arabic sailing vessel that dates from ancient times

difaqane – forced migration by several Southern African tribes in the face of Zulu aggression; also known as *mfeqane*

donga – steep-sided gully caused by soil erosion

dorp – small country settlement in South Africa

drift – river ford; most are normally dry

dumpi – 375ml bottle of beer

duplo – term for a room with twin beds used in Mozambique

dwalas – bald, knoblike domes of smooth rock

eh – (rhymes with 'hay') all-purpose ending to sentences, even very short ones such as 'Thanks, eh?'

euphorbia – several species of cactuslike succulents; most are poisonous to humans

fly camp – temporary camp set up in the bush away from the main camp

fynbos – literally 'fine bush', primarily proteas, heaths and ericas

galabiyya – men's full-length robe

gap it – make a quick exit; often refers to emigration from troubled African countries

garni – hotel in Namibia that lacks a full dining room, but does offer a simple breakfast

gemütlichkeit – distinctly German appreciation of comfort and hospitality

half-bus – Malawian term for a bus with about 30 seats – to distinguish it from big buses or minibuses

heks – entrance gates, farm gates

high season – in most of Southern Africa, this refers to the dry season, from late June to late September; in South Africa's Cape regions, it refers to the dry season,

from late November to early April

highveld – high-altitude grassland

Homelands – formerly self-governing black states (Transkei, Ciskei, Bophuthatswana, Venda etc), which were part of the apartheid regime's plan for a separate black and white South Africa

Incwala – most sacred Swazi ceremony in which the king gives permission to his people to eat the first crops of the new year

inselberg – isolated ranges and hills; literally 'island mountains'

Izzit? – rhetorical question that most closely translates as 'Really?' and is used without regard to gender, person or number of subjects; therefore, it could mean 'Is it?', 'Are you?', 'Is he?', 'Are they?', 'Is she?', 'Are we?' etc; also 'How izzit?' for 'How's it going?'

Jugendstil – German art-nouveau architecture prevalent in Namibia, especially in Swakopmund and parts of Windhoek and Lüderitz

just now – refers to some time in the future but implies a certain degree of imminence; it could be half an hour from now or two days from now

kalindula – rumba-inspired music of Zambia

kampango – catfish in Malawi

kapenta – anchovylike fish (*Limnothrissa mioda*) caught in Lake Kariba and favoured by Zimbabweans

karakul – variety of Central Asian sheep, which produces high-grade wool and pelts; raised in Namibia and parts of Botswana

kgosi – chief in Botswana (Setswana language)

kgotla – village meeting place in Botswana

Khoisan – language grouping taking in all Southern African indigenous languages, including San and Khoikhoi (Nama), as well as the language of the Damara, a Bantu people who speak a Khoikhoi dialect

kizomba – musical style popular in Namibia

kloof – ravine or small valley

kloofing – canyoning into and out of kloofs

kokerboom – quiver tree; grows mainly in southern Namibia and the Northern Cape province of South Africa

konditorei – German pastry shops; found in larger Namibian towns

kopje – pronounced 'koppie'; small hill or rocky outcrop on an otherwise flat plain

kotu – king's court in Zambia

kraal – Afrikaans version of the Portuguese word *curral*; an enclosure for livestock, a fortified village of mud huts, or an Owambo homestead

kwacha – currency in Malawi and Zambia

kwasa kwasa – Congo-style rhumba music

laager – wagon circle

lagosta – crayfish in Mozambique

lapa – large, thatched common area; used for socialising

lekolulo – flutelike instrument played by herd boys in Lesotho

liqhaga – grassware 'bottles'

litunga – king in Zambia

lowveld – see *bushveld*

lupembe – wind instrument made from animal horn

machibombo – large bus in Mozambique

majika – traditional rhythmic sound

makalani – type of palm tree that grows in the Kalahari region; also called *mokolane*

makhosi – Zulu chiefs

malva – apricot pudding of Dutch origin

mapiko – masked dance of the Makonde people

marimba – African xylophone made from strips of resonant wood with various-sized gourds for sound boxes

marrabenta – typical Mozambican music, inspired by traditional *majika* rhythms

mataku – watermelon wine

matola – Malawian term for pick-up or van carrying passengers

mbira – thumb piano; it consists of five to 24 narrow iron keys mounted in rows on a wooden sound board

mealie pap – maize porridge, which is a dietary staple throughout the region; also called *mielie pap*

mfeqane – see *difaqane*

mielie pap – see *mealie pap*

mielies – cobs of maize

miombo – dry, open woodland, also called *Brachystegia* woodland; it's composed mainly of mopane and acacia *bushveld*

mojito – Cuban cocktail made of mint, rum, lime juice, sugar and soda

mokolane – see *makalani*

mokoro – dugout canoe used in the Okavango Delta and other riverine areas; the *mokoro* is propelled by a well-balanced poler who stands in the stern

mopane – hardwood tree native to Southern Africa (also called ironwood), highly resistant to drought

mopane worms – the caterpillar of the moth *Gonimbrasiabelina,* eaten as a local delicacy throughout the region

msasa – small, shrubby tree with compound leaves and small, fragrant flowers

multa – a fine in Mozambique

muti – traditional medicine

nalikwanda – huge wooden canoe, painted with black and white stripes, that carries the *litunga*

Nama – popular name for Namibians of Khoikhoi, Topnaar or Baster heritage

não faz mal – 'no problem' in Portuguese; useful in both Mozambique and Angola

!nara – type of melon that grows in desert areas; a dietary staple of the Topnaar people

nartjie – pronounced 'narkie'; South African tangerine

ncheni – lake tiger fish in Malawi

Ngwenyama – the Lion; term given to the king of Swaziland

nshima – filling maize porridgelike substance eaten in Zambia

nxum – the San people's 'life force'

nyama – meat or meat gravy

oke – term for bloke or guy, mainly heard in South Africa

ondjongo – dance performed by Himba cattle owners to demonstrate the care and ownership of their animals

oshana – normally dry river channel in northern Namibia and northwestern Botswana

oshikundu – tasty alcoholic beverage; popular in traditional areas of northern Namibia

otjipirangi (for men) and **outjina** (for women) – Herero dance in which a plank is strapped to one foot in order to deliver a hollow, rhythmic percussion

pan – dry flat area of grassland or salt, often a seasonal lake-bed

participation safari – an inexpensive safari in which clients pitch their own tents, pack the vehicle and share cooking duties

pensão – inexpensive hotel in Mozambique

peri-peri – see *piri-piri*

pint – small bottle of beer or can of oil (or similar), usually around 300mL to 375mL (not necessarily equal to a British or US pint)

piri-piri – very hot pepper sauce of Portuguese Angolan origin; also known as *peri-peri*

potjie – pronounced *poykee;* a three-legged pot used to make stew over an open fire; the word also refers to the stew itself, as well as a gathering in which a *potjie* forms the main dish

potjiekos – meat and vegetable stew cooked in a *potjie*

praça – town square in Mozambique

praia – beach in Mozambique

pula – the Botswanan currency; means 'rain' in Setswana

pungwe – all-night drinking and music party in Zimbabwe

relish – sauce of meat, vegetables, beans etc eaten with boiled corn meal (*nshima, sadza, mealie pap* etc)

rijsttafel – rice with side dishes

Rikki – small, open van; cross between a taxi and a shared taxi

rondavel – round, African-style hut

rooibos – literally 'red bush' in Afrikaans; herbal tea that reputedly has therapeutic qualities

sadza – maize-meal porridge

San – language-based name for indigenous people formerly known as Bushmen

sandveld – dry, sandy belt

sangoma – witch doctor; herbalist

scud – plastic drink bottle

seif dunes – prominent linear sand dunes, as found in the central Namib Desert

shame! – half-hearted expression of commiseration

shebeen – unlicensed township drinking

establishment (which may also include a brothel)

sibhaca – type of Swazi dance

Sperrgebiet – forbidden area; alluvial diamond region of southwestern Namibia

Strandlopers – literally 'beach walkers'; term used to describe the ancient inhabitants of the Namib region, who may have been ancestors of the San or Nama peoples; occasionally also refers to the brown desert hyena

sua – salt as in Sua Pan, Botswana

swaartgevaar – Afrikaans for the 'black threat'

thomo – stringed instrument played by women in Lesotho

timbila – form of xylophone played by Chope musicians

township – indigenous suburb, typically a high-density black residential area

Trekboers – nomadic pastoralists descended from the Dutch

tufo – traditional dance style from Ilha de Moçambique

tuk-tuk – Asian-style motorised three-wheel vehicle

uitlanders – pronounced 'ait-landers'; foreigners

Umhlanga – reed dance; sacred Swazi ceremony

upshwa – maize- or cassava-based staple in Mozambique

Uri – desert-adapted vehicle produced in Namibia

veld – pronounced 'felt'; open grassland, normally in plateau regions

vlei – pronounced 'flay'; any low, open landscape, sometimes marshy

volkstaal – people's language

Volkstaat – people's state

Voortrekkers – fore-trekkers, pioneers

vundu – Malawian catfish

walende – drink distilled from the *makalani* palm; tastes like vodka

wandelpad – short hiking trail

waterblommetjie bredie – water-flower stew; meat served with the flower of the Cape pondweed

welwitschia – bizarre cone-bearing shrub (*Welwitschia mirabilis*) native to the northern Namib plains

xima – maize- or cassava-based staple in Mozambique, usually served with a sauce of beans, vegetables or fish

LANGUAGE GLOSSARY

behind the scenes

SEND US YOUR FEEDBACK

We love to hear from travellers – your comments keep us on our toes and help make our books better. Our well-travelled team reads every word on what you loved or loathed about this book. Although we cannot reply individually to postal submissions, we always guarantee that your feedback goes straight to the appropriate authors, in time for the next edition. Each person who sends us information is thanked in the next edition – the most useful submissions are rewarded with a selection of digital PDF chapters.

Visit **lonelyplanet.com/contact** to submit your updates and suggestions or to ask for help. Our award-winning website also features inspirational travel stories, news and discussions.

Note: We may edit, reproduce and incorporate your comments in Lonely Planet products such as guidebooks, websites and digital products, so let us know if you don't want your comments reproduced or your name acknowledged. For a copy of our privacy policy visit lonelyplanet.com/privacy.

OUR READERS

Many thanks to the travellers who used the last edition and wrote to us with helpful hints, useful advice and interesting anecdotes:

Hector Arguelles, Emma Beumer, Jochen Fuchs, Pierre Gaspart, Danica Hantke, Lars Hellvig, Andrew Hobson, Jennifer Jader, Beathe Legind, Dan McGovern, Hazel Nelson, Nancy O'Grady, Michal Onderco, Wrelf Rolf, Ellen Van Brandenburg, Katrijn Van Loo, Sandra Van Maarseveen, James Wesson, Kyle Zieba

AUTHOR THANKS

Alan Murphy

A big thanks to my travel companion and friend Smitzy for his patience, advice and adventurous spirit (and for not getting further traffic infringements). In Namibia there are too many to thank but special mention to Almuth Styles in Swakopmund whose assistance was much appreciated, and to the honorary consul in Windhoek for making me legal again after my ID was stolen. Thanks to the numerous CEs at LP that I worked with and to my coauthors whose work on this guide was outstanding. To my gorgeous wife, Alison, whose dancing drives me crazy, but whose strength and spirit inspires me and gives me courage.

Kate Armstrong

A special thanks to the Raw family and Katie McCarthy for their kindness and ongoing help, and to fellow writer Tom Spurling for doing the groundwork in Lesotho. Huge thanks to coordinator Alan and the Lonely Planet team.

Lucy Corne

Thanks to my mum and dad for first introducing me to this wonderful country, and to my husband, Shawn, for finding an excuse to keep us here. Thanks to Kate Armstrong for her KZN tips and to Elmar Neethling and Ed Salomons for all the Durban and Drakensberg insights, to Gary Pnematicatos for bringing me up to speed on Cape Town's nightlife and to my boys for being the best travel companions ever. At Lonely Planet I'd like to say *enkosi* to Alan, Glenn, David, Lucy and Brigitte for their help and support.

Mary Fitzpatrick

Many thanks to all those who helped me with this update, to Alan for being such a great coordinating author and for the extra words, and – most of all – to Rick, Christopher, Dominic and Gabriel for their company, patience and good humour.

Michael Grosberg

Thanks to all those who welcomed me with open arms and shared their insight, experience and knowledge of Zambia: Amy Waldman, Oli Dreike, Andy Hogg, Jess and Ade Salmon, Alec Cole and Emma Wood, Tyrone McKeith, Linda van Heerden, Greg Heltzer, Riccardo Garbaccio, Meegan Treen, Natalie Clark, Adrian Penny, Lynda and Rick Schulz, Glenn Evans, Sheila Donnelly, Ian Stevenson (who let me 'co-spot' on an antipoaching flight over the Lower Zambezi), Mindy Roberts, Nathalie Zanoli and Samrat Datta.

Anthony Ham

Andy Raggett of Drive Botswana was an invaluable source of information at all stages of the journey. Thanks also to Mike Romeo, Will Gourlay, Alan Murphy, Glyn Maude, Keitumetse Ngaka, Olefile Sebogiso, Nick Jacobsen, Monika Schiess and to Jan and Cleo in Khutse. Special thanks to Jan and Ron, and to my three girls Marina, Carlota and Valentina: *Os quiero con todo mi corazon*.

Trent Holden & Kate Morgan

There are some huge thank yous to give out for the help we received while researching. First up thanks to Joy in Victoria Falls, and Kim in Livingstone for all your assistance in getting some of the nitty gritty stuff down pat. The Seremwe brothers, James and George, for all their guidance and assistance.

Sally Wynn for her unparalleled knowledge of Kariba and around, Choice Mushunje from Zimbabwe Parks, Gordon Adams, Ann Bruce and Jane High from the east, and Val from Bulawayo. Thanks also to all the travellers we met, including John and Linda Hutton for all the suggestions. Finally huge thanks to the production team, particularly Will Gourlay, Glenn van der Knijff and coordinating author Alan Murphy.

Richard Waters

My special thanks to Rob and Lindsay McConaghy and their excellent team who provided specialist advice every step of the way; Chris Badger, Zane, and Emma and Chris; Gaye Russell, Kate Webb and my Malawian pal Gareth Watson for keeping me company. Thanks also to James Lightfoot for his valuable help. Finally my gratitude to the people of Malawi who remain in adversity among the most decent I've ever met.

ACKNOWLEDGMENTS

Climate Map Data Climate map data adapted from Peel MC, Finlayson BL & McMahon TA (2007) 'Updated World Map of the Köppen-Geiger Climate Classification', *Hydrology and Earth System Sciences*, 11, 163344.

Cover photograph: Lion in *fynbos* (fine bush) field, South Africa, Hoberman Collection/Corbis©

THIS BOOK

This 6th edition of Lonely Planet's *Southern Africa* guidebook was researched and written by Alan Murphy (coordinating author), Kate Armstrong, Lucy Corne, Mary Fitzpatrick, Michael Grosberg, Anthony Ham, Trent Holden and Kate Morgan, and Richard Waters. David Lukas wrote the text that formed the basis of the Wildlife chapter and Jane Cornwell wrote the Music in Southern Africa chapter. The previous edition was also coordinated by Alan Murphy.

This guidebook was commissioned in Lonely Planet's Melbourne office, and produced by the following:

Commissioning Editor Glenn van der Knijff

Coordinating Editors Alison Ridgway, Saralinda Turner

Coordinating Cartographer Brendan Streager

Coordinating Layout Designer Carol Jackson

Managing Editors Barbara Delissen, Brigitte Ellemor

Managing Cartographers Alison Lyall, Adrian Persoglia

Managing Layout Designer Chris Girdler

Assisting Editors Sarah Bailey, Andrew Bain, Penny Cordner, Kate Daly, Andrea Dobbin, Kate Kiely, Susan Paterson, Erin Richards, Luna Soo, Ross Taylor, Jeanette Wall

Assisting Cartographers Xavier Di Toro, Jolyon Philcox, Peter Shields

Cover Research Naomi Parker

Internal Image Research David Nelson

Language Content Branislava Vladisavljevic

Thanks to Frank Deim, Bruce Evans, Ryan Evans, Larissa Frost, Genesys India, Jouve India, Annelies Mertens, Trent Paton, Kerrianne Southway, Joseph Spanti, Gerard Walker

NOTES

000 Map pages
000 Photo pages

000 Map pages
000 Photo pages

how to use this book

These symbols will help you find the listings you want:

👁 Sights	🎊 Festivals & Events	⭐ Entertainment
🏃 Activities	🛏 Sleeping	🛍 Shopping
🍃 Courses	✗ Eating	ℹ Information/Transport
👉 Tours	🍷 Drinking	

These symbols give you the vital information for each listing:

🕗 Telephone Numbers	@ Internet Access	🚍 Bus
⊙ Opening Hours	📶 Wi-Fi Access	🚢 Ferry
P Parking	🏊 Swimming Pool	Ⓜ Metro
⊖ Nonsmoking	🥗 Vegetarian Selection	Ⓢ Subway
❄ Air-Conditioning	👪 Family-Friendly	🚊 Tram
		ᴿ Train

Look out for these icons:

TOP CHOICE	Our author's recommendation
FREE	No payment required
🍃	A green or sustainable option

Our authors have nominated these places as demonstrating a strong commitment to sustainability – for example by supporting local communities and producers, operating in an environmentally friendly way, or supporting conservation projects.

Map Legend

Sights
- 🏖 Beach
- ☸ Buddhist
- 🏰 Castle
- ✝ Christian
- 🕉 Hindu
- ☪ Islamic
- ✡ Jewish
- ❶ Monument
- 🏛 Museum/Gallery
- ⚱ Ruin
- 🍷 Winery/Vineyard
- 🐾 Zoo
- ● Other Sight

Activities, Courses & Tours
- 🤿 Diving/Snorkelling
- 🛶 Canoeing/Kayaking
- ⛷ Skiing
- 🏄 Surfing
- 🏊 Swimming/Pool
- 🚶 Walking
- 🏄 Windsurfing
- ➕ Other Activity/Course/Tour

Sleeping
- 🛏 Sleeping
- ⛺ Camping

Eating
- ✗ Eating

Drinking
- ☕ Drinking
- ☕ Cafe

Entertainment
- 🎭 Entertainment

Shopping
- 🛍 Shopping

Information
- 🏦 Bank
- 🏛 Embassy/Consulate
- ➕ Hospital/Medical
- @ Internet
- 👮 Police
- ✉ Post Office
- ☎ Telephone
- 🚻 Toilet
- ℹ Tourist Information
- ● Other Information

Transport
- ✈ Airport
- ⊗ Border Crossing
- 🚌 Bus
- ➕Ⓒ➕ Cable Car/Funicular
- ⊙ Cycling
- ⊖ Ferry
- Ⓜ Monorail
- P Parking
- ⛽ Petrol Station
- 🚕 Taxi
- ➕ℝ➕ Train/Railway
- ➕Ⓣ➕ Tram
- Ⓜ Underground Train Station
- ● Other Transport

Geographic
- 🏠 Hut/Shelter
- 🚨 Lighthouse
- 👀 Lookout
- ▲ Mountain/Volcano
- 🌴 Oasis
- 🌳 Park
-)(Pass
- 🧺 Picnic Area
- 💧 Waterfall

Population
- 🟢 Capital (National)
- ◉ Capital (State/Province)
- ● City/Large Town
- ○ Town/Village

Routes
- Tollway
- Freeway
- Primary
- Secondary
- Tertiary
- Lane
- Unsealed Road
- Plaza/Mall
- Steps
- ⊐⊏ Tunnel
- Pedestrian Overpass
- Walking Tour
- Walking Tour Detour
- Path

Boundaries
- --- International
- ---- State/Province
- --- Disputed
- --- Regional/Suburb
- Marine Park
- Cliff
- Wall

Hydrography
- River, Creek
- Intermittent River
- Swamp/Mangrove
- Reef
- Canal
- Water
- Dry/Salt/Intermittent Lake
- Glacier

Areas
- Beach/Desert
- + + + Cemetery (Christian)
- × × × Cemetery (Other)
- Park/Forest
- Sportsground
- Sight (Building)
- Top Sight (Building)

Michael Grosberg

Zambia With a valuable philosophy degree in hand and business experience on a small Pacific island, Michael moved to Durban, South Africa where he wrote about political violence and helped train newly elected government officials. He also found time to travel all over Southern Africa, including forays into Zambia. Later, during his years in graduate school and while teaching in New York City, he fantasised about returning to the region, which he has been fortunate to visit on numerous Lonely Planet assignments and for other publications.

Anthony Ham

Botswana Anthony has been travelling around Africa for more than a decade. A writer and photographer, his past Lonely Planet guidebooks include *Kenya, Botswana & Namibia, Africa, Libya* and *West Africa*. Anthony has written and photographed for magazines and newspapers around the world, among them *Travel Africa* and *Africa Geographic*. When he's not in Africa, Anthony divides his time between Madrid and Melbourne where he lives with his wife and two daughters.

Read more about Anthony at:
lonelyplanet.com/members/anthonyham

Trent Holden

Victoria Falls, Zimbabwe As a regular visitor to Africa, Trent rates Zimbabwe up there with the best of them. It's a nation that first grabbed his attention when it upset Australia in the 1983 cricket World Cup, and it's this underdog quality that continues to bowl him over to this day. World-class sights, amazing wildlife, striking *msasa* trees and friendly down-to-earth people are what makes this place so great. All it needs now is the tourists it deserves. Trent lives in Melbourne, Australia and has worked on more than 10 books for Lonely Planet – most recently *East Africa* and *India*.

Kate Morgan

Victoria Falls, Zimbabwe Having travelled in East and North Africa, tracking mountain gorillas, spotting wildlife and winding though Moroccan medinas, Kate was keen to check out what the southern part of the continent had to offer. She was lucky enough to head off to Zimbabwe and realise a country that's been completely misrepresented. Humbled by the character of Zimbabweans and floored by the glorious Victoria Falls, Kate is hoping to get back there to do it all again soon. Kate is a freelance writer and editor based in Melbourne, and has worked on other titles such as *Philippines, Phuket* and *Japan*.

Richard Waters

Malawi Richard is an award-winning journalist and works for the *Independent, Sunday Times, Wanderlust* and *National Geographic Traveller*. He lives with his fiancé and two kids in the Cotswolds.

Contributing Authors

Jane Cornwell wrote the Music chapter. Jane is a London-based, Australian-born writer, broadcaster and journalist with a long-time interest in African music. She is world music critic for the London *Evening Standard,* a contributing editor on the world-music magazine *Songlines,* a writer for Peter Gabriel's *Real World Records* and for newspapers including the *Times,* the *Telegraph,* the *Guardian* and the *Australian.*

David Lukas wrote the Wildlife chapter. David teaches and writes about the natural world from his home on the edge of Yosemite National Park. He has contributed Environment and Wildlife chapters to more than 25 Lonely Planet guides, including *Tanzania, East Africa, South Africa, Lesotho & Swaziland* and *Botswana & Namibia.*

OUR STORY

A beat-up old car, a few dollars in the pocket and a sense of adventure. In 1972 that's all Tony and Maureen Wheeler needed for the trip of a lifetime – across Europe and Asia overland to Australia. It took several months, and at the end – broke but inspired – they sat at their kitchen table writing and stapling together their first travel guide, *Across Asia on the Cheap*. Within a week they'd sold 1500 copies. Lonely Planet was born.

Today, Lonely Planet has offices in Melbourne, London and Oakland, with more than 600 staff and writers. We share Tony's belief that 'a great guidebook should do three things: inform, educate and amuse'.

OUR WRITERS

Alan Murphy

Coordinating Author, Namibia Alan remembers falling under Southern Africa's ambient spell after bouncing around in the rear of a *bakkie* (pick-up truck) on the way from Johannesburg airport in 1999. Since then he has been back numerous times for Lonely Planet and travelled widely throughout the region, including this trip to Namibia. Alan finds wildlife watching, in particular, exhilarating and he has certainly taken years off his life staking out waterholes. This was Alan's third trip to Namibia, a country custom-built for road trips with landscapes that never cease to inspire. Alan lives with his wife in the Yarra Valley outside Melbourne, which he wishes was just a touch closer to Melbourne airport.

Kate Armstrong

Lesotho, Swaziland Kate was bitten by the Africa bug when she lived and worked in Mozambique, and returns to Southern Africa regularly. For this edition she danced her way through Swaziland, got her car bogged (more than once) and enjoyed hanging out for a day with some black rhinos. When she's not eating, hiking and talking her way around parts of Africa, Europe and South America, she's a freelance writer for newspapers and magazines around the world from wherever she's living at the time. For more of Kate's adventures, see www.katearmstrong.com.au.

Lucy Corne

South Africa Since she first visited South Africa in 2002, Lucy has been hooked and has returned on six occasions, spending time in more than 200 towns across the country. South Africa still manages to deliver firsts at every turn and research for this book brought Lucy her first black rhino sighting (in Addo Elephant National Park), her first full-on conversation in Xhosa and her first experience of brewing *umqhombothi*. Lucy currently lives in Cape Town where she writes about travel and beer.

Read more about Lucy at:
lonelyplanet.com/members/lucycorne

Mary Fitzpatrick

Mozambique A travel writer for more than 15 years, Mary has lived, worked and travelled in Mozambique, returning many times to explore this magnificent country, to enjoy its beaches and to keep in contact with the countless amazing Mozambicans whom she has met along the way. In addition to authoring many Lonely Planet Africa titles, Mary also writes for various newspapers and magazines, focusing on Africa.

OVER MORE
PAGE WRITERS

Published by Lonely Planet Publications Pty Ltd
ABN 36 005 607 983
6th edition – Aug 2013
ISBN 978 1 74179 889 0
© Lonely Planet 2013   Photographs © as indicated 2013
10 9 8 7 6 5 4 3 2 1
Printed in China